Dictionary of Pseudonyms

FIFTH EDITION

Dictionary of Pseudonyms

*13,000 Assumed Names
and Their Origins*

FIFTH EDITON

Adrian Room

McFarland & Company, Inc., Publishers
Jefferson, North Carolina, and London

LIBRARY OF CONGRESS CATALOGUING-IN-PUBLICATION DATA

Room, Adrian.
Dictionary of pseudonyms : 13,000 assumed names
and their origins / Adrian Room.— 5th ed.
p.   cm.
Includes bibliographical references.

ISBN 978-0-7864-4373-4
illustrated case binding : 50# alkaline paper ∞

1. Anonyms and pseudonyms.   I. Title.
Z1041.R66   2010   929.4'03 — dc22   2010021995

British Library cataloguing data are available

Front cover image ©2010 Eyewire

Manufactured in the United States of America

*McFarland & Company, Inc., Publishers
Box 611, Jefferson, North Carolina 28640
www.mcfarlandpub.com*

TABLE OF CONTENTS

Preface
1

Introduction
3

THE DICTIONARY
11

Bibliography
525

PREFACE

This fifth edition of the *Dictionary of Pseudonyms* is a substantially revised and enlarged version of the fourth edition, published in 2004. It has more than 2,000 new entries, making a total of approximately 13,000, and an entirely rewritten Introduction. The entries have been updated and in many cases expanded, whether as original text or by way of quoted material, and the cross-references have been substantially increased in number. Any errors detected in the earlier edition have now been corrected, while a number of names formerly lacking an origin have been supplied with one.

Otherwise, readers familiar with previous editions will find the mixture as before, with an even wider range of writers, actors, dancers, musicians, entertainers, sports personalities, religious figures, and impostors. Anyone known to have adopted a new name, even by the alteration of a single letter, is included, though it will be seen that most newly assumed names differ noticeably from the original.

INTRODUCTION

A *pseudonym* (literally "false name") is a name that differs from an original *orthonym* ("true name"), and as popularly understood is a new name that a person assumes for a particular purpose. Common examples are the pen names taken by writers, or the stage names adopted by actors. Well-known examples are the author Lewis **Carroll** (original name Charles Ludwidge Dodgson) and the actress Marilyn **Monroe** (original name Norma Jean Mortensen). Pseudonyms are also widely found in the world of music, especially among pop and rock performers. Bob **Dylan** (originally Robert Zimmerman) and Elton **John** (Reginald Dwight) are just two of many examples. On a contrasting note, religion has sanctified popes such as **Benedict XVI** (born Joseph Ratzinger) and holy men and women such as Mother **Teresa** (Agnes Bojaxhiu), while Italy has nurtured Renaissance artists such as **Donatello** (Donato de' Bardi), **Giorgione** (Giorgio Barbarelli), and **Tintoretto** (Jacopo Robusti). Elsewhere, the sphere of sport has its rechristened exponents (boxer and prizefighter **Bendigo** began life as William Thompson), while in politics Russia and the Soviet Union gave the world Vladimir **Lenin** (Vladimir Ulyanov), Joseph **Stalin** (Iosif Dzhugashvili), and Leon **Trotsky** (Lev Bronstein).

Within most categories, distinct groups and subgroups are discernible. In former times, a number of women writers adopted male names to find a readership for their work. Although now familiar as Charlotte Brontë, the English author made her debut in print as Currer **Bell**, while her sisters, Ann and Emily, first made themselves known to their readers as Acton **Bell** and Ellis **Bell**. Crime writers are famous adopters

of pseudonyms. Erle Stanley Gardner wrote bestsellers as A.A. **Fair**, while Harry Patterson tok the name Jack **Higgins**.

Stage names were regularly taken up by music-hall artists and comedians as well as serious actors. Among them are such as Marie **Lloyd** (Matilda Wood), Harry **Fragson** (Léon Fragmann), and **Little Tich** (Harry Relph), while the domain of dance has graced the international stage with gifted ballerinas such as Beryl **Grey** (Beryl Groom), Marie **Rambert** (Myriam Ramberg), and Ninette **de Valois** (Edris Stannus).

Historical figures known by new names include certain Roman emperors, such as **Caligula** (Gaius Julius Caesar), **Caracalla** (Marcus Aurelius Severus Antoninus Augustus), and **Nero** (Lucius Domitius Ahenobarbus). The first emperor of all, Caesar **Augustus**, was born Gaius Octavius. Persons prominent in more recent European history include Grigory **Rasputin** (Grigory Novykh) and **Mata Hari** (Margarethe Zelle). The latter adopted her name as a dancer, but became better known as a spy. Secret agents often assumed an alias, among them Rudolf **Abel** (William Fischer) and George **Blake** (Georgy Behar), while activists such as **Cicero** (Elyesa Bazna) and **Cynthia** (Amy Elizabeth Pack) properly bore a code name.

This sampling of pseudonyms suffices to illustrate the different forms they can assume. Some are recognizable as typical first-and-last-name combinations, and this is a regularly adopted type, often with a visible relationship between the old and new names or even with one name remaining unchanged. The connection between the former name and adopted name is not always obvious, however, and it is not immediately apparent, for example, that Lewis **Carroll**'s new first name was created from his original middle name, or that his assumed last name was devised from his given first name. Conversely, there are many cases where a new if conventional-looking pseudonym may differ completely from the bearer's birth name. Ninette **de Valois** is a case in point. In such instances an explanation or etymology is needed, and this is one of the principal aims of the dictionary.

At the other end of the spectrum are names that bear no resemblance to a conventional name at all. **Little Tich** is such a name, as a creation that is half-nickname ("Little" for his small stature), half-adoption (and truncation) of a surname (Tichborne). **Mata Hari** is another well-known example, from a Malay word meaning "sun."

Nicknames play an important role in the creation of pseudonyms. A person is given a nickname and adopts it, or becomes so widely known by it that it replaces the original name. The distinction between an adopted nickname and an adopted new name can be very fine. The criterion is usually whether the person becomes mainly or solely known by the adopted nickname or not. Thus the U.S. pool player Minnsota **Fats** is generally known by his nickname rather than his original formal name, Rudolf Walter Wanderone, Jr. The same goes for the many musical performers nicknamed "Big," such as **Big Bopper**, who was exclusively billed under this name rather than his birth name, Jiles Perry Richardson, Jr.

Like all pseudonyms, nicknames can be in any language, including the two quoted above for Roman emperors. **Caracalla** was so dubbed for a type of cloak he designed, from a Latin word of Gaulish origin, while **Caligula** was given a name meaning "little boots," a nickname bestowed when the emperor-to-be ran around camp as a child. (Two millennia later his Latin name was adopted in its English version by pop singer **Little Boots**, born Victoria Hesketh.)

Single-word pseudonyms are fairly frequently found. The adopted name may be simply an original first name or surname, or a form of it. The painter **Giorgione** already mentioned thus came to be known by a name amounting to "Big George," derived from his given name. Following in his footsteps are a number of modern cartoonists, who intentionally choose a short name as a signature. They include **Jak** (Raymond Jackson), **Low** (David Low), and **Marc** (Mark Boxer). The photographer **Wols** (Alfred Schulze) came by his name when his surname was misspelled in a telegram.

A quite different stratum of single names comprises the many female pop singers who perform under their first name, as **Beyoncé**, **Björk**, **Camille**, **Charlene**, **Cher**, **Jewel**, **JoJo**, **Louise**, **Madonna** (who may have boosted the mode), **Melanie**, **Millie**, **Rihanna**, **Sade**, **Shakira**, **Shannon**, **Sinitta**, **Soraya**, **Tiffany**, and **Yazz**. **CéU** also really belongs here, although the name is not her first name, as do **Dana** and **Lulu**, adopting their respective nicknames, and **Duffy**, whose friendly-sounding surname serves essentially as a nickname.

Cartoonists are not alone in shortening their names for practical purposes. A change in form or spelling of an original name is frequently made on pragmatic grounds. The U.S. aircraft designer Malcolm **Lockheed** thus respelled his original Scottish surname, Loughead, to ensure its correct pronunciation, while the anglicization or simplification of a non–English name is an equally popular resort. The actress Ethel **Merman** began life as Ethel Zimmerman, while the star dancer Fred **Astaire** originally bore the German surname Austerlitz. U.S. actor Walter **Matthau** came into the world with the Slavic surname Matuschanskayasky, and a drastic pruning was an obvious solution.

Matthau was of Jewish parentage, and many Jewish names were anglicized when their bearers left their European homeland to settle in the United States or elsewhere. Thus Hardy Albrecht became Hardie **Albright**, Bella Becker became Belle **Baker**, Herbert Feuermann became Bert **Firman**, and Alan Kniberg became Alan **King**. Alterations of this kind were often made in an arbitrary fashion by immigration officials at Ellis Island, where the photographer who became known as **Weegee** had his original name of Usher changed to Arthur, while the father of actress Anne **Bancroft** had his name noted as Italiano. The latter resulted from a misunderstanding, as he was being asked for his name, not his nationality.

Some of the more unconventional and colorful names are those adopted as recording names by Jamaican musicians, and especially reggae artists. They include **Chicken Chest, Eek a Mouse, Gospel Fish, Honey Boy, Kool Herc, Shabba Ranks, Spragga Benz**, and **Smiley Culture**. Some Jamaican names are prefixed with "Jah," meaning God, while others have "Prince" as the first element. Such names are an insight into Jamaican popular culture.

In the field of "regular" pseudonyms, certain surnames have gained particular popularity. The present dictionary notes more than 30 instances of **Gray**, for example. This may be because it is simply an agreeable name: easy to spell, easy to say, easy to write. The converse of this is a name that although relatively unremarkable in itself came to be adopted by more than one person. Such was the alliterative Peter **Parley**, first assumed by the U.S. bookseller Samuel Goodrich but later taken up by dozens of other writers imitating his style.

The adoption of another's pseudonym borders on plagiarism, but the assumption of a person's real name may be intended as nothing more sinister than a tribute to the individual concerned, especially when a member of the same family. Many adopters of pen names or stage names assumed their mother's maiden name. Examples range from actress Maude **Adams** (Maude Kiskadden) to singer Katy **Perry** (Katheryn Hudson), writer Helen **Campbell** (Helen Weeks) to novelist Elizabeth **Garner** (Elma Napier). In some cases the adopter already bore his or her mother's maiden name as their middle name, which made the transition even more straightforward. The English painter Hercules **Brabazon** (Hercules Brabazon Sharpe) is just one instance of several. A similar adoption

may originate elsewhere in the family. The engraver and publisher Frank **Leslie**, born Henry Carter, thus took his father's middle name as his new surname, while jazz musician Melvin Sokoloff took his brother's first name as his new surname, so becoming Mel **Lewis**.

The adoption of a placename is also not uncommon. The Hungarian church leader József **Mindszenty** (born József Pehm) took his new name from his native village of Mindszent while four centuries earlier the Austrian astronomer known as **Rhäticus** (originally Georg Joachim von Lauchen) came to be known by the name of his native district of Rhaetia. This type of name is evident among a number of artists, such as the Italians **Pontormo** (Jacopo Carucci), named for the village of his birth, and **Veronese** (Paolo Caliari), famed under the name of his native city of Verona.

There are instances when a single pseudonym does duty for more than one person. Caroline **Lewis** (intentionally suggesting Lewis **Carroll**) was the joint name adopted by three English writers. The opposite can also sometimes occur, when a multiple name is borne by a single person. A famous example is (or are) William and Robert **Whistlecraft**, a double name assumed by the single writer John Hookham Frere.

Multiple names of a more conventional sort are the many names assumed by a single person. A famous example is the English thriller writer John Creasey, who authored more than five hundred books under some twenty pen names, including Gordon **Ashe** and Kyle **Hunt**. This was not simply a desire for diversity, for Creasey produced fiction other than thrillers, and reserved different names for distinct genres, including westerns, romantic novels, and children's stories.

A writer may sometimes assume a persona, not simply a different name, and publish a work in the guise of that persona. Washington Irving thus took on the character of a Dutch author named Diedrich **Knickerbocker** for his famous *History of New York*, while Jonathan Swift published *Gulliver's Travels* as if he actually *was*

Lemuel Gulliver, and described himself in the novel's full title as "first a Surgeon, and then a Captain of several Ships." The original edition even had a portrait of the fictional author, aged 58. The French writer Prosper Mérimée went even further in this direction when he published *Le Théâtre de Clara Gazul* under the female name of Clara **Gazul**. A foreword to the work gave a brief biography of the lady author and its frontispiece depicted her portrait, posed for by the young writer.

Such trickery also gave the name of more serious impostors, such as the 16th-century Frenchman Arnault du Tilh, who took the name Martin **Guerre**, that of a soldier who had disappeared and was presumed dead, and in this persona formed a relationship with the latter's wife, who accepted him as her long-lost husband and bore him two children. In similar fashion, cases are on record of women who have joined the army under male guise and name. Mary Anne Talbot was one such, joining the English military as John **Taylor**, while another was Deborah Sampson, who donned male dress and enlisted in the Fourth Massachusetts Regiment as Robert **Shurtleff**. Such adventures or enterprises of course risked exposure at any time, and it is remarkable that the impostures succeeded as long as they did.

A related category, though hardly impostors, is that of transexuals who changed their name on assuming their new gender, whether or not it involved a surgical "reassignment." Male-to-female conversions include April **Ashley** (born George Jamieson), Debra **Bowring** (Peter Compton), Roberta **Close** (Roberto Moreira), Christine **Jorgensen** (George Jorgensen), and Renee **Richards** (Richard Rasking). Lady Colin **Campbell**, writing under her married name, was misdiagnosed male at birth and so was christened George William Ziadie. Female-to-male conversions include Claude **Cahun** (Lucie Schwob), Marcel **Moore** (Suzanne Malherbe), and Brandon **Teena** (Teena Brandon), the latter neatly switching names to denote her new gender.

In a number of cases a new name is gained as a condition of a bequest. The politician John **Barrington**, for example, was born John Shute, but on inheritng the estate of Francis Barrington, husband of his first cousin, adopted the name of the bequeather, while the philanthropist Angela **Burdett-Coutts** added the name Coutts to her original name on inheriting her grandfather's fortune. On similar lines, newspaper editor Geoffrey **Dawson**, originally Geoffrey Robinson, changed his name by royal license following an inheritance from his aunt Margaret Jane Dawson. A bequest of this kind may well tie directly in with a marriage, as when the physician Robert **Clobery**, born Robert Glynn, married his cousin, Lucy Clobery, and took her name on inheriting a property from her father. His is just one example of a man's adoption of his wife's name, rather than that of a woman who takes or adds her husband's name on marriage, as is conventionally more common.

Many name changes, whether resulting from an inheritance or not, are confirmed by the legal process known as a deed poll, a term dating from the days when the document had one edge polled (cut even) rather than being indented, as was more usual.

One pseudonymous sportsman has already been instanced, but there are significant nests of others worth singling out. In the somewhat specialized world of Brazilian football, for example, one finds **Didi**, **Garrincha**, **Jaïrzinho**, **Jorginho**, **Juninho**, **Kaká**, **Pelé**, **Ronaldinho**, **Ronaldo**, **Tostão**, and **Vavá**, among others, while the esoteric arena of sumo wrestling includes such warriors as **Akebono**, **Asahifuji**, **Chiyonofuji**, **Daijuyama**, **Fujinoshin**, **Hananokuni**, **Hananoumi**, **Kokutenyu**, and **Krishima**. The football names are largely nicknames, while the sumo pseudonyms are meaningful Japanese fighting names.

Elsewhere in the world of foreign names a distinctive subgroup is formed by the Russian-style names assumes by dancers. Russia is traditionally regarded as the home and mainspring of ballet, and at one time it was common for ballet dancers to russify their original name wherever possible. Examples of such names are those of Harcourt **Algeranoff**, Sonia **Arova**, Hilda **Butsova**, Anton **Dolin**, Vera **Fredowa**, Margareta **Krasnova**, and Alicia **Markova**. Lydia **Sokolova** actually adopted the name of an earlier Russian dancer. The fashioning of such names is no longer common.

Finally, a curious nucleus of Italian names is found among members of the 18th-century literary circle known as the Academy of Arcadia, which included such classically pastoral poets as Eulibio **Berentiatico**, Aglauro **Cidonia**, Lesbia **Cidonia**, Comante **Eginetico**, Glaucilla **Eurotea**, Tirsi **Leucasio**, Corilla **Olimpica**, Fidalma **Partenide**, and Eterio **Stinfalico**. A variant was created by Maria Antonia Walpurgis, Princess of Bavaria, Electress of Saxony, who came to be known as **ETPA**, an acronym of her Arcadian name, Ermelinda Talea Pastorella Arcada, whose last two words gave the title of "Arcadian Shepherdess."

In areas of activity where the adoption of a pseudonym is common, such as the theater, there are always those who resolutely refuse to adopt a stage name. In such areas, even a real name, especially if unusual, may be wrongly taken as a stage name. Here are some examples:

• U.S. movie actress Sandra **Bullock** (1966–) has resolutely refused to change her name, although one journalist feels she should have: "There is something about the name Sandra Bullock that just isn't Hollywood. It sounds grimly ordinary, plain and tough. It lacks the delicate beauty of a Michelle Pfeiffer, the take-no-prisoners hit of a Jamie Lee **Curtis** or the languorous sexiness of a Kim Basinger. In an industry where changing your name is as routine as changing your socks these things matter. If a name says something about a person, then Sandra Bullock could be an installation artist, a sprint-hurdler or a gum-chewing bully at school. But a Hollywood starlet? Surely not" [Sasha Miller in *Sunday Times Magazine*, September 25, 1994].

• As a child, U.K. actress Frances **Cuka** (1936–) told her ballerina aunt that she wanted to go on stage under the name "Gloria La Raine." "What's wrong with Cuka?" retorted

the aunt. "I was Cuka; your aunt Eileen acted under the name Cuka. No one can spell it, no one can pronounce it — but no one will forget it." Said Frances, who pronounces her name "Chewka": "I was too scared to change my name, and I am pleased now I was frightened into keeping it" [*TV Times*, Ferbruary 14–20, 1987].

• U.S. movie actor Bradford **Dillman** (1930–) commented: "Bradford Dillman sounded like a distinguished, phoney, theatrical name, so I kept it" [J.F. Clarke, p. 250].

• U.S. actress Bridget **Fonda** (1964–), daughter of Peter Fonda (1942–) and granddaughter of Henry Fonda (1905–1982), has often been tempted to change her name since childhood, when her father divorced her mother. She acknowledges that bearing this particular name has problems: "I did consider changing my name but it does no good to run away and I am part of the Fonda family" [*The Times*, August 1, 1988].

• U.K. radio and TV presenter Gloria **Hunniford** (1940–) has said: "A lot of people think it's a stage name but it isn't. When my husband told his family he was marrying me, they said: 'No wonder — she wants to change her name!'" [Sachs and Morgan, p. 94].

• "Of course it's my real name," said U.S. TV star Cloris **Leachman** (1926–), when interviewers expressed doubts about it. "Would anyone in his right mind change it *to* Cloris Leachman?" [Andersen, p. 247].

• When a Hollywod executive wanted to change the name of Jack **Lemmon** (1925–2001) to "Lennon," the movie actor replied: "I told him it had taken most of my life to get used to the traumatic effects of beng called Jack U. Lemmon, and that I was used to it now and I wasn't going to change it" [J.F. Clarke, p. 250].

• When Helena **Michell** (1961–), daughter of Australian actor Keith Michell (1926–), appeared with her father in the 1988 movie *The Deceivers*, she was asked how she intended to preserve her distinct identity. Her reply: "What do people want me to do? Change my name? I think my Dad would be upset if I did, as if I were ashamed of it" [*TV Times*, October 22–28, 1988].

• U.K. TV comedian and presenter Bob **Monkhouse** (1928–2003) said of his name: "Americans never get it right, they always call me Mongoose. If I'd had my wits about me I would have changed it at the start. People like Ted **Ray** and **Lulu** had it right" [Sachs and Morgan, p. 199].

• U.S. movie actress Sydne **Rome** (1951–) once inquired at an airport whether she should stop off in Nice. The clerk, on learing her name, reaplied: "Madam, I think you would do well to transfer to Qantas" [*Telegraph Sunday Magazine*, June 3, 1979].

• Popular singer Frank **Sinatra** (1915–1998), at the age of 22, was a singing waiter in New Jersey under the name Frank Trent. He kept this name until it was pointed out to him that his real name was much more musical. From then on he firmly refused to adopt a new name, saying: "You like the voice, you take the name" [1. *Times Literary Suplement*, March 1, 1996; 2. *The Times*, December 6, 2002].

• U.S. actress and singer Barbra (originally Barbara) **Streisand** (1942–) and actor Dustin **Hoffman** (1937–) were just two of the 1960s generation of Hollywood stars who refused to change their names [Charles Derry in Vinson, p. 594].

• South African actress Janet **Suzman** (1939–), when she first went on stage, adamantly refused to accede to suggestions that she change her name because it was too "foreign." Instead, she sent a telegram to the theater director: "Imperative remain Suzman" [*TV Times*, April 9, 1976].

• Anglo–U.S. playwright Timberlake **Wertenbaker** (1945–) found that critics reacted with suspicion to her name, seeing it as some sort of anagram. Yet it is her real name, her first name being a former family surname [*Sunday Times*, April 6, 1986].

Arrangement of Entries

The entries run in alphabetical order and comprise two or more elements, as follows.

1. The name itself, printed in **bold**. This is often a surname but may be a single name or some kind of unconventional name, often consisting of more than one word. Titles such as "Sir" precede the name in square brackets (as for [Sir] Algernon **Methuen**) unless they are assumed as part of the name itself (as for Sir Charles **Morell**). Abbreviations such as "St." (Saint) and "Dr." (Doctor) are treated similarly. Religious titles such as "Father," "Sister," on the other hand, are not enclosed in brackets, nor are words that are military ranks or nicknames such as "Captain," "Kid." Such terms have their own entries as a guide to the alphabetical location of the name they precede, e.g.:

Brother ... For names beginning thus, see the next word, e.g. for Brother Adam see **Adam**, for Brother Antoninus see **Antoninus**, for Brother Daniel see **Daniel**, etc.

The few examples of numeral names are located where the name would fall if spelled out. Thus **50 Cent** comes between W.C. **Fields** and **Figaro**.

2. The person's real name, followed by his or her birth and (if appropriate) death dates, nationality (for the abbreviations used, see below), and a descriptive label such as "writer," "movie actor," "politician," and the like. The type of writer may be specified, as "novelist," "playwright," while a stage actor is usually indicated as such, for distinction from a movie actor, but if the person lived before the motion-picture era, "actor" will mean stage actor.

These two elements are the mimimum present in all entries.

3. Wherever possible, an origin of the pseudonym or assumed name then follows, either as a straightforward account or by means of a quotation, in which case the source of the quote is invariably given, with year of publication for books and date of publication for items from the press. (With regard to the latter, *The Times* means the London newspaper.) Sources given by author name only refer to titles listed in the Bibliography with page number, as "[Marble, p.181]" in the entry for Adair **Aldon**. Where two or more authors share a name, as

Donald Clarke and J.F. Clarke, they are distinguished by their first name or initials. Where a single author published more than one book, the relevant year of publication is added, as Fisher 1976. Where two titles were published by the same author(s) in a single year, they are distinguished as I and II, as Sachs and Morgan II. (Some examples of the treatment occur in the selection of real names above.) Indevitably, some names attract a longer etymology than others, and there may be more than one quotation.

Names mentioned in an entry that have their own individual entries are printed in **bold**. This even applies to names occurring in a quotation. Thus the entry for Susan **Hayward** has a quotation that includes the name of Rita **Hayworth**, and this appears in bold even though not so printed in the original text.

4. There are a number of cross-entries in the book in the format:

Philip **Owen** *see* Hugh **Pentecost**

Abbreviations

The following abbreviations are used for the nationalities or provenance of the subjects of the entries.

Austr.: Austrian
Austral.: Australian
Belg.: Belgian
Br.: British
Bulg.: Bulgarian
Can.: Canadian
Chin.: Chinese
Cz.: Czech
Dan.: Danish
Du.: Dutch
Eng.: English
Finn.: Finnish

Fr.: French
Ger.: German
Gk.: Greek
Hung.: Hungarian
Ind.: Indian
Ir.: Irish
It.: Italian
Jap.: Japanese
Norw.: Norwegian
N.Z.: New Zealand
Pol.: Polish
Port.: Portuguese
Rom.: Romanian
Russ.: Russian
S.A.: South African
Sc.: Scottish
Sp.: Spanish
Swe.: Swedish
Turk.: Turkish
U.K.: United Kingdom
Ukr.: Ukrainian
U.S.: United States

A few standard abbreviations are also used generally, such as:

c. circa (Latin): "about" (used with dates)
DJ: disk jockey
fl. floruit (Latin): "flourished" (used when exact dates are not known)
ibid. (short for Latin *ibidem*): "in the same place" (used in quotations to refer to a source already named)
p.: page
R&B: rhythm and blues
Rev.: Reverend
SF: science fiction
TV: television
vol.: volume

THE DICTIONARY

A.A. *see* Anthony **Armstrong**

Jeppe **Aakjaer:** Jeppe Jensen (1866–1930), Dan. poet, novelist.

Aaliyah: Aaliyah Dana Haughton (1979–2001), U.S. black R&B singer, movie actress. The singer adopted her first name, Arabic for "sublime," "most exalted one," as her professional name.

Willie **Aames:** William Upton (1960–), U.S. TV actor. A new surname that will bring the actor from near the bottom straight to the top of any alphabetical billing.

Els **Aarne:** Elze Janovna Paemurru (1917–1995), Ukr.-born Estonian composer.

Aba-Daba: Carlos Calderón Ramírez (1947–), Mexican comedy magician. A hint of "abracadabra."

Aleksandr **Abasheli:** Aleksandr Vissarionovich Chochiya (1884–1954), Georgian poet.

Francesco **Abati:** William Winwood Reade (1838–1875), Eng. writer. The writer, a nephew of the novelist Charles Reade (1814–1880), used this name for his novel *See Saw* (1865), in which a Catholic narrator is interrupted by Anglican Reade.

Anthony **Abbot:** Charles Fulton Oursler (1893–1952), U.S. journalist, playwright, novelist. The writer was also a magician under the name Samri Frickell.

John **Abbot:** Vernon John (1896–1943), U.S. music-hall singer.

Russ **Abbot:** Russell Allan Roberts (1947–), Eng. TV comedian. A name presumably based on the comedian's real name, although at one time he also had a pop band called The Black Abbots.

Bud **Abbott:** William A. Abbott (1895–1974), U.S. movie comedian, teaming with Lou **Costello.**

Jacob **Abbott:** Jacob Abbot (1803–1879), U.S. educator, author. Abbot added an extra "l" to his family name while attending Bowdoin College, Brunswick, Maine. Many of his brothers did likewise.

John **Abbott** *see* Evan **Hunter**

Philip **Abbott:** Philip Abbott Alexander (1923–1998), U.S. movie actor.

Abd-ru-shin: Oskar Ernest Bernhardt (1875–1941), Ger. cult leader. The founder of the Grail Movement assumed his quasi–Arabic name, which he interpreted as "son of light," after World War I as a result of visits made before the war to the east. He claimed the name came from a former incarnation when, in the time of Moses, he had lived as the prince of an Arabian tribe.

Kareem **Abdul-Jabbar:** Ferdinand Lewis Alcindor, Jr. (1947–), U.S. black basketball player. Lew Alcindor (as he was usually known) adopted his new name in 1971 following his conversion to Islam in 1968, when at the University of California, Los Angeles.

Achmed **Abdullah:** Alexander Nicholayevitch Romanoff (Aleksandr Nikolayevich Romanov) (1881–1945), Russ.-born Br. writer of fantasy fiction. The writer adopted the name Achmed Abdullah Nadir Khan el-Durani el-Iddrissyeh after his parents divorced. He also wrote as A.A. Nadir and John Hamilton.

Ahmed **Abdullah:** Leroy Bland (1946–), U.S. black jazz musician.

Abdullah ibn Buhaina: Art Blakey (1919–1990), U.S. black jazz drummer, bandleader. Blakey adopted his new name on converting to Islam during a visit to Africa in 1948. He never recorded under his Muslim name, although several of his children shared the name with him and he was later known to his musical friends as "Bu."

Ahmed **Abdul-Malik:** Jonathan Timms (1927–1993), U.S. black jazz musician. Timms adopted his Muslim name in the 1950s.

Abe Kobo: Abe Kimifusa (1924–1993), Jap. novelist.

Rudolf **Abel:** William August Fischer (1903–1971), Eng.-born Russ. spy, of Ger. parentage, working in U.S. The Soviet intelligence officer used various aliases in the course of his work. He lived for some time in New York as an artist and photographer called Emil Robert Goldfus, a name apparently in part based on "Rudolf Abel." Some sources give Abel's birthplace as a town on the Volga and his original name as Alexander Ivanovich Belov. To Gordon

Lonsdale he was known as Alec. The name Abel was also used by other Russian spies.

Johann Philip **Abelin:** Johann Ludwig Gottfried (*c.*1600–1634), Ger. historian.

F. **Abell:** [Rev.] Charles Butler Greatrex (?1832–1898), Eng. humorist. The writer's pseudonym suggests "fable." He also wrote as Lindon Meadows and Abel Log.

Raymond **Abellio:** Georges Soulès (1907–1986), Fr. occultist.

Swami **Abhishiktananda:** Henri Le Saux (1910–1973), Fr. priest. Henri le Saux entered the Benedictine order in 1929 but soon developed a desire to fulfill his monastic vocation in India. In 1948 he joined another French priest already in India, Jules Monchanin, and with him founded an ashram in Tamil Nadu, taking the name Abhishiktananda, "bliss of Christ," from Sanskrit *abhishikt*, "anointed," and *ananda*, "bliss." Monchanin himself took the name **Paramarubyananda.** Swami is a title meaning "master," "prince."

Mr. **Abington:** George Alexander Baird (1861–1893), Eng. racehorse owner, jockey. The horseman raced under this name, of unexplained origin.

Ab Ithel: John Williams (1811–1862), Welsh writer. The writer adopted the Welsh form of the surname of his grandfather, William Bethell, itself literally meaning "son of Ithael."

Ab o' th' Yate: Benjamin Brierley (1825–1896), Eng. dialect writer. Brierley was an English weaver who wrote stories and verse in the Lancashire dialect. His early stories were narrated by a character called "Owd Ab" (Old Abe), and this gave his basic pen name, with "Yate" being a Lancashire form of "gate," meaning "street," as in many street names in northern English towns, such as Briggate ("Bridge Street") in Leeds. He was thus "Abe from the street," a typical old-world townee character.

Abraham: Rachel Cuming (1971–), Br. pop singer, songwriter. "Why she calls herself Abraham when she has a perfectly decent name of her own and isn't even a boy is ... unclear. She apparently likes the fact that it has 'significance across so many religions,' and is finding out more about its significance every day" [*The Times Magazine*, March 23, 2002].

Abraham a Sancta Clara: Johann Ulrich Megerle (1644–1709), Ger. Augustinian friar, preacher. The author of popular devotional works, many of them satirical, took a name meaning literally "Abraham of St. Clare."

Lee **Abrams:** Leon Curtis Abramson (1925–1992), U.S. jazz musician, brother of Ray **Abrams.**

Ray **Abrams:** Raymond Joseph Abramson (1920–1992), U.S. jazz musician.

Victoria **Abril:** Victoria Merida Rojas (1959–), Sp. movie actress.

Blanka **Absolon:** Blanka Ocelikova (1944–), Cz. magician, teaming with Karel **Absolon,** her husband.

Karel **Absolon:** Karel Ocelikov (1940–), Cz. magician, teaming with Blanka **Absolon,** his wife.

Abu: Abu Abraham (1924–2002), Ind.-born Br. political cartoonist. The cartoonist's original name was Abraham Mathew. He took his first name, then created a (literal) pen name from this.

Abu Ali Mustafa: Mustafa az-Zibri (1938–2001), Palestinian nationalist.

Abu Amar *see* Yasir **Arafat**

Abu Bakr Suraj ad-Din: Martin Lings (1909–2005), Br. scholar of Islam. Lings converted to Islam after a visit to Egypt in 1939, and adopted his Arabic name (Abu Bakr, "lamp of religion") as the author of *The Book of Certainty: The Sufi Doctrine of Faith, Wisdom, and Gnosis* (1952). (The original Abu Bakr was the first Muslim caliph, reputedly Muhammad's first male convert and his closest companion.)

Abu Iyad: Salah Khalaf (1933–), Palestinian resistance leader. The revolutionary leader, one of the founders of the PLO, took a *nom de guerre* meaning "father of might."

Abu Izzadeen: Trevor Brooks (1975–), Br. Muslim extremist, of Jamaican parentage. The Muslim convert, whose family emigrated to England in the 1960s, originally called himself Omar Brooks before adopting his Muslim name, "father of Izz-ud-Din," an Arabic name meaning "honor of the religion."

Mumia **Abu-Jamal:** Wesley Cook (1954–), U.S. black radio reporter.

Abu Jihad: Khalil Ibrahim Machmud al-Wazir (1936–1988), Palestinian terrorist. The military commander of the PLO, killed by the Israelis, took a literal *nom de guerre* meaning "father of the holy war" and even named his son Jihad.

Abu Musab al-Zarqawi: Ahmad Faadhil al-Khalailah (1966–2006), Jordanian-born Islamic leader, working in Afghanistan. The leader of Islamic terrorists in Iraq assumed a *nom de guerre* meaning "the imposer from Zarqa," referring to his Jordanian birthplace.

Abu Nidal: Sabri Khalil al-Banna (*c.*1937–2002), Palestinian militant. The terrorist took his *nom de guerre*, meaning "father of contest," in the early 1960s, when a member of the PLO, but broke with that organization in 1974 to set up his own group, the more radical Fatah Revolutionary Council.

Abu Qatada: Omar Mohammad Othman (1960–), Jordanian Muslim cleric. The radical Islamist preacher, based in Britain, adopted an Arabic name meaning "father of the qatada" (a hardwood tree).

Abu Yahya al-Libi: Muhammad Hassan Qa'id

(c.1963–), Libyan Islamic militant leader. The militant preacher adopted his alias, referring to his Libyan origin, on joining al-Qaeda in the 1990s. He was also known by several other names, including Abu Yahya al-Sahrawi ("of the desert").

Acanthus: Harold Frank Hoar (1909–1976), Eng. architect, cartoonist. The acanthus is a prickly plant, and the cartoonist presumably regarded himself as a "barbed" commentator and caricaturist.

Stanley **Accrington:** Michael Bray (1951–), Br. folk musician. The musician took his name from the town of Accrington, Lancashire, the county where he began his career as a railroad stationmaster.

Buddy **Ace:** James Lee Land (1936–1994), U.S. R&B guitarist, singer.

Goodman **Ace:** Goodman Aiskowitz (1899–1982), U.S. radio entertainer, of Latvian origin, teaming with Jane Ace, née Epstein (1905–1974), his wife.

Johnny **Ace:** John Marshall Alexander, Jr. (1929–1954), U.S. black rock musician, songwriter. The musician's name was changed in 1952 by David James Mattis, program director at the Memphis all-black radio station WDIA.

Maurice **Achard:** Marcel-Auguste Ferréol (1899–1974), Fr. playwright, screenwriter.

Chinua **Achebe:** Albert Chinualumogu (1930–), Nigerian novelist, poet, critic. The writer abbreviated his surname to serve as a first name and abandoned his original European Christian name for a new African surname.

Acheta Domestica: [Miss] L.M. Budgen (fl.1850s), Eng. writer on floriculture. The writer used this name for such works as *Episodes of Insect Life* (1840), *March Winds and April Showers* (1854), and *May Flowers* (1855). *Acheta domestica* is the scientific name of the house cricket.

Rodney **Ackland:** Norman Ackland Bernstein (1908–1991), Br. playwright.

John **Ackworth:** [Rev.] Frederick R. Smith (1845–?1919), Eng. writer of dialect tales. The Methodist minister would have deemed it prudent to write fiction under a pseudonym.

Acquanetta: Burnu Acquanetta (1921–2004), U.S. movie actress, of Native American origin. The actress, promoted as "The Venezuelan Volcano" at the start of her career in the 1940s, was adopted as a child by a family who renamed her Mildred Davenport.

Alex **Acuna:** Alejandro Neciosup-Acuna (1944–), Peruvian-born U.S. jazz musician.

Cecil **Adair:** Evelyn Ward Everett-Green (1856–1932), Eng. popular novelist, children's writer. The writer used this name for her 41 adult romances. She also wrote as Evelyn Ward.

James **Adair** *see* Abbé **Bossut**

James Makittrick **Adair:** James Makittrick (1728–1802), Sc. medical writer. Makittrick added the name of Adair around 1783: "It was probably his mother's maiden name, but [English writer Philip] Thicknesse asserted that it was stolen from a physician at Spa" [*Dictionary of National Biography*].

Janice **Adair:** Beatrice Duffy (fl.1930s), Br. movie actress, of Ir. parentage.

Jean **Adair:** Violet McNaughton (1873–1953), Can.-born U.S. stage, movie actress.

[St.] **Adalbert:** Vojtech (956–997), Cz. saint, martyr. The bishop of Prague received his name at his confirmation from St. Adalbert (?–981), archbishop of Magdeburg.

Adam: Adam Sobey (1925–). Br. crossword compiler.

Brother **Adam:** Karl Adam Kehrle (1898–1996), Ger.-born Br. Benedictine monk, beekeeper.

Richard **Adama:** Richard Adams (1928–), U.S. ballet dancer. A typical Italianate adaptation for ballet purposes of a standard English (American) name.

Annette **Adams** *see* Fenton **Brockley**

Casey **Adams:** Max Showalter (1917–2000), U.S. movie actor. The actor subsequently reverted to his real name.

Charles **Adams:** Karl Adam Schwanbeck (1845–1895), Ger.-born U.S. soldier, diplomat. Adams' decision to change his name was influenced by his wife, the change itself being ratified by the Colorado legislature in 1871.

Daniel **Adams** *see* Andrew **York**

Derroll **Adams:** Derroll Lewis Thompson (1925–), U.S. popular singer, songwriter. The musician took his new surname from his mother's third husband, George Adams.

Don **Adams:** Donald James Yarmy (1923–2005), U.S. TV actor, comedian. The actor became tired of being called last at auditions, so replaced his "Y" surname with an "A" one.

Donna **Adams** *see* Donna **Reed**

Edie **Adams:** Elizabeth Edith Enke (1927–2008), U.S. movie actress, singer.

Faye **Adams:** Fayle Tuell (c.1925–?), U.S. black blues singer.

James Fenimore Cooper **Adams:** Edward Sylvester Ellis (1840–1916), U.S. writer. This pen name, of obvious origin, was just one of those used by Ellis for his dime novels, others being Latham C. Carleton, Edwin Emerson, Frank Faulkner, Ned Hunter, and Seelin Robins.

Joey **Adams:** Joseph Abramowitz (1911–), U.S. TV, movie comedian.

Julie **Adams:** Betty May Adams (1926–), U.S. movie actress. Universal Pictures changed the actress's first name to Julia on signing her up in 1950, and five years later she modified this to Julie.

Marie **Adams:** Ollie Marie Givens (1925–*c*.1972), U.S. black popular singer ("TV Mama").

Mary **Adams:** Elizabeth Stuart Phelps (1844–1911), U.S. writer. Phelps used this name for *Confessions of a Wife* (1902), a portrayal of a woman's misery in marriage.

Maud **Adams:** Maud Wikstrom (1945–), Swe.-born movie actress.

Maude **Adams:** Maude Ewing Kiskadden (1872–1953), U.S. stage actress. The actress adopted her mother's maiden name from the start of her career.

Nick **Adams:** Nicholas Adamshock (1931–1968), U.S. movie actor.

Stephen **Adams:** Michael Maybrick (1844–1913), Eng. composer. "Appeared as a baritone vocalist in all the leading London and provincial concerts, and also in English opera, etc., for many years; also became popular as a writer of songs, etc., under the name of Stephen Adams" [*Who's Who*].

Adamski: Adam Tinley (1968–), Br. pop singer.

Joy **Adamson:** Friederike Viktoria Gessner (1910–1980), Austr.-born Br. writer, conservationist. The author of *Born Free* (1960), describing the rearing and rehabilitation of an orphaned lion cub, took her new surname from her third husband, British game warden George Adamson, having assumed her new first name while married to her second, Swiss botanist Peter Bally. (She may have based her new English name on her original German one, altering *Friede*, "peace," to give *Freude*, "joy.")

Lydia **Adamson:** Frank King (1936–), U.S. crime writer.

Franz **Adamus:** Ferdinand Bronner (1867–1948), Ger. dramatist.

Nora **Adamyan:** Eleonora Georgiyevna Adamova (1910–), Russ. writer.

Martin **Adán:** Rafael de la Fuente Benavides (1907–1974), Peruvian writer.

Mozis **Addums:** George William Bagby (1828–1883), U.S. journalist, humorist. Bagby used this frivolous name for letters to the *Southern Literary Messenger* in Richmond, Virginia, the first of which appeared in 1858. They were modeled on the speech of backwoods characters Bagby had known in southside Virginia and were addressed to a friend named "Billy Ivvins" in "Curdsville, Va."

King Sunny **Ade:** Prince Sunday Anthony Ishola Adeniyi (1946–), Nigerian rock musician.

Gaye **Adegbalola:** Gaye Todd (1944–), U.S. black blues musician.

[Count] **Adelaer:** Cort Sivertsen (1622–1675), Norw.-born naval commander. Sivertsen entered the Dutch navy in 1639 as a cadet (*adelborst*). In 1642 he moved into Venetian service and became known as Curzio Suffrido Adelborst. He returned to Holland in 1661 but the following year accepted the command of the Danish navy with the title of Count Adelaer, from the Norwegian word for "eagle." This was originally a nickname, given him for his perspicacity and prowess at sea and punning on his original title.

Adele: Adele Laurie Blue Adkins (1988–), Eng. (white) soul singer.

Max **Adeler:** Charles Heber Clark (1841–1915), U.S. journalist, humorist. The writer first used the name John Quill (punning on the flower) before settling on "Max Adeler," the name of a character in a storybook he had enjoyed as a boy.

Adeline: Emily Frances Adeline Sergeant (1851–1904), Eng. novelist.

Ademir: Ademir Marques de Meneses (1922–), Brazilian footballer.

Adeva: Patricia Daniels (1960–), U.S. black R&B singer.

Kamau Muata **Adilifu:** Charles Sullivan (1944–), U.S. black jazz musician.

Irene **Adler:** Catherine Storr (1913–2001), Br. children's writer, psychiatrist. The author of *Marianne Dreams* (1958) and the Clever Polly series used this name for *Freud for the Jung; or, Three Hundred and Sixty Six Hours on the Couch* (1963), presumably taking it from Irene Adler, the American-born opera singer and adventuress ("*the* woman") in Arthur Conan Doyle's Sherlock Holmes story "A Scandal in Bohemia" (1891).

Adolfo: Adolfo Sardiña (1933–), Cuban fashion designer, working in U.S.

Adonis: Ali Ahmad Said Esber (1930–), Lebanese poet, of Syrian origin.

Joe **Adonis:** Giuseppe Antonio Doto (1902–1971), It.-born U.S. gangster. The organized crime leader adopted the name "Adonis" to reflect his good looks. It also echoes his middle name.

Renée **Adorée:** Jeanne de la Fonté (1898–1933), Fr.-born U.S. movie actress. "Renée" suggests "reborn"; "Adorée" suggests both "adored" and "gilded."

Luisa **Adorno:** Mila Curradi (1921–), It. writer.

Theodor **Adorno:** Theodor Ludwig Wiesengrund (1903–1969), Ger.-born philosopher, sociologist, musicologist, working in U.S. The scholar adopted his mother's maiden name as his professional name when his academic writing began to appear in 1938.

Adri: Adrienne Steckling (*c*.1935–), U.S. fashion designer.

Adrian: Adrian Adolph Greenberg (1903–1959), U.S. movie costume designer. The fashion designer's original name is given in some sources as Gilbert Adrian.

Adrian IV: Nicholas Breakspear (*c*.1100–1159), Eng. pope. All popes of this name are also known as Hadrian.

Adrian V: Ottobono Fieschi (*c*.1205–1276), It. pope. The pope took his name from the church of St. Adrian (S. Adriano), Rome, of which he was appointed cardinal deacon in 1251.

Adrian VI: Adrian Florensz Dedal (1459–1523), Du. pope. The last non–Italian pope before 1978 retained his baptismal name.

Iris **Adrian:** Iris Adrian Hostetter (1913–1994), U.S. movie actress.

Jane **Adrian** *see* Jan **Sterling**

John **Adrian:** John Adrian Marie Edward Warne (1938–), Br. singer, dancer.

L.R. **Adrian** *see* Rhys **Adrian**

Max **Adrian:** Max Bor (1903–1973), Ir.-born Br. stage actor.

Rhys **Adrian:** Rhys Adrian Griffiths (1928–1990), Br. radio, TV dramatist, of Welsh parentage. Early in his career the writer used pseudonyms such as L.A. Reece and L.R. Adrian, explaining that he did not wish to be thought of as "just another Welsh playwright."

Jean **Adrienne:** Jean Armstrong (1905–1994), Eng. stage actress.

Adzhzi: Khodzhi Said-Akhmed-khodzha Siddiki (1865–1926), Tajik poet. The poet adopted a symbolic name meaning "helpless."

Æ: George William Russell (1867–1935), Ir. poet, artist. The name represents the first letter of "Æon," a pseudonym used by Russell for his first poems, and itself meaning "eternity," from the Greek. He is said to have chosen the name for the verses "because they seemed to be of yesterday, to-day and forever, in their motives" [Marble, p.155]. The printer had queried the spelling of the name, however, so Russell opted for the digraph alone. The story goes that when the poet was in New York on a reading tour of America, someone asked, "Why did Mr. Russell call himself 'Æ'?" Murray **Hill**, who was present, promptly replied, "Because he did not wish to be called 'I.O.U.'"

Dom **Aelred:** Benjamin Fearnley Carlyle (1874–1955), Eng. religious. The Anglican founder of the Benedictine community of Prinknash Abbey, Gloucestershire, England, took his religious name on being clothed as a Benedictine oblate in 1893. St. Aelred (Ethelred) was a 12th-century Cistercian abbot.

Franz **Aepinus:** Franz Maria Ulrich Theodor Hoch (1729–1802), Ger. physicist. The scientist adopted a classical rendering of his surname, from Greek *aipeinos*, "high" (German *hoch*).

Johannes **Aepinus:** Johannes Hoeck (1499–1553), Ger. theologian. The ecclesiastic adopted a classical rendering of his surname, from Greek *aipeinos*, "high" (German *hoch*).

Yusus **Afari:** J. Sinclair (*c*.1968–), Jamaican dub poet, reggae musician.

Affable Hawk: [Sir] Desmond MacCarthy (1878–1952), Br. dramatic, literary critic. The Native American–style name was chosen by MacCarthy for his articles in the *New Statesman* to match that of his predecessor, Solomon **Eagle**.

Afrika Bambaataa *see* Afrika **Bambaataa**

Afrique: Alexander Witkins (1907–1961), S.A.–born Br. revue artist. The name of the impersonator of celebrities is French for "Africa."

Afrit: Alistair Ferguson Ritchie (1887–1954), Br. crossword compiler. The name partly derives from the initial elements of his real name, partly represents Afrit, a powerful devil in Muslim mythology. A crossword compiler aims to inspire awe in his hapless solvers.

Afro: Afro Basaldella (1912–1976), It. painter, stage designer, brother of **Mirko**.

Yaacov **Agam:** Jacob Gipstein (1928–), Israeli painter, sculptor, of Russ. parentage, working in France.

Agathon: Henri Massis (1886–1970), Fr. literary journalist. The name, Greek for "good," "virtuous," was used by the writer for early coauthored surveys.

Mojola **Agbebi:** David Brown Vincent (1860–1917), Nigerian church leader. In 1894 the former Anglican minister became a Baptist pastor and adopted his African name.

Age: Agenore Incrocci (1919–), It. movie scriptwriter.

Arthur **Aglionby:** Arthur Cooper (1832–1911), Eng. army officer. In 1871 Arthur Cooper married Elizabeth Aglionby, daughter of Charles Fetherstonhaugh, and assumed her name on her death in 1885.

Madame **Agnès:** ? (*fl*.1940s–50s), Fr. fashion designer.

Luigi **Agnesi:** Louis Ferdinand Léopold Agniez (1833–1875), Belg. opera singer. The bass singer italianized his name to accord with his roles in Italian opera.

Spiro **Agnew:** Spiro Theodore Anagnostopoulos (1918–1996), U.S. politician, of Gk. parentage. A sensible shortening of a typically lengthy Greek surname for the U.S. vice president (1969–73), who later in life preferred to be known as Ted.

Agnihotri: Shiv Narayan (1859–1928), Ind. religious leader. The Hindu founder of the Dev Samaj adopted a name relating to the *agnihotra*, the daily ritual of offering food and drink to Agni, the Hindu god of fire.

Shmuel Yosef **Agnon:** Samuel Josef Czaczkes

(1888–1970), Pol.-born Israeli novelist, short-story writer. The writer adopted a Hebrew name taken from the story that was his literary debut, "Agunot" ("Deserted Wives") (1908). Hebrew *agnon* is the singular of *agunot*, and refers to a Jewish woman who although abandoned by her husband is still legally married to him until he is proven dead or until a divorce is finalized. Czaczkes made the pseudonym his family name in 1924, when it symbolized his abandonment of an Eastern European life in favor of new life in the promised land of Israel.

Orme **Agnus**: John C. Higginbotham (?–1919), Eng. rural writer.

Alexander **Agricola**: Alexander Ackermann (*c.*1446–1506), Du. composer. The musician substituted his agricultural name (literally "acreman," meaning a plowman) for one essentially identical in meaning (Latin *agricola*, "plowman," "farmer") when working in Spain. Compare the names below.

Georgius **Agricola**: Georg Bauer (1494–1555), Ger. scholar, humanist. Latin *agricola* means "plowman," "farmer," to which German *Bauer* ("farmer," "smallholder") corresponds.

Johann **Agricola**: Johann Schneider (or Schnitter) (1494–1566), Ger. Lutheran reformer. Schneider first latinized his name as *Sartor* (German *Schneider*, "tailor"), but then adopted the name Agricola, as for Alexander **Agricola**.

Martin **Agricola**: Martin Sore (or Sohr) (1486–1556), Ger. composer, teacher, writer on music. Sore was self-taught, and was thus called to music "from the plow." Hence his adoption of the name Agricola (Latin, "plowman").

Mikael **Agricola**: Mikael Bauer (1509–1557), Finn. bishop, writer. The scholar's Latin name translates his German surname as for Georgius **Agricola**.

Rodolphus **Agricola**: Roelof Huysman (1443–1485), Du. humanist, musician. The Dutch surname means "man of the house," here interpreted through Latin *agricola*, as for Alexander **Agricola**.

Agrippa: Henricus Cornelius Agrippa von Nettesheim (1486–1535), Ger. occultist

Ahad Ha'am: Asher Hirsch Ginzberg (1856–1927), Russ.-born Jewish writer, philosopher. The Zionist leader adopted a Hebrew name meaning "one of the people" (*ahad*, "one," + *ha*, "the," + *'am*, "people").

Eden **Ahbez**: Robert Botsin (1908–1995), U.S. beatnik songwriter, poet.

Ernst **Ahlgren**: Victoria Maria Benedictsson, née Bruzelius (1850–1888), Swe. writer.

Philip **Ahn**: Pil Lip Ahn (1905–1978), U.S. movie actor, of Korean parentage.

Juhani **Aho**: Johannes Brofeldt (1861–1921), Finn. novelist, short-story writer. The writer's name is a Finnish equivalent of his Swedish name, with Juhani corresponding to Johannes (John) and Finnish *aho*, "clearing," "glade," replacing Brofeldt, literally "broad field."

Ah Wah Cous: Charles Marion Russell (1864–1926), U.S. artist, writer. The artist depicted several scenes from cowboy life, and adopted this pseudonym following his visit to the Blood Indians in 1888: "At the time of Russell's visit ... he was wearing a pair of pants reinforced in the seat with buckskin, a common practice in those days. His appearance from the rear reminded the Indians of the white rump of an antelope and they promptly called Russell 'Ah Wah Cous,' their name for the animal. The artist occasionally signed his letters with his Indian name" [Frederick G. Renner, *Charles Russell*, 1969].

AI: Florence Anthony (1947–), U.S. poet.

Berkley **Aikin**: Fanny Aikin Kortright (1821–1900), U.S.-born Br. novelist, journalist.

Gustave **Aimard**: Olivier Gloux (1818–1883), Fr.-born U.S. adventure novelist.

Anouk **Aimée**: Françoise Sorya Dreyfus (1932–), Fr. movie actress. The actress named herself after a servant girl that she played in her first movie, *La Maison sous la mer* (1947), in which she was billed as simply Anouk. She began to appear under her full name in the mid–1950s.

Arthur **Ainslie**: Arthur Wellesley Odell Pain (1871–1940), Br.-born magician. The conjuror, specializing in magic for children, also performed as F.M. Archer.

Herbert **Ainslie**: Edward Maitland (1824–1897), Eng. writer of mystical novels. Maitland used this name for an autobiographical novel, *The Pilgrim and the Shrine: Passages from the Life and Correspondence of Herbert Ainslie, B.A., Cantab.* (1867). The academic title referred to his attendance of Cambridge University, from where he graduated B.A. in 1847.

Patricia **Ainsworth**: Patricia Nina Bigg (1932–), Austral. writer.

Ruth **Ainsworth**: Ruth Gilbert (1908–), Br. children's writer.

Catherine **Aird**: Kinn Hamilton McIntosh (1930–), Eng. mystery writer.

Catherine **Airlie**: Jean Sutherland MacLeod (1908–), Sc. writer.

Harriot **Airy**: Mary Darwall, née Whately (1738–1825), Eng. poet.

Aisha: Pamela Ross (*c.*1967–), Br. black reggae singer. The singer, also known as "Sister Aisha," assumed an Arabic name meaning "living," "flourishing."

Jonas **Aistis**: Jonas Aleksandravicius (1904–1973), Lithuanian poet.

Émile **Ajar** *see* Roman **Gary**

Ajit: Hamid Ali Khan (1922–1998), Ind. movie actor.

Aka Gündüz: Enis Avni (1885–1958), Turk. writer. Turkish *gündüz* means "daytime," presumably here in some significant sense.

Martin Akakia: Martin Sans-Malice (1539–1588), Fr. medical writer. The writer changed his French name, meaning "without guile," to its Greek equivalent (*akakia*, "guilelessness," from *a-*, "not," and *kakos*, "bad"). **Voltaire** wrote a prose satire entitled *Diatribe du docteur Akakia, médecin du pape* ("Diatribe of Dr. Akakia, Doctor to the Pope") (1752), in which he ridiculed the views of the mathematician Pierre-Louis Moreau de Maupertuis (1698–1759), president of the Berlin Academy.

Akebono: Chadwick Haheo Rowan (1969–), Hawaiian-born Jap. sumo wrestler. The Japanese name means "the dim light of the morning."

Alan Burt **Akers:** Henry Kenneth Bulmer (1921–2005), Eng. SF writer. Bulmer also wrote as Dray Prescot.

Floyd **Akers:** Lyman Frank Baum (1856–1919), U.S. novelist, children's writer. Other names used by the author of the *The Wonderful Wizard of Oz* (1900) were Laura Bancroft, John Estes Cooke, Hugh Fitzgerald, Suzanne Metcalf, Schuyler Staunton (for adult novels), and Edith Van Dyne (stories for girls). At one time Baum was on the stage as George Brooks.

Akhenaten: Amenhotep IV (*fl.*14th century BC), Egyptian pharaoh. The "heretic" king was the son of Amenhotep III and originally bore the same name as his father, meaning "Amun is content," from *amen*, "Amun," and *hotep*, "to be satisfied." In his fifth regnal year he changed his name to Akhenaten, "glory of Aten," from *akhen*, "to derive pleasure," and *aten*, "Aten," and began to build a new capital city called Akhetaten, "horizon of Aten." Worship of the sun god Aten (a name meaning literally "sun disk") was subsequently disavowed by his son-in-law, **Tutankhamun**, who reintroduced the worship of Amun, the ram-headed god (more commonly known as Ammon) identified by the Greeks with Zeus.

Anna **Akhmatova:** Anna Andreyevna Gorenko (1889–1966), Russ. poet. When Anna Gorenko was 17, and an aspiring poet, her father objected to her writings, calling her a "decadent poetess," and saying she would shame the family name. Anna retorted, "I don't need that name," and instead chose a Tatar name, that of her great-grandmother. The southern Tatars had always seemed mysterious and fascinating to the young woman who came to be one of Russia's greatest modern poets [Amanda Haight, *Anna Akhmatova: A Poetic Pilgrimage*, 1976].

Akinoshima: Yamanaka Katsumi (1967–), Jap. sumo wrestler.

Pheeroan **Aklaff:** Paul Maddox (1955–), U.S. jazz drummer.

Boris **Akunin:** Grigory Shalvovich Chkhartishvili (1956–), Georgian-born Russ. writer of detective fiction. The author, a philologist and Japanese translator, adopted a name that not only evoked the Russian anarchist Mikhail Bakunin (1814–1876) but could be read as Japanese *akunin*, "villain."

Alachini: Bronislaw Szymanski (1895–1970), Pol. magician.

Johnny **Aladdin:** John ("Jack") Randall (1919–), U.S. illusionist, hypnotist, teaming with **Taki**, his first wife.

Alafon: Owen Griffith Owen (1847–1916), Welsh poet. The name is a local placename.

Alaïa: Azzedine Alaïa (*c.*1935–), Tunisian fashion designer, working in France.

Alain: Émile-Auguste Chartier (1868–1952), Fr. philosopher, essayist. The writer took his pseudonym from his medieval namesake, the poet Alain Chartier (*c.*1385–*c.*1430).

Alain-Fournier: Henri Alban Fournier (1886–1914), Fr. novelist. The novelist took his new name in order to be distinguished either from his fellow writer Édouard Fournier (1819–1880) or, according to some, from two contemporary Frenchmen named Henri Fournier, one an admiral, the other a cycling champion. He first used the name in 1907.

Jamil Abdullah **al-Amin:** H. Rap Brown (1943–), U.S. black activist. The political activist and writer converted to the Islamic faith following his imprisonment in 1974 and adopted a Muslim name accordingly. Of the three Arabic names, Jamil means "handsome," Abdullah means "servant of Allah," and al-Amin, the name of a 9th-century Abbasid caliph, means "the faithful."

Susan **Alamo:** Edith Opal Horn (1925–1982), U.S. TV, radio evangelist. The Pentecostal minister, a convert from Judaism, took her new name from street evangelist Tony Alamo (Bernie Lazar Hoffman), whom she married as her third husband in 1966.

A.J. **Alan:** Leslie Harrison Lambert (1883–1941), Br. broadcaster, storyteller.

Alan **Alan:** Alan Rabinowitz (1926–), Br.-born magician.

Don **Alan:** Donald Alan McWethy (1926–1999), U.S. magician, writer.

Jane **Alan:** Lillian Mary Chisholm (1906–?), Eng. short-story writer. The author also wrote as Anne Lorraine.

Alastair: Hans Henning Voigt (1887–1969), Ger.-born Br. writer, illustrator, dancer. Voigt claimed to be the illegitimate offspring of a Bavarian prince and an Irish girl, but such an origin is as suspect as his assumed title of "Baron."

Vagram **Alazan:** Vagram Martirosovich Gabuzyan (1903–1966), Armenian writer.

Alazonomastix Philalethes: [Dr.] Henry More (1614–1687), Eng. philosopher. More used this mock–Greek name, meaning "impostor Philalethes," for an attack on the alchemical work *Anthroposophia Theomagica* by **Eugenius Philalethes.**

Maria **Alba:** Maria Casajuana (1905–1999), Sp. stage, movie actress, dancer.

Antony **Alban:** Antony Allert Thomson (1939–), Br. writer.

[Dame] Emma **Albani:** Marie Louise Cécile Emma Lajeunesse (1847–1930), Can. opera singer. Mme. Albani, as she was generally known, is said to have taken her professional name from Albany, New York, where she moved with her parents in 1865. But according to another theory, she assumed it on making her debut as Amina in Bellini's opera *La Sonnambula* in Messina, Sicily, in 1870, when "on the advice of her Italian elocution master, Delorenzi, she adopted the name of 'Albani,' the patronymic of an old Italian noble family, practically extinct" [*Dictionary of National Biography*].

James **Albany** *see* Robert **Crawford**

Joe **Albany:** Joseph Albani (1924–1988), U.S. jazz pianist.

Father **Alberik:** Joseph Zwyssig (1808–1854), Swiss priest, organist, composer.

Albert: Albert Rusling (1944–), Eng. cartoonist.

Don **Albert:** Albert Dominique (1908–1980), U.S. jazz trumpeter.

Eddie **Albert:** Edward Albert Heimberger (1906–2005), U.S. stage, movie, TV actor. The actor is said to have adopted the name because he grew tired of announcers referring to him as "Eddie Hamburger."

Konrad **Alberti:** Konrad Sittenfeld (1862–1918), Ger. writer

Sister **Albertina:** Ellen Albertina Pollyblank (1840–1930), Eng.-born U.S. Anglican sister, educator, working in Hawaii.

Albert L'Ouvrier: Alexandre Martin (1815–1895), Fr. mechanic. The socialist leader adopted this name, meaning "Albert the worker," when he was elected to the provisional French government in 1848.

Al Berto: Alberto Pidwell Tavares (1948–1997), Port. poet.

Henricus **Albicastro:** Heinrich Weissenburg del Biswang (*c.*1680–*c.*1738), Swiss composer. The musician italianized his German name to give a Latin equivalent (German *weiss*, Latin *albus*, "white"; German *Burg*, Latin *castrum*, "castle").

Herbert **Albini:** Abraham Laski (1860–1922), Pol.-born magician.

Albius *see* Thomas **Blacklow**

Marietta **Alboni:** Maria Anna Marzia (1823–1894), It. opera singer.

Martha **Albrand:** Heidi Huberta Freybe Loewengard (1914–1981), Ger.-born U.S. spy novelist. The writer's new surname is that of her great-grandfather.

Bernard **Albrecht** *see* Barney **Sumner**

Hardie **Albright:** Hardy Albrecht (1903–1975), U.S. movie actor, of Sc. Jewish parentage.

William Foxwell **Albright:** William Thomas Albright (1891–1971), U.S. biblical archaeologist. Albright changed his middle name to his mother's maiden name when studying at Johns Hopkins University, Baltimore, in the 1910s.

Dennis **Alcapone:** Dennis Smith (1947–), Jamaican DJ, popular musician. The name seems to commemorate the U.S. gangster Al Capone, since the singer was born in the year of the latter's death. But Alcapone himself has a more subtle explanation: "It all started the night I went to the movies at Majesty Theatre and I was laughing. And the guy say to me: 'Look how him going like a pocony.' Whatever pocony is, I don't know. Then someone change it to Me Capone and then Macaroni until someone just start calling me Capone. Then I pick up Alcapone from that. And it just stick" [Chris Salewicz and Adrian Boot, *Reggae Explosion: The Story of Jamaican Music*, 2001].

Alceste: (1) Louis Belmontet (1799–1879), Fr. writer; (2) Edouard Laboulaye (1811–1883), Fr. writer; (3) Alfred Assolant (1827–1886), Fr. writer; (4) Hippolyte de Castille (*fl.*1840s), Fr. writer. Doubtless one or more of these derive from the character of this name in Molière's *Le Misanthrope*, the misanthropic hero who scorns the civilities of life and the shams of society.

Alcibiades: (1) Albert, Margrave of Brandenburg (1522–1557), Ger. prince; (2) George Villiers, Duke of Buckingham (1627–1688), Eng. courtier; (3) Alfred, Lord Tennyson (1809–1892), Eng. poet. Tennyson used this name for *Literary Squabbles*, published in the February and March, 1846, numbers of *Punch*. The original Alcibiades was a 5th-century BC Athenian general.

Alcipe: Leonor de Almeida de Portugal, Marquesa de Alorna (1750–1839), Port. poet. The poet's classical-style name was suggested to her by Filinto **Elísio.**

Bronson **Alcott:** Amos Bronson Alcox (1799–1888), U.S. educator, mystic. The father of Louisa May Alcott (1832–1888), author of the bestselling novel *Little Women* (1868), changed the family name from Alcox to Alcott because of the original name's indecent associations, especially in spoken form.

Alan **Alda**: Alphonso d'Abruzzo (1936–), U.S. stage actor. The actor created his new surname from the first syllables of his two original names, as did his father, Robert **Alda**.

Frances **Alda**: Frances Jeanne Adler, née Davies (1883–1952), N.Z.–born U.S. opera singer.

Robert **Alda**: Alphonso Giuseppe Giovanni Roberto d'Abruzzo (1914–1986), U.S. movie actor, of It. parentage, father of Alan **Alda**. The actor created his new surname from the first two letters of his first name (Alphonso) and last name (d'Abruzzo).

M.A. **Aldanov**: Mark Aleksandrovich Landau (1889–1957), Russ. writer. A name that is a near anagram of the writer's surname, while also containing letters in his patronymic (middle name).

Jean François **Alden** see Mark **Twain**
Richard **Alden** see Tom **Drake**
Peter **Alding** see Roderic **Graeme**

Richard **Aldington**: Edward Godfree Aldington (1892–1962), Eng. poet, novelist, husband of **H.D.** The writer adopted his new first name as a boy.

Aldini: Alex Weiner (1917–1989), U.S. magician, writer.

G.R. **Aldo**: Aldo Rossano Graziati (1902–1953), It. cinematographer.

Adair **Aldon**: Cornelia Lynde Meigs (1884–1973), U.S. novelist, children's writer. The author used the name for her earlier stories. Asked if it was some sort of pun, she replied: "I have no very subtle explanation to give. I used it for my first story of adventure for boys as I wished to keep that kind of tale separate from the historical stories I was writing at that time. The name Adair was current — not precisely in my own family, but in one with which I have close connection. As it would apply either to a man or a woman I thought it useful for my purposes and took the name Aldon to go with it, as I liked alliterative names. On the strength of the masculinity a boy's [sic] camp wrote to me and asked me to spend the summer with them as they liked one of Adair Aldon's books so much. I never felt sufficient courage to disillusion them in the matter, so I had to reply that circumstances over which I had no control prevented my visiting them" [Marble, p.181].

Louis **Aldrich**: Louis Lyon (1843–1901), U.S. actor. The actor adopted his new name in 1858 on joining the Robert G. Marsh troupe of juvenile players.

Alec: Alec E. Wiles (1924–), Eng. cartoonist, illustrator.

O **Aleijadinho**: Antônio Francisco Lisbôa da Costa (c.1738–1814), Brazilian sculptor, architect. The artist was born deformed, and his name is Portuguese for "the little cripple."

Aleksandr **Aleksandrov**: (1) Aleksandr Artemyevich Martirosyants (1891–1955), Russ. ballet dancer; (2) Aleksandr Nikolayevich Fedotov (1903–1971), Russ. circus performer.

Grigory **Aleksandrov**: Grigory Vasilyevich Mormonenko (1903–1983), Russ. movie director.

Vladimir **Aleksandrov**: Vladimir Borisovich Keller (1898–1954), Russ. literary critic.

Aleksandra **Aleksandrova-Kochetova**: Aleksandra Dormidontovna Kochetova, née Sokolova (1833–1902), Russ. opera singer, musicologist. When actually performing, the singer used the name Aleksandra Aleksandrova, basing the surname on her own first name.

Aleksey I: Sergey Vladimirovich Simansky (1877–1970), Russ. churchman. The head of the Russian Orthodox Church assumed his name on taking monastic vows in 1902.

Aleksey II: Aleksey Mikhaylovich Ridiger (1929–2008), Estonian-born Russ. churchman. The head of the Russian Orthodox Church, elected in 1990, retained his original name, unlike **Aleksey I**.

Aleksandr **Aleksidze**: Aleksandr Georgievich Songulashvili (1874–1934), Georgian ballet dancer.

Jean le Rond d'**Alembert**: Jean-le-Rond Destouches (1717–1783), Fr. mathematician. Destouches was the illegitimate son of the hostess Mme. de Tencin and one of her lovers, the chevalier Destouches. As a baby, he was abandoned on the steps of the Paris church of Saint-Jean-le-Rond, and this gave his first name. However, he was enrolled in school as Jean-Baptiste Daremberg, and the latter name was altered for reasons of euphony to give "d'Alembert."

Sibilla **Aleramo**: Rina Pierangeli Faccio (1876–1960), It. feminist writer. The writer's pseudonym was suggested by her lover, Giovanni Cena.

Tony **Aless**: Anthony Alessandrin (1921–1985), U.S. jazz pianist.

Alexander: Calude Alexander Conlin (1880–1954), U.S. magician, "mentalist."

Alexander II: Anselm (?–1073), It. pope.

Alexander III: Orlando Bandinelli (c.1105–1181), It. pope.

Alexander IV: Rinaldo dei Segni (c.1199–1261), It. pope.

Alexander V: Pietro di Candia (originally Petros Philargos) (c.1339–1410), It. antipope.

Alexander VI: Rodrigo de Borja y Borja (or Rodrigo Borgia) (1431–1503), Sp.-born It. pope. The pope took his new name in honor of Alexander the Great, king of Macedonia, whose conquering prowess he admired. "An odd hero for a pope to have, to be sure, but not inappropriate, as the new pontiff's subsequent career would show" [Coulombe, p.239].

Alexander VII: Fabio Chigi (1599–1667), It. pope.

Alexander VIII: Pietro Vito Ottoboni (1610–1691), It. pope.

Ben **Alexander:** Nicholas Benton Alexander (1911–1969), U.S. movie actor.

Bill **Alexander:** William Alexander Paterson (1948–), Eng. theatrical director.

Dair **Alexander:** Christine Campbell Thomson (1897–1985), Br. author. Other names used by the writer were Molly Campbell, Christine Hartley, and Flavia Richardson.

[Sir] George **Alexander:** George Alexander Gibb Samson (1858–1918), Br. stage actor, theater manager.

Henry **Alexander:** Alexander McAllister (1877–1944), Ir. playwright, novelist.

Jane **Alexander:** Jane Quigley (1939–), U.S. movie, TV actress.

Jason **Alexander:** Jay Scott Greenspan (1959–), U.S. movie actor.

Joan **Alexander:** Joan Pepper (1920–), Br. author.

John **Alexander:** John Taylor (1580–1653), Eng. poet ("The Water Poet"). Taylor used the name *John Alexander, a Joyner* for *Love One Another; A Tub Lecture preached at Watford in Hartfordshire at a Conventicle on the 25th of December last* (1642).

Maev **Alexander:** Maev Alexandra Reid McConnell (1948–), Sc. TV actress.

Mrs. **Alexander:** Annie Hector, née French (1825–1902), Ir.-born Br. popular novelist. The author took her name from that of her husband, Alexander Hector, a wealthy merchant who disapproved of her writing. She adopted the name only after his death in 1875.

Shana **Alexander:** Shana Ager (1925–2005), U.S. journalist, writer.

Alexander the Corrector: Alexander Cruden (1701–1770), Sc. bookseller. The author of the famous *Concordance to the Holy Scriptures* (1737) so called himself. "There was a double meaning in this designation, with which he seems to have been greatly pleased; for it might be interpreted, either as referring to his old occupation as a [proof] corrector of the Press, or to the new office which he supposed himself to sustain, as corrector of the manners and morals of the People. Of this ambiguity he availed himself with much adroitness, as circumstances seemed to dictate" [Rev. Jabez Bunting, "Memoir of Mr. Alexander Cruden," prefaced to 7th edition of the *Concordance*, 1815].

Alexandre de Paris: Louis Alexandre Raimon (1922–2008), Fr. hair stylist.

Lorez **Alexandria:** Dolorez Alexandria Nelson, née Turner (1929–), U.S. black jazz singer.

Willibald **Alexis:** Georg Wilhelm Heinrich Häring (1798–1871), Ger. writer, critic. The writer first used this name for his novel *Cabanis* (1832).

Alfonsina: Alfonsina Storni (1892–1938), Argentinian poet, playwright.

Kenneth J. **Alford:** [Major] Frederick Joseph Ricketts (1881–1945), Br. composer, bandmaster. The composer of the march "Colonel Bogey" (1914), familiar from the movie *The Bridge on the River Kwai* (1957), adopted his mother's maiden name. He used the name W.V. Richards for the march "Namur."

Michael **Alford:** Michael Griffiths (1587–1652), Eng. Jesuit, church historian.

Alfred: Frances McCollin (1892–1960), U.S. organist, pianist, composer. The musician was as prolific in her choice of pseudonyms as in her compositions. Others include Atticus, Awbury, Canonicus, Garrett, Karlton, Mayfair, Pastor, Pilgrim, Selin, Wendel, and Wheelwright.

Harcourt **Algeranoff:** Harcourt Algernon Essex (1903–1967), Br. ballet dancer, working in Australia, husband of Claudie **Algeranova**. The dancer assumed his Russian-style name, based on his middle name, on joining Anna Pavlova's company in 1921.

Claudie **Algeranova:** Claudie Leonard (1924–), Fr.-born Br. ballet dancer. The dancer took her name from that of her husband, Harcourt **Algeranoff**.

Nelson **Algren:** Nelson Ahlgren Abraham (1909–1981), U.S. writer.

Father **Algy:** William Strowan Amherst Robertson (1894–1955), Eng. religious. The head of the Anglican Society of St. Francis was for some reason nicknamed "Algy" when a Cambridge university student and kept the name in religion.

Muhammad **Ali:** Cassius Marcellus Clay, Jr. (1942–), U.S. black boxer. The boxer adopted his new name in 1964 on joining the Black Muslim movement after becoming the new world heavyweight champion as a result of his contest against Sonny Liston. The name was given him by Elijah **Muhammad**, leader of the Black Muslims in the U.S. "Changing my name was one of the most important things that happened to me in my life. It freed me from the identity given to my family by slavemasters. If Hitler changed the names of people he was killing, and instead of killing them made them slaves, after the war those people would have changed their slave names. That's all I was doing. People change their names all the time, and no one complains. Actors and actresses change their names. The pope changes his name. Joe **Louis** and Sugar Ray **Robinson** changed their names. If I changed my name from Cassius Clay to something like Smith or Jones because I wanted a name that white people thought was more American, nobody would have complained. I was honored that

Elijah Muhammad gave me a truly beautiful name. 'Muhammad' means one worthy of praise. 'Ali' was the name of a great general [a cousin of the Prophet Muhammad, and the third Caliphate after the death of the Prophet]. I've been Muhammad Ali for twenty-six years. That's four years longer than I was Cassius Clay" [Thomas Hauser with the co-operation of Muhammad Ali, *Muhammad Ali: His Life and Times*, 1997].

Noble Drew **Ali:** Timothy Drew (1886–1929), U.S. black religious leader. The names of Ali's parents are unknown, but he grew up with the name Timothy Drew. He regarded himself as a prophet of Allah and claimed that he was named "Ali" during a visit to the holy Muslim city of Mecca.

Rashied **Ali:** Robert Patterson (1933–2009), U.S. black jazz drummer. When the musician's father changed his name to Rashied Ali, Robert Patterson, Jr., followed suit.

Ali Bey: David Charles Lemmy (1905–1975), Br. magician. The name has a generally oriental flavor.

Ali Bongo: William Wallace (1929–2009), Eng. TV magician. The magician took his quasi–Arabian stage name from a character he played in a national youth club pantomime as a teenager.

Cousin **Alice:** Emily Bradley Neal Haven (1827–1863), U.S. writer, editor. In the early 1840s Emily Bradley sent a story she had written to *Neal's Saturday Gazette* under the pseudonym Alice Gordon Lee. The editor, Joseph C. Neal, accepted it, and in correspondence with the author told her how much he liked the name Alice Gordon Lee because it sounded Scottish and his mother was a Scot. On learning her real name from a subscriber, Neal asked if he might continue to call her "Alice." The correspondence led to marriage in 1846, after which Emily Neal wrote for children as "Cousin Alice." Neal, who was more than twice Emily's age, died suddenly in 1847, and in 1853 she married Samuel H. Haven.

Alidad: Alidad Mahloudji (1954–), Iranian-born Br. interior designer.

Alien: Louisa Alice Baker, née Dawson (1858–?1903), N.Z. novelist, working in U.K. The writer used this name for serials written in Britain but set in New Zealand, presumably inspired by the example of Ralph **Iron**.

Abdulla **Alish:** Abdulla Bariyevich Alishev (1908–1944), Russ. (Tatar) writer.

May **Alix** *see* Josephine **Beatty**

Ibrahim **al-Jaafari:** Ibrahim al-Ashaiqir (1947–), Iraqi politician. The former physician was the leader of the Islamic Da'wah Party, an underground movement opposed to the regime of Saddam Hussein. When Saddam decreed that membership of the party was punishable by death, Jaafari fled to Iran, where the fear of retaliation against his family in Iraq forced him to change his name. Following Saddam's overthrow in 2003, Jaafari returned to Iraq and was elected prime minister two years later.

Alkan: Charles-Henri-Valentin Morhange (1813–1888), Fr. pianist, composer, of Jewish parentage. The composer adopted the first name of his father, as did his six siblings, all also musicians.

Santeri **Alkio:** Santeri Filander (1862–1930), Finn. writer, politician.

Allan: Albin Neumann (1909–?), Austr. magician, writer on gambling fraud.

Elkan **Allan:** Elkan Philip Cohen (1922–2006), Br. TV producer, journalist. The broadcaster's father, Allan Cohen, adopted his first name as the family name in place of his Jewish surname in the 1930s.

George **Allan:** Mite (or Marie) Kremnitz, née Marie von Bardeleben (1852–1916), Ger. writer.

Johnnie **Allan:** John Allan Guillot (1938–), U.S. pop musician.

Maud **Allan:** Ula Maude Durrant (1873–1956), Can.-born U.S. ballet dancer, choreographer. The dancer adopted her father's middle name as her stage name.

Sidney **Allan:** Carl Sadakichi Altmann (1867–1944), Jap.-born U.S. art critic, writer.

Paula **Allardyce:** Ursula Torday (*fl.*1960s), Eng. crime, mystery writer. Other names used by the author were Charity Blackstock, Lee Blackstock, and Charlotte Keppel.

Henri **Alleg:** Henri Jean Salem (1921–), Algerian writer, working in France.

Chesney **Allen:** William Ernest Chesney Allen (1896–1982), Br. music-hall comedian, teaming with Bud **Flanagan**.

Corey **Allen:** Alan Cohen (1934–), U.S. movie actor, director.

Dave **Allen:** David Tynan O'Mahony (1936–2005), Ir. TV comedian. When the comic began his career and was eager for engagements, he was told he would have to change his name, as not many English people would know how to pronounce "O'Mahony." He came to the same conclusion. "I tried 'Dave O'Mahony,' and I'd arrive at places and it would be spelt [on the playbills] 'Dave O'Mally' or 'Dave Maloney' or 'O'Maloney.' So I thought, well, 'Tynan' is simple enough, so I tried 'Tynan,' but 'Tynan,' for whatever reason, became 'Tyrone' and 'Tannen' and 'Tinnen,' and so I never knew who the bloody hell I was! By then I had an agent, Richard Stone, and I was sitting looking at his list of clients, and there was nobody with an 'A,' so I thought, well, if I had a surname beginning with 'A' I'd be top of the list. So I changed my name to Allen" [Dave Allen, interviewed by Paul Jackson, *Talking Comedy*, BBC Radio 4, April 6, 2000, quoted in Graham McCann, ed., *The Essential Dave Allen*, 2005].

(Major) E.J. **Allen:** Allan Pinkerton (1819–1884), Sc.-born U.S. detective.

Elizabeth **Allen:** Elizabeth Allen Gillease (1934–), U.S. stage, movie actress.

Eric **Allen:** Eric Allen Ballard (1908–1968), Eng. children's writer. The author also wrote as Paul Dallas and Edwin Harrison.

F.M. **Allen:** Edmund Downey (1856–1937), Ir. publisher, novelist. The writer adopted his wife's maiden name as his pen name. He used the name Dan Banim for comic histories told in Irish English.

Fred **Allen:** John Florence Sullivan (1894–1956), U.S. radio comedian, movie actor. Sullivan was at first a juggler, billed as Freddy James. He became Fred Allen in 1918 after tiring of telling people that he was not a member of the Jesse James Gang. His new name, he said, was a tribute "to [frontiersman] Ethan Allen who had stopped using the name after the revolution." The name was actually created for him by a William Fox Agency booking agent, Edgar Allen, who wanted to conceal from the Keith-Albee vaudeville booking office that Allen was performing in a competing New York theater.

Gene **Allen:** Eugene Sufana (1928–), U.S. jazz musician.

Jay Presson **Allen:** Jacqueline Presson (1922–), U.S. screenwriter. Presson married British-born movie director Lewis Allen (1905–2000).

Macon Bolling **Allen:** A. Macon Bolling (1816–1894), U.S. lawyer, judge. The lawyer's birth name is given in some sources as Malcolm B. Allen. He changed his name to Macon Bolling Allen by act of the Massachusetts legislature in 1844.

Mel **Allen:** Melvin Allen Israel (1913–1996), U.S. sports broadcaster.

Peter **Allen:** Peter Allen Woolnough (1942–1992), Austral. popular singer, songwriter.

Phog **Allen:** Forrest Clare Allen (1885–1974), U.S. basketball coach. Allen adopted his nickname, given him by sportswriters for his "foghorn" voice, which he used during games.

Robert **Allen:** Irving Theodore Baehr (1906–1998), U.S. movie actor.

Roland **Allen:** Alan Ayckbourn (1939–), Br. playwright. The dramatist used this name, partly from his own first name, partly from his wife's maiden name (Roland), for his first three plays, but thereafter wrote under his real name.

Rosalie **Allen:** Julie Marlene Bedra (1924–), U.S. country singer, of Pol. descent.

Sarah A. **Allen:** Pauline E. Hopkins (1859–

1930), U.S. black editor, novelist. The writer often published under her mother's name.

Terry **Allen:** Edward Albert Govier (1924–1987), Br. boxer. Govier gave two accounts of his new name. "Mate of mine called Terry Allen got killed, so I took his name for boxing. Sort of keeps it goin,' like," was his original version. Later, however, he recalled how, when on the run from the Navy, he stole the identity card of an Islington, London, newspaper boy called Terry Allen. His birth date, which many of the record books have accepted as Govier's own, was August 11, 1925 [*The Times*, April 9, 1987].

Tim **Allen:** Timothy Allen Dick (1953–), U.S. comic movie actor.

William **Allen:** Edward Sexby (?–1658), Eng. soldier. Sexby used this name for his pamphlet *Killing No Murder* (1657), advocating the assassination of Oliver Cromwell (to whom the work was ironically dedicated). The assumed name was that of a member of Cromwell's cavalry.

Woody **Allen:** Allen Stewart Konigsberg (1935–), U.S. stage, TV, movie actor, director. In 1952, when he had started sending jokes to New York newspapers, the future actor decided to become a comedy writer under a new name. But what? "He liked Allan and thought the more commonly spelled Allen made a good last name. But what of a first one? He thought of Max, after the writer Max Shulman.... He thought of Mel, but Mel **Allen** was the broadcaster for the New York Yankees. Eventually he thought of Woody and settled on it because it had, he says, 'a slightly comic appropriateness and is not completely off the tracks.' Contrary to the popular belief that his choice was an *hommage* to one musician or another, it was, he insists, purely arbitrary and wholly unrelated to Woody **Herman**, Woody Guthrie, Woody Woodpecker, or even Woodrow Wilson" [Eric Lax, *Woody Allen*, 1991].

Frank **Allenby:** Francis Gatehouse (1898–?), Austral.-born Br. stage actor. The actor adopted his mother's maiden name as his stage name.

G. **Allenby** *see* Ann **Bridge**

Alfred **Allendale:** Theodore Edward Hook (1788–1841), Eng. novelist, humorist. For *Tentamen* (1820) (its title from a Latin word meaning "trial") Hook wrote as Vicesimus Blinkingsop, LL.D., while for *Exchange no Robbery* (1820) he was Richard Jones. He also wrote as Mrs. Ramsbottom and simply T.E.H. "The clever farce 'Exchange no Robbery' [was] so unluckily suggestive in title that that it had to be brought out under the pseudonym of 'Richard Jones'" [*Dictionary of National Biography*].

Bert **Allerton:** Albert Allen Gustafson (1889–1958), U.S. magician.

Mary **Allerton:** Mary Christine Govan (1897–

?), U.S. novelist. The writer also used the name J.N. Darby.

Ellen **Alleyn:** Christina Georgina Rossetti (1830–1894), Eng. poet, of It. parentage. The sister of Dante Gabriel **Rossetti** first used this name for seven poems appearing in the Pre-Raphaelite journal *The Germ* in 1850.

Clay **Allison** *see* Wes **Hardin**

Peter **Allison** *see* J.P. **McCall**

Sister **Allison:** Allison Colleen Mason (1969–), Br. black radio DJ, popular singer.

Claud **Allister:** William Claud Michael Palmer (1891–1970), Eng. stage, movie actor.

Mary **Allitsen:** Mary Frances Bumpus (1849–1912), Eng. songwriter.

Alli-Vad: Aleksandr Alekseyevich Vadimov-Markelov (1895–1967), Russ. circus artist, conjuror.

Alltud Eifion: Robert Isaac Jones (1815–1905), Welsh poet, editor. The writer's name means "Alltud of Eifionydd," this being a historic district of northwest Wales, the homeland of many poets.

David **Allyn:** Albert DiLello (1923–), U.S. popular singer.

June **Allyson:** Eleanor Geisman (1917–2006), U.S. dancer, singer, movie actress. The actress's new surname derived from the pet form of her first name.

Alma: Charlotte Mary Yonge (1823–1901), Eng. novelist, writer. In her own *History of Christian Names* (1863), Yonge interprets the name Alma as meaning either "fair" or "all good," and perhaps she intended this sense for herself. But she also rightly relates the name to the Battle of Alma (1854), the first of the Crimean War, and possibly she adopted the pen name at about this time for her early writing.

E.M. **Almedingen:** Martha Edith von Almedingen (1898–1971), Russ.-born Eng. novelist, poet, biographer. The initials are those of the writer's two first names, reversed.

John **Almeida:** John Meade (1572–1653), Eng. Jesuit missionary, working in Brazil.

A.L.O.E.: Charlotte Maria Tucker (1821–1893), Br. children's writer, missionary. The initials were intended to stand for "A Lady of England," and the suggestion of "aloe" (the plant, with its bitter drug) appears to be merely coincidental. "This Aloe is not at all in keeping with her cognomen, for she has produced upwards of fifty pieces ... under the above initials, and we commend them to the reader as of exceeding beauty" [Hamst, p.11].

Alicia **Alonso:** Alicia Ernestina de la Caridad del Cobre Martínez del Oyo (1921–), Cuban ballet dancer. The dancer took her surname from her first husband, Fernando Alonso, also a dancer.

V. **Alov:** Nikolay Vasilyevich Gogol (1809–1852), Russ. novelist, playwright. Gogol used the name, apparently formed from letters in his full name, for his early poem of German idyllic life, *Hanz Küchelgarten* (1828), published at his own expense. When it was derided by the critics, he bought up all the copies and destroyed them. At least he had preserved his true identity.

Wanda **Alpar:** Rosalind Isabel Appleton-Collins (1927–2009), Eng. vaudeville dancer. The dancer adopted her stage name when training with the Polski Ballet of Poland.

Alpha: James Fitton (1899–1982), Eng. painter, illustrator, cartoonist.

Alpha of the Plough: Alfred George Gardiner (1865–1946), Br. essayist. The pen name is primarily of astronomical origin, referring to the brightest star (Alpha Ursae Majoris) in the Plough (Big Dipper), the formation in the constellation of Ursa Major (Great Bear). But there are certain other links, which may or may not have been intentional. "Alpha" suggests "Alfred," and the name George, meaning "farmer," appears to be echoed in the "Plough," while even Gardiner has a similar rustic association.

The celestial source was suggested to the writer to accord with the title of his editor's paper: "'As for your name, I offer you the whole firmament to choose from.' In that prodigal spirit the editor of the *Star* invites me to join the constellation that he has summoned from the vasty deeps of Fleet Street" [Alpha of the Plough, "On Choosing a Name," *Selected Essays*, 1920]. After considering names such as "Orion," "Arcturus," and "Vega," Gardiner makes his choice: "My eye roves northward to where the Great Bear hangs head downwards as if to devour the earth. Great Bear, Charles's Wain, the Plough, the Dipper, the Chariot of David.... There at the head of the Plough flames the great star that points to the pole. I will hitch my little wagon to that sublime image. I will be Alpha of the Plough" [ibid.].

Mother **Alphonsa:** Rose Lathrop, née Hawthorne (1851–1926), U.S. writer, nun, medical worker. The daughter of novelist Nathaniel Hawthorne took this name after joining the Dominican Order, following the breakup of her marriage in 1895.

William **Alston:** William Allston (1757–1839), U.S. planter, legislator. Alston first spelled his surname with a single "l" in about 1790 to avoid being taken for his cousin, William Allston.

Al. **Altayev:** Margarita Vladimirovna Yamshchikova (1872–1959), Russ. children's writer, biographer. The author adopted her new surname from that of a character in *A Widow's Story* by the Russian poet Yakov Polonsky, who had encouraged her when she was a promising young writer.

Peter **Altenberg:** Richard Engländer (1859–1919), Austr. writer.

Althea: Althea Braithwaite (1940–), Br. children's writer, illustrator.

Libero **Altomare:** Remo Mannoni (1883–1966), It. Futurist poet. The heroic pseudonym can be taken to mean "free (on the) high seas."

Delia **Alton** *see* **H.D.**

John **Alton:** Janos (or Jacob) Altman (1901–1996), Hung.-born U.S. movie actor.

Robert **Alton:** Robert Alton Hart (1897–1957), U.S. stage, movie choreographer, movie director.

Alun: John Blackwell (1797–1840), Welsh poet, prose writer. The name is bardic. Blackwell was born in Flintshire, and the Welsh forename Alun is associated with the name of the Alyn River, which flows through that county.

Alun Cilie: Alun Jeremiah Jones (1897–1975), Welsh poet. The poet took his second name from the farm, Y Cilie, on which he was born. He was the twelfth child of a family of poets who lived here.

Francesco **Alunno:** Francesco del Bailo (*c.*1485–1556), It. mathematician, philologist. The scholar's adopted name is Italian for "pupil."

Luigi **Alva:** Luis Ernesto Alva-Tolledo (1927–), Peruvian opera singer, working in Italy.

Alvar: Eduarda Mansilla de García (1838–1892), Argentinian writer. The author used this name for chronicles published in *El Plata Illustrado* over the period 1871–72.

Don **Alvarado:** Joseph Paige (1904–1967), U.S. movie actor, father of Joy **Page**. The silent screen actor's name, given him by Jack L. **Warner**, accorded with his "Latin lover" roles, in the style of Rudolph **Valentino**. "Jack had given Alvarado his stage name. When the actor had auditioned as Joseph Paige, Jack said, 'You look Spanish, you need a Latin name.' The only Spanish Jack knew was Alvarado, the name of a Los Angeles street" [Cass Warner Sperling and Cork Millner, *Hollywood Be Thy Name: The Warner Brothers Story*, 1994].

Albert **Alvarez:** Raymond Gourron (1861–1933), Fr. opera singer.

Max **Alvary:** Maximilian Achenbach (1856–1898), Ger. opera singer.

Betti **Alver:** Elizabet Lepik (1906–1989), Estonian writer, translator.

Danny **Alvin:** Danny Viniello (1902–1958), U.S. jazz drummer.

Burt **Alvord** *see* Wes **Hardin**

Carl **Alwin:** Oskar Pinkus Alwin (1891–1945), Ger. pianist, conductor, composer.

Kenneth **Alwyn:** Kenneth Alwyn Wetherell (1925–), Br. conductor, composer.

Alyett: Alfred Auzet (1885–1975), Fr. illusionist.

Kirk **Alyn:** John Feggo, Jr. (1910–1999), U.S. movie actor.

Samuil **Alyoshin:** Samuil Iosifovich Kotlyar (1913–), Russ. playwright.

Bill **Amac:** Robert William Macfarland (1890–1961), Br. magician.

Amalfi: William F. Tunnah (?–), Br. magician.

Lucine **Amara:** Lucine Armaganian (1927–), U.S. opera singer, of Armenian descent.

Giuseppe **Amato:** Giuseppe Vasaturo (1899–1964), It. movie producer.

Miles **Amber:** Ellen Melicent Sickert, née Cobden (*c.*1848–1914), Eng. novelist. The writer used this name for the tragic novel *Wistons* (1902).

George **Amberg:** Hans Aschaffenburg (1901–1971), Ger.-born U.S. dance critic. Of Jewish origin, Amberg fled Hitler's Germany in 1933 under the name de Spina, an old French Huguenot name in his mother's family. He immigrated to the U.S. in 1941 and became an American citizen in 1946.

Richard **Amberley:** Paul Bourquin (1916–), Br. writer.

Victor **Ambroise** *see* Horatio **Nicholls**

Ambrose: (1) Andrey Yushkevich (1690–1745), Russ. preacher; (2) Andrey Stepanovich Zertis-Kamensky (1708–1771), Russ. church dignitary, writer; (3) Andrey Podobedov (1742–1818), Russ. preacher; (4) Avraam Serebrennikov (or Serebryakov) (1745–1792), Russ. preacher; (5) Aleksey Ivanovich Protasov (1762–1841), Russ. preacher; (6) Andrey Antipovich Ornatsky (1778–1827), Russ. religious writer; (7) Aleksandr Mikhaylovich Grenkov (1812–1891), Russ. monk; (8) Aleksey Iosifovich Klyucharev (1821–1901), Russ. religious writer; (9) Baruch Ambrose (1896–1971), Br. bandleader. All of the Russian prelates assumed their monastic name (in Russian Amvrosy) in honor of St. Ambrose, 4th-century bishop of Milan. The name in each case retains the initial letter of the original first name.

Don **Ameche:** Dominic Felix Ameche (1908–1993), U.S. movie actor, of It./Ir.–Ger. parentage. Ameche's Italian father had changed the spelling of his name from an original "Amici" to "Ameche" on immigrating to the U.S., the aim being to prompt an accurate pronunciation.

Amedeo: Amedeo Vacca (1890–1974), It.-born magician.

A-Mei: Sherry Chang Huei-Mei (1972–), Chin. popular singer.

Carl **Amery:** Christian Anton Mayer (1922–), Ger. writer, translator. An altered first name and an anagrammatized surname.

Jean **Améry:** Hans Mayer (1912–1978), Austr. Jewish writer. The pioneer of Holocaust survival literature evolved his pen name by a roundabout route. "Having played variations on the name he was born with several times — Hans Mayer, Hanns Mayer,

Hans Maier — and having awarded himself an entirely spurious doctorate, this Austrian émigré ... finally took the decision to frenchify his name (actually an angaram of Mayer) only after the War. Améry was more than a *nom de plume*, less than a *nom de guerre*. It was, perhaps, a *nom de paix*. Yet he continued to write in German rather than French" [Daniel Johnson, review of Irene Heidelberger-Leonard, *Jean Améry, Times Literary Supplement*, October 1, 2004]

Adrienne **Ames:** Adrienne Ruth McClure (1907–1947), U.S. movie actress.

Ed **Ames:** Ed Ulrick (1927–), U.S pop singer.

Gerald **Ames:** Gerald Otto (1906–1993), U.S. children's writer on science and magic.

Jennifer **Ames** *see* Maysie **Greig**

Leon **Ames:** Leon Waycoff (1903–1993), U.S. stage, movie, TV actor. The actor adopted his new name in 1935, after being billed in early movies under his real name.

Ramsay **Ames:** Ramsay Phillips (1919 or 1924–1998), U.S. movie actress.

Amicus Curiae: John Payne Collier (1789–1883), Eng. literary scholar, forger. Collier began his career as a law reporter on *The Times* and used this name, a Latin legal term (literally "friend of the court") for an impartial adviser in a court case, for an early work, *Criticisms on the Bar* (1819).

Jean (earlier John) **Amila:** Jean Meckert (1910–1995), Fr. novelist. The writer used this name for a series of thrillers, beginning with the American-style *Y'a pas de bon Dieu* ("There Is No God") (1950).

Johari **Amini:** Jewel Christine McLawler (1935–), U.S. black writer. McLawler changed her name after her consciousness-raising by the future Haki R. **Madhubuti** whom she met as a 32-year-old freshman. "Hohari" is Swahili for "Jewel," while "Amini" is Swahili for "honesty and fidelity." "Amini believes that the meaning of a name becomes an inherent part of the person carrying that name, and she wanted names that would reflect her personality and her values of honesty and fidelity — values that she lived by and that she wanted her writings to convey" [Andrews, Foster, and Harris, p.5].

Meir **Amit:** Meir Slutzky (1921–2009), Israeli intelligence chief, soldier.

Amnon: Rees Jones (1797–1844), Welsh poet. The poet appears to have adopted the name of the biblical Amnon, the eldest of David's sons.

Tori **Amos:** Myra Ellen Amos (1963–), U.S. rock singer, of part–Sc. parentage. The singer adopted her new first name in 1985, supposedly when a friend's boyfriend commented that she "didn't look much like an Ellen, more like a Tori."

Kamal **Amrohi:** Syed Amir Haider Kamal (1918–1993), Ind. writer, poet, movie director. The writer was born in Amroha, Uttar Pradesh.

Alfred **Amtman-Briedit:** Alfred Fritsevich Amtmanis (1885–1966), Latvian theatrical director, actor.

Arthur **Amyand:** [Major] Edward Arthur Haggard (1860–1925), Br. novelist, historian. The writer used this name for his first novel, *Only a Drummer Boy* (1894). Later works appeared under his real name, with the pseudonym in brackets. Some sources misattribute the pseudonym to Haggard's brother, Lieutenant-Colonel Andrew Charles Parker Haggard (1854–1923), also a novelist and historian. Both were brothers of the better-known adventure novelist Henry Rider Haggard (1856–1925), author of *King Solomon's Mines* (1885), *She* (1887), and *Allan Quatermain* (1887).

Gerhard von **Amyntor:** Dagobert von Gerhardt (1831–1910), Ger. soldier, novelist. Amyntor was a warrior in Greek mythology.

Ana-Alicia: Ana Alicia Ortiz (1957–), Mexican-born U.S. TV actress.

Anacharsis Cloots *see* Anacharsis **Cloots**

Michael **Anagnos:** Michael Anagnostopoulos (1837–1906), Gk.-born U.S. educator of the blind. Anagnos shortened his original name soon after his marriage in 1870 to Julia Romana Howe, daughter of Julia Ward Howe, author of "The Battle Hymn of the Republic."

Ananda Metteya: Charles Henry Allan Bennett (1872–1923), Eng. Buddhist missionary. Ill health prompted the first British *bhikkhu* (fully ordained Buddhist monk) to travel to the East, first to Ceylon (Sri Lanka), then to Burma (Myanmar), where he was ordained in 1903. Continuing poor health later obliged him to disrobe and return to Britain, although he continued Buddhist propaganda work, which he attempted to finance by his own inventions. Ananda was the name of a cousin of the Buddha.

Anastacia: Anastacia Lyn Newkirk (1973–), U.S. soul singer.

Anastasia *see* Anna **Anderson**

Albert **Anastasia:** Umberto Anastasio (1902–1957), U.S. gangster.

Anastasius IV: Corrado (di Suburra) (*c.*1073–1154), It. pope.

Dulce **Anaya:** Dulce Esperanza Wöhner de Vega (1933–), Cuban ballet dancer.

Jorge **Anders:** Jorge Etzensberger (1939–), Argentinian-born U.S. jazz musician.

Merry **Anders:** Mary Anderson (1932–), U.S. movie actress. "Mary" often sounds like "Merry" on an American tongue.

Lale **Andersen:** Lale Wilke, née Bunterberg (1910–1972), Ger. popular singer, of Dan. parentage.

Andersen gained international fame for her recording of "Lili Marleen" (*see* Marlene **Dietrich**).

Martin **Andersen-Nexö:** Martin Andersen (1869–1954), Dan. writer. The writer originally used the pseudonym Nexö, taking this from the town on the island of Bornholm where his father was born. He later joined it to his surname, if only for distinction from the many other Andersens in Denmark.

Anna **Anderson:** Franziska Schankowska (1896–1984), Pol.-born U.S. impostor. The claimant to the person and title of Grand Duchess Anastasia Nikolayevna Romanova (1901–1918), youngest daughter of Czar Nicholas II of Russia, adopted her new name when in Germany. In 1969, after a visit to America, she married history professor John Manahan and moved to the USA. The similarity of her adopted name to that of the Russian heiress was presumably intentional rather than purely coincidental.

Broncho Billy **Anderson:** Max Aronson (1882–1971), U.S. movie actor. The western film hero originally changed his name to Gilbert Anderson, then adopted his new first name from Broncho Billy, a character who featured in a story by Peter B. Kyne in the *Saturday Evening Post*. Anderson produced and directed a series of films starring him, playing the part himself when unable to find a suitable actor.

Captain Lindsay **Anderson:** Alexander Christie (1841–1895), Sc. writer. The writer was a captain in the merchant marine and used this name in retirement for three tales of seafaring life: *Among Typhoons* (1891), *A Cruise in an Opium Clipper* (1891), and *Allan Gordon* (1892).

Daphne **Anderson:** Daphne Carter, née Scrutton (1922–), Eng. stage, movie actress.

Diana **Anderson:** Adrienne Ralston Fox (1928–), U.S. artist. The only daughter of movie actress Joan Bennett (1910–1990) assumed the first name Diana early in life. In 1936 her surname became Markey, after her mother divorced Seattle lumberman John Fox and married writer Gene Markey (who later married Hedy **Lamarr** and Myrna **Loy**). In 1945 it became Wanger, after her mother married Walter **Wanger**. It became Anderson in 1948, when she herself married real estate agent John Hardy Anderson, former brother-in-law of Gloria Somborn, elder daughter of Gloria **Swanson**.

[Dame] Judith **Anderson:** Frances Margaret Anderson (1898–1992), Austral.-born U.S. movie actress. The actress appears to have selected a new first name to match those of her parents, James and Jessie.

R. **Andom:** Alfred Walter Barrett (1869–1920), Eng. humorist. A rather transparent pun for a humorous writer. He also expanded the name to Robert Andom.

Fern **Andra:** [Baroness] Fern Andra von Weichs (1893–1974), Ger.-born U.S. movie actress.

Eugénio de **Andrade:** José Fontinhas (1923–2005), Port. poet.

Annette **André:** Annette Andreallo (1939–), Austral. ballet dancer, movie actress, working in U.K.

Andrea del Castagno: Andrea di Bartolo de Bargilla (*c.*1421–1457), It. painter. The artist was born near Castagno San Godenzo, Florence, and took his name from there.

Andrea del Sarto: Andrea d'Agnolo di Francesco (1486–1530), It. painter. The artist's family had been craftsmen and tradesmen, and his father was a tailor. Hence "del Sarto," from Italian *sarto*, "tailor."

Lycosthenes Psellionores **Andreopediacus:** Wolfhart Spangenberg (*c.*1570–1636), Ger. poet, theologian. The scholar's pseudonym is a literal Greek rendering of his original name, with the third word representing his birthtown, Mansfeld, as follows (in order Greek, German, English): *lykos*, *Wolf*, "wolf," *sthenos*, *Härte*, "strength"; *psellion*, *Spange*, "bracelet," *oros*, *Berg*, "mountain"; *andro-*, *Mann*, "man," *pedion*, *Feld*, "field."

Brother **Andrew:** Ian Travers-Ball (1928–2000), Eng. priest. After training with the Jesuit mission in India, the gambler-turned-priest set up a charity with Mother **Teresa**, taking his new name in 1966.

Stephen **Andrew:** Frank G. Layton (1872–1941), Eng. novelist.

Thomas **Andrew:** Edward Thomas Andrulewicz (1932–1984), U.S. ballet dancer, choreographer.

Corinne **Andrews** *see* Rebecca **West**

Dana **Andrews:** Carver Daniel Andrews (1912–1992), U.S. movie actor, brother of Steve **Forrest**.

[Dame] Julie **Andrews:** Julia Elizabeth Wells (1935–), Eng. movie actress. The actress assumed the name of her stepfather, Ted Andrews, a Canadian singer. In 1969 she married her second husband, U.S. director Blake **Edwards**, and added his name to hers as Julie Andrews Edwards for her books *Mandy* (1972) and *The Last of the Really Great Whangdoodles* (1973).

Ruby **Andrews:** Ruby Stackhouse (1947–), U.S. R&B singer.

Tige **Andrews:** Tiger Androwaous (1920–), Lebanese-born U.S. movie actor.

V.C. **Andrews:** Virginia Cleo Andrews (?1923–1986), U.S. Gothic horror novelist. Andrews' editors decided to publish her fiction under her initials in order to mask her gender. She is recorded as saying: "Without the initials, I think it's very likely that I would be discriminated against as a woman in a man's field" [Douglas Winter, *Faces of Fear: Encounters with the Creators of Modern Horror*, 1985],

Pierre **Andrezel:** Karen Christentze Blixen, née

Dinesen (1885–1962), Dan. writer, working in Kenya. The author, also writing as Isak **Dinesen**, used the male French name for her book *Gengoedelsens Beje* (translated as "The Angelic Avengers") (1944), criticizing the German occupation of Denmark. Andrezel is the name of a village east of Paris.

Phil **Andro:** Samuel Morris Steward (1909–1993), U.S. writer. The writer's Greek-based pen name, meaning "man lover," was that of the hero of several collections of short stories dealing with gay male sex. Steward began his career as a teacher, but in 1952 became a tattooist under the name Phil Sparrow. In 1958 he turned to writing, using at least ten pseudonyms.

Andronicus: John William Jones (1842–1895), Welsh essayist. The writer presumably took his name from one of the early Greek poets or philosophers, such as Andronicus of Rhodes, the 1st-century commentator on Aristotle.

Olga **Androvskaya:** Olga Nikolayevna Shults (Schultz) (1898–1975), Russ. movie actress.

Bob **Andy:** Keith Anderson (1944–), Jamaican reggae musician.

Horace **Andy:** Horace Hinds (1951–), Jamaican reggae singer. Hinds was nicknamed Andy as a tribute to fellow songwriter Bob **Andy** by reggae musician Coxsone Dodd, and adopted his name accordingly.

Zigmas **Angaretis:** Zigmas Ionovich Aleksa (1882–1940), Lithuanian revolutionary.

Ange de St. Joseph: Joseph Labrosse (1636–1697), Fr. missionary, working in Persia. The scholar's name means literally "Angel of St. Joseph."

Ange de St. Rosalie: François Raffard (1655–1726), Fr. historian. The scholar's name means literally "Angel of St. Rosalia," after a 12th-century Sicilian anchorite.

Mother **Angela:** Eliza Marie Gillespie (1824–1887), U.S. educator, religious. Gillespie received the habit of the Marianites of Holy Cross in 1853 and was given the religious name of Sister Mary of St. Angela. She subsequently became mother superior of the community under the single name Angela.

Pier **Angeli:** Anna Maria Pierangeli (1932–1971), It. movie actress, working in U.S., twin sister of Marisa **Pavan**. The actress's family name conveniently divides to form a new first and last name.

Fra **Angelico:** [Fra] Giovanni da Fiesole (*c.*1400–1455), It. painter. The Renaissance painter's original (lay) name was Guido di Pietro, and his religious name, as a Dominican friar, is thus the one given here, with "Fra" meaning "brother." It originated as a nickname, "Beato Angelico," (literally "blessed angelic one"), because of the beauty of his character. This name became established only after

his death. He was beatified as a saint in 1960 and was effectively canonized in 1984 on being declared patron of artists.

Angelina: Harriet Martineau (1802–1876), Eng. author.

[Sir] Norman **Angell:** Ralph Norman Angell Lane (1873–1967), Eng. publicist. The author of the influential *The Great Illusion* (1910) published *Patriotism under Three Flags* (1903) under his original name, but thereafter dropped "Lane."

Jean **Angelo:** Jean Barthélémy (1875–1933), Fr. stage, movie actor.

Battista **Angeloni:** John Shebbeare (1709–1788), Eng. political writer. Shebbeare used the Italian-style name for his political satire, purporting to be a translation, attacking the Duke of Newcastle. Its full title was *Letters on the English Nation, by Battista Angeloni, a Jesuit resident in London* (1756).

Maya **Angelou:** Marguerite Annie Johnson (1928–), U.S. black poet, playwright. The writer's surname is that of a Greek husband, Tosh Angelos, while her forename was originally a pet name given her by her brother Bailey.

Muriel **Angelus:** Muriel Angelus Findlay (1909–2004), Sc. movie actress.

Angelus à Sancto Francisco: Richard Mason (1601–1678), Eng. Franciscan priest. The name can be understood as "angel of St. Francis."

Angelus Silesius: Johannes Scheffler (1624–1677), Ger. religious poet. The poet was a native of Silesia. Hence the Latin name that he took in 1653 on converting from Lutherism to Catholicism, meaning "Silesian messenger."

Kenneth **Anger:** Kenneth Wilbur Anglemyer (1927–), U.S. moviemaker.

Margit **Angerer:** Margit von Rupp (1905–1978), Hung.-born Austr. opera singer.

Gasparo **Angiolini:** Domenico Maria Angiolo Gasparini (1731–1803), It. choreographer, composer.

Anglus *see* Thomas **Blacklow**

Angoulevant: Nicolas Joubert (?–before 1623), Fr. jester, poet. Angoulevant was jester to Henri IV.

Antonio **Aniante:** Antonio Rapisarda (1900–1983), It. writer.

Anis: Mir Babar Ali (1801–1874), Ind. poet. The poet's adopted name means "friendly."

Anise: Anna Louise Strong (1885–1970), U.S. poet, journalist. A name formed from the writer's first two names.

Jennifer **Aniston:** Jennifer Anistonapoulos (1969–), U.S. TV actress.

Anita Louise: Anita Louise Fremault (1915–1970), U.S. stage, movie actress. The actress was first billed under her shortened name as a juvenile in the silent movie *Square Shoulders* (1929).

Morris **Ankrum:** Morris Nussbaum (1896–1984), U.S. stage, movie actor.

Mother **Ann:** Ann Lee (1736–1784), U.S. mystic, founder of Shaker movement.

Annabella: Suzanne Georgette Charpentier (1909–1996), Fr. movie actress. The actress was given her new name by the French movie director Abel Gance, who took it from Edgar Allan Poe's lyrical ballad *Annabel Lee* (1849).

Annabelle: Annabelle Moore, later Whitford, then Buchan (c.1878–1961), U.S. skirt dancer, movie actress.

Anna Livia: Anna Livia Julian Brawn (1955–), Ir.-born Br. fiction writer. As a personal name, Anna Livia is a folk name of the Liffey River, eastern Ireland, as a corruption of Irish *Abha na Life*, "river (of) Liffey." James Joyce personified the river as Anna Livia Plurabelle in *Finnegans Wake* (1939).

Anna Matilda: (1) Hester Lynch Piozzi, née Salusbury (1741–1821), Eng. writer; (2) Hannah Cowley, née Parkhouse (1743–1809), Eng. dramatist, poet. The same name was used by both women in their correspondence with the Della Cruscans (*see* **Della Crusca**). Hester Piozzi, better known as Mrs. Thrale, after her first husband, was called "Matilda" by William Gifford in his two satires, *The Baviad* (1791) and *The Maeviad* (1795), both directed against the Dellacruscan school of English poetry. Today, "the name 'Anna Matilda' has passed into a synonym of namby-pamby verse and sentimental fiction" [Smith, p.60].

Barbara **Annandale** *see* Avon **Curry**

Annette: Annette Funicello (1942–), U.S. movie actress, singer.

Ann-Margret: Ann-Margret Olsson (1941–), Swe.-born U.S. movie actress. "I made my decision to drop my last name and simply go by Ann-Margret. It wasn't an affectation. Nor was it an attempt to be different. I didn't know of any performers who went by one name. It was just my way of ensuring that my parents were not hurt, embarrassed, or bothered by anything that might happen as a result of my being in show business. And so it was. Not Ann. Not Miss Margaret. But Ann-Margret" [Ann-Margret with Todd Gold, *Ann-Margret*, 1994].

Anodos: Mary Elizabeth Coleridge (1861–1907), Eng. poet. The great-niece of poet Samuel Taylor Coleridge used this name, Greek for "way up," for two books of verse, *Fancy's Following* (1896) and *Fancy's Guerdon* (1897).

Freddie **Anoka:** Janine Baganier (1924–), Fr. composer.

Another Lady: Marie Dobbs, née Catton (c.1920–), Austral. author. The name was used by Dobbs for her completion (published 1975) of Jane Austen's unfinished novel *Sanditon* (written 1817), so that the combined authorship was credited to "Jane Austen and Another Lady," in the style of Jane Austen's day. Marie Dobbs also wrote as Anne Telscombe.

Anouk *see* Anouk **Aimée**

Père **Anselme:** Pierre de Guibours (1625–1694), Fr. genealogist, friar.

S. **Ansky:** Solomon Zanvel Rappoport (Shloyme Zaynvl Rapoport) (1863–1920), Russ. Jewish author, folklorist, writing in Yiddish. The original form of the pseudonym, which had several variants, was "S. An — sky," implying missing letters.

F. **Anstey:** Thomas Anstey Guthrie (1856–1934), Eng. author, children's writer. The writer intended his pseudonym to be "T. Anstey," from his first two names. A printer misprinted this as "F. Anstey," which he allowed to remain. It has been pointed out that this suggests "fantasy," appropriately for the author of *Vice Versa* (1882), telling how a father and son change bodies with the aid of a magic stone.

Gilbert **Anstruther:** Russel S. Clark (1909–?), Austral. writer of popular fiction.

Adam **Ant:** Stuart Leslie Goddard (1954–), Br. rock singer. Goddard was at the Hornsey College of Art, London, when he asked a friend to design a tattoo for his upper left arm. This was a heart pierced with a dagger, the word ADAM on top, PURE and SEX on either side, the whole thing set just above his vaccination mark. From then on, he called himself "Adam." "When I had the tattoo done," he said, "I really went in for it. Adam is a very strong name; it's the *first* name — you know — the Garden of Eden. I associate it with strength." The strength was further incorporated by adding "ant" to make "adamant," and "Ant" thus became his surname. ("Mr. Ant for you," said the girl on the telephone.) He soon adopted the surname for the group of four he sang with, so that he was "Adam and the Ants" [*Observer Magazine*, January 10, 1982].

Ant and Dec: Anthony McPartlin (1975–), Br. TV presenter + Declan Donnelly (1975–), Br. TV presenter.

Franz **Antel:** François Legrand (1913–), Austr. movie director, producer.

Anthony: Anthony Hutchings (1946–), Eng. cartoonist, illustrator.

[Metropolitan] **Anthony:** Andrey Borisovich Bloom (1914–2003), Swiss-born Russ. prelate, working in U.K.

C.L. **Anthony:** Dorothy Gladys Smith (1896–1990), Eng. playwright, novelist. As a teenager, Smith sold a screenplay, *Schoolgirl Rebels* (1915), under the male name Charles Henry Percy. Her first play, *Au-*

tumn Crocus (1931), was written as C.L. Anthony, and she continued to use this name until 1935. She then wrote as Dodie Smith, using the pet form of her first name.

David **Anthony:** Wiliam Dale Smith (1929–1986), U.S. detective novelist.

Evelyn **Anthony:** Evelyn Bridget Patricia Ward-Thomas (1928–), Br. mystery novelist.

Jack **Anthony:** John Anthony Herbertson (1900–1962), Sc. comedian.

John **Anthony:** Ronald Brymer Beckett (1891–1970), Eng. writer, civil servant.

Joseph **Anthony:** Joseph Anthony Deuster (1912–1993), U.S. stage, movie actor, director, screenwriter.

Julie **Anthony:** Julie Nutt, née Lush (1952–), Austral. cabaret singer, dancer.

Lysette **Anthony:** Lysette Chodzka (1963–), Br. TV actress, of Pol. descent. The actress gave the following account of the evolution of her name: "My father appeared with Ivor **Novello** in *King's Rhapsody* and decided that Chodzki was no good as a stage name: so he became Michael **Anthony**. When I first went to school at a convent I was asked my name and got terribly confused. I said my father's name was Michael Anthony, my mother was Bernadette Milnes and my name was Lysette Chodzka — the female version of the [Polish] family name. That was complicated enough, but then when I was ten I played a precocious kitten in *Pinocchio* in the West End and decided to call myself Lysette Elrington, after my grandmother. But at 16 I started fashion modeling and adopted my father's stage name and became Lysette Anthony — anyway, if your name starts with letter A you are always first in the casting directories" [*Telegraph Sunday Magazine*, April 17, 1983].

Mark **Anthony:** Marco Antonio Muñiz (1969–), U.S. salsa musician. The singer's Puerto Rican parents named him after a Mexican singer, and he adopted the name in an English equivalent.

Michael **Anthony:** Michael Adam Anthony Chodzko (1911–1998), Br. stage actor, of Pol. descent, father of Lysette **Anthony**.

Mike **Anthony:** Michael Joseph Logiudice (1930–1999), U.S. songwriter.

Piers **Anthony:** Piers Anthony Dillingham Jacob (1934–), Eng.-born U.S. SF writer.

Ray **Anthony:** Raymond Antonini (1922–), U.S. pop musician.

Richard **Anthony:** Richard Anthony Bush (1938–), U.S. pop musician.

Sister **Anthony:** Mary O'Connell (1814–1897), Ir.-born U.S. nurse, religious. O'Connell emigrated to the U.S. following her mother's death in about 1825 and entered the Sisters of Charity community ten years later, receiving the name Sister Anthony.

[St.] **Anthony of Padua:** Fernando (1195–1231), Port. Franciscan friar, churchman.

Anthropos: Robert David Rowland (*c.*1853–1944), Welsh journalist, poet. The writer's Greek name means simply "human being."

Dr. Pessimist **Anticant:** Thomas Carlyle (1795–1881), Sc. philosopher, writer. "Anticant" means "anticant."

L'**Antico:** Pier Jacopo di Antonio Alari Bonacolsi (*c.*1460–1528), It. sculptor. The artist came to be known by his nickname, meaning "the ancient one," with reference to his classically inspired statuettes, many of which were versions of famous antique statues.

Antoine: Antek Cierplikowski (1884–1977), Pol.-born Fr. hairdresser.

Father **Antoine:** Francisco Antonio Ildefonso Moreno y Arze (1748–1829), Sp.-born U.S. Roman Catholic priest. The cleric was originally known as Antonio de Sedella (for his birthplace) in his native Spain, but then became Father Antoine after taking a post as a missionary priest in Louisiana in 1781.

Anton: Beryl Botterill Yeoman, née Thompson (1907–1970), Austral.-born Br. cartoonist. The artist originally shared this name with her brother, Harold Underwood Thompson (1911–1996), for the cartoons they published jointly from 1937. He explained: "Beryl, a name she hated, had recently converted to Roman Catholicism and had adopted the name Antonia. I thought 'J. Anton' had a sophisticated continental ring that the editorial staff would appreciate. We worked out the style and submitted some drawings which were accepted, but with the 'J.' dropped from the name" [*Punch*, October 12–18, 1996].

Brother **Antoninus:** William Oliver Everson (1912–1994), U.S. poet, Dominican lay brother.

Antonio: (1) Antonas Ignosovich Markunas (1915–1977), Latvian circus artist; (2) Antonio Lopez (1943–1987), Puerto Rican–born U.S. fashion illustrator. Lopez "dropped his surname only when his fame was sufficient to allow him to do so" [*Sunday Times*, February 23, 1997].

António: António Ruíz Soler (1922–1996), Sp. ballet dancer, choreographer.

Father **Antony:** Joseph McCabe (1867–1955), Eng. writer. As a boy, the writer was led to believe he had a religious vocation. At the age of 15 he accordingly entered a monastery to become a Franciscan monk and in due course a priest, when he was known as the Very Rev. Father Antony, O.S.F. He later realized he was mistaken in his calling and left the Church in 1896 to pursue a career under his original name as an author, journalist, and lecturer.

Hilda **Antony:** Hilda Antonietti (1886–?), Br. stage actress, of Eng.-It. parentage.

Peter **Antony:** [Sir] Peter Levin Shaffer (1926–), Eng. playwright + Anthony Joshua Shaffer (1926–2001), Eng. playwright, his twin brother. The twins also used this name for some early novels.

Scott **Antony:** Anthony Scott (1950–), Br. movie actor.

Christopher **Anvil:** Harry C. Crosby, Jr. (*fl.*1970s), U.S. SF writer.

Mme. **Aorena:** Liliuokalani (1838–1917), queen of Hawaii. Named Lydia Kamakeaha Paki by her adoptive parents, the last sovereign queen of Hawaii used this pseudonym for her musical compositions.

Apache Indian: Steve Kapur (1967–), Br. reggae musician, of Ind. parentage.

Ape: Carlo Pellegrini (1839–1889), It. caricaturist, working in England. The artist chose his pen name to reflect the essentially mischievous nature of his work, since a caricature "apes" its subject. Ape's first effort, drawn over the name "Singe" (French for "monkey"), was a caricature of Disraeli published in the fashionable magazine *Vanity Fair* in 1869. Another contributor to this journal was **Spy.**

Aper: Alec P.F. Ritchie (1869–1918), Sc.-born Br. political cartoonist, caricaturist. The name actually represents the cartoonist's initials (adding a lower bar to the "F"), while a caricaturist is essentially an "aper" anyway, as notably was **Ape.**

Apex: Eric Chalkley (1917–2006), Eng. crossword compiler. In typical cryptic crossword fashion, the name has a double sense, indicating not only a "top" compiler but one who aimed to "ape X," that is, to imitate **Ximenes.**

Aphex Twin: Richard D. James (1972–), Ir.-born Br. "ambient techno" rock musician. The name suggests "effects" rather than "affects." The experimental musician has recorded under a variety of surreal names, among them Caustic Window, GAK, Blue Calx, and PCP.

Petrus **Apianus:** Peter Bienewitz (1501–1552), Ger. astronomer, geographer. The scholar adopted a Latin equivalent of his German name, based on Latin *apis*, German *Biene*, "bee."

Apis: Dragutin Dimitrijevic (1876–1917), Serbian solder, intriguer. A founder of the secret society Crna Ruka ("Black Hand"), Col. Dimitrijevic adopted a Latin "underground" name meaning "The Bee."

Ap Neurin: [Dr.] Rowan D. Williams (1950–), Welsh prelate. The Archbishop of Wales (from 2003 Archbishop of Canterbury) was inducted into the Gorsedd of Bards under this name in 2002. The name means "son of Aneurin," referring both to his father, Aneurin Williams, and to the 6th-century Welsh poet Aneurin. Dr. Williams had referred jokingly to himself as a "hairy lefty," meaning a bearded Labour supporter, resulting in media taunts that the bardic name actually paid homage to the Welsh Labour politician Aneurin Bevan (1897–1960), creator of Britain's innovatory National Health Service.

Guillaume **Apollinaire:** Wilhelm Apollinaris de Kostrowitzki (1880–1918), Fr. poet, art critic, of It.-Pol. parentage. The poet adopted his pseudonym in 1902, some two years after settling in Paris.

App: Barry Ernest Appleby (1909–1996), Eng. cartoonist.

Johnny **Appleseed:** John Chapman (1774–1845), U.S. nurseryman, folk hero. The name, properly a nickname, was given to the man who planted apple seedlings for the frontier settlers in Pennsylvania, Ohio, Indiana, and Illinois. He adopted it, however, so it can legitimately be included here.

Fiona **Apple:** Fiona Apple McAfee-Maggart (1977–), U.S. rock singer, pianist.

Victor **Appleton:** Edward L. Stratemeyer (1862–1930), U.S. writer. The Stratemeyer Literary Syndicate set up in 1906 used this name for stories about the boy-hero Tom Swift.

Apsīšu Jēkabs: Jānis Jaunzemis (1858–1929), Latvian writer. The writer took his new first name from Latvian *apse*, "aspen," referring to the tree in front of his study window. The second word of the name is the equivalent of Jacob.

Mr. **Aptommas:** John Thomas (1826–1913), Welsh harpist. The musician used this name for his definitive work, *A History of the Harp*, published in New York in 1864. Hamst comments: "This gentleman *Welshified* his name, probably for the sake of euphony" [p.18]. "Aptommas" would mean "son of Thomas."

Ap Vychan: Robert Thomas (1809–1880), Welsh theologian, writer. The writer's name means "little son" (Welsh *ap*, "son," and *bychan*, "little").

Serafino **Aquilano:** Serafino Ciminelli (1466–1500), It. poet. The poet's adopted name comes from his birthplace, the town of L'Aquila in central Italy.

Arachnophilus: Adam White (1817–1879), Sc. naturalist. An official in the zoological department of the British Museum, White adopted this Greek name, meaning "spider lover," for *A Contribution towards an Argument for the Plenary Inspiration of Scripture; Derived from the Minute Historical Accuracy of the Scriptures of the Old Testament, as Proved by Certain Ancient Egyptian and Assyrian Remains Preserved in the British Museum* (1851).

Yasir **Arafat:** ar-Rachman 'abd ar-Ra'uf Arafat al-Qudwah al-Husayni (1929–2004), Palestinian resistance leader. The exact form of the PLO leader's original name is uncertain, but Israeli intelligence files suggest it was as given here. Early in life Arafat dropped his last two names (those of his family and clan) and changed his first name to Yasir. This was a surprising decision, as he was a relative of the grand mufti of Jerusalem, Haj Amin al-Husayni (1893–1974), who was himself a direct descendant of Hussein (Hasan) (624–680), grandson of the prophet Muhammad, and thus from one of the most famous families in all Islam. According to Neil C. Livingstone and David Halevy, *Inside the PLO* (1991), the dropping of the name may have had something to do with the fact that al-Husayni had collaborated with Adolf Hitler during World War II. Arafat itself is the name of a valley around 12 miles from Mecca where a special ceremony is held by Muslims during a hajj (pilgrimage to Mecca). The name derives from Arabic *'arafa*, "to learn," "to know," and the place is mentioned in the Koran: "When you come running from Arafat remember God as you approach the sacred monument" (2:198).

Arafat used various names to conceal his identity as a revolutionary, one of the most regular being Abu Amar, which he subsequently adopted as his *nom de guerre*. *Abu* means "father" (in the literal or figurative sense) and *al-amar* means "the command of God," with reference to a passsage in the Koran: "They put questions to you about the Spirit. Say: 'The Spirit is at my Lord's command'" (17:85). The name Yasir means "rich," "easy." Of his original names, ar-Rachman means "the most gracious" and ar-Ra'uf "the compassionate," both epithets of Allah.

Aragon: Richard Rogan (1961–), Br. crossword compiler. The setter's pseudonym is apparently not derived from letters in his real name but from the French poet Louis **Aragon**.

Louis **Aragon:** Louis Andrieux (1897–1982), Fr. Surrealist poet, Communist writer, Resistance fighter. The poet and patriot was the illegitimate son of Marguerite Toucas and Louis Andrieux, a former *préfet de police* and ambassador to Spain, who named him Aragon for the historic Spanish kingdom. The quest for legitimacy and identity was one of the major themes of Aragon's work. The poet himself occasionally used pseudonyms. His poem *Panopticum* (1943), for example, an exposé of Hitler's henchmen, was signed François la Colère, as if to mean "angry France."

Shio **Aragvispireli:** Shio Zakharyevich Dedabrishvili (1867–1926), Georgian writer. The writer took his name from the Aragvi River by which he was raised.

Dmitry Ignatyevich **Arakishvili:** Dmitry Ignatyevich Arakchiev (1873–1953), Georgian composer. The musician substituted the Georgian patronymic ("son of") suffix *-shvili* for the Russian *-ev*.

Charlotte **Arand:** Leopold von Sacher-Masoch (1836–1895), Austr. writer. The man who gave the world the word "masochism" sometimes wrote under this name, as well as that of Zoë von Rodenbach.

Araphil: William Habington (1605–1654), Eng. poet. The name may mean "loving the altar," i.e. marriage, from Latin *ara*, "altar," and Greek *-phil*. If so, it would relate to his wife, Lucy Herbert, daughter of the first Baron Powis, whom he praises in a collection of love poems called *Castara* (1634), a name perhaps meaning "sacred altar" (Latin *casta*, "chaste," "sacred"). In this work, Habington "dwells upon Castara's chastity with wearisome iteration" [*Dictionary of National Biography*].

Araucaria: [Rev.] John Graham (1924–), Eng. crossword compiler. The setter of cryptic puzzles in *The Guardian* appropriately adopted the botanical name of the monkey puzzle tree, *Araucaria araucana*.

Arazi: Movses Melikovich Arutyunyan (1878–1964), Armenian writer. The writer's pseudonym represents the Armenian name of the Araks River. This flows along the border between Iran and Azerbaijan, south of Georgia, where he was born.

Ilya **Arbatov:** Ilya Ilyich Yagubyan (1894–1967), Armenian ballet dancer.

Thoinot **Arbeau:** Jehan Tabourot (1519–1595), Fr. priest, writer on dancing. The name is a precise anagram, taking "j" as "i."

Stella **Arbenina:** Stella Meyendorff, née Whishaw (1887–1976), Russ.-born Br. stage, movie actress.

Nelly **Arcan:** Isabelle Fortier (1973–2009), Can. novelist. The French-Canadian writer adopted a new name on first assuming a new persona as an explicit recorder of her sexual experiences.

Father **Archangel:** John Forbes (1571–1606), Sc. friar. Protestant John Forbes joined the Catholic Capuchin order in Belgium and took the same religious name as his elder brother William (?–1591).

Anne **Archer:** Anne Bowman (1945–), U.S. movie actress, daughter of John **Archer**.

F.M. **Archer** *see* Arthur **Ainslie**

Harry **Archer:** Harry Auracher (1888–1960), U.S. popular composer, musical director.

John **Archer:** Ralph Bowman (1915–1999), U.S. movie actor. A synonymous name change.

Richard Dacre **Archer-Hind:** Richard Dacre Hodgson (1849–1910), Eng. classical scholar. The scholar's father changed the family name to Archer-Hind on succeeding to his brother's estate in 1869.

Archibald: Leon T. Gross (1912–1973), U.S. popular pianist. The musician gained the nickname

"Archie Boy" during years of playing at parties and brothels, and this gave his stage name.

Jules François **Archibald:** John Feltham Archibald (1856–1919), Austral. journalist, of Ir. descent. Archibald was a Francophile, and assumed his French first names in the 1870s.

Archimedes: [Sir] James Edward Edmonds (1861–1956), Eng. military historian.

Ardelia: Anne Finch, née Kingsmill (1661–1720), Eng. poet. The name occurs in earlier English literature, but Finch may have specifically adopted it from a poem, "A Retir'd Friendship. To Ardelia," by Katherine Philips ("the Matchless **Orinda**") (1632–1648).

Don **Arden:** Harry Levy (1926–), Eng. rock music manager, father-in-law of Ozzy **Osbourne**. Arden adopted his new name in 1944 on beginning a career as a stand-up comic and singer.

Elizabeth **Arden:** Florence Nightingale Graham (1878–1966), Can.-born U.S. cosmetician. A cosmetician needs a carefully selected and suitable name. Graham's original name was felt to be not sufficiently glamorous. She rather liked the name Elizabeth Hubbard, which was that of the original owner of the New York salon where she set up her business. (The name was still on the window, although the lady herself had moved two doors further down Fifth Avenue.) But "Elizabeth Graham" did not sound quite right, so she instead chose Elizabeth Arden. She is popularly said to have taken the name from a favorite book and a favorite poem, *Elizabeth and her German Garden*, by **Elizabeth**, and *Enoch Arden* by Tennyson. But would she have been so closely familiar with these Victorian works? She reputedly made the final choice of name after posting letters to Elizabeth Arden "in care of Graham" to see what impact the name made on the envelope. Her rival in the cosmetic field was Helena Rubinstein. Elizabeth Arden was thus the "Miss" of the cosmetics world, Rubinstein the "Madame," and Coco **Chanel** the "Mademoiselle" [Margaret Allen, *Selling Dreams*, 1981].

Eve **Arden:** Eunice West, née Quedens (1912–1990), U.S. stage, movie, TV comedienne. The actress is said to have adopted her name after looking over the cosmetics "Evening in Paris" (giving "Eve") and "Elizabeth **Arden**" (giving "Arden"). Some accounts, however, say she took "Eve" from the heroine of a book she was reading at the time.

Mordecai **Ardon:** Max Bronstein (1896–1992), Pol.-born Israeli painter. The artist adopted his new name in 1926 on moving to Munich, Germany. In 1933 he fled to Jerusalem to escape Nazi persecution.

Tina **Arena:** Filippina Lydia Arena (1967–), Austral. popular singer, of It. descent. The singer was known at home as Pina (short for Filippina), so she was Pina Arena. She altered the first letter of this to become Tina Arena, and early in her singing career was originally billed as "Tiny Tina."

Pietro **Aretino:** ? (1492–1556), It. satirist, dramatist. The writer's original name is unknown. "Aretino" means "of Arezzo," his native town. He also wrote under the anagrammatical name Partenio Etiro.

Imperio **Argentina:** Magdalena Nile del Río (1906–2003), Argentine-born Sp. movie actress, singer.

La **Argentina:** Antonia Mercé y Luque (1890–1936), Argentine-born Sp. ballet dancer.

La **Argentinita:** Encarnación Lopez Julvez (1895–1945), Argentine-born Sp. ballet dancer. La Argentinita was younger than La **Argentina**, so took a diminutive form of the name, "the little Argentinian."

Tudor **Arghezi:** Ion N. Teodorescu (1880–1967), Rom. lyric poet.

Argo: Abram Markovich Goldenberg (1897–1968), Russ. poet, playwright. A name formed from letters in the writer's full name, while also suggesting "argot," as one who enjoyed manipulating words. Goldenberg wrote both for the music hall and the circus.

Pearl **Argyle:** Pearl Wellman (1910–1947), S.A.-born Br. ballet dancer, stage actress.

Carina **Ari:** Carina Janssen (1897–1970), Swe. ballet dancer. An unusual extraction of a surname from an existing forename.

Imanol **Arias:** Manuel Arias Domínguez (1956–), Sp. movie actor.

India **Arie:** India Simpson (*c.*1970–), Ind. pop singer. The singer was given her second name by her mother. (She was named India as she was born on Gandhi's birthday.) She also presents her name in the form India.Arie, like a dotcom name.

José **Arigó:** José Pedro de Freitas (1918–1971), Brazilian native healer.

Arion: William Falconer (1732–1769), Eng. "sailor poet." Falconer went to sea as a boy and was the only officer to survive from the *Britannia* when she was wrecked off Cape Colonna, Greece. The experience forms the basis of his poem *The Shipwreck* (1762). Ironically, he was drowned at sea. According to legend, the ancient Greek poet Arion was cast into the sea by mariners but subsequently brought back to land by a dolphin.

Ariosto: [Rev.] Edward Irving (1792–1834), Sc. clergyman, founder of the Holy Catholic Apostolic Church. The name of the epic Italian poet Lodovico Ariosto (1474–1533) was widely adopted by "great" men, or used as a nickname for important writers of the 18th and 19th centuries. Goethe, for example, was

"The Ariosto of Germany," and Walter Scott "The Ariosto of the North." Possibly Irving had the latter specifically in mind.

Arkan: Zeljko Raznatovic (1952–2000), Serbian paramilitary leader.

Alan Wolf **Arkin:** Roger Short (1934–), U.S. movie actor, director.

Harold **Arlen:** Hyman Arluck (1905–1986), U.S. songwriter.

Leslie **Arlen** *see* Andrew **York**

Michael **Arlen:** Dikran Kuyumdjian (1895–1956), Bulg.-born Br. novelist, of Armenian parentage, working in U.K., U.S. In the preface to his first book, the semiautobiographical *London Venture* (1920), the writer told his readers that he was changing his name to Michael Arlen in order to deprive them "of their last excuse for my obscurity."

Richard **Arlen:** Cornelius Richard Van Mattimore (1898–1976), U.S. movie actor. The actor adopted his new name in 1924, after originally being billed as Van Mattimore. (Van was his mother's maiden name.)

Arletty: Léonie Bathiat (1898–1992), Fr. stage, movie actress. The actress took her stage name in memory of Arlette, a character in Maupassant's novel *Mont-Oriol* (1887), as this is set in the Auvergne, near Lake Tazenat, where Bathiat's grandmother had lived. For some reason she then decided that an English final "y" was more chic than a French "e."

Arley: Miles Peter Andrews (?–1814), Eng. dramatist, politician.

Joyce **Arling:** Joyce Bell, née Burge (1911–), U.S. stage actress.

George **Arliss:** George Augustus Andrews (1868–1946), Eng. stage, movie actor, working in U.S., father of Leslie **Arliss**. The actor took his stage name from his father, William Joseph Arliss Andrews.

Leslie **Arliss:** Leslie Andrews (1901–1988), Br. movie director, son of George **Arliss**.

Arlodhes Ywerdhon: Margaret Pollard, née Steuart Gladstone (1903–1996), Eng. scholar. Pollard settled in Cornwall following her marriage in 1928 and was made a bard of the Gorseth Kernow (Cornish Gorsedd) in 1938. Her bardic name means "the Irish lady," reflecting her dedication to things Celtic.

Arman: Armand Pierre Fernandez (1928–2005), Fr.-born U.S. artist. In 1957 the artist decided he wanted to be known by his first name alone. The final "d" is missing through a printer's error on the cover of a catalog.

Armand: Friedrich August Strubberg (1808–1889), Ger.-born author, working in U.S.

Armando: H.D. van Dodeweerd (1929–), Du. artist.

Mkrtich **Armen:** Mkrtich Grigoryevich Arutyunyan (1906–1972), Armenian writer. The writer's pen name emphasizes his nationality.

Armida: Armida Vendrell (1911–1989), Mexican movie actress.

Armillita Chico: Miguel Espinosa Menéndez (1958–), Mexican bullfighter. The matador took his name from his famed father, Fermín Espinosa Saucedo (1911–1978), who in turn took it from his brother, Juan Espinosa Saucedo. The name, found also for other bullfighters, means "little armed one."

Jacobus **Arminius:** Jakob Hermandszoon (or Harmensen) (1560–1609), Du. theologian, Protestant churchman. A conventional latinization of the minister's original surname.

Armonie: John Dawson (1946–), Br. crossword compiler. The setter's pseudonym alludes to his love of early music.

John **Armour** *see* Mark **Carrel**

Anthony **Armstrong:** George Anthony Armstrong Willis (1897–1976), Can.-born Br. humorist, novelist. From 1925 to 1933 Willis made a weekly contribution to *Punch* as simply A.A.

Henry **Armstrong:** Henry Jackson, Jr. (1912–1988), U.S. boxer. The boxer first bore the ring name Melody Jackson, given by a former boxer, Harry Armstrong, after he heard him singing in the shower. He then took his regular name, basing it on the boxer who had coached him.

Robert **Armstrong:** Donald Robert Smith (1890–1973), U.S. movie actor.

Dudley (or Ernest) **Armytage:** William Edward Armytage Axon (1846–1913), Eng. journalist, writer.

Georges **Arnaud:** Henri Girard (1918–), Fr. novelist, dramatist.

Desi **Arnaz:** Desiderio Alberto Arnaz y Acha III (1917–1986), Cuban-born U.S. movie, TV actor.

Peter **Arne:** Peter Arne Albrecht (1920–1983), Br.–U.S. movie actor.

James **Arness:** James Aurness (1923–), U.S. movie, TV actor.

Achim von **Arnim:** Karl Joachim Friedrich Ludwig von Arnim (1781–1831), Ger. writer.

Ed **Arno:** Arnold Edelstein (1916–2008), Austr.-born U.S. cartoonist. Like his pseudonymous namesake, Peter **Arno**, Ed Arno's work appeared in the *New Yorker*, although not until after the other Arno's death. "In the 1930s Arnold had contracted his name to Ed Arno. He was unaware that Curtis Arnoux Peters had done something similar in 1925 and become Peter Arno" [*The Times*, July 19, 2008].

Peter **Arno:** Curtis Arnoux Peters, Jr. (1904–1968), U.S. cartoonist, illustrator. The artist, whose work appeared in the *New Yorker*, took a new name for distinction from his identically named father. Lois

Long, Arno's first wife (married 1927, divorced 1931), wrote for the same magazine as "Lipstick."

Sig Arno: Siegfried Aron (1895–1975), Ger. movie comedian, working in U.S.

Cecile Arnold: Cecile Laval Arnoux (or Arnole) (*c*.1895–1931), U.S. movie comedienne, of Fr.–U.S. parentage. The actress subsequently changed her screen name to Arley.

Danny Arnold: Arnold Rothman (1925–), U.S. movie producer.

Edward Arnold: Guenther Edward Arnold Schneider (1890–1956), U.S. movie actor, of Ger. parentage.

Harry Arnold: Harry Arnold Persson (1920–1971), Swe.-born U.S. bandleader.

Margot Arnold: Petronelle Marguerite Mary Cook (1925–), U.S. crime writer.

Maurice Arnold: Maurice Arnold Strothotte (1865–1937), U.S. movie music composer.

Wallace **Arnold** *see* Craig **Brown**

Charles Arnold-Baker: Wolfgang Charles Werner von Blumenthal (1918–2009), Ger.-born Br. historian, writer. The scholar adopted his new name when his English mother married Percy Arnold-Baker as her second husband.

Françoise Arnoul: Françoise Annette Marie Mathilde Gautsch (1931–), Algerian-born Fr. movie actress.

Sidney J. Arodin: Sidney J. Arnondrin (1901–1948), U.S. jazz musician.

Sonia Arova: Sonia Errio (1927–2001), Bulg.-born Br. ballet dancer. The dancer's adopted surname is a russianized version of the Bulgarian original.

Bill Arp: Charles Henry Smith (1826–1903), U.S. humorist. The name is almost certainly intended to suggest a comic rendering of "Wyatt Earp," the famous lawman of the Wild West. "Bill Arp" began his career in 1861 when he sent a letter to the *Southern Confederacy*, a Rome, Georgia, newspaper, addressed to "Mr. Abe Linkhorn," this being a similar eccentric spelling of a famous name.

Arrago: Roman Semyonovich Levitin (1883–1949), Russ. circus artist, "memory man."

Claude Arrieu: Louise Marie Simon (1903–1990), Fr. composer. It is tempting to see the musician's adopted name as a variation on that of her coeval, Chilean-born U.S. pianist Claudio Arrau (1903–1991).

Cletto Arrighi: Carlo Righetti (1830–1906), It. journalist, novelist. A purely anagrammatic name.

Don Arrol: Donald Angus Campbell (1929–1967), Sc. comedian.

Arrow: Alphonsus Cassell (1954–), West Indian calypso musician.

Emmanuelle Arsan: Marayat Rollet-Andriane, née Bibidh (1932–), Thai-born Fr. author + Louis-Jacques Rollet-Andriane (?–), Fr. author, her husband. The pen name was adopted by the writers for their pornographic novel *Emmanuelle* (1959).

Pavel Arsky: Pavel Aleksandrovich Afanasyev (1886–1967), Russ. writer.

Artemas: Arthur Telford Mason (*fl.*1920s), Br. author. The name, formed from the first syllables of the writer's full name, is also a proper first name, as for the U.S. Revolutionary commander Artemas Ward (*see* Artemus **Ward**) or the rather obscure St. Artemas. Mason's *The Book of Artemas* (1919) was popular in its day.

Artemisia: [Lady] Mary Wortley Montagu (1689–1762), Eng. writer of letters, poems. Artemisia was the name of queens of Asia Minor, one being the sister (and wife) of King Mausolus, to whom she erected the famous tomb known as the Mausoleum.

Artemus: Arthur Hull Hayes (1890–1986), Ir.-born U.S. conjuror.

Arthénice: Catherine de Vivonne, Marquise (Madame) de Rambouillet (1588–1665), Fr. social leader. The classical-looking name is an exact anagram of "Catherine."

Bea Arthur: Beatrice Arthur, née Bernice Frankel (1922–2009), U.S. movie, TV actress. The actress's first marriage to Robert Alan Arthur ended in divorce in 1950, when she married Gene Saks.

George K. Arthur: George K. Arthur Brest (1899–1985), Sc. movie actor.

Jean Arthur: Gladys Georgianna Greene (1900–1991), U.S. movie actress.

Johnny Arthur: John Lennox Arthur Williams (1883–1951), U.S. movie actor.

Julia Arthur: Ida Lewis (1869–1950), Can.-born U.S. stage actress. The actress first appeared under her stage name in 1891, taking her surname from her mother's maiden name.

Peter Arthur: Arthur Porges (1915–), U.S. writer of detective stories, SF, horror fiction.

Peter M. Arthur: Peter McArthur (1831–1903), Sc.-born U.S. labor leader. A payroll error listed the engineer's name as "Peter M. Arthur" and he adopted the name thereafter.

Robert Arthur: (1) Robert Arthur Feder (1909–1986), U.S. movie producer; (2) Robert Arthaud (1925–), U.S. movie actor, previously radio announcer.

Ruth M. Arthur: Ruth Mabel Arthur Higgins (1905–1979), Br. writer of fantasy fiction, children's author.

Arudra: Bhagvathula Shankara Sastry (1925–1998), Ind. poet, movie songwriter.

Mark **Arundel** *see* G.N. **Mortlake**

Arvonius: Thomas Roberts (*c*.1765–1841),

Welsh pamphleteer. The writer's name is a latinized form of Arfon, the historic region of northwest Wales that gave the name of Carnarvonshire, the former county in which Roberts was born. He used it for a pamphlet of 1806 defending the Methodists in response to a libellous pamphlet of 1797 by **Siamas Gwynedd**.

Nikolay **Arzhak:** Yuly Markovich Daniel (1925–1988), Russ. poet, short-story writer. The Soviet writer used this name for anti–Stalinist poems published in Paris, France, in 1962.

Joe **Arzonia:** Arthur Longbrake (1881–1953), Eng. songwriter.

George **Asaf:** George Henry Powell (1880–1951), Eng. songwriter.

Shoko **Asahara:** Chizuo Matsumoto (1955–), Jap. religious leader. The founder of the Aum Shinrikyo ("Supreme Truth") sect in 1986 was sentenced to death in 2004 following the group's gas attack on the Tokyo subway system in 1995.

Asahifuji: Masaya Suginomori (1960–), Jap. sumo wrestler. The wrestler based his fighting name, meaning "sunrise over Fuji," on that of his master, Asahikuni ("sunrise country," from Japanese *asahi*, "morning sun," and *kuni*, "country").

Tadanobu **Asano:** Tadanobu Sato (1973–), Jap. movie actor.

Oscar **Asche:** Thomas Stange Heiss (1871–1936), Austral.-born Br. stage actor, of Scandinavian descent.

Ascot: Allan Scott (1946–), Br. crossword compiler. A pseudonym representing the setter's real name.

Dougie **Ascot:** Douglas Frederick Hayes (1892–?), Austral. comedian, dancer.

Asdreni: Aleks Stavri Drenova (1872–1947), Albanian poet. The name is formed from letters in the poet's full name.

Fenton **Ash:** Francis Harry Atkins (1840–1927), Eng. writer.

Marvin **Ash:** Marvin Ashbaugh (1914–1974), U.S. jazz pianist.

Mary Kay **Ash:** Mary Kathlyn Wagner (1918–2001), U.S. entrepreneur.

Stephanie **Ash** *see* Olivia **Darling**

Ashanti: Ashanti Douglas (1980–), U.S. black hip-hop, R&B singer.

Richard **Ashby:** Richard Thimelby (1614–1680), Eng. Jesuit, theological writer.

Clifford **Ashdown:** Richard Austin Freeman (1862–1943), Eng. mystery writer + John James Pitcairn (1860–1936), Eng. mystery writer.

Gordon **Ashe:** John Creasey (1908–1973), Br. crime novelist. Creasey used around two dozen pen names. Others were Margaret Cooke, M.E. Cooke,

Henry St. John Cooper, Norman Deane, Elise Fecamps, Robert Caine Frazer, Patrick Gill, Michael Halliday, Charles Hogarth, Brian Hope, Colin Hughes, Kyle Hunt, Abel Mann, Peter Manton, J.J. Marric, James Marsden, Richard Martin, Rodney Mattheson, Anthony Morton, Ken Ranger, William K. Reilly, Tex Riley, and Jeremy York.

Max **Asher:** Max Ascher (1879 or 1880–1957), U.S. movie comedian. "Max seems to have amended the spelling of his Germanic surname even before the widespread Germanophobia induced by the Great War compelled several other screen stars to follow suit" [Mitchell, p.19].

Renée **Asherson:** Renée Ascherson (1920–), Eng. stage, movie actress.

Jeffrey **Ashford** *see* Roderic **Graeme**

[Sri] Madhava **Ashish:** Alexander Phipps (1920–1997), Br.-born Hindu monk, hill farmer.

Ashley: Ashley Eldrid Havinden (1903–1973), Eng. designer, typographer, painter. The artist signed his work with his first name alone.

April **Ashley:** George Jamieson (1935–), Eng. transexual. The fashion model changed her name following her sex change operation in 1960. "April" was the month of her birth, and "Ashley" came from Ashley Wilkes in *Gone with the Wind*, as for Elizabeth **Ashley**.

Caroline **Ashley:** Caroline Smith (1958–), Sc. TV actress. Smith changed her name to avoid confusion with an identically named actress. She adopted her new name from the Laura Ashley fashion shops.

Edward **Ashley:** Edward Ashley Cooper (1904–2000), Br. movie actor.

Elizabeth **Ashley:** Elizabeth Ann Cole (1939–), U.S. movie actress. The actress took her new surname from Ashley Wilkes, played by Leslie **Howard** in the motion picture of Margaret Mitchell's novel, *Gone with the Wind* (1936), first screened in the year of Cole's birth.

Merrill **Ashley:** Linda Michelle Merrill (1950–), U.S. ballet dancer.

Ted **Ashley:** Theodore Assofsky (1922–2002), U.S. motion picture executive. The future Warner Brothers chairman and CEO changed his name on establishing a talent agency early in his career.

Thomas Clarence **Ashley:** Clarence Earl McCurry (1895–1967), U.S. folksinger, instrumentalist. The musician took his mother's maiden name when still a boy.

Bill **Ashton:** William Richard Allingham (1936–), Eng. jazz musician.

John **Ashton:** John Groves (1950–), Eng. stage, movie, TV actor.

Teddy **Ashton:** Charles Allen Clarke (1863–1935), Eng. journalist, writer. The Lancashire writer used this name for his popular weekly *Teddy Ashton's Magazine.*

Lena Ashwell: Lena Margaret Pocock (1872–1957), Br. stage actress, theatrical manager. The actress adopted her stage name from the second name of her father, Captain Charles Ashwell Botelar Pocock.

Leon Askin: Leo Aschkenasy (1907–2005), Austr.-born U.S. movie actor.

Joseph Askins: Thomas Haskey (1771–?), Eng. ventriloquist.

Grégoire Aslan: Kridor Aslanian (1908–1982), Fr.-Turk. movie actor. A French version of the Turkish name, with "Aslan" (meaning "lion") retained from the original name.

Asmik: Tagush Sergeyevna Akopyan (1879–1947), Armenian movie actress.

Asmus: Matthias Claudius (1740–1815), Ger. journalist, writer. Claudius adopted this name for his contributions to the newspaper *Der Wandsbecker Bothe,* of which he became editor in 1771.

Aspazija: Elza Rozenberga (1868–1943), Latvian poet. The poet, wife of Jaanis **Rainis,** adopted the name of Aspasia, the 5th-century BC Greek courtesan and mistress of Pericles, renowned for her beauty and intelligence.

Asper: Samuel Johnson (1709–1784), Eng. lexicographer, critic. Latin for "rough," "severe," as a critic can be.

Orsola (or Ursula) **Aspri** (or Asperi): Adelhaide Appignani (1807–1884), It. conductor, composer.

Assiac: Heinrich Fraenkel (1897–1986), Ger.-born Eng. journalist, writer on chess. The pseudonym is a reversal of "Caissa," the name of the muse of chess, first appearing in a poem of 1763 by Sir William Jones.

Adele Astaire: Adele Austerlitz (1898–1981), U.S. dancer, actress, singer, sister of Fred **Astaire.**

Fred Astaire: Frederick Austerlitz (1899–1987), U.S. dancer, stage, movie actor. The name change was made by the dancer's parents, Frederick and Ann Geilus Austerlitz, when the future movie star was only two years old. "There is something very suggestive of Americana in the way a Napoleonic battle is turned into a name without roots or etymology. Yet how evocative that name is: run the parts together and the result is as rhythmic as [the song] Frenesi; separate them and it could be Fred a Star or Fred on a staircase, astride the stair—thus Astaire, *l'esprit d'escalier*" [Thomson 2003, p. 33].

Mikhail Astangov: Mikhail Fedorovich Ruzhnikov (1900–1965), Russ. stage, movie actor.

Juliet Astley: Norah Lofts, née Robinson (1904–1983), Eng. historical novelist. The writer also used the male name Peter Curtis for a number of mystery novels.

Anne Aston: Anne Lloyd (1948–), Sc. TV hostess.

James Aston: Terence Hanbury White (1906–1964), Br. novelist.

Adelaide Astor: Gertrude Grossmith, née Rudge (*fl.*1900s), Eng. stage actress, wife of actor manager and playwright George Grossmith, Jr. (1874–1935).

Mary Astor: Lucile Vasconcellos Langhanke (1906–1987), U.S. movie, TV actress, of Ger./U.S.-Port. parentage. The actress was given her new name at age 15 on signing with Famous Players–Lasky (the future Paramount Pictures).

Astraea: Aphra Behn, née Johnson (1640–1689), Eng. playwright, poet. The name, meaning "starry" (Greek *astraia*), had earlier been used by the French writer Honoré d'Urfé for the heroine of his pastoral romance *L'Astrée* (1607–27), while in classical mythology Astraea was the Roman goddess of justice. Behn originally used the name when employed as a secret agent for the government in the Netherlands.

Astrophel *see* **Stella**

Atano III: Mariano Juaristi Mendizábal (1904–2001), Sp. Basque pelota player.

Mustafa Kemal Atatürk: Mustafa Kemal (1881–1938), Turk. soldier, statesman. The president of the Turkish Republic adopted his surname in 1934, when he made surnames compulsory for all Turkish citizens. (Most Muslim Turks were then known only by their forenames.) "Mustafa Kemal thought long and hard about the surname he should adopt. Finally ... he chose for himself the name Atatürk, literally Father Turk—that is, father of the Turks. It shed light on his state of mind: the innovator was now 53 years old and felt paternally middle-aged. With no children of his own, he could be father to all Turks" [Andrew Mango, *Atatürk*, 1999].

Atatürk was born simply Mustafa, an Arabic name meaning "chosen," one of the titles of the prophet Muhammad. He received his second name, Kemal, when at military preparatory school (1891–95). He was gifted at mathematics, and his knowledge soon equalled that of his teacher. "'The teacher's name was Mustafa. One day he turned to me and said: "My boy, your name is Mustafa and so is mine. This won't do. There must be some distinction. From now on you'll be called Mustafa Kemal." And that's how I've been known ever since'" [ibid.]. Other sources, however, claim that Atatürk added the name for distinction from a classmate, or adopted it as a tribute to the patriotic poet Namik Kemal (1840–1888). The name itself is Turkish for "perfection."

Muhammad Atef: Sobhi Abu Sitta (?1944–2001), Egyptian-born Islamist militant. The al-Qaeda strategist also used the noms de guerre Abu

Hafs al-Misri ("son of Hafs the Egyptian") and Abu Khadijah ("son of Khadijah," the first wife of the prophet Muhammad).

Georgios **Athanas**: Georgios Athaniasiadis-Novas (1893–1987), Gk. poet.

William **Atheling**: Ezra Pound (1885–1972), U.S. poet. Pound used this name when writing for *New Age Magazine.*

William **Atheling, Jr.**: James Blish (1921–1975), U.S. novelist, short-story writer, working in U.K. Blish adopted this name, from William **Atheling**, for his fanzine columns.

Athenagoras I: Aristokles Spyrou (1886–1972), Gk. churchman. The archbishop of Constantinople adopted the name of the 2d-century AD Christian philosopher Athenagoras. His own name means "Athens marketplace," implying one who is important or influential in Greek society.

William **Atherton**: William Atherton Knight (1947–), U.S. TV actor.

Acharya **Athreya**: Kilambi Narasimhacharyulu (1921–1989), Ind. poet, playwright, movie songwriter.

Cholly **Atkins**: Charles Sylvan Atkinson (1913–2003), U.S. black dancer, choreographer. The dancer took his new first name from the society columnist Cholly **Knickerbocker**.

Tommy **Atkins**: Ruth Buckley (?–), U.S. magician.

Dr. **Atl**: Gerardo Murillo (1875–1964), Mexican painter, writer, revolutionary. The painter's Aztec name is the Aztec (Nahuatl) word for "water." He adopted it in 1902 in order to repudiate his Spanish heritage on the one hand and demonstrate his pride in his Mexican Indian ancestors on the other.

Atlas: William Hedley Roberts (1864–1946), Welsh variety artist, "society athlete," teaming with **Vulcana**, his common-law wife.

Charles **Atlas**: Angelo Siciliano (1893–1972), It.-born U.S. physical culturist. When Siciliano started bodybuilding, neighborhood friends compare his physique to a statue of the Greek god Atlas on a local bank. He adopted the name, combining it with the regular form of his existing nickname of "Charley."

Philip **Atlee**: James Atlee Philips (1915–1991), U.S. mystery novelist.

Atma Ram: Atmaram Padukone (1930–1994), Ind. movie director.

Kiyoshi **Atsumi**: Yasuo Tadokoro (1926–1996), Jap. comic movie actor.

Abe **Attell**: Albert Knoehr (1884–1970), U.S. boxer, of Russ. Jewish parentage. The fighter's adopted name may have been intended to suggest "a battle." Two of his brothers, Monte and Caesar, followed him into the ring and also assumed the name Attell.

Joseph **Atterley**: George Tucker (1775–1861), U.S. essayist, satirist.

Atticus: (1) Joseph Addison (1672–1719), Eng. poet, dramatist; (2) **Junius**; (3) Richard Hebes (1773–1833), Eng. bibliomaniac. The name of Atticus, a Roman literary patron of the 2d century BC, has been adopted by many writers and diarists.

Attila the Hun: Raymond Quevedo (1892–1962), Trinidadian calypso singer.

Moshe **Atzmon**: Moshe Groszberger (1931–), Hung.-born Israeli orchestral conductor.

Lenore **Aubert**: Eleanore Maria Leisner (1913–1993), Yugoslav movie actress, working in U.S.

Lucie **Aubrac**: Lucie Simon, née Bernard (1912–2007), Fr. Resistance fighter. In 1939 Simon married Raymond Samuel, a civil engineer, and the following year joined a resistance group he had set up in southern France. The couple then changed their Jewish surname to a purely French *nom de guerre.*

Aubrey: James Crabe (1931–), U.S. TV illusionist.

Gus **Aubrey**: Edward Brown (1909–?), Eng. transvestite comedian.

James **Aubrey**: James Aubrey Tregidgo (1947–2010), Br. movie, TV actor.

Cécile **Aubry**: Anne-Marie-José Bénard (1929–), Fr. movie actress.

Michel **Auclair**: Vladimir Vujovic (1922–1988), Ger. movie actor, of Serbian-Fr. parentage, working in France.

Auctor: Paul McKenna (1961–), Br. crossword compiler. The setter's pseudonym is Latin for "author."

Audi Alteram Partem: [General] Thomas Perronet Thompson (1783–1869), Eng. soldier, political reformer. In 1822, following army service in India, Thompson devoted himself to writing and politics. As Member of Parliament for Bradford, Yorkshire, he used this pseudonym for letters to his constituents criticizing the measures adopted to suppress the Indian Mutiny (1857). The Latin phrase means "Hear the other side," a quotation from St. Augustine, who insisted that there are two sides to every question.

Eleanor **Audeley**: Eleanor Audeley Douglas, earlier Davies (1590–1652), Ir. writer. The prophetic writer was the daughter of George Touchet, Baron Audeley, and this gave her basic writing name, which in her first work, *A Warning to the Dragon and all his Angels* (1625), she expanded to "Eleanor Audeley, Reveale O'Daniel," the second half of which was an anagram of the first (with "v" for "u" and "i" for "y"). It remained her signature in many of her treatises and expressed her conviction that her family name possessed hidden properties linking her to the prophet Daniel.

Maxine **Audley:** Maxine Hecht (1923–1992), Eng. stage actress.

Stéphane **Audran:** Colette Suzanne Jeannine Dacheville (1932–), Fr. movie actress.

Audreus: Audrey Young, née Jones (1921–), Welsh crossword compiler. A classical-looking male pseudonym for a female setter, based on her first name.

Mischa **Auer:** Mischa Ounskowsky (1905–1967), Russ.-born U.S. movie actor. The actor took the name of his maternal grandfather, Leopold Auer, a violinist, who adopted him and brought him to the U.S. in 1920.

Berthold **Auerbach:** Moyses Baruch Auerbacher (1812–1882), Ger. Jewish novelist, short-story writer. For his first work, a biography of Frederick the Great, Auerbach used the name Theobald Chaubert, an anagram of his adopted pseudonym.

Haydon **Augarde** *see* Horatio **Nicholls**

Markos **Augeres:** Georgos Papadopulos (1884–?), Gr. writer, critic.

Edwin **August:** Edwin August Philip von der Butz (1883–1964), U.S. movie actor, director.

Jan **August:** Jan Augustoff (1912–1976), U.S. popular pianist.

John **August:** Bernard Augustine DeVoto (1897–1955), U.S. editor, essayist, writer.

Joseph **August:** Joseph Augustus (1931–1992), U.S. R&B singer.

Madame Brasileira **Augusta** *see* Madame Floresta A. **Brasileira**

Mlle. **Augusta:** Caroline Augusta Joséphine Thérèse Fuchs, Comtesse de Saint-James (1806–1901), Fr. ballet dancer. Mlle. Augusta was probably right to select her second name as the most prestigious and "international" for professional use. The name itself, meaning "consecrated," "venerable," has a classical pedigree, as "a title conferred by the Roman emperors on their wives, sisters, daughters, mothers, and even concubines. It had to be conferred; for even the wife of an Augustus was not an Augusta until after her coronation" [E. Cobham Brewer, *The Reader's Handbook*, 1882]. *See also* Caesar **Augustus**.

Auguste: Auguste Poireau (*c.*1780–1844), Fr.-born Russ. ballet dancer, director. Poireau emigrated to St. Petersburg in 1798 and was formally known by the Russian name of Avgust Leontyevich Ogyust.

George **Auguste:** George Edward Read (1911–?), Br. trapeze artist. Auguste was long a standard name for a circus clown, through French *auguste* from German *der dumme August*, "the circus clown," itself presumably from the personal name *August*, "Augustus." A popular account of the origin is as follows: "The name is supposed to have come about this way: A century ago an English clown, playing in Germany, had the novel idea ... of going into the circus with a battered hat and his clothes all wrong. The audience began shouting out 'August!' 'August!' (The German phrase, 'dumme August' is equivalent to our word 'zaney' or 'addlepate.') And the name has stuck to this day" [*The Observer*, December 15, 1935].

Sister **Augustine:** Amalie von Lasaulx (1815–1872), Ger. abbess. Sister Augustine was superior of the Johannes Hospital in Bonn.

Caesar **Augustus:** Gaius Octavius (63 BC–AD 14), Roman emperor. The first of the Roman emperors was born Gaius Octavius, the son of the niece of Julius Caesar. When Caesar adopted him in 44 BC he became Caius Julius Caesar Octavianus, otherwise Octavian. In this name, according to the Roman naming system, Caius was his *praenomen*, or forename, Julius Caesar was the name of his adoptive father, and Octavianus was his *cognomen*, or extra personal name, here the adjectival form of his original *nomen*, his *gens* (clan) name. In 27 BC the Senate conferred on Octavian the imperial title Augustus, meaning "consecrated," "venerable," after which he was known by this name alone. (It was subsequently adopted as a title by all other Roman emperors and was even given to military units and cities, some of which, such as Augst, Switzerland, still bear it.)

The Roman historian Suetonius (*c.*69–*c.*140) explained Octavian's new name as follows: "He adopted the surname Caesar to comply with the will of his mother's uncle, the Dictator; and then the title Augustus after a motion to that effect had been introduced by Munatius Plancus. Some senators wished him to be called Romulus, as the second founder of the city [of Rome]; but Plancus had his way. He argued that 'Augustus' was both a more original and a more honourable title, since sanctuaries and all places consecrated by the augurs are known as 'august'" [*The Twelve Caesars*, translated by Robert Graves, 1957].

Georgie **Auld:** John Altwerger (1919–1990), Can. jazz musician.

Marie **Ault:** Mary Cragg (1870–1951), Eng. stage, movie actress. The actress adopted her mother's maiden name as her stage name.

Charles **Aumont:** Charles Solomon (*fl.*1890s), Fr. theatrical entrepreneur, working in Russia. The movie show organizer adopted his stage name from his original surname, less its first syllable.

Jean-Pierre **Aumont:** Jean-Pierre Philippe Salomons (1911–2001), Fr. movie actor, working in U.S. The actor formed his new name on the same lines as those of Charles **Aumont**.

Aunt ... For names beginning thus, see the next word, e.g. for Aunt Charlotte see **Charlotte**, for Aunt Effie see **Effie**, etc.

Aura: Aura Lewis (*c.*1958–), S.A. black jazz musician, working in Jamaica.

Aurangzeb: Muhi-ud-Din Muhammad (1618–1707), Ind. emperor. The last of the great Mogul emperors surrounded his royal presence with pomp and luxury. Hence his assumed name (or title), meaning "beauty of the throne." On succeeding to the throne itself in 1658 he took the equally grandiose kingly title of Alamgir, "conqueror of the universe."

Johann **Aurifaber:** Johannes Goldschmied (1519–1575), Ger. theologian. The Latin name translates the German (literally "goldsmith").

Dominique **Aury:** Anne Desclos (1907–1998), Fr. writer, editor. The writer based her pen name on the maiden name of her mother, Louise Auricoste. She later gained notoriety for the erotic international bestseller *L'Histoire d'O* (1954), published under the pseudonym Pauline Réage. This name in turn referred to two of Aury's heroines: Pauline Borghese, sister of Napoleon and wife of the Italian nobleman Camillo Borghese (1775–1832), and the French feminist Pauline Roland (1805–1852). The book had a preface written by Desclos' lover, literary editor Jean Paulhan, leading many to suppose that he was the actual author.

Auseklis: Mikelis Krogzemis (1850–1879), Latvian poet. The writer's poetic name means "break of day," "morning light."

Charlotte **Austen:** Charlotte Auerbach (1899–1994), Ger.-born Sc. geneticist. The scientist adopted this name as author of a book of fairy stories, *Adventures with Rosalind* (1947).

Charles **Austin:** Charles Reynolds (1879–1942), Eng. music-hall comedian.

Frank **Austin** *see* Max **Brand**

Frederick **Austin** *see* Baron **Corvo**

Gene **Austin:** Eugene Lucas (1900–1972), U.S. popular singer.

Johnny **Austin:** John A. Augustine (1910–1983), U.S. jazz musician.

Lovie **Austin:** Cora Calhoun (1887–1972), U.S. black jazz pianist. "Lovie" is said to have been a nickname given the future jazzwoman by her grandmother. Her new surname is that of her second husband, vaudeville performer Austin of the team Austin and Delaney.

Steve **Austin:** Steve Williams (1964–), U.S. wrestler ("Stone Cold").

Florence **Austral:** Florence Wilson (1894–1968), Austral. opera singer. The soprano adopted her patriotic name at the start of her stage career, which opened at Covent Garden, London, in 1922.

Frankie **Avalon:** Francis Thomas Avallone (1939–), U.S. pop singer, movie actor.

Claude **Aveline:** Eugène Avtsine (1901–1992), Fr. novelist.

Hanoch **Avenary:** Herbert Loewenstein (1908–1994), Israeli musicologist.

Aventinus: Johannes Thurmayr (or Turmaier) (1477–1534), Ger. historian, humanist. The historian was a native of Abensberg, and adopted its Latin name (Aventinum) as his professional name.

Richard **Avery:** Edmund Cooper (1926–), Eng. SF writer, reviewer.

Tex **Avery:** Frederick Bean Avery (1907–1980), U.S. movie animator. Like many people so nicknamed (such as Tex **Ritter**), Avery was born in Texas. To 1941 he was credited as Fred Avery.

Avi: Edward Irving Wortis (1937–), U.S. writer of fantasy, horror fiction for teenagers. The writer's adopted name is pronounced "Ah-vee."

Menaham **Avidom:** Menaham Mahler-Kalkstein (1908–1995), Pol.-born Israeli composer.

Shaul **Avigur:** Shaul Meirov (1899–1978), Russ.-born Israeli political leader. The head of Mossad, the Israeli state intelligence service, adopted his new name, meaning "father of Gur," after the tragic death of his son, Gur.

Kofi **Awoonor:** George Kofi Awoonor Williams (1935–), Ghanaian poet, novelist.

Axe: Alun Evans (1949–), Welsh crossword compiler. The former businessman took his pseudonym from his last company's password. It can also be read as the "cross" (X) of "crossword," with the compiler's initials either side of this.

Gabriel **Axel:** Gabriel Axel Mørch (1918–), Dan. movie director, working in France.

Axel **Axgil:** Axel Johannes Lundahl Madsen (1915–), Dan. gay activist. Madsen adopted his new name in 1956, as did his companion, Eigil Axgil (1922–1995).

Axiologus: William Wordsworth (1770–1850), Eng. poet. This name, Greek for "worthy of mention," was adopted by the then youthful poet for his "Sonnet, on seeing Miss Helen Maria Williams weep at a tale of Distress," published in *The European Magazine* in 1787.

Aybek: Musa Tashmukhamedov (1904–1968), Uzbek writer, translator. The writer adopted a poetic name meaning "knight of the moon." It arose from his childhood memories, one of the most vivid being that of a moonlit night. In his own words: "A full white moon sailed in the sky and it seemed so beautiful that I held out my little arms to it and kept saying, 'Momma, give me the moon!' I still sense the ecstasy that I experienced in those times" [Dmitriyev, p.141].

Catherine **Aydy:** Emma Christina Tennant (1937–), Br. novelist, journalist. The writer claims she got her name from an Ouija board. She used it for her first novel, *The Colour of Rain* (1964). The book had a mixed reception, however, and she dropped the name.

Aydyn: Manzura Sabirova (1906–1953), Uzbek poet. The writer chose a pen name meaning "bright."

Dan **Aykroyd:** Daniel Agraluscasacra (1951–), Can. movie actor.

Richard **Aylett:** Richard Argall (*fl.* 1621), Eng. poet. Argall is generally said to have assumed this form of his name for a second edition in 1654 of a volume of religious poems first published in 1621. But there is doubt regarding which name was the original and even whether Argall actually existed.

[Sir] Felix **Aylmer:** Felix Edward Aylmer-Jones (1889–1979), Br. stage, movie actor.

Allan **Aynesworth:** Edward Abbot-Anderson (1864–1959), Eng. stage actor, brother of Louis **Goodrich**.

Ayni: Sadriddin Said-Murodzoda (1878–1954), Tajik writer. The writer has described how he finally arrived at his pseudonym: "In my early years [at a Muslim college] in Bukhara some people, especially the mullahs, used to make me feel small. So I at first chose the name Sifli, i.e. belittled one. But as time went on I no longer liked the name. They might demean me, but why should I regard myself as demeaned? ... So I dropped the pseudonym Sifli and chose a new name — Mukhtodzhi, i.e. impoverished one. But I began to tire of that name in turn. 'I am hard up, it's true — I said to myself— but why should I broadcast my poverty to all and sundry?' So I dropped that name as well.

Some people, noticing my rather odd behavior, would say, 'He's a bit crazy!' As a result of those remarks I chose the name Dzhununi, i.e. madman. But I soon grew sick of that pseudonym. After all, I wasn't crazy!

Discovering that I wrote poetry, people began asking about my pseudonym and its meaning. I decided to find a name that would be as meaningful as possible. Leafing through the dictionary to that end, I came across the word 'ayni'; it had 48 meanings, of which the best known — eye, source, sun — were very suitable as a pseudonym. So I chose the name Ayni. If anyone now asked me what my name meant, I replied: 'It has forty-eight meanings, so look it up in the dictionary and find out for yourself.' That soon silenced the questioners" [Dmitriyev, pp.111–12].

Agnes **Ayres:** Agnes Hinkle (1896–1940), U.S. movie actress. The actress was originally billed as Agnes Ayars.

Lew **Ayres:** Lewis Frederick Ayer III (1908–1996), U.S. movie actor.

Paul **Ayres** *see* Edward **Ronns**

Mitchell **Ayres:** Mitchell Agress (1910–1969), U.S. jazz musician.

Hertha **Ayrton:** Phoebe Sarah Marks (1854–1923), Eng. physicist, inventor. As a teenager, Sarah took the name Hertha after the Germanic earth goddess and became an agnostic. In 1885 she married the English physicist William Ayrton (1847–1908) as his second wife.

J. Calder **Ayrton:** Mary Frances Chapman (1838–1884), Ir.-born Br. novelist. The writer's first novel, *Mary Bertrand*, begun when she was 15, was published in 1860 under the name Francis Meredith, a pseudonym based on her first two names. Her last novel, *The Gift of the Gods* (1879), was the only one published under her real name.

Michael **Ayrton:** Michael Gould (1921–1975), Eng. artist, writer. The artist adopted his mother's maiden name as his professional name.

John **Ayscough:** [Rt. Rev. Mgr. Count] Francis Browning Drew, later Bickerstaffe-Drew (1858–1938), Eng. writer of religious novels. The Roman Catholic prelate had the original name of Bickerstaffe, but assumed his mother's maiden name of Drew (which he already bore) as an additional surname on coming of age in 1879.

Azamat Batuk: [M.] Thiebland (*fl.*1870), Br. journalist. The supposed Turk adopted this name as a war correspondent of the *Pall-Mall Gazette*. The Muslim name Azamat means "majesty," "pride."

Brother **Azarias:** Patrick Francis Mullany (1847–1893), Ir.-born U.S. educator, writer.

Azed: Jonathan Crowther (1942–), Eng. crossword compiler. The setter's cryptic crossword clues cover "A to Z" (with "z" as British "zed" rather than American "zee"), while at the same time being tortuous, or even torturous, like Don Diego de Deza, the Spanish grand inquisitor whose name is reversed here. This association is all the more meaningful when it is known that Crowther succeeded **Ximenes** as chief compiler for the *Observer*. Earlier, he had set puzzles for other publications as "Gong," an early childhood attempt at his first name.

Maria **Azevedo:** Francisca Júlia (1871–1920), Brazilian poet.

Mohamed **Aziza:** Chems Nadir (1940–), Tunisian poet, working in French.

Kaifi **Azmi:** Athar Husain Rizvi (*c.*1920–2002), Ind. poet, movie songwriter, scenarist.

Charles **Aznavour:** Shahnour Varenagh Aznavurjan (1924–), Fr. movie actor, singer, of Armenian parentage.

Azorín: José Augusto Trinidad Martínez Ruiz (1873–1967), Sp. novelist, literary critic. The writer took his pen name from the hero of his autobiographical novel *António Azorín* (1902), with the name itself from the Spanish for "hawklike."

Agnès **b:** Agnès Bourgeois, née Troublé (1941–), Fr. fashion designer. On opening her first fashion shop in Paris in 1975, the designer saw that her real name was hardly suitable. She therefore needed a new name. She considered her married name (Bourgeois), but her former husband "had a certain notoriety in the publishing world," which did not seem compatible with her work. She therefore just kept the initial, "lower case, because it suits me better" [*The Times*, January 8, 1996].

Anthony **B**: Anthony Blair (*c*.1976–), Jamaican reggae musician. The musician first struck fame in the 1990s, when he wisely decided not to record under his real name, Tony Blair.

Derek **B**: Derek Boland (1965–2009), Br. black rapper.

Lisa **B** *see* **Elisa**

Baal Shem Tov: Israel ben Eliezer (*c*.1700–1760), Pol. Jewish mystic, folk healer. The founder of Hasidism came to be known by a Hebrew name or title meaning "master of the good name" (*ba'al*, "master," + *shem*, "name," + *tov*, "good"), implying that he had gained the secret of God's hidden name and thus won supernatural powers. The Besht, as he was known acronymically, had a reputation as a healer, who worked using herbs, talismans, and the like inscribed with the divine name.

Baantjer: Albert Cornelis Baantjer (1923–), Du. crime writer.

Johannes Theodor **Baargeld**: Alfred Emanuel Ferdinand Grünwald (1892–1927), German photographer. Other names used by the photographer were Zentrodada, for his connection with the Dada art movement, and Jesaias.

Lida **Baarova**: Ludmilla Babkova (1914–2000), Cz. movie actress, working in Germany, Italy.

Bab: [Sir] William Schwenk Gilbert (1836–1911), Eng. playwright, comic poet, illustrator. The writer, librettist of the Gilbert and Sullivan operettas, used this name for his *Bab Ballads* (1866–71). The name originated as nickname given Gilbert as a child by his parents.

The **Bab**: Ali Muhammad (1819–1850), Persian religious leader. Ali Muhammad claimed to be a gateway to the Hidden Imam, a new messenger of Allah who was to come. Hence his title, adopted in 1844, from the Arabic word for "gate." Some years after the Bab's execution, his work was taken up by the "Hidden Imam" in question, **Baha-'Allah**.

Babette: Elizabeth H. McLaughlan (1925–1999), Sc. music-hall dancer, teaming with **Raoul**, her husband. "Babette" is a French pet form of "Elizabeth."

Gracchus **Babeuf**: François Noël Babeuf (1760–1797), Fr. revolutionary. The protocommunist adopted as his new first name that of the 2d-century BC agrarian reformer Gaius Sempronius Gracchus, who also gave the name of Julien **Gracq**. He later ef-

fectively adopted the name as a whole, calling himself "Caius-Gracchus, Tribun du peuple."

Jean **Babilée**: Jean Gutmann (1923–), Fr. ballet dancer, choreographer, actor. The dancer adopted his mother's maiden name for his professional career.

Alice **Babs**: Alice Nilsson Sjöblom (1924–), Swe. popular singer, movie actress.

Marian **Babson**: Ruth Stenstreem (1929–), U.S.–born Br. crime writer.

Master **Babua**: Prosanta Kumar Roy (1947–), Ind. child movie actor. The name is simply a Hindi term of endearment for a son.

Babybird: Stephen Jones (1962–), Eng. rock musician. Originally Baby Bird, the musician settled to present his name in the distinctive form *baby*bird, also adopted for his band, formed in 1996.

Babyface: Kenneth Edmonds (1959–), U.S. black R&B musician. The musician adopted his nickname, given him for his youthful looks.

Baby Huey: James Ramey (1944–1970), U.S. R&B singer.

Baby Laurence: Laurence Donald Jackson (1921–1974), U.S. black jazz tap dancer.

Baby LeRoy: Ronald LeRoy Winebrenner (1932–), U.S. child movie actor. Some sources give the actor's original name as Le Roy Overacker.

Baby Madge: Margherita Evans (1909–1981), U.S. child movie actress. As an adult, the actress was billed as Madge Evans. In 1938 she deserted the screen altogether for the theater.

Baby Peggy: Peggy Montgomery (1917–), U.S. child movie actress.

Baby Sandy: Sandra Lee Henville (1938–), U.S. child movie actress.

Lauren **Bacall**: Betty Joan Perske (1924–), U.S. stage, movie actress. The actress's mother left Romania for America when she (the mother) was only a year or two old, together with her own parents. On arriving at the immigration office on Ellis Island, the family gave their name, Weinstein-Bacal, meaning "wineglass" in German and Russian. The immigration officer must have written just the first half of the name, so that the husband and wife were Max and Sophie Weinstein (Lauren's grandparents), with their daughters Renee and Nathalie (her mother) and their son Albert. Nathalie married William Perske, but soon divorced him, and then took instead the second half of the original "double" name for herself and her daughter. Then when Lauren was eight years old, her mother became Nathalie Bacal, and the little girl was Betty Bacal. By this time Betty had added another "l" to her name, as "there was too much irregularity of pronunciation. Some people rhymed the name with "cackle" while others pronounced it "Bacahl." She felt the second "l" would ensure that the second syllable of the name would be pronounced correctly, as in "call."

When Lauren began her movie career, director Howard Hawks wanted to find a good name to go with her surname, and asked if there was a suitable one somewhere in her family. Betty's grandmother's name, Sophie, did not seem to be quite right, and Hawks said he would think of something. Later, over lunch one day with her, he said he had found a name. It was "Lauren," and he was going to tell everyone that it was an old family name of hers, even that it had been her great-grandmother's. "What invention!" exclaimed the actress, who was said to dislike the name [Lauren Bacall, *By Myself*, 1979].

Barbara Bach: Barbara Goldbach (1947–), U.S. movie actress.

Dr. Charlotte Bach: Karoly Mihaly Hajdu (1920–1981), Hung.-born transvestite academic, entrepreneur, working in England. In 1942 Hajdu forged a birth certificate in which he renamed himself as Karoly Mihaly Balazs Agoston Hajdu, son of the Baron of Szadelo and Balkany. In 1948 he emigrated to England, where he anglicized his name as Carl Hajdu and assumed the title of "Baron Balkanyi." In 1951 he found a job as a barman in London and two years later married a Welshwoman, Phyllis Mary Rodgers. In 1957 he set himself up in London as a hypnotherapist named Michael B. Karoly, a name devised by anglicizing his middle name, switching it with his first name, and inserting a middle initial that stood, he claimed, for "Blaise." His writing paper soon added a string of bogus qualifications: "Michael B. Karoly, Sc.Sc. (Budapest), D.Psy., C.P.E. (Cantab.), M.B.S.H."

Hajdu had long had transvestite leanings, and in 1963 he was arrested for walking into a hotel dressed as a woman. By 1969 he was living permanently as a woman and on April 1 (April Fools' Day), 1970, he changed his name by deed poll from Carl Michael Blaise Augustine Hajdu to Charlotte Maria Beatrix Augusta Hajdu. She (as Hajdu now was) never used her real surname, however, and embarked on an academic career as Dr. Charlotte M. Bach. Soon after, she also set up business as a "spanking madam" (dominatrix) named Daphne Lyell-Manson [Francis Wheen, *Who Was Dr Charlotte Bach?*, 2002].

P.D.Q. Bach: Peter Schickele (1935–), U.S. composer, writer. The musician adopted the name of a fictional son of J.S. Bach for humorous works written in mock-18th-century style, among them operas such as *The Stoned Guest* and *The Abduction of Figaro* (1984). His selection of the initials P.D.Q. (usually taken to mean "pretty damn quick") imitated those of the (real) musical sons of J.S. Bach, such as C.P.E. Bach and J.C.F. Bach.

Sebastian Bach: Sebastian Bierk (1968–), U.S. rock singer. An apparent tribute or at least acknowledgment to the German composer.

Amitabh Bachchan: Amit Shrivastava (1942–), Ind. movie actor.

Richard Bachman: Stephen Edwin King (1947–), U.S. horror novelist. King first used this pseudonym for his novel *Rage* (1977), but his true identity, which many had long suspected, became public knowledge following the publication of *Thinner* in 1984.

The pen name lay behind a rounded personification. "Richard Bachman — born in 1942, a graduate of the University of New Hampshire, a Vietnam veteran, window washer, commercial fisherman, private security guard, and most recently a dairy farmer and part-time writer — died a sudden death of what King termed 'cancer of the pseudonym' on January 9, 1985" [George Beahm, *The Stephen King Story*, 1992].

King wanted to resurrect the Bachman name for a later novel, *The Dark Half* (1989), which he submitted for publication as a "collaboration" by Stephen King and Richard Bachman (appropriately, as the story is about a writer's pen name that comes back to life), but his publishers rejected the idea.

Il Baciccia: Giovan Battista Gaulli (1639–1709), It. painter. The artist's name probably arose as a childish pronunciation of the second half of his first name, which literally means "John the Baptist." Compare **Battistello**.

Backsight-Forethought: [Sir] Ernest Dunlop Swinton (1868–1951), Br. army officer, writer. Major-General Swinton used this name for his treatise on minor tactics entitled *The Defence of Duffer's Drift* (1904), subsequently recommended reading for young officers. His better-known pen name was **Ole Luke-Oie**.

George Bacovia: George Vasiliu (1881–1957), Rom. Symbolist poet. The poet took his name from his birthplace, the Romanian city of Bacau.

Angela Baddeley: Madeleine Angela Byam Shaw, née Clinton-Baddeley (1904–1976), Eng. stage, movie actress, sister of Hermione **Baddeley**.

Hermione Baddeley: Hermione Willis, née Clinton-Baddeley (1906–1986), Eng. stage, movie actress.

Baden Powell: Roberto Baden Powell de Aquino (1937–2000), Brazilian guitarist. The musician was originally named in honor of Robert Baden-Powell (1857–1941), English founder of the Boy Scouts.

Badinguet: Napoleon III (1808–1873), Fr. emperor. The name is that of the workman in whose clothes Louis Napoleon escaped to England disguised as a mason from the castle of Ham, northern France, in 1846. After his escape, the future emperor adopted the name of Comte Arenenberg, after the castle in Switzerland where he had lived with his mother. He was known by a number of nicknames (rather than actual assumed names), one being Boustrapa, from *Bou*logne, *Stras*bourg, and *Pa*ris, the towns where he had attempted a coup (respectively in 1840, 1836, and 1851, the third successfully).

Badly Drawn Boy: Damon Gough (1970–), Br. rock musician. The singer is popularly said to have named himself after the main character in the children's TV cartoon *Sam and His Magic Ball*, who was dissatisfied with his creator's art. On the other hand: "A long-time admirer of the *Viz* adult comic, he loved May 1983's one-off *Badly Drawn Man*, with all the jokes stemming from the dashed-off delineation" [Beech, p. 30].

Erykah **Badu:** Erica Wright (1971–), U.S. black soul singer. The singer saw "Erica" as a slave name so altered the spelling to "Erykah," saying the *kah* meant "inner self." Her new surname represented the sounds she made when scatting, her voice imitating the sound of the instrument, but she later associated it with an Arabic word meaning "truth," "light."

George **Bagby** *see* Hampton **Stone**

Eduard **Bagritsky:** Eduard Georgiyevich Dzyubin (1895–1934), Russ. revolutionary poet. The poet based his name on that of the princely Bagratid dynasty of Armenia and Georgia, and so on that of one of their descendants, the Russian general and hero of the Napoleonic Wars Prince Bagration (1765–1812). He himself commented on his new name: "It smacks of war, and has something of the flavor of my writing." Bagritsky published an early volume of poems, *Auto in Trousers* (1915), under the name Nina Voskresenskaya. His readers were sure it was by a woman, for one poem began with the line, "I am in love with him," while another, naming an Odessa street, ended, "So Deribasovskaya has its poetess!"

Elisaveta **Bagryana:** Elisaveta Belcheva (1893–1991), Bulg. lyric poet. The poet's adopted name means "crimson."

Baha-'Allah: Huseyn Ali Nuri (1817–1892), Persian religious leader. The founder of the Baha'i faith was a follower of the **Bab** who at some point in the 1860s proclaimed himself "Him whom God shall make manifest," a divine spirit foretold by the Bab. Hence his Arabic name, meaning "Glory of God" (*baha,'* "splendor," + *allah,* "God"). The keystone of Baha'i belief is thus that the Bab and Baha-'Allah are manifestations of God, and that when the latter proclaimed himself, the Bab's mission was fulfilled.

Bill **Bailey:** Mark Bailey (1965–), Br. comedian. The stand-up comic was nicknamed "Bill" at school from the popular song of the turn of the 20th century, "Won't You Come Home Bill Bailey," and he adopted it. "His mother ... never got used to the name. 'People would ring asking for Bill. She'd say: "There's no Bill here. Would you like to speak to Mark?"'" [*The Times*, November 11, 2008].

Guy **Bailey:** [Professor] Cedric Keith Simpson (1907–1985), Eng. pathologist, forensic expert. "Guy" is a reference to Guy's Hospital, London, where Simpson was head of the department of forensic medicine; "Bailey" refers to the Old Bailey, London, the Central Criminal Court of England.

Harry **Bailey:** Harry Daniels (1910–1989), Ir. comedian.

James Anthony **Bailey:** James Anthony McGinniss (1847–1906), U.S. circus owner. The future showman began his circus career at age 13, doing odd jobs for Frederick H. Bailey, the advance man of the Robinson and Lake Circus. Bailey took to the young lad, asked him to become his protégé on the road, and had him adopt his name. In 1881 Bailey joined with P.T. Barnum to form the famous Barnum and Bailey circus.

Mildred **Bailey:** Mildred Rinker (1907–1951), U.S. jazz singer, movie actress, wife of Red **Norvo**.

Bill **Baird:** William Keckritz (1914–1978), U.S. illusionist.

Ba Jin: Li Yao-tang (later Li Fei-han) (1904–2005), Chin. anarchist writer. The writer created his pseudonym from the Chinese forms of the first syllable of the surname of Mikhail Bakunin (1814–1876) and the last of that of Peter Kropotkin (1842–1921), two Russian anarchists that he admired.

Art **Baker:** Arthur Shank (1898–1966), U.S. movie actor.

Asa **Baker** *see* Brett **Halliday**

Belle **Baker:** Bella Becker (1895–1957), U.S. vaudeville singer, actress, of Russ. Jewish parentage. By 1909 Baker had formed a double act with her future husband, Lew **Leslie**.

Bonnie **Baker:** Evelyn Nelson (1918–), U.S. popular singer

Charles **Baker:** David Lewis (1617–1679), Eng. Jesuit.

Cheryl **Baker:** Rita Maria Crudgington (1955–), Eng. pop singer, TV presenter.

Eddie **Baker:** Edward King (1897–1968), U.S. movie actor.

Josephine **Baker:** Freda Josephine McDonald (1906–1975), U.S.–born Fr. black dancer, singer. The dancer's original name is given thus in several sources. The last name is that of her mother, Carrie McDonald, who married Eddie Carson, a musician. Her new surname is that of her second husband, William Baker, whom she married in 1921 at the age of 15.

LaVern **Baker:** Dolores Williams (1928–1997), U.S. black blues singer. Williams renamed herself for the dancer Josephine **Baker**, whom she claimed as a relative.

Lefty Baker: Eustace Britchforth (1942–1971), U.S. guitarist, banko player.

Bakhori: Abdumalik Rakhmanov (1927–), Tajik poet. The writer's adopted name means "of the spring," "vernal."

Léon Bakst: Lev Samoylovich Rosenberg (1866–1924), Russ. graphic artist, stage designer, working in France. The artist's adopted name was that of his grandfather.

Balabrega: John Miller (1857–1906), Swe.-born magician.

George Balanchine: Georgy Melitonovich Balanchivadze (1904–1983), Russ.-born U.S. ballet choreographer, of Georgian descent. When in France in the 1920s, Balanchivadze was prevailed upon by the Russian impresario Sergey Diaghilev to modify his name in deference to Western audiences. He originally altered his first name to the French equivalent Georges, but in English programs this became George, while his surname was sometimes spelled Balanchin.

Béla Balász: Herbert Bauer (1884–1949), Hung. writer, movie director.

Rev. Edward Baldwin: William Godwin (1756–1836), Eng. philosopher, novelist, dramatist. The writer, husband of the moral writer Mary Wollstonecraft, mother-in-law of the poet P.B. Shelley, used this as his main pen name. Originally a Nonconformist minister, he adopted it on becoming an atheist in 1783, rejecting "God-" in favor of "Bald-." He also wrote as Theophilus **Marcliffe**.

William Bales: William Bialystotsky (1910–1990), U.S. dancer, of Russ. Jewish parentage.

Neil Balfort: Robert Lionel Fanthorpe (1935–), Eng. SF writer. A name based on the author's original name, as were many of his other pseudonyms, such as Erle Barton (presumably suggested by the name of the Northamptonshire village Earls Barton), Thornton Bell, Phil Nobel, and Olaf Trent.

Clara Balfour: Felicia Dorothea Hemans, née Browne (1793–1835), Eng. poet.

James Balfour: William Bruce Hepburn (1925–1992), Eng. doctor, novelist.

Bal Gandharva: Narayanrao Rajhans (1888–1967), Ind. female impersonator, singer. The performer's new name relates to the Gandharv, a mythological community of heavenly singers.

Geeta Bali: Harikirtan Kaur (1930–1965), Ind. dancer, movie actress, singer. The performer's adopted name is Sanskrit for "young singer."

Balilla: Giovanni Battista Perasso (1729–1781), It. militant leader. The name, a childish form of "Battista," is traditionally that of the teenager who led a popular uprising in Genoa against Austrian domination in 1746. His (supposedly) true identity was established only some time later, and his name was subsequently adopted as a Fascist symbol of youthful ardor and patriotism.

Ina Balin: Ina Rosenberg (1937–1990), U.S. movie actress.

Marty Balin: Martyn Jerel Buchwald (1942–), U.S. rock singer.

Bobby Ball: Robert Harper (1944–), Eng. TV comedian, teaming with Tommy **Cannon**.

Harry Ball: William Henry Powles (1841–1888), Eng. music-hall singer, father of Vesta **Tilley**.

Hank Ballard: John H. Kendricks (1927–2003), U.S. singer, songwriter.

Kaye Ballard: Catherine Gloria Balotta (1926–), U.S. movie comedienne, singer.

Carl Ballantine: Meyer Kessler (?–), U.S. comedy magician, actor.

Balthus: [Count] Baltucz (or Balthasar) Klossowski de Rola (1908–2001), Fr. painter, of Pol. parentage. The artist's aristocratic title was self-assumed. "He forced his friends to accept his claim to a bogus Polish title ... and denied his descent from Jews on his mother's side (Elizabeth Klossowska, née Spiro, known as Baladine, was the daughter of Abraham Bear Spiro, a cantor in Breslau)" [*Times Literary Supplement*, April 5, 2002].

Baltimora: James McShane (1957–1995), Northern Ireland-born pop singer, working in Italy.

Juozas Baltùsis: Albertas Juozenas (1909–1991), Lithuanian writer. The writer adopted his name from Lithuanian *baltas*, "white."

Micah Balwhidder *see* Rev. T. **Clark**

Honoré de Balzac: Honoré Balssa (1799–1850), Fr. novelist. Balzac's father was Bernard-François Balssa. Wishing to "improve" on the name's peasant connotations, the writer changed this to Balzac in 1821 and added the honorific particle "de," possibly in imitation of the writer Jean-Louis Guez de Balzac (1595–1654). According to D'Israeli, the latter was also a pseudonym: "*Guez* (a beggar) is a French writer of great pomp of style, but he felt such extreme delicacy at so low a name, that to give some authority to the splendour of his diction, he assumed the name of his estate, and is well known as Balzac" [p.201].

Balzac wrote a number of *genre* novels early in his career as Horace de Saint-Aubin and Lord R'Hoone, the latter name being an anagram of his first name. "The works — mainly bad sensational novels — of 'Horace de Saint-Aubin' filled sixteen volumes in a collected edition of 1836–40" [Harvey and Heseltine, p.647].

Afrika Bambaataa: Kevin Donovan (1960–), U.S. black soul musician, rapper. The rap-music pioneer took his name, translating as "chief affection," from a 19th-century Zulu chief, with the name itself being inspired by the 1964 movie *Zulu* and the code of honor and bravery of its black participants. Bambaataa's alternate African name is Khayan Aasim.

Bam Bam: Peter Poulton (1970–), Br. radio DJ.

Toni Cade **Bambara:** Toni Cade (1939–1995), U.S. black writer, moviemaker. The writer published as Toni Cade from 1959 to 1970, when she changed her surname to Bambara, a name she discovered as a signature in a sketchbook found in a trunk of her grandmother's belongings.

Bamboccio: Pieter van Laer (?1599–1642), Du. painter, working in Italy. The artist's Italian nickname means "clumsy doll," "big baby," from *bambino*, "child," and the "plump" suffix *-occio*. His scenes of low life were known as *bambocciate*, and his Dutch followers in Italy were called *bambroccianti*.

Peter **Bamm:** Curt Emmrich (1897–1975), Ger. essayist.

Eric **Bana:** Eric Banadinovich (1968–), Austral. movie actor.

D.R. **Banat:** Ray Douglas Bradbury (1920–), U.S. SF writer.

Anne **Bancroft:** Anna Maria Louise Italiano (1931–2005), U.S. stage, movie actress. The actress was born in New York as the daughter of Italian immigrants, and even her original name came as the result of a misunderstanding. Her father, asked his name on his arrival at Ellis Island, thought he was being asked his nationality and said "Italiano, Italiano." Bancroft began her career on TV in 1950 as Ann Italiano. She then signed for Twentieth Century–Fox, when producer Darryl F. Zanuck, fearing she might end up playing nothing but Italians, told her she had to take a new name. "'He gave me a list of names,' she said. 'They sounded like strippers' names. Bancroft was the only one with any dignity'" [*The Times*, June 9, 2005]. She made her movie debut under the name in *Don't Bother to Knock* (1952).

Francis **Bancroft:** Frances Charlotte Slater (1892–1947), Eng. novelist.

Laura **Bancroft** *see* Floyd **Akers**

[Sir] Squire **Bancroft:** Sydney Bancroft Butterfield (1841–1926), Eng. stage actor, theatrical manager. The actor assumed his new name in 1867.

Albert **Band:** Alfredo Antonini (1924–2002), It.-born movie director, producer, working in U.S.

Baccio **Bandinelli:** Bartolomeo Brandini (1488–1560), It. sculptor, painter. The artist changed his name in 1530 to receive the Order of the Knights of Santiago, which was restricted to the nobility.

Billy **Bang:** William Vincent Walker (1947–), U.S. black jazz musician. Walker was fond of playing on the bongos as a young boy, but switched to the violin when he was 12.

Dan **Banim** *see* F.M. **Allen**

Archibald **Banks** *see* John **Dangerfield**

Darrell **Banks:** Darrell Eubanks (1937–1970), U.S. pop musician.

Monty **Banks:** Mario Bianchi (1897–1950), It.-born U.S. movie comedian, director. Bianchi was discovered and renamed by fellow comedian Fatty Arbuckle (*see* William B. **Goodrich**). The name appropriately suggests a "mountebank" or buffoon.

Banksy: Robin Gunningham (1974–), Br. graffiti artist. The identity of the secretive artist remains uncertain. Some sources give his real name as Robin Banks, but this is probably a pun (like that of Rob da Bank). "'Is it true that your real name is Robin Gunningham, and that you are a public schoolboy from Bristol? No lies, please.' 'My job occasionally requires a little light law-breaking, so I've never confirmed or denied my identity'" [Interview by e-mail, *Sunday Times*, June 14, 2009].

Vilma **Banky:** Vilma Lonchit (or Konsics) (1898–1991), Austr.-Hung. movie actress.

Angela **Banner:** Angela Mary Maddison (1923–), Br. children's writer. The writer's name appears to match the insect characters Ant and Bee that first featured in her stories for young children in 1950.

Margaret **Bannerman:** Margaret Le Grand (1896–1976), Can. stage actress.

R.C. **Bannon:** Daniel Shipley (1945–), U.S. country musician. The musician adopted his new name in 1968 as a DJ in Seattle, basing it on the commercial product RC Cola.

Anna **Banti:** Lucia Longhi Lopresti (1895–1985), It. novelist, short-story writer.

Buju **Banton:** Mark Anthony Myrie (1973–), Jamaican reggae musician. The nickname "Buju," meaning "breadfruit," was given Myrie by his mother for his chubbiness as a baby. "Banton" compliments the talented DJ Burro Banton (*c.*1960–), famous for his chanting at the mike, his own name a Jamaican-patois term for a DJ "full of lyrics."

Mega **Banton:** Garth Williams (*c.*1973–), Jamaican reggae musician. Williams continued the style of lyrics initiated by Burro Banton, who in turn inspired Buju **Banton**.

Starkey **Banton:** David Murray (1962–), Br. black reggae musician. Murray first performed as "Starkey Super," but then changed his name to Banton after Burro Banton, who inspired Buju **Banton**.

Banx: Jeremy Banks (1959–), Eng. cartoonist.

Bao Dai: Nguyen Vinh Thuy (1913–1997), Vietnamese ruler. The last reigning emperor of Vietnam succeeded to the throne in 1926 and assumed a name (or title) meaning "keeper of greatness."

Father **Baptist:** [Rev.] Richard Baptist O'Brien (1809–1885), Ir. writer. O'Brien used this name for poems published in *The Nation*.

R. Hernekin **Baptist:** Ethelreda Lewis (1875–1946), Eng.-born S.A. novelist. The writer used this name for four novels published in the 1930s.

Baptiste: (1) Nicolas Anselme (1761–1835), Fr. sentimental comedy actor; (2) Jean-Gaspard Deburau (originally Jan Kašpar Dvořák) (1796–1846), Fr. pierrot, of Bohemian parentage.

Bapu: Sattiraju Lakshminarayana (1933–), Ind. cartoonist, designer, movie director. The artist's new name is Sanskrit for "father."

Theda **Bara:** Theodosia Burr Goodman (1885–1955), U.S. stage, movie actress. Goodman was the daughter of Bernard Goodman, a Polish Jew, and Pauline Louise de Coppet, a French immigrant. In 1917, Goodman's parents legally changed their name to Bara, after de Coppet's Swiss father, Francis Bara de Coppet. Goodman thus first came on stage under the name Theodosia de Coppet. Then in 1914 she was cast as the vampire in the movie *A Fool There Was* (1915), directed by Frank Powell, who renamed her Theda Bara for the part. For publicity purposes, as the first "vamp," Goodman was said to be the love child of a French artist and his Egyptian mistress, her name a near-reversal of "Arab death." "The anagrammatic connection between Theda Bara and Arab Death so often evoked in awed tones is today like an archaeological find, proving only that we live in a different culture" [Thomson 2003, p. 50].

Ehud **Barak:** Ehud Brog (1942–), Israeli politician, of Lithuanian parentage. Israel's prime minister from 1999 to 2001 changed his name on being drafted into the Israel Defense Forces in 1959.

Amiri **Baraka:** Everett LeRoy (later LeRoi) Jones (1934–), U.S. black writer. The writer changed his name in 1968 on converting to Islam, at first often prefixing it with the title Imamu ("imam"). Amiri (originally Ameer) means "prince," "ruler," and Baraka "shining," "lustrous."

Timir **Baran:** Timirbaran Bhattacharya (1904–1987), Ind. composer of movie music.

Galerana **Baratotti** (or Barcitotti): Arcangela Tarabotti (1604–1652), It. satirist, polemicist.

Porfirio **Barba Jacob:** Miguel Angel Osorio Benítez (1883–1942), Colombian poet.

Barbara: Monique Serf (1930–1997), Fr. popular singer, songwriter, of Pol.-Russ. Jewish parentage.

Paola **Barbara:** Paolina Prato (1912–), It. movie actress.

La **Barbarina:** Barbara Campanini (1721–1799), It. ballet dancer.

Paolo **Barbaro:** Ennio Gallo (1922–), It. writer.

Johannes **Barbarus:** Johannes Varesh (1890–1946), Estonian poet. The writer's name arose in his school days, when he distributed a hectographed magazine in Russian, Estonian, and Latvian. It included his first poems and articles. He could not put his name to them, however, for that would have risked expulsion. He recalled: "I needed a pen name. One of the teachers called me a barbarian because I was once late for a lesson. I translated the word into Latin, and that gave my pseudonym, which I have used all my life" [Dmitriyev, p.96].

Barbecue Bob: Robert Hicks (1902–1931), U.S. black blues musician. Hicks adopted the nickname given him by Columbia Records for his day job as a chef in a barbecue restaurant.

John Henry **Barbee:** John Henry Barbee (1905–1964), U.S. black blues musician. Barbee told researchers that his real name was William George Tucker but in 1937 applied for social security as John Henry Barbee, naming his father as Beecher Barbee.

W.N.P. **Barbellion:** Bruce Frederick Cummings (1889–1919), Eng. essayist, diarist, naturalist. The writer adopted this name, taken from the front of a confectioner's shop in Bond Street, London, when he published entries from his diary in book form under the title *The Journal of a Disappointed Man* (1919). He claimed that the initials stood for "Wilhelm Nero Pilate," all men of bravado.

Antonia **Barber:** Barbara Anthony, née Wilson (*c.*1935–), Br. children's writer.

Glynis **Barber:** Glynis van der Riet (1955–), S.A.–born TV, movie actress, working in U.K., wife of Michael **Brandon**.

Barbette: Van der Clyde Broodway (1899–1972), U.S. music-hall female impersonator. The artist made his debut in the circus dressed as one of the Alfaretta Sisters, but subsequently developed his own individual act as an aerialist (trapeze artist) named Barbette.

Ion **Barbu:** Dan Barbilian (1895–1964), Rom. lyric poet.

Ann **Barclay** *see* Maysie **Greig**

David **Barclay:** David Poole Fronabarger (1912–1969), U.S. stage actor.

Eddie **Barclay:** Edouard Ruault (1921–2005), Fr. music producer. The record producer adopted a name that he reckoned would play much better when he went to the U.S. to do business there. In 1949 he set up his first record label, Blue Star, and Barclay Records followed it in 1955.

Tessa **Barclay** *see* Avon **Curry**

Roy **Barcroft:** Howard H. Ravenscroft (1901–1969), U.S. movie actor.

Countess Hélène **Barcynska:** Marguerite Florence Barclay, later Evans, née Jervis (1894–1964),

Eng. romantic novelist. The writer assumed a fictional identity to match her books, claiming her first husband, Armiger Barclay, was the son of a Polish count called Barcynski. Her second husband was Caradoc **Evans**. Her (male) writing name was Oliver **Sandys**.

Samuel A. **Bard:** Ephraim George Squier (1821–1888), U.S. archaeologist, traveler, author. The writer used this name for a romantic and largely autobiographical novel, *Waikna, or Adventures on the Mosquito Shore* (1855).

The **Bard:** Edward Jerringham (1727–1812), Eng. poet, dramatist of the Della Cruscan school.

Wilkie **Bard:** William Augustus Smith (1870–1944), Eng. music-hall comedian. The actor had a high, domed forehead, like that of Shakespeare. Hence his nickname and subsequent stage name, which was originally Will Gibbard when he made his debut in 1895.

Y **Bardd Cloff:** Thomas Jones (1768–1828), Welsh poet. The poet's name means "the lame poet," referring to an accident he had as a child.

Y **Bardd Coch o Fôn:** Hugh Hughes (1693–1776), Welsh poet. The poet's name means "the red poet of the bottom."

Y **Bardd Cocos:** John Evans (1827–1888), Welsh poetaster. The rhymester earned a living by selling cockles. Hence the name by which he became known, meaning "the cockles poet." Local wags gave him the Welsh title *Archfardd Cocysaidd Tywysogol*, "Royal High Cockle-Poet."

Y **Bardd Crwst:** Abel Jones (1829–1901), Welsh balladist. The singer's name means literally "the crust poet," implying one who earns his daily bread by his street performances.

Bardd Gwagedd: Richard Williams (*c.*1805–*c.*1865), Welsh balladist. The singer's name means literally "vanity poet," alluding to his reputation as "the king of all the ballad singers" in southern Wales.

Bardd Nantglyn: Robert Davies (1769–1835), Welsh poet. The poet took his name from his birthplace, Nantglyn near Denbigh.

Bardd y Brenin: Edward Jones (1752–1824), Welsh musician, writer. The writer was appointed bard (court poet) to the Prince of Wales. Hence his bardic Welsh name or title, meaning "King's Poet." The appointment was an honorary one.

Bardd yr Haf: Robert Williams Parry (1884–1956), Welsh poet. The poet won the chair at the 1910 National Eisteddfod with his poem *Yr Haf*, "The Summer," and so came to be known as "poet of the summer."

Shlomo **Bardin:** Shlomo Bardinstein (1898–1976), Ukr.-born Jewish educator, working in U.S. Bardinstein probably shortened his name on com-

pleting his education in 1918, when he left Russia for Palestine.

John **Bardon:** John M. Jones (1939–), Eng. movie, TV actor.

Brigitte **Bardot:** Brigitte Bardot (1934–), Fr. movie actress. Many sources give the actress's original name as Camille Javal, but this is the character she played in the 1963 Franco-Italian movie *Le Mépris* (English title *Contempt*), based on the 1954 novel *Il Disprezzo* (English title *A Ghost at Noon*) by Alberto **Moravia** [Jeffrey Robinson, *Bardot: An Intimate Portrait*, 1994]. *See also* **B.B.**

Lynn **Bari:** Marjorie Schuyler Fisher (1913–1989), U.S. movie actress. The actress once explained that she created her new name by combining those of actress Lynn Fontanne and dramatist James Barrie.

Max **Baring:** Charles Messent (1857–?), Eng. short-story writer.

Norah **Baring:** Norah Baker (1907–), Br. movie actress.

Dave **Barker:** David Collins (*c.*1952–), Jamaican reggae musician.

Megan **Barker** *see* Rosalind **Erskine**

Victor **Barker:** Valerie Arkell-Smith (1895–1960), Eng. adventuress. Following her successive marriages to two Australians, Arkell-Smith assumed a male identity and rank as Colonel Victor Barker, as whom she married Elfrida Haward in 1923. Seven years later she downgraded her rank and expanded her name to become Captain Leslie Ivor Victor Gauntlett Bligh Barker. Her true sex was revealed when she was arrested and jailed on a bankruptcy charge.

Charles **Barling** *see* Pamela **Barrington**

Edward **Barlow:** Edward Booth (1639–1719), Eng. priest, horological inventor. Booth took his new name from his uncle, Edward Barlow (1587–1641), a Benedictine monk known as Ambrose, executed for being a Roman Catholic priest "unlawfully abiding in England" [*Dictionary of National Biography*].

Viktor **Barna:** Győző Viktor Braun (1911–1972), Hung.-born Br. table-tennis player. The sportsman changed his name to avoid antisemitism in the years before World War II. After the war he became a British citizen.

A.M. **Barnard:** Louisa May Alcott (1832–1888), U.S. novelist, short-story writer. Alcott adopted this name for a number of adventure thrillers published in the "Flag of Our Union" series.

Barney **Barnato:** Barnett Isaacs (1852–1897), Eng. financier, diamond magnate. The speculator adopted the name of the Barnato Brothers, which he and his brother had used in London as vaudeville entertainers.

Louis **Barnaval:** Charles De Kay (1848–1935), U.S. editor, writer.

Binnie **Barnes:** Gitelle Gertrude Maude Barnes (1903–1998), Eng. movie actress, working in U.S.

Jimmy **Barnes:** James Swan (1956–), Sc. rock musician.

John **Barnett:** John Barnett (1802–1890), Eng. composer, of Ger. Jewish/Hung. parentage. Although born in England, Barnett was the son of a family whose original name was Beer, and he was a second cousin of the German composer Giacomo **Meyerbeer**, whose original name was also Beer.

L. David **Barnett:** Barnett D. Laschever (1924–), U.S. journalist, writer.

Esdras **Barnivelt, Apothecary:** Alexander Pope (1688–1744), Eng. poet. This name was used for a key to Pope's *The Rape of the Lock* (1714), published a year after the poem itself. Although the poet is generally reckoned to be the author, it has also been attributed to the Scottish physician and writer John Arbuthnot (1667–1735).

Baron: Baron de V. Nahum (1906–1956), Eng. photographer.

Alexander **Baron:** Alec Bernstein (1917–1999), Eng. novelist, TV writer.

David **Baron:** Harold Pinter (1930–2008), Eng. playwright. The dramatist adopted this name in his early career as an actor when touring Ireland in the 1950s.

Michel **Baron:** Michel Boyron (1653–1729), Fr. actor, dramatist.

Jacques **Baroncelli:** Jacques Baroncelli-Javon (1881–1951), Fr. movie director.

Baron de Bookworms *see* **Toby, M.P.**

Baron Korff: Harry Domela (1903–?), Ger. impostor. Homeless and unemployed after World War I, during which he lost his faher and brothers, Domela decided to enter society. He first assumed the name and title of Baron Korff, then the royal persona of Prince Lieven of Latvia. In this latter role, he befriended young aristocrats in military circles, who decided there was more to him than met the eye. They did not penetrate his impersonation, even so, but instead decided that he was actually Prince Wilhelm of Hohenzollern, the Kaiser's grandson, in disguise. Domela threw himself gleefully into the part, so that he was the heir to the throne in the event of a restoration of the monarchy. He soon sensed, however, that detectives were after him, and fled to France with the aim of joining the Foreign Legion. There the long arm of the law fell on his shoulder, and he was jailed for imposture. At his trial seven months later, all of the witnesses affirmed that Domela's imposture had been harmless, and he was freed.

Billy **Barr:** Walter Shufflebottom (1897–?), Eng. comedian, impersonator.

Cecil **Barr:** Jack Kahane (1887–1939), Eng. writer, publisher, working in France, father of Maurice **Girodias**. Kahane settled in Paris, where in 1929 he founded the Obelisk Press. His first successful title was *Daffodil* (1931), by an author named Cecil Barr, otherwise Jack Kahane. His great discovery was Henry Miller, whose *Tropic of Cancer* arrived in 1932 from the literary agent of an author who signed himself "Anonymous," but which he eventually published under the author's real name two years later.

Donald **Barr:** Charles Leslie Barrett (1879–1959), Austral. children's writer.

Ida **Barr:** Maud Barlow (1882–1967), Eng. music-hall comedienne. The artist made her music-hall debut in 1897 under the name Maud Laverne. She adopted her regular stage name 11 years later.

Richard **Barr:** Richard Baer (1917–1989), U.S. theater director, producer.

Ray **Barra:** Raymond Martin Barallobre (1930–), U.S. ballet dancer.

Edith **Barrett:** Edith Williams (1906–1977), U.S. stage, movie actress. The actress adopted her mother's maiden name as her stage name.

Judith **Barrett:** Lucille Kelly (1914–2000), U.S. movie actress.

Rona **Barrett:** Rona Burnstein (1934–), U.S. gossip columnist.

Syd **Barrett:** Roger Keith Barrett (1946–2006), Br. rock musician. The Pink Floyd founder took his new first name from his nickname, after a dummer of the same name, as a teenager at a local jazz club.

Odoardo **Barri:** Edward Slater (1844–1920), Ir. popular composer.

Amanda **Barrie:** Shirley Anne Broadbent (1939–), Eng. stage, movie, TV actress. The actress changed her name on being accepted for a part in the revue *Five Past Eight,* produced by Freddie Carpenter. "He insisted that I change my name. 'You'll never be taken seriously in this business with a name like that,' he told me firmly.... However, finding a new name wasn't easy. I picked Barrie with a pin from the phone book, and was pleased with my chance choice because of its connection with J.M. Barrie, the writer of *Peter Pan.* I thought of Amanda because of my lifelong devotion to Gertrude **Lawrence**, who always wanted to be called Amanda, as indeed she was in [Noel Coward's] *Private Lives....* But I thought that would be too pretentious so picked Lynne instead. Then [actors' union] Equity turned that down because there was already a Lynne Barrie listed, so I asked a friend to choose a book for me and open it at random. The book was *Rival Experiments*, by H.G. Wells, and it opened at two pages that were blank except for a one-word chapter heading 'Amanda.' I reckoned that was a message from Gertie, and

Amanda Barrie I became" [Amanda Barrie with Hilary Bonner, *It's Not a Rehearsal*, 2002].

"Lynne Barrie" may have actually been Lynn **Bari**, while Wells's Amanda was probably really Amanda Benham in Wells's *The Research Magnificent* (1915).

Barbara **Barrie:** Barbara Ann Berman (1931–), U.S. movie actress.

J.J. **Barrie:** Barry Authors (1933–), Can. pop musician.

Mona **Barrie:** Mona Smith (1909–1964), Austral. movie actress, working in U.S.

Scott **Barrie:** Nelson Clyde Barr (1941–1993), U.S. black fashion designer.

Wendy **Barrie:** Marguerite Wendy Jenkins (1912–1978), Br. movie actress. Marguerite Jenkins was the goddaughter of J.M. Barrie, author of *Peter Pan* (1904), and she took her new name from him. She was already named Wendy, after the play's young heroine, Wendy Darling.

E. **Barrington:** Eliza Louisa Moresby Adams Beck (?1862–1931), Eng. romantic, historical novelist, working in Canada. The writer used the name Lily Adams Beck for books about oriental culture and also wrote under the male name Louis Moresby. "I chose Louis Moresby as pseudonym because two of my names — I have a good many — are Louisa Moresby. As to 'E. Barrington,' I wanted the initials E.B. because two of my names are those initials —*i.e.*, E.B." [Marble, p.197].

George **Barrington:** George Waldron (1755–1804), Ir. writer, adventurer. Waldron ran away from school at the age of 16 and joined a group of strolling players, changing his name to Barrington to encourage confusion with an existing actor named John Barrington. He subsequently turned to crime, and as a persistent pickpocket was deported in 1790 to Botany Bay, Australia, where he reformed and wrote interesting accounts of his experiences. A popular verse was current following his conviction:

> Two namesakes of late, in a different way,
> With spirit and zeal did bestir 'em;
> The one was transported to Botany Bay,
> The other translated to Durham.

The namesake was Shute Barrington (1734–1826), bishop of Durham, son of John Shute **Barrington**.

John Shute **Barrington:** John Shute (1678–1734), Eng. politician. In 1710 the future Viscount Barrington inherited the estate of Francis Barrington, husband of his first cousin, and according to the terms of the will adopted the name and arms of the bequeather.

Pamela **Barrington:** Muriel Vere Mant Barling (1904–1986), Eng. detective novelist. Barrington also wrote under the name of her husband, Charles Barling.

Rutland **Barrington:** George Rutland Barrington Fleet (1853–1922), Eng. actor, singer.

Desmond **Barrit:** Desmond Brown (1944–), Br. stage, movie actor.

Blue **Barron:** Harry Friedland (1911–), U.S. trombonist, bandleader.

Chris **Barron:** Christopher Barron Gross (1968–), U.S. rock musician.

Rev. S. **Barrow** *see* Abbé **Bossut**

A.J. **Barrowcliffe:** Albert Julius Mott (*fl.*1850–1870), Eng. writer. Mott lived near Liverpool, and his pen name may have had some local significance.

Charles **Barry:** Charles Bryson (1887–1963), Eng. detective novelist.

Christine **Barry:** Grace Underwood (1911–1964), Br. stage actress.

David **Barry:** Meurig Wyn Jones (1943–), Welsh-born Br. TV actor.

Don "Red" **Barry:** Donald Barry de Acosta (1912–1980), U.S. movie actor.

Gene **Barry:** Eugene Klass (1919–2009), U.S. movie, TV actor.

Jack **Barry:** Jack Barasch (1918–1984), U.S. TV personality, producer.

James **Barry:** Margaret Bulkley (*c.*1790–1865), Sc. medical officer, reformer. Margaret Bulkley adopted this male name when registering for a medical degree at Edinburgh University in 1809, claiming a birth date of 1799. She then retained the name and male guise for a career in military medicine.

Joan **Barry:** Joan Tiarks, née Bell (1901–1989), Eng. stage, movie actress, society hostess.

Jocelyn **Barry** *see* Avon **Curry**

Joe **Barry:** Joseph Barrios (1939–2004), U.S. blues singer, songwriter.

John **Barry:** Jonathan Barry Prendergast (1933–), Eng. movie music composer.

Len **Barry:** Leonard Borrisoff (1942–), U.S. pop singer.

Michael **Barry:** (1) James Barry Jackson (1910–), Eng. musician, writer; (2) Michael John Bukht (1941–), Br. food writer.

Diana **Barrymore:** Diana Blanche Barrymore Blyth (1921–1960), U.S. movie actress, daughter of John **Barrymore** (by his second wife, Michael **Strange**).

Ethel **Barrymore:** Ethel Mae Blyth (1879–1959), U.S. stage, movie actress. Both Ethel Blyth and her brothers John and Lionel Blyth adopted the name of their father, Maurice **Barrymore**.

John **Barrymore:** John Sidney Blyth (1882–1942), U.S. stage, movie actor, father of actor John

Drew Barrymore (John Barrymore, Jr.) (1932–2004), grandfather of movie actress Drew Blyth Barrymore (1975–). The Drew name came from the actor's mother, actress Georgie Barrymore, née Georgiana Emma Drew (1856–1893), herself the daughter of Irish-born actor John Drew (1827–1862).

Lionel **Barrymore:** Lionel Herbert Blyth (1878–1954), U.S. stage, movie actor.

Maurice **Barrymore:** Herbert Arthur Chamberlayne Hunter Blyth (1849–1905), Eng. actor, father of Ethel, John, and Lionel **Barrymore.** Maurice Barrymore adopted his stage name from an old playbill hanging in the Haymarket Theatre, London. It was in turn adopted by his three children, who made their name on the American stage, where Maurice himself first appeared in 1874.

Michael **Barrymore:** Michael Keiran Parker (1952–), Eng. TV entertainer. The celebrity was obliged to find another name early in his career as there was already a Michael Parker in show business. The story usually told is that his agent renamed him after the U.S. actor Lionel **Barrymore.** But such a link seems unlikely, and has been refuted in informed media profiles. "He acquired his new name from a married couple who decided to manage him. He had never heard of the Barrymores, the royal family of the theatre. 'I thought, "Oh well, any name'll do"'" [*Sunday Times*, September 15, 2002].

Louis **Barsac:** Ernest James Oldmeadow (1867–1949), Br. journalist, writer.

Jean **Bart:** Eugen Botez (1874–1933), Rom. writer. Many of the writer's works have the sea as their setting. Hence his pen name, that of the French naval commander Jean Bart (1650–1702).

Lionel **Bart:** Lionel Begleiter (1930–1999), Br. composer, songwriter. The musician adopted his new name from Bart's, the popular name of St. Bartholomew's hospital, London. Begleiter (whose real name happens to be German for "musical accompanist") changed his name by deed poll. "I was called Big Lighter and Bagel Eater, but the main problem was that I got fed up with having to spell it out. I was on a bus going past Bart's hospital when I got the idea" [*Sunday Times*, April 4, 1999].

Freddie **Bartholomew:** Frederick Llewellyn (1924–1992), Br. child movie actor, working in U.S. The actor was raised by an aunt, Millicent Bartholomew, and adopted her name.

Bartimeus: [Captain Sir] Lewis Anselmo Ritchie (1886–1967), Br. writer of naval stories. The writer's original surname was Ricci, but he altered this to Ritchie by deed poll in 1941. The biblical Bartimaeus was a blind beggar cured by Jesus (Mark 10), and Ritchie's use of the name presumably has a personal reference. He joined the Royal Navy as a teen-ager in 1901 and served for a short time in home waters before being obliged to transfer to the paymaster branch because of poor eyesight.

Sy **Bartlett:** Sacha Baraniev (1909–1978), Russ.-born U.S. screenwriter, movie producer. The writer's full adopted name was Sydney S. Bartlett.

Eva **Bartok:** Eva Martha Sjöke (1926–1998), Hung.-born Br. movie actress.

Fra **Bartolommeo:** Bartolommeo di Pagolo del Fattorino (or Baccio della Porta) (1472–1517), It. painter.

Archie **Barton:** ? (1936–2008), Austral. indigenous campaigner. The names of Barton's parents are unknown, and his surname was the name of the railroad siding on the edge of the Great Victoria Desert in South Australia where he was born to an Aboriginal mother following her conception by a white man.

Buzz **Barton:** William Lamarr (1914–1980), U.S. juvenile movie actor.

Erle **Barton** *see* Neil **Balfort**

Richard **Barton:** Richard Bradshaigh (or Bradshaw) (1601–1669), Eng. Jesuit.

Billy **Barty:** William John Bertanzetti (1924–2000), U.S. dwarf movie actor.

Ganna (Hanna) **Barvinok:** Aleksandra Mikhaylovna Belozerskaya-Kulish (1828–1911), Ukr. writer. Russian *barvinok* is the periwinkle (the flowering plant *Vinca minor* or *Vinca herbacea*).

Georg **Baselitz:** Hans-Georg Kern (1938–), Ger. painter, sculptor. The avant-garde artist began his training in East Berlin but in 1956 moved to West Berlin, when he adopted his new name, from his birthplace, Deutschbaselitz, Saxony.

Matsuo **Basho:** Matsuo Munefusa (1644–1694), Jap. haiku poet. The poet's pen name is the Japanese word for the banana tree, alluding to the simple hut by such a tree where he liked to retreat from society.

Basia: Basia Trzetrzelewska (1956–), Pol.-born U.S. rock singer.

Count **Basie:** William Basie (1904–1984), U.S. black jazz musician. Basie first called himself "Count" in 1928, adopting a regal title of the type favored by other jazz musicians, such as Duke **Ellington**.

Basil: Richard Ashe King (1839–1932), Ir. cleric, novelist, biographer. King took the name Desmond B. O'Brien for his writings in *Truth* magazine, of which he was literary editor.

Theodore **Basil:** Thomas Becon (1512–1567), Eng. Protestant clergyman, writer.

Ivan **Baskoff:** Henri Meilhac (1832–1897), Fr. dramatist, author. The writer used this name for contributions to *La Vie Parisienne*.

Lina **Basquette:** Lena Baskette (1907–1994), U.S. movie actress. The actress adopted the modified form of her name in 1927, two years after marrying Sam Warner, elder brother of Jack L. **Warner**.

Ralph **Bass**: Ralph Basso (1911–1997), U.S. R&B producer.

Kingsley **Bass, Jr.**: Ed Bullins (1935–), U.S. black playwright. Bullins adopted this pseudonym for the publication of *We Righteous Bombers* in the anthology *New Plays from the Black Theatre* (1969).

Jacopo **Bassano**: Jacopo da Ponte (*c.*1515–1592), It. painter. The painter took his name from his birth town of Bassano, northern Italy. His four painter sons, Francesco, Gerolamo, Giovanni Battista, and Lerandro, adopted the name in turn.

Jack **Bassett** *see* Fenton **Brockley**

Hogan "Kid" **Bassey**: Okon Bassey Asuquo (1932–1998), Nigerian boxer. "Hogan" from "Okon."

Ugo **Bassi**: Giuseppe Bassi (1801–1849), It. cleric, religious writer. The priest and preacher changed his first name in honor of the poet and patriot Ugo Foscolo (1778–1827).

Batata: Paulino Salgado Valdez (1929–2004), Colombian drummer, singer.

Reg **Batchelor** *see* Mark **Carrel**

Florence **Bates**: Florence Rabe (1888–1954), U.S. movie actress. The actress took her screen name from the character of Miss Bates that she played in a 1935 stage adaptation of Jane Austen's novel *Emma*.

Deacon L.J. **Bates**: Blind Lemon Jefferson (1897–1929), U.S. black blues guitarist, singer. The musician used this name, based on his initials, for some gospel and spiritual songs.

Bat for Lashes: Natasha Khan (1979–), Br. pop singer, of Pakistani-Eng. parentage. The singer's name seems to suggest a flirtatious girl who "bats her lashes" or flutters her eyelids. Its creator denies a meaningful origin. "The words 'bat' and 'lashes' cane into Natasha Khan's mind as she was working out the visual and audio concepts for her 2006 debut *Fur and Gold*. 'It just sounds like the music,' she said in an interview. The words were 'chosen simply because they sounded unusual together'" [Beech, p.33].

Oliver **Bath**: Hardinge Goulburn Giffard, 2d Earl of Halsbury, Viscount Tiverton (1880–1943). The son of the three-times lord chancellor of England adopted this name, a reversal of "Bath Oliver," a type of biscuit or cookie invented by a Dr. Oliver, as writer of the lyrics for the musical comedy *Naughty Nancy* (1902), a gift for his fiancée Esme Wallace, whom he married five years later.

Jane **Bathori**: Jeanne-Marie Berthier (1877–1970), Fr. concert singer.

[Sir] Brian **Batsford**: Brian Caldwell Cook (1910–1991), Br. publisher. The painter, publisher, and politician adopted his mother's maiden name by deed poll in 1946.

Batt: Oswald Barrett (1892–1945), Br. illustrator.

Battistello: Giovanni Battista Caracciolo (1578–1635), It. painter. The artist's name is a diminutive of the second word of his first name, which literally translates as "John the Baptist." Compare **Baciccia**.

Battling Siki: Louis Phal (1897–1925), Senegalese boxer, working in U.S.

Nikolay **Baturin**: Nikolay Nikolayevich Zamyatin (1877–1927), Russ. Communist activist, historian.

Steven **Bauer**: Steven Echevarria (1956–), Cuban-born U.S. movie actor.

Willy **Bauer**: Willy Benedikt Gegen-Bauer (1937–), Ger.-born Br. hotelier.

Roger **Bax** *see* Andrew **Garve**

Beryl **Baxter**: Beryl Gross, née Ivory (1926–), Br. stage, movie actress.

Geoffrey **Baxter** *see* J.P. **McCall**

George Owen **Baxter** *see* Max **Brand**

Hazel **Baxter** *see* Fenton **Brockley**

Jane **Baxter**: Feodora Kathleen Alice Forde (1909–1996), Br. stage, movie actress. The playwright James Barrie advised the actress early in her career that Feodora Forde was not a good stage name. She therefore chose a new name, taking it from a character in Booth Tarkington's novel *Seventeen* (1916).

Keith **Baxter**: Keith Stanley Baxter-Wright (1933–), Welsh stage actor.

Maurice **Baxter**: [Sir] Joseph Compton Rickett (1847–1919), Eng. industrialist, politician, writer. Rickett used this name for his poetry and fiction.

Valerie **Baxter** *see* A. Stephen **Tring**

Nathalie **Baye**: Judith Mesnil (1945–), Fr. movie actress.

Sylvia **Bayer**: John Glassco (1909–1981), Can. author, poet. Other names used by the writer include Jean de Saint-Luc, Silas M. Gooch, and Miles Underwood, this last for *The English Governess* (1960), also published as *Harriet Marwood, Governess*, a parody of Victorian pornography.

Nora **Bayes**: Theodora Goldberg (1880–1928), U.S. singer, comedienne. The singer had already taken her stage name when appearing in 1898 at the Hyde and Behman vaudeville theater in Chicago.

William **Baylebridge**: Charles William Blocksidge (1883–1942), Austral. poet, short-story writer. The writer adopted his pen name from about 1925. It is uncertain to what extent the new surname is a meaningful alteration of the original.

Beverly **Bayne**: Pearl von Name (1894–1982), U.S. movie actress.

Vladimir **Bazarov**: Vladimir Aleksandrovich Rudnev (1874–1939), Russ. philosopher, economist. The socialist philosopher appears to have adopted the name of Bazarov, the nihilist hero of Turgenev's novel *Fathers and Sons* (1862), especially as his original name suggests the writer's earlier novel *Rudin* (1856).

Hervé **Bazin:** Jean-Pierre-Marie Hervé-Bazin (1911–1996), Fr. poet, novelist, short-story writer.

B.B. (1) Lewis **Carroll**; (2) Denys James Watkins-Pitchford (1905–1990), Eng. writer on the countryside; (3) Brigitte **Bardot**.

Watkins-Pitchford first used the initialism for *The Sportsman's Bedside Book* (1937), deriving it from the size of lead shot he used for shooting wild geese (BB is 0.18 in. in diameter). He illustrated his own books, whose title pages invariably read "by 'B.B.,' Illustrated by D.J. Watkins-Pitchford." "The oddest thing about BB is that he became a moderately successful writer despite the difficulties raised by deciding to write under a pseudonym chosen not because it made him sound intriguing or mysterious but based on the size of lead shot he used to shoot geese" [Tom Quinn, *BB Remembered: The Life and Times of Denys Watkins-Pitchford*, 2006].

Bardot's own initials are of course B.B., and "BB" was first used in print for her appearance as a cover girl on the French magazine *Elle* in 1948. The initials have added point when it is remembered that in French they are pronounced the same as *bébé*, "baby." Bardot was in her early teens at the time.

Beachcomber: (1) Dominic Bevan Wyndham Lewis (1891–1969), Br. humorous columnist; (2) John Cameron Andrieu Bingham Michael Morton (1893–1979), Br. humorous columnist. The name was passed down by (1) to (2) in 1924, when Morton succeeded Lewis as columnist on the *Daily Express*. The columnists hunted out interesting news items, just as a beachcomber searches the shore for valuables. Lewis's original first name was actually Llewelyn, but he dropped this in favor of Dominic on being received into the Catholic Church in 1921.

John **Beal:** James Alexander Bliedung (1909–1997), U.S. stage, movie actor.

Abraham D. **Beame:** Abraham David Birnbaum (1906–2001), U.S. politician. Beame was born the son of a Polish revolutionary who had fled Warsaw for New York. His mother stayed in London, England, where he was born, before continuing to America, where the family adopted their new name, a form of English *beam*, rendering the latter half of the original family name. Beame was mayor of New York City 1974–77.

Orson **Bean:** Dallas Frederick Burroughs (1928–), U.S. stage actor, comedian. Burroughs began his stage career as a magician, and chose this randomly humorous name for his act.

Pierre **Béarn:** Louis-Gabriel Besnard (1902–2004), Fr. writer, activist.

Allyce **Beasley:** Allyce Schiavelli, formerly Sansocie, née Tannenberg (1954–), U.S. movie, TV actress.

Beatmaster V: Victor Ray Wilson (1959–1996), U.S. rock drummer. "V" for "Victor."

Beato Angelico *see* Fra **Angelico**

George **Beaton:** Edward Fitzgerald ("Gerald") Brenan (1894–1987), Br. writer, working in Spain.

Beatrice: Anne Manning (1807–1879), Eng. novelist, miscellaneous writer.

Dona **Béatrice:** Kimpa Vita (c.1682–1706), Congolese religious leader. Declaring herself to be the reincarnation of the Portuguese St. Anthony, Dona Béatrice founded the Antonian church in 1703. She was burned at the stake as a heretic for preaching that Christ was of Congolese origin.

Sister **Beatrice:** Elizabeth Ann Rogers (1829–1921), Eng.-born U.S. educator, religious. Rogers took her religious name in 1867, when she was received into the first order of the Society of the Most Holy Trinity, an Anglican sisterhood with a mission field in Hawaii.

Josephine **Beatty:** Albert Hunter (1895–1984), U.S. black blues singer. Hunter recorded over 50 songs in the 1920s under her own name and various pseudonyms, including this one, her sister's name. Other names were May Alix and Alberta Prime.

Warren **Beatty:** Henry Warren Beaty (1937–), U.S. movie actor. Beaty made a minor adjustment to his real name by doubling a letter for his screen name. His sister, Shirley **MacLaine**, made a similar modification.

Philip **Beauchamp:** George Grote (1794–1871), Eng. historian.

Beauchâteau: François Chastelet (*fl.*1625–1665), Fr. actor.

Douglas **Beaufort:** Douglas Broad (1864–1939), Eng. magician.

John **Beaufort:** John Thelwall (1764–1834), Eng. poet, politician, writer. Thelwall took his pen name from Beaufort Buildings, Strand, London, where he lived for a time.

Beau Jocque: Andrus Espre (1952–1999), U.S. black blues musician. The zydeco artist adopted his nickname, meaning "big handsome guy."

Balthasar de **Beaujoyeux:** Baldassare di Belgiojoso (?–1587), It. violinist, composer. A name that is part rendered, part translated, from Italian to French.

Pierre-Augustin Caron de **Beaumarchais:** Pierre-Augustin Caron (1732–1799), Fr. dramatist. Beaumarchais took his writing name from that of a small property in Brie owned by his first wife. There are several villages of the name (meaning "beautiful marsh") to be found in the north of France.

Mlle. **Beauménard** *see* Mme. **Bellecour**

André **Beaumont:** Jean Conneau (1880–1937), Fr. aviator.

Averil **Beaumont:** Margaret Hunt, née Raine (1831–1912), Eng. novelist.

Charles **Beaumont:** Charles Leroy Nutt (1929–1967), U.S. SF writer.

Susan **Beaumont:** Susan Black (1936–), Br. movie actress.

Beauval: Jean Pitel (*c.*1635–1709), Fr. actor.

Roger de **Beauvoir:** Eugène-Auguste-Roger de Bully (1806–1866), Fr. novelist.

Bebeto: José Roberto Gama de Oliveira (1964–), Brazilian footballer. The sportsman's nickname evolved as a pet form of his second name.

Gilbert **Bécaud:** François Gilbert Silly (1927–2001), Fr. popular singer, songwriter.

Domenico **Beccafumi:** Domenico di Pace (*c.*1486–1551), It. painter, sculptor. The artist adopted the name of his patron, Lorenzo Beccafumi.

Beck: Beck David Hansen (1970–), U.S. rock musician.

Christopher **Beck:** Thomas Charles Bridges (1868–1944), Eng. writer of stories for boys. Bridges also wrote as Martin Shaw and John Stanton.

K.K. **Beck:** Kathrine Kristine Beck (1950–), U.S. crime writer. The novelist was born Kathrine Marris but legally changed her name to that of her pseudonym.

Lily Adams **Beck** *see* E. **Barrington**

[Sir] Edmund **Beckett:** Edmund Beckett Denison (1816–1905), Eng. lawyer, architect, horologist. Beckett's father, also Sir Edmund Beckett (1787–1874), assumed the additional surname Denison by royal tetters patent in the year of his son's birth under the terms of his wife's great-great aunt's will, but reverted to his original surname of Beckett by the same process on succeeding to the baronetcy of Grimthorpe in 1872. His son in turn succeeded to the baronetcy on the death of his father, when he followed the latter's example and dropped his second surname.

Walter **Beckett** *see* Martin **Mills**

Grania **Beckford** *see* Rosalind **Erskine**

Gustavo Adolfo **Bécquer:** Gustavo Adolfo Domínguez Bastida (1836–1870), Sp. poet. The poet adopted his father's middle name as his new surname.

Cuthbert **Bede:** [Rev.] Edward Bradley (1827–1889), Br. humorist. The author of *The Adventures of Mr. Verdant Green* (1853) attended the University of Durham, and took his name from the two patron saints of that city, St. Cuthbert and the Venerable Bede.

Bonnie **Bedelia:** Bonnie Bedelia Culkin (1946–), U.S. movie actress, singer, dancer, aunt of U.S. juvenile actor Macaulay Culkin (1980–).

Donald **Bedford:** Henry James O'Brien Bed-ford-Jones (1887–1949), Can.-born U.S. writer of historical adventures.

Kenneth **Bedford** *see* Mark **Carrel**

Demyan **Bedny:** Yefim Alekseyevich Pridvorov (1883–1945), Russ. Socialist poet. Pridvorov's pen name derives from Russian *bedny*, "poor," reflecting the conditions of the peasants and working classes before the 1917 Revolution. Compare the name of Maxim **Gorky**. It was originally a nickname. He had brought a poem entitled "Demyan Bedny, the Harmful Peasant" to his editors, and when he next visited the office they exclaimed "It's Demyan Bedny!" Demyan (English Damian) was actually the first name of his uncle, who was a peasant. The poet would also have certainly wished to avoid the aristocratic associations of his real surname, Pridvorov, which suggests *pridvorny*, "of the court."

Widow **Bedott:** Frances Miriam Whitcher (1814–1852), U.S. humorous writer.

Auntie **Bee:** Bertha Henry Buxton, née Leupold (1844–1881), Eng. writer. Buxton used this name for her children's books.

Jimmie **Bee:** James O'Farrell (1934–1993), U.S. pop musician.

Jon **Bee:** John Badcock (*fl.*1816–1830), Br. sporting writer. Badcock also used the name John Hinds. His best-known work was *Slang. A Dictionary of the Turf, the Ring, the Chase, the pit of bon-ton, and the varieties of Life, forming the completest Lexicon Balatronicum of the Sporting World* (1823). A *Lexicon Balatronicum* is a "Babblers' Dictionary."

Kenny **Bee:** Zhang Chentau (1953–), Hong Kong movie actor, singer.

Henry Knowles **Beecher:** Henry Knowles Unangst (1904–1976), U.S. medical researcher. The future professor of research in anesthesia entered Harvard Medical School in 1928 but before leaving adopted his new name, which he felt would be more widely recognized and admired in Boston than Unangst. He was in fact related to the famous abolitionist Beecher clan through his maternal grandmother, Maria Kerley, whose maiden name was Beecher.

Janet **Beecher:** Janet Beecher Meysenburg (1884–1955), U.S. movie actress, of Ger.–U.S. parentage.

Francis **Beeding:** John Leslie Palmer (1885–1944), Br. thriller writer + Hilary Aidan St. George Saunders (1898–1951), Br. thriller writer. A single name for a two-man writing partnership. Palmer had always liked the name Francis; Saunders had once owned a house in the Sussex village of Beeding.

Captain **Beefheart** *see* **Captain Beefheart**

Beenie Man: Anthony Moses Davis (1973–), Jamaican DJ, ragga musician.

Lou **Bega:** David Loubega (1975–), Ger. pop musician, of Ugandan-Sicilian parentage.

J. & W. **Beggarstaff:** [Sir] William Newzam Prior Nicholson (1872–1949), Eng. poster artist + James Pryde (1866–1941), Eng. poster artist, his brother-in-law. Nicholson explains the duo's choice of name: "Pryde and I came across it one day in an old stable, on a sack of fodder. It is a good, hearty, old English name, and it appealed to us, so we adopted it immediately" [Chilvers 2004, p.64]. After a time, people started referring to the "Beggarstaff Brothers," but the artists themselves did not care for this version.

Bei Dao: Zhao Zhenkai (1949–), Chin. writer. This pen name, meaning "North Island," was one of several the underground poet and writer of fiction adopted in the 1970s.

Lenny **Beige:** Stephen Furst (1968–), Br. entertainer. The comedian's professional name is reflected (almost literally) in the beige sequined costume that he affects when on stage.

Maurice **Béjart:** Maurice-Jean Berger (1927–2007), Fr. dancer, choreographer.

Belcampo: Herman P. Schönfeld Wichers (1902–1990), Du. writer. The writer, by profession a doctor, took for his pen name an Italian-style translation of his middle name, literally "beautiful field."

Aunt **Belinda** see Lady Caroline **Lascelles**

Belita: Belita Gladys Olive Lyne Jepson-Turner (1923–2005), Br. ice skater, dancer, movie actress.

Ivan Petrovich **Belkin:** Aleksandr Sergeyevich Pushkin (1799–1837), Russ. poet, dramatist. Pushkin used the name for the supposed narrator of his *Tales of the Late Ivan Petrovich Belkin* (1831), and in a preface, "From the Editor," "A.P." gives a brief account of "the life, occupations, disposition and physical appearance of my late friend and neighbour," telling how he was "born of honourable parentage in the year 1798," that he "joined a chasseur regiment ... in which he remained throughout his service until the year 1823," that he "caught an extremely severe cold which developed into a fever, and died" in 1828, and that he "was of medium height, and he had grey eyes, fair hair, and a straight nose" [Alexander Pushkin, *The Tales of Belkin*, translated by Gillon Aitken and David Budgen, 2000].

Acton **Bell:** Ann Brontë (1820–1849), Eng. novelist, poet, sister of Currer **Bell**.

Carey **Bell:** Carey Bell Harrington (1936–2007), U.S. blues harmonica player.

Currer **Bell:** Charlotte Brontë (1816–1855), Eng. novelist, sister of Acton **Bell** and Ellis **Bell**. When the three daughters of Patrick **Brontë** first published some poems in 1846, they named themselves as "Currer, Ellis, and Acton Bell," leading many people to think that the authors were three brothers, and therefore writing to them as men. Charlotte Brontë later gave the following account of the assumption of these names: "Averse to personal publicity, we veiled our own names under those of Currer, Ellis, and Acton Bell; the ambiguous choice being dictated by a sort of conscientious scruple at assuming Christian names positively masculine, while we did not declare ourselves women, because — without at that time suspecting that our mode of writing and thinking was not what is called 'feminine' — we had a vague impression that authoresses are liable to be looked on with prejudice" [Charlotte Brontë, "Biographical Notice of Ellis & Acton Bell," 1850]. Charlotte Brontë's *Jane Eyre* (1847) was originally published as by Currer Bell, and that same year Emily Brontë's *Wuthering Heights* also appeared, with the author given as Ellis Bell. Their guise was soon penetrated, however, and when Charlotte Brontë received a letter from her contemporary, Harriet Martineau, it began "Dear Madam," although "Currer Bell, Esq." appeared on the envelope.

The choice of the respective first names and the surname has been a matter of much speculation. Charlotte Brontë is said to have chosen the name Bell because it was the middle name of Arthur Bell Nicholls, her father's curate and her future husband. Currer is a Yorkshire surname and was familiar to the Brontës as that of a local benefactor, Frances Richardson Currer. Ellis is also a Yorkshire name, and was that of a local family of mill owners. Acton was a name Anne Brontë would have known from her time as governess to a family at Thorp Green Hall, near York. All three names preserved their bearers' original initials [Juliet Barker, *The Brontës*, 1994].

Ellis **Bell:** Emily Brontë (1818–1848), Eng. novelist, sister of Currer **Bell**.

Frank **Bell** see Carolyn **Keene**

Freddie **Bell:** Freddie Bello (1931–2008), U.S. rock'n'roll singer, songwriter, of It.–U.S. parentage.

Josephine **Bell:** Doris Bell Ball, née Collier (1897–1987), Eng. detective novelist, physician. Doris Ball created her pseudonymous persona as a female equivalent of Dr. Joseph Bell (1837–1911), the Scottish surgeon and professor who was Arthur Conan Doyle's model for Sherlock Holmes.

Marie **Bell:** Marie-Jeanne Bellon-Downey (1900–1985), Fr. stage, movie actress, theater manager.

Marjorie **Bell** see Marge **Champion**

Neil **Bell** see Stephen **Southwold**

Paul **Bell:** Henry Fothergill Chorley (1808–1872), Eng. journalist, novelist, music critic. Chorley adopted a pen name for his fiction that honored the Brontë sisters (see Currer **Bell**).

Rex **Bell:** George Francis Beldam (1905–1962), U.S. movie actor.

Solomon **Bell:** William Joseph Sneling (1804–1848), U.S. writer, journalist. Snelling adopted his mother's maiden name for several volumes of travel and adventure tales for children.

Thornton **Bell** *see* Neil **Balfort**

William **Bell:** William Yarborough (1939–), U.S. soul singer.

Bellachini: Samuel Berlach (1828–1885), Pol.-born magician.

George **Bellairs:** Harold Blundell (1902–1982), Eng. mystery novelist.

Madge **Bellamy:** Margaret Philpott (1903–1990), U.S. movie actress.

Bellecour: Jean-Claude-Gilles Colson (1725–1778), Fr. playwright, comic actor, husband of Madame **Bellecour.**

Madame **Bellecour:** Rose-Perrine le Roy de la Corbinaye (1730–1799), Fr. actress. The actress left home when she was 13 and took up with an itinerant comic actor called Beauménard. She adopted his name and calling and thus became known as Mlle. Beauménard. Later she married the actor **Bellecour**, and became known by his name as Madame Bellecour.

Belle de Jour: Brooke Magnanti (1975–), Br. writer. The identity of the author of *The Intimate Adventures of a London Call Girl* (2003) was long a mystery, although it was clear the pseudonym came from the 1967 French movie so titled, about a surgeon's wife who takes on afternoon work in a brothel. (French *belle-de-jour*, literally "daytime beauty," is a name for the convolvulus, a plant whose flower closes at sunset.) Professionally a research scientist, Magnanti used her book to describe her own short-lived experiences as a prostitute. She eventually decided to unmask herself, saying she had grown tired of her self-imposed anonymity [*The Sunday Times*, November 15, 2009].

Belleroche: Raymond Poisson (*c.*1630–1690), Fr. actor.

Bellerose: Pierre Le Messier (*c.*1592–1670), Fr. actor.

Belleville *see* **Turlupin**

Saul **Bellow:** Solomon Bellows (1915–2005), Can.-born U.S. novelist.

Dormont de **Belloy:** Pierre-Laurent Buirette (1727–1775), Fr. dramatist.

Louie **Bellson:** Luigi Paolino Alfredo Francesco Antonio Balassoni (1924–2009), U.S. jazz drummer, bandleader, of It. parentage.

Bessie **Bellwood:** Elizabeth Ann Katherine Mahony (1847–1896), Ir. music-hall performer. The artist made her debut on the music-hall stage under the name Signorina Ballantino.

Anatoly **Belov:** Anatoly Antonovich Dubin (1925–), Russ. ballet dancer.

Albert **Bels:** Janis Cirulis (1938–), Latvian writer.

Belsaz: John C. Green (1866–1951), Can. magician, showman.

Vizma **Belševica:** Vizma Elsberga (1931–), Latvian poet.

N. **Beltov:** Georgy Valentinovich Plekhanov (1856–1918), Russ. Marxist revolutionary. Plekhanov adopted the name of the central character of Herzen's novel *Who Is to Blame?* (1841–46). He also wrote as Volgin (*see* Vladimir Ilyich **Lenin**).

Lola **Beltran:** Maria Lucial Beltran Ruiz (1932–1996), Mexican popular singer.

Richard **Belvoir** *see* Geoffrey **Crayon, jun.**

Andrey **Bely:** Boris Nikolayevich Bugayev (1880–1934), Russ. symbolist poet, writer, critic. When Bugayev wished to publish some poetry as a student, in 1901, his father objected. The pseudonym Andrey Bely was thus proposed for him by his editor, M.S. Solovyov, who devised it simply for its euphony, even though Russian *bely* means "white." Bugayev had initially preferred the name "Boris Burevoy" ("Boris Blustery"). But Solovyov said that people would only pun on the name, seeing it as *Bori voy*, "Borya's howl." So Andrey Bely it was.

Ben: Benjamin Vautier (1935–), Fr. artist.

Lisa **Ben:** Edith Eyde (1921–), U.S. gay activist. Eyde settled in Los Angeles in 1945, when she created a new name for herself from the letters in "lesbian."

Yitzhak **Ben-Aharon:** Yitzhak Nussboim (1906–2006), Israeli politician.

Shek **Ben Ali:** Mohari Alli (1912–1978), Ind.-born Br. magician. "Ben Ali" and "Ali Bey" are stock stage names for a magician, as **Ben Ali Bey.**

Ben Ali Bey: Max Auzinger (1839–1928), Ger. magician.

Jacob **Ben-Ami:** Yakov Shchirin (1890–1977), Belorussian-born U.S. stage actor, working in Yiddish. It is not known when the actor adopted his new surname, which is Hebrew for "son of my people."

Pat **Benatar:** Patricia Andrzejewski (1953–), U.S. rock singer. The singer's professional name is that of her first husband, Dennis Benatar, whom she married in 1977. They soon divorced, but she kept the name following her second marriage in 1982 to Neil Giraldo since by then she was an established artist.

Benauly: Benjamin Vaughan Abbott (1830–1890), U.S. author + Austin Abbott (1831–1896), U.S. author + [Rev.] Lyman Abbott (1835–1922), U.S. author. The composite name consists of the first syllables of each of the three brothers' forenames, in strict order of seniority.

Bendigo: William Thompson (1811–1880), Br. boxer, prizefighter. The name is a corruption of

"Abednego," one of the three "certain Jews" (Shadrach, Meshach and Abednego) who according to the Bible story were ordered to be cast into King Nebuchadnezzar's burning fiery furnace for not serving his gods or worshiping his golden image. But why Abednego? "According to one account, he was one of triplets, whom a jocular friend of the family nicknamed Shadrach, Meschach, and Abed-Nego, the last of whom was the future celebrity.... The rival theory is that, when he was playing in the streets and his father appeared in the offing, his companions used to warn him by crying 'Bendy go!' This theory disregards the assertion of the 'oldest inhabitant' that the great man was never called Bendy" [Ernest Weekley, *The Romance of Words*, 1922].

Alexander **Bendo:** Robert Carr, Viscount Rochester, Earl of Somerset (?1589–1645), Sc. politician, favorite of James I.

Benedetta: Benedetta Cappa (1899–1977), It. novelist, painter, writer.

Benedict VIII: Theophylactus (or Teofilatto) (*c.*980–1024), It. pope.

Benedict IX: Theophylactus (or Teofilatto) (?–*c.*1055), It. pope. The pontiff adopted the name of his uncle, **Benedict VIII**, whose original name he also shared.

Benedict X: Giovanni Mincio (?–*c.*1080), It. antipope. Giovanni took the name of pope **Benedict IX**.

Benedict XI: Niccolò Boccasini (1240–1304), It. pope. The pontiff assumed the original name, Benedict (Benedetto), of his predecessor, **Boniface VIII**.

Benedict XII: Jacques Fournier (*c.*1280–1342), Fr. pope.

Benedict XIII: (1) Pedro de Luna (*c.*1328–1423), Sp. antipope; (2) Pietro Francesco Vincenzo Maria Orsini (1649–1730), It. pope. The pontiff had joined the Dominican order at an early age, and assumed his papal name in honor of **Benedict XI**, who had also been a Dominican.

Benedict XIV: Prospero Lorenzo Lambertini (1675–1758), It. pope. The pontiff chose his papal name as a tribute to his friend and patron **Benedict XIII**, who had created him cardinal in 1728.

Benedict XV: Giacomo della Chiesa (1854–1922), It. pope.

Benedict XVI: Joseph Alois Ratzinger (1927–), Ger. pope. When the newly-elected pope gave his acceptance speech in 2005 he explained that he wished to inherit the mantle of **Benedict XV**, who was a moderate after **Pius X** and who enjoyed only "a short reign" (1914–22), as Ratzinger believed he might. He added that to have taken the name John Paul III, following his popular predecessor, **John Paul II**, would have been "presumptuous."

Dirk **Benedict:** Dirk Niewoehner (1944–), U.S. TV actor.

Leopold **Benedict** *see* Morris **Winchevsky**
Peter **Benedict** *see* Ellis **Peters**

Richard **Benedict:** Riccardo Benedetto (1916–1984), U.S. movie actor.

David **Ben-Gurion:** David Gruen (1886–1973), Pol.-born Israeli prime minister. David Gruen adopted the ancient Hebrew name of Ben-Gurion when working as a farmer in northern Palestine, where he came in 1906. The name means "son of a lion" (or "son of strength"), and assimilates well to his former surname, which means "green." The specific reference is to Joseph ben Gurion, head of the independent Jewish state in ancient Palestine at the time of the revolt of the Jews against the Romans. Itzhak **Ben-Zvi** emigrated to Palestine in 1907, soon after Ben-Gurion. Compare the name of Micah **Bin Gorion**.

Paul **Ben-Haim:** Paul Frankenburger (1897–1984), Ger.-born Israeli composer, conductor. The musician's adopted name means "son of life."

Benito: Eduardo García Benito (1892–1953), Sp. fashion illustrator, working in France.

Paul **Benjamin:** Paul Auster (1947–), U.S. novelist, poet.

Georgi **Benkowsky:** Gavril Khlytev (*c.*1841–1876), Bulg. revolutionary.

Bruce **Bennett:** Herman Brix (1906–2007), U.S. movie actor. The former world-class athlete adopted his new name when he became so closely linked with the role of the ape-man Tarzan in the 1930s that he found it difficult to get other good roles. He explained: "I realized the name Herman Brix was associated with Tarzan, so I made up a list of seven or eight names and asked people which they liked best. Bruce Bennett was the name I came up with" [*The Times*, April 12, 2007].

Compton **Bennett:** Robert Compton-Bennett (1900–1974), Eng. movie director.

Harve **Bennett:** Harvey Fischman (1930–), U.S. TV series producer.

Lennie **Bennett:** Michael Berry (1938–2009), Eng. stage, TV entertainer.

Lou **Bennett:** Jean-Louis Benoit (1926–), U.S. jazz musician, of part–Martiniquan parentage.

Michael **Bennett:** Michael Bennett Di Figlia (1943–1987), U.S. ballet dancer, choreographer.

Tony **Bennett:** Anthony Dominick Benedetto (1926–), U.S. popular singer, of It. parentage. When the singer began his career at age 19 in New York night clubs, he called himself Joe Bari, after his father's hometown in Italy. One night in 1949, Bob **Hope** came into the club and engaged Bennett to join his touring show. "There was one condition. 'Joe

Bari' should change his name to something a little classier. 'Let's call you Tony Bennett,' Hope proposed. Newly reincarnated, Bennett soon got ... a recording contract with Columbia Records" [*The Times Magazine*, December 14, 1996].

Nelly Jane **Benneweis:** Annette Otto Benneweis, née Jensen (1934–2009), Dan. circus ringmistress. Jensen originally changed her name on taking up a career as a variety theater dancer.

Jack **Benny:** Benjamin Kubelsky (1894–1974), U.S. stage, radio, TV comedian. When Kubelsky first appeared on stage under his own name, Czech-born Hungarian concert violinist Jan Kubelik threatened to sue if he did not change his name. He accordingly called himself Ben K. Benny. But this in turn was too close to the name of bandleader Ben **Bernie,** so after World War I he changed again to Jack Benny, taking his new first name from Jack Osterman, a popular comic. He found it odd at first to see his name in lights: "I got the strangest feelings ... as if this wasn't me and I was an impostor and someday the audience would find me out" [Irving A. Fein, *Jack Benny: An Intimate Biography*, 1976].

Beno: Nikolay Konstantinovich Sheskin (?–1942), Russ. circus artist, acrobat.

Alain de **Benoist:** Fabrice Laroche (1943–), Fr. journalist, essayist.

Henry **Benrath:** Albert Henry Rausch (1882–1949), Ger. lyric poet, novelist.

Al **Benson:** Arthur Learner (1908–1978), U.S. black popular singer.

Carl **Benson:** Charles Astor Bristed (1820–1874), U.S. essayist.

Robby **Benson:** Robert Segal (1956–), U.S. movie actor.

Steve **Benson** *see* Joe **D'Amato**

Bent Fabric: Benjamin Fabricius Bjerre (1924–), Dan. jazz pianist, music publisher.

Brook **Benton:** Benjamin Franklin Peay (1931–1988), U.S. black popular singer.

Karla **Benton** *see* Fenton **Brockley**

Eliezer **Ben-Yehuda:** Eliezer Yitzchak Perelman (1858–1922), Lithuanian Jewish lexicographer. The initiator of the *Great Dictionary of the Ancient and Modern Hebrew Language* has a name meaning "Son of Judah," emphasizing his dedication to Judaism and to the promotion of the Hebrew language.

Itzhak **Ben-Zvi:** Isaac Shimshelevich (1884–1963), Ukr.-born Israeli politician. Israel's second president (1952–63) emigrated to Palestine in 1907, soon after David **Ben-Gurion,** with whom he became closely associated. His adopted name means "son of a deer."

André **Beranger:** George André de Berganger (1895–1973), Austral. stage, movie actor.

Jane **Berbié:** Jeanne Marie-Louise Bergougne (1934–), Fr. opera singer.

Tom **Berenger:** Thomas Moore (1949–), U.S. movie actor.

Bernard **Berenson:** Bernhard Valvrojenski (1865–1959), Lithuanian-born U.S. art historian, working in Italy. After immigrating to Boston in 1875, the Valvrojenskis changed their surname to Berenson ("son of Bernard").

Eulibio **Berentiatico:** Paolo Rolli (1687–1765), It. poet. The poet's pseudonym is his Arcadian name (*see* Aglauro **Cidonia**).

Jack **Beresford:** Jack Beresford Wiszniewski (1899–1977), Br. rower, of Pol. origin.

Max **Beresford:** Annie E. Lee-Hamilton, née Eliza Ann Holdsworth (1860–1917), Eng. novelist, short-story writer.

Jack "Kid" **Berg:** Judah Bergman (1909–1991), Br. boxer.

Philip **Berg:** Feivel Gruberger (1929–), U.S.-born Jewish biblical scholar.

Teresa **Berganza:** Teresa Vargas (1935–), Sp. opera singer. Spanish *varga* means "hill," and doubtless the singer chose a name that presented this in a more familiar form, through Germanic *berg*.

Edgar **Bergen:** Edgar John Berggren (1903–1978), U.S. actor, ventriloquist, of Swe. parentage.

Polly **Bergen:** Nellie Paulina Burgin (1930–), U.S. stage, radio, TV singer, movie actress. For her first movie, *Across the Rio Grande* (1949), the actress was billed as Polly Burgin.

Veritas Leo **Bergen:** Irma von Troll-Vorostyani (1847–1912), Austr. writer, feminist.

Augustin **Berger:** Augustin Razesberger (1861–1945), Cz. ballet master.

E. **Berger:** Elizabeth Sara Sheppard (1830–1862), Eng. novelist, of Jewish descent. Sheppard published two volumes of tales and fables under this name (French for "shepherd"). She also wrote as Mme. Kinkel and Beatrice Reynolds.

Helmut **Berger:** Helmut Steinberger (1944–), Austr. movie actor.

Ludwig **Berger:** Ludwig Bamberger (1892–1969), Ger. movie director.

Elisabeth **Bergner:** Elisabeth Ettel (1897–1986). Pol.-born Br. movie actress, working in U.S.

Elio **Berhanyer:** Eliseo Berenguer (1931–), Sp. fashion designer.

Fred **Berk:** Fritz Berger (1911–1980), Austr.-born U.S. dancer, of Viennese Jewish origin.

Anthony **Berkeley:** Anthony Berkeley Cox (1893–1971), Br. writer of detective fiction. Cox also wrote as Francis Iles and A. Monmouth Platts.

Ballard **Berkeley:** Ballard Blascheck (1904–1988), Eng. stage, movie, TV actor.

Busby **Berkeley:** William Berkeley Enos (1895–1976), U.S. stage, movie choreographer, director. Berkeley adopted his new first name from Amy Busby, a popular Broadway star at the turn of the 20th century who toured with Berkeley's parents as part of the Tim Frawley Repertory Company.

Helen **Berkley** *see* Henry C. **Browning**

Steven **Berkoff:** Leslie Steven Berks (1937–), Eng. playwright, stage actor, director, of Russ. descent. "Steven was christened Leslie, which he loathed almost as much as Berks. He switched to his middle name, adding 'Off' to his surname to preserve the ethnic ring without reverting to Berkovitch, which [his father] Albert had abbreviated to assimilate in the adopted country of his Russian forebears" [*The Times*, March 21, 2009].

Milton **Berle:** Mendel Berlinger (1908–2002), U.S. TV, stage, movie comedian. Until Berlinger was 12 he performed under his family name, but in 1920 he teamed up in a vaudeville act with a girl named Kennedy. The two trisyllabic names hardly tripped off the tongue, however, so "Berlinger" became "Berle."

Irving **Berlin:** Israel Baline (1888–1989), Russ.-born U.S. composer, songwriter. Baline, the son of a penniless itinerant synagogue cantor, published his first sheet music in 1907, when the printer misprinted his surname as "Berlin." The composer kept it that way, altering "Israel" to "Irving."

Bartolomé **Bermejo:** Bartolomé de Cárdenas (*c*.1440–1499), Sp. painter. The artist's nickname means "ginger," "reddish," describing his hair.

Paul **Bern:** Paul Levy (1889–1932), Ger.-born U.S. movie director.

Victoria **Bern:** M.F.K. Fisher (1908–1992), U.S. writer + Dillwyn Parrish (1894–1941), U.S. painter. The two friends used this name for a light-hearted novel, *Touch and Go* (1939), written while living together at Vevey, near Bern, Switzerland. In 1940 they returned to California and married, both having divorced their original spouses. Fisher was born Mary Frances Kennedy but always used her masculine-sounding initials in her writing, whether novels or books on culinary subjects.

Pierre **Bernac:** Pierre Bertin (1899–1979), Fr. concert singer.

[St.] **Bernadette:** Marie-Bernarde Soubirous (1844–1879), Fr. peasant girl, visionary. The saint's name derives from the second part of her own Christian name, with -*ette* a diminutive suffix. The first half would have given "St. Mary," which would have been unacceptable.

Bert **Bernard:** Herbert James Maxwell (1918–2004), U.S. vaudeville performer.

Charles de **Bernard:** Charles-Bernard du Grail de la Villette (1805–1850), Fr. journalist, novelist.

Eric **Bernard:** Bernard Ciocci (1943–1991), U.S. interior designer.

Jay **Bernard** *see* Colin **Forbes**

Jeffrey **Bernard:** Jerry Joseph Bernard (1932–1997), Eng. journalist. The columnist, famous for his bohemian lifestyle, begged his mother to change his first name at the age of eight. He recounts: "I got teased a lot at school in the war ... because Jerries were Germans — and chamberpots were jerries.... My mother said, 'Well, we'll call you something else beginning with J,' and she chose Jeffrey" [Graham Lord, *Just the One: The Wives and Times of Jeffrey Bernard*, 1992]. Bernard's mother was the opera singer Fedora **Roselli**, and his family name was originally West. It was changed to Bernard, after a French aunt, by Jeffrey's paternal grandfather, Charles West, a music-hall impresario.

Sam **Bernard:** Samuel Barnett (1863–1927), Eng.-born U.S. vaudeville comedian.

Bernard-Lazare: Lazare Bernard (1865–1902), Fr. polemicist, antisemitist.

Bernardo: Boris Mikhaylovich Mukhnitsky (?–1918), Russ. circus artist, clown.

Bernardon: Johann Josef Felix von Kurz (1717–1783), Austr. actor, playwright. The actor took his stage name from a character that he created.

Carlo **Bernari:** Carlo Bernard (1909–1992), It. novelist, of Fr. origin. The writer was obliged to change the spelling of his name under Fascism.

Antonia **Bernasconi:** Antonia Wagele (?1741–?1803), Ger. opera singer. The soprano adopted the name of her stepfather, Italian composer Andrea Bernasconi (?1706–?1784), in whose opera *Temistocle* she made her debut in 1762.

Lord **Berners:** [Sir] Gerald Hugh Tyrwhitt-Wilson (1883–1950), Br. musician, artist, writer. The eccentric Englishman, invariably known by his baronial title, which he inherited from his uncle in 1918, was born Gerald Hugh Tyrwhitt but added the name Wilson by royal license in 1919.

Carl **Bernhard:** Andreas Nicolai de Saint-Aubin (1798–1865), Dan. novelist, chronicler.

Göran **Bernhard:** Göran Streijflert (1932–), Dan. child movie actor.

Clyde Edric Barron **Bernhardt:** Clyde Edric Barnhardt (1905–1986), U.S. black jazz trombonist, singer. Bernhardt added the name Barron when a child because his grandmother in slavery had been lent to a family named Barron who treated her kindly. He changed the spelling of his surname in 1930 on the advice of a psychic.

Sarah **Bernhardt:** Sarah-Marie-Henriette-Rosine Bernard (1844–1923), Fr. stage tragedienne. Bernhardt was born the illegitimate daughter of Judith Van Hard, a Dutch courtesan who had settled in Paris, and Édouard Bernard, a law student. Her Germanic-style surname was devised to reflect the names of both.

Ben **Bernie:** Benjamin Woodruff Anzelevitz (1891–1943), U.S. bandleader.

L'Abbé **Bernier:** Paul-Henri Thiry, baron d'Holbach (1723–1789), Fr. materialist, atheist writer. The philosopher and encyclopedist used the name cynically for his *Théologie portative, ou Dictionnaire abrégé de la religion chrétienne* (1786). Holbach also wrote as Nicolas **Boulanger** and Jean **Mirabaud**.

Léon **Bernoux:** Amélie Perronnet (*c.*1831–?), Fr. librettist, composer.

Bert **Berns:** Bert Russell (1929–1967), U.S. pop writer, producer.

BeRo: Barry Rose (1941–), Br. crossword compiler. A pseudonym based on the setter's real name.

François **Béroalde de Verville:** François Brouart (1556–*c.*1629), Fr. writer.

Claude **Berri:** Claude Berel Langmann (1934–2009), Fr. movie director, producer, of East European Jewish descent.

Judith M. **Berrisford:** Mary Lewis (1921–), Eng. children' writer + Clifford Lewis (1912–), Eng. children's writer, her husband. The writers of animal books for cbildren based their joint name on the maiden name, Berrisford, of Mary Lewis's mother.

Dave **Berry:** David Holgate Grundy (1941–), Eng. pop musician. Berry found success in 1963 with a version of Chuck Berry's "Memphis Tennessee" and adopted the U.S. musician's name in his honor.

Helen **Berry** *see* Fenton **Brockley**

John **Berry:** Jack Szold (1917–1999), U.S. movie director, working in France.

Jules **Berry:** Jules Paufichet (1883–1951), Fr. movie actor.

Berryman: Royden Herbert Frederick Ullyett (1914–2001), Eng. sports cartoonist. The artist used this name for his contributions to the *Sunday Pictorial* until 1953.

John **Berryman:** John Allyn Smith, Jr. (1914–1972), U.S. poet. The poet's father committed suicide in 1926 and his mother then married John McAlpin Berryman, whose name passed to the boy.

Ivan **Bersenev:** Ivan Nikolayevich Pavlishchev (1889–1951), Russ. stage, movie actor, theatrical director.

Louky **Bersianik:** Lucille Durand (1930–), Can. poet, novelist, playwright, writing in French. The feminist writer assumed the Slavic name to break free from her patriarchal lineage.

Bertall: Charles Albert d'Arnoux (1820–1893), Fr. illustrator.

Jean **Bertheloy:** Berthe Roy de Clotte le Barillier (1868–1927), Fr. poet, novelist.

Marina **Berti:** Elena Maureen Bertolini (1924–), It. movie actress, of part Eng. parentage. In 1951 Berti went to Hollywood, where she adopted the name Maureen Melrose. "There were some who reproached her for having changed her name to Maureen Melrose from sheer servility towards the allies. To them, Marina explained that Maureen was her real name and Melrose that of an actress grandmother in England" [Masi and Lancia, p.150].

Francesca **Bertini:** Elena Seracini Vitiello (1888 or 1892–1985), It. movie actress.

Vic **Berton:** Victor Cohen (1896–1951), U.S. jazz drummer.

Charles **Bertram:** James Bassett (1853–1907), Eng. magician. Bassett probably adopted the name of the English literary forger Charles Bertram (1723–1765), who sometimes called himself Charles Julius.

Noel **Bertram:** [Rev.] Joseph Noel Thomas Boston (1910–1966), Eng. writer of ghost stories.

Mary **Berwick:** Adelaide Anne Procter (1825–1864), Eng. poet, daughter of Barry **Cornwall**. The writer contributed to Charles Dickens's periodical *Household Words* under this name. "Dickens ... was her father's friend, and she adopted the policy of anonymity because she did not wish to benefit by his friendly partiality" [*Dictionary of National Biography*].She seems to have chosen a name that contrasted geographically to that of her father. The county of Cornwall is in the extreme southwest of England, while the town of Berwick is in the extreme northeast, on the Scottish border.

Besht *see* **Baal Shem Tov**

Besiki: Besarion (Vissarion) Zakharievich Gabashvili (1750–1791), Georgian poet. The poet's adopted name is a diminutive of his first name.

Pavel **Besposhchadny:** Pavel Grigoryevich Ivanov (1895–1968), Russ. poet. The poet began his career as a miner in the Ukraine. The name he adopted means "merciless," "pitiless," describing the conditions he experienced and which were later endured by the miners that he wrote about.

T. Ernesto **Bethancourt:** Tomàs Ernesto Bethancourt Passailaigue (1932–), U.S. writer.

Mongo **Beti:** Alexandre Biyidi (1932–2001), Cameroonian novelist, political writer, working in France. Biyidi used the name Ezra Boto for his first novel, *Ville cruelle* (1954), about the exploitation of peasants, then adopted his regular pen name for his second novel, *Le Pauvre Christ de Bomba* (1956).

Don **Betteridge:** Bernard Newman (1897–1968), Br. novelist, travel writer. Newman used his pen name for some spy novels, beginning with *Scotland Yard Alibi* (1938).

Bettina: Bettina Ehrlich, née Bauer (1903–

1985), Austr.-born Br. children's book illustrator, writer.

Billy Bevan: William Bevan Harris (1887–1957), Austral.-born U.S. movie comedian.

Isla Bevan: Isla Buckley (1910–), Br. movie actress.

Clem Bevans: Clement Blevins (1879–1963), U.S. movie actor.

Ali Bey *see* **Ali Bey**

Turhan Bey: Turhan Gilbert Selahattin Sahultavy (1920–), Austr.-born U.S. movie actor, of Turk.-Cz. parentage. The actor's new name represents the Turkish word for "prince."

John Beynon *see* John **Wyndham**

Beyoncé: Beyoncé Giselle Knowles (1981–), U.S. black pop singer.

Petr Bezruč: Vladimír Vašek (1867–1958), Cz. poet. The name adopted by the poet means literally "without responsibility." He also wrote as Ratibor Suk.

Master Bhagwan: Bhagwan Abhaji Palav (1913–), Ind. movie actor, director.

A.C. Bhaktivedanta: Abhay Charan De (1896–1977), Indian spiritual leader, working in U.S. After beginning his career as a chemist, the founder of the International Society for Krishna Consciousness met his spiritual master, Bhaktisiddhanta Sarasvati Thakura, in 1922, became his formal disciple in 1932, and in the 1950s was given the name Abhay Charanaravinda Bhaktivedanta Swami. His name means "devotion to the Vedanta," from Hindi *bhakti*, "devotion," and *Vedanta*, "end of the Veda," the latter being the system of Hindu philosophy founded on the Veda, the ancient holy books of the Hindus.

Subramania C. Bharati: Subramania C. Iyer (1882–1921), Ind. writer, translator. The Tamil poet's adopted surname derives from Bharat, the Hindi name of India.

Bharatidasan: Kanaka Subburathnam (1891–1964), Ind. poet, playwright, movie scenarist. The writer changed his name in 1908 to Bharatidasan, "disciple of Bharati," in honor of his mentor, Subramania C. **Bharati**.

Adoor Bhasi: K. Bhaskaran Nair (1929–1990), Ind. movie actor.

Bhaskar: Bhaskar Roy Chowdhury (1930–), Indian ballet dancer, teacher, working in U.S.

Ernesto Bianco: Oscar Ernesto Pelicori (1923–1977), Argentinian stage actor.

Bibbiena: Bernardo Dovizi (1470–1520), It. cardinal, writer. The ecclesiastic came to be known by the name of his birthplace, Bibbiena, near Arezzo in central Italy.

Marthe-Lucile Bibesco: Lucile Decaux (1888–1973), Fr. writer, of Rom. origin.

Le **Bibliophile Jacob:** Paul Lacroix (1806–1884), Fr. bibliographer, cataloger, novelist.

Bi-Bo-Bi: Émile Descheemaeker (?–1928), Belg. music-hall musician. The artist's name represents the sound of the tuned bells he played.

John Bickerdyke: Charles Henry Cook (1858–1933), Eng. novelist, writer on angling.

Isaac Bickerstaff: (1) Jonathan Swift (1667–1745), Ir.-born Br. satirist, cleric; (2) [Sir] Richard Steele (1672–1729), Ir. essayist, dramatist; (3) Benjamin West (1730–1813), U.S. mathematician. Swift used the name for a pamphlet of 1708 attacking the almanac-maker John Partridge. Steele used it for launching *The Tatler* the following year. West adopted it for a series of almanacs published in 1768 in Boston. Swift was thus the first to use the name, and he is said to have taken it from a smith's sign, adding the common first name Isaac. There was an Irish playwright Isaac Bickerstaffe (1733–after 1808), with a final "e," but he lived after both Steele and Swift so the name could hardly have derived from him. But possibly he adopted it from them? "The libretto [of *Thomas and Sally*] is the earliest work by the well-known Irish dramatist, Isaac Bickerstaffe.... That his name — Isaac Bickerstaffe — was assumed cannot be entirely outruled, for the same name had earlier been used as a pseudonym both by Sir Richard Steele and Dean Swift" [T.J. Walsh, *Opera in Dublin 1705–1797*, 1973].

Biddeshagor: Ishshorchondro Shorma (1820–1891), Ind. writer, translator. The scholar's honorary name translates as "ocean of knowledge."

Bigas Luna: José Juan Bigas Luna (1946–), Sp. writer, movie director.

Big Bad Smitty: John Henry Smith (1941–2002), U.S. black blues musician.

Big Bopper: Jiles Perry Richardson, Jr. (1930–1959), U.S. rock singer, songwriter. The musician so nicknamed himself for his ample size.

Big Boy Henry: Richard Henry (1921–2004), U.S. blues musician.

Big Daddy: Shirley Crabtree (1930–1997), Eng. heavyweight wrestler. The wrestler began his career as "Shirley Crabtree, The Blond Adonis," as well as simply "Mr. Universe." By the time he was in his early 30s, he was wrestling as "The Battling Guardsman." It was then that he met and married his wife Eunice, and she suggested a new name to improve his "bad guy" image, as she knew he had a gentle side. In 1975 "The Battling Guardsman" thus became the softer, cuddlier "Big Daddy" [*TV Times Magazine*, October 16–22, 1982]. The name itself was said to come from Big Daddy in Tennessee Williams's play *Cat on a Hot Tin Roof* (1955). More recently the name became familiar as the nickname of the U.S. heavyweight boxer Riddick Bowe (1967–), reputedly a hamburger junkie.

Big Daddy Kane: Antonio M. Hardy (1969–), U.S. black rapper. The self-styled "black gentleman vampire" cliamed that his new name was an acronym for "King Asiatic Nobody's Equal."

Biggie Smalls *see* **Notorious B.I.G.**

Biggins: Christopher Biggins (1948–), Br. TV actor. Far into his career, the actor decided to be professionally known by his surname alone. "First there was **Madonna**, then **Prince**. Now Christopher Biggins is joining the list of celebrities whose global fame requires them to be known by a single name" [*The Times*, July 28, 2009].

Big Joe: Joseph Spalding (*c.*1955–), Jamaican reggae musician.

Big Joe Louis: Alasdair Blaazer (1961–), Jamaican blues musician, working in U.K. The blues and gospel artist presumably patterned himself on the boxer Joe **Louis**.

Big L: Lamont Coleman (1974–1999), U.S. black rapper.

Hosea **Biglow:** James Russell Lowell (1819–1891), U.S. humorist, satirist, poet. Lowell used the name for the purported author, a young New England farmer, of *The Biglow Papers*, two series of satirical verses in Yankee dialect published in the mid–1840s.

Cantell A. **Bigly:** George Washington Peck (1817–1859), U.S. writer, editor. Peck adopted this name as author of *Aurifodina; or, Adventures in the Gold Region* (1849), a fictional account of a journey to a land of gold.

Big Maceo: Major Meriweather (1905–1953), U.S. blues singer.

Big Maybelle: Mabel Louise Smith (*c.*1920–1972), U.S. black blues, jazz singer.

Big Punisher: Christopher Carlos Rios (1971–2000), U.S. rapper, of Puerto Rican descent. The musician was originally known as Big Moon Dog before adopting the stage name Big Pun, a short form of Big Punishment, itself referring to his weight problems. He died young of a heart attack.

Big Time Sarah: Sarah Streeter (1953–), U.S. black blues singer.

Big Twist: Larry Nolan (1937–1990), U.S. black blues musician.

Big Youth: Manley Augustus Buchanan (1949–), Jamaican pop singer, DJ.

Bilitis *see* Pierre **Louÿs**

Acker **Bilk:** Bernard Stanley Bilk (1929–), Eng. jazz clarinetist. The musician was born in Somerset, where he was nicknamed "Acker," a local friendly form of address that he adopted as his first name.

Vladimir **Bill-Belotserkovsky:** Vladimir Naumovich Belotserkovsky (1884–1970), Russ. dramatist. English speakers have long had problems with Russian names, and when Belotserkovsky was in the USA, Americans gave up on his surname and called him by its first syllable, as "Bill." The writer liked this, and added it to his existing name, thus unwittingly exaggerating the problem.

Bud **Billiken:** Willard Francis Motley (1909–1965), U.S. black novelist. Motley adopted this name for an early column that he wrote for the *Chicago Defender*.

Josh **Billings:** Henry Wheeler Shaw (1818–1885), U.S. humorist. Shaw used the name for his first book, *Josh Billings, Hiz Sayings*, publication of which was arranged in 1865 by C.F. Browne (*see* Artemus **Ward**). The name is not as crackpot as most of Shaw's writings, which incorporate a fine display of absurd spellings, grotesque grammar, and surrealistic statements. He wrote standard English as Uncle Esek, and his "Uncle Esek's Wisdom" column ran in *Century Illustrated Monthly Magazine* from 1884 to 1888, "Esek" being a form of "Isaac." Shaw's first comic lecture, in Napoleon, Indiana, was delivered under the name Mordecai David, and he initially wrote for Poughkeepsian newspapers as Si Sledlength before settling on Josh Billings, a name that presumably implies "joke business."

Peter **Billingsley:** Peter Michaelson (1972–), U.S. juvenile movie actor

Billy the Kid: Henry McCarty (1859–1881), U.S. western outlaw. In 1873 McCarty's mother married William Henry Antrim, whereupon he became Henry Antrim. Later, for reasons that are obscure, he adopted the name William H. Bonney. As a teenager he was called "Kid" but was not known as "Billy the Kid" until the final months of his life.

Bim: Ivan Semyonovich Radunsky (1872–1955), Russ. circus clown, teaming with **Bom**. Bim was always accompanied by Bom, and Bom always went with Bim. The team of *Bim-Bom*, in fact, was a single interdependent entity: a pair of Russian clowns who first performed under the name in 1891. (The name is meaningless, but suggests something like "bing-bang" or "boom-boom"). There was always a single *Bim* in the person of Ivan Radunsky, a Pole by origin, but there were no less than four *Boms*: a russianized Italian named Cortesi, a fellow Pole called Stanevsky, a Czech (or another Pole) by the name of Wilczak, and finally a Russian named Kamsky. The duo began as an eccentric but versatile couple, both amusing and acrobatic, lively and highly literate (they spoke "proper" Russian, as distinct from the broken Russian affected by a number of clowns). After the tragic death by drowning of Cortesi in 1897, the second Bom presented a different image, dressing not as a conventional clown but as a chic "man about town," wearing evening dress, complete with top hat and buttonhole chrysanthemum. The pair now played down the acrobatics in favor of verbal satire. In the early 20th century the two toured Europe. After the Revolution, Stanevsky emigrated to his native Poland, and Bim followed suit. He returned in 1925, however, and in partnering Wilczak now concentrated on the musical aspect of his turns. (The third Bom was an accomplished if unorthodox musician. One of his specialties was playing two concertinas simultaneously.) Bim finally teamed up with Kamsky in World War II. The early 1920s produced a number of Bim-Bom imitators, notably Bib-Bob (G.L. Rashkovsky and I.A. Vorontsov), but also Viys-Vays (V.A. Sidelnikov and M.I. Solomenko), Din-Don, Rim-Rom, Fis-Dis and the like [Shneyer, p.67].

Satané **Binet:** Francisque Sarcey (1828–1899), Fr. dramatic critic, novelist.

Bingi Bunny: Eric Lamont (*c*.1956–), Jamaican reggae musician. Lamont began his career as "Bunny," working with Bongo Herman, and later adopted a new first name that matched the other's.

Micah Joseph **Bin Gorion:** Micah Joseph Berdichevsky (1865–1921), Russ. Jewish writer. The writer's adopted name is of the same origin as that of David **Ben-Gurion**.

Bing Xin: Hsieh Wan-Ying (1900–1999), Chin. (female) writer of sentimental stories, poems. The writer's adopted name means "pure in heart."

Bint ash-Shatt: Aisha Abd ar-Rahman (1916–), Egyptian writer, academic. The writer was born in Dumyat (Damietta), an old port at the mouth of the Nile. Hence her pen name, Arabic for "daughter of the beach."

William **Birchley:** John Austin (1613–1669), Eng. religious writer.

Billie **Bird:** Bird Bernice Sellen (1908–2002), U.S. vaudeville entertainer.

Richard **Bird:** William Barradell-Smith (1885–?), Sc. writer of stories for boys. The name was presumably meant to evoke "dicky bird," as a teller of tales ("A dicky bird told me"). The name itself was perhaps suggested by the author's original surname. (Some sources give this as Barradale-Smith, his first name as Walter, and his birth year 1881.)

W. **Bird:** Jack Butler Yeats (1871–1957), Ir. painter, illustrator, writer. The younger brother of the poet W.B. Yeats used this name for his cartoons published in *Punch* from 1910 to 1941.

Cleo **Birdwell:** Don DeLillo (1936–), U.S. novelist, playwright. The writer used this name for his 1980 novel *Amazons*.

Tala **Birell:** Natalie Bierle (1908–1959), Pol.-Austr. movie actress, working in U.S.

George A. **Birmingham:** [Rev.] James Owen Hannay (1865–1950), Ir.-born Br. author of light novels. James Hannay chose the pen name "Birmingham" not because he had some connection with that city, but simply because it was (and still is) a fairly common name in Co. Mayo, where he was rector in the town of Westport. A more common spelling of the Irish surname is Bermingham.

Miervaldis **Birze:** Miervaldis Berzins (1921–2000), Latvian writer. The writer's new name, while suggesting his original name, translates as "grove."

Bishi: Bishnupriya Bhattacharya (1983–), Br. DJ, pop musician, of Bengali parentage.

Bernice Pauahi **Bishop:** Pauahi (1831–1884), U.S. philanthropist. The native Hawaiian high chiefess was originally known by the single name Pauahi, meaning "the fire is out," given to honor her maternal aunt, who had been badly burned by a gunpowder explosion as a child. She was then named Bernice by the American missionary couple with whom she stayed as a teenager. She finally received her surname on marrying Charles Reed Bishop, an American businessman, in 1850.

Joey **Bishop:** Joseph Abraham Gottlieb (1918–2007), U.S. TV, movie comedian, of Central European Jewish parentage. The actor adopted the name of his roadie, Glenn Bishop.

Julie **Bishop:** Jacqueline Wells Brown (1914–), U.S. movie actress. The actress began her career in 1923 as a child star under her original name of Jacqueline Brown. She changed this to Jacqueline Wells in 1931, then signed for Warner Bros. in 1941, who renamed her Julie Bishop. For the 1932 serial *Heroes of the West* she was billed as Diane Duval.

Stacey **Bishop:** George Antheil (1900–1957), U.S. novelist, opera composer. Stacey can be either a man's or a woman's name, and the writer does not seem to have been seeking any special ambiguity in choosing it.

Stephen **Bishop-Kovacevich:** Stephen Bishop (1940–), U.S. pianist, of Yugoslav descent. The musician added his Yugoslav name in 1975 and subsequently came to be known by it alone.

Zoubida **Bittari:** Louise Ali-Rachedi (1937–), Algerian novelist, working in France.

Arthur **Bitter:** Samuel Haberstich (1821–1872), Ger. writer, satirical magazine editor.

Billy **Bitzer:** Johann Gottlieb Bitzer (1872–1944), U.S. movie cameraman. Bitzer changed his two German baptismal names, recorded on his birth record as John William, to George William, although he was always known professionally as G.W. or Billy, the latter as a pet form of William.

George **Bizet:** George Tulloch Bisset-Smith (1863–1922), Sc. sociologist, writer. The name presumably puns on that of the composer Georges **Bizet**

Georges **Bizet**: Alexandre-César-Léopold Bizet (1838–1875), Fr. composer.

Biz Markie: Marcel Hall (1964–), U.S. black hip-hop musician.

Brynjolf **Bjarme**: Henrik Ibsen (1828–1906), Norw. poet, dramatist. Ibsen used this name early in his career.

Björk: Björk Guðmundsdóttir (1965–), Icelandic pop singer, songwriter, movie actress.

Dinna **Bjørn**: Dinna Bjørn Larsen (1947–), Dan. ballet dancer, choreographer.

Black: Colin Vearncombe (1951–), Br. rock singer.

Benjamin **Black**: John Banville (1945–), Ir. novelist. The writer adopted his pen name for a series of detective novels, beginning with *Christine Falls* (2006).

Cilla **Black**: Priscilla Maria Veronica White (1943–), Eng. popular singer, TV presenter. The singer explains how she came by her name: "My mum's name is Priscilla as well and she was always known as Big Priscilla whereas I was Little Priscilla. I lived in a very tough area [in Liverpool] and to have a posh name like that was very embarrassing. Luckily the kids called me Cilla at school. The Black bit came when a local paper, called The Mersey Beat, had a misprint. They knew my surname was a colour and guessed wrong. My manager Brian Epstein quite liked it, though, and put it into my contract. My dad went spare [was furious] because he didn't think any of his mates down at the docks would believe I was his daughter" [Sachs and Morgan II, p.26].

Denise **Black**: Denise Nixon (1958–), Eng. TV actress.

Don **Black**: Donald Blackstone (1938–), Br. lyricist.

Frank **Black**: Charles Michael Kitteridge Thompson IV (1965–), U.S. rock musician. Thompson first called himself Black Francis on founding the Pixies in Boston, Massachusetts, in 1986. He adopted the present form of the name for his first solo album (1993): "I wanted something a bit more basic. A little more straight ahead. Something with a little more oomph" [*The Times*, February 17, 2001].

Gavin **Black**: Oswald Morris Wynd (1913–1998), Sc. thriller writer.

Ivory **Black**: Thomas Allibone Janvier (1849–1913), U.S. novelist.

Jimmy Carl **Black**: James Carl Inkanish (1938–2008), U.S. rock musician. The drummer with the Mothers of Invention, whose skin color came from his Cheyenne mother, is remembered for his repeated satirical one-liner on the band's 1968 album *We're*

Only in it for the Money: "Hi boys and girls, I'm Jimmy Carl Black and I'm the Indian of the group!"

Karen **Black**: Karen Blanche Ziegler (1942–), U.S. movie actress. "Black" from "Blanche" (a name that properly means "white").

Laura **Black** *see* Rosalind **Erskine**

Lionel **Black**: Dudley Barker (1910–1980), Eng. novelist, nonfiction writer.

Mansell **Black** *see* Elleston **Trevor**

[Sir] Misha **Black**: Moisey Cherny (1910–1977), Br. architect, industrial designer, of Russ. parentage. The architect's father translated his Russian name to Black when the boy was barely a year old, and the latter's first name was subsequently altered from Jewish Moisey (Moses) to Russian Misha (Michael).

Sonny **Black**: Bob Boazman (1946–), Br. blues musician.

Black Ace: Babe Karo Lemon Turner (1905–1972), U.S. black blues musician.

Black Bart: Charles E. Boles (*fl.*1875–1888), U.S. stagecoach robber. The highwayman took the name "Black Bart" from a character in a story he had read.

E. Owens **Blackburne**: Elizabeth Owens Blackburne Casey (1848–1894), Ir. novelist, journalist.

Black Francis: Charles Michael Kitteridge Thompson IV (1965–), U.S. rock musician.

Thomas **Blacklow**: Thomas White (1593–1676), Eng. philosopher. The controversial writer was ordained a Roman Catholic priest under this name in 1617. "Black-" clearly opposes his original name, while "-low" may come from the maiden name of his mother, Mary Plowden. Some of his Latin works were published under the name Albius, corresponding to his English surname, while for others he was Anglus. One such work, published in 1660, was stated to be "authore T. Anglo ex Albiis East-Saxonum" ("by the author T. Anglus of the Whites of the [kingdom of the] East Saxons"), this last being the Latin name of his native county of Essex.

Bernard **Blackmantle**: Charles Molloy Westmacott (1787–1868), Eng. journalist, writer. The author also wrote as Abel Funnefello.

Black Stalin: Leroy Calliste (1941–), Trinidad calypso singer.

Charity **Blackstock** *see* Paula **Allardyce**

Lee **Blackstock** *see* Paula **Allardyce**

Harry **Blackstone**: Harry Boughton (1885–1965), U.S. magician. The illusionist altered his original surname to Bouton in 1910 when performing a double comedy act with his brother, Pete Bouton (1888–1968). He then appeared under a succession of names: Martin, The Great Stanley, Francisco, Harry Careejo, Mr. Quick, C. Porter Newton, LeRoy Boughton, Beaumont the Great, Fredrik the Great, and finally Harry Blackstone in 1918. ("Fredrik" had to be abandoned because of anti–German sentiment.) The magician explained the source of his final name variously: either it was his grandmother's maiden name, or it came from the Blackstone Hotel, Chicago, or he took it from a billboard advertising Blackstone cigars. Blackstone's first wife, Inez Nourse, claimed the third of these was correct, the billboard in question being in Wapakoneta, Ohio [Fisher 1987]. He was succeeded by his son, Harry Blackstone, Jr. (1934–1997).

The **Black Tarantula:** Kathy Acker (1944–1997), U.S. novelist, short-story writer. Acker used this pseudonym for her first novel, *The Childlike Life of the Black Tarantula, by the Black Tarantula* (1975).

Mr. **Blackwell:** Richard Sylvan Selzer (1922–2008), U.S. fashion designer.

Scrapper **Blackwell:** Frankie Black (1903–1962), U.S. black jazz guitarist.

Matty **Blag:** Matthew Roberts (1964–2000), U.S. punk rock musician.

Hal **Blaine:** Harold Simon Belsky (1929–), U.S. drummer.

Jan **Blaine** *see* Jane **Langford**

Vivian **Blaine:** Vivienne Stapleton (1921–1995), U.S. movie actress, singer.

Betsy **Blair:** Elizabeth Winifred Boger (1923–2009), U.S. movie actress. The actress is said to have adopted the name of a boy she fancied at Blair Academy, New Jersey. She became active in politics, and on one occasion was invited to Thailand by an official who mistook her for Cherie Blair, wife of former U.K. prime minister Tony Blair. (As a lawyer, Cherie Blair retained her maiden name, Cherie Booth.)

David **Blair:** David Butterfield (1932–1976), Eng. ballet dancer.

Emma **Blair:** Iain Blair (1942–), Sc. writer. Blair adopted this female name at the suggestion of his publishers for his romantic novels.

Isla **Blair:** Isla Jean Baxter (1944–), Br. stage, TV actress. The actress's original surname was Blair Hill, "Hill" having been added to the Scottish family name of Blair in about 1880. She dropped the "Hill" when she left the Royal Academy of Dramatic Art (RADA), since "Blair Hill seemed a mouthful" [personal fax from Isla Blair, March 22, 1996].

Janet **Blair:** Martha Janet Lafferty (1921–2007), U.S. movie actress. The actress was born in Altoona, Blair County, Pennsylvania, and took her stage name from her home county.

Joyce **Blair:** Joyce Sheridan Taylor, née Ogus (1932–2006), Br. stage actress, sister of Lionel **Blair**.

Lionel **Blair:** Henry Lionel Ogus (*c*.1931–), Can.-born Br. entertainer, dancer, of Pol.-Russ. Jewish descent, brother of Joyce **Blair**.

Rev. David **Blair** *see* Abbé **Bossut**

Anne **Blaisdell** *see* Dell **Shannon**

Immodesty **Blaize:** Kelly Fletcher (1977–), Br. burlesque performer. The erotic dancer and comedian acquired her stage name from a gas fitter. "'He appeared at my door to fix the boiler, and told me I looked like the cartoon character Modesty Blaise. I was like: "Yeah, sure, Immodesty Blaize, more like!"'" [*Sunday Times Magazine*, April 17, 2005]. The character in question was created for the London *Evening Standard* in 1963 as a sort of female James Bond, with her adventures published in a series of novels by her creator, Peter O'Donnell.

Amanda **Blake:** Beverly Louise Neill (1929–1989), U.S. stage, movie actress.

Bobby **Blake:** Michael James Vijencio Gubitosi (1933–), U.S. child movie actor. The member of the "Our Gang" series performed as Mickey Gubitosi until 1942.

Captain Wilton **Blake** *see* Morton **Pike**

George **Blake:** Georgy Ivanovich Behar (1922–), Du.-born Br. traitor, Russ. double agent, of Du.-Egyptian Jewish (naturalized Br.) parentage. Blake adopted his new name in World War II when he escaped to England as a member of the Dutch resistance and volunteered for the Royal Navy.

Jerry **Blake:** Jacinto Chabania (1908–*c*.1961), U.S. jazz musician.

Marie **Blake:** Blossom MacDonald (1896–1978), U.S. movie actress.

Nicholas **Blake:** Cecil Day-Lewis (1904–1972), Ir.-born Br. writer. Day-Lewis used this name for his detective fiction, taking it from his son, Nicholas, and one of his mother's family names. (She was born Kathleen Blake Squires.) The first novel written under the name was *A Question of Proof* (1935).

Whitney **Blake:** Nancy Baxter (1925–2002), U.S. movie, TV actress.

Blakitny-Ellan: Vasily Mikhaylovich Yelannsky (1894–1925), Ukr. poet, politician. The first part of the writer's name, prefixed to a form of his original surname, means "blue," contrasting symbolically with the "red" socialist stance taken by many of his contemporaries at the time of the Russian Revolution (1917).

Blam: Edmund Blampied (1886–1966), Br. cartoonist, illustrator.

Anna **Blaman:** Johanna Petronella Vrugt (1905–1960), Du. novelist.

Mel **Blanc:** Melvin Jerome Blank (1908–1989), U.S. voice artist.

Neltje **Blanchan:** Nellie Blanchan Doubleday, née de Graff (1865–1918), U.S. writer on nature subjects.

Pierre **Blanchar:** Pierre Blanchard (1892–1963), Fr. stage, movie actor.

Robert **Blanchard** *see* McDonald **Hobley**

Alexander **Bland:** Nigel Gosling (1909–1982), Eng. ballet critic + Maude Gosling, née Lloyd (1908–), S.A.-born Br. ballet dancer, critic, his wife.

Fabian **Bland:** Hubert Bland (1856–1914), Br. writer + E. **Nesbit**, Br. writer, his wife. The joint pseudonym was used for the novel *The Prophet's Mantle* (1889), with "Fabian" a reference to the Fabian Society, of which Bland was a prominent member.

Jennifer **Bland** *see* Avon **Curry**

Ana **Blandiana:** Otilia Valeria Coman Rusan (1942–), Rom. lyric poet.

Ralph **Blane:** Ralph Uriah Hunsecker (1914–1995), U.S. movie music composer, lyricist.

Sally **Blane:** Elizabeth Jane Young (1910–1997), U.S. movie actress, sister of Loretta **Young**.

Caroline **Blangy:** Marie Félicie Clémence de Reiset, vicomtesse de Grandval (1830–1907), Fr. composer.

Docteur **Blasius:** Paschal Grousset (1845–1919), Fr. writer. The Communist journalist used this name for articles in the newspaper *Figaro*, while for his adventure novels he wrote as André Laurie.

Blas Roca: Francisco Vilfredo Calderio (1908–1987), Cuban Communist official.

Christopher **Blayre:** Edward Heron-Allen (1861–1943), Eng. writer of fantasy fiction.

Henri **Blaze:** Ange Henri Blaze de Bury (1813–1888), Fr. author.

Oliver **Bleeck:** Ross E. Thomas (1926–1995), U.S. mystery writer.

Blek le Rat: Xavier Prou (1952–), Fr. graffiti artist. "His splendid nom de guerre was carefully chosen.... Like all graffiti artists working in the streets at night, he needed to find another name, because you don't leave your real name at the bottom of your illegal pictures for the police to trace. Instead, you come up with something else that's catchy and punchy and cool.... He settled on Blek le Rat for a couple of reasons. As a kid, he'd been a fan of some comic books set in the war of American independence featuring the antics of a character called Blek le Roc, a thorn in the side of the British. Also, if you jumble up the letters of the word 'rat' you get 'art.' *Voilà*" [*Sunday Times Magazine*, June 8, 2008].

Emile **Blémont:** Léon-Emile Petitdidier (1839–1927), Fr. critic, dramatist, writer.

Carla **Bley:** Carla Borg (1938–), U.S. jazz, rock composer. The musician's performing name is that of her first husband, Paul Bley, although she used her maiden name initially.

Rose **Blight:** Germaine Greer (1939–), Austral.-born Br. literary critic, reviewer, journalist. The writer used this punning name for *The Revolting Garden* (1979).

Mathilde **Blind:** Mathilde Cohen (1841–1896), Ger.-born Br. poet, translator. The writer adopted the name of her stepfather, Karl Blind (1826–1907), who came to England as a political refugee in 1852. She used the name Claude Lake for *Poems* (1867).

Blind Boy Fuller *see* Blind Boy **Fuller**

Belinda **Blinders:** Desmond F.T. Coke (1879–1931), Br. army officer, schoolmaster, novelist. Coke used this name for *Sandford of Merton* (1903), a parody of Thomas Day's instructional storybook *The History of Sandford and Merton* (1783–9), the standard children's book of its day. He also wrote as Charbon (French for "coal," punning on his surname) for articles in *Hearth and Home* magazine.

Blind Tom: Thomas Grimes (1849–1908), U.S. black pianist, composer. Grimes was blind from birth.

Blinkhoolie: William Allison (1851–1925), English sporting writer. The writer used this name for various novels about hunting and horses. The name is that of a celebrated racehorse, foaled in 1864 and winner of the Gimcrack Stakes, Queen Alexandra Stakes, and Ascot Gold Vase.

Vicesimus **Blinkingsop, LL.D.** *see* Alfred **Allendale**

Helen **Bliss:** Helena Louise Lipp (1917–), U.S. stage actress, singer.

Reginald **Bliss:** Herbert George Wells (1866–1946), Eng. novelist, sociological writer. Wells used the name for his novel *Boon* (1915), in which Reginald Bliss is the friend and literary executor of the main character, George Boon, a popular playwright and novelist.

Luther **Blissett:** Roberto Bui, It. author + Giovanni Cattabriga, It. author + Luca Di Meo, It. author + Federico Guglielmi, It. author. The authorial quartet, of uncertain birthdates, became famous for their novel *Q* (1999), for which they adopted the name of Jamaican-born British footballer Luther Blissett (1958–). In 2000 they were joined by a fifth writer, Riccardo Pedrini, wherupon they changed their collective name to Wu Ming, a Chinese pseudonym that can mean either "anonymous" or "five names," depending on how it is pronounced. Luca Di Meo left the group in 2008.

Blitz: David Batents (?–1889), U.S. magician. The entertainer adopted the name of Signor **Blitz**.

Signor **Blitz:** Antoni van Zandt (1810–1877), Eng.-born U.S. magician. Many other magicians tried to capitalize on Signor Blitz's popularity by adopting his name, as for one did **Blitz**. His son, Harry Blitz, who died in 1915, performed as "Haba-Haba," a name on the lines of that of **Aba-Daba**.

Levi **Blodgett:** Theodore Parker (1810–1860), U.S. religious writer.

Pyotr Grigoryevich **Blokhin:** Grigory Iosifovich Sverdlin (1887–1942), Russ. revolutionary.

Jan **Blom:** Breyten Breytenbach (1939–), S.A. writer. The name suggests that of Jan Bloem, said by some to have given the name of the South African city of Bloemfontein.

Leonard **Blomefield:** Leonard Jenyns (1800–1893), Eng. naturalist. "In 1871, through his connection with the Chappelow family, the descendants of Edward Chappelow of Diss, whose sister married Francis Blomefield, the historian of Norfolk, a considerable property devolved upon him, and he adopted the name of Blomefield" [*Dictionary of National Biography*].

Max **Blonda:** Gertrud Schoenberg, née Kolisch (*c.*1894–1967), Austr. musician. The musician was the second wife of the Austrian-born U.S. composer Arnold Schoenberg, whom she married in 1924. She used this name as librettist of his comic opera *Von Heute auf Morgen*, composed in 1928–29. The name itself appears to pun vaguely on that of her husband, with Schoenberg literally meaning "beautiful hill." Reading from right to left, the final -*a* can be seen as representing his first name, *blond* as meaning "fair," "beautiful," and *max* as denoting something high or lofty, like a hill.

Charles **Blondin:** Jean-François-Emile Gravelet (1824–1897), Fr. funambulist. The tightrope walker took his name from his tutor in the art, Jean Ravel Blondin.

Alpha **Blondy:** Seydou Kone (1953–), Ivorian reggae singer, bandleader. The West African musician interpreted his recording name as "First Bandit."

Johnny **Blood:** John Victor McNally (1904–1985), U.S. American football player. When at college, McNally and his friend Ralph Hanson decided to set up a semipro football team. In order to play for the semipros, yet protect their eligibility for collegiate teams, they knew they would have to use assumed names. The story goes that on their way to the tryouts they passed a movie theater showing *Blood and Sand*. "There are our names," said McNally, "I'll be Blood and you be Sand." It is not known what became of Sand.

Matthew **Blood** *see* Brett **Halliday**

Buster **Bloodvessel:** Douglas Trendle (1958–), Br. rock singer.

Claire **Bloom:** Patricia Claire Blume (1931–), Eng. stage, movie actress, of Pol.-Latvian descent.

Hyman **Bloom:** Hyman Melamed (1913–2009), Latvian-born U.S. painter, of East-European Jewish descent. In 1920, together with his parents and brother Bernard, Melamed emigrated to the U.S, where he adopted the same surname as that already taken by his two eldest brothers who had preceded him.

Luka **Bloom:** Barry Moore (1955–), Ir. folk singer, working in U.S. The musician adopted his new name to be distinguished from his elder brother, Irish folk singer Christy Moore (1945–), taking Luka from Suzanne Vega's 1987 hit so titled and Bloom from Leopold Bloom, the central character of James Joyce's novel *Ulysses* (1922).

Mrs. H. Hilton **Bloom:** Harriott Horry Rutledge Ravenel (1832–1912), U.S. writer. Ravenel adopted this name in 1879 on entering the *Charleston News and Courier* contest for the best fiction story. Her entry, "Ashurst," won the $100 gold prize.

Fannie **Bloomfield:** Fannie Zeisler, née Blumenfeld (1863–1927), Austr.-born U.S. concert pianist. The pianist performed under this name until her marriage (1885), after which she appeared under her married name.

Cheese **Blotto:** Keith A. Stevenson (1956–1999), U.S. rock bassist. "Cheese" from "Keith."

Kurtis **Blow:** Kurt Walker (1959–), U.S. black rock singer, rapper. The musician first made his name as a DJ, calling himself Kool DJ Kurt. He was then convinced by Russel Simmons, brother of Run DMC rapper Joe Simmons, to change his name to Kurtis Blow.

Ben **Blue:** (1) Benjamin Bernstein (1901–1975), Can. vaudeville comedian, dancer; (2) S. David Cohen (1941–1982), U.S. pop-music writer. Cohen was renamed by his friend Bob **Dylan**.

David **Blue:** Stuart David Cohen (1941–1982), U.S. folk-rock musician.

"Little" Joe **Blue:** Joseph Valery (1934–1990), U.S. black blues musician

Miss **Bluebell:** Margaret Leibovici, née Murphy, originally Kelly (1910–2004), Ir. dancer, teacher. The founder in 1932 of the Bluebell Girls dance troupe, performing in nightclubs and cabarets, was born in Dublin to a Mrs. Kelly. Only a fortnight after the birth, however, her mother gave away her baby to a spinster, Mary Murphy, who would raise the child. "A sickly toddler, she was taken by her adoptive mother to a doctor, who was struck by the child's piercing blue eyes. 'If I was her mother,' he said, 'I'd call her Bluebell.' The nickname stuck" [*The Times*, September 14, 2004]. Margaret Murphy adopted the name for herself and passed it on to her dancers.

Blue Boy: Austin Lyons (1955–), Trinidadian calypso singer.

Jake **Blues:** John Belushi (1949–1982), U.S. soul singer.

Peter **Blume:** Piotr Sorek-Sabel (1906–1992), Russ.-born U.S. painter.

James **Blunt:** James Hillier Blount (1979–), Eng. pop singer, songwriter.

Eduard **Blutig:** Edward St. John Gorey (1925–2000), U.S. writer, illustrator. The name is a sort of Germanic form of the original, as German *blutig* means "bloody," "gory." Gorey was famous for his anagrammatic pseudonyms based on his first and last names: Mrs. Regera Dowdy, Wardore Edgy, Raddowy Gewe, Aedwyrd Gore, Redway Grode, Ogdred Weary, Garrod Weedy, Madame Groeda Weyrd, Dreary Wodge, Dogear Wryde.

Nellie **Bly:** Elizabeth Jane Seaman, née Cochran (1864–1922), U.S. reporter. At age 15, Elizabeth Jane went to Indiana (Pennsylvania) Normal School, adding an "e" to her surname. At age 18 she joined the staff of the *Pittsburgh Dispatch*, when editor George Madden named her "Nellie Bly" from the character (properly "Nelly Bly") in the popular Stephen Foster song (1850).

Larry **Blyden:** Ivan Lawrence Blieden (1925–1975), U.S. stage actor, director.

Oliver **Blyth** *see* Brinsley **MacNamara**

Betty **Blythe:** Elizabeth Blythe Slaughter (1893–1972), U.S. movie actress.

Jimmy **Blythe:** Sammy Price (1901–1931), U.S. black jazz pianist.

Capel **Boake:** Doris Boake Kerr (1895–1944), Austral. novelist.

Tim **Bobbin:** John Collier (1708–1786), Eng. writer, caricaturist. The writer used this name for satirical poems in the Lancashire dialect, the first being *The Blackbird* (1740).

Bobèche: Jean-Antoine-Aimé Mardelard (or Mandelard) (1791–c.1840), Fr. comic actor, teaming with **Galimafré**. French *bobèche* is a slang word for "head," so can be understood as something like "nut," "noddle."

Willie **Bobo:** William Correa (1934–1983), U.S. jazz musician, of Puerto Rican parentage. The musician was nicknamed "Bobo" by jazz pianist Mary Lou Williams during a recording session in 1951.

Bob Tai'r Felin: Robert Roberts (1870–1951), Welsh folksinger. The singer's name means "Bob of the millhouse," referring to his home near Bala, northwest Wales.

Bocage: Pierre-Martinien (or François) Touzé (1797–1863), Fr. actor.

Maxwell **Bodenheim:** Maxwell Bodenheimer (1893–1954), U.S. poet, critic, novelist. In 1909 Bodenheimer joined the army, rejected his Jewish heritage, and shortened his name.

Bhikkhu **Bodhi:** Jeffrey Block (1944–), U.S.-born Buddhist, of Jewish parentage, working in Sri Lanka. Bodhi is the Sanskrit word for "perfect knowledge" (related to the name of the Buddha). Bhikkhu, literally "beggar," is the term for a fully ordained Buddhist monk.

Bo Diddley: Otha Elias Bates, later McDaniel (1928–2008), U.S. black blues musician, songwriter. The musician's mother was too poor to raise him and he was adopted by her cousin, Gussie McDaniel, a Sunday school teacher in Chicago, whose name he subsequently adopted. The origin of his performing name is disputed. Some take it from "bo diddley," the name of a one-stringed African guitar. He acquired the name while competing in boxing competitions, and according to another theory, "[it] derived from the Southern putdown 'you ain't bo diddley,' meaning 'you're nothing,' but also carrying the sense of 'bad bo diddley,' implying someone it would be foolish to cross" [*The Times*, June 3, 2008]. "Otha Ellas [*sic*] Bates was never going to make it on a theatre hoarding but Bo Diddley ... there's a name to build a myth upon" [Russell and Smith, p.54].

Mrs. **Bogan of Bogan:** Carolina Oliphant, née Nairne (Baroness Nairne) (1766–1845), Sc. songwriter.

[Sir] Dirk **Bogarde:** Derek Jules Gaspard Ulric Niven van den Bogaerde (1921–1999), Br. stage, movie actor, of Du. descent.

Neil **Bogart:** Neil Bogatz (1941–1982), U.S. rock singer, record executive. The singer launched his career in 1961 as Neil Scott, then acted for a time as Wayne Roberts before returning to music.

Aleksandr **Bogdanov:** Aleksandr Aleksandrovich Malinovsky (1873–1928), Russ. socialist writer, Proletkult leader.

V. **Bogucharsky:** Vasily Yakovlevich Yakovlev (1861–1915), Russ. revolutionary historian. The writer also used the name B. Bazilevsky.

Edmund **Boisgilbert:** Ignatius Loyola Donnelly (1831–1901), U.S. writer, politician. Donnelly used this name for his social novel *Caesar's Column* (1890).

Maurice **Boissard:** Paul Léautaud (1872–1956), Fr. novelist, essayist. The writer used this name as a drama critic.

Bojangles: Bill (originally Luther) Robinson (1878–1949), U.S. black tap dancer. The dancer came to be so called because he was a "jangler" or contentious person.

Hannes **Bok:** Wayne Woodard (1914–1964), U.S. artist, writer, astrologer.

Ray **Bol** *see* Don Juan **Cardoza**

Marc **Bolan:** Mark Feld (1947–1977), Br. pop musician, of Pol.-Russ. descent. Feld cut his first disk in 1965 as Mark Bowland, a name said to have been given him by his recording company, Decca. That same year he made this more distinctive as Marc Bolan. However, according to another account, he took his new name from the first and last syllables of the name of Bob **Dylan**. He had earlier called himself Mark Riggs, after Riggs O'Hara, an actor friend, while as a teenage model he took the name Toby Tyler, after the young waif who is the central character in James Otis's 1881 novel for boys so titled.

Rolf **Boldrewood:** Thomas Alexander Browne, originally Brown (1826–1915), Eng.-born Austral. romantic novelist. The writer took his pseudonym from a placename mentioned in the Introduction to Canto I in Sir Walter Scott's poem *Marmion* (1808): "Through Boldrewood the chase he led."

Richard Valentinovich **Boleslavsky:** Boleslaw Ryszart Srzednicki (1889–1937), Pol.-born U.S. stage director. Boleslavsky adopted his stage name in 1908 on being accepted as a student at the Moscow Art Theatre and retained it on immigrating to the United States in 1922.

Bogdan **Boleslawita:** Józef Ignacy Kraszewski (1812–1887), Pol. novelist.

William **Bolitho:** William Bolitho Ryall (1831–1930), S.A.–born Br. journalist, author.

Florinda **Bolkan:** Florinda Suarez Bulcão (1941–), It. movie actress, of Brazilian-Ind. parentage.

Yammie **Bolo:** Rolando Ephraim McClean (1970–), Jamaican reggae singer.

Isabel **Bolton:** Mary Britton Miller (1883–1975), U.S. poet, novelist. Possibly the writer's middle name suggested her adopted surname.

Michael **Bolton:** Michael Bolotin (1953–), U.S. rock balladist. The musician slightly adjusted his name because his original surname "sounded too Russian."

Bom: (1) F. Cortesi (?–1897), It.-born Russ. circus clown, teaming with **Bim**; (2) Mechislav Antonovich Stanevsky (1879–1927), Russ. clown, of Pol. parentage, teaming with Bim; (3) Nikolay Iosifovich Wilczak (1880–1960), Russ. clown, of Cz. (or Pol.) parentage, teaming with Bim; (4) N.A. Kamsky (1894–1966), Russ. clown, teaming with Bim.

Bombardinio: William Maginn (1793–1842), Ir. journalist, poet, writer.

L.-A.-C. **Bombet** *see* **Stendhal**

Bombita: Ricardo Torres (1879–1936), Sp. bullfighter. The matador's name means "bulb" (as in "light bulb"), appropriately for his *traje de luces* or bullfighter's costume (literally "suit of lights").

Fortunio **Bonanova:** Luis Moll (1895–1969), Sp. movie actor, singer.

Father **Bonaventura:** Charles Edward Stuart (1720–1788), Sc. prince ("Bonnie Prince Charlie"). The Young Pretender adopted this name on visiting England from France incognito in 1753.

[St.] **Bonaventure** (or Bonaventura): Giovanni di Fidanza (*c*.1217–1274), It. theologian, scholar, mystic. The saint is said to have been given his new name, meaning "good fortune," by St. **Francis of Assisi**, whose order he joined around 1243.

Steve **Bond:** Shlomo Goldberg (1953–), U.S. juvenile movie actor.

Beulah **Bondi:** Beulah Bondy (1892–1981), U.S. movie actress.

Manik **Bondopadhai:** Probodhkumar (1908–1956), Ind. novelist, short-story writer.

Gary U.S. **Bonds:** Gary Anderson (1939–), U.S. rock composer. The musician's new name originated with his first manager, Frank Guida, who sent copies of his first single "New Orleans" to radio stations in sleeves marked "Buy U.S. Bonds," hoping DJs would take this to be a public service announcement.

Margaret **Bonds:** Margaret Jeannette Allison Majors (1913–1972), U.S. black composer, pianist. The musician and teacher adopted her mother's maiden name in her professional life.

Egon **Bondy:** Zbynek Fiser (1930–2007), Cz. writer.

Captain Ralph **Bonehill:** Edward L. Stratemeyer (1863–1930), U.S. writer. Stratemeyer used this name for his "Flag of Freedom" (1899–1902), "Mexican War" (1900–02), and "Frontier" (1903–07) series of stories for boys.

Richard **Bonelli:** Richard Bunn (1887–1980), U.S. opera singer. The tenor adopted an Italian name similar to the American original.

Bon Gaultier: William Edmonstone Aytoun (1813–1865), Sc. poet + [Sir] Theodore Martin (1814–1909), Sc. poet. The name was first used for the joint work, *Bon Gaultier Ballads* (1845), in which the poets parodied the verse of the day. It originated with Rabelais, who uses it in a favorable sense: "I truly hold it for an honour and praise to be called and reputed a frolic Gaulter [*sic*] and a Robin Goodfellow" [Author's Prologue to *Gargantua*, translated by Thomas Urquhart and Peter Motteux, 1653]. Gaultier itself is the French equivalent of English Walter.

Ali **Bongo** *see* **Ali Bongo**

Omar **Bongo:** Albert-Bernard Bongo (1935–2009), Gabonese head of state. The president of Gabon changed his French Christian name to Omar on converting to Islam in 1973.

Jacques **Bonhomme:** Guillaume Cale (or Caillet) (?–1358), Fr. peasant leader. The generic name (something like "Jack Goodfellow") was one given to the peasantry in the 14th century. Its sense was derogatory, however, not approbatory, and it implied serfdom.

[St.] **Boniface:** Wynfrith (or Winfrid) (*c*.675–754), Eng. missionary, martyr. The "Apostle of Germany" was renamed by pope Gregory II in 719 for the 3d-century saint Boniface who had been martyred at Tarsus.

Boniface VIII: Benedetto Caetani (*c*.1235–1303), It. pope. This pope's original name was adopted as a papal name by his successor, **Benedict XI.**

Boniface IX: Pietro Tomacelli (*c.*1350–1401), It. pope.

Bonita: Pauline Hall (*c.*1885–?), U.S. music-hall artist.

Jon **Bon Jovi:** John Francis Bongiovi, Jr. (1962–), U.S. rock musician, movie actor.

Egomet **Bonmot** *see* Herr Cornelius van **Vinkbooms**

Issy **Bonn:** Benjamin Levin (1903–1977), Eng. radio comedian, singer. A typical Jewish nickname for the Jewish comedian, who was popular on radio in the 1930s. He also occasionally appeared in the movies as Benny Leven. "Issy" implies Israel, and "Bonn" represents Benjamin.

Blaise **Bonnain** *see* George **Sand**

Frank **Bonner:** Frank Boers, Jr. (1942–), U.S. TV actor.

Sherwood **Bonner:** Katherine Sherwood Bonner Macdowell (1849–1883), U.S. short-story writer.

Hugh **Bonneville:** Hugh Richard Bonneville Williams (1963–), Br. stage, TV actor. When the actor began his career in 1986 he felt it prudent to adopt a new name so as not to evoke an association with the actor Hugh Williams (1904–1969), who though no longer alive was still remembered by many. He thus decided to use his two middle names, Richard Bonneville. "However, my family and friends still called me Hugh, so when I worked with actors who were also friends no-one knew *what* to call me. I battled on for nine years, trying to explain to each bemused new acquaintance just who the hell I was — until last year, when I finally gave up the fight and changed my [actors' union] Equity forename to Hugh. Beats me why I didn't go with this in the first place" [personal fax from Hugh Bonneville, March 26, 1996]. The form of the actor's third name on his birth certificate is actually Bonniwell.

Bill **Bonney** *see* Wes **Hardin**

William H. **Bonney** *see* **Billy the Kid**

Bono: Paul David Hewson (1960–), Ir. rock singer. The U2 lead singer originally used the name Bono Vox, from Bonavox, a hearing-aid shop in O'Connell Street, Dublin. At first he was not keen on the name, but then saw it could be taken as Latin for "good voice." He later settled to Bono alone. "I can't remember when [wife] Ali started calling me Bono. I was 16, I'd say. Before Bono, I was Steinvic von Huyseman, and then just Huyseman, and then Houseman, then Bon Murray, Bono Vox of O'Connell Street, and then just Bono" [Bono, *Bono on Bono: Conversations with Michka Assayas*, 2005].

Chaz **Bono:** Chastity Bono (1969–), U.S. writer. The oldest child of **Sonny** and **Cher** adopted a male version of his original first name in 2009 after on undergoing gender reassignment surgery. "I've felt male as far back as I can remember," he said, speaking on ABC's *Good Morning America* show.

Jessie **Bonstelle:** Laura Justine Bonesteele (1871–1932), U.S. stage actress, theater manager. Justine was called "Jessie" by her family and altered the spelling of her surname as her stage name early in her career.

Giovanni Andrea **Bontempi:** Giovanni Andrea Angelini (1624–1705), It. composer, singer. The musician adopted the name of his patron, Cesare Bontempi.

Roger **Bontemps:** Roger de Collerye (?1470–1540), Fr. poet.

Betty **Boo:** Alison Moira Clarkson (1970–), Br. pop singer, of Sc.-Malayan parentage. The singer adopted her stage name from the cartoon character Betty Boop.

Johnny **Booker:** John Martyn (1923–2007), Br. skiffle singer. The singer took his new name from the title of a traditional American folk song.

Books-Nabonag: [Comte] Georges Libri-Bagnano (*fl.*1830), Belg. journalist, forger. The literary figure translated the first part of his hyphenated name into English, then anagrammatized the second.

Dany **Boon:** Daniel Hamidou (1966–), Fr. stage, movie comedian.

William **Boot** *see* Tom **Stoppard**

Adrian **Booth:** Virginia Mae Davis, née Pound (1918–), U.S. movie actress. Originally a singer under the name Ginger Pound, the actress first appeared in the movies in 1937 as Virginia Pound. She was then billed as Lorna Gray from 1930 through 1946, when she made a fresh start as Adrian Booth. In 1949 she married David **Brian**.

Edwina **Booth:** Josephine Constance Woodruff (1909–1991), U.S. movie actress. The actress took her stage name from the tragedian and theatrical manager Edwin Booth (1833–1893), the first American actor to make his reputation in Europe.

James **Booth:** James Geeves (1927–2005), Eng. stage, movie actor, working in U.S.

Karin **Booth:** Katharine Hoffman (1919–1992), U.S. movie actress. The actress was Katharine Booth before progressing to Karin Booth in 1947.

Shirley **Booth:** Thelma Booth Ford (1898–1992), U.S. stage, movie actress. The actress adopted her stage name in the 1930s when touring with the Poli Stock Company and other theatrical troupes.

Wee Bea **Booze:** Muriel Nicholls (1920–1975), U.S. black blues musician.

Georg **Borchardt:** Georg Hermann (1871–1943), Ger. Jewish novelist.

Cornell **Borchers:** Cornelia Bruch (1925–), Ger. movie actress.

Olive **Borden:** Sybil Tinkle (1909–1947), U.S. movie actress.

Giovanni **Bordoni:** Catterina Vizzani (1719–1743), It. retainer. Vizzani assumed male dress and identity in her work as a retainer for a Perugian priest, who chid "him" for constantly chasing women.

Petrus **Borel:** Joseph-Pierre Borel d'Hauterive (1809–1859), Fr. poet, novelist. The writer, associated with melodramatic horror novels such as *Madame Putiphar* (1839), came to be known as *Le Lycanthrope*, "The Wolf-Man," apparently with reference to the classic saying, "Man is a wolf to man."

Victor **Borge:** Boerge Rosenbaum (1909–2000), Dan.-born U.S. comic pianist.

Scipione Caffarelli **Borghese:** Scipione Caffarelli (1576–1633), It. cardinal, art patron. The churchman was the son of Ortensia Caffarelli, sister of Camillo Borghese, the future pope **Paul V**, who adopted him and gave him his name

Ernest **Borgnine:** Ermes Effron Borgnino (1917–), U.S. movie actor, of It. parentage. The actor's new English first name is similar only in sound to his original Italian forename, the equivalent of "Hermes."

Il **Borgognone:** Jacques Courtois (1621–1676), Fr. painter, working in Italy. The painter of battle scenes was born in Burgundy (Italian *Borgogna*). Hence his nickname, meaning "the Burgundian."

Lucrezia **Bori:** Lucrezia Borja y Gonzalez de Rianche (1887–1960), Sp. opera singer.

Inge **Borkh:** Ingeborg Simon (1917–), Ger. opera singer.

Stefan **Born:** Stefan Buttermilch (1824–1898), Ger. political reformer.

Ludwig **Börne:** Juda Löw Baruch (1786–1837), Ger. political writer, satirist. Baruch took his new name on converting from Judaism to Christianity in 1817 with the aim of qualifying for public service.

Eduard **Bornhöhe:** Eduard Brunberg (1862–1923), Estonian historical novelist. The writer adopted a name that means more or less the same (literally "well height") as his original name.

George **Borodin** *see* George **Sava**

Mikhail **Borodin:** Mikhail Markovich Gruzenberg (1884–1951), Russ. Communist official, newspaper editor.

Havel **Borovsky:** Karel Havlícek (1821–1856), Cz. journalist.

Borra: Borislav Milojkowic (1921–), Yugoslav-born Austr. magician, working in U.K.

Francesco **Borromini:** Francesco Castelli (1599–1667), It. architect. The architect adopted his new name in around 1627.

Bos: Thomas Peckett Prest (1809–1879), Eng. author of stories for boys. Prest, and others like him, originally intended to ascribe their virtual piracies of writings by Dickens to "Boaz," after Dickens's own pen name **Boz**. This was ruled out, however, as being rather too close, and also rather too biblical. The genre of Prest's particular fiction came to be known as the "penny dreadful."

Hieronymus **Bosch:** Jerom van Aeken (*c*.1450–1516), Du. painter. Bosch took his new surname from his birthplace, the town of 'sHertogenbosch, and his new first name as the Greek form of Jerom(e).

Michel **Bosquet** *see* André **Gorz**

Abbé **Bossut:** [Sir] Richard Phillips (1767–1840), Eng. journalist, writer of educational books. Phillips was a noted pseudonymist. He used "Abbé Bossut" (after the genuine French mathematician of the name, his near contemporary) for a series of French, Italian, and Latin word books and phrase books. Names adopted for other writings include James Adair, Rev. S. Barrow, Rev. David Blair, Rev. C.C. Clarke, Rev. J. Goldsmith (for geographical and scientific works), and Mrs. (or Miss) Margaret Pelham.

The **Boston Bard:** Robert Stevenson Coffin (1797–1827), U.S. journalist, poet. The writer used this name for such works as *The Miscellaneous Poems of the Boston Bard* (1818).

A **Bostonian** *see* Edgar A. **Perry**

Connee **Boswell:** Constance Foore Boswell (1907–1976), U.S. jazz singer. The popular artist spelled her first name "Connie" until 1941. The change came about because when signing autographs she never dotted the "i," so that on receiving fan mail addressed to "Connee" she decided to adopt this form.

Eve **Boswell:** Eva Keleti (1922–1998), Hung.-born Br. popular singer. The singer's nationality made her an alien when touring Britain with her family in 1939, so she and they emigrated to South Africa, where they joined Boswell's Circus. There Eva fell in love with Trevor McIntosh, stepson of the circus owners. They eloped and married in 1944, and McIntosh changed his wife's name to Eve Boswell, for the circus. She made her singing debut in England in 1949 with the British bandleader **Geraldo**.

Frank **Bosworth** *see* Mark **Carrel**

Ezra **Boto** *see* Mongo **Beti**

Sandro **Botticelli:** Alessandro di Mariano dei Filipepi (1445–1510), It. painter. The artist is said to have adopted the nickname given to his elder brother Giovanni, a rotund pawnbroker. "Botticello" means "little barrel" (Italian *botte*, "barrel"). According to Giorgio Vasari's *Lives of the Artists* (1550), however, the painter was apprenticed to a goldsmith named Botticelli and adopted his name.

Francesco **Botticini:** Francesco di Giovanni (*c*.1446–1497), It. painter. The artist took his name from his more illustrious contemporary, Sandro **Botticelli**, on whom he based his style.

Anthony **Boucher:** William Anthony Parker White (1911–1968), U.S. editor, SF, detective story writer.

Charles **Boucheron:** Charles James (1906–1978), Eng.-born U.S. fashion designer. James opened a hat shop in Chicago under this name in 1926 before moving to New York two years later to take up dress designing.

Barbara **Bouchet:** Barbara Gutscher (1943–), Ger.-born U.S. movie actress, working in Italy.

Chili **Bouchier:** Dorothy Irene Boucher (1909–1999), Br. movie actress. The actress was given her new first name by a boyfriend. "'I love my Chili Bom Bom,' he said to my retreating back. I turned, intrigued. 'What do you mean?' He told me that on the previous evening he had seen a revue called 'The Punch Bowl' in which Sonnie **Hale** had sung a song called 'I Love My Chili Bom Bom' to a girl who looked like me.... From then on, he ... called me Chili Bom Bom, gradually reducing it to just 'Chili.' And so Chili was born" [Chili Bouchier, *Shooting Star: The Last of the Silent Film Stars*, 1995].

She modified her surname herself. "The first photograph of me ever published had somebody else's name underneath and the second called me Chili Poucher. Even if my name had been spelt correctly I still thought it looked rather ugly. So I put an 'i' in Boucher and made it Bouchier — hoping that it would be pronounced the French way. I did not succeed in this for ages and ages for everybody thought I was the daughter of the famous actor-manager, Arthur Bourchier [(1864–1927)], who pronounced his name as Boucher to rhyme with voucher" [ibid.].

Dion **Boucicault:** Dionysius Lardner Boursiquot (1820–1890), Ir.-born U.S. actor, dramatist. The actor, who was of Huguenot extraction, began his career under the name of Lee Morton in 1838. He adopted the French-style spelling of his original name in 1841, after the success (in London) of his play *London Assurance*.

Louis Boudinoff **Boudin:** Louis Boudinoff (1874–1952), Ukr.-born U.S. political theorist. On emigrating to New York in 1891, Boudinoff took a shortened form of his original name as his surname.

Elias **Boudinot:** Galagina (?1804–1839), U.S. tribal leader. Boudinot was the son of a Cherokee warrior and the daughter of a white trader and Cherokee woman. From 1811 to 1818 he attended the Moravian mission school in the Cherokee nation and in 1817 replaced his original name (meaning "Buck") with the name of the president of the American Bible Society, Elias Boudinot (1740–1821).

Daniel **Boukman:** Daniel Blérald (1936–), Martinique-born Fr. dramatist, journalist.

Nicolas **Boulanger:** Paul-Henri Thiry, baron d'Holbach (1723–1789), Fr. materialist, atheist writer. Holbach used this name for his antireligious work *Le Christianisme dévoilé* (1761), taking it from the French philosopher Nicolas-Antoine Boulanger, who had died two years earlier. Holbach also wrote as L'Abbé **Bernier** and Jean **Mirabaud**.

Ingrid **Boulting:** Ingrid Munnik (1947–), S.A. movie actress.

Houari **Boumédienne:** Mohammed Ben Brahim Boukharrouba (1927–1978), Algerian head of state. The military leader adopted his new name as a *nom de guerre* when he joined a guerrilla unit in 1955. "Boumédienne" is the French spelling of Arabic Bum-ed-Din, literally "owl of religion."

Benjamin **Bounce:** Henry Carey (1685–1743), Eng. poet, composer. Carey used the exuberant name for his equally lively dramatic burlesque *Chrononhotonthologos*, "the Most Tragical Tragedy that ever was Tragediz'd by any Company of Tragedians" (1734). In this, Chrononhotonthologos is the king of Queerummania, while two other characters are Aldiborontiphoscophornia and Rigdum-Funnidos, names which Sir Walter Scott later gave to his printer and publisher, the brothers James and John Ballantyne, for the pomposity of the former and the cheerfulness of the latter.

Bounty Killer: Rodney Basil Price (1972–), Jamaican ragga musician. The lyrics of many ragga hits relate to guns. Hence the musician's recording name. (His big 1993 hit, "Down in the Ghetto," describes how guns and drugs reached the ghettos sanctioned by corrupt government officials, and includes the lines: "Down in the ghetto where the gun have a ting — and the politician is the guns them a bring — hey — and the crack and the coke them a support the killing — me check it out the whole a dem ah the same ting.") The name itself presumably puns on "bounty hunter," as a nickname for someone who pursues wanted criminals for the sake of the reward offered.

Nicolas **Bourbaki:** Henri Cartan (1904–2008), Fr. mathematician + Claude Chevalley (1909–1984), Fr. mathematician + Jean Dieudonné (1906–1992), Fr. mathematician + André Weil (1906–1998), Fr. mathematician. The named men were the nucleus of a group formed in 1933 to represent the essential "contemporary mathematician." Their group pseudonym, chosen humorously, was that of a French general, Charles Bourbaki (1816–1897), whose attempts to bridge the Prussian line during the Franco-German War (1870–1) ended in a humiliating disaster. The name is chiefly associated with the group's huge reference work, *Éléments de mathématiques*, published over many years from 1939.

Maurice **Bourgès-Maunoury**: Maurice Jean-Marie Bourgès (1914–1993), Fr. Resistance leader, politician. The politician, briefly prime minister (1957), added the name of his maternal grandfather to his original name. His code name as a Resistance leader in World War II was "Polygone."

Margaret **Bourke-White**: Margaret White (1904–1971), U.S. photographer. In 1926, following a brief marriage, White added her mother's maiden name to her original surname.

George **Bourne**: George Sturt (1863–1927), Eng. writer of books on rural subjects. Sturt took his pen name from his birthplace, Lower Bourne, Farnham, Surrey.

Peter **Bourne** *see* Bruce **Graeme**

Sam **Bourne**: Jonathan Saul Freedland (1967–), Br. journalist, novelist. The writer created this pseudonym for his thriller *The Righteous Men* (2006) for distinction from his real name as a journalist. He based it on the name of his young son, Sam, and a billboard he saw advertising the movie *The Bourne Supremacy* (2004). "I liked it instantly. It made the connection with my son even stronger: after all, the book was hatched in 2004, and when was Sam born? (Sam Bourne — get it?) And I thought he sounded like a thriller writer. My own name is somehow too convoluted, too polysyllabic, with difficult 'fr' and 'th' sounds. Sam Bourne is altogether shorter and sharper" [*The Guardian*, March 29, 2006].

Bourvil: André Raimbourg (1917–1970), Fr. movie comedian. The actor's screen name came from the village of Bourville, northwest of Paris, where he was raised. At the same time it half suggests the latter half of his real surname.

Pete **Bouton** *see* Harry **Blackstone**

Bartholomew **Bouverie**: William Ewart Gladstone (1809–1898), Br. prime minister, author.

John **Bowe**: John Wilson (1950–), Br. stage, TV actor.

Jim **Bowen**: James Whittaker (1937–), Eng. TV gameshow presenter.

Marjorie **Bowen**: Margaret Gabrielle Vere Long, née Campbell (1888–1952), Eng. novelist, biographer. The writer created her pen name from a variant of her first name and her great-grandfather's surname. She used many other (mostly male) pseudonyms, of which the best known are Robert Paye, George R. Preedy, Joseph Shearing, and John Winch.

David **Bowie**: David Robert Hayward-Jones (1947–), Eng. rock musician. The singer changed his name to Bowie in 1966 so as not to be confused with Davy Jones of The Monkees, with his new name allegedly for the bowie knife. As to pronunciation:

"Since the bowie knife was popularised by the frontiersman Jim Bowie, ... the pop star's name should most accurately be pronounced David Bo-hie, or even the down south pronunciation of Jim's name, Boo-ie" [Paul Gambaccini, *Masters of Rock*, 1982].

Bowie's son, movie director Duncan Jones (1971–), began life as Zowie Bowie but later reverted to the original family name. "He adopted the more prosaic name on his passport when he realised that he didn't want to be in the shadow of his rather famous father David" [*The Times*, July 15, 2009].

Mark **Bowland** *see* Marc **Bolan**

Debra Louise **Bowring**: Peter John Compton (1938–), Br. movie producer. The producer, a transexual, explains the choice of three new names as follows: "The name of Debra was chosen as I just liked it, Louise was an old family name, and Bowring likewise as my father's family surname was Bowring Compton" [personal letter from Debra Bowring, September 14, 1995].

Emmanuel **Bove**: Emmanuel Bobonikov (1898–1945), Fr. writer.

Charles-Samuel **Bovy-Lysberg**: Charles-Samuel Bovy (1821–1873), Swiss pianist, composer. The musician added the name of his birthplace, Lysberg, near Berne.

Edgar **Box**: Gore Vidal (1925–), U.S. novelist, playwright, writer. The writer reserved this name for three detective novels: *Death in the Fifth Position* (1952), *Death before Bedtime* (1953), and *Death Like It Hot* (1954). Vidal kept this pseudonym secret for many years, although he did confide it to one or two literary colleagues.

Boxcar Willie: Lecil Travis Martin (1931–1999), U.S. country musician. Martin took his name after being impressed by the way in which, during the Depression, unemployed men would climb onto the roofs of boxcars so as to travel aross the States by freight train. His own father was a railroad man, and the family house lay only a few feet from the track. (According to one account, he called himself Willie on seeing a hobo who resembled an old friend of this name.) On assuming the name, Martin adopted the stage guise of an unshaven, unkempt, cigar-chompin' hobo in a battered hat. Earlier, as an adolescent, he had performed under the name Marty Martin.

Boy: Tadeusz Żeleński (1874–1941), Pol. writer, translator, literary critic. The writer, murdered by political opponents, used this name for his "Library of Boy," a series of around 400 translations of the classics of French literature (works by Rabelais, Villon, Montaigne, Molière, Montesquieu, Rousseau, Diderot, Beaumarchais, Stendhal, Mérimée, Balzac, etc.).

Candy **Boyd**: Marguerite Dawson (1947–), U.S. black educator, children's writer.

John **Boyd:** Boyd Bradfield Upchurch (1919–), U.S. SF writer.

Margot **Boyd:** Beryl Billings (1913–2008), Br. stage, TV actress.

Nancy **Boyd:** Edna St. Vincent Millay (1892–1950), U.S. poet.

Stephen **Boyd:** William Millar (1928–1977), Ir. movie actor, working in U.S.

Boy George: George Alan O'Dowd (1961–), Eng. pop singer. The singer adopted the name in 1982, when he first began appearing, dressed as a girl (or at least androgynously), with his group Culture Club. He had himself billed as "Boy George" on the sleeve of his first single in order to answer the inevitable initial question, "Is it a boy or a girl?" The name would ensure that the apparent "she" was correctly identified as a "he" [*Pop Focus*, 1983].

Katie **Boyle:** Caterina Irene Helen Imperiali di Francavilla (1926–), It.-born Eng. TV panelist, writer, columnist. "Katie" for Caterina, and "Boyle" for her first husband (married 1947, divorced 1955), Richard Bentinck Boyle, Viscount Boyle (1924–), subsequently Earl of Shannon.

Oswald **Boyle:** Alfred Austin (1835–1913), Eng. writer. The future Poet Laureate (from 1896) used this name for a melodramatic novel, *Jessie's Expiation* (1867), as well as other fiction.

René **Boylesve:** René-Marie-Auguste Tardiveau (1867–1926), Fr. novelist. The writer adopted his mother's maiden name as his pen name.

Boz: Charles Dickens (1812–1870), Eng. novelist. Dickens used this name (pronounced "Boze") in reports of debates in the House of Commons in *The Morning Chronicle* (1835) and in his collection of articles entitled *Sketches by Boz* (1836–37). He explained: "Boz, my signature in the 'Morning Chronicle,' ... was the nickname of a pet child, a younger brother [Augustus (died 1827)], whom I had dubbed Moses, in honour of the 'Vicar of Wakefield' [by Goldsmith, in which Moses Primrose is the vicar's son], which being facetiously pronounced through the nose, became Boses, and being shortened, Boz. Boz was a very familiar household word to me, long before I was an author, and so I came to adopt it" [preface to *Pickwick Papers*, 1847 ed.]. A humorous verse of the day ran: "Who the dickens 'Boz' could be / Puzzled many a learned elf; / But time revealed the mystery, / And 'Boz' appeared as Dickens' self." Some contemporary writers sought to emulate Dickens by adopting names such as "Bos," "Pos," and "Poz." Dickens finally dropped the name with *Dombey and Son* (1847).

Bozhidar: Bogdan Petrovich Gordeyev (1894–1914), Russ. poet. The poet's adopted name relates to his original first name: Bogdan literally means "given by God," while Bozhidar means "gift of God."

Hercules Brabazon **Brabazon:** Hercules Brabazon Sharpe (1821–1906), Eng. painter. The artist adopted his mother's maiden name, his own middle name, as a condition of inheriting the family estates in Ireland in 1847.

James **Brabazon:** Leslie James Seth-Smith (1923–2007), Br. writer, TV producer.

Hugh Henry **Brackenridge:** Hugh Montgomery Breckenridge (1748–1816), Sc.-born U.S. novelist, prose writer, poet. The writer changed his middle name to Henry and and altered the spelling of his surname "because I found the bulk of the same stock spelt it so."

George **Braddin** *see* George **Sava**

Jesse **Bradford:** Jesse Bradford Watrouse (1979–), U.S. movie actor.

Edward P. **Bradley:** Michael Moorcock (1939–), Eng. SF writer.

Will **Bradley:** Wilbur Schwichtenberg (1912–1989), U.S. jazz trombonist. The musician changed his name because his original surname was too cumbersome for billings.

Scott **Brady:** Gerard Kenneth Tierney (1924–1985), U.S. movie actor.

June **Brae:** June Bear (1917–2000), Eng. ballet dancer. The dancer adopted her anagrammatic stage name when invited to guest with the Ballet Rambert early in her career.

Eric **Braeden:** Hans Gudegast (1942–), Ger. movie actor.

Braguinha: Carlos Alberto Ferreira Braga (1907–2006), Brazilian songwriter. When Braga first began writing songs as a student of architecture he adopted the name João de Barro to hide his musical activity from his father, who disapproved of his son's musical ambitions.

John **Braham:** John Abraham (1774–1856), Eng. opera singer.

May **Brahe:** Mary Hannah Morgan (1885–1956), Austral. composer.

Otto **Brahm:** Otto Abrahamsohn (1856–1912), Ger. stage director, literary critic.

Caryl **Brahms:** Doris Caroline Abrahams (1901–1983), Eng. writer, songwriter. The writer adopted her new name as a student in order to conceal her literary activities from her parents, "who envisaged a more domestic future for her" [*Dictionary of National Biography*].

Stan **Brakhage:** Robert Sanders (1933–2003), U.S. filmmaker.

Ernest **Bramah:** Ernest Brammah Smith (1868–1942), Br. writer. The writer used this pseudonym for all of his books, and even his *Who's Who* entry appears under the name. Brammah was his mother's maiden name.

Bramantino: Bartolomeo Suardi (*c.*1460–1530), It. painter. The name effectively means "little Bramante," referring to the artist Donato Bramante (1444–1515), whose disciple he was.

Tabitha **Bramble:** Mary Robinson, née Darby (1758–1800), Eng. actress, writer. The actress best known as **Perdita** had many pseudonyms. She adopted this one for some poems, taking it from the "maiden of forty-five, exceedingly starched, vain and ridiculous" in Tobias Smollett's novel *Humphry Clinker* (1771). "There could hardly be a wittier pen name for the woman once described as the most beautiful woman in England" [Paula Byrne, *Perdita: The Life of Mary Robinson*, 2004].

Branco: Claudio Ibrahim Vaz Leal (1964–), Brazilian footballer.

Christianna **Brand:** Mary Christianna Lewis (1907–1988), U.K. thriller writer.

Max **Brand:** Frederick Schiller Faust (1892–1944), U.S. novelist, short-story writer. Other names used by Faust, a prolific contributor to pulp magazines, include Frank Austin, George Owen Baxter, Walter C. Butler, George Challis, Peter Dawson, Evan Evans, John Frederick, Frederick Frost, David Manning, and Peter Henry Morland.

John **Brandane:** John MacIntyre (1869–1947), Sc. dramatist.

Klaus Maria **Brandauer:** Klaus Maria Steng (1944–), Austr. stage, movie actor.

Georg **Brandes:** Morris Cohen (1842–1927), Dan. literary critic, historian, of Jewish parentage.

Henry **Brandon:** Henry Kleinbach (1912–1990), U.S. movie actor.

Michael **Brandon:** Michael Feldman (1945–), U.S. movie, TV actor, husband of Glynis **Barber**.

Ivan **Brandt:** Roy Francis Cook (1903–), Eng. stage actor. Cook began his career as an architect, and took his new name when first appearing on the stage in 1927.

Marianne **Brandt:** Marie Bischof (1842–1921), Austr. opera singer.

Willy **Brandt:** Herbert Ernst Karl Frahm (1913–1992), Ger. politician. The future West German chancellor took his new name for articles that he wrote after joining the Socialist Workers' Party in 1931, and retained it on fleeing to Norway in 1933.

Brandy: Rayana Norwood (1979–), U.S. R&B singer.

Lewis **Brant** *see* Fenton **Brockley**

Floresta Augusta **Brasileira** *see* Madame Floresta A. **Brasileira**

Madame Floresta A. **Brasileira:** Nísia Floresta (1810–1885), Brazilian poet, novelist, essayist. Other pseudonyms used by the writer include Une Brésilienne, Telesilla (Portuguese for "chairlift"), Floresta Augusta Brasileira, Madame Brasileira Augusta, and N.F.B.A. (initials of her original and adopted names). For ten years she owned a school called Augusto in Rio de Janeiro.

Brassaï: Gyula Halász (1899–1984), Hung.-born Fr. photographer, writer. The photographer adopted his name in 1925 from that of his native city, Brassó, Hungary (now Braşov, Romania), the Hungarian suffix giving the sense "of."

Pierre **Brasseur:** Pierre-Albert Espinasse (1905–1972), Fr. stage, movie actor, playwright. The actor adopted his mother's maiden name as his stage name.

Johannes **Brassicanus:** Johannes Alexander Kohlburger (1500–1539), Swiss poet, philosopher. The writer's original name can be punningly understood to mean "cabbage-town dweller," for which the Latin equivalent would be *brassicanus*.

Sasthi **Brata:** Sasthibrata Chakravarti (1939–), Ind.-born Br. writer.

Ivan **Bratanov:** Ivan Marinov (1920–1968), Bulg. movie actor.

Mz **Bratt:** Cleopatra Humphrey (1992–), Br. (white) rapper.

Wellman **Braud:** Wellman Breaux (1891–1966), U.S. black jazz bassist.

Linda **Brava:** Linda Lampenius (1971–), Finn. violinist. "This nice middle-class girl from suburban Helsinki is groomed for success Hollywood style. It is a metamorphosis straight from Ovid. It began six months ago with her name: she is now Linda Brava, an all-purpose brand name aimed Exocet-like at the American heartland.... The shift also avoids the snigger-inducing problem of the last two syllables of her surname" [*Sunday Times*, July 20, 1997]. In 2002, however, the player resumed her original name.

Nikolay **Bravin:** Nikolay Mikhaylovich Vasyatkin (1883–1956), Russ. opera singer. The baritone's new name was perhaps meant to suggest *bravo* or *bravura*, with the same sense in Russian as in English.

Danny **Bravo:** Daniel Zaldivar (*c.*1947–), U.S. juvenile movie actor.

Alison **Bray** *see* Fenton **Brockley**

William **Brayce** *see* Fenton **Brockley**

George **Brecht:** George MacDiarmid (1926–2008), U.S. conceptual artist, sculptor.

Brécourt: Guillaume Marcoureau (1638–1683), Fr. actor, dramatist.

Hans **Breitmann:** Charles Godfrey Leland (1824–1903), U.S. humorous writer, editor. Leland had received a university education in Germany, and from 1857 he used the name for his amusing dialect poems, collected in *Hans Breitmann's Ballads* (1914).

Carl **Brema:** Karl Brehmer (1864–1942), Ger.-born U.S. magician, entertainer.

Marie **Brema:** Minny Fehrman (1856–1925). Br. opera singer, of Ger.–U.S. parentage. The singer took her professional name from the city of Bremen, the birthplace of her German father.

Brenda: Georgina Castle Smith, née Meyrick (1845–1933), Br. children's writer.

Edith **Brendall:** Eddy Charly Bertin (1944–), Ger.-born Belg. writer of horror stories.

Michel **Brenet:** Antoinette Christine Marie Bobillier (1858–1918), Fr. musical biographer.

Matthew **Brenher:** Matthew Alexander Benham (1961–), Eng. movie, TV actor.

Máire **Brennan:** Máire Ní Bhraonáin (1952–), Ir. popular singer, harpist. The musician, formerly a member of the group Clannad, adopted the English form of her Irish name (in which Ní is "daughter").

Tim **Brennan:** Jack Conroy (1899–1990), U.S. writer. The leftist writer, born John Wesley Conroy, also used the pseudonym John Norcross.

Arvid **Brenner:** Fritz Helge Heerberger (1907–1975), Swe. writer, of Ger.-Swe. parentage.

Victor David **Brenner:** Victor David Barnauskas (1871–1924), Lithuanian-born U.S. medalist, sculptor.

Adolf **Brennglas:** Adolf Glassbrenner (1810–1876), Ger. journalist.

Evelyn **Brent:** Mary Elizabeth Riggs (1899–1975), U.S. movie actress. The actress was initially billed as Betty Riggs before assuming her later name.

George **Brent:** George Brendan Nolan (1904–1979), Ir.-born U.S. movie actor.

Linda **Brent:** Harriet Jacobs (*c*.1813–1897), U.S. black writer, reformer. The former slave used this name for her autobiography, *Incidents in the Life of a Slave Girl: Written by Herself* (1861).

Romney **Brent:** Romulo Larralde (1902–1976), Mexican-born U.S. stage, movie actor, dramatist.

Tony **Brent:** Reginald Bretagne (1926–1993), Br. popular singer.

Elinor M. **Brent-Dyer:** Gladys Eleanor May Dyer (1894–1969), Eng. writer of books for girls.

Brent of Bin Bin: Stella Maria Sarah Miles Franklin (1879–1954), Austral. novelist. The author's pseudonym is said to represent the name of a kindly elderly gentleman writing about his experiences of Australian bush life, "Bin Bin" being a typical outback placename. The name was originally "Brand of Bin Bin," but the first word of this was altered following a typing error. Franklin used the name for six chronicle novels of pioneer years in Australia: *Up the Country* (1928), *Ten Creeks Run* (1930), *Back to Bool Bool* (1931), *Prelude to Waking* (1950), *Cockatoos* (1954), and *Gentlemen at Gyang Gyang* (1956).

Edmund **Breon:** Edmund MacLaverty (1882–1951), Sc. stage, movie actor, working in U.S., U.K.

John **Brereley, Priest:** James Anderton (*fl.*1604–24), Eng. Roman Catholic writer. Little is known about the controversialist, and the identity of Brereley with Anderton is uncertain. The Rev. Charles **Dodd**, in his *Church History of England, Chiefly with Regard to Catholics* (1737–42) states that "John Brereley" is "either a fictitious name, or at least assumed by James Anderton ... to conceal his person."

Ford **Brereton:** Samufel Rutherford Crockett (1860–1914), Sc. novelist, journalist. The writer used this name for *Dulce Cor* (1886), an early book of poems.

Une **Brésilienne** *see* Madame Floresta A. **Brasileira**

Jeremy **Brett:** Peter Jeremy William Huggins (1935–1995), Eng. stage, movie actor. Huggins changed his name at his father's insistence to hide the social disgrace of having an actor in the family. He is said to have taken the name from the label in his first suit: "Brett & Co."

Lucienne **Bréval:** Berthe Agnès Lisette Schilling (1869–1935), Swiss-born Fr. opera singer.

Teresa **Brewer:** Theresa Veronica Breuer (1931–2007), U.S. popular singer.

Otokar **Březina:** Václav Ignác Jebavý (1868–1929), Cz. poet.

David **Brian:** Brian Davis (1914–1993), U.S. movie actor.

Havergal **Brian:** William Brian (1876–1972), Eng. composer. The prolific symphonic composer adopted his new first name in 1899, when he had begun to gain fame as a church organist. He probably took it from William Henry Havergal (1793–1870), English hymn composer.

James **Brian:** Arthur George Street (1892–1966), Eng. farmer, writer of books on country life. A.G. Street, as he usually signed himself, used this name for a late book, *Fair Enough* (1962).

Mary **Brian:** Louise Byrdie Dantzler (1906–2002), U.S. movie actress.

Fanny **Brice:** Fania Borach (1891–1951), U.S. singer, comedienne. Fania Borach grew so weary of having her name mispronounced as "Bore-ache" and "Bore-act" that she changed it to something simpler. Lauren **Bacall** had similar problems.

Bricktop: Ada Beatrice Queen Victoria Louise Virginia Smith (1894–1984), U.S. black entertainer, nightclub operator. The entertainer's lengthy original name was given her by parents who did not wish to disappoint the many people who had made suggestions for naming her. She was nicknamed "Bricktop" for her red hair when she was in her late 20s by Harlem nightclub owner Barron Wilkins. The name passed to the chic Chez Bricktop club in the Rue Pigalle, Paris, where she was the proprietress and where she entertained many famous expatriate U.S. writers.

Ann **Bridge:** [Lady] Mary Dolling O'Malley, née Sanders (1889–1974), Eng. historical novelist. Ann Bridge took her pen name from the hamlet of Bridge End, Surrey, where she and her husband, Sir Owen Sinclair O'Malley, had rented a house for their family. Reverse the two halves of the name to give "End Bridge" and so "Ann Bridge." (In the writer's day, "Ann" would have sounded more like "Enn" in educated English speech.) Another name was G. Allenby, adopted for poetry published in *The Spectator*.

Bonar **Bridge** *see* **Orion** (1)

Beau **Bridges:** Lloyd Vernet Bridges III (1941–), U.S. movie actor.

Dee Dee **Bridgewater:** Denise Garrett (1950–), U.S. black jazz singer, working in France. The singer married Cecil Bridgewater in 1970 and kept his name after divorcing him a few years later.

James **Bridie:** Osborne Henry Mavor (1888–1951), Sc. playwright. As a physician, Mavor needed a pseudonym for his distinctive dramatic writing. His first play was *The Sunlight Sonata* (1928), which he wrote under the name of Mary Henderson. He subsequently adopted his maternal grandmother's surname for later plays, with the first under the Bridie name being *The Anatomist* (1930). He continued in general medical practice until 1938.

Brigadier Jerry: Robert Russell (1957–), Jamaican DJ, brother of Sister **Nancy.**

Bright Eyes: Susette La Flesche (1854–1903), Native American physician, tribal leader. Susette was the daughter of Omaha chief Joseph La Flesche, also known as Inshtamaza (Iron Eye), who was himself the son of a French trader and an Omaha woman. She took the name Bright Eyes, as the English version of her Native American name, Inshtatheamba, when she became involved in a group called the Indian Ring, which advocated fair treatment for Native Americans.

Lee **Brilleaux:** Lee Green (1952–1994), Eng. rock musician.

Jean **Brioché:** Pierre Datelin (?–1671), Fr. mountebank. The Parisian street entertainer was famous for his marionettes and for his costumed monkey called Fagotin.

Pete **Briquette:** Patrick Cusack (1954–), Ir. rock musician. The Boomtown Rats member, a cousin of Johnny **Fingers,** was given a meaningful name change: "We changed Pat Cusack's name because we thought it sounded too Irish. We made it more Irish. We changed it to Pete Briquette, which was a pun on the fuel cakes made in Ireland from compressed peat" [Bob Geldof, *Is That It?*, 1986].

Jules **Brissac:** Emma Marie MacFarren, née Bennett (1824–1895), Eng. concert pianist, composer.

Carl **Brisson:** Carl Pedersen (1895–1958), Dan. movie actor, working in U.K.

Elton **Britt:** James Britt Baker (1917–1972), U.S. country singer, yodeler.

May **Britt:** Maybritt Wilkens (1933–), Swe. movie actress.

Morgan **Brittany:** Suzanne Cupito (1951–), U.S. child movie, TV actress. The actress took her screen name from the lead character in a paperback novel titled *Blood Ties* that she picked up at an airport. Taken individually, the two names have a common Celtic connection.

Barbara **Britton:** Barbara Brantingham Czukor (1919–1980), U.S. movie actress.

Colonel **Britton:** Douglas Ernest Ritchie (1905–1967), Br. radio director. The broadcaster first used his patriotic byname in 1941, when he was appointed assistant director of BBC European broadcasts.

Jack **Britton:** William James Breslin (1885–1962), U.S. boxer. The boxer was nicknamed "Britain" for his former home city, New Britain, Connecticut. He altered this to "Britton" for use in the ring.

William **Brocius:** William Graham (1851–1882), U.S. gunman, cattle rustler ("Curly Bill").

Lynn **Brock** *see* Anthony **Wharton**

Rose **Brock** *see* James **Colton**

Fenton **Brockley:** Donald Sydney Rowland (1928–), Eng. SF writer. Rowland has used over 50 male and female pen names, not all of them for SF. Others are Annette Adams, Jack Bassett, Hazel Baxter, Karla Benton, Helen Berry, Lewis Brant, Alison Bray, William Brayce, Oliver Bronson, Chuck Buchanan, Rod Caley, Roger Carlton, Janita Cleve, Sharon Court, Vera Craig, Wesley Craile, John Dryden, Freda Fenton, Charles Field, Graham Garner, Burt Kroll, Helen Langley, Henry Lansing, Harvey Lant, Irene Lynn, Stuart McHugh, Hank Madison, Chuck Mason, Edna Murray, Lorna Page, Olive Patterson, Alvin Porter, Alex Random, W.J. Rimmer, Donna Rix, Matt Rockwell, Charles Roscoe, Minerva Rossetti, Norford Scott, Valerie Scott, Bart Segundo, Frank Shaul, Clinton Spurr, Roland Starr, J.D. Stevens, Mark Suffling, Kay Talbot, Will Travers, Elaine Vinson, Rick Walters, and Neil Webb.

Lea **Brodie:** Lea Dregham (1951–), Eng. TV actress. Lea Dregham came to adopt her husband's former pseudonym for her professional work.

Steve **Brodie:** John Stevens (1919–1992), U.S. movie actor.

Harold **Brodkey:** Aaron Roy Weintraub (1930–1996), U.S. writer. Weintraub's mother died when he was 17 months old, following which he was adopted by his father's cousins, Joseph and Doris Brodkey. They gave him his new surname, with "Harold" formed from "Aaron."

Brok: Tamara Timofeyevna Sidorkina (1910– 1975), Russ. circus artist, juggler, lion tamer. An adoption of the familiar clown name "Brock," as used in England by the partner of Brick, whose own later partner was **Grock**.

James **Brolin:** James Bruderlin (1940–), U.S. movie, TV actor.

Josh **Brolin:** Joshua Bruderlin (1968–), U.S. movie, TV actor, son of James **Brolin**.

John **Bromfield:** Farron Bromfield (1922–), U.S. movie actor.

Henry **Bromley:** Anthony Wilson (*fl.*1793), Eng. art historian. The publisher of *A Catalogue of Engraved British Portraits* (1793) may have been connected with the Wilson family of Kendal, Westmorland, which intermarried with the Bromley family.

June **Bronhill:** June Gough (1929–2005), Austral. opera singer. The soprano based her stage name on that of her home town, Broken Hill, New South Wales.

Charles **Bronson:** (1) Charles Dennis Bunchinsky (1921–2003), U.S. movie actor; (2) Michael Gordon Peterson (1952–), Eng. criminal. The actor's grandfather, Charles Dennis Bunchinsky, was the son of Russian immigrants from Lithuania. The family dropped the middle "n," and Buchinsky became "Bronson" for his third movie, *Drum Beat* (1954). "With the hounds of McCarthyville skulking round Hollywood, Slavic names didn't seem so fashionable," he reasoned [David Downing, *Charles Bronson*, 1982]. He is said to have taken the name from Bronson Avenue, an entry way to the Paramount studios in Hollywood.

Peterson, in and out of jail since 1974, when he was sentenced for armed robbery, adopted the actor's name at the age of 35 on taking up prize fighting. "My gaffer [manager] chose my name ... Charles Bronson. I don't think I've ever seen a Charles Bronson film ... I actually wanted to be called Jack **Palance** after the great actor, who in his early years won prize money boxing. But Bronson it was — and Bronson stuck" [Charles Bronson with Robin Ackroyd, *Bronson*, 2002].

Oliver **Bronson** *see* Fenton **Brockley**

[Rev.] Patrick **Brontë:** Patrick Prunty (1777– 1861), Ir.-born Anglican clergyman, writer, working in England. The father of the Brontë sisters (*see* Currer **Bell**) adopted the variant form of his family name shortly before leaving Ireland for England in 1802 to study at Cambridge University. "He took to spelling his name as Bronte with some kind of accent over the last letter in order to signify that it was not

silent. Throughout his life he used a variety of marks over the 'e,' never consistently using the form Brontë which his printed works carry, and which his children were to use exclusively" [Brian Wilks, *The Brontës*, 1975]. According to one account, he adopted this particular spelling because the English naval hero, Lord Nelson, was created Duke of Bronte (in Sicily) by Ferdinand I of Naples in 1799. There is no evidence, however, that he did so in order to imply that his and Nelson's families were related. He may equally have been struck by the suggestion of Greek *brontē*, "thunder," perhaps with a biblical reference.

Bronterre: James O'Brien (1805–1864), Ir. journalist, politician. O'Brien used this name from 1831 for his contributions to the *Poor Man's Guardian* and *Poor Man's Conservative* and later added the name to his own, as James Bronterre O'Brien. The name itself seems to be a blend of Greek *brontē* and French *tonnerre*, both meaning "thunder."

Il **Bronzino:** Agnolo di Cosimo (1503–1572), It. painter. The origin of the artist's assumed nickname, meaning "bronzed," is uncertain. It probably refers to his dark complexion.

Brook: Richard Brookes (1948–), Welsh-born Br. political cartoonist.

Kelly **Brook:** Kelly Parsons (1979–), Eng. model, TV presenter, actress. The model was given her name by *Daily Star* glamor photographer Jeany Savage. "'She was the first person to take me under her wing. She just decided I couldn't be Parsons, and Brook was more pin-up.' Kelly Brook does sound like a glamour pin-up, halfway between [U.S.–born British model and actress] Kelly LeBrock and [U.S. movie actress] Louise Brooks. It has a kind of sleekness and it was a world Kelly Parsons couldn't wait to sheen into" [*Sunday Times Magazine*, June 29, 2003].

· Lesley **Brook:** Lesley Learoyd (1916–), Br. movie actress. The actress (not to be confused with Leslie **Brooks**) adopted the middle name of her father, Reginald Brook Learoyd, as her screen name.

Gwydion **Brooke:** Frederick James Gwydion Holbrooke (1912–2005), Br. bassoonist.

Hillary **Brooke:** Beatrice Sofia Mathilda Peterson (1914–1999), U.S. movie actress.

Magdalen **Brooke:** Harriet Mary Capes (*fl.*1890s), Eng. writer. The author adopted this name for *The Story of Eleanor Lambert* (1891) and other novels.

Harris **Brookes:** Giorgio (later George) Loraine Stampa (1875–1951), Turk.-born Br. cartoonist, illustrator, of It. descent. The artist sometimes used this name for his cartoons for *Punch*.

Albert **Brooks:** Albert Einstein (1947–), U.S. movie director, screenwriter, actor, son of **Parkyakarkus**. "It's a subject for Woody **Allen**: you have this very smart, anxiety-ridden comedian ... who takes the prudent early step of changing his name. Because how can anyone else get away with being Albert Einstein? So he becomes Albert Brooks — as in Brooks Brothers, mainstream" [Thomson 2003, p.111].

Beverley **Brooks:** Patricia Evelyn Beverley Brooks, née Matthews (1929–1992), Eng. socialite. The future Viscountess Rothermere, nicknamed "Bubbles," had an early career as a movie actress under this name.

Dennis **Brooks:** James Mealey (1942–1978), U.S. R&B singer.

Elkie **Brooks:** Elaine Bookbinder (1946–), Eng. popular singer. As a youngster, Bookbinder took singing lessons from the cantor of her local synagogue in Lancashire. She chose the name Elkie as a Yiddish equivalent of "Elaine," while simultaneously shortening her lengthy surname to "Brooks" [*The Times*, March 21, 1987]. Her real name gave the title of her 1988 album *Bookbinder's Kid*.

Ferdinand **Brooks:** Hugh Green (?1584–1642), Eng. Roman Catholic martyr.

George **Brooks** *see* Floyd **Akers**

Geraldine **Brooks:** Geraldine Stroock (1925–1977), U.S. movie actress. "Brooks" is a more manageable name than "Stroock," to which it even so retains a kind of resemblance.

Hadda **Brooks:** Hadda Hopgood (1916–2002), U.S. black boogie-woogie pianist.

Harvey **Brooks:** Harvey Goldstein (*fl.*1960s), U.S. electric bassist.

Leslie **Brooks:** Lorraine Gettman (1922–), U.S. movie actress (not to be confused with Lesley **Brook**).

Lonnie **Brooks:** Lee Baker, Jr. (1933–), U.S. black blues musician. Baker originally performed as Guitar Jr., but abandoned the name in 1960 on moving to Chicago, where Luther "Guitar Jr." Johnson was already established.

Mel **Brooks:** Melvin Kaminsky (1926–), U.S. movie comedy writer, producer. Kaminsky changed his name so as not to be confused with jazz trumpeter Max Kaminsky (1908–1994). His new name arose as a contraction of his mother's maiden name, Brookman.

Nikki **Brooks:** Nicola Ashton (1968–), Eng. popular singer, movie, TV actress.

Phyllis **Brooks:** Phyllis Weiler (or Steiller) (1914–1995), U.S. movie actress.

Richard **Brooks:** Ruben Sax (1912–1992), U.S. writer, movie director. "A ... bit of serendipity allowed me to learn that the late writer-director Richard Brooks had invented his own name. A colleague attended his memorial service, where this fact was publicly revealed for the first time; as a result, I believe I am the first to publish his name, Ruben Sax" [Maltin, p.vii].

D.K. **Broster:** Dorothy Kathleen Broster (1878–1950), Eng. writer of historical novels for children. Readers of Broster's books generally assumed the author to be a man, "an impression she took no steps to correct" [Carpenter and Prichard, p.85].

Brother ... For names beginning thus, see the next word, e.g. for Brother Adam see **Adam**, for Brother Antoninus see **Antoninus**, for Brother Daniel see **Daniel**, etc.

Joyce **Brothers:** Joyce Bauer (1928–), U.S. TV psychiatrist.

David **Brough:** David Bingham (1940–1997), Br. spy. The former naval officer, one of Britain's most notorious spies, was jailed for 21 years in 1971 for selling secrets to the Russians and assumed his new identity as David Brough after his release from prison in 1981.

Fanny **Brough** *see* Julia **Marlowe**

John Henri Isaac **Browere:** John Henry Brower (1790–1834), U.S. sculptor. The artist added an "e" to his surname, adopted the French spelling of his middle name, and for some reason added the name Isaac.

Arthur **Brown:** Arthur Wilton (1944–), Eng. rock musician, comedian.

Buster **Brown:** Wayman Glasco (1911–1976), U.S. black blues singer, harmonica player.

Carter **Brown:** Alan Geoffrey Yates (1923–1985), Br.-born Austral. thriller writer. The original form of the pen name was "Peter Carter Brown," but the writer later dropped the first part of this on the basis that "Carter Brown" alone suited his American market better. He used many other names, such as Tom Conway, Caroline Farr, Sinclair MacKellar, Dennis Sinclair, and Paul Valdez, as well as permutations of his original name.

Charles **Brown:** Leslie Uyeda (1962–), U.S. (female) flutist, pianist, composer.

Craig **Brown:** Vernon Rice (1967–), Br. journalist, writer. The writer uses different pen names for different columns. "It can be a funny old business changing your name. When the young Vernon Rice decided to call himself Craig Brown to avoid the accusation that he was cashing in on the fame of his elder brother Tim ... he cannot ... have dreamed that 15 years later the Scottish Football Association would appoint a genuine Craig Brown to manage its national football team and that he would be forced to adopt a series of pseudonyms (Bel Littlejohn, Wallace Arnold, Charlotte Raven, Gary Bushell, Matthew Norman, Peter Hitchens) in order to ply his trade and write his 20 articles a week without being taken for a track-suited tactician" [Jonathan Meades in *The Times Magazine*, August 2, 1997].

Foxy **Brown:** Inga Fung Marchand (1979–),

U.S. black rapper. The singer took her stage name from the central character of the 1974 "blaxploitation" movie of the same name played by Pam Grier.

Georgia **Brown**: Lillian Claire Laizer Gelel Klot (1933–1992), Eng. stage, movie, TV actress, singer. The actress began her career as a jazz singer, and took her stage name from Maceo Pinkard's 1925 song "Sweet Georgia Brown," which featured in her act. The surname was coincidentally appropriate for her long dark hair and dark brown eyes.

Harriet **Brown** *see* Greta **Garbo**

Herbert **Brown**: Herbert Brovarnik (1912–2004), Br.-born U.S. chemist, of Ukr. parentage.

Irving **Brown** *see* Oliver **Optic**

John **Brown**: Thomas Jefferson Hogg (1792–1862), Eng. lawyer, writer. P.B. Shelley's friend and biographer used this name for his novel *Memoirs of Prince Alexy Haimatoff* (1813), stated on the title page to be "translated from the original Latin MS. under the immediate inspection of the Prince by John Brown, esq."

Lew **Brown**: Louis Brownstein (1893–1958), Ukr.-born U.S. songwriter.

Michael **Brown**: Michael Lookofsky (1949–), U.S. rock musician.

Nappy **Brown**: Napoleon Brown Goodson Culp (1929–2008), U.S. black blues singer.

Roy "Chubby" **Brown**: Royston Vasey (1945–), Br. movie actor, comedian. Brown's real name, Royston Vasey, was chosen as the name of a fictitious town in northern England that was the setting of the British TV comedy series *The League of Gentlemen*, first screened in 1999. Brown himself appeared in the series as a guest character, Mayor Vaughan.

Teddy **Brown**: Abraham Himmebrand (1900–1946), U.S. music-hall instrumentalist.

Vanessa **Brown**: Smylla Brind (1928–1999), Austr.-born U.S. movie actress. "Brown" evolved from "Brind."

VV **Brown**: Vanessa Brown (1984–), Br. pop singer, songwriter, of Jamaican/Puerto Rican parentage. The initials evolved as a nickname based on the singer's first name.

Coral **Browne**: Coral Edith Brown (1913–1991), Austral. stage, movie actress, working in U.K.

Henriette **Browne**: Sophie de Saux, née de Boutellier (1829–1901), Fr. painter, etcher.

Matthew **Browne**: William Brighty Rands (1823–1882), Br. writer of poems, fairy tales for children. Rands also wrote as Timon Fieldmouse and Henry Holbeach.

Henry C. **Browning**: Anna Cora Mowatt (1819–1870), U.S. actress, writer. Mowatt used a number of pseudonyms in her career as a writer. This male name was for a biography, *The Life of Goethe* (1844), while

for the novel *The Fortune Hunter* (1844) she was Helen Berkley. For an earlier work, the epic poem *Pelayo: or, The Cavern of Cavadonga* (1836), she took the name Isabel. The first literary work to appear under her real name was *Evelyn* (1845). She then turned to acting.

Sterry **Browning** *see* Leo **Grex**

Henry **Brownrigg** *see* Paul **Prendergast**

Thomas **Brown, the Younger**: Thomas Moore (1779–1852), Ir. poet, satirist. This is the best-known of the poet's pseudonyms. Others include An Irish Gentleman, Thomas **Little**, One of the Fancy, Captain Rock, and Trismegistus Rustifucius, D.D. (Captain Rock was the name assumed by the leader of a group of Irish insurgents in 1822. Trismegistus, "thrice greatest," was the Greek title of the Egyptian Hermes, the god Thoth. Rustifucius is a comic latinization of English *rusty-fusty*.)

Hedin **Brú**: Hans Jakob Jacobsen (1901–1987), Dan. (Faroese) writer.

Bruce: Bruce Angrave (1912–1983), Eng. cartoonist, writer.

Arthur Loring **Bruce**: Francis Welch Crowninshield (1872–1947), U.S. editor, writer.

Carlton **Bruce** *see* **Old Humphrey**

David **Bruce**: Andrew McBroom (1914–1976), U.S. movie actor.

Jack **Bruce**: John Symon Asher (1943–), Sc. jazz, rock musician.

Lenny **Bruce**: Leonard Alfred Schneider (1925–1966), U.S. nightclub comedian.

Leo **Bruce**: Rupert Croft-Cooke (1903–1979), Br. detective novelist.

Peter **Bruce**: Peter Robinson (1960–), Sc. TV actor. The actor took a new (typically Scottish) name to avoid confusion with another actor who bore his original name.

Virginia **Bruce**: Helen Virginia Briggs (1910–1982), U.S. movie actress.

Bruce of Los Angeles: Bruce Harry Bellas (1909–1974), U.S. photographer.

Edith **Bruck**: Edith Steinschreiber (1932–), Hung. author, writing in Italian.

Ferdinand **Bruckner**: Theodor Tagger (1891–1958), Austr. playwright, of Austr.-Fr. parentage.

Cathal **Brugha**: Charles William St. John Burgess (1874–1922), Ir. revolutionary. The future Minister of Defence in the first Irish parliament replaced English "Charles" by Irish "Cathal" and substituted Irish "Brugha" for equivalent English "Burgess."

John **Bruin**: Dennis Brutus (1924–), S.A. writer, critic.

Henri **Brûlard** *see* **Stendhal**

Christian **Brulls** *see* Georges **Sim**

Brummie: Eddie James (1941–), Br. crossword

compiler. The setter was born in Birmingham, a city whose inhabitants are colloquially known as "Brummies."

Gabrielle **Brune:** Gabrielle Hudson (1912–), Eng. stage actress, singer. The actress adopted the maiden name of her mother, actress and singer Adrienne (originally Phyllis Caroline) Brune, as her stage name.

G.E. **Brunefille:** [Lady] Gertrude Elizabeth Campbell, née Blood (1857–1911), Ir. writer, art critic. Before her marriage to Lord Colin Campbell in 1881, Gertrude Blood used this name for a children's story, *Topo* (1878).

Carla **Bruni:** Carla Bruni Tedeschi (1968–), It. model.

Georg **Brunis:** George Clarence Brunies (1900–1974), U.S. trombonist. Brunies modified his first and last names on the advice of a numerologist.

Bruno de Jésus-Marie: Jacques Froissart (1892–1962), Fr. priest, writer on religious psychology.

Paul **Brunton:** Raphael Hurst (1898–1981), Eng.-born mystic, writer on mysticism, working in U.S. The writer, who introduced Indian mysticism to the West, revealed little about his personal life, and it is not clear why he adopted this particular name: "Evidently he was born with the name Raphael Hurst, and took, first Brunton Paul, then Paul Brunton as a pen name" [Jeffrey Masson, *My Father's Guru*, 1993].

Bruscambille: Jean Deslauriers (*fl.*1610–1634), Fr. comic actor. The name appears to represent French *brusque en bille*, "abrupt in the head," with *bille* a slang word for "head," something like English "nut," "noddle."

Brutus: David Owen (1795–1866), Welsh preacher, teacher, editor. This is the writer's best-known pseudonym, used for the satirical tale *Wil Brydydd y Coed* ("Wil the Rhymester of the Woods") (1863–65), among other writings. The name alludes to Brutus, the legendary progenitor of the British.

David **Bryan:** David Bryan Rashbaum (1962–), U.S. rock musician.

Dora **Bryan:** Dora May Lawton, née Broadbent (1923–), Eng. stage, movie, TV comedienne. Dora Broadbent's surname was "not a name for the stage," as Noel Coward put it. She therefore looked for an alternative, which would at the same time suggest the original. At first she selected "Bryant," from the match manufacturers, Bryant & May, but when the program arrived from the printers, the final "t" was missing and she settled for "Bryan" instead.

Hal **Bryan:** Johnson Clark (1891–1948), Eng. stage actor.

Jane **Bryan:** Jane O'Brien (1918–2009), U.S. movie actress.

Michael **Bryan:** Brian Moore (1921–1999), Ir.-born Can. novelist. Moore also wrote as Bernard Mara.

Rudy **Bryans:** Bernard Godet (*c.*1945–), Fr. ballet dancer.

Beulah **Bryant:** Blooma Walton (1918–1988), U.S. black popular singer.

Chris **Bryant:** Christopher Brian Spencer Dobson (1936–2008), Eng. screenwriter, teaming with Allan **Scott**. "Dobson adopted the name Chris Bryant as his professional showbiz name, though when he was unhappy with the way directors treated his work he would use a third name, Bradley T. Winter, an anagram of 'Badly Rewritten'" [*The Times*, November 29, 2008].

Dan **Bryant:** Daniel Webster O'Brien (1833–1875), U.S. actor, musician.

Felice **Bryant:** Matilda Genevieve Bryant, née Scaduto (1925–2003), U.S. songwriter, teaming with Boudleaux Bryant, her husband.

Louise **Bryant:** Anna Louise Mohan (1885–1936), U.S. journalist. Louise's parents divorced when she was four and her mother then married Sheridan Bryant, who gave her her name.

James **Bryce:** Alexander Anderson (1862–1949), Sc. novelist.

Brychan: John Davies (*c.*1784–1864), Welsh poet. The name is that of the 5th-century saint and king Brychan, who gave the name of the historic region of Brycheiniog and former county of Breconshire, in which the poet was born.

Rob **Brydon:** Robert Brydon Jones (1965–), Welsh TV writer, actor.

Bryfdir: Humphrey Jones (1867–1947), Welsh poet.

Bryher: Annie Winnifred Ellerman (1894–1983), Eng. novelist. The novelist took her name from the island of Bryher, one of the Isles of Scilly, which she visited in 1919 with her intimate friend, **H.D.**

Brynfab: Thomas Williams (1848–1927), Welsh poet. The name means "son of the hill." Williams was a hillside farmer for most of his life.

Delme **Bryn-Jones:** Delme Jones (1935–2001), Welsh baritone. Aware that there are hundreds of Welsh people named Jones, the singer added Bryn for distinction, this being the first syllable of his birthplace, Brynamman, near Swansea.

Yul **Brynner:** Yuly Borisovich Bryner (1915–1985), Russ.-born U.S. movie actor. The actor chose to cloak his family origins in mystery, at one time claiming that he was really Taidje Khan and of Swiss-Japanese parentage. On immigrating to America in 1941, he initially spelled his name "Youl Bryner," but a New York theatrical agent told him that "Youl" sounded too much like "you-all" and "Bryner" as though he was soaked in brine and pickled. To clarify the pronunciation, the actor respelled his name as Yul Brynner, pronounced "Yool Brinner" [Jhan Robbins, *Yul Brynner: The Inscrutable King*, 1988].

Karl Pavlovich **Bryullov**: Charles Bruleau (1799–1852), Russ. painter. The artist was of French descent and the family name was russified only in 1821, the year that Bryullov graduated from the St. Petersburg Academy of Fine Arts.

Mohammed **Bu Amama**: Mohammed Hajj ben Larbi (1840–1908), Algerian tribal leader. The leader of a tribal uprising in French Algeria in 1881 adopted his nickname, meaning "turban wearer."

Bubbles: John William Sublett (1902–1986), U.S. black tapdancer. While working at a bowling alley, Sublett met Ford Lee Washington. In 1915 they formed a vaudeville act called "Buck and Bubbles," with Sublett taking the the name "Bubbles" (a near anagram of his original name) and Washington becoming "Buck." They worked together until Washington's death in 1955.

Barney **Bubbles**: Colin Fulcher (1942–1983), Br. record album cover designer.

Charlie **Bubbles**: Charles Sistovaris (1971–), Br. movie actor. Charlie Chaplin's grandson explains his name: "I don't have the Chaplin name. Although my mother [Josephine] is a Chaplin, my father was Nicolas Sistovaris, so I'm really Charlie Sistovaris. It was Annie [his actress aunt] who first called me Charlie Bubbles. When I drank from my bottle I always blew milk bubbles" [*Sunday Times Magazine*, March 28, 1993]. Presumably Aunt Annie got the nickname from the 1968 movie *Charlie Bubbles*.

Buccaneer: Andrew Bradford (*c.*1974–), Jamaican DJ, ragga musician. The musician's adopted name alludes to Jamaica's past reputation as a pirate haven, and he dressed the part with an eye patch and a hairstyle displaying a bleach ring.

Martin **Bucer**: Martin Kuhhorn (1491–1551), Ger. Protestant reformer. In the fashion of his time, the theologian translated his German name (literally "cow horn") into Greek, with "Bucer" the latinized form of Greek *boukeros* (from *bous*, "ox," and *keras*, "horn"). The name is pronounced "Bootser."

Buchan: James E. Boswell (1906–1971), N.Z.-born Br. painter, cartoonist, writer, of Sc. descent. The artist used this name for antifascist drawings published in the *Daily Worker* in the 1930s.

Chuck **Buchanan** *see* Fenton **Brockley**

David **Buckingham**: David Hugh Villiers (1921–1962), Br crime writer. The link between the writer's family name and pen name was presumably suggested by the English courtier and politician George Villiers, 1st duke of Buckingham (1592–1628)

or his son George Villiers, 2nd duke of Buckingham (1628–1887).

Henrietta **Buckmaster**: Henrietta Henkle (*c.*1909–1983), U.S. writer, editor.

J.E. **Buckrose**: Annie Edith Jameson, née Foster (1868–1931), Eng. novelist.

Buckwheat Zydeco: Stanley Dural, Jr. (1947–), U.S. accordion player. Dural first earned "Buckwheat" as a nickname, taken from a *Little Rascals* character, then adopted the second word of his name for his special interest in zydeco, a type of Afro-American accordion-led dance music from southern Louisiana, his own place of origin.

Z. **Budapest**: Zsuzsanna Mokcsay (1940–), Hung-born U.S. writer, witch. The founder of the woman-centered religion Dianic Wicca was born in Budapest, Hungary.

Buddhadassa Bhikkhu: Ngeurm Panich (1906–1993), Thai Buddhist monk. When the Buddhist scholar became a monk, he adopted the name Buddhadassa, meaning "slave of the Buddha" (Sanskrit *dasa*, "servant," "slave"). Bhikkhu is the title of a fully ordained monk.

Buddug *see* **Gweirydd ap Rhys**

Budgie: Peter Edward Clarke (1957–), Br. rock drummer. Presumably a nickname, perhaps from the performer's initials, suggesting "peck" (the action of a budgerigar, or budgie).

Algis **Budrys**: Algirdas Jonas Budrys (1931–), U.S. SF writer, editor, of Lithuanian origin. The writer's surname may be a shortening of an original longer name. Budrys used a variety of pseudonyms for magazine stories in the early years of his career, among them David C. Hodgkins, Ivan Janvier, Robert Marner, William Scarff, John A. Sentry, and Albert Stroud.

Buffalo Bill: William Frederick Cody (1846–1917), U.S. scout, showman. Cody was so named by Ned **Buntline** because he provided buffalo meat for rail construction crews. *See also* Lord George **Sanger**.

Bufo: Peter Rhodes (1945–), Br. crossword compiler. The setter's pseudonym is Latin for "toad," presumably because the English word is suggested by letters in his real name.

Harry T. **Buford**: Loreta Janeta Velasquez (1842–?), Cuban-born U.S. adventuress. According to her widely-read autobiography, *The Woman in Battle* (1876), Velasquez married a young American officer in 1856 and eloped to the U.S. When her husband enlisted at the outbreak of Civil War, she took the *nom de guerre* of Lieutenant Harry T. Buford in the Confederate army and was involved in a number of military incidents. She finally retired from active service and became a spy. Doubts have been expressed about the veracity of some of the exploits she describes, and it is even possible Velasquez never existed.

Jan **Bugay:** Krzystof Kamil Baczynski (1921–1944), Pol. poet. The poet published two slim volumes of verse under this name shortly before his early death in the Warsaw Uprising of 1944.

Ken **Bugul:** Marietou Mbaye (1948–), Senegalese writer. When the writer's French-language publishers, Les Nouvelles Éditions Africaines, insist she use a pseudonym for her fictionalized autobiography, *Le Baobab fou* ("The Mad Baobab") (1982), this was her answer, Wolof for "nobody wants it."

bülbül *see* **Byul-Byul**

Kir **Bulychyov:** Igor Vsevolodovich Mozheyko (1934–), Russ. SF writer.

Bulyga Kurtsevich: Aleksandr Aleksandrovich Fadeyev (1901–1956), Russ. writer. An early pseudonym used by the Soviet novelist.

Bumble Bee Slim: Amos Easton (1905–1968), U.S. black blues musician.

Ted **Bundy:** Theodore Robert Cowell (1946–1989), U.S. lawyer, serial killer. Cowell's mother married Johnnie Bundy in 1951 and young Theodore (Ted) took his stepfather's name. In 1974 he began a series of some 40 murders for which he was brought to trial in 1977. Escaping from custody, he fled to Florida and assumed the name of Christopher Hagen. He subsequently murdered a 12-year-old girl, was brought to trial in Miami in 1979, and executed ten years later.

Douglas **Bunn:** Douglas Henry David Honeybunn (1928–), Br. equestrian.

Bunny: Carl Emil Schultze (1866–1939), U.S. cartoonist.

Bunthorne: Bob Smithies (1934–), Br. crossword compiler. The setter selected a pseudonym that reflected his liking for Gilbert and Sullivan operettas, with Bunthorne a character in *Patience* (1881).

Ned **Buntline:** Edward Zane Carroll Judson (1823–1886), U.S. adventurer, writer. The future author of dime novels ran away to sea as a cabin boy and at age 14 enlisted in the U.S. Navy, where he would have encountered the maritime term that he took for his pen name, with "Ned" a pet form of his first name, Edward. (A buntline is a line for restraining the loose center of a sail while it is hauled up for furling.) Ned Buntline named **Buffalo Bill**, and depicted him in his writings.

John **Buonarroti:** John Papworth (1775–1847), Eng. architect. "In 1815 he produced a fine design for a 'Tropheum' to commemorate the victory of Waterloo.... His artistic friends were reminded by its boldness of Michael Angelo [**Michelangelo**], and he thereupon added 'Buonarroti' to his name" [*Dictionary of National Biography*].

Il **Burchiello:** Domenico di Giovanni (1404–1449), It. poet. The poet took his name from the poems he wrote *alla burchia*, meaning in a deliberately casual fashion.

[Baroness] Angela Georgina **Burdett-Coutts:** Angela Georgina Burdett (1814–1906), Eng. philanthropist. Burdett added the name Coutts to her own in 1837 on inheriting the fortune of the banker Thomas Coutts (1735–1822), her grandfather.

Eleanor **Burford:** Eleanor Alice Hibbert, née Burford (1906–1993), Eng. novelist. The writer was here simply using her maiden name. Her best-known pseudonym was Jean **Plaidy**.

David **Burg:** Alexander Dolberg (1933–), Russ.-born Eng. writer, translator.

Annekatrin **Bürger:** Annekatrin Rammelt (1937–), Ger. movie actress.

Hugo **Bürger:** Hugo Lubliner (1846–1911), Ger. playwright. An early pseudonym used by the popular dramatist.

Ann Marie **Burgess** *see* Samuel **Edwards**

Anthony **Burgess:** John Burgess Wilson (1917–1993), Eng. novelist, critic. Burgess explained how he came by his pen name in his autobiography: "I was christened John Burgess Wilson and was confirmed in the name of Anthony. When I published my first novel I was forced to do so in near-disguise. I was an official of the Colonial Office at the time, and it was regarded as improper to publish fiction under one's own name. So I pulled the cracker of my total name and unfolded the paper hat of Anthony Burgess ... Burgess was the maiden name of the mother I never knew ... a dancer and singer ... named the Beautiful Belle Burgess on music hall posters. She married a Manchester Wilson but was right to insist that her slightly more distinguished surname get on to my baptismal certificate. There have always been too many plain Wilsons around" [Anthony Burgess, *Little Wilson and Big God*, 1986]. Burgess used the name Joseph Kell for *One Hand Clapping* (1961) and *Inside Mr Enderby* (1963).

Michael **Burgess** *see* Samuel **Edwards**

Trevor **Burgess** *see* Elleston **Trevor**

Jules **Burgmein:** Giulio Ricordi (1840–1912), It. music publisher, composer. The musician composed under this name as well as his real name.

Betty **Burke:** Charles Edward Stuart (1720–1788), Sc. prince ("The Young Pretender"). One of the prince's many disguise names, in this instance when rescued by Flora Macdonald after the Battle of Culloden (1746) and taken secretly by her to the Isle of Skye disguised as her maid. The prince was 26 at the time, and Flora two years younger.

Billie **Burke:** Mary William Ethelbert Appleton Burke (1885–1970), U.S. stage, movie actress. The actress adopted a colloquial form of her second name, itself that of her father, William (Billy) Burke, a circus clown. Billie is a female name in its own right, and was popular among chorus girls at one time.

Fielding **Burke:** Olive Dargan, née Tilford (1869–1968), U.S. poet, novelist.

Marie **Burke:** Marie Holt (1894–1988), Br. stage actress.

Ray **Burke:** Raymond N. Barrois (1904–1986), U.S. jazz musician.

Vinnie **Burke:** Vincenzo Bucci (1921–), U.S. jazz musician.

Jonathan **Burn:** Henry Jonas Jonathan Burn-Forti (1939–), Eng. stage, TV actor.

Vincent Justus **Burnelli:** Vincent Justus Buranelli (1895–1964), U.S. aircraft designer. The reason for the changed spelling of the designer's surname is unknown.

Sheila **Burnes** *see* Lozania **Prole**

Andreas **Burnier:** Catharina Irma Dessaur (1931–), Du. writer.

Burning Spear: Winston Rodney (1948–), Jamaican rock musician. The musician took his name from that additionally adopted by Kenyan president Jomo **Kenyatta** for his study of the Kikuyu, *Facing Mount Kenya* (1938), by "Jomo (Burning Spear) Kenyatta."

Bobby **Burns:** Robert Müller (*c*.1920–), Ger. child movie actor. Any connection between the name and the Scottish poet Robert **Burns** (or the Bobby Burns cocktail called after him) is unsubstantiated.

George **Burns:** Nathan Birnbaum (1896–1996), U.S. stage, TV comedian, teaming with U.S. radio, movie, TV comedienne Gracie Allen (1895–1964), his second wife.

Katherine **Burns:** Katharine Hepburn (1907–2003), U.S. stage, movie actress. Hepburn used this name for her first stage performance in New York, when she appeared in *Night Hostess* (1928). Her movie debut followed only four years later.

Rex **Burns:** Raoul Stephen Sehler (1935–), U.S. crime writer.

Robert **Burns:** Robert Burness (1759–1796), Sc. poet. The poet's ancestors were named Campbell, from Burnhouse (a common Scottish placename meaning "house by the stream") near Loch Etive. They moved to Forfar, where they were known as the Campbells of Burness (a form of "Burnhouse"). On publishing his first volume of verse, *Poems Chiefly in the Scottish Dialect* (1786), Burns adopted the familiar spelling of the surname.

Tex **Burns** *see* Louis **L'Amour**

Tommy **Burns:** Noah Brusso (1881–1955), Can. heavyweight boxer.

Burnum **Burnum:** Henry James Penrith (1936–1997), Austral. Aboriginal political activist.

Henry **Burr:** Harry H. McClaskey (1882–1941), U.S. popular singer. McClaskey used several pseudonyms. Another was Irving Gillette.

Augusten **Burroughs:** Chris Robinson (1965–), U.S. memoirist.

Abe **Burrows:** Abram Solman Borowitz (1910–1985), U.S. librettist.

Malandra **Burrows:** Malandra Elizabeth Newman (1966–), Eng. TV actress. The actress's regular but uncommon first name combines those of her parents, Malcolm and Sandra.

Ellen **Burstyn:** Edna Rae Gillooly (1932–), U.S. stage, movie actress, of Ir. parentage. The actress began her career as a model under the name Edna Rae. She was then a dancer in a Montreal nightclub as Keri Flynn before becoming Erica Dean for a screen test in the mid–1950s. She appeared as Ellen McRae in the Broadway comedy *Fair Game* (1957) and kept that name until the mid–1960s, when she finally became Ellen Burstyn, from her third husband, Neil Burstyn (married 1960, divorced 1971).

Hermann **Burte:** Hermann Strübe (1879–1960), Ger. painter, writer. The writer fashioned his new surname out of his original one.

Alfred **Burton:** John Mitford (1782–1831), Eng. mariner, journalist, writer. Mitford used this name for *The Adventures of Johnny Newcome in the Navy, a Poem in four Cantos* (1818).

[Sir] Montague **Burton:** Meshe David Osinsky (1885–1952), Lithuanian-born Br. clothing manufacturer, retailer, of Jewish parentage. The noted businessman, who used the full name Montague Maurice Burton, is said to have adopted his English name from a public house, perhaps itself called the Montague Arms and obtaining its beer from the brewery town of Burton-on-Trent. He took it in 1904.

Richard **Burton:** Richard Walter Jenkins (1925–1984), Welsh stage, movie actor. When a schoolboy in Port Talbot, southern Wales, Jenkins showed signs of promise as an actor. As such, he became the protégé of the English teacher and school play producer Philip H. Burton, who made the 18-year-old his legal ward and gave him his name. The document that spelled out the change was dated December 17, 1943. Philip Burton would have adopted his pupil if it had been legally possible, but the difference between their ages was 20 days short of 21 years, the minimum required by law at that time. This ruled out official adoption. Instead, an agreement was drawn up between Philip Burton and the real father making the "infant" a ward until he reached the age of 21. Part of the document declared that Richard Jenkins shall "absolutely renounce and abandon the use of the surname of the parent and shall bear and use the surname of the adopter and shall be held out to the world and in all respects treated as if he were in fact the child of the adopter" [Paul Ferris, *Richard Burton*, 1981].

Aleksandr Borisovich **Bushe:** Aleksandr Ksenofontovich Gnusov (1882–1970), Russ. circus artist, ringmaster.

Gary **Bushell** *see* Craig **Brown**

Bushman: Dwight Duncan (1973–), Jamaican DJ. The musician interprets his recording name as an African term meaning "medicine man."

Darcey **Bussell:** Marnie Crittle (1969–), Br. ballerina. The dancer's Australian father, John Crittle, deserted the family when she was young, and her mother renamed her Darcey to erase all traces of the name Marnie Crittle. Her new surname was that of her stepfather, Phillip Bussell, an English dentist.

Christine **Busta:** Christine Dimt (1915–1987), Austr. poet.

[Sir] Alexander **Bustamante:** William Alexander Clarke (1884–1977), Jamaican prime minister. Clarke, the son of an Irish planter father and Jamaican mother, went to New York in 1932 in the guise of a Spanish gentleman named Alejandro Bustamante. He adopted the name William Alexander Bustamante by deed poll in 1943 when forming the Jamaica Labour Party in order to avoid disqualification from nomination as a candidate under a name that was not legally his. The name itself was that of the Cuban lawyer and politican Antonio Sánchez de Bustamante y Sirvén (1865–1951), who drew up the Bustamante Code dealing with international private law.

Walter **Busterkeys** *see* **Liberace**

The **Busy-Body:** Benjamin Franklin (1706–1790), U.S. statesman, scientist, philosopher. Franklin used the name for articles written in 1728.

Brett **Butler:** Brett Anderson (1958–), U.S. TV actress. A name presumably suggested by that of Rhett Butler, Scarlett O'Hara's third husband in Margaret Mitchell's novel *Gone With the Wind* (1936).

Richard **Butler:** Theodore Edward Le Bouthillier Allbeury (1917–2005), Eng. thriller writer. Allbeury was so prolific, at one time producing four novels a year, that he also wrote under this name and that of Patrick Kelly.

Walter C. **Butler** *see* Max **Brand**

Hilda **Butsova:** Hilda Boot (*c.*1897–1976), Eng. ballet dancer. A "Russian" form of the English name.

Nathan **Butt** *see* Rev. T. **Clark**

William **Butterworth:** Henry Schroeder (1774–1853), Eng. topographer, engraver. Schroeder used this name for his engravings and for his written work *Three Years' Adventures of a Minor in England, Africa,* *the West Indies, South Carolina, and Georgia, by William Butterworth, Engraver* (1822).

Myra **Buttle:** Victor William Williams Saunders Purcell (1896–1965), Br. author of books on China. The writer used this name for *The Sweeniad* (1958), a parody of T.S. Eliot, with his pen name intended to be read as "my rebuttal."

Red **Buttons:** Aaron Chwatt (1919–2006), U.S. stage, movie, TV comedian. At the age of 16, Chwatt was a singing bellhop at Dinty Moore's City Island Tavern in the Bronx. For this job he had to wear a uniform with 48 brass buttons. He had red hair, so was nicknamed after these two distinctive features. Maltin disputes this: "Believe it or not, he took his stage name not from his hair, but from the uniform he wore as a bellboy!" (p.118). Buttons later adoped the name in place of his Jewish immigrant name.

Richard **Buxton:** Edward Shanks (1892–1953), Eng. writer.

Zmitrok **Byadulya:** Samuil Yefimovich Plavnik (1886–1941), Belorussian writer. The writer came from a needy family. Hence his adopted name, meaning "poor one."

A.S. **Byatt:** [Dame] Antonia Susan Byatt, née Drabble (1936–), Eng. novelist, sister of novelist Margaret Drabble (1939–).

Max **Bygraves:** Walter William Bygraves (1922–), Eng. TV entertainer. On his first night in the Royal Air Force, aged 17 (and having lied about his age to enlist), Bygraves impersonated his idol, Max **Miller**, and thereafter assumed his first name.

Julian **Byng:** Julian Michael Edmund Lafone (1928–), Br. racehorse breeder. Byng assumed his new surname by deed poll in 1952 in place of his original name. His father was (Captain) Michael William Millicent Lafone and his mother (Lady) Elizabeth Alice Lafone, who in accordance with her father's will resumed her maiden name of Byng by deed poll in the same year that her son took that name.

Robert **Byr:** Karl Robert Emmerich von Bayer (1815–1902), Austr. novelist, writer on military subjects.

Bretton **Byrd:** James Thomas Byrd (1904–1959), Br. movie music composer.

Donn **Byrne:** Brian Oswald Donn-Byrne (1889–1928), U.S.–born Ir. novelist.

Evelyn **Byrd** *see* J.P. **McCall**

James **Byrne:** Edward William Garnett (1868–1937), Br. writer, literary adviser.

Edd **Byrnes:** Edward Breitenberger (1933–), U.S. juvenile TV actor.

David **Byron:** David Garrick (1947–), Eng. rock musician.

John **Byron:** John Heanley (1912–), Br. stage actor, dancer.

Kathleen **Byron:** Kathleen Elizabeth Fell (1921–2009), Eng. movie actress. Famous for her scene-stealing performance as the sexually frustrated nun Sister Ruth in Michael Powell and Emeric Pressburger's 1947 movie *Black Narcissus*, the actress changed her name "after it was suggested that her surname made it sound as though she had taken a tumble. Given the nature of the role of Sister Ruth, it was remarkably appropriate" [*The Times*, January 21, 2009].

Marion **Byron:** Miriam Bilenkin (1911–1985), U.S. movie actress.

Walter **Byron:** Walter Butler (1899–1972), Br. movie actor, of Ir. descent.

E. Fairfax **Byrrne:** Emma Frances Brooke (1844–1926), Eng. novelist. An asexual pen name, retaining the writer's initials, with the new surname punning on the original (a burn is a brook).

Byul-Byul: Martuza Rza ogly Mamedov (1897–1961), Azerbaijani opera singer, folk musician. The singer's name means "bulbul," a songbird of the thrush family. (Turkish *bülbül*, "nightingale," is a name imitating the bird's warbling song.) The same name, in its lowercase form bülbül, was adopted by the U.S. feminist cartoonist Genny Pilgrim, who points out that in Middle Eastern poetry a bülbül is a bird of protest. Of her own use of the name, she says: "I took it as a pen name when my family suffered for my outspoken opinions" [bülbül, *off our backs*, July 1984].

Melanie **C:** Melanie Jayne Chisholm (1974–), Eng. rock singer. As Mel C, the singer was formerly familiar as one of the four Spice Girls. The initial distinguished her from another member, Mel B, otherwise Melanie Janine Brown.

Mr. **C** *see* Mr. **Cee**

Roy **C:** Roy Charles Hammond (1943–), U.S. pop singer. Hammond adopted this short, distinctive name in order not to be confused with either pop musician Roy Hamilton or singer Ray **Charles**.

James **Caan:** James Cahn (1939–), U.S. movie actor.

Fernán **Caballero:** Cecilia Francesca de Arrom, née Böhl de Faber y Larrea (1796–1877), Sp. novelist, of Ger.-Sp. parentage.

Boyd **Cable:** Ernest Andrew Ewart (1878–1943), Br. writer, journalist, screenwriter, army officer. Ewart was a tireless traveler and sea voyager, so that his assumed name may pun on "buoyed cable."

Bruce **Cabot:** Jacques Étienne Pelissier de Bujac (1904–1972), U.S. movie actor, of Fr. descent.

Susan **Cabot:** Harriet Shapiro (1927–1986), U.S. movie actress.

Cabu: Jean Cabut (1938–), Fr. cartoonist.

Cachao: Israel Cachao López (1918–2008), Cuban-born U.S. bassist.

Jean **Cacharel:** Jean Bousquet (1932–), Fr. fashion designer. The stylist adopted his new name, also that of his company, founded in 1962, from the local word for a wild duck from the wetlands of the Camargue, near his hometown of Nîmes.

Robin **Cade** *see* Andrew **York**

Cadence Weapon: Roland Pemberton (1986–), Can. black rapper. The name appears to denote a kind of rhythmic onslaught, aptly for a rap artist.

Cadenus: Jonathan Swift (1667–1745), It. satirist, cleric. The name is an anagram of Latin *decanus* "dean." Swift had become dean of St. Patrick's Cathedral, Dublin, in 1699, hence his common nickname of "Dean" Swift. He used the name Cadenus for his poem *Cadenus and Vanessa* (1713) addressed to Esther Vanhomrigh, thereby incidentally creating the woman's name Vanessa. (Swift formed the name from the first three letters of "Vanhomrigh" plus "Essa," a pet form of Esther.)

Some authorities claim that Swift wrote the poem *before* he became a dean, in which case a different interpretation is needed. It has thus been suggested that the name may be an anagram of Swift's coded phrase *Cad Es Vn*, meaning "familiar spirit of Es[ther] Van[homrigh]."

Cadfan: John Davies (1846–1923), Welsh poet. The poet took his bardic name from his native village of Llangadfan, Montgomeryshire (now Powys), where the parish church is dedicated to the 6th-century St. Cadfan.

Cadrawd: Thomas Christopher Evans (1846–1918), Welsh folklorist. The antiquarian's bardic name means literally "battle troop," from Welsh *cad*, "battle," and *rhawd*, "course," "troop."

George **Cadwalader, Gent.:** George Bubb Dodington, Lord Melcombe (1691–1762), Eng. politician, pamphleteer, verse writer.

Alberto **Caeiro:** Fernando Pessoa (1888–1935), Port. poet. The name is one of the four "heteronyms" (as he called them) that the poet created to represent the different aspects of his work. This one was the pastoral poet. The others were the classicist Ricardo Reis, the futurist Álvaro de Campos, and the symbolist Fernando Pessoa himself. There were also less prominent personae, as António Mora who speculated on metaphysics and Alexander Search who wrote only in English. It has been suggested that the heteronymity was not a deliberate literary device but a symptom of multiple personality disorder.

Caerfallwch: Thomas Edwards (1779–1858), Welsh lexicographer. The writer took his name from the location in Flintshire where he was born.

Irving **Cæsar:** Isidor Keiser (1895–1996), U.S. lyricist, of Rom. Jewish parentage.

Caffarelli: Gaetano Majorano (1710–1783), It.

singer. The male mezzosoprano took his name from that of Caffaro, his teacher in Bari.

Cafu: Marcos Evangelista de Moraes (1970–), Brazilian fotballer. The footballer was so nicknamed because of his speed as he ran up and down the right flank, like that of **Cafutinga**.

Cafutinga: Moacir Fernandes (1948–1991), Brazilian footballer.

Cagancho: Joaquín Rodríguez Ortega (1903–1984), Mexican bullfighter. The matador adopted the name of his horse.

Nicolas **Cage:** Nicholas Kim Coppola (1964–), U.S. movie actor. The actor adopted his new name to avoid any invidious comparison with his uncle, director Francis Ford Coppola (1939–). After considering Nic Blue and Nic Faust, he settled on Cage, taking it from two distinctive Cages: black comic-book hero Luke Cage and idiosyncratic composer John Cage (1912–1992).

Alessandro, conte di **Cagliostro:** Giuseppe Balsamo (1743–1795), It. magician, charlatan, adventurer.

Joe **Cago:** Joseph Valachi (1903–1971), U.S. criminal, Mafia informer.

Holger **Cahill:** Sveinn Kristján Bjarnarson (1887–1960), Icelandic-born U.S. folk-art authority.

Sammy **Cahn:** Samuel Kahn (or Cohen) (1913–1993), U.S. movie lyricist. Cahn tells how he and his friend, composer Saul **Chaplin**, then still Saul Kaplan, came by their names: "When I saw the names on that first copy of [their song] 'Rhythm Is Our Business'—Kahn, Kaplan—I said to him: 'You're going to have to change your name.' He bristled and said, 'Why? It looks good.' I said, 'It doesn't look good at all. Kahn and Kaplan, that's a dress firm.' He said, 'Why don't you change *your* name?' I: 'That's fair. From now on I'll be Cahn with a C.' He: 'Okay, I'll be Caplan with a C.' I said: 'Cahn and Caplan, that's *still* a dress firm. From now on its Cahn and Chaplin'" [Sammy Cahn, *I Should Care*, 1975].

Claude **Cahun:** Lucie Renée Matilde Schwob (1894–1954), Fr. transexual artist, photographer, writer. The niece of writer Marcel Schwob and great-niece of orientalist David Léon Cahun settled on a genderless name after earlier calling herself Claude Courlis (French *courlis*, "curlew") and Daniel Douglas, the latter after Lord Alfred Douglas (1870–1945), friend of Oscar Wilde. Her partner and stepsister was Marcel **Moore**, with whom she shares a grave in Jersey, Channel Islands.

Christopher **Cain:** Bruce Doggett (1943–), U.S. movie director, screenwriter.

Henry **Caine:** Henry Hawken (1888–1962), Br. stage actor. The actor probably formed his new name from the second half of his original surname.

Marti **Caine:** Lynne Denise Ives, earlier Stringer, née Shepherd (1945–1995), Eng. TV singer, comedienne. The entertainer chose her new name in the late 1960s with the help of her first husband, Malcolm Stringer: "I wasn't Marti Caine at that stage. I was Zoe Bond, but only after being Sunny Smith for three weeks. I didn't want to be a 'Julie Rose' or a 'Cindy Summers,' I wanted a name like Kiki **Dee** or Dusty **Springfield** and didn't feel 'Zoe Bond' was quite 'it.' We took a book from a shelf, which happened to be a gardening book. 'O.K.—page seventy-six.' Malc turned to the required page. 'Fourth line down, second word along.' 'Greenfly.' 'O.K. Page thirty four...' and so on until, bored with the game, Malc came across: 'Tomato cane—that'll do, you're built like one. Call yourself Marta Cane.' I rang the club I was appearing at and informed the Con-Sec that Marta Cane would be appearing in place of Zoe Bond who was ill. When I arrived at the club, I found I was billed ... as Marti Caine. I liked it" [Marti Caine, *A Coward's Chronicles*, 1990].

[Sir] Michael **Caine:** Maurice Joseph Micklewhite (1933–), Eng. movie, TV actor, working in U.S. The actor first played bit parts as Michael Scott, his new first name suggested by his regular nickname "Mick," based on his surname. Then in 1954 he was cast for a part as a prison guard in a live televised version of Anouilh's play *The Lark*. But Equity, the actors' union, heard about it, and told his agent that they already had a Michael Scott on their files and that he must find a new name immediately.

"Michael spent the day in turmoil. He had changed his name once, and grown quite attached to Michael Scott. Now he had to go through the whole trauma all over again, and this time it would have to be a name that stuck.... 'All the names anyone could ever think about galloped through my mind ... I spent the day wandering around the West End [in London], and finally decided the only way I could relax was to go to the pictures. *The Caine Mutiny* was playing at the Odeon, Leicester Square.... Afterwards I went across the square to the Forte's coffee bar next to the Ritz. I was sitting in there having a cup of tea and a cigarette, still agonizing over this name—and suddenly I looked up and there it stood in great big red neon lights outside the Odeon ... *The Caine Mutiny*. I thought: That's it. That's the name. It's strong and sharp. That's the one for me'" [William Hall, *Arise, Sir Michael Caine*, 2000]. To his relief, Equity confirmed that they had no Michael Caine on their books.

The actor's choice may have been further motivated by the movie title as a whole. "The fact that he must have responded sympathetically to the social resonance of the word *mutiny* could bring us back to psychoanalysis if we let it" [*Telegraph Sunday Magazine*, May 9, 1982].

Anne Billson, one of Caine's biographers, remarked that by changing his name from Maurice Micklewhite, "Caine hit the jackpot, because it meant that newspaper sub-editors had a deep vein of headlines that they could mine, all the way from 'Caine mutiny' and 'Caine is able' to 'Caine toad' (the lesson here, for aspiring actors, is to change your surname to something such as 'Fantastic' now)" [*The Times*, December 24, 2002].

Cajetan (or Gaetano): Giacomo de Vio (1469–1534), It. theologian. The scholar, who took the name Thomas on entering the Dominican order in 1484, came to be known from his birthplace, Gaeta (in Roman times Caieta), central Italy.

Caju: Francisca Jülia (1871–1920), Brazilian poet. A name created from the last syllable of the writer's first name and the first of her surname.

Aleksandrs **Caks:** Aleksandrs Cadarainis (1902–1950), Latvian poet, short-story writer.

Calamity Jane: Martha Jane Burk, née Cannary (or Canary) (1852–1903), U.S. popular heroine of the West. Calamity Jane was a colorful character who wore men's clothes, carried a gun, indulged in drinking sprees, and generally prophesied "doom and gloom." Hence her nickname, which became the name by which she is generally known today, having featured (in a much more attractive guise) in dime novels of the 1870s and 1880s. "Jane" has long been a nickname for a woman, especially a distinctive or disreputable one. Burk was a prostitute in various frontier towns.

Ettore **Calcolona:** Carlo Celano (1617–1673), It. writer.

Moyra **Caldecott:** Olivia Brown (1927–), S.A. writer of fantasy fiction.

Taylor **Caldwell:** Janet Miriam Taylor Reback, née Caldwell (1900–1985), Eng.-born U.S. novelist. It is not clear whether Caldwell wished to disguise her sex, if at all, or to what extent she wished to be associated with the contemporary novelist, Erskine Caldwell. According to legend, it was Scribner's vice president Maxwell Perkins who suggested Caldwell's book *Dynasty of Death* (1938) would sell better if she dropped the feminine "Janet" and used "Taylor Caldwell" as her pen name. The novelist also wrote as Max Reiner and Marcus Holland.

Caledfryn: William Williams (1801–1869), Welsh poet. The poet, a Nonconformist minister, took his bardic name from the location where he lived. The placename itself literally means "hard hill." His son, a portrait painter, was known as Ab Caledfryn ("son of Caledfryn").

Rod **Caley** *see* Fenton **Brockley**

Louis **Calhern:** Carl Henry Vogt (1895–1956), U.S. stage, movie actor. The actor was obliged to adopt a stage name under pressure from his uncle, who regarded the profession as shameful. His new surname came from a contraction of his first two names; his first name from the city of St. Louis.

Charles **Calhoun:** Jesse Stone (1901–1999), U.S. jazz musician, pop music arranger.

Rory **Calhoun:** Francis Timothy Durgin, later McCown (1922–1999), U.S. movie actor. The actor's new name was created by Henry Willson, who also named Rock **Hudson**, Tab **Hunter**, and many other Hollywood stars. In his earliest movies of the mid–1940s, Calhoun was billed as Frank McCown.

John David **California:** Fredrik Colting (1976–), Swe. writer. Colting adopted his American name as author of *60 Years Later: Coming through the Rye* (2009), a sequel to J.D. Salinger's classic novel *The Catcher in the Rye* (1951).

Randy **California:** Randolph Craig Wolfe (1951–1997), U.S. rock musician. The musician was raised in Los Angeles, California, and named for that state by his first manager, Chas Chandler, bass player of the Animals.

California Joe: Moses Embree Milner (1829–1876), U.S. plainsman, army scout. Milner was born in Kentucky but moved to California with his bride following his marriage in 1850. It is uncertain how he actually acquired the name. The story goes that whenever anyone asked his identity, Milner would say he was called "Joe" and that he came from California.

Caligula: Gaius Julius Caesar (AD 12–41), Roman emperor. The name means "Little Boots," and was the pet name given to Gaius Caesar by his father's soldiers when he ran around the camp as a young boy. It is ironic that such an agreeable name should come to be adopted by such a willful despot. The English form of the name was adopted centuries later by **Little Boots**.

Calixtus II: Guido di Borgogna (*c*.1050–1124), It. pope. Popes of this name are also known as Callistus. The name itself derives from Greek *kallistos*, "the best," "the noblest" (literally "the most beautiful").

Calixtus III: Alfonso de Borja (Borgia) (1378–1458), Sp. pope.

Clinch **Calkins:** Marion Clinch Calkins (1895–1968), U.S. poet, novelist. The writer dropped her first name, in favor of a name that was neither obviously masculine nor feminine, on submitting a poem, "When I Was a Maiden," to a competition in the magazine *Nation*. (The poem won first prize but was not published because it was regarded as too "advanced." It first appeared in print only in 1928.)

Calkins subsequently wrote humorous poems for the *New Yorker* under the name Majollica Wattles.

Peggy Call: Peggy Castle (1926–1973), U.S. movie actress. The actress used this name for her first movie, *When a Girl's Beautiful* (1947).

Michael Callan: Martin Calinieff (1935–), U.S. dancer, movie actor.

Maria Callas: Sophia Cecilia Anna Meneghini, née Kalogeropoulos (1923–1977), U.S. opera singer, of Gk. parentage. In 1926, the singer's parents legally changed the family name to Callas, a name that was shorter and easier to pronounce in an English-speaking land. (Maria was actually registered at her birth in New York City as Sophie Cecilia Kalos, her lengthy surname abbreviated by the immigration authorities when her parents arrived in New York earlier that year.) Although obviously based on the family name, it is possible her parents saw the name as a near anagram of *La Scala*, Milan, Italy's leading opera house. As Greeks, too, they would have made an association with Greek *kallos*, "beauty."

Joseph Calleia: Joseph Alexander Herstall Vincent Spurin-Calleja (1897–1975), Maltese-born U.S. movie actor.

[Sir] Henry Calley: Henry Algernon Langton (1914–1997), Eng. racehorse owner, breeder. In 1974, somewhat late in life, the stud manager adopted his mother's maiden name.

Callimaco: Filippo Buonaccorsi (1437–1496), It. humanist. The scholar adopted a Greek equivalent of his name, from *kallos*, "beauty" + *makhomai*, "to fight" (Italian *buona*, "good" + *accorsi*, "to run up").

Calmac: Michael Macdonald-Cooper (1941–), Sc. crossword compiler. The pseudonym refers both to the popular short name for the Caledonian-MacBrayne ferry service in western Scotland, where the setter was born, and to his own real name.

Il Calmeta: Vincenzo Colli (*c*.1460–1508), It. humanist. The scholar is said to have taken the name by which he became known from the figure of a shepherd in Boccaccio's prose romance *Filocolo* (*c*.1336).

Emma Calvé: Rosa-Noémie Emma Calvet de Roquer (1858–1942), Fr. opera singer.

Charles Stuart Calverley: Charles Stuart Blayds (1831–1884), Eng. poet, parodist. Calverley's father was the Rev. Henry Blayds, and a descendant of the old Yorkshire family of Calverley. The poet assumed the ancient name in 1852, when he became 21 and of full age.

Phyllis Calvert: Phyllis Bickle (1915–2002), Eng. stage, movie, TV actress. Phyllis Bickle was requested to change her name by movie producer Herbert Wilcox. The actress is said to have selected Calvert as she felt it "had a sort of ring to it." "Her professional surname was inherited from a photog-

rapher who took some shots of her [as a young dancer] in her ballet gear, and whose interest in her, she intimated, was not entirely professional" [Matthew Sweet, *Shepperton Babylon*, 2005].

Victor Francis Calverton: George Goetz (1900–1940), U.S. socialist writer, editor, of Ger. descent. The writer adopted a pseudonym to protect his job as a public-school teacher on publishing the first issue of the *Modern Quarterly* in 1923. Born in Baltimore, Maryland, it seems likely that Calverton based his adopted surname on that of George Calvert, 1st Lord Baltimore (?1580–1632), or one of his descendants.

Corinne Calvet: Corinne Dibos (1925–2001), Fr. movie actress.

Robert Calvi: Gian Roberto Calvini (1920–1982), It. banker, financier.

Henry Calvin: (1) Wimberly Calvin Goodman, Jr. (1918–1975), U.S. movie comedian; (2) Clifford Leonard Clark Hanley (1922–1999), Sc. novelist, playwright.

Calvus: Walter Savage Landor (1775–1864), Eng. writer. Landor used this name, Latin for "bald," for *Letters Addressed to Lord Liverpool, and the Parliament, on the Preliminaries of Peace* (1814).

Marie Anne Camargo: Marie Anne Cupis de Camargo (1710–1770), Belg. ballet dancer, of Sp. parentage. The dancer adopted her Spanish mother's maiden name as her professional name.

Camarón de la Isla: José Monge Cruz (1951–1992), Sp. flamenco singer. The singer's stage name, meaning "island shrimp," evolved from the nickname he was given as a child. Because the boy had a pale complexion, his uncle likened him to the big shrimp in the waters around the island of San Fernando, southwestern Spain, where he was born.

Elizabeth Cambridge: Barbara K. Hodges, née Webber (1893–1949), Br. novelist, short-story writer.

Joachim Camerarius: Joachim Liebhard (1500–1574), Ger. classicist, theologian. The scholar changed his name to Camerarius because his ancestors had been chamberlains (German *Kammerer*) to the bishops of Bamberg, his birth town.

John Cameron: Archibald Gordon Macdonell (1895–1941), Sc. crime, mystery writer. The author also wrote as Neil Gordon.

Rod Cameron: Nathan Roderick Cox (1910–1983), Can. movie actor, working in U.S.

Camille: Camille Dalmais (1978–), Fr. pop singer.

Camillus: (1) Alexander Hamilton (1755–1804), U.S. statesman, pamphleteer, author; (2) Fisher Ames (1758–1808), U.S. statesman, orator, political writer. Both men adopted the name of Camillus, the Roman soldier and statesman who saved Rome from the Gauls and who was instrumental in securing the passage of the so-called Licinian laws, introducing measures in favor of the rights of the plebeians.

David **Caminer**: David Treisman (1915–2008), Br. computer software designer.

Achille **Campanile**: Gino Cornabò (1900–1977), It. humorist, writer of brief novels, comedies.

Aline **Campbell**: Merle Montgomery (1904–1986), U.S. pianist, composer.

[Lady] Colin **Campbell**: George William Ziadie, (1949–), Br. writer. The writer, who publishes under her (titled) married name, underwent a sex change operation. "Lady Colin Campbell's original passport had described her as male because she was born with a cosmetic malformation and mistakenly registered as a boy at birth. She was brought up as George William, but at 21 had corrective surgery and was issued with a new birth certificate. Now officially Georgia Arianna, she was able to apply for a new passport which gave her gender as female" [*The Independent*, November 2, 1997].

[Sir] Colin **Campbell**: Colin MacLiver (1792–1863), Sc. soldier. The future field marshal adopted the name of his maternal uncle, Colonel John Campbell, who paid for his education and when he was 15 introduced him to the Duke of York as a suitable army officer. "The commander-in-chief cried out, 'What, another of the clan!' and a note was made of his name as Colin Campbell, and when the boy was about to protest, his uncle checked him and told him that Campbell was a good name to fight under" [*Dictionary of National Biography*].

Helen Stuart **Campbell**: Helen Campbell Weeks, née Stuart (1839–1918), U.S. writer, reformer. The writer adopted her mother's maiden name (her existing middle name) as a pen name for some of her fiction in the 1860s and in 1877 assumed it legally.

Herbert Edward **Campbell**: Herbert Edward Story (1844–1904), Br. music-hall artist.

Judy **Campbell**: Judy Birkin, née Gamble (1916–2004), Eng. stage, screen, TV actress, mother of movie actress Jane Birkin (1946–). The actress adopted the surname assumed by her father, playwright Joseph Arthur Campbell, originally Gamble.

Louise **Campbell**: Louise Weisbecker (1915–), U.S. movie actress.

Maria **Campbell**: June Stifle (1940–), Can. dramatist, children's writer, of Sc./Fr./ Native American ancestry.

Molly **Campbell** *see* Dair **Alexander**

Mrs. Patrick **Campbell**: Beatrice Stella Campbell, née Tanner (1865–1940), Eng. stage actress. The actress was always known by her husband's name. Not really a pseudonym, of course, but even so a distinctive stage name. Tanner eloped when she was 19 to marry Patrick Campbell, a London businessman.

R.T. **Campbell**: Ruthven Todd (1914–1978), Sc. poet, novelist, children's writer, working in U.S. Todd used this name for a number of detective novels, including *Unholy Dying* (1945).

Walter Stanley **Campbell**: Walter Stanley Vestal (1887–1957), U.S. historian, writer. The writer's father died soon after he was born, and he assumed the name of his stepfather, James Robert Campbell, whom his mother married in 1896.

[Sir] Henry **Campbell-Bannerman**: Henry Campbell (1836–1908), Br. politician. The British prime minister (1905–08) added his mother's maiden name of Bannerman to his own in 1872 under the will of her brother, Henry Bannerman.

Sarah **Campion**: Mary Rose Coulton (1906–), Eng.-born N.Z. novelist.

Cristina **Campo**: Vittoria Guerrini (1924–1977), It. poet, essayist. "Cristina Campo's name, like much else about her, was her own creation, a pseudonym which she first enjoyed hiding behind and then later came to identify with. But for her friends throughout her life she also remained Vittoria Guerrini, the daughter of Maestro Guido Guerrini.... She adored her father, though she opted for a pseudonym partly to mark her independence from him" [Peter Hainsworth, review of Cristina De Stefano, *Belinda e il mostro: Vita segreta di Cristina Campo* ("Beauty and the Beast: Secret Life of Cristina Campo"), *Times Literary Supplement*, September 13, 2002].

Álvaro de **Campos** *see* Alberto **Caeiro**

Walter **Camryn**: Walter Cameron (1903–1984), U.S. ballet dancer.

Mario **Camus**: Mario Camus Garcia (1935–), Sp. movie director, screenwriter.

Cañadas: Henry Higgins (1944–1978), Colombian-born Eng. bullfighter, working in Spain. Henry Higgins was the only Englishman to have qualified as a matador in the Spanish bullring. In the bullfighting tradition, he adopted a Spanish ring name. It means "glens," "narrow valleys" (related to English "canyon"). Such valleys are a feature of the countryside around Bogotá, Colombia, where Higgins was born. The Spanish themselves usually referred to him as just *el Inglés*, "the Englishman."

Canaletto: Giovanni Antonio Canal (1697–1768), It. painter. The artist's adopted name means "little Canal." It is uncertain how the painter came to acquire this version of his surname, as he was not noticeably small. Possibly it was to distinguish him from his father, Bernardo Canal, a theatrical scene painter. Giovanni often assisted his father in his work, so that the Italian diminutive suffix *-etto* more or less equated to "Jr."

Chan **Canasta**: Chananel Mifelew (1921–), Pol.-born magician, mentalist.

Candido: Candido Camero de Guerra (1921–), Cuban-born U.S. jazz musician.

Edward **Candy:** Barbara Alison Neville (1925–), Br. novelist.

Icho **Candy:** Winston Evans (*c.*1964–), Jamaican DJ, reggae musician.

Mark **Canfield** *see* Melville **Crossman**

Denis **Cannan:** Denis Pullein-Thompson (1919–), Br. playwright. The writer adopted his mother's maiden name as his pen name, and later officially changed it by deed poll.

Charles **Cannell:** Evelyn Charles Vivian (1882–1947), Eng. writer of adventure, detective stories.

Effie **Canning:** Effie Carlton, née Crockett (1857–1940), U.S. stage actress, composer. At age 15 Effie Crockett composed her famous song "Rock a bye baby," published in 1884 under this pseudonym.

Curt **Cannon** *see* Evan **Hunter**

Dyan **Cannon:** Samille Diane Friesen (1937–), U.S. movie actress. The actress was given her new name by writer-producer Jerry Ward, who arranged her first screen test. The story goes that that one day he looked at her and exclaimed, "I see something explosive. Terrific. Bang. Cannon" [*TV Times*, June 1–7, 1985].

Freddy **Cannon:** Frederick Anthony Picariello (1940–), U.S. rock musician.

Tommy **Cannon:** Thomas Darbyshire (1938–), Eng. TV comedian, teaming with Bobby **Ball**. The two men, formerly Lancashire welders, first performed as the Harper Brothers (after Ball's real name), working in social clubs and cabaret. They changed their joint name to "Cannon and Ball" for an appearance on the TV talent show *Opportunity Knocks* in 1973. Cannon is the bigger and older of the two, with Ball his "feed" (providing his "ammunition," as it were).

Hans **Canon:** Johann von Puschka-Straschiripka (1829–1886), Austr. painter. The artist translated the Slavic first part of his surname to the French equivalent (English "cannon").

Blu **Cantrell:** Tiffanie Cobb (1975–), U.S. R&B singer.

Cantu: Abraham J. Cantu (1896–1949), Mexican illusionist.

Cantinflas: Mario Moreno Reyes (1911–1993), Mexican circus clown, bullfighter, stage, movie comedian. The performer developed a routine that was a blend of gibberish, double-talk, mispronunciation, and pantomime. Hence his Spanish name, from a contraction of a heckler's call: "*En la cantina tu inflas!*" ("You talk big in the barroom!"). He adopted it to hide his identity from his family when he began working in variety in 1930.

Eddie **Cantor:** Edward Israel Iskowitz (1892–1964), U.S. singer, entertainer, movie actor, of Russ.

Jewish parentage. The entertainer was orphaned at the age of three and raised by his grandmother, Meta Kantrowitz, who registered him as "Israel Kantrowitz," but this name was subsequently anglicized as "Isidore Kanter" by a school official. Eddie altered the spelling of his name to "Cantor" on entering show business in 1911.

Terry **Cantor:** K.E. Macnaghten (1912–1979), Eng. comedian.

Monty **Cantsin:** Maris Kundzins (1942–), Latvian poet, working in U.S. The adopted name, coined in 1978 by critic David Zack, is a form of the original that can be read in English as "Monty can't sing."

Janey **Canuck:** Emily Gowan Murphy, née Ferguson (1868–1933), Can. journalist, essayist, judge. "Canuck" is a nickname for a Canadian, and Janey Canuck was the name of the writer's first heroine in a number of popular books, such as *The Impressions of Janey Canuck Abroad* (1901) and *Janey Canuck in the West* (1910). For *The Black Candle* (1922), a book about narcotics, the author was Judge Murphy.

Yakima **Canutt:** Enos Edard Canutt (1895–1986), U.S. movie stuntman, director. Canutt began his career as a rodeo rider, when he gained his nickname as one of Washington state's "Yakima Riders."

Cornell **Capa:** Kornel Friedmann (1918–2008), Hung.-born U.S. photographer, brother of Robert **Capa**.

Robert **Capa:** Endre Ernö Friedmann (1913–1954), Hung.-born U.S. photographer. Friedmann adopted his new name in 1936, when he was publishing his work as simply André. He felt that this made him sound like a hairdresser, however, so he and his girlfriend Gerda Pohorylle (later Gerda **Taro**), who helped him promote this work, devised a different name. This was Robert Capa, supposedly the name of an already successful American photographer who was so rich that he refused to sell his photos at normal prices. The name itself was arbitrary in origin. André (Endre) himself claimed that "Robert" came from the movies, and in particular from Robert **Taylor**, who in 1936 starred as the lover of Greta **Garbo** in *Camille*, although some sources say he adopted the name in admiration of movie director Frank Capra (1897–1991). Either way, both words of the name were easy to pronounce, in many languages, and "Capa" looked like any nationality. Gerda could thus tell French editors that Capa was American, but also tell American editors that the photographer was French. And when the newly christened Capa went to Spain, his surname sounded conveniently Spanish. This ambiguity appealed to André, as did the fact that he was actually confused with the Hollywood director, and the name was perfect for a stateless person. In a letter to his mother soon after, Capa wrote: "I am working under a new name. They call me Robert Capa. One could almost say that I've been born again, but this time it didn't cause anyone any pain" [Richard Whelan, *Robert Capa: A Biography*, 1985].

Judith **Cape**: Patricia Kathleen Page (1916–), Eng.-born Can. artist, poet.

Ally **Capellino**: Alison Lloyd (1956–), Br. fashion designer.

Caper: Jeff Pearce (1957–), Br. crossword compiler. The setter seems to have devised his pseudonym from letters in his surname, with "caper" also describing a tricky crossword.

Wolfgang Fabricius **Capito**: Wolfgang Fabricus Köpfel (1478–1541), Ger. clergyman, reformer. The humanist adopted a Latin equivalent, *capito*, "bigheaded," of his German surname, a derivative (strictly speaking a diminutive) of *Kopf*, "head."

Capleton: Clifton George Bailey III (1967–), Jamaican rapper. The smart-thinking musician was nicknamed after a lawyer in his hometown and adopted the name.

Capnio: Johannes Reuchlin (1455–1522), Ger. humanist. "The celebrated *Reuchlin*, which in German signifies *smoke* [modern *Rauch*], considered it more dignified to smoke in Greek by the name of *Capnio* [from *kapnos*, "smoke"]" [D'Israeli, p.201]. The scholar is now in fact usually known by his real name.

Truman **Capote**: Truman Streckfus Persons (1924–1984), U.S. novelist, short-story writer, playwright. The writer acquired his new surname as a child in 1932 when his mother married Joseph Capote, a Cuban-American textile broker.

Al **Capp**: Alfred Gerald Caplin (1909–1979), U.S. cartoonist. The creator of Li'l Abner adopted "Capp" as his legal name in 1949.

Andy **Capp**: Lynford Anderson (*c*.1948–), Jamaican reggae musician. The former studio engineer adopted the name of the British comic-strip character Andy Capp (punning on "handicap"), a lazy and belligerent working-class antihero created by cartoonist Reg **Smythe**.

Frankie **Capp**: Frank Cappucio (1931–), U.S. jazz drummer.

Caprice: Caprice Bourret (1974–), U.S. model, working in U.K.

Kate **Capshaw**: Katherine Susan Nail (1953–), U.S. movie actress.

Captain ... For names beginning thus, excepting those below, see the following surname, e.g. for Captain Coe see Captain **Coe**, for Captain George North see Captain George **North**, etc.

The **Captain and Tennille**: Daryl Dragon (1942–), U.S. rock musician + Catheryn Antoinette ("Toni") Tennille (1953–), U.S. rock musician, his wife. Dragon was dubbed "Captain Keyboard" because of the naval officer's cap he invariably wore on stage.

Captain Beefheart: Don Van Vliet (1941–), U.S. pop singer. When he was 13, Van Vliet moved with his family from Los Angeles to Lancaster, California, where Frank Zappa, then his classmate at Antelope Valley High School, nicknamed him. "Captain Beefheart came from the beef in my heart about people stealing the land and covering it over; from the beef in my heart about the way people treat animals" [Storm Thorgerson and Peter Curzon, *100 Best Album Covers*, 1999].

Captain Moonlite: Andrew George Scott (1842–1880), Ir.-born Austral. outlaw. "Certainly the Irish were among bushranging's big names and those that have attracted the fame of balladry — Donohue, Doolan, Henry Power, Captain Moonlite..." [Patrick O'Farrell, *The Irish in Australia*, 1987]. The name springs from Captain Moonlight: "In Ireland a mythical person to whom was attributed the performance of atrocities by night especially in the latter part of the 19th century" [*Brewer's Dictionary of Phrase and Fable*, 1989].

Captain Rock *see* Thomas **Brown, the Younger**

Captain Sensible: Raymond Burns (1957–), Eng. pop singer. The singer adopted his name in about 1977. Its origins are somewhat vague, but it appears to have had something to do with his habit of wearing a peaked cap, playing the fool on an airplane trip to France with his punk group, The Damned, and announcing himself as "your captain speaking." He later admitted that he would have preferred a more macho name, "something like Duane Zenith or Bert Powerhouse, but I'm lumbered with Captain Sensible" [*Observer Magazine*, February 3, 1985].

A later account is more specific: "I had got a shirt with epaulettes. I was pretending to be the pilot, and shouting: 'It's all right! Everything's under control! It's on autopilot!' People were getting upset. And someone said: 'Oh, it's Captain Fucking Sensible.' We called ourselves by wacky names, so we could keep signing on the DHSS [Department of Health and Social Security]. I thought it would last five minutes. I didn't know I would still be called Captain Sensible at 35" [Jon Savage, *England's Dreaming*, 1991].

Captain Thunderbolt: Frederick Ward (1835–1870), Austral. bushranger.

Capucine: Germaine Lefebvre (1933–1990), Fr. model, stage, movie actress.

Car: Robert Frederick Goodwin Churchill (1910–), Eng. cartoonist, illustrator. The artist used this name for a weekly strip, "Saturday News Reel," published in the *Evening Standard* from 1945 to 1946. Churchill's father was a pioneer automobile (car) designer and manufacturer. Hence his pen name.

Caracalla: Marcus Aurelius Severus Antoninus Augustus (AD 188–217), Roman emperor. The infamous emperor was originally named Septimius Bassanius, for his father, Lucius Septimius Severus, and his maternal grandfather, Bassanius. He then assumed the name Marcus Aurelius Antoninus and added Caesar because his father wanted to link the family to the famous Antonine dynasty. In 198 he was given the title Augustus. The name by which he is now usually known, Caracalla, is said to refer to a new type of cloak that he designed, from a word of Gaulish origin.

Maria Caradori-Allan: Maria Caterina Rosalbina Allan, née de Munck (1800–1865), It.-born singer, working in England. After the death of her Alsatian father, the soprano added the maiden name of her mother, her sole teacher in the art of singing.

Caran d'Ache: Emmanuel Poiré (1858–1909), Fr. caricaturist. The artist was born in Moscow, and took his name as a French respelling of the Russian word *karandash*, meaning "pencil." Compare the name of **Karandash.**

Caravaggio: Michelangelo Merisi (da Caravaggio) (1573–1610), It. painter. The painter's name is that of his birthplace, Caravaggio, near Bergamo in northern Italy.

Leos Carax: Alexandre Oscar Dupont (1960–), Fr. movie director, screenwriter, actor. The moviemaker's assumed name is an anagram of his first two names (in the form "Alex Oscar").

Harry Caray: Harry Christopher Carabina (?1919–1998), U.S. baseball announcer.

Ethna Carbery: Anna MacManus, née Johnston (1866–1902), Ir. poet, short-story writer.

Francis Carco: François Marie Alexandre Carcopino-Tussoli (1886–1958), Fr. poet, writer.

Vincenzo Cardarelli: Nazareno Caldarelli (1887–1959), It. poet.

Cardini: Richard Valentine Pitchford (1895–1973), Welsh magician, working in U.S. The illusionist was impressed as a boy by the skill of cardsharpers, and made card tricks his own special study. He arrived in the USA in 1926, where he tried a number of stage names, such as Val Raymond, Professor Thomas, and Valentine, before settling on Cardini, a name based on that of **Houdini.** His U.S.–born wife and stage assistant, in her familiar bellhop uniform, was Swan Cardini, née Walker (1903–?).

Don Juan Cardoza: Émile Brazeau (1889–1980), Fr.-born illusionist, working in U.S. The entertainer subsequently changed his legal name to Pierre LeBlanc. He also performed as Ray Bol and Ray Danton.

Peter Cardy: Peter John Stubbings (1947–), Br. charity executive. Cardy assumed his new name by deed poll in 1987.

Careca: Antonio de Oliveira Filho (1960–), Brazilian footballer. The sportsman's name arose as a nickname amounting to "baldie" (Portuguese *carecer*, "to lack").

Christine Carère: Christine de Borde (1930–), Fr. movie actress.

Carette: Julien Carette (1897–1966), Fr. movie actor.

James Carew: James Usselman (1876–1938), U.S. stage, movie actor, working in U.K.

Edwin Carewe: Jay Fox (1883–1940), U.S. movie director.

Joyce Carey: Joyce Lawrence (1898–1993), Eng. stage, movie actress, playwright. Carey used the name Jay Mallory for her play *Sweet Aloes* (1934), in which she herself acted. This was filmed as *Give Me Your Heart* (1936), in which she had no part. Her name should not be mistaken for that of the (male) English novelist Joyce Cary (1888–1957).

Max George Carey: Maximillian Carnarius (1890–1976), U.S. baseball player ("Scoops"). The player took a new name to preserve his amateur status, which he would have lost by playing professional ball.

Jean-Pierre Cargol: Reyes Baliardo (1957–), Fr. juvenile movie actor, of Romany origin.

Tahia Carioca: Badawiyya Muhammad Karim (1919–1999), Egyptian dancer, movie actress.

Carl Carl: Carl Andreas von Bernbrunn (1789–1854), Pol.-born Austr. actor, theatrical director.

Frankie Carle: Francisco Nunzio Carlone (1903–2001), U.S. popular musician.

Richard Carle: Charles Carleton (1871–1941), U.S. movie actor.

Latham C. Carleton *see* James Fenimore Cooper **Adams**

Belinda Carlisle: Belinda Jo Kerzcheski (1958–), U.S. rock singer. The spelling of the Go-Gos singer's original name varies in some sources, and the name itself is entirely absent in most.

Kitty Carlisle: Catherine Carlisle Hart, née Conn (1910–2007), U.S. opera singer, movie actress.

Egbert Carllsen: August Egbert von Derschau (1845–1883), Ger. novelist.

Dr. Carlo: Carlo Sommer (?–), U.S.–born magician.

Carlo-Rim *see* Carlo **Rim**

Wendy Carlos: Walter Carlos (1939–), U.S. keyboardist. The musician underwent a sex change operation and in 1979 legally assumed his new female first name.

Carlos the Jackal: Ilich Ramirez Sánchez (1949–), Venezuelan terrorist. The instigator of various murders, shootings, and bombings in the 1970s and 1980s, born the eldest of three brothers raised as revolutionaries and named respectively Ilich, Lenin, and Vladimir after the Communist leader, is believed to have adopted his alias from the Brazilian urban guerrilla Carlos Marighella, who was probably his mentor. He had several other names. "We have traced five different sets of travel documents used by him. He has been Cenon Clarke of New York; Hector Hugo Dupont, an Anglo-Frenchman; Glenn Gebhard. an American; Adolf Bernal from Chile and Carlos Martinez-Torres, a Peruvian economist. Using these identities he flitted in and out of the country and nobody imagined for a moment that he was a terrorist" [Christopher Dobson and Ronald Payne, *The Carlos Complex*, 1977]. He was nicknamed "the Jackal" by the media when a copy of Frederick Forsyth's 1971 thriller *The Day of the Jackal* (which may also have inspired Francis **Markham**) was found in his belongings.

Carlota: Marie-Charlotte-Amélie-Augustine-Victoire-Clémentine-Léopoldine (1840–1927), Belg.-born empress of Mexico. The wife of Emperor Maximilian adopted a Spanish version of the second word of her seven-part French name as a single name for standard use. Royal personages usually acquire strings of names like this with the aim of preserving the names of earlier family members. Léopoldine, for example, commemorated her father, Leopold I (1790–1865), king of the Belgians.

Richard **Carlson:** Albert Lea (1914–1977), U.S. movie actor, director.

Carlton: Arthur Carlton Philps (1881–1942), Eng. illusionist.

Roger **Carlton** *see* Fenton **Brockley**

Carlyle: Lyle Laughlin (1906–?), U.S. magician.

David **Carlyle** *see* Robert **Paige**

Francis **Carlyle:** Francis Finnernan (1911–1975), U.S. magician.

Il **Carmagnola:** Francesco Bussone (*c.*1380–1432), It. condottiere. The name is that of the mercenary leader's birthplace, Carmagnola, near Turin.

Felix **Carmen:** Frank Dempster Sherman (1860–1916), U.S. poet. The poet's adopted name translates as the Latin for "happy song."

Carmen Marina: Carmen Manteca Gioconda (1936–), Sp. guitarist, singer, composer, working in U.S.

Carmen Sylva: Elisabeth, Queen of Romania, née Pauline Elisabeth Ottilie Luise, Princess of Wied (1843–1916), Ger.-born Rom. verse, prose writer. The pen name, suggested by the queen's physician, reflected Elisabeth's love of singing and of the forest,

from Latin *carmen*, "song," and *silva*, "wood." She revealed her true name in her French-written *Pensées d'une reine* ("Thoughts of a Queen") (1882).

T. **Carmi:** Charmi Charny (1925–1994), U.S.-born Israeli poet, editor.

Harry **Carmichael:** Leopold Horace Ognall (1908–1979), Br. crime novelist. The wrter reserved his pseudonym for his thrillers. He also wrote as Hartley Howard.

Judy **Carmichael:** Judith Lea Hohenstein (1952–), U.S. jazz pianist.

Carmo *see* The **Great Carmo**

Carmontelle: Louis Carrogis (1717–1806), Fr. portraitist, architect, dramatist.

Carol **Carnac:** Edith Caroline Rivett (1894–1958), Br. detective novelist. The writer seems to have based her pen name on reduplicated letters in "Caroline." She also wrote as E.C.R. **Lorac**.

Judy **Carne:** Joyce Botterill (1939–), Eng. TV actress, working in U.S. The actress took her screen name "from a character she played years ago in a school play" [*TV Times Magazine*, June 5–11, 1982].

Marcel **Carné:** Albert Cranche (1906–1996), Fr. movie director.

Dale **Carnegie:** Dale Breckenridge Carnegey (1888–1955), U.S. writer, public speaker. The author modified his name in 1919 in honor of his hero, philanthropist Andrew Carnegie (1835–1919).

Hattie **Carnegie:** Henrietta Kanengeiser (1886–1956), Austr.-born U.S. fashion designer. The designer adopted the surname of philanthropist Andrew Carnegie (1835–1919), perhaps for its connotation of wealth, on opening her first hat shop in New York City in 1909. She married Major John Zanft in 1927 but never used his name publicly or professionally.

Mosco **Carner:** Mosco Cohen (1904–1985), Austr.-born Br. musicologist.

Kate **Carney:** Catherine Mary Pattinson (1868–1950), Br. music-hall singer, comedienne. The performer used her real name on the stage until 1889.

Lesley **Carol** *see* Carole **Lesley**

Martine **Carol:** Marie-Louise-Jeanne Mourer (1922–1967), Fr. movie actress.

Sue **Carol:** Evelyn Jean Lederer (1906–1982), U.S. movie actress.

Terri **Carol:** Ivy Rosina Victoria Moore (1915–2002), Br. variety artist.

Carolina Slim: Edward P. Harris (1923–1953), U.S. blues, country singer. Born in North Carolina, Harris also recorded as Jammin' Jim, Country Paul, and Lazy Slim Jim.

Carolus-Duran: Charles-Auguste-Émile Durand (1837–1917), Fr. painter.

Francis **Carpenter:** Francis Willburn Keef (1911–), U.S. child movie actor.

Carpentras: Elzéar Genet (*c*.1470–1548), Fr. composer. The musician, also known by the equivalent Italian name Il Carpentrasso, took his name from his birthplace, Carpentras, in the south of France.

Catharine Carr: Rosalind Herschel Seymour, née Wade (1909–1989), Eng. novelist.

Eric Carr: Paul Caravello (1950–1991), U.S. rock drummer.

Glyn Carr: Frank Showell Styles (1908–), Br. detective novelist. The writer made his home in Wales, and his pseudonym is a typical Welsh placename, meaning "Carr valley."

Jane Carr: Rita Brunstrom (1909–1957). Br. movie actress, of Swe.-Eng. parentage.

Jolyon Carr *see* Ellis **Peters**

Lodi Carr: Lois Ann Cox-Kasher (1933–), U.S. jazz singer.

Mary Carr: Mary Kennevan (1874–1973), U.S. stage, movie actress.

Michael Carr: Maurice Cohen (1904–1968), Br. songwriter.

Philippa Carr *see* Jean **Plaidy**

Russ Carr: Frederick Russell Parnell (1889–1973), Eng. ventriloquist, son of Fred **Russell**.

Sam Carr: Schmil Kogan (1906–), Ukr.-born Can. Communist official, spy. Kogan adopted his new name on emigrating to Canada in 1924.

Vikki Carr: Florencia Bisenta de Casillas Martinez Cardona (1941–), U.S. pop singer.

Raffaella Carrà: Raffaella Pelloni (1942–), It. ballerina, singer, TV show presenter.

David Carradine: John Arthur Carradine (1936–), U.S. movie actor, son of John **Carradine**.

John Carradine: Richmond Reed Carradine (1906–1988), U.S. movie actor. For five years from 1930 Carradine played under the name John Peter Richmond.

Thomas Carre: Miles Pinkney (1599–1674), Eng. Catholic cleric.

Danny Carrel: Suzanne Chazelles du Chaxel (1935–), Fr. movie actress. The name evolved from the actress's first two names.

Mark Carrel: Lauran Bosworth Paine (1916–), U.S. writer. Paine is chiefly known for his western fiction, but to cover his wide range of literary genres also wrote as John Armour, Reg Batchelor, Kenneth Bedford, Frank Bosworth (from his middle name), Robert Clarke, Richard Dana, J.F. Drexler, Troy Howard, Jared Ingersol, John Kilgore, Hunter Liggett, J.K. Lucas, and John Morgan.

Rudi Carrell: Rudolf Wijbrand Kesselaar (1934–2006), Du.-born Ger. TV personality.

Tia Carrere: Althea Janairo (1967–), Hawaiian-born U.S. movie actress.

Arthur G. Carrick: [Prince] Charles (1948–), Eng. prince. The Prince of Wales is a keen amateur painter, and he adopted this pseudonym when submitting a small watercolor entitled *Farm Buildings in Norfolk* to the 1987 Summer Exhibition of the Royal Academy of Arts, London. His identity was revealed only after the picture was accepted. The Prince's full names are Charles Philip Arthur George, while as Great Steward of Scotland he bears the title Earl of Carrick, this being a region of western Scotland. Prince Charles is also Duke of Cornwall, a county in which Carrick is an administrative district.

Edward Carrick: Edward Anthony Craig (1905–1998), Br. art director, movie actor. "Carrick" means the same as "Craig," that is, "rock," the former name being a Celtic variant of the English.

Robert Carrier: Robert Carrier MacMahon (1923–2006), U.S.–born Br. restaurateur, food writer.

Eva Carrière: Marthe Béraud (1886–?), Fr. medium. The supposed "materializer" is known in research literature as simply "Eva C."

John Carrodus: John Tiplady Carruthers (1836–1895), Br. violinist, teacher.

Norman Carrol: Sydney Edward Brandon (1890–1954), Eng. music-hall comedian.

Andrea Carroll: Andrea Lee DeCapite (1946–), U.S. pop singer.

Barbara Carroll: Barbara Carole Coppersmith (1925–), U.S. jazz pianist, singer.

David Carroll: Nook Schrier (1913–), U.S. orchestra arranger, conductor.

Diahann Carroll: Carol Diann Johnson (1935–), U.S. black TV singer, actress. When they were both 16, the singer and her friend Elissa Oppenheim turned up to audition for the TV show *Arthur Godfrey's Talent Scouts*, calling their act Oppenheim and Johnson. "'Before we take this any further,' the man in charge answered, 'I'd like you to go home and try to find another name. There's no way in the world we can announce, "Ladies and Gentlemen, Oppenheim and Johnson," then have you two march out there.' ... I was crestfallen, but Elissa wouldn't let herself be discouraged. Late that night ... she called with the solution to our problem. 'I've got it!' she proclaimed. 'I'm changing my name to Lisa Collins and you're going to be Diahann Carroll! D-i-a-h-a-n-n C-a-r-r-o-l-l. How does that sound to you? Is it all right?' 'It's fine, Elissa. Just fine,' I mumbled" [Diahann Carroll with Ross Firestone, *Diahann: An Autobiography*, 1986].

Elisabeth Carroll: Elisabeth Pfister (1937–), U.S. ballet dancer.

Joan Carroll: Joan Felt (1932–), U.S. child movie actress. The actress changed her name when she was only eight, choosing a name that seemed "musical."

John **Carroll:** Julian LaFaye (1905–1979), U.S. movie actor, singer.

Lewis **Carroll:** Charles Lutwidge Dodgson (1832–1898), Eng. children's writer. One of the most famous names in 19th-century English literature, that of the author of *Alice in Wonderland* (1865) and *Through the Looking-Glass* (1871), was created by a mathematical lecturer at Oxford University. His pseudonym is a transposition and translation (or rendering) of his first two names: Lutwidge to Lewis and Charles to Carroll. He was requested to produce a pen name by Edmund Yates, editor of the humorous paper *The Train*, to which Dodgson was contributing in 1856. He first offered Yates the name Dares, after Daresbury, his Cheshire birthplace, but Yates thought this "too much like a newspaper signature." So Dodgson tried again, and on February 11, 1856, noted in his diary: "Wrote to Mr. Yates sending him a choice of names: 1. *Edgar Cuthwellis* (made by transposition out of 'Charles Lutwidge'). 2. *Edgar U.C. Westhill* (ditto). 3. *Louis Carroll* (derived from Lutwidge ... Ludovic ... Louis, and Charles). 4. *Lewis Carroll* (ditto)." Yates made his choice, saving all Alice lovers from Edgar Cuthwellis, and on March 1 Dodgson duly recorded in his diary: "Lewis Carroll was chosen."

The name has a royal ring to it, appropriately for the Victorian era in which Dodgson lived, and "Lewis" was long the traditional English spelling for the many French kings named Louis, while "Carroll" suggests Carolus as the Latin equivalent for the French and English kings named Charles.

It was not actually Carroll's first pseudonym, since early contributions to *The Train* were signed as "B.B." (it was this that prompted his editor to ask for a proper *nom de plume*). The precise origin of B.B. is not clear, although Dodgson had shown a fondness for writing over mysterious initials as self-appointed editor of the Dodgson family journal, *The Rectory Magazine* (1845). In this, as a teenager, he contributed pieces as V.X., F.L.W., J.V., F.X., Q.G.—and B.B. Anne Clark (see below) suggests that B.B.—which would appear to be one of the few initialized pseudonyms Dodgson retained for use in adult life— might perhaps stand for "Bobby Burns," since a number of the pieces contributed to *The Rectory Magazine* were mournful ballads in the style of Robert **Burns**. On the other hand in *Poverty Bay: A Nondescript Novel* (1905), by Harry Furniss, the illustrator chosen by Dodgson for *Sylvie and Bruno* (1889), the following is found: "He was known at Eton as 'B.B.,' short for Beau Brummell, the exquisite, whom he was supposed, by the boys at school, to emulate." Furniss was here perhaps consciously or unconsciously using Dodgson's own nickname, which had been confided

to him some years before and which he now remembered. This seems quite a likely explanation for the double-letter name. Reviewing Clark's biography, Francis King commented: "What she does not remark on is the coincidence that in 'The Hunting of the Snark' ... every crew member (Bellman, Barrister, Broker, Billiard-marker, Beaver, etc) begins with the letter B and that even the Snark itself should turn out to be a Boojum" [*Sunday Telegraph*, September 9, 1979].

Dodgson the don deliberately distanced himself from the persona of Lewis Carroll, and a footnote to an enumeration of his factual and fictional writings in Sharp 1904 reads: "It should be noted that Mr. Dodgson states, with reference to this list, that he 'neither claims nor acknowledges any connection with the books not published under his name.'" In other words, the writer of *An Elementary Treatise on Determinants* (1867) is entirely distinct from the author of *Alice in Wonderland* [1. Lewis Carroll, ed., *The Rectory Magazine*, facsimile edition, 1975 (1850); 2. John Pudney, *Lewis Carroll and His World*, 1976; 3. Anne Clark, *Lewis Carroll: A Biography*, 1979; 4. Donald Thomas, *Lewis Carroll: A Portrait with Background*, 1996].

Madeleine **Carroll:** Marie-Madeleine Bernadette O'Carroll (1906–1987), Br.-born U.S. movie actress.

Nancy **Carroll:** Ann Veronica La Hiff (1905–1965), U.S. movie actress. "Ann" gave "Nancy."

Ronnie **Carroll:** Ronald Cleghorn (1934–), Northern Ireland popular singer.

Sydney W. **Carroll:** George Frederick Carl Whiteman (1877–1958), Austral.-born Br. stage actor, critic, theater manager. The actor's middle initial represents his surname, while his new surname is formed from his third name.

Arthur **Carron:** Arthur Cox (1900–1967), Eng. opera singer.

Jasper **Carrott:** Robert Davis (1945–), Eng. comedian, father of TV actress Lucy Davis (1973–). Davis explains how he came by his name: "Jasper is a nickname I picked up when I was nine, I don't know why. There is no reason for it. I added Carrott when I was 17. I was on a golf course with a friend, when he met somebody, and said: 'Oh, this is Jasper.' Carrott was the first name that came into my head. No one since school days has ever called me, or even known me, by my original name, Bob Davis" [*TV Times*, February 15, 1979].

Carrot Top: Scott Thompson (1967–), U.S. stage comedian. The comedian was so nicknamed for his red hair.

Arthur **Carson:** Peter Brooke (1907–), Eng.-born U.S. thriller writer.

Jeannie **Carson:** Jean Shufflebottom (1928–), Br. movie, TV actress.

John **Carson:** John Derek Carson-Parker (1927–), Br. stage, TV actor.

Sunset **Carson:** Michael Harrison (1922–1990), U.S. movie actor. When the actor became a cowboy star in the 1940s, the movie company changed his name to coincide with the fictional western hero he portrayed.

Sylvia **Carson** *see* Brett **Halliday**

John Paddy **Carstairs:** John Keys (1910–1970), Eng. movie director, screenwriter.

Peter **Carsten:** Pieter Ransenthaler (1929–), Ger. movie actor, working in U.S.

Betty **Carter:** Lillie Mae Jones (1929–1998), U.S. black jazz singer. The singer first performed as Lorraine Carter. Jazz musician Lionel Hampton, who employed her from 1948 to 1951, nicknamed her "Betty Bebop" for her style of singing, and although she resented the belittling reference to the cartoon character Betty Boop she none the less adopted the first name and became Betty Carter.

Bo **Carter:** Armenter Chatmon (1893–1964), U.S. black blues musician.

Bob **Carter:** Robert Kahakalau (1922–), U.S. jazz musician, of Hawaiian parentage.

Bruce **Carter:** Richard Alexander Hough (1922–), Eng. children's writer, publisher. The writer used the name Elizabeth Churchill for *Juliet in Publishing* (1956), while for *The Plane Wreckers* (1961) he was Pat Strong.

Carlene **Carter:** Rebecca Carlene Smith (1955–), U.S. country singer. The singer, a granddaughter of Maybelle Carter of the Carter Family, adopted her mother's maiden name as her professional name.

Helen **Carter:** Helen Carter Jones (1927–1998), U.S. country singer.

Helena **Carter:** Helen Rickerts (1923–2000), U.S. movie actress.

Jack **Carter:** John Chakrin (1922–), U.S. TV comic.

Janis **Carter:** Janis Dremann (1917–1994), U.S. movie actress.

Marilyn **Carter** *see* Marilyn **Ross**

Mrs. Leslie **Carter:** Caroline Louise Dudley (1862–1937), U.S. stage actress. An actress who, like Mrs. Patrick **Campbell**, appeared professionally under her husband's name. She took to the stage in 1889, following the breakup of her marriage.

Nell **Carter:** Nell Ruth Hardy (1948–2003), U.S. stage, TV actress, singer.

Nick **Carter:** (1) John R. Coryell (1848–1924), U.S. popular fiction writer; (2) Thomas Chalmers Harbaugh (1849–1924), U.S. popular fiction writer; (3) Frederick Van Rensselaer Day (?1861–1922), U.S. popular fiction writer. The name was adopted by the author (or authors) of a series of detective novels that appeared in the U.S. from about 1870. The character Nick Carter, who gave the name, is said to have been invented by Coryell and passed down by him to the other two.

Anna **Carteret:** Anna Wilkinson (1942–), Br. stage actress. The actress adopted her mother's maiden name as her stage name.

R.C. **Carton:** Richard Claude Critchett (1856–1928), Br. actor, dramatist. Carton was influenced by Charles Dickens, and his stage name may have been taken from Sydney Carton, hero of *A Tale of Two Cities* (1859). Carton's wife was the actress Katherine Mackenzie Compton (1853–1928), stage name "Miss Compton," daughter of Henry **Compton** and aunt of Fay **Compton** and Compton **Mackenzie**.

Louise **Carver:** Louise Spilger Murray (1868–1956), U.S. movie actress.

Lynne **Carver:** Virginia Reid Sampson (1909–1955), U.S. movie actress. The actress began her screen career as Virginia Reid.

Heron **Carvic:** Geoffrey Richard William Harris (1913–1980), Br. crime writer.

Carw Coch: William Williams (1808–1872), Welsh poet. The poet's bardic name means "red deer."

Ivan **Caryll:** Félix Tilkin (1861–1921), Belg. operetta composer, working in U.K., U.S.

Jean **Carzou:** Garnik Zulumyan (1907–2000), Fr. painter, theatrical decorator, of Armenian parentage.

Maria **Casarès:** Maria Casarès Quiroga (1922–1996), Fr. movie actress, of Sp. parentage. The actress came to France with her family when she was 13, at the time of the civil war.

Justin **Case:** Hugh Barnett Cave (1910–), Eng.-born U.S. horror-fiction writer. A corny name, of course, but included here to show that at least one writer actually resorted to it.

Jean **Caselli:** Henri Cazalis (1840–1909), Fr. physician, poet.

Bill **Casey:** William Weldon (1909–), U.S. black blues singer, guitarist.

Alvin **Cash:** Alvin de Forest Welch (1939–1999), U.S. R&B singer.

W.J. **Cash:** Joseph Wilbur Cash (1900–1941), U.S. journalist, writer. For some reason Cash chose to reverse the order of his given names and then call himself by their initials.

Jean **Casimir-Perier:** Jean Perier (1847–1907), Fr. statesman. In 1874 the future French president (1894–95) added the first name of his grandfather, Casimir Perier (1777–1832), head of the Banque de France.

Casina: Wadham Sutton (1945–), Br. crossword

compiler. The setter was allocated his pseudonym when first submitting crosswords to *Country Life* magazine. Its precise significance is obscure, although it may be a variant on "casino," which is a card game, just as a crossword is a word game.

Sir Edwin **Caskoden:** Charles Major (1856–1913), U.S. novelist. The writer adopted his pen name from one of his own fictional characters, the master of the dance at the court of Henry VIII who is the narrator in Major's first and best novel, *When Knighthood Was in Flower* (1898).

Alejandro **Casona:** Alejandro Rodríguez Álvarez (1903–1965), Sp. dramatist.

Cassandra: [Sir] William Neil Connor (1909–1967), Eng. columnist. Connor was columnist for the *Daily Mirror* from 1935, and was noted for his gloomily prophetic articles. His pen name reflects this, for in Greek mythology Cassandra was the daughter of Priam, king of Troy, who received the gift of prophecy from Apollo. However, when she refused the god's advances, he decreed that no one would believe her predictions, although they were invariably true. Her name has thus come to denote any "prophet of doom." The columnist did not choose the name himself, and it was given him by Harry Bartholomew, one of the newspaper's directors. Connor commented: "I was a bit surprised to discover that I had changed my sex; was the daughter of the King of Troy; that I could foretell in the stars when the news was going to be bad; ... that nobody believed me when I spoke the unpleasant truth" [Robert Connor, *Cassandra: Reflections in a Mirror*, 1969].

Cassandre: Adolphe-Jean-Marie Mouron (1901–1968), Fr. graphic artist, stage designer.

Jean-Pierre **Cassel:** Jean-Pierre Crochon (1932–2007), Fr. movie actor.

Butch **Cassidy:** Robert LeRoy Parker (1866–?1909 or ?1937), U.S. outlaw, teaming with the **Sundance Kid**. The Wild Bunch leader was nicknamed "Butch" as he had worked in a butcher's shop for a time in Rock Springs, Wyoming, when on the run from the law. "Cassidy" was an alias adopted from cowhand Mike Cassidy, an older outlaw from whom he learned cattle rustling and gunslinging.

Joanna **Cassidy:** Joanna Virginia Caskey (1944–), U.S. movie actress.

Robert **Cassilis:** Michael Edwardes (1923–), Br. writer.

Billie **Cassin** *see* Joan **Crawford**

Oleg **Cassini:** Oleg Cassini Loiewski (1913–2006), Fr.-born fashion designer, of Russ. parentage, working in U.S.

Lou **Castel:** Luigi Castellato (1943–), It. movie actor.

Giorgione di **Castel Chiuso:** Peter Bayley (1778–1823), Eng. writer. The author used this name for *Sketches from St. George's Fields* (1820), a volume of verse with descriptions of London life. His pen name is an Italian-style rendering, literally meaning "closed castle," of his surname, since English "bailey," as a court in a castle, derives from Old French *baile,* "enclosure."

Leo **Castelli:** Leo Krauss (1907–1999), It.-born U.S. art dealer, of Hung.-It. parentage. The New York dealer adopted his mother's maiden name in 1919.

Castil-Blaze: François-Henri-Joseph Blaze (1784–1857), Fr. ballet critic.

Castine: Noah Brooks (1830–1903), U.S. journalist. Brooks used this name for his contributions to the *Sacramento Union* in the 1860s, taking it from his birthplace, Castine, Maine.

Don **Castle:** Marion Goodman, Jr. (1919–1966), U.S. movie actor.

Frances **Castle:** Evelyn Barbara Leader, née Blackburn (1898–1981), Eng. novelist, playwright.

Irene **Castle:** Irene Foote (1893–1969), U.S. ballroom dancer, teaming with Vernon **Castle,** her husband. She made a number of movies following her husband's death in an air crash.

Lee **Castle:** Aniello Castaldo (1915–1990), U.S. jazz trumpeter.

Vernon **Castle:** Vernon Blythe (1887–1918), Br. ballroom dancer, aviator, teaming with Irene **Castle,** his wife. Blythe immigrated to the United States in 1906 and took the name Castle the following year. He married Irene Foote in 1911.

William **Castle:** William Schloss (1914–1977), U.S. horror-movie director. The English surname translates the German original.

Harry **Castlemon:** Charles Austin Fosdick (1842–1915), U.S. writer of adventure stories for boys.

Victor **Català:** Caterina Albert i Paradís (1869–1966), Catalan writer.

Georgina **Cates:** Clare Woodgate (1975–), Eng. TV, movie actress.

Gilbert **Cates:** Gilbert Katz (1934–), U.S. movie director, uncle of Phoebe **Cates**.

Phoebe **Cates:** Phoebe Katz (1963–), U.S. movie actress, niece of Gilbert **Cates**.

Lois **Catesby:** Lydia Arms Avery Coonley Ward (1845–1924), U.S. poet, philosopher. Ward began her writing career in 1878 under this name.

Ambrosius **Catharinus:** Lancelot Politi (*c.*1484–1553), It. theologian. The scholar entered the Dominican order in 1517 and adopted his religious name in honor of the two Sienese saints of that order, Blessed Ambrosius Sansedone (1220–1286) and St. Catherine (of Siena) (1347–1380).

Helen **Cathcart:** Harold Albert (1909–1997),

Eng. royal biographer. The writer claimed to be the "literary manager" of Helen Cathcart, who was thus supposedly the actual author of biographies of Queen Elizabeth II, Queen Elizabeth, the Queen Mother, and other members of the British royal family. Sometimes "her" books would contain an acknowledgement to "the help given by Harold Albert," and on one occasion the *Daily Mail* sent a reporter to Albert's house to seek details about Mrs. Cathcart, but he would not be drawn. (Albert's father abandoned the family home and his mother married a stepfather whom Harold hated. He therefore renounced the original family name of Kemp and used his middle name, Albert, as his surname.) Albert created Helen Cathcart in the 1950s, "choosing a good Scottish name that had just the right ring to it" [*The Times*, November 4, 1997].

Willa **Cather:** Wilella Cather (1873–1947), U.S. novelist, short-story writer. The writer tried out the full names Willa Love Cather and Willa Lova Cather before settling for Willa Sibert Cather, taking the middle name from an uncle on her mother's side who was killed fighting for the Confederacy. She adopted this name in 1902, three years before publishing her first book of short stories and ten years before her first novel.

[St.] **Catherine:** Alessandra Lucrezia Romola dei Ricci (1522–1590), It. mystic. The saint is known by the name she assumed on entering a Dominican convent at the age of 13. The name itself honors St. Catherine of Siena (Caterina Benincasa) (1347–1380), who is venerated by the Dominican order.

Catherine I: Marta Skawronska (1684–1727), Russ. empress. The Empress of Russia was the daughter of a Lithuanian peasant named Samuil Skawronski. In 1703 she was received into the Russian Orthodox Church and rechristened Yekaterina Alekseyevna. She married Peter the Great in 1712.

Catherine II: Sophie Friederike Auguste von Anhalt-Zerbst (1729–1796), Ger.-born Russ. empress. Catherine the Great, Empress of Russia, was born the daughter of an obscure German prince, Christian August von Anhalt-Zerbst. She assumed the title of Yekaterina Alekseyevna on arriving in Russia in 1744 and married her cousin, the future Peter III, the following year.

[St.] **Catherine of Bologna:** Caterina de'Vigri (1413–1463), It. saint.

[St.] **Catherine of Genoa:** Caterinetta Fieschi (1447–1510), It. mystic.

Cat Iron: William Carradine (*c*.1896–*c*.1958), U.S. blues singer. The musician came by his name as the result of a journalist's mishearing of his surname.

Christopher **Caudwell:** Christopher St. John Sprigg (1907–1937), Br. Marxist writer. The writer adopted his mother's maiden name, first using it for his novel *This My Hand* (1936).

Frank **Cauldwell:** Francis Henry King (1923–), Eng. novelist, short-story writer. King used this name for *The Firewalkers* (1956).

Dr. Christopher **Caustic:** Thomas Green Fessenden (1771–1837), U.S. author, inventor, lawyer. Fessenden first used this name for *Terrible Tractoration!!* (1803), a satirical poem attacking English critics of Elisha Perkins's "Metallic Tractors," a pair of metal pieces supposed to relieve pain by galvanic action when applied to an inflamed spot on the skin.

C.P. **Cavafy:** Konstantínos Pétrou Kaváfis (1863–1933), Gk. poet.

Alberto **Cavalcanti:** Alberto de Almeida-Cavalcanti (1897–1982), Brazilian movie director, of It. origin.

Alain **Cavalier:** Alain Fraissé (1931–), Fr. movie director.

Francesco **Cavalli:** Pier Francesco Caletti-Bruni (1602–1676), It. opera composer. The musician assumed the name of his Venetian patron, Federico Cavalli.

Anna **Cavan:** Helen Ferguson, née Woods (1901–1968), Eng. novelist. The writer adopted the name of one of her own fictional characters. Her first novel following the creation of her new persona had the significant title *Change the Name* (1941).

[St.] Nikolaos **Cavasilas:** Nikolaos Chamaetos (*c*.1320–1395), Gk. theologian, mystical writer. The theologian adopted the name of his uncle, Archbishop Nilus Cavasilas, in place of his own.

Caveat Emptor: [Sir] George Stephen (1794–1879), Eng. writer, lawyer. Stephen used this name, from the Latin tag meaning "Let the buyer beware," for his popular work, *The Adventures of a Gentleman in Search of a Horse* (1835). It appeared in a fifth edition in 1841 under his real name.

Cavendish: Henry Jones (1831–1899), Eng. physician, authority on whist. The writer took his name from his London club, the Cavendish, in Cavendish Square.

Kay **Cavendish:** Kathleen Dorothy Cavendish-Murray (1908–2000), Br. pianist, "croonette," broadcaster.

Cawrdaf: William Ellis Jones (1795–1848), Welsh poet. The poet's bardic name is a local place-name.

Pisistratus **Caxton:** Edward George Earle Lytton Bulwer-Lytton (1803–1873), Eng. novelist, playwright, statesman. One of several pseudonyms used at different times by Bulwer **Lytton**. This one presumably alluded to Pisistratus, the 5th-century BC. "Tyrant of Athens," and William Caxton, the first English printer.

Cazuza: Agenor de Miranda Araújo Neto (1958–1990), Brazilian rock singer, songwriter. The musician adopted the nickname given him by his father, meaning "rascal."

Arthur **Cecil:** Arthur Cecil Blunt (1843–1896), Eng. actor.

Henry **Cecil:** [His Honour] Henry Cecil Leon (1902–1976), Br. judge, playwright. Leon also wrote as Clifford Maxwell.

Mr. **Cee** (or C): Hubert Kyle Church III (1973–1995), U.S. black "gangsta" rapper.

Cee-Lo: Thomas DeCarlo Callaway (1974–), U.S. black rapper.

Ceiriog: John Ceiriog Hughes (1832–1887), Welsh poet, folk musicologist. The poet's middle name and bardic name was that of the village where he was born, Llanarmon Dyffryn Ceiriog, itself named for the river on which it lies.

Celadon: Georg Greflinger (*c.*1620–*c.*1677), Ger. lyric poet. Greflinger first used this name (also spelled Seladon) as a member of the Elbschwanenorden ("Order of Elbe Swans"), a society of poets founded in 1658. This Celadon predates the one who is the lover of Amelia in the "Summer" (1727) section of James Thomson's *The Seasons*. The name subsequently became popular for any rustic lover.

Paul **Celan:** Paul Leo Antschel (1920–1970), Rom.-born Ger. poet, translator, working in France. The writer's adopted surname is an anagram of Ancel, the Romanian spelling of his original surname.

Gabriel **Celaya:** Rafael Múgica (1911–1991), Sp. poet.

Madame **Céleste:** Anastasie Céleste (or Céline) Elliott, née Keppler (1810–1882), Fr. dancer, actress, working in U.S., U.K. Céleste married an American, Henry Elliott, but performed mainly in England.

Celestine II: Guido di Città di Castello (?–1144), It. pope.

Celestine III: Giacinto Orsini (*c.*1106–1198), It. pope. The pontiff took his name from his former fellow-student, **Celestine II**, who had created him cardinal in 1144.

Celestine IV: Goffredo Castiglioni (?–1241), It. pope.

[St.] **Celestine V:** Pietro da Morrone (*c.*1209–1296), It. pope.

Céline: Odette Marie Céline Hallowes, earlier Sansom, then Churchill, née Brailly (1912–1995), Fr.-born Br. wartime agent. This was the code name taken by the World War II agent better known as **Odette:** "Every pupil, student, undergraduate, should choose a name, a Christian name, and during the period of training, she would be known only by that name. Now what name would Mrs. Sansom like? Odette thought for a moment. Her real names were Odette Marie Céline. She said cautiously: 'Would "Céline" do?' 'Certainly. We haven't got a Céline. For purposes of training, you are simply "Céline" from now on'" [Jerrard Tickell, *Odette: The Story of a British Agent*, 1949]. Odette worked for **Raoul**.

Louis-Ferdinand **Céline:** Louis-Ferdinand Destouches (1894–1961), Fr. novelist. The writer adopted the name for his first novel, *Voyage au bout de la nuit* ("Journey to the End of Night") (1932). "That was when he had settled on his pseudonym, Louis-Ferdinand Céline, in hommage [*sic*] to his maternal grandmother, Céline Guillou, i.e., in reference to the past, to the happy or idealized days of his childhood" [Frédéric Vitoux, *Céline*, translated by Jesse Browner, 1992].

Vincenzo **Celli:** Vincenzo Yacullo (1900–1988), It.-born U.S. ballet dancer.

Celt: Edward Morgan Humphreys (1882–1935), Welsh journalist, novelist. Humphreys used this pseudonym as a weekly columnist and reviewer in the *Liverpool Daily Post* and *Manchester Guardian*.

Konrad **Celtis:** Konrad Bickel (1459–1508), Ger. humanist.

Blaise **Cendrars:** Frédéric Louis Sauser (1887–1961), Fr. novelist, poet, of Swiss parentage. Sauser is said to have adopted a name that was a blend of the name of St. Blaise, French *braise*, "embers," French *cendres*, "cinders," and Latin *ars*, "skill," "art," with an overall evocation of lines from Nietzsche: "And everything of mine turns to mere cinders / What I love and what I do."

Cephas *see* **Peter**

Luigia **Cerale:** Luigia Cerallo (1859–1937), It. ballet dancer.

C.W. **Ceram:** Kurt W. Marek (1915–1972), Ger.-born U.S. writer, archaeologist. The writer's pen name reversed his real name.

Il **Cerano:** Giovanni Battista Crespi (1575–1632), It. painter. The artist came to be known from his birthplace, Cerano, near Novara, northwest Italy.

Carolus **Cergoly:** Carlo Luigi Cergozzi Serini (1908–1987), It. poet, novelist.

Ceridwen Peris: Alice Gray Jones (1852–1943), Welsh writer, editor. The writer's new first name is that of the goddess said to have been the mother of the legendary 6th-century poet Taliesin. Her second name comes from Llyn Peris, a lake in northwest Wales. Both names are forenames in their own right. Jones was born at Llanllyfni, less than 10 miles from Llyn Peris.

Frederick **Cerny:** Frederick Guthrie (1833–1886), Eng. physicist. The scientist used his pen name for two poems published early in life.

Giacobbe **Cervetto:** Giacobbe Bassevi (*c.*1682–1783), It. cellist, composer, of Jewish parentage, working in England. The musician adopted his new name before settling in London in 1728.

César: César Baldaccini (1921–1998), Fr. sculptor, of It. parentage.

CéU: Maria do Céu Whitaker Poças (1980–), Brazilian singer, songwriter. The musician adopted (and slightly adapted) one of her original names, itself the Portuguese word for "sky," "heaven," pronounced "Say-oo."

Ceulanydd: John Ceulanydd Wlliams (1847–1899), Welsh poet.

Teobaldo **Ceva:** Giovan Roberto (1697–1746), It. writer.

Jacques **Chaban-Delmas:** Jacques Pierre Michel Delmas (1915–2000), Fr. politician. The future prime minister of France (1969–72) took the first part of his surname as his *nom de guerre* in World War II, when active in the Resistance. The name itself is that of the château of Chaban, at St.-Léon-sur-Vézère in the Dordogne, where he set up a network of underground agents.

M.E. **Chaber** *see* Richard **Foster**

Ivan Ivanitz **Chabert:** Julien Xavier Chabert (1792–1859), Fr.-born U.S. magician.

Chad and Jeremy: Chad Stuart (1943–), Eng. pop musician + Jeremy Clyde (1944–), Eng. pop musician.

Chad Gadya *see* Ephraim **Kishon**

Marc **Chagall:** Mark Zakharovich Segal (1887–1985), Russ.-born Fr. artist, of Jewish parentage.

Francis **Chagrin:** Alexander Paucker (1905–1972), Rom.-born Eng. composer.

Jakov **Chaklan** *see* Jakov **Lind**

Chakrapani: Aluri Venkata Subba Rao (?–1975), Ind. movie scenarist, producer.

George **Challis** *see* Max **Brand**

Cham: [Comte] Amédée de Noé (1819–1879), Fr. political caricaturist. The artist was known for his wit. "As Cham or Ham was the second son and scapegrace of Noah, so Amédée was the second son and scapegrace of the comte de Noé" [E. Cobham Brewer, *The Reader's Handbook*, 1882].

Sidney Joseph **Chamberlain** *see* John **Gilmore**

Marilyn **Chambers:** Marilyn Ann Briggs (1952–2009), U.S. model, porno movie actress. After taking up modeling in her teens, the actress first appeared in the movies in 1970 under the name Evelyn Lang.

Whittaker **Chambers:** Jay Vivian Chambers (1901–1961), U.S. journalist. When the future magazine editor's parents separated in 1908, he called himself David Whittaker, with his mother's maiden name. By the time he graduated from high school, he was calling himself Charles Adams. He subsequently enrolled at Columbia University as Whittaker Chambers, and essentially kept the name, although

also using a number of aliases, such as Karl Phillips and Harold Phillips, when working for the Communist underground.

Nicolas de **Chamfort:** Nicolas-Sébastien Roch (*c*.1740–1794), Fr. moralist.

Claude **Champagne:** Adonaï Desparois (1891–1965), Can. composer.

Champfleury: Jules-François-Félix Husson (1821–1889), Fr. novelist, journalist. Jules Husson was Jules Fleury before he became Champfleury, and the latter name must have evolved from the former. It was probably suggested by *Champfleury* ("Flowery Field"), a work by the 16th-century grammarian Geoffrey Tory, which encouraged the writing of learned works in French instead of the traditional Latin.

Harry **Champion:** William Henry Crump (1866–1942), Br. stage comedian, singer. The performer originally appeared as Will Conray before assuming his regular stage name in 1887.

Marge **Champion:** Marjorie Celeste Belcher (1921–), U.S. movie actress, dancer. The actress was initially billed as Marjorie Bell, based on her maiden name, before taking the name of her dancer, actor, and director husband, Gower Champion, with whom she featured in the 1950s.

La **Champmeslé:** Marie Desmares (1642–1698), Fr. actress. The actress came to be known from the name of her second husband, actor Charles Chevillet Champmeslé, whom she married in 1666.

Jackie **Chan:** Chan Kwong Sang (or Chan Gang-shen) (1954–), Hong Kong movie actor, director.

James **Chance:** James Siegfried (1953–), U.S. rock musician.

John T. **Chance:** John Howard Carpenter (1948–), U.S. movie director, writer. Carpenter edited *Assault on Precinct 13* (1976) under this name, retaining his real name as this movie's director, screenwriter, and music composer. The name itself is that of John **Wayne**'s character in the classic western *Rio Bravo* (1959) on which *Assault on Precinct 13* is ostensibly based. "Pseudonyms are rampant throughout Carpenter's work.... Realising that too many occurrences of the same name in the credits can be detrimental to a film's distribution (because it looks cheap), alter egos begin to emerge" [Colin Odell and Michelle Le Blanc, *John Carpenter*, 2001]. Carpenter was screenwriter of *Prince of Darkness* (1987) as Martin Quatermass, while credited as director under his real name. The movie's storyline has clearly been influenced by the writings of Nigel Kneale, particularly his TV play *Quatermass and the Pit* (1958), and this is probably the source of Carpenter's pseudonym here.

Gene **Chandler:** Eugene Dixon (1937–), U.S.

pop singer, record producer. The musician adopted his new name from that of his favorite actor, Jeff **Chandler**.

Jeff **Chandler**: Ira Grossel (1918–1961), U.S. radio, movie actor.

Lane **Chandler**: Robert Lane Oakes (1899–1972), U.S. movie actor.

Fay **Chandos**: Irene Maude Swatridge, née Mossop (c.1905–1993), Eng. romantic novelist. The writer also published as Theresa Charles, Leslie Lance, and Jan Tempest.

Coco **Chanel**: Gabrielle Bonheur Chanel (1883–1971), Fr. fashion designer. The name adopted by the creator of Chanel No. 5 perfume has been variously explained. "Traditionally, her nickname 'Coco' was earned by her habit of riding in the Bois [de Boulogne] when the cocks were still crowing 'co-corico,' but she later claimed it was merely a respectable version of 'cocotte'" [*The Times*, January 6, 1971]. More likely, it arose as a stage nickname from one of the cabaret songs that she sang, "Ko Ko Ri Ko" ("Cock-a-dooodle-doo") or "Qui qu'a vu Coco dans le Trocadéro?" ("Who has seen Coco at the Trocadero?").

Frances **Chaney**: Fanya Lipetz (1915–2004), U.S. radio actress, of Ukr. parentage.

Lon **Chaney, Jr.**: Creighton Tull Chaney (1906–1973), U.S. movie actor. The actor always harbored a desire to emulate his father Lon (originally Leonidas) Chaney (1883–1930), "The Man of a Thousand Faces," and accordingly adopted his first name. "He often grumbled that he was 'starved' into changing his name to capitalize on his father's stardom, and dropped the 'Junior' from 1942 onward" [Schneider, p. 146].

Henrietta Baker **Chanfrau**: Jeannette Davis (1837–1909), U.S. actress. The actress made her debut in 1854 under the stage name Henrietta Baker. In 1858 she married actor Frank Chanfrau (1824–1884) and after her marriage acted under the name "Mrs. Chanfrau."

Chang: Juan Pablo Jesorum (1889–1972), Chin.-Panamanian illusionist.

Jung **Chang**: Er-hong Chang (1952–), Chin. writer, working in U.K. The doctor attending the writer's birth exclaimed, "Ah, another wild swan is born." Hence her original name, Er-hong, "second wild swan." She acquired her new name at the age of 12, following a comment by a politics teacher that Communist China could change color "from bright red to faded red."

"It so happened that the Sichuan expression 'faded red' had exactly the same pronunciation (*er-hong*) as my name ... I felt I must get rid of my name immediately. That evening I begged my father to give me another name ... I told my father that I wanted 'something with a military ring to it' ... My new name, Jung (pronounced 'Yung'), was a very old and recondite word for 'martial affairs' ... It evoked an image of bygone battles between knights in shining armor, with tasseled spears and neighing steeds. When I turned up at school with my new name even some teachers could not recognize the [Chinese] character" [Jung Chang, *Wild Swans: Three Daughters of China*, 1991].

Stockard **Channing**: Susan Williams Antonia Stockard Channing Schmidt (1944–), U.S. movie, TV actress. The actress born Susan Stockard arrived at her professional identity by combining her surname with that of her first husband, Walter Channing.

Joy **Chant**: Eileen Joyce Rutter (1945–), Br. writer of fantasy fiction.

Mlle. **Chantilly**: Marie-Justine-Benoiste Duronceray (1727–1772), Fr. actress.

Octave **Chanute**: Octave Chanut (1832–1910), Fr.-born U.S. engineer, aeronautical experimenter. Chanut early added an *e* to his name "as a mark of Americanization and a means of suggesting the proper pronunciation of his name" [Tom D. Crouch in Garraty and Carnes, vol. 4, p. 685].

Chapelle: Claude-Emmanuel Lhuillier (1626–1686), Fr. poet. The poet was born in La-Chapelle-Saint-Denis, Paris.

Martin **Chapender**: Harold M. Jones (c.1876–1905), Eng. conjuror.

Saul **Chaplin**: Saul Kaplan (1912–1997), U.S. movie music composer, musical director.

Charbon *see* Belinda **Blinders**

Jacques **Chardonne**: Jacques Boutelleau (1884–1968), Fr. novelist.

Yegishe **Charents**: Yegishe Abgarovich Sogomonyan (1897–1937), Armenian poet. The poet's adopted name means "of indomitable lineage."

Chargesheimer: Karl Heinz Hargesheimer (1924–1971), Ger. photographer. The photographer first used his name in 1948 on submitting work to *Stern* magazine.

Cyd **Charisse**: Tula Ellice Finklea (1922–2008), U.S. movie actress, dancer. The surname by which the actress became known was that of her first husband, dance teacher Nico Charisse, whom she married in 1939. She retained the name although soon divorcing him and marrying actor and singer Tony **Martin**. As a young child she was called "Sid" by her baby brother, his attempt to say "sis." She adopted the name, but respelled it "Cyd." When she first danced as a teenager for the the Ballet Russe de Monte Carlo she was given the pseudo–Russian names Maria Istomina and Felia Sidorova. (Istomina may have been an intentional pun on Russian *istomit,* "to weary," while Felia suggests Finklea, her original name, and Sidorova may have been based on "Cyd.") She started in films in 1943, when she played bit parts as Lily Norwood. She finally became Cyd Charisse when she was put under contract by MGM in 1946.

Charlene: Charlene Duncan (1950–), U.S. pop singer.

Charles XIV: [Count] Jean-Baptiste Bernadotte (1763–1844), Fr.-born king of Sweden. Bernadotte rose to be a high-ranking officer in the French army and was held in favor by Napoleon when campaigning against Sweden in 1809. In 1810 he he was elected Swedish crown prince, mainly through Sweden's wish to retain Napoleon's goodwill, but also as a result of financial promises from Bernadotte himself. He was adopted as son by the elderly childless reigning king, Charles XIII (1748–1818), and took the name of Charles John (Karl Johan). On the death of Charles XIII the prince became king of Sweden and Norway, taking the regnal name and number of Charles XIV John (Karl XIV Johan). His family still reigns today.

Bobby Charles: Robert Charles Guidry (1938–2010), U.S. singer, songwriter.

Don Charles: Walter Stanley Scuffham (1933–2005), Eng. pop singer.

Gerda Charles: Edna Lipson (1914–1996), Eng. novelist, short-story writer. "Gerda" is a blend of "Gertrude," the writer's mother's first name, and "Edna," her own first name, while "Charles" is a family name.

Harold Charles: Robert Charles A. Fawcett (1885–1960), Austral. children's poet.

Hugh Charles: Charles Hugh Owen Ferry (1907–1995), Br. songwriter.

Kate Charles: Carol Ann Chase, née Fosher (1950–), U.S. crime writer.

Maria Charles: Maria Zena Schneider (1929–), Br. movie, TV actress.

Pamela Charles: Pamela Foster (1932–), Eng. stage actress, singer. The actress adopted her father's first name as her stage name.

Ray Charles: Ray Charles Robinson (1930–2004), U.S. black popular singer. Robinson dropped his surname so as not to be confused with the champion boxer Sugar Ray **Robinson**.

Teddy Charles: Theodore Charles Cohen (1928–), U.S. jazz musician.

Aunt Charlotte: Charlotte Mary Yonge (1823–1901), Eng. novelist, children's writer. The author used this name for a series of historical works for children, beginning with *Aunt Charlotte's Stories of English History* (1873).

Charlotte Elizabeth: Charlotte Elizabeth Tonna, earlier Phelan, née Browne (1790–1846), Eng.

writer of evangelical books for children. Tonna published under her first names alone in order to protect her income from the claims of her first husband after the couple separated in around 1824.

John Charlton: Martin Charlton Woodhouse (1932–), Eng. novelist, mystery writer. Woodhouse adopted a family name (his existing middle name) for his "rather violent detective story," *The Remington Set* (1975). This was full of cops and robbers and four-letter words, so a different name was desirable in order not to shock his regular readers.

Lloyd Charmers: Lloyd Tyrell (1938–), Jamaican reggae musician. In 1962 Tyrell formed a ska duo with Roy Willis as the Charmers. When the partnership dissolved in the late 1960s, he adopted the name for himself.

Charo: Maria del Rosario Pilar Martinez Molina Baeza (1948–), Can. folk singer.

Mikhas Charot: Mikhail Semyonovich Kudzelka (1896–1938), Belorussian poet. The poet's adopted plant name means "reed," "rush."

Lidiya Charskaya: Lidiya Alekseyevna Churilova (1875–1937), Russ. writer, actress. An alteration of an awkward-sounding surname to a more euphonious one.

Leslie Charteris: Leslie Charles Bowyer Yin (1907–1993), Singapore-born U.S. thriller writer, of Eng.-Chin. parentage. The creator of the debonair hero Simon Templar (criminal alias "The Saint") adopted his new name by deed poll in 1926, taking it from the colorful Scottish criminal Colonel Francis Charteris (1675–1732).

Charybdis: Chris L. Poole (1951–), Br. crossword compiler. The setter's pseudonym refers to the sea whirlpool of classical mythology, as "sea whirlpool" in its spoken form sounds like "C.L. Poole."

Leon Chasanowitsch: Kasriel Schub (1882–1925), Pol. Jewish publicist, labor leader. The surname is sometimes rendered in the Russian form Kazanovich.

Alida Chase: Alida Anderson (1951–), Austral. ballet dancer.

Beatrice Chase: Olive Katharine Parr (1874–1955), Eng. novelist. Chase was the middle name of the writer's father, Charles Chase Parr.

Bill Chase: William Edward Chiaiese (1934–1974), U.S. jazz trumpeter, composer.

Borden Chase: Frank Fowler (1900–1971), U.S. screenwriter. The writer took his name from the well-known food company (Borden) and bank (Manhattan Chase).

Brandon Chase: Alan Gary Zekley (1943–1996), U.S. rock songwriter.

Charley Chase: Charles Parrott (1893–1940), U.S. movie comedian. Chase also worked as a movie director under his original name, and *Picture Show* reported on December 11, 1926, that he had legally changed his name from Parrott to Chase. His first name was sometimes spelled "Charlie" in billings. The name as a whole suggests "Chase Me Charlie," a popular song of the turn of the 20th century.

Chevy **Chase:** Cornelius Crane Chase (1944–), U.S. movie actor. The actor's grandmother nicknamed him "Chevy" after Chevy Chase, Maryland, the Washington, DC, residential suburb. Its own name is said to derive from a form of French *chevauchée,* "cavalcade," adopted in English for a mounted raid on enemy territory, but is more likely to come from the battle of Chevy Chase (1388), at Otterburn, Northumberland, England, near the Scottish border, when the Scots defeated Henry Percy ("Hotspur"), especially as the skirmish was the (romanticized) subject of the 15th-century *Ballad of Chevy Chase.* The name here is understood as "Cheviot chase," meaning the chase or hunt of the Earl of Douglas among the Cheviot Hills for Percy of Northumberland.

James Hadley **Chase:** René Brabazon Raymond (1906–1985), Eng. crime writer. The American-style name is appropriate for an author whose fiction was set in the United States. Raymond also wrote as James L. Docherty, Ambrose Grant, and Raymond Marshall.

John Baptist Claude **Chatelaine:** Jean-Baptiste Claude Philippe (1710–1771), Eng. draftsman, engraver, of Fr. parentage.

Geoffrey **Chater:** Geoffrey Michael Chater Robinson (1921–), Eng. stage, movie, TV actor.

Theobald **Chaubert** *see* Berthold **Auerbach**

Daniel **Chaucer** *see* Ford Madox **Ford**

Chaval: Yvan Le Louarn (1915–1968), Fr. cartoonist.

Paddy **Chayefsky:** Sidney Aaron Chayefsky (1923–1981), U.S. playwright, screenwriter. Chayefsky was an ill-disciplined and indolent soldier when serving in the army in Germany, and was nicknamed Paddy for his attempts to get out of kitchen duty by saying he had to attend Catholic mass. Some sources give his original surname as Stuchevsky, but that was his mother's maiden name.

Chubby **Checker:** Ernest Evans (1941–), U.S. black pop singer, dancer. The name originated as a punning nickname, comparing the musician to Fats **Domino**, whom he resembled when young ("fat" to "chubby," "domino" to "checker"). The nickname was given him by the wife of U.S. DJ Dick Clark.

Cheech: Richard Anthony Marin (1946–), U.S. stand-up comic, movie comedian, teaming with **Chong.** Marin is said to have earned his nickname

from his fondness for the Chicano food specialty cheecharone (chicharones), a type of crackling. The duo broke in 1985 because of creative differences.

Cheero: George Ernest Studdy (1878–1948), Eng. cartoonist, illustrator. The artist used this name for his drawings for comic postcards.

Chefalo: Ralfo Cefalo (1885–1963), It.-born magician.

Cheiro: William Warner (1866–1936), Ir.-born U.S. writer on palmistry. Warner liked to claim he was really Count Louis le Warner de Hamon. He took his professional name from the Greek element "cheir-" meaning "hand" that gave English "cheiromancy," otherwise palmistry. The title pages of some of Cheiro's books inform readers that the name is "pronounced KI-RO."

Antosha **Chekhonte:** Anton Pavlovich Chekhov (1860–1904), Russ. short-story writer, dramatist. The name was humorously given to the young Anton by Fr. Pokrovsky, his scripture teacher at school in Taganrog, and Chekhov adopted it for several early, lighter writings in various magazines. In 1886 he explained to a journalist: "The pen name 'A. Chekhonte' may seem somewhat weird and wonderful, but it arose back in the hazy days of my youth. I have gotten used to it, and so no longer regard it as strange." It was not Chekhov alone that Pokrovsky selected for this treatment, however, and he liked giving amusing names to his students generally.

Chekhov used the name for his first book, *Tales of Melpomene* (1884), but was advised to use his real name for his second, *Motley Stories* (1886). His response: "I don't see why the public should prefer 'An. Chekhov' to 'A. Chekhonte.' Is there really any difference? ... I have devoted my surname to medicine, which will stay with me to my dying day. Sooner or later I shall have to give up writing anyway. Secondly, there should be different names for medicine, which takes itself seriously, and for the hobby of writing." In the event he used A. Chekhonte for *Motley Stories* but added his real name in brackets. For his third book, *In the Gloaming* (1887), he not only abandoned his pseudonym but gave his full initials, "An. P.," to avoid any confusion with his brother Alexander, also a writer [Dmitriyev, p.95].

Chekhov used over 40 pseudonyms at one time or another, including (in translation) "A Doctor With No Patients," "A Man With No Spleen," "My Brother's Brother," and "A Prosaic Poet."

Joan **Chen:** Chen Chong (1961–), Chin.-born U.S. movie actress. Chinese "Chong" has here become English "Joan."

Pierre **Chenal:** Pierre Cohen (1903–1991), Fr. movie director.

Cher: Cherilyn Sarkisian LaPiere (1946–), U.S.

pop singer, movie actress, formerly teaming with husband **Sonny**.

Marko **Cheremshina:** Ivan Yuryevich Semanyuk (1874–1927), Ukr. writer. The writer adopted a plant name meaning "bird-cherry tree."

Rose **Chéri:** Rose-Marie Cizos (1824–1861), Fr. actress.

Gwen **Cherrell:** Gwen Chambers (1926–), Eng. stage actress.

Neneh **Cherry:** Neneh Mariann Karlsson (1964–), Br. rock singer, of Swe.-African parentage. The singer adopted the name of her stepfather, jazz trumpeter Don Cherry.

C.J. **Cherryh:** Carolyn Janice Cherry (1942–), U.S. SF, fantasy novelist.

Weatherby **Chesney:** Charles John Cutliffe Wright Hyne (1865–1944), Eng. traveler, novelist.

Leonard **Chess:** Lazar Shmuel Czyz (1917–1969), Pol.-born U.S. recording executive. Chess was raised in Chicago, where his immigrant family settled in 1928. In 1946 he and his brother, Phil, founded Aristocrat Records, recording blues artists such as Muddy **Waters**. In 1950 Aristocrat was succeeded by Chess Records. The company was sold off in 1975, and in 1997 Leonard's son, Marshall Chess (1942–), together with a cousin, Kevin Chess, founded Czyz Records.

Betty **Chester:** Elizabeth Grundtvig (1895–1943), Br. stage, movie actress.

Charlie **Chester:** Cecil Victor Manser (1914–1997), Br. stage actor, entertainer.

Norley **Chester:** Emily Underdown (*fl.*1900s), Br. novelist. The writer appears to have taken her genderless name from the village of Norley, Cheshire, and the nearby city of Chester.

Denise **Chesterton** *see* Denise **Robins**

Robert **Chetwyn:** Robert Suckling (1933–), Br. stage actor.

Leslie **Cheung:** Cheung Kwok Wing (1956–2003), Hong Kong movie actor.

Maria **Chevska:** Maria Elizabeth Skwarczewska (1948–), Br. painter.

Peter **Cheyney:** Reginald Evelyn Peter Southouse-Cheyney (1896–1951), Ir. crime novelist.

Minoru **Chiaki:** Katsuji Sasaki (1917–1999), Jap. movie actor.

Walter **Chiari:** Walter Annichiarico (1924–1991), It. movie actor.

Sonny **Chiba:** Sadao Maeda (1939–), Jap. movie actor, martial arts champion.

Chic: Cyril Alfred Jacob (1926–), Eng. cartoonist, illustrator. The artist's signature arose as a contraction of his childhood nickname "Chickabiddy."

Judy **Chicago:** Judy Gerowitz, née Cohen (1939–), U.S. feminist artist. The artist adopted her new name in 1970 from the city of her birth.

Chicken Chest: Alton O'Reilly (1962–), Jamaican pop musician.. On quitting school the future DJ worked at his brother's Fried Chicken restaurant in downtown Kingston, where he often entertained the customers by chanting in a DJ style. This gave his adopted name, which he personified in his one hit, "Ragamuffin Selector," sung while strutting and beating his chest, with the odd crowing thrown in.

El **Chiclanero:** José Redondo (1818–1853), Sp. bullfighter. The matador was born in Chiclana, near Cadiz in southwest Spain, the birthplace of his master, El **Paquiro**, and adopted the name accordingly.

Chief Thundercloud: (1) Victor Daniels (1899–1955), Native American movie actor; (2) Scott Williams (1901–1967), U.S. radio, movie actor, of Native American descent.

Billy **Childish:** William Charles Hamper (1959–), Br. writer, artist, musician. Hampert adopted his new name in 1977 from the nickname he was given as a teenager in a punk band.

Charles B. **Childs:** Charles Vernon Frost (1903–), Eng. mystery writer.

Chim: David Szymin (1911–1956), U.S. photojournalist, of Pol. Jewish parentage. On moving from Poland to France in 1933, Szymin created an abbreviated phonetic form of his surname, originally spelling it "CHIM" (pronounced "Sheem") in capital letters. He later used the name David Seymour as an anglicized form of his original name.

Ching Ling Foo: Chee Ling Qua (1854–1922), Ch.-born magician.

Chinko: Thomas Cromwell-Knox (1880–1943), Eng. stage juggler, brother of Teddy **Knox**.

Will **Chip:** Hannah More (1745–1833), Eng. playwright, religious writer. The author used this name for a tract of 1793 on the reform of the conditions of the poor, with full title: *Village Politics, Addressed to All Mechanics, Journeymen, and Day Labourers in Great Britain. By Will Chip, a Country Carpenter.*

Chipmunk: Jahmaal Noel Fyffe (1991–), Br. black hip-hop, "grime" artist.

Chiquito de Cambo: Joseph Apesteguy (1881–1955), Fr. Basque pelota player. The sportsman adopted his Spanish nickname, meaning "The Kid from Cambo." He was born in the southwest of France near the Spanish border in the small resort town of Cambo-les-Bains.

Chiquito d'Eibar: Indalecio Sarasqueta (1860–1928), Sp. Basque pelota player. The player's name means "The Kid from Eibar," referring to the Basque city in northern Spain where he beat Spain's reigning pelota champion at the young age of 16.

Chiranjeevi: Shivashankara Varaprasad (1955–), Ind. movie actor.

Chiyonofuji: Akimoto Mitsugu (1955–), Jap. sumo wrestler. The champion wrestler was granted a *shikona* (fighting name) meaning "Fuji of a thousand generations" (Japanese *chi*, "thousand" + *yo*, "world," "age," "generation" + *no*, "of ").

Hans **Chlumberg:** Hans Bardach, Edler von Chlumberg (1897–1930), Austr. dramatist.

Chocolat: Rafael Padilla (1868–1917), Cuban circus clown, teaming with George **Footit**. Chocolat was a mulatto, so named for his skin color.

El **Chocolate:** Antonio de la Santisima Trinidad Núñez Montoya (1930–2005), Sp. flamenco singer. The singer adopted his nickname, given him for his warm, rich voice rather than for his dark skin.

Gali **Chokry:** Mukhammetgali Gabdelsalikhovich Kiyekov (1826–1889), Russ. (Bashkir) poet. The writer adopted the name of his native village as his new surname.

Chong: Thomas B. Kin Chong (1938–), Can. stand-up comic, movie comedian, teaming with **Cheech**.

Chop Chop: Alvin H. Wheatley (1901–1964), Austral.-born magician, working in U.S.

Manolo **Chopera:** Manuel Martínez Flamarique (1928–2002), Sp. bullfight promoter. The taurophile was so nicknamed by his father, also in the bullfight business, from his habit of calling into bars up and down Spain and asking for a *chopera*, or glass of wine. "Manolo" is a pet form of "Manuel."

Kuzma **Chorny:** Nikolay Karlovich Romanovsky (1900–1944), Belorussian writer. The writer's adopted surname means "black," presumably referring to his appearance. Compare the name of Sasha **Chyorny**.

Professeur **Choron:** Georges Bernier (1929–2005), Fr. satirical journalist.

George **Chowdharay-Best:** Vijay Chowdharay (1935–2000), Ind.-born Br. lexicographer. After his father died in 1959, the writer was baptized into the Church of England and altered his first name to the Christian name George while adding Best, the name of the girl he hoped to marry, to his surname.

Chris: Ernest Alfred Wren (1908–1982), Eng. cartoonist, illustrator. The artist was nicknamed "Chris Wren" after the architect Sir Christopher Wren (1632–1723), of whom he was a descendant, and derived his pen name from this. He also used the name "Christopher."

Lena **Christ:** Magdalena Benedix, née Bichler (1881–1920), Ger. writer. The writer was illegitimate, and adopted her stepfather's surname.

Ada **Christen:** Christiane Frideriks (1844–1901), Austr. actress, writer.

Christian: Christian Stelzel (1945–), Austr. ma-

gician. The entertainer is usually billed as "Magic Christian," a name perhaps suggested by the 1969 movie *The Magic Christian*.

Linda **Christian:** Bianca Rosa Welter (1923–), Mexican movie actress, of part-Du. parentage.

Neil **Christian:** Christopher Tidmarsh (1943–), Eng. pop musician.

Paul **Christian:** Paul Hubschmid (1917–), Swiss-born movie actor, working in Germany, U.S. The actor took his new name in 1949 when offered work in Hollywood. He returned to Germany a few years later, where he reverted to his original name, but continued to be known as Paul Christian in the English-speaking world on account of his films that had reached the international market.

Christian-Jaque: Christian Albert François Maudet (1904–1994), Fr. movie director, writer.

Lou **Christie:** Lugee Alfredo Giovanni Sacco (1943–), U.S. pop singer.

Tony **Christie:** Anthony Fitzgerald (1944–), Eng. pop musician.

Miss **Christine:** Christine Frka (1950–1972), U.S. rock musician.

Virginia **Christine:** Virginia Christine Kraft (1917–1996), U.S. movie actress.

Christo: Christo Javacheff (1935–), Bulg.-born U.S. artist, teaming with **Jeanne-Claude**, his wife.

Christodoulos: Christos Paraskevaidis (1939–2008), Gk. religious leader.

Christophe: Georges Colomb (1856–1945), Fr. writer, cartoonist.

A.B. **Christopher** *see* Alexandre **Darlaine**

Dennis **Christopher:** Dennis Carelli (1955–), U.S. movie actor.

John **Christopher:** Christopher Samuel Youd (1922–), Eng. SF novelist, children's writer. Other names used by the writer include Hilary Ford, William Godfrey, Peter Graaf, Peter Nichols, and Anthony Rye.

June **Christy:** Shirley Luster (1925–1990), U.S. jazz singer. The singer first used the name Sharon Leslie before settling on the more musical June Christy in 1945.

Chrys: George Fraser Chrystal (1921–1972), Sc. political, sports cartoonist.

Chrysander: Wilhelm Christophe Juste Goldmann (1718–1778), Ger. historian, theologian. The scholar adopted the Greek equivalent of his family name.

Chryssa: Chryssa Vardea Mavromichaeli (1933–), Gk.-born U.S. sculptor.

Chubb Rock: Richard Simpson (1968–), Jamaican rock musician.

Chuckle Brothers: Paul Elliot (?–), Br. TV comedian + Barry Elliot (1944–), Br. TV comedian, his brother. The brothers became popular for their long-running children's TV show *Chucklevision*.

Korney Ivanovich **Chukovsky:** Nikolay Vasilyevich Korneychukov (1882–1969), Russ. literary critic, children's writer. The writer used his surname to form a new first and last name, at the same time adopting a new patronymic (middle name).

Chulpan: Abdul-Khamid Suleyman ogly Yunusov (1893–1937), Uzbek writer. The writer's adopted name means "morning star."

Chung Ling Soo: William Ellsworth Campbell (1861–1918), U.S. conjuror. The artist originally used the name William E. ("Billy") Robinson in the U.S. When in England in 1900, he modeled himself on a real Chinese conjuror, **Ching Ling Foo**, who had toured successfully in the USA. Ching accused Campbell of being an impostor, and he admitted it. However, this impersonation made him all the more popular with his audiences. The name itself was said to mean "very good luck."

Elizabeth **Churchill** *see* Bruce **Carter**

William **Churne of Staffordshire:** [Rev.] Francis Edward Paget (1806–1882), Eng. clergyman, novelist. The rector of Elford, near Lichfield, Staffordshire, wrote several religious books and a work on churches but used this name for *The Hope of the Katzekopfs* (1844), the first published fantasy for children.

Nikolay **Chuzhak:** Nikolay Fyodorovich Nasimovich (1876–1937), Russ. revolutionary, writer, literary critic. The activist's adopted name means "stranger," "alien."

Chyna: Joan Marie Laurer (1970–), U.S. wrestler. Joanie Laurer first entered the ring as Joanie Lee but was renamed Chyna by Hunter Hearst **Helmsley**, who hired her as his bodyguard in 1997. Presumably the name is a short (and respelled) form of "China doll," a slang term for a beautiful woman. (Foxy **Brown**'s second album, released in 1999, was called *Chyna Doll*.)

Sasha **Chyorny:** Aleksandr Mikhaylovich Glikberg (1880–1932), Russ. poet. The poet's adopted surname means "black," presumably referring to his appearance. Glikberg was not too pleased when in the 1910s another writer, the humorist Aleksandr Sokolov, started signing his work with exactly the same name. Compare the name of Kuzma **Chorny**.

La **Cicciolina:** Ilona Staller (1955–), Hung.-born It. porno movie actress, politician. The media personality accepted her (pet) nickname, which means "the little plump one" (Italian *ciccia*, "fat").

Cicero: Elyesa Bazna (1904–1970), Albanian spy. The secret agent, one of the most famous spies of World War II, worked for Nazi Germany while employed as a valet to Sir Hughe Montgomery Knatchbull-Hugessen, British ambassador to neutral Turkey. His code name of Cicero was given him by the former German chancellor, Franz von Papen, "because his information spoke so eloquently." The 1st-century BC Roman statesman Marcus Tullius Cicero was a noted orator. (Compare the entry below.)

Marcus Tullius **Cicero:** William Melmoth the Elder (1666–1743), Eng. religious writer, lawyer. The three-part name was the true one of the 1st-century BC Roman orator. (Compare the entry above.)

Ciceruacchio: Angelo Brunetti (1800–1849), It. revolutionary. The activist adopted his nickname, meaning "crafty Cicero."

The **Cid:** Rodrigo Díaz de Vivar (*c.*1043–1099), Sp. military leader. The Castilian national hero's name, in Spanish *El Cid*, means "the lord" (Arabic *as-saiyid*), the nickname given him by Muslim soldiers, among whom he was very popular. He is also known as *El Campeador*, "the champion."

Aglauro **Cidonia:** Faustina Maratti Zappi (1679–1745), It. poet, wife of Tirsi **Lucasio**. The poet adopted her pseudonym in 1704 on becoming a member of the Academy of Arcadia, the Italian literary circle founded in 1690 with the aim of idealizing pastoral life on classical lines. All of its members assumed pseudonyms, usually consisting of a first name of classical bucolic form and a second name relating to a region of Arcadia in Greece. Her second name was later taken by Lesbia **Cidonia**.

Lesbia **Cidonia:** Paolina Grismondi Secco Suardi (1746–1801), It. poet. The poet adopted this name on entering the Academy of Arcadia (*see* Aglauro **Cidonia**).

Gina **Cigna:** Ginetta Sens, née Cigna (1900–2001), Fr.-born It. opera singer. The soprano made her debut in 1927 as Genoveffa Sens, having married French tenor Maurice Sens in 1923. In 1929 she sang as Gina Cigna, reverting to her maiden name, by which she was known for the rest of her career and long life.

Il **Cigoli:** Ludovico Cardi (1559–1613), It. painter, architect, poet. The artist was named after his birthplace, Cigoli, near Florence.

Cimabue: Bencivieni (or Cenni) di Pepo (*c.*1240–*c.*1302), It. painter, mosaicist. The name reveals something of the artist's proud and impetuous nature. It arose as a nickname, and means effectively "bullheaded," from Italian *cima*, "top," "head," and *bue*, "ox."

Cino da Pistoia: Cino dei Sighibuldi (*c.*1270–1336), It. poet, jurist. The writer is named for his native town of Pistoia, near Florence.

Paul **Cinquevalli:** Emile Otto Lehmann-Braun (1859–1918), Pol.-born U.S. juggler. The performer adopted the name of his tutor in the art, Giuseppe

Chiese-Cinquevalli. His original name is given in some sources as Paul Kestner.

A **Citizen of New York**: Alexander Hamilton (1737–1804), U.S. statesman + James Madison (1751–1836), U.S. president + John Jay (1745–1829), U.S. jurist, statesman. The three men adopted the unified name for their essays in the *Federalist* in favor of the new U.S. Constitution (1787–88). They subsequently adopted the joint name **Publius**.

Louis **CK**: Louis Szekely (1968–), U.S. comedian. The initials represent a simplified form of the comic's original Hungarian surname.

Tim **Cladpole**: Richard Lower (1782–1865), Eng. dialect poet. Lower took this name for *Tom Cladpole's Journey to Lunnon, told by himself, and written in pure Sussex doggerel by his Uncle Tim* (1831). A later composition was *Jan Cladpole's Trip to Merricur, written all in rhyme by his Father, Tim Cladpole* (1844), directed against the evils of slavery.

Mavis **Clair**: Mavis Tunnell (1916–), Eng. stage actress. It is possible the actress took her name from the character Mavis Clair in Marie **Corelli**'s novel *The Sorrows of Satan* (1895).

René **Clair**: René-Lucien Chomette (1898–1981), Fr. movie director. Chomette first adopted the name as an actor in 1920. French *clair* means "clear," "bright," "light," so that the name presumably relates to "Lucien" (Latin *lux, lucis*, "light"). It happens to be suitable for the director's art and style.

Bernice **Claire**: Bernice Jahnigan (1911–), U.S. movie actress.

Ina **Claire**: Ina Fagan (1892–1985), U.S. stage, movie actress. The actress adopted her mother's maiden name as her stage name.

Mlle. **Clairon**: Claire-Josèphe-Hippolyte Léris de la Tude (1723–1803), Fr. tragic actress. The actress's stage name not only echoes her first name but is also the French word for "bugle."

Henrietta **Clandon** *see* John **Haslette**

Eric **Clapton**: Eric Patrick Clapton (1945–), Eng. rock guitarist. The musician's original name is given in many sources as Clapp, but this was the name of Jack Clapp, second husband of his grandmother, Rose, who raised Eric following his birth to Patricia Clapton and a Canadian serviceman.

Ada **Clare**: Jane McElheney (c.1836–1874), U.S. actress, writer. This was the most common pseudonym used by McElheney. She also wrote as Clare and Alastor, and acted as Agnes Stanfield. Her original surname is also given as McEhenney, McElhenney, McElhenny, McEleny, McElhinney, McEthenery, and McEthenney. She actually called herself Ada McElhenny.

Austin **Clare**: Wilhelmina Martha James (c.1845–1932), Eng. writer.

George **Clare**: Georg Klaar (1920–2009), Austr. writer, businessman, of Jewish parentage, working in U.K. After settling in Britain to escape Nazi persecution, the author anglicized his name on joining the Royal Artillery in 1943.

Claribel: Charlotte Barnard, née Alington (1830–1869), Eng. writer of popular ballads. The poet, now remembered only for "Come back to Erin" (1866), formed her name from letters in her real name. "Claribel" also exists as a literary name implying "bright and beautiful," as a poet or singer should be.

Clarín: Leopoldo Enrique García Alas y Ureña (1852–1901), Sp. novelist, critic. The writer's pen name means "bugle," and refers to his prominent critical "voice." Leopoldo Alas (as he was usually known) was a highly influential critic, and his articles were noted for their "bite" and belligerence.

Clarinda: Agnes McLehose, née Craig (1758–1841), Sc. letter writer. In 1787 Mrs. McLehose met Robert Burns at a soirée and began a correspondence with the poet. For the purposes of this he named her Clarinda, while he was **Sylvander**. The name had earlier been adopted by the English poet Sarah Egerton, previously Field, née Fyge (between 1669 and 1672–1722).

Al C. **Clark**: Donald Goines (1937–1974), U.S. black novelist. Goines published under his own name until 1974, when his publishers asked him to adopt a pen name. He chose that of a friend, Al C. Clark.

Buddy **Clark**: Samuel Goldberg (1912–1949), U.S. popular singer.

Dane **Clark**: Bernard Zanville (1913–1998), U.S. movie actor. The actor was billed under his real name until the early 1940s, when he was signed by Warner Bros., who renamed him Dane Clark "in a clear attempt to make him the new John **Garfield**" [Maltin, p.153].

Emily **Clark** *see* Greta **Garbo**

Jean **Clark** *see* Greta **Garbo**

Joan **Clark** *see* Carolyn **Keene**

Ossie **Clark**: Raymond Clark (1942–1996), Eng. fashion designer. The artist's new first name arose as a nickname, itself from the town of Oswaldtwistle, Lancashire, where he was raised in World War II.

Petula **Clark**: Petula Sally Olwen Clark (1932–), Eng. popular singer, movie actress. Many sources give the singer's original name as "Sally Owen" [*sic*].

Susan **Clark**: Nora Golding (1940–), Can.-born U.S. movie actress.

Rev. T. **Clark**: John Galt (1779–1839), Sc. novelist, poet. Galt used this name for *The Wandering Jew; or, The Travels and Observations of Hareach the Prolonged* (1820). For the astute reader, he encoded his real name in the first letters of the sentences in the book's final paragraph: "If," "Over," "History," "Nevertheless," "Greatness," "All," "Literally," "To." (The "I" of "If" is the "J" of "John.") Galt also wrote as Micah Balwhidder, Nathan Butt, Thomas Duffle, Archibald Jobbry, and Samuel Prior.

J.P. Clark-Bekederemo: John Pepper Clark (1935–), Nigerian poet.

George Clarke: George Broome (1886–1946), Eng. stage, movie actor.

John Clarke: Richard Cromwell (1626–1712), Eng. soldier, politician. The eldest son of Oliver Cromwell used this name when living in seclusion in Paris from 1659 to 1680.

Kenny Clarke: Kenneth Clarke Spearman (1914–1985), U.S. black jazz drummer, bandleader. Spearman dropped his surname after moving to New York City in 1935. He was also known by the Muslim name Liaqat Ali Salaam and by the nickname "Klook," short for "Klookmop," referring to his unexpectedly accented beats on the drums. (It is also, of course, close to "Clarke.")

Mae Clarke: Mary Klotz (1907–1992), U.S. movie actress. "Mae" from "Mary" and "Clarke" from "Klotz."

Michael Clarke: Michael James Dick (1946–1993), U.S. rock drummer.

Rev. C.C. Clarke *see* Abbé **Bossut**

Robert Clarke: Robert Graine (?–1675), Eng. priest, writer of Latin poems. The scholar may have adopted a name related etymologically to "cleric," as a clerk was originally a learned or literate person. *See also* Mark **Carrel**.

Shirley Clarke: Shirley Brimberg (1919–1997), U.S. movie director, of Pol. parentage.

Clasio: Luigi Fiacchi (1754–1825), It. poet.

Madame Claude: Fernande Grudet (1924–), Fr. procureuse.

Claude Lorrain: Claude Gellée (1600–1682), Fr. landscape painter. "Lorrain" is not the artist's surname, as sometimes supposed, but represents Lorraine, the region of France where he was born and where, for a short period in 1625, he worked. The name thus means "Claude the Lorrainer," and as such distinguished him from other artists named Claude.

Jean Claudio: Claude Martin (1927–), Fr. juvenile movie actor. The actor was billed as simply Claudio at the start of his career, but then prefixed that with Jean as if it were a surname.

Eduard Claudius: Eduard Schmidt (1911–1976), Ger. writer. The writer adopted his name in honor of the 1st-century AD Roman emperor, scholar, and historian, whom he admired.

H. Clauren: Wilhelm Hauff (1802–1827), Ger. novelist, short-story writer. Hauff used this name for

his novel *Der Mann im Monde* ("The Man in the Moon") (1826), a parody of Heinrich **Clauren**.

Heinrich Clauren: Karl Gottlieb Samuel Heun (1771–1854), Ger. writer. "Clauren" is a near-anagram of "Carl Heun."

Mrs. Mary Clavers: Caroline Matilda Kirkland, née Stansbury (1801–1864), U.S. short-story writer, novelist. The author used this protective name for *A New Home—Who'll Follow?* (1839), a semifictional personal account of Michigan frontier life.

Kate Claxton: Catherine Elizabeth Cone (1848–1924), U.S. actress, theater manager.

Andrew "Dice" Clay: Andrew Clay Silverstein (1958–), U.S. movie comedian.

Bertha M. Clay: Charlotte Monica Braeme (1836–1884), Eng. romantic novelist.

Joe Clay: Claiborne Joseph Cheramie (1939–), U.S. rockabilly guitarist.

Judy Clay: Judy Guions, later Gatewood (1938–2001), U.S. black soul singer. The singer's recording company had wanted to rename her Amanda Knight.

Rosamund Clay: Ann Oakley (1944–), Br. writer.

Tom Clay: Thomas Clayque (1929–1995), U.S. DJ.

Richard Clayderman: Philippe Pages (1953–), Fr. popular pianist. The pianist's original surname was liable to be mispronounced abroad. It was thus altered by composers and record producers Olivier Toussaint and Paul de Senneville to that of his great-grandmother.

Jay Clayton: Judith Colantone (1941–), U.S. jazz singer.

Lou Clayton: Louis Finkelstein (1887–1950), U.S. vaudeville actor.

Lucie Clayton: Evelyn Florence Kark, née Gordine (1928–1997), Eng. fashion designer. The charm-school head assumed the name of the existing Lucie Clayton Model and Charm School founded in 1928 by Sylvia Golledge.

Claudius Clear: [Sir] William Robertson Nicoll (1851–1923), Sc. journalist, editor. The writer used this name for a series of letters published in the *British Weekly*, of which he was editor, as well as for *Letters on Life* (1901). Two further selections of letters appeared subsequently as *The Day Book of Claudius Clear* (1905) and *A Bookman's Letters* (1913). As W.E. Wace he wrote an early (1881) book on Tennyson, while other names were Man of Kent and O.O.

Eddy Clearwater: Edward Harrington (1935–), U.S. blues musician, cousin of Carey **Bell**. The musician turned his nickname into a new surname.

Lucas Cleeve: Adeline Georgina Isabella Kingscote, née Wolff (1860–1908), Eng. novelist.

Jedediah Cleishbotham: [Sir] Walter Scott

(1771–1832), Sc. poet, novelist. One of the humorous pen names devised by the Scottish writer. (Others were Chrystal Croftangry and Captain Cuthbert Clutterbuck.) This particular name was used for the four series of his *Tales of My Landlord* (1816), with the author supposedly a schoolmaster and parish clerk. The name ties in well with these two roles: "Jedediah" is a typical Puritan name, and "Cleishbotham" means "whip-bottom" (Scottish dialect *cleish*, "to whip"). A writer in the January, 1817, number of the *Quarterly Review* commented: "Why he should industriously endeavour to elude observation by taking leave of us in one character, and then suddenly popping out upon us in another, we cannot pretend to guess without knowing more of his personal reasons for preserving so strict an incognito than has hitherto reached us."

Clemens non Papa: Jacob (or Jacques) Clement (*c.*1510–*c.*1556), Flemish composer. The name or nickname by which the composer is generally known may have been intended (if meaning "not the pope") to distinguish him from **Clement VII**, or (if meaning "not Papa") from the Flemish poet Jacobus Papa, who also lived and worked in his birthtown of Ypres. But such a distinction, especially the first, seem unlikely, if only because the name did not appear on publications until 14 years after the pope's death, and "the probability is that it was a joke" [Kennedy, p.179].

Clement II: Suidger (?–1047), It. pope.

Clement III: Paolo Scolari (?–1191), It. pope.

Clement IV: Guy Folques (or Guido Fulconi) (*c.*1195–1268), Fr. pope.

Clement V: Bertrand de Got (*c.*1260–1314), Fr. pope.

Clement VI: Pierre Roger (1291–1352), Fr. pope.

Clement VII: Giulio de' Medici (1478–1534), It. pope. Clement had wished to keep his original name, presumably to become Julius III, but was dissuaded from doing so by the conclave of cardinals, who pointed out that many popes who had preserved their original names had died in the first year of their pontificates. This was true of certain early popes, some of whom were elderly or ill (or both), such as John V and Conon in the 7th century, although some later pontiffs who took new names also had short reigns. It was certainly true of Marcellus II, one of the few popes in modern times to retain his baptismal name, who died after only three weeks in office (April 9–May 1, 1555).

Clement VIII: Ippolito Aldobrandini (1536–1605), It. pope.

Clement IX: Giulio Rospigliosi (1600–1669), It. pope.

Clement X: Emilio Bonaventura Altieri (1590–1676), It. pope. The pontiff assumed his name in honor of his predecessor, **Clement IX**.

Clement XI: Giovanni Francesco Albani (1649–1721), It. pope.

Clement XII: Lorenzo Corsini (1652–1740), It. pope. The pontiff adopted the name of his patron, **Clement XI**, who had created him cardinal in 1706. He himself gave the name of **Clement XIII**.

Clement XIII: Carlo della Torre Rezzonico (1693–1769), It. pope. The pontiff adopted the name of his patron, **Clement XII**, who had created him cardinal in 1737. He in turn gave the name of **Clement XIV**.

Clement XIV: Giovanni Vincenzo Antonio Ganganelli (1705–1774), It. pope. The pontiff adopted the name of his patron, **Clement XIII**, who had created him cardinal in 1759.

Hal **Clement:** Harry Clement Stubbs (1922–2003), U.S. SF writer.

King **Clement** *see* Baron **Corvo**

Arthur **Clements:** Andrew Clement Baker (1842–1913), Eng. journalist, writer. The writer used this name, a variant on his first two names, for articles in the *Illustrated Sporting and Dramatic News*, of which he became editor.

Cleophil: William Congreve (1670–1729), Eng. dramatist, poet. Congreve used this name, Greek for "lover of fame," for his first published work, the novel *Incognita; or Love and Duty Reconciled* (1692).

E. **Clerihew:** Edmund Clerihew Bentley (1875–1956), Eng. writer. The writer's middle name, which has passed into the language as the term for a type of short comic verse, was his mother's maiden name.

N.W. **Clerk:** Clive Staples Lewis (1898–1963), Ir. novelist, poet, children's writer. C.S. Lewis (as he was usually known) used this name for *A Grief Observed* (1961), written following the death of his wife.

Janita **Cleve** *see* Fenton **Brockley**

Jimmy **Cliff:** James Chambers (1948–), Jamaican reggae singer. The musician changed his name in the early 1960s, choosing "Cliff" because it implied the "heights" to which he aspired.

Laddie **Cliff:** Clifford Albyn Perry (1891–1937), Br. stage, movie comedian, composer.

Charles **Clifford:** William Henry Ireland (1777–1835), Eng. Shakespearean forger.

Lucy Lane **Clifford:** Sophia Lucy Clifford, née Lane (1853–1929), Br. novelist, children's writer. The author wrote as Mrs. W.K. Clifford after the death of her husband, mathematics professor William Kingdon Clifford (1845–1879), whom she had married in 1875.

Martin **Clifford** *see* Frank **Richards**

Vivian Erle **Clifford** *see* Marie **Corelli**

Bill **Clifton:** William August Marburg (1931–), U.S. folk musician.

Patsy **Cline:** Virginia Patterson Hensley (1932–1963), U.S. country singer. The singer's new first name came from her middle name, while her new surname was that of her first husband, Gerald Cline (married 1953, divorced 1957).

Bill **Clinton:** William Jefferson Blythe III (1946–), U.S. president. The 42nd president of the United States (1993–2001) took his surname from his stepfather, Roger Clinton. His biological father, William Jefferson Blythe, Jr., died in an auto accident in 1946, three months before his son was born. Clinton's mother, Virginia Dell Blythe, divorced Roger in 1962 but soon after remarried him.

"Shortly before she took Daddy back, I went down to the courthouse and had my name changed legally from Blythe to Clinton, the name I had been using for years. I'm still not sure exactly why I did it, but I know I really thought I should, partly because [younger brother] Roger was about to start school and I didn't want the differences in our lineage ever to be an issue for him, partly because I just wanted the same name as the rest of my family" [Bill Clinton, *My Life*, 2004].

Walter **Clinton:** William Henry Davenport Adams (1828–1891), Eng. editor, writer.

Clio: (1) Joseph Addison (1672–1719), Eng. poet, dramatist, essayist; (2) Thomas Rickman (1761–1834), Eng. bookseller, reformer. The two names have different origins. For Addison, the letters represented *C*helsea, *L*ondon, *I*slington, the *O*ffice, as the places where he lived and worked. (He was a civil servant, so that "Office" means "government office.") But they could equally represent the individual initials that he used when signing letters to the *Spectator*. And of course they also form the name of Clio, the Muse of history, which was the sense chosen by Rickman. It arose as a nickname when he was a student, for his precocity as a poet and his taste for historical subjects.

Clive: Clive Evans (1933–), Eng. fashion designer.

Colin **Clive:** Colin Clive-Greig (1898–1937), Br. movie actor, working in U.S.

John **Clive:** Clive John Hambley (1938–), Br. movie, TV actor, writer.

Kitty **Clive:** Catherine Raftor (1711–1785), Eng. actress. In 1733 the actress married George Clive, a barrister, and although they soon parted she kept his name for her stage appearances.

Robert **Clobery:** Robert Glynn (1719–1800), Eng. physician, poet. Glynn married his cousin, Lucy Clobery, and took her name on inheriting a considerable property from her father.

Clodion: Claude Michel (1738–1814), Fr. sculptor. The artist came to be known by a diminutive form of his first name.

G. Butler **Clonblough:** Gustav von Seyffertitz (1863–1943), Austr.-born U.S. movie actor. The actor assumed this name, almost as esoteric as the original, in World War I with the aim of disguising his Teutonic provenance. He used it as late as 1919 as director of *The Secret Garden*.

Anacharsis **Cloots:** Jean-Baptiste du Val-de-Grâce, Baron de Cloots (1755–1794), Fr. revolutionary. The self-styled "Orator of Mankind," born into a Prussian family of Dutch descent, chose a name that punningly mocked his aristocratic ancestry, since Greek *anacharsis* means "graceless." But he could equally have intended a reference to the 6th-century BC Scythian traveler and philosopher Anacharsis. "The baron wished by the name to intimate that his own object in life was like that of Anacharsis" [E. Cobham Brewer, *The Reader's Handbook*, 1882].

Roberta **Close:** Luiz Roberto Gambine Moreira (1964–), Brazilian transexual model. Close was born a hermaphrodite but was raised as a boy. Her father turned her out of the family home at the age of 14, and she began her career in 1981 when she appeared almost nude in a magazine called *Close*, from which she adopted her new name. She underwent a sex-change operation in 1989 and subsequently moved to Switzerland, where she lived under the name Luiza Gambine.

Upton **Close:** Josef Washington Hall (1894–1960), U.S. journalist, novelist. When the journalist held a government post in Shantung in World War I, he learned of the Japanese invasion and put "up close" on his messages to indicate his position near the front. This notation later produced his pen name.

Henry Rose **Cloud:** Wohnaxilayhunga (1884–1950), U.S. Native American educator, leader. The educator was born on the Winnebago reservation, Nebraska, the son of Chayskagah (White Buffalo) and Aboogenewingah (Hummingbird). His Indian name means Chief of the Place of Fear (i.e. the battleground), but he was named Henry Cloud by a reservation school administrator. While an undergraduate at Yale he was adopted by Dr. and Mrs. Walter C. Rose, who gave him his middle name.

Colin **Clout:** Edmund Spenser (c.1552–1599), Eng. poet. In giving this name to the central character, a shepherd boy, of *The Shepheardes Calender* (1579), published anonymously, Spenser spelled out in a "Glosse" that he was referring to himself: "Colin Clovte is a name not greatly vsed, and yet haue I sene a Poesie of M. Skeltons vnder that title. But indeede the word Colin is Frenche, and vsed of the French Poete Marot ... in a certein Æglogue. Vnder which name this Poete secretly shadoweth himself, as sometime did Virgil vnder the name of Tityrus, thinking it much fitter, then such Latine names, for the great vnlikelyhoode of the language." "Clout" means "cloth," referring to the shepherd's ragged clothes. (Colin, now thought of as an independent name, originated as a pet form of Nicholas.) As Spenser says, the name was used earlier by John Skelton in his *Collyn Clout* (1521), where Colin is a wandering poet. Spenser revived his own Colin Clout in *Colin Clovts Come Home Againe* (1595), but this time naming himself on the title page as "Ed. Spencer."

Cluff: John Longstaff (1949–), Eng. cartoonist.

Captain Cuthbert **Clutterbuck** *see* Jedediah **Cleishbotham**

Frank **Clune:** Francis Patrick (1909–1971), Austral. author.

Clwydfardd: David Griffiths (1800–1894), Welsh poet. The first Archdruid took a bardic name meaning "bard of Clwyd," referring to the historic region of northeast Wales that was his homeland.

June **Clyde:** June Tetrazini (1909–1987), U.S. movie actress, singer, dancer.

Pierre **Coalfleet:** Frank Cyril Shaw Davison (1893–1960), Can. journalist, writer, working in U.K. The author used this name for four novels published in the 1920s.

Phyllis **Coates:** Gipsy Ann Stell (1925–), U.S. movie actress.

Sheila **Coates** *see* Charlotte **Lamb**

Arnett **Cobb:** Arnette Cleophus Cobbs (1918–1989), U.S. black jazz musician.

Lee J. **Cobb:** Leo Jacob Cobb (1911–1976), U.S. stage, movie, TV actor. The actor's new name essentially concertinas his original name.

William **Cobb:** Jules Hippolyte Lermina (1839–1915), Fr. novelist.

Tom **Cobbleigh:** Walter Raymond (1852–1931), Eng. writer on the countryside. Raymond was born in Somerset, in the West Country, where in the neighboring county of Devonshire is the village of Widecombe in the Moor, famed from an old ballad: "Tom Pearse, Tom Pearse, lend me your grey mare, / All along, down along, out along, lee. / For I want for to go to Widdicombe Fair, / Wi' Bill Brewer, Jan Stewer, Peter Gurney, Peter Davey, Dan'l Whiddon, Harry Hawk, / Old Uncle Tom Cobbleigh and all." Compare the name of Jan **Stewer**.

Roberto **Cobo:** Roberto García Romero (1930–2002), Mexican movie actor.

Charles **Coborn:** Colin Whitton McCallum (1852–1945), Br. music-hall comedian. The artist took his name from Coborn Road, in London's East End.

Cobra: Ewart Everton Brown (1968–), Jamaican reggae musician. Brown was nicknamed Cobra after a character in the G.I. Joe comic books.

Merlin **Cocai:** Teofilo Folengo (1491–1544), It.

poet. The macaronic poet was baptized Gerolamo but took the religious name Teofilo (Theophilus) on becoming a Benedictine monk in 1508. He also wrote as Limemo Pitocco, a partial anagram of his pseudonym, as if from Italian *pitocco*, "miser."

Johannes **Cocceius:** Johannes Koch (1603–1669), Ger. theologian. The scholar's adopted name is a latinized equivalent of the original, meaning "cook."

Cochi: Aurelio Ponzoni (1941–), It. comic stage, TV actor.

Johannes **Cochlaeus:** Johannes Dobeneck (or Dobneck) (1479–1552), Ger. Catholic theologian, musical scholar The scholar's adopted name is Latin for "snail shell" (related English *cockle*), as a rendering of the name of his birthplace, Wendelstein, literally "spiral stone."

Eddie **Cochran:** Edward Cochrane (1938–1960), U.S. rock 'n' roll musician.

Steve **Cochran:** Robert Cochran (1917–1965), U.S. movie actor.

Pindar **Cockloft:** William Irving (1766–1821), U.S. poet. Irving used this name for his contributions to *Salmagundi* (1808), in which Cockloft Hall was a locale. For his first name, *see* Peter **Pindar**. Irving was given his name by his brother, Washington Irving, the two joining with James Kirk Paulding under the communal pseudonym Launcelot **Langstaff**.

Coco: Nikolai Poliakov (1900–1974), Russ.-born Eng. circus clown. The clown's ring name represents the "-ko-" syllable that is found in each of his real names. "Coco" has now become a popular name for any clown, both in English-speaking countries and elsewhere, as for **Koko**, for example.

Cocoa Tea: Calvin Scott (1960–), Jamaican reggae singer. The singer's name arose as a nickname.

Codex: Colin Dexter (1930–), Br. crime fiction writer, crossword compiler. Dexter adopted this apt name as a setter of cryptic crosswords, basing it on his real name.

Commander **Cody:** George Frayne (*c.*1940–), U.S. rock musician.

Diablo **Cody:** Brook Busey-Hunt (1978–), U.S. screenwriter. The writer created her name when working in a strip club, then adopted it permanently after a movie producer asked her to try her hand at a screenplay. "Unaware that Diablo was a cyber-pseudonym, he addressed her as such, and the name stuck" [*Sunday Times*, January 20, 2008].

Iron Eyes **Cody:** Oscar DeCorti (1904–1999), U.S. movie actor, of It. parentage. The actor reinvented himself as an American Indian, taking a name to match. According to some sources, however, he was the son of Thomas Long Plume, a Cherokee Indian, and Frances Salpet, a Cree Indian.

Lew **Cody:** Louis Joseph Coté (1884–1934), U.S. movie actor, of Fr. parentage.

Liza **Cody:** Liza Nassim (1944–), Br. crime writer.

Captain **Coe:** (1) Edward Card Mitchell (1853–1914), Eng. sporting writer, editor; (2) Tom Cosgrove (1902–1978), Eng. sporting writer, editor. The name was apparently passed down to Cosgrove by Mitchell.

Tucker **Coe** *see* Richard **Stark**

Brian **Coffey** *see* Leigh **Nichols**

Geoffrey **Coffin:** F. Van Wyck Mason (1901–1978), U.S. suspense writer, author of historical novels. Mason adopted his mother's maiden name for this pseudonym. He also wrote as Ward Weaver.

Joshua **Coffin:** Henry Wadsworth Longfellow (1807–1882), U.S. poet, writer. Longfellow used this name for *A Sketch of the History of Newbury* (1845).

George M. **Cohan:** George Michael Keohane (1878–1942), U.S. stage actor, playwright, director, producer.

Émile **Cohl:** Émile Courtet (1857–1938), Fr. movie cartoonist.

Claudette **Colbert:** Lily Claudette Chauchoin (1903–1996), Fr.-born U.S. stage, movie actress. The actress adopted her new name for her first stage appearance, in *The Wild Westcotts* at the Frazee Theatre, New York, on Christmas Eve, 1923.

Maurice **Colbourne:** Roger Middleton (1939–1989), Eng. TV actor. The actor is said to have taken his stage name from that of a Shakespearean actor whose obituary he had read.

Ann **Cole:** Cynthia Coleman (1934–), U.S. black gospel singer.

Graham **Cole:** Graham Coleman Smith (1952–), Eng. TV actor.

Jack **Cole:** John Ewing Richter (1911–1974), U.S. dancer, choreographer. Richter took his stepfather's name when he became a dancer.

Judson **Cole:** Milton Greishaber (1894–1943), U.S. vaudeville entertainer, comedy magician.

Lester **Cole:** Lester Cohn (1904–1985), U.S. screenwriter, of Pol. parentage.

Nat "King" **Cole:** Nathaniel Adams Coles (1916–1965), U.S. black jazz singer, pianist. The musician's own name, with his nickname of "King," plus the name of his group, the King Cole Trio, resulted in a performing name that was additionally associated with the "Old King Cole" of the children's nursery rhyme. Coles dropped the "s" of his name in 1939, when he formed his trio.

Blanche **Coleman:** Blanche Schwartz (1910–2008), Eng. jazzband leader. The musician may have intended a connection between her original name, meaning "black," and the phrase "black as coal." In retaining her first name Blanche, literally "white," she would have kept the color contrast.

Brunette **Coleman:** Philip Arthur Larkin (1922–1985), Eng. poet. Larkin used this name for two early girls' school stories, *Trouble at Willow Gables* (1943) and *Michaelmas Term at St. Bride's* (1943), the latter an unfinished sequel to the former. Both remained unpublished until 2002. The poet was a jazz enthusiast, and based the name punningly on that of jazzband leader Blanche **Coleman**. "Larkin must have been amused at the later emergence of *Ornette* Coleman, the adventurous alto saxophonist whose 'sonorous bayings' he only grudgingly praised in *All What Jazz*" [Alan Brownjohn in *Times Literary Supplement*, May 17, 2002].

Cy **Coleman:** Seymour Kaufman (1929–2004), U.S. songwriter, composer, of Russ. parentage.

Manning **Coles:** Adelaide Frances Oke Manning (1891–1959), Eng. spy, detective novelist + Cyril Henry Coles (1901–1965), Eng. spy, detective novelist, her husband. A combination of two surnames to make a unified first name and surname.

Colette: Sidonie-Gabrielle Claudine Colette (1873–1954), Fr. novelist. A single name that suggests a first name rather than the surname that it actually is. The writer's four early novels about the young ingénue Claudine (1901–3) were published under the pen name of her husband, **Willy**. She used her own name, in combination with his (as Colette-Willy), for *Dialogues de Bêtes* (1904). She divorced Willy two years later, but went on writing as Colette-Willy until 1916, after which she wrote as Colette alone.

[St.] **Colette:** Nicolette Boylet (1381–1447), Fr. Franciscan nun, reformer.

Bonar **Colleano:** Bonar William Sullivan II (1924–1958), U.S. movie actor. The actor joined the Colleano Circus Family as a child and adopted their name.

Stephen **Collet** *see* Reuben **Percy**

Catrin **Collier** *see* Katherine **John**

Constance **Collier:** Laura Constance Hardie (1878–1955), Eng. stage, movie actress. The actress adopted her mother's maiden name as her stage name.

Joel **Collier:** George Veal (*fl.*1774–1818), Eng. musician. François Fétis's *Biographie universelle des musiciens* (1835–44) gives Collier's original name as John Laurence Bicknell, but this is refuted by the *Dictionary of National Biography*.

Lois **Collier:** Madelyn Jones (1919–1999), U.S. movie actress.

Patience **Collier:** René Collier, née Ritcher (1910–1987), Eng. stage actress.

William **Collier:** William Senior (1866–1944), U.S. stage, movie actor.

Harry **Collingwood:** William Joseph Cosens Lancaster (1851–1922), Eng. author of boys' books.

The writer of juvenile nautical tales based his pen name on that of Lord Cuthbert Collingwood (1748–1810), a hero of British naval history in the Napoleonic Wars.

Hunt **Collins** *see* Evan **Hunter**

John D. **Collins:** John Christopher Dixon (1942–), Eng. TV actor.

Michael **Collins:** Dennis Lynds (1924–), U.S. mystery writer, journalist. The writer adopted the name of the Irish nationalist leader Michael Collins (1890–1922) as his pen name.

Sam **Collins:** Samuel Thomas Collins Vagg (1827–1865), Eng. music-hall artist, manager.

Tom **Collins:** Joseph Furphy (1843–1912), Austral. novelist, of Ir. parentage. At the end of the 19th century "Tom Collins" was a slang term in Australia for a mythical rumormonger. Furphy adopted the name in 1892 and later made Collins a leading character in some of his novels.

The writer's original name is said by some to be the origin of of the Australian slang term "furphy" for a rumor or mythical report, although more generally it is believed to derive from the name of a firm, J. Furphy & Sons Pty. Ltd., who operated a foundry in Shepparton, Victoria, and who manufactured water carts. The name passed to the water carts brought into camps in Egypt in World War I, the drivers of such carts bringing rumors with them. "Furphy worked for 20 years in Shepparton, and it was there that he turned in a serious way to writing, first as a contributor of paragraphs and articles to the Sydney *Bulletin* under the pen-name 'Tom Collins,' which was in those times a synonym for idle rumour; it was an amusing coincidence that during World War I his real name, Furphy, came to mean the same thing" [*Australian Encyclopedia*, 1965].

Tommy **Collins:** Leonard Raymond Sipes (1930–), U.S. country singer.

Carlo **Collodi:** Carlo Lorenzini (1826–1890), It. writer. The author of *Le Avventure di Pinocchio* (1883) took his pen name from his mother's birthplace, a small village in northern Italy. He himself was born in Florence.

Bud **Collyer:** Clayton Johnson Heermanse, Jr. (1908–1969), U.S. TV personality, brother of June **Collyer.**

June **Collyer:** Dorothy Heermanse (1907–1968), U.S. movie actress.

G. **Colmore:** Gertrude Baillie Dunn, later Weaver, née Renton (1855–1926), Eng. novelist. The writer used various pen names, mostly created from her own name and those of her husbands. This one comes from the initial of her first name and the third name of her first husband, Henry Arthur Colmore Dunn.

Denise **Colomb:** Denise Loeb (1902–2004), Fr. photographer. When Loeb and her marine engineer husband, Gilbert Cahen, returned to France from Saigon just before the start of World War II they survived denunciation as Jews by changing their names to Colomb. Loeb later kept the name as a professional photographer.

(La) Marquesa **Colombi:** Maria Antonietta Torriani (1846–1920), It. novelist.

Colombine: Carmen de Burgos Seguí (*c.*1870–1932), Sp. feminist writer.

Colon: Joseph Dennie (1768–1812), U.S. essayist, satirist, collaborating with **Spondee.**

Colonel ... For names beginning thus, see the following name, e.g. for Colonel Britton see **Britton,** for Colonel W. de Basil see **de Basil,** for Colonel Fabien see **Fabien,** etc.

Édouard **Colonne:** Judas Colonna (1838–1910), Fr. orchestral conductor, violinist.

Colourman: Fudel Hugh Henry (*c.*1965–), Jamaican reggae musician.

Ithell **Colquhoun:** Margaret Ithell (1906–1988), Eng. Surrealist artist, poet.

Jessi **Colter:** Miriam Johnson (1943–), U.S. country singer. The singer claimed to have an ancestor Jessi Colter who was a member of the Jesse James Gang. She therefore adopted his name as her stage name.

James **Colton:** Joseph Hansen (1923–2004), U.S. crime writer. Hansen also wrote Gothic novels under the name Rose Brock.

Robbie **Coltrane:** Anthony Robert McMillan (1950–), Sc. TV actor. The actor admired the black U.S. jazz saxophonist John Coltrane (1926–1967) and adopted his name in the 1970s.

Coluche: Michel Gérard Joseph Colucci (1944–1986), Fr. radio, stage, movie comedian, of It. parentage.

Columba: Colin Gumbrell (1961–), Br. crossword compiler. The setter's pseudonym, Latin for "dove," is based on letters in his real name.

Chris **Columbus:** Joseph Christopher Columbus Morris (1902–?), U.S. black jazz drummer, bandleader.

Comale: Therese Emile Henriette aus dem Winkel (1784–after 1850), Ger. harpist. The musician used this name for published articles on the construction of the harp.

Betty **Comden:** Elizabeth Kyle, née Cohen (1917–2006), U.S. lyricist, screenwriter, actress. When a student at New York University the songwriter changed her name to one that was not obviously Jewish. "Comden's original name, she delights in revealing in her memoir, was Basya Astershinsky Simselyevitch-Simselyovitch, which would surely have looked wonderful on a Broadway billboard" [*The Times*, March 4, 2005].

Jan Ámos **Comenius:** Jan Ámos Komenský (1592–1670), Cz. educationist, Moravian bishop.

Cuthbert **Comment, Gent.** *see* Edward **Search**

Common: Lonnie Rashied Lynn (*c.*1971–), U.S. black hip-hop musician. The rapper originally recorded under the name Common Sense, but abbreviated it after losing a court battle to retain his rights to the fuller name.

Perry **Como:** Pierino Roland Como (1913–2001), U.S. crooner, movie actor, of It. descent. The singer initially appeared under the name Nick Perido.

Compay Segundo: Maximo Francisco Repilado Muñoz (1907–2003), Cuban popular musician. In 1942 Muñoz teamed up with Lorenzo Hierrezuelo to form a duo under the name Los Campadres ("The Companions"). As Hierrezuelo was the lead singer, he was known as Compay Primo ("First Friend"), so that Muñoz, singing bass harmonies, was Compay Segundo ("Second Friend"). He adopted the name and in 1950 formed his group, Compay Segundo y Sus Muchachos ("Compay Segundo and His Boys").

Fay **Compton:** Virginia Lilian Emmiline Compton (1894–1978), Br. stage actress, sister of novelist Compton **Mackenzie.**

Frances Snow **Compton:** Henry Brooks Adams (1838–1918), U.S. historian, novelist.

Henry **Compton:** Charles Mackenzie (1805–1877), Eng. actor, grandfather of novelist Compton **Mackenzie** and actress Fay **Compton.** The actor adopted the maiden name of his Scottish paternal grandmother.

Joyce **Compton:** Eleanor Hunt (1907–1997), U.S. movie actress.

Comus: Robert Michael Ballantyne (1825–1894), Sc. novelist for boys. Comus was the name of the pagan god invented by Milton for his pastoral entertainment ("masque") so titled (1634).

Laure **Conan:** Marie-Louise-Félicité Angers (1845–1924), Fr.-Can. novelist.

Arthur **Concello:** Arthur Vasconcellos (1912–2001), U.S. circus trapeze artist. Concello was performing professionally at age 16 and by the time he was 18 had formed his own act, the Flying Concellos. In the 1930s, he and his wife, Antoinette, gained fame for their triple somersaults on the flying trapeze.

Concolorcorvo: Alonso Carrío de la Vandera (1715–*c.*1778), Sp. colonial administrator. The official used this name for *El Lazarillo de ciegos caminantes* ("El Lazarillo: A Guide for Blind Travelers") (1775), an account of his travels from Buenos Aires to Lima. (Lazarillo is a boy who guides the blind in the anonymous novel *Lazarillo de Tormes*, published in 1554.) The work and the name were originally attributed to

his Native American guide, Calixto Carlos Inca Bustamante, but research has revealed that Carrío used the pseudonym to avoid punishment for having criticized the Spanish regime.

Congo Ashanti Roy: Roy Johnson (1941–), Jamaican reggae musician. Johnson took the first word of his name from the Congos, a duo that he originally formed with Cedric Myton. Ashanti is the name of an African people and former West African state.

Chester **Conklin:** Jules Cowles (1888–1971), U.S. movie comedian. The actor should not be confused with movie comedian Charles "Heinie" Conklin (1880–1959), who sometimes acted as Charlie Lynn.

F. Norrys **Connell:** Conal Holmes O'Connell O'Riordan (1874–1948), Ir. dramatist, novelist.

John **Connell:** John Henry Robertson (1909–1965), Br. novelist, biographer.

Marc **Connelly:** Marcus Cook (1890–1980), U.S. playwright, screenwriter, stage director.

Rearden **Conner:** Patrick Reardon Connor (1907–1991), Ir. novelist, short-story writer. The author also wrote as Peter Malin.

J.J. **Connington:** Alfred Walter Stewart (1880–1947), Sc. crime writer.

Elizabeth **Connor:** Una Troy (1913–), Ir. novelist, playwright. The writer used this name for her first two novels, *Mount Prospect* (1936) and *Dead Man's Light* (1938), as well as for four later plays.

Ralph **Connor:** [Rev.] Charles William Gordon (1860–1937), Can. writer of religious novels, of Sc. parentage. The novelist intended to use the pen name "Cannor," from the letter heading "Brit. Can. Nor. West Mission," but his editor copied this as "Connor" and added "Ralph" to give a full name.

Mike **Connors:** Kreker Jay Michael Ohanian (1925–), U.S. movie, TV actor, of Armenian parentage. The actor was billed as Touch Connors for movies in the 1950s before his TV career took off.

George **Conquest:** George Augustus Oliver (1837–1901), Br. actor, theatrical manager. The actor adopted the same name as his father, Benjamin Oliver (1805–1872), also a theatrical manager.

Owen **Conquest** *see* Frank **Richards**

Brenda **Conrad** *see* Leslie **Ford**

Con **Conrad:** Conrad K. Dober (1891–1938), U.S. songwriter.

Jess **Conrad:** Gerald James (1936–), Br. pop singer.

Joseph **Conrad:** Józef Teodor Konrad Korzeniowski (1857–1924), Pol.-born Br. novelist, writing in English. Conrad became a British naturalized subject in 1886 and anglicized his first and third names.

Robert **Conrad:** Conrad Robert Falk (1935–), U.S. TV, movie actor.

William **Conrad:** William Cann (1920–1994), U.S. radio, movie actor.

Will **Conray** *see* Harry **Champion**

Heinrich **Conried:** Heinrich Cohn (1855–1909), Austr.-born U.S. actor, theater director, impresario. It is not known when or why the actor changed his last name.

Jill **Consey:** Margery Edith Felix (1907–?), Eng. music teacher, composer. The musician also used the names Margery Dawe and Carol Medway.

Konstantin **Constans:** Marie Drdova (1889–1970), Cz. composer.

Constant: Constant A. Nieuwenhuys (1920–), Du. painter, sculptor.

Constantia: Judith Sargent Stevens Murray (1751–1820), U.S. writer. Murray used this name for early poems published in various periodicals. Later names were Honora-Martesia or simply Honora.

Constantia *see* **Philenia**

K.C. **Constantine:** Carl Constantine Kosak (1934–), U.S. crime writer.

Michael **Constantine:** Constantine Joanides (1927–), Gk.-born U.S. TV, movie actor.

Murray **Constantine:** Katharine Penelope Burdekin, née Cade (1896–1963), Eng. novelist. The author used this name for four novels published between 1922 and 1940. The identity of the writer behind the pseudonym was discovered only in the 1980s.

Richard **Conte:** Nicholas Conte (1910–1975), U.S. movie actor.

Contessa Lara: Evelina Cattermole Mancini (1849–1896), It. poet, of Eng.-Russ. parentage.

Albert **Conti:** Albert de Conti Cedassamare (1887–1967), Austr. movie actor.

Gloria **Contreras:** Carmen Gloria Contreras Roeniger (1934–), Mexican ballet dancer, teacher.

Blade Stanhope **Conway** *see* Robert **Cummings**

Gary **Conway:** Gareth Carmody (1938–), U.S. movie, TV actor.

H. Derwent **Conway:** Henry David Inglis (1795–1835), Sc. writer, traveler. Inglis used this pseudonym, apparently based on the names of rivers (the Derwent in England, the Conway in Wales), for his first work, *Tales of the Ardennes* (1841).

Hugh **Conway:** Frederick John Fargus (1847–1885), Eng. novelist. The writer took his pen name from the school frigate *Conway*, stationed on the Mersey, which he entered as a 13-year-old naval student.

Peter **Conway** *see* George **Sava**

Russ **Conway:** Trevor Herbert Stanford (1925–2000), Eng. popular pianist, composer. The musician adopted his new name on making his first recording in 1957 at the suggestion of Columbia record producer Norman Newell, who "did not feel that the name Terry Stanford was right for a performer" [*The Times*, November 17, 2000].

Shirl **Conway:** Shirley Crossman (1914–), U.S. TV actress.

Steve **Conway:** Walter James Groom (1920–1952), Eng. popular singer.

Tom **Conway:** Thomas Charles Sanders (1904–1967), Br.-born U.S. movie actor, brother of actor George Sanders (1906–1972).

Tom **Conway** *see* Carter **Brown**

Troy **Conway** *see* Ed **Noon**

William Augustus **Conway:** William Augustus Rugg (1789–1828), Ir. actor.

Pedr **Conwy:** Peter John Mitchell Thomas (1920–2008), Welsh politician. The future secretary of state for Wales and Conservative Party chairman took his bardic name from the Conwy River, on which his birth town of Llanrwst stands, Pedr being the Welsh equivalent of Peter. He was made a life peer in 1987 as Lord Thomas of Gwydir, taking his title from a nearby castle.

Captain **Conyers** *see* Reginald **Wray**

Coo-ee: William Sylvester Walker (1846–1926), Austral. novelist. "Coo-ee" was originally a call used by an Australian Aboriginal to communicate with another at a distance. It was later adopted by settlers and is now widely used as a signal. (The call consists of a long "coo" ending in a sudden higher "ee.")

Doc **Cook:** Charles L. Cooke (1881–1958), U.S. jazz pianist, arranger, bandleader.

Joe **Cook:** Joseph Lopez (1890–1959), U.S. comedian.

Marianne **Cook:** Marianne Koch (1930–), Ger. movie actress. The actress was usually billed under this name in the U.S. and U.K.

John Estes **Cooke** *see* Floyd **Akers**

Margaret **Cooke** *see* Gordon **Ashe**

M.E. **Cooke** *see* Gordon **Ashe**

Ina **Coolbrith:** Josephine Donna Smith (1841–1928), U.S. poet. The writer adopted her new name in the early 1860s, taking her new first name from a pet form of her original name and her surname from her mother's middle name. It was Coolbrith who persuaded the poet Cincinnatus Hiner Miller to adopt the name Joaquin **Miller**.

Susan **Coolidge:** Sarah Chauncy Woolsey (1835–1905), U.S. writer of books for girls. The author of *What Katy Did* (1872) and subsequent stories based her pen name on that of her younger sister, Jane Woolsey Yardley, who had written as "Margaret Coolidge."

Coolio: Artis Leon Ivey, Jr. (1964–), U.S. black rapper, movie actor. The artist's name is obviously based on "cool," but he liked to joke: "My homeboy asked me, 'Who do you think you are, Coolio Iglesias?'" The pun is at the expense of the Spanish romantic singer Julio Iglesias (1943–).

Alice **Cooper:** Vincent Damon Furnier (1948–), U.S. rock singer. The female name was long said to have been chosen by the musician in 1969 to illustrate his theory that "people are both male and female biologically," while a Ouija board supposedly indicated that Alice Cooper had been a 17th-century witch, now reincarnated as Furnier. But when Cooper was asked how he came by it, he replied: "I have no idea. I really don't. It was one day, just [snaps fingers] boom ... I could have said Mary Smith, but I said Alice Cooper.... But think about it — Alice Cooper has the same sort of ring as Lizzie Borden and Baby Jane. 'Alice Cooper.' It's sort of like a little girl with an ax. I kept picturing something in pink and black lace and blood. Meanwhile, people expected a blond folksinger" [Headley Gritter, *Rock 'N' Roll Asylum: Conversations with the Madmen of Music*, 1984].

"Any guy can dress like a girl these days, but it took a real man to change his name to Alice and have it accepted as one of the most masculine monikers in the history of popular culture" [John Lydon (formerly Johnny **Rotten**) on Alice Cooper, interviewed in *Sunday Times*, December 1, 2002].

Frank **Cooper:** William Gilmore Simms (1806–1870), U.S. novelist.

Gary **Cooper:** Frank James Cooper (1901–1961), U.S. movie actor. The metamorphosis of "Coop's" first name was the work of his Hollywood agent, Nan Collins, who came from Gary, Indiana. She explained: "'My home town was named after Elbert H. Gary. I think Gary has a nice poetic sound to it. I'd like to see you take Elbert Gary's last name for your first. 'You mean,' he interrupted, 'Gary Cooper?' 'Yes — Gary Cooper. Say it again. Gary Cooper. Very nice. I like it. Don't you?' Gary Cooper. He ran the name around in his mind a few times. He spoke it again, 'Gary Cooper.' Then he smiled. 'I like it.' 'You see,' Miss Collins said. 'I knew you would. And you'll have to agree, Gary Cooper doesn't sound as tall and lanky as Frank Cooper'" [George Carpozi, Jr., *The Gary Cooper Story*, 1971].

Henry St. John **Cooper** *see* Gordon **Ashe**

Jackie **Cooper:** John Cooperman, Jr. (1921–), U.S. movie actor.

James Fenimore **Cooper:** James Cooper (1789–1851), U.S. novelist. The writer did not add his middle name, his mother's maiden name, until 1826, the year he published *The Last of the Mohicans*.

Jefferson **Cooper:** Gardner Francis Fox (1911–), U.S. writer of historical romances.

Natasha **Cooper:** Idonea Daphne Wright (1951–), Br. crime writer.

Robin **Cooper:** Robert Popper (1968–), Br. humorist, comedy writer. Cooper gained fame for his book *The Timewaster Letters* (2004), in which he made spoof proposals for new products to a number of commercial companies.

William **Cooper:** Harry Summerfield Hoff (1910–2002), Eng. novelist. The writer assumed his pseudonym for his fifth novel, *Scenes from Provincial Life* (1950). He was pursuing a career as a civil servant at the time, and needed to protect the identities of the book's two homosexual characters. Four earlier novels, *Trina* (1934), *Rhea* (1937), *Lisa* (1937), and *Three Marriages* (1946), appeared under his real name (in the form H.S. Hoff).

Joan **Copeland:** Joan Maxine Miller (1922–), U.S. stage actress, singer.

Copi: Raúl Damonte Taborda (1939–1987), Argentinian playwright, humorist.

Aaron **Copland:** Aaron Kaplan (1900–1990), U.S. composer, pianist, of Russ. parentage.

Marc **Copland:** Marc Cohen (1948–), U.S. jazz musician.

David **Copperfield:** David Kotkin (1957–), U.S. magician. The name, which may have arisen as a nickname, is familiar as that of the young hero of Charles Dickens's novel (1849).

Il **Coppetta:** Francesco Beccuti (1509–1553), It. poet.

Giovanni **Coprario:** John Cooper (*c.*1575–1626), Eng. composer. Cooper is described by the 17th-century biographer Anthony Wood as "an Englishman borne, who having spent much of his time in Italy, was there called *Coprario*, which name he kept when he returned into England [in *c.*1604]" [*Dictionary of National Biography*].

Joe **Coral:** Joseph Kagarlitski (1904–1996), Br. bookmaker, of Pol. Jewish origin. The founder of one of Britain's largest chain of betting shops smoothed his name to a word that evokes both decorativeness and durability.

Cora **Coralina:** Ana Lins dos Guimarães Peixoto Bretas (1890–1985), Brazilian writer.

Jean **Coralli:** Giovanni Coralli Peracini (1779–1854), Fr. ballet dancer, of It. parentage.

Coram: Thomas Whitaker (1883–1937), Eng. ventriloquist. Latin *coram* means "openly," "in public." A ventriloquist is a paradoxical performer who conceals his voice for public entertainment.

Glen **Corbett:** Glenn Rothenburg (1929–1993), U.S. movie actor.

Tristan **Corbière:** Édouard Joachim Corbière (1845–1875), Fr. poet.

Le **Corbusier** *see* Le **Corbusier**

Ellen **Corby:** Ellen Hansen (1913–1999), U.S. movie actress.

Alex **Cord:** Alexander Viespi (1931–), It.-born U.S. movie, TV actor.

Maria **Corda:** Maria Farcas (*c.*1902–1965), Hung. movie actress. The actress's screen name is a modified form of the surname of her first husband, movie producer Alexander **Korda.**

Charlotte **Corday:** Marie-Anne-Charlotte de Corday d'Armont (1768–1793), Fr. revolutionary.

Mara **Corday:** Marilyn Watts (1932–), U.S. movie actress. "Mara" from "Marilyn."

Paula **Corday:** Jeanne Paule Teipotemarga (1924–1992), Br.-Swiss movie actress, working in U.S. The actress also used the names Paule Croset and Rita Corday.

Rita **Corday** *see* Paula **Corday**

John **Cordelier:** Evelyn Underhill (1875–1941), Eng. religious writer. A male name used for some of the author's mystical writings, such as *The Path of the Eternal Wisdom* (1911).

Alexander **Cordell:** George Alexander Graber (1914–1997), Br. novelist, settling in Wales.

Denny **Cordell:** Dennis Cordell-Laverack (1943–1995), Argentinian-born U.S. record producer.

Ritchie **Cordell:** Richard Joel Rosenblatt (1943–2004), U.S. songwriter, record producer.

Louise **Cordet:** Louise Boisot (1946–), Eng. popular singer. The singer took her mother's stage name on first signing with Decca Records in 1962.

El **Cordobés:** Manuel Benítez Pérez (1936–), Sp. bullfighter. The matador's ring name means "the Cordovan," although he was not actually born in Córdoba, but in Palma del Río, some 30 miles away. However, the latter town is in Córdoba province, and the name itself is said to come from a monument in the city to the famous **Manolete,** who inspired Benítez to excel in the bullring. The name was subsequently adopted by Benítez's illegitimate son, Manuel Benítez Freysse, who entered the ring in the 1990s. El Cordobés Sr. finally retired in 2002.

Raymond **Cordy:** Raymond Cordiaux (1898–1956), Fr. movie comedian.

Marie **Corelli:** Mary Mackay (1855–1924), Br. novelist. The writer was the illegitimate daughter of Charles Mackay (1814–1889), a poet and journalist, and Mary Mills, a servant, whom Mackay later married following the death of his first wife in 1859. Knowing this origin, Corelli created the myth that Mackay had adopted her. In a letter to a Mrs. Cudlipp of December 23, 1889, she thus wrote: "My name is *not* Mackay, not am I related to the Mackays at all. I was *adopted* by the late Charles Mackay LLD, LSA who lost his own daughter by fever in Italy — but my name is Corelli, and though my mother was Scotch, I am much more Italian than British! I know you will be kind enough to always remember this." Earlier, in a letter of May 25, 1883, accompanying some poems submitted to the editor of *Blackwood's Magazine,* she had written of herself: "Signorina Corelli is a Venetian, and the direct descendant (through a long line of ancestry) of the great Michael Angelo Corelli, the famous composer."

She originally chose the name for a possible musical career, and apparently took it from a young Italian tenor, Signor Corelli, who was appearing at Her Majesty's Theatre, London, in 1874. Her second choice of name at the time was Rose Trevor, taken from one of the main characters in Mackay's epic poem *A Man's Heart* (1860), while earlier she had written as Vivian Erle Clifford. Arcangelo Corelli (1653–1713) was an Italian composer [Teresa Ransom, *The Mysterious Miss Marie Corelli,* 1999].

Jill **Corey:** Norman Jean Speranza (1935–), U.S. pop singer.

Lewis **Corey:** Luigi Carlo Fraina (1892–1953), It.-born U.S. Marxist theorist.

Corinna: Elizabeth Thomas (1675–1731), Eng. poet, letter writer. The poet was given her name by Dryden, who admired two poems she sent him in 1699 and compared her to the 6th-century BC Greek lyric poet of this name. "I would have called you Sapho," he said, "but that I hear you are handsomer." (Contemporary portraits of Sappho depict her as somewhat plain-featured.)

Corisande: Alice Smith, née Jerrold (1849–1872), Eng. writer. Smith appears to have called herself after "La belle Corisande," a name given to the French-woman Diane d'Andouins, mistress of Henri IV.

Corita: Frances Elizabeth Kent (1918–1986), U.S. artist. In 1936 Kent entered the order Sisters of the Immaculate Heart of Mary, taking the religious name Sister Mary Corita. She retained the name for her work as an artist, not all of it religious in nature.

Fernand **Cormon:** Fernand-Anne Piestre (1845–1924), Fr. painter.

Corneille: Cornelis van Beverloo (1922–), Belg. painter, working in France. The artist's name is a French form of his original Flemish name.

Don **Cornell:** Dominico Francisco Connello (1919–2004), U.S. popular singer. Some sources give the singer's original name as Luigi Francisco Varlarlo.

Theresa **Cornelys:** Theresa Pompeati, née Imer (1722–1797), It. singer, working in England. The singer took her stage name from a liaison made in the Netherlands. "When at Amsterdam as a singer she was known as Mme. Trenti, and took the name of Cornelis (or Cornelys) from that of a gentleman at Amsterdam, M. Cornelis de Rigerboos" [*Dictionary of National Biography*].

Kyle **Corning** see A.A. **Fair**

Corno di Bassetto: George Bernard Shaw (1856–1950), Ir. dramatist, critic, novelist. Shaw used the waggish name when writing as a music critic for *The Star* (1888–90). The corno di bassetto is (in its Italian notation, found in music scores) the basset horn, which two words suggest "Bernard Shaw." "It was not until February 1889 that Shaw replaced [E. Belford] Bax completely and, in need of a pseudonym, created his *alter ego*. Corno di Bassetto, after months of anonymity, made his presence known to readers of The Star on 15 February" [Dan H. Lawrence, ed., *Shaw's Music*, 1981].

Barry Cornwall: Bryan Waller Procter (1787–1874), Eng. poet, songwriter, father of Mary **Berwick**. The writer was professionally a lawyer, and originally adopted his near-anagrammatical name to conceal his identity as a law student when contributing poems to the *Literary Gazette*. As a poet, he was probably also attracted to the euphony of the name, which happened to match his modest persona.

Bernard Cornwell: Bernard Wiggins (1944–), Br. historical novelist. The writer's choice of name was neither that of his adoptive parents, Joe and Marjorie Wiggins, nor that of his biological father, a Canadian airman, whose identity (as William Oughtred) he learned at the age of ten and whom he eventually traced in 2001. He explains the origin: "My mother was Dorothy Rose Cornwell, and I decided to take the Cornwell as my nom de plume, partly because Wiggins sounds so ugly, and partly because W is a long way down the alphabetical shelves in bookshops" [*The Times*, November 6, 2002].

Corrado: Corrado Mantoni (1924–1999), It. television presenter, game-show host.

Correggio: Antonio Allegri (da Correggio) (1494–1534), It. painter. As was the custom of his day, the painter adopted the name of his birthtown, Correggio, near Reggio in northern Italy.

Adrienne Corri: Adrienne Riccoboni (1930–), Sc. movie actress, of It. descent. The actress was renamed by Gordon Harbord, who also renamed Laurence **Harvey** and who nearly renamed Diana **Dors**. The letters of "Corri" come from the actress's surname.

Emmett Corrigan: Antoine Zilles (1868–1932), Du.-born U.S. stage, movie actor.

Ray "Crash" Corrigan: Ray Benard (1902–1976), U.S. movie actor. Corrigan was billed as "Crash" for the SF serial *Undersea Kingdom* (1936) so his name would sound like "Flash Gordon."

Bud Cort: Walter Edward Cox (1950–), U.S. movie actor. The actor was obliged to choose a new name because his real name already existed for the U.S. comic actor Wally Cox (1924–1973).

Joaquín Cortés: Joaquín Reyes (1969–), Sp. flamenco dancer. The dancer changed his name in 1990.

Dave "Baby" Cortez: David Cortez Clowney (1938–), U.S. pop musician.

Leon Cortez: Richard Alfred Chalkin (1898–1970), Eng. stage comedian.

Ricardo Cortez: Jacob Kranz (1899–1977), U.S. movie actor, brother of Stanley **Cortez**.

Stanley Cortez: Stanislaus Kranz (1908–1997), U.S. cinematographer.

Jakob Corvinus: Wilhelm Raabe (1831–1910), Ger. novelist. The writer used this name for his first novel, *Die Chronik der Sperlingsgasse* ("The Chronicle of Sperling Street") (1856), with a derivative of Latin *corvus* translating German *Rabe*, "crow," "raven."

Baron Corvo: Frederick William Serafino Austin Lewis Mary Rolfe (1860–1913), Br. writer. The idiosyncratic author claimed to have received the title of Baron Corvo from the Duchess Sforza-Cesarini when living in Italy in the 1880s, a claim that has been neither confirmed nor disproved. The writer himself gave three versions of the origin of his pseudonym: that it was a style offered and accepted for use as a *tekhnikym* or trade name when he denied sacred orders and sought a secular livelihood, that it came from a village near Rome and was assumed when he was made a baron by the Bishop of Emmaus, who was on a visit to Rome, and that it was bestowed by the aforementioned duchess. Rolfe had other pseudonyms, as Frederick Austin, King Clement, and Fr. Rolfe (with "Fr." representing "Frederick" but suggesting a priestly "Father"). He wrote autobiographically as Nicholas Crabbe in *Nicholas Crabbe* (1958) and *The Desire and Pursuit of the Whole* (1934) and as George Arthur Rose in (and as) *Hadrian the Seventh* (1904). *Corvo* is Italian for "raven," moreover, and he had already adopted the raven as a heraldic device. (Possibly Crabbe has a similar symbolic significance.) George Arthur Rose is said to derive from St. George "of the Roses" and Duke Arthur (of Brittany) murdered by King John in 1203. [1. A.J.A. Symons, *The Quest for Corvo*, 1940; 2. Donald Weeks, *Corvo*, 1971].

Caroline **Cory** see Minnie Maddern **Fiske**

Desmond Cory: Shaun Lloyd McCarthy (1928–), Eng. mystery novelist.

Donald Webster Cory: Edward Sagarin (1913–1986), U.S. scholar, of Russ. Jewish parentage. As a gay activist, Sagarin based his pseudonym on André Gide's *Corydon* (1924), a defense of pederasty.

William Johnson Cory: William Johnson (1823–1892), Eng. translator, poet. The academic, long a teacher at Eton College, adopted the name Cory in 1872 after inheriting an estate two years previously.

Coryat Junior: Samuel Paterson (1728–1802), Eng. bookseller, auctioneer. Paterson used this name for *Another Traveller! or Cursory Remarks and Tritical Observations made upon a Journey through part of the Netherlands in 1766* (1767–9), described by the *Dictionary of National Biography* as "sentimental travels in the manner of Sterne, of very poor quality." His pseudonym presumably relates to the English traveler and writer Thomas Coryate (?1577–1617).

Corylus: Chris Feetenby (1940–), Br. crossword compiler. The setter's pseudonym, the botanical Latin name of the hazel, refers punningly to his grandfather, Alfred Heselwood.

Corymbæus: Richard Brathwaite (1588–1673), Eng. poet, writer. Brathwaite used this name, from Latin *corymbus*, "cluster of fruit or flowers," for his best-known work, *Barnabae Itinerarium, or Barnabee's Journal* (1638), a record of English travel written in Latin and English doggerel. Other classical-style names used by him were Blasius Multibibus, Clitus Alexandrinus, Eucapnus Nepenthiacus, Musæus Palatinus, Musophilus, Hesychius Pamphilus, and Philogenes Paledonius.

Howard **Cosell:** Howard William Cohen (1920–1995), U.S. radio, TV sportscaster, of Pol. Jewish parentage. As an undergraduate at New York University, the future sports journalist changed his name of Cohen, given his family by immigration officials, to the original family name of Cosell.

Cosey Fanni Tutti: Christine Carol Newby (1951–), Br. rock musician, artist. The musician was the partner of Genesis **P-Orridge**, founder of the rock group Throbbing Gristle, in which she played guitar. She originally changed her first name to Carol, then after meeting P-Orridge to Cosey. In 1973 she lengthened this name to Cosey Fanni Tutti, as a play on the title of Mozart's opera *Così fan tutte* ("Thus do all women"). The name thus spanned the divide between high opera and pop music while evoking a burlesque link with "cozy," "fanny," "tootie," and "tutti frutti," all words of potential female reference.

Frank **Costa** *see* Frank Donald **Coster**

Gal **Costa:** Maria da Graça Costa Penna Burgos (1946–), Brazilian rock singer. "Gal" is "Girl."

[Sir] Michael **Costa:** Michele Costa (1808–1884), It.-born Br. orchestral conductor, composer. The musician anglicized his full Italian name, Michele Andrea Agniello Costa, as Michael Andrew Agnus Costa.

Costa-Gavras: Konstantinos Costa-Gavras (1933–), Gk.-born Fr. movie director.

Elvis **Costello:** Declan Patrick MacManus (1954–), Br. rock singer, songwriter. When his parents divorced and separated, MacManus took his mother's maiden name, Costello, and moved with her from London to Liverpool. He then returned to London and sang as a solo singer in folk clubs as D.P. Costello. In 1976 Jake Riviera signed him for Stiff Records and gave him the name Elvis, for Elvis Presley, if only so that he could promote him with the Presley slogan, "Elvis is King." Costello's father, big-band singer Ross MacManus, commented: "I didn't like it, then I realised it was probably quite good because he didn't sound anything like Elvis: I could see that Declan MacManus wasn't a very good name for a rock star" [*Sunday Times Magazine*, July 17, 1994].

The musician later resumed his real name. "He explains to me the relationship between Costello and MacManus, but it's not entirely straightforward. Elvis makes the records, clearly; that's him on the label. But even when Declan wrote songs for other people, the singers wanted the composer to be credited as Costello, since MacManus is not a famous name. The driving licence is Costello ... but the passport has changed back to MacManus.... You don't hear of Elton **John** or Cliff **Richard** wanting to become Reg Dwight or Harry Webb again. It's a tricky manoeuvre" [*The Times Magazine*, March 2, 2002].

Frank **Costello:** Francesco Castiglia (1891–1973), It.-born U.S. criminal.

Lou **Costello:** Louis Francis Cristillo (1906–1959), U.S. movie comedian, of It. descent, teaming with Bud **Abbott**.

Pierre **Costello:** Ernest Charles Heath Hosken (1875–1934), Eng. journalist, writer. Hosken used this name for two novels, *A Sinner in Israel* (1910) and *Tainted Lives* (1912), the latter a murder mystery.

Tom **Costello:** Thomas Costellow (1863–1943), Br. music hall comedian, singer.

Al **Coster:** René Cardona III (1960–), Mexican juvenile movie actor.

Frank Donald **Coster:** Philip Mariano Fausto Musica (1884–1936), U.S. fraudster, of It. parentage. Musica used this name, or variations of it, to set up a number of drug companies, both legitimate and illegitimate. As Frank Costa, he opened the Adelphi Pharmaceutical Manufacturing Company of Brooklyn in 1920. Three years later, as Frank D. Coster, he began Girard and Company in Mount Vernon, New York. By 1925 he was calling himself F. Donald Coster. Earlier, as an investigator for the New York district attorney's office, he had worked under the name William Johnson.

Costillares: Joaquín Rodríguez (1729–1800), Sp. bullfighter. The matador's ring name means literally "ribs."

Peter **Cotes:** Sydney Arthur Rembrandt Boulting (1912–1998), Br. stage actor, theatrical producer. The actor's stage name, adopted to avoid confusion with his younger brothers John and Roy Boulting (the Boulting Brothers, known as "the British movie twins"), derived from a house called "Northcotes" where he had lived as a child.

A.V. **Coton:** Edward Haddakin (1906–1969), Eng. ballet critic, writer.

Carolina **Cotton:** Helen Hagstom (1926–1997), U.S. singer, movie actress.

Robert Turner **Cotton:** Edward James Mortimer Collins (1827–1876), Eng. novelist, humorist. Collins used this name for *Mr. Carington* (1873).

Joseph **Cotton:** Silbert Walton (1957–), Jamaican pop singer. Walton originally recorded in 1976 as Jah Walton. He adopted his professional name in the mid–1980s.

Mathilde **Cottrelly:** Mathilde Meyer (1851–1933), Ger.-born U.S. stage actress. The actress adopted the stage name of her husband, English circus acrobat George Cottrell, whom she married at age 16.

François **Coty:** Francesco Giuseppe Spoturno (1874–1934), Corsican-born Fr. perfume manufacturer.

Johnny **Cougar** *see* John **Mellencamp**

Country Jim: Jim Bledsoe (*c.*1925–), U.S. country, blues musician.

Wayne **County:** Wayne Rogers (1947–), U.S. punk musician, working in U.K. There are many U.S. counties named Wayne County, including one in the musician's native Georgia. The transexual singer and songwriter was subsequently known as Jayne County.

Nicole **Courcel:** Nicole Marie-Anne Andrieux (1930–), Fr. movie actress.

Claude **Courlis** *see* Claude **Cahun**

Sharon **Court** *see* Fenton **Brockley**

Georges **Courteline:** Georges-Victor-Marcel Moinaux (1858–1929), Fr. humorist, dramatist.

Peregrine **Courtenay:** Winthrop Mackworth Praed (1802–1839), Eng. poet. The names have an aristocratic ring for a Cambridge man, as Praed was.

Sir William Percy Honeywood **Courtenay:** John Nichols Tom (or Thom) (1799–1838), Eng. impostor. The former liquor dealer from Cornwall became known by his new name and title in 1832, when he sought support among the citizens of Canterbury, Kent, in a bid to improve conditions for the poor. He claimed to be heir to the earldom of Devon, a title which in 1831 had been restored to the 3d Viscount Courtenay, and also claimed the Kentish estates of Sir Edward Hales, who had died in 1829. Other names adopted by the colorful but deluded campaigner were the Hon. Sydney Percy, Count Moses Rothschild, and Squire Thompson. He was shot dead near Boughton, Kent, in a skirmish with the military known as the Battle of Bossenden Wood.

Jacques **Courtin-Clarins:** Jacques Courtin (1921–2007), Fr. businessman. The founder of the luxury cosmetics and perfume firm Clarins Group added the company name to his family name in 1978.

Jerome **Courtland:** Jerome Jourolmon (1926–), U.S. movie actor, first husband of Polly **Bergen**.

Edward **Courtney:** Edward Leedes (?1599–1677), Eng. Jesuit.

Cousin ... For names beginning thus, see the next word, e.g. for Cousin Alice see **Alice**, for Cousin Emmy see **Emmy**, for Cousin Jacques see **Jacques**, etc.

Leonard **Covello:** Leonardo Coviello (1887–1982), It.-born U.S. educator. Coviello's name was adjusted while he was in the public school system.

Don **Covay:** Donald Randolph (1938–), U.S. black soul singer.

John **Coventry:** John Williamson Palmer (1825–1906), U.S. journalist.

Louis George **Cowan:** Louis George Cohen (?1909–1976), U.S. radio, TV producer. Cohen changed his name to Cowan in 1931 on starting a public relations firm.

Cowboy: Robert Keith Wiggins (1960–1989), U.S. black rapper.

Joe **Cowell:** Joseph Leathley Hawkins-Witchett (1792–1863), Eng. stage comic, working in U.S.

Jane **Cowl:** Grace Bailey (1884–1950), U.S. playwright, stage, movie actress. Following the failure of *Information Please* (1918), coauthored with fellow actress Jane Murfin, the two writers penned one of their most popular plays, *Smilin' Through* (1919), under the joint male name Alan Langdon Martin, feeling that the flop of the earlier work was due in part to prejudice against female authors.

Richard **Cowper:** John Middleton Murry (1926–2002), Eng. SF writer, son of critic John Middleton Murry (1889–1957). The writer published four non–SF novels under the name Colin Murry, "Colin" being a nickname, and two autobiographical works, *One Hand Clapping* (U.S. title *I at the Keyhole*) (1975) and *Shadows on the Grass* (1977), as Colin Middleton Murry. He first used the name Richard Cowper for the SF novel *Breakthrough* (1967).

Ida **Cox:** Ida Prather (1896–1967), U.S. black blues singer.

Frank **Coyne:** Josiah Jones (1875–1906), Eng. music-hall artist.

Fred **Coyne:** Frederick Sterling (1845–1886), Eng. music-hall artist.

Peter **Coyote:** Peter Cohon (1941–), U.S. movie actor. The actor changed his name in 1967, allegedly either "after a healing spiritual encounter with ... a coyote" [Maltin, p.178] or as the result of a vision induced by taking the drug peyote.

Buster **Crabbe:** Clarence Linden Crabbe (1908–1983), U.S. movie actor, swimmer. Crabbe adopted his nickname "Buster," given him in high school for his sporting prowess.

Nicholas **Crabbe** *see* Baron **Corvo**

Simon **Crabtree** *see* Michael **Wharton**

Carl **Crack:** Karl Bohm (1971–2001), Swiss-born Ger. "technopop" singer.

Hubert Montague **Crackanthorpe:** Hubert Montague Cookson (1870–1896), Eng. short-story writer. The family name was changed in 1888.

Charles Egbert **Craddock:** Mary Noailles Murfree (1850–1922), U.S. novelist, short-story writer. Mary Murfree, who wrote in dialect, took her (male) name from Egbert Craddock, a character in one of her early stories in *Appleton's Journal*, adding "Charles" as a name that went well with the combination. It was not until 1885, the year after the publication of her first collection of stories, *In the Tennessee Mountains*, that the editor of the *Atlantic Monthly*, to which she contributed, discovered the author of the tales of mountaineers and their pioneer romances to be in reality a frail, crippled spinster. Murfree began her literary career by using the name R. Emmett Dembry for two stories in *Lippincott's Magazine*.

Fanny **Cradock:** Phyllis Nan Sortain Cradock, née Primrose-Pechey (1909–1994), Br. TV chef. The popular broadcaster's surname was that of her third husband, Major John Cradock, who accompanied her in her programs. (They first met in 1939 and although she took his name they did not marry until 1977.) Her new first name was that of a grandmother with whom she went to live at age 15. She used the name Frances Dale as fashion editor of the *Sunday Graphic*, and together with her husband adopted the joint *nom de plume* "Bon Viveur" for a column on travel and food in the *Daily Telegraph*. "The *Telegraph*, sticklers for exactitude, wanted it to be called 'Bon Vivant' but she overruled them" [Christine Hamilton, *The Book of British Battleaxes*, 1997].

A.A. **Craig:** Poul William Anderson (1926–), U.S. SF writer.

Ailsa **Craig:** Edith Ailsa Geraldine Craig (1869–1947), Eng. stage actress, producer The actress was given her stage name by her mother, Ellen Terry (*see* Gordon **Craig**), but used it only early in her career, performing with Henry **Irving** at the Lyceum Theatre, London. "When *Richard III* was revived in 1896 the part of King's Page was played by Edith Craig. 'Ailsa' had vanished for ever from the programmes" [Harcourt Williams, "Bygones," in Eleanor Adlard, ed., *Edy: Recollections of Edith Craig*, 1949].

Alisa **Craig:** Charlotte Matilda Macleod (1922–), Can. thriller writer. The name must surely be based on the Scottish isle of Ailsa Craig, written about by Keats and Wordsworth (*see* Gordon **Craig**).

David **Craig:** Allan James Tucker (1929–), Welsh crime writer. The writer adopted his wife's maiden name as his pen name. He has also written under his real name (as James Tucker).

Douglas **Craig:** Ernest Herbert Douglas Jones (1916–2009), Eng. musical director, singer. The director of the Sadler's Wells Theatre, London, had never been too keen on his original prosaic name, so changed it to one with more distinctive theatrical connections.

Gordon **Craig:** Edward Henry Gordon Godwin (1872–1966), Eng. stage actor, designer, director. Craig was the illegitimate son of actress Ellen Terry (1847–1928) and architect Edward William Godwin (1833–1886). He was thus known as Edward Godwin until 1878, when his mother married actor Charles **Kelly** and he became Edward Wardell, taking the latter's original name. In 1887 his mother gave him the additional names Henry, for his godfather, actor Henry **Irving**, whose leading lady she was, and Gordon, for his godmother, Lady Gordon.

He assumed the name Craig in 1888. "This came about in haphazard fashion when, with his mother, Henry [Irving], and possibly [his sister] Edy, he was on holiday on the west coast of Scotland, driving past a huge dark rock out in the Atlantic. They were intrigued, asked what it was and were told Ailsa Craig. Ellen was delighted, 'What a good stage name! A pity you can't have it, Ted. I shall give it to Edy'" [Moira Shearer, *Ellen Terry*, 1998]. Edy, now aged 19, was thus christened Edith Ailsa Geraldine Craig (*see* Ailsa **Craig**), while 16-year-old Ted became Edward Henry Gordon Craig, "finally settling the uncertainty of Godwin, Terry or Wardell" [ibid.]. He subsequently legalized the name by deed poll. "This shifting-sands character named himself after a rock, to reclaim himself from illegitimacy, and avoid having to take the name of his mother's husband" [Susannah Clapp, review of Michael Holroyd, *A Strange Eventful History: The Dramatic Lives of Ellen Terry, Henry Irving and Their Remarkable Families*, Times Literary Supplement, December 19 & 26, 2008].

James **Craig:** James Henry Meador (1912–1985), U.S. movie actor. The actor took his screen name following his appearance in *Craig's Wife* (1936).

Michael **Craig:** Michael Gregson (1928–), Eng. movie actor.

Vera **Craig** *see* Fenton **Brockley**

Craigfryn: Isaac Hughes (1852–1928), Welsh novelist. The writer assumed a placename meaning literally "rock hill."

Richard **Craig-Hallam:** Horace Ernest Richard Smith (1910–2000), Eng. soldier. Lieutenant-Colonel

Richard Craig-Hallam, last surviving president of a British war crimes court in the Far East, took his new name when he was sent to Germany after the trials to take command of the remains of a former German paratroop battalion.

Mrs. **Craik:** Dinah Maria Craik, née Mulock (1826–1887), Eng. novelist, children's writer. Although the writer's best-known novel, *John Halifax, Gentleman* (1856), was published some time before her marriage in 1865 to George Lillie Craik, its author is still usually known as "Mrs. Craik." Works appearing before her marriage were published as by Dinah Maria Mulock or simply Miss Mulock.

Wesley **Craile** *see* Fenton **Brockley**

Cornelius **Crambo:** William Barnes Rhodes (1772–1826), Eng. banker, burlesque writer. Rhodes used this name for *Eccentric Tales in Verse* (1808).

Tom **Crampton:** Barbara Pym (1913–1980), Eng. novelist. The writer assumed this male name for novels written in the 1960s and 1970s. They were consistently rejected by publishers. She took the name from her mother's maiden name, Thomas, and her father's middle name, Crampton, this also being one of her own names (in full Barbara Mary Crampton Pym).

Lucas **Cranach** (the Elder): Lucas Müller (1472–1553), Ger. painter. The painter adopted the name of his birthtown, Cranach (now Kronach, Germany). He first indicated his adoption of the name by signing his painting *Rest on the Flight into Egypt* (1504) as "LC." His son, Lucas Cranach the Younger (1515–1586), kept the name.

Hart **Crane:** Harold Hart Crane (1899–1932), U.S. poet. Forced to take sides when his parents' marriage began to break down, Crane became increasingly estranged from his father and closer to his mother. He thus honored her maiden name (his existing middle name) by dropping his own first name.

Les **Crane:** Lesley Stein (1933–2008), U.S. talk-show host, computer software tycoon.

Lloyd **Crane** *see* Jon **Hall**

Phyllis **Crane:** Phyllis Francis (1912–), U.S. movie actress.

Vincent **Crane:** Vincent Rodney Cheesman (1943–), Eng. rock musician.

Cranogwen: Sarah Jane Rees (1839–1916), Welsh poet, musician, editor. The poet took her bardic name from her native village of Llangrannog, where the parish church is dedicated to St. Carannog.

John **Cranston:** Christina Jamieson (1864–1942), Sc. writer, suffragist. The writer used this male name for contributions to local papers.

An **Craoibhín Aoibhinn:** Douglas Hyde (1860–1949), Ir. statesman, historian. Ireland's first president was the founder of the Gaelic League and a campaigner for the native Irish language. His name comes from the title of a traditional Irish song, "An craoibhín aoibhinn álainn óg" ("The fair excellent young maid," literally "The fair excellent young little branch"). The name is pronounced approximately "Un creen een." "During the greater part of the struggle [for independence], Douglas Hyde's was the guiding hand and his the biggest influence. The younger Gaels looked up to him as men look up to a prophet. 'An Craoibhín' — the 'Little Branch' — they called him affectionately" [*Irish Press*, 1949].

Darby **Crash:** Jan Paul Beahm (1959–1980), U.S. punk-rock musician.

Arthur **Cravan:** Fabian Lloyd (1887–?1920), Fr. poet, prose writer.

José **Craveirinha:** José G. Vetrinha (1922–), Mozambican poet, writing in Portuguese.

Hawes **Craven:** Henry Hawes Craven Green (1837–1910), Eng. theatrical scene painter.

Henry Thornton **Craven:** Henry Thornton (1818–1905), Eng. actor, playwright.

Anne **Crawford:** Imelda Crawford (1919–1956), Br. movie actress.

Harry **Crawford:** Eugenia Falleni (1875–1938), It.-born Austral. crossdresser. As a young girl, Falleni dressed as a boy and later worked as a man. In 1913 she married Annie Birkett, who disappeared in 1917. In 1919 she married Lizzie Allinson. When questioned by police in 1920, she claimed to be Harry Leon Crawford, a Scot born in Edinburgh. She subsequently admitted she was a woman, was arrested and tried for the murder of her first wife (Birkett), and sentenced to death. After serving 11 years in jail, she obtained early release and lived the rest of her life as Mrs. Jean Ford.

Joan **Crawford:** Lucille Fay LeSueur (1905–1977), U.S. movie actress, of Fr.-Can./Ir.-Scandinavian parentage The actress first played (1925) under her real name (on which a Hollywood producer is said to have commented, "Well, honey, you certainly picked a fancy one"). She would soon become Billie Cassin, however, after Harry Cassin, with whom her mother had formed a liaison. Not long after, she acquired her lasting stage name: "Obviously Lucille LeSueur was a comer. But Pete Smith was convinced she couldn't make it with that name. The [MGM] publicity chief laid his case before Louis Mayer. "'Lucille LeSueur' sounds too stagy, even if it is the girl's name,' argued Smith. 'And it sounds too much like "LeSewer." I think we ought to change it.' Mayer granted permission, and Smith went to work. Why not conduct a nationwide publicity contest to find a name for the promising new actress? A McFadden fan publication, *Movie Weekly*, agreed to sponsor the contest.... The winner was 'Joan Arden,' and Lucille LeSueur became Joan Arden for a few days until a bit player protested that the name belonged to her. The second choice was submitted by Mrs. Marie M. Tisdale ... 'Joan *Crawford!*' the former Lucille complained to her new friend William Haines. 'It sounds like "Crawfish."' '"Crawford's" not so bad,' the actor replied. 'They might have called you "Cranberry" and served you every Thanksgiving with the turkey'" [Bob Thomas, *Joan Crawford*, 1979]. Crawford first married Douglas Fairbanks, Jr. (*see* Douglas **Fairbanks, Sr.**), then actor Franchot Tone (1905–1968), then Phillip **Terry**.

Kathryn **Crawford:** Kathryn Crawford Moran (1908–1980), U.S. movie actress.

Michael **Crawford:** Michael Patrick Smith (1942–), Eng. stage, movie, TV actor. The actor was born the illegitimate son of Doris Smith, née Pike, and an unknown father. In 1945 Doris, whose husband, Sgt. Arthur Dumbell Smith, a Royal Air Force pilot, had been killed in action in 1940, married Lionel Ingram, and her son took his stepfather's name, calling himself Michael Ingram. He then opted for a more distinctive name, and selected "Crawford" from a passing cookie truck on quitting school at age 15. ("Crawford's Crackers" are still well known in Britain.) He subsequently adopted this name legally. Some sources give Crawford's original surname inaccurately as "Dumble-Smith."

Robert **Crawford:** Hugh Crawford Rae (1935–), Sc. crime novelist. Rae also wrote as R.B. Houston, James Albany, and Stuart Stern, while for romantic novels he adopted the female name Jessica Sterling.

Captain Rawdon **Crawley:** George Frederick Pardon (1824–1884), Eng. editor, sporting writer. The writer adopted the name of the son of Sir Pitt Crawley, the coarse, brutal, wife-bullying old man in Thackeray's *Vanity Fair* (1847–8). It is not clear to what extent Pardon actually wished to be identified with the character's disagreeable nature. He used it for several handbooks on different sports and games, many under both his names. "We fear this is a use of a pseudonym we should condemn, for it savours of book-making [i.e. the writing of books for simple commercial gain]" [Hamst, p.36]. Another pen name used by Pardon was George Quiet.

Geoffrey **Crayon:** Washington Irving (1783–1859), U.S. humorous writer. Irving used the name for *The Sketch Book* (1819–20), a collection of familiar essays and tales. The pen name is appropriate for the title of the work.

Geoffrey **Crayon, jun.:** George Darley (1795–1846), Ir. poet, mathematician, writer. Darley adopted this name for *The New Sketch-Book* (1829), a work in the spirit of his U.S. namesake, Geoffrey **Crayon**. He also wrote as Richard Belvoir, John Lacy, Guy Penseval, and Peter Patricius Pickle-Herring.

Pee Wee **Crayton:** Connie Curtis (1914–1985), U.S. blues musician.

Crazy Horse: Ta-sunko-witko (*c.*1842–1877), U.S. Native American chief. The military leader came to be known by the English equivalent of his Sioux name, which he is said to have assumed either after dreaming of horses [Mari Sandoz, *Crazy Horse: The Strange Man of the Oglalas*, 1955] or because a wild horse ran through his camp when he was born [Stoutenburgh, p.81].

Crébillon: Prosper Joliot, sieur de Crais-Billon (1674–1762), Fr. dramatic poet.

Joseph **Crehan:** Charles Wilson (1884–1966), U.S. movie actor.

Adolphe **Crémieux:** Isaac Moïse (1796–1880), Fr. politician, Jewish leader.

Hélisenne de **Crenne:** Marguerite Briet (*c.*1510–*c.*1550), Fr. novelist, translator. The writer took her new name from her husband, a *petit seigneur de Cresnes* ("little lord of Cresnes"). She apparently devised her unusual first name herself, and used it for the semiautobiographical heroine of her novel *Les Angoisses douloureuses qui procèdent d'amours* ("The Grievous Anxieties that Proceed from Love") (1538).

Kid **Creole** *see* August **Darnell**

Charles de **Cresseron:** Joseph Sheridan Le Fanu (1814–1873), Ir. journalist, novelist. Le Fanu used this name for contributions to the *Dublin University Magazine*. He also wrote as Rev. Francis Purcell.

Dormer **Creston:** Dorothy Julia Colston-Baynes (*c.*1900–1973), Br. biographer, writer. The author was born Dorothy Baynes but assumed the additional name of Colston by deed poll in 1946. Her pseudonym appears to be a sexually ambiguous name, perhaps evolving from "Dorothy Colston."

Paul **Creston:** Giuseppe Guttoveggio (1906–1985), U.S. composer, organist, of It. origin.

Creuddynfab: William Williams (1814–1869), Welsh literary critic. The writer took his name from his birthplace, Creuddyn, near Llandudno. The name thus literally means "son of Creuddyn."

J. Hector St. John de **Crèvecoeur:** Michel-Guillaume Jean de Crèvecoeur (1735–1813), Fr.-born U.S. writer. After military service in Canada during the French and Indian War, Crèvecoeur did not return to France with the defeated troops but resigned his commission and took passage to New York, where on arrival in 1759 he changed his name to J. Hector St. John (as he is now usually known in America itself) and his language to English.

Quentin **Crewe:** Quentin Hugh Dodds (1926–1998), Br. writer, traveler. The writer became Crewe by deed poll in 1945 when his mother, Lady Annabel Crewe-Milnes, inherited what remained of the estates of her father, the Marquess of Crewe.

Paul **Creyton:** John Townsend Trowbridge (1827–1916), U.S. novelist, poet, writer of books for boys. The writer used this pseudonym early in his career for such novels as *Father Brighthopes, or an Old Clergyman's Vacation* (1853), *Martin Merrivale, His mark* (1854), and *Hearts and Faces* (1855).

Otis **Criblecolis** *see* W.C. **Fields**

Jimmy **Cricket:** James Mulgrew (1945–), Ir.-born Br. TV entertainer. The comedian presumably based his name on the interjection of surprise, "jiminy cricket!"

Tom **Cringle:** William Walker (1838–1908), Sc.-born Austral. writer. Walker took his pseudonym from *Tom Cringle's Log*, a book of travels by the Scottish writer Michael Scott (1789–1835), published in *Blackwood's Magazine* from 1829 to 1833.

Pietro **Crinito:** Pietro Riccio (1475–1507), It. humanist.

Quentin **Crisp:** Denis Pratt (1909–1999), Eng. writer, performer, artist's model. "Denis Pratt," quipped the gay icon, "as my name was before I dyed it" [Paul Bailey, ed., *The Stately Homo: A Celebration of the Life of Quentin Crisp*, 2001].

Crispa: Margery Ruth Edwards (1918–), Br. crossword compiler. After an unhappy second marriage the setter changed her name to Ruth Crisp. Her pseudonym derives from this, as well as the feminine form of Latin *crispus*, "curled," referring to her former nickname, "Curly," given for her frizzy hair.

Edmund **Crispin:** Robert Bruce Montgomery (1921–1978), Eng. crime, SF writer, composer. The writer composed music under his own name, leaving this pseudonym for his crime and SF fiction. He took his pen name from a character in Michael **Innes**'s early detective novel *Hamlet, Revenge!* (1937).

Peter **Criss:** Peter Crisscoula (1945–), U.S. rock musician.

Linda **Cristal:** Victoria Maya (1936–), Mexican movie actress, working in U.S.

Michael **Cristofer:** Michael Procaccino (1945–), U.S. playwright, screenwriter, movie actor.

Criswell: Charles Criswell King (1907–1982), U.S. psychic.

Estil **Critchie:** Arthur J. Burks (1898–1974), U.S. fantasy-fiction writer.

Job **Crithannah:** Jonathan Birch (1783–1847), Eng. writer, translator. The author used this name, an anagram of his real name, for *Fifty-one Original Fables, with Morals and Ethical Index* (1851).

Criton: Charles Maurras (1868–1952), Fr. political journalist. The writer used this name for polemical articles in the paper *L'Action française*, presumably taking it from the 5th century BC Athenian, better known in English as Crito, who was a friend of Socrates and introduced by Plato in one of his dialogues.

Monsieur **Croche:** Achille-Claude Debussy (1862–1918), Fr. composer. The composer used this name for some of his musical criticisms. He made a selection of these in 1917 and they were published posthumously as by *Monsieur Croche, anti-dilettante* (1921). The name itself translates as "Mr. Quaver" (in the sense "eighth note").

Howard **Crockett:** Howard Hausey (1925–1944), U.S. songwriter.

David **Croft:** David Sharland (1922–), Br. TV scriptwriter. The writer adopted his mother's maiden name as his professional name.

Douglas **Croft:** Douglas Malcolm Wheatcroft (1929–), U.S. juvenile movie actor. The actor's name was originally shortened to Douglas Wheat, but when this proved unsuitable for publicity purposes he replaced it with the more marketable Croft.

Jaq **Croft:** Jacqueline Mycroft (1968–), Br. movie, TV actress.

Nita **Croft:** Nita Pycroft (1902–), Eng. stage actress.

Chrystal **Croftangry** *see* Jedediah **Cleishbotham**

Francis de **Croisset:** Frantz Wiener (1877–1937), Fr. comedy, travel-sketch writer, of Belg. origin. The new name may refer to Croisset, the location of the house outside Rouen where Gustave Flaubert, the "hermit of Croisset," lived and wrote for much of his life.

H. Ripley **Cromarsh:** Bryan Mary Julia Josephine Angell, née Doyle (1877–1927), Eng. writer, sister of Arthur Conan Doyle, creator of Sherlock Holmes.

Deas **Cromarty:** Elizabeth Sophia Watson, née Fletcher (1850–1918), Eng. novelist. The writer used this name for five novels and collections of regional tales set in Scotland. *Deas* is Gaelic for "the South," so that the name perhaps stands for Watson herself, born in London, in the south of England, and for her Scottish husband, Rev. Robert A. Watson (1845–1921), born in Aberdeen, northeastern Scotland, not far from the historic district of Cromarty.

Richmal **Crompton:** Richmal Crompton Lamburn (1890–1969), Eng. children's writer. The author of the stories featuring the schoolboy William Brown adopted her pen name when writing for magazines while teaching classics at a London girls' school. "The High School ... had a rule that their staff should have no other employment without the Headmistress's express permission. Richmal was not sure whether her free-lance writing counted as 'other employment,' but played for safety by not using her full name. She forgot, however, that the annual index to *Punch* used proper names, not noms de plume. Miss Hodge ... send for Richmal, who very nervously went to see her. She was greeted with an excited 'My dear, why didn't you tell me?' Gradually after this the identity of the author of the William stories leaked out to the school" [Mary Cadogan, *Richmal Crompton: The Woman Behind William*, 1986]. The author's unusual first name, which she inherited from her grandmother, led many fans of her scruffy young hero to assume that she was a man. Her stories were regularly illustrated by Thomas **Henry**.

Richard **Cromwell**: (1) Richard Williams (?–?), Welsh great-grandfather of Eng. soldier, statesman Oliver Cromwell; (2) Roy M. Radebaugh (1910–1960), U.S. movie actor. Robert Cromwell, father of Oliver Cromwell (1599–1658), was the "grandson of a certain Richard Williams, who rose to fortune by the protection of Thomas Cromwell, earl of Essex [(?1485–1540)], and adopted the name of his patron" [*Dictionary of National Biography*]. Richard Williams's own father was a Welshman, Morgan Williams, who married Katherine Cromwell, Thomas's elder sister.

Il **Cronaca**: Simone del Pollaiolo (1457–1508), It. architect. According to Giorgio Vasari's *Lives* (1550), the architect was nicknamed "The Chronicler" from his accurate accounts of the marvels of Rome, where he studied. He was not related to the painter Antonio **Pollaiuolo**.

Arthur **Cronquist**: Franklin Arthur Beers (1919–1992), U.S. botanist.

Hume **Cronyn**: Hume Cronyn Blake (1911–2003), Can. movie actor.

Alfred **Croquis**: Daniel Maclise (1806–1870), Ir. painter, caricaturist. The artist used this name for "A Gallery of Illustrious Literary Characters" published in *Fraser's Magazine* in the 1830s. French *croquis* means "sketch."

Bing **Crosby**: Harry Lillis Crosby (1903–1977), U.S. crooner, movie actor. Harry Crosby enjoyed the comic strip "Bingville Bugle" when at grade school, with its hero a character named Bing. Either because of his fondness for this character, or (some say) his resemblance to it, he was nicknamed "Bing" and later adopted the name.

David **Crosby**: David Van Cortland (1941–), U.S. rock singer.

Paule **Croset** *see* Paula **Corday**

Amanda **Cross**: Carolyn Gold Heilbrun (1926–), U.S. feminist literary critic, crime writer, of Russ. Jewish parentage. Heilbrun adopted this name (to protect her academic career at Columbia University) for mystery novels featuring the English feminist detective Kate Fansler. Her true identity was not revealed until 1972.

Christopher **Cross**: Christopher Geppert (1951–), U.S. pop singer. A name playing on "crisscross."

Henri Edmond **Cross**: Henri Delacroix (1856–1910), Fr. neoimpressionist painter. Presumably the artist translated his name to promote his national name internationally.

Mark **Cross**: Archibald Thomas Pechey (1876–1961), Eng. popular songwriter, playwright. Pechey also used the name Valentine, adopting it from his mother's maiden name of Vallentin.

Victoria **Cross**: Annie Sophie Cory (1868–1952), Eng. novelist, sister of Laurence **Hope**. The writer's pen name (originally Victoria Crosse) puns on the gallantry award, popularly known as the V.C. Cory's father, a colonel in the Indian army, was decorated at the siege of Lucknow. After the death of Queen Victoria (1901), she dropped the "e." "She selected as a pseudonym the name of a military decoration, as if to imply that she too had engaged in combat and displayed valor. The initials 'V.C.' corresponded to 'Victoria Cross,' a name she used instead of her birth name, and suggested double meanings: the frankness of her fiction would cross (Queen) Victoria, or make Victoria cross" [Schlueter, p.174].

Crab **Crossbones** *see* **Xariffa**

Melville **Crossman**: Darryl F. Zanuck (1902–1979), U.S. movie producer, film studio head. Zanuck began his career as a screenwriter for Warner Bros., using three pseudonyms so that his name did not appear on too many of the company's films. The other two were Mark Canfield and Gregory Rogers.

Jill **Croston** *see* Lacy J. **Dalton**

Billy **Crotchet**: William Davidson Crockett (1920–), Sc. comedy musician. The British crotchet is the American quarternote.

Christopher **Crowfield**: Harriet Elizabeth Beecher Stowe (1811–1896), U.S. novelist. The author of *Uncle Tom's Cabin* (1851) used this male name for some of her lesser writings.

Aleister **Crowley**: Edward Alexander Crowley (1875–1947), Eng. occultist, writer, poet. Crowley's new first name appeared in 1895, when on entering Trinity College, Cambridge, he signed the register as "Edward Aleister Crowley." There has been much speculation why he chose this name. Crowley mistakenly believed he had Irish ancestry, and he presumably picked what he saw as a Celtic equivalent of "Alexander." (A Scottish Gaelic equivalent would have been Alasdair, and later in life Crowley took on the lifestyle of a Highland laird.) On his initiation in 1898 into the magical society known as the Hermetic Order of the Golden Dawn he was given the magical name Perdurabo, interpreted as "The One Who Will Endure." In 1907 Crowley founded his own society, the Order of the Silver Star, calling himself Frater V.V.V.V.V., the letters standing for Latin *Vi Veri Vniversum Vivus Vici*, "In my life I have conquered the universe with the power of truth." Other names used by Crowley include Khaled Khan, Count Vladimir Svareff, Master Therion, and Soror Vikaram. The penultimate of these derives from Greek *therion*, "beast," matching the title Crowley had taken to himself, "The Beast 666."

Henry **Crown**: Henry Krinsky (1896–1990), U.S. industrialist, of Lithuanian parentage.

Alfred **Crowquill**: Alfred Henry Forrester (1804–1872), Eng. illustrator, comic artist + Charles Robert Forrester (1803–1850), Eng. writer, his brother. Charles Forrester abandoned his literary activities around 1843, after which the name was borne by Alfred alone. A crow quill, originally made from crows' quills, is a special type of artist's pen, capable of drawing very fine lines.

Tom **Cruise**: Thomas Cruise Mapother IV (1962–), U.S. movie actor.

Paul **Crum**: Roger Pettiward (1906–1942), Eng. cartoonist, painter.

Juana Inés de la **Cruz**: Juana Ramírez de Asbaje (1651–1695), Sp.-Mexican poet, nun. Juana was born the illegitimate child of a Spanish captain, Pedro Manuel de Asbaje y Vargas Machuca, and Isabel Ramírez de Santillana. She entered a Carmelite convent at the age of 16 but left a few months later and made her profession in the convent of Jerome under the religious name and title Sor Juana Inés de la Cruz (Sister Joanna Agnes of the Cross).

Penélope **Cruz**: Penélope Cruz Sanchez (1974–), Sp. movie actress, working in U.S.

James **Cruze**: Jens Cruz Bosen (1884–1942), U.S. movie director, of Dan. parentage.

Crwys: William Crwys Williams (1875–1968), Welsh poet. The poet's bardic name means "cross."

Lili **Csokonai**: Péter Esterházy (1950–), Hung. novelist. short-story writer. Esterházy used this name for *Tizenhét hattyúk* ("Seventeen swans") (1987), set in 1980s Hungary but written in 17th-century Hungarian, in which the female narrator tells of her unhappy love. The novel won high critical acclaim and was assumed to be by a new writer. Publication of the second edition revealed the true author.

C3.3: Oscar Fingal O'Flahertie Wills Wilde (1854–1900), Ir. dramatist, poet. The writer used this name for his poem *The Ballad of Reading Gaol* (1898), about his experiences in the jail of the title. The name itself was his prison number (block C, 3d floor, cell #3).

Joe **Cuba**: Gilberto Miguel Calderón (1931–2009), U.S. bandleader, of Puerto Rican parentage. In 1954, after playing in various groups, the salsa musician formed his own band, the Jose Calderon Sextet. On landing a booking at a leading New York Latin music venue, however, the club's owner decided his name was not a crowd-puller and billed him instead as Joe Cuba and his Sextet. The first Calderón knew of his new identity was when he saw the engagement announced in a local paper, leading him to conclude that somebody else had stolen his gig.

Cúchares: Francisco Arjona Herrera (1818–1868), Sp. bullfighter. The name is now borne by the Mexican bullfighter Jorge Benavides (1978–).

Cuey-na-Gael: [Rev. Dr.] John Irwin Brown (*fl*.1908), Sc. minister, writer. Irwin Brown was minister of the Scottish Presbyterian Church in Rotterdam, Netherlands, when he wrote his amusing account *An Irishman's Difficulties with the Dutch Language* (1908), which went into eight editions. His pseudonym means "Hugh the Scotsman," implying a native speaker of Gaelic.

Paul **Cuffe**: Paul Slocum (1759–1817), U.S. black boatbuilder. The Pan-Africanist adopted his father's Akan name, properly "Kofi," meaning "born on Friday."

Xavier **Cugat**: Francisco de Asis Javier Cugat Mingall de Bru y Deulofeo (1900–1990), Sp.-born U.S. bandleader. The musician's original name breaks down into Francisco de Asis ("Francis of Assisi"), Javier (giving Xavier), Cugat (from his father, Juan Cugat) and Mingall de Bru y Deulofeo (his mother).

Countée **Cullen**: ? (?1903–1946), U.S. black poet, playwright. The name of Cullen's father is not known. In 1916 he was enrolled in Public School Number 27 in the Bronx, New York, as "Countee L. Porter," with no accent on the first "e." He was then living with Amanda Porter, who was probably his grandmother. When she died in 1917, he went to live with the Rev. Frederick Asbury Cullen and his wife. Although never formally adopted by them, he claimed them as his natural parents and in 1918 took the name Countée P. Cullen, the middle initial standing for "Porter." He dropped the initial in 1925.

Guy **Cullingford**: Constance Lindsay Taylor (1907–2000), Br. crime writer.

Ridgewell **Cullum**: Sidney Groves Burghard (1867–1943), Br. writer of westerns.

Kathryn **Culver** *see* Brett **Halliday**

Silas Tomken **Cumberbatch**: Samuel Taylor Coleridge (1772–1834), Eng. poet, critic. The poet adopted the name, retaining his initials, on enlisting in the 15th Dragoons in 1793: "No objection having been taken to his height, or age, and being thus accepted, he was asked his name. He had previously determined to give one that was thoroughly Kamschatkian, but having noticed that morning over a door in Lincoln's Inn Fields (or the Temple) the name 'Cumberbatch' (not 'Comberback'), he thought this word sufficiently outlandish, and replied, 'Silas Tomken Cumberbatch,' and such was the entry in the regimental book" [Joseph Cottle, *Early Recollections, chiefly relating to Samuel Taylor Coleridge*, 1837].

Constance **Cummings:** Constance Cummings Levy, née Halverstadt (1910–2005), U.S.–born stage, movie actress, working in U.K. The actress's middle name, which she took as her stage surname, was the maiden name of her mother, concert artist Kate Cummings.

e.e. **cummings:** Edward Estlin Cummings (1894–1962), U.S. poet. Cummings used the lowercase form of his name until the 1930s, although not as regularly or insistently as is sometimes supposed. (Nor did he legally change his name to lowercase letters only, as is also said.) Cummings devised a variety of humorous pseudonyms for his comic contributions to *Vanity Fair*, such as Helen Whiffletree and Professor Dunkell of Colgate University.

Robert **Cummings:** Charles Clarence Robert Orville Cummings (1908–1990), U.S. movie actor. The actor's regular screen name is not as original as the one under which he passed himself off when he went to England to acquire the accent. For this purpose he was Blade Stanhope Conway, and under this name succeeded in obtaining a part in Galsworthy's last play, *The Roof* (1929).

Grace **Cunard:** Harriet Mildred Jeffries (1894–1967), U.S. movie actress.

E.V. **Cunningham:** Howard Fast (1914–2003), U.S. novelist. The author of *Spartacus* (1951) used this pseudonym for detective and police novels. He also wrote three novels as Walter Ericson.

J. Morgan **Cunningham:** Donald E. Westlake (1933–2008), U.S. crime writer. The prolific author of crime fiction used this name for a spoof of Arthur Hailey's novels *Hotel* (1965) and *Airport* (1968) set in a public toilet and called *Comfort Station* (1973). The jacket had a blurb written by Westlake himself saying, "I wish I had written this book." *See also* Richard **Stark**.

Robert **Cunninghame-Graham:** Robert Graham (?–*c*.1797), Sc. songwriter. The writer assumed the additional name of Cunninghame in 1796 on succeeding to the estates of John Cunninghame, 15th (and last) earl of Glencairn. The songwriter's great-grandson and namesake was the writer, politician, and adventurer, Robert Bontine Cunninghame-Graham (1852–1936).

Le **Curé d'Ars:** Jean-Baptiste-Marie Vianney (1786–1859), Fr. priest. The patron saint of parish priests gained his better-known name from the village of Ars-en-Dombes, where he was in charge of the parish from 1817 to the end of his life.

Curnonsky: Maurice Edmond Sailland (1872–1956), Fr. gastronome, cookery writer.

Finlay **Currie:** Finlay Jefferson (1878–1968), Sc. stage, movie actor.

Avon **Curry:** Jean Bowden (1920–), Sc. mystery writer, romantic novelist. Other names used by the writer were Barbara Annandale, Tessa Barclay, Jocelyn Barry, Jennifer Bland, and Belinda Dell.

Kid **Curry:** Harvey Logan (1865–1903), U.S. outlaw. The gunslinger, a member of the Wild Bunch led by Butch **Cassidy**, adopted the name of his uncle, George Sutherland ("Flat Nose") Curry (1841–1882), a notorious cattle rustler, whose own original name is said to have been George Parrott.

Philip **Curtin:** Marie Adelaide Lowndes, née Belloc (1868–1947), Fr.-born Eng. novelist, of Eng.-Fr. parentage. Known generally as Mrs. Belloc Lowndes, the author adopted this name for *Noted Murder Mysteries* (1914), while for *Not All Saints* (1914) she was Elizabeth Rayner.

Alan **Curtis:** Harold Ueberroth (1909–1953), U.S. movie actor, husband of Priscilla **Lawson**. (Some sources misspell Curtis's original name as "Neberroth" by mistranscription of the initial letter.)

Chris **Curtis:** Christopher Crummey (1941–2005), Eng. pop singer.

Dick **Curtis:** Richard D. Dye (1902–1952), U.S. movie actor.

Jamie Lee **Curtis:** Jamie Leigh Curtis (1958–), U.S. movie actress, daughter of Janet **Leigh** and Tony **Curtis**.

Jean-Louis **Curtis:** Louis Laffitte (1917–1995), Fr. novelist, essayist.

Ken **Curtis:** Curtis Gates (1916–1991), U.S. movie, TV actor.

King **Curtis:** Curtis Ousley (1934–1971), U.S. black saxophonist.

Mann **Curtis:** Norman Kurtz, Sr. (1911–1984), U.S. lyricist.

Peter **Curtis** *see* Juliet **Astley**

Tony **Curtis:** Bernard Schwartz (1925–), U.S. movie actor, of Hung. descent. The actor explains: "When I started in movies, I knew I'd have to change my name, and I went through a whole basketful of them — every conceivable kind of name. Steven John, John Stevens.... One of my Hungarian ancestors' names was Kertész, so I thought maybe I'd anglicize it to Curtis. First Jimmy Curtis. Then Johnny Curtis. Finally I hit on Anthony Curtis, and it eventually got shortened to Tony.... Not long after I changed it, I was at a cocktail party with Janet **Leigh**, and there was Cary **Grant**, my idol. Janet said, 'Come on, we'll go over and meet him.' So I went over to meet him and I was so nervous. I said, 'Hi, my name is ... Bernie Schwartz'" [Tony Curtis and Barry Paris, *Tony Curtis: The Autobiography*, 1993].

Michael **Curtiz:** Mihály Kertész Kaminer (1886–1962), Hung.-born U.S. movie director. Curtiz's obituary in *The Times* (April 12, 1962) records that his name "went through a number of transformations and transliterations before reaching its final American form." (But not to an ultimate possible Curtis.)

Clare **Curzon:** Eileen-Marie Duell Buchanan, née Belderson (1922–), Br. crime writer. Buchanan originally wrote as Rhone Petrie, then under forms of her real name (Marie Buchanan, Marie Duell), before settling in the 1970s to the name by which she became known for her short stories.

Cusanino: Giovanni Carestini (*c.*1705–*c.*1758), It. male soprano singer. The singer took his name from the Cusani, the noble Milanese family who were his patrons.

Paul **Cushing:** Roland Alexander Wood-Seys (1854–1919), Eng. novelist. Wood-Seys settled in California to grow olives and write novels, and reviewers often took him to be an American writer.

Bob **Custer:** Raymond Anthony Glenn (1898–1974), U.S. movie actor.

Dom **Cuthbert:** Edward Joseph Aloysius Butler (1858–1934), Ir. religious. The abbot of Downside Abbey, England, took his religious name on entering the Catholic Benedictine novitiate in 1876. St. Cuthbert was a 7th-century bishop of Lindisfarne.

Cybi o Eifion: Ebenezer Thomas (1802–1863), Welsh poet and critic. The writer better known as Eben **Fardd** used this name as a young man. It means "Cybi of Eifionydd," the latter being his native district. (It also gave the name of **Eifionydd**.) Cybi was a 6th-century saint.

Cymro Gwyllt: Richard Jones (1772–1833), Welsh hymnwriter. The writer's assumed name means "wild Welshman." "Wild Wales," as an epithet, became familiar from George Borrow's 1862 book so titled, but the phrase itself dates from medieval times (Welsh *gwyllt Gwalia*).

Cynan: [Rev. Sir] Albert Evans-Jones (1895–1970), Welsh poet. The poet, twice Archdruid of Wales, took his bardic name from that of a Welsh saint or historical figure, such as the 6th-century traditional founder of Brittany who it is said will one day return to restore to the Welsh the right to govern the whole of Britain. The name itself means "chief," "high."

Cynddelw: Robert Ellis (1810–1875), Welsh poet, antiquary. The Baptist minister adopted a traditional bardic name for his poetry. Cynddelw was the name of a famous 12th-century Welsh court poet. The name itself means "chief image."

Cynfaen: John Hugh Evans (1833–1886), Welsh poet. The minister's bardic name means literally "chief stone."

Cynicus: Martin Anderson (1854–1932), Sc. cartoonist, postcard publisher. The artist's name alludes to the satirical nature of his work.

Cynthia: Amy Elizabeth Pack, née Thorpe (1910–1963), U.S. secret agent.

Savinien de **Cyrano de Bergerac:** Savinien de Cyrano (1619–1655), Fr. writer. In 1638 the colorful and controversial writer began adding "de Bergerac" to his original name, taking it from land owned by his family in the Chevreuse valley southeast of Paris. (It is thus not the better-known Bergerac in the Dordogne.) His name became widely known through Edmond Rostand's verse play *Cyrano de Bergerac* (1897), which presents him as a fictional character.

[St.] **Cyril:** Constantine (*c.*827–869), Byzantine missionary. The theologian and scholar for whom the Cyrillic alphabet is named took his religious name on becoming a monk in early 869, shortly before his death. He and his brother Methodius were jointly known as "Apostles of the Slavs."

Miley **Cyrus:** Destiny Hope Cyrus (1992–), U.S. juvenile TV, movie actress, daughter of country singer Billy Ray Cyrus (1961–). The actress first appeared under her birth name, given by her ambitious parents, but in 2008 legally changed her name to Miley Ray Cyrus, her new first name coming from her nickname, "Smiley Miley," given for her sunny disposition. Her new name was also that of the character she played in the TV series *Hannah Montana* (2005), about a schoolgirl called Miley Stewart who disguises herself by night as a glamorous pop singer, Hannah Montana.

Tomasz **Czaszka:** Tadeusz Rittner (1873–1921), Pol. playwright, novelist. The writer's adopted surname is the Polish word for "skull."

Adam **Czepiel:** Stanislaw Brzozowski (1878–1911), Pol. literary critic, philosopher, working in Italy.

Chuck **D:** Carlton Douglas Ridenhour (1960–), U.S. black rapper.

Rob **da Bank:** Robert Gorham (1973–), Eng. radio DJ, record producer. A punning name based on the broadcaster's first name. "I was given the name Rob da Bank when I was 18 and needed a DJ name. My wife says it sounds stupid and I have to agree, but it's my trademark — there's no point in changing it. Even my parents call me it, to humour me" [*Sunday Times*, April 19, 2009].

Da Brat: Shawntae Harris (1974–), U.S. black rapper. The singer adopted a name to fit her foul-mouthed image.

Pierre **Dac:** André Issac (1893–1975), Fr. stage comedian.

Caran **d'Ache** *see* **Caran d'Ache**

Morton **Da Costa:** Morton Tecosky (1914–1989), U.S. stage, musical, movie director.

Charlotte **Dacre:** Charlotte Byrne, née King (?1782–1825), Eng. writer of "Gothic" fiction. Byrne contributed poems to the *Morning Post* newspaper under the name Rose Matilda.

Harry Dacre: Henry Decker (1860–1922), Br. popular composer.

J. Colne Dacre: Mary Stuart Boyd, née Kirkwood (?–1937), Sc.-born N.Z. writer.

Daddy Rings: Everald Dwyer (1972–), Jamaican reggae musician. Dwyer was given his nickname for the flashy rings that he wore.

Daddy Stovepipe: Johnny Watson (1867–1963), U.S. popular musician. The street musician derived his nickname from his tall top hat.

Dafis Castellhywel: David Davis (1745–1827), Welsh teacher, poet. The name means "Davis of Castellhywel," the latter being the location of his famous school, opened around 1782.

Willem Dafoe: William Dafoe (1955–), U.S. movie actor. Dafoe modified his first name to avoid being called "Billy," which he hated. "The name Willem made me feel funny for a while ... because I don't like the idea of having a stage name. But I guess I'm used to it now; I've been Willem longer than I've been Billy" [Cameron-Wilson, p.45].

Asadata Dafora: John Warner Dafora Horton (1890–1965), Sierra Leonean singer, dancer, choreographer, working in U.S. Dafora came to New York in 1929, traveling with other African dancers.

Da Free John: Franklyn Albert Jones (1939–), U.S. religious leader. Following study in India with Swami Rudrananda, Jones founded the Dawn Horse Communion in 1972. In 1975 it became the Free Daist Community, and Jones changed his name first to Bubba ("Brother") Free John, then in 1979 to Da ("Giver") Free John. In the mid–1980s he became known as Heart-Master Da Love Ananda, or Avadhoota Da Love Ananda Hridayam. Each change of name brought a new style of teaching.

Dafydd Ddu Eryri: David Thomas (1759–1822), Welsh poet, bardic teacher. The poet's name means "Black David of Snowdonia." In 1783 he began to establish literary societies in Arfon, the historic district where the well-known mountain region is located.

Dafydd Ddu Feddyg: David Samwell (1751–1798), Welsh surgeon, writer. The name means "Black David of Beddyg," from a local placename.

Dafydd Ionawr: David Richards (1751–1827), Welsh poet. The poet's name means "David January," referring to the month of his birth.

Dafydd Morganwg: David Watkin Jones (1832–1905), Welsh historian, poet. The writer's name means "David of Glamorgan," the latter being his native county.

Dafydd y Garreg Wen: David Owen (c.1711–1741), Welsh harpist. The musician came to be known by the name of his farm, its own name meaning "the white stone."

Stig Dagerman: Stig Halvard Jansson (1923–1954), Swe. writer.

Dagmar: Virginia Ruth Egnor (1921–2001), U.S. TV comedienne.

Dagonet: (1) J.A. Hardwick (1815–1866), Eng. songwriter; (2) George Robert Sims (1847–1922), Eng. journalist, dramatist. Sims used the name for his "Mustard and Cress" column in the *Referee*, from its first issue in 1877. Dagonet was King Arthur's fool in Thomas Malory's *Le Morte d'Arthur* (1470).

Lil Dagover: Marie Antonia Sieglinde Marta Daghofer, née Liletts (1897–1980), Ger. movie actress, of Du. parentage.

Richard Dahen: Clotilde Inez Mary Graves (1864–1932), Ir. verse dramatist, fiction writer.

Daijuyama: Sakatsume Tadaaki (1959–), Jap. sumo wrestler. The wrestler's fighting name means "splendid mountain."

Johan Daisne: Herman Thiery (1912–1978), Belg. novelist, dramatist, writing in French.

Nicolas Dalayrac: Nicolas d'Alayrac (1753–1809), Fr. composer. Although officially favored by the monarchy, the composer had democratic sympathies, and accordingly changed the spelling of his name during the French Revolution in order to remove the aristocratic *d'* prefix.

Julian D'Albie: D'Albiac Luard (1892–1978), Ir.-born Eng. stage, radio, TV actor.

Jehanne d'Alcy: Charlotte-Stéphanie Faes (1865–1956), Fr. stage, movie actress. The actress also went by the name Fanny Manieux.

Alan Dale: (1) Alfred J. Cohen (1861–1928), Eng.-born U.S. theater critic, playwright; (2) Aldo Sigismondi (1925–2002), U.S. popular singer, TV host, of It. parentage. Both names evoke the Allan-a-Dale who was a companion of the legendary English outlaw Robin Hood, and Cohen specifically took his name from the character Alan-a-Dale in Reginald De Koven's popular operetta *Robin Hood* (1890).

Charles Dale: Charles Marks (1881–1971), U.S. vaudeville, movie actor, teaming with Joe **Smith**.

Darley Dale: Francesca Maria Steele (1848–1931), Eng. writer. Steele used this name for her adult and children's fiction, keeping her own name for historical and biographical works of a religious nature. The attractively alliterative name is actually that of a picturesque valley in Derbyshire.

Dick Dale: Richard Anthony Monsour (1937–), U.S. rock musician, "surf guitarist." The musician's new name was suggested to him by T. Texas Tiny, a Texas DJ.

Edwin Dale: Edward Reginald Home-Gall

(1899–after 1980), Br. writer of stories for boys, son of Reginald **Wray**.

Flora **Dale** *see* Rosa **Henderson**

Frances **Dale** *see* Fanny **Cradock**

Jim **Dale**: James Smith (1935–), Br. movie actor, comedian.

Margaret **Dale**: Margaret Bolam (1922–), Br. ballet dancer, choreographer, TV director.

Cass **Daley**: Catherine Dailey (1915–1975), U.S. movie comedienne.

Vernon **Dalhart**: Marion Try Slaughter (1883–1948), U.S. country singer. The singer devised his stage name by combining the names of two small towns in his native Texas.

Dalida: Yolande Christina Gigliotti (1933–1987), Egyptian-born movie actress, singer, of It. parentage, working in France. The singer's stage name presumably derives from that of the biblical Delilah, Samson's mistress, who appears as Dalida in Wyclif's Bible (1380s) and in the early 15th-century *The Court of Love*, doubtfully attributed to Chaucer.

M. **Dalin**: Linda Villari, née White (1836–1915), Eng. novelist, essayist, translator. An anagram of the writer's first name.

Marcel **Dalio**: Israel Mosche Blauschild (1900–1983), Fr. movie comedian, working in U.S. The actor took his screen name from Count Danilo Danilowitsch in Franz Lehár's opera *The Merry Widow* (1905).

John **Dall**: John Jenner Thompson (1918–1971), U.S. movie actor.

Johny **Dallas**: Peter Ross (1929–), Eng. actor, comedian.

Paul **Dallas** *see* Eric **Allen**

Ruth **Dallas**: Ruth Mumford (1919–), N.Z. poet, children's writer. The author adopted the name of her maternal grandmother.

Henri **d'Alleber**: Pierre Henri Victor Berdalle de Lapommeraye (1839–1891), Fr. critic, lecturer. The scholar formed his new surname by inverting the elements of his fourth name.

Toti **dal Monte**: Antonietta Meneghelli (1893–1975), It. opera singer. "Toti" is a pet form of the soprano's first name. "Dal Monte" is the surname of her maternal grandmother, of noble Venetian birth.

Charles **Dalmorès**: Henry Alphonse Brin (1871–1939), Fr. opera singer, working in U.S.

Ksaver Sandor **Dalski**: Ljubo Babic (1854–1935), Croatian writer.

Mamont **Dalsky**: Mamont Viktorovich Neyelov (1865–1918), Russ. actor.

Vladimir **Dalsky**: Vladimir Mikhaylovich Nesterenko (1912–), Russ. artist.

Lacy J. **Dalton**: Jill Byrem (1948–), U.S. coun-try, rock singer. The musician originally used the singing name Jill Croston.

Priscilla **Dalton** *see* Ed **Noon**

Brian **Daly**: John M. East (1932–2003), Eng. movie actor, screenwriter. East adopted this name as screenwriter of the porno movie *Emmanuelle in Soho* (1981), originally titled *Funeral in Soho*. "Over the course of a weekend, East rewrote and retitled the script, assuming the pseudonym of Brian Daly, his grandfather's regular scenarist and greatest friend, dead since 1923" [Matthew Sweet, *Shepperton Babylon*, 2005]. East's grandfather was the stage and movie actor John Marlborough East (1860–1924).

Mark **Daly**: Mark Hobson (1887–1957), Sc. stage. movie actor.

Rann **Daly**: Edward Vance Palmer (1885–1959), Austral. writer.

Damaskinos: Dimitrios Papandreou (1891–1949), Gk. archbishop, regent of Greece. The prelate's religious name relates to the 7th-century monk and theologian John Damascene (John of Damascus).

Gasparino **Damata**: Gasparino da Mata e Silva (1918–*c*.1980), Brazilian writer, gay activist.

Joe **D'Amato**: Aristide Massaccesi (1936–1999), It. movie director. Other pseudonyms used by the director, whose output centered on horror and porno movies, are Steve Benson, Michael Wotruba, David Hills, and Kevin Mancuso, none of which bears any relationship to his real name.

Jacques **d'Amboise**: Jacques Joseph Ahearn (1934–), U.S. ballet dancer, choreographer.

Lucio **d'Ambra**: Renato Eduardo Manganella (1880–1939), It. novelist, comedy writer.

Tadd **Dameron**: Tadley Ewing Peake (1917–1965), U.S. jazz musician.

Dame Shirley: Louise Amelia Knapp Smith Clappe (1819–1906), U.S. writer, humorist. The author assumed this persona for the writer of letters home to New England by a woman who had gone west to California for the gold rush. They were published in collected form as *The Shirley Letters* (1922).

Damia: Louise Marie Damien (1889–1978), Fr. popular singer.

Damian: Damian Davey (1964–), Eng. singer, entertainer.

Father **Damien**: Joseph de Veuster (1840–1889), Belg. missionary. De Veuster took the name Damien when he became a member of the Fathers of the Sacred Heart of Jesus and Mary in 1859. In 1863 he was sent to Hawaii, where he was ordained priest and where from 1873 he worked in a leprosy settlement, himself dying of the disease. He was beatified in 1994 and canonized as a saint in 2009.

Lili **Damita**: Liliane Marie Madeleine Carré (1901–1994), Fr. movie actress. The actress claims she first changed her name after king Alfonso XIII of Spain (who became her lover) saw her on the beach at Biarritz and enquired after the *damita* (young lady) in the red bathing dress [*The Times*, April 4, 1993]. She was thus originally Damita del Rojo, "young lady in red," and then for a while Lily Deslys ("lily of the lilies") before settling for Lili Damita in 1923.

Damita Jo: Damita Jo DuBlanc (1930–1998), U.S. jazz, R&B singer.

Jerry **Dammers:** Gerald Dankin (1954–), Eng. rock musician.

Mark **Damon:** Alan Mark Harris (1933–), U.S. movie actor, producer.

Stuart **Damon:** Stuart Michael Zonis (1937–), U.S. stage, TV actor, director.

Vic **Damone:** Vito Rocco Farinola (1928–), U.S. movie actor, singer.

Claude **Dampier:** Claude Connelly Cowan (1879–1955), Br. stage, movie comedian. The actor first made his name in Australia, where the English buccaneer William Dampier (1652–1715) gave his name to the Dampier Archipelago and Dampier Strait.

Fyodor **Dan:** Fyodor Ilyich Gurvich (1871–1947), Russ. Menshevik leader.

Michael **Dan:** Michael Dorane (1948–), Jamaican-born Br. reggae musician.

Dana: Rosemary Scallon, née Brown (1951–), Northern Ireland pop singer. The singer adopted her school nickname, Irish *dana* meaning "naughty," "mischievous."

Freeman **Dana** *see* Alice **Tilton**

Richard **Dana** *see* Mark **Carrel**

Rose **Dana** *see* Marilyn **Ross**

Viola **Dana:** Violet Flugrath (1897–1987), U.S. movie actress.

Dana International: Yaron Cohen (1972–), Israeli-born transexual pop singer. The winner of the 1998 Eurovision Song Contest began her career as a drag artist named Sharon. She underwent a sex-change operation in 1993 and made her name under the title of her first song, itself not about the Northern Ireland singer **Dana**, as popularly supposed, but a character of that name in the books Israeli children use when learning to read.

Frank **Danby:** Julia Frankau, née Davis (1859–1916), Ir.-born Br. popular novelist, of Jewish parentage, sister of Owen **Hall**, grandmother of Eliot **Naylor**. Frankau used this name for her antisemitic novel *Dr. Phillips, A Maida Vale Idyll* (1887).

Frank **Danby** *see* J.P. **McCall**

Dancourt: Florent Carton, sieur d'Ancourt (1661–1725), Fr. actor, playwright.

Clemence **Dane:** Winifred Ashton (1888–1965), Eng. novelist, playwright. The writer took her name from the London church of St. Clement Danes, itself probably so named as it was built on an ancient Danish burial site. It stood (and stands) in a part of London that she knew well, and was where she lived for most of her life. In reply to a private inquiry she told how she came by the name: "Just chance! I was talking over with a friend the type of name that I thought effective for a pseudonym — and instanced 'Bow Bells,' 'St. Mary Axe,' 'St. Clement Dane' (city churches and names that I knew) and so, in a flash, arrived my own 'umbrella'" [Marble, p.6]. Ashton went on stage in 1913 as Diana Portis.

Hal **Dane:** Haldane M'Fall (1860–1928), Eng. soldier, author, art critic.

Karl **Dane:** Karl Daen (1886–1934), Dan. movie actor.

Mark **Dane** *see* Ed **Noon**

Pascal **Danel:** Jean-Jacques Pascal (1944–), Fr. actor, singer, entertainer. The singer originally adopted his name as a circus performer, taking it from his birthplace, Danel.

William **Danforth:** William Daniels (1869–1941), U.S. movie actor.

D'Angelo: Michael D'Angelo Archer (1974–), U.S. black soul singer.

John **Dangerfield:** Oswald John Frederick Crawfurd (1834–1909), Eng. writer. Crawfurd had several pseudonyms for his different types of writing, others being Archibald Banks, Alex Freke Turner, Joseph Strange, Humphrey St. Kayne, George Windle Sandys, and John Latouche. Using this last in *Country House Essays* (1885) he apologized for the "impertinence of an author in using a feigned name," whether from modesty or from "fear of the possible fierceness of critics" [Marble, p.7].

Rodney **Dangerfield:** Jacob Cohen (1921–2004), U.S. comedian, comedy writer. The actor was originally a standup comic under the name Jack Roy.

Danger Mouse: Brian Burton (1977–), U.S. DJ. Originally performing in mouse costume to disguise his shyness, the musician adopted his name from *Dangermouse*, a popular Brtish TV cartoon series of the 1980s, in which the named character is "the greatest secret agent in the world."

Mlle. **Dangeville:** Marie-Anne Botot (1714–1796), Fr. actress.

Dangle: Alexander Mattock Thompson (1861–1948), Ger.-born Eng. journalist, playwright. Dangle is a character in R.B. Sheridan's play *The Critic*. See *also* **Nunquam**.

Daniel: Eduarda Mansilla de Garcia (1835–1892), Argentinian music critic, singer, composer.

Brother **Daniel:** Oswald Rufeisin (1922–), Pol.-born Israeli Carmelite monk. During the Nazi occupation of Poland, Rufeisin was hidden in a Carmelite convent. He was baptized, became a Carmelite monk under the name Brother Daniel, and in 1958 was sent to the Carmelite monastery on Mount Carmel in Haifa, Israel. He continued to regard himself as a Jew, however, and became an Israeli citizen.

Daniel Daniel: Daniel Markowitz (1890–1981), U.S. sportswriter. The writer adopted his duplicate name in 1913 at a time of strong antisemitic sentiment.

Daniel à Jesu: John Floyd (1572–1649), Eng. Jesuit. Floyd used his religious name for some of his writings, as well as the names Hermannus Lœmelius, George White, and Annosus Fidelis Verimentanus.

Daniele da Volterra: Daniele Ricciarelli (1509–1566), It. painter.

Suzanne Danielle: Suzanne Morris (1957–), Eng. TV actress.

Henry Daniel-Rops: Jean-Charles-Henri Petiot (1901–1965), Fr. writer, church historian.

Bebe Daniels: Phyllis Daniels (1901–1971), U.S. movie actress, of Sc.-Sp. ancestry. Daniels later moved to the U.K., where with her husband, actor Ben Lyon (1901–1979), she appeared on radio and TV, notably in the popular World War II radio show *Hi Gang!* She was called Bebe, Spanish for "baby," from birth.

Maxine Daniels: Gladys Lynch (1930–), Eng. jazz singer.

Lisa Daniely: Elizabeth Bodington (1930–), Br.-Fr. movie, TV actress. The actress used this name for what she defined as "sexy, undistinguished movies." She reverted to her real name in the 1970s with "a new middleaged persona," as she put it.

Daniel y Pant: Daniel Thomas (1851–1910), Welsh storyteller. The teller of tall tales took his name from the farm where he lived, its own name meaning "the valley."

Danilo: Danilo Dixon (1956–), U.S. hairdresser, perruquier.

Mariya Danilova: Mariya Ivanovna Perfilyeva (1793–1810), Russ. ballet dancer.

Frederic Dannay *see* Ellery **Queen**

Sybil Danning: Sybelle Danninger (1950–), Austr.-born movie actress, working in Germany, U.S.

Gabriele D'Annunzio: Gaetano Rapagnetta (1863–1938), It. poet, novelist, dramatist. The writer's father, Francesco Rapagnetta, was adopted at the age of 13 by his uncle, Antonio d'Annunzio, and legally added that name to his own, as later did Gaetano himself. As a child, Gaetano was nicknamed "Gabriele" by his family for his saintly looks, after the archangel Gabriel. He liked the name and adopted it, presumably appreciating the apposite combination "Gabriele d'Annunzio," as if meaning "Gabriel of the Annunciation," referring to the angel

who announces to the Virgin Mary that she will give birth to Jesus (Luke 1:26–31).

Jane Danson: Jane Dawson (1978–), Br. TV actress.

Dante: August Harry Jansen (1883–1955), Dan.-born U.S. conjuror. A name that alludes to the performer's nationality (and also surname) while evoking the famous Italian poet. Jansen assumed the name in 1923 on the suggestion of U.S. conjuror Howard Thurston.

Michael Dante: Ralph Vitti (1935–), U.S. movie actor.

Ron Dante: Carmine Granito (1945–), U.S. popular singer, songwriter.

Louis Dantin: Eugène Seers (1865–1945), Can. author, critic, writing in French.

Helmut Dantine: Helmut Guttman (1917–1982), Austr. movie actor, working in U.S. The actor adopted the stage name, Niki Dantine, of his actress wife, whose original name was Nicola Schenck.

Ray Danton *see* Don Juan **Cardoza**

Caleb D'Anvers: Nicholas Amhurst (1697–1742), Eng. poet, political writer. The writer used the name as editor from 1726 of the *Craftsman*, an influential political journal.

Tony Danza: Anthony Iandanza (1951–), U.S. heavyweight boxer, TV actor.

Ram Da-Oz: Avraham Daus (1929–), Ger.-born Israeli composer.

Lorenzo da Ponte: Emanuele Conegliano (1749–1838), It. poet, librettist, adventurer, working in U.S. The librettist of three of Mozart's best-known operas was born a Jew. On converting in 1763 from Judaism to Catholicism he took the name of the bishop who baptized him, Monsignor Lorenzo da Ponte, as was then the custom. In 1805, when living in London, he was threatened with imprisonment for debt and immigrated to the United States to escape his creditors.

Dappy: Costas Dinos Contostavlos (1987–), Br. rapper, singer, of Gk. origin.

Olu Dara: Charles Jones III (1941–), U.S. black jazz musician. Jones adopted his Yoruba name in 1969.

Mme. d'Arblay: Frances ("Fanny") Burney (1752–1840), Eng. novelist, diarist. The writer's adopted name was that of her husband, General Alexandre d'Arblay, a French refugee in England, whom she married in 1793.

Kim Darby: Deborah Zerby (1947–), U.S. movie actress. The actress was originally a dancer and singer under the name Derby Zerby.

Terence Trent D'Arby: Terence Trent Darby (1962–), U.S. black soul singer. The singer retained his full name, with "Trent" as his middle name, but added an apostrophe to his surname as an affectation.

Mireille **Darc:** Mireille Aigroz (1938–), Fr. movie actress.

Denise **Darcel:** Denise Billecard (1925–), Fr. movie actress, working in U.S. The actress extracted her new surname from her original one.

Hariclea **Darclée:** Hariclea Haricly Hartulari (1860–1939), Rom. opera singer. The soprano's new surname is a French-style derivative of her original name.

Ciro **D'Arco:** Giuseppe Torelli (1816–1866), It. writer, politician. Torelli wrote various papers under this name.

Alex **D'Arcy:** Alexander Sarruf (1908–1996), Egyptian movie actor.

Roy **D'Arcy:** Roy Francis de Giusti (1894–1969), U.S. movie actor.

Dardanelle: Dardanelle Breckenridge (1917–1997), U.S. jazz musician.

Jean-Pierre **Dardenne:** Carl Higgans (1951–), Belg. movie director, working with Luc **Dardenne**, his brother. The brothers' adopted name seems to suggest *d'Ardennes*, "of the Ardennes," for the mountainous area in southeastern Belgium.

Luc **Dardenne:** Eric Higgans (1954–), Belg. movie director, working with Jean-Pierre **Dardenne**, his brother.

Dardmend: Zakir Ramiyev (1859–1921), Russ. (Tatar) poet. The poet's adopted name means "woeful one," alluding to the repression experienced by Tatars under czarism.

Phyllis **Dare:** Phyllis Dones (1890–1975), Eng. musical-comedy actress, sister of Zena **Dare**.

Simon **Dare:** Marjorie Huxtable (1897–?), Br. author of romantic novels. The writer also published as Marjorie Stewart.

Zena **Dare:** Florence Hariette Zena Dones (1887–1975), Br. movie actress, sister of Phyllis **Dare**. The sisters first performed together under their new name in 1899.

Georges **Darien:** Georges Adrien (1862–1921), Fr. novelist, polemicist. A simple anagram.

Bobby **Darin:** Walden Robert Cassotto (1936–1973), U.S. pop singer, movie actor, husband of Sandra **Dee** (married 1960, divorced 1967). The singer was advised to change his name by George Scheck, manager of Connie **Francis**, whom Cassotto was dating at the time. He is said to have found his new name in a phone book, although "reports of how 'Darin' was selected vary widely" [Brenda Scott Royce in Garraty and Carnes, vol. 6, p. 106].

Rubén **Darío:** Félix Rubén García Sarmiento (1867–1916), Nicaraguan poet, essayist. The poet's adopted surname is the Spanish form of "Darius."

Possibly he chose the name for Darius the Great, the ancient king of Persia.

Darkman: Brian Mitchell (*c*.1970–), Br. black reggae musician.

Alexandre **Darlaine:** Alexander D'Arbeloff (1898–1996), Russ.-born (Georgian) U.S. entrepreneur, writer. The writer used this name for two novels, publishing another book, *The Word Accomplished* (1951), under the pseudonym A.B. Christopher.

Candy **Darling:** James Hope Slattery (1949–1974), U.S. transvestite movie actor. A "sweet and sugary" name to match the performer's tacky persona. "At the bar I meet Candy Darling, who is working as a barmaid ... 'Candy is my new name,' she explains in a whispery, soft voice, like a low-volume Kim **Novak**. 'I was born Jimmy Slattery. I'm from Massapequa, Long Island. I belong on the screen. I was born to be a star. I'm in Jackie [Curtis]'s play *Glamour, Glory and Gold*. I inspired her to write it'" [Ultra Violet, *Famous for 15 Minutes: My Years with Andy Warhol*, 1988].

Olivia **Darling:** Chris Manby (1976–), Eng. romantic novelist. The writer, who mostly uses her real name, has also written erotic novels as Stephanie Ash.

William **Darling:** Wilhelm Sandorhazi (1882–1963), Hung.-born U.S. movie art director.

Clark **Darlton:** Walter Ernsting (1920–2005), Ger. SF writer. Ernsting adopted an English name on the grounds that no one would want to read science fiction written by a German. He began his career as a translator of American SF stories, then decided to try his own hand at the genre. On presenting his work to his first publisher, he accordingly told him that he had translated it, not that he was its actual author. His ruse was successful, and his story *UFO in the Night Sky* appeared in German bookstores in 1955.

August **Darnell:** Thomas August Darnell Browder (1951–), U.S. rock singer, of Dominican/Fr.-Can. parentage. The singer is also familiar as Kid Creole, a name referring to his mixed parentage.

Larry **Darnell:** Leo Edward Donald (1929–1983), U.S. popular singer ("Mr. Heart & Soul"). "Darnell" presumably from "Donald," reflecting the name's typical American pronunciation.

Linda **Darnell:** Monetta Eloyse Darnell (1921–1965), U.S. movie actress.

J. Herbert **Darnley:** Herbert McCarthy (1872–1947), Br. songwriter.

George **Darrell:** George Frederick Price (1841–1921), Eng.-born Austral. actor, playwright. The actor changed his name in 1868 on returning to Melbourne from New Zealand, where he had tried his luck as a golddigger.

Maisie **Darrell:** Maisie Hardie (1901–?), Br. stage actress, dancer.

Peter **Darrell:** Peter Skinner (1929–1987), Br. dancer, choreographer.

James **Darren:** James William Ercolani (1936–), U.S. movie actor, pop singer.

Frankie **Darro:** Frank Johnson (1917–1976), U.S. movie actor.

John **Darrow:** Harry Simpson (1907–1980), U.S. movie actor.

Lycette **Darsonval:** Alice Perron (1912–1996), Fr. ballet dancer, choreographer.

Helga **Dart** *see* **H.D.**

Bella **Darvi:** Bayla Wegier (1927–1971), Pol.-Fr. movie actress, working in U.S. The actress's new surname was devised from the first names of movie mogul Darryl F. Zanuck and his wife Virginia, who "discovered" her in Paris in 1951 and made her their protégée. Her new first name is simply a modification of the original.

Jane **Darwell:** Patti Woodward (1879–1967), U.S. movie actress. Woodward claimed to have taken her acting name from "a character in fiction." But who was Jane Darwell?

Silvio **d'Arzo:** Ezio Comparoni (1920–1952), It. writer.

Comtesse **Dash:** Vicomtesse de Pouillöue de Saint-Mars, née Gabrielle-Anna Cisterne de Courtiras (1804–1872), Fr. writer, society leader.

Howard **Da Silva:** Harold Silverblatt (1909–1986), U.S. movie actor, director. A neat conversion of a German Jewish name into a Portuguese-style one.

Marcel **Dassault:** Marcel Bloch (1892–1986), Fr. industrialist. The noted aircraft designer officially change his name to Bloch-Dassault in 1946 and to just Dassault in 1949. Dassault was the Resistance cover name of his brother, General Paul Bloch (1882–1969), who subsequently adopted it as a surname. The name represents French *d'assaut*, as in *char d'assaut*, "tank" (literally "assault car").

Jean **Dauberval** (or d'Auberval): Jean Bercher (1742–1806), Fr. ballet dancer, choreographer.

Sophie **Daumier:** Elisabeth Hugon (1936–2003), Fr. stage, movie actress.

Claude **Dauphin:** Claude Franc-Nohain (1903–1978), Fr. stage, movie actor.

Victor **d'Auverney:** Victor-Marie Hugo (1802–1885), Fr. novelist.

Dauvilliers: Nicolas Dorné (*c.*1646–1690), Fr. actor.

Lewis **Davenport:** George Ryan (1883–1916), Eng. conjuror.

Guido **da Verona:** Guido Verona (1881–1939), It. novelist.

Mildred **Davenport** *see* **Acquanetta**

Davertige: Denis Vilar (1940–), Haitian writer.

Jocelyn **Davey:** Chaim Raphael (1908–1994), Eng. crime novelist. The writer's original surname was Rabinovitch, but he hebraized this by deed poll in 1936.

Nuna **Davey:** Margaret Symonds (1902–1977), Eng. stage actress.

David V: Khariton Dzhiboyevich Devdariani (1903–1977), Georgian catholicos. The head of the Georgian Orthodox Church bore a name, used by four predecessors, that had long been associated with Georgia and Armenia. It is traditionally understood to mean "beloved."

Hugh **David:** David Williams Hughes (1925–1987), Welsh TV director.

Joanna **David:** Joanne Elizabeth Hacking (1947–), Br. stage, movie, TV actress. The actress adopted her stage name from her mother's first name (Davida).

Lolita **David:** Lolita Davidovich (1961–), Can.-born U.S. movie actress, of Serbian parentage. The actress was billed under this name for her early movies in the late 1980s.

Mordecai **David** *see* Josh **Billings**

Moses **David:** David Brandt Berg (1919–1994), U.S. cult leader. The founder in 1968 of the Children of God (later reconstituted as The Family) was known to his followers as simply "Mo."

Thayer **David:** David Thayer Hersey (1926–1978), U.S. movie actor.

David d'Angers: Pierre-Jean David (1788–1856), Fr. sculptor.

Israel **Davidson:** Alter Movshovitz (1870–1939), Lithuanian-born U.S. Hebrew scholar.

Lawrence H. **Davidson:** David Herbert Lawrence (1885–1930), Eng. novelist, short-story writer. Although resembling his real name, this early pen name used by D.H. Lawrence derived from Davidson Road School, Croydon, where the future novelist taught for a brief period. Appropriately, he assumed the name for a school textbook, *Movements in European History* (1921).

Eliza Rhyl **Davies:** William Clark Russell (1844–1911), U.S.–born Br. nautical novelist. Rhyl is a town on the north coast of Wales, and Davies a typical Welsh surname. Russell also wrote as Sydney Mostyn, the latter being a village just along the coast from Rhyl.

Marion **Davies:** Marion Cecilia Douras (1897–1961), U.S. movie actress, of Ir. descent. The actress's three older sisters Reine (originally Irene) (1886–1938), Ethel (1889–1940), and Rose (1895–1963) had already changed their name from Douras to Davies on beginning their stage careers.

Siobhan **Davies:** Susan Davies (1950–), Eng. ballet dancer, teacher, choreographer.

Gordon **Daviot** *see* Josephine **Tey**

Bette **Davis:** Ruth Elizabeth Davis (1908–1989), U.S. movie actress. Bette Davis was known as Betty (a regular pet form of "Elizabeth") as a child. In her high school years she changed the spelling of this after the central character of Honoré de Balzac's novel *La Cousine Bette* (1846).

Billie **Davis:** Carol Hedges (1945–), Eng. (white) soul singer.

B. Lynch **Davis** *see* Honorio Bustos **Domecq**

Danny **Davis:** George Nowlan (1925–), U.S. trumpeter, popular singer.

David **Davis:** William Eric Davis (1908–1996), Eng. broadcaster, children's radio storyteller.

Don **Davis** *see* Brett **Halliday**

Foxcroft **Davis** *see* Vera **Sapoukhyn**

Gail **Davis:** Betty Jeanne Grayson (1925–1997), U.S. movie actress.

James "Thunderbird" **Davis:** James Houston (1938–1992), U.S. blues guitarist, singer.

Maxwell Street Jimmy **Davis:** Charles Thompson (1925–1995), U.S. black blues musician. It is uncertain when Thompson adopted his new name. The first part of the name comes from Maxwell Street, Chicago, where he regularly performed.

Nancy **Davis:** Anne Frances Robbins (1921–), U.S movie actress. "Nancy," a pet form of "Anne," was the actress's nickname from infancy. Davis was the name of her stepfather, a Chicago surgeon. The lady herself took on a new role as Nancy Reagan, wife of U.S. president Ronald Reagan. The two married in 1952 when they were both Hollywood actors.

Noel **Davis:** Edgar Davis (1927–2002), Eng. movie, TV casting director. Davis began his career as an actor on the London stage, and it was then that he adopted his new first name, after actor and dramatist Noël Coward (1899–1973).

Simon **Davis:** Keith Denny (1937–2002), Eng. movie actor, costume designer. Denny used his real name as a movie costume designer after beginning his career as an actor under his screen name.

Skeeter **Davis:** Mary Frances Penick (1931–2004), U.S. country singer. Mary Penick took her singing name from that of her schoolfriend, Betty Jack Davis (1932–1953), with whom she formed the Davis Sisters group in 1953, just before Davis's death in an auto accident, in which she was herself critically injured. Her grandfather nicknamed her "Skeeter" because she was "just like a little ol' water bug, skeeting here and there."

Tyrone **Davis:** Tyrone Branch (1938–2005), U.S. black soul singer.

William **Davis:** Adolf Günther Kies (1933–), Ger.-born Eng. writer, editor.

Peter **Davison:** Peter Moffet (1951–), Br. TV actor.

Bobby **Davro:** Robert Christopher Nankeville (1958–), Eng. stage, TV comedian, impressionist. The entertainer explains his name: "My father needed a name for his [auto dealing] business so he took DAV from my brother David's name and RO from Robert, my first name. I liked the name so much I took it as a stage name" [Sachs and Morgan II, p.54].

Margery **Dawe** *see* Jill **Consey**

Peter **Dawlish:** James Lennox Kerr (1899–1963), Sc. writer of boating stories for boys. Dawlish is a Devonshire coastal resort near the mouth of the Exe River.

Dolly **Dawn:** Theresa Maria Stabile (1916–2002), U.S. popular singer. The singer began her career in her early teens under the name Billie Starr. Bandleader George Hall then changed this to Dolly Dawn. It was a name she came to hate. "It made me sound like a stripper," she said [*The Times*, January 8, 2003].

Elizabeth **Dawn:** Sylvia Butterfield (1939–), Br. TV actress.

Florence **Dawson:** Frances Julia Wedgwood (1833–1913), Eng. writer. The niece of Charles Darwin used this name for her second novel, *An Old Debt* (1858).

Geoffrey **Dawson:** George Geoffrey Robinson (1874–1944), Eng. journalist, newspaper editor. Twice editor of *The Times*, Dawson changed his name by royal license in 1917 following an inheritance from his mother's eldest sister, Margaret Jane Dawson. A quip circulating at the newspaper ran: "It's strange that a deed-poll under the law / Can change a robin into a daw."

Peter **Dawson** *see* Max **Brand**

Pol **Dax** *see* Arthur **Pougin**

Bobby **Day:** Robert James Byrd, Sr. (1930–1990), U.S. "doo-wop" singer, songwriter.

Darren **Day:** Darren Graham (1969–), Eng. actor, singer. Day was asked in an interview whether he changed his name for "showbiz" reasons. "I suppose, in all honesty, I did it because I didn't get on with my father all that well and so didn't feel the desire some people do to carry on the family name. For a while, my cheque book said 'Darren Graham trading as Darren Day,' but that proved just too complicated and, eventually, I changed it by deed poll. Now I feel it's just who I am. There's a drawback to having chosen Day, of course. Doris becomes the obvious nickname!" [*The Times Magazine*, February 26, 2000].

Dennis **Day:** Eugene Denis McNulty (1917–1988), U.S. movie actor, singer, radio, TV entertainer.

Doris **Day:** Doris Mary Ann von Kappelhoff (1924–), U.S. movie actress, singer, of Ger. parentage.

The singer was given her new name by Cincinnati bandleader Barney Rapp. "He didn't think the name [Kappelhoff] sounded very good – and it looked even worse on the marquee outside the restaurant [where she sang]. It had to go. But to what? 'How about La Ponselle,' he suggested, although why can only be guessed at.... He also suggested 'Marmaduke' – which had even less reason behind it. 'Doris Kapp?' well, that might not be a bad idea. It would certainly fit logically with a girl born Doris Kappelhoff.... And then he thought about the first song he had heard her sing on the radio, and the one that had become something of a mascot for her at the restaurant, the one she sang so much, 'Day After Day.' 'We'll call you "Doris Day",' he said. She didn't like it. 'It sounded really cheap,' she would say years later. 'Like a burlesque singer. "Doris Day and her Dove Dance," that sort of thing.' But he was the boss and she was only sixteen.... So Doris Day she became. And that's how it all started" [Michael Freedland, *Doris Day*, 2000]. Her first name is said to have been given as a tribute to silent movie actress Doris Kenyon (1897–1979), whom her mother admired.

Frances Day: Frances Victoria Schenk (1908–1984), U.S. movie actress.

Jill Day: Yvonne Page (1930–1990), Eng. popular singer, stage, movie actress.

Josette Day: Josette Dagory (1914–1978), Fr. movie actress.

Laraine Day: Laraine Johnson (1917–2007), U.S. movie actress. The actress adopted the name of her drama teacher, Elias Day. For her earliest movies in the late 1930s she was billed as Lorraine Hayes.

Margie Day: Margaret Hoeffler (1926–), U.S. R&B singer.

Margie Day *see* Margaret **Lockwood**

Swami Dayananda: Alan Richard Griffiths (1906–1993), Eng. cleric. After joining the Benedictine order under the name Bede Griffiths, the English priest went to India in 1955 where he became known as Dayananda, "bliss of compassion" (Sanskrit *daya*, "compassion" + *ananda*, "bliss"). He would continue the work begun by the two French priests Henri le Saux and Jules Monchanin, respectively known as **Abhishiktananda** and **Paramarubyananda**. Swami is a title meaning "master," "prince."

Dayananda Sarasvati: Mul Shankara (1824–1883), Ind. Hindu ascetic, social reformer. Dayananda took his new name, meaning "bliss of compassion," on being initiated as an ascetic in 1848. The second word of the name honors Sarasvati, the consort of Brahma, the first god of the Hindu Trinity. In 1875 Dayananda founded the Hindu reform movement known as Arya Samaj ("Society of Nobles").

Taylor Dayne: Leslie Wunderman (1963–),

U.S. rock singer. Dee Snider, of the group Twisted Sister, is said to have suggested that Leslie Wunderman change her name into something more glamorous.

De ... Names beginning *de* (less often *De*) not found below should be sought under the word that follows, e.g. Honoré de Balzac under **Balzac**, Nicolas de Chamfort under **Chamfort**, etc.

Eugenia **de Acton:** Alethea Lewis, née Brereton (1749–1827), Eng. didactic novelist.

Dead: Per Yngve Ohlin (1969–1991), Norw. "black metal" singer.

Andrew **Dean:** Cecily Sidgwick, née Ullmann (1852–1934), Eng. novelist, of Ger. Jewish parentage.

Eddie **Dean:** Edgar Dean Glossup (1907–1999), U.S. movie actor.

Erica **Dean** *see* Ellen **Burstyn**

Frances **Dean:** Ruth Elizabeth Grable (1916–1973), U.S. movie actress. Betty Grable, as she was usually known, appeared under this name in some juvenile roles in the early 1930s.

Isabel **Dean:** Isabel Hodgkinson (1918–1997), Eng. stage, movie actress.

Jimmy **Dean:** Seth Ward (1928–2010), U.S. country singer.

Man Mountain **Dean:** Frank Simmons Leavitt (1891–1953), U.S. wrestler.

Mrs. Andrew **Dean:** Cecily Sidgwick, née Ullmann (1852–1934), Eng. novelist, of Ger. Jewish parentage.

Pamela **Dean:** Pamela Dyer-Bennett (1953–), U.S. writer of fantasy fiction.

Eugénio **de Andrade:** José Fontainhas (1923–2005), Port. poet.

Charles **Deane:** Edward Saunders (1866–1910), Eng. music hall singer, songwriter.

Edna **Deane:** Edna Morton Sewell (1905–1995), Br. ballroom dancer, choreographer.

Martha **Deane:** Mary Margaret McBride (1899–1976), U.S. radio talk-show host, writer. The pseudonym was that of the persona, a folksy grandmother, as which McBride was hired by the New York City radio station WOR in 1934. She abandoned the role after a few weeks, claiming that as a single 35-year-old woman it was too difficult for her. She later hosted a show under her real name.

Norman **Deane** *see* Gordon **Ashe**

Mickey **Deans:** Michael DeVinko (1935–2003), U.S. singer, pianist.

Basil **Dearden:** Basil Dear (1911–1971), Br. movie director, producer, screenwriter. The moviemaker changed his name to avoid confusion with director and producer Basil Dean (1888–1978), whose assistant he was.

Max **Dearly**: Lucien-Max Rolland (1874–1943), Fr. actor, variety artist.

Colonel W. **de Basil**: Vasily Grigoryevich Voskresensky (1888–1951), Russ. ballet impresario. The codirector of the Ballets Russes de Monte Carlo was formerly a Cossack officer. "Basil" equates to Russian "Vasily."

Speech **Debelle**: Corynne Elliot (1983–), Br. black rapper. The singer adopted her new surname from her Jamaican grandmother, originally Deeble, a word said to have two meanings. "The second, slang for someone who annoys you, who acts like an idiot, need not detain us here. The first, though, might have been invented for Debelle.... Coined by the American sci-fi writer Roger Zelazny, it means 'to explode with great force.' She is certainly doing that" [*The Sunday Times*, July 26, 2009].

Her new first name arose as a nickname. "Corynne's friends called her Speech because of how she used to talk. She wrote poetry and would be in school debates and had intuition beyond her years. She was almost like a philosopher in the school playground" [Interview with Marylin Dennis, Debelle's mother, in *Sunday Times Magazine*, October 25, 2009].

Anton **de Borca**: A.A. Roback (1890–1965), Pol.-born U.S. psychologist, scholar in Yiddish studies. The academic, whose initials stood for Abraham Aaron, occasionally published under this pseudonym, a near-anagram of his surname.

Abram **Deborin**: Abram Moiseyevich Ioffe (1881–1963), Lithuanian-born Russ. Marxist philosopher.

Pierre **de Boscobel de Chastelard**: William Henry Ireland (1777–1835), Eng. novelist. This was just one pseudonym used by the Shakespeare forger, in this case for the tongue-in-cheek *Effusions of Love from Chatelar to Mary, Queen of Scotland; translated from a Gallic manuscript in the Scotch College at Paris: interspersed with songs, sonnets, and notes explanatory, by the Translator. To which is added, Historical Fragments, Poetry, and Remains of the Amours, of that unfortunate Princess* (1808).

Brian **de Breffny**: Brian Michael Leese (1931–1989), Eng. genealogist. The writer, the son of a Jewish father and an Irish mother, adopted his new name from the maiden name, Breffni, of his great-great-grandmother. He added the aristocratic prefix "de" and also styled himself "Baron," a title that he sometimes varied, so he could be Baron O'Rorke de Breffny one day and Count O'Rourke the next.

Hal **Debrett** *see* Brett **Halliday**

Santi **Debriano**: Alonso Santi Wilson Debriano Santorino (1955–), Panamanian-born U.S. jazz musician.

Jean **Debucourt**: Jean Pelisse (1894–1958), Fr. movie actor.

Jean-Gaspard **Deburau**: Jan Kaspar Dvořák (1796–1846), Fr. pantomime actor, of Cz. parentage. A French rendering (but not translation) of the actor's original Czech name.

A. **De Burgh**: Edward Morgan Alborough (*fl.*1899), Eng. writer. The author used this name, presumably punning on his surname, for *Elizabeth, Empress of Austria* (1899).

Chris **de Burgh**: Christopher John Davison (1948–), Ir.-born Br. pop singer, songwriter. The singer took his wife's maiden name as his stage name. His daughter, beauty queen Rosanna Davison (1984–), followed in his footsteps. "Crowned Miss Ireland and Miss World in 2003, Rosanna, who chose to go by her mother's maiden name to avoid charges of nepotism, recently graduated from University College, Dublin" [*Sunday Times Magazine*, October 8, 2006].

Peter Joseph William **Debye**: Petrus Josephus Wilhelmus Debije (1884–1966), Du.-born U.S. physicist. The scientist modified his Dutch name on leaving the Netherlands to enroll at the Aachen Technical University, Germany, in 1901.

Yvonne **de Carlo**: Margaret Yvonne Middleton (1922–2007), Can.-born U.S. movie actress.

Jeanne **de Casalis**: Jeanne de Casalis de Pury (1896–1966), Eng. radio, movie comedienne.

Eleanora **de Cisneros**: Eleanor Broadfoot (1878–1934), U.S. opera singer.

Arturo **de Cordova**: Arturo Garcia (1908–1973), Mexican movie actor.

Jacques **Decour**: Daniel Decourdemanche (1910–1942), Fr. writer, editor.

Dave **Dee**: David Harman (1941–2009), Eng. pop singer, TV actor. "Dee" represents "David," the singer's first name, originally a school nickname. He first used the name on stage for his group Dave Dee and the Bostons. Later, this same group was reorganized under the cumbersome name of Dave Dee, Dozy, Beaky, Mick and Tich, those being the individual school nicknames of the classmates who formed it. (Dozy was Trevor Davis; Beaky was John Dymond; Mick was Michael Wilson; Tich was Ian Amey.) Dee left the group in 1969, although remaining in the music business.

David **Dee**: David Eckford (*c.*1942–), U.S. blues singer.

Jay **Dee**: James Yancey (1973–2006), U.S. black rapper, hip-hop producer. The musician also recorded under the name J. Dilla.

Joey **Dee**: Joseph DeNicola (1940–), U.S. rock musician.

Kiki **Dee**: Pauline Matthews (1947–), Eng. pop singer, stage actress. "One night in Leeds, a salesman from the Philips record label heard her singing, draped a microphone over the stage and sent the tape to his headquarters. The next thing Pauline Matthews knew she was on a train with her father, heading for London to sign a contract to record her first album, *I'm Kiki Dee* [(1968)]. 'My name was changed by my manager,' she says ... 'The singer Sandra **Dee** was very big at that time – and Kiki was supposed to be a cookie, cutsie version of her'" [*Sunday Telegraph*, September 27, 1998].

Mercy Dee: Mercy Dee Walton (1915–1962), U.S. blues singer, pianist.

Nicholas Dee: Joan Aiken (1924–), Eng. thriller, children's book writer.

Ruby Dee: Ruby Ann Davis, née Wallace (1923–), U.S. black movie actress.

Sandra Dee: Alexandra Cymboliak Zuck (1942–2005), U.S. movie actress, wife of Bobby **Darin** (married 1960, divorced 1967). The actress was still a young child when her mother remarried, and she first performed at the age of eight as Sandra Douvan, after her stepfather, Eugene Douvan. The surname was later abbreviated as "Dee."

Simon Dee: Cyril Nicholas Henty-Dodd (1935–2009), Eng. radio, DJ, talk-show presenter. The popular presenter took his new first name from his son and his surname from the first letter of "Dodd."

André Deed: André Chapuis (1884–1938), Fr. movie comedian. The actor gained a remarkable collection of nicknames in different European languages, once his particular brand of destructive lunacy became popular. In France itself he was known as Boireau (from *boire*, "to drink"), in Italy Beoncelli ("little drunkard," from *beone*, "tippler"), in Spain Sanchez, and so on. When he worked for the Itala Company of Turin, Italy, he gained further names, such as Cretinetti (Italy), Gribouille (France), Toribio (Spain), Glupyshkin (Russia), Foolshead (England), all from words denoting stupidity or dumbness. Compare the different names of his fellow French comedian, **Prince-Rigadin**.

Barbara Deely *see* Barbara **La Marr**

John Peter Deering: John Peter Gandy (1787–1850), Eng. architect. "In 1827 he acquired by bequest from his friend Henry Deering of the Lee, the estate of that name, near Missenden, Buckinghamshire. He assumed the name of Deering, and, gradually renouncing the active practice of his profession, devoted himself to public life and the management of his property" [*Dictionary of National Biography*].

Deeyah: Deepika Thathaal (1977–), Norw.-born Pakistani/Afghan singer, human rights campaigner, working in U.K.

Eduardo De Filippo: Eduardo Passarelli (1900–1984), It. movie actor, director, playwright.

Daniel Defoe: Daniel Foe (1660–1731), Eng. journalist, novelist. It is just possible that the author of *Robinson Crusoe* (1719) was originally Daniel Defoe. But records show that he was probably Daniel Foe, and that he came to be known as "Mr. D. Foe" to distinguish himself from his father, James Foe. The initial then became the aristocratic particle "de."

Louis de Funès: Carlos Louis de Funès de Galarza (1908–1982), Fr. movie actor, comedian, of Port. parentage.

Cherubina de Gabriac: Yelizaveta Ivanovna Vasilyeva, née Dmitriyeva (1887–1928), Russ. poet. When in 1909 the poet submitted a selection of her work to the avant-garde journal *Apollo*, the poet Maksimilian Voloshin proposed this Italian-style pseudonym instead of the writer's unremarkable Russian name. It moreover disguised her modest, unassuming appearance. The journal's editor, S.K. Makovsky, was so entranced by her verse and apparently exotic personality that he quite fell for her. When Voloshin disclosed the writer's true identity, however, he flew into a rage and challenged him to a duel. Some of the poems were in all probability written by Voloshin himself [Dmitriyev, p.189].

Félix de Grand' Combe: Félix Boillot (1880–1961), Fr. army officer. Boillot adopted this name for some of his writings, taking it from his home in the village of Grand' Combe-Châteleu, eastern France.

Terry de Havilland: Terence Higgins (1938–), Eng. footwear designer.

Richard Dehan: Clotilde Inez Augusta Mary Graves (1863–1932), Ir. novelist, playwright. Graves used this name for her historical works, beginning with *The Dop Doctor* (1911), a story of South Africa.

John Dehner: John Forkum (1915–1992), U.S. movie actor.

Elmyr de Hory: Palmer Hoffer (1906–1976), Hung. copier of master painters. The painter's assumed name is more or less a reworking of his original name, allowing for artistic license.

Desmond Dekker: Desmond Adolphus Dacres (1941–2006), Jamaican singer, songwriter.

Maurice Dekobra: Ernest Maurice Tessier (1885–1973), Fr. novelist. The writer claimed his pen name punned on French *deux cobras*, "two cobras."

Buatier de Kolta: Joseph Buatier (1847–1903), Fr. magician, working in U.S., U.K.

E.M. Delafield: Edmée Elizabeth Monica Dashwood, née de la Pasture (1890–1943), Eng. novelist, of Fr.-Eng. parentage. The writer's new surname, which she assumed to avoid confusion with her mother, also a novelist (as Mrs. Henry de la Pasture), is a sort of English equivalent of the French, perhaps partly prompted by the familiar misquotation

"To fresh fields and pastures new" (Milton's "To fresh woods and pastures new").

Theodore **de la Guard**: Nathaniel Ward (*c.*1578–1652), Eng. Puritan cleric, poet, novelist. Ward emigrated to Massachusetts in 1634 and settled as a minister at Agawam (now Ipswich). In 1645 he wrote *The Simple Cobler of Aggawam* under this pseudonym, which he formed by translating his first name from its Hebrew original into Greek (they both mean "gift of God") and his surname from English to French. He then returned to England, where the work was published in 1647.

Jo **Delande**: Christiane-Josée Vigneron-Ramakers (1914–), Belg. organist, pianist, composer. The musician used her pseudonym for light compositions and literary works.

Delaney and Bonnie: Delaney Bramlett (1939–2008), U.S. rock musician + Bonnie Lynn Bramlett, née O'Farrell (1944–), U.S. rock musician, his wife.

Pierre **Delanoë**: Pierre Charles Marcel Napoléon Leroyer (1918–2006), Fr. songwriter. The lyricist first began writing songs when working in a tax office and adopted his grandmother's name to prevent identification by his employers.

Jeames **de la Pluche** *see* C.J. **Yellowplush**

Adelina **de Lara**: Adelina Tilbury (1872–1961), Eng. pianist, composer.

Isidore **de Lara**: Isidore Cohen (1858–1935), Eng. opera composer.

Mazo **de la Roche**: Mazo Roche (1879–1961), Can. novelist. The added particle *de la* falsely implied that the author was of aristocratic French descent, although her father, William Richmond Roche, was an Irishman. Her first name Mazo is a form of "Maisie."

Abbé **de la Tour**: Isabelle de Charrière, née Isabella Agneta Elisabeth van Tuyll van Serooskerken (1740–1805), Du.-born Swiss novelist, autobiographer. The novelist seems to have devised a pen name that worked on more levels than one. As it stands, it translates as "abbot of the tower." But "Abbé" could equally well represent "Isabelle" (or "Isabella"), and "Tour" may have evolved from "Tuyll." In other words, "Abbé de la Tour" is a sort of meaningful "Isabella van Tuyll." Serooskerken is a Dutch placename, "Seroos' church," also suggesting a holy man and a tower. The author also wrote as **Zélide**.

Vicomte Charles **de Launay**: Delphine de Girardin, née Gay (1804–1855), Fr. writer. Mme. de Girardin, wife of journalist Émile de Girardin (1806–1881), adopted the male name in the 1830s for a weekly gossip column in her husband's paper, published in book form in 1842 as *Lettres parisiennes*.

Sonia **Delaunay-Terk**: Sonia Delaunay, née Stern (1885–1979), Russ. painter, designer, working in France. The artist adopted the name Terk from the wealthy uncle who raised her in St. Petersburg. In 1910 she married the French painter Robert Delaunay (1885–1941).

Barbu **Delavrancea**: Barbu Stefanescu (1858–1918), Rom. writer, playwright.

Hugo **Del Carril**: Piero Bruno Ugo Fontana (1912–1989), Argentinian movie actor, director, of It. parentage.

Liviu **Deleanu**: Lipa Samuilovich Kligman (1911–1967), Moldavian poet, children's writer.

[Lord] Bernard **Delfont**: Boris (later Barnet) Winogradsky (1909–1994), Ukr.-born Br. theatrical impresario, TV manager, presenter. Winogradsky began his career as a dancer, changing his name to avoid being confused with his brother, Lew **Grade**.

Junior **Delgado**: Oscar Hibbert (1958–2005), Jamaican reggae singer, working in U.K. The singer adopted his long-standing nickname, from Spanish *delgado*, "thin," "slim."

Délia: Maria Benedita Câmara de Bormann (1853–1895), Brazilian novelist.

Jean **de L'Isle**: Alphonse Daudet (1840–1897), Fr. novelist, short-story writer.

Frederick **Delius**: Fritz Theodor Albert Delius (1862–1934), Eng.-born composer, of Ger. parentage, working in U.S., Germany, U.K., France. The composer published his works under the name Fritz Delius until around 1904. He lived in France from 1897 and died there, but was reinterred in 1935 in England. His father had been naturalized as an Englishman in 1850.

Alan **Dell**: Alan Creighton Mandell (1924–1995), S.A.-born Br. broadcaster, dance-band authority.

Belinda **Dell** *see* Avon **Curry**

Claudia **Dell**: Claudia Del Smith (1910–1977), U.S. movie actress.

Denis **D'Ell**: Denis James Dalziel (1943–2005), Eng. pop musician. The singer and harmonica player respelled his surname to show its pronunciation, i.e. as "Dee-ell."

Dorothy **Dell**: Dorothy Goff (1915–1934), U.S. movie actress.

Gabriel **Dell**: Gabriel Del Vecchio (1919–1988), U.S. movie actor.

Myrna **Dell**: Marilyn Dunlap (1924–), U.S. movie actress.

Peggy **Dell**: Peggy Tisdall (*c.*1905–1979), Ir. pianist, entertainer.

Della Crusca: Robert Merry (1755–1798), Eng. poet. Merry was the leader of the so-called Della Cruscans, a band of poets who produced affected, sentimental verse in the latter half of the 18th century. They took their name (and so therefore did he) from the Della Crusca, the literary academy established in Florence in 1582 with the aim of purifying the Italian language. The name literally means "of the chaff," referring to the "sifting" process to which the academy submitted the language. Merry mainly used the name for his poetic correspondence in the *World* with **Anna Matilda**.

Mario **dell'Arco:** Mario Fagiolo (1905–1996), It. poet.

Florian **Deller:** Florian Drosendorf (1729–1773), Austr. violinist, composer.

Francesca **Dellera:** Francesca Cervellera (1966–), It. movie actress.

Delly: Jeanne Marie Petitjean de la Rosière (1875–1949), Fr. romantic novelist + Frédéric Petitjean de la Rosière (1876–1947), Fr. romantic novelist, her brother. The name appears to have been created from the aristocratic *de la* particle.

Florentina **del Mar:** Carmen Conde Abellán (1907–1996), Sp. poet, novelist, short-story writer. Carmen Conde used this name for children's books, biographies, and historical works, while her writings on religious subjects appeared under the name Magdalena Noguera.

Nathalie **Delon:** Francine Canovas (1938–), Fr. movie actress.

Danièle **Delorme:** Gabrielle Girard (1926–), Fr. movie actress.

Joseph **Delorme:** Charles-Augustin Sainte-Beuve (1804–1869), Fr. literary critic. The writer used this name for his *Vie, Poésie et Pensées de Joseph Delorme* (1829), a collection of romantic autobiographical poems. The name is said to be that of a friend of Sainte-Beuve who had died young as a medical student.

Victoria **de los Angeles:** Victoria de los Ángeles López García (1923–2005), Sp. opera singer. Some sources give the singer's original name as Victoria Gómez Cima.

Carla **Del Poggio:** Maria Luisa Attanasio (1925–), It. movie actress.

Lester **del Rey:** Ramon Felipe San Juan Mario Silvio Enrico Smith Heathcourt-Brace Sierra y Alvarez del Rey y de los Verdes (1915–1993), U.S. SF writer, editor, of Sp. descent. The writer helpfully shortened his lengthy original name to something much more manageable. He also wrote under several other pseudonyms, such as Philip St. John, Erik van Lhin, Wade Kaempfert, Philip James, Edson McCann, and Kenneth Wright. (The first of these is an English version of his second and third names.)

Dolores **Del Rio:** Lolita Dolores Martinez Asunsolo Lopez Negrette (1905–1983), Mexican movie actress. The actress's screen name is that of her first husband, Jaime Del Rio, and she continued to use it after his death in 1928.

Delta: David MacBeth Moir (1798–1851), Sc. physician, essayist. The writer used this name, in the form of a Greek capital letter (Δ), standing for his first name, for his contributions to *Blackwood's Magazine*. "From this signature he was wont to be called the Pyramid or the Triangle by his mirthful literary companions" [Robert Chambers, *A Biographical Dictionary of Eminent Scotsmen*, 1855].

Michael **Delving:** Jay Williams (1914–1978), U.S. mystery writer.

Alice **Delysia:** Alice Kolb-Bernard, née Lapize (1889–1979), Fr. stage, movie actress, singer, working in U.K.

Jean **Delysse:** Marguerite Sara Roesgen-Champion (1894–1976), Swiss harpsichordist, composer.

R. Emmett **Dembry** *see* Charles Egbert **Craddock**

Maria **de Medeiros:** Maria de Almeida (1965–), Port. movie actress.

Angela **Demello:** Angela Joy Cox (1959–), Eng. ballet dancer. The dancer adopted her stage name in 1983 from her first husband, a Brazilian. She found it more suitable than her maiden name, which she frequently had to spell out. It was also more "international," and so appropriate for a dancer. Her subsequent partner was the dancer Kevin Richmond [personal telephone call from Angela Demello, March 22, 1996].

Helen **Demidenko:** Helen Darville (1971–), Austral. writer. The writer won Australia's leading literary prize in 1995 for her novel, *The Hand That Signed the Papers*, dealing with the Ukrainian massacre of Jews during World War II. She claimed to be the daughter of an illiterate Ukrainian taxi driver and a poor Irish mother, but in reality her parents were middle-class English immigrants. The imposture naturally involved a new name. She explained: "I changed my name to protect my family and friends as well as my sources." The hoax set the Australian literary establishment in considerable disarray [*The Times*, August 23, 1995].

Nikita **Demidov:** Nikita Demidovich Antufyev (1656–1725), Russ. ironmaster. The first of the distinguished Demidov family, a Tula blacksmith, adapted his patronymic (middle name) as his surname in 1702, presumably on the grounds that its initial *De-* gave it an aristocratic air. It seemed to work, for in 1720 Peter the Great made him a nobleman.

Katherine **De Mille:** Katherine Lester (1911–1995), U.S. movie actress. The actress was an orphan and took her name from director Cecil B. De Mille, who adopted her when she was nine.

Democritus Junior: Robert Burton (1577–1640), Eng. writer. The author used this apt name for *The Anatomy of Melancholy* (1621), about the "disease" of melancholy. The reference is to the 5th-century BC Greek philosopher Democritus, known as the "laughing philosopher" by contrast with the melancholy Heraclitus, the "weeping philosopher." The name is included in the Latin epitaph which Burton composed for himself on his monument in Christ Church Cathedral, Oxford: "Paucis notus, paucioribus ignotus, hic jacet Democritus Junior, cui vitam dedit et mortem Melancholia" ("Known by a few, unknown by even fewer, here lies Democritus Junior, to whom Melancholy gave life and death").

Mylène **Demongeot:** Marie-Hélène Demongeot (1936–), Fr. movie actress. For her earliest movies, in the mid–1950s, the actress was billed as Mylène Nicole, then for a while as Mylène-Nicole Demongeot. The "Nicole" was subsequently dropped.

Louis **de Montalte:** Blaise Pascal (1623–1662), Fr. philosopher, physicist. Pascal's pen name contains a latinized reference to the "high mountain" of Puy-de-Dôme, near Clermont-Ferrand, where he conducted several of his scientific experiments into atmospheric pressure.

Rebecca **De Mornay:** Rebecca George (1961–), U.S. movie actress.

Peter **de Morny:** Dorothy Estelle Esmé Wynne-Tyson, née Ripper (1898–1972), Eng. novelist, dramatist, critic. From 1909 to 1920 the writer was an actress under the name Esmé Wynne. She then left the stage to concentrate on a literary career.

Jack **Dempsey:** William Harrison Dempsey (1895–1983), U.S. heavyweight boxer. Dempsey took his ring name from the boxer Nonpareil Jack **Dempsey**. He first boxed as Kid Blackie.

Nonpareil Jack **Dempsey:** John Edward Kelly (1862–1895), Ir.-born U.S. boxer. Kelly assumed the name of his American stepfather, Patrick Dempsey, adding "Nonpareil" (meaning "unequaled") as the sobriquet given him for his many victories in the ring.

Carl **De Muldor:** Charles Henry Miller (1842–1922), U.S. artist, writer. Miller used this name, that of his father's Dutch ancestors, for *The Philosophy of Art in America* (1885).

[Colonel] Robert **Denard:** Gilbert Bourgeaud (1929–2007), Fr. mercenary.

Terry **Dene:** Terence Williams (1938–), Eng. rock singer. The singer, who first gained recognition in the late 1950s, renamed himself after the legendary U.S. movie actor James Dean (1931–1955).

Catherine **Deneuve:** Catherine Fabienne Dorléac (1943–), Fr. movie actress. The actress adopted her mother's maiden name as her screen name to avoid confusion with her elder sister Françoise Dorléac (1942–1967), also an actress.

[Sir] James Steuart **Denham:** James Steuart (1712–1780), Sc. economist. The noted lawyer obtained his new name in 1733, when his father inherited the estates of his uncle, Sir Archibald Denham, on condition that he and his father adopt Denham as a surname.

Sergei **Denham:** Sergei Dokuchayev (1897–1970), Russ.-born U.S. ballet impresario.

Denim: Frederick Joss (*c.*1909–1967), Austr.-born Br. political cartoonist, writer. Joss's original name was Fritz Josefowitsch.

Julio **Denis:** Julio Cortázar (1914–1984), Argentinian novelist, short-story writer, working in France.

María **Denis:** Maria Esther Beomonte (1916–2004), Argentinian-born It. movie actress.

Adolphe Philippe **d'Ennery:** Adolphe Philippe Dennery (1811–1899), Fr. playwright, librettist. The writer legally adopted the (supposedly aristocratic) spelling of his name in 1858.

Richard **Denning:** Ludwig (later Louis) Albert Heinrich Denninger, Jr. (1914–1998), U.S. movie actor. Paramount Studios is said to have changed the actor's name as it sounded similar to that of U.S. outlaw John Dillinger (1903–1934).

Denny **Dennis:** Ronald Dennis Pountain (1913–1993), Br. dance band vocalist.

Eugene **Dennis:** Francis Xavier Waldron, Jr. (1905–1961), U.S. Communist leader, of Ir.-Norw. descent. Waldron adopted his party name in 1935 on returning to the United States from the Soviet Union, where he had fled to avoid imprisonment in 1930.

Les **Dennis:** Leslie Heseltine (1953–), Eng. TV comedian, teaming with Dustin **Gee**.

Will **Dennis:** Stephen Townesend (?–1914), Eng. surgeon, writer. The writer used this name for a limited but successful stage career.

Willie **Dennis:** William DeBerardinis (1926–1965), U.S. jazz trombonist.

Reginald **Denny:** Reginald Leigh Daymore (1891–1967), Br. stage, movie actor.

Robert **Dentry:** Osmar Egmont Dorkin White (1909–1991), Austral. writer. White also wrote as E.M. Dorkin (from his middle name) and Maros Gray (with an anagram of his first name).

John **Denver:** Henry John Deutschendorf, Jr. (1943–1997), U.S. country singer, songwriter. The musician, born in New Mexico, moved to Los Angeles in the mid–1960s and adopted the name of the capital of Colorado, a state whose natural beauty he greatly admired.

Karl **Denver:** Angus McKenzie (1931–1998), Sc. pop musician.

Lee **Denver** *see* Leo **Grex**

Robert **Denvers:** Robert Nennertheim (1942–), Belg. ballet dancer.

Rossy **De Palma:** Rosy Garcia (1965–), Sp. movie actress.

Lynsey **De Paul:** Lynsey Reuben (1948–), Br. popular singer, songwriter.

Filippo **de Pisis:** Filippo Filippo Tibertelli (1896–1956), It. painter, writer.

Madame Marguerite **de Ponti:** Stéphane Mallarmé (1842–1898), Fr. poet. The symbolist poet used this name when acting as editor of the fashion magazine *La Dernière Mode* (1897).

A.J. **DePre** *see* Ed **Noon**

Lya **De Putti:** Amalia Putty (1901–1931), Hung. movie actress.

Dan **De Quille:** William Wright (1829–1898), U.S. humorist, historian of the Far West. There is a pun here on "quill" and "write," appropriately for a pen name.

Thomas **de Quincey:** Thomas Quincey (1785–1859), Eng. essayist. There is some uncertainty whether the writer added the aristocratic "de" himself, to claim Norman descent, or whether his father was already named De Quincey. According to the *Dictionary of National Biography*, the author liked to alphabetize his name under "Q," which seems to suggest otherwise.

Jacques **Deray:** Jacques Desrayaud (1929–2003), Fr. movie director.

Jane **Derby:** Jeanette Barr (1895–1965), U.S. fashion designer.

Derek: Peter Chamberlain (1947–), Br. crossword compiler. The setter adopted the name of his younger son as his pseudonym.

Bo **Derek:** Mary Cathleen Collins (1957–), U.S. movie actress. "Bo" was a childhood nickname, and Bo Shane an early screen name. The actress married John **Derek** as his third wife.

John **Derek:** Derek Harris (1926–1998), U.S. movie actor, director, husband of Bo **Derek**.

Tristan **Derème:** Philippe Huc (1889–1942), Fr. poet.

Maya **Deren:** Eleanora Derenkowsky (1917–1961), Ukr. Jewish-born U.S. filmmaker, wife of Alexander **Hammid**. The Derenkowsky family immigrated to the United States in 1922 and changed their name to Deren in 1928. Eleonora, a lover of the exotic, adopted the first name Maya in 1943, apparently after the goddess Maya, mother of the Buddha.

Jean **De Reszke:** Jan Mieczyslaw (1850–1925), Pol. opera singer. The tenor made his debut in Italy in 1874 as Giovanni di Reschi. His brother, bass opera singer Édouard De Reszke (1853–1917), adopted the same name.

José **de Rivera:** José A. Ruiz (1904–1985), U.S. sculptor. The artist adopted his maternal grandmother's name.

Édouard **Dermithe:** Antoine Dhermitte (1925–1995), Fr. movie actor, painter.

Portia **de Rossi:** Amanda Rogers (1973–), Austral.-born U.S. movie, TV actress. The actress adopted her more exotic-sounding name at the age of 14.

Louis **de Rougemont:** Henri Grin (1847–1921), Swiss-born Eng. impostor. "[He was] an adventurer who decided at the age of 16 to see the world. He began as a footman to [actress] Fanny Kemble, touring through Europe and America, and eventually became butler to the governor of Australia. After spending many years there he contributed to *Wide World Magazine* in 1898 sensational articles relating to his extraordinary, mostly bogus, voyages and adventures in search of pearls and gold, where he encountered an octopus with tentacles 75 feet long and rode turtles in the water" [Drabble, p.880]. Among his other Australian adventures, de Rougemont claimed to have married an Aboriginal wife, Yamba, and to have rescued two young white women, kept as "wives" by a native chief, who identified themselves as Blanche and Gladys Rogers, daughters of a sea captain. The names were those of Grin's own daughters. The self-styled explorer's imposture was exposed by the *Daily Chronicle*, and he died in poverty.

Frances **Derrick:** Frances Eliza Millett Notley, née Thomas (1820–1912), Eng. novelist.

Rick **Derringer:** Rick Zehringer (1947–), U.S. rock musician. The new name implies a reference to the derringer pistol.

Derry Down Derry: Edward Lear (1812–1888), Eng. artist, nonsense poet. Lear used this name for his first book of nonsense poems, *A Book of Nonsense* (1846). The name is (appropriately) a meaningless phrase in the refrain of a popular song, and hence a ballad or set of verses.

Lavinia **Derwent:** Elizabeth Dodd (1909–1989), Sc. children's writer, broadcaster.

Rósza **Déryné:** Rósza Schenbach (1793–1872), Hung. actress, opera singer. Schenbach was the German form of the singer's original surname. The Hungarian form was Széppataki.

Louis Charles Antoine **Desaix:** Louis Charles Antoine Des Aix (1768–1800), Fr. general.

Sugar Pie **DeSanto:** Umpeylia Marsema Balinton (1935–), U.S. black pop singer. The singer was nicknamed "Little Miss Sugar Pie" by Johnny **Otis** and adopted this as her performing name.

Marceline **Desbordes-Valmore:** Marceline Félicité Joséphine Desbordes (1786–1859), Fr. poet. The poet married an actor, Prosper Lanchantin, and added his stage name, Valmore, to her maiden name.

Jackie **De Shannon:** Sharon Lee Myers (1944–), U.S. pop musician.

Father **Desiderius:** Peter Lenz (1832–1928), Ger. artist, architect. Desiderio da Settignano was a famous 15th-century Florentine sculptor. Lenz, however, probably based his name on that of "Monsu" Desiderio, the pseudonym of a painter active in Naples in the 17th century. Works grouped under this name are now known to belong to at least three separate artists, including François Nomé, a painter noted for his ghostly architectural fantasies, and Didier Barra, who painted topographical views.

Jules **De Sivrai:** Jane Roeckel, née Jackson (1834–1907), Eng. pianist, music teacher, composer.

Martin **Desjardins:** Martin van den Bogaert (1640–1694), Du.-born Fr. sculptor. The French name essentially translates the Dutch, literally "of the orchard."

Gaby **Deslys:** Gabrielle Caïre (1881–1920), Fr. stage actress, revue artist.

Astra **Desmond:** Gwendolyn Mary Thomson (1893–1973), Br. opera singer.

Eric **Desmond:** Matthew Reginald Sheffield-Casson (1901–1957), Br.-born U.S. stage, movie actor. As a child performer, the actor was billed as Reggie Sheffield, but changed his name to Eric Desmond, possibly for the Earls of Desmond, in 1913, when he played the title role in *David Copperfield*. In some of his later movies, however, he is billed as Reginald Sheffield.

Florence **Desmond:** Florence Dawson (1905–1993), Eng. revue artiste, impersonator. The actress was renamed as a child dancer by a matron overseeing the group she was in at the time.

Johnny **Desmond:** Giovanni Alfredo di Simone (1920–1985), U.S. actor, singer. "Johnny" as an equivalent of "Giovanni" and "Desmond" from "di Simone." The date of the name change is unknown.

Paul **Desmond:** Paul Emil Breitenfeld (1924–1977), U.S. jazz saxophonist.

William **Desmond:** William Mannion (1878–1949), Ir. movie actor, working in U.S.

Jerry **Desmonde:** James Robert Sadler (1908–1967), Eng. music-hall comedian.

Ivan **Desny:** Ivan Desnitzky (1922–), Russ. movie actor, working in France, Germany.

Oleksa **Desnyak:** Aleksey Ignatovich Rudenko (1909–1942), Ukr. novelist, short-story writer.

Desperdicios: Manuel Domínguez (1816–1886), Sp. bullfighter. The matador's ring name, meaning "refuse," "garbage," has a memorably vivid origin. "He acquired this gruesome nickname in a *corrida* in Puerta de Santa Maria on 1 June 1857, when a bull gored him in the eye, which he promptly tore out and cast disdainfully away [like garbage] before continuing his performance" [Arnott, p.258].

Des'ree: Des'ree Weekes (1968–), Br. rock singer, of West Indian parentage. A shortened form of "Desiree" ("Désirée"), pronounced "Dezza-*ray*" by Americans but "Day-*zee*-ray" by the British.

Gilbert **des Roches:** [Baroness] Julie Legoux (1842–1891), Fr. composer.

Jean **Dessès:** Jean Dimitré Verganie (1904–1970), Egyptian-born fashion designer, of Gk. parentage, working in France.

Emmy **Destinn:** Emilie Pavlína Kittlová (1878–1930), Cz. opera singer. The soprano adopted the name of her teacher, Marie Loewe-Destinn. In sympathy with the Czech national movement in World War I, she adopted the name Ema Destinnová, but was interned on her Bohemian estate for her pains.

Philippe **Destouches:** Philippe Nicolas Néricault (1680–1754), Fr. comic playwright. The writer adopted his aunt's name.

B.G. **DeSylva:** George Gard DeSylva (1895–1950), U.S. lyricist, screenwriter, movie producer. DeSylva was popular known as "Buddy," and this gave the initial "B."

Determine: Rohan Bennett (*c.*1972–), Jamaican reggae musician.

Andre **de Toth:** Endre Antal Mihály Sásvári Farkasfalvi Tóthfalusi-Tóth (1913–2002), Hung. movie director, working in U.S.

Detroit Junior: Emery Williams, Jr. (1931–2005), U.S. black blues musician. Williams was born in Arkansas and settled in Chicago, but at one time lived in Detroit.

Gene **Detroy:** Samuel Wood (1909–1986), Br. animal trainer. The entertainer gained world fame for his act with Marquis the Chimp.

Cristina **Deutekom:** Christine ("Stientje") Engel (1932–), Du. opera singer.

Jacques **Deval:** Jacques Boularan (1890–1972), Fr. playwright, working in U.S.

William **Devane:** William Devaney (1937–), U.S. movie actor.

David **Devant:** David Wighton (1868–1941), Eng. magician. The illusionist was the son of a Scottish landscape painter, and the artistic connection may have had some bearing on his new name. As a boy, the story goes, he visited an art gallery and admired there a biblical painting by a French artist entitled *David Devant Goliath* ("David Before Goliath"). Young Wighton mistook the second word for the subject's name and "filed it away mentally for professional purposes in later life" [Fisher 1987, p.118].

Robert **Deverell:** Robert Pedley (1760–1841), Eng. writer.

Ananda **Devi:** Ananda Devi Nirsimloo-Anenden (1957–), Mauritian writer, working in French.

Anjali **Devi:** Anjani Kumari (1927–), Ind. movie actress.

Indra **Devi:** Eugenie Vasilievna Peterson (1899–2002), Latvian-born movie actress, yoga teacher, of Swe.-Pol. parentage. The first Western woman to enter an Indian ashram originally made her name as a film actress, playing the part of the goddess Devi in an early movie. She adopted the name for her later calling as a yoga teacher or guru, adding the name Indra, normally a male Indian name, that of the god of the sky, but here perhaps standing for the female Indira, a name of Lakshmi, wife of the god Vishnu.

Saraswati Devi: Khorsheed Manchershah Minocher-Homji (1912–1980), Ind. movie music director. India's first female movie music director was forced to change her name to avoid the wrath of her community when she and her sister, Manek, joined the film studio Bombay Talkies, founded in 1934.

Seeta Devi: Renee Smith (1912–), Ind. movie actress. In Hindu mythology, Seeta (Sita) is regarded as an incarnation of the goddess Lakshmi, while Devi, as for the names above, is a generic name for a female deity as well as a specific name of the wife of Shiva (Siva), the great god of generation.

Sophie Devienne: Jeanne Françoise Thevenin (1763–1841), Fr. actress.

Willy DeVille: William Borsay (1950–2009), U.S. rock singer, of Native American descent. The musician based his stage name on that of his band, Mink DeVille.

Mlle. de Villedieu: Marie Catherine H. Desjardins (1631–1683), Fr. author.

Justin de Villeneuve: Nigel Jonathan Davies (1939–), Br. photographer. The former manager of **Twiggy** has taken on many roles, including a spell as hairdresser under the name Christian St. Forget.

Andy Devine: Jeremiah Schwartz (1905–1977), U.S. movie comedian.

Dominic Devine: David McDonald Devine (1920–1980), Eng. thriller writer.

Magenta Devine: Kim Taylor (1960–), Br. TV presenter.

Devlo: Cyril Shaw (1910–), Eng. magician. The name may be based on that of David **Devant**.

Dorothy Devore: Inez Williams (1899–1976), U.S. movie comedienne.

Howard Devoto: Howard Trafford (*c.*1955–), Eng. punk rock musician. The Buzzcocks member was inspired to take his new name in 1976 after seeing the Sex Pistols, with their own outlandish names. "Devoto" was taken from U.S. writer Bernard DeVoto (*see* John **August**), referred to by Trafford's philosophy lecturer.

Patrick Dewaere: Jean-Marie Bourdeau (1947–1982), Fr. movie actor. The actor adopted his grandmother's surname at the start of his career in 1968. He also appeared under the name Patrick Maurin.

Dewi Dywyll: Dafydd Jones (1803–1868), Welsh poet. The balladeer was blind. Hence his name, meaning "Blind David." He was also known as Deio'r Cantwr, "Dafydd the Singer."

Dewi Emlyn: David Davies (1817–1888), Welsh-born U.S. poet. The poet's name means "David of Emlyn," the latter being the historic region in which he was born.

Dewi Emrys: David Emrys James (1881–1952), Welsh poet.

Dewi Havhesp: David Roberts (1831–1884), Welsh poet. The poet took his bardic name, meaning "David of Havhesp," from a stream by his home near Bala.

Dewi Hefin: David Thomas (1828–1909), Welsh poet. The poet's name means "David of Hefin," this presumably being a local placename.

Dewi Môn: David Rowlands (1836–1907), Welsh poet. The poet's name means "David of Môn," this being the Welsh name of the island of Anglesey, where he was born.

Hildegard Dewitz: Hildegard Kazoreck (1911–), Ger. composer. The musician also used the name Diana Monti.

Dewi Wyn o Eifion: David Owen (1784–1841), Welsh poet. The poet's name means "Fair David of Eifionydd," the latter being the historic region in northwest Wales where he was born and where many poets lived.

Billy de Wolfe: William Andrew Jones (1907–1974), U.S. stage, movie comedian, of Welsh parentage. Bill Jones (as he was usually known) was told by a theater manager that his real name would not do for a star. He therefore simply adopted the manager's own name.

Al Dexter: Albert Poindexter (1902–1984), U.S. country singer, songwriter.

Anthony Dexter: Walter Reinhold Alfred Fleischmann (1913–2001), U.S. movie actor.

Aubrey Dexter: Douglas Peter Jonas (1898–1958), Br. stage, movie, TV actor.

Brad Dexter: Boris Milanovich (1917–2002), U.S. movie actor, producer, of Serbian parentage. Dexter at first appeared regularly on stage and on radio under the name Barry Mitchell.

William Dexter: William T. Pritchard (1909–), Eng. SF writer.

Agyness Deyn: Laura Hollins (1983–), Br. model. The supermodel's new name, in full Agyness G. Deyn, with middle initial, was devised for her by a self-proclaimed name analyst, who said that her career was hampered by the "u" in "Laura." The new name seems to suggest a corruption of Latin *Agnus Dei*, "Lamb of God," referring to Christ.

Lodewijk van Deyssel: Karel Joan Lodewijk Alberdingk Thijm (1864–1952), Du. writer, critic.

Augusto D'Halmar: Augusto Thomson (1882–1950), Chilean writer.

Guy d'Hardelot: Helen Rhodes, née Guy

(1858–1936), Fr.-born Br. composer, singer, of Fr.-Eng. parentage. The musician was born in the Château Hardelot, Boulogne-sur-Mer, France.

Anagarika **Dharmapala:** Don David Hewavitarne (1864–1933), Ceylonese Buddhist leader. The Buddhist pioneer and preacher adopted his new name in his late teens. Dharmapala means "guardian of the dharma," this being the Sanskrit word for "law," that is, the ideal truth as set forth in the teachings of the Buddha. Anagarika, literally "houseless one" (from Sanskrit *anagara*, "houseless," from *an-*, "not," and *agara*, "house"), is the title of a celibate fulltime roving worker for Buddhism. Dharmapala was the first *anagarika* in modern times, and took his vow of celibacy (*brahmacharya*) at the age of eight.

Robert **Dhéry:** Robert Léon Fourrey (1921–2004), Fr. movie actor, director. The actor took his name from his birthplace, the small town of Héry, so that he was "Robert d'Héry."

I.A.L. **Diamond:** Itek Dommnici (1920–1988), Rom.-born U.S. screenwriter. Diamond chose his new name when working on the campus newspaper at Columbia University. Tongue firmly in cheek, he claimed that the initials stood for Interscholastic Algebra League, of which he had been champion in 1936 and 1937.

Neil **Diamond:** Neil Diamond (1941–), U.S. popular singer. Many sources give the musician's real name as Noah Kaminsky. However: "Neil Diamond says he was born Neil Diamond, has never toned down his heritage, and many reports and books are wrong that he was Noah Kaminsky" [Beech, p.96].

Alela **Diane:** Alela Diane Menig (1983–), U.S. folksinger, songwriter, of Sc.-Ger. descent.

Willy **Dias:** Fortuna Morpurgo (1872–1956), It. writer of romantic fiction.

Fra **Diavolo:** Michele Pezza (1771–1806), It. brigand chief. The legendary guerrilla leader adopted his nickname, meaning "Brother Devil," given him by victimized peasants on account of his ferocity. It was rumored, moreover, that Pezza had originally been a monk named Fra Angelo ("Brother Angel").

Ottone **di Banzole:** Alfredo Oriani (1852–1909), It. novelist, essayist. The writer used this name for early fiction.

Thomas John **Dibdin:** Thomas John Pitt (1771–1833), Eng. actor, playwright. The actor was illegitimate, so adopted his mother's maiden name.

Ivan Osipovich **Dic:** Jon Dicescu (1893–1938), Rom. socialist activist.

Dic Aberdaron: Richard Robert Jones (1780–1843), Welsh scholar. The eccentric linguist adopted a name meaning "Dick of Aberdaron," the latter being his birthplace.

Roberta **di Camerino:** Giuliana Coen Camerino (1920–), It. fashion designer.

Dic Dywyll: Richard Williams (*c.*1805–*c.*1865), Welsh poet. The balladeer's name means "Blind Dick." He is not actually known to have been blind, but he would put his pinkie in the corner of his eye when singing his ballads.

Angie **Dickinson:** Angeline Brown (1931–), U.S movie actress. The name is that of the actress's first husband, Gene Dickinson.

Sandra **Dickinson:** Sandra Searles (1940–), U.S.-born Br. TV actress.

Carr **Dickson:** John Dickson Carr (1905–1977), U.S. journalist, crime writer. The writer also used the name Carter Dickson, as well as the quite distinct Roger Fairbairn.

Carter **Dickson** *see* Carr **Dickson**

Gloria **Dickson:** Thais Dickerson (1916–1945), U.S. movie actress.

Dic Tryfan: Richard Hughes Williams (*c.*1878–1919), Welsh journalist, short-story writer. The writer's name means "Dick of Tryfan," the latter being a mountain near his birthplace in northwest Wales.

Dida: Nelson de Jesus Silva (1973–), Brazilian footballer.

Bo **Diddley** *see* **Bo Diddley**

P. **Diddy:** Sean Combs (1970–), U.S. black rapper, clothes designer, movie actor. The musician was at first known as "Puffy" from his habit of puffing up his chest during football practice. "He has more sides to him than he has names. On the confusing, what-to-call-him front, there's Sean Combs, the official name he was born with. Puff Daddy, the fancy hip-hop name from his days of dating Jennifer Lopez, the singer and Hollywood queen. Puffy, the nickname given to the schoolboy who puffed out his chest at sports. And not forgetting P-Diddy, the ridiculous tag he adopted as a joke and then decided it suited his post-trial [on firearms charges], post–J-Lo self. Four names, then, for a star.... As for the old name of Puff Daddy: 'We ran that name into the ground. It's all played out. You can call me whatever name best rolls off your tongue.' I opt for Puffy, the name he seems most comfortable with" [*Sunday Times Magazine*, September 30, 2001].

His multiple names and roles continue to fascinate. "Here I am in Copenhagen to talk to and ... to watch Diddy—aka P. Diddy, Puffy, Puff Daddy, Sean, Jack Johnson, Mr. Combs or just Da Man" [*Sunday Times Magazine*, November 11, 2006]. "He was Puff Daddy, a music producer and party promoter.... He then became P. Diddy, a rapper.... On his way to dropping the P—'it got between me and my fans'—and becoming, in the US at least, simply

Diddy, he has transformed himself into the front man for his own fashion label, Sean Jean, and is now an actor" [*The Times*, December 31, 2008].

Didi: Waldir Pereira (1928–2001), Brazilian footballer. A pet form of the player's first name.

Dido: Florian Cloud de Bounevialle Armstrong (1971–), Eng. popular singer. The singer was so nicknamed as a young girl, after the mythological queen and founder of Carthage, familiar from Virgil's *Aeneid* and Purcell's opera *Dido and Aeneas*. At first she hated the name, with its fusty classical connections, but she later accepted it as neat and individualistic.

Babe **Didrikson:** Mildred Ella Didriksen (?1914–1956), U.S. sportswoman, of Norw. parentage. The athlete was the sixth child in her family, so was nicknamed "Baby." Later, this became "Babe" because, like Babe Ruth, she hit tape-measure home runs. She herself changed the Scandinavian "-sen" of her surname to an English-style "-son."

Diego of Cadiz: José Francisco Lopez Camoño (1743–1801), Sp. preacher. Lopez Camoño took the name Diego after joining the Capuchin order in 1759.

Vin **Diesel:** Mark Vincent (1967–), U.S. movie actor, of multiracial origin. The actor long concealed his true identity. His first name is a short form of his original name. His last name came from a nickname given by friends for his nonstop energy, making him look as if he ran off diesel.

Marlene **Dietrich:** Maria Magdalene Dietrich (1901–1992), Ger.-born U.S. movie actress, singer. The actress's first name is a telescoped form of "Maria Magdalene." Her father was Louis Erich Otto Dietrich, and her mother Wilhelmina Elisabeth Josephine Felsing. A year or two after her birth, Maria's family moved from Berlin to Weimar, where her mother married Edouard von Losch. In the popular mind, the name of Marlene Dietrich is associated with that of Lili Marlene, the girl in the song that became popular in World War II, as Dietrich herself was.

The original poem "Lili Marleen" [*sic*] was written by the German Hans Leip in 1915, telling the story of the love of a soldier for his girl. The name combined that of his girlfriend, Lili, and a young nurse named Marleen. The poem was set to music in 1938 by Norbert Schultze and first recorded in 1939 by Lale **Andersen**. It became popular among German troops in World War II and British troops then adopted it in a translated version titled "Lili Marlene." This version was used as a signature tune by Anne **Shelton** in her radio show *Introducing Anne* and was later sung by Dietrich herself.

Dieudonné: Dieudonné M'Bala M'Bala (1966–), Fr. movie actor, satirist.

Laura **Di Falco:** Laura Carpinteri (1910–), It. novelist, painter.

Edoardo **di Giovanni:** Edward Johnson (1878–1959), Can.-born U.S. opera singer, impresario. Johnson adopted this Italian form of his name when studying and singing in Italy from 1908 to 1919.

Bobby **Digital:** Robert Dixon (*c.*1960–), Jamaican reggae musician. Dixon was nicknamed "Digital" because his arrival on the reggae scene in 1985 coincided with the rise of computerized rhythm tracks.

Irasema **Dilian:** Irasema Warschalowska (1924–), It. movie actress. The actress is billed as Eva Dilian in the credits of her first movie, *Maddalena ... zero in condotta* (1940).

Phyllis **Diller:** Phyllis Driver (1917–), U.S. movie actress, comedienne.

Dillinger: Lester Bullocks (1953–), Jamaican rock musician. Bullocks was named for U.S. mobster John Dillinger (1903–1934) by Lee "Scratch" Perry. "'At first I was trying to sound like Dennis **Alcapone**,' said Dillinger. 'When I was going to the studio, I was saying, "My name is Alcapone Junior," but when Scratch Perry take me to the studio at Dynamic, and when I come to do my track, he say, "What is your name?" I say, "I am Alcapone Junior." He say, "No, you are not, you are Dillinger." Scratch give me that name'" [Chris Salewicz and Adrian Boot, *Reggae Explosion: The Story of Jamaican Music*, 2001].

Clarence **Dillon:** Clarence Lapowski (1882–1979), U.S. investment banker. Lapowski's father, a Polish Jew, took his mother's maiden name around 1900.

Dimitry: John Frederick Grimshaw (1950–), Eng. crossword compiler. The pseudonym has multilayered meanings, referring both to the first name of the setter's favorite composer, Shostakovich, and to False Dmitry, the impostor in Russian history who claimed to be the son of Czar Ivan IV. (A deviser of cryptic crosswords is also a "false pretender.") Again, it can be read as "(being) dim, I try" and, as a cryptic clue, "I'm into dirty tricking," with IM inserted into a "tricking" (anagram) of DIRTY. Grimshaw further points out that his full name is an anagram of "charming, if shrewd, joker."

Penelope **Dimont** *see* Ann **Temple**

Isak **Dinesen:** Karen Christentze Blixen-Finecke, née Dinesen (1885–1962), Dan. writer, broadcaster, working in Kenya. The author adopted her new first name, mindful of its traditional Hebrew meaning "laughter," for *Seven Gothic Tales* (1934), written in English. She also wrote as Pierre **Andrezel**, Tania B., and Osceola, the last for various Danish periodicals.

Ding: Jay Norwood Darling (1876–1962), U.S. cartoonist. A shortening of his surname.

Ding Ling: Jiang Weizhi (Chiang Wei-chih) (1904–1986), Chin. feminist writer, Communist activist.

Júlio **Dinis:** Joaquim Guilherme Gomes Coelho (1839–1871), Port. poet, playwright, novelist. The writer was of English descent on his mother's side.

Francisco **di Nogero:** Emilie Frances Bauer (1865–1926), U.S. pianist, composer, of Fr. parentage, sister of composer Marion Eugenie Bauer (1887–1955).

Ronnie James **Dio:** Ronald Padavona (1942–2010), U.S. rock singer.

Diocletian: Diocles (245–316), Roman emperor. The emperor's eventual full name, as found in official inscriptions, was Gaius Aurelius Valerius Diocletianus. Gaius was his *praenomen*, or forename, Aurelius his *nomen*, or *gens* (clan) name, Valerius his *cognomen*, or additional name (from his daughter, Valeria), and Diocletianus his second *cognomen*, created as an adjectival form of his own original name, Diocles (itself meaning "fame of Zeus").

Diogenes: William John Brown (*c.*1895–1960), Eng. trade union advisor, journalist, writer. Brown adopted this name for contributions to *Time and Tide.*

Dion: Dion DiMucci (1939–), U.S. rock musician.

Dionigi da Piacenza: Flaminio Carli (1637–1695), It. missionary. Flaminio Carli, born in Piacenza, took the name Dionigi on entering the Capuchin order in 1652.

Diplodocus: Roy Dean (1927–), Br. crossword compiler. The setter chose a pseudonym (the scientific name of the dinosaur) that referred to his aging status and old-fashioned methods of compilation, without the use of a computer.

Dirceu: Tomás Antônio Gonzaga (1744–1810), Port. poet, of Brazilian parentage. The romantic name derives from Gonzaga's book of pastoral love lyrics, *Marília de Dirceu* (1792).

Dirtsman: Patrick Thompson (1966–1993), Jamaican reggae musician, brother of **Papa San.**

Discobolus: Donald Williams Aldous (1914–before 1995), Eng. writer on sound recording, engineering. The writer's name is Latin (from Greek) for "discus thrower," or in modern terms "disk thrower" (that is, one who "throws" disks on to a record player, or who records on such disks). The name is familiar from *Discobolus*, a statue of a discus thrower by the 5th-century BC Greek sculptor Myron.

Dick Distich: Alexander Pope (1688–1744), Eng. poet. Pope used this pseudonym for writing in the *Guardian*, a distich being a verse couplet.

Dito und Idem: Elisabeth, Queen of Romania (1843–1916), Ger.-born Rom. verse, prose writer +

Mite (or Marie) Kremnitz (1852–1916), Ger. writer. This was the joint pseudonym used by the already pseudonymous Carmen **Sylva** and George **Allan** when the two ladies wrote as coauthors. The words (respectively in Italian, German, and Latin) translate punningly as "the same and the same."

Carl **Ditters von Dittersdorf:** Carl Ditters (1739–1799), Ger. violinist, composer. The Vienna-born musician was ennobled in 1773 and adopted his aristocratic augmentation then.

Divine: Harris Glen Milstead (1945–1988), U.S. transvestite movie actor. The "screen goddess" name was created for the larger-than-life actor by director John Waters, whose star performer he became.

Father **Divine:** George Baker (?1877–1965), U.S. black evangelist. According to one account, the founder of the Peace Mission movement adopted the name Major J. Devine soon after moving to New York from Georgia in 1915. This name was soon popularly modified to Divine, with "Father" indicating his leadership status. He was originally known as The Messenger, and as another explanation recounts: "About this time [1917], the Messenger adopted a new name, the Reverend Major Jealous Divine, implying religious and military authority, the jealousy of the biblical God, and his own divinity. His flock shortened this to Father Divine and chanted, 'God is here on earth today. Father Divine is his name'" [Elizabeth Abbott, *A History of Celibacy*, 2001].

Dorothy **Dix:** (1) Elizabeth Gilmer, née Meriwether (1861–1951), U.S. journalist, women's rights pioneer; (2) Jean Nicol (?–1986), Eng. journalist. Gilmer joined the New Orleans *Picayune* in 1894 and took the name soon after when writing an advice column for women called "Sunday Salad." Nicol took the name when employed by the *Daily Mirror* at the start of her career in the 1930s. The name itself was presumably borrowed from the U.S. social reformer Dorothea Dix (1802–1887).

Richard **Dix:** Ernest Carlton Brimmer (1894–1949), U.S. movie actor.

Marmaduke **Dixey:** [His Honour] Geoffrey Howard (1889–1973), Eng. judge, novelist, poet.

Denver **Dixon:** Victor Adamson (1901–1972), N.Z.–born U.S. movie actor, producer, director. The star of silent westerns also acted under the names Art James and Art Mix. The latter name was later adopted by two other western actors, George Kesterson and Bob Roberts.

Floyd **Dixon:** Jay Riggins, Jr. (1929–2006), U.S. black R&B pianist.

Franklin W. **Dixon:** Edward L. Stratemeyer (1862–1930), U.S. writer. The Stratemeyer Literary Syndicate set up in 1906 used this name for stories for boys about the Hardy Boys, juvenile detectives.

Jean **Dixon:** Marie Jacques (1894–1981), U.S. stage, movie comedienne.

Diz: Edward Jeffrey Irving Ardizzone (1900–1979), Br. cartoonist, illustrator.

Lefty **Dizz:** Walter Williams (1937–1993), U.S. black blues guitarist. Williams played a right-handed Stratocaster guitar with the strings reversed. This gave his new first name. His second name came following a spell as a trumpeter (like Dizzy Gillespie).

Dizzee Rascal *see* Dizzee **Rascal**

Assia **Djebar:** Fatima-Zohra Imalayène (1936–), Algerian novelist, moviemaker.

DJ Minute Mix: Jarrett Cordes (1968–), U.S. black hip-hop musician, turntable artist (mixer). The musician, nicknamed "J.C. the Eternal," is the brother of **Prince Be**.

DJ Quik: David Blake (1970–), U.S. black DJ, rapper.

DJ Screw: Robert Earl Davis, Jr. (1971–2000), U.S. record producer.

DJ Shadow: Josh Davis (*c.*1972–), U.S. hip-hop musician.

DJ SS: Leroy Small (1971–), Br. black hip-hop musician.

Art **D'Lugoff:** Athur Joshua Dlugoff (1924–2009), U.S. nightclub owner. The impresario slightly modified the spelling of his name for ease of pronunciation.

[St.] **Dmitry Donskoy:** Dmitry Ivanovich (1350–1389), Russ. prince. The grand prince of Vladimir and Moscow was given his name, meaning "of the Don," for his victory over the Golden Horde near the Don River at the Battle of Kulikovo in 1380. He was canonized in 1988.

[St.] **Dmitry Rostovsky:** Daniil Savvich Tuptalo (1651–1709), Russ. ecclesiastic, poet, playwright, of Ukr. origin. The writer took monastic vows in 1668 and was appointed metropolitan of Rostov (hence his title) in 1702.

Duke **D'Mond:** Richard Edward Palmer (1943–2009), Eng. pop singer. The Barron Knights lead singer was given his unconventional name by Les Perrin, the group's publicist.

DMX: Earl Simmons (*c.*1970–), U.S. black rapper. The musician took his name from the DMX digital sound machine, but liked to interpret the letters as "Dark Man X."

Anatoly **Dneprov:** Anatoly Petrovich Mitskevich (1919–), Russ. SF writer.

D-Nice: Derrick Jones (1970–), U.S. black rock musician.

I. **Dniprovsky:** Ivan Danilovich Shevchenko (1895–1934), Ukr. writer. The writer took his pen name from the Dnieper River, near which he was born.

Don Leucadio **Doblado** *see* Joseph Blanco **White**

Issay **Dobrowen:** Ishok Israelevich Barabeychik (1891–1953), Russ. conductor, pianist, working in Germany, Sweden. The musician took the name that his orphaned mother had adopted from a relative.

Doc: Tom Johnson (1947–), Br. crossword compiler.

James L. **Docherty** *see* James Hadley **Chase**

Lew **Dockstader:** George Alfred Clapp (1856–1924), U.S. vaudeville artist, blackface minstrel. The singer took the name Lew Dockstader in 1873. He subsequently formed a partnership in a minstrel troupe with Charles Dockstader, who despite his name was not related. When Charles died in 1883, Clapp kept the name, even after the troupe had disbanded.

[Rev.] Charles **Dodd:** Hugh Tootel (1672–1743), Eng. Catholic historian, theologian. The cleric used this name for all of his writings, notably his *Church History of England* (1737–43).

John Bovee **Dods:** Johannes Dods Bovee (1795–1872), U.S. writer on spiritualism. The author modified his name after serving in the War of 1812, "probably out of respect for the maternal uncle who cared for him after his father's untimely death" [Bret E. Carroll in Garraty and Carnes, vol. 6, p. 697).

Meg **Dods:** Christian Isobel Johnstone, earlier M'Leish, née Tod (1781–1857), Sc. cookery writer, novelist. The writer made her name with *The Cook and Housewife's Manual* (1826), by "Mistress Margaret (Meg) Dods," popularly known as *Meg Dods' Cookery*, supposedly written by the landlady of the Cleikum Inn, St. Ronan's. The name is actually that of a character in Sir Walter Scott's novel *St. Ronan's Well* (1824).

John **Doe** *see* Elmer **Ellsworth, Jr.**

Theo van **Doesburg:** Christian Emil Marie Kupper (1883–1931), Du. painter, designer, writer. The artist renamed himself after his stepfather. In 1923 he exhibited as a Dadaist under the name J.K. Bonset.

Q.K. Philander **Doesticks, P.B.:** Mortimer Neal Thomson (1831–1875), U.S. humorist. The name is simply a frivolous one, although Thomson claimed that "P.B." stood for "Perfect Brick." "Doesticks" may be a humorous alteration of "doeskins." His 29 letters under the name, mostly appearing in the *Detroit Daily Advertiser*, were collected in *Doesticks: What He Says* (1855). He also used the name for *Plu-ri-bus-tah, a Song That's-by-No-Author* (1856), a parody of Longfellow's *Hiawatha*. Thomson was the son-in-law of Fanny **Fern**.

Sir Iliad **Doggrel:** [Sir] Thomas Burnet (1694–1753), Eng. writer + George Duckett (?–1732), Eng.

writer, politician. The two men used this name for their *Homerides*, a criticism of Pope's neoclassical translation of the *Iliad* (1715).

Fritz **Döhring:** Carl Busse (1872–1918), Ger. poet. An occasional pseudonym.

Ştefan Augustin **Doinaş:** Ştefan Popa (1922–), Rom. poet.

Dolbokov: Hannes Vayn Bok (1914–1964), U.S. SF writer, artist + Boris Dolgov (?–?), U.S. artist.

Thomas **Dolby:** Thomas Morgan Robertson (1958–), Br. rock musician, producer. The musician was nicknamed "Dolby" at school by classmates impressed by his keen interest in electronics, including the Dolby noise-reduction system for audiotapes. In 1987 Dolby Laboratories reportedly tried to sue Robertson for trademark infringement. The musician won the case, however, on the grounds that the company could not stop anyone called Dolby from using the name.

R. **Doleman:** Robert Parsons (1546–1610), Eng. Jesuit missionary, plotter. Parsons, who founded the English province of the Society of Jesus, used this name for *A Conference about the Next Succession to the Crown of England* (1594). He had several other pseudonyms, many of them simply initials.

Georg **Doleschal:** Oskar Welten (1844–1894), Ger. writer.

Anton **Dolin:** Sydney Francis Patrick Chippendall Healey-Kay (1904–1983), Eng. ballet dancer, choreographer. Patrick Healey-Kay assumed his stage name in 1923, on joining Diaghilev's Ballets Russes: "As the programmes were being printed Pat suddenly conceived the idea of disguising himself under a Russian name. 'It will be an excellent joke. It is sure to mystify all my friends and annoy some of them intensely. What shall I be?' He reached for a volume of Tchekov. 'Anton, at any rate, is a good beginning.' The rest was not so easy. Most of the names were difficult to pronounce, and still more difficult to remember. Someone ... hit upon Dolin. 'It is simple and will look well in print. I can already hear the public calling out: "Dolin! Bravo, Dolin!"'" They did the very next night" [Arnold Haskell, *Balletomania*, 1934]. Dolin is not only a genuine Russian name, appropriate for a ballet dancer, but equally suggests the common Irish surname Dolan. Healey-Kay's mother, née Healey, was Irish. An earlier name used by the dancer was Russian-style Patrikéeff, from his first (originally third) name.

Tiny **Doll:** Elly Schneider (1914–2004), Ger.-born U.S. circus performer, movie actress. The actress was a member of the leading family of midgets in American showbiz, performing with her elder brother and two sisters, who adopted the same surname for obvious reasons (Tiny herself was only 39 inches tall)

and changed their original German first names to the English names Harry, Gracie, and Daisy.

Jim **Dollar:** Marietta Sergeyevna Shaginyan (1888–1982), Russ. writer, playwright, literary critic. The writer used this name for her popular adventure story *Mess Mend: Yankees in Petrograd* (1923), a parody of Western detective fiction set in Russia and an imaginary New York.

Johnny **Dollar:** John L. Sibley (1941–), U.S. black blues musician.

Jenny **Dolly:** Janszieka Deutsch (1892–1941), Hung.-born U.S. movie actress, singer, teaming with twin sister Rosy **Dolly**.

Rosy **Dolly:** Roszicka Deutsch (1892–1970), Hung.-born U.S. movie actress, singer, teaming with twin sister Jenny **Dolly**. Although the duo were billed as "The Dolly Sisters" from the first, they continued to use the European forms of their first names for several years.

Evsey David **Domar:** Evsey David Domashevitsky (1914–1997), Pol.-born U.S. economist.

Arielle **Dombasie:** Sonnery de Fromental (1955–), U.S.–born Fr. movie actress.

Honorio Bustos **Domecq:** Adolfo Bioy Casares (1914–1999), Argentinian writer + Jorge Luis Borges (1899–1986), Argentinian writer. Other joint pseudonyms used by the writers for satirical works were B. Suárez Lynch and B. Lynch Davis.

Domenichino: Domenico Zampieri (1581–1641), It. painter. The artist's name is a diminutive of his first name, so means "little Domenico."

Dominguín: Domingo del Campo (1873–1905), Sp. bullfighter. The name passed to the matador's son, Luis Miguel Gonzáles Lucas (1926–1996).

Hilde **Domin:** Hilde Löwenstein (1909–2006), Ger. poet. The writer took her name from the Dominican Republic, to which, as German Jews, she and her husband emigrated in 1940. They returned to their native Germany from their country of exile in 1954.

Rey **Domini:** Audre Lorde (1934–1992), U.S. black feminist writer. The writer was born Audrey Geraldine Lorde, so that "Rey" is a pet form of her first name and "Domini" presumably a Latin-style translation of her surname.

R.B. **Dominic** *see* Emma **Lathen**

Léon **Dominique:** Léon Aronson (1893–1984), Russ.-born Fr. restaurateur, drama critic. Aronson adopted the name of the Russian restaurant he founded (in 1927) in Paris, the Dominique, as a pseudonym for his second profession as drama critic.

Domino: Shawn Ivy (*c.*1972–), U.S. black rapper.

Fats **Domino:** Antoine Domino (1928–), U.S. black jazz musician. The musician's surname is his real one. "Fats" was the (descriptive) nickname given him by band leader Bill Diamond when he first started playing, as a ten-year-old, at the Hideaway Club, New Orleans. In 1949 his first record was called "The Fat Man." He was the inspiration for the name of Chubby **Checker**.

Sam **Donahue:** Samuel Koontz (1918–1974), U.S. saxophonist, bandleader.

Tom **Donahue:** Thomas Coman (1928–1975), U.S. rock musician, radio station manager.

Troy **Donahue:** Merle Johnson, Jr. (1936–2001), U.S. movie actor. The actor was given his screen name by Henry Willson, the agent who had earlier transformed Roy Harold Scherer into Rock **Hudson**. Johnson soon took to his new name: "It was part of me ten minutes after I got it."

Pauline **Donalda:** Pauline Lightstone (1882–1970), Can. opera singer.

Donatello: Donato di Niccolò de' Bardi (*c.*1386–1466), It. sculptor. The artist's adopted name arose as an affectionate nickname, "little Donato."

Lonnie **Donegan:** Anthony James Donegan (1931–2002), Sc.-born pop musician, of Ir. descent The "King of Skiffle" took his new first name from U.S. blues musician Lonnie Johnson (1889–1970), with whom an MC confused him when the two men were on the same London bill.

Richard **Donner:** Richard Donald Schwartzberg (1930–), U.S. movie actor.

Donovan: Donovan Philip Leitch (1946–), Sc. rock musician, father of Ione **Skye**.

Dick **Donovan:** Joyce Emmerson Preston Muddock (1843–1934), Eng. journalist, detective fiction writer. The writer took his name from one of the 18th-century Bow Street runners (a precursor of the London Metropolitan Police).

Don Yute: Jason Andrew Williams (1974–), Jamaican DJ.

Mr. **Dooley:** Finley Peter Dunne (1867–1936), U.S. humorist. Mr. Dooley, in a series of the writer's works, was a typical Irish saloon keeper with a typical Irish name.

Rupert **Doone:** Ernest Reginald Woodfield (1903–1966), Br. ballet dancer, choreographer.

Daniela **Dor:** Barbara Kaufman (1912–), Hung.-born Israeli violinist, composer. The musician used this name for popular music and songs.

Milo **Dor:** Milutin Doroslovac (1923–), Serbian writer.

Madame **D'Ora:** Dora Kallmus (1881–1963), Austr. photographer.

Sister **Dora:** Dorothy Wyndlow Pattison (1832–1878), Eng. medical missionary. The former schoolteacher adopted her religious name, based on her own first name, on becoming a member of the Sisterhood of the Good Samaritan in 1864.

Dora d'Istria: [Princess] Elena Koltsov-Massalsky, née Ghika (1828–1888), Rom. writer, of Albanian origin. The daughter of Prince Alexander Ghika (1795–1862), hospodar of Wallachia, used this name, meaning "Dora of Istria," for *Women in the East; Les Femmes en Orient. Par Mme. la Comtesse Dora d'Istria*, published simultaneously in Zürich and London in 1861.

Mary **Doran:** Florence Arnott (1907–1995), U.S. movie actress.

Jean **Dorat:** Jean Dinemandi (1508–1588), Fr. humanist, poet, translator. The scholar's change of name is explained not entirely accurately by D'Israeli: "Dorat, a French poet, had for his real name *Disnemandi*, which, in the dialect of the Limousins, signifies one who dines in the morning: that is, one who has no other dinner than his breakfast. This degrading name he changed to *Dorat*, or gilded, a nickname which one of his ancestors had for his fair tresses" [p.201]. The writer actually adopted the name of his birthplace, Le Dorat, near Limoges. D'Israeli goes on to tell how Dorat's daughter married a man named Goulu, "glutton" (compare La **Goulue**), so that "in spite of her father's remonstrances, she once more renewed his sorrows in this alliance!"

Roland **Dorgelès:** Roland Lecavelé (1886–1973), Fr. novelist, short-story writer.

Clara **Doria:** Clara Kathleen Rogers, née Barnett (1844–1931), Eng. singer, composer, working in U.S. The singer first used her stage name in 1863 for her debut at Turin, Italy, as Princess Isabella in Meyerbeer's opera *Robert le Diable*. She emigrated to the United States in 1871.

Angela **Dorian:** Victoria Vetri (1944–), U.S. movie actress, model, of It. parentage. Vetri was given her new name as *Playboy*'s September 1967 "Playmate of the Month." "Being named for a shipwreck doesn't sound appealing, but a young actress named Victoria Vetri went for the idea, which was hatched by an agent who must have been haunted by the sinking of the Italian liner *Andrea Doria* [in 1956]" [Gretchen Edgren, *The Playmate Book*, 1996].

John **Dormer:** John Huddleston (1636–1700), Eng. Jesuit. "He was generally known by the name of Dormer, but he occasionally assumed the *alias* of Shirley" [*Dictionary of National Biography*].

Dolores **Dorn:** Dolores Dorn-Heft (1935–), U.S. stage, movie actress.

Philip **Dorn:** Hein van der Niet (1901–1975), Du. stage, movie actor, working in U.S. The actor appeared in early movies as Frits van Dongen, and some sources give this as his real name.

Sandra **Dorne:** Joanna Smith (1925–1992), Br. movie actress.

Marie **Doro:** Marie Kathryn Stewart (1882–1956), U.S. stage, movie actress. The actress adopted the stage name "Doro" from a youthful nickname, "Adorato."

Rheta Childe **Dorr:** Reta Louise Child (1866–1948), U.S. journalist, feminist. Reta Child altered the spelling of her first and last names before marrying John P. Dorr in 1892 (separated 1898).

Diana **Dors:** Diana Mary Fluck (1931–1984), Eng. stage, movie, TV actress. The actress was nearly called Diana Scarlett, a name proposed by her agent, Gordon Harbord, who also named Laurence **Harvey** and Adrienne **Corri.** But Diana was not keen on this, and her final stage name came about as described in her autobiography: "To be born with the name of Fluck, particularly if one is a girl, can be nothing less than disastrous. Originally my reason for changing it was no more than a young girl's ambition to become a film star with a beautiful name which would look good in twinkling lights, but when I was cast in my first film the director tried gently to explain that the second part of my name would have to be altered because people might try to place a vulgar intonation [*sic*] on it! I was only fourteen and did not quite understand his well meant reasoning then, but as I wished to call myself something much more exotic anyway, I agreed willingly, and the search for a new surname was on! My agent had suggested Scarlett ... and I toyed with that for a while. My own fantasy of Diana Carroll also seemed a possibility but my father was incensed that the family name was not to be used.... Finally my mother in a moment of brilliance decided that I *would* stick to a family name after all, and because my grandmother's maiden name had been Dors, she felt it sounded good to have two names with the same initial. So Dors it was and we were all happy!" [Diana Dors, *Behind Closed Dors*, 1979].

Fifi **D'Orsay:** Angelina Yvonne Cecil Lussier D'Sablon (1904–1983), Can.-born U.S. stage, movie actress. The actress claimed that her new name was adopted from a bottle of French perfume, and that "Fifi" was what other girls called her when in the Greenwich Village Follies chorus in the 1920s.

M.L. **D'Orsay:** Maria Luisa Ponsa (1878–1919), Sp. pianist, composer.

Ruth **Dorset** *see* Marilyn **Ross**

St. John **Dorset:** Hugo John Belfour (1802–1827), Eng. poet. The writer first used this name for *The Vampire, a Tragedy in five acts* (1821), published when he was 18.

Marie **Dorval:** Marie Thomase Amélie Delaunay (1798–1849), Fr. actress. The actress's stage name is that of her husband, actor-manager Allan Dorval, whom she married at 15. He died five years later.

Gabrielle **Dorziat:** Gabrielle Sigrist Moppert (1886–1979), Fr. movie actress.

Stanislav **Dospevski:** Zafir Zograf (1823–1878), Bulg. painter.

Carlo **Dossi:** Carlo Alberto Pisani Dossi (1849–1910), It. writer.

Dosso **Dossi:** Giovanni di Luteri (*c.*1490–1542), It. painter. The artist's name, which is not documented before the 18th century, probably comes from Dosso, near Mantua, where he is first recorded in 1512.

Dottsy: Dorothy Brodt (1954–), U.S. country singer.

Felia **Doubrovska:** Felizata Dluzhnevskaya (1896–1981), Russ.-born ballet dancer, working in France, U.S.

Catherine **Doucet:** Catherine Green (1875–1958), U.S. stage, movie actress.

Doug E. **Doug:** Douglas Bourne (1970–), U.S. movie actor, rap artist.

Douglas: Thomas Douglas England (1891–1971), Eng. cartoonist, commercial artist.

Craig **Douglas:** Terence Perkins (1941–), Eng. popular singer.

Daniel **Douglas** *see* Claude **Cahun**

Donald **Douglas:** Douglas Kinleyside (1905–1945), U.S. movie actor.

Donna **Douglas:** Doris Smith (1933–), U.S. TV actress.

Edith **Douglas:** Clara Louise Root Burnham (1854–1927), U.S. novelist. The writer occasionally used this name for early stories and poems submitted to magazines.

Ellen **Douglas:** Josephine Haxton, née Ayres (1921–), U.S. novelist, short-story writer.

Felicity **Douglas:** Felicity Dowson, née Tonlin (1910–), Eng. stage, movie, TV, radio author.

George **Douglas:** (1) [Lady] Gertrude Georgina Douglas (1842–1893); Eng. novelist; (2) George Douglas Brown (1869–1902), Sc. novelist. After publishing a book for boys, *Love and a Sword* (1899), as Kennedy King, George Douglas Brown produced the bestselling novel *The House with the Green Shutters* (1901) under the name that brought him fame.

Jack **Douglas:** Jack Roberton (1927–2008), Eng. comic TV actor.

[Sir] Kenneth **Douglas:** Kenneth Mackenzie (1754–1833), Sc. soldier. Mackenzie spent the whole of his military career, rising to the rank of lieutenant general, under his original family name. In 1831, at the age of 77, he adopted the name Douglas by royal license on being created a baronet.

Kirk **Douglas:** Issur (later Isidore) Danielovitch Demsky (1916–), U.S. movie actor, of Russ. Jewish parentage. The actor chose his new first name because he felt it was "snazzy," and his surname out of his admiration for Douglas Fairbanks, Jr., son of Douglas **Fairbanks, Sr.**

Melvyn **Douglas:** Melvyn Edouard Hesselberg (1901–1981), U.S. stage, movie actor, producer, director, of Russ. Jewish parentage. The actor adopted his new name from a forebear in his mother's old Kentucky family.

Mike **Douglas:** Michael Delaney Dowd, Jr. (1925–2006), U.S. TV presenter, singer.

O. **Douglas:** Anna Masterton Buchan (1877–1948), Sc. novelist, sister of novelist John Buchan (1875–1940). The writer took her new name for her first book, *Olivia in India: The Adventures of a Chota Miss Sahib* (1913), based on her experiences while visiting her younger brother William in Calcutta in 1907: "I did not want to use my name as (in my opinion) John had given lustre to the name of Buchan which any literary efforts of mine would not be likely to add to, so I called myself 'O. Douglas'" [Anna Buchan, *Unforgettable, Unforgotten*, 1945]. A "Chota Miss Sahib" (in the book title) is a young unmarried lady.

Robert **Douglas:** Robert Douglas Finlayson (1909–1999), Br. stage, movie actor, working in U.S.

Scott **Douglas:** James Hicks (1927–1996), U.S. ballet dancer.

Steve **Douglas:** Steven Kreisman (1938–1993), U.S. saxophonist.

Theo **Douglas:** Henrietta Dorothy Everett, née Huskisson (1851–1923), Br. writer of fantasy fiction.

Wallace **Douglas:** Wallace Finlayson (1911–), Can. stage director.

Walter Sholto **Douglas:** Mary Diana Dods (*c*.1790–*c*.1830), Sc. writer, crossdresser. The writer began her literary career under the male name David Lyndsay. In 1827 she took to wearing male dress and styled herself Mr. Walter Sholto Douglas, her "wife" being the Englishwoman Isabella Robinson, with whom she had formed a relationship.

Frederick **Douglass:** Frederick Augustus Washington Bailey (1818–1895), U.S. black abolitionist, writer. The human rights leader escaped from slavery in Baltimore, Maryland, in 1838 and settled with his wife, Anna Murray, in New Bedford, Massachusetts, where he changed his name to disguise his background and confuse slavecatchers.

Stephen **Douglass:** Stephen Fitch (1921–), U.S. stage actor, singer. The actor adopted his mother's maiden name.

Billie **Dove:** Lillian Bohny (1900–1997), U.S. movie actress, of Swiss parentage. The actress was nicknamed "Billie" as a child and to this she later added "Dove." (According to one account, she was nicknamed "The Dove" for her gentle features when employed as an artist's model.) Her new first name was adopted by jazz singer Billie **Holiday**.

Dovima: Dorothy Virginia Margaret Juba (1927–1990), U.S. model, of Pol.-Ir. parentage. When the future model was confined to bed with rheumatic fever for seven years as a child she occupied herself by drawing, signing her pictures with a name formed from the first syllables of her three forenames. She kept the name in her professional career.

Peggy **Dow:** Margaret Josephine Varnadow (1928–), U.S. movie actress.

Mrs. Regera **Dowdy** *see* Eduard **Blutig**

Dow, Jr.: Elbridge Gerry Paige (1816–1859), U.S. humorist. The writer used this name for *Short Patent Sermons* (1875).

Eddie **Dowling:** Joseph Nelson Goucher (1894–1976), U.S. stage actor, producer, playwright. The future actor adopted his mother's maiden name as an 11-year-old cabin boy on the Fall River Line.

Charles **Downing:** Charles James Frank Dowsett (1924 —1998), Br. academic. Professor of Armenian Studies at Oxford University from 1965 to 1991, Dowsett adopted his pen name for some children's books, beginning with *Russian Tales and Legends* (1956).

Major Jack **Downing:** Seba Smith (1792–1868), U.S. humorist. Jack Downing was the supposed name of a "Down East" Yankee who in 1830 began to publish letters in the *Portland Courier*, founded by Smith the year before. His comic turn of speech and homespun sagacity soon won him popularity among his readers.

Dox: Jean Verdi Solomon Razkandrainy (1913–1978), Malagasy lyric poet. The poet adopted his pen name from the last syllable of *paradox*, reflecting both the indigenous and (French) colonial background against which his writing is set as well as his leading theme of love, with its duality of joy and sadness, beauty and melancholy.

Lynn **Doyle:** Leslie Alexander Montgomery (1873–1961), Ir. humorous writer. "His pseudonym was typical of his sense of fun — early in his writing career, he happened to notice a can marked *Linseed Oil* in a grocer's shop, and so 'Lynn C. Doyle' was born. Later he dropped the 'C'" [Introduction to Lynn Doyle, *An Ulster Childhood*, 1985]. "His pseudonym ... is a pun on what humour can do to ease life's frictions" [Sam Burnside in Brian Lalor, gen. ed., *The Encyclopaedia of Ireland*, 2003].

Martin **Doyle:** William Hickey (1787–1875), Ir. writer, philanthropist. Hickey used this name for a number of publications on agricultural topics.

Dr. ... For names beginning thus, see the next word, e.g. Dr. **Dre**, Dr. **Feelgood**, Dr. **John**, etc.

Billy **Drago:** William Burrows (1949–), U.S. movie actor.

Edward **Dragonet** see S.S. **Smith**

Crescent **Dragonwagon:** Ellen Zolotow (1952–), U.S. children's writer. The writer legally adopted her pseudonym, with "Crescent" meaning "The Growing." She has also written as Ellen Parsons.

Rade **Drajnac:** Radojko Jovanovic (1899–1943), Serbian writer, journalist.

Alfred **Drake:** Alfredo Capurro (1914–1992), It.-born U.S. stage singer, dancer.

Charles **Drake:** Charles Ruppert (1914–1994), U.S. movie actor.

Charlie **Drake:** Charles Edward Springall (1925–2006), Eng. TV, movie, stage comedian. The actor adopted his mother's maiden name early in his career.

Dona **Drake**: Rita Novella (1920–1989), Mexican singer, dancer, movie actress. An early name used by the singer was Rita Rio.

Fabia **Drake:** Fabia Ethel McGlinchy (1904–1990), Br. movie actress. The actress took her name from her Irish father, Alfred Drake. Her mother, Annie McGlinchy, née Dalton, was Scottish.

Frances **Drake:** Frances Dean (1908–2000), U.S. movie actress.

Samuel **Drake:** Samuel Drake Bryant (1768–1854), Br.-born U.S. actor-manager.

Tom **Drake:** Alfred Alderdice (1918–1982), U.S. movie actor. The overt "maleness" of the actor's new names may have been intended for his "boy next door" roles of the 1940s. He began his career with the screen name Richard Alden.

Dranem: Armand Ménard (1869–1935), Fr. comic singer. A simple reversal of the entertainer's name.

Dranmor: Ferdinand von Schmid (1823–1888), Swiss poet.

Hastings **Draper** see Roderic **Graeme**

M.B. **Drapier:** Jonathan Swift (1667–1745), Ir. satirist, cleric. A "nonce" pseudonym adopted by the author of *Gulliver's Travels*. He used the name for *The Drapier's Letters* (1724), written in the guise of a Dublin draper (which Swift elected to spell "drapier"). A patent had been granted to the Duchess of Kendal for supplying copper coins for use in Ireland, and this she sold to one William Wood for £10,000. The profit on the patent would have been, it is said, around £25,000, and Swift published four letters prophesying ruin to the Irish if "Wood's half-pence" were admitted into circulation. The letters were effective, and the government was forced to abandon the plan and to compensate Wood.

The first pamphlet was titled *A Letter to the Shop-Keepers, Tradesmen, Farmers, and Common-People of Ireland concerning the Brass Half-Pence coined by Mr. Woods*, and the next one provoked the following proclamation from the Lord Lieutenant and Council of Ireland, dated October 27, 1724: "Whereas a Wicked and Malicious Pamphlet, Intituled, *A Letter to the whole People of* Ireland, by *M.B. Drapier, Author of the Letters to the Shopkeepers,* &c. ... in which are contained several Seditious and Scandalous Paragraphs highly Reflecting upon His Majesty and His Ministers.... We the Lord Lieutenant and Council do hereby Publish and Declare, That in Order to Discover the Author of the Said Seditious Pamphlet, We will give the necessary orders for the Payment of Three Hundred Pounds *Sterling*."

Sir Alexander **Drawcansir:** Henry Fielding (1707–1754), Eng. novelist, playwright. Fielding used the pseudonym as editor of *The Covent-Garden Journal* (1752). The original Drawcansir was the burlesque tyrant in George Villiers, Duke of Buckingham's farcical comedy *The Rehearsal* (1672), caricaturing the knight errant Almanzor in Dryden's *The Conquest of Granada* (1670). The name itself puns on "Almanzor," while perhaps also implying someone who likes to *draw* a *can* of liquor.

Buckingham's Drawcansir has only three lines in the play, of which two are: "He that dares drink, and for that drink dares die, / And, knowing this, dares yet drink on, am I." This parodied Almanzor's: "He who dares love, and for that love must die, / And, knowing this, dares yet love on, am I."

Alfred **Drayton:** Alfred Varick (1881–1949), Br. movie actor.

Dr. **Dre:** Andre Ramelle Young (1965–), U.S. black "gangsta" rapper.

Judge **Dread** see **Judge Dread**

Mikey **Dread:** Michael Campbell (c.1958–), Jamaican reggae DJ, "toaster." The musician was named after his Rastafarian dreadlocks, "the longest in Jamaica."

Carl **Dreadstone:** John Ramsey Campbell (1940–), Eng. writer of horror fiction.

Lydia **Dreams:** Walter H. Lambert (1869–1949), Eng. drag artist, ventriloquist.

Sonia **Dresdel:** Lois Obee (1908–1976), Eng. stage, movie actress.

Louise **Dresser:** Louise Kerlin (1878–1965), U.S. movie actress.

Paul **Dresser:** John Paul Dreiser, Jr. (1857–1906), U.S. songwriter. The future songwriter changed his name to Dresser when he ran away from home to join a traveling show at age 16.

Marie **Dressler:** Leila Marie von Koerber (1869–1934), Can.-born U.S. stage, movie actress, comedienne. The actress adopted her new name, from an aunt, when she ran away from home at 14 to join a traveling stock theater company. The change was necessary because, as she wrote in her autobiography *My Own Story* (1934), her father said he would "never drag the name of von Koerber through the mud by showing off behind the footlights."

Ellen **Drew:** Esther Loretta Ray (1914–2003), U.S. movie actress. The actress first adopted the screen name Erin Drew before becoming Ellen Drew.

Reginald **Drew** *see* Reginald **Wray**

Richard **Dreyfuss:** Richard Stephen Dreyfus (1947–), U.S. movie actor.

Nancy **Drexel:** Dorothy Kitchen (1910–), U.S. movie actress.

J.F. **Drexler** *see* Mark **Carrel**

Étienne **Drian:** Étienne Adrien (1885–1961), Fr. fashion illustrator.

Driftin' Slim: Elmon Mickle (1919–1977), U.S. harmonica player, singer.

Jimmy **Driftwood:** James Corbett Morris (1907–1998), U.S. country singer. The singer's adopted name reflected his background as a teacher in a backwoods high school, touring folk festivals and performing his own songs.

Adam **Drinan:** Joseph Todd Gordon Macleod (1903–1984), Sc. author, play producer, radio newsreader. The writer chose the name for three books of verse about the Hebrides, selecting the pseudonym because some of his ancestors had come from Drinan in the Isle of Skye.

John **Drinkrow:** Michael John Drinkrow Hardwick (1924–1991), Eng. literary reference writer. The author of books on Charles Dickens and Sherlock Holmes used this name for *The Vintage Operetta Book* (1972) and *The Vintage Musical Comedy Book* (1973).

D-Roc: Dennis L. Miles (1959–2004), U.S. rock guitarist.

Droch: (1) Robert Seymour Bridges (1844–1930), Eng. poet; (2) Robert Bridges (1858–1941), U.S. literary adviser. The poet's early pen name is a Celtic rendering of his surname, as is that of his American namesake. (Scottish Gaelic *drochaid* is "bridge.") The poet also wrote as Broch, from the Scottish word (related to English "borough") for a round stone castle.

Dromio: William John Townsend Collins (1868–1952), Br. journalist, local historian. The writer used this name for his publications on rugby football. Dromio is a messenger in Shakespeare's *Comedy of Errors*, his own name coming from Greek *dromos*, "running." Rugby is a game in which speed is of the essence.

Juliette **Drouet:** Julienne Gauvain (1806–1883), Fr. actress, mistress of novelist Victor Hugo.

Joanne **Dru:** Joanne Letitia La Cock (or La Coque) (1923–1996), U.S. movie actress, sister of Peter **Marshall**. When a stage actress (briefly), Joanne La Cock performed as Joanne Marshall. She selected

the name of Dru from a Welsh ancestor after director Howard Hawkes encouraged her to change her name. "It is a sign of the times that this ... actress saw fit to change her name. Twenty years later, anyone called Letitia La Cock would have been welcomed rapturously at the [Andy] **Warhol** factory and could hardly fail to have been lit up with the Day-Glo camp of the name. Her invented name sounded much more plausible" [Thomson 2003, pp. 253–4].

The **Druid:** Henry Hall Dixon (1822–1870), Eng. sporting writer. Dixon first wrote for the *Sporting Magazine* as "General Chassé," but then adopted the name by which he became familiar to his readers. It may have been suggested by **Stonehenge**, himself named after a monument associated with the Druids.

Johnny **Drummer:** Thessex Johns (1938–), U.S. black blues musician. The artist was a drummer before he became a singer.

Bill **Drummond:** William Butterworth (1953–), S.A.–born Br. rock musician.

Ivor **Drummond** *see* Rosalind **Erskine**

Dryasdust *see* M.Y. **Halidom**

The Rev. Dr. **Dryasdust:** [Sir] Walter Scott (1771–1832), Sc. novelist. Scott used this mock self-deprecatory name for the person who introduces several of his novels, or to whom they are introduced. Thus *Ivanhoe* (1820) mentions "the venerable name of Dr. Jonas Dryasdust," while the "Introductory Epistle" to *The Fortunes of Nigel* (1822) is from "Captain Clutterbuck to the Reverend Dr. Dryasdust."

John **Dryden** *see* Fenton **Brockley**

Leo **Dryden:** George Dryden Wheeler (1862–1939), Eng. songwriter.

Doggrel **Drydog:** Charles Clark (1806–1880), Br. farmer, publisher, satirist, sporting writer. Clark used other names, such as Chilly Charley, Charles William Duckett, Thomas Hood the Younger, Pe-Gas-Us, and Quintin Queerfellow, this last for *A Doctor's "Do"-ings, or the entrapped Heiress of Witham* (1848), a self-published satirical poem of racy content intended for private circulation.

Edward **Dryhurst:** Edward Roberts (1904–1989), Br. movie producer, actor.

dsh: [Dom] Sylvester Houedard (1924–1992), Br. poet, priest, scholar. The Benedictine monk used this lowercase initialism for over 1,000 so-called "typetracts" published in the 1960s and 1970s.

César **Duayen:** Ema de la Barra de Llanos (1861–1947), Argentinian novelist, painter, singer. The artist used this (male) name for her writing.

Sieur **du Baudrier:** Jonathan Swift (1667–1745), Ir. satirist, cleric. Swift used the name for his *New Journey to Paris* (1711).

Alice **Dubois:** Louise de Bettignies (1880–1918),

Fr. spy. The former governess adopted this cover name when working as an Allied agent in German-occupied Lille during World War I.

Ducange Anglicus: Bernard Quaritch (1819–1899), Ger.-born Eng. antiquarian bookseller. The name means "English Ducange," referring to the famous French historian and antiquarian Charles Du Fresne, seigneur Du Cange (1610–1688).

Paul **Ducelle:** Carrie William Krogmann (1943–), U.S. composer.

Raymond **Duchamp-Villon:** Raymond Duchamp (1876–1918), Fr. sculptor. The sculptor was the brother of the artists Marcel Duchamp (1887–1968) and Jacques **Villon.**

Jacques **Duchesne:** Michel Jacques Saint-Denis (1897–1971), Fr.-born Eng. stage actor, director. This was the *nom de guerre* under which the director headed a team that broadcast from London to their compatriots over the BBC's French service during World War II.

Père **Duchesne:** Jacques-René Hébert (1757–1794), Fr. political journalist. The writer began his career as the author of a series of sacrilegious satires, adopting the name for his own persona and for the title of his journal, *Le Père Duchesne,* which first appeared in 1790 and which was the most successful periodical of the French Revolution. The name itself was that of a legendary Parisian character, well known long before the Revolution, whose name was synonymous with crude, down-to-earth statements. He was portrayed at the head of Hébert's paper, at first with a pipe in his mouth and a shag of tobacco in his right hand, but later with mustaches and two pistols in his belt, and with the tobacco replaced by an ax, which he brandished over a kneeling *abbé* (representing the ecclesiastical writer and politician, the abbé Maury). The wording beneath this vignette was: "*Je suis le véritable Père Duchesne, foutre*" ("I am the real Father Duchesne, dammit"). Inevitably, his virulent leftism led his alter ego to the guillotine.

Duck: Don Manley (1945–), Br. crossword compiler. An obvious pseudonym for someone named Donald.

Thomas **du Clévier:** Bonaventure Des Périers (*c.*1500–1543), Fr. storyteller, humanist. The writer used the name for his *Cymbalum Mundi* (1537), four satirical dialogues in the style of Lucian. Du Clévier is an anagram of French *incrédule* ("unbeliever"), with Thomas alluding to the biblical Doubting Thomas. The work was supposedly translated by du Clévier, and sent by him to his friend Tryocan. But the latter was also a pseudonym used by Des Périers, and is an anagram of *croyant* ("believer"). The work is an attack on the Christian faith and its liturgy and discipline. It was officially suppressed, and only one copy survived.

Mlle. **Duclos:** Marie-Anne de Châteauneuf (1668–1748), Fr. actress.

Dave **Duddley:** David Darwin Pedruska (1928–2003), U.S. country singer.

Arthur **Dudley** *see* Hans **Werner**

Dave **Dudley:** David Pedruska (1928–), U.S. country musician.

Ernest **Dudley:** Vivian Ernest Coltman-Allen (1908–2006), Eng. writer, broadcaster. The host of the popular radio series *Armchair Detective* took his professional name from his birth town, Dudley, near Birmingham.

Pete **Duel:** Peter Deuel (1940–1972), U.S. movie actor.

Thomas **Duffle** *see* Rev. T. **Clark**

Duffy: Aimée Duffy (1984–), Welsh pop singer. The singer is said to use her surname alone to avoid comparison with the controversial star Amy Winehouse, whose first name and voice are similar. "To which Duffy has a simple reply: she dropped her first name when she was 19, since she had always been called Duffy by schoolmates and friends.... Not everyone has been persuaded by those arguments. Winehouse burst onto the music scene in 2003.... In 2004 Duffy released an EP of Welsh ballads under her full name, before executing an abrupt change of style and moniker" [*Sunday Times*, January 4, 2009].

Dufresne: Abraham-Alexis Quinault (1693–1767), Fr. actor.

Dugazon: Jean-Baptiste-Henri Gourgaud (1746–1809), Fr. actor.

Jacques François **Dugommier:** Jacques François Coquille (1736 or 1738–1794), French general.

Doris **Duke:** Doris Curry (1945–), U.S. black soul singer.

Raoul **Duke:** Hunter S. Thompson (1937–2005), U.S. writer. The maverick author submitted his seminal novel *Fear and Loathing in Las Vegas* to *Rolling Stone* magazine under this name in 1970. It appeared in book form under his real name two years later.

Vernon **Duke:** Vladimir Aleksandrovich Dukelsky (1903–1969), Russ.-born U.S. composer. In 1921 Dukelsky arrived in New York with his mother and brother and soon after met George **Gershwin,** who encouraged him to write popular music and suggested the American version of his name. The two sides of Dukelsky's musical personality evolved during a subsequent visit to Europe, so that Vladimir Dukelsky composed classical music while Vernon Duke honed his skills as a popular songwriter. In 1929 Duke returned to the States and in 1936 legalized the name on becoming an American citizen.

Germaine **Dulac:** Charlotte Elisabeth Germaine Saisset-Schneider (1882–1942), Fr. movie director, actress. The actress adopted the name of her husband, engineer and novelist Marie-Louis Albert-Dulac, whom she married in 1905.

Benson Dulay: William Dooley (1899–1991), Br. illusionist. The entertainer began his career as a comedy conjuror under the name Billy Dooley, but then appeared in the revue *Why Go to Paris?*, when he was advised to make his name sound more French.

Alexandre Dumas: Alexandre Davy de la Pailleterie (1802–1870), Fr. novelist, playwright. The author of *The Three Musketeers* (1844), known as Dumas *père*, took his name from his West Indian grandmother, and it was his father, Thomas-Alexandre Davy de la Pailleterie, natural son of the Marquis de la Pailleterie and Marie Cessette Dumas, who adopted the name in 1786. His identically named son (1824–1895), known as Dumas *fils*, author of *La Dame aux camélias* (1848), was also illegitimate.

Mlle. Dumesnil: Marie-Françoise Marchand (1712–1803), Fr. tragic actress.

Carlotta Dumont: Clorinda Matto de Turner (1909–), Peruvian writer. A name created using letters from the writer's original name.

Henry Du Mont: Henry de Thier (1610–1684), Belg. composer, organist.

Margaret Dumont: Marguerite Baker (1889–1965), U.S. comic stage, movie actress. Baker first appeared appeared on the stage in minor singing and comedy roles under the name Daisy Dumont. Later, as a dedicated comedienne in Marx Brothers movies, she was regularly Margaret Dumont.

Charles François Dumouriez: Charles François Du Périer (1739–1823), Fr. general.

Dumpynose: Chris Brougham (1947–), Br. crossword compiler. The setter's pseudonym does not allude to his appearance but is an appropriate anagram of "pseudonym."

Steffi Duna: Stephanie Berindey (1913–1992), Hung. dancer, movie actress.

Irma Duncan: Irma Dorette Henriette Ehrich-Grimme (1897–1977), Ger.-born U.S. ballet dancer, teacher. Irma was trained as a child by the dancer Isadora **Duncan** and, like Maria-Theresa **Duncan**, took her name.

Isadora Duncan: Angela Duncan (1877–1927), U.S. dancer, choreographer. The dancer took her new first name in 1894, and six of her child pupils became known as the "Isadorables." In 1920 she adopted all six, of which three, including Irma **Duncan** and Maria-Theresa **Duncan**, took her name.

Jane Duncan: Elizabeth Jane Cameron (1910–1976), Sc. novelist. The writer took her new first name from her own middle name and her surname from the first name of her father, Duncan Cameron.

She also wrote as Janet Sandison, her mother's maiden name.

Julia K. Duncan *see* Carolyn **Keene**

Maria-Theresa Duncan: Maria-Theresa Kruger (1895–1987), Ger.-born U.S. concert dancer. Maria was trained by the dancer Isadora **Duncan** as a child and, like Irma **Duncan**, legally adopted her name.

Richard Duncan: Richard Duncan Rudin (1957–), Br. writer, broadcaster.

Robert Edward Duncan: Edward Howard Duncan (1919–1988), U.S. poet. The future poet was adopted in the year of his birth by Edwin Joseph Symmes and Minnehaha Harris, who renamed him Robert Edward Symmes. On discharge from the army in 1941, the poet combined his original surname and adopted first and middle names to form his regular name.

Trevor Duncan: Leonard Charles Trebilco (1924–), Br. popular composer.

Chris Dundee: Cristofo Mirena (1907–1998), U.S. fight promoter.

Johnny Dundee: Giuseppe Carrora (1893–1965), It.-born U.S. featherweight boxer ("The Scotch Wop"). Carrora was given his ring name by boxing manager William "Scotty" Montieth, a Scotsman.

James Dundonald: John James Lawlor (1918–1999), Eng. academic. Professor of English Language and Literature at Keele University from 1950 to 1980, Lawlor adopted this name as author of *Letters to a Vice-Chancellor* (1962).

Elaine Dundy: Elaine Brimberg (1921–2008), U.S. writer, of Jewish parentage. In 1946, the future author of the bestselling *The Dud Avocado* (1958) and of a biography of Peter **Finch** (see his entry) entered the Jarvis Theatre School, Washington, DC, run by an Englishman of the same name. "One day, after doing a scene, Mr Jarvis looked at me thoughtfully ... 'Your name doesn't suit you,' he said finally. 'You should change it.' 'To what?' I asked. He said he'd think about it and let me know tomorrow. The next day he said Elaine Dundy. Instantly I knew it was right. Lighthearted, playful yet forceful, serious – I read all sorts of adjectives into it. The important thing was that it seemed to reflect the person I saw in the mirror" [Elaine Dundy, *Life Itself!*, 2001].

Dunga: Carlos Bledorn Verri (1963–), Brazilian footballer.

David Dunham: David Eugene Smith (1860–1944), U.S. writer on the history of mathematics. An occasional pseudonym ued by the scholar for some of his books.

Colonel Walter B. Dunlap: Sylvanus Cobb, Jr. (1823–1887), U.S. writer. Cobb used this name for travel and adventure sketches that he contributed to the *New York Ledger*.

Jane **Dunlap:** Adelle Davis (1904–1974), U.S. nutritionist. Mainly a cookbook writer, Davis took this name for a quite different book, *Exploring Inner Space: Personal Experiences under LSD-25* (1961).

Kaye **Dunn:** Katherine Dunham (1909–2006), U.S. black dancer, choreographer. The dancer sometimes used the pseudonym for her wrtten work.

Michael **Dunn:** Gary Neil Miller (1934–1973), U.S. dwarf movie actor.

Irene **Dunne:** Irene Marie Dunn (1898–1990), U.S. stage, movie actress. The actress added the "e" to her name on entering show business in 1922, but was alternately billed "Dunn" and "Dunne" until 1930.

Philip Hart **Dunning:** Philip Hart Dunn (?1891–1968), U.S. playwright, producer. The writer modified his name in the 1920s in order to be distinguished from his brother, Caesar Dunn, also a playwright.

Augustus **Dun-shunner:** William Edmonstone Aytoun (1813–1865), Sc. poet. The writer used this name for his contributions to *Blackwood's Magazine*. A "dun" is a debt collector, so that a "dun-shunner" is someone who avoids debt collectors or creditors. *See also* **Bon Gaultier.**

Amy **Dunsmuir:** Margaret Oliphant Oliphant, née Wilson (1828–1897), Sc. novelist, historical writer. (Margaret Wilson married her cousin, Francis Wilson Oliphant. Hence the double "Oliphant.") The pen name was used for *Vida: The Story of a Girl* (1880), but *Claire* (1889) was "by the author of Vida."

T. E. **Dunville:** Thomas Edward Wallen (1868–1924), Eng. music hall comedian, singer.

La **Du Parc:** Thérèse de Gorle (1633–1668), Fr. actress, mistress of the dramatist Racine. The actress married a comic actor, René Berthelot (*c.*1630–1664), whose stage name was Du Parc.

Marie **Duplessis:** Alphonsine Plessis (1824–1847), Fr. courtesan ("La Dame aux camélias"). Born into a poverty-stricken home in Normandy, Plessis entered fashionable society at the age of 18, "nobilizing" her name and sporting a corsage of fresh camellias on first nights at the Opéra. Her fame and nickname made her the prototype for Marguerite Gautier, the central character in Alexandre Dumas *fils'* novel, *La Dame aux camélias* (1848), which in turn was the inspiration for Verdi's opera *La traviata* (1853).

David **Durand:** David Durrant (1921–), U.S. juvenile movie actor.

Jean **Durand:** Andrée Rochat (1900–?), Swiss pianist, composer.

Don **Durant:** Donald Allison Durae (1932–2005), U.S. TV actor.

Henry Fowle **Durant:** Henry Welles Smith (1822–1991), U.S. attorney. In 1847 Smith moved from Lowell, Massachusetts, to Boston, where he was prompted to change his name in order to avoid confusion with 11 other lawyers named Smith.

Marguerite **Duras:** Marguerite Donnadieu (1914–1996), French novelist, playwright, moviemaker. The writer adopted her pseudonym in the 1940s from a wine-growing village near Bordeaux where her father had once owned a house.

Leon **Duray:** George Stewart (1894–1956), U.S. racecar driver. Stewart adopted his new name as a tribute to fellow driver Arthur Duray (1882–1954).

Deanna **Durbin:** Edna Mae Durbin (1921–), Can. movie actress, singer. The actress juggled the letters of her fairly common first two names and came up with the more esoteric "Deanna," counting "m" as "n" and losing the "y" in the process.

Jane **Durrell** *see* Jane **Wyman**

Luc **Durtain:** André Nepveu (1881–1959), Fr. writer.

Guru **Dutt:** Gurudatta Padukone (1925–1964), Ind. movie director, actor.

Theodora **Dutton:** Blanch Ray Alden (1934–), U.S. pianist, composer.

Olav **Duun:** Ole Julius Raabye (1876–1939), Norw. novelist.

Diane **Duval** *see* Julie **Bishop**

Enna **Duval:** Anne Hampton Brewster (1818–1892), U.S. writer. Brewster used her pen name for the short stories that she began publishing in 1845. She abandoned the name in 1860.

Frank **Duveneck:** Frank Decker (1848–1919), U.S. painter, etcher, sculptor, of Ger. parentage. The artist adopted the name of his stepfather, Joseph Duveneck, also of German origin.

Henri **Duvernois:** Henry Schwabacher (1875–1937), Fr. novelist, playwright.

Duy Tan: Vinh San (1899–1945), Vietnamese emperor. The emperor assumed his new name on his succession in 1907. It means "reform," and as written in Chinese characters was the same as the name of the Duy Tan Hoi ("Reformation Society"), a radical nationalist organization founded around the same time.

Ann **Dvorak:** Anna McKim (1911–1979), U.S. movie actress. The actress adopted a family name on her mother's side. She was the daughter of silent actress Anna Lehr, and in her earliest movies, as a child player, was billed as Baby Anna Lehr.

Michel **Dvorsky:** Josef Hofmann (1876–1957), Pol.-born U.S. pianist, composer. The musician used this name for compositions. It equates to the original, as Slavic *dvor* and German *Hof* both mean "court."

Deanna **Dwyer** *see* Leigh **Nichols**

K.R. **Dwyer** *see* Leigh **Nichols**

Gilbert **Dyce:** Percy Hetherington Fitzgerald (1834–1925), Ir. novelist.

David Ochterlony **Dyce-Sombre:** David Ochterlony Dyce (1808–1851), Eng. eccentric. Dyce's great-grandfather, Walter Reinhard, had served as a soldier in India, where he was nicknamed "Sombre" for his constantly serious or somber expression. In 1836, on inheriting a large legacy through his family's maternal line, Dyce appended his forebear's nickname to his own surname.

Anson **Dyer:** Ernest Anson-Dyer (1876–1962), Eng. movie cartoonist.

Dyfed: Evan Rees (1850–1923), Welsh poet. The poet and archdruid took his bardic name from the ancient province (and former modern county) of Dyfed, southwest Wales, where he was born.

Dyfnallt: [Rev.] John Owen (1873–1956), Welsh poet. The poet and archdruid took his bardic name from a favorite locality. The name itself means "deep wood."

Bob **Dylan:** Robert Allen Zimmerman (1941–), U.S. songwriter, singer, of East European Jewish origin. It is usually said that Dylan adopted the name of the Welsh poet Dylan Thomas (1914–1953) because he admired him. But he has flatly denied this: "No, God, no. I took the name Dylan because I have an uncle named Dillon. I changed the spelling, but only because it looked better. I've read some of Dylan Thomas's stuff, and it's not the same as mine." The notion persisted, however, prompting Dylan to ask Robert Shelton, author of *No Direction Home: The Life and Music of Bob Dylan* (1986), to "straighten out in your book that I did not take my name from Dylan Thomas" [Dolgins, p.74].

Alternate accounts exist. "As Bob became more serious about his music it was clear to him that he needed a stage name. Most of the performers he liked had a name they adopted because it was catchy, and Zimmerman was not that. There has been much speculation over how Bobby Zimmerman became Bob Dylan, and Bob has given several confusing statements, none of which tallies with the version his friends remember. The clearest answer he gave was that he originally wanted to call himself Dillion, after an uncle of that name. In truth, there was no Dillion in the family. However, the name *Dillon* was familiar to Bob. James Dillon was one of the earliest settlers of [Dylan's boyhood town] Hibbing, and a family of that name owned a farm on Dillon Road. One of the best-known football players in Minnesota was Bobby Dillon. A popular television show of the time, *Gunsmoke*, featured a character named Matt Dillon. Any or all of these associations could have brought the name to his attention. Still, Bob chose to spell the name differently" [Howard

Sounes, *Down the Highway: The Life of Bob Dylan,* 2001].

But Dylan Thomas cannot be ignored. "In the spring of 1958 ... Bob drove up in his Ford convertible. [His girlfriend] Echo met him in the yard. He was excited. 'I've got my name,' he said. 'I know what my name's gonna be now.' When he told her, Echo asked, 'Do you mean, D-i-l-l-o-n, like Matt Dillon?' 'No, no, no, like this, D-y-l-a-n.' Bob had a book under his arm and he showed it to Echo. It was a book of poems by the Welsh poet Dylan Thomas" [ibid.]. Dylan adopted the name legally in 1962.

Osip **Dymov:** Osip Isidorovich Perelmann (1878–1959), Russ. Jewish writer, working in U.S.

Adolf **Dymsza:** Adolf Baginski (1900–1975), Pol. movie actor.

Ms. **Dynamite:** Niomi McLean-Daley (1981–), Br. black hip-hop, soul singer. The name reflects the explosively expressed emotions of the singer's lyrics, which "fire broadsides at wife-beaters, drug-dealers, black-on-black violence and feckless former lovers" [*Sunday Times*, August 18, 2002].

Dzerents: Ovsep Shishmanyan (1822–1888), Armenian historical novelist. The writer's name is the Armenian equivalent of Terence (as for the Roman poet).

Dzhivani: Serob Levonyan (1846–1909), Armenian poet. The poet's assumed name, meaning "handsome," was originally his father's nickname for him as a child.

Sheila **E.:** Sheila Escovedo (1959–), U.S. rock singer, percussionist, songwriter.

Jeanne **Eagels:** Amelia Jean Eagles (?1894–1929), U.S. stage actress. It is uncertain when or why the actress changed the spelling of her surname.

Vince **Eager:** Roy Taylor (1940–), Eng. pop singer. The singer was renamed in 1958 by manager and impresario Larry Parnes. "'He seems very eager to get on,' I heard Larry say to someone over the phone. 'Eager, yes, that describes him, yes, I'll call him Eager.' With that Larry put down the phone, looked at me and said: 'You're a very eager young man aren't you?' 'Am I?' I asked. 'Yes, you'll be Eager. What would you like for a first name,' enquired Larry. 'I don't know, Larry, I like Roy.' 'No, no,' replied Larry ... 'Don't you have a favourite singer?' My liking for Gene **Vincent** and Lonnie **Donegan** met with an unfavourable silence. 'Gene? Lonnie? Neither of those are suitable,' replied Larry. 'What about Vince? Short for Vincent,' I asked. 'My brother's middle name is also Vincent.' A smile of approval greeted my suggestion. 'Yes, Vince Eager. That's good,' said Larry. 'That's very good.' And so Vince Eager was born" [Vince Eager, *Vince Eager's Rock n' Roll Files,* 2007].

Solomon Eagle: [Sir] John Collings Squire (1884–1958), Br. poet, essayist, short-story writer.

Ronnie Earl: Ronald Earl Horvath (1953–), U.S. blues guitarist.

Jean Earle: Doris Burge, née Stanley (1909–2002), Eng. poet, writer.

Sullivan Earle: [Sir] John William Kaye (1814–1876), Eng. army officer, civil servant. The writer used this name for his fiction.

Earl Sixteen: Earl Daley (1958–), Jamaican reggae musician. After winning local talent shows, Daley embarked on his fulltime musical career at age 16.

Virgil **Earp** *see* Wes **Hardin**

Rachel **East** *see* Rebecca **West**

Edward Eastaway: Edward Thomas (1878–1917), Eng. poet, writer, of Welsh parentage. Thomas used this name for a collection of poems published posthumously in 1917.

Sheena Easton: Sheena Shirley Orr (1959–), Sc. rock singer. The singer's new surname was that of her first husband, Sandy Easton.

Easy Baby: Alex Randle (1934–), U.S. black blues musician.

Eazy-E: Eric Wright (1963–1995), U.S. black "gangsta" rapper. "E" stood for "Eric," though Wright, who in 1985 set up his own record company with profits from drug dealing, liked to claim it stood for "entrepreneur."

Abba Eban: Aubrey Solomon Meir (1915–2002), S.A.–born Israeli diplomat, political leader. The Israeli foreign minister's father died when he was only a few months old. Some years later his mother married Isaac Eban. When Eban settled in Israel and became a politician he adopted the Hebrew word *even*, "stone," as his surname, resulting in media reports that he had changed his name to Evans.

Eben Fardd: Ebenezer Thomas (1802–1863), Welsh poet, critic. The poet's bardic name means simply "Ebenezer the bard."

Buddy Ebsen: Christian Rudolph Ebsen (1908–2003), U.S. movie actor, dancer.

Eccles: Frank Hilton Brown (1926–1986), Eng. political cartoonist. The artist used this name for his contributions to the *Daily Worker* (later renamed *Morning Star*) from 1952.

Johann Eck: Johann Maier (1486–1543), Ger. theologian. Martin Luther's leading Roman Catholic opponent adopted his name early in his theological career from his native village of Eck (or Egg).

Johnnie Eck: John Eckhart (1909–1991), U.S. performer. The actor, born with a body that ended at the waist, exhibited himself as a "Living Half-Man" and starred in the classic horror movie *Freaks* (1932).

Billy Eckstine: William Clarence Eckstein (1914–1993), U.S. popular singer, bandleader. The singer changed the spelling of his name as a young adult at the suggestion of a nightclub owner, who thought his name looked too Jewish.

Jenny Eclair: Jennifer Claire Hargreaves (1960–), Br. comedian, TV personality. The celebrity adopted a whimsical version of her two first names for her professional name.

Barbara Eden: Barbara Jean Moorhead, later Huffman (1934–), U.S. movie actress.

Sir John **Edgar:** [Sir] Richard Steele (1672–1729), Eng. essayist, dramatist. Steele used this name as editor of *The Theatre* (1720), the first English theatrical periodical.

Damon Edge: Thomas Wise (1950–1995), U.S. rock musician.

The Edge: David Evans (1961–), Welsh rock guitarist. The U2 musician is said to have been named by the group's lead singer, **Bono**, after a hardware store that the latter passed on his way into Dublin city center. But there are other explanations. "The name was apparently chosen because it matched the shape of his head, although it was a very appropriate description of the original, angular way in which he approached the guitar" [Dave Bowler and Bryan Dray, *U2: A Conspiracy of Hope*, 1993]. Further theories attribute the name to Evans's position as an outsider in the band, the only Welshman among Irishmen, or to his love of walking on the edges of high walls and buildings. The Edge himself comments: "Just about everybody calls me Edge, or The Edge if it's a formal occasion. I'm only David Evans to people who don't know me well, immigration officers and the like" [Beech, p. 110]. Whatever the origin, "Evans the Edge" has the ring of a typical Welsh nickname.

Rosemary Edghill: Eluki Bes Shahar (1956–), U.S. SF writer. The writer adopted a more conventional name at the suggestion of her publisher on beginning her career as a historical novelist.

Wardore **Edgy** *see* Eduard **Blutig**

Edílson: Edílson da Silva Ferreira (1970–), Brazilian footballer.

Edmílson: Edmílson José Gomes de Moraes (1976–), Brazilian footballer.

Paul **Edmonds** *see* C.L. **Moore**

G.C. Edmondson: José Mario Garry Ordonez Edmondson y Cotton (1922–), Guatemalan-born U.S. SF writer. Edmondson wrote westerns under the names Kelly P. Gast, J.B. Masterson, and Jake Logan.

William Edmunds: William Weston (?1550–1615), Eng. Jesuit. The ecclesiastic adopted his new name in 1575 as a tribute to his fellow Jesuit, Edmund Campion (1540–1581). He was sometimes also known by the surname Hunt.

Willie Edouin: William Frederick Bryer (1846–

1908), Eng. comic actor. "Willie" from his own first name, and "Edouin" from the middle name of his father, John Edwin Bryer.

Robert Edric: Gary Edric Armstrong (1956–), Eng. novelist.

Kasimir Edschmid: Eduard Schmid (1890–1966), Ger. writer. The writer adopted his pseudonym as his official name in 1947.

Albert Edwards: Arthur Bullard (1879–1929), U.S. journalist, writer.

Blake Edwards: William Blake McEdwards (1922–), U.S. movie producer, director. Some sources give the filmmaker's original name as William Blake Crump.

Gus Edwards: Gustave Edward Simon (1881–1945), U.S. songwriter, entertainer.

Henry Edwards: Ethelbert Edwards (1882–1952), Eng. stage, movie actor. Edwards is said to have been given his new first name by British producer-director Cecil Hepworth, who also renamed the actor's wife, Chrissie **White**. "Ethelbert Edwards, a successful stage actor who had given over 600 performances as the hero of *Robin Hood*, appeared in Hepworth's films as Henry Edwards, and lived under the name until his death" [Matthew Sweet, *Shepperton Babylon*, 2005].

Neely Edwards: Cornelius Limbach (1883 or 1889–1965), U.S. movie comedian.

Penny Edwards: Millicent Edwards (1928–1998), U.S. movie actress.

Samuel Edwards: Noel Bertram Gerson (1914–1988), U.S. journalist, writer. Gerson adopted several pseudonyms for the various facets of his prolific output, including this one for two novels, *The Naked Maja* (1759) and *55 Days at Peking* (1963). Other pen names were Ann Marie Burgess, Michael Burgess, Paul Lewis, Leon Phillips, and Carter A. Vaughan, while for "Wagons West" and "White Indian," two series for juvenile readers, he was respectively Dana Fuller Ross and Donald Clayton Porter

Vince Edwards: Vincenzo Edoardo Zoino (1928–1996), U.S. movie actor, of It. parentage.

Eek A Mouse: Ripton Joseph Hylton (1957–), Jamaican reggae singer. Hylton took his name from a racehorse on which he frequently lost money. (On the one occasion he refused to back it, it naturally won.)

Jean Effel: François Lejeune (1918–1982), Fr. cartoonist. The artist's new surname represented his initials, "F.L.," pronounced in French as in English. He preceded this with the most common French forename, Jean. The name overall was shorter than the original, and so more suitable for signatures on his cartoons.

Aunt Effie: Jane Euphemia Browne (1811–1898), Br. children's writer.

Philippe Egalité: Louis Philippe Joseph, duc d'Orléans (1747–1793), Fr. statesman. The duke assumed his (literally) egalitarian name in order to court the favor of the people when he became Deputy for Paris (1792) in the *Convention Nationale*. In the *Convention* he voted for the death of Louis XVI, his cousin, but was himself executed the following year. So much for egalitarianism.

Lesley Egan *see* Dell **Shannon**

Willie Egans: Willie Lee Egan (1933–2004), U.S. R&B singer.

H.M. Egbert: Victor Rousseau Emanuel (1879–1960), Eng.-born U.S. pulp-magazine writer.

George Egerton: Mary Chavelita Dunne (1857–1945), Austral.-born novelist, of Ir.-Welsh parentage, daughter of **Hi-Regan**. After eloping to Norway in 1887 with a married American, H.H.W. Melville (died 1889), and an affair with the Norwegian writer Knut **Hamsun**, in 1891 Dunne married a Canadian, Egerton Clairmonte, then in 1901 Reginald Golding Bright (1874–1941). Her pen name derives from her mother's maiden name and the first name of her Canadian husband.

Georg Egestorff: Georg, Freiherr von Ompteda (1863–1931), Ger. novelist.

Comante Eginetico: Carlo Innocenzo Frugoni (1692–1768), It. poet. This was the poet's Arcadian pseudonym, based on the Greek island of Aegina (Italian *Egina*) (*see* Aglauro **Cidonia**).

Werner Egk: Werner Mayer (1901–1983), Ger. opera, ballet-music composer. The musician apparently adopted his name as a tribute to Johann **Eck**, who originally had the same surname.

John Eglinton: William Kirkpatrick Magee (1868–1961), Ir. essayist, poet, biographer.

Eglwysbach: John Evans (1840–1897), Welsh preacher, writer. The name is that of the village in Denbighshire (now Conwy) where the Wesleyan minister was born. Aptly, it means "little church."

Eha: Edward Hamilton Aitken (1851–1909), Br. writer on India, natural history, of Sc. parentage. An initialism.

Ehedydd Iâl: William Jones (1815–1899), Welsh poet. The name means "lark of Iâl," the latter being the historic region of northeast Wales where the poet was born.

Gustave Eiffel: Gustave Bonickausen (1832–1923), Fr. engineer. The engineer's father immigrated from Germany to Paris, France, in around 1710, adding as a memento the name of his home country, the Rhineland region of Eifel (as it is now usually spelled). His son kept the German name until 1880, only nine years before the Universal Exposition of 1889 for which the famous Eiffel Tower was built.

Eifion Wyn: Eliseus Williams (1867–1926),

Welsh poet. The poet took his bardic name from the historic region of Eifionydd where he was born, as were many other poets. "Wyn" means "white," "fair," "pure." Compare the next name below.

Eifionydd: John Thomas (1848–1922), Welsh journalist, editor. The writer took his name from the historic region of Eifionydd, northwest Wales, famous for its literary and cultural associations. It was itself named for the 5th-century ruler Eifion.

John **Eilian:** John Tudor Jones (1904–1985), Welsh poet, editor. The writer took his name from his birthplace, the village of Llaneilian ("St. Eilian's church"), Anglesey.

Eilir: William Eilir Owen (1852–1910), Welsh poet. The poet's bardic name means "butterfly."

C. Wilkins **Eimi:** Charles Wilkins Webber (1819–1856), U.S. writer, adventurer. Webber used this name for "Shot in the Eye," a story of Texas border life published in 1845.

Einhart: Heinrich Class (1868–1953), Ger. writer. Class used this name for his nationalistic work *Deutsche Geschichte* ("German Story") (1908).

Nikolay **Ekk:** Nikolay Vladimirovich Ivakin (1902–1976), Russ. movie director.

Britt **Ekland:** Britt-Marie Eklund (1942–), Swe. movie actress.

Elaheh: Bahar Gholam Hosseinin (1934–2007), Iranian singer, working in U.S.

Elangovan: T.K. Thanikachalam (1913–1971), Ind. scriptwriter.

Lile **Elbe:** Einar Wegener (1886–1931), Dan. painter. Born male, the artist adopted her new name after undergoing a gender reassignment operation.

Abulfaz **Elchibey:** Abulfaz Kadyrgula-ogly Aliyev (1938–2000), Azerbaijani nationalist leader. The first president of the Republic of Azerbaijan, elected in 1989, assumed his new name, meaning "envoy of the people," in the late 1980s. He was succeeded in 1993 by his namesake, Geidar Aliyev.

Florence **Eldridge:** Florence McKechnie (1901–1988), U.S. stage actress.

Carmen **Electra:** Tara Leigh Patrick (1972–), U.S. model, TV actress.

Gus **Elen:** Ernest Augustus Elen (1862–1940), Eng. music-hall artist, singer of Cockney songs.

Elephant Man: O'Neil Bryan (1977–), Jamaican dancehall musician. The musician adopted the nickname given him for his large ears.

Elerydd: William John Gruffydd (1916–), Welsh poet, novelist, short-story writer. The writer's name is presumably a local placename.

Elfed: Howell Elvet Lewis (1860–1953), Welsh poet, hymnwriter. The poet and archdruid took his bardic name from his native village of Cynwyl Elfed, Carmarthenshire.

Elfyn: Robert Owen Hughes (1858–1919), Welsh poet. In Welsh folklore, Elfyn or Elffyn ap Gwyddno is the character who fostered the legendary 6th-century poet Taliesin as a child.

Elfynydd: James Kenward (*fl.*1834–1868), Eng. poet, of Welsh affinity.

Avril **Elgar:** Avril Williams (1932–), Eng. stage actress. The actress assumed her father's third name as her stage name.

El Hakim: Barry Walls (1937–), Eng. circus fakir. The name is a stock one for fake fakirs, and is Arabic for "the wise one." The entertainer used other names for his various acts. "Barry turns the pages of his scrap-book — a catalogue of his sundry disguises: Sai-Wen the illusionist; Vulcan the fire-eater; Psychos; the Great Zeus In His Bed Of Pain; The Human Pin-Cushion. It was his father who gave him the name El Hakim when he was 18; that and Otaki are the only pseudonyms he has used since joining the circus seven years ago, as a painter and fire-eater, only drawing on his full repertoire of effects when the previous fakir got bitten by a bear" [*Sunday Times*, October 8, 1978].

Elia: Charles Lamb (1775–1834), Eng. writer, poet. The writer first used the name in his *Essays of Elia*, which appeared in the *London Magazine* in 1820–23. "In a letter, dated July 30, 1821, to John Taylor, senior partner in the firm of Taylor and Hessey, Publishers, of Fleet St., Lamb related the circumstances under which he came to adopt the *nom de guerre* of Elia. 'The fact is, a person of that name, an Italian, was a fellow clerk of mine at the South-Sea House [head office of the South Sea Company, Threadneedle Street, London], thirty (not forty) years ago ... but had left it like myself many years; and I having a brother now there, and doubting how he might relish certain descriptions in it, I clapt down the name of Elia to it, which passed off pretty well ... I went the other day (not having seen him for a year) to laugh over with him at my usurpation of his name, and found him, alas! no more than a name, for he died ... eleven months ago ... so the name has fairly devolved to me, I think'" [Thomas Hutchinson, ed., *The Works of Charles Lamb*, 1908]. The name is now usually pronounced "Eelia."

Elidir Sais: William Hughes Jones (1885–1951), Welsh literary critic. The writer adopted the name of a 13th-century Welsh court poet. His own name meant "Elidir the Englishman," from his exile in that country. Jones was originally so called by way of a nickname, since he habitually spoke English to his Welsh-speaking friends.

Donna **Elidora:** Caroline Wuiet (Vuyet) (1766–1835), Fr. pianist, composer, writer. The musician married in 1807 and accompanied her husband to Portugal, where she assumed her pseudonym.

Elin-Pelin: Dimitar Ivanov Stojanov (1877–1949), Bulg. short-story writer. Stojanov's stories express the bitterness of his time. (He has been called a "singer of rural wretchedness.") Hence his pen name, meaning "wormwood" (Bulgarian *pelin*), with Elin a jingling prefix.

Eliodd: Elisabetta Oddone Sulli-Rao (1878–1972), It. organist, singer, composer. The musician created her pseudonym from the first syllables of her first two names.

George **Eliot:** Mary Anne (later Marian) Evans (1819–1880), Eng. novelist. The writer took her male first name from her lover, philosopher and writer George Henry Lewes (1817–1878), who himself wrote as Slingsby **Lawrence**. She may have also been influenced by the new first name of George **Sand**. As she later explained to her husband, American banker John Walter Cross: "George was Mr. Lewes's Christian name, and Eliot was a good, mouth-filling, easily pronounced word" [J.W. Cross, *George Eliot's Life as Related in her Letters and Journals*, 1885]. She first used the name for her novel *Scenes of Clerical Life* (1858).

"Why, then, did George Eliot adopt a male pseudonym? Like Currer **Bell** ... she might have wished to avoid the condescension of male critics towards female writers.... A more persuasive cause is that she had already created a body of intellectual work in her journalism that she chooses to exempt from the new and risky creative venture of novel writing. If George Eliot fails, Marian Evans remains intact.... She liked the name. She leaves parental authority. She 'makes a name for herself.' She chooses her own patronymic. For the time being, she casts the 'author' as a male origin for the text" [Gillian Beer, *George Eliot*, 1986].

Max **Eliot:** [Mrs.] Anna M.B. Ellis (?–1911), U.S. journalist, writer, drama critic.

Elisa: Lisa Barbuscia (1970–), U.S. pop singer, of Puerto Rican/It.-Ir. parentage. The singer began her career as a model, and at first sang as Lisa B. Her comment on her new name: "It's like a plague of Lisas out there ... Lisa Stansfield, Lisa M, **Lisa Lisa**, **Wendy and Lisa**, **Lisa Marie**..." [*Sunday Times Magazine*, October 4, 1992]. Hence the choice of something a little more original.

Elisheva: Yelizaveta Ivanovna Zirkova (1888–1949), Russ. Jewish poet, working in Palestine. The writer's pen name is the Hebrew form of her Russian first name (English Elizabeth).

Filinto **Elísio:** [Fr.] Francisco Manuel do Nascimento (1734–1819), Port. poet. Elisio was the last of the Portuguese Neoclassical poets and a member of the literary society known as the Arcádia Lusitana. Hence his Arcadian name, meaning "Elysium."

Elis o'r Nant: Ellis Pierce (1841–1912), Welsh novelist. The writer's pen name means "Ellis of the brook."

Eliza: Elizabeth Carter (1717–1806), Eng. poet. The name was used by other women writers called Elizabeth, including the unidentified author of *Eliza's Babes; or, The Virgins-Offering* (1652).

Elizabeth: (1) Mary Annette, Gräfin von Arnim-Schlagenthin, later Countess Russell, née Beauchamp (1866–1941), Austral.-born Br. author; (2) Mary Elizabeth Jenkin (1892–1979), Eng. children's radio producer. The countess assumed her mother's first name for her novels, and it occurs in the title of her best-known work, *Elizabeth and Her German Garden*, published anonymously in 1898.

K. **Elkan:** Wilhelm Dilthey (1833–1911), Ger. philosopher. Dilthey used this name for an early work, *Lebenskämpfe und Lebensfriede* ("Life Struggles and Life Peace") (1865).

Ella: Margaretta Van Wyck Bleecker Faugères (1771–1801), U.S. poet, playwright, essayist.

Henry **Ellen:** James Barron Hope (1829–1887), U.S. poet. Hope adopted this name for poems published in the *Southern Literary Messenger* and other periodicals.

John Lodge **Ellerton:** John Lodge (1801–1873), Eng. composer. The prolific composer added the name Ellerton around 1845, apparently basing it on that of the concert director John Ella (1802–1888).

Duke **Ellington:** Edward Kennedy Ellington (1899–1974), U.S. black jazz musician. "Duke" has long been used in the U.S. as a nickname for a smart or accomplished person, especially one who dresses and behaves stylishly. This certainly suited the most prolific jazz musician of the 20th century.

Cass **Elliot:** Ellen Naomi Cohen (1941–1974), U.S. pop singer. The singer was nicknamed "Cass" by her father after the Trojan prophetess Cassandra (*see* **Cassandra**). Cass herself took the name Elliot to honor a friend who had been killed in an auto accident.

[Sir] John **Elliot:** John Elliot Blumenfeld (1898–1988), Br. railroad manager. "Knowing the disadvantage of having a German name, he had changed his name by deed poll in 1922, taking his second forename as his surname" [*Dictionary of National Biography*].

Chick **Elliott:** Violet Wooll (1900–?), Austral. blackface comedienne, working in England. The singer may have taken her stage name from the English singer and dancer G.H. Elliott (1884–1962), who had a similar act (but varied it with chocolate-colored makeup, as distinct from conventional black).

Don **Elliott:** Don Elliott Helfman (1926–1984), U.S. jazz musician.

Gertrude **Elliott:** May Gertrude Dermot (1874–1950), U.S. stage actress, sister of Maxine **Elliott**.

Laura **Elliott** *see* Kasey **Rogers**

Maxine **Elliott:** Jessica Dermot (1869–1940), U.S. stage actress. Dermot studied acting with Dion **Boucicault**, and devised her stage name with his help. Her younger sister was the actress Gertrude **Elliott**, who married the English actor Johnston Forbes-Robertson (*see* under Bryan **Forbes**).

Missy "Misdemeanor" **Elliott:** Melissa Elliott (1971–), U.S. black pop, R&B singer.

Ramblin' Jack **Elliott:** Elliott Charles Adnopoz (1931–), U.S. folksinger. The singer was embarrassed by his family name and at first called himself Buck Elliott before adopting the more homely "Jack." He was "ramblin'" because he was constantly traveling.

William ("Wild Bill") **Elliott:** Gordon Nance (1903–1965), U.S. movie actor. The western star was long billed as Gordon Elliott in movies of the 1920s and 1930s. He was Bill Elliott in the early 1940s, then Wild Bill Elliott, with subsequent parts under either of these names or as William Elliott.

Alexander John **Ellis:** Alexander John Sharpe (1814–1890), Eng. philologist. "He adopted the name of Ellis by royal license in 1825 in consequence of the bequest of a relative, who wished to enable him to devote his life to study and research" [*Dictionary of National Biography*]. He did not disappoint.

Alice Thomas **Ellis:** Anna Margaret Haycraft, née Lindholm (1932–2005), Br. novelist. The writer published her first novel, *The Sin Eater* (1977), under this name "to make myself anonymous, but of course it didn't at all. Now I'm stuck with it" [*The Times*, March 3, 2001].

E. **Ellis:** Elizabeth Wolstenholme-Elmy (1834–1913), Eng. essayist, poet. A name concocted from the first half of the writer's original first name and second part of her surname. She also wrote as Ellis Ethelmer.

John Fanshawe **Ellis** *see* **Speranza**

Mary **Ellis:** Mary Elsas (1897–2003), U.S. movie actress, singer.

Patricia **Ellis:** Patricia Gene O'Brien (1916–1970), U.S. movie actress.

Robert **Ellis:** Robert Ellis Reel (1892–1974), U.S. movie actor, director, screenwriter.

Cary **Ellison:** Ellison Bayles (1915–2002), Eng. theatrical talent scout. The talent spotter began his career on the stage himself, when he was advised by a fellow actor, Alexander Gauge, to take the rather more glamorous name of Cary Ellison, with its subtle suggestion of Greek *Kyrie eleison*, "Lord, have mercy," a prayer in the Roman Mass.

James **Ellison:** James Ellison Smith (1910–1994), U.S. movie actor.

Grace **Elliston:** Grace Rutter (1878–1950), U.S. stage actress. The actress first assumed her stage name for her part in *The Idol's Eye* (1897).

Elmer **Ellsworth, Jr.:** Tiffany Ellsworth Thayer (1902–1959), U.S. novelist, advertising copywriter. Thayer adopted this name, his father's first and middle names, for a number of novels. He also wrote as John Doe.

Ellyay: Serafim Romanovich Kulachikov (1904–1976), Russ. (Yakut) poet.

Ziggy **Elman:** Harry Aaron Finkelman (1914–1968), U.S. jazz trumpeter, bandleader. The musician's nickname "Ziggy" is said to have come from the name of entertainment impresario Florenz Ziegfeld, of the Ziegfeld *Follies*, allegedly given him by Atlantic City showgirls in mocking response to his high aspirations for a showbusiness career. "Elman" came from his original surname.

Martin **Elmer:** Robert Carl Berg (1930–), Dan. author, journalist. The writer changed his name in 1953 to Robert Cecil Martin Elmer Berg, then adopted the third and fourth of these names.

Belle **Elmore** *see* Mr. and Master **Robinson**

Elphin: Robert Arthur Griffith (1860–1936), Welsh poet. The poet's bardic name is a variant spelling of Elfyn or Elffyn, who gave the name of **Elfyn**.

Leslie **Elphinstone:** Sidney Leslie Elphinstone Ollif (*fl.* 1910), Br. writer.

Isobel **Elsom:** Isobel Reed (1893–1981), Br. stage, movie actress, working in U.S.

Willem **Elsschot:** Alfons de Ridder (1882–1960), Belg. novelist, writing in Flemish. Elsschot used his real name for a book about Stijn **Streuvels**, published in 1908.

Julian **Eltinge:** William Julian Dalton (1883–1941), U.S. vaudeville artist, female impersonator. The entertainer's new surname (rhyming with "melting") came from a boyhood friend in Butte, Montana.

Anthony **Elton:** Anthony Williams (1935–), Eng. composer, pianist. The musician adopted the middle name of his father, Jack Elton Williams, as his new surname.

Geoffrey Rudolph **Elton:** Gottfried Rudolf Otto Ehrenberg (1921–1994), Ger.-born Eng. historian. The Tudor historian, writing as simply G.R. Elton, changed his name to Elton in 1944, in World War II, under an Army Council Instruction.

Paul **Éluard:** Eugène-Émile Paul Grindel (1895–1952), Fr. Surrealist poet. Grindel adopted his maternal grandmother's name as his pen name. His only children's book, *Grain d'aile* ("Wing Seed") (1951), is about a young girl of this name, a phonetic variant of his original name.

Maurice **Elvey:** William Seward Folkard (1887–1967), Br. movie director.

Violetta **Elvin:** Violetta Prokhorova (1925–), Russ. ballet dancer. The dancer's professional name is that of her English husband, Harold Elvin, a member of the British Embassy in Moscow, with whom she went to Britain in 1946.

Ely: (1) Elisha Hall (*fl.* 1562), Eng. fanatic, impostor; (2) Adam Asnyk (1838–1897), Pol. poet, dramatist. Hall, a self-declared prophet, claimed to write books by direct inspiration. "On his appearance in London he was brought before Grindal, bishop of London, on 12 June 1562 for examination. He asserted that in 1551 he heard a voice say 'Ely, arise, watch and pray; for the day draweth nigh,' and that in April 1552 he was absent from earth two days while he saw heaven and hell" [*Dictionary of National Biography*]. His adopted name comes from his first name.

Ron **Ely:** Ronald Pierce (1938–), U.S. athlete, TV actor.

Odysseus **Elytis:** Odysseus Alepoudhelis (1911–1996), Gk. poet. The poet changed his name as a young man to dissociate himself from the family soap business. His new surname has a range of modern Greek allusions: *Hellas* ("Greece"), *elpida* ("hope"), *eleutheria* ("freedom"), *Heleni* ("Helen"), and *alētēs* ("wanderer"). This last is the word used by Homer to describe Odysseus (for whom the poet was already named). The sea is a common motif in the works of Elytis.

Arnold **Elzey:** Arnold Elzey Jones (1816–1871), U.S. army officer. Jones dropped his surname in 1837 on being commissioned in the Second U.S. Artillery, presumably for purposes of distinctiveness.

Jacob Israel **Emden:** Jacob ben Zebi (1697–1776), Ger. rabbi, Talmudic scholar. The rabbi took his name from the city in which he served four years.

Louis **Emerick:** Louis Emerick Grant (1953–), Br. black movie, TV actor.

Alice B. **Emerson** *see* Carolyn **Keene**

Edwin **Emerson** *see* James Fenimore Cooper **Adams**

Jane **Emerson** *see* Greta **Garbo**

Gilbert **Emery:** Gilbert Emery Bensley Pottle (1875–1945), U.S. stage, movie actor, playwright, of Br. parentage.

Gevorg **Emin:** Karlen Grigoryevich Muradyan (1919–), Armenian poet.

Eminem: Marshall Bruce Mathers III (1972–), U.S. (white) rapper, movie actor. The controversial performer is said to have derived his stage name not simply from his initials ("M and M") but "from his cannabis-induced cravings for the M&M sweet" [*Sunday Times*, February 2, 2001]. But the former

and obvious origin is surely the right one: "'Eminem' comes from the initials of his real name, Marshall Mathers III, which displays a curiously all–American enthusiasm for dynastic lineage given that he never knew his father" [*Sunday Times*, January 12, 2003]. The artist's fictional alter ego is Slim Shady, a name that he says "just popped into my head" and is his "dark, evil, creatively sick part" [Beech, p. 253].

Mihail **Eminescu:** Mihail Eminovici (1850–1889), Rom. poet.

Emin Pascha: Eduard Schnitzer (1840–1892), Ger. explorer, colonial official. While serving the Ottoman governor of Albania in 1870–4, Schnitzer adopted a Turkish mode of living and took the Islamic name Mehmed. He later served General Charles Gordon in Khartoum as medical officer, and became known as Emin Effendi, the latter word being a title of respect (literally "master") for an educated person. In 1878 Gordon appointed him governor of Equatoria with the title of bey, and he was subsequently promoted to the rank of pasha. Hence his eventual name and title, Emin meaning "honorable," "trustworthy."

Emma: Emilia Ferretti Viola (1844–1929), It. novelist, essayist.

Pierre **Emmanuel:** Noël Jean Mathieu (1916–1984), Fr. religious poet. The writer chose a name that epitomized the role he envisaged for a poet, who was both priest (St. Peter, founder of the Christian church) and prophet (Emmanuel, Christ as the coming Messiah).

Sœur **Emmanuelle:** Madeleine Cinquin (1908–2008), Belg. nun, humanitarian, of Belg.-Fr. parentage, working in Egypt.

Emmepì: Marco Praga (1862–1929), It. playwright. The writer used this name, representing his initials (M.P.), for his contributions to *L'Illustrazione italiana.*

Father **Emmerich:** Johann Anton Sinelli (or Sennel) (1622–1685), Austr. Capuchin dignitary.

Emmwood: John Bertram Musgrave-Wood (1915–1999), Eng. political cartoonist, painter.

El **Empecinado:** Juan Martín Díaz (1775–1825), Sp. revolutionary. The activist adopted his nickname, meaning "the stubborn one."

Caveat **Emptor** *see* **Caveat Emptor**

Emrys: William Ambrose (1813–1873), Welsh poet. The poet adopted the Welsh equivalent of his surname as his bardic name. Compare the next entry below.

Emrys ap Iwan: Ambrose Jones (1851–1906), Welsh poet, writer, nationalist. The poet's bardic name is the Welsh equivalent of his English name (literally "Ambrose son of John").

Emu: William Henry Dyson (1880–1938), Austral. cartoonist, working in U.K. The artist used this name for his caricatures. The emu is a distinctive Australian bird.

Cousin **Emmy:** Cynthia May Carver (1903–1980), U.S. country singer. The singer began using her stage name (presumably from her middle name) in 1937.

Enazakura: Toru Hayakawa (1960–), Jap. sumo wrestler.

Frederick **Engelheart:** Lafayette Ronald Hubbard (1911–1986), U.S. SF writer. As founder of the Church of Scientology (1954), the writer's real name is more familar in the form L. Ron Hubbard.

Edward **England:** Edward Seegar (*fl.*1720), Eng. pirate.

S. **England:** Richard Porson (1759–1808), Eng. Greek scholar. Porson used this name when writing to the *Morning Chronicle.*

Harold **English** *see* Colin **Forbes**

Isobel **English:** June Guesdon Braybrooke, earlier Orr-Ewing, née Joliffe (1920–1994), Br. novelist, short-story writer.

Enigma: Simon Martin (1950–), Br. crossword compiler. A fairly obvious pseudonym for a setter of cryptic crosswords and also a rather obvious anagram of "I am Eng."

Envy: Nicola Varley (19??–), Br. (white) rapper, MC. A pun on the musician's initials.

Enya: Eithne Ní Bhraonáin (1961–), Ir. popular singer. The name of the former member of the family band Clannad represents a phonetic spelling of her Irish first name. Máire **Brennan** is a relative.

Eos Ceiriog: Huw Morys (1622–1709), Welsh poet. The poet's name means "nightingale of Ceiriog," the latter being the name of the district where he lived. Compare the next two entries below.

Eos Eyas: James Rhys Parry (*c.*1570–*c.*1625), Welsh poet. The poet's name means "nightingale of Eyas," from the parish where he lived.

Eos Gwynfa: Thomas Williams (*c.*1769–1848), Welsh poet, songwriter. The writer's name means "nightingale of Gwynfa," the latter from the name of the village, Llanfihangel-yng-Ngwynfa ("St. Michael's church in paradise") where he lived. He was also known as Eos y Mynydd, "nightingale of the mountain."

Ephelia: Joan Phillips (*fl.*1678–1682), Eng. poet. This the traditional identification of the author of *Female Poems on Several Occasions* (1679), although other writers have been proposed, among them Mary Stuart, née Villiers, Duchess of Richmond and Lennox (1622–1685). "By making herself the dedicatee of her own book, clever Lady Villiers hid in plain sight and also executed the genius stroke that assured her pseudonymity and kept researchers fum-

bling these three centuries" [Maureen E. Mulvihill, *Restoration*, 1995]. The name itself may have been intended as a feminine form of Greek *ephelix*, a synonym of *ephebos*, "of age," "near maturity."

Ephemera: Edward Fitzgibbon (1803–1857), Eng. journalist, writer of books on angling. There is a pleasant pun here: "ephemera" on the one hand denotes something short-lived, such as journalists write about; on the other hand it is a term for the mayfly, an artificial form of which is used as bait by anglers.

Rust **Epique:** Charles Anthony Lopez (1968–2004), U.S. rock guitarist.

Epsilon: James Baldwin Brown (1785–1843), Eng. lawyer, writer. Epsilon, the fifth letter of the Greek alphabet, transliterated "e," must have had some particular significance here.

Desiderius **Erasmus:** Gerhard Gerhards (or Geert Geerts) (?1466–1536), Du. humanist, theologian. The general explanation of the scholar's name is as follows. He was born as the second child of Margaret, a physician's daughter, and Roger Gerhard (or Geert), a priest. He was thus illegitimate, or a "love child," and the name that he adopted reflects this, as both Desiderius and Erasmus means "desired one," that is, "loved one," from Latin *desiderare*, "to want," "to desire" and Greek *erasmios*, "beloved." (Compare the name below.)

According to D'Israeli, the literal meaning of the original name played its part: "*Desiderius Erasmus* was a name formed out of his family name *Gerard*, which in Dutch signifies amiable; or GAR *all*, AERD *nature*. He first changed it to a Latin word of much the same signification, *desiderius*, which afterwards he refined into the Greek *Erasmus*, by which names he is now known" [p.201]. This explanation is negated, however, by the misinterpretation of "Gerard," which actually means "brave spear."

Thomas **Erastus:** Thomas Lieber (or Liebler) (1524–1583), Ger.-Swiss theologian, physician. "Erastus" translates the scholar's real name, which literally means "lover." (Compare the name above.)

Erckmann-Chatrian: Émile Erckmann (1822–1899), Fr. writer + Charles-Louis-Alexandre Chatrian (1826–1890), Fr. writer. The two men used this joint name for popular historical novels set in Alsace.

Werner **Erhard:** John Paul Rosenberg (1935–), U.S. "New Age" cultist.

Eric: Carl Oscar August Erickson (1891–1958), U.S. fashion illustrator, of Swe. parentage.

Leif **Erickson:** William Wycliff Anderson (1911–1986), U.S. movie actor. Presumably the actor based his name on that of the Norwegian explorer Leif Eriksson, who in 1000 landed in Vinland, often identified as America.

John **Ericson:** Joseph Meibes (1926–), Ger.-born U.S. movie actor.

Walter **Ericson** *see* E.V. **Cunningham**

Erik **Erikson:** Erik Salomonsen (1902–1994), Ger.-born U.S. psychoanalyst, writer. The name of the scholar's father is unknown, and he was originally named after his Danish mother's first husband. When the latter died, she married a German, Theodor Homburger, and her son accordingly became Erik Homburger. As he grew up, Erik underwent an identity crisis: was he Jew or Gentile, Dane or German? Who was his real father? He solved this dilemma in 1939 on finalizing his application for U.S. citizenship. He became Erik Erikson, that is, Erik's son, so that he was his own father.

Erinni: Maria Borgese Freschi (1881–1947), It. poet, novelist. The writer's occasional pen name is the Italian for "Erinyes," the Furies of Greek mythology.

Laurajean **Ermayne:** Forrest J. Ackerman (1916–2008), U.S. SF writer. Ackerman used this name for a number of lesbian-themed novels, as a result of which he was voted an "honorary lesbian" by the Daughters of Bilitis (*see* Pierre **Louÿs**), the first lesbian rights group to be founded in the U.S.

George **Ernest:** George Hjorth (1921–), U.S. juvenile movie actor, of Dan. parentage.

Otto **Ernst:** Otto Ernst Schmidt (1862–1926), Ger. writer.

Erratic Enrique: Henry Clay Lukens (1838–1900), U.S. humorous writer, poet, journalist. The humorist also wrote as Heinrich Yale Snekul, each of these names being a variant of some kind on his real full name.

Erró: Gudmundur Gudmundsson (1932–), Icelandic painter.

Malcolm J. **Errym:** James Malcolm Rymer (1804–1884), Sc. writer of "penny dreadfuls." This is just one of the mainly anagrammatic pseudonyms adopted by Rymer. Another was Malcom J. Merry.

Margaret **Erskine:** Margaret Wetherby Williams (1901–1984), Can.-born Br. crime novelist.

Rosalind **Erskine:** Roger Erskine Longrigg (1929–2000), Sc.-born Br. author. Longrigg put himself over as a 17-year-old schoolgirl who launched herself onto the literary scene in 1962 with a novel about a group of boarding-school girls who turn their gym into a brothel. He also wrote as Laura Black, Ivor Drummond, Megan Barker, Grania Beckford, Frank Parish, and Dominic Taylor, each name having its own style and persona. Laura Black, for example, wrote romantic historical novels, while Ivor Drummond penned thrillers set in the jet-set world of luxury yachts, race meetings, and African safaris.

Erté: Romain de Tirtoff (1892–1990), Russ.-born Fr. costume designer. The designer's brief pseudonym, suitable for signing, derives from his initials "R.T." pronounced (approximately) in Russian and French as "air-tay." He first used it when sketching women's fashions for the Russian magazine *Damsky Mir* ("Ladies' World"), and in France first in 1913 in the magazine *La Gazette du Bon Ton.*

Ertis: [Countess] Alexandrine Esterhazy (*c.*1849–1919), Austr. opera composer.

Patrick **Ervin:** Robert E. Howard (1906–1936), U.S. SF writer.

Janus Nicius **Erythraeus:** Gian Vittorio Rossi (1577–1647), It. biblical scholar. The scholar adopted a classical form of his name for his Latin writings: Janus from Gian (John), Nicius (Greek *nikē,* Italian *vittoria,* "victory") from Vittorio, and Erythraeus (Greek *erythros,* Italian *rosso,* "red") from Rossi.

L. **Escardot:** Carmen Karr y de Alfonsetti (1865–?), Sp. playwright, writer, composer. The musician composed Catalan songs under this name.

Christoph **Eschenbach:** Christoph Ringmann (1940–), Ger. pianist, orchestral conductor.

Uncle **Esek** *see* Josh **Billings**

Levi **Eshkol:** Levi Shkolnik (1895–1969), Ukr.-born Israeli politician. Israel's prime minister (1963–69) hebraized his Slavic name when Israel became independent in 1948.

Carl **Esmond:** Wilhelm Eichberger (1906–2004), Austr. movie actor, working in U.K., U.S.

Henry Vernon **Esmond:** Henry Vernon Jack (1869–1922), Eng. stage actor, manager, dramatist. The actor appears to have been influenced in his choice of professional name by that of the central character in Thackeray's *Henry Esmond.*

El **Espartero:** Manuel García Cuesta (1865–1894), Sp. bullfighter. The matador was nicknamed after his father's esparto grass holding near Seville.

Dr. **Esperanto:** [Dr.] Lazar Ludwik Zamenhof (1859–1917), Pol. doctor, inventor of Esperanto. The linguist's name translates (in Esperanto) as "Dr. Hoping One." He used it for his book introducing the language, *Langue Internationale: Préface et Manuel Complet* (1887). He also sometimes used the anagrammatic pseudonyms Gamzefon and Gofzamen.

Don Manuel Alvarez **Espriella:** Robert Southey (1774–1843), Eng. poet. In 1807 Southey published *Letters from England, by Don Manuel Alvarez Espriella,* a three-volume work purporting to be the translation of an account by a young Spaniard of life and manners in England. A genuine translation, *Chronicle of the Cid,* followed a year later.

Esquerita: Esker Reeder, Jr. (1952–1986), U.S. black pop pianist.

Esquivel: Juan Garcia Esquivel (1931–2002), Mexican popular pianist, working in U.S.

David **Essex:** David Albert Cook (1947–), Eng. pop singer. The singer gained his new name early in his career. "Around this time [manager] Derek [Bowman] had applied for David Cook to join Equity (the actor's [*sic*] union), but there was already a member called David Cook so we had to think of a new name. It was important for me to join — no union meant no work. Derek rang me and suggested David Essex, as I was now living in [the county of] Essex. I wasn't too sure, but as usual I went along with it, and now I'm just glad I wasn't living in Middlesex!" [David Essex, *A Charmed Life*, 2002].

Mary **Essex** *see* Lozania **Prole**

Martin **Esslin:** Martin Julius Pereszlenyi (1918–2002), Br. radio producer, drama critic, of Austr.-Hung. parentage.

Luc **Estang:** Lucien Bastard (1911–1992), Fr. Catholic novelist, poet, critic.

Estelle: Estelle Swaray (1980–), Br. black R&B singer, of Senegalese parentage.

La **Esterella:** Esther Mathilda Lambrechts (1916–), Du.-born variety singer, working in U.K. The stage name is presumably from Spanish *estrella*, "star," which "Esther" is also popularly said to mean.

John **Esteven:** Samuel Shellabarger (1888–1954), U.S. novelist, biographer. Shellabarger used this name for a mystery thriller, *Door of Death* (1928), a romantic adventure, *The Black Gale* (1929), a murder mystery, *Voodoo* (1930), and one final mystery, *Assurance Doubly Sure* (1939). He was Peter Loring for a romance, *Grief Before Night* (1938), and an adventure story, *Miss Rolling Stone* (1939). The aim in each case was to keep his scholarly biographies distinct from his creative writing. From 1938 to 1946, when he was headmaster of the Columbus, Ohio, School for Girls, he wrote under his real name.

Esther John: Qamar Zia (1929–1960), Ind. missionary. Zia adopted her new name after becoming a Christian in the 1950s.

Jean **Estoril:** Mabel Esther Allan (1915–1998), Eng. children's writer. Other names used by the prolific writer were Priscilla Hagon and Anne Pilgrim. Allan reserved the name Jean Estoril for a series of stories about Drina, a teenage ballerina. Estoril is the name of a town in Portugal.

Eta Delta: Evan Davies (1794–1855), Welsh temperance campaigner. The name represents the Greek letters equating to the minister's initials.

Jean-Jacques **Etchévéry:** Marie-Ernest-Jean-Jacques de Peyre-Chappuis (1916–), Fr. ballet dancer, director.

Ellis **Ethelmer** *see* E. **Ellis**

Père **Étienne:** Étienne Pierre François de Paule Malmy (1744–1840), Fr. religious community founder. In 1816 Père Étienne and 14 companions reestablished and rebuilt the ruined Cistercian monastery at Aiguebelle, near Montélimar in the south of France.

Étienne-Martin: Étienne Martin (1913–1995), Fr. sculptor.

Partenio **Etiro** *see* Pietro **Aretino**

Robert **Eton** *see* A. Stephen **Tring**

ETPA: Maria Antonia Walpurgis, Princess of Bavaria, Electress of Saxony (1724–1780), Ger. composer, artist, writer, patron. The eldest daughter of Karl Albert, Elector of Bavaria, later Emperor Karl VII, used this name as the writer of the words for her own operas. The initials stand for Ermelinda Talea Pastorella Arcada, denoting her affiliation to the Academy of Arcadia (*see* Aglauro **Cidonia**). The last two words of her pseudonym mean "Arcadian Shepherdess."

Etteila: Jean-François Aliette (1738–1791), Fr. fortuneteller. The tarot practitioner's name is a reversal of his original name.

Eudocia: Athenais (401–465), Byzantine princess. Before marrying the Eastern Roman emperor Theodosius II in 421, Athenais renounced paganism, was baptized a Christian, and adopted a Greek name meaning "goodwill."

Eugen: Eugen Pillatt (1879–1943), Ger. circus artist, clown, working in Russia.

Eugene: Hugo Arnot (1749–1846), Sc. historical writer.

Eugenius III: Bernardo Paganelli (or Pignatelli) (?–1153), It. pope.

Eugenius IV: Gabriele Condulmaro (*c*.1383–1447), It. pope.

Eugenius Philalethes: Thomas Vaughan (1622–1666), Eng. alchemist, twin brother of **Silurist**. The mock–Greek name literally means "noble-born truth-lover," and was used by Vaughan for the majority of his works. The name should not be confused with that of Eirenaeus Philalethes, another 17th-century alchemist of uncertain identity, whose own name means "peaceful truth-lover." There were a number of other writers calling themselves Philalethes, including at least four Philalethes Cantabrigiensis (from Cambridge) and several named Phileleutharus followed by a Latin adjectival placename, as **Phileleutharus Devoniensis** and **Phileleutharus Norfolciensis**.

Arthur Fritz **Eugens:** Arthur Fritz Schumacher (1930–), Ger. juvenile movie actor.

Eulalie: Eulalie Banks (1895–after 1997), U.S. illustrator, working in U.K.

Sandro **Euli:** Aleksandr Kishvardovich Kuridze (1890–1965), Georgian poet. The poet took a name meaning "Sandro the lonely," alluding to his sense of isolation.

Eurialo d'Ascoli: Aurello Morani de Guiderocchi (*c*.1485–1554), It. humanist.

Euronymous: Oystein Aarseth (1968–1993), Norw. "black metal" musician. A name perhaps intended as a blend of "European" and "anonymous."

Glaucilla Eurotea: Diodata Saluzzo Roero (1775–1840), It. poet. The poet's pseudonym is her Arcadian name (*see* Aglauro **Cidonia**).

Eusebia: (1) Frances Seymour, Countess of Hertford (1699–1754), Eng. poet, letter writer; (2) Mary Hays (1760–1843), Eng. novelist, polemical writer. The Countess of Hertford used this name, Greek for "reverence," "piety," for some verses published in 1734. Mary Hays used it for her pamphlet entitled *Cursory Remarks on an Enquiry into the Expediency and Propriety of Public or Social Worship* (1792), replying to Gilbert Wakefield's attack on dissenting public worship.

Eusébio: Eusébio Ferreira da Silva (1942–), Mozambiquan-born Port. footballer (the "Black Panther").

Eusebius: (1) Edmund Rack (?1735–1787), Eng. writer; (2) Robert Schumann (1810–1856), Ger. composer. Rack used this name, that of various early Greek theologians, for *Reflections on the Spirit and Essence of Christianity* (1771). Schumann used it as a pseudonym for his critical writings. It expressed the feminine or contemplative side of his personality, as distinct from a contrasting character, Florestan, who was masculine and impetuously romantic. The use of fictitious personae to express his duality in this way was inspired by **Jean Paul**, whose unfinished novel *Flegeljahre* (literally "uncouth years," meaning the awkward age of adolescence) (1804–5) contained the contrasting twins Vult and Walt. Schumann's two characters are musically represented in his suite of piano pieces *Carnaval* (1834–5).

Robert Eustace: Robert Eustace Barton (1868–1943), Eng. physician, crime novelist.

Eva: Mary Anne O'Doherty, née Kelly (1825–1910), Ir. poet. The writer used this name for her poems published in the weekly cultural and political journal *The Nation*. A collected edition, *Poems by "Eva" of "The Nation,"* appeared in San Francisco in 1877.

Caradoc Evans: David Evans (1878–1945), Welsh short-story writer, novelist, husband of Countess Hélène **Barcynska**. Evans first published some stories under the name D. Evans-Emmott, then took his distinctive first name, after the 1st-century British chieftain Caratacus, known in Welsh as Caradog.

Dale Evans: Frances Octavia Smith (1912–2001), U.S. movie actress, singer. The actress, "Queen of the Cowgirls" and wife (from 1947) of movie actor Roy **Rogers**, "King of the Cowboys," changed her name in 1933 at the suggestion of a radio station manager.

Evan Evans *see* Max **Brand**

Gil Evans: Ian Ernest Gilmore Green (1912–1988), Can.-born U.S. jazz arranger, bandleader, of Austral. parentage. The musician adopted his stepfather's name.

Joan Evans: Joan Eunson (1934–), U.S. movie actress.

Linda Evans: Linda Evanstad (1943–), U.S. TV actress, of Norw. descent.

Margiad Evans: Peggy Eileen Arabella Williams, née Whistler (1909–1958), Eng. novelist, poet. The writer was raised and educated near the Welsh border, and took a name to reflect her links with Wales. Her new first name is a Welsh diminutive of "Margaret," and thus the equivalent of Peggy. Her surname she adopted from her paternal grandmother.

Robert Evans: Robert Shapera (1930–), U.S. movie producer.

Eve: Eve Jihan Jeffers (1979–), U.S. black rapper.

Judith Evelyn: Judith Evelyn Allen (1913–1967), U.S. stage, movie actress.

Chad Everett: Raymond Lee Cramton (1937–), U.S. TV, movie actor.

Kenny Everett: Maurice James Christopher Cole (1944–1995), Eng. radio, TV DJ, entertainer, presenter. Maurice Cole was working for a pirate radio station when the program controller, Ben Tony, told all on board the ship that they must change their names for legal purposes. The DJ explains how he made his own choice: "I think I'd just seen a movie with an actor called Edward Everett Horton ... I quite liked the name Everett so that came first, followed straightaway by Kenny" [Kenny Everett, *The Custard Stops at Hatfield*, 1982]. Edward Everett Horton (1887–1970) was a U.S. movie comedian.

Leon Everette: Leon Everette Baughman (1948–), U.S. country musician.

Evoe: Edmund George Valpy Knox (1881–1971), Eng. essayist, humorist. The writer's pseudonym is a blend of the initials of two of his names and the Latin cry *evoe* (from Greek *euoi*), used as an exclamation of joy in Bacchic rites. The name had the practical purpose of distinguishing Knox from the writer E.V. Lucas (1868–1938), a fellow contributor to the magazine *Punch*, of which Knox subsequently became editor (1932–49).

Tom Ewell: Samuel Yewell Tompkins (1909–1994), U.S. movie comedian, stage actor. The actor adopted a form of his mother's maiden name, which he already bore as his middle name.

Express: Simon Francis (*c.*1967–), Br. black hip-hop musician.

Ex-Private X: Alfred McLelland Burrage (1889–1956), Eng. novelist, fantasy story writer.

Clive **Exton:** Clive Jack Montague Brooks (1930–2007), Eng. actor, playwright. The dramatist changed his name by deed poll in the 1950s to avoid confusion with the actor Clive Brook (1887–1974). "I chose Exton by the dodgy expedient of sticking a pin in a Shakespeare concordance and happening on Sir Piers of Exton in Richard II" [personal fax from Clive Exton, March 23, 1996].

Gnassingbé **Eyadéma:** Étienne Eyadéma (1935–2005), Togolese politician. The Togolese president changed his French colonial first name to a native name as part of an africanization program.

An **Eye-Witness:** Charles Lamb (1775–1834), Eng. essayist, critic, poet. The writer, whose best-known pseudonym was **Elia**, used this pen name for his verses entitled *Satan in Search of a Wife* (1831).

Miss **F:** Ann Thicknesse, née Ford (1737–1824), Eng. autobiographer. This is the tentative identity of the author of *A Letter from Miss F addressed to a Person of Distinction, with a New Ballad to an old tune. Sent to the author by an unknown hand* (1761), describing Miss F's life and the loss of her reputation through the wickedness of Lord — —. The "Person of Distinction" may have been William Villiers, Earl of Jersey.

Johannes **Faber:** Johannes Heigerlin (1478–1541), Ger. theologian.

Fabian: Fabiano Forte Bonaparte (1943–), U.S. pop singer, movie actor. Fabian was "discovered" in 1957 by two talent scouts in Frankie **Avalon**'s Philadelphia youth club Teen and Twenty, and it was they who shortened his name. His movie roles from the 1970s were as Fabian Forte.

Françoise **Fabian:** Michèle Cortès de Leone y Fabianera (1932–), Sp. movie actress. A French name that is more of an international draw than the Spanish original.

Warner **Fabian:** Samuel Hopkins Adams (1871–1958), U.S. writer. Adams used this name for a series of Jazz Age novels, beginning with *Flaming Youth* (1923).

Colonel **Fabien:** Pierre Georges (1919–1944), Fr. Resistance agent. The name may have intentionally alluded to the 3d-century BC Roman general Fabius ("Cunctator"), who advocated delaying tactics in battle.

Nanette **Fabray:** Ruby Bernadette Nanette Fabares (1920–), U.S. movie comedienne, singer.

Philippe **Fabre d'Eglantine:** Philippe-François-Nazaire Fabre (1755–1794), Fr. playwright, revolutionary politician. The writer assumed this name after winning the *Prix de l'églantine* ("Wild Rose Prize") at the *Jeux Floraux* of Toulouse in his youth, although some say he won by a false claim.

Napoleon **Fabri:** Avgust Fransuazovich Pyubaset (Puybasset) (1869–1932), Fr.-born Russ.

circus artist, horseman, clown. The performer took his name from the Italian Fabri troupe with whom he trained as an acrobat.

Georg **Fabricius:** Georg Goldschmied (1516–1571), Ger. scholar. The scholar's assumed name is a latinization of his real name, which means "goldsmith." Compare the next two names below.

Barent **Fabritius:** Barent Pieterz (1624–1673), Du. painter, brother of Carel **Fabritius**.

Carel **Fabritius:** Carel Pieterz (1622–1654), Du. painter, brother of Barent **Fabritius**. Both brothers adopted the name Fabritius as a reference to their previous trade as carpenters (Latin *faber*, "carpenter"). Compare the name of Georg **Fabricius**.

The **Fabulous Moolah:** Lillian Ellison (*c.*1930–), U.S. wrestler. Ellison began her career in the ring in the 1950s as the "prop" of a wrestler named Elephant Boy. It was tour organizer Jack Pfefer who gave her her first big break. When he asked her why she wanted to become a wrestler, she is said to have replied, "For the moolah [money], of course." Pfefer started calling her Moolah and the name stuck, later gaining the enhanced form "The Fabulous Moolah." She realized her ambition, and in the 1970s claimed to be earning more than $100,000 a year.

Max **Factor:** Max Faktor (?1872–1938), Pol.-born U.S. cosmetician. The adjustment of the cosmetician's name was made in 1904 during immigrant processing at Ellis Island.

Aleksandr **Fadeyev:** Aleksandr Aleksandrovich Bulyga (1901–1956), Russ. novelist. The writer would have readily shed a surname that is a Russian dialect word for a lout or boor.

Frederick **Fag:** James Johnson (1777–1845), Ir. physician, medical writer. Johnson adopted this name for *The Recess* (1834).

Fagus: George Faillet (1872–1933), Fr. poet. The poet's adopted name is the Latin word for "beech," which perhaps he imagined to be the origin of his real name.

Sammy **Fain:** Samuel Feinberg (1902–1989), U.S. composer of musicals, movie music.

A.A. **Fair:** Erle Stanley Gardner (1889–1970), U.S. crime novelist. This is Gardner's best-known pseudonym, adopted for 29 novels written between 1939 and 1970. Other names include Kyle Corning, Charles M. Green, Grant Holiday, Carleton Kendrake, Charles J. Kenny, and Robert Parr.

Douglas **Fairbanks, Sr.:** Douglas Elton Thomas Ulman (1883–1939), U.S. movie actor. The actor was the son of Hezekiah Charles Ulman and Ella Adelaide Marsh, whose first husband was John Fairbanks. On his death in 1873, Ella turned for financial assistance to Ulman, who married her as her third husband. (Her second was Edward Wilcox.) When Douglas was five, Ulman deserted the family and his mother then changed her son's Jewish-sounding name to that of her first husband. Ulman legally adopted the name himself in 1900 and passed it on to Douglas Fairbanks, Jr. (1909–2000), his only child by his first wife, Anna Beth Sully. In 1920 Douglas Sr. married Mary **Pickford** as his second wife.

Sydney **Fairbrother**: Sydney Tapping, later Parselle (1873–1941), Eng. movie actress. The actress adopted her great-grandmother's name as her screen name.

Mindy **Fairchild**: Mahinder Singh Rupal (1964–), Ind.-born Br. fraudster. The bank robber and credit-card heister changed his name, not necessarily with criminal intent, in order to "sound more English."

Morgan **Fairchild**: Patsy Ann McClenny (1950–), U.S. TV actress. The actress's name, perhaps intentionally, evokes that of Morgan le Fay, the beautiful young woman ("fair child") who is King Arthur's sister in the Arthurian romances.

Beatrice **Fairfax**: Marie Manning (1868–1945), U.S. advice columnist. In 1898 Manning started an advice column in the *Evening Journal* for which she was already a feature writer, creating her name from a combination of Dante's Beatrice and Fairfax County, Virginia, where her family owned property. On her death, her role under this name was taken over by Marion Clyde McCarroll (1891–1977).

Flora **Fairfield**: Louisa May Alcott (1832–1888), U.S. children's writer. The author of *Little Women* (1868) used this flowery name for some early adult stories published in *Peterson's Magazine* and the *Saturday Evening Post*.

Mr. **Fairie**: Alfred W. Cox (1857–1919), Eng. racehorse owner, jockey. "For some reason, never divulged, he elected to race under the *nom de course* of 'Mr Fairie'" [Roger Mortimer, Richard Onslow, Peter Willett, *Biographical Encyclopaedia of British Flat Racing*, 1978].

Frank **Fairleigh**: Francis Edward Smedley (1818–1864), Eng. novelist. The writer adopted the name of the fictional hero of his own novel, *Frank Fairleigh* (1850), as editor of *Sharpe's London Magazine*.

Benjamin F. **Fairless**: Benjamin Franklin Williams (1890–1962), U.S. industrialist. The future president of U.S. Steel changed his name as a young boy to that of his adopted parents.

Michael **Fairless**: Margaret Fairless Barber (1869–1901), Eng. nature writer, mystic. Barber, who as a young child renamed herself Marjorie, partly preserved her own name in her pseudonym, with the initial "M" of "Michael" from "Margaret" and "Fairless," as her middle name, from her father, Fairless

Barber. "Michael" was also the name of a young boy who often spent his summer vacation with her family. He was Michael McDonnell (1882–1956), later Sir Michael and chief justice of Palestine in the 1930s. In the last years of her life, Fairless was informally adopted by her physician, Mary Emily Dowson (born 1848), author of mystical works under the name William Scott Palmer, and adopted her family name.

Mrs. **Fairstar**: Richard Henry (or Hengist) Horne (1803–1884), Eng. traveler, poet. Horne used this name as the supposed editor (in fact writer) of the popular children's book *Memoirs of a London Doll, Written by Herself, Edited by Mrs. Fairstar* (1846). He also wrote as Sir Julius Cutwater, Bart., K.C.B., Prof. Grabstein, Phil. D., of Gottingen, Sir Lucius O'Trigger (a character in R.B. Sheridan's play *The Rivals*), Ben Uzair Salem, and Ephraim Watts.

Sidney **Fairway**: Sidney Herbert Daukes (1879–1947), Eng. physician, writer. Daukes adopted this pen name for his novels, written in retirement. Fairway was the name of his house in Worthing, Sussex.

Adam **Faith**: Terence Nelhams (1940–2003), Eng. pop singer, actor. When Nelhams appeared on British television's first teenage pop-music show, *Six-Five Special* (1957–8), program producer Jack Good wanted to give him a solo spot. "First, though, he'd have to find a new name; Terry Nelhams sounded like a Fourth Division Footballer. On a Sunday afternoon in Good's Chiswick flat the name problem was tackled with the help of a 'Choose A Name For Your Baby' book. The first page of boys' names, under A, produced Adam. The fifth page of girls' names, under F, produced Faith. Yeah, great. Adam Faith. Terrific" [*Sunday Times Magazine*, September 21, 1980]. Faith himself wrote: "I liked the sound of Adam. Adam, the first man. Short. Sweet. Easily memorized" [Adam Faith, *Poor Me*, 1961]. On the name as a whole: "I liked the note of courage in it. Adam Faith. Yes, they seemed to match up" [ibid.].

Falco: Johann Hölzel (1957–1998), Austr. rock singer.

Edmund **Falconer**: Edmund O'Rourke (1814–1879), Ir. poet, playwright.

Lanoe **Falconer**: Mary Elizabeth Hawker (1848–1908), Sc.-born Eng. novelist. It has been suggested that the writer created her new first name as an anagram of "alone," but it is more probable that she took it from the third name of her father, Peter William Lanoe Hawker. Her surname was a punning allusion to her family name, and may also have been inluenced by the hero of her favorite book, George MacDonald's *Robert Falconer* (1868). After many rejections from publishers, she finally broke into print with *Mademoiselle Ixe* (1890), the first novel in T. Fisher Unwin's "Pseudonym Library" series.

Johan **Falkberget:** Johan Petter Lillebakken (1879–1967), Norw. writer. The novelist took his pen name from the farm where he was born in the central eastern mountains of Norway.

Konrad **Falke:** Karl Frey (1880–1942), Ger. writer.

Jinx **Falkenburg:** Eugenia Falkenburg (1919–2003), U.S. movie actress. The actress adopted her playful nickname, based on her original first name.

Marcus **Fall:** Richard Dowling (1846–1898), Ir. writer. Dowling also wrote as Emanuel Kink.

Hans **Fallada:** Wilhelm Friedrich Rudolf Ditzen (1893–1947), Ger. novelist. Following a scandalous boyhood, involving a spell in a sanitarium, Ditzen was persuaded by his father to adopt a pseudonym for his writing in order to prevent further disgrace to the family name. He took it from two characters in *Grimms' Fairy Tales* (1812–22): the hero of "Hans im Glück" ("Lucky Hans") and the talking horse Falada (wih one "l") in "Die Gänsemagd" ("The Goose Girl").

Martin **Fallon** *see* Jack **Higgins**

Mary **Fallon:** Kathleen Mary Berriman, née Denman (1951–), Austral. writer. The writer adopted her grandmother's name as her pen name.

Georgie **Fame:** Clive Powell (1943–), Eng. pop musician. The name was given to the singer by the impresario Larry Parnes, who allegedly said: "The next kid to walk through my door, I'm gonna call Georgie Fame." The next kid to do so was Powell, and Parnes hired him as a member of the Blue Flames, the backing band assigned to Billy **Fury** on a 1960 tour. There is evidence that the name first proposed by Parnes for Powell was actually Lance **Fortune**.

Violet **Fane:** [Lady] Mary Montgomerie Currie, earlier Singleton, née Lamb (1843–1905), Eng. novelist, verse writer. The author selected her new name, that of a character in Benjamin Disraeli's first novel, *Vivian Grey* (1827), for her first publication, a volume of verse entitled *From Dawn to Noon* (1872). She adopted the pseudonym to conceal her writing from her parents.

Aunt **Fanny:** Frances Elizabeth Barrow (1822–1894), U.S. children's writer.

U.A. **Fanthorpe:** Ursula Askham Fanthorpe (1929–2009), Eng. poet. The use of initials may have arisen as much from the poet's natural modesty as from the wish to mask her gender.

Alioum **Fantouré:** Mohamed Touré (1938–), Guinean economist, writer.

Faraway: Clement Hobson (1877–1952), Eng. racehorse breeder, racecar driver, working in France. Hobson used this name as French racing correspondent of *Horse and Hound*.

Don **Fardon:** Don Maughn (*c.*1943–), Eng. pop singer.

Farfa: Vittorio Tommasini (1879–1964), It. Futurist poet, painter.

Donna **Fargo:** Yvonne Vaughn (1949–), U.S. country singer.

Princess **Farida:** Safina Zulfikar (1920–1988), Egyptian queen. Safina changed her first name (Iranian for "pure rose") to Farida ("precious") in 1938, when she married King Farouk (1920–1965). The change complied with a tradition that all members of the Egyptian royal family must have names beginning with the same initial. (His father was King Fuad, and his sister, who married the Shah of Persia, Fawziya.) Farouk divorced her in 1948, however, when she failed to produce an heir to the throne, and she went to live in France with her three daughters. Farouk obtained a son and heir, Fuad II, from his second marriage, in 1951, to Narriman Sadek.

Farinelli: Carlo Broschi (1705–1782), It. castrato singer. The singer adopted the surname of his benefactors, the brothers Farina. According to some accounts, he may have been their nephew. The brothers were of French origin, and appear to have been originally named Farinel.

Giuseppe **Farinelli:** Giuseppe Francesco Finco (1769–1836), It. opera composer.

El Nino **Farini:** Samuel Wasgate (1855–1939), Br. aerialist. The tightrope artist began his career at an early age, when he was adopted by one William Hunt, whose original Italian name was Guillermo Antonio Farini (1838–1929), from whom he took his name. At first he was carried along the rope on Hunt's back, but from 1870, aged 16, performed independently under the name Mlle. Lu-Lu ("The Beautiful Girl Aerialist and Circassian Catapultist"). The artist's real gender was revealed in 1878, to the dismay of his many male fans, who had quite fallen for the lithe and graceful female performer.

Mukhiddin **Farkhat:** Mukhiddin Khasanov (1924–) Tajik poet. The poet's pen name means "joy."

John Murphy **Farley:** John Murphy Farrelly (1842–1918), Ir.-born U.S. archbishop. The future Archbishop of New York modified his name on being appointed secretary to Cardinal McCloskey in 1872.

Ralph Milne **Farley:** Robert Sherman Hoar (1887–1963), U.S. SF writer.

Chris **Farlowe:** John Henry Deighton (1940–), Eng. pop singer. The singer took his name from the U.S. jazz guitarist Tal Farlowe.

A.W. **Farmer:** Samuel Seabury (1729–1796), U.S. cleric. The first American Episcopalian bishop used this name for a series of pamphlets in 1775 defending the English Crown. The name stood for "A

Westchester Farmer," as at the time Seabury was rector of St. Peter's Church in Westchester, New York.

Ferdinand **Farmer:** Ferdinand Steinmeyer (1720–1788), Ger.-born Jesuit missionary, working in U.S.

Marianne **Farningham:** Mary Anne Hearn (1834–1909), Eng. religious writer, hymnwriter. The writer combined her first two names to form a single Christian name, then changed her surname to that of the Kent village where she was born.

Martha **Farquharson:** Martha Farquharson Finley (1828–1909), U.S children's writer.

Caroline **Farr** *see* Carter **Brown**

Jamie **Farr:** Jameel Joseph Farah (1934–), U.S. movie, TV actor.

Walli **Farrad:** Wallace D. Fard (*c*.1877–?1934), U.S. Black Muslim leader. This is one of the many names assumed by the founder of the Nation of Islam in the U.S. He is now revered by Black Muslims as Master Wallace Fard Muhammad, and all the attributes of God (Allah) are assigned to him, so that he is referred to as "Creator of Heaven and Earth, Most Wise, All Knowing, Most Merciful, All Powerful, Finder and Life-Giver, Master of the Day of Judgment." Understandably, one of the criticisms leveled at the Black Muslims by orthodox Muslims is that they worship Wallace Fard rather than Allah of the "true" Islam. Among other names used by Fard were Professor Ford, Farrad Mohammed, F. Mohammed Ali, Wallace Fard Muhammad, and God (Allah). More importantly for our purposes, he gave his followers Arabic names to replace those that had originated in slavery and that were of Christian origin. His divinity was reinforced by his mysterious disappearance in 1934. One of Farrad's influential followers was Elijah Muhammad, father of W.D. **Mohammed**.

Louis **Farrakhan:** Louis Eugene Walcott (1933–), U.S. Black Muslim leader. The advocate of black separatism was originally a calypso performer under the name of Prince Charmer before being converted to the Nation of Islam in the mid–1950s by Malcolm X. His name at first was accordingly Louis X. After the death in 1975 of Elijah **Muhammad**, leader of the Nation of Islam, he fell out with Elijah's son, assumed his present name, and formed his own Nation of Islam.

Edward **Farran:** Edward John Elias (1937–2003), U.S. rock musician.

Joe **Farrell:** Joseph Carl Firrantello (1937–1986), U.S. jazz musician.

M.J. **Farrell:** Mary ("Molly") Nesta Keane, née Skrine (1904–1996), Ir. novelist, playwright. Mary Skrine began to write during a long spell in bed with suspected tuberculosis. The result was a romantic tale

titled *The Knight of Cheerful Countenance* (1926), written when she was 17. For this she selected the pen name M.J. Farrell, taking it from a bar she passed one day when returning home from the hunting field. She said, "I had to keep it a secret as long as I possibly could. Young men in that circle would have been afraid of you if they thought you read, let alone wrote" [*Sunday Times Magazine*, August 24, 1986].

Nicholas **Farrell:** Nicholas Frost (1955–), Br. stage, movie actor.

Perry **Farrell:** Peretz Bernstein (1959–), U.S. rock musician. The original singer took his brother's first name as his new surname, so that the name as a whole sounds like "peripheral."

Suzanne **Farrell:** Roberta Sue Ficker (1945–), U.S. ballet dancer.

Wes **Farrell:** Wes Fogel (1939–1996), U.S. songwriter, music publisher.

Claude **Farrère:** Frédéric Charles Bargone (1876–1957), Fr. novelist.

Geoffrey **Farrington:** Geoffrey Smith (1955–), Br. writer of fantasy fiction.

Mia **Farrow:** Maria de Lourdes Villiers-Farrow (1945–), U.S. movie actress.

Fatboy Slim: Quentin Leo Cook (1963–), Br. DJ. This is the most familiar of the names adopted by the big-beat pioneer. "He is Norman Cook, aka Fatboy Slim, aka Pizzaman, aka Beats International, aka Freakpower. Oh, and aka Quentin Cook, the name his parents actually gave him, but which he dropped beause he was called a poofter [homosexual] at school. He changed it to Norman because it's, well, normal" [*Sunday Times Magazine*, December 12, 1999]. Cook is said to have taken the second name of his oxymoronic creation from that of **Bumble Bee Slim**.

Jane **Fate:** Lisa Garston (1935–), It. movie actress, working in U.K. The actress was billed under this name for some movies in the mid–1960s, by which time she had returned to Italy.

Father ... For names beginning thus, see the next word, e.g. for Father Algy see **Algy**, for Father Baptist see **Baptist**, for Father Damien see **Damien**, etc.

Fat Pat: Patrick Hawkins (1971–1998), U.S. black rapper.

Minnesota **Fats:** Rudolf Walter Wanderone, Jr. (1913–1996), U.S. American pool player. The player's name alludes directly to his impressive dimensions: at only 5 ft 10 in tall, he weighed 300 pounds. He originally called himself New York Fats, but altered the first word following his depiction in the 1961 movie *The Hustler*, in which he is played by Jackie **Gleason**.

Sheikh **Fattelal:** Yashin Mistri (1897–1964), Ind. movie director. The director's adopted surname is also spelled Fatehlal, while his alternate first name (or title) is Sahebmama.

Frank **Faulkner** *see* James Fenimore Cooper **Adams**

William **Faulkner**: William Cuthbert Falkner (1897–1962), U.S. short-story writer, novelist. Faulkner added the "u" to his name when *The Marble Faun*, his first book of poems, was published in 1924, claiming that his great-grandfather, Colonel William Clark Falkner (1825–1889), had deleted the letter.

William Alfred **Faversham**: William Jones (1868–1940), Eng.-born U.S. stage actor.

Catherine **Fawcett**: Catherine Cookson (1906–1998), Eng. novelist. *See also* Katie **McMullen**.

Eric **Fawcett**: Eric Burbidge (1904–?), Br. stage actor, singer.

George **Fawcett**: George Deneal Fawsett (1860–1939), U.S. stage actor. The actor modified the spelling of his surname after going on the stage.

Marion **Fawcett**: Katherine Roger Campbell (1886–1957), Sc. stage actress.

Farrah **Fawcett-Majors**: Farrah Fawcett (1947–2009), U.S. model, TV actress. The star of *Charlie's Angels* was billed under her hyphenated name following her marriage to actor Lee **Majors** in 1973.

Guy **Fawkes**: Robert Benchley (1889–1945), U.S. humorist, drama critic. Benchley adopted the name of the 17th-century English "Gunpowder Plot" conspirator for "The Wayward Press" column that he contributed to the *New Yorker* from 1925.

Dorothy **Fay**: Dorothy Alice Fay Southworth (1915–2003), U.S. movie actress. The actress became Dorothy Fay Ritter after marrying her costar Tex **Ritter** in 1941.

Erica **Fay** *see* G.N. **Mortlake**

Frank **Fay**: Francis Anthony Donner (1897–1961), U.S. stage, movie comedian.

Alice **Faye**: Alice Fay Leppert (1912–1998), U.S. movie actress, singer.

Joey **Faye**: Joseph Anthony Palladino (1910–1997), U.S. stage comedian.

Frank **Faylen**: Frank Ruf (1905–1985), U.S. movie actor.

Eleanor **Fayre**: Eleanor Mary Tydfil Smith-Thomas (1910–), Welsh stage actress, singer.

Fayruz: Nouhad Haddad (1935–), Lebanese (female) popular singer. The singer's Arabic name means "turquoise" (the gem).

Irving **Fazola**: Irving Henry Prestopnik (1912–1949), U.S. jazz clarinetist. The musician's new name is said to derive from the three musical notes *fa* (F), *soh* (G), and *la* (A). One motive for a name change may well have been that his Slavic surname means "criminal."

F.B. *see* R.E.H. **Greyson**

Fearless Nadia: Mary Evans (1908–1996), Austral.-born movie actress, of Br.-Gk. parentage, working in India. The actress, originally a circus and variety performer, was "fearless" in her stunts.

Daniel **Featley**: Daniel Fairclough (1582–1645), Eng. cleric. The religious controversialist was the first of his family to adopt the modified form of his name. In 1661 his nephew, John Featley, published a brief biography of his uncle, explaining that "His right name was Faireclough ... but this then varied and altered from Faireclough to Faircley, then to Fateley and at length to Featley."

Justinus **Febronius**: Johann Nikolaus von Hontheim (1701–1790), Ger. Roman Catholic bishop. The ecclesiastic used this name for his principal work, *De statu ecclesiae et legitima potestate Romani Pontificis* ("On the State of the Church and the Legitimate Authority of the Roman Pontiff") (1763), attacking the temporal power gained by medieval popes. The pseudonym gave the name of Febronianism, a movement against the claims of the papacy. The name itself seems to imply a "just cleansing," in allusion to Februus, the Roman god of purification.

Elise **Fecamps** *see* Gordon **Ashe**

Daniele Teofilo **Fedele**: Daniel Gottlieb Treu (1695–1749), Ger. violinist, composer. From 1716 to 1725 the musician was a pupil of Antonio Vivaldi in Venice, Italy, where he was known by the Italian equivalent of his German name.

Camillo **Federici**: Giovanni Battista Viassolo (1749–1802), It. playwright, actor.

Dr. **Feelgood**: William Lee Perryman (1911–1985), U.S. blues singer. As a player the singer used the name **Piano Red**.

Hans **Fehér**: Johann Anton Weiss (1922–1958), Austr. juvenile movie actor, working in U.S. The actor's new surname is the Hungarian equivalent of his German original, meaning "white." He emigrated with his family to Britain in 1933 and to the USA three years later.

Fela: Fela Anikulapo Kuti (1939–1997), Nigerian afro-beat musician, activist.

Charles K. **Feldman**: Charles Gould (1904–1968), U.S. movie producer.

Félix: Félix Fernandez García (*c.*1896–1941), Sp. ballet dancer.

María **Félix**: María de los Ángeles Félix Güereña (1914–2002), Mexican movie actress.

N. **Felix**: Nicholas Wanostrocht (1807–1876), Eng. schoolmaster, writer on cricket. The teacher and cricketer used his pen name for his writings on the "great game," including the primer *Felix on the Bat* (1845), a book sometimes found in the natural history section of public libraries. He was equally "N. Felix" when playing cricket, and is stated to have adopted this name "in deference, it is supposed, to the feelings of parents" [*Dictionary of National Biography*].

Seymour **Felix:** Felix Simon (1892–1961), U.S dance movie director.

Anne **Fellowes** *see* Jane **Langford**

Elisaveta **Fen:** Lydia Jackson, née Jiburtovich (1900–1983), Russ.-born Eng. writer, translator.

Freddy **Fender:** Baldemar G. Huerta (1937–2006), U.S. country singer. The musician adopted his new name on signing with Imperial Records in 1959. He explained: "Since I was playing a Fender guitar and amplifier, I changed my name to Freddy Fender" [*The Times*, October 16, 2006].

Edwige **Fenech:** Edwige Sfenek (1948–), It. movie actress, of Sicilian-Maltese parentage.

John **Fennell:** Francis Walsingham (1577–1647), Eng. Jesuit, Roman Catholic writer.

Frank **Fenton:** Frank Fenton-Morgan (1906–1957), U.S. movie actor.

Freda **Fenton** *see* Fenton **Brockley**

Lavinia **Fenton:** Lavinia Beswick (1708–1760), Eng. actress, singer. The actress, later the mistress, then the second wife, of the Duke of Bolton, adopted the name of her stepfather.

Shane **Fenton** *see* Alvin **Stardust**

Ferdausi (or Firdausi): Abu ul-Qasem Mansur (*c*.935–*c*.1020), Persian poet. The poet took his name from the garden of Ferdaus, owned by the governor of Khorasan, the region (now in northeastern Iran) in which he lived. He was thus "of Ferdaus." The garden name itself means "paradise" (the English word is related), and in turn represents Middle Persian *pardez*, related to Avestan *pairidaeza*, "enclosure," "park," in other words "garden," a compound of *pairi-*, "around" (Greek *peri-*), and *daeza*, "wall." Greek *paradeisos*, from the same source, is used in the Bible for the Garden of Eden.

H-Bomb **Ferguson:** Robert Ferguson (1929–2006), U.S. black blues musician. The singer adopted his nickname, given him for his "explosive" stage shows and booming voice.

Luisa **Ferida:** Luisa Monfrino Farnet (1914–1945), It. movie actress. Ferida was the only Italian motion picture actress executed by the partisans at the end of World War II for her Fascist affiliations.

Lawrence **Ferlinghetti:** Lawrence Ferling (1919–), U.S. poet, writer. Born the fifth son in the family of Charles Ferling, an Italian immigrant, Ferlinghetti adopted the original form of the family name on becoming a poet.

Fanny **Fern:** Sarah Payson Parton, née Willis (1811–1872), U.S. novelist, columnist; (2) Voltairine de Cleyre (1866–1912), U.S. anarchist writer. Sarah Parton made her name with the bestselling *Fern*

Leaves from Fanny's Portfolio (1853), a collection of her pieces in various magazines, but she was already writing articles for the *New York Musical World and Times* as "Fanny Fern" in 1852 and apparently first used the name for a piece in a small Boston newspaper, the *Mother's Assistant*, in 1851. De Cleyre published her first essays and stories in the *Progressive Age* under the name in the 1880s, at the same time modifying her original name of De Claire to de Claire and eventually to de Cleyre.

Fernandel: Fernand-Joseph-Désiré Contandin (1903–1971), Fr. movie comedian. The mother-in-law of the future comedian used to refer to him as *Fernand d'elle*, "*her* Fernand," as he was more attentive to her daughter than to herself. This is said to be the origin of the name.

Wilhelmenia **Fernandez:** Wilhelmenia Wiggins (1949–), U.S. opera singer.

Alonso **Fernández de Avellaneda:** ?, Sp. writer. The identity of the author of the continuation of the first volume of Cervantes' *Don Quixote*, published in 1614, is uncertain. It may have been Fray Luis de Aliaga, confessor of Philip III, or Lope de Vega, or even Cervantes himself, who in fact mocks the book in chapter 59 of the second volume of his famous work.

Carl **Fernau:** Sebastian Franz Daxenberger (1809–?), Ger. poet.

Adriana **Ferrarese Del Bene:** Adriana Gabrielli (*c*.1755–after 1799), It. singer. As an orphan in Venice the soprano was called Ferrarese, "(one) from Ferrara." Del Bene was presumably the name of her husband.

Lolo **Ferrari:** Eve Vallois (1970–2000), Fr.-born porno star. Famous for her grossly enhanced bust (said to be the largest in Europe and the fourth largest in the world), the former nightclub singer and model based her new name on French slang *lolo*, "boob," and the prestigious surname Ferrari. She used the latter for a line of underwear, resulting in an action brought by the Italian automobile manufacturer, who nevertheless allowed her to continue using the name in her stage shows.

E.X. **Ferrars:** Morna Doris Brown, née MacTaggart (1907–1995), Br. writer of detective fiction. The writer adopted her Anglo-German mother's maiden name. She also wrote as Elizabeth Ferrars.

Jean **Ferrat:** Jean Tenenbaum (1930–2010), Fr. singer.

Edoardo **Ferravilla:** Edoardo Villani (1846–1916), It. actor, comedy writer.

José **Ferrer:** José Vicente Ferrer de Otero y Cintrón (1909–1992), Puerto Rican–born U.S. stage, movie actor.

Anna Maria **Ferrero:** Anna Maria Guerra (1931–),

It. movie actress. The actress adopted her screen name in honor of her godfather, conductor and composer Willy Ferrero.

Arthur Ferres: John William Kevin (?1843–1903), Ir.-born Austral. children's writer.

Ernst Fest: Eduard Heinrich Mayer (1821–1907), Ger. poet. The pen name could have a German significance, as *ernst* is "serious" and *fest* is "solid."

Afanasy Fet: Afanasy Afanasyevich Shenshin (1820–1892), Russ. poet. The poet was the illegitimate son of a German mother, Charlotte Fet (or Foeth), and a Russian landowner named Shenshin. He adopted his mother's name for his writing and legally assumed it in 1876.

Stepin Fetchit: Lincoln Theodore Monroe Andrew Perry (1902–1985), U.S. black movie actor. The actor, who made his name as a slow-moving, slow-witted black servant, originally adopted the stage name of "Skeeter" (which he wasn't). This became "Stepin Fetchit," however, when he was near destitute on one occasion, and bet his clothes against $30 on a horse of this name at an Oklahoma race. He won, saved his clothes, and would soon write a comical song about his equine savior, whose own name implies "Step and fetch it," otherwise "Run fast and win the prize."

The name may have had a less specific origin, however. "*Stepin Fetchit*, ... stage name of a black American vaudeville actor who played the role of a shuffling, grinning, eye-rolling character in Hollywood films of the 1920's and 1930's, probably adopted from *Step-an'-fetch-it*, a nickname for any slow or lazy person" [Robert K. Barnhart, Sol Steinmetz, Clarence L. Barnhart, *Third Barnhart Dictionary of New English*, 1990].

Edwige Feuillère: Caroline Vivette Edwige Cunati-Kœnig (1907–1998), Fr. stage, movie actress, of Fr.-It. parentage. The actress's screen name was that of her former husband, Pierre Feuillère (married 1929, divorced 1933). She began her stage career as Cora Lynn (from her first name, Caroline).

Jacques Feyder: Jacques Frédérix (1885–1948), Belg.-born Fr. movie director. A simplification of the director's original rather awkward surname, and perhaps originating from a slurred pronunciation of this.

Michael ffolkes: Brian Davis (1925–1988), Eng. cartoonist. The artist explains how he got his name: "I've always had a kind of attraction for multiple identity. I got ffolkes from *Burke's Peerage*. As an unusual name it has been very valuable. It was about the time of Sprods and Trogs [*see* **Trog**] and Smilbys [*see* **Smilby**]. I wanted a distinctive name. I don't think *Punch* knows, actually.... Originally I wanted to write and called myself Brian Chorister, horrible

name. Then I tried using the name Dedalus, based on the James Joyce character.... I had just read Joyce. It shows a tendency to want to get away from the ordinariness of being Davis. Davis, plain Davis, is one of the commonest names in the country" [Michael Bateman, *Funny Way to Earn a Living*, 1966]. Sprod, mentioned above, was the real name of Australian-born cartoonist George Napier Sprod (1919–2003).

I.D. Ffraid: John Evans (1814–1876), Welsh translator, lexicographer. The writer and scholar took his name from the village where he was born, Llansanffraid Glan Conwy. The significance of the initials is uncertain. He also published a number of letters as Adda Jones, where the first name is the Welsh equivalent of Adam.

Padraic Fiacc: Patrick Joseph O'Connor (1924–), Ir. poet.

Allan Field *see* Lester **Wallack**

Charles Field *see* Fenton **Brockley**

Chelsea Field: Kim Botfield (1957–), U.S. movie actress.

Joanna Field: Marion Milner (1900–1998), Br. writer, psychoanalyst.

John Field: John Greenfield (1921–1991), Eng. ballet dancer, director.

Martyn Field: Frederick William Horner (1854–?), Eng. politician, administrator, author. The writer took his name from the London church of St. Martin-in-the-Fields, where he was chairman of the works committee.

Michael Field: Katherine Harris Bradley (1846–1914), Eng. poet, playwright + Edith Emma Cooper (1862–1913), Eng. poet, playwright, her niece. The pair chose a male name for their joint writings because "we have many things to say that the world will not tolerate from a woman's lips." Once their identities were revealed, their output received little attention. When writing individually they used the respective pseudonyms Arran Leigh and Isla Leigh, both forenames being adopted from Scottish islands. The name Michael Field was first used for two tragic dramas, *Callirrhoë* and *Fair Rosamund* (both 1884).

Sally Field: Sally Field Mahoney (1946–), U.S. movie actress.

Shirley Ann Field: Shirley Bloomfield (1936–), Br. movie actress. The actress aded an "e" to "Ann" from 1960.

Sylvia Field: Harriet Johnson (1901–1998), U.S. stage actress. The actress was given her stage name by her first manager, Winthrop Ames, for her maiden appearance at the age of 16 at the Shubert Theatre, New York.

Virginia Field: Margaret St. John Field (1917–1992), Eng. movie actress, working in U.S. Some sources have the actress's original middle name as

Cynthia, presumably a mishearing of "St. John," as a family name usually pronounced "Sinjun."

Ann Mary **Fielding:** Anita Mostyn, née Fielding (1907–1993), Eng. novelist. Although Fielding was the writer's genuine family name, she consciously adopted a pen name that honored her ancestor, the novelist Henry Fielding (1707–1754), especially as she was born in the bicentennial year of his birth. Compare the next entry below.

Gabriel **Fielding:** Alan Gabriel Barnsley (1916–1986), Br. novelist. The writer assumed his mother's maiden name, not as a compliment to her, since she dominated his childhood, but to honor the novelist Henry Fielding (1707–1754), of whom he was a descendant. Compare the entry above.

Timon **Fieldmouse** *see* Matthew **Browne**

Benny **Fields:** Benjamin Geisenfeld (1894–1959), U.S. movie actor, singer.

[Dame] Gracie **Fields:** Grace Stansfield (1898–1979), Eng. popular singer, comedienne. The singer began her career as a teenager in her native town of Rochdale, Lancashire. After a performance one day, she raised the matter of her name. "'Mumma,' said Grace, as they walked home together after the second house, 't' manager says Grace Stansfield's a bit long as names go.' Mumma who was glowing inside with secret pride, tried it out for sound. Yes, it might be a bit costly to put a name like that up in lights. She wondered whether they should cut the name in half. 'How about, Fields?' she suggested. 'But let's get sommat posh to put in front, like Stana, or Anna!' 'What's wrong with Grace, Mumma?' Mumma rolled it over her tongue. 'Grace Fields! Bit too stiff-like. Now what about ... Gracie. That's it, Gracie Fields!' The thirteen-year-old, newly-christened Gracie Fields gave a whoop of joy" [Muriel Burgess with Tommy Keene, *Gracie Fields*, 1980].

Jackie **Fields:** Jacob Finkelstein (1908–1987), U.S. boxer. As a youth, the boxer was trained by a former fighter, Marty Fields. He adopted his name, thus finding a simpler alternative to his original Jewish surname.

Lew **Fields:** Lewis Maurice (earlier Moses) Schoenfeld (1867–1941), Pol.-born U.S. stage comedian, teaming with Joe Weber (1867–1942).

Stanley **Fields:** Walter L. Agnew (1884–1941), U.S. movie actor, former prizefighter.

Tommy **Fields:** Thomas Stansfield (1908–1988), Eng. music-hall comedian, brother of Gracie **Fields**.

Totie **Fields:** Sophie Feldman (1930–1978), U.S. nightclub, TV comedienne. "Totie" was presumably a childish pronunciation of "Sophie."

W.C. **Fields:** William Claude Dukenfield (1880–1946), U.S. movie comedian. This was the comedian's standard screen name. But he famously de-vised many others, either as film character or screenwriter, among them Primrose Magoo, Mahatma Kane Jeeves, Otis Criblecolis, Ampico J. Steinway, Felton J. Satchelstern, Egbert Sousé, Eustace McGargle, J. Frothingham Waterbury, Ogg Ogilvie, Filthy McNasty, Ouliotta Haemoglobin, E. Snoopington Pinkerton, Elmer Prettywillie, T. Frothingwell Bellows, A. Pismo Clam, Ambrose Wolfinger, Egbert Sousé, Cuthbert J. Twillie, and Larson E. Whipsnade. He first used W.C. Fields in 1893. Claude was a name that he had always hated, and the villains in his movies were often called Claude. Many of the names he subsequently adopted were based on the names used by Charles Dickens, whose books he admired [Carlotta Monti with Cy Rice, *W.C. Fields and Me*, 1974].

50 Cent: Curtis James Jackson III (1975–), U.S. black rapper. The musician called himself after a Brooklyn robber, Kelvin Martin, who was so known. "I'm the same kind of person 50 Cent was," he said. "I provide for myself by any means."

Figaro: Henry Clapp (1814–1875), U.S. journalist, editor. The name has been popular with many journalists and columnists. Another was Mariano Jose de Larra (1809–1837), the Spanish satirist and dramatist, who used the pseudonym for the contribution of humorous articles to various periodicals. *Le Figaro* is itself a leading French daily newspaper, founded in 1825. The name comes from the hero of Beaumarchais's *Le Barbier de Séville* (1775) and *Le Mariage de Figaro* (1784), where Figaro is a barber-turned-doorkeeper. Barbers (and doorkeepers), of course, hear all the gossip. The ultimate source of the name may be in Spanish *hígado*, "liver," in the sense of someone who has "pluck" and spirit.

Filandre: Jean-Baptiste Monchaingre (or Jean Mathée) (1616–1691), Fr. actor-manager. The Greek name literally means "lover of men."

Filaret: (1) Fyodor Nikitich Romanov (*c*.1554–1633), Russ. churchman, patriarch of Moscow and All Russia; (2) Vasily Mikhaylovich Drozdov (1782–1867), Russ. churchman, metropolitan of Moscow. The name is of Greek origin (properly Philarethes) and means "lover of virtue." It was assumed by each man on taking monastic vows (Romanov in 1601, Drozdov in 1808). There are several other Orthodox churchmen who assumed the name.

Filarete: Antonio di Pietro Averlino (*c*.1400–*c*.1469), It. sculptor, architect, writer. The artist adopted his nickname, which derives from the Greek and means either "lover of virtue" (as for **Filaret**) or, more precisely in his case, "lover of virtu," the latter being a collective term for objects of art or antiquity.

Filia: Sarah Anne Ellis Dorsey (1829–1879), U.S. writer. Dorsey took her pen name from the

Latin byname, "Filia Ecclesiae" ("Daughter of the Church"), given her by the editors of the *Churchman* when she responded to a request in that magazine for information on music in church services.

Fillia: Luigi Colombo (1904–1936), It. Futurist poet, painter, dramatist.

Fillmore Slim: Clarence Sims (1935–), U.S. black blues musician.

Quirico **Filopanti:** Giuseppe Barilli (1812–1894), It. writer, patriot.

Fin-Bec: William Blanchard Jerrold (1826–1884), Eng. playwright, novelist. French *fin-bec* (literally "fine beak") means "gourmet." Jerrold lived as much in Paris as in London, and was himself a gourmet, publishing the *Epicure's Year-Book* in 1867 and (as Fin-Bec) gastronomic works such as *Knife and Fork* (1871), *The Dinner Bell* (1878), and the like.

Peter **Finch:** Peter George Ingle Finch (1916–1977), Eng. stage, movie actor. The actor's name is as given here, and not William Mitchell, as stated in many otherwise reliable sources. The misnomer seems to have been initiated in Finch's obituary in *The Times* of January 15, 1977, which had: "Peter Finch, whose real name was William Mitchell, ..." The mixup arose from an incident when Finch was visiting Rome with the real William Mitchell, a Canadian movie actor. Mitchell became involved in a barroom brawl and the two men were taken to the police station, where they were charged. Finch had his passport but Mitchell did not. Mitchell was thus taken to be Finch, and Finch as Mitchell. The incident was picked up by the British press, and later led to the obituary error [Elaine Dundy, *Finch, Bloody Finch*, 1980].

Herman **Finck:** Herman van de Vinck (1872–1939), Eng. composer of comic operas, conductor.

Richard **Findlater:** Kenneth Bruce Findlater Bain (1921–1985), Engl. theater critic, historian.

Larry **Fine:** Louis Feinberg (1911–1975), U.S. movie comedian. Fine joined Moe and Shemp **Howard** in the early 1920s as a member of the future "Three Stooges" comedy team.

Johnny **Fingers:** John Moylett (1956–), Ir. rock musician. The Boomtown Rats member, a cousin of Pete **Briquette**, was so named for the nimbleness of his fingers on the keyboard.

Alejandro **Finisterre:** Alejandro Campos Ramírez (1919–2007), Sp. poet, editor. The writer, famous as the inventor of table football, was born in Fisterra, northwestern Spain, and adopted the Castilian name of his native town on starting his studies in Madrid.

[Sir] Moses I. **Finley:** Moses Finkelstein (1912–1986), U.S.–born Br. classical historian. The academic adopted his new name around 1936. He had no actual middle name, but simply used the initial "I." He emigrated to England in 1954 and became a British subject in 1962.

Jack **Finney:** Walter Braden Finney (1911–1995), U.S. SF writer.

Fiore della Neve: Martinus Gesinus Lambert van Loghem (1849–1934), Du. poet, fiction writer. The writer's Italian-style name means "flower of the snow."

Fiorello: Rosario Fiorello (1960–), It. popular singer, TV presenter, introducer of karaoke to Italy.

Firdausi *see* **Ferdausi**

Alice **Firefly:** Alice Newton (1977–), Br. street performer. The entertainer explains: "Firefly is one of the two characters I've developed. A friend came up with the name as a perfect way to explain my act: I do fire juggling in bright, iridescent costumes and I do trapeze work" [*The Times*, May 12, 1999].

Bert **Firman:** Herbert Feuermann (1906–1999), Br. danceband leader. The musician, born into a large Jewish family, anglicized his name, as did his brothers, pianist John and violinists Sam and Sidney.

David **Firth:** David Firth Coleman (1945–), Br. stage, TV actor. The actor adopted his father's (and his own) middle name as his stage name.

Ruth **Fischer:** Elfriede Eisler (1895–1961), Ger.-born U.S. Communist activist. The political activist apparently adopted her new name from those of her parents, Rudolf Eisler and Maria Ida Fischer.

Fish: Derek William Dick (1958–), Sc. rock musician. When Dick was working in the Scottish village of Fochabers he lodged with a landlady who objected to the number of baths he took and the time he spent in the bathtub. But the more she protested, the more he defied her, taking in beer, radio, and books for hours. "One night a friend hung about waiting for me to come out of the bath and he said: 'Are you some sort of fish or something?' and I said: 'That's it.' I just could not imagine being introduced on stage as Derek William Dick" [Beech, p.122].

Bud **Fisher:** Harry Conway (1885–1954), U.S. strip cartoonist.

Clay **Fisher** *see* Will **Henry**

Fred **Fisher:** Alfred Breitenbach (1875–1942), Ger.-born U.S. popular composer, lyricist. The musician adopted his new name on settling in Chicago in 1900.

John **Fisher:** John Percy (1569–1641), Eng. Jesuit.

Nicholas **Fisk:** David Higginbottom (1923–), Eng. children's writer.

John **Fiske:** Edmund Fisk Green (1842–1901), U.S. philosopher, historian. In 1855, when he was 13, the future historian agreed to his grandmother's request that he legally adopt her father's name, John

Fisk. He added an "e" to the surname in 1860, when he was 18.

Minnie Maddern **Fiske:** Marie Augusta Davey (1865–1932), U.S. stage actress. The actress made her stage debut with her parents at the age of three under her mother's maiden name of Maddern, with "Minnie" referring to her smallness. She continued as Minnie Maddern until 1890, when she married her second husband, playwright Harrison Grey Fiske, after which she performed as Minnie Maddern Fiske.

Mary **Fitt:** Kathleen Freeman (1897–1959), Br. classical scholar, novelist. The writer used this name for her detective novels. She also wrote as Caroline Cory and Stuart Mary Wick.

Roger **Fitzalan** *see* Elleston **Trevor**

Edward **Fitzball:** Edward Ball (1792–1873), Eng. popular dramatist. The playwright added his mother's maiden name of Fitz to his existing name. This makes sense when it is remembered that Fitz means "son."

George Savage **Fitz-Boodle:** William Makepeace Thackeray (1811–1863), Eng. novelist. The writer used this name for the supposed author of *The Fitz-Boodle Papers*, appearing in *Fraser's Magazine* (1842–3), Fitz-Boodle being a pipe-smoking bachelor clubman. The pseudonym is thus based on the names of London clubs: the Savage Club and Boodle's still flourish. Thackeray himself was a member of the Garrick.

Barry **Fitzgerald:** William Joseph Shields (1888–1961), Ir. stage, movie actor, working in U.S. When Shields began his acting career, he was working full time as a civil servant. Another name for his stage appearances was therefore needed, and he chose a typical Irish name. By day he was thus William Shields, and by night, when on stage, Barry Fitzgerald.

Hugh **Fitzgerald** *see* Floyd **Akers**

Walter **Fitzgerald:** Walter Fitzgerald Bond (1896–1977), Eng. stage, movie actor.

Sir Thomas **Fitzosborne:** William Melmoth (1710–1799), Eng. classical scholar, writer. Melmoth used this name for his first book, *Letters on Several Subjects* (1742).

John **Fitzvictor:** Percy Bysshe Shelley (1792–1822), Eng. poet. Shelley used this name for *Posthumous Fragments of Margaret Nicholson* (1810), published in the same year as *Original Poetry by Victor and Cazire*, written jointly with his sister, Elizabeth.

Fix: Felix Runcie (1916–after 1988), N.Z.–born Br. cartoonist, illustrator.

Paul **Fix:** Paul Fix Morrison (1901–1983), U.S. movie actor.

Francis **Flagg:** Henry George Weiss (1898–1946), U.S. SF writer.

Ric **Flair:** Richard Fliehr (1949–), U.S. wrestler.

Bud **Flanagan:** Chaim Reuben Weintrop (1896–1968), Eng. stage, movie comedian, of Pol. Jewish parentage, teaming with Chesney **Allen**. The actor first trod the boards of the London music hall as Fargo the Boy Conjuror. At the age of 13 he emigrated with his family to the United States and, after a brief interlude as a boxer with the ring name of Luke McGluke, tried his fortune on the vaudeville stage as Bobby Wayne. Back in Britain again at the start of World War I he joined the army as Driver Robert Winthrop.

The name Flanagan was inherited from his army years. Apparently a mean sergeant-major seemed to have it in for the future singer, and when Driver Winthrop was wounded in 1918 and left the service, his last words to his sergeant-major were, "I'll remember your name as long as I live." He took the name on resuming his career on the stage. (Later the sergeant-major became a barman in London, and Bud and he were reconciled.) After Flanagan and Allen's popular song "Underneath the Arches" was published in 1932 the profits began to roll in. With his share, Bud bought a house in the village of Angmering, Sussex, and named it "Arches." His first break in show business was given him by Florrie **Forde** [Bill McGowran, "You See Him Everywhere," in *Late Extra: A Miscellany by "Evening News" Writers, Artists, & Photographers*, c.1952].

Flavius Josephus: Joseph ben Matthias (AD 37–100), Jewish historian, general. The historian originally had the Hebrew name Yosef ben Mattityahu, "Joseph son of Matthew." He added Flavius to this when the Roman emperor Titus Flavius Vespasianus (better known as Vespasian) granted him the rights of a Roman citizen and appointed him historiographer of the Flavius *gens* (clan).

Marty **Flax:** Martin Flachsenhaar (1924–1972), U.S. jazz musician.

Fléchelles *see* **Gaultier-Garguille**

[Sir] Peter Hesketh **Fleetwood:** Peter Hesketh (1801–1866), Eng. entrepreneur. The founder in 1836 of the Lancashire town and port of Fleetwood added his mother's maiden name to his existing surname in 1831.

Edmond **Fleg:** Edmond Flegenheimer (1974–1963), Fr. writer.

Bryant **Fleming** *see* Gig **Young**

George **Fleming:** Julia Constance Fletcher (1858–1938), U.S. novelist, playwright.

Gerald **Fleming:** Gergard Flehinger (1921–2006), Ger.-born war historian, working in England.

Ian **Fleming:** Ian Macfarlane (1888–1969), Austral.-born Br. stage, movie actor.

Oliver **Fleming:** Philip MacDonald (1900–

1981), Eng. mystery writer. The writer used this name for novels written jointly with his father, Ronald MacDonald (1860–1933). He wrote independently under the names Anthony Lawless and Martin Porlock.

Rhonda **Fleming**: Marilyn Lewis (or Louis) (1922–), U.S. movie actress.

Waldo **Fleming** *see* S.S. **Smith**

Herb **Flemming**: Arif Nicolaiih El-Michelle (1898–1976), U.S. jazz musician, of Tunisian parentage.

Robert de **Flers**: Marie-Joseph-Louis-Camille-Robert Pellevé de la Motte-Ango, marquis de Flers (1872–1927), Fr. comedy writer.

George U. **Fletcher**: Fletcher Pratt (1897–1956), U.S. naval, American history, fantasy writer.

Robert **Fletcher**: Robert Fletcher Wycoff (1923–), U.S. theater designer.

Fleury: Abraham-Joseph Bénard (1750–1822), Fr. comic actor.

Richard **Flexmore**: Richard Flexmore Geatter (1824–1860), Eng. pantomime artist.

Arnold **Flint** *see* J.P. **McCall**

Flood: Mark Ellis (1960–), Eng. rock-group producer. The musician's unusual name is said to have arisen from his willingness to make the tea when working in a recording studio. A fellow technician was nicknamed "Drought."

Evangeline **Florence**: Evangeline Crerar, née Houghton (1873–1928), U.S. opera singer.

William Jermyn **Florence**: Bernard Conlin (1831–1891), U.S. actor, playwright, of Ir. parentage.

Florence and the Machine: Florence Mary Leonine Welch (1986–), Br. pop singer, of U.S.–Br. parentage. The singer began her career in 2006 as Florence Robot Is a Machine, the "machine" being drums, and this gave her later name.

Lola **Flores**: Dolores Flores Ruiz (1923–1995), Sp. flamenco dancer, movie actress.

Raúl **Flores Canelo**: Raúl Flores González (1929–1992), Mexican ballet dancer, choreographer.

Florestan *see* **Eusebius** (2)

Floridor: Josias de Soulas, Sieur de Prinefosse (?1608–1671), Fr. actor.

Cornelis **Floris**: Cornelis de Vriendt (1514–1575), Flemish architect, sculptor, brother of Frans **Floris**.

Frans **Floris**: Frans de Vriendt (1515–1570), Flemish painter, brother of Cornelis **Floris**.

Florizel *see* **Perdita** (2)

Flotsam: Bentley Collingwood Hilliam (1890–1968), Eng. composer, pianist, entertainer, teaming with **Jetsam**. The comic singers always signed off their act with the phrase, "Yours very sincerely, Flotsam and Jetsam." Flotsam was a countertenor, as fit-

ting for his name (flotsam *floats* on the surface of the water), while Jetsam was a bass (jetsam often *sinks* when thrown overboard).

Barbara **Flynn**: Barbara Joy McMurray (1948–), Eng. stage, TV actress.

Keri **Flynn** *see* Ellen **Burstyn**

Josiah **Flynt**: Josiah Flint Willard (1869–1907), U.S. writer on life as a hobo.

Nina **Foch**: Nina Consuelo Maud Fock (1924–2008), Du.-born U.S. stage, movie actress.

Gorch **Fock**: Hans Kinau (1880–1916), Ger. writer. The writer's adopted surname is the German word for "foresail," denoting the seafaring theme that runs through his books.

Jonathan Lituleson **Fogarty**: James T. Farrell (1904–1979), U.S. novelist, critic.

Michel **Fokine**: Mikhail Mikhailovich Fokin (1880–1942), Russ.-born U.S. ballet dancer, choreographer. The dancer adopted a French form of his original Russian name.

Helen **Foley**: Helen Rose Fowler, née Huxley (1917–), Eng. novelist. The writer attended Newnham College, Cambridge, and adopted the name of an earlier Newnham student, poet Helen Foley (1896–1937). The name happens to represent the first part of her married name and last part of her maiden name.

Luciano **Folgore**: Omero Vecchi (1888–1966), It. Futurist poet. The poet's name may have been suggested by his medieval predecessor, Iacopo di Michele (*c*.1270–*c*.1330), known as Folgore da San Gimignano, from his nickname, Folgore, literally "thunderbolt," implying a poetic luminary. "Luciano" would accord with this to mean "light" (Italian *luce*).

Signor **Foli**: Allan James Foley (1835–1899), Ir.–U.S. opera singer. The bass adopted an italianized form of his name.

Regina **Fong**: Reginald Bundy (1945–2003), Br. drag artist, female impersonator. The gay icon, who trained as a dancer, assumed the royal title "Her Imperial Highness the Grand Duchess Regina Fong."

Joan **Fontaine**: Joan de Havilland (1917–), Eng.-born U.S. stage, movie actress. The actress originally toured with regional theater groups under the name Joan Burfield, and made her screen debut as such in *No More Ladies* (1935). She adopted the name Joan Fontaine in 1937, following her mother's divorce and subsequent remarriage to George M. Fontaine. The aim of the name change was to avoid being confused with her actress sister, Olivia de Havilland (1916–).

Wayne **Fontana**: Glyn Geoffrey Ellis (1945–), Eng. rock musician. Ellis adopted his stage name in honor of Elvis Presley's 1950s drummer, D.J. Fontana, some time before he signed a contract with the coincidentally named Philips' Fontana label for his first recording in 1963, a version of "Road Runner," by **Bo Diddley**.

Moderata **Fonte**: Modesta Pozzo de'Zorzi (1555–1592), It. poet, religious writer.

[Dame] Margot **Fonteyn**: Peggy Hookham (1919–1991), Eng. ballet dancer. "You couldn't succeed with such a suburban moniker as Peggy Hookham. The inspired Nita [Hookham, Fonteyn's mother] wrote to her paternal family (wealthy Brazilians by the name of Fontes) for permission to use their name. As staunch Catholics, they responded with a resounding 'No'; a relative in the theatre would bring disgrace. Instead the 's' became an 'n' and with the addition of the 'y' the fledgling dancer sounded properly foreign. It seems ridiculous today, but 70 years ago, with English ballet in its infancy, it was necessary to be thought Russian or Italian or anything uncommon" [*Sunday Times*, October 24, 2004].

George **Footit**: Tudor Hall (1864–1921), Eng. circus clown, teaming with **Chocolat**.

Dick **Foran**: John Nicholas Foran (1910–1979), U.S. movie actor, singer. Foran's first screen appearance was in the 1934 musical *Stand Up and Cheer*, in which he sang to the child star Shirley Temple under the name Nick Foran. He changed "Nick" to "Dick" on signing with Warner Bros. later in the decade.

Athol **Forbes**: [Rev.] Forbes Alexander Phillips (1866–1917), Eng. playwright, novelist. The name seems to have a Scottish reference.

Brenda **Forbes**: Brenda Taylor (1909–1996), Eng. stage actress. The actress adopted her mother's maiden name as her stage name.

Bryan **Forbes**: John Theobald Clarke (1926–), Eng. movie actor, screenwriter, producer. The actor's name was chosen for him at the start of his stage career: "[BBC radio producer] Lionel Gamlin ... announced that it would be necessary for me to change my name. Another young actor, ahead of me in the game, was also named John Clarke.... He elaborated on the surname first. 'Forbes has a good theatrical ring to it,' he said. 'Forbes-Robertson, you know.' I nodded. I hadn't the vaguest idea what he was talking about. [He was talking about Johnston Forbes-Robertson (1853–1937), London actor and theater manager, whose second wife was the U.S. actress Gertrude Elliott, sister of Maxine **Elliott**. English actress Meriel **Forbes** was his grandniece.] Had he suggested I call myself Joseph Stalin I would have agreed without a murmur ... Forbes it was, and then Lionel began to juggle with Christian names to go with it. 'You want a good sounding name,' he said, 'and one that *looks* right on the bills. These things are important' ... I dimly comprehended that Lionel was asking if I would accept Brian. 'Bryan with a Y, I think.' He

wrote it down ... 'How does that strike you?' ... I managed to blurt out my grateful acceptance of the miracle. 'Fine, that's it, then,' Lionel went on. 'From now onwards you're Bryan Forbes'" [Bryan Forbes, *Notes for a Life*, 1974].

Colin **Forbes**: Raymond Harold Sawkins (1923–2006), Eng. thriller writer. This was the author's main pseudonym. He also wrote as Richard Raine, Jay Bernard, and Harold English.

Meriel **Forbes**: Meriel Forbes-Robertson (1913–2000), Eng. stage, movie actress, grandniece of Johnston Forbes-Robertson (*see* under Bryan **Forbes**), wife of actor Sir Ralph Richardson (1902–1983).

Miranda **Forbes**: Maddalena Stephanie Weet (1946–), Br. movie, TV actress.

Ralph **Forbes**: Ralph Taylor (1902–1951), Br. movie actor, working in U.S.

Stanton **Forbes**: Deloris Stanton Forbes (1923–), U.S. mystery writer.

Charles Henri **Ford**: Charles Henry Ford (1908–2002), U.S. writer. The free-living poet and novelist modified the spelling of his middle name for distinction from the automobile manufacturer Henry Ford (1863–1947) and the latter's grandson Henry Ford II (1917–1987).

Clinton **Ford**: Ian George Stopford Harrison (1931–2009), Eng. showbusiness performer. The musician adopted his American-style name early in his career after forming his own skiffle group.

Elbur **Ford** *see* Jean **Plaidy**

Emile **Ford**: Emile Sweetman (1937–), Bahamanian rock singer.

Ford Madox **Ford**: Ford Hermann Hueffer (1873–1939), Br. novelist, editor. The writer, grandson of the painter Ford Madox Brown (1821–1893), was baptized a Roman Catholic with the additional Christian names Joseph Leopold. In 1915 he changed his name by deed poll to Ford Madox Hueffer, then in 1919, embarrassed by his German surname, to Joseph Leopold Ford Hermann Madox Ford. On the title pages of his books his name alternated between Ford Madox Ford and Ford Madox Hueffer, the former for his sequence of war novels with main character Christopher Tietjens as well as for travel books and reminiscences. Earlier, for *The Questions at the Well; With Sundry Other Verses for Notes of Music* (1893) he was Fenil Haig, while for *The Simple Life Limited* (1911) and *The New Humpty-Dumpty* (1912) he was Daniel Chaucer. "Although Ford's change of name may register the wish to escape, it also recognises the impossibility of escaping, revisiting as it does its origin, and recreating the self in the process" [Max Saunders, *Ford Madox Ford: A Dual Life*, Vol. I, 1996].

Francis **Ford**: Francis O'Fearna (1883–1953), U.S. movie actor, brother of John **Ford**.

Frankie **Ford**: Francis Guzzo (1939–), U.S. rock singer.

Gerald R. **Ford, Jr.**: Leslie Lynch King, Jr. (1913–2006), U.S. president. When the 38th president of the United States was still an infant, his parents divorced and his mother moved from Omaha, Nebraska, to Grand Rapids, Michigan, where she married Gerald R. Ford, Sr., who adopted the boy and gave him his name.

Glenn **Ford**: Gwyllyn Samuel Newton Ford (1916–2006), Can.-born U.S. movie actor. The actor's new first name was an americanized form of his birth name, which reflected his mother's Welsh origins.

Hilary **Ford** *see* John **Christopher**

James William **Ford**: James William Foursche (1893–1957), U.S. black labor leader, Communist party official. James's family took a new surname soon after his birth, when a white policeman questioning his father said that "Foursche" was too difficult to spell and changed the name to Ford.

John **Ford**: Sean Aloysius O'Fearna (1895–1973), U.S. movie director, of Ir. parentage. When Sean O'Fearna graduated from high school in 1913, his elder brother, Francis **Ford**, was working as a director and actor in Hollywood and had already adopted the name Ford. Sean took the same name when he joined him, calling himself Jack Ford. Some sources give the director's original name as John Martin Feeney, an English equivalent of the Irish (but with Martin as a middle name).

Keeley **Ford**: Mair Davies (1948–), Br. popular radio singer.

Leslie **Ford**: Zenith Brown, née Jones (1898–1983), U.S. detective novelist. The writer also used the names Brenda Conrad and David Frome.

Mary **Ford**: Iris Colleen Summer (1928–1977), U.S. country singer, teaming with Les **Paul**. The singer was given her stage name by Paul, whom she married in 1949 (but divorced in 1964).

Paul **Ford**: Paul Ford Weaver (1901–1976), U.S. comic stage, movie, TV actor. The actor adopted his mother's maiden name, which was already his middle name.

Wallace **Ford**: Samuel Jones Grundy (1897–1966), Eng.-born U.S. movie actor. The actor assumed the name of a friend killed in a railroad accident.

Webster **Ford** *see* Dexter **Wallace**

Florrie **Forde**: Florence Flanagan (1876–1940), Austral.-born Br. music-hall singer.

Walter **Forde**: Thomas Seymour (1896–1984), Br. movie director.

Keith **Fordyce**: Keith Marriott (1928–), Eng. radio, TV interviewer, DJ.

Nikolay **Foregger**: Nikolay Mikhaylovich Greyfenturn [Greifenturn] (1892–1939), Russ. ballet producer, teacher.

Antonia **Forest**: Patricia Giulia Caulfield Tate Rubinstein (1915–2003), Br. children's novelist, of Russ. Jewish parentage.

Mark **Forest**: Lou Degni (1933–), U.S. movie actor.

Cecil Scott **Forester**: Cecil Lewis Troughton Smith (1899–1966), Br. novelist, working in U.S. The writer, who signed himself simply C.S. Forester, took his new name for professional purposes in 1923. It was an elaboration of the middle name of his father, George Foster Smith.

Fanny **Forester**: Emily Chubbuck Judson (1817–1854), U.S. novelist. Following the publication of a number of children's books under her maiden name, Emily Chubbuck changed direction. In June 1844 she wrote an amusing letter to the *Mirror*, a popular New York weekly, offering her services as a regular contributor and signing herself "Fanny Forester," a name that may have been suggested by that of Frank **Forester**. The editors took her on and her pseudonym soon became familiar to the public.

Frank **Forester**: Henry William Herbert (1807–1858), Eng. author, editor, working in U.S. Herbert began writing articles about horses, hunting, and fishing in the 1830s, adopting the name Harry Archer. In 1842 he edited a collection of sketches by a friend, William P. Haws, who wrote under the psudonym J. Cypress, Jr., and followed these up with pieces of his own under the name Frank Forester. The name was suggested to him by William T. Porter, U.S. editor of the sporting newspaper *Spirit of the Times*.

Frank **Forester** *see* Lieutenant **Murray**

Forez: François Mauriac (1885–1970), Fr. novelist, playwright, poet. When working for the French Resistance, Mauriac wrote *Cahier Noir* (1943), choosing for this the name of the mountainous region in the Massif Central that Resistance workers found so suitable for cover.

James **Forman**: James Rufus (1928–2005), U.S. civil rights activist.

George **Formby**: George Hoy Booth (1904–1961), Eng. movie comedian, singer, ukelele player. The comedian, whose middle name, Hoy, was his mother's maiden name, took the same stage name as his father, music-hall artist James Lawler Booth (1877–1921). How did Booth Senior come to acquire his name? As a young millworker, James would supplement his small wages by singing in the street, where he was "discovered" by a Mr. Brown, together with another boy who had teamed up with him, and sent to different towns in the north of England to earn a shilling or two for his "manager." Mr. Brown would pay James threepence a week and the other boy sixpence. To cut his expenses, Mr. Brown transported the boys in the traveling props basket, with the lid down, to avoid paying their train fares.

"On one occasion, when they were travelling from Manchester to Bury, Jimmy happened not to be in the basket and sat watching coal wagons go by. A sign on one of the wagons showed that it came from Formby, Lancashire. The name appealed to him. He preferred it, in a theatrical sense, to his own name of Booth and decided there and then to make it his own. But Jimmy or James did not go with it. Beginning with the first letter of the alphabet he went through in his mind all the names he could think of and stopped when he got to 'G' and George. That was it — George Formby. It sounded right. It suited him. His change of name coincided with his desire to end the singing partnership" [Alan Randall and Ray Seaton, *George Formby*, 1974].

Alan **Forrest**: Allan Forrest Fisher (1889–1941), U.S. stage, movie actor.

David **Forrest**: David Denholm (1924–), Austral. novelist, short-story writer.

George **Forrest, Esq., M.A.**: [Rev.] John George Wood (1827–1889), Eng. naturalist, writer. The writer used this pen name, of obvious but appropriate derivation, for the highly popular *Every Boy's Book* (1855).

George "Chet" **Forrest**: George Forrest Chichester, Jr. (1915–1999), U.S. lyricist, composer.

Helen **Forrest**: Helen Fogel (1918–1999), U.S. jazz singer. The singer began her career under various assumed names, among them Bonnie Blue, The Blue Lady, and Marlene.

Sally **Forrest**: Katharine Scully Feeney (1928–), U.S. movie actress.

Sam **Forrest**: Simon Mordecai Lazarus (1870–1944), U.S. stage director, of Russ. Jewish parentage.

Sidney **Forrest**: Louise E. Stairs (1892–?), U.S. organist, pianist, conductor, composer.

Steve **Forrest**: William Forrest Andrews (1924–), U.S. movie actor.

Helen **Forrester**: June (or Jamunadevi) Bhatia (1919–), Eng.-born Can. novelist.

John **Forsell**: Carl Johan Jacob (1868–1941), Swe. opera singer.

Willi **Forst**: Wilhelm Anton Frohs (1903–1980), Austr. movie actor.

Friedrich **Forster**: Waldfried Burggraf (1895–1958), Ger. stage actor, playwright.

Robert **Forster**: Robert Foster, Jr. (1941–), U.S. movie actor.

Bruce **Forsyth**: Bruce Joseph Forsyth-Johnson (1928–), Br. entertainer, TV host.

Jean **Forsyth**: Jean Newton McIlwraith (1859–1938), Can. novelist, biographer, of Sc. parentage.

John **Forsythe**: John Lincoln Freund (1918–2010), U.S. stage, movie actor.

Paul **Fort**: Frank Richard Stockton (1834–1902), U.S. novelist. Paul Fort (1872–1960) happens to be the name of a French poet, but Stockton took his pseudonym before the Frenchman had made his mark. Stockton's niece, Mrs. MacAllister, explained the likely origin of the name in a letter to Alice Marble: "My father's name was Paul, and Uncle Frank always had a liking for the name. *Fort* was a name running through a branch of the Evans family in the south and Fort Evans was Aunt Marian's [Stockton's wife's] cousin" [Marble, p.178].

George **Forth** *see* Harold **Frederic**

Franco **Fortini**: Franco Lattes (1917–1994), It. poet, essayist.

Fortis: Leslie Forse (1907–1978), Eng. journalist, editor.

Fortuna: Diego Mazquiarán (1895–1940), Sp. bullfighter.

Dion **Fortune**: Violet Mary Firth (1890–1946), Br. writer of occult novels. The writer created her pseudonym from the Firth family motto, "Deo, Non Fortuna" ("By God, not Fortune").

Lance **Fortune**: Chris Morris (1940–), Br. pop. singer. The singer's name was given him by impresario Larry Parnes, who had originally intended it for the future Georgie **Fame**.

Lukas **Foss**: Lukas Fuchs (1922–2009), Ger.-born U.S. composer, conductor.

Dianne **Foster**: Dianne Laruska (1928–), Can. movie actress, working in U.S.

Frank **Foster**: Daniel Puseley (1814–1882), Eng. writer.

Jodie **Foster**: Alicia Christian Foster (1962–), U.S. movie actress. Jodie Foster was given her new first name as a child by her three older siblings.

Norman **Foster**: Norman Hoeffer (1900–1976), U.S. movie actor.

Phil **Foster**: Fivel Feldman (1914–1985), U.S. TV comedian.

Phoebe **Foster**: Phoebe Eager (1896–?), U.S. stage actress.

Richard **Foster**: Kendell Foster Crossen (1910–1981), U.S. crime, SF writer. Crossen also wrote as M.E. Chaber, Christopher Monig, and Clay Richards.

Susanna **Foster**: Suzanne DeLee Flanders Larson (1924–), U.S. movie actress. The actress began her career as an opera singer and took her professional name from that of Stephen Foster and his song "Oh, Susanna." Compare the name of Nelly **Bly**.

Fougasse: Cyril Kenneth Bird (1887–1965), Eng. artist, cartoonist, editor. Bird adopted his unusual name in order to avoid confusion with another artist calling himself W. **Bird**. He later explained that "fougasse" was an old technical term for a small anti-personnel landmine which "might or might not go off," and modestly thought the same could apply to his cartoons. (He had himself been injured by a shell in World War I.) He was the only cartoonist to be editor of *Punch*, succeeding **Evoe** in 1949.

Adam **Fouleweather**: Thomas Nashe (1567–1601), Eng. satirical pamphleteer, dramatist. The satirist used this name for *A wonderful, strange, and miraculous Astrologicall Prognostication for this year of our Lord God 1591, by Adam Fouleweather, student in Asse-tronomy* (1591), in which he replied to the savage attack on him by Richard Hervey, the astrologer. His best-known pseudonym was **Pasquil**.

Hugh **Foulis**: Neil Munro (1864–1930), Sc. writer. Munro used this name for humorous stories of life in western Scotland, keeping his real name for Highland romances.

Oliver **Foulis**: David Lloyd (1635–1692), Welsh biographer. The writer used this name for *Cabala; or the History of Conventicles unvail'd* (1664).

Bud **Fowler**: John Jackson (1858–1913), U.S. black baseball player. It is not known why the player adopted his new name (formally John W. Fowler).

Gene **Fowler**: Eugene Devlan (1890–1960), U.S. journalist, writer, dramatist. Devlan adopted his stepfather's surname.

Imro **Fox**: Isador Fuchs (1862–1910), Ger.-born U.S. magician.

James **Fox**: William Fox (1939–), Eng. movie actor, brother of movie actor Edward Fox (1937–). Fox began his career as a child actor in 1950 under his original name. Later, in the 1960s, he changed his first name to James on discovering another British actor called William Fox.

Michael J. **Fox**: Michael Andrew Fox (1961–), Can. movie, TV actor, working in U.S. "Along with a new country, new city, new job, new apartment, and new chair, I'd also picked up a new identity. The Screen Actors Guild prohibits any two members from working under the same stage name, and they already had a 'Michael Fox' on the books. My middle name is Andrew, but 'Andrew Fox' or 'Andy Fox' didn't cut it for me. 'Michael A. Fox' was even worse.... And then I remembered one of my favorite character actors, Michael J. **Pollard**.... I stuck in the *J*, which I sometimes tell people stands for either *Jenuine* or *Jenius*, and resubmitted my forms" [Michael J. Fox, *Lucky Man: A Memoir*, 2002].

Rock **Fox**: Charles Meredith (1933–), Ir. jazz musician. The musician adopted his stage name in 1952, when his apprenticeship as a solicitor (lawyer) prohibited him from taking another job.

Sidney **Fox**: Sidney Liefer (1910–1942), U.S. movie actress.

Steven **Fox**: Jules G. Furthman (1888–1966), U.S. screenwriter. Furthman signed his earliest films by his full name, Julius Grinnell Furthman, but in 1918 adopted the name Steven Fox, probably as a consequence of general anti–German feeling at that time. Two years later, however, his name on the credits was Jules Furthman, a slightly modified form of the original, and remained as such.

William **Fox**: Wilhelm Fried Fuchs (1879–1952), Hung.-born U.S. movie executive, of Ger. Jewish parentage. The name of the movie mogul, the Fox of "Twentieth Century–Fox," was americanized when his family immigrated to the USA in 1880.

Fanne **Foxe**: Annabel Battistella (1936–), Argentinian striptease artist. The stripper's stage name seems to suggest "foxy fanny."

Jamie **Foxx**: Eric Morlon Bishop (1967–), U.S. stand-up comedian. The comedian adopted his gender-neutral name in 1989 on discovering that it was easier for women to get stage time at "open mics," when members of the public were encouraged to perform. "The way I looked at it was," he said at the time, "if I fail as Jamie Foxx I'll just change my name and come back as somebody else."

John **Foxx**: Dennis Leigh (*c*.1950–), Eng. rock musician.

Redd **Foxx**: John Elroy Sanford (1922–1991), U.S. movie, TV comedian. The comedian, a fan of the Chicago Red Sox baseball team, was already known by his nickname "Chicago Red," partly in reference to his red hair. He added an extra "d" to the second word of this and took his new surname from the baseball star Jimmie Foxx (1907–1967), who at one time played for that team. The name as a whole was further suggested by the red fox featuring in children's books.

Nita **Foy**: Anita Fay Tipping (*c*.1910–1930), Eng. stage, movie actress.

Eddie **Foy**: Edwin Fitzgerald (1856–1928), U.S. comedian. The comic changed his name at age 16 because he felt that his original surname sounded too Irish. Two of the 11 children born to four-times-married Foy were the movie actors Bryan Foy (1896–1977) and Eddie Foy, Jr. (1910–1983).

F.P.A.: Franklin Pierce Adams (1881–1960), U.S. journalist, humorist. The writer usually signed his columns with his initials.

Fra ... For names beginning thus, see the next word, e.g. for Fra Angelico see **Angelico**, for Fra Bartolommeo see **Bartolommeo**, for Fra Diavolo see **Diavolo**, etc.

Frack *see* **Frick**

Harry **Fragson**: Léon Vince Philippe Pott (originally Fragmann) (1869–1913), Eng. music-hall comedian, singer, of Belg. parentage. "He first chose the stage name Frogson, which he later diplomatically changed to Fragson" [Jacques Pessis and Jacques Crépineau, *The Moulin Rouge,* 1990].

Janet **Frame:** Janet Paterson Frame Clutha (1924–2004), N.Z. novelist. The writer legally adopted the additional surname of Clutha, taking it from a river that was important in her childhood. (It enters the sea south of Dunedin, where she was born.)

Maud Jeanne **Franc:** Matilda Jane Evans (1827–1886), Eng.-born Austral. children's writer.

Celia **Franca:** Nita Celia Franks (1921–2007), Eng. ballet dancer, choreographer, working in Canada.

Pietro **Francavilla:** Pierre de Francheville (*c.*1548–1615), Fr. sculptor, working in Italy. The artist came to be known by the Italian equivalent of his French name.

Alexis **France:** Alexis McFarlane (1906–), Rhodesian-born Br. stage actress.

Anatole **France:** Jacques-Anatole-François Thibault (1844–1924), Fr. novelist, poet, dramatist. The writer assumed his pseudonym not so much to emphasize his nationality as to mark the fact that his father, François-Noël Thibault, who owned a bookshop, was called "Monsieur France" by his customers, this being a local form of François. (When he opened the shop in 1839 he called it the "Librairie politique de France Thibault," a name which in 1844 became "Librairie politique ancienne et moderne de France," as if referring to the country.)

Victor **Francen:** Victor Franssen (1888–1977), Belg. movie actor, working in U.S.

Paula **Frances:** Paula Frances Muldoon (1969–), Br. TV actress.

Mother **Frances Mary Theresa:** Frances Ball (1794–1861), Eng. religious founder of Loretto nuns, Ireland.

Franco **Franchi:** Franco Benenato (1922–1992), It. movie comedian, teaming with Ciccio Ingrassia (1923–).

Francesco **Francia:** Francesco di Marco di Giacomo Raibolini (*c.*1450–1517), It. painter.

Franciabigio: Francesco di Cristofano (1484–1525), It. painter.

Tony **Franciosa:** Anthony George Papaleo (1928–2006), U.S. movie actor, of It. origin.

Arlene **Francis:** Arlene Francis Kazanjian (1907–2001), U.S. TV personality, of Armenian parentage.

Arthur **Francis:** Ira Gershwin (1896–1983), U.S. songwriter. Ira **Gershwin** used this name when, after an abortive literary start, he began writing the lyrics for his brother George's songs in the 1920s.

Connie **Francis:** Concetta Rosa Maria Fran-

conero (1938–), U.S. pop singer, movie actress, of It. descent. The singer appeared as an 11-year-old on Arthur Godfrey's TV talent show, and he suggested her new name as her existing name was long to remember and difficult to pronounce.

Doris **Francis:** Doris Akast (1903–?), Br. stage actress, singer.

Joan **Francis:** Joan Francis Willi (1920–1995), Eng. actress.

Kay **Francis:** Katherine Edwina Gibbs (1899 or 1903–1968), U.S. stage, movie actress. The actress's stage name came from that of her first husband, James Dwight Francis (married 1922).

Matthew **Francis:** Francis Edwin Matthews (1953–), Br. theatrical producer.

M.E. **Francis:** Mary Elizabeth Blundell, née Sweetman (1859–1930), Ir. novelist. The writer adopted the first name of her husband, Francis Nicholas Blundell (1853–1884).

Jan **Francisci:** Janko Rimavský (1822–1905), Slovakian writer, journalist, patriot.

Franciscus a Sanctâ Clarâ: Christopher Davenport (1598–1680), Eng. theologian. The Franciscan friar took a name for his missionary work meaning "Francis of St. Clare," referring to St. **Francis of Assisi** and his follower and helper, St. Clare.

[St.] **Francis of Assisi:** Giovanni di Pietro di Bernadone (1182–1226), It. monk, preacher. The generally accepted origin of the saint's name is as follows. His father was away on business in France at the time of his son's birth and on his return changed the baby's name to Francesco (Francis), partly as a memorial to his visit, but also because the child's mother was a Frenchwoman, from Provence.

"According to one tale, which if not true would be none the less typical, the very name of St. Francis was not so much a name as a nickname. There would be something akin to his familiar and popular instinct in the notion that he was nicknamed very much as an ordinary schoolboy might be called 'Frenchy' at school. According to this version, his name was not Francis at all but John; and his companions called him 'Francesco' or 'The little Frenchman' because of his passion for the French poetry of the Troubadours. The more probable story is that his mother had named him John in the absence of his father, who shortly returned from a visit to France, where his commercial success had filled him with so much enthusiasm for French taste and social usage that he gave his son the new name signifying the Frank or Frenchman. In either case the name has a certain significance, as connecting Francis from the first with what he himself regarded as the romantic fairyland of the troubadours" [G.K. Chesterton, *St. Francis of Assisi,* 1923].

Franco: Franco l'Okanga La Ndju Pene Luambo Makiadi (1938–1989), Zaïrian guitarist, bandleader. The musician's original name was Okanga Luambo Makiadi. He then expanded this as above in the 1970s following President Mobutu's *authenticité* (indigenization) campaign, which involved the renaming of the country (from Congo) together with its main provinces and cities. In 1981 he converted to Islam and adopted the name Aboubakar Sidiki.

Harry Franco: Charles Frederick Briggs (1804–1877), U.S. journalist, author.

André François: Andre Farkas (1915–2005), Rom.-born Fr. cartoonist, illustrator. The artist adopted a typically unobtrusive French name on becoming a French citizen in the 1930s.

M. François: Alexandrine Sophie Bawr (1773–1860), Fr. pianist, writer, composer. The daughter of the Marquis Goury de Champgrand used this name for her literary works (novels, short stories, children's stories), keeping Mme. de Saint Simon and Mme. de Bawr for her musical compositions (romances, comedies, melodramas). The latter two names refer to her two husbands: Frenchman Claude-Henry de Rouvroy, Comte de Saint-Simon, and Russian officer Baron de Bauer.

Jacob Frank: Jacob Leibowicz (1726–1791), Pol. Jewish false messiah.

Pat Frank: Harry Hart Frank (1907–1964), U.S. novelist.

Melvin Franklin: David English (1942–1995), U.S. black Motown singer.

Sydney Franklin: Sydney Frumkin (1903–?), U.S. bullfighter, movie actor. The actor should not be confused with the U.S. movie producer and director Sidney Franklin (1893–1972).

Frankmusik: Vincent Frank (1985–), Br. pop musician.

Mary Frann: Mary Luecke (1943–1998), U.S. TV actress.

Dennis Franz: Dennis Schlachta (1944–), U.S. TV actor.

Emma Franz: Marie von Pelzeln (1830–1894), Austr. writer.

Robert Franz: Robert Franz Knauth (1815–1892), Ger. composer.

Frascuelo: Salvador Sánchez Povedano (1842–1898), Sp. bullfighter. The name, a pet form of Francisco (Francis), was later taken by other matadors, such as Carlos Escolar Martín (1948–).

James Fraser: Alan White (1924–), Eng. crime novelist, journalist. White also wrote under the names Alec Haig and Alec Whitney.

Liz Fraser: Elizabeth Winch (1933–), Eng. movie, TV actress. The actress originally played

under her real name. She then took the name Elizabeth Fraser, but finally adopted the short form of her first name.

Jane Frazee: Mary Jane Frehse (1918–1985), U.S. singer, movie actress. A phonetic modification of a European name for the benefit of an English-speaking audience.

Robert Caine Frazer *see* Gordon **Ashe**

Philip Frazier: Philip Fraser (*c.*1958–), Jamaican reggae singer.

Freaky Tah: Raymond Rodgers (1971–1999), U.S. black rapper.

Fred: Othon Aristides (1931–), Fr. cartoonist.

John Fred: John Fred Gourrier (1941–2005), U.S. black blues singer.

Frédéric: Pierre Frédéric Malaverne (1810–1872), Fr. ballet dancer, director, teacher, working in Russia.

Harold Frederic: Harold Henry Frederick (1856–1898), U.S. journalist, novelist. Frederick dropped the final "k" from his surname early in his career in order to present himself as a distinctive writer. He used the pseudonym George Forth for the novel *March Hares* (1896) so as not to upset sales of *The Damnation of Theron Ware*, his best-known work, published that same year.

Frédérick: Antoine-Louis Prosper Lemaître (1800–1876), Fr. actor. The actor adopted his grandfather's name as his stage name.

John Frederick *see* Max **Brand**

Pauline Frederick: Beatrice Pauline Libbey (1883–1938), U.S. stage, movie actress.

Vera Fredowa: Winifred Edwards (1896–1989), Eng. ballet dancer, teacher. A Russian-style name created from the dancer's original first name.

Free I: Jeff Samuel Dixon (1946–1987), Jamaican radio broadcaster, reggae musician.

Nicolas Freeling: Nicolas Davidson (1927–2003), Br. novelist, detective-story writer.

Mrs. Freeman: Sarah Churchill, Duchess of Marlborough (1660–1744), Eng. aristocrat. This was the significant name adopted by the duchess for her correspondence with Queen Anne (Mrs. **Morley**).

Cynthia Freeman: Beatrice Cynthia Feinberg, née Freeman (?1915–1988), U.S. romantic novelist, of Ger. Jewish parentage. Following a career in interior design, Freeman turned to writing novels, first using her pseudonym (her middle name and maiden name) for *A World Full of Strangers* (1975).

Joseph Freeman: Joseph Lvovovitch (1897–1965), Ukr.-born U.S. writer. Freeman's father changed the family's Jewish name following their immigration to the United States in 1904.

Fréhel: Marguerite Boulc'h (1891–1951), Fr. music-hall singer, movie actress. The actress was of

Breton origin and took her stage and screen name from Cape Fréhel, Brittany.

Bruno **Frei:** Benedikt Freistadt (1897–1988), Austr. journalist, writer.

Olive **Fremstad:** Olivia Rundquist (1871–1951), Swe. opera singer. The singer took the name of her adoptive parents, with whom she emigrated to the U.S. when in her early teens. She subsequently became an American citizen.

Ashley **French** *see* Denise **Robins**

Charles K. **French:** Charles E. Krauss (1860–1952), U.S. movie actor.

Nicci **French:** Nicci Gerrard (1958–), Eng. crime novelist + Sean French (1959–), Eng. crime novelist, her husband. The authors of psychological thrillers also write individually.

Peter **French:** John Nicholas ffrench (1935–), Welsh stage, TV actor.

Mirella **Freni:** Mirella Fregni (1935–), It. opera singer. The soprano adopted a simplified spelling of her name for international use.

Pierre **Fresnay:** Pierre-Jules-Louis Laudenbach (1897–1975), Fr. stage, movie actor.

Sami **Frey:** Samuel Frei (1937–), Fr. movie actor.

Frick: Werner Fritz Groebli (1915–2008), Swiss-born U.S. ice-skating comedian. Groebli formed a partnership with Hansruedi Mauch and the two regularly teamed together as Frick and Frack, "Clown Kings of the Ice." After Mauch died in 1979, Groebli performed alone as Mr. Frick.

Samri **Frickell** *see* Anthony **Abbot**

Janie **Frickie:** Jane Fricke (1947–), U.S. country singer. The singer adjusted the spelling of her name to avoid any mispronunciation.

Jan **Fridegard:** Johan Fridolf Johansson (1897–1968), Swe. writer.

Egon **Friedell:** Egon Friedmann (1878–1938), Austr. stage actor, writer.

Donald **Friend:** Donald Stuart Leslie Moses (1915–1989), Austral. painter, illustrator, writer. The artist adopted his mother's maiden name following a family quarrel in the 1920s.

Aunt **Friendly:** Sarah S.T. Baker (1824–1906), Br. children's writer.

Fred **Friendly:** Ferdinand Wachenheimer (1915–1998), U.S. TV producer.

William **Friese-Greene:** William Edward Green (1855–1921), Eng. photographer, inventor. The motion-picture pioneer married Victoria Marina Friese as his first wife in 1874 and joined her name to his own, adding an "e" to his surname to match the one ending hers.

Trixie **Friganza:** Brigid O'Callaghan (or Delia O'Callahan) (1870–1955), U.S. actress, singer, of Sp.-

Ir. origin. The entertainer adopted her mother's maiden name as her stage name.

Freddie **Frinton:** Frederick Hargate (1911–1968), Eng. stage, TV, movie comedian.

Joe **Frisco:** Louis Wilson Joseph (*c*.1890–1958), U.S. vaudeville, movie actor.

Frisco Kid: Stephen Wray (*c*.1970–), Jamaican DJ, reggae musician.

Willy **Fritsch:** Wilhelm Egon Fritz (1901–1973), Ger. movie actor.

Joachim **Frizius:** Robert Fludd (1574–1637), Eng. physician, Rosicrucian writer. He also wrote as Rudolf Otreb, an anagram of his name in the variant spelling Robert Floud.

Gert **Fröbe:** Karl-Gerhart Froeber (1913–1988), Ger. movie actor.

David **Frome** *see* Leslie **Ford**

Frost: Arturo Molina, Jr. (1964–), U.S. rapper, of Mexican descent. The musician originally performed as Kid Frost, but dropped the prefix in 1995.

Frederick **Frost** *see* Max **Brand**

Sadie **Frost:** Sadie Liza Vaughan (1967–), Br. movie, TV actress.

Fru-Fru: Teresa de la Parra (1889–1936), Fr.-born Venezuelan novelist, short-story writer. The writer's full original name was Ana Teresa Parr Sanojo, but she adopted the pseudonym Fru-Fru, from a Spanish equivalent of French *froufrou*, a word used to imitate the rustling of a dress. Presumably this came from a (possibly childhood) nickname.

Christopher **Fry:** Christopher Fry Harris (1907–2005), Eng. playwright. The writer adopted his middle name, his maternal grandmother's maiden name, on becoming a schoolteacher at age 18.

John **Fubister:** Isabelle Gunn (1781–1861), Sc. adventuress. Gunn adopted this male name in 1806 when signing on with the Hudson's Bay Company as part of a crew that in 1807 set sail aboard the *Prince of Wales* for the Nor' West. Her sex was revealed when she gave birth to a son at the company post, and in 1809 she and her infant returned to Scotland, where she resumed the name of Gunn.

Elmer **Fudpucker:** Hollis Champion (1935–), Can. country & western singer, comedian.

Fujinoshin: Yagi Tesuya (1960–), Jap. sumo wrestler. The wrestler's fighting name means "true Fuji" (Japanese *Fuji* + *no*, "of" + *shin*, "true").

Fulcanelli: Jean-Julien Champagne (1877–1932), Fr. alchemist.

Sarah Jane **Fulks** *see* Jane **Wyman**

Blind Boy **Fuller:** Fulton Allen (1908–1941), U.S. blues singer. The blind singer based his name on his physical condition and his original first name.

Fu Manchu: David Bamberg (1904–1974), U.S. magician, son of **Okito**. Fu Manchu is the Chinese master villain in the stories by Sax **Rohmer**, beginning in 1912.

Joseph **Fume** *see* Stephen **Oliver**

Abel **Funnefello** *see* Bernard **Blackmantle**

Sofia **Fuoco**: Maria Brambilla (1830–1916), It. ballet dancer. Fuoco was a lively dancer, justifying her stage name, from Italian *fuoco*, "fire," "vigor."

Furkat: Zakirdzhan Khalmukhamedov (1858–1909), Uzbek poet, polemicist. The writer was obliged to resettle in Kashgaria (Chinese Turkistan) in order to escape reprisals following his mockery of the authorities. Hence his adopted name, meaning "separation," "alienation."

Robin **Furneaux**: Frederick William Robin Smith, 3d Earl of Birkenhead (1936–1985), Br. author, historian.

Yvonne **Furneaux**: Yvonne Scatcherd (1928–), Fr. movie actress, working in U.K.

Andrew **Furuseth**: Anders Andreassen (1854–1938), Norw.-born U.S. labor leader. "Furuseth" was the name of the cottage in which Andreassen was born.

Füruzan: Füruzan Yerdelen, née Selçuk (1935–), Turk. novelist. The writer adopted her first name as her pen name following the failure of her marriage.

Billy **Fury**: Ronald Wycherley (1941–1983), Eng. pop singer. The singer was renamed by impresario Larry Parnes, whose career in British rock and roll management began with his promotion of Tommy **Steele**. "Larry first asked Ronnie if he would like to be a professional singer, to which the shy young man simply replied, 'Yes.' 'Tell me again, what was your second name,' asked Larry. 'Wycherley' mumbled Ronnie. 'Well,' said Larry, ... 'we have to find a suitable name for you. Ronnie Wycherley is a nice name but doesn't really describe you. I think you look furious at times when you're singing. So Fury should perhaps be your second name. As for your first name, you have a boy next-door appeal, so we need something like Tommy, but you can't use that because of Tommy Steele. Maybe Bobby or Billy. Yes, Billy describes you perfectly. Billy. Billy Fury, we'll call you Billy Fury.' Already I was jealous of him. What a great name. Why couldn't Larry have christened me Billy Fury?" [Vince Eager, *Vince Eager's Rock n' Roll Files*, 2007].

Fusbos: Henry Edward Doyle (1827–1892), Ir.-born Br. painter, cartoonist. The artist presumably adopted the name of Fusbos, minister of state to Artaxaminous, king of Utopia, in William B. Rhodes's farce *Bombastes Furioso* (1810).

Henry **Fuseli**: Johann Heinrich Füssli (1741–1825), Swiss-born Br. painter, writer on art. The artist settled in England in 1764 and at first adjusted his name to Fusseli, a variant of Fuessli, an alternate spelling of his original German name. In 1770 he went to Italy, where he further altered his name to Fuseli, to match the Italian pronunciation, and retained this spelling on returning to England in 1779.

Futabatei Shimei: Hasegawa Tatsunosuke (1864–1909), Jap. novelist, translator.

Frances **Fyfield**: Frances Hegarty (1948–), Br. crime writer.

Rose **Fyleman**: Rose Amy Feilmann (1877–1957), Br. children's writer, of Ger. Jewish-Russ. parentage.

Bobby **G**: Robert Gubby (1953–), Eng. pop singer.

Gina **G**: Gina Gardner (1970–), Austral.-born Br. pop singer.

Johnny **G**: John Gotting (1949–), Eng. folk, pub rock singer.

Kenny **G**: Kenneth Gorelick (1956–), U.S. jazz saxophonist.

Warren **G**: Warren Griffin III (1970–), U.S. black "gangsta" rapper, half-brother of Dr. **Dre**.

Franceska **Gaal**: Fanny Zilveritch (1904–1972), Hung. movie actress, working in U.S.

Jean **Gabin**: Jean Alexis Moncorgé (1904–1976), Fr. movie actor. The actor adopted the same professional name as that of his father, a café entertainer.

Naum **Gabo**: Naum Neemia Pevsner (1890–1977), Russ.-born U.S. sculptor. The artist adopted a family name in 1915 for distinction from his brother, sculptor and painter Antoine Pevsner (1886–1962).

Dennis **Gabor**: Dénes Gábor (1900–1979), Br. electrical engineer, physicist, of Hung. origin. The inventor of holography was the son of Bertalan Günsberg, a Hungarian of Russian and Spanish Jewish origin, who changed his name to Gábor in 1899, the year he married an actress, Adrienne Kálmán.

Zsa Zsa **Gabor**: Sari Gabor (1923–), Hung. movie actress, working in U.S. "Zsa Zsa," a pet form of "Sari" (English "Sarah"), is pronounced "Za Za" by English speakers but "Zha Zha" (as in the Russian name "Zhukov") by Hungarians.

Gabriel: (1) James Friell (1912–1997), Sc. cartoonist, journalist; (2) Joseph Gabriel Wierzbicki (1958–), U.S. magician. Friell first used the name for political cartoons in the *Daily Worker* (from 1936).

Juan **Gabriel**: Alberto Aguilera Valadés (1950–), Mexican songwriter.

Gabrielle: Louise Gabrielle Bobb (1970–), Br. soul singer.

Gabrielli: Mary Meeke (?–?1816), Eng. novelist, translator. The pen name may be the maiden name of the writer, who was perhaps the wife of the Rev. Francis Meeke, whose widow died in 1816. If so, it suggests she was of Italian descent.

Gabriel of St. Mary Magdalen: Adrian Devos

(1893–1953), Belg. Discalced Carmelite, writer on mysticism, working in Italy.

Steve Gadd: Stephen K. Gadda (1945–), U.S. jazz drummer.

Antonio Gades: Antonio Estevez Ródenas (1936–2004), Sp. movie actor, flamenco dancer.

Mazhit Gafuri: Gabdulmazhit Nurganiyevich Gafurov (1880–1934), Russ. (Bashkir) writer.

Zoë Gail: Zoë Margaret Stapleton (1920–), S.A. stage actress, dancer, working in U.K.

Bessie Gaines: Bessie Ginzberg (1890–1973), U.S. concert pianist, painter. Gaines's father, Bernard Himmelhoff, originally from Russia, assumed the name Ginzburg around 1870. In 1909 she married Jesse L. Lasky, of Famous Players-Lasky, who gave Mary **Astor** her screen name.

Sarah Gainham: Sarah Rachel Ames (1922–), Br. novelist.

Serge Gainsbourg: Lucien Ginzburg (1928–1991), Fr. popular singer, songwriter, of Russ. Jewish parentage. The singer changed his first name, which he regarded as that of a typical hairdresser ("Lucien coiffeur pour hommes"). He had never liked it, anyway. He converted his Jewish surname to a French-style equivalent [Lucien Roux, *Serge Gainsbourg*, 1986]. His daughter, movie actress Charlotte Gainsbourg (1971–), kept the name.

Gais: R.G. Gaisford (1913–after 1958), Eng. cartoonist.

Nick Gaitano: Eugene Izzi (1953–1996), U.S. crime writer

Radola Gajda: Rudolf Gejdl (1892–1948), Cz. counterrevolutionary.

Gala Galaction: Grigore Pişculescu (1879–1961), Rom. novelist, theologian.

June Gale: June Gilmartin (1917–1996), U.S. movie actress, singer.

Philipp Galen: Ernst Philipp Karl Lange (1813–1899), Ger. novelist. An anagrammatic name that happens to suggest that of the 2d-century Greek physician Galen.

Vincenzo Galeotti: Vincenzo Tomaselli (1733–1816), It. ballet dancer, teacher, working in Denmark.

Fra Galgario: Vicente Ghislandi (1655–1743), It. painter.

Galib Dede: Mehmed Esad (1758–1799), Turk. poet. The writer's adopted name means "Grandfather Galib," the personal name meaning "victor," "conqueror." He also wrote as Seyh Galib, from his title as sheikh (superior) of the Galata monastery in Constantinople.

Leonora Galigai: Leonora Dora (c.1571–1617), It. adventuress.

Luxor Gali-Gali: Mahguob Mohammed Hanafi (1902–?), Egyptian-born U.S. magician.

Galimafré: Auguste Guérin (1790–1870), Fr. comic actor, teaming with **Bobèche**. The actor's stage name means "hotchpotch" (modern French *galimafrée*).

Boris Galin: Boris Abramovich Rogalin (1904–), Russ. writer.

Anna Galina: Evelyne Cournand (1936–), U.S. ballet dancer. The name perhaps combines those of two noted Russian artists, the dancer Anna Pavlova and the singer Galina Vishnevskaya.

G.A. Galina: Glafira Adolfovna Guseva-Orenburgskaya, earlier Einerling, née Mamoshina (c.1870–1942), Russ. poet, children's writer. A name created from the writer's initials and first name.

Shaukat Galiyev: Shaukat Galiyevich Idiatullin (1928–), Russ. (Tatar) poet.

Amelita Galli-Curci: Amelita Galli (1882–1963), It.-born U.S. opera singer. The second half of the singer's surname is that of her first husband, Luigi Curci (married 1908, divorced 1920). She became an American citizen in 1921.

Junius Gallio: Lucius Annaeus Novatus (c.5 BC–AD 65), Roman consul. Famous for dismissing the charges brought by the Jews against the apostle Paul (Acts 18:12–17), Novatus assumed his new name following his adoption by the senator Junius Gallio.

El Gallo: Rafael Gómez (1882–1962), Sp. bullfighter, brother of **Joselito**. The matador's ring name means "the cockerel."

William Galt: Luigi Natoli (1857–1941), It. novelist, journalist. The writer used this name for several historical novels, set in his native Sicily.

Galyorka: Mikhail Stepanovich Aleksandrov (1863–1933), Russ. revolutionary, writer, historian. This was a prerevolutionary name adopted by the activist better known as Mikhail **Olminsky**. It means "the gallery," as the writer explained at the end of his first published article: "I finished the article and thought: what pseudonym shall I use? ... I am a theater lover, and for some reason always end up in the gallery. I like being with the gallery audience, and feel at home among such people. And it is to you, my gallery-going colleagues, ... that I shall address my final words: I ask you to excuse me for daring to sign my personal article with our general collective name: Galyorka" [Dmitriyev, p.117].

Rita Gam: Rita Mackay (1928–), U.S. movie actress, of Fr. and Rom. descent.

Geoffrey Gambado: Henry William Bembury (1750–1811), Eng. artist, caricaturist.

Kenyon Gambier: Lorin Andrews Lathrop (1859–1929), U.S. diplomat, novelist. Lathrop was born in Gambier, Ohio, where his grandfather and father had attended Kenyon College. Before World War I, Lathrop used the name Andrew Loring for serial writing in magazines. When war broke out, "he wished to write on certain political subjects more freely than a member of the consular service could readily do. It became necessary to adopt another pen name, and thus 'Kenyon Gambier' came into being" [Tom Stamp, "Who was Kenyon Gambier?" in *Kenyon College Alumni Bulletin*, Summer/Fall 1997].

Abram **Games**: Abraham Gamse (1914–1996), Br. graphics designer, poster artist, of Latvian-Pol. Jewish parentage. The artist's father, a photographer, emigrated to London in 1904 and in 1926 changed the family name by simply transposing the last two letters. Games himself whimsically explained that he cut the "ham" from his first name because it wasn't kosher.

Gamgyusar: Aliguli Alikper Nadzhafov (1880–1919), Azerbaijani satirical poet, journalist. The writer's name means "woe," "sorrow," referring to the state of the capitalist and colonialist world as he saw it.

GAN: Gösta Adrian-Nilsson (1884–1965), Swe. painter. The artist was usually known by this initialism.

Peter **Gan**: Richard Moering (1894–1974), Ger. lyric poet, writer.

Zan **Ganassa**: Alberto Naselli (*c*.1540–*c*.1584), It. actor, theatrical company manager. The actor assumed the name of a character that he invented.

Abel **Gance**: Eugène Alexandre Péréthon (1889–1981), Fr. movie director. The moviemaker was the illegitimate son of a physician, Abel Flamant, and took his legal name from his mother, Françoise Péréthon, and his professional name from her boyfriend (later husband), Adolphe Gance.

Ganconagh: William Butler Yeats (1865–1939), Ir. poet, dramatist. Yeats adopted this name for the novella *John Sherman* and the short story *Dhoya*, published together in 1891. The ganconagh or ganconer is an amorous leprechaun-like fairy of Irish mythology, sometimes known in English as the "love talker."

Sir Gregory **Gander**: George Ellis (1753–1815), Eng. author. The writer used the name for *Poetical Tales by Sir Gregory Gander* (1778), which were immediately identified as coming from his pen.

Gandolin: Luigi Arnaldo Vassallo (1852–1906), It. satirical journalist, writer.

Gemini **Ganesan**: Rawamswamy Ganesh (1920–2005), Ind. movie actor. The actor took his screen name from the Gemini Studios, Madras (now Chennai), which he joined in 1946 as a casting assistant.

Sivaji **Ganesan**: Villupuram Chinniah Pillai Ganesan (1927–2001), Ind. movie actor. The actor took his screen name from the 17th-century emperor Sivaji, founder of the Maratha kingdom of India,

played by Ganesan as the central character of C.N. Annadurai's play *Sivaji Kanda Indhu Rajyam*.

Ganpat: Martin Louis Alan Gompertz (1886–1951), Eng. soldier, travel writer. A form of the writer's last name.

Joe **Gans**: Joseph Gant (1874–1910), U.S. black lightweight boxer. The boxer was said to be the son of an African-American baseball player, Joseph Butts. He was adopted at age four by Maria Gant and her husband. It is not clear why he altered her name to "Gans." It is possible this was her original name, misspelled "Gant" in sources.

Pedro de **Gante**: Peeter van der Moere (*c*.1486–1572), Belg. monk, missionary, working in Mexico. The Franciscan monk came to be known by a Spanish name meaning "Peter of Ghent," the latter being his birth town in what was then Flanders.

Kurt **Gänzl**: Brian Roy Gallas (1946–), N.Z. writer on music.

Ilija **Garasanin**: Ilija Savić (1812–1874), Serbian prime minister.

Henri **Garat**: Henri Garascu (1902–1959), Fr. movie actor, singer.

Garbo: Juan Pujol García (1912–1988), Sp. spy, working in U.K. The double agent, who was first taken on by the Germans in World War II to spy on the British, then by the British to work against the Germans, was given his British codename after Greta **Garbo** for his acting skills. He was known to the Abwehr as "Anabel." He had a number of imaginary agents, one being "Wren," after the acronymic nickname for a member of the Women's Royal Naval Service.

Greta **Garbo**: Greta Lovisa Gustafsson (1905–1990), Swe.-born U.S. movie actress. The star's original name is in no doubt. How she acquired her screen surname is less certain. The name is generally thought to have been given to her by the Swedish movie director Mauritz Stiller. But how did he devise it? One version says that he "toyed with Gabor after Gabor Bethlen, an ancient Hungarian king, then settled on the variation, Garbo" [Norman Zierold, *Garbo*, 1970].

A detailed account of the name origin is given by one of Garbo's many biographers: "The name, which became so memorable, was the invention of Mauritz Stiller, who had long cherished it and was determined to bestow it on an actress worthy of it. In his imagination the name suggested fairyland, romance, beauty, everything he had associated in his childhood with the utmost happiness and the wildest dreams. Many explanations were later offered to explain the name. Someone wrote that he derived it from the first letters of a sentence he wrote describing Greta Gustafsson: *Gör alla roller berömvärt opersonligt*

("Plays all roles in a commendably impersonal fashion"). Others remembered that *garbo* in Spanish and Italian is a rarely used word describing a peculiar kind of grace and charm. Still others imagined it was derived from the name of Erica Darbo, a famous Norwegian singer of the time. A more plausible explanation can be found in the *garbon*, a mysterious sprite that sometimes comes out at night to dance to the moonbeams. This elfin creature was a descendant of the dreaded *gabilun* of Swedish and German folklore, who was killed by Kudrun. The *gabilun* breathed fire from its nostrils and could assume any shape at will, and some memory of his ancient power remained in the *garbon*, just as Robin Goodfellow retains some features of the Great God Pan. No one knows the true origin of the word. When asked about it, Stiller simply looked up in the air, smiled, and said, 'I really don't know. But it's right, isn't it?'" [Robert Payne, *The Great Garbo*, 1976].

This does not exhaust the theories. Another is that Greta had visited some relatives who lived on a farm called "Garboda," and that may be the source [Frederick Sands and Sven Broman, *The Divine Garbo*, 1979]. A more recent biographer claims Stiller took it from Polish *wygarbować*, "to tan" (as in making leather): "'When I saw you for the first time, you were beautiful, but your beauty was not refined.... I said to myself, I must *wygarbować* this girl'" [Antoni Gronowicz, *Garbo*, 1990]. This origin is dismissed as "absurd" by a later writer, who offers his own theory. Stiller wanted a name that was "modern and elegant and international [and] says just as clearly who she is in London and Paris as in Budapest and New York." His assistant, Arthur Nordén, suggested "Mona Gabor," deriving it from Gábor Bethlen, a 17th-century Hungarian king. "Stiller rather liked it but kept trying out different variations: Gábor, GabOR, Gabro ... Garbo!" [Barry Paris, *Garbo: A Biography*, 1995]. Which is where we came in...

Garbo used other pseudonyms, among them Harriet Brown (her favorite), Gussie Berger, Mary Holmquist, Jean Clark, Karin Lund, Miss Swanson (surely misleading?), Emily Clark, Jane Emerson, Alice Smith, and the unexpected male name Karl Lund.

José Luis **Garci:** José Luis Garci Monoz (1944–), Sp. movie director, screenwriter.

Andy **Garcia:** Andrés Arturo García Menéndez (1956–), Cuban-born U.S. movie actor.

Jules Auguste **Garcin:** Jules Auguste Salomon (1830–1896), Fr. orchestral conductor. The musician adopted the name of his maternal grandmother.

Joyce **Gard:** Joyce Reeves (1911–), Br. children's writer, sister of poet James (originally John Morris) Reeves (1909–1978).

Carlos **Gardel:** Charles Romuald Gardés (1890–1935), Fr.-born movie actor, working in Argentina.

Helen Hamilton **Gardener:** Alice Chenoweth (1853–1925), U.S. writer, suffragist. The writer used various pseudonyms for her short stories and essays before finally settling on this name.

Vincent **Gardenia:** Vincent Scognamiglio (1922–1992), It.-born U.S. movie actor. The actor began his career at the age of five as the main character in *The Shoeshine Boy*, an Italian play presented by the Gennaro Gardenia Company, his father's group, who performed in Italian for Italian-American audiences.

Arthur **Gardner:** Arthur Goldberg (1910–), U.S. movie producer.

Ava **Gardner:** Ava Lavinia Gardner (1922–1990), U.S. movie actress. A number of sources give the actress's "real" name as Lucy Johnson. But she was born the daughter of Jonas Bailey Gardner and Mary Elizabeth Balcer, of Brogdon, North Carolina [1. John Daniell, *Ava Gardner*, 1982; 2. Ava Gardner, *Ava: My Story*, 1990].

Ed **Gardner:** Edward Poggenberg (1901–1963), U.S. TV actor.

Noel **Gardner** *see* C.L. **Moore**

S.S. **Gardons:** William De Witt Snodgrass (1926–), U.S. poet. The pseudonym is an obvious anagram of the poet's surname.

Allen **Garfield:** Allen Goorwitz (1939–), U.S. movie actor. From 1978 through 1983 the actor was billed under his real name.

John **Garfield:** Jacob Julius Garfinkle (1913–1952), U.S. stage, movie actor. The actor used the stage name Jules Garfield until Warner Bros. changed "Jules" to "John" in 1938.

N. **Garin:** Nikolay Georgiyevich Mikhaylovsky (1852–1906), Russ. novelist. The writer was obliged to take a new name to be distinguished from his near namesake, Nikolay Konstantinovich Mikhaylovsky, editor of *Russkoye bogatstvo* ("Russian Riches"), the magazine in which he was first published. For his first article, "A few words about the Siberian railway," he thus took the name *Inzhener-praktik*, "Practicing Engineer." But this would obviously not be suitable for a fictional work, for which he adopted a name based on Garya, the diminutive form of Georgy, his son's name. He later joined his new name to the original, giving the surname Garin-Mikhaylovsky [Dmitriyev, p.73].

Robert **Garioch:** Robert Garioch Sutherland (1909–1981), Sc. poet, translator.

Troy **Garity:** Troy Fonda (1974–), U.S. movie actor. The son of Jane Fonda (1937–), grandson of Henry Fonda (1905–1982), nephew of Peter Fonda (1939–), and cousin of Bridget Fonda (1964–) was given a new surname by his parents, that of his paternal grandmother, in a bid to protect his anonymity as a member of the famous acting dynasty.

Beverly **Garland:** Beverly Lucy Fessenden (1926–), U.S. movie, TV actress. The actress was billed as Beverly Campbell in her debut in the thriller *D.O.A.* (1949).

Judy **Garland:** Frances Ethel Gumm (1922–1969), U.S. movie actress, singer. The actress made her stage debut at the age of three, appearing with her two older sisters, Mary Jane and Dorothy Virginia, as the Gumm Sisters. When she was 12, they were renamed by their agent, George Jessel. "He had only one problem with the Gumm sisters. When he introduced them, he noticed that their name, which rhymed with words like 'bum,' 'crumb,' 'dumb' and 'scum,' made the audience snicker. 'These kids should have a new name!' he told Ethel [Gumm, Judy's mother]. 'I think so too,' she replied, and happily accepted his alternative: Garland, after Jessel's friend Robert Garland, the drama critic of the *New York World-Telegram*. Though Ethel used 'Gumm' a few more times — a typographical error found one theater advertising the Glum Sisters — the Garland Sisters they now were, and the Garland Sisters they remained" [Gerald Clarke, *Get Happy: The Life of Judy Garland*, 2000].

The following year, Judy adopted her new first name. "Babe had never liked either her given name, Frances, or her nickname, Babe ... and in the summer of 1935 she renamed herself Judy, after a Hoagy Carmichael and Sammy Lerner song about a girl with a voice as fresh as spring. From then on she stubbornly refused to respond to 'Babe' or 'Frances' ... 'Judy' was the only name she answered to, and it was for Judy — Judy Garland — that Hollywood finally opened its doors" [ibid.]. The song opens with: "If her voice can bring / Every hope of spring, / That's Judy, / My Judy," and ends with: "If she seems a saint / And you find that she ain't, / That's Judy." The words would have appealed to the young star.

Elizabeth **Garner:** Elma Napier, earlier Gibbs, née Gordon-Cumming (1892–*c*.1975), Sc.-born novelist, short-story writer, working in Dominica. The writer adopted her mother's maiden name for her novels, set in Dominica.

Graham **Garner** *see* Fenton **Brockley**

James **Garner:** James Scott Baumgarner (1928–), U.S. movie actor.

Garofalo: Benvenuto Tisi (?1481–1559), It. painter. The artist came to be known by his nickname, said to derive from his inclusion of a gillyflower (Italian *garofano*) in a corner of his paintings.

Garou: Pierre Garand (1972–), Fr.-Can. popular singer.

Andrew **Garran:** Andrew Gamman (1825–1901), Eng.-born Austral. journalist, politician.

Edward **Garrett:** Isabella Mayo, née Fyvie (1843–1914), Br. novelist, of Sc. parentage. The writer took her occasional pen name from the elderly main characters, brother and sister Edward and Ruth Garrett, in her first novel, *The Occupations of a Retired Life* (1868).

Leif **Garrett:** Leif Per Nervik (1961–), U.S. rock singer, movie actor.

John **Garrick:** Reginald Dandy (1902–1966), Br. stage, movie actor, singer. The actor's name presumably commemorates the famous English actor David Garrick (1717–1779).

Garrincha: Manoel Francisco dos Santos (1933–1983), Brazilian footballer. The sportsman adopted his childhood nickname, the word for a small bird. "Mané was a sweet child. As small as a wren, a *garrincha*, said his big sister Rosa, and the nickname stuck. Later he would be compared to a little bird for the way he flew past defenders" [Bellos, p. 97].

Charles **Garry:** Garabed Hagop Robutlay Garabedian (1909–1991), U.S. lawyer, of Armenian parentage.

[Sir] Richard **Garth:** Richard Lowndes (1820–1903), Eng. colonial lawyer. The chief justice of Bengal changed his name at the same time as his father, who did so on succeeding to the property of his mother, née Elizabeth Garth, in 1837.

Tishka **Gartny:** Dmitry Fyodorovich Zhilunovich (1887–1937), Belorussian revolutionary writer. The writer based his new name on *gart*, "tempering" (as of steel).

Andrew **Garve:** Paul Winterton (1908–2001), Eng. journalist, crime novelist. The writer used three pseudonyms for his crime fiction. He produced six books as Roger Bax between 1938 and 1951, then was Paul Somers for a time in the late 1950s. He adopted his best-known name in 1950 for *No Tears for Hilda*, the first of almost 30 domestic dramas.

Gary: Gary James Smith (1963–), Eng. cartoonist.

Romain **Gary:** Roman Kacewgary (later Kassevgari) (1914–1980), Fr. novelist, of Georgian Jewish origin. Gary devised a literary double for himself as Émile Ajar, under which name he won the Prix Goncourt in 1975 for *La Vie devant soi* ("The Life Before One").

"In 1977, [Barbara] Wright reviewed for the *TLS* the new work in French by Émile Ajar, at that time a sensation but also an enigma, since he refused to appear in public. The novel was teasingly called *Pseudo*. 'Who is Émile Ajar?' Wright asked. His books had been attributed to Roman Gary, who, Wright told readers, was Ajar's 'distant cousin.' In *Pseudo*, it happened that Ajar gave an account of his 'love-hate relationship with his ever-helpful cousin,' referred to by the sobriquet 'Tonton Macoute.' What's more, the narrator of a previous Ajar novel was a man called Cousin. Was it all a game on the part of Barbara Wright, intended to prompt readers of the *TLS* to deduce that Gary and Ajar were one and the same? In fact, the world learned the secret of Ajar's identity only after Gary's suicide in 1980" [*Times Literary Supplement*, March 20, 2009].

Pierre **Gascar:** Pierre Fournier (1916–1997), Fr. novelist, short-story writer.

Jonathan **Gash:** John Grant (1933–), Br. crime, mystery writer. The writer adopted his pseudonym from the slang word meaning "worthless," "superfluous."

A.P. **Gaskell:** Alexander Gaskell Pickard (1913–2006), N.Z. writer.

El **Gaskoina:** Jean Erratchun (1817–1859), Fr. Basque pelota player. The player's name means "The Gascon."

Gassendi: [Abbé] Pierre Gassend (1592–1655), Fr. philosopher, mathematician.

Kelly P. **Gast** *see* G.C. **Edmondson**

Peter **Gast:** Johann Heinrich Köselitz (1854–1918), Ger. composer.

Giacomo **Gates:** Giacomo Agostini (1950–), U.S. jazz singer.

Pearly **Gates:** Viola Billups (1946–), U.S. black popular singer. The singer was so named by her manager, Bruce Welch, who told her she had "better learn how to spell it." But how else could you spell such a heavenly name?

Gath: George Alfred Townsend (1841–1914), U.S. journalist, war correspondent, fiction writer. The name represents the writer's initials with also, one suspects, an oblique pun on the biblical exhortation, "Tell it not in Gath" (2 Samuel 1:20).

Henri **Gaudier-Brzeska:** Henri Gaudier (1891–1915), Fr. sculptor. The artist added the name of his Polish companion, Sophie Brzeska, to his own, as she added his to hers.

Gaultier-Garguille: Hugues Guéru (*c*.1573–1633), Fr. actor. The actor took this name for his parts in farces. For his less frequent appearances in serious plays his stage name was Fléchelles.

Paul **Gavarni:** Sulpice-Guillaume Chevalier (1804–1866), Fr. lithographer, painter. The artist acquired his "canvas name" by an unusual error. He once sent his drawings to a Paris exhibition from the picturesque Pyrenean village of Gavarnie. When displayed, the paintings were labeled as being by "Gavarnie," this name having appeared on the container. The exhibition was a success, and with a minor adjustment of spelling, the artist assumed the name attributed to him.

Yury Petrovich **Gaven:** Jan Ernestovich Dauman (1884–1936), Latvian Communist official.

Kid **Gavilan:** Gerardo González (1926–2003), Cuban-born U.S. boxer.

John **Gavin:** Jack Golenor (1928–), U.S. movie actor.

John **Gawsworth:** Terence Ian Fytton Armstrong (1912–1970), Eng. poet, critic, editor, horror-story writer.

William **Gaxton:** Arturo Antonio Gaxiola (1893–1963), U.S. stage actor, singer. The name appaers to have been suggested by the English printer William Caxton, with the first half of the actor's surname retained for distinction.

Francis **Gay:** Herbert Leslie Gee (1901–1977), Eng. "inspirational" writer, children's author. The northcountry writer, famous for *The Friendship Book* and his regular feature in newspapers such as the Scottish *Sunday Post*, selected a name that matched his "couthy [friendly], heart-warming" style. His new surname also reflects his original name (another book was titled *Gay Adventure*), while "Francis" was perhaps meant to suggest "Friendship." *The Friendship Book* still appears annually, and his feature weekly, although obviously both are now written or compiled by others. A companion publication to *The Friendship Book* is *The Fireside Book* of David **Hope**.

John **Gay:** Hans Gohler (1909–1999), Ger.-born Br. photographer.

Joseph **Gay:** John Durant Breval (?1680–1738), Eng. writer. There is evidence that the poet assumed the name, or was assigned it by the publisher Edmund Curll, to suggest an affinity or even identity with the well-known poet and playwright John Gay (1685–1732).

Maisie **Gay:** Maisie Munro-Noble (1883–1945), Eng. revue, movie actress.

Noel **Gay:** Reginald Moxon Armitage (1898–1954), Eng. popular songwriter, music publisher. The musician adopted the name when he was director of music and organist at St. Anne's Church, London. The aim was to avoid embarrassment to the church authorities, who might not have been too pleased to discover their director writing musicals. The name itself is a sort of reversal of "Merry Christmas," though this may not have been the composer's intention.

Peter **Gay:** Peter Froelich (1923–), Ger.-born U.S. historian. The future historian emigrated to the U.S. as a teenager and translated his name to the English equivalent.

Julián **Gayarré:** Gayarré Sebastián (1844–1890), Sp. opera singer.

Arkady **Gaydar**: Arkady Petrovich Golikov (1904–1941), Russ. writer. There is some doubt concerning the origin of the novelist's name. Shortly before his untimely death in World War II, he is said to have told his fellow combatants how he came by it in the final stages of the Civil War when serving on the Mongolian border: "A Mongolian would often run up to me, waving his cap and shouting 'gay-dar! gay-dar!' This was translated for me from the Mongolian to mean an outrider. So that was what my mates began calling me. It meant a lot to me, that word, it really did.... So you see, lads, I didn't take that name just because it sounded good!"

According to another theory, however, the name is a cryptonym, as follows: *G* is the initial of his original surname, *ay* represents the first and last letters of Arkady, and *dar* is a shortening of *d'Arzamas*, "of Arzamas," in the French manner (like d'Artagnan), meaning the town where Golikov was raised [Dmitriyev, pp.250–1].

Lisa **Gaye**: Lisa Griffin (1935–), U.S. movie actress, sister of actress Debra **Paget**

Marvin **Gaye**: Marvin Pentz Gay, Jr. (1939–1984), U.S. black Motown singer. The musician is said to have added "e" to his surname to ward off homosexual jibes. The altered spelling first appeared in 1961 in the credits of his first single, "Let Your Conscience Be Your Guide."

Catherine **Gayer**: Catherine Ashkenasi (1937–), U.S. opera singer.

Crystal **Gayle**: Brenda Gail Webb (1951–), U.S. country singer. After graduating in the late 1960s, Brenda Webb signed with USA Decca, the record label owned by her sister, country singer Loretta Lynn (1935–). As the label already had Brenda **Lee**, a new name was needed. The story goes that as the sisters drove past a sign for Krystal hamburgers, Lynn said, "That's your name. Crystals are bright and shiny, like you." Her new surname is a respelling of her middle name.

Newton **Gayle**: Muna Lee (1895–1965), U.S. poet + Maurice Guinness (1897–?), Ir. writer. The two authors collaborated under this name to write five mystery novels in the 1930s.

George **Gaynes**: George Jongejans (1917–), Finn. movie actor, working in U.S.

Gloria **Gaynor**: Gloria Fowles (1949–), U.S. pop singer.

Janet **Gaynor**: Laura Augusta Gainer (or Gainor) (1906–1984), U.S. movie actress. Laura's stepfather encouraged her to enter show business and is said to have suggested her screen name.

Mitzi **Gaynor**: Francesca Mitzi Marlene de Charney von Gerber (1930–), U.S. movie actress, singer, dancer. The actress is said to be a descendant of the Hungarian aristocracy. Hence the wealth of original names. Some sources give her real name as simply Francesca Mitzi Gerber.

Gayrati: Abdurakhim Abdullayev (1905–?), Uzbek poet. The writer's adopted name means "energetic," "lively."

Eunice **Gayson**: Eunice Sargaison (1931–), Br. movie, stage actress.

Ibragim **Gazi**: Ibragim Zarifovich Mingazeyev (1907–1971), Russ. (Tatar) writer.

Clara **Gazul**: Prosper Mérimée (1803–1870), Fr. novelist, historian. In 1825 Mérimée published *Le Théâtre de Clara Gazul*, a selection of six plays set in Spain. A foreword by one "Joseph Létrange" gave a biographical backgound to the lady and a portrait of her formed the frontispiece to the work. But the attractive female figure was really that of the 22-year-old author wearing a mantilla and a necklace.

Georg **Gé**: Georg Herman Grönfeldt (1893–1962), Finn. ballet dancer, choreographer.

Ged: Gerard Melling (1934–2007), Sc. cartoonist. The shortened form of the cartoonist's first name, adopted for his signature, was pronounced "Jed."

Nicolai **Gedda**: Nicolai Ustinov (1925–), Swe. opera singer, of Russ.-Swe. parentage. The tenor adopted his mother's maiden name.

Norman Bel **Geddes**: Norman Melancton Geddes (1893–1958), U.S. stage designer, architect. In 1916 Geddes married Helen Belle Sneider and added a masculine form of her middle name to his own. One of their two daughters was the Broadway actress Barbara Bel Geddes (1922–2005).

Dustin **Gee**: Gerald Harrison (1942–1986), Eng. TV comedian, teaming with Les **Dennis**.

Robbie **Gee**: Robert Grant (1970–), Br. black stage, TV actor.

Gee Bee: George Goodwin Butterworth (1905–1988), Eng. cartoonist, illustrator. The artist first used this name, representing his initials, for sports cartoons published in the *Daily Dispatch* from 1932.

Will **Geer**: Willem Aughe Ghere (1902–1978), U.S. stage, movie actor.

Frank **Gehry**: Ephraim Owen Goldberg (1929–), Can.-born U.S. architect. Goldberg changed his name after an architecture professor told him he was no good, a judgment he regarded as as anti–Semitic.

Max **Geldray**: Max van Gelder (1916–2004), Du. harmonica player, working in France, U.K., U.S.

Agnes **Gelencsér**: Agnes Körtvélyes (1927–), Hung. balletmistress, critic.

Otto **Gelsted**: Ejnar Jeppesen (1888–1968), Dan. poet.

Firmin **Gémier**: Firmin Tonnerre (1869–1933), Fr. stage actor, manager, director.

[Dame] Adeline **Genée:** Anina Margarete Kirstina Petra Jensen (1878–1970), Dan.-born Br. ballet dancer. The dancer adopted the stage name of her uncle, Alexander Genée, a ballet master and choreographer, while he chose her new first name for her, in honor of the singer Adelina Patti (1843–1919) (whose original first name was actually Adela).

Mme. **Geneive:** Selina Powell, née Hunt (1827–1863), Eng. circus artist, tightrope walker.

Pietro **Generali:** Pietro Mercandetti (1773–1832), It. opera composer.

General Kane: Mitch McDowell (1954–1992), U.S. black rapper. The musician originally recorded as General Caine, after an officer who had encouraged his talent when he was at military school.

Dee **Generate:** Roger Bullen (*c*.1961–), Eng. punk rock drummer.

Genêt: Janet Flanner (1892–1978), U.S. journalist, novelist, art critic. Flanner was resident in Paris, France, from 1922 and became noted for her biweekly "Letter from Paris" in the *New Yorker*, containing comments on French society and politics. Hence her French-style name, representing her first name.

Genghis Khan: Temujin (or Temuchin) (1162–1227), Mongol conqueror. The warrior-ruler adopted the title Genghis (or Chingis), meaning "perfect warrior," in 1206, adding "Khan" to mean "lord."

Marcelle **Geniat:** Eugénie Martin (*c*.1879–1959), Russ.-born Fr. stage actress. A name loosely based on the actress's two original names.

Orazio **Gentileschi:** Orazio Lomi (1563–1639), It. painter.

Johnny **Gentle:** John Askew (1941–), Eng. pop singer. The singer was given his new name by impresario Larry Parnes, whose career in rock and roll management began with his promotion of Tommy **Steele**.

A **Gentleman of the University of Oxford:** Percy Bysshe Shelley (1792–1822), Eng. poet. Shelley used this name or title for his early "Gothic horror" verses, *St. Irvyne, or the Rosicrucian* (1811), published privately when he was a student at Oxford University.

A **Gentleman who has left his Lodgings:** [Lord] John Russell (1792–1878), Eng. poet. The earl adopted this *nom de plume* for his *Essays and Sketches of Life and Character* (1820). The preface of this work is signed "Joseph Skillet," this being the supposed lodging-house keeper, who published the letters to pay the rent the "gentleman" had forgotten.

A **Gentleman with a Duster:** Harold Begbie (1871–1929), Eng. novelist, biographer, religious writer. The writer used this name for his analyses of political leaders, whom he aimed to "show up."

Bobbie **Gentry:** Roberta Lee Streeter (1944–), U.S. pop musician, of Port. descent. The singer took her stage name from the 1952 movie *Ruby Gentry*, with Bobbie a pet form of her first name.

Mme. **Geoffrin:** Marie-Thérèse Rodet (1699–1777), Fr. literary patron.

George I: William (1845–1913), Dan.-born king of Greece. Prince William (Vilhelm) of Denmark took the name George (Georgios) on becoming king of the Hellenes in 1863.

Ann **George:** Ann Snape (1903–1989), Eng. singer, TV actress. The actress adopted the first name of her first husband, George Snape, as her stage surname.

Chief Dan **George:** Geswanouth Slaholt (1899–1981), Can. Native American chief, movie actor.

Daniel **George:** Daniel George Bunting (1890–1967), Br. essayist, critic, anthologist.

Eliot **George:** Gillian Freeman (1929–), Eng. writer. The author used this name (presumably a reversal of George **Eliot**) for the novel *The Leather Boys* (1961). For the suspense thriller *Love Child* (1984) she wrote as Elaine Jackson.

Gladys **George:** Gladys Anna Clare (?1894–1954), U.S. stage, movie actress. The actress's stage career began at an early age, touring as a member of the vaudeville trio "The Three Clares," which became "Little Gladys George and Company" to boost her popularity as a child star. (Her commonly stated birth year of 1900 was probably the result of a promotional device to extend her years as such.)

Grace **George:** Grace Doughtery (1879–1961), U.S. stage actress, director. Doughtery changed her name in 1892 for professional purposes.

Heinrich **George:** Heinrich Georg Schulz (1893–1946), Ger. stage, movie actor.

Mlle. **George:** Marguerite-Joséphine Weymer (1787–1867), Fr. actress.

Screaming Mad **George:** Joji Tani (1956–), Jap.-born movie director, special-effects makeup artist.

Jim **Gérald:** Jacques Guenod (1889–1958), Fr. stage, movie actor.

Geraldo: Gerald Walcan-Bright (1904–1974), Br. danceband leader. The musician added the "o" to his first name in 1930 on his return to London after a visit to Argentina and Brazil to study Latin American music.

Paul **Géraldy:** Paul Lefèvre (1885–1983), Fr. writer.

E.D. **Gerard:** Emily Jane de Laszowski, née Gerard (1849–1905), Sc. novelist + Dorothea Mary Stanislaus Longard de Longgarde, née Gerard (1855–1915), Sc. novelist, her sister. The sisters first used this pseudonym, combining the initials of their first names, in 1879, before either were married.

Morice **Gerard:** [Rev.] John Jessop Teague (1856–1929), Eng. writer of historical romances.

Gerardo: Gerardo Mejia III (1965–), Ecuadorean-born U.S. rapper.

Steve **Geray:** Stefan Gyergyay (1899–1974), Hung. movie actor, working in U.K., U.S.

William **Gerhardie:** William Alexander Gerhardi (1895–1977), Russ.-born Eng. novelist. The writer added an "e" to his name in the 1960s, saying that Dante, Shakespeare, Racine, Goethe, and Blake had "e's" so why not he? [*The Times,* July 16, 1977].

Karl **Germain:** Charles Mattmueller (1878–1959), U.S. magician, of Ger. parentage. The illusionist took his name from the mysterious Comte de Saint-Germain (*c.*1707–1784), a French adventurer of unknown origin who was employed by Louis XV as a diplomat on confidential missions and who made a special study of the occult.

St. **Germaine:** Germaine Cousin (*c.*1579–1601), Fr. mystic.

[Sir] Edward **German:** Edward German Jones (1862–1936), Br. light opera composer. The composer dropped his surname, presumably for distinctiveness, some time in the 1880s, when a student at the Royal Academy of Music.

Geronimo: Goyahkla (*c.*1823–1909), Native American war leader. The chief of the Bedonkohe Apache was given his familiar name by the Spanish following his persistent raids into Mexico, presumably as a corruption of his battle cry rather than of his original name, which means "one who yawns." (Geronimo is actually an Italian equivalent of English Jerome.)

Gene **Gerrard:** Eugene Maurice O'Sullivan (1892–1971), Br. music-hall comedian, movie actor.

Wirt **Gerrare:** William Oliver Greener (1862–1946), Eng. novelist. The writer presumably based his pen name on his original name.

Kurt **Gerron:** Kurt Gerso (1897–1944), Ger. movie actor, director.

Squire **Gersh:** William Hirsback (1913–), U.S. bassist.

Karen **Gershon:** Karen Tripp, née Loewenthal (1923–1993), Ger.-born poet, novelist, working in England. The poet was Jewish, and at age 15 was sent to England for her own safety by her parents, who subsequently perished in the Holocaust. Her new name expressed her feeling of alienation, and was the name given by Moses to a son born in Midian as a "stranger in a strange land" (Exodus 2:22).

George **Gershwin:** Jacob Gershvin (1898–1937), U.S. composer, of Russ. Jewish parentage, brother of Ira **Gershwin**. Gershwin's father changed the original family name of Gershovitz to Gershvin, then to Gershwin.

Ira **Gershwin:** Israel Gershvin (1896–1983), U.S. lyricist, brother of George **Gershwin**.

Gérson: Gérson de Oliveira Nunes (1941–), Brazilian footballer.

Gersonides *see* **Ralbag**

John **Gerstad:** John Gjerstad (1924–), U.S. stage actor, producer, director, playwright.

Gertrude: Jane Cross Simpson, née Bell (1811–1886), Sc. poet, hymnwriter.

Sylvia **Geszty:** Sylvia Witkowsky (1934–), Hung. opera singer.

Estelle **Getty:** Estelle Scher Gettleman (1923–2008), U.S. movie, TV actress.

Stan **Getz:** Stanley Gayetzby (1927–1991), U.S. jazz saxophonist.

Tamara **Geva:** Tamara Zheverzheyeva (1908–1997), Russ. ballet dancer, working in U.S. The ballerina was billed under the name Sheversheieva for her first London performance in 1924. Her original name is spelled in some sources as "Gevergeyeva."

Raddowy **Gewe** *see* Eduard **Blutig**

Kofi **Ghanaba:** Kpakpo Akwei (1923–2008), Ghanaian drummer, bandleader. The musician's adopted name means "Friday son of Ghana," the African name Kofi denoting a person born on that day. In the 1960s and early 1970, when playing jazz in Chicago and London, Ghanaba called himself Guy Warren of Ghana.

Michel de **Ghelderode:** Adémar Adolphe Louis Martens (1898–1962), Belg. dramatist, prose writer.

Henri **Ghéon:** Henri Léon Vangéon (1875–1944), Fr. playwright.

René **Ghil:** René-François Guilbert (1862–1925), Fr. poet.

Domenico **Ghirlandaio:** Domenico di Tommaso Bigordi (1449–1494), It. painter. The artist's professional name denotes his early skill in making metal garlands (Italian *ghirlanda*).

Giacomino: Giacomo Cireni (1884–1956), It. circus artist, clown.

Gian Dauli: G. Ugo Nalato (1884–1945), It. novelist, publisher.

Joey **Giardello:** Carmine Orlando Tilelli (1930–2008), U.S. boxer.

Matthew **Gibb:** Matiozas Waytkeviczia (1920–2008), Sc.-born Royal Air Force navigator, of Lithuanian parentage.

Lewis Grassic **Gibbon:** James Leslie Mitchell (1901–1935), Sc. novelist, short-story writer. The writer adopted his mother's maiden name for his Scottish tales, keeping his real name for scientific and historical works. He first used it for *Sunset Song* (1932), the first in a trilogy of novels.

Georgia **Gibbs:** Freda Gibbons (1920–), U.S. pop singer.

Henry **Gibbs:** Henry St. John Clair Rumbold-Gibbs (1910–1975), Br. spy novelist.

Joe **Gibbs:** Joel Gibson (1940–2008), Jamaican reggae musician, record producer.

Michael **Gibbs:** Michael Clement Irving (1937–), S.A.–born composer, bandleader, working in U.S.

Terry **Gibbs:** Julius Gubenko (1924–), U.S. jazz musician.

Gibby: Leebert Morrison (*c.*1959–), Jamaican reggae musician.

Kahlil **Gibran:** Gibran Khalil Gibran (1883–1931), Lebanese poet, painter, working in U.S. Gibran's original name was formed by prefacing the name of his father, Khalil Gibran, with the surname of his paternal grandfather. In 1895 his mother left his father and took her children to Boston, Massachusetts, and when he started school there later that year a teacher shortened and misspelled his name as "Kahlil Gibran," which he adopted as his pen name.

Chloë **Gibson:** Chloë Cawdle (1899–?), Eng. stage director.

Harry **Gibson:** Harry Raab (1914–1991), U.S. jazz musician ("The Hipster").

Helen **Gibson:** Rose August Wenger (1892–1977), U.S. movie actress, of Swiss descent. The actress's screen surname is that of her husband, Hoot **Gibson.**

Hoot **Gibson:** Edmund Richard Gibson (1892–1962), U.S. cowboy movie actor. Gibson's nickname "Hoot" is said to derive from his boyhood habit of hunting owls, although an alternate account traces its origins to his time working as a bicycle messenger in California for the Owl Drug Company.

Madeline **Gibson:** Madeline Stride (1909–), Br. stage actress.

Tim N. **Gidal:** Ignaz Nahum Gidalewitsch (1909–1996), Israeli photographer, of Russ. Jewish parentage, working in Germany and U.S. The photographer adopted his professional name after one of his pictures was accepted by the German magazine *Münchner Illustrierte Presse* in 1929.

Charles Lewis **Giesecke:** Johann Georg Metzler (1761–1833), Ger. mineralogist, working in Ireland. The expert began his career as a composer and librettist, changing his name to Karl Ludwig Giesecke in 1781. He later settled in Ireland and anglicized his first two names.

John **Gifford:** (1) John Richards Green (1758–1818), Eng. writer; (2) Edward Foss (1787–1870), Eng. jurist, biographer. Green took his new name in 1781 on fleeing to France to escape his creditors. He retained it for all of his writings, including an abridgment of William Blackstone's *Commentaries on the Laws of England* (1765–70), which he did not live to complete. Foss took over the work and published his

own abridgment under the same name in 1820. Hamst was bemused by the situation: "It is most extraordinary that two persons should, about the same time, write abridgments of the same work, under the same pseudonym. But another extraordinary point is that John Richard [*sic*] Green died in 1818, five [*sic*] years before his abridgment was published!" [p.53]. Green also wrote as Humphrey Hedgehog.

Theo **Gift:** Theodora Boulger, née Havers (1847–1923), Eng. writer of children's stories, fantasy fiction. The writer's pen name is a part-translation of her first name Theodora, meaning "God's gift."

Marnix **Gijsen:** Joannes Alphonsius Albertus (or Jan-Albert) Goris (1899–1984), Belg. author, writing in Flemish.

Gilberto **Gil:** Gilberto Passos Gil Moreira (1942–), Brazilian popular musician.

Anthony **Gilbert:** Lucy Beatrice Malleson (1899–1973), Eng. writer of detective novels, short stories.

[Sir] Arthur **Gilbert:** Arthur Bernstein (1913–2001), Br. art collector, of Pol. parentage. In 1934 Bernstein married a dressmaker, Rosalinde Gilbert, went into business with her, and adopted her surname.

Billy **Gilbert:** William Gilbert Baron (1893–1971), U.S. movie actor.

E. Jayne **Gilbert** *see* **Rita**

George David **Gilbert:** Mary Lucy Arthur (*c.*1882–1919), Br. writer of historical romances, of Ir. descent.

Jean **Gilbert:** Max Winterfield (1879–1942), Ger. operetta composer.

John **Gilbert:** (1) John Gibbs (1810–1889), U.S. actor; (2) John Pringle (1895–1936), U.S. movie actor. Pringle adopted his stepfather's surname as his screen name.

Lou **Gilbert:** Lou Gitlitz (1908–1978), U.S. stage actor.

Paul **Gilbert:** Paul MacMahon (1917–1976), U.S. movie comedian, dancer.

Ray **Gilbert:** Ray Kalin (1912–1976), U.S. composer of popular songs, lyricist, of Russ. Jewish/Swe. parentage.

Gilbert & George: Gilbert Proesch (1943–), It.-born Br. painter, performance artist + George Passmore (1942–), Br. painter, performance artist, his partner.

Gilderoy: Patrick Macgregor (?–1638), Sc. robber, cattlestealer. The criminal's assumed name was perhaps ironically taken by him on the understanding that it meant "servant of the king," as if from Gaelic *gille,* "lad," "servant," and French *du roy,* "of the king." It actually represents Gaelic *gille ruadh,* "ruddy-faced (or red-haired) fellow." He was hanged in the year stated, thus giving the expression "to be hung higher than Gilderoy's kite," meaning "to be punished more severely than the worst criminal." The gallows outside Edinburgh where Gilderoy met his fate were 30 feet high.

Rex **Gildo:** Ludwig Alexander Hirtreiter (1936–1999), Ger. pop singer.

Giles: Carl Ronald Giles (1916–1995), Br. cartoonist.

Jack **Gilford:** Jacob Gellman (1907–1990), U.S. movie comedian.

Lord **Gilhooley:** Frederick Henry Seymour (1850–1913), U.S. humorist.

André **Gill:** Louis-André Gosset de Guines (1840–1885), Fr. caricaturist. The artist's original name was Louis-André Gosset, to which he added "de Guines" in the belief that he was the illegitimate son of the Comte de Guines.

Bartholomew **Gill:** Mark McGarrity (1943–), It.-born U.S. crime writer. McGarrity adopted his pen name from his maternal grandfather.

B.M. **Gill:** Barbara Margaret Trimble (1921–), Br. crime writer.

John **Gill:** John Russell Gillies (1920–2009), N.Z. crime, mystery novelist.

Patrick **Gill** *see* Gordon **Ashe**

Mildred **Gillars:** Mildred Elizabeth Sisk (1900–1988), U.S. Nazi radio propagandist ("Axis Sally"). When Mildred was seven her parents divorced, and soon after her mother married Robert Bruce Gillars, who gave her new surname.

Aidan **Gillen:** Aidan Murphy (1968–), Ir. movie, TV actor.

Daniel **Gillès:** Daniel Gillès de Pelichy (1917–1981), Belg. writer.

Geneviève **Gilles:** Geneviève Gillaizeau (1946–), Fr. movie actress.

Susan **Gillespie:** Edith Constance Turton-Jones (1904–1968), Br. novelist.

Irving **Gillette** *see* Henry **Burr**

Ann **Gillis:** Alma O'Connor (1927–), U.S. child movie actress.

Werner **Gillon:** Werner Goldman (1905–1996), Ger.-born Br. art historian, of Jewish parentage.

Ann **Gilmer** *see* Marilyn **Ross**

John **Gilmore:** Willi Hirsch (1908–*c*.1961), Ger.-born Russ. spy, working in U.S. The future Soviet agent adopted this name in 1932 on marrying an American, Dorothy Baker, in Philadelphia. When sent to Moscow as art editor of the magazine *Soviet Russia Today* in 1936 he traveled with a false passport in the name of Sidney Joseph Chamberlain, presumably cocking a snook at the British colonial secretary Joseph Chamberlain (1835–1914).

Virginia **Gilmore:** Sherman Virginia Poole (1919–1986), U.S. movie actress, of Br. parentage.

Barbara **Gilson:** Charles Gibson (1878–1943), Eng. soldier, writer of children's stories. Although mainly a writer of stories for boys, Gibson used the female name for adventure tales for girls.

Maria **Ginanni:** Maria Crisi (1892–1953), It. poet, novelist, playwright. The writer took her pen name from that of her husband, the futurist painter Arnaldo Ginna (originally Arnaldo Ginanni-Corradini).

Ginuwine: Elgin Baylor Lumpkin (1975–), U.S. black R&B musician. A "genuine" name.

Aleksandr **Ginzburg:** Aleksandr Arkadyevich Galich (1919–1977), Russ. satirical songwriter.

Vivi **Gioi:** Vivian Trumphey (1919–), It. movie actress, of part-Norw. parentage.

Giorgione: Giorgio Barbarelli (da Castelfranco) (1477–1510), It. painter. The painter's name, with its Italian augmentative suffix, means "big George." Giorgio Vasari's *Lives* (1550) notes: "Because of his physical appearance and his moral and intellectual stature he later came to be known as Giorgione."

Virgilio **Giotti:** Virgilio Schönbeck (1885–1957), It. poet, writing in Triestine dialect.

Albert **Giraud:** Marie Emile Albert Kayenbergh (1860–1929), Belg. poet, playwright, critic.

Girodet-Trioson: Anne-Louis Girodet de Roucy (1767–1824), Fr. painter, illustrator. The artist's adopted name was a combination of his own surname and that of a benefactor, one Dr. Trioson.

Maurice **Girodias:** Maurice Kahane (1919–1990), Fr. publisher. The founder in 1953 of the Olympia Press, notorious for publishing books of merit that were banned or censored in other countries, such as Vladimir Nabokov's *Lolita* (1955), was the son of an English Jewish father, Jack Kahane, and a French non–Jewish mother, Marcelle Girodias. He adopted his mother's maiden name during World War II.

Françoise **Giroud:** Françoise Gourdji (1916–2003), Fr. journalist, feminist, politician. The writer modified her surname after being rejected by her Turkish father.

E.X. **Giroux:** Doris Shannon, née Giroux (1924–), Can.-born U.S. crime writer. The pseudonym refers to the writer's maiden name, as after marriage she was "ex-Giroux."

Gisander: Johann Gottfried Schnabel (1692–?1750), Ger. writer. The author used this name for *Die Insel Felsenburg* ("Mountain Fortress Island") (1731–43), a four-part adventure in the style of *Robinson Crusoe*. According to the work's full descriptive title, the actual author was Eberhard Julius, and Gisander merely the editor. The name itself seems to derive from Schnabel's birthplace, Sandersdorf, near Bitterfeld, with "Gi-" representing the reversed initials of his first two names ("J" giving "i").

Dorothy **Gish:** Dorothy Elizabeth Gish (1898–1968), U.S. movie actress. Some sources give the actress's original name as de Guiche, as they do for her better-known sister Lillian **Gish**, but evidence seems to show that her father was actually James Lee Gish.

Lillian **Gish:** Lillian Diana Gish (1893–1993), U.S. movie actress. The actress's *Who's Who* entry gives her original name as de Guiche, as do some sources for her sister, Dorothy **Gish**.

Amos **Gitai:** Amos Weinraub (1950–), Israeli movie director.

Gertie **Gitana:** Gertrude Mary Ross, née Astbury (1887–1957), Br. music-hall singer. The singer derived her second name from the Spanish for "gypsy," referring both to her appearance (small, dark-haired, with ringlets) and to the pierrot costume she wore in her act. She was already performing as Little Gitana at the age of five. At about the age of 15 she substituted an alliterative "Gertie" for "Little," and became established under this name.

Giulio Romano: Giulio Pippi (*c.*1499–1546), It. painter, architect. The artist was born in Rome and came to be known by the name of his native city.

Gizziello: Gioacchino Conti (1714–1761), It. singer. The male soprano was so named after his teacher, Domenico Gizzi.

Ksaver Šandor **Gjalski:** Ljubomir Babic (1854–1935), Croatian poet.

Glamma Kid: Iyael Constable (1978–), Br. black reggae musician.

Glanffrwd: William Thomas (1843–1890), Welsh local historian. The scholar adopted a placename meaning literally "bank of the stream."

Glanmor: John Williams (1811–1891), Welsh antiquarian. The cleric's bardic name represents a placename meaning literally "big bank."

Brian **Glanville:** Brian Goldberg (1931–), Br. writer, sports columnist. In 2003 Glanville's son, opera singer Mark Glanville, published his memoirs under the punning title *The Goldberg Variations*.

Christine **Glanville:** Nancy Fletcher (1924–1999), Br. TV puppeteer.

Henricus **Glareanus:** Heinrich Loris (1488–1563), Swiss humanist, poet, musician. The scholar took his Latin name from his native canton of Glarus.

John **Glashan:** John McGlashan (1927–1999), Sc. cartoonist, painter. The artist began his career in London as a portrait painter, but finding work hard to come by dropped the "Mc" from his name and became a more financially rewarding cartoonist and illustrator.

Hannah **Glasse:** Hannah Glasse (*fl.* 1746), Eng. cookbook writer. In 1746 appeared *The Art of Cookery, Made Plain and Easy; which far exceeds any Thing ever yet Published. By a Lady*, long attributed to the writer John Hill (1716–1775) (who called himself "Sir" as a member of the Swedish order of Vasa). But the true author is now thought to be Mrs. Glasse.

Glasynys: Owen Wynne Jones (1828–1870), Welsh historian, writer. The writer adopted a placename meaning "green island" as his pen name.

Hertha **Glaz:** Hertha Glatz (1908–2006), Austr.-born U.S. opera singer.

Jackie **Gleason:** Herbert John Gleeson (1916–1987), U.S. movie comedian.

Joanna **Gleason:** Joanna Hall (1950–), Can. movie actress.

Gleb **Glebov:** Gleb Pavlovich Sorokin (1899–1967), Belorussian stage actor.

Igor **Glebov:** Boris Vladimirovich Asafyev (1884–1949), Russ. composer, musicologist. The musician used his pseudonym for musical criticism and books on individual composers.

Arlette **Glenny** *see* Marie **Glory**

Glenroy: Glen Mead Royston (1887–1919), U.S. magician. The dwarf magician was usually billed as "Glenroy the Midget."

Gary **Glitter:** Paul Francis Gadd (1944–), Eng. pop singer. According to some accounts, the singer's performing name originated as a nickname (with "Gary" suggested by his surname). Gadd began his recording career as Paul Raven, probably referring to his thick, black hair. In the late 1960s, he toured clubs in Frankfurt and Hamburg, Germany, under the name of Paul Monday. After considering other alliterative names such as Davey Dazzle, Horace Hydrogen, Turk Thrust, Terry Tinsel, Stanley Sparkle, and Vicky Vomit, he and his writer/producer Mike **Leander** settled on "Gary Glitter" in 1971.

Marie **Glory:** Raymonde Louise Marcelle Toully (1905–2009), Fr. movie actress. Gloty began her career in the days of the silent screen, and until 1927, when she took her regular name, she was billed as Arlette Glenny.

Fidenzio **Glottocrisio Ludimagistro:** Camillo Scroffa (*c.*1526–1565), It. poet. Scroffa used this mock-classical name for his *Amorosa elegia di un appassionato pedante al suo amatissimo Camillo* ("Amorous Elegy of a Passionate Pedant to his Most Beloved Camillo") (1562), parodying classicism.

Gluck: Hannah Gluckstein (1895–1978), Br. painter. The artist adopted her monosyllabic name because she regarded the sex of the painter as irrelevant. "On the backs of photographic prints of her paintings, sent out for publicity purposes, she always wrote in her elegant handwriting: 'Please return in good condition to Gluck, no prefix, suffix, or quotes.' She pronounced her chosen name with a short vowel to rhyme with, say, cluck, or duck" [Diana Souhami, *Gluck*, 1988].

Alma **Gluck:** Reba Fiersohn (1884–1938), Rom.-born U.S. opera singer. In 1902 the soprano married Bernard Glick, whose surname was an anglicization of German Glück. She first used the name Alma Gluck for a concert performance with the Metropolitan Opera Company at the New Theatre, New York, on November 16, 1909, in which she sang Sophie in Massenet's *Werther.* The surname was her preferred form of her married name, while her new first name was simply one that she liked.

Howard **Glyndon:** Laura Catherine Redden Searing (1840–1923), U.S. journalist, writer. Laura C. Redden, as she then was, adopted this male name for her contributions in the late 1850s to the *St. Louis Presbyterian* and *St. Louis Republican.* In 1861 she wrote an article ridiculing the repudiation by Missouri's secessionist governor Claiborne Fox Jackson of President Abraham Lincoln's call for 50,000 troops for the Union army. When editors of a St. Louis Confederate newspaper sought out "Howard Glyndon," discovered the writer's true identity, and ridiculed a mere "school girl" for interfering in politics, she replied with "An Appeal from Judge to Jury," urging Missouri to side with the Union. She long retained the male pen name, using it for her last book, *El Dorado* (1897).

Angela **Glynne:** Angela West (1933–), Br. stage actress. The actress took her mother's maiden name as her stage name.

Mary **Glynne:** Mary Aitken (1898–1954), Welsh-born Br. stage actress.

William **Glynne-Jones:** William Glyn Jones (1909–1977), Welsh novelist.

Gary **Go:** Gary Baker (1984–), Br. rock singer, songwriter. A dynamic name for a musical entrepreneur.

Tito **Gobbi:** Tito Weiss (1913–1984), It. opera singer.

Paulette **Goddard:** Pauline Marion Levy (1910–1990), U.S. movie actress. The actress adopted her divorced mother's maiden name as her screen name.

Thomas **Godden:** Thomas Tylden (1624–1658), Eng. Roman Catholic priest, polemicist.

John **Godey:** Morton Freedgood (1912–2006), U.S. crime, mystery writer.

Charles **Godfrey:** Paul Lacey (1851–1900), Eng. music-hall artist.

Elizabeth **Godfrey:** Jessie Bedford (?1854–1918), Eng. writer of romantic fiction.

Hal **Godfrey:** Charlotte O'Conor Eccles (1863–1911), Ir. journalist, novelist. The writer used this male name for her amusing novel *The Rejuvenation of Miss Semaphore* (1897).

William **Godfrey** *see* John **Christopher**

Mary **Godolphin:** Lucy Aikin (1782–1864),

Eng. writer. Aikin used this name late in life for some versions for young children of literary classics such as Aesop's *Fables* and Defoe's *Robinson Crusoe.*

Gog: Gordon Hogg (1912–1973), Eng. cartoonist. The artist was also racing and sports cartoonist on *The Sun* newspaper, for which he used the name Gay Gordon.

Y **Gohebydd:** John Griffith (1821–1877), Welsh journalist. The writer became the London correspondent of the Welsh newspaper *Baner Cymru* ("Banner of Wales"). Hence his byline, meaning "the correspondent."

Ziya **Gökalp:** Mehmed Ziya (1876–1924), Turk. sociologist, writer.

Menahem **Golan:** Menaheim Globus (1929–), Israeli movie producer, director, screenwriter.

Salomon von **Golaw:** Friedrich Freiherr von Logau (1604–1655), Ger. epigrammatist. The writer used this anagrammatic name for *Salomons von Golaw Deutscher Sinn-Getichte Drey Tausend* ("Salomon von Golaw's Three Thousand German Epigrams") printed in three volumes in 1654 as an enlarged and improved edition of a work originally published in 1638.

Harry **Gold:** Heinrich Golodnitsky (1910–1972), Russ.-born U.S. spy. Gold was taken to the United States in 1914 and became a U.S. citizen in 1922. He worked for Soviet intelligence in World War II.

Jimmy **Gold:** James McGonigal (1886–1967), Sc. comedian, teaming with Charles Naughton (1887–1976), Sc. comedian (as "Naughton and Gold").

Michael **Gold:** Itzok Isaac Granich (1894–1967), U.S. socialist writer, critic, of Rom.-Hung. Jewish parentage. The radical intellectual chose the name Michael Gold for the sake of anonymity during the government attack on radicals led by Alexander Palmer in the "Red Scare" period 1919–21.

Sid **Gold:** Solomon Borisovich Goldin (1887–1990), Russ. revolutionary, watchmaker, working in U.K. "Sid Gold ... adopted a prosaic English name which concealed a past lived in ... an atmosphere of plots, intrigues, bombs and revolution" [*The Times,* April 1, 1990].

Goldberg: William Scott Goldberg (1966–), U.S. wrestler.

Sonja **Goldberg:** Draga Balenovic (1947–), Austr. singer, writer, composer.

Whoopi **Goldberg:** Caryn Elaine Johnson (1955–), U.S. black movie actress, comedienne. A probably apocryphal story tells how movie colleagues nicknamed the actress Whoopi Cushion because of her problems with flatulence. She herself claims that she took her new name when "a burning bush with a Yiddish accent" suggested that her real name was boring and that she should change it [Blackwell, p.217]. Her new surname is that of her first husband.

Jack **Goldbird**: Drafi Deutscher (1946–2006), Ger. pop composer, of Hung. descent. This is just one of the many pseudonyms taken by the musician, both as performer and composer, in his desire to avoid personal publicity. Others were Baby Champ, Big Wig Wam, Ironic Remark, and Hektor von Usedom.

Harry **Golden**: Herschel Goldhirsch (1902–1981), U.S. journalist, of Austr. Jewish parentage. The journalist's family name was changed by immigration officials when they came to the United States in 1904. Herschel americanized his first name as Harry on graduating from public school in 1917.

Golden Gorse: Muriel Wace (1881–1968), Eng. children's writer. The identity of the author of *Moorland Mousie* (1929), the story of an Exmoor pony, was long a mystery. The book itself, heavily influenced by Anna Sewell's *Black Beauty* (1877), started a trend for anthropomorphized pony stories.

Abraham **Goldfaden**: Abraham Goldenfoden (1840–1908), Russ. Jewish poet, playwright, writing in Hebrew, Yiddish, working in U.S.

Emil Robert **Goldfus** *see* Rudolf **Abel**

Goldie: Clifford Joseph Price (1965–), Br. black rock musician, movie actor, of Jamaican-Sc. parentage. The musician was called Goldilocks as a child because of his blond dreadlocks. When he had them cropped, he shortened this nickname to "Goldie." But early in his career Price stayed for a time in his father's home in Miami, where he earned his living making and selling gold tooth caps. He took to wearing them himself, so that his original nickname acquired a different application, especially as in later life he had no locks at all.

Don **Goldie**: Donald Elliott Goldfield (1930–1995), U.S. jazz trumpeter.

GoldieLocks: Sarak Awkisome (19??–), Br. (white) MC, rapper. The name describes the musician's long blond hair.

Horace **Goldin**: Hirsh (or Hyman) Goldstein (1873–1939), Pol.-born U.S. magician.

Paul **Goldin**: Ronald Paul Gold (1928–), Br. stage hypnotist.

Olivia **Goldsmith**: Randy Goldfield (1949–2004), U.S. novelist.

Peter **Goldsmith**: John Boynton Priestley (1894–1984), Eng. novelist, essayist, dramatist + George Billam (?–?), Eng. writer. The two authors used this name for their cowritten play *Spring Tide* (1936).

Rev. J. **Goldsmith** *see* Abbé **Bossut**

Horace **Goldwin**: Hyman Goldstein (1873–1939), Polish-born U.S. illusionist.

Samuel **Goldwyn**: Shmuel Gelbfisz (1882–1974), U.S. movie producer, of Pol. Jewish parentage. When the future producer came to England in the 1890s, he anglicized his name as Samuel Goldfish. In 1916, he and his two brothers Edgar and Arch Selwyn formed the Goldwyn Pictures Corporation, its name formed from the first half of Goldfish and last half of Selwyn. He himself then adopted this name. (The other way around he would have been "Samuel Selfish.") In 1918 he officially adopted the name Samuel Goldwyn [A. Scott Berg, *Goldwyn: A Biography*, 1989].

Golia: Eugenio Colmo (1885–1967), It. caricaturist, painter, illustrator. The artist's assumed name is Italian for "Goliath," the biblical giant.

Ivan **Goll**: Isaac Lang (1891–1950), Ger. Jewish writer, working in France, U.S. Lang also used the pseudonym Iwan Lassang.

Mikhail **Golodny**: Mikhail Semyonovich Epshteyn (Epstein) (1903–1949), Russ. poet. The writer's new name means "hungry," relating to the period of deprivation in which he lived.

Golyddan *see* **Gweirydd ap Rhys**.

Gomer: Joseph Harris (1773–1825), Welsh writer. The Baptist minister's bardic name came from the chapel where he preached, Capel Gomer, Swansea. The name is biblical, as that of one of the grandsons of Noah (Genesis 10:2).

Agapy **Goncharenko**: Andrey Onufriyevich Gumnitsky (1832–1916), Ukr. writer, working in U.S.

Gong *see* **Azed**

Babs **Gonzales**: Lee Brown (1919–1980), U.S. black jazz singer. The singer is said to have chosen the name Gonzales so that he could claim to be Hispanic and so avoid Jim Crow laws while on tour, although another account says he picked it while acting as chauffeur for actor Errol Flynn in 1943. His new first name arose as a nickname. He and his brothers played basketball at a time when there was a star player called Big Babbiad. The three were thus Big Babs, Middlesized Babs, and (he) Little Babs.

Chilly **Gonzales**: Jason Beck (1971–), Can.-born (white) rapper, working in Germany. The name may pun on the spicy dish "chilli con carne," or on the Pat Boone hit song "Speedy Gonzales" (1962), the latter by way of a nickname.

Nelson **Gonzalves**: António Gonzalves Sobral (1919–1998), Brazilian crooner.

Silas M. **Gooch** *see* Sylvia **Bayer**

Lemmie B. **Good**: Limmie Snell (*c*.1945–), U.S. pop singer. A plainly punning name similar to that of William B. **Goodrich**.

Louis **Goodrich**: Louis Abbot-Anderson (*c*.1873–1945), Eng. stage, movie actor, brother of Allan **Aynesworth**.

William B. **Goodrich:** Roscoe ("Fatty") Arbuckle (1887–1933), U.S. movie comedian, director. Arbuckle adopted this name (implying "Will B. Good") on attempting to take up directing again after a ban of 11 years resulting from a scandal in 1921 in which a young actress, Virginia Rappé (1895–1921), was raped and died. Arbuckle was acquitted of his alleged crime less than a year later, but his reputation was ruined, and his career never recovered its former success. "No pseudonym was deemed necessary when the campaign to reinstate Arbuckle manifested itself in restaurant ventures and ... appearances in vaudeville" [Mitchell, p.17].

Goodwin: Robert Frederick Goodwin Churchill (1910–), Eng. cartoonist, illustrator.

Sam **Goody:** Samuel Gutowitz (1904–1991), U.S. record store entrepreneur. Gutowitz founded the record chain Sam Goodys, opening his flagship store in Manhattan in 1945.

Julie **Goodyear:** Julie Kemp (1942–), Eng. TV actress. The actress's parents separated when she was still a toddler, and when her mother later married Bill Goodyear, Julie adopted his name.

Goofy: Chad Simpson (1974–), Jamaican reggae musician.

Googoosh: Faegheh Atashin (1950–), Iranian pop singer.

Gregory **Goosequill** *see* **Orion** (1)

Gopi: V. Gopinathan Nair (1937–), Ind. movie actor, director.

Claudio **Gora:** Emilio Giordana (1913–1998), It. movie actor, screenwriter, director.

Ivan **Gorbunov-Posadov:** Ivan Ivanovich Gorbunov (1864–1940), Russ. writer, publisher. The writer was born in the *posad* (suburb) of Kolpino, near St. Petersburg, and added a name based on this word to his surname.

El **Gordito:** Antonio Carmona y Luque (1862–1920), Sp. bullfighter. The matador's ring name means "The Darling."

Gordius: David Moseley (1930–), Br. crossword compiler. The pseudonym names the king of ancient Phrygia who was famed for tying an intricate knot (which a setter of cryptic puzzles also aims to do).

C. Henry **Gordon:** Henry Gordon Racke (1883–1940), U.S. movie actor.

Gale **Gordon:** Gaylord Aldrich (1906–1995), U.S. TV actor.

Janet **Gordon:** Cecil Blanche Woodham-Smith, née Fitzgerald (1896–1977), Welsh novelist, historian.

Leon **Gordon:** (1) Judah Loeb (1830–1892), Russ. Jewish poet, novelist, writing in Hebrew; (2) Leon Lilly (1884–1960), Eng. stage actor, playwright.

Mack **Gordon:** Morris Gittler (1904–1959), Polish-born U.S. songwriter.

Marjorie **Gordon:** Marjorie Kettlewell (1893–?), Br. stage actress, singer. The actress adopted her mother's maiden name as her stage name.

Mary **Gordon:** Mary Gilmour (1882–1963), Sc. movie actress, working in U.S.

Max **Gordon:** (1) Mechel Salpeter (1892–1978), U.S. theater manager, producer, of Pol. Jewish parentage; (2) Morris Gittler (1904–1959), U.S. lyricist. Mechel adopted the same surname as his elder brother, a vaudeville comedian performing under the name Cliff Gordon.

Millard Verne **Gordon** *see* David **Grinnell**

Neil **Gordon** *see* John **Cameron**

Rex **Gordon:** Stanley Bennett Hough (1917–), Br. SF writer.

Richard **Gordon:** Gordon Ostlere (1921–), Br. comic novelist.

Robert **Gordon:** Robert Gordon Duncan (1895–1971), U.S. movie actor.

Ruth **Gordon:** Ruth Gordon Jones (1896–1985), U.S. stage, movie actress, screenwriter.

Waxey **Gordon:** Irving Wexler (1888–1952), U.S. bootlegger, of Pol. Jewish parentage. Irving's skill as a pickpocket earned him the nickname "Waxey" (meaning "smooth-fingered"), although the term may equally have been suggested by his surname. "Gordon" was one of the aliases he gave the police.

Aedwyrd **Gore** *see* Eduard **Blutig**

Lesley **Gore:** Lesley Goldstein (1946–), U.S. pop singer, songwriter.

Eli **Goren:** Eli Alexander Gruenberg (1923–1999), Austr-born Br. violinist. The founder of the Allegri String Quartet changed his name when playing with the Jerusalem Symphony Orchestra to a more Hebrew, less German-sounding surname. This would also help in later years to avoid confusion with his younger brother, violinist Erich Gruenberg of the London String Quartet.

Gorgeous George: George Raymond Wagner (1915–1963), U.S. wrestler. The wrestler was noted for his grand entrance into the ring, wearing long blond hair and a lace- or fur-trimmed robe. He would be preceded by his valet, bearing a silver-plated tray with a small mat and a Flit-type gun full of perfume-scented disinfectant. The valet would part the ropes so that George did not have to bend too far to come into the ring, where he would wipe his dainty white shoes on the mat. He would then order the valet to spray here and there to purify the contaminated atmosphere. The announcer would finally introduce him as "The Human Orchid, The Toast of the Coast — Goooorrrrrrgeous George!" "'I do not think I'm gorgeous,' he would say, 'but what's my opinion against millions of others?'" [Jares, p.17].

Arshile **Gorky:** Vosdanik Manoog Adoian (1904–1948), Armenian-born U.S. painter. The artist's adopted first name represents the Armenian form of "Achilles," the Greek mythological hero. His second name honors the Russian writer Maxim Gorky, to whom he claimed to be related. (He may also have known that the latter's name means "bitter.") He first used the name on moving from Boston to New York City in 1924.

Maxim **Gorky:** Aleksey Maksimovich Peshkov (1868–1936), Russ. writer. Early in his career, the writer identified with ordinary Russians, and for some time lived "among the people," sharing their poverty and hardship. He first used the name for his story *Makar Chudra* (1892), which he submitted to a local newspaper in Tiflis (Tbilisi), Georgia: "A journalist asked him what name he wanted to use for his first published piece of writing. Alexey hesitated; his real name, Peshkov, suggested the idea of abasement and humility to him, since the Russian word *peshka* means 'pawn' ... He remembered that because of his 'sharp tongue' his father had been nicknamed Bitter, *gorky* in Russian. That would be a wonderful pseudonym for a young writer rebelling against society. So he chose Gorky, 'Bitter,' as his last name, and Maxim [from his patronymic] as his first" [Henri Troyat, *Gorky: A Biography*, translated by Lowell Blair, 1986].

Eydie **Gorme:** Edith Gormenzano (1932–), U.S. popular singer.

Jay **Gorney:** Daniel Jason Gornetzky (1896–1990), Russ.-born U.S. popular composer.

Goronva Camlann: Rowland Williams (1817–1870), Welsh-born Br. theologian, poet. Goronva is a form of the first name now more familiar as Goronwy. (Compare the next name below.) Camlann or Camlan is the name of a legendary battle of *c.*539 in which King Arthur and the traditional hero Medrod are said to have been killed. The name was associated by early Welsh poets with a terrible or futile slaughter, and Welsh *cadgamlan* (*cad*, "battle" + *Camlan*) came to mean "rabble," "confusion." Williams adopted the name for *Lays from the Cimbric Lyre* (1846).

Goronwy Ddu o Fôn: Goronwy Owen (1723–1769), Welsh poet. The poet's bardic name means "Black Goronwy of Anglesey," the latter being the island where he was born. The name itself was probably adopted from the 14th-century poet Gronw Ddu o Fôn, especially as Owen's father was Owen Gronw.

Rita **Gorr:** Marguérite Geirnaert (1926–), Belg. opera singer.

Tobia **Gorrio:** Arrigo Boito (1842–1918), It. composer, librettist. An anagrammatic name. The composer's full original name was Enrico Giuseppe Giovanni Boito. "Arrigo" is a pet form of "Enrico."

Suren **Gorsky:** Suren Grigoryevich Ter-Gevondyan (1903–), Georgian ballet dancer, director.

Sirak **Goryan:** William Saroyan (1908–1981), U.S. novelist, short-story writer, of Armenian parentage. An early pseudonym used by the writer for stories published in the 1930s.

André **Gorz:** Gérard Hirsch (1923–2006), Austr.-born Fr. philosopher. In 1930 Hirsch's Jewish father converted to Catholicism and changed the family name to Horst. In 1949 Horst, as he now was, married Doreen Keir, an Englishwoman, and the couple moved to France, where his wife changed her first name to Dorine, its French equivalent. While awaiting his French naturalization papers, Horst decided that it would be safer to write under a pseudonym. He chose the name Gorz, that of the Austrian town where his father's spectacles had been manufactured. As a journalist, Gorz wrote under the French name Michel Bosquet, the surname translating German *Horst* ("thicket," "grove").

Gospel Fish: Everald Thomas (*c.*1965–), Jamaican DJ, reggae musician. Fellow DJ Jimmy Crazy gave Thomas his nickname after watching him singing in the local church choir.

Gotlib: Marcel Gotlieb (1934–), Fr. cartoonist.

Jeremias **Gotthelf:** Albert Bitzius (1797–1854), Swiss novelist, short-story writer. The writer was a pastor, with strong Christian principles. He thus changed his name in order to express his convictions, with "Jeremias" for the Old Testament prophet (whose own name means "God raise up") and "Gotthelf" as the German for "God's help." The name itself originated as that of the central character (and supposed narrator) of his story of Swiss peasant life, *Der Bauernspiegel* ("The Peasants' Mirror") (1837).

Olympe de **Gouges:** Marie-Olympe Gouze (1748 or 1755–1793), Fr. writer, revolutionary.

Bernard **Gould:** [Sir] Bernard Partridge (1861–1945), Br. actor, cartoonist.

Elliott **Gould:** Elliott Goldstein (1938–), U.S. stage, movie actor. The actor was given this simpler version of his name by his mother.

Robert **Goulet:** Stanley Applebaum (1933–), Can. singer, movie, TV actor.

La **Goulue:** Louise Weber (or Wébert) (*c.*1865–1929), Fr. cancan dancer. "She was called La Goulue (The Glutton) because, ever since her adolescence, she had been in the habit of draining glasses dry in bars" [Jacques Pessis and Jacques Crépineau, *The Moulin Rouge*, 1990].

Henri **Goupillier:** Henri Desmarets (1661–1741), Fr. composer. Desmarets used this name for church music written early in his career.

Govinda: Govind Ahuja (1963–), Ind. movie actor, dancer.

Lama Anagarika Govinda: Ernst Lother Hoffman (1898–1985), Ger. Buddhist, working in India. Precise details of the Buddhist proselytizer's life are uncertain, but he adopted his new name around 1928, when he moved from Capri, where he had gone to live after World War I, to Ceylon (Sri Lanka). In 1947, following internment in World War II, he married a Parsi photographer, Li Gotami, and took Indian nationality. Govinda, a Sanskrit name meaning literally "(one good at) finding cows," is an epithet of the Hindu god Krishna. Govinda was strongly influenced by Tibetan Buddhism. Hence his title of lama (monk, priest). Anagarika, literally "homeless one" (from Sanskrit *anagara*, "homeless," from *an-*, "not," and *agara*, "house"), is the title of a celibate fulltime roving worker for Buddhism.

Peter Graaf *see* John **Christopher**

Axel Graatkjær: Axel Sørensen (1885–1969), Dan. moviemaker.

Graban: [Sir] Granville Bantock (1868–1946), Eng. composer. The musician used this name, from the first three letters of his first name and surname, for some popular songs.

Charles Emmanuel Grace: Marceline Manoel da Graca (1881–1960), Cape Verde-born U.S. religious leader, of Port.-African ancestry ("Bishop Grace"). The original name of the church leader, whose self-proclaimed title was "Boyfriend of the World," is believed to have been as stated here.

Sister Grace: Grace Thyrza Kimmins, née Hannam (1870–1954), Eng. charity worker, writer. Grace Kimmins, who devoted her life to helping disadvantaged children, was known by the full name Sister Grace of the Bermondsey Settlement by the time she wrote *Polly of Parker's Rents* (1899).

Charlie Gracie: Charles Anthony Graci (1936–), U.S. popular guitarist, songwriter.

Julien Gracq: Louis Poirier (1910–2007), Fr. novelist, essayist. The writer took his new first name from Julien Sorel, the ambitious young hero of Stendhal's *Le Rouge et le Noir* (1830), and his last name from the Gracchi (the brothers Gaius Sempronius Gracchus and Tiberius Sempronius Gracchus), the reformist tribunes of ancient Rome.

[Baron] Lew Grade: Louis Winogradsky (1906–1998), Russ.-born Br. movie, TV producer. The show-business tycoon, brother of Bernard **Delfont**, changed his name in the 1920s, when he entered dancing competitions in London at the height of the Charleston craze. He won several prizes, and became an increasingly popular attraction. Soon realizing that his original name was "too much of a mouthful," he shortened it to "Louis Grad." Subsequently, he be-

came a professional dancer, and went on to perform at the Moulin Rouge, Paris. "A few days before my opening night, a big article appeared about me in the *Paris Midi* newspaper. It was great publicity, but the writer had spelt my name incorrectly. Instead of Louis Grad it came out as Lew Grade. I liked the look and sound of it — and Lew Grade it has been ever since" [Lew Grade, *Still Dancing*, 1987].

A Graduate of Oxford: John Ruskin (1819–1900), Eng. artist, art critic. Newly graduated from Oxford University, Ruskin published the first two volumes of *Modern Painters* (1843, 1846) under this name. The remaining three volumes (1856, 1860) followed under his real name.

Bruce Graeme: Graham Montague Jeffries (1900–1982), Eng. crime, mystery writer. Jeffries also wrote as Peter Bourne.

Joyce Graeme: Joyce Platt (1918–1991), Br. ballet dancer.

Roderic Graeme: Roderic Graeme Jeffries (1926–), Eng. crime, mystery writer. Other names used by the writer are Peter Alding, Jeffrey Ashford, Hastings Draper, and Graham Hastings.

Boothby Graffoe: James Rogers (1962–), Eng. comedian. The entertainer was born in the city of Hull, East Yorkshire, and took his stage name from the village of Boothby Graffoe, in the neighboring county of Lincolnshire.

Augustus Graham: Richard King (1776–1851), Eng.-born U.S. philanthropist. It is not known why King took this name on emigrating to the United States, where he became an American citizen in 1808.

Bill Graham: Wolfgang Wolodia Grajonca (1931–1991), Ger.-born U.S. rock-music promoter, of Russ. Jewish parentage.

Ennis Graham: Mary Louisa Molesworth, née Stewart (1839–1921), Br. novelist, of Sc. parentage. Down to 1874 the writer used this name, that of a female friend who died in Africa, for her novels directed at adults. Subsequent children's books were published as by simply "Mrs. Molesworth."

Harvey Graham: Harvey Flack (1912–1966), Eng. surgeon, medical historian. Flack used this name for "numerous publications in the lay and magazine press" [*Who's Who*].

James Graham *see* Jack **Higgins**

Kenny Graham: Kenneth Thomas Skingle (1924–1997), Eng. jazz musician.

Sheilah Graham: Lily Shiel (1904–1988), Eng. writer, biographer. In 1926 the future companion (1937–40) to F. Scott Fitzgerald married Major John Graham Gillam, 25 years her senior, in London, England, and went to Hollywood, where she became a gossip columnist. Her new name, adopted for a planned stage career, was created from a form of her original surname and her husband's middle name. She once said, "The name Lily Shiel, to this day, horrifies me to a degree impossible to explain."

Virginia **Graham:** Virginia Komiss (1912–1998), U.S. TV personality, actress.

Viva **Graham:** Edith Anna Œnone Somerville (1858–1949), Ir. novelist + Martin **Ross**, her cousin. The coauthors, writing as Somerville and Ross, were assigned this name by their publisher for the second edition of *An Irish Cousin* (1889). Expecting the name to be "Giles Logan," Ross expressed her displeasure in a letter to Edith dated August 21, 1889: "I am awfully disgusted with Bentley for his meanness or carelessness in the matter of Viva Graham [and I told him] that I feared you would be much disappointed, and that we certainly understood the name was to be Giles Logan — I do not regret the loss of Giles, but *Viva*! It is hard luck, but if it be any consolation, I mind it as much as you do." Earlier suggestions for a name, all wisely rejected, were Peg o' the Purlieu, Miss B. O'Hemia, and Sister Chimpan. The name assigned for the first edition of the book was Geilles **Herring**.

Alec **Grahame:** James Alexander Pratchett (1926–2001), Eng. revue writer. The writer adopted his stage name on entering the theater in the late 1940s.

Gloria **Grahame:** Gloria Hallward (1923–1981), U.S. stage, movie actress, of Eng. descent. The actress's new surname was the professional name of her mother, Jean McDougall, who acted under the name Jean Grahame on the British stage. Grahame's grandfather, Reginald Francis Hallward (1858–1948), was an illustrator and friend of Oscar Wilde, who adopted his surname for Basil Hallward, the painter in his story *The Picture of Dorian Gray* (1891).

Corney **Grain:** Richard Corney (1844–1895), Br. entertainer, writer, composer. A name that probably originated as a (corny) nickname.

Donald **Gramm:** Donald Grambasch (1927–1983), U.S. opera singer.

Grammont: Guillaume Antoine Nourry (1750–1794), Fr. actor, political agent.

Otis **Grand:** Fred Bishti (1950–), Lebanese blues guitarist, working in U.S. The musician's new first name pays tribute to two of his influences, Otis Rush and Johnny **Otis**.

Sarah **Grand:** Frances Elizabeth Bellenden McFall, née Clarke (1854–1943), Ir.-born Br. novelist. Having initially published anonymously, the writer first used her pseudonym for her bestselling novel *The Heavenly Twins* (1893), claiming the name was "simple, short and emphatic — not easily forgotten."

Grandfather Greenway: Charles James Cannon (1800–1860), U.S. writer, of Ir. parentage. Cannon adopted this name for *Ravellings from the Web of Life*, a collection of tales published in 1855.

Grandmaster Flash: Joseph Saddler (1958–), West Indian-born U.S. hip-hop DJ. The artist adopted the nickname given him for his rapid hand movements when "seguing" from one record to another on the turntables, with "grandmaster," originally the title of a high-ranking chess player, a general term for any good player.

His group, the Furious Five, contained five rappers all known by different names: Cowboy (Keith Wiggins), Melle Mel (Melvin Glover), Kid Creole (Danny Glover), Mr. Ness (Eddie Morris), and Rahiem (Guy Williams). "His publicists issue a daunting list of do's and don'ts. Do address him as Flash. Don't describe him as a rapper: he is a DJ and producer" [*The Times*, March 7, 2009].

D.St. **Grandmixer:** Derek Howells (1960–), U.S. black hip-hop musician, scratch DJ. His first name represents the abbreviation of Delancey Street, New York, where he added to his collection of fashion wear. His last name alludes to his talent as a DJ.

Grandville: Jean-Ignace-Isidore Gérard (1803–1847), Fr. illustrator, caricaturist.

Peter **Grange** *see* Andrew **York**

Stewart **Granger:** James Lablache Stewart (1913–1993), Eng. movie actor, working in U.S. The actor changed his name in the late 1930s to avoid confusion with U.S. movie actor James Stewart (1908–1997). As a British actor, he was anyway governed by the rules of Equity, the actors' union, which states that no two actors can have the same name. Granger became an American citizen in 1956.

Daniil **Granin:** Daniil Aleksandrovich German (1919–), Russ. novelist, short-story writer.

[Baron] Albert **Grant:** Abraham Gottheimer (1831–1899), Ir. businessman, of Ger. Jewish parentage. Gottheimer changed his name on going to London to embark on a career as a company promoter.

Ambrose **Grant** *see* James Hadley **Chase**

Cary **Grant:** Archibald Alexander Leach (1904–1986), Eng. movie actor, working in U.S. The actor adopted his new name in 1931. "I changed my name at the behest of the [Paramount] studio. They said Archie Leach had to go. John Monk Saunders, a friend and the author of *Nikki*, a play I'd done in New York, suggested I take the name of the character I played in the show: Cary Lockwood. Well, Cary was all right, but Lockwood wasn't; there was already an actor named Harold Lockwood under contract to the studio. What went with 'Cary'? It was an age of short names — Gable, Brent, Cooper.... A secretary came with a list and put it in front of me. 'Grant' jumped out at me, and that was that" [Nancy Nelson, *Cary Grant*, 1991].

"It would be many years ... before he could begin to separate the two identities of Archie Leach and Cary Grant and there are those who believe he never quite reconciled himself to this self-determined schizophrenia" [Gary Morecambe and Martin Sterling, *Cary Grant: In Name Only*, 2001].

Gogi **Grant:** Myrtle Audrey Arinsberg (1924–), U.S. pop singer. The singer's name is said to come from a New York restaurant called Gogi's La Rue. She first used the names Audrey Brown and Audrey Grant.

Hector **Grant** *see* J.P. **McCall**

Jan **Grant:** Jan Jekabson (1909–1970), Latvian novelist, short-story writer.

Joan **Grant:** Joan Kelsey, née Marshall (1907–1989), Eng. novelist, occultist. The writer adopted the name of her first husband, Arthur Leslie Grant.

John **Grant:** Paul le Page Barnett (1949–), Sc. editor, novelist.

Kathryn (or Kathy) **Grant:** Olive Kathryn Grandstaff (1933–), U.S. movie actress.

Kirby **Grant:** Kirby Grant Hoon (1911–1985), U.S. movie actor, of Du.-Sc. parentage. The former bandleader was billed as Robert Stanton in a couple of early movies.

Landon **Grant** *see* Leo **Grex**

Lee **Grant:** Lyova Haskell Rosenthal (1927–), U.S. stage, movie actress.

Richard E. **Grant:** Richard Grant Esterhuysen (1957–), Br. movie actor, novelist.

Ted **Grant:** Isaac Blank (1913–2006), S.A.–born Br. revolutionary politician, of Russ. parentage. The founder of the Militant Tendency political faction is said to have adopted his new name from a crew member of the ship he sailed in from South Africa to England in the 1930s.

Ulysses S. **Grant:** Hiram Ulysses Grant (1822–1885), U.S. president. In 1839 the future 18th president of the United States was appointed to West Point where he registered as Ulysses Hiram Grant, reversing his first two names, as he did not wish to have the initials H.U.G. The congressman who had nominated him, however, had in haste given Grant's first names as Ulysses Simpson, the second of these being his mother's maiden name. An adjutant at the academy refused to correct the error, so that Grant's classmates inevitably read his initials U.S. as "Uncle Sam" and accordingly nicknamed him "Sam."

Charles **Granville:** Francis Charles Granville Egerton, Earl of Ellesmere (1847–1914), Eng. novelist.

Christine **Granville:** Krystyna Starbeck, née Gyzicka (?–1952), Pol.-born Br. spy.

Gravelot: Hubert-François Bourguignon (1699–1773), Fr. engraver, painter. The artist's

adopted name derived, presumably by way of a nickname, from French *graver*, "to engrave."

Peter **Graves:** Peter Aurness (1926–2010), U.S. movie actor, brother of James **Arness**.

Ralph **Graves:** Ralph Horsburgh (1900–1977), U.S. movie comedian.

Rob **Graves:** Robert Ritter (*c.*1960–1990), U.S. punk musician.

Fernand **Gravet** (or Gravey): Fernand Martens (1904–1970), Belg.-born Fr. movie actor, working in U.S.

Caroline **Gravière:** Estelle Marie Louise Ruelens, née Crèvecoeur (1821–1878), Belg. novelist.

Gray: Gray Jolliffe (1937–), Eng. cartoonist, illustrator.

Allan **Gray:** Josef Zmigrod (1902–1973), Austr.-born movie music composer, working in U.K.

Annabel **Gray:** [Mrs.] Anne Cox (1853–?), Eng. novelist.

Arvella **Gray:** Walter Dixon (1906–1980), U.S. blues guitarist.

Barry **Gray:** Robert Barry Coffin (1826–1886), U.S. journalist, poet, writer.

Caroline **Gray** *see* Andrew **York**

Coleen **Gray:** Doris Jensen (1922–), U.S. movie actress, of Dan. descent.

Dobie **Gray:** Leonard Victor Ainsworth (1942–), U.S. soul singer.

Donald **Gray:** Eldred Tidbury (1914–1979), Eng. movie, TV actor.

Dulcie **Gray:** Dulcie Winifred Catherine Denison, née Bailey (1919–), Eng. stage, movie actress, novelist. The actress tells how she came by her stage name: "I ... had to change my name from Bailey as there was another Dulcie Bailey on the stage ... I found it hard to think of a good name. At one time I decided to call myself Angela Botibol — every tube [subway] station in London had an Angel Botibol tobacconist's kiosk and I thought at least the critics wouldn't for better or worse be able to overlook me. But I eventually took my mother's maiden name of Gray" [Dulcie Gray, *Looking Forward—Looking Back*, 1991].

E. Conder **Gray** *see* H.A. **Page**

Edith **Gray** *see* **H.D.**

Eileen **Gray:** Kathleen Eileen Moray Smith (1879–1976), Ir. designer, architect. The designer's mother inherited the title of Baroness Gray in 1895, and in 1897 her father changed his name by royal license to Smith-Gray. From that time on, when Eileen was 18, all the children took the surname Gray.

Elizabeth Janet **Gray:** Elizabeth Gray Vining (1902–1999), U.S. children's writer.

Ellington **Gray:** Naomi Ellington Jacob (1884–1964), Eng. actress, popular novelist. The writer's mother, Nina Ellington, née Collinson, wrote novels as Nina Abbott.

George Kruger **Gray:** George Edward Kruger (1880–1943), Br. designer. The artist added Gray to his surname on his marriage in 1918 to Audrey Gordon Gray.

Gilda **Gray:** Marianna Michalska (1899–1959), Pol. dancer, movie actress, working in U.S. The dancer originally adopted the stage name "May Gray" but Sophie **Tucker** convinced her to change "May" to "Gilda." "She never heard of the name Gilda until I gave it to her. I was going up to Hartford to visit the family and in the Grand Central I bought a ten-cent magazine of short stories to kill the two-and-a-half-hour train ride. The first story I turned to started off: 'Gilda Gray was a fascinating blonde.' The minute I got back to New York from Hartford ... I rushed up to May's room ... May was sound asleep. 'Wake up!' I yelled. 'I've got a new monniker [*sic*] for you — Gilda Gray! You'll never make a cent with a name like May Gray. It sounds just as tough as you are. But Gilda is class!'" [Sophie Tucker, *Some of These Days: An Autobiography*, 1948].

Glen **Gray:** Glen Gray Knoblaugh (1906–1963), U.S. saxophonist, bandleader.

Harriet **Gray** *see* Denise **Robins**

James **Gray:** Hannah Snell (1723–1792), Eng. adventuress. In 1744, Snell married a Dutch sailor, James Summs, who left her six months later. Keen to find him, she borrowed a suit from her brother-in-law, took his name, James Gray, and in 1745 enlisted. Later, while working as a sailor, she discovered that James Summs had died and retired from sea in 1750, whereupon she resumed her female identity.

Jennifer **Gray:** Jennifer Skinner (1916–1962), Br. stage actress.

Jerry **Gray:** Generoso Graziano (1915–1976), U.S. jazz musician, bandleader.

Linda **Gray:** Linda Baxter (1910–), Eng. stage actress, singer. The actress took her mother's maiden name as her stage name. She should not be confused with U.S. actress Linda Gray (1942–).

Lorna **Gray** *see* Adrian **Booth**

Macy **Gray:** Natalie Renee McIntyre (1970–), U.S. black soul singer. The singer adopted the name of a man her father played poker with as her professional name.

Mary **Gray:** Elizabeth Stuart Ward, née Phelps (1844–1911), U.S. novelist, daughter of novelist Elizabeth Wooster Phelps (1815–1852).

Maxwell **Gray:** Mary Gleed Tuttiett (1847–1923), Eng. novelist, poet.

Michael **Gray:** Michael Grealis (1947–), Eng. TV reporter.

Nadia **Gray:** Nadia Kujnir-Herescu (1923–1994), Russ.-Rom. movie actress.

Rowland **Gray:** Lilian Kate Rowland-Brown (1863–1959), Eng. writer of romantic fiction.

Sally **Gray:** Constance Vera Stevens (1916–2006), Eng. movie actress.

Simon **Gray:** [Sir] Alexander Boswell (1775–1822), Eng. antiquary, poet.

Victor **Gray** *see* Ted **Pauker**

David **Grayson:** Ray Stannard Baker (1870–1946), U.S. journalist, essayist. The writer is said to have chosen this name when he recalled having heard it "once when I was in the South" [Marble, p.94]. He used it for nine volumes published between 1907 and 1942, beginning with *Adventures in Contentment*, in which David Grayson is a farmer-philosopher who hymns the beauty and peace of the countryside, by contrast with the noise and turmoil of urban life. The pseudonym long mystified the public, but the identity of its bearer was revealed in 1916 following the appearance of an impostor who claimed to be "David Grayson."

Diane **Grayson:** Diane Guinibert (1948–), Flemish-born Eng. stage, movie, TV dancer, actress.

Kathryn **Grayson:** Zelma Kathryn Elizabeth Hedrick (1922–2010), U.S. movie actress, singer.

Larry **Grayson:** William White (1923–1995), Eng. TV entertainer. An illegitimate child, Grayson first started acting in the music hall at the age of 14 under the name of Billy Breen. In 1956 he was spotted by agent Evelyn Taylor at London's Nuffield Centre. She signed him up, and began looking for a new name for him. "We sat there for ages going through different names. First we settled on Larry. And at the time there was a very popular Hollywood singing star Kathryn **Grayson**. 'That's it,' said Eve, 'Larry Grayson — write it down.' He did, liked it and has written it many thousands of times on autograph books since" [*TV Times*, August 20–26, 1983]. "Grayson" also suggests a kinship with original "White."

Richard **Grayson:** Richard Frederick Grindal (1922–), Sc.-born Br. crime novelist.

Bettina **Graziani:** Simone Micheline Bodin (1925–), Fr. fashion model. When Bodin was invited by Christian Dior to join him in his fashion house, she refused, choosing instead to work for Jacques Fath, and it was he who renamed her, telling her: "We already have a Simone; you look to me like a Bettina" [Michael Gross, *Model*, 1995].

Rocky **Graziano:** Thomas Rocco Barbella (1919–1990), U.S. boxer, TV actor. The boxer adopted the name of his sister's boyfriend, Tommy Rocky Graziano, in order to avoid detection when an army deserter in 1942. It was Graziano who popularized the name Rocky for boxers, and who was the model for the "Rocky" movies starring Sylvester Stallone. (Perhaps for this reason, and the similarity of name, he is apt to be confused with Rocky **Marciano**.)

The **Great Cardo:** Shree Probhat Kumar Chatterjee (1901–?), Ind.-born Br. magician. The name alludes to the playing cards that are every illusionist's stock in trade.

The **Great Carmo:** Harry Cameron (1881–1944), Austral.-born Br. magician. "Carmo" is obviously extracted from "Cameron."

The **Great Khali:** Dalip Singh Rana (1972–), Ind.-born U.S. wrestler. The wrestler originally battled as The Giant Singh but then settled on The Great Khali, after Kali, the Hindu goddess of destruction.

The **Great Lafayette:** Sigmund Neuberger (1871–1911), Ger.-born U.S. magician, working in U.K. The illusionist's early stage acts were rehearsed and produced along military lines. Hence his name, from the Marquis de Lafayette (1757–1834), the French statesman and soldier who fought against Britain in the American Revolution. He adopted the name legally by deed poll and always signed his initials "T.G.L."

The **Great Leon:** Leon H. Levy (1876–1951), U.S. magician. The illusionist also staged an oriental act under the name Chunda Hula or, subsequently, Kadan Sami.

The **Great Lester:** Marian Czajkowski (c.1880–1956), Pol.-born U.S. ventriloquist. The performer also appeared under the name Harry Lester.

The **Great Levante:** Leslie George Vante Cole (1892–1978), Austral. magician. Although clearly based on his first and third names, the magician's name evokes the mystery of the Levant or east.

The **Great Macdermott:** Gilbert Hastings Farrell (1845–1901), Br. music-hall artist.

The **Great Nicola:** William Mozart Nicol (1880–1946), U.S. illusionist. The name would have been pronounced "Ni-*co*-la," rhyming with "Lola," not like the modern female forename Nicola.

The **Great Omani:** Ronald Cunningham (1915–2007), Eng. stuntman, escapologist.

The **Great Ovette:** Giuseppe Olivio (1885–1946), It.-born magician, working in U.S. The artist also performed as Joseph Ovette, and perfected an oriental act under the name Lung Tchang Yuen.

The **Great Soprendo:** Geoffrey Durham (c.1950–), Br. magician. The magician produced surprises, as his name indicates (Spanish *sorprendo*, "I surprise"). Durham studied Spanish at university and his act was as a Spaniard. He married TV entertainer Victoria Wood (1953–) in 1980 and retired in 1989.

Harry **Greb:** Edward Henry Berg (1894–1926), U.S. boxer ("The Human Windmill"). A simple surname reversal.

Il **Grechetto:** Giovanni Benedetto Castiglione (c.1616–1670), It. painter, etcher. The artist's name is Italian for "the little Greek," given him for his fine coloring, in the manner of El **Greco**.

El **Greco:** Domenikos Theotokopoulos (1541–1614), Gr.-born Sp. painter, sculptor, architect. The artist usually signed his paintings with his Greek name. He was known in Spain as *El Griego*, "the Greek," and gained his familiar name only after his death, from Spanish *el*, "the," and Italian *greco*, "Greek," the latter language coming from his time in Italy, where he is believed to have been until 1577.

Al **Green:** Al Greene (1946–), U.S. soul, gospel singer. The singer formed a group, The Creations, in the mid–1960s and in 1967 set up the Hot Line Music Journal record label to release "Back Up Train." It was a one-off hit, however, and the label folded, whereupon Greene dropped the final "e" of his name and embarked on a solo career.

Charles M. **Green** *see* A.A. **Fair**

Hannah **Green:** Joanne Greenberg (1932–), U.S. writer. When she wrote *I Never Promised You a Rose Garden* (1964), a story of schizophrenia, Greenberg adopted a pseudonym in order to protect her sons from the stigma that their mother had at one time been hospitalized with mental illness.

Harry **Green:** Henry Blitzer (1892–1958), U.S. stage, movie comedian.

Henry **Green:** Henry Vincent Yorke (1905–1973), Br. novelist.

Hugo **Green:** Hugo Gryn (1930–1998), Br. broadcaster, of Hung. Jewish parentage. The rabbi and broadcaster became known under his original name, but after emigrating to Britain in 1946 called himself Hugo Green until he was naturalized in the mid–1950s as a U.S. citizen, as related in his daughter's introduction to his autobiography: "My father ... used to tell the story of how, when he first arrived in Britain in February 1946, the immigration officer had asked him for his name. In those days he spoke no English at all, but understood the sentiment. 'Gryn,' he said. G-R-E-E-N, wrote the official. '*Nem*,' said my father, '*ipsilon*,' and pointed vigorously at this unfamiliar spelling of his family name. *Ipsilon*. Hungarian for 'y.' Bemused, the official led him by the hand and showed him to the toilet" [Hugo Gryn with Naomi Gryn, *Chasing Shadows*, 2000].

Green was named Hugo (properly Hugó) because his mother was reading Victor Hugo's *Les Misérables* at the time. His Jewish name was Zvi-Hirsh, Hebrew and Yiddish for "deer," after his maternal great-grandfather, Reb Zvi-Hirsh Neufeld.

Joseph **Green:** Joseph Greenberg (1900–1996), Pol.-born Yiddish movie director, working in U.S.

Martyn **Green:** William Martyn-Green (1899–1975), Eng. light opera singer, stage actor, working in U.S.

Mitzi **Green:** Elizabeth Keno (1920–1969), U.S. child movie actress. The actress adopted her mother's maiden name as her screen name.

Peter **Green:** Peter Greenbaum (1946–), Br. blues, rock musician.

Olive **Green:** Myrtle Reed (1874–1911), U.S. writer. Reed used this rather corny name for a series of 10 cookbooks, beginning with *What to Have for Breakfast* (1905).

Rosa **Green** *see* Rosa **Henderson**

Max **Greene:** Mutz Greenbaum (1896–1968), Ger. cinematographer, working in U.K.

Shecky **Greene:** Fred Sheldon Greenfield (1925–), U.S. TV comedian.

Elizabeth **Greenhill:** Christine Elizabeth Florence Grünhold (1907–2006), Br. bookbinder, of Germ. parentage. The artist's family adopted an anglicized version of their name during World War I, as did many other British families with German surnames.

Sonny **Greenwich:** Herbert Lawrence Greenidge (1936–), Can. jazz guitarist.

Grace **Greenwood:** Sara Jane Lippincott, née Clarke (1823–1904), U.S. poet, journalist. Lippincott first used her pen name in 1844 when contributing letters to the New York *Mirror and Home Journal*. She also began using it socially then. She was soon writing for other periodicals, and in 1850 published a collection of her contributions under the title *Greenwood Leaves*.

Richard **Greenwood:** Richard Peirse-Duncomb (c.1959–), Welsh-born Br. TV actor.

[Sir] Ben **Greet:** Philip Barling Greet (1857–1936), Br. stage actor, theater manager. The actor first appeared on the stage in 1879 as Philip Ben, the nickname "Benjamin" having been given to him as the youngest of eight children. He later adopted the name Ben in place of his original first names.

Carlotta **Greet:** Josephine Frey Herbst (1892–1969), U.S. novelist, biographer. Herbst used this name for her first story, "The Elegant Mr. Gason," published in the early 1920s.

Bernadette **Greevy:** Bernadette Tattan (1940–), Ir. opera singer.

Greg: Michel Régnier (1931–), Belg. cartoonist.

W.S. **Gregg:** Frances Mabel Robinson (?1855–?1911), Eng. novelist.

Gregory V: Bruno (di Carinzia) (972–999), Ger.-born It. pope. The first German pope adopted

the name of St. Gregory the Great (c.540–604), whom he regarded as his exemplar.

Gregory VI: Giovanni Graziano (Johannes Gratianus) (?–?1048), It. pope. This Gregory is said to have been given his name by popular acclaim, presumably in honor of St. Gregory the Great (c.540–604).

[St.] **Gregory VII:** Hildebrand (c.1020–1085), It. pope. The pontiff took his name in honor of St. Gregory the Great (c.540–604).

Gregory VIII: Alberto de Morra (?1110–1187), It. pope.

Gregory IX: Ugo (or Ugolino) (dei Conti di Segni) (c.1155–1241), It. pope.

Gregory X: Tedaldo (or Tebaldo) Visconti (c.1210–1276), It. pope.

Gregory XI: Pierre Roger de Beaufort (1329–1378), Fr. pope.

Gregory XII: Angelo Correr (c.1325–1417), It. pope.

Gregory XIII: Ugo Buoncompagni (1502–1585), It. pope. It was this Gregory that gave the name of the Gregorian calendar, instituted by him.

Gregory XIV: Niccolò Sfondrati (1535–1591), It. pope. The pontiff took the name of his patron, **Gregory XIII**, who had created him cardinal in 1583.

Gregory XV: Alessandro Ludovisi (1554–1623), It. pope.

Gregory XVI: Bartolomeo Alberto Cappellari (1765–1846), It. pope. The future pontiff took the name Mauro, for one of the early saints so called, on becoming a Benedictine monk at the age of 18. In 1805 he became abbot of San Gregorio al Celio, and may have taken his papal name from this.

Gregory XVII: Clemente Domínguez y Gomez (1946–), Sp. antipope. On the death of Pope **Paul VI** in 1978, Bishop Clemente Domíngez, founder in 1975 of the Carmelite Order of the Holy Face, declared himself his successor in Bogotá, Colombia, and was soon after crowned "pope" in Seville, Spain. The sect has its headquarters at Palmar de Troya, near Seville, where four young girls are said to have had heavenly visions in 1968. The actual pope to succeed Paul VI was the briefly reigning **John Paul I**.

Bryan **Gregory:** Gregory Becker (1955–2001), U.S. "psychobilly" musician.

Father **Gregory:** Edward Leslie Dudding (1930–2009), N.Z.–born religious community superior. Dudding went to England and there joined the Community of the Servants of the Will of God in 1962, becoming the Anglican community's superior in 1973.

Frederick **Gregory:** Fritz Gugenheim (1893–1961), Br. plant physiologist, of Ger. Jewish origin. The scientist was exempted from military service in

World War I on medical grounds, and began his plant studies then at an experimental station. He was subjected to abuse because of his German name, as "Fritz" was a common derogatory nickname for Germans at this time, and his experimental records were sabotaged. The experience led him to change his name by deed poll in 1916.

Paul **Gregory**: Jason Lenhart (*c*.1905–), U.S. impresario, movie producer.

Simon **Gregson**: Simon Alan Gregory (1974–), Br. TV actor. The actor originally played under his real name, but changed his surname to Gregson in 1991 to avoid confusion with another actor named Simon Gregory.

Martin **Greif**: Friedrich Hermann Frey (1839–1911), Ger. lyric poet.

Maysie **Greig**: Maysie Sopoushek, earlier Murray, née Greig-Smith (1901–1971), Austral.-born journalist, writer, working in U.K. The romantic novelist also wrote as Jennifer Ames, Ann Barclay, and Mary Douglas Warre.

Anna **Greki**: Colette Anna Melki, née Grégoire (1931–1966), Algerian poet, writing in French.

I. **Grekova**: Yelena Sergeyevna Ventsel (Wenzel) (1907–?), Russ. mathematician, writer. The scholar used this name as a fiction writer, basing it on Russian *igrek* (from French *i grec*, "Greek i," the name of the letter "y"), as she was an "unknown quantity" (like algebraic *y*) in this capacity.

Gren: Grenfell Jones (1934–), Welsh cartoonist, illustrator.

Stephen **Grendon**: August William Derleth (1909–1971), U.S. writer of horror fiction.

Madame **Grès**: Germaine Émilie Krebs (1903–1993), Fr. fashion designer. Grès was originally a signature name used by the designer's husband, Russian artist Serge Czerefkov, who formed it by reversing his first name.

Henry **Gréville**: Alice Marie Céleste Fleury Durand-Gréville, née Fleury (1842–1902), Fr. writer of novels and short stories about Russian society.

Leo **Grex**: Leonard Reginald Gribble (1908–1985), Eng. crime, western novelist. Other names used by the writer were Sterry Browning, Lee Denver, Landon Grant, Louis Grey, and Dexter Muir. Some of these vaguely relate to his original name.

Al **Grey**: Albert Thornton (1925–2000), U.S. jazz trombonist.

Anne **Grey**: Aileen Ewing (1907–1998), Br. movie actress.

[Dame] Beryl **Grey**: Beryl Svenson, née Groom (1927–), Br. ballet dancer, artistic director. When Beryl Groom was beginning her dancing career at the age of 14, Ninette **de Valois** suggested this new name for her. "I called her Beryl Grey because there was an easy flow to it. If she had remained Groom people would have called her Broom or something. It's not a ballet name." Dame Ninette also suggested "Iris Grey," but Beryl resisted this. It took her around twenty years to get used to her new name [David Gillard, *Beryl Grey: A Biography*, 1977].

Denise **Grey**: Edouardine Verthiey (1896–1996), Fr. stage, movie actress.

Joel **Grey**: Joel Katz (1932–), U.S. stage, movie actor, singer, dancer. The actor's father formed a group called Mickey Katz and His Kittens. When the father changed this name to Mickey Kats and His Kosher Jammers, Joel Katz went on the stage alone as Joel Kaye, later changing this to Joel Grey [*The Times*, May 15, 1976]. Movie actress Jennifer Grey (1960–) is Grey's daughter.

Katherine **Grey**: Katherine Best (1873–1950), U.S. stage actress.

Lita **Grey**: Lillita MacMurray (1908–1995), U.S. juvenile movie actress.

Louis **Grey** *see* Leo **Grex**

Mary **Grey**: Ada Bevan ap Rees Bryant (1878–1974), Welsh stage actress.

Nan **Grey**: Eschal Loleet Grey Miller (1918–1993), U.S. movie actress, wife of Frankie **Laine**.

Rowland **Grey**: Lilian Kate Rowland Brown (1863–1959), Eng. novelist, journalist. A change of color here.

Sasha **Grey**: Maria Ann Hantzis (1988–), U.S. porno movie actress. Hantzis is said to have taken her new first name from Sasha Konietzko of the rock band KMFDM and her surname from Oscar Wilde's story *The Picture of Dorian Gray* (1891). "The Grey mythology states that, when she was choosing her professional name, she originally considered the name Anna **Karina** in homage to Jean-Luc Godard's wife and muse" [*The Times*, November 27, 2009].

Zane **Grey**: Pearl Zane Gray (1875–1939), U.S. author of romantic novels about the American West. The writer grew up in Zanesville, Ohio, founded in 1797 by his pioneer great-great-grandfather, Ebenezer Zane (1747–1812), and this gave his middle name. He was usually known as "Pearl," a name then found for men as well as women (his mother was aware that Queen Victoria's favorite color was pearl gray), but dropped this when he overheard two young women on a train discussing his work and referring to him as "she." At the same time he modified the spelling of his last name from Gray to Grey [Jane Tompkins, Introduction to 1990 edition of *Riders of the Purple Sage*, 1912].

Grey Owl: Archibald Stansfeld Belaney (1888–1938), Eng.-born Can. writer. The writer is best known for his autobiography, *Pilgrims of the Wild* (1934). He was the son of an English father who had married, in the U.S., a woman said by him to be of Native American descent. His pen name, which he took in 1920 when he was adopted as a blood brother by the Ojibwa, was that of a Native American chief, and was an English equivalent of the original, Washaguonasin, "He Who Walks by Night." Grey Owl lived with the Ojibwa for 37 years and married an Indian, who bore him a daughter, "Little Dawn."

R.E.H. Greyson: Henry Rogers (1806–1877), Eng. reviewer, theologian. The writer's pen name is an anagram of his real name. He used it for two volumes of imaginary letters, *Selections from the Correspondence of R.E.H. Greyson, Esq.* (1857). His main work, *The Eclipse of Faith, or a Visit to a Religious Sceptic* (1852), was published as "by F.B."

Gridiron Gabble: Joseph Haslewood (1769–1833), Eng. historian, writer. Haslewood used this name for the alliteratively titled (and alphabetically subtitled) *Green-Room Gossip; or Gravity Gallinipt: A Gallimawfry, Consisting of Theatrical Anecdotes, Bon Mots, Chit-Chat, Drollery, Entertainment, Fun, Gibes, Humour, Jokes, Kickshaws, Lampoons, Mirth, Nonsense, Oratory, Quizzing, Repartee, Stories, Tattle, Vocality, Wit, Yawning, Zest... Gathered and Garnished by Gridiron Gabble, Gent., Godson to Mother Goose* (1809). In theatrical parlance, the gridiron is "the arrangement of beams over a theater stage supporting the machinery for flying scenery" [*Webster's Third New International Dictionary*].

Sydney Carlyon **Grier:** Hilda Caroline Gregg (1868–1933), Eng. novelist, writer.

Francis **Grierson:** Benjamin Henry Jesse Francis Shepard (1848–1927), Eng.-born U.S. writer, musician, mystic. Shepard took his pseudonym in 1899, while living in London, England, combining one of his given names with his mother's maiden name. He presumably aimed to distinguish his work as a writer from the fame (or infamy) he had gained as a musician and mystic.

Ethel **Griffies:** Ethel Woods (1878–1975), Eng. stage, movie actress, working in U.S.

Arthur **Griffinhoofe:** George Colman [the Younger] (1762–1836), Eng. dramatist. The pseudonym perhaps puns on Griffinfeet, a name of the marks by which the Desert Fairy was known in the Comtesse d'Aulnoy's fairy tale "The Yellow Dwarf" (1698).

Corinne **Griffith:** Corinne Scott (1898–1979), U.S. movie actress.

George **Griffith:** George Chetwynd Griffith-Jones (1857–1906), Eng. travel, early SF writer.

Kenneth **Griffith:** Kenneth Griffiths (1921–2006), Welsh-born Br. movie actor, documentary filmmaker. Griffith dropped the "s" from his surname when he became an actor, having been told at school that it was an anglicism.

Fred **Griffiths:** Frederick George Delaney (1856–1940), Eng. music-hall artist.

Ieuan **Griffiths:** David Matthew Williams (1900–1970), Welsh playwright.

Gritsko **Grigorenko:** Aleksandra Yevgenyevna Sudovshchikova-Kosach (1867–1924), Ukr. short-story, children's writer. The writer adopted a typical (male) Ukrainian name. It was used before her by another writer, Grigory Aleksandrovich Kushelev-Bezborodko (1832–1870).

Romayne **Grigorova:** Romayne Austin (1926–), Eng. ballet dancer, teacher. The dancer's name is not a contrived Slavic-style one, but her own married name, that of Grigor Grigorov, a Bulgarian journalist whom she married in 1960. "At our wedding reception several colleagues suggested I use Grigorova all the time, as it would look good on the programmes: Romayne Grigorova, Ballet Mistress to the Covent Garden Opera" [personal letter from Romayne Grigorova, November 15, 1982].

Roman **Grigoryev:** Roman Grigoryevich Katsman (Katzman) (1911–1972), Russ. movie director.

Sergey **Grigoryev:** Sergey Timofeyevich Grigoryev-Patrashkin (1875–1953), Russ. children's writer.

Dod **Grile:** Ambrose Gwinett Bierce (1842–?1914), U.S. short-story writer. The writer used this name for three collections of vitriolic sketches and witticisms published in the 1870s. The name looks like (but is probably not) an anagram ("Gold Ride," "Idler Dog," "Old Ridge," etc.).

Laurentius **Grimalus:** Wawrzyniec Goslicki (c.1530–1607), Pol. bishop, diplomat. The prelate used the Latin pseudonym for his principal work, *De optimo senatore* ("The Best Senator") (1568).

Aleksandr **Grin:** Aleksandr Stepanovich Grinevsky (1880–1932), Russ. novelist, short-story writer. The writer adopted a name that was originally his school nickname. For some early stories he used the name A. Stepanov, and for one or two adopted female names, among them Elsa Moravskaya and Victoria Klemm. See also the next entry below.

Elmar **Grin:** Aleksandr Vasilyevich Yakimov (1909–), Russ. writer. When his father died, the writer adopted the surname of his Estonian mother, and his first stories were published as by "Al. Grin." Later editors advised him to adopt a new first name to avoid confusion with Aleksandr **Grin.** "I had no time to think," he explained. "I suggested the first thing that came to mind. That was how I was landed with an Estonian name" [Dmitriyev, p.73].

Carleton **Grindle:** Gerald W. Page (1939–), U.S. SF, horror-fiction writer, editor.

Miron **Grindon:** Mondia Miron Grunberg (1909–1995), Rom.-born editor.

Harry **Gringo**: Henry Augustus Wise (1819–1869), U.S. author of melodramatic novels. Wise had been in the Mexican War, and recounted some of his experiences in *Los Gringos; or, An Inside View of Mexico and California, with Wanderings in Peru, Chile, and Polynesia* (1849). "Gringo" is a nickname used in Spanish-speaking countries for an English speaker. There may have been an implicit pun on the writer's surname, as Spanish *gringo* means "gibberish," "nonsense," the converse of "wise."

David **Grinnell**: Donald A. Wollheim (1914–1990), U.S. SF, fantasy writer, publisher. Wollheim also wrote as Millard Verne Gordon and Martin Pearson.

Juan **Gris**: José Victoriano González (1887–1927), Sp. Cubist painter, working in France. The artist had already adopted his pseudonym by around 1905.

Iosif **Grishashvili**: Iosif Grigoryevich Mamulaishvili (1889–1965), Georgian poet. The poet adopted a Georgian form of his patronymic, itself deriving from his father's first name Grigory (pet form Grisha). (The Georgian suffix *-shvili* corresponds to Russian *-ovich* or *-evich*, meaning "son of.")

Bruce **Grit**: John E. Bruce (1856–1924), U.S. black columnist. Bruce first used his pen name in 1884 when he began writing for the *Cleveland Gazette* and the *New York Age*.

Zanis **Griva**: Zanis Karlovich Folmanis (1910–1982), Latvian novelist. The writer's adopted name means "river mouth," denoting his birthplace near Tukums, west of Riga.

Grock: Charles Adrien Wettach (1880–1959), Swiss circus clown. Wettach had originally been a partner of another clown named Brick, whose own partner was Brock. Wettach took Brock's place when the latter left to carry out military service. "Grock" went well with "Brick" but was distinctive from "Brock." For a similar pairing of clown names, *see* **Bim**.

Redway **Grode** *see* Eduard **Blutig**

Charles **Grodin**: Charles Grodinsky (1935–), U.S. movie actor.

Ferde **Grofé**: Ferdinande Rudolf von Grofe (1892–1972), U.S. composer, conductor.

Grooverider: Raymond Bingham (1968–), Br. black dance-music DJ. The name is appropriate for a DJ, who "rides grooves" or plays records.

Winston **Groovy**: Winston Tucker (1946–), Jamaican reggae musician.

Gros-Guillaume: Robert Guérin (*fl.*1598–1634), Fr. actor. The name, meaning "Fat William," described the actor's appearance. He accentuated his rotundity by strapping two belts around his middle

so that he resembled a walking barrel. He used the name for farces, but in serious plays was **La Fleur**.

Danny **Grossman**: Daniel Williams (1942–), U.S. ballet dancer.

Valerie **Grosvenor Myer**: Valerie Winifred Godwin (1925–2007), Eng. novelist, biographer, editor. The writer took her new surname by adding the maiden name of both of her great-grandmothers to that of her husband, Michael Myer.

George **Grosz**: Georg Ehrenfried Groß (1893–1959), Ger.-born U.S. painter. Together with John **Heartfield**, the artist anglicized his name in 1917 as an expression of his antiwar sentiments.

Anton **Grot**: Antocz Franziszek Groszewski (1884–1974), Pol. movie art director, working in U.S.

Frederick Philip **Grove**: Felix Paul Greve (1879–1948), Ger.-born Can. novelist. The writer adopted his new name in 1913 when he faked his suicide in Germany and reappeared in Canada as a teacher named Fred Grove.

Hal **Groves** *see* B. **Traven**

Growling Tiger: Neville Marcano (1915–1993), Trinidadian calypso singer.

René **Gruau**: [Conte] Renato Zavagli Ricciardelli delle Caminate (1909–2004), It. graphic desgner, illustrator. The artist took his new surname from the maiden name of his French mother, Marie Gruau de la Chesnaie.

Grubendol: Henry Oldenburg (?1615–1677), Ger.-born natural philosopher, working in England. The scholar used this anagrammatical name for some of his writings.

Victor David **Gruen**: Viktor David Grünbaum (1903–1980), Austr.-born U.S. architect, planner. Grünbaum lost his Viennese architectural practice in 1938, following the *Anschluss*, and emigrated to the United States, where he became a naturalized citizen and in 1943 shortened his name to Gruen.

Nora **Gruhn**: Nora Grunebaum (1905–?), Eng. opera singer, of Ger. descent.

Anastasius **Grün**: Anton Alexander, Graf von Auersperg (1806–1876), Austr. poet, statesman. The writer first used his pseudonym for *Der letzte Ritter* ("The Last Knight") (1830), a cycle of poems on the career of the emperor Maximilian I.

Matthias **Grünewald**: Matthis Gothardt (*c.*1470–1528), Ger. painter. The artist's name arose from a 17th-century misprinting of "Gothardt" as "Grünewald," and this is now the standard form of his name.

Sergey **Grustny**: Sergey Mikhaylovich Arkhangelsky (1859–1921), Russ. poet. The poet's new name means "sad," "melancholy." It summarized his writing, as is evident from the following verse (translated by A.R.) from one poem, "On Sleepless Nights" (1908):

The constant voice of woe unending,
The constant moan of heart that's numb.
The constant chains of iron unbending
Band hands around with shackles dumb.

Ellova **Gryn:** Montague Eliot (1870–1960), Eng. writer. Eliot used this punning name as the author of *Too Weak* (1907), a parody of Elinor Glyn's popular novel *Three Weeks* (1907).

Andreas **Gryphius:** Andreas Greif (1616–1664), Ger. poet, dramatist.

Kit **Guard:** Christen Klitgaard (1894–1961), Dan.-born U.S. stage, movie comedian.

Nathaniel **Gubbins:** Edward Spencer Mott (1844–1910), Eng. sporting writer. Presumably the writer based his pen name on "gubbins" as a slang word for miscellanea or oddments, although Gubbins is in fact a surname in its own right. He also used the friendly "Gub-Gub."

Hilde **Güden:** Hilde Herrmann (1917–1988), Austr. opera singer.

Guerau de Liost: Jaume Bofill y Mates (1878–1933), Sp. (Catalan) poet.

Il **Guercino:** Giovanni Francesco Barbieri (1591–1666), It. painter, illustrator. The artist's name is Italian for "the squinting one," referring to an eye defect. His strabismus does not seem to have affected the quality of his work.

Martin **Guerre:** Arnault du Tilh (*fl.*1550s), Fr. impostor. Martin Guerre was a soldier living in southern France who disappeared around 1548. His family presumed him dead, but four years later he turned up again. His appearance had changed somewhat, but he was accepted by Bertrande, his wife of ten years, who lived happily with him for three years and bore him two children to add to the son she had before Martin had gone away. Then the real Martin Guerre turned up, albeit minus a leg, and the impostor was exposed. The motive for his impersonation remains uncertain. He was sent to the gallows, while Bertrande and the real Martin were reconciled in a marriage that produced another son. The story was the subject of an acclaimed French movie, *Le Retour de Martin Guerre* (1982).

Guerrita: Rafael Guerra Bejarano (1862–1941), Sp. bullfighter.

Jules **Guesde:** Mathieu Jules Basile (1845–1922), Fr. socialist leader, popularizer of Marxism. The politician adopted his mother's maiden name.

George **Guess:** Sequoyah (?1770–1843), Native American language teacher, writer. The half-breed Cherokee, who devised a system of writing for his tribe, was probably the son of a British trader named Nathaniel Guess (or Gist). His native name (in the spelling Sequoia) was given to the giant redwoods of California and to Sequoia National Park in that state.

Georges **Guétary:** Lambros Woorlou (1915–1997), Fr. singer, variety artist, of Gk.-Egyptian origin. The musician based his professional name on the Basque town of Guéthary.

Che **Guevara:** Ernesto Guevara de la Serna (1928–1967), Argentinian-born guerrilla leader. Many Argentines have a verbal mannerism in that they punctuate their speech with the interjection ¡che! Guevara did this, and the word became his nickname, which he subsequently adopted as a first name. He regarded his new name as "the most important and cherished part of my life," adding: "Everything that came before it, my surname and my Christian name, are minor, personal, and insignificant details."

Jean-Pierre **Guignon:** Giovanni Pietro Ghignone (1702–1774), It.-born Fr. violinist, composer. The musician gallicized his Italian name on settling in France.

Yvette **Guilbert:** Emma Laure Esther Guilbert (1865–1944), Fr. diseuse. The singer was advised at the start of her career to take a new first name: "A name, it was explained to her, was important: it should have a 'ring' to it, and a 'ring' the prosaic combination of 'Emma Guilbert' clearly lacked.... A young man who happened to know Guy de Maupassant offered to ask that celebrity's opinion. Within a few days came a laconic reply: 'Tell her to call herself Yvette,' the great man counselled. Yvette Guilbert. Completely satisfying, everyone agreed. Here was a name with a ring to it" [Bettina Knapp and Myra Chipman, *That Was Yvette*, 1966].

Robert **Guillaume:** Robert Peter Williams (1937–), U.S. movie, TV actor.

Tata **Guines:** Aristides Soto Alejo (1930–2008), Cuban percussionist. The musician took his stage name from his home neighborhood of Guines, near Havana.

[Sir] Alec **Guinness:** Alec Guinness de Cuffe (1914–2000), Br. stage, movie actor. "My birth certificate registers me as Alec Guinness de Cuffe, born in Marylebone, London, 2nd April 1914. My mother at the time was a Miss Agnes Cuffe; my father's name is left an intriguing, speculative blank. When I was five years old my mother married an army Captain, a Scot named David Stiven, and from then until I left my preparatory school I was known as Alec Stiven (a name I rather liked, although I hated and dreaded my stepfather). At fourteen I was told, quite casually, that my real name was Guinness and that de Cuffe and Stiven were obliterated" [Alec Guinness, *Blessings in Disguise*, 1985].

Bonnie **Guitar:** Bonnie Buckingham (1923–), U.S. country musician. Buckingham adopted her new name in the mid-1950s, when she worked as a session guitarist in Los Angeles.

Johnny **Guitar:** John Byrne (1939–1999), Br. pop musician. The cofounder of the band Rory **Storm** and the Hurricanes took his performing name from the 1953 western movie so titled.

Guitar Curtis: Curtis Colter (1940–1995), U.S. guitarist.

Guitar Gable: Gabriel Perrodin (1937–), U.S. guitarist.

Guitar Gabriel: Robert Jones (1925–1996), U.S. black blues musician. The artist gained his new name while playing with a fair, although when recording in Pittsburgh in 1970 he was renamed Nyles Jones by his producer.

Guitar Nubbit: Alvin Hankerson (1923–), U.S. guitarist. "Nubbit" was a nickname given the player following the loss of the tip of his right thumb at the age of three.

Guitar Shorty: (1) John Henry Fortescue (1923–1976), U.S. guitarist, street singer; (2) David William Kearney (1939–), U.S. black blues musician.

Guitar Slim: Eddie Jones (1926–1959), U.S. black blues guitarist, singer.

Guitar Slim, Jr.: Rodney Armstrong (1951–), U.S. black blues guitarist, singer, son of **Guitar Slim**.

Lemuel **Gulliver:** Jonathan Swift (1667–1745), Ir.-born satirist, clergyman, of Eng. parentage. Swift used this name as the supposed author of *Gulliver's Travels* (1726), of which the full title was: *Travels into several Remote Nations of the World. In four parts. By Lemuel Gulliver, first a Surgeon, and then a Captain of several Ships.* The original edition has a portrait of the fictional author at the age of 58, Swift's own age at the time of writing, captioned: "CAPTAIN LEMUEL GULLIVER OF REDRIFF. ÆTAT. SUÆ LVIII." (Redriff is modern Rotherhithe, London.) The reason for Swift's choice of this name for his hero is uncertain. According to Paul Turner, editor of the work in the 1971 "World's Classics" edition, "Gulliver" is probably meant to suggest gullibility, while "Lemuel," meaning literally "devoted to God," should be taken ironically.

Friedrich **Gundolf:** Friedrich Gundelfinger (1880–1931), Ger. literary historian, poet.

Yilmaz **Güney:** Yilmaz Pütün (1937–1984), Turk. movie director.

Judy **Gunn:** Judy Winfindale (1914–), Br. stage actress. The actress adopted her mother's maiden name as her stage name, no doubt for reasons of brevity as much as anything.

Thom **Gunn:** William Guinneach Gunn (1929–2004), Eng. poet, of Sc. origin. The poet changed his name by deed poll in 1949, shortly before completing service in the Royal Army Educational Corps. In so doing, he replaced Guinneach, a Gaelic form of his surname, with a form of his mother's maiden name, Thomson. Commentators have suggested that the new name represented Gunn's rejection of his father in favor of his mother. "There were many reasons why the name seemed appropriate: for one thing it virtually rhymes with 'John Donne,' who was Gunn's first important poetic model ... and for another, the poet who as a boy had delighted in Robert Louis Stevenson ... would have enjoyed the echo of Ben Gunn from *Treasure Island*. In a writer preoccupied with soldiers, moreover, the hint of a firearm behind the forceful spondee seems more than fitting, and indeed, during his teens, he published a poem as 'Tommy Gunn'" [Clive Wilmer, "The self you choose," *Times Literary Supplement*, April 25, 2008].

Kristjana **Gunnars:** Kristjana Gunnarsdóttir (1948–), Icelandic-born Can. writer. The writer emigrated to the U.S. in 1964, then settled in Canada. She dropped the *-dóttir*, "daughter," that all Icelandic women have in their surname, whether married or not. (The first part of the surname is the forename of the bearer's father, in this case Gunnar.)

Norman **Gunston:** Garry McDonald (1948–), Austral. TV comedian.

Shusha **Guppy:** Shamsi Assar (1935–2008), Iranian singer, writer. At age 17 the singer emigrated to France, where she adopted the artistic name Shusha, after the ancient city of Susa (biblical Shushan) in southwestern Iran. Her second name is that of the English geographer and art dealer Nicholas Guppy, whom she went to London to marry in 1961. The marriage was dissolved in 1976.

Sigrid **Gurie:** Sigrid Gurie Haukelid (1911–1969), Norw.-born U.S. movie actress.

Yelena **Guro:** Yelena Genrikhovna Notenberg (1877–1913), Russ. writer.

Gus: George William Smith (1915–1999), Eng. cartoonist. The artist's signature represents his initials, the "W" becoming "U."

Sergey Ivanovich **Gusev:** Yakov Davidovich Drabkin (1874–1933), Russ. Communist official.

Angelina **Gushington:** Charles Wallwyn Radcliffe-Cooke (1841–1911), Br. agriculturist, writer. The author used this name for *Thoughts on Men and Things; A Series of Essays* (1868).

Hon. Impulsia **Gushington:** Helena Selina Sheridan (1806–1867), Ir. song, ballad writer. Helena Sheridan, granddaughter of the playwright Richard Brinsley Sheridan, who was in turn Mrs. Blackwood, Lady Dufferin, and the Countess of Blackwood, used this name for *Lispings from Low Latitudes; or Extracts from the Journal of the Hon. Impulsia Gushington* (1863), written as a widow when she accompanied her son, Frederick Temple Blackwood, Lord Dufferin, on his travels up the Nile. The title of her work contrasts with her son's *Letters from High Latitudes* (1859), an account of his yachting voyage to Iceland.

Philip **Guston:** Philip Goldstein (1913–1980), Can.-born U.S. artist, of Russ. Jewish parentage.

Johannes **Gutenberg:** Johann Gensfleisch (*c.*1398–1468), Ger. printing pioneer. The inventor exchanged his original name, meaning "gooseflesh," for that of a property owned by his second wife, Else Wilse, the *Haus zum Gutenberg* ("house by the good hill") in Mainz.

Albert Paris von **Gütersloh:** Albert Konrad Kiehtreiber (1887–1973), Austr. painter, writer. The artist adopted this name for his writing, and took Gütersloh as his official name in 1921. He was earlier an actor and stage designer under the name Albert Matthäus.

Ramsay **Guthrie:** [Rev.] John George Bowran (1869–1946), Eng. Methodist minister, writer.

Guto Nyth Bran: Griffith Morgan (1700–1737), Welsh athlete. The champion runner's first name is a form of his original name, Griffith, while the rest of the name is that of the farm, Nyth Bran, where he lived.

Gutyn Peris: Griffith Williams (1769–1838), Welsh poet. The writer's new first name is a form of his original name, Griffith, while his second name, a forename in its own right, derives from Llyn Peris, the lake in northwest Wales by which he spent his boyhood.

Billy "Bip" **Guy:** Frank William Phillips, Jr. (1936–2002), U.S. R&B singer.

Gwallter Mechain: Walter Davies (1761–1849), Welsh poet. The poet took his bardic name from his native village of Llanfechain (probably originally meaning "little church," but popularly understood as "Mechain's church"), Montgomeryshire (now Powys).

Gweirydd ap Rhys: Robert John Pryse (1807–1889), Welsh writer, historian. The writer's new surname is a Welsh form of his original name, meaning literally "son of Rhys." His son, John Robert Pryse (1840–1862), known as Golyddan, and daughter, Catherine Prichard (1842–1909), known as Buddug, were both poets. The latter name means "victorious," and is related to that of Queen Boudicca (Boadicea).

Gwenallt: David James Jones (1899–1968), Welsh poet, critic, scholar. The writer was born in the village of Alltwen, near Swansea, and took a bardic name that reversed the two elements of this. The name itself means "white hill" or "white wood."

Edmund **Gwenn:** Edmund Kellaway (1875–1959), Welsh movie actor, working in U.S.

Gwili: John Jenkins (1872–1936), Welsh poet. The poet and archdruid took his bardic name from the Gwili River, Carmarthenshire, where he was born.

Gwilym Callestr: William Edwards (1790–1855), Welsh poet. The poet came from Flintshire. Hence his name, Welsh *callestr* meaning "flint."

Gwilym Cyfeiliog: William Williams (1801–1876), Welsh poet. The poet's name means "William the accompanist."

Gwilym Deudraeth: William Thomas Edwards (1863–1940), Welsh poet. The writer was raised in the town of Penrhyndeudraeth. Hence his bardic name, meaning "William of Deudraeth." (This part of the placename means "two beaches.") Compare the names below.

Gwilym Gellideg: William Morgan (1808–1878), Welsh poet, musician. The writer spent most of his life in Gellideg, near Merthyr Tydfil. Hence his name, meaning "William of Gellideg."

Gwilym Hiraethog: William Rees (1802–1883), Welsh poet, preacher. The poet was born near Llansannan, Denbighshire (now Conwy), in a village below a mountain named Hiraethog. Hence his bardic name, "William of Hiraethog."

Gwilym Lleyn: William Rowlands (1802–1865), Welsh bibliographer, editor. The writer's name means "William of Lleyn," from the region in northwest Wales where he was born.

Gwilym Marles: William Thomas (1834–1879), Welsh poet. The writer adopted the name of his paternal uncle. (The poet Dylan Thomas was given his middle name, Marlais, in honor of the same man.)

Gwilym Morgannwg: Thomas Williams (1778–1835), Welsh poet. The writer's name means "William of Glamorgan," referring to the historic region (and county) in which he spent his childhood.

Gwilym Pant Taf: William Parry (1836–1903), Welsh poet. The writer's name means "William of Taff Valley," referring to the river that flows through the historic region of Glamorgan where he was born.

Gwilym Teilo: William Davies (1831–1892), Welsh poet, historian. The writer was born near the town of Llandeilo, and thus has a name deriving from this, meaning "William of Teilo." The town's own name means "(St.) Teilo's church."

Gwydderig: Richard Williams (1842–1917), Welsh poet. The writer took his bardic name from that of a river in his native Carmarthenshire.

Gwylfa: Richard Roberts (1871–1935), Welsh poet. The Congregational minister took a bardic name from a local placename meaning "watching place."

Gwyndaf: Evan Gwyndaf Evans (1913–1986), Welsh poet. The poet adopted the name of a Celtic saint as his bardic name.

Anne **Gwynne:** Marguerite Gwynne Trice (1918–2003), U.S. movie actress.

Arthur **Gwynne:** Gwynfil Evans (1898–1938),

Welsh-born Br. writer of stories for boys. The writer also used the name Barry Western.

Paul **Gwynne**: Ernest Slater (?–1942), Eng. electrical engineer, novelist. "Spent many years on engineering schemes abroad, chiefly in Spain and Mexico, and under the above pseudonym has specialized in works of fiction with Spanish and French setting, generally Spanish" [*Who's Who*].

Gwynoro: John Davies (1855–1935), Welsh poet, patriot. The poet adopted the name of an early saint as his bardic name.

Gwyrosydd: Daniel James (1847–1920), Welsh poet. The writer adopted a local placename as his bardic name.

Greta **Gynt**: Margrethe Woxholt (1916–2000), Norw.-born Br. movie actress. The actress began her career as a dancer in London, England, and her name was changed because her surname sounded too much like the London district of Vauxhall. "Gynt was settled upon while listening to a four-piece orchestra at Clifton Court in Baker Street playing Grieg's *Peer Gynt* suite" [*The Times*, April 4, 2000].

Gyp: Sibylle-Gabrielle Marie-Antoinette de Riquetti de Mirabeau, Comtesse de Martel de Janville (1849–1932), Fr. novelist. The writer is said to have taken her name from Jip, the little dog in Charles Dickens's *David Copperfield*. She pronounced the name "Zheep." When making her writing debut in 1879 she originally called herself "Scamp." For her own illustrations to her novels she signed herself "Bob." Her mother had earlier written stories in the journal *La Vie Parisienne* under the name "Chut!"

"Gyp" was a male name, the persona of a military officer. "Although she let it be known that she wrote all night in a négligé using purple ink, Gyp also insisted on the maleness of her literary persona; Gyp was a 'man of letters,' always 'to be spoken of in the *masculine*'" [*Times Literary Supplement*, January 19, 1996].

Haakon VII: Christian Frederik Carl Georg Valdemar Axel (1872–1957), Norw. king. The king was originally Prince Carl (Charles) of Denmark. When elected to the throne in 1905, as the first king of Norway following the restoration of the country's independence, he took the Old Norse name of Haakon, not used as a royal name since the 14th century. His son, **Olaf V**, was similarly renamed at the time of his father's coronation.

ha-Ari: Isaac ben Solomon Luria (1534–1572), Jewish kabbalist. The name by which Luria came to be known, Hebrew for "the lion," is an acronym of *ha*-Elohi *Rabbi Yitzhak*, "the Divine Rabbi Isaac."

Hans **Habe**: Hans Békessy (1911–1977), Hung.-born Ger. writer, journalist.

Jeanne **Hachette**: Jeanne Laisné (or Fourquet)

(1456–?), Fr. heroine. Jeanne Hachette defended the city of Beauvais when it was besieged by Charles the Bold, Duke of Burgundy, in 1472. Her name is said to have arisen from the ax (French *hachette*) that she used to repel the assailants.

Buddy **Hackett**: Leonard Hacker (1924–2003), U.S. movie comedian.

Albert **Haddock**: [Sir] Alan Patrick Herbert (1890–1971), Eng. journalist, writer. "A.P.H.," as he was usually known, used this name when he wanted to refer to himself in comic articles in *Punch*.

Christopher **Haddon**: John Leslie Palmer (1885–1944), Eng. novelist, theater critic.

Peter **Haddon**: Peter Tildsley (1898–1962), Br. stage, movie actor.

Shafi **Hadi**: Curtis Porter (1929–), U.S. black jazz musician.

Reed **Hadley**: Reed Herring (1911–1974), U.S. movie actor. The actor began his career on stage and was on radio as Red Ryder.

Hafetz Hayyim: Israel Meir Kagan (originally Poupko) (1838–1933), Lithuanian Jewish writer. The Talmudic and Rabbinic scholar came to be known by the title of his first book, which he published anonymously in 1873. It means "delighteth in life," a phrase from the Bible: "What man is he that delighteth in life, and loveth many days, that he may see good?" (Psalm 34:12).

Hafez (or Hafiz): (1) Muhammad Shams ud-Din (*c*.1325–1389), Persian poet; (2) Thomas Stott (1755–1829), Ir. poet. The Persian poet's adopted Arabic name means "one who remembers," that is, a Muslim who can recite the Koran by heart. Stott adopted his name when contributing poetry to the *Northern Star*.

Sebastian **Haffner**: Raimund Pretzel (1907–1999), Ger. writer, working in U.K. The former lawyer fled to Britain in 1939 and soon learned English. To protect his family in the Third Reich he adopted a new name: "Sebastian" from Johann Sebastian Bach, "Haffner" from Mozart's symphony so titled.

Christopher **Hagen** *see* Ted **Bundy**.

Jean **Hagen**: Jean Shirley Verhagen (1923–1977), U.S. movie actress.

William **Haggard**: Richard Henry Michael Clayton (1907–1993), Eng. author of spy, mystery novels. The writer assumed his mother's maiden name as his pen name.

Bob **Haggart**: Robert Sherwood (1914–1998), U.S. jazz musician.

Larry **Hagman**: Larry Hageman (1931–), U.S. movie, TV actor.

Priscilla **Hagon** *see* Jean **Estoril**

ha-Gra: Elijah ben Solomon Zalman (1720–

1797), Lithuanian Jewish scholar. The name is an acronym of *ha-Gaon Rabbi* Eliyahu, "the Gaon Rabbi Elijah." *Gaon* ("pride," "excellence") is an honorific title of the heads of Jewish academies in Babylonia.

Alec **Haig**   *see*   James **Fraser**

Fenil **Haig**   *see*   Ford Madox **Ford**

Jack **Haig:** Jack Coppin (1913–1989), Eng. stage comedian, TV actor.

Kevin **Haigen:** Kevin Higgenbotham (1954–), U.S. ballet dancer.

Bernard **Haigh:** Clara Edwards (1887–1974), U.S. pianist, singer, composer.

Haile Selassie: Tafari Makonnen (1892–1975), emperor of Ethiopia. The name adopted by the former Ras ("Prince") Tafari, on being crowned emperor in 1930, is effectively a title, meaning "Might of the Trinity." It was the emperor's princely name that gave the title of the Rastafarians, the Jamaican sect who believe that Ras Tafari was divine and that he would secure their repatriation to their African homeland.

Connie **Haines:** Yvonne Marie Antoinette Jamais (1921–2008), U.S. cabaret singer. The singer was given her stage name by bandleader Harry James, who in 1939 overheard her demonstrating songs for music publisher Larry Shayne. James offered her a job as his singer, starting the same night. "She did not know that he had rechristened her Connie Haines until she read her name in lights outside the Benjamin Franklin Hotel, where the band was appearing. James later explained that her full name would not fit on the billboard, and he had come up on the spur of the moment with something that more or less rhymed with James" [*The Times*, October 4, 2008].

Sadik **Hakim:** Argonne Thornton (1922–1983), U.S. black jazz pianist. The musician adopted his Muslim name after converting to Islam in 1947.

Talib Rasul **Hakim:** Stepehen Alexander Chambers (1940–1988), U.S. black musician. Chambers became interested in Sufism in the 1960s and adopted his Arabic name then.

Hala: Robert Barton (*fl.*1880–1908), Eng. trapeze artist.

Ann **Halam:** Gwyneth A. Jones (1952–), Eng. fantasy, SF, children's writer. Jones adopted this name for her fiction for children.

John **Halas:** John Halasz (1912–1995), Hung.-born Br. animated cartoon producer, teaming with Joy Batchelor (1914–1991), Eng. animated cartoon producer, his wife.

Olivér **Halassy:** Olivér Haltmayer (1909–1946), Hung. water-polo player.

Emanuel **Haldeman-Julius:** Emanuel Julius (1889–1951), U.S. writer, publisher, of Ukr. Jewish parentage. In 1916 Julius (from a family whose original name was Zolajefsky) married Anna Marcet Haldeman, each adding the other's name to their original name.

C.F. **Haldenby:** [Rev.] Erskine Neale (1804–1883), Eng. religious novelist.

Henry **Haldin:** Henry Hyman Haldinstein (1863–1931), Br. lawyer. The authority on Stock Exchange law modified his German Jewish name during World War I, when he was "authorised to use and bear the name of Haldin by Royal Licence granted 15 June 1915" [*Who's Who*].

Alan **Hale:** Rufus Alan McKahan (1892–1950), U.S. movie actor.

Arthur William **Hale:** Arthur William Glunt (1896–1971), U.S. radio news broadcaster. Glunt assumed his more media-friendly surname in 1935 when Transradio Press Service chose him to be newscaster for its 11:00 P.M. spot on radio station WOR, whose staff he had joined five years earlier.

Binnie **Hale:** Bernice Mary Hale-Monro (1899–1984), Eng. stage comedienne, sister of Sonnie **Hale**.

Creighton **Hale:** Patrick Fitzgerald (1882–1965), U.S. movie actor.

Jonathan **Hale:** Jonathan Hatley (1891–1966), Can.-born U.S. movie actor.

Katherine **Hale:** Amelia Beers Warnock (1878–1956), Can. poet, music critic, writer. The writer adopted the first two names of her mother, Katherine Hale Warnock, née Bayard.

Keron **Hale**   *see*   G.B. **Lancaster**.

Sonnie **Hale:** John Robert Hale-Monro (1902–1959), Eng. stage, movie comedian, brother of Binnie **Hale**.

Fromental **Halévy:** Jacques-François-Fromental Élie Lévy (1799–1862), Fr. composer, of Jewish parentage. The first two added letters of the composer's surname are the initials of his original first names *Henry Aron*. In Hebrew, *ha-lewi* means "the Levite" (*ha*, "the," + *lewi*, "Levite").

Rodolfo **Halffter:** Rodolfo Escriche (1900–1987), Sp. composer, working in Mexico. Rodolfo's brother, composer and conductor Ernesto Halffter (1905–1989), adopted the same name.

Half Pint: Lyndon Roberts (*c.*1962–), Jamaican reggae singer. The musician adopted his nickname, given him for his diminutive size.

Hugh **Haliburton:** James Logie Robertson (1846–1922), Sc. poet, prose writer.

M.Y. **Halidom:** ? (*fl.*1890s–1900s), Br. horror-story writer(s). The identity of the writer(s) is still uncertain, although the assumed name clearly derives from the oath "by my halidom," "halidom" being an old word for "holiness." Halidom also wrote as Dryasdust, under which name appeared the three-volume *Tales of the Wonder Club* (1899–1900), with stories of the supernatural.

Robert **Halifax:** Robert Edwin Young (1870–?) Eng. novelist.

Adam **Hall** *see* Elleston **Trevor**

Anmer **Hall:** Alderson Burrell Horne (1863–1953), Br. stage actor, theatrical director.

Aylmer **Hall:** Norah Eleanor Lyle Hall, née Cummins (1914–), Br. children's writer. For her new first name the writer adopted the middle name of her husband, Robert Aylmer Hall, and the complete name was originally used for stories written jointly with him.

Daryl **Hall:** Daryl Hohl (1949–), U.S. rock musician, teaming with John Oates (1949–).

Frank **Hall:** Herbert Stewart (1836–1898), Eng. popular songwriter.

Gus **Hall:** Arvo Kusta Halberg (1910–2000), U.S. Communist leader, of Finn. parentage. The future secretary-general of the Communist Party of the United States based his new name on his middle name and surname.

Holworthy **Hall:** Harold Everett Porter (1887–1936), U.S. novelist, short-story writer.

Huntz **Hall:** Henry Hall (1920–1999), U.S. movie actor.

James **Hall:** James Brown (1900–1940), U.S. movie actor.

James **Hall** *see* C.L. **Moore**

Jon **Hall:** Charles Hall Locher (1913–1979), U.S. movie actor. The actor began his film career as Charles Locher, then changed his name to Lloyd Crane in 1936 before finally becoming Jon Hall in 1937.

Monty **Hall:** Monty Halparin (1924–), Can. TV personality.

Owen **Hall:** James Davis (1848–1907), Ir. playwright, songwriter. Actress Ada **Reeve** had a story about Davis's pen name: "Originally he intended to call himself Owen May. This caused his witty novelist sister, Frank **Danby** ... to remark: 'Jimmie, ... you must be doing well if you are only owing in May.' After that he adopted the name of Hall, and it is on record that he and a friend collaborated under the [punning] pen-names of Owen Hall and Payne Nunn" [Ada Reeve, *Take It For A Fact*, 1954].

Patricia **Hall:** Maureen O'Connor (1940–), Br. crime writer.

Pauline **Hall:** Pauline Fredericka Schmidgall (or Schmitgall) (1860–1919), U.S. singer.

Radclyffe **Hall:** Marguerite Antonia Radclyffe-Hall (1886–1943), Eng. novelist, poet. The lesbian author of *The Well of Loneliness* (1928) personally preferred to be known as "John."

Ruth **Hall:** Ruth Hale Ibanez (1912–), U.S. movie actress.

[Sir] Charles **Hallé:** Karl Halle (1819–1895), Ger.-born Br. pianist, orchestral conductor. The musician settled in England in 1848 and ten years later founded the symphony orchestra named for him.

Joseph **Haller:** Henry Nelson Coleridge (1798–1843), Eng. lawyer, writer. The nephew of Samuel Taylor Coleridge (*see* Silas Tomkyn **Cumberbatch**) used this name in the *Quarterly Magazine*.

Andrew **Halliday:** Andrew Halliday Duff (1830–1877), Sc. journalist, essayist, dramatist.

Brett **Halliday:** Davis Dresser (1904–1977), U.S. author of "private eye" stories. The writer's new surname came from the name of the detective in his first novel. His publisher, however, had not liked the name Halliday and had changed it to Burke. The publisher's own name was Brett, and this was the one adopted by Dresser as his new forename. Among other names used by Dresser for pulp magazine short stories were Matthew Blood, Peter Shelley, Anthony Scott, Don Davis, Anderson Wayne, Hal Debrett (jointly with Kathleen Rollins), Asa Baker (for his first mystery), Sylvia Carson, and Kathryn Culver.

James **Halliday:** David Symington (1904–1984), Eng. writer on India, Africa.

Michael **Halliday** *see* Gordon **Ashe**

James Orchard **Halliwell-Phillipps:** James Orchard Halliwell (1820–1889), Eng. scholar. The Shakespearean scholar added the name of his wife, née Henrietta Phillipps, to his own following her incapacitation as the result of a riding accident in 1872.

Johnny **Hallyday:** Jean-Philippe Smet (1943–), Fr.-Belg. pop singer. The singer was virtually abandoned by his parents, and was raised by his aunt, Hélène Mar, wife of U.S. singer and dancer Lee Halliday. As a boy he accompanied his relatives on all their tours around Europe, and in due course adopted the name Halliday, but with a small change in spelling. In 2004 he applied for Belgian citizenship.

Friedrich **Halm:** Eligius Franz Joseph, Freiherr von Münch-Bellinghausen (1806–1871), Ger. playwright. Münch first used his pen name in 1834.

Brett **Halsey:** Charles Hand (1933–), U.S. movie actor.

Margaret **Halstan:** Margaret Hertz (1879–1967), Br. stage actress.

Halston: Roy Halston Frowick (1932–1990), U.S. fashion designer. Halston's single name, originally his middle name, was that of his maternal grandfather, Halston Holmes.

Hersch **Hamel:** Herschel Himmelstein (1928–), U.S. bassist.

Asger **Hamerik:** Asger Hammerich (1843–1923), Dan. composer, of Ger. parentage. Asger's son, composer and conductor Ebbe Hamerik (1898–1951), adopted the same name.

Robert **Hamerling:** Rupert Johann Hammerling (1830–1889), Austr. poet.

Sufi Abdul **Hamid:** Eugene Brown (1903–1938), U.S. black religious, labor leader. Hamid claimed to have been taken to Egypt at the age of nine, then to Greece for schooling before returning to the United States in 1923. He then joined the Ahamidab movement, an Islamic organization, changing his name to Bishop Conshankin. In 1930 he moved to New York and founded the International Islamic Industrial Alliance (later Negro Industrial and Clerical Alliance), a boycott organization, under the name Sufi Abdul Hamid. "Sufi" is properly the title of a Muslim mystic, while Abdul Hamid is a regular Islamic proper name (that of two Ottoman sultans).

Cicely **Hamilton:** Cicely Mary Hammill (1872–1952), Eng. novelist, playwright, stage actress, of Eng./Sc.-Ir. parentage. The writer first adopted the name for the stage. She also acted as Elfreda Salisbury.

Clive **Hamilton:** Clive Staples Lewis (1898–1963), Br. writer on literary, religious subjects, novelist, children's writer. C.S. Lewis adopted his mother's maiden name for his long narrative poem *Dymer* (1926).

Cosmo **Hamilton:** Cosmo Gibbs (1879–1942), Eng. playwright, novelist. The writer adopted his mother's maiden name as his pen name.

David **Hamilton:** David Pilditch (1939–), Eng. radio, TV announcer, presenter. The broadcaster adopted his mother's maiden name (his own middle name) when he began his career in radio. At the time he was carrying out his statutory national service in the Royal Air Force at the base at Compton Bassett, Wiltshire, where John Dightam, the corporal who ran the services broadcasting station, Compton Forces Network, suggested he change his name. "Pilditch is too unusual. You'll need something people will remember easily if you ever make it to BFN [British Forces Network]" [David Hamilton, *The Music Game: An Autobiography*, 1986].

Dorothy **Hamilton:** Dorothy Jones (1897–?), Br. stage actress. The actress seems to have adopted a variant of Hampton, her mother's maiden name.

[Lady] Emma **Hamilton:** Amy Lyon (1765–1815), Eng. society leader, mistress of naval hero Horatio Nelson. In 1781, when she was 16, Amy Lyon was calling herself Emily Hart when she began to live with Charles Francis Greville, nephew of the man who ten years later, when she was 26, became her husband, 61-year-old Sir William Hamilton.

Gail **Hamilton:** Mary Abigail Dodge (1833–1896), U.S. popular writer, essayist. The writer, associated with women's issues, adapted her second name to provide her first name, taking her new surname from Hamilton, her Massachusetts hometown.

Hervey **Hamilton** *see* Denise **Robins**

John **Hamilton** *see* Achmed **Abdullah**

M. **Hamilton:** Mary Spotswood Luck, née Ash (1866–1952), Ir. novelist.

Russ **Hamilton:** Ronald Hulme (1933–), Eng. popular singer, songwriter.

Edith **Hamlet:** Edith Lyttelton, née Balfour (1873–1945), Austral.-born N.Z. novelist, dramatist.

Paul **Hamlyn:** Paul Bertrand Hamburger (1926–2001), Br. publisher. The publisher came to Britain as a German Jewish refugee from Berlin in 1933, when he was only seven. He changed his name because as a child he did not like being nicknamed "Sausage" and "Wimpy" at school. His elder brother was the poet and translator Michael Hamburger (1924–2007).

M.C. **Hammer:** Stanley Kirk Burrell (1963–), U.S. black rapper. The rap artist, born in Oakland, California, was nicknamed "Little Hammer" in his teens from his resemblance to Oakland A's big hitter, "Hammerin' Hank" Aaron. He later called himself "M.C. Hammer," the initials being the standard abbreviation for "master of ceremonies." (A DJ could make himself MC by means of his rapping. Hence the many rappers and rap groups using the initials.) The name happens to suggest that of Mike Hammer, the tough tec of Mickey Spillane's thrillers. From 1991 Burrell called himself simply Hammer, but reverted to M.C. Hammer for his 1995 album *Inside Out*.

Will **Hammer:** William Hinds (1897–1957), Br. movie producer, a founder (1947) of Hammer Movies, noted for their horror content. Hinds was originally a jeweler in Hammersmith, London, and appears to have taken his new name from there.

Hans **Hammergafferstein:** Henry Wadsworth Longfellow (1807–1882), U.S. poet. The poet used this name for a minor work, *Nights Revealings from the Ancient Sclavonian, etc.*, following it up, as "H.W.L.," with *Nights Revealings from the Ancient Sclavonian of Hans Hammergafferstein*.

Nicky **Hammerhead:** John Scott Pallotta (1960–1992), Br. rock drummer, stage actor.

Alexander **Hammid:** Alexander Hackenschmied (1907–2004), Cz. photographer, documentary director, working in U.S., first husband of Maya **Deren**.

Kay **Hammond:** Dorothy Katherine Clements, earlier Leon, née Standing (1909–1980), Eng. stage, movie actress. The actress adopted the pseudonym of her mother, née Dorothy Plaskitt, as her stage name.

Keith **Hammond** *see* C.L. **Moore**

Pierre **Hamp:** Henri Louis Bourillon (1876–1962), Fr. novelist.

Walter **Hampden:** Walter Hampden Dougherty (1879–1955), U.S. stage, movie actor.

John **Hampson:** John Simpson (1901–1955), Br. novelist.

Robert **Hampton:** Robert Paul Toop (1962–), Sc. ballet dancer.

Hamsalekha: Govindaraju Gangaraju (1951–), Ind. movie music composer, songwriter.

Olphar **Hamst:** Ralph Thomas (*fl.*1850–1880), Eng. bibliographer. The anagrammatic pseudonym masks the name of one of the leading pseudonymists of his day, professionally a lawyer, and for the purposes of this book the important author of a *Handbook of Fictitious Names* (see Bibliography, p.525).

Knut **Hamsun:** Knut Pedersen (1859–1952), Norw. novelist. The writer had intended to adopt Hamsund as his pen name, as the name of the estate on the island of Hamarøy, near Narvik, where his family moved when he was four years old. When a printer omitted the final "d," however, he assumed the reduced name instead.

Hananokuni: Akihiro Noguchi (1959–), Jap. sumo wrestler. The wrestler's fighting name means "land of blossoms" (Japanese *hana*, "flower," "blossom" + *no*, "of" + *kuni*, "land," "country").

Hananoumi: Ken Sawaishi (1960–), Jap. sumo wrestler. The wrestler's fighting name means "sea of blossoms" (Japanese *hana*, "flower," "blossom" + *no*, "of" + *umi*, "sea," "ocean").

George Frideric **Handel:** Georg Friedrich Händel (1685–1759), Ger.-born Eng. composer. The composer went to England in 1710 and anglicized his name, with its unconventional spelling of "Frederick," five years later. He became a British subject in 1726.

Johnny **Handle:** John Alan Pandrich (1935–), Br. folk musician. No doubt the musician evolved his new name by way of a nickname "Panhandle," punning on his surname.

George Joseph **Handy:** George Joseph Hendleman (1920–1997), U.S. jazz musician.

Justin **Hannaford:** Shafto Justin Adair Fitz-Gerald (1859–1925), Br. novelist, dramatist.

Lance **Hannibal** *see* Tito **Simon**

Ezra **Hannon** *see* Evan **Hunter**

Hansi: Jean-Jacques Waltz (1873–1951), Fr. writer, caricaturist.

Gladys **Hanson:** Gladys Cook, née Snook (1887–1973), Eng. stage actress. The actress seems to have adapted her father's middle name, Harrison, as her stage name.

James Christian Meinich **Hanson:** Jens Christian Meinich Hansen (1864–1943), Norw.-born U.S. librarian.

John **Hanson:** John Stanley Watts (1922–1998), Can.-born Br. stage actor, singer.

Han Suyin: Elizabeth Rosalie Matthilde Clare Comber, née Kuanghu Chou (1917–), Br. novelist, of Chin.-Belg. parentage. The writer assumed a pseu-

donym meaning roughly "little voice of China," first using it for her novel *Destination Chungking* (1953), paying tribute to the stoicism of Chinese peasants in the face of poverty and the Japanese invasion. Her original Chinese name means "Moon Guest."

Erik Jan **Hanussen:** Herschel Steinschneider (1889–1933), Austr. "mentalist." Some German sources give the clairvoyant's professional name as Erik van Hanussen.

Abdul **Haq:** Humayoun Arsala (1957–2001), Afghan resistance leader. The guerrilla commander adopted his *nom de guerre* after joining Afghanistan's war against the Soviet Union in 1977.

Setsuko **Hara:** Masai Aida (1920–), Jap. movie actress.

Otto **Harbach:** Otto Abels Hauerbach (1873–1963), U.S. librettist, lyricist.

Robert **Harbin:** Edward Richard Charles Williams (1909–1978), S.A.–born Br. conjuror. The illusionist was obliged to take another name for distinction from the British conjuror Oswald Williams (1881–1937).

Robert **Harbinson:** Robert Harbinson Bryans (1928–), Ir. short-story writer.

E.Y. "Yip" **Harburg:** Isidore Hochberg (1896–1981), U.S. lyricist, librettist, of Russ. Jewish parentage. The musician's boyhood nickname was "Yipsel," a Yiddish word meaning "squirrel." He later adopted the first name Edgar and the initials E.Y. to represent this and the nickname.

Harcourt: Harcourt Dennis Mallet (1909–1988), Eng. cartoonist, writer.

Charles **Harcourt:** Charles Parker Hillier (1838–1880), Eng. actor.

Henry **Harcourt:** Henry Beaumont (1612–1673), Eng. Jesuit.

James **Harcourt:** James Hudson (1873–1951), Eng. stage actor.

Thomas **Harcourt:** Thomas Whitbread (1618–1679), Eng. Jesuit.

William **Harcourt:** (1) William Waring (1610–1679), Eng. Jesuit; (2) William Aylworth (1625–1679), Eng. Jesuit. Waring was also known by the name Barrow.

Ephraim **Hardcastle:** William Henry Pyne (1769–1843), Eng. painter, author. The artist used his pseudonym for his literary activities, which he began by way of a series of anecdotes on art and artists in the 1820s.

Theo **Hardeen:** Theodore Weiss (1876–1944), U.S. illusionist, brother of **Houdini**.

Maximilian **Harden:** Maximilian Felix Ernst Witkowski (1861–1927), Ger. political journalist. Harden also used the pseudonyms Kent, Apostata, Proteus, and Kunz von der Rosen.

Kate **Hardie:** Kate Oddie (1968–), Br. movie, TV actress. The actress is the daughter of the former TV comedian Bill Oddie. She changed her name to be dissociated from her father when making her first movie in 1983: "'I wasn't going to be known as Bill Oddie's bloody daughter, you could forget that!'" [*Sunday Times Magazine*, December 12, 1993]. Her new surname is a blend of those of her (separated) parents, her mother being Jean Hart, a former jazz singer.

Ty **Hardin:** Orson Whipple Hungerford II (1930–), U.S. TV, movie actor. The actor legally adopted his screen name. "Ty" was a boyhood nickname.

Wes **Hardin:** Henry John Keevill (1914–1978), Eng. writer of westerns. Other names used by Keevill are Clay Allison, Burt Alvord, Bill Bonney, Virgil Earp, Frank McLowery (the name of one of the victims of the celebrated O.K. Corral shootout in 1881), Burt Mossman, Johnny Ringo, and Will Travis.

Ann **Harding:** Dorothy Walton Gatley (1901–1981), U.S. stage, movie actress.

Duncan **Harding** *see* Leo **Kessler**

John Wesley **Harding:** Wesley Harding Stace (1965–), Br. folk-rock musician. Stace took his stage name from Bob **Dylan**'s 1968 album, *John Wesley Harding*.

Ernst **Hardt:** Ernst Stöckhardt (1876–1947), Ger. writer, translator.

Laura **Hardy** *see* Charlotte **Lamb**

Oliver **Hardy:** Oliver Norvell Hardy (1892–1957), U.S. movie comedian, teaming with Stan **Laurel**. Hardy was originally known by the maiden name of his mother, Emily Norvell, but later chose to be called by the name of his father, Oliver Hardy.

Cyril **Hare:** Alfred Alexander Gordon Clark (1900–1958), Eng. crime novelist. The writer, professionally a barrister (lawyer) and judge, took his name from Cyril Mansions, Battersea, London, where he settled after his marriage (1933), and his Temple chambers, Hare Court, where he worked.

David **Hare:** David Rippon (1947–), Br. playwright. The dramatist adopted his mother's maiden name as his professsional name.

[Sir] John **Hare:** John Fairs (1844–1921), Br. stage actor, theater manager.

Martin **Hare:** Zoë Zajdler, née Girling (*c.*1907–), Ir. journalist, writer.

Isser **Harel:** Isser Halperin (1912–2003), Israeli spymaster.

Yossi **Harel:** Yosef Hamburger (?1918–2008), Israeli intelligence officer.

Henry **Harford:** William Henry Hudson (1841–1922), Eng. naturalist, writer. W.H. Hudson, as he was usually known, used this name for a three-volume novel, *Fan: The Story of a Young Girl's Life* (1892).

Leonie **Hargreave:** Thomas M. Disch (1940–2008), U.S. novelist. Disch adopted this name for the "Gothic" novel *Clara Reeve* (1975).

Nick **Harkaway:** Nicholas Cornwell (1973–), Br. novelist, son of John **le Carré**. The author of *The Gone-Away World* (2008) took his pen name from Jack Harkaway, the famous hero of Victorian boys' fiction. "I settled on Harkaway ... I liked the way it sounded: far-off places, feats of daring. Maybe it's appropriate for a son looking to make his way in the world — and Jack Harkaway, after many years, ends up a father himself, which can't be all bad" [*Daily Telegraph*, June 28, 2008].

Caroline **Harker:** Caroline Owens (1966–), Br. movie, TV actress, sister of Susannah **Harker**. The sisters, born within 11 months of each other, are the daughters of actors Richard Owens and Polly Adams. Their parents separated when they were four and five, and on taking up their acting career they adopted the name of their actress grandmother, Joan Harker.

Susannah **Harker:** Susannah Owens (1965–), Br. movie, TV actress, sister of Caroline **Harker**.

Marion **Harland:** Mary Virginia Terhune, née Hawes (1830–1922), U.S. novelist, domestic expert. Hawes's first publications began to appear under a male pseudonym when she was 15 or 16. In 1854, not yet married, her first novel, *Alone*, was published as by Marion Harland and became a bestseller. Marion Harland's son was the writer Albert Payson Terhune (1872–1942), best known for his dog stories.

Steve **Harley:** Steven Nice (1951–), Eng. pop musician.

Renny **Harlin:** Lauri Harjula (1959–), Finn. movie director, working in U.S.

Harry Frederick **Harlow:** Harry Frederick Israel (1905–1981), U.S. comparative psychologist. The scientist gained a Ph.D. in 1930 when at Stanford University and in view of the anti–Semitic climate of the day was recommended by faculty advisers to change his surname. "Harlow" was the result.

Jean **Harlow:** Harlean Harlow Carpenter (1911–1937), U.S. movie actress. The actress was given her stage name in 1928 when she was hired by Fox Studios, with her new first name that of her mother and her surname her existing middle name.

Anthony **Harmer:** Henry Wharton (1664–1695), Eng. theologian. Wharton used this name for *A Specimen of Some Errors and Defects in the Reformation of the Church of England wrote by Gilbert Burnet, D.D.* (1693), pointing out errors (some of them by copyists) in the named bishop's work, the first two volumes of which appeared respectively in 1679 and 1681.

Harmonica Fats: Harvey Blackston (1927–2000), U.S. black blues harmonica player.

Harmonica Slim: Richard Riggins (1921–), U.S. black blues harmonica player. Compare the name of **Slim Harpo**.

Haro: Haro Reginald Victor Hodson (1923–), Sc.-born Br. cartoonist.

Rolf **Harolde:** Rolf Harolde Wigger (1899–1974), U.S. movie actor.

Charlie **Harper:** David Charles Perez (1944–), Eng. pop musician.

Tess **Harper:** Tessie Jean Washam (1950–), U.S. movie actress.

James **Harpole:** James Johnston Abraham (1876–1963), Ir. surgeon, writer. The medical specialist used this name for some of his writings.

George G. **Harrington:** William Mumford Baker (1825–1883), U.S. cleric, novelist.

Barbara **Harris:** Sandra Markowitz (1935–), U.S. movie actress.

Don "Sugarcane" **Harris:** Donald Bowman (1938–1999), U.S. blues-rock violinist.

Frank **Harris:** James Thomas Harris (1856–1931), Eng. journalist, biographer, writer, of Welsh parentage.

Jed **Harris:** Jacob Hirsch Horowitz (1900–1979), Austr.-born U.S. theatrical impresario.

Johana **Harris:** Beula Aleta Duffey (1912–1995), Can.-born U.S. pianist. The pianist's surname was that of her husband, composer Roy Harris. She assumed her new first name in honor of Johann Sebastian Bach. The single "n," instead of the expected two, was selected for numerological reasons.

Johnson **Harris** *see* John **Wyndham**

Jonathan **Harris:** Jonathan Charasuchin (1914–2002), U.S. movie, TV actor.

Lester **Harris:** Harry Lester (1920–1953), U.S. R&B musician.

MacDonald **Harris:** Donald William Heiney (1921–1993), U.S. writer, academic.

Mae **Harris** *see* Rosa **Henderson**

Mark **Harris:** Mark Finkelstein (1922–2007), U.S. novelist, short-story writer.

Peppermint **Harris:** Harrison D. Nelson, Jr. (1925–1999), U.S. black blues singer. The singer is said to have gotten his name when Bob Shand, his record manager, could not remember his real name. Harris kept the name so his religious family would not know that he sang that kind of music.

Edwin **Harrison** *see* Eric **Allen**

Michael **Harrison:** Maurice Desmond Rohan (1907–1991), Br. fantasy writer.

[Sir] Rex **Harrison:** Reginald Carey Harrison (1908–1990), Eng. stage, movie actor. Harrison adopted his new first name as a child: "At the early age of six or seven [I] decided that I was not a Reggie or a Reginald, and asked my mother if she would be so kind as to address me as Rex in future.... It would be nice to think that this regal choice was influenced by the heroic deeds of some ancient king or other.... It might even be amusing to think that perhaps I'd passed some early picture palace or place of entertainment called The Rex. Alas, I believe it was but a childish, arbitrary choice, which may, at best, have occurred because I heard someone calling his dog to heel" [Rex Harrison, *A Damned Serious Business*, 1990].

Uncle **Harry:** John Habberton (1842–1921), U.S. journalist, writer.

Jodie **Harsh:** Jay Clarke (1984–), Br. transvestite. The socialite's name puns on that of the English model and TV personality Jodie Marsh (1978–). "Jay Clarke is better known as Miss Jodie Harsh: drag queen extraordinaire, self-publicist without parallel and unrivalled queen bee of the party scene" [*Sunday Times*, August 26, 2007].

Alvin Youngblood **Gart:** Gregory Edward Hart (1963–), U.S. black blues musician.

Charley **Hart:** William Clarke Quantrill (1837–1865), U.S. guerrilla leader. Quantrill used this alias on moving in 1860 from Stanton, Kansas, to Lawrence, where he became a jayhawker (proslavery raider).

Dolores **Hart:** Dolores Hicks (1938–), U.S. movie actress.

Freddie **Hart:** Fred Segrest (1926–), U.S. country musician.

Gary **Hart:** Gary Warren Hartpence (1936–), U.S. political leader. The Democrat senator shortened his name when he was 25 and already married. He had tired of his real name at Yale Law School, where he was known by the nickname "Gary Hotpants."

Tony **Hart:** Anthony Cannon (1855–1891), U.S. actor, of Ir. parentage. Cannon changed his name to Hart in 1871 on teaming with Ned Harrigan (1844–1911) to tour as the vaudeville act Harrigan and Hart.

Bret **Harte:** Francis Brett Harte (1836–1902), U.S. short-story writer.

John **Hartford:** John Cowan Harford (1937–2001), U.S. country singer.

C. Gasquoine **Hartley:** Ada E. Gallichan, née White (1866–after 1911), Eng. writer, first wife of Geoffrey **Mortimer**.

Christine **Hartley** *see* Dair **Alexander**

Marsden **Hartley:** Edmund Hartley (1877–1943), U.S. painter. The artist adopted his stepmother's maiden name as his new first name.

Phil **Hartman:** Philip Edward Hartmann (1948–1998), Can.-born U.S. TV actor, comedian.

Simon **Harvester:** Henry St. John Clair Rumbold-Gibbs (1910–1975), Br. crime writer.

Caroline **Harvey:** Joanna Trollope (1943–), Eng. romantic novelist. The author used this name for *Charlotte, Alexandra* (1980) and later novels of the 1990s.

Jack **Harvey:** Ian James Rankin (1960–), Sc. novelist. The author mostly writes under his real name but devised this pseudonym for certain novels, taking it from the name of his first son and his wife's maiden name. "The marketing folk were pleased, reckoning that a name beginning with H could only be good, since it planted the book in the middle of the shelf, where the shopper's eye would easily find it. Rankin himself confesses to a more mischievous thought: 'Maybe fans of Jack **Higgins** would be tricked into buying my titles instead of his'" [*The Guardian*, March 29, 2006].

Laurence **Harvey:** Larushka Mischa Skikne (1928–1973), Lithuanian-born movie actor, working in U.K., U.S. The actor's name was changed by his agent, Gordon Harbord, who also created the name of Adrienne **Corri** and proposed Diana Scarlett for Diana **Dors.** His first name should be changed to "Laurence," he decided, while "Skikne" was "much too continental." "He always asked actors their mothers' names or the names of their relatives. Larry Skikne's mother's name had been Zotnik. That would never do. The most English name he could think of was Harvey, as in the solid Knightsbridge store, Harvey Nichols. Not so English as Harrods perhaps, but they could hardly call him Laurence Harrods. Harbord was quite pleased with the name Laurence Harvey. 'But we have to be careful,' he told Skikne. Together they searched the pages of the theatrical directory, but they found no other actor named Harvey" [Des Hickey and Gus Smith, *The Prince, Being the Public and Private Life of Larushka Mischa Skikne, a Jewish Lithuanian Vagabond Player, otherwise known as Laurence Harvey*, 1975].

Lilian **Harvey:** Helene Lilian Muriel Pape (1906–1968), Br. movie actress, of Ger. parentage.

Paul **Harvey:** Paul Harvey Aurandt (1918–2009), U.S. radio journalist.

Rachel **Harvey** *see* Lozania **Prole**

Ronald **Harwood:** Ronald Horwitz (1934–), Br. stage, TV actor, writer.

John **Haslette:** John George Haslette Vahey (1881–1938), Ir. writer of crime fiction. Other names used by Vahey were John Mowbray, Vernon Loder, Walter Proudfoot, Henrietta Clandon, and Anthony Lang.

Signe **Hasso:** Signe Larsson (1910–2002), Swe. movie actress.

Graham **Hastings** *see* Roderic **Graeme**

Hudson **Hastings** *see* C.L. **Moore**

Hugh **Hastings:** Hugh Williamson (1917–), Austral. stage actor, dramatist.

William **Hatfield:** Ernest Chapman (1892–1969), Eng.-born Austral. writer.

Henry **Hathaway:** Marcus Henri Leopold de Fiennes (1898–1985), U.S. movie director, of Belg. descent. The director adopted his mother's maiden name, as later did the rest of his family.

Aunt **Hattie** *see* Mrs. Madeline **Leslie**

G. Noel **Hatton:** Alice Mona Henryson-Caird (1858–1932), Eng. novelist, of Sc. parentage. The writer adopted her gender-neutral name for her earlier novels. Its origin is uncertain.

Minnie **Hauk:** Amalia Mignon Hauck (1851–1929), U.S. opera singer.

Kaspar **Hauser** *see* Ignaz **Wrobel**

June **Haver:** June MacMurray, née Stovenour (1925–2005), U.S. movie actress.

Phyllis **Haver:** Phyllis O'Haver (1899–1960), U.S. movie actress.

Jack H. **Haverly:** Christopher Heverly (1837–1901), U.S. minstrel showman. The showman adopted his name from a printer's error of his original surname on a batch of posters.

June **Havoc:** Ellen Evangeline Hovick (1913–2010), U.S. stage, movie actress, writer, sister of Gypsy Rose **Lee.**

Colonel **Hawari:** Abdullah abd al-Hamid Labib (*c.*1942–), Palestinian resistance leader. The head of Al Fatah's special operations group took his *nom de guerre* while training in Algeria in the 1960s, apparently adopting it from Colonel (later President) Houari **Boumédienne.**

Jeremy **Hawk:** Cedric Lange (1918–2002), S.A.–born Br. movie actor, TV quiz show host, father of Belinda **Lang.**

Simon **Hawke:** Nicholas Valentin Yermakov (1951–), U.S. fantasy writer. The writer legally adopted his pen name.

Dale **Hawkins:** Delmar Allen Hawkins (1938–), U.S. rock musician.

Allan **Hawkwood:** Henry James O'Brien Bedford-Jones (1887–1949), Can.-born U.S. historical fiction, fantasy writer.

Jack **Hawley:** Lionel Scott Pilkington (1828–1875), Eng. horseman. The eccentric sportsman, known in the stables as "Jack," adopted the name of Sir Joseph Hawley (1813–1875), a famous figure of the racing field, whom he had served as groom.

Alice **Hawthorne:** Septimus Winner (1827–1902), U.S. popular composer, songwriter. The writer adopted the name of Nathaniel **Hawthorne,** an ancestor on his mother's side, for many of his songs.

Nathaniel **Hawthorne:** Nathaniel Hathorne

(1804–1864), U.S. novelist, short-story writer. The writer adjusted the spelling of the family name as a young man to reflect its pronunciation. His grandfather was the Revolutionary hero Daniel Hathorne (1731–1796).

Rainey **Hawthorne** *see* F.G. **Trafford**

Charles **Hawtrey:** George Frederick Joffre Hartree (1914–1988), Eng. stage, radio, movie actor. According to Sally and Nina Hibbin, *What a Carry On: The Official Story of the Carry on Film Series* (1988), Hawtrey, who regularly starred in the series, was "the son of the light-comedy actor-manager, Sir Charles Hawtrey [(1858–1923)], who was celebrated for his immaculate man-about-town roles and won his knighthood for services to the theatre. Charles Hawtrey is immensely proud of his father and ... delights in tellings anecdotes about him. Well into middle age he was still billed as Charles Hawtrey, Jnr, in deference to his father's memory." But he was actually the son of William John Hartree, an engineer, and the bogus link was made when Hawtrey began his career in a production of J.M. Barrie's *Peter Pan* (1931), overseen by Barrie himself [Roger Lewis, *The Man Who Was Private Widdle*, 2001].

Elzey **Hay:** Eliza Frances Andrews (1840–1931), U.S. author. The writer and educator adopted this name for a number of articles and poems written early in her career, taking her new first name from her original name and her last name from Hayworth Plantation, her birthplace near Washington, Georgia.

Ian **Hay:** John Hay Beith (1876–1952), Sc. novelist. Scottish "Ian" corresponds to English "John."

Timothy **Hay** *see* Golden **MacDonald**

Marcia **Haydée:** Marcia Haydée Salaverry Pereira de Silva (1939–), Brazilian ballet dancer.

Linda **Hayden:** Linda Mary Higginson (1951–), Br. movie, TV actress.

Melissa **Hayden:** Mildred Herman (1923–), Can.-born U.S. ballet dancer, teacher.

Robert Earl **Hayden:** Asa Bundy Sheffey (1913–1980), U.S. black poet. The poet was left as a baby with neighbors, William and Sue Ellen Hayden, also black, who raised him and gave him his new name.

Russell **Hayden:** Pate Lucid (1912–1981), U.S. movie actor.

Sterling **Hayden:** Sterling Relyea Walter (1916–1986), U.S. movie actor. Sterling was nine years old when his father died, and four years later his mother married James Watson Hayden, who gave the boy his new surname. Paramount initially billed him as Stirling Hayden when signing him up in 1940.

Julie **Haydon:** Donella Lightfoot Donaldson (1910–), U.S. stage, movie actress.

Helen **Haye:** Helen Hay (1874–1957), Br. stage, movie actress.

Salma **Hayek:** Salma Hayek Jiminez (1966–), Mexican movie actress, of part-Lebanese parentage.

Allison **Hayes:** Mary Jane Hayes (1930–1977), U.S. movie actress.

Evelyn **Hayes:** Mary Ursula Bethell (1874–1945), Br.-born N.Z. poet. The writer used this name for her early work.

Helen **Hayes:** Helen Hayes MacArthur, née Brown (1900–1993), U.S. stage, movie actress. The actress adopted her mother's maiden name, her own middle name, as her stage name.

Henry **Hayes:** Ellen Warner Kirk, née Olney (1842–1928), U.S. popular fiction writer.

Lorraine **Hayes** *see* Laraine **Day**

Peter Lind **Hayes:** Joseph Conrad Lind (1915–1998), U.S. radio, TV comedian, actor. The entertainer adopted his mother's maiden name as his stage name.

Giant **Haystacks:** Martin Austin Ruane (1946–1998), Br. wrestler, actor, of Ir. parentage. The wrestler's name is descriptive of his size and height, but at the same time suggests an inner softness. (Though feared for his supposed viciousness, he was in fact a shy and religious man.) Haystacks was famed for his battles with **Big Daddy**.

Joan **Haythorne:** Joan Mary Shankland, née Haythornthwaite (1915–1987), Eng. stage, movie actress.

O.B. **Hayve** *see* Gideon **Wurdz**

Louis **Hayward:** Seafield Grant (1909–1985), S.A.–born Br. movie actor, working in U.S. The actor became a U.S. citizen in 1941.

Susan **Hayward:** Edythe Marrener (1918–1975), U.S. movie actress. How come this particular metamorphosis? Here's how Warner Bros. talent executive Max Arnow and talent agent Benny Medford brought it about, after Marrener's screen test for the role of Scarlett O'Hara in *Gone with the Wind* (1939) (in which she lost out to Vivien **Leigh**): "The first item on the agenda was to change her name. Edythe was far too sedate for the screen image they had in mind. Edythe herself suggested the name of her grandmother, Katie Harrington, but Arnow felt it smacked of burlesque; so the brainstorming began. Another up-and-coming actress from Brooklyn, Margarita Cansino, had been doing rather well under the name Rita **Hayworth**. Hayworth, Haywood.... Arnow tossed it about in his mind. He had been working a lot lately with superagent Leland Hayward, and liked the sound of the name. Medford agreed. From his private garden of favorite names, Medford plucked Susan, and Susan Hayward was born ... Edythe viewed her name change with equanimity. It was, after all, a necessary step toward stardom" [Christopher P. Anderson, *A Star, Is a Star, Is a Star! The Lives and Loves of Susan Hayward*, 1981].

Richard **Haywarde:** Frederick Swartwout Cozzens (1818–1869), U.S. humorist.

Rita **Hayworth:** Margarita Carmen Cansino (1918–1987), U.S. stage, movie actress. Cansino's first husband, Edward Judson, who became her agent, created her new name in 1937 when introducing her to Columbia Pictures boss Harry Cohn: "The signing of Rita Cansino couldn't have been a less significant event. Cohn took no interest at all in the unknown who had already flopped at Fox — except for her name. 'Latin types are out. She sounds too Mexican,' Cohn argued, even though she had been cast as a Spanish dancer in her first Columbia programmer. 'How about her mother's maiden name?' Judson asked. 'Her uncle Vinton has done okay at RKO.' Vinton Haworth ... was by this time a successful character actor and radio star ... 'Haworth. If it's pronounced Hayworth,' said Cohn, 'why the hell isn't it spelled that way?' They added the 'y' and Rita Hayworth was born" [Edward Z. Epstein and Joseph Morella, *Rita: The Life of Rita Hayworth*, 1983].

Désiré **Hazard:** Octave Feuillet (1821–1890), Fr. novelist, dramatist.

Robert **Hazard:** Robert Rimato (1948–2008), U.S. pop musician, songwriter.

Hy **Hazell:** Hyacinth Hazel O'Higgins (1920–1970), Br. musical comedy, movie actress. The actress was billed as Derna Hazell for two early movies: *The Dummy Talks* and *My Learned Friend* (both 1943).

Yusuf **Hazziez** *see* Joe **Tex**

H.B.: John Doyle (1797–1868), Ir. caricaturist, painter. The initials are in fact the artist's, represented by the letters JD written one on top of the other. The top and bottom Js represent the lefthand upright of the H. The downstrokes of the Ds form both the righthand upright of the H and the downstroke of the B. The crossbar of the H and "belt" of the B form the dividing line between the top and bottom letters JD.

H.D.: Hilda Doolittle (1886–1961), U.S. poet, novelist, moviemaker. The writer was a pupil (and briefly the fiancée) of Ezra Pound, and it was he who named and promoted her as "H.D., Imagiste," after three of her Imagist poems appeared in *Poetry* in 1913. She also wrote as Delia Alton, Helga Dart, Edith Gray, John Helforth, and Rhoda Peter, among other names.

Matthew **Head:** John Edwin Canaday (1907–1985), U.S. art critic, mystery novel writer.

Lian **Hearn:** Gillian Rubenstein (1942–), Austral. children's author. The writer of teenage fantasy adopted her pen name for *Across the Nightingale Floor* (2001), an adventure set in medieval Japan, the first in a series of novels overall titled *Tales of the Orori*. "'Hearn is derived from "heron," one of the key sym-bols in the books,' she says, though she was also thinking of Lafcadio Hearn, one of the earliest European popularisers of Japanese culture.... The pseudonym came about simply because she wanted to start [writing] again without being pigeon-holed" [*The Times*, September 16, 2006].

John **Heartfield:** Helmut Herzfelde (1891–1968), Ger. painter, working in U.K. Like his compatriot, George **Grosz**, the artist anglicized his name in World War I as a protest against German nationalistic fervor.

Nita **Heath:** Gwen Kelly, née Smith (1922–), Austral. novelist, poet. The writer adopted her mother's maiden name as her pen name.

Claude **Heathcote:** James Harwood Panting (*fl.*1910), Eng. writer of stories for boys.

William Least **Heat Moon:** William Trogdon (1939–), U.S. memoirist, of Eng./Ir.-Native American ancestry. The writer adopted his Native American name in translated form ("Least Heat Moon").

Mark **Hebden:** John Harris (1916–1991), Br. crime writer.

Eileen **Heckart:** Anna Eckart Herbert (1919–), U.S. stage, movie actress.

Joseph **Heco:** Hamada Kikozo (1837–1897), Jap.-born U.S. government interpreter, publisher. Hamada was rescued from a drifting ship in 1850 and brought to America, where he received a Catholic education and in 1854 was baptized under his new name.

Andrew **Hedbrook** *see* Anthony **Morehead**

Hedd Wyn: Ellis Humphrey Evans (1887–1917), Welsh poet. The bardic name means "blessed peace." In the event it was ironic, for the poet was killed in World War I within days of winning the chair at the 1917 National Eisteddfod.

David **Hedison:** Ara Heditsian (1926–), U.S. movie, TV actor.

Tippi **Hedren:** Nathalie Kay Hedren (1935–), U.S. movie actress.

Jack **Hedley:** Jack Hawkins (1930–), Br. movie, TV actor.

Mr. Michael **Heffernan:** [Sir] Samuel Ferguson (1810–1886), Ir. lawyer, poet. The writer used this name for "Father Tom and the Pope," a burlesque on Irish Catholicism contributed to *Blackwood's Magazine* in 1838.

Van **Heflin:** Emmett Evan Heflin, Jr. (1910–1971), U.S. stage, movie actor.

Humphrey **Hedgehog** *see* John **Gifford**

W. **Heimburg:** Bertha Behrens (1850–1912), Ger. novelist.

Heintje: Hein Nicolaas Theodoor Simons (1955–), Du. child pop singer, juvenile movie actor.

The name is a diminutive of the artist's first name, to which he added his surname for his (German) movie roles.

Heinz: Heinz G. Burt (1942–2000), Ger.-born Br. pop bassist, singer.

Gerard **Heinz:** Gerard Hinze (1903–1972), Ger. stage actor, working in U.K.

Amalie **Heiter:** Amalie Friederike Marie Auguste (1794–1870), Ger. aristocrat, dramatist. The Duchess of Saxony's assumed surname means "happy," "cheerful."

Heldau: [Colonel] Jules-Clément-Ladislas Subanski (1854–1907), Fr. writer of military romances. The author also wrote as Jean Star.

Helen: Helen Richardson (1940–), Ind.-born dancer, movie actress, of Burmese-Sp. parentage, working in India.

[St.] **Helena:** Olga (c.890–969), Russ. saint. The first saint of the Russian Orthodox Church, wife of Prince Igor of Kiev, was baptized at Constantinople under this name but is still regularly known as St. Olga. (She is not to be confused with the Roman empress St. Helena, mother of Constantine the Great.)

Ernest **Helfenstein:** Elizabeth Oakes Smith (1806–1893), U.S. popular novelist, magazine writer.

John **Helforth** see **H.D.**

Heliogabalus: Sextus Varius Avitus Bassanius (204–222), Roman emperor. The emperor, known to his men as Marcus Aurelius Antoninus, adopted the byname Elagabalus, that of the sun god who was the local god of Emesa, the Syrian town where he was born. This name, meaning "god of the mountain" (Hebrew *el*, "god," and Arabic *jabal*, "mountain"), was prefixed by that of the Greek sun god, Helios (or by Greek *helios*, "sun"), to give the name as it is now usually known.

Richard **Hell:** Richard Myers (1949–), U.S. punk rock musician. The musician's new name reflected his "hell-raising" character and spiky hairstyle.

Theodor **Hell:** Karl Gottlieb Theodor Winkler (1775–1856), Ger. publicist, translator.

Franz **Hellens:** Frédéric van Ermenghem (1881–1972), Belg. novelist, poet, writing in French.

Frank **Heller:** Gunnar Martin Serner (1886–1947), Swe. writer.

Robert **Heller:** William Henry Palmer (c.1830–1878), Eng. magician, working in U.S. The illusionist may have adopted a name that was a variant on that of **Robert-Houdin**, whom he greatly admired when young.

Brigitte **Helm:** Brigitte Eva Gisele Schittenhelm (1906–1996), Ger. movie actress.

Hunter Hearst **Helmsley:** Jean-Paul LeVesque (c.1965–), U.S. wrestler. Known for short as Triple H, the wrestler first entered the ring for World Championship Wrestling in 1992 as Terra Ryzing (say it). He then left the WCW for the World Wrestling Federation. "Looking for a clean start in his new federation, LeVesque decided to go with a new ring name. He chose Hunter Hearst Helmsley as his moniker.... He chose the 'Hearst' part of his name in tribute to the egotistical billionaire William Randolph Hearst and the 'Helmsley' part was taken from Leona Helmsley, the stuffy millionaire heiress of the Helmsley hotel fortune" [Picarello, p.156].

Helvidius: James Madison (1751–1836), U.S. president. The fourth president of the United States used this name, that of a Roman praetor, when replying to the letters of **Pacificus**.

John **Hely-Hutchinson:** John Hely (1724–1794), Ir. politician. In 1751 the statesman married Christina Hutchinson, niece and heiress of Richard Hutchinson, and added her family name to his.

Percy **Hemingway:** William Percy Addleshaw (1866–1916), Eng. writer.

Anouska **Hempel:** Ann Geissler (1941–), N.Z.-born Br. hotelier, fashion designer, of Russ.-Ger. descent. The former movie actress adopted the name of her first husband, Constantine Hempel (died 1973). In 1980 she married Sir Mark Weinberg to become formally Lady Weinberg.

Yr **Hen Broffwyd:** Edmund Jones (1702–1793), Welsh writer, preacher. The name by which the pious writer and zealous preacher was known means "the old prophet." He accepted and approved the nickname. Compare the name of Yr **Hen Ficer**.

Henriette **Hendel:** Johanne Henriette Rosine Schüler (1772–1849), Ger. actress, ballet dancer.

Mary **Henderson** see James **Bridie**

Paul **Henderson:** Ruth France (1913–1968), N.Z. novelist, poet.

Ray **Henderson:** Raymond Brost (1896–1970), U.S. songwriter, pianist. The musician adopted his professional name in 1920.

Rosa **Henderson:** Rosa Deschamps (1896–1968), U.S. vaudeville artist, blues singer. The performer had many aliases. The best known was taken from her husband and stage partner, Douglas "Slim" Henderson. Others included Flora Dale, Rosa Green, Mae (or Mamie) Harris, Sara Johnson, Sally Ritz, Josephine Thomas, Gladys White, and Bessie Williams.

Jimi **Hendrix:** James Marshall (originally Johnny Allen) Hendrix (1942–1970), U.S. black rock musician. On being discharged from the U.S. paratroopers in 1963 for medical reasons, Hendrix first played under the name Jimmy James. He then adopted his better-known name, which became prominent in 1966 on the formation of his group, the Jimi Hendrix Experience.

Yr **Hen Ficer:** Rhys Prichard (1579–1644), Welsh clergyman, poet. The popular preacher accepted his nickname, meaning "the old vicar."

Paul **Henreid:** Paul George Julius von Hernreid (1908–1992), Austr.-born U.S. stage, movie actor.

Robert **Henri:** Robert Henry Cozad (1865–1929), U.S. painter, writer. The artist adopted his French-style name, identifying with his Huguenot forebears, after his father killed a man in self-defense in 1882. He insisted (with little success) that his new surname be given the "American" pronunciation "Hen-rye."

Émile **Henriot:** Émile Maigrot (1889–1961), Fr. writer. The writer have may wished to avoid the suggestion of *maigriot*, "skinny."

Buck **Henry:** Buck Henry Zuckerman (1930–), U.S. movie actor, screenwriter, director.

Gale **Henry:** Gale Trowbridge (1893–1972), U.S. movie comedienne.

John **Henry, Jr.:** Don Marion Davies (1917–), U.S. child movie actor. The actor was billed under this name for a series of Mack **Sennett** comedies from 1919 to 1922. He later acted as Don Marion.

Les **Henry:** Henry Leslie (1920–2007), Br. harmonica player, comedian. The musician reversed his original names on turning professional.

O. **Henry:** William Sydney Porter (1862–1910), U.S. short-story writer. Porter first used the name (sometimes misprinted "O'Henry") for his story "Whistling Dick's Christmas Stocking" (1899) written in prison at Columbus, Ohio, where he was serving a sentence for embezzlement (as a result of obtaining money for his sick wife). The pseudonym is sometimes said to have been taken from one of the prison guards, Orrin Henry, but the commonly accepted version of the origin takes it from the name of a French pharmacist, Étienne-Ossian Henry, found in the *U.S. Dispensatory*, a reference work used by Porter when employed as a prison pharmacist.

Paul **Henry:** Paul Henry Smith (1947–), Br. TV actor.

Thomas **Henry:** Thomas Henry Fisher (1881–1964), Br. illustrator, cartoonist. The artist was particularly associated with the novels by Richmal **Crompton** featuring the naughty schoolboy William.

Will **Henry:** Henry Wilson Allen, Jr. (1912–1991), U.S. novelist, short-story writer. Allen wrote so fast and so well that he decided to adopt both this pen name and that of Clay Fisher. He later admitted that this was a professional mistake, since the adoptions long fragmented critical response to his work.

Henry IX: Henry Benedict Maria Clement Thomas Francis Xavier Stuart, Cardinal Duke of York (1725–1807), Sc. royal claimant. Stuart proclaimed himself king of Great Britain under this name in 1788 on the death of his brother, Charles Edward Stuart, the "Young Pretender," and retained the title for the rest of his life. (The real king of Great Britain over this period was George III, who ascended the throne in 1760 and reigned until his death in 1820.)

Gladys **Henson:** Gladys Gunn (1897–1983), Ir. stage, movie actress.

Audrey **Hepburn:** Edda Kathleen van Heemstra Hepburn-Ruston (1929–1993), Belg.-born U.S. movie actress, of Eng.-Du. parentage. Hepburn's father was Joseph Victor Anthony Hepburn-Ruston, an English banker. Her mother was a Dutch baroness, Ella van Heemstra. "Audrey" evolved from "Edda."

Anne **Hepple:** Anne Hepple Dickinson, née Batty (1877–1959), Eng. novelist, short-story writer.

Charles **Herbert:** Charles Herbert Saperstein (1948–), U.S. child movie actor.

Evelyn **Herbert:** Evelyn Houstellier (1898–?), U.S. stage actress, singer.

Holmes **Herbert:** Edward Sanger (1882–1956), Br. stage, movie actor. The actor adopted his name from the Sherlock Holmes movies in which he had small parts.

Mort **Herbert:** Morton Herbert Pelovitz (1925–1983), U.S. jazz musician.

Herblock: Herbert Lawrence Block (1909–2001), U.S. cartoonist. The political cartoonist adopted his pen name at his father's suggestion after joining the *Chicago Daily News* at the age of 19.

Hergé: Georges Rémi (1907–1983), Belg. cartoonist. The creator of Tintin, the boy detective, used a name that was simply the reversal of his initials in their French pronunciation ("R.G." gives "Hergé").

Philippe **Hériat:** Raymond Gérard Payelle (1898–1971), Fr. writer. The writer was originally an actor, and adopted his stage name as his pen name.

Jeanie **Hering:** Marion Adams-Acton, née Hamilton (1846–1928), Sc. novelist. The Scottish-sounding pseudonym, apparently the name of her adoptive parents, is appropriate for a writer born on the island of Arran, off the west coast of Scotland.

Eileen **Herlie:** Eileen Herlihy (1919–), Sc. stage, movie actress.

Herman: Peter Blair Denis Bernard Noone (1947–), Eng. pop singer. The lead singer of the group Herman's Hermits, formed 1963, owed his name to a nickname. Members of the local Manchester group, the Heartbeats, with whom he sang previously, claimed that Noone resembled Sherman of the *Rocky and Bullwinkle* TV cartoon series. This name was then slightly shortened to "Herman" and used to blend in nicely with that of his own band. Noone performed under his real name from 1970.

Andrew **Herman** *see* Theodore Moses **Tobani**

Pee-wee Herman: Paul Reubens, earlier Rubenfeld (1952–), U.S. movie, TV comedian. According to the actor himself: "'I had a little one inch harmonica that said "Pee-wee" on it. I just loved the way it sounded…. Growing up I knew a kid who was extremely obnoxious … and his last name was Herman'" [Blackwell, p.258]. The name is that of the character he played in the movies *Pee-Wee's Big Adventure* (1985) and *Big Top Pee-Wee* (1988) and the TV children's show *Pee-Wee's Playhouse* (1986–91).

Père Herman: Louis Joseph Macagge (1751–1828), Belg. cleric, poet.

Pete Herman: Peter Gulotta (1896–1973), U.S. prizefighter. The boxer adopted the ring name of a popular lightweight of the day, Kid Herman.

Woody Herman: Woodrow Charles Thomas Herrmann (1913–1987), U.S. jazz bandleader.

Hermes: Benjamin Lumley, originally Levy (1811–1875), Eng. SF writer, of Can. Jewish parentage. Lumley used this name for *Another World* (1873), a utopian vision of civilization on an alien planet.

Stefan Hermlin: Rudolf Leder (1915–1997), Ger. writer, translator.

James A. Herne: James A'Herne (1839–1901), U.S. actor, playwright, of Ir. parentage. The actor adjusted his name when a theater manager suggested that removing the apostrophe would make his name more suitable for the stage.

E. & H. Heron: [Major] Hesketh Vernon Prichard (1876–1922), Eng. writer, traveler, cricketer + Kate O'Brien Prichard, née Ryall (1851–1935), Eng. writer, his mother.

Robert Heron: John Pinkerton (1758–1826), Sc. writer. Pinkerton adopted his mother's maiden name for *Letters of Literature* (1785), introducing a new system of English grammar and spelling.

Geilles Herring: Edith Anna Œnone Somerville (1858–1949), Ir. novelist + Martin **Ross**, Ir. novelist, her cousin. The coauthors, later writing as Somerville and Ross, adopted this name for the first edition of *An Irish Cousin* (1889). "It is possibly worth mentioning that the mothers of the two 'Commencing Authors' held, very firmly, with the convention of their period, that to write for publication — and possibly for payment — was a pursuit not to be approved of for *Jeunes filles bien élevées* and they insisted on the concealment of a fact that they considered to be discreditable, if not disreputable. For my cousin a simple *nom de plume* presented itself, by treating her surname as a Christian name, and joining it with the name of her home, Ross. For me the question was less easily disposed of. Finally, 'Geilles Herring' was exhumed from an ancestral record, and was inflicted on me and the title page by my mother.… It may be recorded

that when the 2nd edition, also 500 copies, appeared, the name 'Geilles Herring' was, without reference to E.Œ.S., changed to the more elegant soubriquet of 'Viva **Graham**,' 'Grilled Herring' having — not without justification — assumed to be the name of one of the authors" [Elizabeth Hudson, *A Bibliography of the First Editions of the Works of E.Œ. Somerville and Martin Ross*, compiled and edited by Elizabeth Hudson with explanatory notes by E.Œ. Somerville, 1942].

James Herriot: James Alfred Wight (1916–1995), Eng. writer. The Yorkshire veterinarian, who first began to publish his popular books only in 1970, when he was over 50, took his pen name ingenuously: "I had to have one because I didn't want to be accused of advertising by the Royal College of Veterinary Surgeons. And I was watching the telly one night when this footballer came on. He was the goalkeeper for Bristol City, I think. He was called James Herriot and I thought: 'That's a nice name.' So I used it" [*Telegraph Sunday Magazine*, June 7, 1981]. The player was in fact the Scottish footballer Jim Herriot, goalkeeper for Birmingham City.

Max Herrmann-Neisse: Max Herrmann (1886–1941), Ger. poet. The writer added the name of his birthplace, Neisse, to his surname.

Herrmann the Great: Alexandre Herman (1843–1896), Fr. magician, working in U.S.

Barbara Hershey: Barbara Herzstein (1947–), U.S. movie actress. Barbara Hershey gained fame as the Hollywood actress who in 1973 changed her name to Barbara Seagull, after accidentally killing a seagull and claiming that its spirit had entered her. She subsequently threw off her image as a typecast flowerchild actress, and settled to the name of Hershey in 1975.

François Hertel: Rodolphe Dubé (1905–1985), Can. author, writing in French.

Carl Hertz: Leib (or Louis) Morgenstern (1859–1924), U.S. magician, working in U.K.

Henrik Hertz: Henrik Heyman (1797–1870), Dan. lyric poet, dramatist.

Hervé: Florimond Ronger (1825–1892), Fr. composer, organist, conductor. The musician used this name for his many operettas.

Mlle. Hervé: Geneviève Béjart (c.1622–1675), Fr. actress. The actress adopted her mother's maiden name as her stage name.

Grant Hervey: George Henry Cochrane (1880–1933), Austral. novelist, forger.

Irene Hervey: Irene Herwick (1910–1998), U.S. movie actress.

Aleksandr Ivanovich Herzen (or Gertsen): Aleksandr Ivanovich Yakovlev (1812–1870), Russ. revolutionary, writer, philosopher. The writer was an illegitimate child, the son of a rich Russian merchant (Ivan Alekseyevich Yakovlev) and a poor German mother (Luise Haag). He was thus a "love child," and his new name, devised by his father, reflected this, from German *vom Herzen*, "from the heart." Herzen used Iskander, the Turkish form of his first name, as a pseudonym for *Notes of a Young Man* (1840) and other writings. Compare **Skanderbeg**.

Werner **Herzog:** Werner Herzog Stipetic (1942–), Ger. movie director.

Catherine **Hessling:** Andrée Madeleine Heuschling (1899–1979), Fr. movie actress.

Eobanus **Hessus:** Helius Eobanus Koch (1488–1540), Ger. humanist, poet. The poet adopted a latinized form of the name of Hesse, the region of his birth in southwestern Germany.

Charlton **Heston:** John Charles Carter (1924–2008), U.S. stage, movie actor. The actor's stage name was adopted from that of his stepfather, Chet Heston.

Frederik **Hetmann:** Hans-Christian Kirsch (1934–), Ger. writer, editor.

Martin **Hewitt:** Arthur Morrison (1863–1945), Eng. novelist, journalist. The writer adopted the name of the hero of his own detective stories, which were collected into three volumes: *Martin Hewitt, Investigator* (1894), *Chronicles of Martin Hewitt* (1895), and *Adventures of Martin Hewitt* (1896).

Sherrie **Hewson:** Sherrie Lynn Hutchinson (*c.*1945–), Eng. TV actress. The actress changed her name in the 1970s on being advised that her surname was too long for billing purposes.

Harrington **Hext:** Eden Phillpotts (1862–1960), Eng. novelist, poet, essayist, playwright. The novelist used the pen name for his mystery stories.

Stefan **Heym:** Helmut Flieg (1913–2001), Ger. novelist, journalist, working in U.S. The writer changed his name to protect his family from reprisals following his emigration to Czechoslovakia in 1933. He is said to have chosen the name on the spur of the moment, basing it on German *Heim*, "home," reflecting his homesickness. Heym gives a full account of his name change in *Nachruf* ("Obituary") (1988), his lengthy autobiography.

Piet **Heyn** (or Hein): Pieter Pieterszoon (1577–1629), Du. admiral.

Anne **Heywood:** Violet Pretty (1932–), Eng. movie actress.

Ezra Hervey **Heywood:** Ezra Hervey Hoar (1829–1893), U.S. social reformer. The family name was changed to Heywood in 1848, presumably for reasons of propriety. Ezra's parents were devout Baptists.

Jean **Heywood:** Jean Murray (1921–), Eng. TV actress.

H.H.: Helen Hunt Jackson (1830–1885), U.S. poet, novelist, children's writer. This was one of Jackson's most commonly used pseudonyms, as the initials of her first two names. (She was born Helen Maria Fiske and her middle name is that of her first husband, Edward Bissell Hunt.) She also wrote as Saxe **Holm**.

Ruth **Hiatt:** Ruth Redfern (1908–), U.S. movie actress.

William **Hickey:** Tom Driberg (1905–1976), Eng. journalist. Driberg joined the *Daily Express* in 1928 and started a gossip column signed with the name of William Hickey (?1749–1830), a racy diarist. The name later passed to other social diarists, among them Compton Miller (*see* Bibliography, p.525) and gossip columnist Nigel Dempster (1941–2007). In 1987 the newspaper's editor, Sir Nicholas Lloyd, killed off Hickey on the grounds that a pseudonymous diarist could not be interviewed on television.

Mrs. Murray **Hickson:** Mabel Kitcat, formerly Hickson, née Greenhow (1859–1922), Eng. author. Mabel Kitcat wrote a number of articles, short stories, and verses under the name of her first husband.

Hedvig **Hidas:** Hedvig Bruckner (1915–), Hung. ballet dancer.

Harry **Hieover:** Charles Bindley (1795–1859), Eng. sporting writer. Both names suggest English field sports, involving harrying and hunting. "Hieover" suggests both "hie over" (hurry over) or "high over" (of a leaping horse). "Hie" is also a command to a horse to turn. Bindley was noted for his extroversion and exuberance, and "seemed to write under the same exhilaration of spirits as he might have felt when going across country" [*Dictionary of National Biography*].

Nehemiah **Higginbottom:** Samuel Taylor Coleridge (1772–1834), Eng. poet, critic. The poet used this name for his contributions to the *Monthly Review*, in which he parodied his own style.

Jack **Higgins:** Harry Patterson (1929–), Eng. thriller writer. The novelist is said to have taken his best-known pen name from a deceased relative. He has also written as Martin Fallon, James Graham, and Hugh Marlowe. "He had to resort to multiple identities because he was simply too prolific, sometimes producing a book every three months. Publishers were wary of flooding the market, so they pretended he was five different men, each turning out a new title every year" [*The Guardian*, March 29, 2006].

Monk **Higgins:** Milton Bland (1930–1986), U.S. R&B musician.

Patricia **Highsmith:** Patricia Plangman (1921–1995), U.S. crime novelist. The writer was the daughter of Jay Bernard Plangman and Mary Coates, respectively of German and Scots-English descent, who separated before her birth. She was accordingly raised by her grandparents until the age of six, then lived with her mother and stepfather, Stanley Highsmith, whose name she adopted. She published a lesbian novel, *The Price of Salt* (1952), under the name Claire Morgan.

Hildebrand: Nicolaas Beets (1814–1903), Du. clergyman, writer. The author used this name for the Dutch classic *Camera Obscura* (1839), a collection of tales and sketches of life and manners in Holland.

Hildegarde: Hildegarde Loretta Sell (1906–2005), U.S. popular singer, pianist. The singer's name, shortened by impresario Gus Edwards, is said to have originated the style of being known by one name.

Addlestone **Hill:** [Lady] Mary Anne Duffus Hardy, née MacDowell (1824–1891), Eng. novelist. The London-born writer may have taken her name from the Surrey village of Addlestone, which has a noted hill near it.

Arthur **Hill**   *see*   **Orion** (1)

Benny **Hill:** Alfred Hawthorne Hill (1925–1992), Br. TV comedian. The comic took his new first name from the U.S. comedian Jack **Benny**, an idol of his, although it was not his first choice. "To begin with he called himself Alf Hill, but 'that sounded too much like a Cockney turn. So I changed it to Leslie Hill, only that seemed more like a cocktail pianist. Eventually, being an admirer of Jack Benny, I took his name'" [*Daily Telegraph*, April 22, 1992, quoted in Massingberd 1997].

Chippie **Hill:** Bertha Hill (1905–1950), U.S. black dancer, singer. The dancer began her career in 1919 at Leroy's Club, Harlem, whose owner nicknamed her "Chippie" for her youth, a name she adopted.

Dana **Hill:** Dana Goetz (1964–1996), U.S. movie actress.

Faith **Hill:** Audrey Faith Perry (1967–), U.S. country singer.

Harry **Hill:** Matthew Hall (1964–), Br. stage, TV comedian. The popular comic, originally a physician, does not stick solely to his stage name. "Sometimes I'm Matthew Hall. Having two names allows you to segregate your life. My friends know me as Matthew. I've never struggled with the idea of being two people. Now it feels as if we've merged" [*The Times*, November 19, 2005].

Headon **Hill:** Francis Edward Grainger (1857–1927), Eng. romantic novelist, detective fiction writer. The author appears to have taken his name from Headon Hill, on the Isle of Wight, and indeed one of his early novels of espionage is *The Spies of the Wight* (1899).

James **Hill:** Storm Jameson (1891–1986), Eng. novelist. The writer used this name for a couple of novels published in the 1930s. Another occasional name was William Lamb.

Jenny **Hill:** Elizabeth Jane Woodley, née Pasta (1851–1896), Br. music-hall artist ("The Vital Spark").

Joe **Hill:** (1) Joel Emanuel Hägglund (1879–1915), Swe.-born U.S. labor leader, songwriter; (2) Joseph Hill King (1972–), U.S. novelist. Hägglund first changed his name to Joseph Hillstrom, presumably as part of his americanization process. King, son of Stephen King (*see* Richard **Bachman**), who dedicated his classic horror novel *The Shining* (1976) to "Joe Hill King," used his name for his first novel, *Heart-Shaped Box* (2007). He explained: "I didn't want someone to publish my book because of who my dad was or what my last name was" [*The Times*, September 25, 2008]. There is a link between Joe Hill (1) and Joe Hill (2) here, as King's mother, also a novelist, named her son after the labor leader.

John **Hill**   *see*   Leigh **Nichols**

Murray **Hill:** Robert Cortes Holliday (1880–1947), U.S. essayist, biographer.

Oliver **Hill:** Oliver White (1907–2007), U.S. lawyer.

Robin **Hill:** Robert Young (1811–1908), Eng. poet.

Steven **Hill:** Solomon Berg (1924–), U.S. stage, movie actor. The actor translated his German surname into English.

Terence **Hill:** Mario Girotti (1939–), It. movie actor, of Ger. descent.

Thelma **Hill:** Thelma Hillerman (1906–1938), U.S. movie comedienne.

Z.Z. **Hill:** Arzel Hill (1941–1984), U.S. black blues singer. The initials highlight the "z" of "Arzel."

William **Hillcourt:** Vilhelm Hans Bjerregaard-Jensen (1900–1992), Dan.-born U.S. Boy Scout leader. In 1926 the pioneer left his job as a newspaper reporter in his native Denmark to travel the world. Soon after, he settled in America, where he legally changed his name. He became a naturalized U.S. citizen in 1939.

Einar **Hille:** Carl Einar Heuman (1894–1980), U.S. mathematician, of Swe. parentage. The scholar's new surname was a mistranslation of Heuman, presumably taken to mean "high man," in the sense "hill dweller."

Wendy **Hiller:** Wendy Margaret Gow, née Watkin (1912–2003), Eng. stage, movie actress. The actress adopted her mother's maiden name as her stage name.

Harriet **Hilliard:** Peggy Lou Snyder (1909–1994), U.S. movie, TV actress.

Kate **Hillier:** Kate Hill (1970–), Eng. TV actress.

Hillo: José Delgado Guerra (1754–1801), Sp. bullfighter.

Morris Hillquit: Morris Hillkowitz (1869–1933), Latvian-born U.S. lawyer, socialist leader. Morris's family immigrated to the United States in 1886 and soon after modified their name to Hillquit.

David Hills *see* Joe **D'Amato**

Kate Hilpern: Justine East (1970–), Br. journalist. Kate Justine Hilpern explains how she came by her name: "I was born Justine East but I was adopted and renamed Katherine Fawsett. After I met my birth family I decided to pick a name from each. Hilpern was the surname of my natural father. My adoptive parents were upset and I sometimes regret it, but Kate Hilpern is who I am now" [*The Times*, January 13, 2007].

John Buxton Hilton: John Greenwood (1921–1986), Eng. crime writer.

Perez Hilton: Mario Armando Lavandeira, Jr. (1978–), U.S. gossip columnist. The writer, famous (or infamous) for his celebrity blogs, based his journalistic name on that of the U.S. socialite Paris Hilton (1981–). "Lavandeira calls himself Perez Hilton because he's a Latino from Miami and he thought the name brought together the two worlds of his background and his first and most enduring love: celebrity" [*SundayTimes Magazine*, July 29, 2007].

Roger Hilton: Roger Hildesheim (1911–1975), Eng. painter. The artist's family changed their name from Hildesheim to Hilton in 1916 as a result of anti-German sentiment in World War I.

Ronnie Hilton: Adrian Hill (1926–2001), Br. romantic singer, broadcaster. The singer may have loosely based his new name on his original names, perhaps partly for distinction from his namesake, artist Adrian Hill (1895–1977). He first performed under his new name in 1954.

Thomas Hinde: [Sir] Thomas Willes Chitty (1926–), Br. novelist. The writer adopted his mother's maiden name as his pseudonym.

John Hinds *see* Jon **Bee**

Jerome Hines: Jerome Albert Link Heinz (1921–2003), U.S. opera singer.

Martina Hingis: Martina Hingisová-Moltorová (1980–), Cz.-born U.S. tennis player. The prodigy ace was given her first name after her compatriot, Martina **Navratilova**, by her tennis-loving parents.

Mary Hinton: Emily Rachel Forster (1896–?), Eng. stage actress.

Père Hippolyte: Pierre Hélyot (1660–1716), Fr. religious, historian. Hélyot adopted his name on becoming a Franciscan monk in 1683, presumably adopting it from the 3d-century saint Hippolytus.

Hi-Regan: [Captain] John Joseph Dunne (1837–1910), Ir. traveler, journalist, writer on sporting

subjects, father of George **Egerton**. Dunne used this name for *How and Where to Fish In Ireland* (1886).

Hiro: Hiro Wakabayashi (1930–), Chin. fashion photographer.

Hiromix: Hiromi Toshigawa (1977–), Jap. photographer. When asked why she had adopted the name Hiromix, the artist explained she had been told to do so in a dream. "It was a divine message" [*Sunday Times*, November 28, 1999].

Ando Hiroshige: Ando Tokutaro (1797–1858), Jap. painter, wood engraver.

Damien Hirst: Damien Steven David Brennan (1965–), Eng. painter, installation artist. The artist was born to an unmarried mother, Mary Brennan, and a father whose name was left blank on his birth certificate. A year after his birth his mother married William Hirst and he took his stepfather's name.

Hugo Hirst: Hugo Hirsch (1863–1943), Ger.-born Br. electrical engineering entrepreneur. The family of the founder of the General Electric Company (in 1889) emigrated from Munich to London in 1880 and anglicized their name soon after.

Peter Hitchens *see* Craig **Brown**

Shere Hite: Shirley Diana Gregory (1942–), U.S. sexologist. The writer's professional name, prone to journalistic joshing, is her married name, with Shere, pronounced "Sherry," a pet form of her first name.

Adolf Hitler: Adolf Hitler (1899–1945), Ger. Nazi leader. Many otherwise reliable sources give the dictator's "real" name as Schicklgruber (or "Schickelgruber"), a cacophonous name that was put to regular satirical use by English speakers in World War II. This was in fact the original name of Hitler's father, Alois Hitler (1837–1903), an Austrian customs officer, who was the illegitimate son of Anna Maria Schicklgruber. Alois's father was Johann Georg Hiedler, a miller, and in 1876 he adopted a variant form of this. Adolf Hitler's mother, Klara Poelzl, was the daughter of a Frau Hüttler, herself the daughter of Johann Nepomuk Hüttler, the brother of Johann Georg Hiedler, the two names being registered under their respective variant forms.

Heinrich Hitzinger: Heinrich Himmler (1900–1945), Ger. Nazi leader. This was the name and identity that Himmler adopted from a dead village policeman on hoping to escape arrest immediately after World War II. His nerve failed him at a routine check by British military police, however, and he admitted to being Himmler. He was thus arrested after all, but took poison before he could be interrogated.

H.L.L.: Jane Laurie Borthwick (1813–1897), Sc. hymnwriter. Together with her sister, Sarah Findlater, née Borthwick (1823–1907), Jane Borthwick made a series of translations (1854–62) from the German, entitled the work *Hymns from the Land of Luther*, and used the initials of this to give her own pen name.

George V. **Hobart:** George Vear Hobart Philpot (1867–1926), Can.-born U.S. playwright, librettist.

Rose **Hobart:** Rose Kéfer (1906–2000), U.S. movie actress.

Hobart Pasha: Augustus Charles Hobart-Hampden (1822–1886), Eng. naval commander, adventurer. Hobart-Hampden served in the Royal Navy during the American Civil War, writing an account of his adventures in *Never Caught* (1867) under the pseudonym "Captain Roberts." In the year of its publication he was appointed naval adviser to the Turkish sultan and gained the title of "Pasha."

Robin **Hobb:** Margaret Astrid Lindholm Ogden (1952–), U.S. fantasy, SF writer. Ogden adopted the name Megan Lindholm for fantasy novels such as *The Wizard of the Pigeons* (1986).

Meindert **Hobbema:** Meyndert Lubbertsz (or Lubbertszoon) (1638–1709), Du. painter. The artist adopted his new surname as a young man.

John Oliver **Hobbes:** Pearl Mary-Teresa Craigie, née Richards (1867–1906), U.S.-born Br. novelist. The writer, often referred to as simply Mrs. Craigie, chose the name Hobbes because it was "homely," suggesting "hob by the hearth" and the like, or according to the *Dictionary of National Biography* because it was "the homely surname of the great philosopher [Thomas Hobbes] whose severe dialectic she admired." John was the name of her father and son, while Oliver was a reference to "warring Cromwell," as she put it. She first used the name for *Some Emotions and a Moral* (1891), published in T. Fisher Unwin's "Pseudonym Library" (in which all writers were obliged to appear under a pen name).

Aspasia **Hobbs:** Elbert Green Hubbard (1856–1915), U.S. writer, publisher. Hubbard used this female name for his first book, *The Man: A Story of Today* (1891).

Owen **Hobbs** *see* Fred **Leslie**

McDonald **Hobley:** Dennys Jack Valentine McDonald-Hobley (1917–1987), Br. TV presenter. In an earlier stage career, McDonald-Hobley used the name Robert Blanchard.

Polly **Hobson:** Julia Evans (1913–), Eng. children's writer.

Ho Chi Minh: Nguyen Tat Thanh (1890–1969), North Vietnamese president. The politician first became an active socialist in France in 1917 under the name of Nguyen Ai Quoc, "Nguyen the patriot." In 1942 he assumed the name by which he came to be best known, Ho Chi Minh, "Ho who enlightens." He also had several party aliases in the course of his life.

Stephen **Hockaby:** Gladys Maude Winifred Mitchell (1901–1983), Eng. crime novelist, children's writer. Another male name used by the writer was Malcolm Torrie.

Jakob van **Hoddis:** Hans Davidsohn (1887–1942), Ger. poet. "Van Hoddis" is an anagram of the writer's original surname.

Johnny **Hodges:** Cornelius Hodges (1907–1970), U.S. saxophonist.

David C. **Hodgkins** *see* Algis **Budrys**

John **Hodgkinson:** John Meadowcroft (1767–1805), Br. actor, working in U.S. Meadowcroft was apprenticed to a Manchester manufacturer as a boy but ran away to Bristol when he was 14 or 15, changing his name to escape detection.

Dennis **Hoey:** Samuel David Hyams (1893–1960), Eng. stage, movie actor, working in U.S.

Monckton **Hoffe:** Reaney Monckton Hoffe-Miles (1880–1951), Ir. playwright, screenwriter.

E.T.A. **Hoffmann:** Ernst Theodor Wilhelm Hoffmann (1776–1822), Ger. writer, composer. Around 1813, the writer changed his third name to Amadeus out of respect for the composer Wolfgang Amadeus Mozart (1756–1791).

Professor **Hoffmann:** Angelo Lewis (1839–1919), Eng. magician. By profession, under his real name, the magician was a lawyer and journalist. He wrote several books on magic, using both his real and his assumed name.

Hulk **Hogan:** Terry Bollea (1953–), U.S. wrestler, movie actor. Bollea originally entered the ring as Sterling Golden and Terry Boulder. In 1979 he was "discovered" by Vince McMahon, Sr., owner of the World Wrestling Federation, who named him Terry Hogan, an Irish villain. Bollea soon dropped his first name in favor of "Hulk," after the popular TV show *The Incredible Hulk*. Hogan explained: "When I first started wrestling, the wrestling world was very territorial. They had Italian wrestlers, and they had Native Americans and they had wrestlers for the Polish people. They said [to me], 'You should be Hogan. Yeah,' they said, 'you should be Hulk Hogan'" [Picarello, p.64].

Charles **Hogarth** *see* Gordon **Ashe**

Cervantes **Hogg, F.S.M.:** Eaton Stannard Barrett (1786–1820), Eng. poet, novelist. Barrett used this name for *The Rising Sun; A Serio-comic Romance* (1807). (Hamst hazards that the initials stand for "Fellow of the Swinish Multitude.") As Polypus he wrote *All the Talents! A Satirical Poem in Three Dialogues* (1807), ridiculing the government of the day.

Hokutenyu: Katsuhiko Chiba (1960–), Jap. sumo wrestler. The wrestler's fighting name means "heavenly help from the north" (Japanese *hoku*, "north" + *ten'yu*, "divine help").

Hokutoumi: Hoshi Nobuyoshi (1963–), Jap. sumo wrestler. The wrestler's fighting name means "northern victory sea" (Japanese *hoku*, "north" + *to*, "victory" + *umi*, "sea").

Henry **Holbeach** *see* Matthew **Browne**

Fay **Holden:** Dorothy Fay Hammerton (1894–1973), Br. stage, movie actress, working in U.S. The actress played her first stage part at the age of ten under the name Gaby Fay.

Jan **Holden:** Valerie Jeanne Wilkinson (1931–2005), Eng. stage, movie, TV actress.

Joyce **Holden:** Jo Ann Heckert (1930–), U.S. movie actress.

Stanley **Holden:** Stanley Waller (1928–), Eng. ballet dancer.

William **Holden:** William Franklin Beedle, Jr. (1918–1981), U.S. movie actor. A Paramount executive said that the actor's real name "sounds like an insect," so renamed him in 1938 after a newspaper friend.

Ephraim **Holding** *see* **Old Humphrey**

Billie **Holiday:** Eleanora Gough McKay, née Fagan (1915–1959), U.S. black jazz singer. The singer took her new first name from the actress Billie **Dove**. Her parents, who apparently never married, were Clarence Holiday (1900–1937), a musician, and Sadie Fagan.

Grant **Holiday** *see* A.A. **Fair**

Clive **Holland:** Charles James Hankinson (1866–1959), Eng. writer.

Marcus **Holland** *see* Taylor **Caldwell**

Vyvyan **Holland:** Vyvyan Oscar Beresford Wilde (1886–1967), Eng. writer. The writer was the younger son of Oscar Wilde, and his name was changed when he was still at school to avoid association with his father following the latter's conviction for homosexual offenses in 1895. Holland was an old family name on the side of the boy's mother, Constance Mary Wilde, née Lloyd. Vyvyan's elder brother Cyril, killed in World War I, underwent the same name change.

Judy **Holliday:** Judith Tuvim (1922–1965), U.S. stage, movie actress. Twentieth Century–Fox requested Tuvim to change her name when offering her a movie contract in 1943. She obliged by translating her Hebrew name to its English equivalent.

Michael **Holliday:** Norman Milne (1928–1963), Eng. popular singer. The singer adopted his mother's maiden name as his stage name.

Earl **Holliman:** Anthony Numenka (1928–), U.S. movie actor.

Buddy **Holly:** Charles Hardin Holley (1936–1959), U.S. songwriter, singer, guitarist. The small difference between the musician's professional name and his original name arose when his surname was misspelled on his first recording contract in 1956, and he did not bother to have the error corrected [John J. Goldrosen, *Buddy Holly: His Life and Music*, 1979].

Claudius **Hollyband:** Claude de Sainliens (died 1597), Fr.-born bibliographer. The scholar translated his French name into English, from *saint*, "holy," and *lien*, "band," "tie." When writing in Latin he was similarly Claudius a Sancto Vinculo, from *sanctus*, "holy," and *vinculum*, "band," "bond."

Hollywood Fats: Michael Mann (1953–1986), U.S. black blues guitarist.

Hanya **Holm:** Johanna Kuntze, née Eckert (1893–1992), Ger.-born U.S. choreographer, dancer. The dancer changed her name in 1923, with "Hanya" a pet form of "Johanna" and "Holm" chosen for its alliteration and its connotation of strength and security ("home").

[Sir] Ian **Holm:** Ian Holm Cuthbert (1931–), Eng. stage, movie, TV actor.

Saxe **Holm:** Helen Hunt Jackson (1830–1885), U.S. poet, novelist, children's writer. Jackson used this name for her earliest writings, after the death in 1863 of her first husband, Edward Bissell Hunt. She also wrote as **H.H.**

Libby **Holman:** Elsbeth Holzman (1904–1971), U.S. stage actress, singer.

Gordon **Holmes:** Louis Tracy (1863–1928), Eng. journalist, fiction writer + Matthew Phipps Shiel (1865–1947), Br. SF writer. The two men used this joint name for their detective fiction.

H.H. **Holmes:** (1) Herman Webster Mudgett (1860–1895), U.S. mass murderer; (2) William Anthony Parker White (1911–1968), U.S. thriller writer. White adopted the serial killer's alias for his pen name.

Leon **Holmes:** Leon Sederholm (1913–), U.S. child movie actor.

Michelle **Holmes:** Corinne Michelle Cunliffe (1967–), Eng. movie, TV actress.

Stuart **Holmes:** Joseph von Liebenben (1887–1971), Ger.-born U.S. movie actor.

Mary **Holmquist** *see* Greta **Garbo**

Bjarne P. **Holmsen:** Arno Holz (1863–1929), Ger. writer + Johannes Schlaf (1862–1941), Ger. writer. The two friends used this name for their joint work *Papa Hamlet* (1889), three stories alleged to be a German translation from a Norwegian original by the named author. The choice of name reflects the prestige that Scandinavian writers enjoyed at this time, following the success of Ibsen and Bjørnson.

Gustav **Holst:** Gustavus Theodore von Holst (1874–1934), Eng. composer, of Swe. origin.

Claire **Holt:** Claire Bagg (1901–1970), Latvian-born U.S. specialist on Indonesia. The journalist took her pen name, which she later legally adopted, when writing for the *New York World* from 1928 to 1930.

She was also that paper's dance critic under the name Barbara Holveg.

Gavin Holt *see* Eliot **Reed**

Jack Holt: Charles John Holt II (1888–1951), U.S. movie actor, father of Tim **Holt** and Jennifer **Holt**.

Jany Holt: Ekaterina Rouxandra Vladesco-Olt (1911–2005), Rom.-born movie actress, working in France.

Jennifer Holt: Elizabeth Holt (1920–1997), U.S. movie actress, brother of Tim **Holt**, daughter of Jack **Holt**. The actress began her movie career in the 1940s under the name Jacqueline Holt.

Patrick Holt: Patrick Parsons (1912–1993), Br. movie actor.

Tim Holt: Charles John Holt III (1918–1973), U.S. movie actor, brother of Jennifer **Holt**, son of Jack **Holt**.

Victoria Holt *see* Jean **Plaidy**

Holte: Trevor Holder (1941–), Eng. cartoonist, illustrator.

Gary Holton: Wayne Winston Norris (1952–1985), Br. rock singer, stage, TV actor.

Leonard Holton *see* Patrick **O'Connor**

Barbara Holveg *see* Claire **Holt**

Cecil Home: Julia Augusta Webster, née Davies (1837–1894), Br. poet, dramatist. The writer used this name, based on her mother's maiden name of Hume, for her only novel, *Lesley's Guardians* (1864).

Edwin Home *see* Reginald **Wray**

Evelyn Home: Peggy Makins, née Carn (1916–?), Br. advice columnist. Evelyn Home was the long-serving "agony aunt" in *Woman* magazine from 1937 through 1974. The name was one that Peggy Carn inherited on the magazine, deriving from Eve, symbolizing womanhood, and (obviously) Home, suggesting domestic happiness. The name itself was first chosen by a German Jewish woman psychologist who was writing for *Woman* when Peggy Carn took over. The columnist later wrote: "The 'Evelyn' contained Eve, the archetypal mother, the temptress, the sexy side of woman; the 'home' was what every woman is supposed to want. At the time I thought the name too phony to be taken seriously ever; I was totally mistaken" [Peggy Makins, *The Evelyn Home Story*, 1975]. The name was abandoned in 1974, when Peggy Makins was succeeded in turn by Anna **Raeburn**.

Homer and Jethro: Henry D. Haynes (1920–1971), U.S. comedy country singer + Kenneth C. Burns (1920–1989), U.S. comedy country singer. The pair began to work together in 1932 on WNOX Knoxville, where they were given their names by program director Lowell Blanchard.

Geoffrey Homes: Daniel Mainwaring (1902–1978), U.S. mystery novelist, screenwriter.

Homesick James: John William Henderson (?1910–2007), U.S. black blues musician. The musician's real name is often cited as James Williamson but is now generally recognized to be as given here.

Mrs. Prudentia Homespun: Jane West, née Iliffe (1758–1852), Eng. novelist, dramatist, poet. Jane West used this transparently moralistic name for her first novel, *The Advantages of Education; or, The History of Maria Williams* (1793).

Home T: Michael Bennet (*c.*1962–), Jamaican reggae singer. The singer began his career as a vocalist in the quartet Home T4.

L'Homme Masqué: José Antenar de Gago (1835–1913), Peruvian magician, working in France. The magician's name, meaning "The Masked Man," referred to the mask that he always wore, not only during his performances but also generally in public.

Elizabeth Honey: Elizabeth Madden Clarke (1947–), Austral. illustrator, children's writer.

Honey Boy: Keith Williams (*c.*1955–), Jamaican reggae musician. Williams adopted his nickname, given him because his singing was regarded as being "sweeter than honey."

Harry Honeycomb: James Henry Leigh Hunt (1784–1859), Eng. essayist, poet. The poet used this semiserious name, based on his second name and surname, for contributions to various journals, such as the *New Monthly Magazine*.

William Honeycomb: Richard Gardiner (1723–1781), Eng. writer. "His unsuccessful suit to a young lady led him to publish in 1754 'The History of Pudica, a Lady of N-rf-lk, with an account of her five lovers, by William Honeycomb.' One of the lovers, named 'Dick Merryfellow,' was intended for himself" [*Dictionary of National Biography*]. The latter name was subsequently applied to Gardiner.

Honora *see* **Constantia**

Honora-Martesia *see* **Constantia**

Honoria: Marguerite Agnes Power (?1815–1867), Eng. novelist, poet. The writer used this name for *The Letters of a Betrothed* (1858).

Honorius II: Lamberto Scannabecchi (?–1130), It. pope.

Honorius III: Cencio Savelli (?–1227), It. pope. **Honorius IV** was this pope's grandnephew.

Honorius IV: Giacomo (or Jacomus) Savelli (1210–1287), It. pope. The pontiff adopted the name of his granduncle, **Honorius III**.

Percy Honri: Percy Henry Thompson (1874–1953), Eng. music-hall instrumentalist. The artist adopted the misprinted version of his earlier stage name, Percy Henry, that appeared in a French billing.

Darla Hood: Dorla Hood (1931–1979), U.S. movie actress. The child actress gained her new first name when her original name of Dorla, invented by her mother, was misspelled on a contract.

bell **hooks:** Gloria Jean Watkins (1952–), U.S. black feminist poet, critic. The writer adopted (and lowercased) the name of her great-grandmother, Bell Hooks, early in her career.

Anthony **Hope:** [Sir] Anthony Hope Hawkins (1863–1933), Eng. historical novelist, playwright. The author of *The Prisoner of Zenda* (1894) wrote the popular romantic adventure novel while practicing as a barrister in London. He therefore adopted a pseudonym, using his first two names only. The book was such a success that it enabled him to give up the law as a career and become a fulltime novelist.

Ascott R. **Hope:** Ascott Robert Hope-Moncrieff (1846–1927), Br. editor, author of books for boys.

Bob **Hope:** Leslie Townes Hope (1903–2003), Eng.-born U.S. movie comedian. In 1925 the actor adopted the name Lester T. Hope, reasoning: "I thought that was a little more manish [*sic*] ... I found a lot of girls would call me Leslie and I'd call them Leslie, and there was a sort of conflict of interests there so I changed it to 'Lester.'" He then felt that this name "still looked a little ginger around the edges," so in 1929 changed "Lester" to "Bob." "I thought that was more chummy and audiences would get to like me" [Charles Thompson, *Bob Hope: The Road from Eltham*, 1981].

But there was more to "Bob" than that. "In his younger days he'd been a fan of automobile racing, one of his idols being the race-car driver Bob Burman. It was from Burman that he took his new first name. Now he was really on his way as a solo act: new name, new image, new everything. And, most of all, new Hope" [Lawrence J. Quirk, *Bob Hope: The Road Well-Traveled*, 1998].

Brian **Hope** *see* Gordon **Ashe**

David **Hope:** Douglas Jamieson Fraser (1910–1989), Sc. "inspirational" poet. The poet became associated with *The Fireside Book*, a selection of poems still published annually as a companion to *The Friendship Book* of Francis **Gay**, although now obviously compiled by others. The soothing-sounding name "David Hope" also suggests "day of hope."

Douglas **Hope:** Matilda Ellen Wilson (1860–1918), Eng. singer, composer. The musician used this name for her songs.

Edward **Hope:** Edward Hope Coffey (1896–1958), U.S. author, screenwriter.

F.T.L. **Hope:** Frederick William Farrar (1831–1903), Eng. schoolmaster, writer. Farrar used this name for a novel, *The Three Homes; A Tale for Fathers and Sons* (1873), contributed to *The Quiver*.

Graham **Hope:** Jessie Hope (?–1920), Eng. novelist, reformer. The author of such novels as *The Lady*

of Lyte (1904) and *The Honour of X* (1908) appeared under her male pen name alone in *Who's Who*.

Laura Lee **Hope:** Edward L. Stratemeyer (1863–1930), U.S. writer. The Stratemeyer Literary Syndicate set up in 1906 used this name for stories for girls about the Bobbsey Twins. The name itself was presumably random, but any name in "Hope" suggests wholesome ambition and enterprise.

Laurence **Hope:** Adela Florence Nicolson, née Cory (1865–1904), Br. poet. "Laurence" may have come from "Florence." Nicolson first used the name for *The Garden of Kāma and Other Love Lyrics from India, Arranged in Verse by Laurence Hope* (1901), which readers took to be written by a man.

Mark **Hope:** Eustace Clare Grenville Murray (1824–1881), Eng. journalist, satirist. The writer was a diplomat, and published accounts of his travels in Turkey as The Roving Englishman, but was Trois-Étoiles for his novel *The Member for Paris: A Tale of the Second Empire* (1871), and Silly Billy for some articles in *Vanity Fair*. Trois-Étoiles, literally "three stars," is the French term for a pseudonym (or more precisely anonym) consisting of three asterisks, typically printed in the form *Monsieur* ***. Mark Hope was the father of James Brinsley **Richards**.

Richard **Hope:** Richard John Hope Walker (1953–), Eng. stage, movie, TV actor.

Stan **Hope:** William Stanley Hope Winfield (1933–), U.S. black jazz musician.

Teri **Hope:** Teri Garr (1949–), U.S. movie actress. The actress was billed under this name for her teenage roles in the first half of the 1960s.

Antony **Hopkins:** Antony Reynolds (1921–), Eng. composer, broadcaster on music. The musician's father died when the family was in Italy in 1925 and he was adopted by a Major Hopkins and his wife, whose name he assumed. He is apt to be confused with the Welsh actor (Sir) Anthony Hopkins (1937–).

DeWolf **Hopper:** William D'Wolf Hopper (1858–1935), U.S. stage actor, singer. The actor dropped his first name and for practical purposes slightly respelled his inheritance of his mother's maiden name. "I thought D'Wolf, my middle name, *distingué*," he said.

Hedda **Hopper:** Elda Furry (1890–1966), U.S. movie actress, gossip columnist. The actress's second name is that of her husband, musical comedy performer William DeWolf Hopper, whom she married in 1913 as his fifth wife. His four previous wives had been named Ella, Ida, Edna, and Nella, and in view of the similarity of Elda's own name to these, a numerologist was consulted. He recommended "Hedda."

Trader **Horn:** Alfred Aloysius Smith (1861–1931), Eng. traveler. When living in a South African doss house in 1926, Smith made the acquaintance of a local novelist, Ethelreda Lewis, who discovered that the old man had a traveler's tale to tell. She transcribed his illiterate account of his adventures in Equatorial Africa and found a publisher for them the following year. First, however, she changed his name to protect his respectable Catholic family in England: "His first names were retained and seemed symbolic. There was 'Alfred,' a name steeped in pre–Norman days.... And there was 'Aloysius,' a saint's name.... His surname had to go, however, and Mrs. Lewis cast about for a substitute. She chose 'Horn,' a name evocative of the wildness of animals, of the southern point of America and the north-eastern tip of Africa" [Tim Couzens, *Tramp Royal: The True Story of Trader Horn*, 1992]. "Trader" was thus a descriptive nickname, for when in West Africa Smith had traded in ivory.

Adam **Hornbook:** Thomas Cooper (1805–1892), Eng. politician, novelist. The writer's pen name seems to suggest Adam as the first man and "hornbook" as a child's first reading aid in former times.

Horace **Hornem:** George Gordon Byron (1788–1824), Eng. poet. Byron used this name for *The Waltz; an Apostrophic Hymn* (1813). The poet was reluctant to admit authorship of this work and wrote to a friend: "I fear that a certain malicious publication on waltzing is attributed to me. This report, I suppose you will take care to contradict; as the author I am sure would not like that I should wear his cap and bells" [Hamst, p.60]. The poem is prefaced by a "Note to the Publisher" in which Hornem describes himself as "a country gentleman of a midland county" who had married "a middle-aged maid of honour" and now had daughters of "a marriageable (or, as they call it, *marketable*) age." Byron also wrote as **Quevedo Redivivus.**

Vladimir **Horowitz:** Vladimir Gorovitz (1904–1989), Ukr.-born U.S. pianist.

Harry **Horse:** Richard Horne (1960–2007), Br. political cartoonist, children's writer. The precise origin of the author's adopted surname is uncertain. Horne himself liked to say that it came from his bad handwriting at school. But he would also say that the name came from the Damon Runyon character Harry the Horse. His new first name was that of his grandfather, who featured in his stories.

Horst P. **Horst:** Horst Paul Albert Bohrmann (1906–1999), Ger.-born U.S. photographer. The photographer became an American citizen at the outbreak of World War II and changed his name to dissociate himself from Hitler's deputy, Martin Bormann. He was generally known simply as Horst.

Hortencia: Hortencia Maria de Fatima Marcari Oliva (1959–), Brazilian basketball player.

Isaac **Hortibonus:** Isaac Casaubon (1559–1614), Swiss theologian, critic. The scholar seems to have devised his pseudonym to complement his real surname, with "Casaubon" (which actually means "in good state") interpreted as "good house." "Hortibonus" or "Hortusbonus," as he sometimes spelled it, thus meant "good garden."

Robert **Hossein:** Robert Hosseinhoff (1927–), Fr. stage, movie actor, director.

Harry **Houdini:** Ehrich Weiss (1874–1926), Hung.-born U.S. magician, escapologist. The artist was keen to escape from the ties of his real name. He adopted his new surname from his admiration of the French illusionist **Robert-Houdin**, while his new first name evolved from "Erie," a pet form of his original name.

Michel **Houellebecq:** Michel Thomas (1956–), Fr. writer. The author's true identity was revealed in 2005 by a French journalist, Denis Demonpion, in *Le Point* magazine.

Félix **Houphouët-Boigny:** Dia Houphouët (?1905–1993), Ivorian politician. Africa's longest-serving head of state, from 1960 to his death, changed his first name from Dia ("divine healer") to Félix ("happy") following his conversion to Catholicism at the age of 11. In 1946 he was elected to the French National Assembly, and added Boigny ("ram") to his surname.

John **Houseman:** Jacques Haussmann (1902–1988), Rom.-born stage, movie director, of Fr. Jewish-Br. parentage, working in U.S. Houseman adopted the anglicized form of his name in 1943 when he became a naturalized U.S. citizen.

Arsène **Houssaye:** Arsène Housset (1815–1896), Fr. writer.

Cissy **Houston:** Emily Drinkard (1933–), U.S. black popular singer, mother of pop and soul singer Whitney Houston (1963–), aunt of Dionne **Warwick**.

R.B. **Houston** *see* Robert **Crawford**

Renée **Houston:** Katherina Houston Gribbin (1902–1980), Sc. vaudeville artist, movie actress.

Gérard d'**Houville:** Marie Louise Antoinette de Régnier, née de Heredia (1875–1963), Fr. poet, novelist. The writer based her pseudonym on the name of a Norman ancestor, Girard d'Ouville.

Edward **Hovell-Thurlow:** Edward Thurlow (1781–1829), Eng. poet. "In commemoration of the descent of his grandmother from Richard Hovell, esquire of the body to Henry V, he prefixed to Thurlow the additional surname Hovell by royal license dated 8 July 1814" [*Dictionary of National Biography*].

Adrian **Hoven:** Wilhelm Arpad Peter Hofkirchner (1922–1981), Austr. movie actor, director.

J. **Hoven:** Johann Vesque von Püttlingen (1803–1883), Austr. composer, of Belg. descent.

The **Howadji:** George William Curtis (1824–1892), U.S. travel writer, newspaper correspondent. The author used this name for his travel writings, such as *Nile Notes of a Howadji* (1851) and *The Howadji in Syria* (1852). The name itself was probably a corruption of Arabic *khawaja*, a form of respectful address approximating to "Sir," used especially for Christians and Westerners.

Ann **Howard:** Ann Pauline Swadling (1936–), Br. opera singer.

Arliss **Howard:** Leslie Howard (1954–), U.S. movie actor.

Bob **Howard:** Howard Joyner (1906–1986), U.S. jazz musician.

Curly **Howard:** Jerome Horwitz (1906–1952), U.S. comedy actor, brother of Moe **Howard** and Shemp **Howard**, together the "Three Stooges."

Cy **Howard:** Seymour Horowitz (1915–1993), U.S. movie director.

David **Howard:** David Paget Davis III (1896–1941), U.S. movie director.

Don **Howard:** Donald Howard Koplow (1935–), U.S. popular singer.

Elizabeth Jane **Howard:** Elizabeth Jane Liddon (1923–), Eng. writer, editor, reviewer. The writer adopted her mother's maiden name as her pen name.

Harriet **Howard:** Elizabeth Ann Haryett (1823–1869), Eng. socialite. The future mistress of Louis-Napoleon, nephew of Napoleon, renamed herself to avoid family shame when she ran off with English jockey Jem Mason as a teenager. Perhaps intentionally, her assumed name echoes that of Henrietta Howard (1681–1767), mistress of George II.

Hartley **Howard** *see* Harry **Carmichael**

H.L. **Howard:** Charles Jeremiah Wells (1800–1879), Eng. poet. The writer used this name for his formerly famous dramatic poem *Joseph and his Brethren* (1823).

John **Howard:** John R. Cox, Jr. (1913–1995), U.S. movie actor.

Keble **Howard:** John Keble Bell (1875–1928), Eng. playwright, journalist. The writer, editor of *The Sketch*, changed his name in order to be distinguished from his brother, R.S. Warren Bell (1871–1921), editor of *The Captain*, a magazine for boys.

Leslie **Howard:** Leslie Howard Stainer (1893–1943), Br. stage, movie actor, of Hung. descent, working in U.S., father of Ronald **Howard**. According to some sources, the actor's name is an anglicized form of his original Hungarian name, László Horváth.

Mary **Howard:** Mary Mussi (1907–1991), Br. romantic novelist.

Moe **Howard:** Moses Horwitz (1897–1975), U.S. movie comedian, brother of Curly **Howard** and Shemp **Howard**.

Peter **Howard:** Howard Weiss (1927–2008), U.S. musical conductor, dance-music arranger.

Ronald **Howard:** Ronald Howard Stainer (1916–1996), Br. movie actor, son of Leslie **Howard**.

Shemp **Howard:** Samuel Horwitz (1891–1955), U.S. movie comedian, brother of Curly **Howard** and Moe **Howard**.

Susan **Howard:** Jeri Lynn Mooney (1943–), U.S. movie, TV actress.

Thomas **Howard:** Jesse Woodson James (1847–1892), U.S. desperado. This pseudonym was used by the (in)famous Jesse James in his final days while living at St. Joseph, Missouri. It seems to have been simply an "innocuous" name.

Trevor **Howard:** Trevor Wallace Howard-Smith (1913–1988), Eng. movie actor.

Troy **Howard** *see* Mark **Carrel**

Willie **Howard:** William Lefkowitz (1886–1949), Ger.-born U.S. theatrical performer. Willie and his brother Eugene took their new name in 1903 when touring as the comedy duo Howard and Howard.

Henry **Howe:** Henry Howe Hutchinson (1812–1896), Eng. actor.

Irving **Howe:** Irving Horenstein (1920–1993), U.S. literary critic, historian.

James Wong **Howe:** Wong Tung Jim How (1899–1976), Chin.-born U.S. cinematographer.

Frankie **Howerd:** Francis Alick Howard (1917–1992), Eng. stage, movie comedian. The actor chose the smallest of changes when adopting his stage name: "It seems [*sic*] to me that there were too many Howards: among them Trevor, Sidney [*sic*] and Arthur [i.e. actors Trevor **Howard**, Sydney Howard (1884–1946), and Arthur Howard (1910–1995), brother of Leslie **Howard**]. So how to stay Howard, yet alter it? I hit on the idea of a change of spelling: Howerd — which, I argued, would have the added advantage of making people look twice because they assumed it to be a misprint" [Frankie Howerd, *On the Way I Lost It*, 1976]. As an aspiring comedian, Howard had earlier tried out the name Ronnie Ordex.

Howlin' Wolf: Chester Arthur Burnett (1910–1976), U.S. black blues singer, songwriter. The musician's name refers to his early singing style, with his hoarse voice and eerie "howling." According to some accounts, he was already nicknamed "The Wolf" as a child for his bad behavior, afteer the wicked wolf in the story of Little Red Riding Hood.

Margaret **Howth:** Rebecca Blaine Harding Davis (1831–1910), U.S. novelist. The writer adopted the name of the heroine of her own novel, *Margaret Howth* (1862).

John **Hoyt:** John Hoysradt (1904–1991), U.S. movie actor.

Jeno **Hubay:** Eugen Huber (1858–1937), Hung. violinist, composer.

Lotti **Huber:** Lotti Goldman (1912–1998), Ger. dancer, movie actress, cabaret performer.

Wilfred Hudleston **Hudleston:** Wilfred Hudleston Simpson (1828–1909), Eng. geologist. Wilfred's mother was heiress through her own mother, Eleanor Hudleston, of the family of Hudleston of Hutton John, Cumberland, and in 1867, together with the rest of his family, he assumed the name of Hudleston by royal license.

Rock **Hudson:** Roy Harold Fitzgerald, originally Roy Scherer, Jr. (1925–1985), U.S. movie, TV actor. Born Roy Scherer, the actor subsequently took the name of his stepfather, Wallace Fitzgerald, whom his mother married when he was eight. Hudson had a more or less standard story to account for his screen name, which he said had been given him by his first agent, Henry Willson. The following is one version: "Henry thought he knew what was best for me. I remember he said, 'we have to change your name.' 'Why?' I asked. 'I don't want one of those silly names.' 'You have to,' he said, 'so it looks good on the marquee. Roy Fitzgerald is too long.' 'What about Geraldine Fitzgerald? Is that too long?' But Henry insisted. He hit me with Hudson. Then he had some really macho, cockamamie first names. Like Dirk. Lance. Finally he said, 'What about Rock?' That clicked. 'Yeah, that sounds pretty good,' I said. It was not too far from Roy, and no one else had it. So that was it." (According to one account, Willson specifically took "Rock" from the Rock of Gibraltar and "Hudson" from the river.) In fact it was actually Ken Hodge, Rock Hudson's lover, who gave him his name, with "Rock" for strength, and "Hudson" from the Long Beach phone book. Even so, Willson *did* rename several famous actors, to many of whom he gave similar names. They included Rory **Calhoun**, Troy **Donahue**, Tab **Hunter**, and Rip **Torn** [Rock Hudson and Sara Davidson, *Rock Hudson: His Story*, 1986].

Francis **Hueffer:** Franz Hüffer (1845–1889), Ger.-born Br. music critic.

Jean **Hugard:** John G. Boyce (1872–1959), Austral. magician.

Adrian **Hughes:** Stanley Hockey (1964–), Br. TV actor, SF scriptwriter, working in U.S.

Billie **Hughes:** William Keith Jones (1948–1998), U.S. songwriter, rock musician.

Colin **Hughes** *see* Gordon **Ashe**

Cyril **Hughes:** Cyril Hodges (1915–1974), Welsh poet. The writer clearly preferred a recognizably Welsh name for his contributions in verse and prose to various magazines.

Hazel **Hughes:** Hazel Heppenstall (1913–1974), S.A. stage actress. The actress adopted her mother's maiden name as her stage name.

Kathleen **Hughes:** Betty von Gerlean (1928–), U.S. movie actress.

Sean **Hughes:** John Patrick (*c*.1965–), Br. stage, movie, TV, comedian, scriptwriter.

Ian **Hugo:** Hugh Parker Guiler (1898–1985), U.S. movie director, cinematographer.

Richard **Hugo:** Richard Franklin Hogan (1923–1982), U.S. poet. The poet's adopted name was that of his stepfather, Herbert Franklin James Hugo, whom his mother married when he was four. He began to use it when he was in eighth grade.

Hulda: Unnur Benediktsdóttir Bjarkling (1881–1946), Icelandic lyric poet. The Scandinavian name means "sweet," "lovable."

Richard **Hull:** Richard Henry Sampson (1896–1973), Eng. crime novelist.

Félicité **Hullin-Sor:** Félicité Virginie Richard (1805–*c*.1860), Fr.-born Russ. ballet dancer. The second part of the dancer's name is that of her husband, Spanish classical guitarist Fernando Sor (1778–1839).

Martin Andrew Sharp **Hume:** Martin Andrew Sharp (1843–1910), Eng. historian, explorer, writer on Spain. Hume was Sharp's mother's maiden name, and a branch of her family had settled in Spain around the end of the 18th century. "The last of the Spanish Humes, a lady advanced in years, died in 1876, bequeathing her property to Martin Sharp, and in August 1877, in compliance with her wish, he assumed the name of Hume" [*Dictionary of National Biography*].

Humilis: Germain Nouveau (1851–1920), Fr. poet. The writer's adopted name is Latin for "humble."

Engelbert **Humperdinck:** Arnold George ("Gerry") Dorsey (1936–), Eng. popular singer. In 1965 Dorsey's career was flagging, and his manager, Gordon Mills, felt a change of name might help. "It was not uncommon for showbiz people to have two names — their real name and a professional one. Anthony Benedetto ... shortened his name to the snappier Tony **Bennett**; and John **Wayne** ... had shed ... his birth name of Marion Morrison.... 'You are *now*,' Gordon said, giving me a dramatic stage pause: Engelbert Humperdinck.' 'Engawhat?' I exclaimed aghast.... 'ENG-EL-BERT, HUM-PER-DINCK — got it?' ... Gordon had to spell Engelbert Humperdinck three times while I rolled it around my tongue and wrote it down on a piece of paper" [Engelbert Humperdinck with Katie Wright, *Engelbert: What's in a Name?*, 2004]. Thus did the singing star, known as "Enge" to his fans, assume the clunky name of Engelbert Humperdinck (1854–1921), the

German composer famed for his fairy opera *Hansel and Gretel* (1893).

Humph: Humphrey Richard Adeane Lyttelton (1921–2008), Eng. jazz trumpeter, cartoonist. The musician used this name, by which his friends knew him, for cartoons published in the *Daily Mail* from 1949 through 1953.

Fritz **Hundertwasser:** Friedrich Stowasser (1928–2000), Austr. painter, architect. The artist adopted his new name in 1949, taking the initial "Sto-" as the Czech word for "hundred" and translating it into German. From about 1969 he signed his work Friedensreich Hundertwasser, the first name (ostensibly based on his real name) meaning "kingdom of peace," and representing his claim to lead the observer into a new realm of peace and happiness. He often added "Regenstag" ("rainy day") to this, making the full name Friedensreich Hundertwasser Regenstag, on the basis that he felt happy on rainy days because colors glowed and sparkled then. "This exaggerated concern with the name is a symptom of the braggadocio, conceit, and talent for self-advertisement that are apparent in his work as well as his life" [Chilvers 2004, p.350].

Sammo **Hung:** Hong Jinbao (1950–), Hong Kong movie director, screenwriter, actor.

Kyle **Hunt**   *see* Gordon **Ashe**

Alan **Hunter:** Alan John Moore (1952–), Eng. TV actor.

Evan **Hunter:** Salvatore Albert Lombino (1926–2005), U.S. crime, SF writer, of It. parentage. Lombino first took to pseudonyms on joining the Scott Meredith literary agency, New York, in 1951, and it was there that he started selling stories to pulp magazines. Some magazines published several of his works in the same issue, unaware they were by the same author. One day, exploiting his position as literary editor, he sent a mystery novel by Evan Hunter to a major publishing house. "The editor liked it and asked to meet Evan Hunter. The young literary agent took the author to meet the editor. The editor asked, 'Where is Evan Hunter?' The young literary agent replied, 'I am Evan Hunter!' The startled editor advised the fledgling novelist that, because of the prejudice against Italian-Americans, Evan Hunter would 'sell a lot more tickets' than Salvatore Lombino" [James Bone, "Adventures in Copland," *The Times Magazine*, April 18, 1998].

Lombino took the name from Hunter College, New York, from which he had graduated with an English degree in 1950. Two years later he adopted it as his legal name in place of his family name. As he pursued his writing career, his best-known pseudonym became Ed **McBain**, while other pen names were Curt Cannon, Ezra Hannon, John Abbott, Hunt Collins, and Richard Marsten.

Jeffrey **Hunter:** Henry Herman McKinnies, Jr. (1925–1969), U.S. movie actor.

Kim **Hunter:** Janet Cole (1922–2002), U.S. stage, movie actress. The actress's name was changed by producer David O. Selznick, who told her that Janet Cole could be anyone, but that Kim Hunter had individuality, and with a name like that she would go far.

Mollie **Hunter:** Maureen Mollie McIlwraith (1922–), Sc. writer of fantasy fiction for children.

Ned **Hunter**   *see* James Fenimore Cooper **Adams**

Ross **Hunter:** Martin Fuss (1916–1996), U.S. movie actor, producer. It looks as if "Fuss" became "Ross," while "Martin" turned into "Hunter."

Russell **Hunter:** Russell Ellis (1925–2004), Sc. movie, TV actor

Tab **Hunter:** Arthur Andrew Kelm (1931–), U.S. movie actor. Kelm originally used his mother's maiden name, Gelien, until 1948, when he was spotted working at a stable by talent scout Dick Clayton. Clayton introduced him to Henry Willson, Rock **Hudson**'s Hollywood agent, who said, "We've got to tab you something," then named him Tab Hunter, his new surname referring to his horse-riding skills.

Clinham **Hunter, M.D.**   *see* Oliver **Optic**

Frances E. **Huntley:** Ethelind Frances Colburn Mayne (1865–1941), Ir. short-story writer, novelist, working in U.K. Mayne used this name for 1890s stories in *The Yellow Book* and *Chapman's Magazine*.

Helen **Huntley:** Nancy Hayes Van de Vate (1930–), U.S. pianist, composer. The musician also used the name William Huntley.

Peter **Hurkos:** Pieter van der Hurk (1911–1988), Du.-born U.S. clairvoyant.

Veronica **Hurst:** Patricia Wilmshurst (1931–), Br. movie actress.

Mary Beth **Hurt:** Mary Beth Supinger (1948–), U.S. movie actress. The actress's professional name is that of her former husband, actor William Hurt (1950–).

Ruth **Hussey:** Ruth Carol O'Rourke (1911–2005), U.S. movie actress.

Wayne **Hussey:** Jerry Lovelock (1958–), U.S. rock musician.

Hustlebuck: Clarence Lawson Wood (1878–1957), Eng. painter, cartoonist. The artist used this name for cartoons published jointly with his son-in-law Keith Sholto Douglas. The name itself is presumably a blend of "hustle" (or "hustle-bustle") and "buck up." Cartoonists often have to work hurriedly or hastily.

Walter **Huston:** Walter Houghston (1884–1950), Can.-born U.S. stage, movie actor. The actor changed the spelling of his surname as a young man to simplify its pronunciation.

Johnny **Hutch:** John Hutchinson (1913–2006), Eng. acrobat.

Willie **Hutch:** William McKinley Hutchinson (1944–2005), U.S. black Motown producer, soul singer.

Betty **Hutton:** Elizabeth June Thornburg (1921–2007), U.S. movie actress, singer. In 1937 Detroit bandleader Vincent Lopez changed the singer's name to Betty Darling after consulting a numerologist. She subsequently assumed the name by which she became famous, as did her sister Marion **Hutton.**

Ina Ray **Hutton:** Odessa Cowan (1916–1984), U.S. jazz singer, bandleader (the "Blonde Bombshell of Rhythm").

Marion **Hutton:** Marion Thornburg (1920–1987), U.S. singer, movie actress, sister of Betty **Hutton.**

Robert **Hutton:** Robert Bruce Winne (1920–1994), U.S. movie actor.

Craig **Huxley:** Craig Hundley (1953–), U.S. jazz musician, TV music composer, producer.

Joris Karl **Huysmans:** Charles-Marie-Georges Huysmans (1848–1907), Fr. novelist, of Fr.-Du. parentage. The writer adopted the Dutch equivalents of his first and last forenames, reversing their order.

Hviezdoslav: Pál Orsz·gh (1849–1921), Slovak poet. The poet's assumed name means "glory of the stars."

Ketil **Hvoslev:** Ketil Saeverud (1939–), Norw. composer. The musician adopted his mother's maiden name in 1980.

Hwfa Môn: Rowland Williams (1823–1905), Welsh poet. The writer took his bardic name from Rhostrehwfa on the island of Anglesey, where his parents moved in 1828. *Môn* is the Welsh name of Anglesey.

Père **Hyacinthe:** Charles-Jean-Marie Loyson (1827–1912), Fr. priest, writer.

Robin **Hyde:** Iris Guiver Wilkinson (1906–1939), S.A.-born N.Z. novelist, poet, of Eng.-Austral. parentage. The writer adopted the name of her (illegitimate) first baby son, Christopher Robin Hyde, stillborn in 1926.

Diana **Hyland:** Diana Gentner (1936–1977), U.S. stage, TV actress.

Jack **Hylton:** Jack Hilton (1892–1965), Br. danceband leader, composer.

Jane **Hylton:** Gwendoline Clark (1927–1979), Br. movie actress.

Ronald **Hynd:** Ronald Hens (1931–), Eng. ballet dancer, choreographer, director, husband of Annette **Page.**

Hypnos: Philip Marlow (1965–), Br. crossword compiler. The setter's pseudonym is the name of the Greek god of sleep, obliquely referring to Raymond

Chandler's novel *The Big Sleep* (1939), in which the central character, private eye Philip Marlowe, has a name virtually identical to that of the compiler.

Dorothy **Hyson:** Dorothy Wardell Heisen (1914–1996), U.S. stage, movie actress.

Iaco ap Dewi: James Davies (1648–1722), Welsh copyist. The scholar adopted a name that is the Welsh equivalent of the original. His surname literally means "son of David."

Iago ap Ieuan: James James (1833–1902), Welsh musician. The composer of the Welsh national anthem (known in English as "Land of My Fathers") adopted a name that means "James son of Evan." It alludes to his father, **Ieuan ap Iago,** who wrote the words.

Janis **Ian:** Janis Eddy Fink (1951–), U.S. pop singer, song writer. The singer adopted her brother's middle name for her new surname.

Scott **Ian:** Scott Rosenfeld (1963–), U.S. rock guitarist.

Ian and Sylvia: Ian Tyson (1933–), Can. folksinger + Sylvia Tyson, née Fricker (1940–), Can folksinger, his wife.

Ianthe: Emma Catherine Embury (1806–1863), U.S. novelist. The writer used this name for her contributions to various periodicals, perhaps borrowing it from one of the many literary Ianthes, such as the maiden in Shelley's *Queen Mab* or the young girl to whom Byron dedicated *Childe Harold's Pilgrimage.*

Juana de **Ibarbourou:** Juanita Fernández Morales (1895–1979), Uruguayan poet.

Abdullah **Ibrahim:** Adolphe Johannes "Dollar" Brand (1934–), S.A. black jazz pianist, composer. The musician converted to Islam in 1968 and was known by his Muslim name from the mid–1970s.

Iceberg Slim: Robert Maupin Beck III (1918–1992), U.S. "blaxploitation" writer. Beck's pen name was originally his street name as a Chicago pimp, when it reflected his ability to be emotionally frigid and physically brutal to the women who worked as prostitutes for him.

Ice Cube: O'Shea Jackson (1969–), U.S. black "gangsta" rapper, movie actor.

Ice-T: Tracy Marrow (1958–), U.S. black rapper, movie actor. The rap artist, a former gang member in Los Angeles, took a name that not only punned on "iced tea" but honored the black writer **Iceberg Slim,** with "T" for "Tracy."

Kon **Ichikawa:** Uji Yamada (1915–), Jap. movie director.

Billy **Idol:** William Michael Albert Broad (1955–), Eng. punk-rock singer. Music reviewer David Toop comments: "Punk pseudonyms do not mature well, as a rule, but William Broad made an inspired choice when he reinvented himself as Billy

Idol. The implications of the name are simultaneously cynical, ironic and starstruck, and that sums up the contradictions of his music and career" [*The Times*, May 4, 1990]. Idol's own comment: "It's a joke, right, but it's smart, and it's better than [Sid] **Vicious**, or [Dee] **Generate**" [Jon Savage, *Time Travel*, 1996].

Idris: Arthur Mee (1860–1926), Welsh journalist, writer. The compiler of *Who's Who in Wales* (1920) took his name from the Celtic giant said to have given the name of Cader Idris ("Seat of Idris"), a mountain ridge in southern Wales.

Thomas **Idris:** Thomas Howell Williams (1842–1925), Welsh chemist. The pharmacist lived much of his life in southern Wales near Cader Idris, and took his name from that mountain ridge (*see* **Idris**). He adopted the name on marrying in 1873 and that year set up as a mineral water manufacturer, so that the name became associated with his product. He legally assumed Idris as an additional surname in 1893.

Idrisyn: John Jones (1804–1887), Welsh biblical scholar. The writer based his name on that of Cader Idris, a mountain in southern Wales named for a legendary giant (*see* **Idris**). The suffix *-yn* is a diminutive, so that the name is effectively "Little Idris."

Ieuan ap Iago: Evan James (1809–1878), Welsh poet. The writer of the words of the Welsh national anthem (known in English as "Land of My Fathers") adopted the Welsh equivalent of his name, literally "Evan son of James." He was the father of **Iago ap Ieuan**, who wrote the music.

Ieuan Brydydd Hir: Evan Evans (1731–1788), Welsh poet, scholar. The writer earned his name as a nickname, "Evan the tall poet." He was also known as Ieuan Fardd, "Evan the bard."

Ieuan Glan Alarch: John Mills (1812–1873), Welsh musician, writer. The writer took his name from a local placename, with his new first name the Welsh equivalent of the original.

Ieuan Glan Geirionydd: Evan Evans (1795–1855), Welsh poet. The writer took his name from a local placename, with his new first name the Welsh equivalent of the original. (Evan and John are related names.)

Ieuan Gwyllt: John Roberts (1822–1877), Welsh musician, writer. The hymnwriter's adopted name means literally "wild John," denoting religious fervor.

Ieuan Gwynedd: Evan Jones (1820–1852), Welsh poet, journalist. The poet was born near Dolgellau, Merionethshire, in the historic kingdom of Gwynedd (a name adopted in recent times for the modern county in this part of Wales). Hence his bardic name, meaning "Evan of Gwynedd."

Ieuan Lleyn: Evan Prichard (1769–1832),

Welsh poet. The writer took his name from his native district of Lleyn, northwest Wales.

Ifor Ceri: John Jenkins (1770–1829), Welsh musicologist. The musician adopted a name meaning "Ifor of Ceri," the latter (also known as Kerry) being the village where he was vicar from 1807.

Father **Ignatius:** Joseph Leycester Lyne (1837–1908), Eng. mission preacher. The cleric, a self-appointed Benedictine monk, took his "monastic" name and title in 1862 in the course of his campaign to revive the Benedictine order in the Anglican Church.

Ivan **Ignatyev:** Ivan Vasilyevich Kazansky (1892–1914), Russ. poet.

Nina **Ignatyeva:** Nina Aleksandrovna Sergeyeva (1923–), Russ. movie critic.

Ignotus: James Franklin Fuller (1835–1924), Ir. architect, writer. The author used this name, Latin for "unknown," "obscure," for some of his writings.

Witi **Ihimaera:** Witi Tame Smiler (1944–), N.Z. writer, of Maori descent. The writer adopted the Maori transliteration of Ishmael, his great-grandfather's first name, as his new surname.

Ika: Albertina Fredrika Peyron (1845–1922), Swe. pianist, composer. A name from the tail end of the musician's middle name.

Rev. **Ike**   *see*   **Reverend Ike**

Lewis **Ilda:** Irwin Dash (?–1984), Br. music publisher.

Francis **Iles**   *see*   Anthony **Berkeley**

I. **Ilf:** Ilya Arnoldovich Faynzilberg (Feinsilberg) (1897–1937), Russ. satirical writer, teaming with Ye. **Petrov**. The writer added the initial of his surname to the first syllable of his first name. The two men became so closely associated in the public mind that they ceased to sign their names separately. They were simply "Ilf and Petrov." At an early stage they wrote jointly as Tolstoyevsky, a humorous blend of the names of Tolstoy and Dostoevsky.

Iliya II: Irakly Georgiyevich Gudushauri-Shioloshvili (1933–), Georgian catholicos. The head of the Georgian Orthodox Church received his name in 1957 on taking monastic vows. The name itself corresponds to English Elijah, traditionally interpreted as "Jehovah is God."

Margaret **Illington:** Maude Ellen Light (1879–1934), U.S. stage actress. The actress's stage name was coined for her by Daniel Frohman, the theater manager who engaged her. He "upgraded" Maude to Margaret and formed her new surname from syllables of her home town and state, Bloomington, Illinois.

M. **Ilyin:** Ilya Yakovlevich Marshak (1895–1953), Russ. writer. The writer was the brother of Yelena **Ilyina**.

Yelena **Ilyina:** Liya Yakovlevna Preys (Preis)

(1901–1964), Russ. children's writer. The writer was the sister of M. **Ilyin**.

Iman: Iman Mohamed Abdulmajid (1955–), Somalian model, wife of rock musician David **Bowie** (married 1992). The Muslim name itself means "belief," i.e. faith in Allah.

Immerito: Edmund Spenser (?1552–1599), Eng. poet. This was the name, Latin for "undeservedly," under which Spenser published his first major work, *The Shepheardes Calender* (1579). He used it to sign the dedication ("To His Booke"), with its opening lines: "Goe little booke: thy selfe present, / As child whose parent is vnkent."

John Ince: John Edwards (1887–1947), U.S. movie actor.

Fay Inchfawn: Elizabeth Rebecca Ward (1881–?), Br. popular verse writer.

Index: Dafydd Rhys Williams (1851–1931), Welsh editor, working in U.S. Williams was the editor of *Y Drych* ("The Mirror"), the leading newspaper for Welsh expatriates in North America, published in Utica, New York, from 1860, and earlier in New York City itself. Latin *index* literally means "informer."

Robert Indiana: Robert Clark (1928–), U.S. pop art painter. The artist took the name of his native state as his professional name.

Juozas Indra: Juozas Stasevich Podletskis (1918–1968), Lithuanian composer, conductor. The musician adopted his new name in 1943.

Ilse Indrane: Undina Jatniece (1927–), Latvian writer.

Frieda Inescort: Frieda Wightman (1900–1976), Sc.-born movie actress, working in U.S. The actress adopted her mother's maiden name as her screen name.

Jared Ingersol *see* Mark **Carrel**

Colonel Frederic Ingham: Edward Everett Hale (1822–1909), U.S. author, editor, Unitarian clergyman. The prolific author used the name for *The Ingham Papers* (1870) and other writings.

Mona Inglesby: Mona Vredenburg (1918–), Br. ballet dancer.

Kathleen Inglewood: Kate Isitt (1876–?), N.Z. novelist, working in England.

John Inglis: Sophia Lucy Jane Clifford, née Lane (1849–1929), Eng. novelist.

Ingoldsby: [Rev.] James Hildyard (1809–1897), Eng. classical scholar. The writer adopted the name of the Lincolnshire village where he had his living as a clergyman (from 1846). Compare the entry below.

Thomas Ingoldsby: [Rev.] Richard Harris Barham (1788–1845), Eng. writer, antiquary. The author of *The Ingoldsby Legends* (1837) (full title *The Ingoldsby Legends: or Mirth and Marvels, by Thomas Ingoldsby Esquire*), took his name from the Lincolnshire village of Ingoldsby, although he never held a living there, as did James Hildyard (*see* **Ingoldsby**). (The *Legends* tell how Thomas's ancestor, Peter de Ingoldsby, was killed at the Battle of Lincoln in 1141, and how his grandson, Sir Ingoldsby Bray, who assumed his mother's name, founded Ingoldsby Abbey in Kent in 1202.) Barham adopted the name to distinguish his lively, exuberant writing from his more temperate commitments as a clergyman.

Rex Ingram: Reginald Ingram Montgomery Hitchcock (1893–1950), Ir.-born U.S. movie director. He should not be confused with the U.S. movie actor Rex Ingram (1895–1969).

Michael Innes: John Innes Mackintosh Stewart (1906–1994), Sc. crime writer. Professionally a lecturer in English literature and literary critic, Stewart used this name for his detective fiction. He took it from the first names of two of his three sons.

Innocent II: Gregorio Papareschi dei Guidoni (?–1143), It. pope.

Innocent III: Giovanni Lotario dei Conti di Segni (1161–1216), It. pope.

Innocent IV: Sinibaldo Fieschi (?–1254), It. pope.

Innocent V: Pierre de Tarentaise (*c.*1224–1276), Fr. pope.

Innocent VI: Étienne Aubert (1282–1362), Fr. pope.

Innocent VII: Cosimo Gentile de' Migliorati (*c.*1336–1406), It. pope.

Innocent VIII: Giovanni Battista Cibò (1432–1492), It. pope. The pontiff assumed his name in honor of **Innocent IV**, a fellow-Genoese.

Innocent IX: Giovanni Antonio Facchinetti (1519–1591), It. pope.

Innocent X: Giovanni Battista Pamfili (1574–1655), It. pope.

Innocent XI: Benedetto Odescalchi (1611–1689), It. pope. The pontiff took the name of his patron, **Innocent X**, who had created him cardinal in 1645. He in turn gave the name of **Innocent XII**.

Innocent XII: Antonio Pignatelli (1615–1700), It. pope. The pontiff took the name of his patron, **Innocent XI**, who had created him cardinal in 1681 and whom he regarded as his exemplar.

Innocent XIII: Michelangelo dei Conti (1655–1724), It. pope. The pontiff adopted the name of **Innocent III**, from whose family he was descended.

Ismet İnönü: Mustafa Ismet (1884–1973), Turk. statesman, army officer. The statesman adopted his surname in 1934 from his victories in the two battles of İnönü, near Ankara, in 1921.

Intelligent Hoodlum: Percy Chapman (*c.*1968–), U.S. black rapper. Chapman's early life centered on crime and drugs. "The Intelligent Hoodlum moniker indicated a path for the future, renouncing his illegal moves but acknowledging the necessary part his criminal past had played in his development. The intelligent prefix inferred [*sic*] his desire to learn, and use his new-found wisdom for the benefit of himself and others" [Larkin, p. 646].

Yiorgos Ioannou: Yiorgos Soroloi (1927–1985), Gk. author. The writer formally adopted his new surname in 1955.

Ioan Pedr: John Peter (1833–1877), Welsh scholar. The Nonconformist minister took a name that was the Welsh equivalent of the original.

Ioan Siengcin: John Jenkin (1716–1796), Welsh poet. The writer's name is the Welsh equivalent of the English original.

Ioan Tegid *see* **Tegid**

Iolann Fionn: Seosamh Mac Grianna (1900–1990), Ir. writer.

Iolo Carnarvon: John John Roberts (1840–1914), Welsh poet. The writer's name means "Iolo of Carnarvon," from his native county of Carnarvonshire, now part of Gwynedd.

Iolo Morganwg: Edward Williams (1746–1826), Welsh poet, antiquary. The poet was born (and died) in the historic county of Glamorganshire. Hence his bardic name, "Iolo of Glamorgan."

Ionicus: Joshua Charles Armitage (1913–1998), Eng. painter, illustrator. The artist took his pen name from a set of Ionic columns on a concert hall in the background of his first cartoon for *Punch* in 1944.

Ionoron Glan Dwyryd: Rowland Walter (1819–1884), Welsh poet, working in U.S. The writer's new first name means "January," presumably because he was born in that month. The rest of the name is a local placename.

Iorwerth Glan Aled: Edward Roberts (1819–1867), Welsh poet. Iorwerth is regarded as a Welsh equivalent of Edward, although properly the two names are quite unrelated. The rest of the poet's name is a local placename.

Iota: Kathleen Mannington Caffyn, née Hunt (1853–1926), Ir.-born Br. novelist.

Mikhail Ippolitov-Ivanov: Mikhail Mikhaylovich Ivanov (1859–1935), Russ. composer.

Bodil Ipsen: Bodil Louise Jensen (1889–1964), Dan. stage, movie actress. The actress's name pays tribute to Henrik Ibsen, whose heroines she played.

Miroslav Irchan: Andrey Dmitriyevich Babyuk (1897–1937), Ukr. writer.

Francis Ireland: Francis Hutcheson (1721–1780), Ir. physician, amateur composer.

Michael Ireland: Darrell Figgis (1882–1925), Ir. poet, novelist, playwright.

Patrick Ireland: Brian O'Doherty (1930–), Ir.

artist, writer. The artist adopted his (quintessentially Irish) name in 1972 as a protest against the shooting of unarmed civil rights protesters in Londonderry on January 30 that year ("Bloody Sunday"), resolving to keep the name until the British presence was removed from Northern Ireland.

Irenaeus: Samuel Irenaeus Prime (1812–1885), U.S. clergyman, author.

Irene: Irene Lentz Gibbons (1907–1962), U.S. costume designer.

Sister Irene: Catherine FitzGibbon (1823–1896), Eng.-born U.S. philanthropist. FitzGibbon emigrated with her parents to the USA at the age of nine and in 1850 joined the Sisters of Charity at Mount St. Vincent, New York, when she took her religious name of Irene (partly preserving her original name of Catherine).

Paul Iribe: Paul Iribarnegaray (1883–1935), Fr. fashion illustrator.

William Irish: Cornell George Hopley-Woolrich (1903–1968), U.S. mystery writer.

An Irish Gentleman *see* Thomas **Brown, the Younger**

Ralph Iron: Olive Emilie Albertina Schreiner (1855–1920), S.A. novelist, of Ger.-Eng. parentage. Schreiner adopted the male name for her feminist novel, *The Story of an African Farm* (1883). She is said to have taken "Ralph" as a homage to U.S. philosopher and poet Ralph Waldo Emerson (1803–1882), whose writings she admired. "Iron" may have had a symbolic sense.

Nestor Ironside: [Rev.] Samuel Croxall (?–1752), Eng. writer. The author took this name for *An Original Canto of Spenser* (1713), supposedly an unpublished poem by Edmund Spenser but in reality a satirical piece of verse attacking the Earl of Oxford. He seems to have assumed the name adopted by Sir Richard Steele when he started *The Guardian* periodical that same year.

I-Roy: Roy Samuel Reid (1944–1999), Jamaican reggae singer, DJ. The musician adopted his new name when working as a DJ in Kingston clubs, basing it on that of the earlier reggae star **U-Roy**.

George Irving: George Irving Shelasky (1922–), U.S. stage actor, singer.

[Sir] Henry Irving: John Henry Brodribb (1838–1905), Eng. actor. Brodribb changed his name to avoid embarrassing his parents, who were ashamed of his profession. "How would he style himself? ... Various ideas were whittled down to two, Baringtone and Irving; the first an amalgam of a great City name [bankers Baring Brothers] with [John Baldwin] Buckstone [(1802–1879)], a leading comedian of the day, and the second from Edward Irving [(1792–1834)], the eloquent evangelist ... and Washington

Irving ([1783–1859)], whose stories he had loved as a boy. Finally, he chose Irving—Baringtone, tried out on many pieces of paper, looked altogether too pompous" [Moira Shearer, *Ellen Terry*, 1998].

"The idea of making a name could have been invented for the man who was born John Brodribb—and briefly toyed with calling himself Baringtone—but who hit the boards as Henry Irving" [Susannah Clapp, review of Michael Holroyd, *A Strange Eventful History: The Dramatic Lives of Ellen Terry, Henry Irving and Their Remarkable Families*, *Times Literary Supplement*, December 19 & 26, 2008].

John **Irving**: John Wallace Blunt, Jr. (1942–), U.S. novelist. The writer's parents divorced when he was two and he adopted the name of his stepfather, Colin Irving.

Jules **Irving**: Jules Israel (1925–), U.S. stage director.

Big Dee **Irwin**: DiFosco Ervin (1939–1995), U.S. "doo-wop" singer.

May **Irwin**: Georgina May Campbell (1862–1938), Can.-born U.S. music-hall artist, of Sc. descent. Georgina made her professional debut at age 13 with her older sister Ada, originally Adeline Flora Campbell (*c*.1859–1930), at the Theatre Comique in Rochester, New York, billed by manager Daniel Shelby as "May and Flo, the Irwin Sisters." They appeared together under this name until 1883, when they split. Many sources misidentify the sisters, naming May as Ada and Flo as Georgina (or Georgia).

Isa: Isa Craig Knox (1831–1903), Sc. writer. Mrs. Knox used her first name alone for poems contributed to the *Scotsman*.

Isabel *see* Henry C. **Browning**

Isfoel: Dafydd Jones (1881–1968), Welsh poet. The poet took his name from a local placename, itself meaning "under the hill."

Ish Kabibble: Merwyn Bogue (1908–1994), U.S. jazz musician, comedian. The performer adopted the nickname given him after his comedy rendering of the Yiddish novelty song "Isch Ka Bibble (I Should Worry)." The phrase itself, perhaps an alteration of Yiddish *nisht gefidlt*, was popularized by Fanny **Brice** in her role as Baby Snooks, a character based on **Baby Peggy**.

Iskander *see* Aleksandr Ivanovich **Herzen**
Yusuf **Islam** *see* Cat **Stevens**

Islwyn: William Thomas (1832–1878), Welsh poet. The poet took his bardic name from Mynydd Islwyn ("Underbush Mountain"), southern Wales, near which he was born.

Isola *see* Norman **Stuart**

Bogdan **Istru**: Ivan Spiridonovich Bodaryov (1914–), Moldavian poet. The writer appears to have extracted his name from that of his native village, Pistrueni.

Itai: Keisuke Itai (1956–), Jap. sumo wrestler.

Juzo **Itami**: Yoshihiro Ikeuchi (1933–1997), Jap. movie director, screenwriter.

Ivanay: Rosalin Thompson (1972–), Jamaican reggae singer. The singer adopted her new name in 1997 to emphasize her individuality.

Mar **Ivanios**: Givergis Thomas Panikervitis (1882–1953), Ind. archbishop. The Syrian-Jacobite archbishop took his new name on being appointed bishop in 1925. "Mar" is an honorific title of Aramaic origin given to saints and higher clergy in the Nestorian and Jacobite churches.

Miki **Iveria**: [Princess] Gayane Mikeladze (1910–1994), Russ.-born Br. movie actress.

Burl **Ives**: Burl Icle Ivanhoe Ives (1909–1995), U.S. stage, movie actor, folk, country singer. The singer's screen name is his real name, which some sources give incorrectly as Burl Icle Ivanhoe.

Viktor **Iving**: Viktor Petrovich Ivanov (1888–1952), Russ. ballet critic.

Ryurik **Ivnev**: Mikhail Aleksandrovich Kovalyov (1891–1981), Russ. poet.

Maria **Ivogün**: Ilse Kempner (1891–1987), Hung.-born Ger. opera singer. The soprano created her new name by taking letters from the full maiden name of her mother, Ida von Günther.

Ub **Iwerks**: Ubbe Ert Iwwerks (1901–1971), U.S. movie animator, director.

Harry **J**: Harry Johnson (*c*.1945–), Jamaican reggae musician, record producer.

Tony **Jaa**: Panom Yeerum (1976–), Thai movie actor, martial arts choreographer.

Daniel **Jablonski**: Daniel Ernst Figulus (1660–1741), Ger. Protestant theologian. The future Moravian bishop adopted his new name in 1685.

Jac Glan-y-gors: John Jones (1766–1821), Welsh satirical poet, working in England. The writer took his name from the farm where he was born, Glan-y-gors ("bank by the marsh"), near Ruthin, Denbighshire.

Beau **Jack**: Sidney Walker (1921–2000), U.S. black lightweight boxer.

Nat **Jackley**: Nathaniel Jackley-Hirsch (1909–1968), Eng. movie comedian.

Zenda **Jacks**: Suzie McClosky (1955–), Br. popular singer.

Aunt Molly **Jackson**: Mary Magdalene Garland (1880–1960), U.S. folksinger.

Elaine **Jackson** *see* Eliot **George**

Joe **Jackson**: Josef Francis Jiranek (?1880–1942), Austr.-born U.S. pantomime artist.

Preston **Jackson**: James Preston McDonald (1902–1983), U.S. jazz trombonist. The musician adopted his stepfather's surname.

Sam **Jackson** *see* Robert **Rich**

Wanda **Jackson:** Wanda Goodman (1937–), U.S. pop singer.

Lou **Jacobi:** Louis Harold Jacobovitch (1913–2009), Can. Jewish actor.

Walter **Jacobs** *see* Walter **Vincson**

Cousin **Jacques:** Louis Abel Beffroy de Reigny (1757–1811), Fr. playwright, composer. The writer used this name for satirical operettas that were popular during the French Revolution.

Sister **Jacques-Marie:** Monique Bourgeois (1921–2005), Fr. nun, former artist's model.

Frank **Jacson:** Ramon Mercader (1914–1978), Sp. assassinator of Leon **Trotsky**. Mercader had earlier called himself Jacques Mornard at a time when his mistress was Sylvia Agelof, a New York Trotskyist whose sister did secretarial work for Trotsky at his home in Mexico City, and it was she who enabled him to gain entrance to Trotsky's house and become acquainted with the members of his household.

Dean **Jagger:** Dean Jeffries (1903–1991), U.S. movie actor.

Jadwiga **Jagiello:** Jadwiga Brzowska-Mejean (1830–1886), Pol. pianist, composer.

Jago: James Coulson (1951–), Br. crossword compiler. The setter's pseudonym punningly refers to the name of the Spanish grand inquisitor Don Diego de Deza (whose reversed name gave that of **Azed**). The Spanish name Diego is also (via Santiago, "St. James") associated with the compiler's real name.

Jahangir: [Prince] Salim (1569–1627), Ind. emperor. The Mogul emperor's adopted name or title, which he assumed in 1605 on his accession to the throne of Delhi, means "conqueror of the world."

Jah Jerry: Jerome Hines (1921–2007), Jamaican reggae guitarist. The musician's name was given him by his Rastafarian brethren. ("Jah" is a Rastafarian name for God, as a contraction of Jehovah.)

Jah Lion: Pat Francis (*c.*1950–), Jamaican reggae musician. Francis has recorded under a number of names, others being Jah Lloyd and the Black Lion of Judah.

Jahmali: Ryan Thomas (1972–), Jamaican reggae singer.

Jah Screw: Paul Love (*c.*1955–), Jamaican record producer.

David **Jahson:** Everald Pickersgill (1954–), Jamaican reggae singer, working in UK. The musician's new surname can be understood as "Son of God."

Jah Stitch: Melbourne James (1949–), Jamaican DJ, reggae musician.

Jah Stone: Gladstone Fisher (*c.*1953–), Jamaican DJ, reggae musician.

Jah Wobble *see* Jah **Wobble**

Jah Woosh: Neville Beckford (1952–), Jamaican reggae musician.

Jaïrzinho: Jaïr Ventura Filho (1944–), Brazilian footballer. A diminutive form of the player's first name.

Jak: Raymond Allen Jackson (1927–1997), Eng. cartoonist, illustrator.

Jussi **Jalas:** Jussi Blomstedt (1908–), Finn. orchestral conductor.

Ahmad **Jamal:** Fritz Jones (1930–), U.S. black jazz pianist. The musician took his new name on converting to Islam in the early 1950s. His original name remains uncertain. "The faint aura of mystery that surrounds him even extends to his name. Every reference book I have ever seen states that before he converted to Islam half a century ago ... his original name was Fritz Jones. Yet when I mention this he goes to some lengths to deny it. The mistake originated, he claims, with the late Leonard Feather, doyen of jazz writers. 'I was never called Fritz Jones,' says Jamal, who clearly does not even like to utter the words. So what was his name? Somehow he never gets round to explaining. At one point he seems to indicate that the 'Jones' part may have been correct, but there is a mischievous twinkle in his eye as he speaks. By the time we part I am still not sure of the answer" [Clive Davis, "Twilight of an American Classicist," *The Times*, April 3, 2002].

Khan **Jamal:** Warren Robert Cheeseboro (1946–), U.S. black jazz musician.

Art **James** *see* Denver **Dixon**

Bill **James:** Allan Jams Tucker (1929–), Welsh crime writer.

Brian **James:** (1) John Tierney (1892–1972), Austral. novelist, short-story writer; (2) Brian Robertson (1955–), Eng. punk-rock guitarist.

Dennis **James:** Demie James Sposa (1917–1997), U.S. TV game-show host.

Dick **James:** Richard Leon Isaac Vapnick (1919–1986), Eng. popular singer, music promoter, of Pol. Jewish parentage. The musician began his career as a dance-band singer under the name Lee Sheridan.

Donald **James:** Donald Wheal (1931–2008), Br. novelist, screenwriter.

Elmore **James:** Elmore Brooks (1918–1963), U.S. black blues musician. Brooks adopted the surname of his stepfather, Joe Willie James.

Eric **James:** Eric James Barker (1913–2006), Eng. popular pianist, composer.

Ethan **James:** Ralph Burns Kellogg (1946–2003), U.S. rock musician.

Etta **James:** Jamesetta Hawkins (1938–), U.S. black soul, blues singer.

Francis **James:** Francis Jacobs (1907–), Austral.-born Br. stage actor.

Freddy **James** *see* (1) Fred **Allen**; (2) Teddy **Powell**

Geraldine **James:** Geraldine Blatchley, née Thomas (1950–), Br. stage, TV actress.

James **James:** Arthur Henry Adams (1872–1936), N.Z. novelist, poet, playwright.

Jimmy **James:** (1) James Casey (1892–1965), Eng. music-hall comic; (2) James Plott (1940–2009), U.S. circus clown, ringmaster. Casey changed his name when working in Wales, on being told that his original name would not be popular there.

Jimmy **James** *see* Jimi **Hendrix**

Joni **James:** Joan Carmello Babbo (1930–), U.S. popular singer.

Marian **James:** Emily Jolly (*c.*1822–1900), Eng. novelist, short-story writer.

Mary **James** *see* M.E. **Kerr**

P.D. **James:** [Baroness] Phyllis Dorothy James, née White (1920–), Eng. crime novelist.

Philip **James** *see* Lester **del Rey**

Polly **James:** Pauline Devaney (1941–), Eng. stage, TV actress.

Rick **James:** James Ambrose Johnson, Jr. (1948–2004), U.S. black "punk funk" musician.

Roderick **James:** Ethan Coen (1958–), U.S movie director, screenwriter + Joel Coen (1955–), U.S movie director, screenwriter, his brother. The Coens adopted this name as editor(s) of the movies they produce, write, and direct between them.

Russell **James:** Russell James Vincent Crickard Logan (1942–), Br. crime writer.

Sid **James:** Sidney James Cohen (1913–1976), S.A. comedy movie actor, working in U.K.

Sonny **James:** James Loden (1929–), U.S. country singer.

Tommy **James:** Thomas Gregory Jackson (1947–), U.S. rock singer.

Will Roderick **James:** Joseph Ernest Nephtali Dufault (1892–1942), Can. writer of westerns, working in U.S. The author is notorious for his bogus autobiography, *Lone Cowboy: My Life Story* (1930), in which he claims he was born in Montana, the son of a Texan cattle drover, William James, and a Spanish/Scottish-Irish Californian mother, Bonnie James, while his middle name, Roderick, came from Rodriguez, his mother's maiden name. In reality he remained in Montreal, Canada, until 1907, when he became a cowboy, then called himself C.W. Jackson, W.R. James, and finally Will R. James. The mendacity of his account was not exposed until 1967.

Jam Master Jay: Jason Mizell (1965–2002), U.S. black DJ. In 1982, Mizell joined Joseph "Run" Simmons (1964–) and Darryl McDaniels ("D.M.C.") (1964–) to form the popular rap group Run-D.M.C.

Jan and Dean: Jan Berry (1941–), U.S. surf musician + Dean Torrence (1941–), U.S. surf musician.

Laurence M. **Janifer:** Larry Mark Harris (1933–), U.S. SF writer, musician, of Pol. descent. The writer reverted to his original family name, which had been changed by an immigration officer when Harris's grandfather had entered the USA from Poland.

Byron **Janis:** Byron Yankelevitch (1928–), U.S. concert pianist. The musician originally shortened his surname to Yanks, then reformed this as Janis.

Dorothy **Janis:** Dorothy Jones (1912–), U.S. movie actress.

Elsie **Janis:** Elsie Jane Bierbower (1889–1956), U.S. variety actress, writer. Bierbower began her formal stage career as a nine-year-old under the name "Little Elsie." She later adopted the name Elsie Janis when a theatrical photographer dispensed with her surname and modified her middle name.

Emil **Jannings:** Theodor Friedrich Emil Janenz (1884–1950), Swiss-born Austr. movie actor, of U.S.–Ger. parentage.

Janosch: Horst Eckert (1931–), Ger. illustrator of children's books.

Louise **Jansen:** Rida Johnson Young (1875–1926), U.S. playwright, lyricist. Before becoming an fulltime playwright, Young was an actress, adopting this name for her last stage appearance in 1904.

Steve **Jansen:** Stephen Batt (1959–), Eng. rock drummer. The Japan member is the brother of that group's lead singer, David **Sylvian**.

David **Janssen:** David Harold Meyer (1931–1980), U.S. movie, TV actor. The actor's screen name is that of his stepfather, Eugene Janssen.

Ivan **Janvier** *see* Algis **Budrys**

Sébastien **Japrisot:** Jean-Baptiste Rossi (1931–2003), Fr. novelist, translator. The writer fashioned his new name as an anagram of his original full name.

Jaque-Catelan: Jacques Guerin-Castelain (1897–1965), Fr. movie actor.

Paul **Jarrico:** Israel Shapiro (1915–1997), U.S. screenwriter.

Hans **Järta:** Hans Hierta (1774–1847), Swe. politician. The political activist, a member of a noble family, was a leader of the coup that overthrew Gustav IV, king of Sweden, in 1809, having changed his name and renounced his title nine years earlier as a protest against the absolutist Swedish regime.

Ja Rule: Jeff Atkins (1976–), U.S. black rapper. "Ja" is a form of "Jah," as for **Jah Lion**.

Bruno **Jasienski:** Bruno Zyskind (1901–1939), Pol. writer.

Jasmin: Jacques Boé (1798–1864), Fr. dialect (Gascon) poet, "troubadour."

Jasmuheen: Ellen Greve (1957–), Austral. spiritualist, "breatharian."

[Sir] David **Jason:** David John White (1940–), Br. TV actor. The actor was obliged to choose another name as there was an existing actor David White. He accordingly changed his surname to Jason, the first name of his twin brother, who died at birth. More colorfully, some sources claim he took his new name from his favorite movie, *Jason and the Argonauts* (1963).

Leigh **Jason:** Leigh Jacobson (1904–1979), U.S. movie director.

Jassef: James Francis Sullivan (1853–1936), Eng. cartoonist, caricaturist. The artist's name represents "Jas. F.," his abbreviated first name and middle initial, with an inserted "s" for "Sullivan."

Jeremy **Jaunt** *see* **Old Humphrey**

Jauran: Rodolphe de Repentigny (1926–1959), Can. abstract painter.

Peju **Javorov:** Peju Kracholov (1877–1914), Bulg. writer.

Simon **Jay:** Colin James Alexander (1920–2007), Eng.-born N.Z. crime, mystery writer.

W.M.L. **Jay:** Julia Louisa Matilda Woodruff, née Curtiss (1833–1909), Eng. writer. The author's pen name consists of a reversal of her initials, with the "J" of "Julia" forming a surname.

Jennifer **Jayne:** Jennifer Jayne Jones (1932–), Br. movie, TV actress.

Michael **Jayston:** Michael James (1935–), Eng. stage, movie, TV actor.

Jay-Z: Shawn Carter (1969–), U.S. black rapper. The artist is said to have taken his name from the J/Z Brooklyn subway lines, although it could equally have originated as "Jazzy," a childhood nickname.

Jazzie B: Beresford Romeo (1963–), Br. black rapper, of Antiguan parentage.

Samuel **Jeake, Jr.:** Conrad Aiken (1889–1973), U.S. writer, critic. Aiken adopted this name while living in England for the "London Letter" column that he wrote for the *New Yorker* in the mid–1930s, taking it from Jeake's House, his home in Rye, Sussex.

Gloria **Jean:** Gloria Jean Schoonover (1926–), U.S. movie actress.

Jeanbon Saint-André: André Jeanbon (1749–1813), Fr. politician, pastor.

Jeanne-Claude: Jeanne-Claude Denat de Guillebon (1935–2009), Fr.-born U.S. artist, teaming with **Christo,** her husband.

Jean Paul: Johann Paul Friedrich Richter (1763–1825), Ger. novelist, didactic writer. The writer's adoption of the French form of his first two names is said to have expressed his admiration for the French writer Jean-Jacques Rousseau (1712–1778).

Ursula **Jeans:** Ursula Livesey, née McMinn (1906–1973), Eng. stage actress.

Jeetendra: Ravi Kapoor (1942–), Ind. movie actor. The actor's screen name, also spelled Jitendra as a personal name, means literally "one who has conquered Indra," implying one who is so powerful that he has conquered Indra, the god of the sky.

Mahatma Cane **Jeeves** *see* W.C. **Fields**

Anne **Jeffreys:** Anne Carmichael (1923–), U.S. stage actress, singer.

Fran **Jeffries:** Frances Makris (1939–), U.S. movie producer, singer.

Herb **Jeffries:** Umberto Balentino (1911–), U.S. black movie actor, jazz singer ("The Bronze Buckaroo").

Ladislav **Jégé:** Ladislav Nádasi (1866–1940), Slovakian novelist, short-story writer.

Jehoash: Solomon Blumgarten (1871–1927), Lithuanian-born U.S. Yiddish poet, translator. Jehoash (or Joash) is a biblical king of Judah. The scholar is also known as Yehoash Shloyme Blumgartn.

Allen **Jenkins:** Alfred McGonegal (1900–1974), U.S. comic movie actor.

Elijah **Jenkins:** John Mottley (1692–1750), Eng. dramatist, historical writer. Mottley used this name for his classic jestbook, *Joe Miller's Jests; or, The Wits Vade-Mecum* (1739). Earlier, he had edited John Stow's *Survey of the Cities of London and Westminster* (1734) under the name Robert Seymour.

Jacquetta Agneta Mariana **Jenks:** William Beckford (1760–1844), Eng. writer. The eccentric builder of Fonthill Abbey adopted this female name, adding the title "of Belgrove Priory in Wales," for *Azemia; A Descriptive and Sentimental Novel, Interspersed with Poetry* (1797). It followed a similar burlesque, *Modern Novel Writing; or, The Elegant Enthusiast; and Interesting Emotions of Arabella Bloomville: A Rhapsodical Romance; Interspersed with Poetry* (1796), written as the Rt. Hon. Lady Harriet Marlow.

Si **Jenks:** Howard Jenkins (1876–1970), U.S. movie actor.

Caryl **Jenner:** Pamela Penelope Ripman (1917–), Eng. stage director, theater manager.

Jenneval: Hippolyte Louis Alexandre Dechet (1801–1830), Fr. comedian, poet.

Jennifer: Elizabeth Kenward, née Kemp-Welch (1906–2001), Eng. society columnist. Betty Kenward wrote her first piece for the *Tatler* in 1942. She became their full-time diarist in 1944, and the following year adopted the name Jennifer for her regular column "Jennifer's Diary." She kept the name when moving to *Queen*, then to *Harpers & Queen*, where she wrote her last piece in 1991. In her autobiography, Kenward tells how she was given her name by *Tatler* subeditor John Mann: "The following day my editor came to see me and said that to him I looked like a Jennifer, and would I agree to 'Jennifer writes her Social Journal' heading my pages. As I knew that no member of my family was called Jennifer, and as it seemed to me a simple old-fashioned name, I readily agreed" [Betty Kenward, *Jennifer's Memoirs: Eighty-five Years of Fun and Functions*, 1992].

Claudia **Jennings**: Mimi Chesterton (*c*.1950–1979), U.S. movie actress. The future actress adopted her new name for her appearance as a centerfold model ("Miss November 1969") in *Playboy*.

Kid **Jensen**: David Allen Jensen (1950–), Can.-born Eng. radio, TV DJ, compère. The radio and TV personality began working as a DJ when he was only 16. In 1968 he started working for Radio Luxembourg, where he was nicknamed "Kid" for his youth and youthful appearance. He adopted the name instead of his first name until about 1980, when he felt sufficiently mature to revert to "David." Even so, he still features as David "Kid" Jensen in later reference and publicity sources.

Ron **Jeremy**: Ronald Jeremy Hyatt (1953–), U.S. porno movie actor.

Chris **Jericho**: Chris Irvine (*c*.1965–), U.S. wrestler.

Maria **Jeritza**: Marie Marcellina Jedlitzková (1887–1982), Moravian-born U.S. opera singer.

Jerome K. **Jerome**: Jerome C. Jerome (1859–1927), Eng. writer. Jerome's middle initial stood for "Klapka," leading many to suppose that he was named for the Hungarian general György Klapka (1820–1892), to whom his father played host in the 1850s. In fact he was christened Jerome Clapp Jerome, with the identical name of his father, but altered his middle name as he did not regard it as appropriate.

Suzie **Jerome**: Suzanne Willis (1960–1986), Br. movie, TV actress.

Mary **Jerrold**: Mary Allen (1877–1955), Br. movie actress.

Siegfried **Jerusalem**: Siegfried Salem (1940–), Ger. opera singer.

Jeru the Damaja: Kendrick Jeru Davis (*c*.1971–), U.S. black rapper. The artist is the son of a Rastafarian, and his full stage name is Jeru the Damaja: D Original Dirty Rotten Scoundrel. Damaja was the "first god" who was the son of the Egyptian deities Osiris and Isis.

Paul **Jesson**: Paul Jackson (1946–), Br. stage, movie, TV actor.

Jesulín de Ubrique: Jesús Janeiro Bazán (1974–), Sp. bullfighter. The matador's first name is a diminutive of his original name. The rest of his name means "of Ubrique," referring to his native town.

Jetsam: Malcolm McEachern (1884–1945), Austral. singer, stage, radio entertainer, teaming with **Flotsam**. As the entry for the latter explains, the two names are essentially opposites.

Joan **Jett**: Joan Larkin (1960–), U.S. rock singer.

Jewel: Jewel Kilcher (1974–), U.S. pop singer.

Jimmy **Jewel**: James Arthur Thomas Marsh (1909–1995), Eng. music-hall, radio, TV comedian, teaming with Ben Warriss (1909–1993), his cousin. Jimmy Jewel explains the genesis of his name: "We were really a family called Marsh, but father always worked as Jimmy Jewel. He wouldn't let me call myself Jimmy Jewel, Jr., so for years I worked as Maurice Marsh because I was always doing [Maurice] Chevalier impressions; then we kept changing our names on the bills so the audience wouldn't know it was all one family" [*The Times*, August 3, 1983].

James Jershom **Jezreel**: James White (1840–1885), Eng. religious sect leader. In 1875 White, then serving as an army private, became a member of a sect called "The New House of Israel." (Its followers were known as "Joannas," after the religious fanatic Joanna Southcott, and it was actually a development of the "Christian Israelites," founded in 1822 by John Wroe.) He soon left, however, and with other members founded "The New and Latter House of Israel." Back on military service in India, he bought himself out of the army in 1876 and returned to England under the name James Jershom Jezreel, "an appellation probably derived from the prophet Hosea, but his initials J.J.J. were supposed to represent Joanna Southcott, John Wroe, and James White" [*Dictionary of National Biography*]. (Hosea prophesied that the nation of Israel would be finally destroyed in the valley of Jezreel.) In 1879, declaring himself a messenger of God, Jezreel married Clarissa Rogers (1860–1888), who took the name and title "Esther, Queen of Israel." The sect attained its apotheosis shortly before Jezreel's death.

Jiang Qing: Luan Shumeng (1914–1991), Chin. politician. The wife of Mao Zedong began her career as a movie actress with the screen name Lan Ping ("Green Apple"). In 1936 she married Mao Zedong as her third husband and he rechristened her Jiang Qing ("Azure River").

Jillana: Jillana Zimmermann (1936–), U.S. ballet dancer.

Ann **Jillian**: Ann Jura Nauseda (1951–), U.S. TV actress.

Jingaku: Nakayama Takashi (1959–), Jap. sumo wrestler.

João do Rio: Paulo Alberto Coelho Barreto (1880–1921), Brazilian writer. The writer was born in Rio de Janeiro. Hence his pseudonym, one of several, meaning "John of Rio."

Archibald **Jobbry** *see* Rev. T. **Clark**

Jobriath: Bruce Wayne Campbell (1946–1983), U.S. "glam rock" singer.

Jodelet: Julien Bedeau (*c*.1595–1660), Fr. comic actor, brother of **L'Espy**.

Cousin **Joe:** Pleasant Joseph (1907–1989), U.S. black blues musician.

Robert **Joffrey:** Abdullah Jaffa Anver Bey Khan (1930–1988), U.S. ballet dancer, choreographer, of Afghan-It. parentage.

Frank **Joglar:** Christopher Milbourne (1914–1984), U.S. conjuror, writer. The entertainer used this name for a column in *Magic Monthly*. The name is itself a trick, to be understood as "candid magician."

Johannes Secundus: Jan Nikolai Everaerts (1511–1536), Du. poet. The poet wrote in Latin. Hence his name, meaning "John (or Jan) the Second."

John II: Mercurius (?–535), It. pope. Because he bore the name of a pagan god (Mercury), the pope adopted the name of John I (martyred 526). He was the first pope to assume a different name (in 533).

John III: Catelinus (?–574), It. pope.

John XII: Ottaviano (Octavian) (*c.*937–964), It. pope. Elected at age 18, John XII was the second pope in history to change his name, the first being **John II**.

John XIV: Pietro Canepanova (?–984), It. pope. This pope took a new name to avoid repeating the name of St. Peter, leader of the apostles and first bishop of Rome.

John XXI: Pedro Julião (Peter of Spain) (*c.*1210 or 1220–1277), Port. pope. Like **John XIV**, this pope took a new name to avoid that of St. Peter, first bishop of Rome.

John XXII: Jacques d'Euse (or Duèse) (*c.*1244–1334), Fr. pope.

John XXIII: Angelo Giuseppe Roncalli (1881–1963), It. pope. Aside from its biblical pedigree (John the Baptist, John the Evangelist), the name John was specially meaningful for Roncalli because it was his father's name, it was the dedication of the village church in Lombardy where he was baptized, as well as of many cathedrals worldwide, including the Lateran basilica of San Giovanni in Rome, and it was the name of 22 of his papal predecessors. The same name and number was earlier assumed by the antipope Baldassare Cossa (*c.*1370–1415).

Alix **John:** Alice Jones (1853–1933), Can. writer, working in France.

Dr. **John:** Malcolm John ("Mac") Rebennack (1941–), U.S. rock musician. Although his own middle name, the musician's stage name evolved from Dr. John Creux, The Night Tripper, the voodoo persona he created in the mid–1960s, itself based on one established by Prince Lala (Lawrence Nelson).

[Sir] Elton **John:** Reginald Kenneth Dwight (1947–), Eng. pop musician. Reg Dwight changed his name by deed poll, adopting his new first name from Elton Dean, saxophonist for the soul group Bluesology, and his surname from rock singer Long John Baldry. The musician's *full* stage name is in Elton Hercules John, the middle name added later since, as he explained, "It gave me something to look up to and to remind me always to be strong." The singer felt that his original name "sounded like a cement mixer" [Gerald Newman with Joe Bivona, *Elton John*, 1976].

Evan **John:** Evan John Simpson (1901–1953), Br. playwright, novelist.

Graham **John:** Graham John Colmer (1887–?), Eng. playwright, lyricist.

Jasper **John:** Rosalie Muspratt Jones (1913–), Br. movie, stage actress. The actress's name is not likely to have been suggested by that of the U.S. artist Jasper Johns (1930–), internationally known only from the mid–1950s.

Katherine **John:** Karen Watkins, née Jones (1948–), Welsh crime writer. A version of the writer's maiden name for her new surname. She also writes as Catrin Collier.

Michael **John:** John Michael Briggs (1927–2003), Br. session singer. The singer simply reversed his first two names to create his professional name.

Mr. **John:** Hansi Harberger (1906–1993), Austr.-born U.S. milliner. Mr. John's mother opened a millinery shop in New York City when the family immigrated to the United States after World War I. Some time later, Harberger started a millinery business which later, with partner Frederic Hirst, became John Frederics. In 1948 the business dissolved, and Mr. John continued on his own. He is said to have originally changed his name because Americans kept referring to him as "Hamburger."

Robert **John:** Robert John Pedrick, Jr. (1946–), U.S. pop singer.

Rosamund **John:** Nora Rosamund Jones (1913–1998), Br. movie actress.

Simon **John:** Simon John Bedford (1966–), Br. photographer.

Johnny Alf: Alfredo José da Silva (1929–), Brazilian popular musician.

John of Saint-Samson: Jean du Moulin (1571–1636), Fr. Carmelite mystic.

John of Saint Thomas: Juan Poinsat (1589–1644), Port.-born Sp. philosopher, theologian. After entering the Dominican order in Madrid, John (Juan) assumed the religious name John of Saint Thomas (Juan de Santo Tomás) in 1610 in honor of St. Thomas Aquinas (*c.*1225–1274), whose thought he championed.

[St.] **John of the Cross:** Juan de Yepes y Álvarez (1542–1591), Sp. mystic, poet. The saint's title refers directly to his poetry, and in particular to his poem

Noche oscura del alma ("Dark night of the soul"), in which he describes how the human soul sheds its attachment to everything and finally passes through a personal experience of the Crucifixion to attain the glory of Christ.

John o'London: Wilfred Whitten (1864–1942), Eng. journalist, writer. Whitten was editor of the periodical *John o'London's Weekly* from 1919 to 1936.

John Paul I: Albino Luciani (1912–1978), It. pope. The briefly reigning pope (August 26-September 28, 1978) chose a name that is said to have expressed his wish to combine the progressive and traditional qualities of **John XXIII** and **Paul VI**, his two predecessors. *See also* **Gregory XVII**.

John Paul II: Karol Jozef Wojtyła (1920–2005), Pol. pope. Wojtyła, elected pope in 1978, at first considered the name Stanislaus, after the patron saint of Poland, St. Stanislaus of Krakow (1010–1079), the city where he had been archbishop since 1964. In the end he followed the example of his predecessor, **John Paul I**. "[On being elected] he was then asked to choose a name. In honour of his predecessors, he said he would be known as John Paul II. The College of Cardinals burst into applause at the choice" [*The Times*, April 1, 2005].

Foster Johns: Gilbert Vivian Seldes (1893–1970), U.S. journalist, drama critic, writer.

Milton Johns: John Robert Milton (1938–), Br. stage, TV actor.

Stratford Johns: Alan Edgar Stratford Johns (1925–2002), Br. stage, TV, movie actor.

Crockett Johnson: David Johnson Leisk (1906–1975), U.S. cartoonist, children's writer. In view of the artist's original first name, his pseudonym may have been based on a nickname ("Davy Crockett").

Don Johnson: Donald Wayne (1950–), U.S. TV actor.

Jimmy Johnson: James Thompson (1928–), U.S. blues musician, brother of Syl **Johnson**.

J.J. Johnson: James Louis Johnson (1924–2001), U.S. black jazz trombonist.

John Johnson: Guy (or Guido) Fawkes (1570–1606), Eng. conspirator. The name was assumed by Fawkes when he hired a house next to the Houses of Parliament with the aim of constructing a gunpowder mine in its cellars (the "Gunpowder Plot") so as to blow up the House of Lords while King James was present there for the official opening of parliament. "John Johnson" was to be the servant of one of the conspirators, Thomas Percy. The name seems arbitrary.

Kay Johnson: Catherine Townsend (1904–1975), U.S. movie actress.

Ken "Snake Hips" Johnson: Kendrick Reginald Huymans (1917–1941), Guyanan bandleader, dancer, working in U.K.

Lady Bird Johnson: Claudia Alta Johnson, née Taylor (1912–2007), U.S. first lady. The wife of President Lyndon B. Johnson (1908–1973) was so nicknamed by her nurse, Alice Tittle, who said of her two-year-old charge, "Why, she's as pretty as a ladybird!" She thus grew up to be known as Lady Bird Taylor, and (in 1934) happened to marry a man whose first names had the same initials as her own. After her husband's death she maintained her bank account in the name of Mrs. L.B. Johnson and continued to sign her correspondence Lady Bird Johnson. The initials were further preserved in the names of the couple's two daughters, Lynda Bird Johnson (1944–) and Luci Baines Johnson (1947–).

Nkosi Johnson: Xolani Nkosi (1989–2001), South African activist.

Richard Johnson: Richard White (1604–1687), Eng. Roman Catholic priest, religious writer. White adopted his new name in 1623 on entering the English College at Douai, France, to train as a priest.

Rita Johnson: Rita McSean (1912–1965), U.S. movie actress. The actress "translated" her Gaelic surname into English to provide her stage name, "McSean" meaning "son of John."

Sara Johnson *see* Rosa **Henderson**

Syl Johnson: Sylvester Thompson (1936–), U.S. blues musician, brother of Jimmy **Johnson**.

Tor Johnson: Tor Johansson (1903–1971), Swe.-born U.S. movie actor.

Van Johnson: Charles Van Johnson (1916–2008), U.S. movie actor.

W. Bolingbroke Johnson: Morris Gilbert Bishop (1893–1973), U.S. writer. Bishop, a university professor, used this name for a mystery novel, *The Widening Stain* (1942), for distinction from the light verse that he published under his real name.

Wilko Johnson: John Wilkinson (1947–), Eng. rock guitarist.

William Johnson *see* Frank Donald **Coster**

Benjamin F. Johnson of Boone: James Whitcomb Riley (1854–1916), U.S. poet, journalist.

JoJo: Joanne Levesque (1991–), U.S. pop singer. The singer first signed a record contract in 2003, when barely in her teens.

Jo-Jo: Leon Laurence (1931–2009), Eng. circus clown. A reduplicated name in the style of clowns such as **Coco** and **Koko**.

Betsy Jolas: Elizabeth Illous (1926–), Fr. composer, of U.S. parentage.

Angelina Jolie: Angelina Jolie Voight (1975–), U.S. movie actress, daughter of movie actor Jon Voight (1938–). The former model dropped her family name in order to remain anonymous when she enrolled in acting class at the age of 16. Inevitably, her identity was soon revealed.

Frédéric **Joliot-Curie:** Jean-Frédéric Joliot (1900–1958), Fr. physicist. In 1926 Joliot married a fellow physicist, Irène Curie (1897–1956), daughter of the Polish-born physicist Marie Curie, née Maria Sklodowska (1867–1934), whereupon each added the other's surname. Their collaboration resulted in their joint award of the Nobel Prize for chemistry in 1935 for making the first artifical radioisotope.

Pete **Jolly:** Peter A. Ceragioli (1932–), U.S. jazz musician.

Al **Jolson:** Asa Yoelson (1886–1950), U.S. singer, stage, movie actor, of Lithuanian Jewish parentage. The singer first changed his forename Asa to Al when his elder brother changed his own name, Hirsh, to Harry. Later, in 1899, Fred E. Moore, an electrician in New York's Dewey Theatre, suggested he join him in a singing act as Harry Joelson. Eventually, in 1903, the printer shortened "Joelson" to "Jolson" as the actor's original name seemed "long, foreign sounding" [Michael Freedland, *Al Jolson*, 1971].

Jon: William John Philpin Jones (1913–1992), Welsh-born Br. political cartoonist.

Victorin de **Joncières:** Félix Ludger Rossignol (1839–1903), Fr. composer.

Adda **Jones** *see* I.D. **Ffraid**

Annie **Jones:** Annika Jasko (*c.*1967–), Austral. TV actress, of Hung. parentage.

Buck **Jones:** Charles Frederick Gebhardt (1889–1942), U.S. movie actor.

Candy **Jones:** Jessica Wilcox (1925–1990), U.S. model, writer on fashion. The story goes that Wilcox was renamed Candy Johnson by her agency but misremembered her name and gave it as Jones.

Carolyn **Jones:** Carolyn Baker (1929–1983), U.S. movie actress.

Casey **Jones:** John Luther Jones (1864–1900), U.S. railroader. The folk hero was nicknamed Casey from the town of Cayce, Kentucky, where he and his family moved when he was in his teens.

Clay **Jones:** David Clay-Jones (1923–1996), Welsh broadcaster on gardening. The horticulturist adopted the name by which he was known at school in order to be distinguished from the other 13 Joneses in his class of 33, many of them also David. Clay, his mother's maiden name, was a coincidentally apt name for a gardener.

Duncan **Jones** *see* David **Bowie**

Grace **Jones:** Grace Mendoza (1948–), Jamaican-born U.S. pop musician, movie actress.

Jennifer **Jones:** Phylis Selznick, earlier Walker, née Isley (1919–2009), U.S. movie actress. The actress was given her new name by producer David O. Selznick, who was not keen on "Phylis Walker." He liked the name Jennifer, but it took around three months before someone came up with the alliterative "Jones." Jennifer Jones was introduced under her new name in January 1942 as Selznick's latest "discovery," and in 1949 she married him as her second husband.

John **Jones:** Henry Cecil, 10th Earl of Exeter, Lord Burghley (1754–1804), Eng. aristocrat. The nephew and heir of the 9th Earl of Exeter adopted this name when living apart from his first wife, born Emma Vernon, who had eloped with a clergyman. He married Sarah Hoggins, a farmer's daughter, under this name when she was 17 and he 36, and subsequently obtained a divorce to legitimize the children she bore him. He abandoned his alias on succeeding to the peerage as 10th Earl (from 1801 1st Marquess) of Exeter, when his wife became a countess. The tale is touchingly told in Tennyson's poem "The Lord of Burleigh" (1842) ("He is but a landscape-painter, / And a village maiden she").

John Aelod **Jones:** John Roberts Williams (1914–), Welsh journalist, broadcaster, writer. A substitution of one common Welsh name for another.

John Paul **Jones:** (1) John Paul (1747–1792), Sc.-born U.S. naval hero; (2) John Baldwin (1946–), Br. rock bassist. Following a ship's mutiny in which he killed a man, John Paul fled from Tobago to Virginia in 1773 and became "Mr. John Jones." He later rose to "John Paul Jones Esq." as a first lieutenant in the U.S. Navy. The Paul Jones ballroom dance is said to be named for him.

Johnny **Jones:** Charles Edward Peil (1907–1962), U.S. juvenile movie actor. The actor appeared under this name in a series of two-reelers in 1920–1 entitled *The Adventures and Emotions of Edgar Pomeroy*. As the son of movie actor Edward J. Peil (1888–1958), he subsequently appeared as Edward Peil, Jr.

L.Q. **Jones:** Justus Ellis McQueen (1927–), U.S. movie actor. The initials represents the actor's original middle name and surname. His new surname came from the character he played in his first movie, *Battle Cry* (1955).

Major **Jones:** William Tappan Thompson (1812–1882), U.S. journalist, humorist. The writer used this name for a supposed upper-middle-class planter from Pineville, Georgia, who wrote dialect letters sketching Georgia-Florida backwoodsmen. The first such letter appeared in the *Family Companion and Ladies' Mirror* in 1842 and a collection of 16 letters was published as *Major Jones's Courtship* (1843).

Paul **Jones:** Paul Pond (1942–), Eng. actor, former pop musician.

Richard **Jones** *see* Alfred **Allendale**

Sheridan **Jones:** Ada Elizabeth Chesterton, née Jones (1870–1962), Br. journalist, philanthropist. Sheridan was a family name on the paternal side, used by the writer for many of her journalistic contributions. Among her family and close friends she was known as "Keith," for the writer Gilbert Keith Chesterton (1874–1936), her brother-in-law. She also wrote under the male name John Keith Prothero.

Sissieretta **Jones:** Matilda Sissieretta Joyner (1868–1933), U.S. black opera singer.

Spike **Jones:** Lindley Armstrong Jones (1911–1965), U.S. bandleader. The musician, famous for his "City Slickers," came by his nickname at about the age of 11 when a telegrapher called him "Spike" as he was always hanging around the railroad tracks.

[Sir] Tom **Jones:** Thomas Jones Woodward (1940–), Welsh popular singer. The singer was originally renamed Tommy Scott when he joined a group called the Senators. Their bass guitarist Vernon Hopkins gave the name: "We were thinking of a name when he joined the Senators and I thought I'd nip out to a telephone box and pick up the directory. I thought something with S maybe and saw the name Scott. I went back in and said 'Tommy Scott and the Senators' and they said 'Great.'" It turned out there was another singer Tommy Scott, however, so in 1964 Woodward's manager, Gordon Mills, gave him the name by which he became famous, taking it from the eponymous hero of Henry Fielding's novel (1749), or, rather, from its movie version (1963), in which Tom Jones, who undergoes many sexual escapades, is played by Albert Finney [Stafford Hildred and David Gritten, *Tom Jones: A Biography*, 1990].

T. Percy **Jones:** William Edmondstoune Aytoun (1813–1865), Sc. humorous writer. Aytoun used this name for *Firmilian, or The Student of Badajoz: A Spasmodic Tragedy* (1854), a satire on the writings of a group of minor poets dubbed by him the "spasmodic school" for their outbursts of romantic passion.

Raymond **Jonson:** Carl Raymond Johnson (1891–1982), U.S. painter, theater graphic designer. The artist modified his surname in mid-career to reflect the Swedish spelling.

Spike **Jonze:** Adam Spiegel (1969–), U.S. movie director. The former photographer presumably adopted (and adapted) the name of bandleader Spike Jones although his own "Spike" was was a nickname given him when he turned up for work at the BMX store in his birthplace of Rockville, Maryland, with his hair all spiky after skateboarding.

Jordan: Catherine ("Katie") Price (1978–), Eng. model, popular author. "[Model agent] Sam[antha Bond] told me that I was going to have to think of a different name to use because doing Page 3 [shoots in *The Sun* newspaper] can stop you getting other work. I could hear her asking round the office for suggestions. The only name I could think of was Emily — it doesn't exactly scream glamour model,

does it? Fortunately, after some frantic brainstorming, Sam's assistant Paul came up with the name Jordan. It was different and I liked the way it sounded. So I said yes" [Katie Price, *Being Jordan*, 2004].

"'Jordan is for glamour work and the male fans. Katie Price is for the books and TV and female fans,' Jordan/Price explained" [*The Times*, May 15, 2009].

Mrs. Dorothy **Jordan:** Dorothea Bland (1762–1816), Ir. comedy actress. The actress was the illegitimate daughter of Grace Phillips, also known as Mrs. Frances, by a man named Francis Bland, and she first went on the stage as "Miss Francis." In 1780 she was engaged by Irish theater manager Richard Daly, for the Smock Alley Theatre, Dublin, but after an affair with him fled two years later to England with her mother and sister. There, although clearly pregnant (but not married), she successfully auditioned for theater manager Tate Williamson, who renamed her for a biblical allusion: "You have crossed the water [i.e. the Irish Sea],"said Tate, so I'll call you 'Jordan.'" By Daly, Jordan had a daughter who became an actress under the name "Miss Jordan." She then had four children by (Sir) Richard Ford, whose name she bore for some years. She finally became the mistress of the Duke of Clarence, the future William IV, by whom she had ten children, all known by the surname Fitzclarence. (Old French *fitz*, "son," implies an illegitimate child.)

Robert **Jordan:** James Oliver Rigney, Jr. (1948–2007), U.S. fantasy fiction writer. Rigney wrote dance reviews as Chang Lung and early novels as Regan O'Neal.

Sheila **Jordan:** Sheila Jeanette Dawson (1928–), U.S. (white) jazz singer.

Steve **Jordan:** Steven Giordano (1919–1993), U.S. guitarist, of Ir.-It. parentage.

Jordi: Johan Jordi Cruyff (1974–), Du. footballer. Jordi is the son of the famous footballer Johan Cruyff (1947–), who named him after the patron saint of Catalonia, Spain.

Christine **Jorgensen:** George William Jorgensen, Jr. (1926–1989), U.S. transexual. Following her gender reassignment operation in 1952, Jorgensen took the first name Christine as a tribute to Christian Hamburger, the Danish physician who had consented to treat her free of charge.

Jorginho: Jorge Amorin Campos (1964–), Brazilian footballer. A diminutive form of the sportsman's first name, amounting to "Georgie."

Asger **Jorn:** Asger Oluf Jørgensen (1914–1973), Dan. painter, sculptor, writer, working in France.

Joselito: José Gómez Ortega (1895–1920), Sp. bullfighter. The matador's name means "Little José."

Chief **Joseph:** Hin-mut-too-yah-lat-kekht (*c*.1840–1904), U.S. Native American leader. The

Nez Percé leader, whose Indian name means "Thunder Rolling in the Mountains," came to be known as Joseph or Young Joseph after his father, Old Joseph (originally Tu-eka-kas), so named by American missionaries.

Nerious Joseph: Nereus Mwalimu (c.1962–), Jamaican reggae musician. The singer began his career with UK-based Fashion Records, who suggested a name change on the basis that "Nerious" rhymes with "serious," and would therefore be easier to pronounce.

Père Joseph: François Joseph Leclerc du Tremblay (1577–1638), Fr. religious reformer. The friar is also known by his nickname of *L'Éminence Grise*, "Gray Eminence," referring to his gray habit, by contrast with Cardinal Richelieu, *L'Éminence Rouge*, "Red Eminence," who made him his secretary.

Joséphine: Marie-Josèphe Tascher de La Pagerie (1763–1814), Martinique-born Fr. empress. Marie-Josèphe first married the Vicomte de Beauharnais in 1779, by whom she had two children, Eugène and Hortense. Following his execution (1794) she married the Emperor Napoleon in 1796. Their marriage, being childless ("Not tonight, Josephine"), was dissolved in 1809, but she retained the title of empress.

Flavius Josephus *see* **Flavius Josephus**

Josh: Samuel Langhorne Clemens (1835–1910), U.S. humorist, writer, lecturer. The writer best known as Mark **Twain** used this name early in his career for humorous letters to the *Virginia City Territorial Enterprise*, where he was offered a staff position.

Joshua II: Franz Edmund Creffield (1875–1906), U.S. cult leader, "messiah," of Ger. descent.

Josiah Allen's Wife: Marietta Holley (1836–1926), U.S. writer. In the humorist's writings, much of the homely philosophizing by Samantha Smith Allen, wife of Josiah Allen, served as propaganda for temperance and female suffrage. The first of the books under the pen name was *My Opinions and Betsey Bobbet's* (1873), the named character being a spinster spokeswoman for gentility.

Maria Jotuni: Maria Kustaava Tarkiainen (1880–1943), Finn. novelist, playwright.

Louis Jourdan: Louis Gendre (1919–), Fr. movie actor. Presumably "Jourdan" from "Gendre."

Jovanotti: Lorenzo Cherubini (1966–), It. popular singer, rap artist. The musician began his career as a teenage radio and television DJ. Hence his stage name, based on Italian *giovanotto*, "young man."

William Jovanovich: Vladimir Jovanovich (1920–2001), U.S. publisher.

Leatrice Joy: Leatrice Joy Zeidler (1894–1985), U.S. movie comedienne.

Brenda Joyce: Betty Graffina Leabo (1917–2009), U.S. movie actress.

Thomas Joyce: Arthur Joyce Lunel Carey (1888–1957), Ir. novelist.

Col. Joye: Colin Jacobsen (1937–), Austral. popular musician.

JR: ? (1984–), Fr. street artist, of Tunisian-East European origin. The former graffiti artist refuses to reveal his identity, saying, "Knowing my full name would add nothing."

J.R. Tryfanwy: John Richard Williams (1867–1924), Welsh poet. The poet took his name from his initials and the name of his birthplace, Rhostryfan, Carnarvonshire (now in Gwynedd).

J.S. of Dale: Frederic Jesup Stimson (1855–1943), U.S. lawyer, writer. The initials presumably represent the author's middle name and surname.

Juan de Mervinia: John Roberts (1576–1610), Welsh Roman Catholic martyr. Roberts joined the Benedictine Order in 1598 and took a Spanish name meaning "John of Merioneth" in honor of his native county. In 1970 he was canonized as one of the Forty Martyrs of England and Wales.

Juanes: Juan Estebán Aristizábal Vásquez (1972–), Colombian singer, songwriter.

Juanita: Joy Ganjou (1912–1992), Br. variety artist, dancer.

Ashley Judd: Ashley Ciminella (1968–), U.S. movie actress. The actress adopted the name of her mother, country singer Naomi Judd (1946–).

Francis K. Judd *see* Carolyn **Keene**

Judge Dread: Alex Hughes (1945–1998), Eng. (white) reggae singer. When asked about his Jamaican-sounding stage name, the portly singer merely replied, "Well, a man my size couldn't call himself the Magical Cabbage, could he?" [*The Times*, March 16, 1998]. The name was directly borrowed from the title of a ska song by Prince **Buster**, but was also probably influenced by the British SF comic-strip character Judge Dredd.

Judge Jules: Julius O'Rearden (1965–), Eng. DJ, remixer. The musician was nicknamed "Judge" in the mid–1980s, when he was studying law at the London School of Economics.

Judic: Anne-Marie-Louise Damiens (1850–1911), Fr. comic actress, singer.

Anodea Judith: Judith Ann Mull (1952–), U.S. witch, writer, healer. After undergoing a spiritual transformation in 1975, the then artist adopted the name Anodea, interpreted as "One of the Goddess," meaning the goddess who embodies the essence of witchcraft as the "Great Mother" or "Mother Nature."

Aunt Judy: Margaret Gatty, née Scott (1809–1873), Eng. children's writer. In 1858 Margaret Scott brought out *Aunt Judy's Tales*, taking the name "Aunt Judy" from the pet name of her daughter, Juliana

Horatia Ewing, née Gatty (1841–1885), a children's author in her own right. In 1866 Scott founded the popular children's periodical *Aunt Judy's Magazine*, which her daughter took over after her death.

Juh: Tandinbilnojui (*c.*1825–1883), U.S. American Indian chief. The Apache chief and war leader came to be known by the last syllable of his Indian name, meaning "He Brings Many Things with Him."

Julevno: Jules Eveno (1845–1915), Fr. occultist.

Raul **Julia:** Raúl Rafael Carlos Julia y Arcelay (1940–1994), Puerto Rican-born U.S. movie actor. Not a pseudonym in the strict sense of the word but a simplified form of a typical lengthy Hispanic name.

Sister **Julia:** Susan McGroarty (1827–1901), Ir.-born U.S. philanthropist. Susan McGroarty and her family emigrated to the USA in 1831. In 1846 she entered the Belgian order of Notre Dame de Namur in Cincinnati and took the religious name Sister Julia.

Julia Matilda: Julia Clara Byrne, née Busk (1819–1894), Eng. writer.

Rupert **Julian:** Percival T. Hayes (1879–1943), N.Z.-born movie director, working in U.S.

Julinho: Julio Botelho (1929–2003), Brazilian footballer. The name is a diminutive form of the player's first name.

Julius II: Giuliano della Rovere (1443–1513), It. pope. The pontiff's new name (in Italian, Giulio) is a form of his original name.

Julius III: Giovanni Maria Ciocchi del Monte (1487–1555), It. pope. The pontiff took the name of **Julius II**, to whom he had been chamberlain as a young man.

Louis **Jullien:** Louis Georges Maurice Adolphe Roch Albert Abel Antonio Alexandre Noé Jean Lucien Daniel Eugène Joseph-le-brun Joseph-Barême Thomas Thomas Thomas-Thomas Pierre-Cerbon Pierre-Maurel Barthélemi Artus Alphonse Bertrand Dieudonné Emanuel Josué Vincent Luc Michel Jules-de-la-plane Jules-Bazin Julio César Jullien (1812–1860), Fr. orchestral conductor, composer, impresario, working in England. An impressive string of names that the composer put to practical use.

"The good curé insisted that the child should be baptised, and [his father] Antonio thought it would be only polite to ask one of the members of the Philharmonic Society to stand as godfather. A difficulty arose when every member claimed this privilege, for there were thirty-six of them. So after much discussion it was decided that the baby should be held at the font by the secretary, and that he should be christened with the names of all the members of the society. Thus it was that the future great conductor acquired the long string of Christian names which in the future he found so useful when he required pseu-

donyms under which to publish some of his musical compositions" [Adam Carse, *Life of Jullien*, 1951].

June: June Howard Tripp (1901–1985), Br. revue actress, singer, working in U.S.

Jennie **June:** Jane Cunningham Croly (1829–1901), Eng.-born U.S. writer, women's club leader. The writer's pen name was presumably an embroidered alliteration of her original first name.

Heinrich **Jung-Stilling:** Johann Heinrich Jung (1740–1817), Ger. mystic, writer. The writer is famous for a progressive autobiography, the first volume of which, *Heinrich Stillings Jugend* ("Heinrich Stilling's Youth"), appeared in 1777. Four more volumes followed, the five being published together as *Heinrich Stillings Leben* ("Heinrich Stilling's Life") in 1806. A sixth volume, *Heinrich Stillings Alter* ("Heinrich Stilling's Old Age"), closed the series in 1817.

Juninho: Osvaldo Giroldo Júnior (1973–), Brazilian-born Br. footballer. The sportsman's name, based on his last name, means "little one." "When Juninho was transferred back to Brazil [from England] he became known as Juninho Paulista—*Juninho from São Paolo*—because his team contained another Juninho, who became Juninho Pernambuco—*Juninho from Pernambuco*" [Bellos, p. 228].

Juninho Paulista *see* **Juninho**

Júnior: Jenílson Ângelo de Souza (1973–), Brazilian footballer. The name happens to reflect the player's first name.

Detroit **Junior:** Emery Williams, Jr. (1831–2005), U.S. black blues pianist. The bluesman took his professional name from the city where he had cut his musical teeth.

Alex **Juniper:** Janette Turner Hospital (1942–), Austral. novelist, short-story writer. The author used this name for *A Very Proper Death* (1990).

Junius: [Sir] Philip Francis (1740–1818), Ir. politician, writer. The named writer is generally believed to be the author of a series of letters that appeared in the *Public Advertiser* between January 21, 1769, and January 21, 1772, attacking, among others, the Duke of Grafton, Lord Mansfield, and even George III himself. If the reference is not to a particular Roman of note, such as one of the conspirators Lucius Junius Brutus or Marcus Junius Brutus, who plotted to kill Caesar, the aim may be to indicate a young or *junior* person. Compare the next two entries below.

E. **Junius:** Adrien Emmanuel Rouquette (1813–1887), U.S. poet, novelist. The writer used the name for his *Critical Dialogue Between Aboo and Caboo* (1880), denouncing the depiction of Creoles in George Washington Cable's novel, *The Grandissimes* (1880). Rouquette, who was the son of a Creole mother, based his pen name on that of **Junius**, with "E." presumably for "Emmanuel."

Junius Americanus: Arthur Lee (1740–1792), U.S. diplomat. The diplomat, who used the name for some letters he published, adopted the pseudonym made famous by **Junius**.

Katy Jurado: María Cristina Estella Marcella Jurado García (1924–2002), Mexican movie actress, working in U.S.

Curd Jürgens: Curd Gustav Andreas Gottlieb Franz Jürgens (1915–1982), Ger. movie actor. Jürgens was usually billed as "Curt" in English-language films.

Vic Juris: Victor E. Jurusz, Jr. (1953–), U.S. jazz guitarist.

John Justin: John Justinian de Ledesma (1917–2002), Br. movie actor, of Argentinian parentage.

Justinian I: Petrus Sabbatius (483–565), Roman emperor. The emperor, whose full Latin name was Flavius Justinianus, took his new name from his uncle, Justin I (c.450–527), who preceded him and promoted him.

Just Jack: Jack Allsopp (1975–), Br. pop singer. The name reflects the singer's "ordinary guy" image. "Even his stage name ... underlines his lack of pop-star pretension" [*The Times*, November 11, 2009].

Leila K: Leila el-Khalifi (c.1972–), Swe. rapper, of Arabic descent.

Tonio K: Steve Krikorian (1950–), U.S. rock singer, songwriter.

Vasily Kachalov: Vasily Ivanovich Shverubovich (1875–1948), Russ. stage actor.

János Kadár: János Czermanik (or Csermanek) (1912–1989), Hung. Communist leader, premier.

Kadyr-Gulyam: Vladislav Konstantinovich Yanushevsky (1886–1970), Russ. circus artist, acrobat, athlete, husband of **Nedin**. The performer adopted an Arabic-style name that could be loosely interpreted as "powerful young man" (although in Arabic the adjective, here *kadir*, properly follows the noun).

Wade **Kaempfert** *see* Lester **del Rey**

Madeline **Kahn:** Madeline Gail Wolfson (1942–1999), U.S. movie actress.

Uuno Kailas: Frans Uuno Salonen (1901–1933), Finn. poet.

Kaimen: Elsa Marianne Stuart-Bergstrom (1889–1970), Swe. pianist, music critic, composer.

Meiko Kaji: Masako Ota (1947–), Jap. movie actress.

Kaká: Ricardo Izecson dos Santos Leite (1982–), Brazilian footballer. The player owes his sports name to his younger brother, Rodrigo, who instead of "Ricardo" could only manage "Caca."

Hilda Maria **Käkikoski:** Hilda Maria Sjöström (1864–1912), Finn. writer. The writer moved to Helsinki at the age of 14 and changed her Swedish name, meaning "sea river," to a Finnish one, meaning "cuckoo falls."

Kako: Francisco Angel Bastar (c.1937–), Puerto Rican popular musician, band leader. A pet name based on the musician's first name.

Kal: Kevin Kallaugher (1955–), U.S.–born Br. political cartoonist.

Kalanag: Helmut Schreiber (1893–1963), Ger. illusionist. The magician adopted the name from Rudyard Kipling's *Jungle Book*, where it is that of an elephant, meaning "Black Snake."

Ossip **Kalenter:** Johannes Burckhardt (1900–1976), Ger. writer.

Bertha **Kalich:** Beylke Kalakh (1872–1939), Pol.-born U.S. actress of the Yiddish stage.

Kalki: Ramasami Krishnamurthy (1899–1954), Ind. writer. The writer adopted the name of the Hindu horse god Kalki, the final avatar of Vishnu.

Taustan **Kalle** *see* Teuvo **Pakkala**

Valdis **Kalnroze:** Valdis Karlovich Rosenberg (1894–1993), Latvian painter. The artist adopted a Latvian equivalent of his original name (meaning "rose hill"). His grandson is the German artist Wolf Wonder (1947–).

Sabine **Kalter:** Sabine Aufrichtig (1889–1957), Pol. Jewish opera singer.

Kam: Craig Miller (c.1971–), U.S. black rapper. The Muslim musician's stage name presumably represents a shortened form of "Kamal."

Galiaskar **Kamal:** Galiaskar Kamaletdinov (1878–1933), Russ. (Tatar) writer.

Sharif **Kamal:** Sharif Baygildiyev (1884–1942), Russ. (Tatar) writer, playwright. The writer adopted his father's name as his pen name.

Kamehameha I: Paiea (c.1758–1819), Hawaiian king. The king and conqueror's original name meant "hard-shelled crab." His new name, which passed to his sucessors in the dynasty he founded, means "very lonely one," "one set apart." The dynasty ended in 1872 with the death of Kamehameha V.

Lev Borisovich **Kamenev:** Lev Borisovich Rozenfeld (Rosenfeld) (1883–1936), Russ. revolutionary, opponent of **Stalin**. The revolutionary's name is based on Russian *kamen'*, "stone," so that he was a "man of stone," while Stalin was a "man of steel." Stalin eventually crushed him, proving that steel is stronger than stone.

Boris **Kamkov:** Boris Davidovich Kats (Katz) (1885–1938), Russ. Socialist Revolutionary leader.

Kamo: Simon Arshakovich Ter-Petrosyan (1882–1922), Georgian revolutionary.

Bob **Kane:** Robert Kahn (1915–1998), U.S. cartoonist, movie animator.

Eden **Kane:** Richard Graham Sarstedt (1942–), Eng. pop singer. The singer is said to have derived his name from the Orson Welles movie *Citizen Kane* (1941). He used it from the early 1960s, although he also featured briefly in 1973 with his brothers Robin and Peter Sarstedt under his own name, as the Sarstedt Brothers.

Gil Kane: Eli Katz (1926–2000), Latvian-born U.S. comic-book artist.

Helen Kane: Helen Schroeder (1903–1966), U.S. singer, movie actress.

John Kane: John Cain (1860–1934), Sc.-born U.S. artist.

Julia Kane *see* Denise **Robins**

Peter Kane: Peter Cain (1918–1991), Br. boxer.

Richard Kane: Richard George Wright (1938–), Br. stage, TV, radio actor.

Karl Kani: Carl Williams (1968–), U.S. black sportswear entrepreneur.

Kannadasan: A.S. Muthaiah (1927–1981), Ind. poet, movie songwriter.

Kapilavaddho: William Purfurst (1906–1971), Eng. Buddhist. The founder of the English Sangha Trust became deeply interested in Buddhism after World War II and adopted the status of anagarika (*see* **Dharmapala**), later taking the name Samanera Dhammananada, meaning "he who spreads the dhamma or dharma," i.e. the universal truth of Buddhism. Samenera is the title of a Buddhist novice who has not as yet received full ordination. In 1954 Purfurst received such ordination in Thailand, adopting the name Kapilavaddho, based on Kapilavatthu (now usually spelled Kapilavastu), the Buddha's native town in southern Nepal. Its own name means literally "brown thing," from Sanskrit *kapila*, "brown" (from *kapi*, "monkey"), and *vastu*, "thing," "object." He then returned to England where in 1957, due to ill health, he disrobed and adopted the name Richard Randall, marrying Ruth Lester. After 10 years in obscurity, he robed once again, but finally disrobed in 1971 to marry Jacqueline Gray.

Fanny Kaplan: Feyda Khaimovna Roitblat (Reutblat) (1887–1918), Russ. revolutionary. Executed for her attempt to assassinate **Lenin**, Kaplan had the full cover name Fanni Yefimovna Kaplan.

Nadezhda Kapustina: Nadezhda Alekseyevna Yergandzhieva (1907–), Russ. ballet dancer.

Karandash: Mikhail Nikolayevich Rumyantsev (1901–1983), Russ. circus clown. The clown's name is the Russian word for "pencil." He adopted it in 1934 when appearing in Leningrad, taking it from the French cartoonist **Caran d'Ache**. Rumyantsev had earlier worked as a commercial artist. Hence the attraction of this particular name.

Allan Kardec: Hippolyte Léon Denizard Rivail (1804–1869), Fr. occultist. The Breton name was given the spiritualist by a female medium, who told

him that in a previous existence he had been a Druid called Allan Kardek. The name probably derives from Breton *kard*, "quarter," denoting a fourth child.

Kardoma: Leonard Crompton Clifford (1891–1959), Eng. magician. The name is that of a famous diamond, itself said to derive from Tibetan *mKha'. 'Gro.Ma*, "sky-walking woman."

Karekin I: Nishan Sarkissian (1932–1999), Armenian churchman. Karekin I took his religious name in 1952 on being ordained priest. In 1995 he succeeded **Vazgen** as head of the Armenian Church.

Sigfrid Karg-Elert: Siegfried Theodor Karg (1877–1933), Ger. composer. In 1902 the musician took up a post at the Magdeburg Conservatory, whose director advised him to adopt a more distinctive name. He duly added his mother's maiden name to his existing surname. Later, the Norwegian composer Edvard Grieg recommended he alter the spelling of his first name to "Sigfrid."

Anna Karina: Hanne Karen Blarke Bayer (1940–), Dan. movie actress, working in France, U.S. The actress's name comes from her two first names, coincidentally evoking Tolstoy's Anna Karenina.

Barbara Karinska: Varvara Zhmoudska (1886–1983), Russ.-born ballet designer, costume maker, working in France, U.S.

Miriam Karlin: Miriam Samuels (1925–), Br. revue actress, movie, TV comedienne.

Boris Karloff: William Henry Pratt (1887–1969), Eng. movie actor, working in Canada, U.S. The actor, famous as the monster in the classic horror movie *Frankenstein* (1931), derived his Slavic-sounding name from an early family member. "I dredged up 'Karloff' from Russian ancestors on my mother's side, and I picked 'Boris' out of the chilly, Canadian air," he explained.

Phil Karlson: Philip N. Karlstein (1908–1985), U.S. movie director.

Karlstadt: Andreas Bodenstein (*c*.1480–1541), Ger. religious reformer. The theologian is so known from his birthtown, Karlstadt.

C. Karlweis: Karl Weiß (1850–1901), Austr. comedy writer.

Dun Karm: Carmelo Psaila (1871–1961), Maltese poet.

Mick Karn: Anthony Michaelides (1958–), Br. rock saxophonist.

Jurgis Karnavicius: Yury Lavrovich Karnovich (1884–1941), Lithuanian ballet dancer.

Maria Karnilova: Maria Dovgolenko (1920–2001), U.S. ballet dancer, of Russ. parentage. The dancer adopted (and adapted) her stage name from her mother's maiden name, which was Karnilovich.

Fred Karno: Frederick John Westcott (1866–1941), Eng. music-hall comedian. The artist adopted his name in 1887 when he and two gymnast colleagues filled in at a London music hall for a troupe called The Three Carnos. His agent, Richard Warner, suggested they change the "C" to a more distinctive "K" [J.P. Gallagher, *Fred Karno, Master of Mirth and Tears*, 1971].

Yodi **Karone:** Alain Ndongo Ndiye (1954–), Cameroonian writer, working in France.

S. **Karonin:** Nikolay Yelpidiforovich Petropavlovsky (1853–1892), Russ. writer.

Ivan **Karpenko-Kary:** Ivan Karpovich Tobilevich (1845–1907), Ukr. dramatist, actor, brother of Nikolay **Sadovsky** and Panas **Saksagansky**. The writer took the first part of his name from his father's first name, Karp (itself giving his own patronymic of Karpovich). The second part came from Gnat Kary, a character in Taras Shevchenko's poetic drama *Nazar Stodolya*.

Karro: Aleksandr Georgiyevich Karashkevich (1893–1945), Russ. circus artist, dog trainer.

Jan **Karski:** Jan Kozeliewski (1914–2000), Pol. Resistance hero. Karski was naturalized a U.S. citizen in 1954 and worked for the United States Information Service.

Marie Luise **Kaschnitz:** Freifrau Marie Luise von Kaschnitz-Weinberg, née von Holzing-Bersteet (1901–1974), Ger. writer. The writer's adopted name is the first half of that of her husband, whom she married in 1925.

Arnold **Kashtanov:** Arnold Lvovich Epshteyn (Epstein) (1938–), Russ. writer.

Harold **Kasket:** Harold Basket (1926–2002), Br. movie actor, of mixed descent. The actor's screen name suggests "casket," which is a sort of small basket. But this may be purely a coincidence.

Garry **Kasparov:** Garri (or Harry) Kimovich Weinstein (1963–), Azerbaijani-born Russ. chess player. The world chess champion was born to a Jewish father and Armenian mother, née Gasparyan. He gained his new name at the age of seven following the death of his father in a road accident: "Many people wonder why I changed my name from Weinstein to Kasparov. After my father died I went to live with my mother's parents. It seemed natural to use the name Kasparov, particularly as they had three daughters and no son" [Garry Kasparov with Donald Trelford, *Unlimited Challenge*, 1990]. Kasparov adopted his new name after his chess teacher, world champion Mikhail Botvinnik, "added that it wouldn't hurt my chances of success in the USSR not to be named Weinstein" [Daniel Johnson, review of Garry Kasparov, *How Life Imitates Chess*, *Times Literary Supplement*, April 13, 2007].

Kasugafuji: Shoki Iwanaga (1966–), Jap. sumo wrestler. The wrestler took his name from his *beya* (stable), Kasugayama, and Mt. Fuji.

Kurt S. **Kasznar:** Kurt Serwischer (1913–1979), Austr. stage, movie actor, working in U.S.

Kurt **Katch:** Isser Kac (1896–1958), Pol. movie actor, working in U.S.

Cousin **Kate:** Catharine Douglass Bell (?–1861), Sc. novelist. The writer used this homely name, in the manner of her day, for *Set About It At Once, or Cousin Kate's Story* (1847) and later tales.

Shintaro **Katsu:** Toshio Okumura (1931–1997), Jap. movie actor, producer.

Anna **Kavan:** Helen Emily Edmonds, earlier Ferguson, née Woods (1901–1968), Fr.-born novelist, short-story writer, working in U.S., U.K. The writer adopted her pen name in 1940 from one of her own fictional characters, the heroine of *Let Me Alone* (1930) and *A Stranger Still* (1935), written as Helen Ferguson. Her first book as Anna Kavan was *Asylum Piece and Other Stories* (1940).

Dan **Kavanagh:** Julian Patrick Barnes (1946–), Eng. novelist. The writer's novels usually appear under his real name, but he adopted this pen name for his detective fiction, taking it from his wife, literary agent Pat Kavanagh (1940–2008). He has also written for the *New Review* as Edward Pygge and for *The Tatler* as Basil Seal, the latter name that of the central character in novels by Evelyn Waugh.

Venyamin **Kaverin:** Venyamin Aleksandrovich Zilberberg (Silberberg) (1902–1989), Russ. writer.

Charles **Kay:** Charles Piff (1930–), Eng. stage actor.

Connie **Kay:** Conrad Henry Kirnon (1927–1994), U.S. jazz drummer.

Janet **Kay:** Janet Kay Bogle (1958–), Br. black reggae singer.

Jay **Kay:** James Kay (*c*.1969–), Br. rock musician. Kay, the son of Karen **Kay**, has a name that seems to reflect that of his funk group, Jamiroquai, although the band is actually named after the Iroquois tribe whose pantheism inspired him.

John **Kay:** Joachim F. Krauledat (1944–), Ger.-born U.S. rock musician.

Karen **Kay:** Adrienne Judith Pringle (1947–), Eng. TV entertainer, singer.

Kathie **Kay:** Connie Wood (1919–2005), Sc. radio singer, TV entertainer.

Cab **Kaye:** Augustus Kwamlah Quaye (1921–2000), Br. jazz musician, of Ghanaian parentage. Kaye based his new name on that of his father, jazzman Caleb Quaye, who was killed in a railroad accident when his son was only four months old.

Carol **Kaye:** Carol Lindsey Young (1930–2006), Br. popular singer, stage, TV actress. The singer took her name from the Kaye Sisters, the vocal trio to which she belonged. (The three were not real sisters, but looked and dressed alike on the stage. They took their name from their manager, Carmen Kaye.)

Danny **Kaye:** David Daniel Kominski (1913–1987), U.S. stage, movie, TV actor, of Ukr. parentage. The popular performer legally adopted his stage name in 1943.

Darwood **Kaye:** Darwood Smith (1929–2002), U.S. child movie actor.

Eff **Kaye** *see* Lorin **Kaye**

Lorin **Kaye:** Lorin Andrews Lathrop (1858–1929), U.S. novelist + [Miss] F. Konstam (*fl.* 1897), U.S. novelist. The writers used this joint pseudonym for their novel *A Drawing-Room Cynic* (1897), "Kaye" being the second part of Miss Konstam's individual pen name, Eff Kaye, from her initials.

M.M. **Kaye:** Mary Margaret Kaye (1908–2004), Eng. writer, illustrator. Kaye wrote children's fiction as Mollie Kaye and also used the name Mollie Hamilton, her married surname.

Nora **Kaye:** Nora Koreff (1920–1987), U.S. ballet dancer, of Russ. parentage. The dancer changed her Russian name to Kaye because "an American dancer ought to have an American name."

Sammy **Kaye:** Samuel Zarnocay, Jr. (1910–1987), U.S. bandleader, of Cz. parentage.

Stubby **Kaye:** Bernard Kotzin (1918–1997), U.S. stage, TV actor. The actor's stage name was formed from a nickname given him for his ample girth and the first letter of his surname.

Howard **Kaylan:** Howard Kaplan (1947–), U.S. rock musician.

Cyril **Kay-Scott** *see* Evelyn **Scott**

[Sir] James **Kay-Shuttleworth:** James Phillips Kay (1804–1877), Eng. educationist. The founder of the English system of publicly financed elementary education added the second part of his name in 1842 on marrying Janet Shuttleworth, daughter and heiress of Robert Shuttleworth.

Elia **Kazan:** Elias Kazanjoglou (1909–2003), Turk.-born U.S. movie director, of Gk. parentage. The future director was taken by his family to the U.S. when he was only four, and they then shortened their name to Kazan. Later, when he was established in Hollywood, an unsuccessful attempt was made to change his name yet again to "Cezanne."

Aleksandr **Kazbegi:** Aleksandr Chopikashvili (1848–1893), Georgian writer. The writer renamed his family for nearby Mt. Kazbek.

Ernie **K-Doe:** Ernest Kador, Jr. (1936–2001), U.S. black R&B singer. The singer signed with the Minit label in 1960, when on the suggestion of record boss Joe Banashak he changed his name to its familiar eye-catching variant.

Kea: Roger Phillips (1960–), N.Z.-born Br. crossword compiler. The setter's pseudonym names the parrot that is native to New Zealand.

Kemble **Kean:** Thomas William Bourne (1899–?), Eng. music-hall comedian. The artist took his name from the two famous actors John Philip Kemble (1757–1823) and Edmund Kean (*c.*1789–1833), often mentioned in the same breath.

Constance **Keane** *see* Veronica **Lake**

Jack **Kearns:** John Leo McKernan (1882–1963), U.S. boxing manager, promoter. McKernan began his boxing career under the ring name Young Kid Kearns.

Edward **Kearsley:** S. Weir Mitchell (1828–1914), U.S. physician, writer, father of John Philip **Varley**. Mitchell used this pseudonym, based on his father's middle name, for his early poetry and fiction in order to keep his literary and medical careers separate, but reverted to his real name after the publication of *Hepzibah Guiness* (1880).

Buster **Keaton:** Joseph Francis Keaton (1895–1966), U.S. movie comedian. It remains uncertain how the actor came by his nickname. The popular account is that it was given him by Harry **Houdini** after seeing the baby boy Keaton tumble unharmed down a flight of stairs during a family act. Or there may be a link with the comic-strip character Buster Brown. He was unrelated to Diane **Keaton**.

Diane **Keaton:** Diane Hall (1946–), U.S. stage, movie actress. The actress adopted her mother's maiden name of Keaton as there was already a Diane Hall as a member of the actors' union, Equity, which rules that no two members must have the same name. Her real name, with the pet form of her first name by which she is known, was that of the lead character that she played in *Annie Hall* (1977), a movie written for her by Woody **Allen**.

Michael **Keaton:** Michael John Douglas (1951–), U.S. movie, TV actor, comedian. The actor changed his name to avoid confusion with Michael Douglas (1944–), actor son of Kirk **Douglas**. He took his new name from Diane **Keaton** on seeing her picture in the *Los Angeles Times*.

Viola **Keats:** Viola Smart (1911–), Sc. stage actress. The actress adopted her mother's maiden name as her stage name.

Keb' Mo': Kevin Moore (1951–), U.S. black blues musician. The musician's performing name, originally a nickname, is in the idiom of his blues persona.

Howard **Keel:** Harry Clifford Keel (1919–2004), U.S. stage, movie actor, singer. Several sources give Keel's original surname as Leek, but it apparently remained unchanged.

Ruby **Keeler:** Ethel Hilda Keeler (1909–1993), Can.-born U.S. movie actress.

Malcolm **Keen:** Malcolm Knee (1887–1970), Br. movie, stage actor, theater manager.

Carolyn **Keene:** Edward L. Stratemeyer (1863–1930), U.S. writer. The Stratemeyer Literary Syndicate set up in 1906 used this name for stories for girls about Nancy Drew, the teenage detective. Stratemeyer's daughter, Harriet Stratemeyer Adams (1894–1982), was a noted contributor to the series, and others who wrote under the name were Mildred Wirt Benson (1905–2002), Leslie McFarlane (1903–1977), Michael Dennis McQuay (1949–), and Sharon Blythe Wagner (1936–). Benson used a host of other pseudonyms for her prolific children's stories, including Frank Bell, Joan Clark, Julia K. Duncan, Alice B. Emerson, Francis K. Judd, Don Palmer, Helen Louise Thorndyke, Dorothy West, Ann Wirt, and Mildred Wirt. But might not Carolyn Keene have been a better name for the feisty detective herself?

Laura **Keene:** Mary Frances Moss (?1820–1873), Eng.-born U.S. actress, theater manager. There is some dispute about the actress's original name and date of birth, but the particulars are probably as here.

Thomas Wallace **Keene:** Thomas R. Eagleson (1840–1898), U.S. actor. The stage name was adopted by Eagleson as a professional actor in his teens.

Tom **Keene:** George Duryea (1896–1963), U.S. movie actor.

Oliné **Keese:** Caroline Woolmer Leakey (1827–1881), Eng. novelist, poet. The writer lived for a time in Tasmania, Australia, and used this name, loosely based on her real name, for *The Broad Arrow* (1859), a novel based on her experiences there.

Keith: James Barry Keefer (1949–), U.S. pop singer. The name presumably originated as a nickname based on the singer's surname.

David **Keith:** Francis Steegmuller (1906–1994), U.S. novelist, literary critic. The author of serious literary and biographical studies used this name for his crime fiction. He used the name Byron Steel for his lesser critical studies.

Ian **Keith:** Keith Ross (1899–1960), U.S. movie actor. The actor took his mother's maiden name as his screen name.

Leslie **Keith:** Grace Leslie Keith Johnston (?1843–1929), Sc. novelist. The writer extracted the sexually ambiguous name from her original name, in which Keith was her grandmother's maiden name.

Penelope **Keith:** Penelope Timson, née Hatfield (1940–), Eng. TV actress. The actress adopted her mother's maiden name.

Herbert **Kelcey:** Herbert Kelcey Lamb (1856–1917), Eng.-born U.S. actor. Lamb dropped his family name when he became an actor in 1877.

Kéler-Béla: Adalbert von Keler (1820–1882), Hung. composer. The musician took the Hungarian equivalent, Béla, of German Adalbert, then inverted first and last names to form a single new name.

Kelis: Kelis Rogers (1980–), U.S. black hip-hop singer, R&B artist. The singer pronounces her name "Keleece."

Joseph **Kell** *see* Anthony **Burgess**

Harry **Kellar:** Heinrich Keller (1849–1922), U.S. magician.

Will P. **Kellino:** William P. Gislingham (1873–1958), Br. circus clown, movie actor, director. The performer's new surname was loosely based on his original name.

Kathleen **Kellow** *see* Jean **Plaidy**

Charles **Kelly:** Charles Clavering Wardell (1839–1885), Eng. actor.

George "Machine Gun" **Kelly:** George Kelly Barnes, Jr. (1895–1954), U.S. gangster. Kelly was so nicknamed by his wife after he allegedly "wrote" his name on a barn wall with bullets from a machine gun she had bought for him from a pawnbroker in Fort Worth, Texas.

Patrick **Kelly** *see* Richard **Butler**

Petra **Kelly:** Petra Karin Lehmann (1947–1992), Ger. politician. The cofounder of the Green Party (*Die Grünen*) took her new name from her stepfather, with whom she and her stepmother moved to the USA in 1960.

R. **Kelly:** Robert Kelly (1969–), U.S. black R&B singer.

Kelly Marie: Jacqueline McKinnon (1957–), Sc. pop singer. "Kelly" from "Jacqueline."

Kem: Kimon Evan Marengo (1904–1988), Egyptian-born Br. political cartoonist, of Gk. parentage. A neat combination of the artist's initials and a shortened form of his first name.

Kemine: Mamedveli (*c*.1770–1840), Turkmen satirical poet. The poet's assumed name means "submissive one."

Ed **Kemmer:** Edward Kemmerer (1920–2004), U.S. TV, movie actor.

[Sir] James **Kemnal:** James Hermann Rosenthal (1864–1927), Br. engineering equipment manufacturer. The head of Babcock & Wilcox, established in 1891 as a independent British firm from the U.S. original, adopted his new name in 1915 when German names fell from favor, taking it from the family estate at Chislehurst, Kent.

Jeremy **Kemp:** Edmund Jeremy James Walker (1935–), Eng. movie, TV actor. The actor adopted his mother's maiden name as his screen name.

Mirdza **Kempe:** Mirdza Yanovna Naykovskaya (1907–1974), Latvian poet.

Kempferhausen: Robert Pearse Gillies (1788–1858), Sc. littérateur, autobiographer. The writer adopted the name under which he featured in the series of dialogues known as the *Noctes Ambrosianae* published in *Blackwood's Magazine* between

1822 and 1835. Compare the name of Christopher **North**.

Joan **Kemp-Welch**: Joan Green (1906–1999), Eng. stage actress, theater director. The actress took her mother's maiden name for her stage name, rather unusually preserving its lengthy (for theatrical purposes) "double-barreling."

Jaan **Kenbrovin**: James Kendis (1883–1946), U.S. songwriter.

Geoffrey **Kendal**: Geoffrey Bragg (1909–1998), Br. stage actor, theater manager As a young man, Bragg was dismissed from his job as an engineering apprentice, and decided instead to try his luck on the stage with his name changed to Kendal, that of his home town in the English Lake District. Bragg was then a name of little charisma, although today it is familiar from the English novelist and broadcaster Melvyn Bragg (1939–), to whom Kendal may have been distantly related. Kendal was the father of TV actress Felicity Kendal (1947–) and movie actress Jennifer Kendal (1934–1984).

[Dame] Madge **Kendal**: Margaret Shafto Robertson (1849–1935), Br. stage actress, The actress was the wife of William Hunter **Kendal** and adopted his stage name as her own. The couple often acted together and starred at the Haymarket, London, as "the Kendals."

William Hunter **Kendal**: William Hunter Grimston (1843–1917), Br. stage actor, theater manager. The actor assumed the name Kendal for his theatrical debut as Louis XIV in *A Life's Revenge* (1861), possibly basing it on the name Kemble, that of a noted acting family, whose prominent members were Charles Kemble (1775–1854), his daughter Frances Anne "Fanny" Kemble (1809–1893), and his elder brother John Philip Kemble (1757–1823).

Gordon **Kendall**: Shariann Lewitt (1954–), U.S. SF writer + Susan M. Shwartz (1949–), U.S. SF writer. The two writers adopted this male name for their acclaimed novel *White Wing* (1985).

Kay **Kendall**: Justine Kay Kendall McCarthy (1926–1959), Eng. movie actress.

Suzy **Kendall**: Frieda Harrison (1944–), Eng. movie actress.

Carleton **Kendrake** *see* A.A. **Fair**

Kennedy: Lisa Kennedy Montgomery (1972–), U.S. video jockey.

A.L. **Kennedy**: Alison Louise Kennedy (1965–), Sc. novelist. "Alison Louise Kennedy says that she writes under her initials because the authors she first admired—J.R.R. Tolkien, C.S. Lewis and E. **Nesbit**—had done so" [*The Times* January 23, 2008].

Merna **Kennedy**: Maude Kahler (1908–1944), U.S. movie actress.

Milward **Kennedy**: Milward Rodon X. Burge (1894–1968), Eng. journalist, mystery writer.

Rudy **Kennedy**: Rudy Karmeinsky (1927–2008), Ger. Jewish scientist. The Holocaust survivor, who led a (largely unsuccessful) battle for compensation fought by British survivors of Nazi death camps, was liberated by British troops and in 1946 permitted to go to London because he had an aunt there. Safely in England, he adopted the name of the British officer who had informed his aunt of his survival.

Tamara **Kennedy**: Tamara Brooks (1962–), Sc. TV actress.

X.J. **Kennedy**: Joseph Charles Kennedy (1929–), U.S. poet, children's author. The writer prefixed his name with "X" in order to avoid a spurious connection with U.S. businessman and diplomat Joseph P. Kennedy (1888–1969).

Kenneth: Kenneth Battelle (1927–), U.S. hairdresser.

Dee Dee **Kennibrew**: Delores Henry (1945–), U.S. pop singer. "Dee Dee" from "Delores."

Charles J. **Kenny** *see* A.A. **Fair**

Barbara **Kent**: Barbara Klowtman (1906–), Can.-born U.S. movie actress.

Barry **Kent**: Barry Sautereau (1932–), Eng. stage actor.

Bruce **Kent**: William Butters (1912–1995), Eng. stage singer.

Jean **Kent**: Joan Mildred Summerfield (1916–), Eng. movie actress. The actress began her movie career as Joan Summerfield, then switched to Jean Carr for a couple of films before assuming her regular screen name in the 1940s.

Kim **Kent**: Knud Rame (1935–), Dan. publisher, astrologer. Rame adopted his pseudonym in 1958 on first publishing the gay monthly magazine *Eon*.

Richard **Kent**: Frank Owen (1893–1968), Eng. writer of "oriental" mystery fiction.

Nan **Kenway**: Helen Hemmings McCartney (1905–2001), Austral.-born Br. radio comedienne, pianist. The entertainer went to England in 1924 and adopted her stage name soon after.

Jomo **Kenyatta**: Kamau wa Ngengi (?1894–1978), Kenyan statesman, nationalist leader. Kenya's first president was orphaned early and was raised first by his uncle, Ngengi, then by his grandfather, Kongo wa Magana. He was baptized in 1914 as Johnstone Kamau, with "Jomo" a pet form of this name. His second name derived from a Kikuyu word for a fancy belt that he affected.

Robert O. **Kenyon** *see* C.L. **Moore**

Kenzo: Kenzo Takada (1939–), Jap. fashion designer, working in France.

Charlotte **Keppel** *see* Paula **Allardyce**

Susan Alice **Kerby**: Alice Elizabeth Burton

(1908–1952), Br. writer of fantasy fiction, working in Canada.

Alfred Kerr: Alfred Kempner (1867–1948), Ger. writer, theater critic. Kempner's pseudonym was adopted by his descendants.

Anita Kerr: Anita Kerr Grob (1927–), U.S. popular singer.

Deborah Kerr: Deborah Kerr Trimmer (1921–2007), Sc.-born movie actress, working in U.K., U.S.

Frederick Kerr: Frederick Grinham Keen (1858–1933), Br. stage, movie actor.

Howard Kerr: [Major] Alexander John Dawson (1872–1952), Eng. writer.

Jean Kerr: Bridget Jean Collins (1923–2003), U.S. humorist, playwright. The writer took her name from that of her husband, drama critic Walter Francis Kerr (1913–).

M.E. Kerr: Marijane Meaker (1927–), U.S. novelist, writer of teenage fiction. The name as a whole represents the writer's surname. She has also written as Mary James and Vin Packer.

Orpheus C. Kerr: Robert Henry Newell (1836–1901), U.S. humorous journalist. The name puns on "office seeker," and was suggested by the many political aspirants at the time of Abraham Lincoln's inauguration (1861). It later came to be used as the name of a stock character for political lampooning.

John Kerrigan *see* Leo **Kessler**

W. Kerrigan *see* Horatio **Nicholls**

George Kerris: George Chakiris (1933–), U.S. dancer, movie actor. The actor used this name for certain movies in the 1950s.

Norman Kerry: Arnold Kaiser (1889–1956), U.S. movie actor.

Willette Kershaw: Willette Mansfield (1890–1960), U.S. stage actress, theatrical producer.

Platon Kerzhentsev: Platon Mikhaylovich Lebedev (1881–1940), Russ. Communist, historian. The publicist took his name from the Kerzhenets River, a tributary of the Volga.

Ke$ha: Kesha Sebert (1987–), U.S. pop singer. A monetary amendation of the singer's first name.

Leo Kessler: Charles Whiting (1926–2007), English novelist, military historian. Whiting's other aliases include Duncan Harding, John Kerrigan, and Klaus Konrad.

Stanley Ketchel: Stanislaus Kiecal (1886–1910), U.S. middleweight boxer, of Pol. descent. The Michigan boxer's family name was changed to Ketchel and his first name to "Stanley" before he left home at age 15 to work as a bellboy and bouncer in Montana.

Richard Keverne: Clifford James Wheeler Hosken (1882–1950), Eng. writer.

Mr. Conny Keyber: Henry Fielding (1707–1754), Eng. novelist. Fielding used this name for his novel *Shamela*, in full *An Apology for the Life of Mrs. Shamela Andrews* (1741), a travesty of Samuel Richardson's epistolary novel *Pamela* (1740–1). The pseudonym and the title of the novel allude to Colley Cibber's autobiography *An Apology for the Life of Mr. Colley Cibber, Comedian* (1740).

Alicia Keys: Alicia J. Augello-Cook (1981–), U.S. black R&B singer, songwriter, of mixed European-Jamaican descent.

Khaled: Khaled Hadj Brahim (1960–), Algerian singer ("king of rai").

Chaka Khan: Yvette Marie Stevens (1953–), U.S. black rock singer. The singer adopted her name in the late 1960s, when she was working on the Black Panthers' breakfast program, with "Chaka" an African name meaning "fire." It was that of the chief Shaka (*c.*1787–1828), founder of the Zulu nation.

Mehboob Khan *see* **Mehboob**

Rahila Khan: [Rev.] Toby Forward (1950–), Eng. clergyman. The Anglican vicar adopted this female Muslim name for his collection of stories *Down the Road, World Away* (1987), purporting to give an insight into the contemporary lives of teenage Asian girls. A note explained that the author was born in 1950, married in 1971, and began writing in 1986. When Forward was revealed as the real author, he was baffled by the critical publicity, explaining that Rahila Khan was just one of the pseudonyms under which he liked to write. The names, he said, "released me from the obligation of being what I seem to be so that I can write as I really am" [*London Review of Books*, February 4, 1988].

Steve Khan: Steven Harris Cahn (1947–), U.S. jazz guitarist, son of lyricist Sammy **Cahn**.

Phra Khantipalo: Lawrence Mills (1932–), Eng. Buddhist, scholar. Mills became interested in Buddhism after being given a book on the religion while serving with the British army in the Middle East at the time of the Suez crisis (1956). He joined the Buddhist Society in London and three years later went to India to study Pali. He was ordained in Bangkok, where he took his new name, Phra being a Thai equivalent of Hindi Thera, meaning "elder."

Daniil Kharms: Daniil Ivanovich Yuvachyov (1905–1942), Russ. children's writer. The writer's assumed name was presumably intended to suggest English *charms* rather than *harms*. He also wrote as Shusterling (seemingly German *Schusterling*, "little cobbler") and Shardam (apparently French *chardon*, "thistle"). Another name was Dandan (perhaps French *dindon*, "turkey"). He obviously enjoyed playing games with his young readers.

Sister Khema: Ilse Ledermann (1923–), Ger. Buddhist. Ledermann's Jewish origins obliged her to leave Germany in 1938. After a long spiritual search, with much traveling, she was ordained a Buddhist nun in Sri Lanka in 1979 under her new name.

Sergey Aleksandrovich **Khudyakov:** Armenak Artyomovich Khanferyants (1901–1950), Azerbaijani-born Russ. army commander. The conscript joined the Red Army in February 1918 and adopted the full name of his commanding officer, killed defending Baku in the Civil War later that same year.

Tagir **Khuryugsky:** Tagir Alimov (1893–1958), Russ. (Lezgin) poet. The poet's adopted name is that of his birthplace, the village of Khuryug, Dagestan.

Mikola **Khvylevoy:** Mikola (or Nikolay) Grigoryevich Fitilyov (1893–1933), Ukr. poet. The poet adopted the adjectival form of Ukrainian *khvilya*, "wave" (of the sea), as his pen name.

Leo **Kiacheli:** Leon Mikhaylovich Shengelaya (1884–1963), Georgian novelist.

Omar **Kiam:** Alexander Kiam (1894–1954), Mexican fashion designer, working in U.S. The designer decided that it made sense to associate his name with that of the Persian poet Omar Khayyám (*c*.1048–*c*.1142), popularized by Edward Fitzgerald's free translation *The Rubáiyát of Omar Khayyám* (1859).

Talib **Kibwe:** Eugene Ludovic Rhynie (1953–), U.S. black jazz musician. Talib Kibwe is also known as T.K. Blue.

Kid ... For names beginning thus, excepting those below (which do not have a conventional surname), see the name which follows, e.g. Kid **Curry**, Kid **Jensen**, Kid **McCoy**, etc.

Kid Creole *see* August **Darnell**

Johnny **Kidd:** Frederick Heath (1939–1966), Eng. rock singer.

Michael **Kidd:** Milton Greenwald (1915–2007), U.S. dancer, choreographer, of Russ. parentage. The dancer took his stage name from the hero of the work in which he had his first leading role, the cowboy ballet *Billy the Kid* (1938), choreographed by Eugene **Loring** to music by Aaron **Copland**.

Kid Frost: Arturo Molina, Jr. (1962–), U.S. hip-hop musician. The performer saw himself as a younger version of **Ice-T**.

Kid Loco: Jean-Yves Prieur (1963–), Fr. (white) DJ, record producer. Prieur originally played in punk bands under the name Kid Bravo. He adopted the name Kid Loco in 1996 for the *Blues Project* EP on France's Yellow Productions.

Kid Rock: Robert James Richie (1971–), U.S. (white) hip-hop musician. "It is not entirely clear whether he earned the name from his prowess as a DJ, or from an apprenticeship in the retail side of the local freebase cocaine business" [Larkin, p.696]. "Rock" is just one of several slang terms for cocaine.

Udo **Kier:** Udo Kierspe (1944–), Ger. movie actor.

Kiki de Montparnasse: Alice Ernestine Prin (1901–1953), Fr. model, singer. Prin posed for many artists and photographers, such as **Man Ray** in *Le Violon d'Ingres* (1924), depicting her with a violin's two *f*-holes on her naked back, and **Brassaï** in *Kiki chantant au Cabaret de Fleurs* (1933). Kiki is a French pet name. Montparnasse (not to be confused with Montmartre) is a noted Paris artists' quarter.

Kiko: Francesco Narvaez Machon (1972–), Sp. footballer. A pet form of the sportsman's first name.

Terry **Kilburn:** Terence Kilbourne (1926–), Br. child movie actor.

John **Kilgore** *see* Mark **Carrel**

Volter **Kilpi:** Volter Adalbert Erikson (1874–1939), Finn. novelist, social critic. Finnish *kilpi* means "shield," "coat of arms," perhaps significantly here.

Kim: Kim Casali (1941–1997), N.Z. cartoonist, working in U.K. The artist, famous for her "Love is..." cartoons, was born Marilyn Judith Grove. In 1971 she married an Italian computer engineer, Roberto Casali, and adopted the new first name Kim.

Bobby **Kimball:** Robert Toteaux (1947–), U.S. rock singer.

Bobbie **Kimber:** Ronald Victor Robert Kimberley (1918–1993), Eng. ventriloquist, female impersonator.

Viktor **Kin:** Viktor Pavlovich Surovikin (1903–1937), Russ. writer. A truncation of the writer's original surname.

Jamaica **Kincaid:** Elaine Potter Richardson (1949–), West Indian-born U.S. writer. Born in Antigua, Richardson was sent to the USA at a young age as an au pair and changed her name in 1973 when she began to write, mainly because she didn't want her folks at home to know she was writing, but also more specifically because it was "a way for [her] to do things without being the same person who couldn't do them — the same person who had all these weights [of her past]" [Leslie Gris, "Through West Indian Eyes," *New York Times Magazine*, October 4, 1990]. Renaming is a theme in Kincaid's works, both fiction and nonfiction, and is used by the writer as a metaphor for conquest and colonial dominance. Her new first name is for the island. When asked why she had not chosen an African name, she replied that the sole connection she had with Africa was the color of her skin, which in itself was not enough to justify the adoption of an African name.

Marien **Kind:** Enrica von Handel-Mazzetti (1871–1955), Austr. writer of Catholic historical novels. Given the theme of the author's writing, it seems reasonable to interpret her German pen name as "Mary's child," referring to the mother of Jesus.

Alan **King**: Irwin Alan Kniberg (1927–2004), U.S. cabaret comedian, movie actor, of Russ. Jewish parentage.

Albert **King**: Albert Nelson (1923–1992), U.S. black blues singer, guitarist. The musician took his stage name from King Records, for whom he recorded in the 1960s.

Andrea **King**: Georgette Andrée Barry (1919–2003), Fr.-born U.S. stage, movie actress. Barry first appeared on Broadway in 1933 under the name Georgette King.

Anna **King**: Anna Delores Williams (1937–2002), U.S. black R&B singer.

B.B. **King**: Riley B. King (1925–), U.S. black blues musician. King acquired his new first name (as initials) on becoming a DJ in Memphis in 1948. "He needed a catchy name that would give him an image and stick in the minds of his listeners.... Variations based on Beale Street, the main symbol of blues, were bandied about; 'Beale Street Blues Boy' won out.... It was a little clumsy, and it excluded his own proper name; later he was called 'Blues Boy King'; finally that was shortened to 'B.B. King'" [Charles Sawyer, *The Arrival of B.B. King*, 1980].

"While staying at a Holiday Inn in Utah, B.B. King is using the pseudonym Pump Davidson. 'I use a different name just so I can retain a bit of privacy from my fans,' explains the 83-year-old King of the Blues. 'It was my great grandfather's name. He was a slave'" [*The Times*, June 20, 2009].

Ben E. **King**: Benjamin Earl Nelson (1938–), U.S. black soul singer. The musician's new name reflected his role as lead singer in the band The Five Crowns.

Carole **King**: Carole Klein (1942–), U.S. pop singer.

Claire **King**: Claire Seed (1963–), Br. TV actress, presenter. To the dismay of her parents, the actress changed her name as a teenager in honor of Elvis Presley, known as "The King (of Rock 'n' Roll)."

Dennis **King**: Dennis Pratt (1897–1971), Eng. opera singer, movie actor. The actor adopted his mother's maiden name as his stage name.

Earl **King**: Earl Silas Johnson IV (1934–2003), U.S. black R&B singer, songwriter.

Edith **King**: Edith Keck (1896–1963), U.S. stage actress. A name change presumably felt to be just as necessary as that made by Dennis **King**.

Freddie **King**: Billy Myles (1934–1976), U.S. black blues musician. The singer and guitarist adopted his mother's maiden name.

Gilbert **King**: Susan Frances Harrison (1859–1935), Can. pianist, poet, composer.

Godfrey Ray **King**: Guy Warren Ballard (1878–1939), U.S. spiritual leader. The controversial founder, with his wife Edna Anne Wheeler Ballard, of the "I AM" religious movement used this name for two books, *Unveiled Mysteries* (1934) and *The Magic Presence* (1935).

Joe **King**: Cecil Emmott (1900–1967), Eng. music-hall comedian. A name of obvious origin.

John "Dusty" **King**: Miller McLeod Everson (1909–1987), U.S. movie actor.

Kennedy **King** *see* George **Douglas** (2)

Larry **King**: Lawrence Zeiger (1933–), U.S. journalist, radio, TV presenter.

Little Freddie **King**: Fread [*sic*] E. Martin (1940–), U.S. black blues musician. King became Little Freddie King in the 1960s.

Little Jimmy **King**: Manuel Gales (1968–2002), U.S. black blues musician. King adopted his new name from his two biggest influences: Jimi **Hendrix** and Albert **King**, the latter being his adopted "grandfather." Like them, he was a left-handed guitarist, playing his instrument upside down.

Martin Luther **King**: Michael King, Jr. (1929–1968), U.S. black civil rights leader, Baptist minister. In 1934 the activist's father, Baptist pastor Michael King (1897–1984), on the request of his own dying father, changed his son's and his own first name to honor Martin Luther (1483–1586), the German founder of Protestantism.

Nosmo **King**: Vernon Watson (?1887–1949), Eng. stage comedian. The comic entered the stage through double doors on which the warning NO SMOKING appeared in large letters. Five letters were on the left-hand door and four on the right, and this made the performer's agreeable stage name.

Pee Wee **King**: Julius Frank Anthony Kuczynski (1914–2000), U.S. country, pop musician, of Pol. parentage. The player was given the nickname "Pee Wee" for his small stature (5 ft 6 in) and adopted it as a first name.

Robert A. **King**: Robert Keiser (1862–1932), U.S. popular composer.

Sid **King**: Sidney Erwin (1936–), U.S. "rockabilly" singer.

Solomon **King**: Allen Levy (1931–2005), U.S. popular singer, working in U.K. The singer's adopted name looks like a reversal of King Solomon, the Old Testament king of Israel.

W. Scott **King**: [Rev.] William Kingscote Greenland (1868–1957), Eng. Wesleyan minister, journalist, novelist. The writer reversed the two halves of his middle name (his mother's maiden name) to form his pseudonym.

Zalman **King**: Zalman King Lefkowitz (1941–), U.S. erotic movie director.

King Biscuit Boy: Richard Alfred Newell (1944–2003), Can. blues musician. Newell's stage name arose as a nickname given him in 1967 for his ability to play the guitar like Sonny Boy Williamson, host of the radio program *King Biscuit Flour Hour* at KFFA in Helena, Arkansas.

Alice **Kingsley:** [Lady] Alice Mary Rothenstein, née Knewstub (1867–1957), Eng. stage actress. The actress adopted this name for a short stage career before her marriage in 1899 to the artist Sir William Rothenstein.

[Sir] Ben **Kingsley:** Krishna Bhanji (1943–), Br. movie actor, of Ind.-Russ. Jewish descent. The actor, famous for his role in (and as) *Gandhi* (1982), reversed his Hindu names and then anglicized them. His father, Rahimtulla Harji Bhanji, was nicknamed Ben at school in London, England, so that his choice of name was not arbitrary. "My father said it would be a good idea to have the kind of name that would broaden the horizons, and he meant it purely pragmatically" [*The Times*, December 28, 2000].

Mary **Kingsley:** Maud Arncliffe Sennett, née Sparagnapane (1862–1936), Br. stage actress, of Eng.-It. parentage.

Sidney **Kingsley:** Sidney Kirschner (1906–1995), U.S. stage, movie actor, playwright.

Hugh **Kingsmill:** Hugh Kingsmill Lunn (1889–1949), Br. novelist, short-story writer, biographer. The writer's first novel, *The Will to Love*, published in 1919, appeared under his original name. He then adopted his first two names as a pen name, partly to be distinguished from his elder brother, skiing pioneer Sir Arnold Lunn (1888–1974), partly to distance himself from his father, with whom he was on strained terms following the failure of his marriage in 1927.

King Sporty: Noel Williams (*c*.1945–), Jamaican DJ, reggae musician, working in U.S.

Julian **Kingstead:** Francis J. de M. Cunynghame (1884–?), Eng. novelist. The author used this name for *Chloris and Zephyrus: A Late-Spring Idyll. In Verse* (1906). A connection between the new name and the original is detectable.

Gertrude **Kingston:** Gertrude Silver, née Konstam (1866–1937), Eng. stage actress, theater manager. The actress's stage name was formed from her maiden name.

King Tubby: Osbourne Ruddock (1941–1989), Jamaican rock musician, recording engineer.

Emanuel **Kink** *see* Marcus **Fall**

Mme. **Kinkel** *see* E. **Berger**

Kinoarashi: Ishiyama Kazutoshi (1961–), Jap. sumo wrestler.

W. **Kinsayder:** John Marston (1576–1634), Eng. dramatist, cleric. Two early satirical works by Marston, *The Metamorphosis of Pigmalions Image* and *The Scourge of Villanie* (both 1598), were published as respectively by "W.K." and "W. Kinsayder."

Sophie **Kinsella:** Madeleine Wickham, née Townley (1969–), Br. romantic novelist. "The rather gentle Madeleine Wickham developed a spikier, harder edge when she became the chick-lit bestseller Sophie Kinsella" [*The Guardian*, March 29, 2006].

Klaus **Kinski:** Nikolaus Günther Nakszynski (1926–1991), Pol.-born Ger. stage, movie actor, father of movie actress Nastassja Kinski (1959–).

Emil **Kio:** Emil Teodorovich Girshfeld-Renard (Hirschfeld-Renard) (1894–1965), Russ. circus artist, magician. The performer adopted his name from an illuminated sign "KINO" (Russian for "movie theater"), in which the letter "N" was unlit. His name and profession passed down to his sons, Emil Emilyevich Kio (1938–) and Igor Emilyevich Kio (1944–2006).

Bruno **Kirby:** Bruno Giovanni Quidaciolu, Jr. (1949–2006), U.S. movie actor.

Jack **Kirby:** Jacob Kurtzberg (1917–1994), U.S. cartoonist, comic-book artist.

Kirill: Vladimir Mikhaylovich Gundyayev (1946–), Russ. churchman. Appointed to succeed **Aleksey II** in 2009, Kirill was the first head of the Russian Orthodox Church to be elected after the collapse of the Soviet Union in 1991. His religious name is significant to Russians as that of St. **Cyril**.

Kirishima: Kazumi Yoshinaga (1959–), Jap. sumo wrestler. The wrestler's *shikona* (fighting name) means "misty island" (Japanese *kiri*, "fog," "mist" + *shima*, "island"). Hence his nickname, "The Fog."

Phyllis **Kirk:** Phyllis Kirkegaard (1926–), U.S. movie actress.

Edmund **Kirke:** James Roberts Gilmore (1822–1903), U.S. businessman, author.

Sergey **Kirov:** Sergey Mironovich Kostrikov (1886–1934), Russ. statesman, Communist leader. The politician had a party name picked for him in 1912 in the office of the Vladikavkaz newspaper *Terek* by selecting the rare first name Kir (from Greek *kyrios*, "lord") from a church calendar. He had previously signed himself S. Mironov, from his patronymic (middle name), but this was regarded as not being sufficiently "secret."

Helene **Kirsova:** Ellen Wittrup Hansen (*c*.1911–1962), Dan. ballet dancer.

Louise **Kirtland:** Louise Isabel Jelly (1905–?), U.S. stage actress.

Ephraim **Kishon:** Ferenc Hoffmann (1924–2005), Hung.-born Israeli satirist. The writer changed his name on moving from Hungary to Israel in 1949. The procedure was not exactly straightforward. "Arriving in Haifa aboard a refugee ship, he identified himself as Ferenc Kishont — with a new, Israeli-sounding name rather than his native Hoffmann. Through a typing error by an immigration official, the 25-year-old Kishont was registered without a final T and his Hungarian name of Ferenc disappeared altogether. 'There's no such name,' said the same official, arbitrarily assigning to him the Hebrew name of Ephraim" [*The Times*, February 2, 2005].

Once settled in Israel, Kishon began writing for both Hungarian and Hebrew newspapers, using the name Chad Gadya for the latter. According to his obituary in *The Times* (as quoted above), the name means "Liitle Lamb," but a reader's letter published on February 8 comments: "The pseudonym Chad Gadya does not mean "Little Lamb," but is the Aramaic for "One Little Kid." It refers to the popular Passover song ... and reflects the hope that the Jewish people, like the little pet goat, ... will be saved by God Almighty from the wicked forces of the world."

Kissy Sell Out: Tommy Bisbee (1985–), Eng. (white) DJ, pop producer. The musician claims he took his stage name from a post-nuclear movie, *Kissy*, he saw in a recurring dream. "The 'Sell Out' part is an ironic declaration of integrity — and a kind of note-to-self not to do so" [*Sunday Times*, June 14, 2009].

Kitakachidoki: Kuga Hayato (1966–), Jap. sumo wrestler.

Lord **Kitchener:** Aldwyn Roberts (1922–2000), West Indian calypso singer. The singer was so named by his patron, fellow calypsonian **Growling Tiger**. The real Lord Kitchener, "Kitchener of Khartoum" (1850–1916), was the British soldier noted for his army recruitment campaign for World War I.

Aunt **Kitty:** Maria Jane McIntosh (1803–1878), U.S. novelist, children's writer. The writer used this name for her children's stories, keeping her real name for her adult fiction.

Aleksis **Kivi:** Aleksis Stenvall (1834–1872), Finn. novelist, playwright. The writer's new name means "rock," not only as an allusion to the barrenness of his native region but also as a rough translation of his original Swedish name, which literally means "stone bank."

Kjarval: Jóhannes Sveinsson (1885–1972), Icelandic painter.

Alf **Kjellin:** Christian Keleen (1920–1988), Swe. movie actor, working in U.S.

Klabund: Alfred Henschke (1890–1928), Ger. poet, playwright, novelist. The writer's pseudonym represents a blend of German *Klabautermann*, "hobgoblin," and *Vagabund*, "vagabond." Henschke felt such a name would be apt for the eternally seeking, wandering poet that he envisaged himself to be.

Ivan **Klecevski:** Wilfrid Voynich (1865–1930), Lithuanian-born Br. bibliographer, working in U.S., husband of Ethel Voynich, née Boole (1864–1960), Ir. novelist, radical activist. Voynich's origins are

doubtful. "Let us begin with what we can be sure of. There was a man called Voynich, Wilfrid Voynich, later Ivan Klecevski. Before he was called Wilfrid he was, maybe, Michal Wojnics from the town of Kaunas or Kovno, or rather the town of Telschi in the province of Kaunas or Kovno. He may have been a Lithuanian.... Certainly he was a Polish nationalist" [*Times Literary Supplement*, November 19, 2004]. In *Who's Who* he is entered as "Voynich, Wilfrid Michael (in Polish, Habdank-Woynicz)."

Henkie **Klein:** Heinrich Kleinmann (1921–), Du. child movie actor, working in Germany. The actor had the same name as his father, who moved to Germany in the early 1920s and directed films under the name Henk Kleinman.

Paul **Klenovsky:** [Sir] Henry Wood (1869–1944), Eng. orchestral conductor, organist. Wood took this name (to tease the critics) for his 1929 orchestral transcription of Bach's Toccata and Fugue in D minor. Russian *klën* means "maple," which of course is a wood. He adopted the name from the Russian conductor Nikolay Klenovsky (1857–1915), about whom he had learned from the composer Alexander Glazunov.

Kleo Dorotti: Klavdiya Georgiyevna Karasik (1900–1974), Russ. illusionist.

Paul **Kletzki:** Pawel Klecki (1900–1973), Pol.-born Swiss orchestral conductor, violinist.

Tristan **Klingsor:** Léon Leclère (1874–1966), Fr. poet, art critic. The poet loved legends and adopted the names of two legendary medieval characters. Tristan (Tristram) fell in love with Iseult (Ysolde) after they both mistakenly drank a love potion; Klingsor was an evil magician in German legend.

Tuifelermaler Kassian **Kluibenschädel:** Rudolf Greinz (1866–1942), Ger. novelist, short-story writer. Greinz used this name when writing for the journal *Jugend* ("Youth").

Sergey **Klychkov:** Sergey Antonovich Leshenkov (1889–1940), Russ. writer.

Hildegarde **Knef:** Hildegard Frieda Albertine Knef (1925–2002), Ger. movie actress, working in U.S. The actress was originally brought to Hollywood in 1947 by producer David O. Selznick, who suggested she change her name to Gilda Christian and present herself as Austrian-born. She refused.

[Sir] Godfrey **Kneller:** Gottfried Kniller (1646–1723), Ger.-born Eng. portraitist.

Cholly **Knickerbocker:** Igor Cassini (1916–2002), U.S. gossip columnist, of Russ.-It descent, brother of U.S. fashion designer Oleg Cassini (1913–2006). The columnist's pseudonym evokes that of Diedrich **Knickerbocker**, with Cholly (a form of Charley) a slang term of black origin for a dollar bill.

Diedrich **Knickerbocker:** Washington Irving

(1783–1859), U.S. humorist. The writer used this name for the supposed Dutch author of his *History of New York from the Beginning of the World to the End of the Dutch Dynasty* (1809), planned with his brother, Dr. Peter Irving (1772–1838). He is said to have taken the name from that of a Dutch family who came to live in Albany County around 1674. The family name, which may originally have been Knickerbacker, probably meant "baker of knickers," these being clay marbles. Irving's pseudonym became popular from the illustrations to his work drawn by George Cruickshank, showing Dutchmen in wide, loose knee breeches. Hence the adoption of "knickerbockers" (later "knickers") as a word for breeches, or trousers (pants), whether outerwear or underwear.

Evel **Knievel**: Robert Craig Knievel (1938–2007), U.S. stuntman. How did the motorcyle daredevil come by his nickname? "While in custody in 1956 he was reputedly penned with a prisoner named Knofel, prompting one of the jailers to joke: 'Double the guard! We got Evil Knievel and Awful Knofel here tonight.' The nickname stuck, but when Knievel was later pressed to use it on his show billings, he preferred the misspelt 'Evel'" [*The Times*, December 3, 2007].

Curtis **Knight**: Curtis McNear (1929–1999), U.S. rock musician.

David **Knight**: David Mintz (1927–), U.S. stage, movie actor. The actor's stage name is his mother's maiden name.

Edward **Knight**: Edward Austen (1767–1852), Eng. landowner, brother of Jane Austen (1775–1817). The novelist's brother was adopted as a teenager by Thomas and Catherine Knight, childless cousins of the Austens, and in 1797 he took their name on inheriting their estate at Godmersham, Kent.

June **Knight**: Margaret Rose Valliquietto (1911–), U.S. stage actress, dancer.

Sonny **Knight**: Joseph Coleman Smith (1934–1998), U.S. black R&B musician.

Ted **Knight**: Tadeusz Wladyslaw Konopka (1923–1986), U.S. TV actor.

Terry **Knight**: Richard Terrance Knapp (1943–2004), U.S. DJ, pop musician.

Anne **Knish**: Arthur Davison Ficke (1883–1945), U.S. lawyer, poet. Ficke adopted this name for *Spectra: A Book of Poetic Experiments* (1916), coauthored as a literary hoax with Emanuel **Morgan**.

Edward **Knoblock**: Edward Knoblauch (1874–1945), U.S. dramatist, working in U.K.

Edward **Knott**: Matthew Wilson (1582–1656), Eng. cleric. The disputatious Jesuit priest took his new name in 1602 when entering the English College at Rome. He subsequently kept it for the rest of his life.

Patric **Knowles**: Reginald Knowles (1911–1995), Br.-born U.S. movie actor.

Cleone **Knox**: Magdalen King-Hall (1904–1971), Eng. author. The writer created a stir in 1926 with *The Diary of a Young Lady of Fashion (1764–1765), edited by her kinsman, Alexander Blacker Kerr*. She followed it up the following year with some fictional memoirs, *I Think I Remember; Being Random Recollections of Sir Wickham Woolicomb*. In 1929 she married Patrick Perceval-Maxwell.

Gilbert **Knox**: Madge Hamilton MacBeth (*c*.1881–1965), U.S.-born Can. novelist, historian. The writer also used the name W.S. Dill.

Teddy **Knox**: Albert Edward Cromwell-Knox (1896–1974), Eng. stage comedian, teaming with Jimmy **Nervo**.

Johnny **Knoxville**: Philip John Clapp (1971–), U.S. TV presenter, movie actor. The performer took his name at age 18 on moving to Los Angeles from his native Knoxville, Tennessee.

Ronald **Koal**: Robert Gooslin, Jr. (1959–1993), U.S. rock musician.

Koba *see* Joseph **Stalin**

John **Kobal**: Ivan Kobaly (1940–1991), Austr.-born Can. film historian.

Ruth **Kobart**: Ruth Maxine Kohn (1924–2002), U.S. stage actress, singer.

John **Kobbler**: John Kelso Hunter (1802–1873), Sc. artist, writer. As a self-taught portrait painter, Hunter's main trade was as a cobbler. Hence his pseudonym.

Koboyama: Misuyoshi Hasuda (1957–), Jap. sumo wrestler. The wrestler's name means "far-seeing mountain."

Rachiya **Kochar**: Rachiya Kocharovich Gabrielyan (1910–1965), Armenian writer. The writer took his father's first name (already present in his patronymic) as his new surname.

Josua von **Kochertal**: Josua Harrsch (1669–1719), Ger.-born U.S. Lutheran clergyman. Harrsch was born in the Kocher Valley (German *Kochertal*), east of Stuttgart. Hence his assumed name.

Jack **Kodell**: John Koudelka (1929–), U.S. magician,

Lydia **Koidula**: Lydia Emilie Florentine Jannsen (1843–1886), Estonian poet, playwright. The writer was given her name, meaning "singer of the dawn," by the Estonian scholar and patriot Carl R. Jakobson.

Yakumo **Koizumi**: Lafcadio Hearn (1850–1904), Gk.-born Ir. writer, orientalist. Following a career as an itinerant journalist in the U.S., in 1890 Hearn went to Japan, where he married a local woman, Setsu Koizumi, and adopted a Japanese name based on her family name.

Kojak: Floyd Anthony Perch (1959–), Jamaican DJ, reggae singer. Perch began his musical career as Pretty Boy Floyd, basing his image on that of the American gangster Charles Arthur Floyd (1901–1934), much in the manner of Dennis **Alcapone** and **Dillinger**. He then became Nigger Kojak, from a nickname given him by his followers, with reference to the bald-headed New York cop played by Telly Savalas in the TV show *Kojak* (1973–7). Perch emulated the star, complete with bald head and often sucking the obligatory lollipop. By 1982 Perch had become Papa Kojak, and after that simply Kojak. A duo formed by Perch with a female singer was Kojak and Liza, the latter being Beverly Brown or Jacqueline Boland.

Alexandre **Kojève:** Aleksandr Kozhevnikov (1902–1968), Russ.-born Fr. philosopher.

N. **Kokhanovskaya:** Nadezhda Stepanovna Sokhanskaya (1825–1884), Russ. writer. The writer appears to have based her pen name on her original name.

Koko: Alfons Frantsevich Luts (1885–1945), Russ. circus artist, clown. The name is the same as that of **Coco**, though not for the same reason.

Kokomo: Jimmy Wisner (1931–), U.S. jazz musician. The musician presumably took his name from Kokomo, Indiana, although he himself was born in Philadelphia.

Yakub **Kolas:** Konstantin Mikhaylovich Mitskevich (1882–1956), Belorussian revolutionary writer. The writer adopted a new name in order to avoid association with the Polish revolutionary poet Adam Mickiewicz (1798–1855).

Walter **Kolbenhoff:** Walter Hoffmann (1908–1993), Ger. novelist.

Kilian **Koll:** Walter Julian Bloem (1868–1951), Ger. novelist, playwright.

René **Kollo:** René Kollodziewski (1937–), Ger. opera singer.

Gertrud **Kolmar:** Gertrud Chodziesner (1894–1943), Ger. lyric poet, of Jewish parentage.

Wendo **Kolosoy:** Antoine Kalosoyi (1925–2008), Congolese popular singer. The African singer, born in the former Belgian Congo, originally took the name Wendo Sor Kolosoy, altering the spelling of his surname and adopting a new first name, later shortened to Wendo, that was said to be a tribute to the Duke of Windsor. "The reason for the homage is unclear, although the Duke was a close friend of the Belgian monarch, Léopold III" [*The Times,* August 2, 2008].

Kolpetti: Pyotr Andreyevich Grudzinsky (1884–1960), Russ. circus artist, clown. The performer originally used the name for a joint musical comedy act with a clown named Nikolay Morozov. Hence the name, formed from the pet names of both men, Kolya (Nikolay) and Petya (Pyotr). From 1923 he teamed with his brother, Dmitry Andreyevich Gruzinsky (1889–1944), under the same name. The name itself also happens to suggest Italian *colpetti,* "taps," "raps," "pats."

Mikhail **Koltsov:** Mikhail Yefimovich Fridlyand (Friedland) (1898–1942), Russ. writer, journalist, magazine editor.

Komar and Melamid: Vitaly Komar (1933–), Russ.-born U.S. artist + Alexander Melamid (1945–), Russ.-born U.S. artist. The team of artists, specializing in "Sots art" (an evolution of Socialist Realism), left the Soviet Union in 1977 and settled in the USA, where they became American citizens in 1988.

Nikolay Pavlovich **Komarov:** Fyodor Yevgenyevich Sobinov (1886–1937), Russ. Communist official.

Krzysztof **Komeda:** Krzysztof Trzcinski (1931–1969), Pol. composer, jazz musician. The musician began using the name Komeda to protect himself in his medical profession, since the Polish government frowned on jazz.

Komitas: Sogomon Gevorkovich Sogomonyan (1869–1935), Armenian composer, choral conductor, musicologist, working in France. The musician adopted the name of a 7th-century Armenian hymn writer.

Anny **Konetzni:** Anny Konerczny (1902–1968), Austr. opera singer, sister of Hilde **Konetzni**.

Hilde **Konetzni:** Hilde Konerczny (1905–1980), Austr. opera singer, sister of Anny **Konetzni**.

Konimo: Daniel Amponsah (1934–), U.S. popular musician.

Konishiki: Salevaa Fuaili Atisanoe (1963–), Hawaiian sumo wrestler, of Samoan descent. The wrestler's fighting name means "little brocade," implying "trophy" (Japanese diminutive prefix *ko-* + *nishiki,* "brocade").

Klaus **Konrad** *see* Leo **Kessler**

Wellington **Koo:** Ku Wei-chun (1888–1985), Chin. diplomat. The diplomat was the son of a wealthy merchant whose hero was said to be the first Duke of Wellington. Hence his name.

Kooky: Andy Stevens (1942–), Eng. circus clown. The name, while meaning "crazy," is close to those of two other famous clowns, **Coco** and **Koko**.

Kool Herc: Clive Campbell (1955–), Jamaican-born U.S. hip-hop musician. "He had been given his nickname, Hercules, for his physical build, but he didn't like that name so he shortened it to 'Herc,' adding 'Kool' when he became a graffiti artist" [Haskins, p.45].

Koos: Koos van den Akker (*c.*1932–), Du. fashion designer, working in U.S.

Raymond **Kopa**: Raymond Kopaczewski (1931–), Fr. footballer, of Pol. parentage.

Rutger **Kopland**: R.H. van den Hoofdakker (1934–), Du. psychiatrist, poet. The professor of psychiatry at Groninger University adopted this pseudonym for his literary work.

Erland **Kops**: Erland Olsen (1937–), Dan. badminton player.

Al **Koran**: Edward Doe (1916–1972), Br. conjuror, "mentalist." The illusionist seems to have chosen a name that simply means "The Koran," otherwise the holy book of Islam, taking the Arabic definite article as the English name "Al" (for "Albert" or "Alfred"). He intended no disrespectful reference.

Janusz **Korczak**: Henryk Goldszmidt (1878–1942), Pol. writer, educator, doctor.

Mira **Kord**: Miroslava "Slavka" Vorlova, née Johnova (1894–1973), Cz. pianist, conductor, composer.

Alberto **Korda**: Alberto Díaz Gutiérrez (1928–2001), Cuban photographer. The photographer, famous for his iconic 1960 portrait of Che **Guevara**, adopted his new name early in his career from the Hungarian-born moviemaker Alexander **Korda**.

[Sir] Alexander **Korda**: Sándor László Kellner (1893–1956), Hung.-born Br. movie producer, of Jewish parentage, brother of directors Vincent **Korda** and Zoltán **Korda**. At the age of 15, Kellner moved from the Hungarian countryside to Budapest, the capital, where he was befriended by a Catholic priest who got him a job on a local paper. As the boy was legally below employment age, he had to find a new name for himself. He chose Sándor Korda, basing this, as a compliment to his patron, on the Latin phrase *Sursum Corda*, "Lift up your hearts," from the Roman Mass. This had the further advantage of being close to his original name (Hungarian Sándor equates to English Alexander) [Michael Korda, *Charmed Lives*, 1980].

Vincent **Korda**: Vincent Kellner (1897–1979), Hung.-born movie art director.

Zoltán **Korda**: Zoltán Kellner (1895–1961), Hung.-born movie director.

Korelli: Aleksandr Vasilyevich Peshkov (c.1880–1930), Russ. circus performer, trapeze artist.

David **Koresh**: Vernon Wayne Howell (1959–1993), U.S. religious leader. Howell's adopted name implied that he was a spiritual heir of the biblical King David and that he, like Koresh (the Hebrew equivalent of Cyrus, the ancient Persian king), was a messianic figure, since Cyrus the Great is the only non–Jew to whom the title "messiah" ("anointed one") is given in scripture: "Thus saith the Lord to his anointed, to Cyrus" (Isaiah 45:1). Koresh himself claimed that the name was the "surname of God,"

and that it meant "death." He changed his name in 1990, at a time when he was already leader of the Branch Davidian cult, an offshoot of the Davidian Seventh Day Adventists.

The name was used before him by another U.S. cult leader, Dr. Cyrus Reed Teed (1839–1908), who founded the Koreshan Unity in Chicago in 1888 and who was known to his followers as Koresh. In his case the name matched his original first name.

Koringa: Renée Bernard (1913–1976), Fr. variety artist ("La Femme Fakir").

Alexis **Korner**: Alexis Koerner (1928–1984), Fr.-born jazz and pop musician, working in U.S., U.K.

Harry **Korris**: Henry Corris (1888–1971), Br. music-hall comedian.

Fritz **Kortner**: Fritz Nathan Kohn (1892–1970), Austr. stage, movie actor.

Sonia **Korty**: Sophia Ippar (1892–1955), Russ. ballet dancer, choreographer, teacher.

Charles **Korvin**: Geza Korvin Karpathi (1907–1998), Cz.-born U.S. movie actor.

Jerzy Nikodem **Kosinski**: Jerzy Nikodem Lewinkopf (1933–1991), Pol.-born U.S. novelist. When the writer's family moved from Łódź to Sandomierz in 1939 to escape the Nazi threat, his father began to change the family name from Lewinkopf to Kosinski to disguise their Jewish identity.

Martin **Kosleck**: Nicolai Yoshkin (1907–1994), Ger.-born Russ. movie actor, working in U.S.

Theodore **Kosloff**: Fyodor Mikhailovich Kozlov (1882–1956), Russ.-born U.S. ballet dancer, movie actor.

Kostandi: Yury Konstantinovich Tolchi-ogly (1876–1933), Russ. circus artist + Vladimir Konstantinovich Tolchi-ogly (1878–1915), Russ. circus artist, his brother. The brothers, who teamed as clowns and comic acrobats, adopted their ring name from their patronymic (middle name).

Henry **Koster**: Hermann Kosterlitz (1905–1988), Ger. movie director, working in U.S.

Kotofuji: Kobayashi Takaya (1964–), Jap. sumo wrestler. Wrestlers from the Sadogatake *heya* (stable) prefix their fighting names with Japanese *koto*, "harp," "lyre." The rest of the name is from Mt. Fuji.

Kotogaume: Kitayama Satoshi (1963–), Jap. sumo wrestler. Wrestlers from the Sadogatake stable prefix their fighting names with *koto* (*see* **Kotofuji**). The latter part of the name comes from Umegatani, the name of two famous master wrestlers, with Japanese *ume* meaning "plum."

Kotoinazuma: Shozo Tamura (1962–), Jap. sumo wrestler. Wrestlers from the Sadogatake stable prefix their fighting names with *koto* (*see* **Kotofuji**). The rest of the name means "lightning" (Japanese *inazuma*).

Kotonishiki: Hideyuki Matsuzawa (1968–), Jap. sumo wrestler. Wrestlers from the Sadogatake stable prefix their fighting names with *koto* (*see* **Kotofuji**). The rest of the name means "brocade" (Japanese *nishiki*), denoting an award or trophy, as for **Konishiki**.

Serge Koussevitzky: Sergey Aleksandrovich Kusevitsky (1874–1951), Russ.-born U.S. orchestral conductor, composer. The musician adopted a French form of his original Russian name.

Marian Koval: Marian Viktorovich Kovalyov (1907–1971), Russ. composer.

Vasily Koval: Vasily Petrovich Kovalyov (1907–1937), Belorussian writer.

Kenneth Kove: John William Stevenson Bridgewater (1893–1965), Eng. stage, movie actor.

"Killer" Kowalski: Edward Walter Spulnik (1926–2008), Can.-born U.S. wrestler, of Pol. parentage. Initially billed as Tarzan Kowalski, the giant bruiser legally adopted his surname in the 1960s, by which time he had already acquired his nickname, given for his brutal manhandlings and manglings in the ring.

Jan Kowski: Harold Lionel Kellaway (1902–1990), Eng.-born Austral. ballet dancer.

Barbara Krafftówna: Barbara Kraft-Gazda (1928–), Pol. movie actress.

Billy J. Kramer: William Howard Ashton (1943–), Eng. pop singer. The singer chose a name that he hoped would suggest he was of stateside origin.

Kondrat Krapiva: Kondrat Kondratyevich Atrakhovich (1896–1991), Belorussian satirical writer, linguist. The writer's aptly chosen plant name means "nettle."

Ivan Krasko: Ján Botto (1876–1958), Slovakian poet.

Lee Krasner: Lenore Krassner (1908–1984), U.S. Abstract Expressionist painter, of Russ. Jewish parentage. The artist adopted her new first name in childhood. She dropped the second "s" from her surname around 1943.

Vladimir Krasnopolsky: Vladimir Arkadievich Krasnopolsky-Ledov (1933–), Russ. movie director.

Margareta Krasnova: Margaret Craske (1892–1990), Eng.-born U.S. ballet dancer. Craske took this Russian version of her name when dancing with Serge Diaghilev's Ballets Russes in the early 1920s.

Alfredo Kraus: Alfredo Kraus Trujillo (1927–1999), Sp. opera singer, of Austr. descent

David Krech: Itzhok-Eizik Krechevsky (1909–1977), Russ.-born U.S. professor of psychology. Krech went with his family to the United States when he was four and after graduating from high school anglicized his name to Isadore Krechevsky. He adopted the name David Krech for his academic publications after World War II.

Kreskin: George Joseph Kresge, Jr. (1935–), U.S. conjuror, "mentalist."

V. Krestovsky: Nadezhda Dmitriyevna Zayonchovskaya, née Khvoshchinskaya (1824–1889), Russ. writer. The writer had already published a number of stories under her (male) pen name, when a real author Vsevolod Krestovsky became increasingly known. From then on, she signed her work as "V. Krestovsky (pseudonym)."

Vincas Kreve: Vincas Mickevicÿius (1884–1954), Lithuanian writer, folklorist, working in U.S. (from 1947).

Andreas Krieger: Heidi Krieger (1966–), Ger. sportswoman. Following the fall of the Berlin Wall in 1989, the former champion East German shotputter discovered that from the age of 16 she had been fed huge doses of testosterone (dressed up as "vitamins") to enhance her performance. These so altered her body that in 1997 she underwent a sex-change operation and changed her name from Heidi to Andreas.

Krik: Henry G. Crickmore (*fl.*1870s), U.S. writer on racing.

Krishnakant: Krishnakant Maganlal Bukhanwala (1922–), Ind. movie actor, director.

Krishna Venta: Francis Pencovic (1911–1958), U.S. cult leader. The founder of the Fountain of the World cult changed his name on leaving the army after World War II. "Krishna" (Sanskrit, "dark one") is the name of a famous Hindu deity. "Venta" apparently relates to Ventura County, California, where the cult settled. Krishna Venta himself claimed to have been born in a valley in Nepal.

Walter G. Krivitsky: Samuel Ginsberg (1899–1941), Russ. counterspy, of Pol. Jewish origin, working in U.S. Ginsberg posed as an Austrian antiquarian bookdealer named Dr. Martin Lessner when working in the Netherlands in the 1930s.

Krizia: Mariuccia Mandelli (1935–), It. fashion designer. Mandelli took her name from *Critias* (Italian *Crizia*), the title of Plato's unfinished dialogue on women's vanity, but spelled it with a "K" to look more exotic. Plato's Critias is a man who squanders all his riches on jewelry and clothing for beautiful and compliant women. The name passed to that of the designer's fashion house.

Helen Kroger: Leoninta ("Lona") Cohen, née Petka (1913–1992), U.S.–born Soviet spy, working with Peter **Kroger**, her husband.

Peter Kroger: Morris Cohen (1910–1995), U.S.–born Soviet spy, of Russ. Jewish parentage, working with Helen **Kroger**, his wife. Cohen fought on the Communist side in the Spanish Civil War under the name Israel Altman. On hearing that the spy couple Julius and Ethel Rosenberg were about to be arrested by the FBI in 1950, he and his wife hastily fled from New York to London, where they reappeared in 1954 under the Kroger name, taking this from a couple who had died in New Zealand.

Burt **Kroll** *see* Fenton **Brockley**

A. **Kron:** Aleksandr Aleksandrovich Kreyn (Krein) (1909–1983), Russ. writer, playwright.

Emil **Krotky:** Emmanuil Yakovlevich German (Herman) (1892–1963), Russ. satirical poet. The writer's adopted name means "mild," "meek," a sense that he intended ironically. Maxim **Gorky** said: "How could he be called mild? He's brusque and brazen!" [Dmitriyev, p.161].

KRS-One: Lawrence Krisna Parker (1965–), U.S. black hip-hop musician.

Kruger: Tom Reynolds (1952–), Br. crossword compiler. The setter took his pseudonym from his dog, a golden retriever, itself so named after the Krugerrand, the gold coin of South Africa.

Diane **Kruger:** Diane Heidkrueger (1977–), Ger.-born U.S. movie actress.

Gustav **Krupp:** Gustav von Bohlen und Halbach (1870–1950), Ger. industrialist. In 1906 the former diplomat married Bertha Krupp (1886–1957), heiress of the Krupp family of arms manufacturers, and by special imperial edict was allowed to adopt her name, inserting it before the "von." It was Bertha Krupp who gave the nickname of "Big Bertha," the howitzer that shelled France in World War I.

Yury **Krymov:** Yury Solomonovich Beklemishev (1908–1941), Russ. writer. The writer was very attached to the Crimea (Russian *Krym*). Hence his name.

Kryztal: Henry Buckley (1972–), Jamaican-born U.S. R&B, ragga musician.

Rachid **Ksentini:** Rachid Billakadar (1887–1944), Algerian stage actor, director, playwright.

Felix **Kshessinsky:** Felix Ivanovich Krzesinski-Neczuj (1823–1905), Pol.-born Russ. ballet dancer, father of Russ. ballerina Mathilda Kshessinska (Mathilda-Maria Feliksovna Kshesinskaya) (1872–1971).

Kuba: Kurt Bartel (1914–1967), Ger. poet, writer. A name formed from the first syllables of the writer's original name.

Aryeh Leon **Kubovy:** Aryeh Leon Kubowitzki (1896–1966), Israeli lawyer, diplomat.

Georgy **Kuchishvili:** Georgy Andukaparovich Chkheidze (1886–1947), Georgian poet.

Johann **Kunau:** Johann Kuhn (1660–1722), Bohemian composer, lawyer.

Kukryniksy: Mikhail Vasilyevich Kupriyanov (1903–1991), Russ. satirical cartoonist + Porfiry Nikitich

Krylov (1902–1990), Russ. satirical cartoonist + Nikolay Aleksandrovich Sokolov (1903–2000), Russ. satirical cartoonist. The three artists adopted a collective name comprising elements from each of their respective names, adding the Russian plural ending (-*y*).

Henry **Kulky:** Henry Kulkavich (1911–1965), U.S. movie actor.

Ashok **Kumar:** Kumudlal Kunjilal Ganguly (1911–2001), Ind. movie actor. "Kumar" in this name and those below is Hindi for "boy," "son."

Dilip **Kumar:** Yusuf Khan (1922–), Ind. movie actor. The actor was renamed by the Hindi novelist Bhagwati Charan Varma.

Manoj **Kumar:** Haris Krishna Goswami (1937–), Ind. movie actor, director, producer.

Rajendra **Kumar:** R.K. Tuli (1929–), Ind. movie actor.

Uttam **Kumar:** Arun Kumar Chatterjee (1926–1980), Bengali movie actor.

Meena **Kumari:** Mahajabeen Bux (1933–1972), Ind. movie actress. The actress first appeared in movies at the age of six under the name Baby Meena. She was renamed Meena Kumari for the musical *Baiju Bawra* (1952), in which she played Baiju's self-sacrificing sweetheart, Gauri. "Kumari" is Hindi for "girl," "daughter."

Kumbel: Piet Hein (1905–1996), Dan. poet, designer. The writer and inventor's pseudonym is an Old Norse word for a gravestone.

Hermann **Kunst** *see* **Orwell**

Yanka **Kupala:** Ivan Dominikovich Lutsevich (1882–1942), Belorussian poet. The writer's new first name is a Belorussian form of Ivan, his original name. The name as a whole refers to the annual summer holiday, of religious origin, known in Russian as *Ivan Kupala*, literally "John the Bather," i.e. John the Baptist. This was held on St. John the Baptist's Day (Midsummer Day, June 24), and was marked with country customs such as leaping over a bonfire (whoever leaped highest would have the richest harvest), bathing, etc. (According to popular belief, it was on this day that John the Baptist drove evil spirits out of the water.) The rites were accompanied by singing and dancing. Hence the poetic association.

Oskar **Kurganov:** Oskar Iyeremeyevich Esterkin (1907–), Russ. writer, screenwriter.

Kushimaumi: Kushimaumi Keita (1965–), Jap. sumo wrestler.

Mitrush **Kuteli:** Dhimitër Pasko (1907–1967), Albanian writer, critic.

Leonid **Kvinikhidze:** Leonid Aleksandrovich Faintsimmer (Feinzimmer) (1937–), Russ. movie director.

Grigory **Kvitka-Osnovyanenko:** Grigory Fyodorovich Kvitka (1778–1843), Ukr. writer. The writer first used the pen name Gritzko Osnovyanenko, from a colloquial form of his own first name and the name of the village of his birth, Osnova. He later added the latter to his original surname.

Stanley **Kwan:** Guan Jinpeng (1957–), Hong Kong movie director.

Kwame **Kwei-Armah:** Ian Roberts (1967–), Br. black TV actor, playwright. When the actor adopted an African name after a visit to Ghana, he realized he had hurt his parents by rejecting the name they had given him. "But my first son was born on a Saturday, which is what my name means, and I took it as confirmation from the gods that I'd done the right thing" [*The Times*, March 3, 2007].

Thomas **Kyd:** Alfred Bennett Harbage (1901–1976), U.S. educator, Shakespeare scholar, detective-story writer. Thomas Kyd was a 16th-century English dramatist.

Duncan **Kyle:** John Franklin Broxholme (1930–2001), Eng. thriller writer.

Elisabeth **Kyle:** Agnes Mary Robertson Dunlop (1910–1982), Sc. novelist, children's writer. The writer also used the name Jan Ralston.

Robert **Kyle:** Robert Terrall (1914–2009), U.S. crime novelist.

Ky-mani: Ky-mani Marley (*c.*1975–), Jamaican reggae musician. Ky-mani is the son of Bob Marley (1945–1981), of Bob Marley and the Wailers, but he refused to capitalize on his father's name, despite the title of his debut album, *Like Father Like Son* (1997).

Herbert **Kynaston:** Herbert Snow (1835–1910), Eng. cleric, classical scholar. The headmaster of Cheltenham College adopted his mother's maiden name in 1875.

Machiko **Kyo:** Motoko Yamo (1924–), Jap. movie actress.

Kyokudozan: Kazuyasu Hata (1964–), Jap. sumo wrestler.

Barbara **Laage:** Claire Colombat (1925–1988), Fr. movie actress.

Rudolf von **Laban:** Rudolf Laban de Varalja (1879–1958), Hung. ballet dancer, choreographer.

Théodore **Labarre:** Théodore-François-Joseph Berry (1805–1870), Fr. composer of comic operas.

Louise **Labé:** Louise Charlin Perrin (1524–1566), Fr. poet. The poet was known as *la Belle Cordière*, "the Beautiful Ropemaker," because of her lovely looks and the occupation (*cordier*) of both her father and her husband, Ennemond Perrin. Her pseudonym arose as an abbreviation of this. "Her anagram was *Belle à Soy* ["Beautiful in herself"]. — But she was *belle* also for others" [D'Israeli, p. 135].

Sleepy **La Beef:** Thomas Paulsley La Beff (1935–), U.S. black guitarist, singer. The musician adopted the nickname "Sleepy," given him for his drooping eyelids.

Patti **LaBelle:** Patricia Louise Holt (1944–), U.S. black rock singer. The singer's professional name arose simultaneously with that of her group, later known as LaBelle but formed in 1961 as Patti LaBelle and the Blue Belles.

[St.] Catherine **Labouré:** Zoé Labouré (1806–1876), Fr. mystic. The former peasant girl took the name Catherine soon after joining the Sisters of Charity of St. Vincent de Paul in 1830, the year that she claimed to have seen the first of many visions of the Virgin Mary in the convent chapel.

William **Lacey:** William Wolfe (1584–1673), Eng. Jesuit.

Simon **Lack:** Simon Macalpine (1917–1980), Sc. stage actor. The actor created his stage surname from a reversal of the *-cal-* in his original name.

Wilton **Lackaye:** William Andrew Lackey (1862–1932), U.S. stage actor, of Ir. parentage.

Paul **Lacôme:** Paul-Jean-Jacques Lacôme-d'Estalenx (1838–1920), Fr. operetta composer.

Lactilla: Ann Yearsley, née Cromartie (1752–1806), Eng. poet. Like her mother, the poet delivered milk from door to door, and accordingly adopted a latinized form of the term for this occupation as her pen name.

Ed **Lacy:** Leonard S. Zinberg (1911–1968). U.S. mystery writer.

John **Lacy** *see* Geoffrey **Crayon, jun.**

Steve **Lacy:** Steven Norman Lackritz (1934–2004), U.S. jazz saxophonist. The musician's surname was corrupted by cornetist Rex Stewart when he played in swing bands as a teenager.

Walter **Lacy:** Walter Williams (1809–1898), Eng. actor.

Paula **La Dare:** Paul Rising (1918–2002), Eng. drag artist.

Cheryl **Ladd:** Cheryl Jean Stoppelmoor (1951–), U.S. TV actress. The actress's first television work involved providing one of the singing voices for the cartoon *Josie and the Pussycats* (1970–2), under the name Cherie Moore. She then appeared on TV under her maiden name until she was cast in *Charlie's Angels* (1976), for which she used her married name. Her husband (married 1974, divorced 1980) was David Ladd, son of movie star Alan Ladd by his second wife, Sue **Carol.**

Diane **Ladd:** Rose Diane Ladner (1932–), U.S. movie actress.

Léon **Ladulfi:** Noël du Fail (1520–1591), Fr. writer. Crossword buffs will readily spot the anagram here.

Lady Anne: Anne Smith (*c.*1960–), Jamaican reggae singer.

Lady Bianca: Bianca Thornton (1955–), U.S. black blues musician.

Lady G: Janice Fyffe (*c*.1974–), Jamaican DJ, reggae singer.

Lady Gaga: Stefani Joanne Angelina Germanotta (1986–), U.S.–It. pop singer. The singer's stage name pays tribute to rock band Queen's 1984 hit "Radio Ga-Ga." "Lady GaGa is loath to give her real name, insisting friends and family refer to her only by her stage name" [*Sunday Times*, December 14, 2008].

Ladyhawke: Pip Brown (1981–), N.Z. pop singer. The singer took her name from the 1985 movie so titled, about a pair of boy and girl lovers who are changed respectively into a wolf and a hawk.

A Lady of Quality: Enid Algerine Bagnold (1889–1981), Eng. novelist, playwright. An earlyish pseudonym used by the writer who became a genuine "lady of quality" in 1920 when she married Sir Roderick Jones.

Lady Saw: Marion Hall (1969–), Jamaican reggae singer. The singer took her stage name from her idol, DJ **Tenor Saw.**

Lady Sheba: Jessie Wicker Bell (1920–2002), U.S. witch. Lady Sheba was initiated as a witch in the 1930s and came to prominence in the 1960s and 1970s. Her new name "came from an inner awareness early in life that, in addition to her family name, she had always been 'Sheba,' perhaps in a former life" [Guiley, p.191].

Lady Sovereign: Louise Harman (1986–), Br. (white) rapper. Colloquially known as "Sov," the musician adopted her nickname, given for the big ornamental rings she formerly wore on her fingers.

Philip Lafargue: Joseph Henry Philpot (1850–1939), Eng. writer. By profession an obstetrician, Philpot used this name for his fiction. The name itself was perhaps suggested by that of the French politician Paul Lafargue (1842–1911), his contemporary, with "Philip" from his original surname.

La Fleur: Robert Guérin (*fl*.1598–1634), Fr. actor. The actor used this name for his tragic roles, keeping his other name of **Gros-Guillaume** for farce. His son-in-law, François Juvenon (*c*.1623–1674), adopted the same name when he played the parts of kings in succession to **Montfleury.** Juvenon's son, also an actor, was **La Tuillerie.**

George Lafollette: George Rushling (1886–1960), U.S.–born magician. The entertainer posed as an oriental performer called Rush Ling Toy, a role he maintained off the stage as well as on.

Thomy Lafon: Thomy Foucher (or Laralde) (1810–1893), U.S. black real estate broker, philanthropist. Lafon probably took his name from the French-born architect Barthélémy Lafon, who settled in New Orleans around 1789. The connection between the two men is unclear, however.

Paul Anton de Lagarde: Paul Bötticher (1827–1891), Ger. Protestant theologian. The biblical scholar adopted his maternal grandfather's name in 1845.

Lago: Laura Netzel, née Pistolekors (1839–1927), Swe. concert pianist, singer, composer.

La Grange: Charles Varlet (1639–1692), Fr. actor.

La Hire: Étienne de Vignolles (*c*.1390–1443), Fr. captain, comrade-in-arms of Joan of Arc.

Jean Lahor: Henri Cazalis (1840–1909), Fr. poet.

Bert Lahr: Irving Lahrheim (1895–1967), U.S. stage, movie comedian.

[Dame] Cleo Laine: Clementina Dinah Campbell (1927–), Br. jazz singer, actress, of Jamaican-Eng. parentage. When the singer joined the group of vocalists known as the Johnny Dankworth Seven, founded by her future husband, the men decided she needed a new name, and came up with "Laine."

Denny Laine: Brian Arthur Haynes (or Hines) (1944–), Eng. R&B musician.

Frankie Laine: Francis Paul LoVecchio (1913–2007), U.S. popular singer, actor, of It. parentage. The singer was "discovered" entertaining in a Hollywood spa by Hoagy Carmichael, who persuaded him to adopt an anglicized *nom de théâtre*.

Papa Jack Laine: George Vetiala Lane (1873–1966), U.S. jazz musician, bandleader.

Hugh Laing: Hugh Morris Alleyne Skinner (1911–1988), Barbadian-born U.S. ballet dancer, of Eng. extraction. The dancer's stage name presumably evolved from his mother's maiden name of Alleyne.

Clara Lair: Mercedes Negron Muñoz (1895–1973), Puerto Rican poet.

Arthur Lake: Arthur Silverlake (1905–1987), U.S. movie actor.

Claude Lake *see* Mathilde **Blind**

Deryn Lake: Dinah Lampitt (1937–), Br. historical novelist.

M.D. Lake: James Allen Simpson (1934–), U.S. mystery novelist. The writer of novels featuring security cop Peggy O'Neill was advised by his editor to choose a genderless pseudonym so that readers would not realize he was a man writing from a woman's viewpoint. The name he devised referred to Medicine Lake, Minnesota, a suburb of Minneapolis, where his wife's family lived, with the initials M.D. representing the abbreviated title of a Doctor of Medicine.

Veronica Lake: Constance Frances Marie Ockelman (1919–1973), U.S. movie actress. The actress made her debut as Constance Keane in *Sorority House* (1939), taking this name from her stepfather. She was given her regular professional name by Paramount producer Arthur Hornblow, Jr., in 1940 for the movie

I Wanted Wings (1941). She tells how the name came about: "'Believe me' [said Hornblow], 'the right name, a name that the public can latch on to and remember can make all the difference. It isn't just a matter, though, of creating a name that can be remembered. If that were all it took, we'd just name you Maude Mudpie or Tilly Tits or something and they'd remember the name.... Picking a name involves coming up with something that associates in the fan's mind the person attached to that name. The name has to... well, it has to be the person, or at least what the fan thinks that person is ... Connie, here's how I came to choose your new name. I believe that when people look into those navy blue eyes of yours, they'll see a calm coolness — the calm coolness of a lake.' The first thing that crossed my mind was that I was going to be named Lake something or other. That doesn't sound very outlandish these days with Tab [**Hunter**] and Rock [**Hudson**], but in those days names stuck closer to the norm ... 'And your features, Connie, are classic features. And when I think of classic features, I think of Veronica.' Lake Veronica! Oh! Veronica Lake. Of course. And then it hit me. My mother was sometimes called Veronica. Of all the goddamn names in the world to choose ... I broke down and bawled like a baby into the couch cushions" [Veronica Lake with Donald Bain, *Veronica*, 1969].

Alice **Lakwena:** Alice Auwa (1956–2007), Ugandan religious leader. The founder of the Holy Spirit Movement, self-titled "Her Holiness," took a name which in the Acholi language means "messenger."

Luc **Lalain:** Suzanne Daneau (1901–1971), Belg. pianist, composer.

Domenico **Lalli:** Niccolò Sebastiano Biancardi (1679–1741), It. poet, librettist. In 1709 Biancardi was charged with theft, whereupon he changed his name and left his native Naples, eventually settling in Venice to begin a literary career.

Lamar: Lale Marinov Ponchev (1898–1974), Bulg. poet. The writer created his name from the initial syllables of his first two names.

La Mara: Marie Lipsius (1837–1927), Ger. writer. The author used this name for various books on musical composers, mainly of a romantic biographical nature.

Barbara **La Marr:** Rheatha Watson (1896–1926), U.S. movie actress. The actress was at first billed as Barbara Deely or Barbara LaMarr Deely.

Hedy **Lamarr:** Hedwig Eva Maria Kiesler (1913–2000), Austr. movie actress, working in U.S. The actress was given her screen name by MGM's Louis B. **Mayer**, after "the most beautiful star he had ever seen," which was Barbara **La Marr**. He reportedly made the change because Hedy Kiesler's original name was too close to *kiester*, a Yiddish slang term for "buttocks."

Mark **Lamarr:** Mark Jones (1967–), Br. TV comedian, presenter.

Charlotte **Lamb:** Sheila Ann Mary Holland, née Coates (1937–2000), Eng. novelist. The writer, famous for her rapidly-written romances, was best known as Charlotte Lamb, but she also also published as Sheila Coates (her maiden name), Sheila Lancaster, Victoria Woolf, and Laura Hardy, the latter two names suggesting those of the novelist Virginia Woolf and the movie comedians **Laurel** and **Hardy**. Charlotte Lamb was perhaps suggested by the character of this name in Ivy Compton-Burnett's novel *Manservant and Mainservant* (U.S. title *Bullivant and the Lambs*) (1947).

Sir James **Lamb:** James Bland Burges (1752–1824), Eng. politician, poet, dramatist. The writer took his new name only late in life. "In 1821 Burges came into possession of the estate of his friend John Lamb, and assumed by royal license the name of Sir James Lamb" [*Dictionary of National Biography*].

William **Lamb** *see* James **Hill**

Peter **Lambda:** Peter Levy (1911–1994), Hung.-born Br. sculptor. The artist's name is the word for the Greek letter L, the initial of his surname. His father had used the same name as a writer.

Gerald **Lambert:** Gerald Flamberg (1922–2007), Br. boys club founder. The entrepreneur was obliged to change his name to ensure his family's safety after World War II, when his opposition to Oswald Mosley's Fascist movement made him a likely target.

John **Lambert:** John Nicholson (?–1538), Eng. Protestant martyr.

Louis **Lambert:** Patrick Sarsfield Gilmore (1829–1892), Ir.-born U.S. bandmaster. Gilmore used this name for various short pieces, including the familiar "When Johnny Comes Marching Home" (1863).

S.H. **Lambert** *see* Stephen **Southwold**

Elli **Lambeti:** Elli Loukou (1926–1983), Gk. movie actress.

La Meri: Russell Meriwether Hughes (1898–1988), U.S. dance artist, educator. The dancer's name, from the first part of her middle name, was given her by a local journalist while she was taking lessons in Spanish dance in Mexico City in the mid–1920s.

Lamia: Alfred Austin (1835–1913), Eng. poet. The poet used this name for some of his autobiographical writing, as when he edited *The Poet's Diary* (1904). He presumably took it with reference to the witch of the name, who was said to suck the blood of children, and who is the subject of Keats's poem *Lamia* (1820).

Dorothy **Lamour:** Mary Leta Dorothy Slaton (1914–1996), U.S. movie actress. Sources give different original names for the actress, including Mary Leta Dorothy Kaumeyer and Mary Dorothy Stanton (presumably a misprint). Evidence seems to suggest, however, that she was really Mary Leta Dorothy Slaton, but that she then took the surname of her mother's second husband, Clarence Lambour, and altered this to "Lamour" [Dorothy Lamour and Dick McInnes, *My Side of the Road*, 1980]. The name of course evokes French *l'amour*, "love."

Maltin relates: "While I was waiting to interview Dorothy Lamour several years ago, the actress' assistant said to me, 'You know, almost every reference book has her real name wrong.' I asked how that was, and she explained that Lamour's first husband was a bandleader who used the stage name Herbie Kaye. His real name was Kaumeyer, and somewhere along the line someone printed this as Lamour's maiden name. In fact, she was born Slaton. Only a chance conversation enabled me to avoid the error in this volume" [pp.vi–vii].

Louis **L'Amour:** Louis Dearborn LaMoore (1908–1988), U.S. novelist. The writer of western novels also used the pen names Tex Burns (for novels about Hopalong Cassidy, as a pastiche of those originally written by Clarence E. Mulford) and Jim Mayo.

Isadore **Lampe:** Isadore Lampkowitz (1906–1982), Eng.-born U.S. radiologist, of Russ.-Pol. Jewish parentage. When Lampkowitz entered medical school in Cleveland in 1927, his classmates nicknamed him "Lamp." After some thought, he legally changed the family name to Lampe.

Lamya: Lamya Al Mulghiery (1974–), Kenyan-born Br. soul singer, working in U.S.

Lana: Alan Kemp (1938–), Eng. female impersonator. By respelling his (male) first name, the performer created his (female) stage name.

Isabel **Lancashire** *see* Rebecca **West**

G.B. **Lancaster:** Edith Joan Lyttleton (1874–1945), Austral.-born N.Z. writer, of Sc.-Can. descent. The author first wrote as Keron Hale, then adopted her regular pen name, as her family "hated publicity in men and denied it to women." "Writing under a pseudonym which implies masculinity meant that Lyttleton ... wrote stories which focused on the activities and society of men" [Buck, p.767].

Sheila **Lancaster** *see* Charlotte **Lamb**

William P. **Lancaster** *see* George F. **Preston**

Lancelot: Abel Hermant (1862–1950), Fr. novelist. The writer used this name for studies on grammar and style printed in the newspaper *Le Temps*.

Elsa **Lanchester:** Elizabeth Sullivan (1902–1986), Br. stage, movie actress, working in U.S. The actress adopted her mother's maiden name as her stage name.

Jon **Land:** Nicholas Febland (1960–), Eng. popular musician.

Harald **Lander:** Alfred Bernhardt Stevnsborg (1905–1971), Dan.-born Fr. ballet dancer, teacher.

Ann **Landers:** Esther Pauline Friedman Lederer (1918–2002), U.S. journalist. The advice columnist inherited her journalistic byname from a previous Ann Landers, competing with her twin "sob sister," Abigail **Van Buren**.

Lew **Landers:** Louis Friedlander (1901–1962), U.S. movie director.

Elissa **Landi:** Elisabeth-Marie-Christine Kühnelt (1904–1948), It. movie actress, novelist, of Austr. parentage. The actress's new name came from that of her Italian stepfather, Count Carlo Zanardi-Landi.

Stefano **Landi:** Stefano Pirandello (1895–1972), It. comedy writer, son of dramatist Luigi Pirandello (1867–1936).

Carole **Landis:** Frances Lillian Mary Ridste (1919–1948), U.S. movie actress.

Jessie Royce **Landis:** Jessie Royce Medbury (1904–1972), U.S. stage, movie actress.

Jane **Landon:** Frances Jane Leach (1947–), Austral. ballet dancer.

Michael **Landon:** Eugene Maurice Orowitz (1936–1991), U.S. movie, TV actor, producer. The actor originally chose Michael Lane as his stage name, but on discovering that another actor was already using that name, he selected "Landon," the name above "Lane" in the Los Angeles phone book.

Avice **Landone:** Avice Spitta (1910–1976), Eng. stage actress.

Allan ("Rocky") **Lane:** Harold Albershart (1904–1973), U.S. movie actor.

[Sir] Allen **Lane:** Allen Lane Williams (1902–1970), Eng. publisher. In 1919, at age 16, Williams was sent to the London publishers Bodley Head, where he was apprenticed to a distant cousin, John Lane. Lane was childless but keen for the family name to be associated with the firm. He therefore stipulated that Williams change his name to Lane on joining him. From then on he was known as Allen Lane, and his parents, two brothers, and sister also adopted the name.

Burton **Lane:** Burton Levy (1912–1997), U.S. composers of musicals.

Carla **Lane:** Romana Barrack (1937–), Eng. TV comedy writer, animal rights campaigner.

Charles **Lane:** Charles Gerstle Levison (1905–2007), U.S. movie actor.

Christy **Lane:** Eleanor Johnston (1940–), U.S. country singer.

Jackie **Lane:** Jocelyn Bolton (1937–), Austr.-

born Br. movie actress, working in U.S. The actress was credited as Jocelyn Lane from the mid–1960s, on moving to Hollywood.

Jane Lane: Elaine Dakers, née Kidner (?–1978), Eng. writer of historical novels, children's books, biographies. The writer adopted her grandmother's maiden name as her pen name.

Jerry Lane *see* Miska **Miles**

Jocelyn Lane *see* Jackie **Lane**

Lois Lane: Lois Wilkinson (1944–), Eng. popular singer. The singer came to be known by the name of the girl reporter in the *Superman* comics.

Lola Lane: Dorothy Mullican (1909–1981), U.S. movie actress, sister of Priscilla **Lane** and Rosemary **Lane**. The actress is said to have taken her new name from a Los Angeles phone book.

Lupino Lane: Henry George Lupino (1892–1959), Br. stage, movie comedian, of It. descent. The actor adopted the surname of his actress great-aunt Sara Lane (1823–1899) as his new surname, using his own surname as his new first name. This conversion of his surname to a forename was his way of paying tribute to the elder Lupinos, and the result was inherited by his son, comedian and actor-manager Lauri Lupino Lane (1922–1986). His Italian ancestors were originally named Luppino, and the first member of the clan to make his mark in the theater was George Richard Escourt Luppino (1710–1787). Other noted members of the theatrical family were the revue and movie comedian Stanley Lupino (1893–1942) and his actress daughter Ida Lupino (1918–1995), who went to Hollywood in 1933.

Maryon Lane: Patricia Mills (1931–2008), S.A.-born Br. ballet dancer.

Nathan Lane: Joseph Lane (1956–), U.S. actor. When the actor was about to join Actors' Equity, he discovered that there was already a Joe Lane as a member, so instead adopted the first name of Nathan Detroit, a character he had played in the musical *Guys and Dolls*.

Priscilla Lane: Priscilla Mullican (1915–1995), U.S. movie actress, sister of Lola **Lane** and Rosemary **Lane**.

Rosemary Lane: Rosemary Mullican (1914–1974), U.S. movie actress, sister of Lola **Lane** and Priscilla **Lane**.

Temple Lane: Mary Isabel Leslie (1899–1978), Ir. novelist.

Wycliffe Lane: Elizabeth Janet Jenings, née Plues (*fl.*1860s), Eng. novelist. The writer used this name for her novel *My Good-for-Nothing Brother* (1862).

Anthony Lang *see* John **Haslette**

Belinda Lang: Belinda Lange (1955–), Eng. TV actress, daughter of Jeremy **Hawk**.

Eddie Lang: Salvatore Massaro (1902–1933), U.S. jazz guitarist, of It. parentage.

Evelyn Lang *see* Marilyn **Chambers**

Frances Lang *see* Jane **Langford**

Jonny Lang: Jon Gordon Langseth (1981–), U.S. blues musician.

June Lang: Winifred June Vlasek (1915–2005), U.S. movie actress.

k.d. lang: Kathryn Dawn Lang (1961–), Can. country singer, lesbian icon. The singer prefers the lowercase version of her name. She explains: "I decided to change my name because Kathy is really mundane. k.d.'s genderless — it's a name, not a sexuality" [*Sunday Times Magazine*, May 3, 1992].

Pearl Lang: Pearl Lack (1921–2009), U.S. dancer, choreographer.

Ronnie Lang: Ronald Langinger (1927–), U.S. jazz musician.

Mary Langdon: Mary Hayden Green Pike (1824–1908), U.S. novelist. Pike adopted this name for *Ada May* (1854), a counterpoint to Harriet Beecher Stowe's *Uncle Tom's Cabin* (1852), in which the title character is a *white* girl sold into slavery. She followed this with *Caste: A Story of Republican Equality* (1856), written under the pseudonym Sydney A. Story, Jr.

Michael Langdon: Frank Birtles (1920–1991), Eng. opera singer.

Dorothea Lange: Dorothea Margretta Nutzhorn (1895–1965), U.S. photographer. The artist adopted her mother's maiden name as her professional name.

Hope Lange: Hope Ross (1931–), U.S. movie actress.

Frances Langford: Frances Newbern (1914–2005), U.S. movie actress, singer.

Jane Langford: Winifred Langford Mantle (1911–1983), Eng. writer of romantic novels, juvenile fiction. Mantle used this name for a number of early novels, taking it from her middle name (also that of her father). A later adopted name was Frances Lang, from the same source, while further occasional names were Jan Blaine and Anne Fellowes, the latter based on her mother's maiden name of Fellows.

Helen Langley *see* Fenton **Brockley**

Ilse Langner: Ilse Siebert (1899–1988), Ger. playwright, poet, novelist.

Lawrence Langner: Lawrence Freedman (1890–1962), Welsh-born U.S. patent agent, playwright. Freedman adopted his mother's maiden name as his professional name.

Launcelot Langstaff: Washington Irving (1783–1859), U.S. story writer, essayist, historian + William Irving (1766–1821), U.S. politician, satirist, his brother + James Kirk Paulding (1778–1860), U.S. writer. The joint name was used by the three men for the satirical essays and poems published as *Salmagundi; or, the Whim-Whams and Opinions of Launcelot Langstaff, Esq. & Others* (1808). The name perhaps implied a punning reference to the satirist who uses his pen as a "lance" or a "staff" to point his barbs.

Lillie Langtry: Emilie Charlotte Le Breton (1853–1929), Eng. stage actress (the "Jersey Lily"). The actress's new first name is a pet form of her original name. Her surname is that of her first husband, Edward Langtry (married 1874, died 1897). In 1899 she married Sir Hugo de Bathe. Her nickname, alluding to her birthplace, Jersey, Channel Islands, derives from the title of Millais's portrait of her at age 25, *A Jersey Lilly* [*sic*], in which she is shown holding a Jersey lily (*Amaryllis belladonna*). Her name was later adopted by Lillie Langtry (1877–1965), a music-hall artist originally named Galimberti.

Josef Lanik *see* Rudolf **Vrba**.

E.B. Lanin: Emile Joseph Dillon (1854–1933), Ir.-born Br. newspaper correspondent. The writer's name is a reference to his native Dublin, kown as "Eblana" by the media and in literary imprints, this being the city's name as originally recorded by the geographer Ptolemy in the 2d century AD.

Jörg Lanner: Jörg Langenstrass (1939–), Ger. ballet dancer.

Henry Lansing *see* Fenton **Brockley**

Joi Lansing: Joyce Wassmansdoff (1928–1972), U.S. movie actress. The actress based her screen name on that of her first husband, actor Lance Fuller (1928–).

Robert Lansing: Robert H. Brown (1929–1994), U.S. movie, TV actor.

Meyer Lansky: Meyer Suchowljansky (1902–1983), U.S. bootlegger, of Pol. Jewish parentage. The gambling entrepreneur did not adopt the shorter version of his Polish name himself at the start of his law-breaking career, as popularly supposed, since he was already known as Lansky on his school record card. The new form of the name was adopted by his father, Max Suchowljansky, on bringing his family to the U.S. from Europe in 1911 [Robert Lacey, *Little Man: Meyer Lansky and the Gangster Life*, 1991].

Harvey Lant *see* Fenton **Brockley**

Mario Lanza: Alfredo Arnold Cocozza (1921–1959), U.S. opera singer, movie actor, of It. parentage. The singer took his first name from the hero of his favorite opera, Puccini's *Tosca* (1900), in which Floria Tosca falls in love with Mario Cavaradossi, and his second name from his mother's maiden name.

Lanza del Vasto: Giuseppe Giovanni di Trabia Branciforte (1901–1981), It. mystic, working in France.

Josef Lapid: Tomislav Lampel (1931–2008), Yugoslav-born political journalist, of Hung. Jewish parentage. Lapid, popularly known as "Tommy," became Israeli justice minister under Ariel **Sharon**.

Ruth Laredo: Ruth Meckler (1937–2005), U.S. pianist. The musician adopted her husband's name.

Derek Laren: Else Antonia van Epen-de Groot (1919–), Du. pianist, conductor, composer.

Eddie Large: Edward Hugh McGinnis (1942–), Sc.-born Br. TV comedian, teaming with Syd **Little** (as "Little and Large").

Yu. Larin: Mikhail Zalmanovich (or Aleksandrovich) Lurye (1882–1932), Russ. revolutionary.

Pierre de Larivey: Pierre de Giunti (*c*.1540–1619), Fr. comic playwright, of It. descent. The writer's name puns on his Italian family name. Giunti means "they who have arrived," so that Larivey is a version of what in modern French would be *l'arrivé*, "he who has arrived."

Pete La Roca: Peter Sims (1938–), U.S. jazz musician. The musician took his new name when his professional work was with Latin bands.

Scott LaRock: Scott Sterling (1962–1987), U.S. black rapper, DJ.

Frankie LaRocka: Frank LaRocca (1954–2005), U.S. rock musician.

Rod La Rocque: Rodrique la Rocque de la Rour (1896–1969), U.S. movie actor.

Laroque: Pierre Régnault Petit-Jean (*c*.1595–1676), Fr. actor.

Rose La Rose: Rosina Dapelle (1913–1972), U.S. entertainer.

La Roux: Elly Jackson (1988–), Eng. pop singer. The singer named herself for her red hair.

Rita La Roy: Ina Stuart (1907–1993), Fr. movie actress, of Eng. descent.

Larry: Terence Parkes (1927–2003), Eng. cartoonist. The artist's name arose in the 1950s when he taught art at Lincoln Road Secondary Modern School, Peterborough. The students there nicknamed him after a movie showing locally, *The Jolson Story* (1946), in which Larry **Parks** played Al **Jolson**. "Recalling the incident, Larry said: 'I've been Larry ever since. Besides, it's nice and short, so it saves time when it comes to signing your drawings'" [*The Times*, June 27, 2003].

Keith Larsen: Keith Larsen Burt (1925–), U.S. movie actor.

Nella Larsen: Nellie Walker (1891–1964), U.S. black novelist. In 1894 Nellie's mother, Mary Hanson Walker, married a Danish man, Peter Larson, who changed the spelling of his name to Larsen. The future novelist adopted this spelling of her surname when in high school, at the same time modifying her first name to Nella. In 1919 she married Dr. Elmer Samuel Imes, and soon after published two children's stories under the name Nella Larsen Imes. A reversal of her married name gave Allen Semi as the name under which she then wrote two pulp-fiction stories.

Jukka **Larsson:** Pirkko Helena Saisio (1949–), Finn. writer, playwright. The writer adopted the male pseudonym for her trilogy *Kiusaaja* ("The Tempter") (1986), *Viettelijä* ("The Seducer") (1987), and *Kantaja* ("The Carrier") (1991). She has also written as Eva Wein, a name which to a Finnish ear suggests *Eva vain*, "just Eve."

Danny **La Rue:** Daniel Patrick Carroll (1927–2009), Ir.-born Br. revue artist, female impersonator. The actor was given his name by comedian and producer Ted Gatty for his revue *Men Only* (1954). He described the procedure in his autobiography: "When I arrived at the Irving Theatre for rehearsals that night there was a large poster on display and the name DANNY LA RUE caught my eye. 'Who's that?' I asked Ted Gatty ... 'You,' came the reply. 'Danny La Rue?' 'Yes. You *had* to have a name and a billing ... so I made it up.' 'But why *Danny La Rue?*' I was intrigued, but I rather liked it. 'Well,' he said, you are very glamorous and very tall.... You look wonderful in costume and you remind me of Paris, like the Follies. You are also long and lean like a lovely French street, so I thought I would call you Danny the Street — *Danny La Rue*' ... It was a glamorous made-up name for a glamorous made-up person" [Danny La Rue, *From Drags to Riches*, 1987].

Jack **La Rue:** Gaspare Biondolillo (1903–1984), U.S. movie actor.

Denise **Lasalle:** Denise Craig (*c.*1947–), U.S. pop singer, songwriter.

Lady Caroline **Lascelles:** Mary Elizabeth Maxwell, née Braddon (1835–1915), Eng. novelist. The author usually wrote under her maiden name, but used this pseudonym for an early novel, *The Black Band* (1861), written some years before her marriage. She may have adopted it from Lady Caroline Lascelles, eldest daughter of George Howard, 6th Earl of Carlisle (1773–1848), and mother of the diplomat Sir Frank Cavendish Lascelles (1841–1920). Braddon also wrote as Babington White, using her mother's maiden name, and published the novel *The Good Hermione* (1886) as Aunt Belinda. At age 19 she began her career as an actress under the name Mary Seyton, but left the stage soon after.

Prince **Lasha:** William B. Lawsha (1929–), U.S. jazz musician.

Marghanita **Laski:** Esther Pearl Laski (1915–1988), Br. writer, broadcaster. The writer's adopted first name was originally given her by her father when she was a child as an exotic variation of her middle name of Pearl. (The linguistic link is Latin *margarita*, "pearl.") She used the name Sarah Russell for her novel *To Bed with Grand Music* (1946).

Maiju **Lassila:** Algot Untola Tietäväinen (1868–1918), Finn. writer.

Orlando di **Lasso** (or Orlande de Lassus):

Roland Delattre (?1532–1594), Flemish composer, working in Italy. Some older reference sources give the composer's original name as above, although others dispute this. It may have arisen in the belief that his more familiar Italian name was a latinized version of a French original, with the "real" name reconstructed accordingly, "Orlando" giving "Roland" and "di Lasso" giving "Delattre." "As he was a Flemish master and lived in Italy a comparatively short time, there is no good reason for keeping to the Italian form of his name, familiar as it is" [Blom, p.306].

Yusef **Lateef:** William Evans (1920–), U.S. jazz musician. Evans changed his name on adopting the Muslim faith in the 1950s. Lateef represents Arabic *al-latif,* "the kind," an attribute of Allah.

Lyle **Latell:** Lyle Zeiem (1905–1967), U.S. movie actor.

Emma **Lathen:** Mary Jane Latsis (1927–1997), U.S. mystery writer + Martha B. Henissart (1929–), U.S. mystery writer. Both women originally worked in corporate finance (Latsis trained as an economist, Henissart as a lawyer) and adopted their joint name to avoid upsetting the sensibilities of their security-conscious clients. They did so by taking the first two letters of their first names to give "Emma" and combining the first three letters of their surnames to make "Lathen." Their pseudonym long disguised their true identities, and famously led British novelist C.P. Snow to comment that Emma Lathen was "the best living writer of American detective stories." They used the joint name R.B. Dominic for *Murder Sunny Side Up* (1968) and other books featuring Ohio congressman Ben Safford.

Frank **Latimore:** Frank Kline (1925–1998), U.S. movie actor.

Henri de **Latouche:** Hyacinthe Thabaud de Latouche (1785–1851), Fr. poet.

John **Latouche** *see* John **Dangerfield**

La Tuillerie: Jean-François Juvenon (1650–1688), Fr. actor, dramatist, grandson of **Gros-Guillaume.**

Horst **Laubenthal:** Horst Rüdiger Neumann (1938–), Ger. opera singer. The singer took his name from his adoptive father, tenor Rudolf Laubenthal (1886–1971), whose sole pupil he was.

Afferbeck **Lauder:** Alistair Ardoch Morrison (1911–1999), Austral. writer. The writer devised "Strine" as a term for the characteristic Australian pronunciation of English. "Strine" is "Australian" in Strine, and "Afferbeck Lauder" is "alphabetical order." He originally used the name as part of a mock academic title for the author of "papers" in the *Sydney Morning Herald* (1965). In full he was thus Professor Afferbeck Lauder, Professor of Strine Studies at the University of Sinny [Sydney].

Estée **Lauder:** Josephine Esther Mentzer (1906–2004), U.S. cosmetician, of Hung. Jewish parentage. The founder of the cosmetics company that bears her name had her second name altered to its French equivalent by a teacher at the school she attended. In 1930 she married Joe Lauter, who later changed the spelling of his surname to Lauder.

Roger **Laugier:** Roger Krebs (*c.*1931–), Fr. juvenile movie actor. The actor dropped his Germanic-sounding surname to replace it with the name of the character he portrayed in his first movie, *La Cage aux rossignols* ("The Cage of Nightingales") (1943), for which he was himself billed as "Le Petit Krebs."

Friedrich **Laun:** Friedrich August Schulze (1770–1849), Ger. popular novelist, short-story writer.

Rose de **Launay:** Marguerite-Jeanne Cordier (*c.*1684–1750), Fr. playwright, correspondent. The writer adopted the name of her mother's family. In 1735, unwillingly, she was married to the baron de Staal to enhance her rank and privileges, as a result of which she became known as Madame de Staal.

Laura Maria *see* **Perdita** (2)

Eugene **Laurant:** Eugene Greenleaf (1875–1944), U.S. magician.

Mae **Laurel:** Mae Charlotte Dahlberg (1888–1969), Austral. movie comedienne, common-law wife of Stan **Laurel**, working in U.S.

Stan **Laurel:** Arthur Stanley Jefferson (1890–1965), Eng. movie comedian, working in U.S., teaming with Oliver **Hardy**. The "thin one" of the comic pair originally appeared on the stage as Stan Jefferson. The story goes that one day in 1912, when touring the U.S. with Fred **Karno**, he realized that his name had 13 letters, so decided to change it. The shorter and more obviously propitious name "Laurel" is said to have been suggested by his common-law wife Mae **Laurel**, who joined him to form a duo in 1917. She recalled: "I was in the dressing-room ... looking at an old history book that someone in the previous week's show must have left ... I opened it up casual like, and I came to an etching or a drawing of a famous old Roman general, Scipio Africanus Major.... Around his head he wore a laurel, a wreath of laurel.... That word stayed with me. I said it aloud, Laurel. Laurel. Stan Laurel. Stan looked up from what he was doing and he said, 'What?' ... 'How about that for a name?' He repeated it aloud, too. 'Stan Laurel. Sounds very good'" [Fred Lawrence Guiles, *Stan*, 1980].

Ralph **Lauren:** Ralph Lipshitz (1939–), U.S. fashion designer. Lipschitz adopted his new name on starting his own fashion business in 1967.

Paula **Laurence:** Paula de Lugo (1916–), U.S. stage actress.

William Leonard **Laurence:** William Leonard Siew (1888–1977), Lithuanian-born U.S. science writer. Raised in an Orthodox Jewish family, Siew fled to Berlin in 1905 to escape a political purge and from there made his way to the United States, where the following year he settled in Boston, Massachusetts, and renamed himself after the street where he lived.

Daniel **Laurent:** Elsa Triolet (1896–1970), Fr. writer, of Russ. origin. The lifelong partner of Louis **Aragon** used this name for her novel *Les Amants d'Avignon* ("The Lovers of Avignon") (1943).

André **Laurie** *see* Docteur **Blasius**

Annie **Laurie:** Winifred Sweet Black (1863–1936), U.S. journalist. Black was hired by the *San Francisco Examiner* in 1890 and as it was then customary for women reporters to take a pseudonym called herself Annie Laurie, after the well-known song of this name that her mother used to sing.

Piper **Laurie:** Rosetta Jacobs (1932–), U.S. movie actress, of Pol. Jewish/Russ.–U.S. parentage. Laurie was named by Universal Studios, who signed her as a contract player when she was 17. "Somewhere deep down in the Hollywood papers (all the reports, all the stories), there may be an explanation of how the name 'Piper Laurie' came to be, and even a joyful self-tribute from the person who came up with the fabrication. What does it say? Cute, tomboyish, melodious. Scots perhaps? And what warning signs were there, in the late forties, in an actress named 'Rosetta Jacobs'? The young woman from Michigan may have hated the name, eventually, yet she never changed it" [Thomson 2003, p.502].

Jay **Laurier:** Jay Chapman (1879–1969), Eng. music-hall artist.

Giacomo **Lauri-Volpi:** Giacomo Volpi (1892–1979), It. opera singer.

[Metropolitan] **Laurus:** Vasili Mihailovich Skurla (1928–2008), Slovakian-born Russ. church leader. The head of the Russian Orthodox Church Outside Russia, based in the U.S. at Jordanville, New York, adopted his monastic name (Russian Lavr) on taking his vows in 1948.

Comte de **Lautréamont:** Isidore Ducasse (1846–1870), Fr. poet. The poet adopted, and slightly adapted, the name and title of the eponymous hero of the historical novel *Latréaumont* (1837) by Eugène **Sue**. The reason for the adoption is unknown, and many details of the poet's brief life remain uncertain.

René **Lavand:** Renato Lavandeira (?–), Argentinian-born U.S. magician.

Christine **Lavant:** Christine Habernig, née Thonhauser (1915–1973), Ger. lyric poet.

Charlie **LaVere:** Charles Levere Johnson (1910–1983), U.S. jazz musician.

Maud **Laverne** *see* Ida **Barr**

Betty **Lavette:** Betty Haskin (1946–), U.S. soul singer. The singer adopted her stage name for the 1962 R&B hit "My Man — He's a Loving Man."

Daliah (or Dahlia) **Lavi:** Daliah Levenbuch (1940–), Israeli movie actress.

Héctor **Lavoe:** Héctor Pérez (1946–), Puerto Rican popular singer, bandleader.

Lavrenty **Lavrov:** Lavrenty Nikitich Selyakhin (1868–1958), Russ. circus artist. The performer's ring name, based on his first name, was passed down to his children, who like him were clowns and acrobats.

Pyotr **Lavrov:** Pyotr Lavrovich Mirtov (1823–1900), Russ. Socialist philosopher. There is an apparent pun here, since Lavrov suggests Russian *lavr*, "laurel," "bay," while Mirtov evokes *mirt*, "myrtle." Both laurel and myrtle are evergreen shrubs specially honored by the Romans.

Leonid **Lavrovsky:** Leonid Mikhaylovich Ivanov (1905–1967), Russ. ballet dancer, choreographer.

John **Law:** Margaret Elise Harkness (1854–1923), Eng. novelist. Harkness probably took her pen name from her great-grandfather, G.H. Law (1761–1845), bishop of Bath and Wells, or else from John Law of Lauriston (1671–1729), French finance minister, a distant relation, to whom she dedicated her tragic novel *Out of Work* (1888).

Peter **Lawford:** Peter Sydney Vaughn Aylen (1923–1984), Br. movie actor, working in U.S. The actor adopted the name of his stepfather, Lieutenant-General Sir Sydney Lawford (1866–1953).

Jody **Lawrance:** Josephine Lawrence Goddard (1930–1986), U.S. movie actress.

Arnie **Lawrence:** Arnold Lawrence Finkelstein (1938–), U.S. jazz musician.

Elliot **Lawrence:** Elliot Lawrence Broza (1925–), U.S. jazz musician.

Florence **Lawrence:** Florence Bridgewood (1886–1938), Can.-born U.S. stage, movie actress. After graduating from high school, Florence took to performing with a touring company run by her mother, née Charlotte Dunn, an actress under the stage name Lotta Lawrence, and adopted her name.

Gertrude **Lawrence:** Gertrud Alexandra Dagmar Lawrence-Klasen (1898–1952), Br. revue artist, movie actress.

Jack **Lawrence:** Jacob Lawrence Schwartz (1912–2009), U.S. songwriter, of Russ. Jewish parentage.

Jerome **Lawrence:** Jerome Lawrence Schwartz (1915–), U.S. dramatist, screenwriter.

Josie **Lawrence:** Wendy Lawrence (1959–), Br. TV actress.

Lars **Lawrence:** Philip Stevenson (1896–1965), U.S. writer.

Lee **Lawrence:** Leon Siroto (*c.*1921–1961), Eng. popular singer.

Louise **Lawrence:** Elizabeth Rhoda Wintle Holden (1943–), Br. SF, fantasy writer.

Marc **Lawrence:** Max Goldsmith (1910–2005), U.S. movie actor.

Peter Lee **Lawrence:** Karl Hirenbach (1943–1973), Ger.-born movie actor.

Slingsby **Lawrence:** George Henry Lewes (1817–1878), U.S. philosopher, literary critic. This was the name used by Lewes, lover of George **Eliot**, for adaptations of French plays. Slingsby seems to have been a popular pseudonym with 19th-century writers. Others who used it (but as a surname) include Jonathan Freke **Slingsby** and Philip **Slingsby**. Its origin may be in the village schoolmaster Slingsby in Washington Irving's *Bracebridge Hall* (1823).

Steve **Lawrence:** Sidney Leibowitz (1935–), U.S. pop singer. The singer borrowed the first names of his two nephews for his professional name, with "Lawrence" also not too far removed from "Leibowitz."

Charles **Lawson:** Quintin Charles Devenish (1959–), Ir.-born Br. stage, movie, TV actor.

[Sir] Edward Levy **Lawson:** Edward Levy (1833–1916), Br. newspaper proprietor, of Jewish parentage. The owner of the *Daily Telegraph* took his new name in 1875 by royal license "in respect of a deed of gift from his uncle Lionel, who had also added Lawson to his surname" [Lord Burnham, *Peterborough Court: The Story of the Daily Telegraph*, 1955]. In a Jewish context, Lawson can be regarded as an equivalent of Levison, i.e. "son of Levy."

Henry Hertzberg **Lawson:** Henry Hertzberg Larsen (1867–1922), Austral. poet, short-story writer.

Priscilla **Lawson:** Priscilla Shortridge (1915–1958), U.S. movie actress.

W.B. **Lawson:** George Charles Jenks (1850–1929), Br. printer, journalist, fiction writer, working in U.S.

Wilfrid **Lawson:** Wilfrid Worsnop (1900–1966), Br. stage, movie actor.

Yank **Lawson:** John Rhea Lauson (1911–1995), U.S. jazz trumpeter.

Frank **Lawton:** Frank Lawton Mokeley, Jr. (1904–1969), Br. movie, stage actor.

Halldór **Laxness:** Halldór Kiljan Guðjónsson (1902–1998), Icelandic poet, novelist, playwright. The writer adopted the name of his father's farm near Reykjavík, where he was raised.

Dilys **Laye:** Dilys Lay (1934–2009), Eng. stage, movie, TV actress. The actress added an "e" to her original name on taking up a stage career.

Evelyn **Laye:** Elsie Evelyn Lay (1900–1996), Br. stage singer, movie actress.

Nikolay **Layne:** Nikolay Grigoryevich Gippiyev (1920–), Russ. (Karelian) poet. The writer's adopted name means "wave" (of the sea).

George **Layton:** George Löwy (1942–), Br. TV actor, of Austr. parentage. The actor's father changed his German Jewish name from Fritz Löwy to Freddie Layton on becoming a naturalized British citizen in 1947, although at the time did not change the names of the rest of his family.

Irving **Layton:** Israel Pincu Lazarovici (1912–2006), Rom.-born Can. poet, of Jewish parentage.

Joe **Layton:** Joseph Lichtman (1931–1994), U.S. choreographer, stage director.

Lazdinu Peleda: Sofia Ivanáuskaite-Psibiláuskene (1867–1926), Lithuanian writer + Maria Ivanáuskaite-Lastáuskene (1872–1957), Lithuanian writer, her sister. The sisters' joint pen name means "owl in the hazel grove," alluding to the rural themes and settings of their stories.

Lazy Lester: Leslie Johnson (1933–), U.S. black blues musician. Johnson adopted his performing name from a nickname given him in the early 1950s by record producer J.D. Miller for his slow-moving, laid-back ways.

Ivan **Le:** Ivan Leontyevich Moysya (1895–1978), Ukr. writer. The writer gained his pen name by chance. On submitting his first piece to a local newspaper in 1913 he signed it with his name. His signature proved difficult to read, however, and the contribution appeared as by "Ivan Le...," which was all the editor could make out. The piece itself aroused the wrath of a local dignitary, who said, "If I knew who wrote it, I'd tan the hide off him!" The young author, learning of this fearful threat, instantly appreciated the benefit of a pseudonym, and used this one from then on [Dmitriyev, pp.93–4].

Barbara **Lea:** Barbara Leacock (1925–), U.S. jazz singer, of Fr. descent. The singer is a descendant of the French composer Charles Lecocq (1832–1918).

Leadbelly: Hudson ("Huddie") William Ledbetter (1889–1949), U.S. black folk, blues singer. An obvious pun on the musician's surname, but also an allusion to his strength. It originated as a nickname given by his fellow convicts while serving a prison sentence for violent crimes.

Mike **Leander:** Michael Farr (1941–1996), Eng. pop music composer, producer. The composer is chiefly known for his promotion of the rock star Gary **Glitter,** whose name he helped select.

Zarah **Leander:** Zarah Hedberg (1900–1981), Swe. stage, movie actress, singer.

Leander à Sancto Martino: John Jones (1575–1636), Welsh monk. Jones took his religious name, meaning "Leander of St. Martin," on being admitted into the Benedictine monastery of San Martín Pinario

at Santiago de Compostela, Spain, in 1599. St. Leander was a 6th-century bishop of Seville.

Leandro: José Luiz Costa (1961–1998), Brazilian country singer, teaming with brother Leonardo.

Léar: Albert Kirchner (*fl.*1890s), Fr. producer of religious and pornographic movies.

Amanda **Lear:** Amanda Tapp (1941–), Br. rock singer, of Russ. descent.

Evelyn **Lear:** Evelyn Schulman (1928–), U.S. opera singer.

Otis **Leavill:** Otis Leavill Cobb (1937–2002), U.S. soul singer, producer.

Vasily **Lebedev-Kumach:** Vasily Ivanovich Lebedev (1898–1949), Russ. satirical poet. The poet added to his name his early pseudonym of Kumach, from Russian *kumach*, a word of Turkish origin used for a kind of red calico cloth. As he himself explained, writing about his work in the immediate postrevolutionary period: "The heroic spirit of those days, the *kumach* armbands worn by the Red Army, the *kumach* ribbons and flags, suggested my literary pseudonym of Kumach, which became permanently part of my name" [Dmitriyev, p.119].

Pavel **Lebedev-Polyansky:** Pavel Ivanovich Lebedev (1881–1948), Russ. literary specialist. The revolutionary writer adopted the name Valerian Polyansky as both a politicial and literary name. On returning to Russia in 1917 from emigration in Geneva, he added Polyansky to his original surname.

Peter **Leberecht:** Ludwig Tieck (1773–1853), Ger. writer. Tieck used this name for his *Volksmärchen* ("Folk Tales") (1789), taking it from the main character of an earlier novel, *Peter Leberecht, eine Geschichte ohne Abenteuerlichkeiten* ("Peter Leberecht, a Story without Improbabilities") (1795).

Pierre **LeBlanc** *see* Don Juan **Cardoza**

Marius-Ary **Leblond:** Georges Athenas (1877–1955), Fr. writer + Aimé Merlo (1880–1958), Fr. writer.

Fred **Lebow:** Fischl Lebowitz (1932–1994), Rom.-born U.S. sports personality.

John **Le Breton:** Thomas Murray Ford (1854–?), Eng. novelist + Alice May Harte-Potts (*fl.*1905), Eng. novelist.

Benat **LeCagot** *see* **Trevanian**

Major **Le Caron:** Thomas Miller Beach (1841–1894), Br. secret agent, working in U.S. In 1861, at the outbreak of the American Civil War, Beach enlisted with the Federalists in the 8th Pennsylvanian Reserves under the name Henri Le Caron, later attaining the rank of major in the Andersen Cavalry.

John **le Carré:** David John Moore Cornwell (1931–), Eng. spy novelist. When starting his career as a writer, Cornwell was employed as a civil servant by the Foreign Office, and was advised to adopt another name, as it would have been frowned on for a serving diplomat to publish novels under his own name. The story goes that Cornwell saw the name on a London shopfront when riding on a bus, and decided to adopt it, although he was later recorded as saying: "I have grown sick of saying I don't know where it comes from, so I usually say I saw it on a shoe shop." He first used it for *A Perfect Spy* (1962).

Jean-Paul Le Chanois: Jean-Paul Dreyfus (1909–1985), Fr. movie director. During World War II the actor was with the French Resistance, and adopted the undercover name Le Chanois. After 1945, he retained this as his professional name.

Jan Lechon: Leszek Serafinowicz (1899–1956), Pol. poet, working in France, U.S.

Ginette Leclerc: Geneviève Manut (1912–1992), Fr. movie actress.

Philippe Leclerc: Jacques-Philippe-Marie de Hauteclocque (1902–1947), Fr. general. The army officer, a major in World War II, adopted his name in order not to jeopardize the lives of his family in German-occupied France when escaping to England to join the "Fighting French."

Charles-Marie-René Leconte de Lisle: Charles-Marie-René Leconte (1818–1894), Fr. poet. The poet was born on the island of Réunion. Hence his added surname de Lisle, "of the island."

Le Corbusier: Charles-Édouard Jeanneret (1887–1965), Swiss-born Fr. architect. The artist signed his work "Jeanneret" until 1920, when he adopted (and adapted) the name of his maternal grandmother, Lecorbésier. It also punned on a nickname, *Le Corbeau* ("The Raven"), given him for his supposed facial resemblance to this bird.

Olivier Le Dain (or Le Daim): Olivier Necker (?–1484), Fr. royal favorite, of Flemish origin. According to D'Israeli, Louis XI's counsellor underwent several changes of name. "The king's barber was named *Olivier le Diable* [Oliver the Devil]. At first the king allowed him to get rid of the offensive part by changing it to *le Malin* [The Sly], but the improvement was not happy, and for a third time he was called *Le Mauvais* [The Bad]. Even this did not answer his purpose; and as he was a great racer, he finally had his majesty's ordinance to be called *Le Dain* [The Deer], under penalty of law if any one should call him *Le Diable, Le Malin,* or *Le Mauvais*" [p.200].

Jacques Ledoux: Jacques Silberberg (1921–1988), Pol.-born Belg. film archivist.

Alexandre Auguste Ledru-Rollin: Alexandre Auguste Ledru (1807–1874), Fr. politician.

Alice Gordon Lee *see* Cousin **Alice**

Amber Lee: Faith Baldwin, later Cuthrell (1893–1978), U.S. novelist. An occasional pseudonym used by the popular writer.

Andrew Lee: Louis (Stanton) Auchinloss (1917–), U.S. novelist.

Anna Lee: Joanna Boniface Winnifrith (1913–2004), Br. movie actress, working in U.S. The actress is said to have based her screen name on the blended names of Tolstoy's heroine Anna Karenina, movie actress Anna May **Wong**, and Confederate general Robert E. Lee, although "Anna" may well have been a short form of her original first name.

Arthur Lee: Arthur Lee Porter (1945–2006), U.S. black rock musician.

Billy Lee: William Lee Schlenaker (1929–1989), U.S. juvenile movie actor.

Bonnie Lee: Jessie Lee Frealls (1931–), U.S. black blues singer.

Brandon Lee: Brian MacKinnon (1961–), Sc. impostor. In 1993, desperate to gain the academic qualification that would enable him to study medicine at university, 32-year-old MacKinnon managed to gain admission to his old school, Bearsden Academy, Glasgow, under the guise of a Canadian teenager named Brandon Lee (a name perhaps inspired by the son of Bruce **Lee**). Although twice as old as his classmates, his ruse succeeded for over a year before his duplicity was discovered. When put on the spot, MacKinnon burst out: "To fuck with identity. It's just a name. I know who I am" [Burton, p.128].

Brenda Lee: Brenda Mae Tarpley (1944–), U.S. country singer. "Lee" represents the "-ley" of the singer's surname. She was given her new name at age 12, when she began her recording career and was promoted as "Little Miss Brenda Lee."

Bruce Lee: (1) Jun Fan Li (1940–1973), U.S. movie actor, martial arts exponent, of Chin. parentage, father of actor Brandon Lee (1964–1993); (2) Peter Dinsdale (1960–), Eng. criminal. The actor was born in San Francisco to Grace Li, wife of Li Hoi Cheun, a comic actor with Hong Kong's Cantonese Opera. To confuse unfriendly spirits, he was at first given a girl's name, Sai Fon ("Small Phoenix"), but his mother then renamed him Jun Fan ("Return Again"), because she felt that one day he might return to his birthplace. (He did, emigrating to the USA in 1959.) The supervising physician, Mary Glover, nicknamed the boy "Bruce," which he kept, and he later anglicized his family name to Lee. He played his first professional role at the age of six in *The Birth of Mankind* (1946) under the name Lee Siu Lung, "Lee Little Dragon," the name by which he became known in Asia [Bruce Thomas, *Bruce Lee: Fighting Spirit*, 1997]. Dinsdale, sentenced in 1981 to detention in a special hospital for the manslaughter of 26 people and on 10 charges of arson, changed his name in 1979 to Bruce Lee after his kung-fu hero.

Canada **Lee**: Leonard Lionel Cornelius Canegata (1907–1952), U.S. black stage, movie actor. The actor began his career as a boxer and adopted his name when veteran fight announcer Joe Humphries had difficulty pronouncing "Lee Canegata" and introduced him as "Canada Lee."

Dickie **Lee**: Richard Lipscombe (1941–), U.S. pop singer. "Lee" from the singer's original surname.

Dixie **Lee**: Wilma Wyatt (1911–1952), U.S. movie actress.

Dorothy **Lee**: Marjorie Millsap (1911–1999), U.S. movie actress.

Frances **Lee**: Myrna Tibbetts (1908–?), U.S. movie comedienne.

Gaby **Lee** *see* Abbey **Lincoln**

Gwen **Lee**: Gwendolyn Le Pinski (1904–), U.S. movie actress.

Gypsy Rose **Lee**: Rose Louise Hovick (1911–1970), U.S. striptease artist, sister of June **Havoc**. The dancer took the name "Gypsy" for her burlesque acts, with "Rose Lee" based on her two first names. Her stage mother in her act was Madame Rose, and Rose was also her real mother's first name.

Holme **Lee**: Harriet Parr (1828–1900), Eng. novelist. Parr, who wrote around 30 "refined" but sentimental novels, adopted a *nom de plume* that was intended to be understood as "homely." She first used it for the novel *Maud Talbot* (1854).

Jackie **Lee**: Earl Nelson (1828–2008), U.S. black soul singer. Nelson, who had hits under many different names and guises, used this name in the mid–1960s for his novelty dance number "The Duck."

Johnny **Lee**: John Lee Ham (1946–), U.S. country singer.

Laura **Lee**: Laura Lee Rundless (1945–), U.S. black gospel singer.

Leapy **Lee**: Lee Graham (1942–), Eng. pop singer.

Lila **Lee**: Augusta Appel (1902–1973), U.S. movie actress.

Lovie **Lee**: Eddie ("Lovie") Lee Watson (1917–1997), U.S. black blues musician.

Margaret **Lee**: Margaret Lightfoot (1909–?), U.S. movie actress. This Margaret Lee should not be confused with the British movie actress Margaret Lee (1943–).

Michael **Lee**: Michael Gary Pearson (1969–2008), Br. rock drummer.

Michele **Lee**: Michele Lee Dusiak (1942–), U.S. movie actress, singer.

Patty **Lee**: Alice Cary (1820–1871), U.S. poet, novelist.

Peggy **Lee**: Norma Deloris (or Dolores) Egstrom (1920–2002), U.S. nightclub singer, movie

actress, of Scandinavian descent. When Egstrom found work as a teenager singing on the radio station WDAY, manager Ken Kennedy nicknamed her "Peggy Lee," presumably for the contemporary singer.

Pinky **Lee**: Pincus Leff (1908–1993), U.S. children's TV entertainer.

Sammy **Lee**: Samuel Levy (1890–1968), U.S. stage, movie dance director. The actor adopted his new name at the age of 11 on making his debut at Miner's Bowery Theatre, New York.

Spike **Lee**: Shelton Jackson Lee (1957–), U.S. black moviemaker. The filmmaker replaced his original first name with the nickname by which his mother dubbed him for his feistiness.

Stan **Lee**: Stanley Martin Lieber (1922–), U.S. comic-book writer, of Rom. parentage. Marvel Comics editor Lee gained fame as the creator of the Incredible Hulk and Spiderman. "So prolific, so varied was his talent, that I assumed Stan Lee was a nom-de-plume for a factory of writers ... I tell him that as a boy I thought Stan Lee was a made-up name. 'It was,' he reminds me" [Andrew Billen in *The Times*, June 17, 2002].

Steve **Lee**: Michael Patrick Parry (1947–), Eng. writer, anthologist.

Tony **Lee**: Anthony Leedham (1934–2004), Br. jazz pianist.

Vanessa **Lee**: Winifred Ruby Moule (1920–1992), Eng. stage actress, singer. When the actress first met Ivor **Novello**, he suggested she change her name. The story goes that when she arrived one day at the Hippodrome Theatre, London, he told her he had written three names on his dressing-room mirror and asked her what names she had herself chosen. She opened her handbag and showed him the three she had written: Vanessa, Virginia, and Sharon. These were identical to the ones he had written on his mirror, and she adopted the first choice [*The Times*, March 16, 1992]. Novello had earlier named Vivien **Leigh**, "and it was Lee again, although spelt differently, that he bestowed on this new find" [W. Macqueen-Pope, *Ivor: The Story of an Achievement*, 1951].

Vernon **Lee**: Violet Paget (1856–1935), Fr.-born Eng. essayist, art critic, novelist, working in Italy. The writer adopted her pseudonym in her teens, taking "Lee" from the surname of her stepmother, Matilda Lee-Hamilton, whom her father married in 1855, when he was tutor to her son, Eugene Lee-Hamilton (1845–1907), poet, novelist, and professional invalid. "Vernon" came from her first name. Lee's father was the son of a French nobleman named De Pagnier who had been forced to flee Poland and who came to be known as Henry Ferguson Paget, the latter being the maiden name of his first wife.

William **Lee:** William S. Burroughs (1914–1997), U.S. novelist. Burroughs used this pen name for *Junkie* (1953), his frank account of his life as a drug addict. He continued the account under his real name in *The Naked Lunch* (1959).

Richard **Leech:** Richard Leeper McClelland (1922–2004), Ir. stage, movie, TV actor.

Andrea **Leeds:** Antoinette M. Lees (1914–1974), U.S. movie actress.

Herbert I. **Leeds:** Herbert I. Levy (?1900–1954), U.S. movie director.

Thomas **Leer:** Thomas Wishart (*c.*1955–), Sc. new wave singer.

Lees: Peter Lees Walmesley (*c.*1908–1942), Eng. cartoonist.

Benjamin **Lees:** Benjamin Lysniansky (1924–), U.S. composer, of Russ. parentage.

Tamara **Lees:** Tamara Mappleback (1920–), It. movie actress, of Russ.-Eng. parentage.

Johnny **Leeze:** John Glen (1941–), Eng. movie, TV actor.

Richard **Le Gallienne:** Richard Thomas Gallienne (1866–1947), Eng. poet, literary critic. "He came of an old seafaring family in the Channel Islands and the prefix 'Le' which he added to his surname on the title-page of his first published poems [*My Ladies' Sonnets* (1887)] was in the style of his forebears" [*Dictionary of National Biography*].

Ethel **Leginska:** Ethel Liggins (1886–1970), Eng. pianist, conductor, composer, working in U.S. The musician's Slavic-style pseudonym was given her as a child by Lady Maud Warrender, who believed that a Polish-looking name would help Ethel's artistic career.

Marshall **Leib:** Marshall Philip Leibovitz (1939–2002), U.S. pop musician.

Arbor **Leigh:** Louisa Sarah Bevington (1845–1895), Eng. essayist, poet. Bevington used this name, based on Elizabeth Barrett Browning's *Aurora Leigh* (1857), for *Key Notes* (1876), verses on evolution.

Arran **Leigh** *see* Michael **Field**

Carolyn **Leigh:** Carolyn Paula Rosenthal (1926–1983), U.S. songwriter.

Dorian **Leigh:** Dorian Elizabeth Leigh Parker (1917–2008), U.S. model, sister of Suzy **Parker**. The model shortened her name because of her parents: "My mother and father thought modeling was so low-class that I shouldn't use the last name Parker" [Michael Gross, *Model*, 1995].

Gracie **Leigh:** Gracie Ellis (*c.*1875–1950), U.S. vaudeville artist.

Isla **Leigh** *see* Michael **Field**

Janet **Leigh:** Jeanette Helen Morrison (1927–2004), U.S. movie, TV actress, wife of Tony **Curtis**, mother of Jamie Lee **Curtis**.

Jennifer Jason **Leigh:** Jennifer Lee Morrow (1962–), U.S. movie actress. The actress adopted her new middle name in honor of the actor Jason Robards (1922–2000), a family friend.

Mitch **Leigh:** Irwin Mitchnick (1928–), U.S. popular composer, arranger.

Vivien **Leigh:** Vivian Mary Hartley (1913–1967), Eng. stage, movie actress, working in U.S. The actress took her new surname from her first husband, Herbert Leigh Holman (married 1932, divorced 1940). The change was not immediate. Her first agent, John Gliddon, to whom she signed in 1934, told her she would need a new name: "She said immediately that she'd prefer a stage name like 'Suzanne Stanley.' 'Too cold ... too hard. What's your maiden name?' 'Hartley ... How about Mary Hartley?' Gliddon turned it down on the spot. Cockney would soon make that into 'Mary 'artley.'" Later, theater manager Gordon Courtney suggested "April Morn," which Gliddon said he would bear in mind. He consulted with manager Ivor **Novello**, who said, "Why not call her Vivian Leigh—half her own name and half her husband's. They can't fall out over that." Impresario Sydney **Carroll** modified Leigh's first name in 1935 on casting her for a part in Ashley Dukes's play *The Mask of Virtue*: "He didn't like her first name. '"Vivian"— it's neither one thing nor the other. It'll confuse people. They won't know if you're a man or a woman. Will you agree to spelling it "Vivien"?' 'I changed my name again today,' she told her husband that evening" [Alexander Walker, *Vivien: The Life of Vivien Leigh*, 1987].

Eino **Leino:** Armas Eino Leopold Lönnbohm (1878–1926), Finn. poet, brother of Kasimir **Leino**.

Kasimir **Leino:** Kasimir Araton Lönnbohm (1866–1918), Finn. poet, brother of Eino **Leino**.

Erich **Leinsdorf:** Erich Landauer (1912–1993), Austr.-born U.S. orchestral conductor, pianist.

Murray **Leinster:** William Fitzgerald Jenkins (1896–1975), U.S. SF writer.

Nate **Leipzig:** Nathan Leipziger (1873–1939), Swe.-born magician.

Lillian **Leitzel:** Lillian Alize Elianore (1892–1931), Ger.-born U.S. circus performer, gymnast. The performer's new surname was based on her existing middle name. There is some uncertainly regarding her original name, with her given names recorded in varying spellings. Leitzel never used her father's name for any length of time during her life, and some sources give her original name as Leopoldina Alitza Pelikan, after Elinor Pelikan, her mother.

Lekain: Henri-Louis Caïn (1729–1778), Fr. tragic actor.

Leksa Manush: Aleksandr Dmitriyevich Belugin (1942–), Russ. Romany (Gypsy) poet. The poet's new first name is a Romany form of his original first name. His second name means "man," so that he is "Alex (the Gypsy) man."

L.E.L.: Laetitia Elizabeth Landon (1802–1838), Eng. poet, novelist. Landon's first poem, "Rome," was published in 1820 as by simply "L.," presumably standing for her first name rather than her last. "Publishing ... under her initials 'L.E.L.' enabled her to assume the literary persona of an innocent, gentle, and devoted but rejected female lover, such that the initials themselves acquired a kind of feminine enchantment in the eyes of the reading public" [Birch, p.570].

Sara **Leland:** Sally Harrington (1941–), U.S. ballet dancer.

Lele: Leanne Jackson (1988–), Br. (white) MC, rapper. A pet form of the musician's first name.

[Sir] Peter **Lely:** Pieter van der Faes (1618–1680), Du. portrait painter, working in England. Although doubt remains regarding the origin of the painter's name, one account tells how his father, a military captain, was known by the nickname of "Lely" for the prominent lily on the house where he was born. The son is then said to have adopted the name as his new surname.

Louis-Isaac **Le Maître de Saci:** Louis-Isaac Le Maître (1613–1684), Fr. priest, religious translator. The director at the Port-Royal convent embellished his name with a near-anagram of his first name Isaac.

Francis **Lemarque:** Nathan Korb (1917–2002), Fr. popular singer, songwriter, of Pol.-Lithuanian Jewish parentage. The singer's new name evolved from that of "Les Frères Marc," a duo formed with his elder brother Maurice ("Marc") in 1934.

Mr. **Lemon:** James Leonard (1940–), Br. crossword compiler. The setter's pseudonym represents a corruption of his real name, used jokingly by some friends as a form of address.

John **Le Mesurier:** John Halliley (1912–1983), Eng. movie, TV actor. The actor adopted his mother's maiden name as his professional name. "[The feature] didn't even know the half of how posh Le Mesurier was, when it discovered that Le Mesurier was christened John Charles Elton Le Mesurier De Somerys Halliley" [*The Times*, June 19, 2009].

Lemmy: Ian Kilminster (1945–), Eng. punk rock musician. The musician's stage name is said to represent his formerly frequent urgent request, "Lend me a fiver!" "No one calls me by my real name, Ian, except my mum" [*The Observer Magazine,* November 10, 2002].

Aïcha **Lemsine:** Aïcha Laïdi (1942–), Algerian novelist, working in Mexico. The writer's surname represents the Arabic letters *lem* (L) and *sin* (S), presumably the initials of her married name and maiden name.

Le Myosotis: Charles Ratsarauelina (1910–), Malagasy poet. Although writing in Malagasy, the poet has a French name meaning "the forget-me-not."

Lenare: Leonard Green (1883–after 1930), Eng. society photographer. Lenare opened his studio in 1923. Since in those days a French-sounding name was the fashion for dressmakers and photographers, he took the first syllable of "Leonard" and added what he believed to be a French-style ending. When asked about the origin of the name, he would point to his bald head and say, "Look, Len no 'air" [*Sunday Times Magazine*, November 13, 1977].

Nikolaus **Lenau:** Nikolaus Franz Niembsch von Strehlenau (1802–1850), Hung.-born Austr. poet.

Leonid **Lench:** Leonid Sergeyevich Popov (1905–1991), Russ. writer, dramatist. The writer regarded his surname as too ordinary, so a member of the editorial staff of the magazine where he worked, the Krasnodar *Krasnoye Znamya* ("Red Banner"), devised the name "Lench" from "Lenchik," one of the diminutive forms of his first name.

Madeleine **L'Engle:** Madeleine L'Engle Camp Franklin (1918–2007), U.S. children's writer.

Paul **Leni:** Paul Josef Levi (1885–1929), Ger.-born movie director, working in U.S.

Vladimir Ilyich **Lenin:** Vladimir Ilyich Ulyanov (1870–1924), Russ. revolutionary leader. "What's in a name? Much pseudo-psychological speculation has been focussed on Ulyanov's choice of 'Lenin' as a pseudonym. Was he inspired by the Siberian river Lena? Or was Lena the name of an early girlfriend? Or was it that the Slavonic etymological root of Lenin implies laziness [Russian *len*] and that Vladimir Ulyanov ... wanted to remind himself constantly that effort was needed?" [Robert Service, *Lenin: A Biography*, 2000].

The origin of the first Soviet premier's name remains uncertain. Lenin first used it in 1901 for an article in the revolutionary journal *Iskra* ("Spark"), then published in Munich. The usual explanation is that the name derives from the river Lena, Siberia, where there had been disturbances. Ulyanov had been exiled to Siberia, although not to the Lena but to the village of Shushenskoye, on the Yenisey. So why this particular river? According to one authority, the choice was more or less random: he would have chosen a name based on the Volga, but this was already "bespoke" (as Volgin) by the Marxist Plekhanov (*see* **Simplicissimus**). He thus took the next big river to the east [Louis Fisher, *The Life of Lenin*, 1966].

The mystery of the name's origin is deepened by the one person who should have known its derivation — Lenin's wife, Nadezhda Krupskaya. In 1924, the year of his death, she wrote a reply to the magazine *Komyacheyka*: "Dear Comrades, I don't know why Vladimir Ilyich took the name 'Lenin'; I never asked him about it. His mother was named Mariya Aleksandrovna, his late sister Olga. The events on the Lena happened after he took his pseudonym. He was never in exile on the Lena. The name was probably a random choice" [Dmitriyev, p.44]. Another tentative explanation is that the name came from a girl classmate, Lena, though this seems unlikely, given the meaningful party pseudonyms adopted by most leading activists and revolutionaries of the day.

Other pseudonyms used by Lenin include William Frey, Vladimir Ilyin, K. Ivanov, N. Konstantinov, Jacob Richter (on registering at the British Museum, London), R. Silin, and K. Tulin, as well as various generic translatable names (Observer, Outsider, Reader, etc.) and a string of initialisms, such as B.B., B.G., F.F., I.V., K.O., M.B., M.M., N.N., T.P., and the like.

[Sir] John Edward **Lennard-Jones:** John Edward Jones (1894–1954), Eng. physicist, administrator. In 1925 Jones married Kathleen Mary Lennard, and added his wife's name to his own.

Ann **Lenner:** Ann Green (1912–1997), Br. danceband singer. The singer took her stage name from her parents, Arthur and Florence Green, who performed under the name of Lenner. She and her four sisters, Judy, Rosa, Ivy, and Shirley, sang together as the Lenner Sisters until Ivy married.

Charles **Lennox:** Charles Fitzroy (1672–1723), Eng. aristocrat. The first Duke of Richmond was the illegitimate son of Charles II and Louise de Kéroualle, Duchess of Portsmouth. As such, he was surnamed Fitzroy, "son of the king." He was made Duke of Lennox in the peerage of Scotland at the age of three, and subsequently adopted his title as a surname.

Dan **Leno:** George Wilde Galvin (1860–1904), Eng. music-hall artist. The performer was trained for the stage at an early age by his parents, who were professionally known as Mr. and Mrs. Johnny Wilde. He made his debut when he was only four, appearing as "Little George, the Infant Wonder, Contortionist and Posturer." His father died soon after, and his mother remarried another artist, whose stage name was Leno and real name Grant. Together with his mother and stepfather, George and his brother toured the country as acrobats under the billing "The Great Little Lenos." George's first name subsequently became Dan "owing to a misapprehension on the part of either the printer or deviser of a playbill. The boy's stepfather appreciated the accidental change and saw the value of it, and as Dan Leno the stage name was crystallised" [*Dictionary of National Biography*].

Jean **Lenoir:** Jean Neuberger (1891–1976), Fr. popular composer.

Sidney **Lens:** Sidney Okun (1912–1986), U.S. radical, trade unionist, of Russ. Jewish parentage. Lens adopted his new name in the 1930s after being blacklisted for his labor organizing.

Rula **Lenska:** [Countess] Rozamaria Laura Leopoldyna Lubienska (1947–), Pol.-born Br. TV actress.

Julian **Lenski:** Julian Leszczynski (1889–1937), Pol. revolutionary.

Aleksandr **Lensky:** Aleksandr Pavlovich Vervitsiotti (1847–1908), Russ. actor, theatrical director. The actor probably adopted the name of Pushkin's Lensky, as for Dmitry **Lensky.**

Dmitry **Lensky:** Dmitry Timofeyevich Vorobyov (1805–1860), Russ. writer, actor. The writer adopted the name of Lensky, the young romantic poet in Alexander Pushkin's *Eugene Onegin* (1833).

Lotte **Lenya:** Karoline Wilhelmine Charlotte Blamauer (1898–1981), Austr. stage actress, opera singer, working in U.S. "Lotte" comes from "Charlotte." "Lenya" was inspired by the character Yelena Andreyevna, Professor Serebryakov's young second wife in Chekhov's play *Uncle Vanya* (1896).

[St.] **Leo IX:** Bruno von Egisheim und Dagsburg (1002–1054), Alsatian pope. The pontiff adopted a name that recalled the ancient, pure church, as it was under St. Leo the Great (died 461).

Leo X: Giovanni de' Medici (1475–1521), It. pope, uncle of **Leo XI.**

Leo XI: Alessandro Ottaviano de' Medici (1535–1605), It. pope. The pontiff adopted the name of his uncle, **Leo X.**

Leo XII: Annibale Sermattei della Genga (1760–1829), It. pope. The pontiff came of a family ennobled by **Leo XI** in 1605 and took his papal name in honor of their patron.

Leo XIII: Vincenzo Gioacchino Pecci (1810–1903), It. pope. The pontiff adopted his name in honor of **Leo XII,** whom he had always admired and whose aims and interests he hoped to emulate.

André **Léo:** Léodile Champseix, née Béra (1824–1900), Fr. novelist, journalist. The writer adopted the first names of her two sons as her pseudonym.

Arakel **Leo:** Arakel Grigoryevich Babakhanyan (1860–1932), Armenian historian, writer.

[Dame] Sister Mary **Leo:** Kathleen Agnes Niccol (1896–1989), N.Z. religious, singing teacher.

Leo Africanus: Al-Hasan ibn Muhammad al-Wazzan al-Zaiyati (*c.*1485–*c.*1554), Arab traveler, geographer. In 1519 the intrepid traveler was captured by Venetian pirates and taken first to Naples, then to Rome, where he was presented to pope **Leo X,** who baptized him and named him after himself as Leo Giovanni, combining his papal name and his birth name. This later settled to simply Leo, with Africanus added to distinguish him from any other Leo and to mark his travels through northern Africa. The name overall translates from Latin as "the African lion," as if a title of nobility.

Leolinus Siluriensis *see* Arthur **Machen**

Leon: (1) William Downing Evans (1811–1897), Welsh poet; (2) Leon Preston Robinson IV (1962–), U.S. black movie actor, singer. The poet took his name from his hometown of Caerleon, Monmouthshire (now Newport).

Leonard: Leonard Lewis (1938–), Eng. hairdresser.

Benny **Leonard:** Benjamin Leiner (1896–1947), U.S. lightweight boxer, of East European Jewish parentage. Leiner originally adopted his ring name in a vain attempt to keep his parents from knowing that he was a boxer.

Eddie **Leonard:** Lemuel Gordon Tooney (1875–1941), U.S. vaudeville actor, songwriter.

Hugh **Leonard:** John Keyes Byrne (1926–2009), Ir. playwright. The writer, always known in Ireland as Jack Byrne, was illegitimate, his middle name being that of his adoptive father, Nicholas Keyes. He took his pen name from that of the central character of his unpublished play *The Italian Road* (1954).

Jack E. **Leonard:** Leonard Lebitsky (1911–1973), U.S. nightclub comedian.

Priscilla **Leonard:** Emily Perkins Bissell (1861–1948), U.S. writer. In the midst of her main occupation as a volunteer social worker, Bissell was the author of a number of magazine stories published from 1894 in *Outlook* and *Harper's Bazaar* under her pen name.

Sheldon **Leonard:** Sheldon Leonard Bershad (1907–1997), U.S. movie actor, TV producer.

Leoncillo: Leoncillo Leonardi (1915–1968), It. sculptor, ceramicist.

Tea **Léoni:** Elizabeth Téa Pantaleoni (1966–), U.S. movie, TV actress. Producer Aaron Spelling told the actress to shorten her name, saying it was not a real star's name.

Leónidas: Leónidas da Silva (1913–2004), Brazilian footballer.

Leonid **Leonidov:** Leonid Mironovich Volfenzon (Wolfensohn) (1873–1941), Russ. stage actor, director.

Anna **Leonowens:** Ann Harriett Edwards (1831–1914), Ind.-born U.S. travel writer. The writer took her name from that of her husband, Thomas Leon Owens, whom she married in 1849. As governess in the 1860s to the royal children of King Mongkut of Siam, Anna Leonowens was the subject of Margaret Landon's popular book *Anna and the King of Siam* (1944), on which was based the musical by Richard

Rodgers and Oscar Hammerstein II, *The King and I* (1951). According to her own account, still found in some sources today, Leonowens was born in Wales in 1834 with the original surname Crawford.

Paul **LePaul:** Paul Braden (1900–1958), U.S. magician.

Baby **LeRoy** *see* Baby **LeRoy**

Tina **Leser:** Christine Wetherill Shilland-Smith (1910–1986), U.S. fashion designer.

Phil **Lesh:** Philip Chapman (1940–), U.S. rock musician.

Theo **le Sieg** *see* Dr. **Seuss**

Carole **Lesley:** Maureen Carole Lesley Rippingdale (1935–1974), Br. movie actress. The actress worked under the name of Lesley Carol before settling to the name by which she is best known.

Amy **Leslie:** Lillie West (1855–1939), U.S. stage actress, drama critic. Lillie West first used her new name for a review of Gustave A. Kerker's *Castles in the Air* that she sold to the *Chicago Daily News*.

Frank **Leslie:** Henry Carter (1821–1880), Eng. engraver, publisher, working in U.S. The artist used the name early in his career when he was being trained by his father and uncle in their glove-making business, and he did not wish to incur their wrath by his taste for drawing, sketching, and engraving. He emigrated to New York in 1848 and changed his name legally in 1857 to Frank Leslie, the surname being his father's middle name. After his death, his wife, Miriam Florence Leslie, née Follin (1836–1914), took over his publishing business and herself legally changed her name to Frank Leslie in 1881.

Fred **Leslie:** Frederick Hobson (1855–1892), Eng. musical comedy actor. As an amateur actor early in his stage career Hobson used the name Owen Hobbs. He later wrote burlesques under the transparently fictitious name of A.C. Torr.

Joan **Leslie:** Joan Agnes Theresa Sadie Brodel (1925–), U.S. movie actress. The actress began her career as a child performer under her real name. In 1941 she joined Warner Bros. and changed her name to escape the suggestion of "broad" in her surname, as did Amanda **Barrie** and Dora **Bryan**.

John **Leslie:** John Stott (1965–), Br. TV presenter. The presenter abandoned his original surname when a television executive advised that foreign viewers might have difficulty pronouncing it.

Lew **Leslie:** Lev Lessinsky (1890–1963), U.S. vaudeville artist, theatrical producer. By 1909 Leslie had a double act with his first wife, Belle **Baker** (divorced 1919).

Mrs. Madeline **Leslie:** Harriette Newell Woods Baker (1815–1893), U.S. children's writer. The author also wrote as Aunt Hattie, after her real first name, and as simply H.N.W.B.

Natasha **Leslie:** Nathalie Krassovska (strictly Krasovskaya) (1919–), Russ.–U.S. ballet dancer. The dancer reverted to her Russian name in 1952.

Sharon **Leslie** *see* June **Christy**

Sylvia **Leslie:** Sylvia Ward (1900–?), Eng. stage, movie actress. For her stage name, the actress adopted the first name of her father, the illustrator **Spy.**

L'Espy: François Bedeau (?–1663), Fr. actor, brother of **Jodelet.**

Bruce **Lester:** Bruce Lister (1912–), S.A. movie actor, working in U.S., U.K.

Claude **Lester:** Claude Forrester (1893–1955), Eng. comedian.

John **Lester** *see* Lester **Wallack**

Ketty **Lester:** Revoyda Frierson (1934–), U.S. popular singer, movie actress.

Mark **Lester:** Mark Letzer (1958–), Br. movie actor.

David **L'Estrange** *see* Ivor **Novello**

Daniel **Lesueur:** Jeanne Lapauze, née Loiseau (1860–1920), Fr. writer.

Marian **Le Sueur:** Marian Lucy (1877–1954), U.S. radical politician.

Ada Miller **Leswy:** Corín Tellado (1927–2009), Sp. writer of romantic fiction. Tellado used this name for a series of erotic novels. Her full original name was María del Socorro Tellado López, with Corín a diminutive form of Soccorín, as she was called at home. (María del Socorro means "Mary of Aid," an epithet of the Virgin Mary.)

Letine: George Gorin (1853–1880), Eng. music-hall artist, trick cyclist.

Tirsi **Leucasio:** Giovan Battista Felice Zappi (1667–1719), It. poet. The poet was one of the founders of the Academy of Arcadia and this was his Arcadian name as the husband of Aglauro **Cidonia.**

Aleksandr **Levada:** Aleksandr Stepanovich Kosyak (1909–?), Ukr. writer.

Larry **Levan:** Lawrence Philpot (1954–1992), U.S. black DJ.

Daniel **Levans:** Daniel Levins (1953–), U.S. ballet dancer.

Michael **Le Vell:** Michael Turner (1964–), Br. TV actor. To avoid confusion with another actor of the same name, Turner took his mother's maiden name, Levell, and split it into two.

Benny **Leven** *see* Issy **Bonn**

Phoebus Aaron Theodor **Levene:** Fishel Aaronovich Levin (1869–1940), Russ.-born U.S. biochemist. Levin adopted his new name after immigrating to New York in 1891 as a result of rising anti–Semitism.

Sam **Levene:** Samuel Levin (1905–1980), Russ.-born U.S. stage, movie actor.

Ethel **Levey:** Ethelia Fowler (1881–1955), U.S. stage actress, singer, dancer.

Richard Michael **Levey:** Richard Michael O'Shaughnessy (1811–1899), Ir. composer.

Éliphas **Lévi:** Alphonse Louis Constant (1810–1875), Fr. magician, mystic. The occultist's assumed name represents a hebraicized form of his original first two names.

Ijahman **Levi:** Trevor Sutherland (1946–), Jamaican-born Br. reggae musician. Sutherland adopted his Rastafarian religious name in 1972.

Robert **Le Vigan:** Robert Coquillaud (1900–1972), Fr. movie actor.

Ivan **Levitsky:** Ivan Nechuy-Levitsky (1838–1918), Ukr. novelist.

Vasil **Levski:** Vasil Ivanov Kunchev (1837–1873), Bulg. revolutionary. The patriot was nicknamed Levski ("Lion-like") for his leading role in the struggle to free Bulgaria from Ottoman rule. The lion is the official symbol of Bulgaria, and the country's standard monetary unit is the *lev* ("lion").

Al **Lewis:** Albert Meister (1923–2006), U.S. radio, TV, movie actor, of Pol.-Ger. Jewish origin.

Alun **Lewis:** Alun Bennett (*c.*1947–), Welsh-born Br. TV actor. The actor took his mother's maiden name as his professional name.

Caroline **Lewis:** Harold Begbie (1871–1929), Eng. writer + M.H. Temple (*fl.*1902), Eng. writer + J. Stafford Ransome (1860–1931), Eng. illustrator. The three men used this collective name for two political parodies, *Clara in Blunderland* (1902) and *Lost in Blunderland* (1903), written in the style of Lewis **Carroll**'s *Alice in Wonderland.* The skits were directed against prime minister A.J. Balfour and his government's failure to resolve the Boer War. Begbie also wrote as A **Gentleman with a Duster.**

David **Lewis:** (1) David Levy (1823–1885), Br. department store owner, of Jewish parentage; (2) David Levy (1903–1987), U.S. stage actor, movie producer, of Jewish parentage. Lewis has long been a stock English-speaking substitute for Levy and similar Jewish names.

Gary **Lewis:** Gary Levitch (1946–), U.S. pop musician, son of Jerry **Lewis.**

George **Lewis:** George Joseph François Louis Zeno (1900–1968), U.S. jazz clarinetist. The musician's new surname was the English form of Louis, his father's middle name and his own fourth name. The family name was originally Zenon.

Huey **Lewis:** Hugh Cregg III (1950–), U.S. rock musician.

James **Lewis:** James Lewis Deming (*c.*1837–1896), U.S. comic actor.

Jerry **Lewis:** Jerome Levitch (1926–), U.S. movie comedian, teaming with Dean **Martin.** Lewis used the same surname as the one adopted by his parents, who were also in show business. "How could anyone called Levitch get laughs?" he asked.

Joe E. **Lewis:** Joseph Kleevan (1910–1971), U.S. nightclub comedian.

Mel **Lewis:** Melvin Sokoloff (1929–1990), U.S. jazz drummer. The musician adopted his brother's first name as his new surname.

Oscar **Lewis:** Oscar Lefkowitz (1914–1970), U.S. anthropologist, of Belorussian Jewish parentage. Lewis legally changed his name in 1940.

Paul **Lewis** *see* Samuel **Edwards**

Richard **Lewis:** Thomas Thomas (1914–1990), Br. opera singer, of Welsh parentage.

Shari **Lewis:** Shari Hurwitz (1934–1998), U.S. TV ventriloquist (with glove puppet "Lamb Chop").

Smiley **Lewis:** Overton Amos Lemons (1913–1966), U.S. black blues musician. Lemons began recording for Deluxe Records, New Orleans, in 1947 under the name Smiling Lewis. "If anyone called Overton Amos Lemons by his real name, he became very unsmiley" [Russell and Smith, p.391].

Strangler **Lewis:** Robert H. Friedricks (1891–1966), U.S. professional wrestler. Friedricks originally changed his name to Ed Lewis to hide his occupation from his parents, who disapproved of wrestling. He later added "Strangler" in honor of a former famous wrestler, Evan "Strangler" Lewis. His powerful headlock made this adopted nickname more than appropriate.

Ted **Lewis:** Theodore Leopold Friedman (1890–1971), U.S. bandleader, entertainer, movie actor.

Ted "Kid" **Lewis:** Gershon Mendeloff (1894–1970), Br. boxer.

Val **Lewton:** Vladimir Ivan Leventon (1904–1951), Russ.-born U.S. horror movie director, novelist.

Ben **Lexcen:** Robert Miller (1936–1988), Austral. yachtsman, marine architect.

Edward **Lexy:** Edward Gerald Little (1897–1970), Eng. stage, movie actor.

Pío **Leyva:** Wilfredo Pacual (1917–2006), Cuban singer.

Lezz: Leslie Alfred Barton (1923–), Eng. cartoonist. An occasional name used by the artist as a phonetic representation of the pet form (Les) of his first name.

Josef **Lhévinne:** Iosif Arkadyevich Levin (1874–1944), Russ.-born U.S. pianist

Jet **Li:** Li Lianjie (1963–), Chin. movie actor, working in U.S.

Liala: Amalia Liana Cambiasi Negretti (1897–1995), It. writer of sentimental novels. The writer's adopted name presumably arose as a pet form of her first name(s).

Liaqat Ali Salaam *see* Kenny **Clarke**

Liberace: Wladziu Valentino Liberace (1919–1987), U.S. popular pianist, movie actor, entertainer, of It.-Pol. parentage. "Call me Lee," the "Casanova of the Keyboard" would say. And somehow his real surname, which he used as his professional name, perfectly suited him, with its suggestion of "libertine." He originally dubbed himself Walter Busterkeys when playing as a minor attraction in Las Vegas in the 1930s. But he soon reverted to his real name, which became well known with his TV appearances. "Perhaps to lend himself an air of ruggedness with which nature had not chosen to endow him, he adopted the stage name 'Walter Busterkeys' when he embarked on his early career in a dance band, but swiftly changed hats, calling himself simply 'Liberace'" [*Daily Telegraph*, February 5, 1987, quoted in Massingberd 1997].

David **Lichine:** David Liechtenstein (1910–1972), Russ.-born U.S. ballet dancer, choreographer. Lichine's father, Michael Liechtenstein, was a composer professionally known as Mikhail Olshansky.

C.H. **Liddell** *see* C.L. **Moore**

Lidiya **Lidina:** Lidiya Stepanovna Koshkina (1900–1976), Russ. circus performer, trapeze artist.

Serge **Lido:** Serge Lidov (1906–1984), Russ. ballet photographer, working in France. Lido, whose name was shortened by the editor of *Vogue* magazine, married the Russian émigré dance writer and presenter Irène Lidova, née Irina Kaminskaya (1907–2002).

Lieutenant Stitchie: Cleveland Laing (*c.*1960–), Jamaican reggae singer. The musician was originally nicknamed Citchie for his love of citrus fruit. This was subsequently misspelled "Stitchie" on a record label, and he kept the name.

Caterina **Ligendza:** Kattarina Beyron (1937–), Swe. opera singer.

Hunter **Liggett** *see* Mark **Carrel**

Winnie **Lightner:** Winifred Josephine Reeves (1899–1971), U.S. vaudeville comedienne.

Lightnin' Slim: Otis Hicks (1913–1974), U.S. black guitarist, blues singer. The musician was given his performing name by producer Jay Miller, who first recorded him in 1954.

Leonid **Likhodeyev:** Leonid Izraylovich Lides (1921–), Russ. writer. The writer, presumably intentionally, adopted a name suggesting both Russian *likhodey*, "evildoer," and his original name.

Rosa **Liksom:** ? (1958–), Finn. writer. The writer's real name is uncertain, but her pseudonym represents Swedish *rosa*, "rose," and *liksom*, "like." She is thus "roselike," perhaps in a way relating to her original name.

Lil Bow Wow: Shad Moss (1987–), U.S. black

rapper. Moss made his debut at the age of six with a guest appearance on an album by **Snoop Dogg**, and it was he who gave the youngster his name.

Li'l Brian: Brian Terry (1972–), U.S. black blues musician.

Nikolai **Liliev:** Nikolai Popivanov (1885–1961), Bulg. lyric poet. The poet based his new surname on Bulgarian *liliya*, "lily."

Mariya **Lilina:** Mariya Petrovna Perevoshchikova (1866–1943), Russ. actress. The actress was the wife of the actor and theatrical director Konstantin **Stanislavsky**.

Li'l Kim: Kimberly Denise Jones (1975–), U.S. black rapper. The self-proclaimed "Queen Bee of hip-hop" adopted a name that described her small stature.

Beatrice **Lillie:** Constance Sylvia Munston (1894–1989), Can.-born Br. revue artist. Some sources give the performer this birth name, but in all probability she was really born Beatrice Gladys Lillie.

Lily Elsie: Lily Elsie Cotton (1886–1962), Br. musical comedy actress, singer

Limahl: Christopher Hamill (1958–), Eng. pop singer. An anagrammatic adaptation for the lead singer of the group Kajagoogoo, which split up in 1986.

Luke **Limner:** John Leighton (1822–1912), Sc. satirist, artist, writer on art. The writer used this name for *London Cries and Public Edifices* (1847), *Suggestions in Design* (1852), and other works. A limner is a portrait painter.

Frank **Lin:** Gertrude Franklin Atherton, née Horn (1857–1948), U.S. novelist.

Nora **Lin:** Dora Alonso (1910–), Cuban writer.

Abbey **Lincoln:** Anna Marie Wooldridge (1930–), U.S. black movie actress, singer. The singer originally performed in nightclubs under her real name, Anna Marie. She then sang as Gaby Lee before changing her name in 1956 at the suggestion of promotion people to Abbey Lincoln, in tribute to Abraham Lincoln. In the 1970s she traveled and performed in Africa, where she took the name Aminata Moseka, in allusion to her roots. (The two names were conferred on her by leaders in Guinea and Zaïre respectively.) She then faded from the professional scene until the 1990s, when her career revived.

Andrew **Lincoln:** Andrew Clutterbuck (1973–), Eng. TV actor.

Charley **Lincoln:** Charles Hicks (1900–1963), U.S. black blues musician, brother of **Barbecue Bob**.

Elmo **Lincoln:** Otto Elmo Linkenhelter (1889–1952), U.S. movie actor.

Trebitsch **Lincoln:** Ignatz Timotheus Trebitsch (1879–?1943), Hung.-born Ger. spy, working in U.K. The agent for German intelligence added "Lincoln" to his name when in England in 1905 and changed his first two names to Ignatius Timothy. His death was reported by Japanese radio in 1943 but he was said to be "alive and kicking" several years later.

A **Lincolnshire Grazier:** [Rev.] Thomas Hartwell Horne (1780–1862), Eng. biblical scholar, bibliographer. Horne adopted this name as a penurious legal clerk for a work of the same title compiled in 1805, but with the publisher taking half of his earnings. "The circumstances under which this pseudonym was employed, if they were not rather distressing, would be highly amusing" [Hamst, p.10].

Jakov **Lind:** Heinz Landwirth (1927–2007), Austr. writer, artist. The future writer was abandoned as a boy in his native Vienna when his parents went to Palestine. He joined a children's transport to the Netherlands, where he escaped detection as a Jew, then found work on a German river freighter, where he took the Dutch name Jan Overbeek. After World War II he changed his name again to Jakov Chaklan, then made his way to Palestine, where he rejoined his parents using the second name Lind.

Edward **Lindall:** Edward Ernest Smith (1915–1978), Austral. writer.

Harrie Thomas **Lindeberg:** Harry Thomas Lindberg (1879–1959), U.S. architect, of Swe. parentage. The architect made minor but distinctive artistic adjustments to his original first and last names.

Kelvin **Lindemann:** Alexis Hareng (1911–), Dan. writer.

Anya **Linden:** Anya Sainsbury, née Eltenton (1933–), Eng. ballet dancer.

Hal **Linden:** Harold Lipshitz (1931–), U.S. stage actor, singer.

Max **Linder:** Gabriel-Maximilien Leuvielle (1883–1925), Fr. movie comedian, working in U.S. Linder was originally a stage actor under his real name, and adopted his screen name when entering the movies with Pathé. A new name was desirable as the theatrical world then despised the new medium. Jack Spears, in *Hollywood: The Golden Era* (1971), suggests that the name may have been based on those of two friends and fellow actors, Max **Dearly** and Marcelle Lender, the latter famously portrayed by Toulouse-Lautrec (*Marcelle Lender en buste*, 1895).

Viveca **Lindfors:** Elsa Viveca Torstendotter (1920–1995), Swe. movie actress, working in U.S.

Berit **Lindholm:** Berit Maria Jonsson (1934–), Swe. opera singer.

Megan **Lindholm** *see* Robin **Hobb**

Harry **Lindsay:** Harry Lindsay Hudson (1858–1926), Eng. writer, journalist.

Howard **Lindsay:** Herman Nelke (1889–1968), U.S. playwright, stage actor. The actor adopted his grandmother's name as his stage name.

Margaret **Lindsay:** Margaret Kies (1910–1981), U.S. movie actress.

Mayne **Lindsay:** [Mrs.] Clarke (*fl*.1910s), Eng. novelist. There is doubt concerning the gender and nationality of this writer, whom many sources refer to as "he" and who may have actually been Australian.

Robert **Lindsay:** Robert Lindsay Stevenson (1949–), Eng. stage, movie actor.

Vachel **Lindsay:** Nicholas Vachel Lindsay 1879–1931), U.S. poet. Lindsay regularly used his first name for his poetry until 1915, when his publisher, Macmillan, suggested he drop it.

Vera **Lindsay:** Vera Poliakoff (1911–), Russ.-born Br. stage actress.

David **Line:** Lionel Davidson (1922–2009), Br. crime novelist, children's writer. The author reserved his pseudonym, formed by a rough reversal of his original names, for his children's stories.

Hip **Linkchain:** Willie Richard (1936–1989), U.S. blues musician. Richard adopted his father's stage name, itself referring to one of his tools as a logger. "Hip" is a shortening of "Hipstick," a childhood nickname, based on "dipstick," a slang term for a foolish person.

Bambi **Linn:** Bambi Linnemeier (1926–), U.S. stage actress, dancer.

Carolus **Linnaeus:** Carl Nilsson Ingemarsson (1707–1778), Swe. botanist. The name Linnaeus was adopted by the botanist's father, taking it from Swedish *lind,* "lime tree." The allusion was to an ancient tree, said to have magic properties, on the family estate. The name became official, for in 1761 the botanist was granted a patent of nobility, antedated to 1757. He then became known as Carl von Linné.

Johannes **Linnankoski:** Johannes Vihtori Peltonen (1869–1913), Finn. novelist, journalist. The writer adopted a local placename, itself meaning "castle falls."

Lin Yutang: Lin Ho-lok (1895–1976), Chin. novelist, linguist, working in U.S. At age 17 the writer changed his given name, meaning "peaceful and happy," to Yutang, meaning "elegant language."

Lios: Luisa, Countess Erdoedy, née Drasche-Wartingerg (1853–?), Austr. pianist, composer.

Lisa Lisa: Lisa Velez (1967–), U.S. rock singer. The Cult Jam singer patterned her performing name on Full Force's U.T.F.O. hit "Roxanne, Roxanne" (1985).

Lisa Marie: Lisa Marie Smith (*c*.1957–), U.S. model, movie actress.

Iakinte **Lisashvili:** Iakinte Barnabovich Khomeriki (1897–1972), Georgian writer.

Virna **Lisi:** Virna Lisa Pieralisi (1937–), It. movie actress.

Il **Lissandrino:** Alessandro Magnasco (1667–1749), It. painter. The name by which the artist came to be known is a colloquial diminutive form of his first name.

El **Lissitzky:** Lazar Markovich Lisitsky (1890–1941), Russ. painter, designer, architect. "El" is a shortening of Eliezar, the Hebrew equivalent of the artist's first name by which he was known.

Emanuel **List:** Emanuel Fleissig (1890–1967), Austr.-born U.S. opera singer.

Lance **Lister:** Solomon Lancelot Inglis Watson (1901–), Br. stage actor.

Wanda **Liszt:** Sven Omann (1950–), Dan. theater manager. The gay activist adopted his new name, perhaps punning on "wanderlust," in 1976.

Little ... for names beginning thus followed by first name and last name, as typically for blues musicians, see the last name, e.g. for Little Freddie King *see* **King**

Frances **Little:** Fannie Macaulay, née Caldwell (1863–1941), U.S. novelist.

Syd **Little:** Cyril John Mead (1942–), Eng. TV comedian, teaming with Eddie **Large** (as "Little and Large"). The pair have descriptive names: Eddie Large is plump and taller than Syd Little, who is thin and bespectacled.

Thomas **Little:** Thomas Moore (1779–1852), Ir. poet, satirist. The author used this name, denoting his small stature, for *The Poetical Works of the Late Thomas Little,* titled in some editions *Juvenile Poems* (1801). (A "Preface by the Editor" notes that "Mr. Little died in his one-and-twentieth year" and adds: "Where Mr. Little was born, or what is the genealogy of his parents, are points in which very few readers can be interested.") Byron referred to Moore by the name in *English Bards and Scotch Reviewers* (1809): "Who in soft guise, surrounded by a choir / Of virgins melting, not to Vesta's fire, / With sparkling eyes, and cheek by passion flush'd, / Strikes his wild lyre, whilst listening dames are hush'd? / 'Tis Little! young Catullus of his day, / As sweet, but as immoral, in his lay!" Moore's best-known pen name was Thomas **Brown, the Younger**.

Little Anthony: Anthony Gourdine (1941–), U.S. pop singer.

Little Boots: Victoria Hesketh (1984–), Eng. "electropop" singer. "Why does this artist ... call herself Little Boots? 'I wanted a name for this project because I see it as this whole world. And my [real] name's crap and not catchy. And I didn't want it to sound like a singer-songwriter thing. So a friend and I went through all my old nicknames. They were all size-related — Titch, Shortarse....' Then 5ft Hesketh's friend happened to watch the film *Caligula* [about the Roman emperor **Caligula**] — a name which translates as 'little boots.' 'That seemed appropriate 'cause

I'm little, it's interesting and I was wearing boots a lot. Not because I'm a mad sex-crazed dictator'" [*The Times Magazine*, May 30, 2009].

Little Egypt: Farida Mazar Spyropoulos (1873–1916), U.S. dancer, of Syrian parentage. The dancer, famous for the hootchy-cootchy, adopted a stage name that suggested an oriental origin.

Little Emmie: Emma Coates, formerly Rivers (1896–1994), Br. singer, dancer. The dancer's original name was that of the children's ballet producer Madame Pauline Rivers, who gave her her stage name and eventually adopted her. Coates was her married name.

Little Eva: Eva Narcissus Boyd (1943–2003), U.S. black pop singer. The singer was so nicknamed for her diminutive size, with an additional literary reference to Little Eva St. Clair, the saintly child in Harriet Beecher Stowe's novel *Uncle Tom's Cabin* (1852).

Little Hatch: Provine Hatch, Jr. (1921–), U.S. black blues harmonica player.

Little Joe Blue: Joseph Valery (1934–1990), U.S. black blues musician.

Little John: John McMorris (*c*.1970–), Jamaican reggae musician.

Bel **Littlejohn** *see* Craig **Brown**

Johnny **Littlejohn:** John Funches (1931–1994), U.S. black blues musician.

Little Milton: Milton James Campbell, Jr. (1934–2005), U.S. black blues musician.

Little Miss Cornshucks: Mildred Cummings (1923–1999), U.S. R&B singer. The singer's name tied in with the "country bumpkin" dress and straw hat she wore on stage.

Cornelius **Littlepage:** James Fenimore Cooper (1789–1851), U.S. novelist. The writer used this name for the *Littlepage Manuscripts*, three novels attacking the Anti-Rent War, *Satanstoe* (1845), *The Chainbearer* (1845), and *The Redskins* (1846), in which the central characters are respectively Corny Littlepage, his son, Mordaunt, and Mordaunt's grandson, Hugh.

Little Richard: Richard Wayne Penniman (1932–), U.S. black rock musician. Penniman was "little" when he began singing at age 14.

Little Roy: Earl Lowe (*c*.1950–), Jamaican reggae musician.

Little Sonny: (1) Johnny Jones (1931–1989), U.S. black blues singer; (2) Aaron Willis (1932–), U.S. black blues musician.

Little Tich: Harry Relph (1868–1928), Br. music-hall comedian. The dwarfish entertainer was nicknamed Little Tich as a child because he resembled the portly so-called "Tichborne claimant," one Arthur Orton, who in 1866 claimed to be Roger **Tichborne**, the heir to an English baronetcy, who

had been lost at sea. There is a further nuance to the name: "Harry Relph adopted this stage name because he was a claimant to theatrical fame, just as Arthur Orton was a claimant to the Tichborne estates and title" [Eric Partridge, *Here, There and Everywhere*, 1950]. In assuming the name Little Tich, Relph bequeathed the words "titch" and "titchy" to the English language (in mainly British use), as applied to a small thing or person.

Mark **Littleton:** John Pendleton Kennedy (1795–1870), U.S. politician, educationist, author. The writer used this pseudonym for historical novels, such as *Swallow Barn* (1832), a series of Virginia sketches.

Little Walter: Marion Walter Jacobs (1930–1968), U.S. black blues harmonica player.

Little Willie John: William John Woods (1937–1968), U.S. soul singer.

Marie **Litton:** Marie Lowe (1847–1884), Eng. actress.

Félia **Litvinne:** Felya Vasilyevna Litvinova, née Françoise-Jeanne Schütz (1861–1936), Russ.-born Fr. opera singer, teacher. The soprano was taken to France as a child.

Maksim Maksimovich **Litvinov:** Meir (or Max) Wallach (1876–1951), Russ. revolutionary, diplomat, of Pol. Jewish parentage. The Soviet politician used the name Litvinov as one of several party cover names. Others were Papasha ("Daddy"), Maximovich, and Felix.

Livs **Liv:** Egon Gutmanis (1924–), Latvian writer. The writer's adopted name means "Livonian," referring to the historic Finno-Ugric people who settled where Latvia is today.

Jay **Livingston:** Jacob Harold Levison (1915–2001), U.S. composer.

Jerry **Livingston:** Jerome Levinson (1909–1987), U.S. movie music composer, songwriter.

Robert **Livingston:** Robert E. Randall (1906–1988), U.S. movie actor.

Belle **Livingstone:** Isabelle Graham (?1875–1957), U.S. showgirl, adventuress. Livingstone was a foundling, and her original name was given her by a couple named Graham. Her stage name, which she took to avoid embarrassing her adoptive parents, was inspired by the explorer David Livingstone.

Dandy **Livingstone:** Robert Livingstone Thompson (1944–), Jamaican reggae musician.

Mary **Livingstone:** Sadya Marks (1908–1983), U.S. radio, TV comedienne, teaming with Jack **Benny**, her husband. Sadya (later Sadie) Marks came by her professional name in 1933, when she stood in for an actress who was due to mimick the voice of a 17-year-old girl named Mary Livingstone in a skit on one of Benny's radio programs but who did not show up.

Emma **Livry:** Emma-Marie Emarot (1842–1863), Fr. ballet dancer.

Michael **Lland:** Holland Stoudenmire (1924–1989), U.S. dancer, ballet master.

L.L. Cool J.: James Todd Smith (1968–), U.S. black rapper. The singer explains that his name should be understood to mean "Ladies Love Cool James."

Richard **Llewellyn:** Richard Dafydd Vivian Llewellyn Lloyd (1906–1983), Eng. novelist, dramatist, of Welsh descent. The genuine Welsh pedigree of the author of the bestselling *How Green Was My Valley* (1939) is disputed, and some sources give his original name as Richard Herbert Vivian Lloyd.

Michael Gareth **Llewelyn:** Frederic Evans (1888–1958), Welsh novelist, son of **Cadrawd**.

Llewelyn Ddu o Fôn: Lewis Morris (1701–1765), Welsh scholar, poet. The writer's name means "Black Llewelyn of Anglesey," referring to the island where he was born.

Llew Llwyfo: Lewis William Lewis (1831–1901), Welsh poet, novelist, journalist. The writer took his name from the Welsh equivalent of his first name and the name of his birthplace, Llanwenllwyfo, Anglesey.

Llew Tegid: Lewis Davies Jones (1851–1928), Welsh conductor. The musician was born near Bala, a town on Lake Bala, which is known in Welsh as Llyn Tegid. This gave his name, with his new first name a Welsh equivalent of "Lewis."

Llig: Jack Gill (1930–), Br. crossword compiler. The pseudonym reverses the setter's surname.

Llinos: Maria Jane Williams (1795–1873), Welsh singer, folksong collector. The singer's name is Welsh for "linnet."

Charles **Lloyd:** [Sir] Charles Lloyd Birkin (1907–), Eng. horror-story writer.

Emily **Lloyd:** Emily Lloyd Pack (1971–), Eng. movie actress, working in U.S.

Frank **Lloyd:** Franz Kurt Levai (1911–1998), Austr.-born international art dealer. At the time of the *Anschluss* in Austria, the art collector and dealer, like many other prosperous Jews, left for Paris, France. He was interned on the German invasion of France in World War II, but soon escaped to London, where he enlisted in the British Army, anglicizing his name to Francis Kenneth Lloyd.

Lucy Vaughan **Lloyd:** John Keats (1795–1821), Eng. poet. An unexpected name used by the poet for an unfinished poem, *The Cap and Bells* (1820). The adoption of a pseudonym by Keats when he was already well established suggests that he intended the poem to be somehow directed against the Lake Poets. It has been pointed out that Lucy suggests Wordsworth ("Lucy" was the subject of a number of Wordsworth's poems), while Charles Lloyd (1775–1839) was a poet and neighbor of Wordsworth. Keats's poem written under the pseudonym was first published posthumously only in 1848 [Robert Gittings, *John Keats*, 1968].

Manda **Lloyd:** Mary Jane Mander (1877–1949), N.Z. novelist.

Marie **Lloyd:** Matilda Alice Victoria Wood (1870–1922), Eng. music-hall artist. The performer first used the name Bella Delmere when she began her stage career at the age of 14. This name probably evolved from that of the Fairy Bell Minstrels, a troupe of little girl singers and actresses that she formed when herself only a young child. Six weeks later, she adopted the name Marie Lloyd, taking this from the journal *Lloyds Weekly News*.

"It was while she was appearing at Sebright's [Music Hall] that the music-hall agent ... George Ware first saw her and decided to take her on. At the time her stage name was Bella Delmeyer — or variations of it — which sounded cosmopolitan to a girl who had never left Hoxton. However, George said Bella was not memorable enough and had to go. They found a suitable replacement simply by looking around them: 'Lloyd' appeared everywhere ... to advertise a range of products including a popular newspaper. She opted for 'Marie,' simply because she liked it and pronounced it *Mar*-ee as in 'starry'" [Midge Gillies, *Marie Lloyd: The One and Only*, 1999].

Llucen: [Rev.] John Cullen (1836–1912), Eng. cleric, writer, traveler. An obvious anagram.

Llwyd o'r Bryn: Robert Lloyd (1888–1961), Welsh bardic adjudicator. The writer and orator's name means "Lloyd of the hill."

Llyfrbryf: Isaac Foulkes (1836–1904), Welsh publisher, writer. The writer's adopted name means "bookworm."

Llysor: William Richard Philip George (1912–2006), Welsh lawyer, poet. The poet served as Archdruid of Wales from 1990 to 1993, taking as his bardic name an old Welsh word meaning "lawyer."

L.N.R.: Ellen Henrietta Ranyard, née White (1810–1879), Eng. religious writer. A combination of the writer's first name (pronounced as letters) and the initial of her married surname. The founder of the Female Bible Mission adopted it for *The Book and its Story, a Narrative for the Young, on occasion of the Jubilee of the British and Foreign Bible Society. By L.N.R., with an Introductory Preface by the Rev. Thomas Phillips, Jubilee Secretary* (1852).

Kenneth **Lo:** Hsiao Chien Lo (1913–1995), Chin.-born Br. chef, restaurateur. Lo acquired his new first name on his first visit to England in 1919. The doctor treating him and his two brothers for flu was unable to spell or pronounce their names and for simplicity's sake decided to label their medicines

Charles, Kenneth, and Walter. "Kenneth" was thus created from "Chien" [*The Times*, August 14, 1995].

Mrs. Olinthus Lobb: Louisa Sarah Ann Parr, née Taylor (?1848–1903), Eng. novelist. The writer first used the name for a story, "How It All Happened," published in the evangelical magazine *Good Words* in 1868.

Lobo: Kent Lavoie (1943–), U.S. pop guitar player, singer, of Fr.-Native American descent. The singer took the name, Spanish for "wolf," when he first recorded "Me and You and a Dog Named Boo," reasoning that he could hide behind his anonymity if he failed to make the charts. The record was in fact a smash hit on both sides of the Atlantic in 1971. Thereafter he kept the name.

Josef Locke: Joseph McLaughlin (1917–1999), Ir. popular singer, movie actor. The singer is said to have been renamed by bandleader-turned-theatrical producer Jack **Hylton**, who found his charge's original name too long to be squeezed onto a bill at the Victoria Palace, London. "Locke" represents the accented syllable of the singer's surname.

Frederick Locker-Lampson: Frederick Locker (1821–1895), Eng. poet. The writer added the surname of his second wife to his own in 1885.

Calvin Lockhart: Bert Cooper (1934–2007), West Indian-born U.S. stage, movie actor.

Malcolm Lockheed: Malcolm Loughead (1887–1958), U.S. aircraft executive. Brothers Malcolm and Allan Haines Loughead (1889–1969) jointly founded the Loughead Aircraft Manufacturing Company in 1916, after which Malcolm vanished from public life. Allan then cofounded the Lockheed Aircraft Company in 1926, the new spelling of his Scottish name reflecting its proper pronunciation. (People persisted in saying "Log-head" or "Loaf-head"). He legally changed it in 1934.

Fred Locks: Stafford Elliot (*c.*1955–), Jamaican reggae musician. Elliot adopted the nickname given him for his unusually long Rastafarian dreadlocks.

Gary Lockwood: John Gary Yusolfsky (1937–), U.S. movie, TV actor.

Margaret Lockwood: Margaret Mary Lockwood (1916–1990), Eng. movie, TV actress. The actress's original name is given in many sources as Margaret Day. But this relates to her temporary stage name, Margie Day, that she based on a family name on quitting school at age 14.

Locum: Geoff Adams (1943–), Br. crossword compiler. The pseudonym arose when the setter stood in for **Doc** after the latter was taken ill.

Loda: Geoffrey Loder (1947–), Br. crossword compiler. A straightforward pseudonym.

John Loder: John Muir Lowe (1898–1988), Br. movie actor.

Vernon Loder *see* John **Haslette**

Charles Martin Loeffler-Tornow: Charles Martin Loeffler (1861–1935), Ger.-born U.S. composer. The musician used this name for his earliest works, adding the pseudonym Tornow adopted by his father, Dr. Karl Löffler, an agricultural chemist and writer. He emigrated to the U.S. in 1881 and became an American citizen in 1887.

Cissie Loftus: Marie Cecilia Loftus Brown (1876–1943), Sc. stage, movie actress, working in U.S.

Séan Dublin Bay Rockall Loftus: Séan Loftus (1927–), Ir. politician, environmentalist. The politician legally changed his name in the 1980s to boost his campaign against the proposed building of an oil refinery in Dublin Bay, off the east coast of Ireland, and his support for Irish ownership of the Atlantic island of Rockall, northwest of Ireland, which stands on the site of potential oil and gas reserves.

Abel Log *see* F. **Abell**

Ella Logan: Georgina Armour Allan (1913–1969), Sc.-born U.S. singer, movie actress. The entertainer was briefly known as Daisy Mars before adopting her regular performing name in her late teens. She was based in Hollywood from 1935.

Jake Logan *see* (1) G.C. **Edmondson**; (2) Martin Cruz **Smith**

Jimmy Logan: James Short (1928–2001), Sc. stage, TV actor, comedian. The entertainer and his four siblings performed as children as the Logan Family, a better name than the "Short Family." His name was a tribute to Ella **Logan**. One of Logan's sisters was the jazz singer Annie **Ross**.

Mark Logan *see* Andrew **York**

Logodaedalus: Donald George Putnam (1930–), Br. crossword compiler. The setter took as an appropriate pseudonym a learned term for a person skilled in the manipulation of words.

Log-roller: Richard Thomas Le Gallienne (1866–1947), Eng. journalist, poet, novelist. The writer used this name for his book reviews in the *Star* from 1891, when "log-rolling" already existed as a colloquialism for "mutual puffing in literary publications" [*Oxford English Dictionary*], on the basis of "You roll my log and I'll roll yours."

Jermain Walter Loguen: Jarm Logue (*c.*1813–1872), U.S. black clergyman, abolitionist. The future bishop of the African Methodist Episcopal Zion Church added an "n" to his name to distinguish it from that of his white slavemaster father, David Logue.

François L'Olonnais: Jean David Nau (1630–1668), Fr. buccaneer. Nau was born at Les Sables d'Olonne, a port on the coast of western France. Hence his name, "François from Olonne," his new first name denoting his nationality.

Herbert **Lom:** Herbert Charles Angelo Kuchačevič ze Schluderpacheru (1917–), Cz. stage, movie actor, working in U.K.

Carole **Lombard:** Jane Alice Peters (1908–1942), U.S. movie comedienne. According to one account, the actress took her name from the Carroll, Lombardi Pharmacy on Lexington Avenue and East 65th Street, New York. According to another, "Lombard" was the name of a friend of her mother. She originally spelled her first name "Carol," but an "e" was mistakenly added to this in a billing for the movie *Fast and Loose* (1930) and she kept it.

Louise **Lombard:** Louise Maria Perkins (1970–), Eng. TV actress.

Nap **Lombard:** Pamela Hansford Johnson (1912–1981), Eng. novelist. Johnson used this name for two novels of the early 1940s, written in collaboration with her first husband, Neil Stewart.

Peter **Lombard:** [Rev.] William Benham (1831–1910), Eng. cleric, religious writer. The writer used this name for his contributions to the *Church Times*. The name itself came from the address of his London parish, St. Edmund the King with St. Nicholas Acons, Lombard Street.

George **London:** George Burnstein (1919–1985), Can. opera singer, of Russ.–U.S. Jewish parentage. The singer made his debut under the name George Burnson in Albert Coates's *Gainsborough's Duchess* at the Hollywood Bowl, Los Angeles, in 1941. He then continued his career under his distinctive name.

Jack **London:** John Griffith Chaney (1876–1916), U.S. novelist, short-story writer. London was the illegitimate son of William Henry Chaney, an itinerant astrologer, and Flora Wellman. Nine months after his birth, Wellman married Civil War veteran John London and changed her son's surname from "Chaney" to "London."

Jean "Babe" **London:** Jean Glover (1901–1980), U.S. movie comedienne.

Julie **London:** Julie Webb, later Troup, née Peck (1926–2000), U.S. movie actress, singer.

Lonesome Sundown: Cornelius Green (1938–1995), U.S. black blues musician.

Professor **Longhair** *see* **Professor Longhair**

Pietro **Longhi:** Pietro Falca (1702–1785), It. painter. The artist apparently adopted the name of the well-known family of Italian architects, Longhi (or Lunghi).

Long Lance: Sylvester Clark Long (1890–1932), U.S. writer, actor, impostor. Of mixed racial background, Long enlisted in the Canadian Expeditionary Force in World War I and after the war assumed the persona of an Oklahoma Cherokee named Long Lance. He worked as a reporter for the Calgary *Herald* from 1919 to 1922, then left Calgary, having in the meantime been adopted as a Blood Indian and given the name Buffalo Child by the old warrior Mountain Horse. He now wrote articles for various Canadian newspapers and magazines, calling himself Chief Buffalo Long Lance. Throughout 1927 he worked on what he claimed was his autobiography, entitled *Long Lance*, with its opening sentence: "The first thing in my life that I can remember is the exciting aftermath of an Indian fight in northern Montana." (He was actually born in Winston, now Winston-Salem, North Carolina.) Soon after, he took the leading role in *The Silent Enemy* (1930), a movie about the Indians of northern Canada. In 1931, his brother Walter contacted him in New York City and told him the family desperately needed money, as his father was seriously sick in Winston-Salem. Long agreed to send money, but not to return himself and risk the disclosure that his family was classified as "colored." He became increasingly unstable, and in 1932 shot himself. The *New York Times* report began: "Chief Buffalo Long Lance, 36-year-old [*sic*] Indian author, was found shot to death yesterday" (March 21, 1932).

Christian **Longomontanus:** Christian Severin (1562–1647), Dan. astronomer, astrologer. The astronomer adopted a Latin form of the name of his birthplace, Longberg, as his surname.

A. Huge **Longway:** Andrew Lang (1844–1912), Sc. folklorist, poet. The writer used this punning name for his novel *Much Darker Days* (1884).

Frederick **Lonsdale:** Lionel Frederick Leonard (1881–1954), Eng. playwright, screenwriter. The writer adopted the name Lonsdale by deed poll in 1908, apparently basing it on his original surname.

Gordon **Lonsdale:** Konon Trofimovich Molody (1922–1970), Russ.-born Can. spy, working in U.K. Molody posed as a Canadian businessman, Gordon Arnold Lonsdale, a name obtained by Soviet espionage operatives from the birth record and passport of a child who had been born in Canada and taken by his mother to Finland, where he died, perhaps in the Finno-Soviet War (1939–40).

Fred **Lookout:** Why-hah-shah-shin-kah (1865–1949), U.S. Native American leader. The Osage warrior accompanied his father on buffalo hunts when young and was given his Indian name, meaning Little Eagle That Gets What He Wants. "Lookout" came from a casual interpretation of this name, which describes a perched eagle gazing into the distance and dreaming. English "Fred" was added later.

Eddie **Lopat:** Edmund Walter Lopatynski (1913–1992), U.S. baseball player.

Benedikt **Lopwegen:** [Sister] Leonora (originally Marie-Cécile) Jenny (1923–), Swiss violinist, conductor, composer.

E.C.R. **Lorac:** Edith Caroline Rivett (1894–1958), Eng. writer of detective novels. The writer devised her pen name from her initials and a reversal of the first part of her middle name.

Violet **Loraine:** Violet Mary Tipton (1886–1956), Eng. variety actress, singer.

Stefan **Lorant:** Istvan Lorant (1901–1997), Hung.-born U.S. editor, writer.

Jack **Lord:** John Joseph Patrick Ryan (1920–1998), U.S. stage, movie, TV actor.

Jeremy **Lord:** Ben Ray Redman (1896–1961), U.S. journalist, writer.

Lord Creator: Kentrick Patrick (*c.*1940–), Trinidadian reggae musician. As his imperious name suggests, Patrick began his career as a calypso singer.

Lord Pretender: Aldric Farrell (1917–2002), Trinidadian calypso singer.

Traci **Lords:** Nora Louise Kuzma (1968–), U.S. porno movie actress. The actress took her new name from Tracy Lord, the character played by Katharine Hepburn in *The Philadelphia Story* (1940), with the surname also a tribute to her favorite actor in her favorite TV show, Jack **Lord** in *Hawaii Five-0* (1968).

Loredana: Loredana Padoan (1924–), It. movie actress.

Sophia **Loren:** Sofia Villani Scicolone (1934–), It. movie actress, working in U.S. The actress was the illegitimate daughter of Riccardo Scicolone and Romilda Villani. When people pointed out that her surname "sounded like a chunk of Italian sausage," she duly adopted her familiar name, popularly supposed to have been chosen by her husband Carlo Ponti, whom she married in 1957.

A biography of Loren suggests otherwise, however. A photoplay magazine editor had originally named her Sofia Lazzaro, from the biblical story of Lazarus (with a symbolic reference to a "rebirth"). Then the boss of Titanus Productions, Gustavo Lombardo, said that "Sofia Lazzaro" was too much like other names. "'We've got to change it.' 'My name is really Scicolone.' 'That's even worse — sounds like you belong in a circus. No, we've got to find you a new name. Something not so Italian — short, clean, easy to remember.'" Lombardo had been working with the Swedish actress Marta Toren. "'That's it, Toren!' and he started down the alphabet — Boren, Coren, Doren — until he got to Loren, which struck him just right. Sofia Loren. 'No,' he said, 'I don't like the spelling of Sofia. Outside of Italy they will think it's a misspelling of Sophia, so we'll change it to Sophia. All right with you?' I readily agreed, but in Italian, *ph* is not pronounced *f* but *p*, so for a long time the people I knew ... wondered why I wanted to be called Sopia" [A.E. Hotchner, *Sophia: Living and Loving: Her Own Story*, 1979]. Loren's first movie

under the new name was *Africa sotto i mari* ("Africa under the seas") (1952).

Pilar **Lorengar:** Pilar Lorenza García (1928–1996), Sp. opera singer. The singer formed her new surname from elements of her original names.

Lorenzo Monaco: Pietro di Giovanni (*c.*1370–*c.*1424), It. painter. The artist became a monk of the Camaldolese order in 1391 and came to be known by his religious name ("Laurence the Monk").

Adam **Lorimer:** William Lorimer Watson (?–1921), Eng. writer. Watson's best-known book under this name was *An Author's Progress; or, The Literary Book of the Road* (1906).

Eugene **Loring:** Leroy Kerpestein (1911–1982), U.S. ballet dancer, choreographer.

Francis **Loring:** [Sir] Francis Loring Gwynne-Evans (1914–1993), Eng. singer. In 1943 the son of Sir Evan Gwynne Gwynne-Evans assumed by deed poll the name of Francis Loring Gwynne Evans-Tipping, the latter name coming from the family of his first wife, Elizabeth Fforde, daughter of J. Fforde Tipping, whom he had married in 1937. On their divorce in 1958, he reverted by deed poll to his patronymic, which he retained (as Francis Loring) for his career as a professional singer.

Peter **Loring** *see* John **Esteven**

Diana **Loris:** Gina Lollobrigida (1927–), It. movie actress. The actress adopted this name when modeling for magazine picture stories early in her career.

Hieronymus **Lorm:** Heinrich Landesmann (1821–1902), Austr. (blind and deaf) poet, philosopher.

Lorna: Jane T. Stoddart (?–1944), Sc. writer on religious subjects. The writer, professionally on the staff of the *British Weekly* from 1890 to 1937, took a typically Scottish name for some of her writings.

Constance **Lorne:** Constance MacLaurin (1914–), Sc. stage actress.

Marion **Lorne:** Marion Lorne MacDougall (1886–1968), U.S. stage, movie comedienne.

Tommy **Lorne:** Hugh Gallagher Corcoran (1890–1935), Sc. music-hall comedian.

Claude **Lorrain** *see* **Claude Lorrain**

Jean **Lorrain:** Paul Duval (1855–1906), Fr. novelist. The writer adopted his pen name on abandoning the study of law to take up a literary career.

Anne **Lorraine** *see* Jane **Alan**

Lillian **Lorraine:** Eulallean De Jacques (1892–1955), U.S. singer, stage actress.

Louise **Lorraine:** Louise Escovar (1901–1981), U.S. movie actress.

Peter **Lorre:** László Loewenstein (1904–1964), Hung.-born U.S. movie actor.

Harry **Lorrequer:** Charles James Lever (1806–1872), Ir. novelist. The author took his pen name from the central character of his first major novel, published in the *Dublin University Magazine* in 1837.

Joan **Lorring:** Magdalen Ellis (1926–), Eng.-Russ. movie actress, working in U.S.

Lucille **Lortel:** Lucille Wadler (1900–1999), U.S. theatrical producer. The "Queen of Off-Broadway" changed her name after attending the American Academy of Dramatic Arts when her sister and a friend decided that actresses should have alliterative names. Lortel made her Broadway debut in 1925 with Helen **Hayes** as Cleopatra and Lionel Atwill as Caesar in G.B. Shaw's *Caesar and Cleopatra*.

Victoria de **los Angeles** *see* Victoria **de los Angeles**

Louis **Lothar:** Paul Dupin (1865–1949), Fr. composer.

Rudolf **Lothar:** Rudolf Spitzer (1865–1943), Hung.-born Ger. playwright, librettist.

Amy **Lothrop:** Anna Bartlett Warner (1827–1915), U.S. novelist, sister of Elizabeth **Wetherell**.

Pierre **Loti:** Louis-Marie-Julien Viaud (1850–1923), Fr. traveler, writer. The writer's tours of duty as a naval officer took him to Tahiti, where women in the court of Queen **Pomare IV** nicknamed him "Loti," from the name of a local flower, a type of rose. He adopted the name professionally.

Lenny **Lottery:** Aidan McGurran (1963–), Br. media lottery correspondent. McGurran, a newspaper reporter, changed his name by deed poll after he was appointed lottery correspondent of *The Sun* in 1994, his task being to report on National Lottery winners. In 1997 he moved to *The Mirror*. The original character Lenny Lottery was created by Stuart Higgins, editor of *The Sun*.

Mariella **Lotti:** Anna Maria Pianotti (1921–), It. movie actress.

Miss **Lou:** Louise Bennett-Coverly (1919–2006), Jamaican folklorist, poet.

Lisa **Loud:** Lisa McKay (1968–), Br. DJ.

Father M. **Louis:** Thomas Merton (1915–1968), U.S. religious, writer, of N.Z.–U.S. parentage. The author of the classic of spiritual autobiography, *The Seven Storey Mountain*, published under his secular name in 1948, took the name Louis in the Trappist monastery near Bardstown, Kentucky, that he entered in 1941. He died on a visit to Bangkok, where his grave bears his name in religion, Fr. Louis Merton.

Jean **Louis:** Jean-Louis Berthault (1907–1997), Fr.-born U.S. costume designer.

Joe **Louis:** Joseph Louis Barrow (1914–1981), U.S. black heavyweight boxer ("The Brown Bomber"). The boxer unintentionally omitted his surname when filling out an amateur application card. From then on he was always known in boxing circles as simply "Joe Louis."

Joe Hill **Louis:** Lester (or Leslie) Hill (1921–1957), U.S. black blues musician. The musician was nicknamed after Joe **Louis** when he outfought a local tearaway and he adopted this as his stage name.

Morris **Louis:** Morris Louis Bernstein (1912–1962), U.S. painter, of Russ. Jewish parentage. Louis legally changed his name in 1936 on moving to the Chelsea district of New York City.

Viktor **Louis:** Vitali Yevgeniyevich Lui (1928–1992), Russ. journalist, working in England.

Louisa: Elizabeth Boyd (*fl.*1727–1745), Eng. poet, artist.

Aunt **Louisa:** Laura B.J. Valentine (1814–1899), Br. children's writer.

Louise: Louise Elizabeth Nurding (1974–), Eng. pop singer, dancer.

Anita **Louise** *see* **Anita Louise**

Tina **Louise** *see* **Tina Louise**

Louiseboulanger: Louise Boulanger, née Melenot (1878–*c*.1950), Fr. fashion designer.

Louisiana Red: Iverson Minter (1932–), U.S. black blues musician.

Louis of Besse: Alphonse Éliséus Chaix (1831–1910), Fr. Capuchin friar. Louis de Besse, as the pioneer of the social apostolate is known in French, was born in Besse-sur-Issole in the south of France.

Louis of Casoria: Arcangelo Palmentieri (1814–1885), It. Franciscan friar. Luigi da Casoria, as the founder of the Brothers of Charity is known in Italian, was born in Casoria, near Naples.

Eddy **Louiss:** Édouard Louise (1941–), Fr. jazz musician.

Ira **Louvin:** Ira Lonnie Loudermilk (1924–1965), U.S. country musician. Ira and his brother Charlie performed together and in 1946 changed their surname to Louvin by taking the first three letters of "Loudermilk" and adding a simple suffix.

Pierre **Louÿs:** Pierre Félix Louis (1870–1925), Belg.-born Fr. poet, novelist. The modified spelling and added dieresis were an appropriately poetic touch. In 1894 Louÿs published *Les Chansons de Bilitis* ("The Songs of Bilitis"), a collection of prose poems supposedly translated from the writings of a 6th-century BC Greek poetess. According to Louÿs, her tomb had been discovered by a Dr. Heim, an archaeologist, and subsequent editions of the *Chansons* even contained a "portrait" of Bilitis herself. But it was all a hoax: Bilitis had never existed, there was no Dr. Heim, and the portrait was simply a copy of a statue in the Louvre. The poems themselves were written by Louÿs in the style of Sappho.

Bessie **Love:** Juanita Horton (1898–1986), U.S. movie actress, working in U.K. The actress was renamed by Frank Woods, head of scenario for D.W. Griffith, right before the cast of her first movie, *The Flying Torpedo* (1916): "Bessie, because any child can pronounce it; and Love, because we want everyone to love her!" [*Sunday Times Magazine*, September 18, 1977].

Courtney **Love**: Love Michelle Harrison (1965–), U.S. rock singer, guitarist. The musician was renamed Courtney Michelle Harrison as a baby by her mother after the latter's separation from her father, when presumably "love" no longer seemed appropriate. She later combined the two first names, which coincidentally suggest "courtly love" as a term for medieval poetry that idealized women.

Darlene **Love**: Darlene Wright (1938–), U. S. pop singer, movie actress. The singer has also recorded under her real name, but her adopted name presumably means what it looks and sounds as if it does.

Mabel **Love**: Mabel Watson (1874–1953), U.S. stage actress. The actress adopted her mother's maiden name as her stage name. It was also the name of her grandfather, William Edward Love, a popular entertainer in his time.

Monie **Love**: Simone Johnson (1970–), Eng.-born U.S. black rapper. "Monie" from "Simone."

Mrs. Solomon **Lovechild**: [Lady] Eleanor Fenn, née Frere (1743–1813), Eng. writer of educational books for children. The writer, who had no children of her own, found some solace in her pen name, with "Solomon" presumably implying wisdom. She also wrote as Mrs. Teachwell.

Linda **Lovelace**: Linda Marchiano, formerly Traynor, née Boreman (1949–2002), U.S. porno movie actress, writer. The actress was given her screen name by Gerry Damiano, director of her best-known movie, *Deep Throat* (1972). He "came up with the name Linda Lovelace for the character in his movie. There had been a BB [Brigitte **Bardot**] and an MM [Marilyn **Monroe**] and now he wanted an LL." She commented: "In time I came to dislike the name, Linda Lovelace, because of what it stood for" [Linda Lovelace with Mike McGrady, *Ordeal*, 1981]. Lovelace was the dashing rake who loves Clarissa Harlowe in Samuel Richardson's novel *Clarissa* (1748). It is a real surname, famous as that of the handsome and elegant courtier and poet Richard Lovelace (1618–?1657), and originated as a nickname for a philanderer, who is "loveless" and so "fancy free" (though suggesting one who "loves lace").

Patty **Loveless**: Patricia Lovelace, née Ramey (1957–), U.S. country musician. The singer changed the spelling of her married name to avoid any connection with porn star Linda **Lovelace**.

Katharine **Lovell**: Margaret Olive Hubicki (1905–), Eng. pianist, violinist, composer.

Mark **Lovell**: David Tollemache (?–1918), Sc. writer, journalist. The writer used this name for his short stories published in periodicals.

Jay **Lovestone**: Jacob Liebstein (1898–1990), Lithuanian-born U.S. political activist. The future fanatical anti–Communist anglicized his name when he first took up far-left politics.

Lene **Lovich**: Lili Marlene Premilovich (1949–), Br. rock singer, of Eng.-Yugoslav parentage. The singer's alliterative stage name abbreviates her original name.

Low: [Sir] David Alexander Cecil Low (1891–1963), N.Z.–born Br. cartoonist, caricaturist, of Sc.-Ir. parentage. The artist was fortunate to have a brief surname to serve as a readymade signature.

Gardner **Low** *see* Eliot **Reed**

Robert **Lowery**: Robert Lowery Hanks (1916–1971), U.S. movie actor.

Woytec **Lowski**: Wojciech Wiesidlowski (1939–), Pol. ballet dancer.

Violet **Loxley**: Violet Humphreys (1914–), Br. stage actress.

Mina **Loy**: Mina Gertrude Lowy (1882–1966), Br.-born U.S. poet, artist. Lowy changed the spelling of her name in 1903 following her marriage to Stephen Haweis, an art student. It was a change, she later recalled, that she "adopted in a spirit of mockery" in response to her husband's old and distinguished family name, which was pronounced "Hoyes."

Myrna **Loy**: Katerina Myrna Adele Williams (1905–1993), U.S. movie actress. The actress took her new name in 1932 when she felt that "the plain old Welsh name of Williams just didn't seem flossy enough." She made the change at the suggestion of Rudolf **Valentino**, who thought it exotic. She commented: "I didn't intend to keep it very long. But then I signed a contract and I was stuck with it."

Lobby **Loyde**: John Baslington Lyde (1951–2007), Austral. rock musician.

A. **Lozovsky**: Solomon Abramovich Dridzo (1878–1952), Russ. revolutionary, historian.

Antonella **Lualdi**: Antonietta de Pascale (1931–), It.-Gk. movie actress.

Samuel **Lubell**: Samuel Lubelsky (?1911–1987), Pol.-born U.S. writer, political analyst.

Arthur **Lucan**: Arthur Towle (1887–1954), Eng. music-hall female impersonator, movie actor. The comedian was on tour in 1913 at the Lucan Dairy, Dublin, Ireland, and this provided a handy stage name for the creator of his famous character, Old Mother Riley, who engaged in boisterous banter with her "daughter" (actually his wife), Kitty McShane (1897–1964).

J.K. **Lucas** *see* Mark **Carrel**

Victoria **Lucas:** Sylvia Plath (1932–1963), U.S. poet. The poet adopted this name for her semiautobiographical novel *The Bell Jar* (1963), reissued three years later under her own name. Plath was devastated when her pseudonym was revealed in the original year of publication.

William **Lucas:** William Thomas Clucas (1925–), Br. stage, movie, TV actor.

Lucas van Leyden: Lucas Hugenz (or Lucas Jacobsz) (1494–1533), Du. painter, engraver. The artist adopted the name of his birthplace (and also the place of his death), the Dutch town of Leiden.

Lucebert: Lubertus Jacobus Swaanswijk (1924–1994), Du. lyric poet.

Sister **Luc-Gabrielle:** Jeanine Deckers (1933–1985), Belg. popular singer ("The Singing Nun"). Three years after her 1963 hit song, "Dominique," the singer left the Dominican order to which she belonged and resumed her original name.

Yanka **Luchina:** Ivan Lyutsianovich Neslukhovsky (1851–1897), Belorussian poet. The writer based his pen name on a colloquial form of his first name and patronymic (middle name), the latter itself corresponding to English Lucian.

Luciano: Jepther McClymont (*c*.1960–), Jamaican DJ, reggae singer. The musician adopted the name of the Mafia enforcer Lucky **Luciano.**

Lucky **Luciano:** Salvatore Lucania (1897–1962), It.-born founder of the Mafia in the United States. Lucania's family immigrated to the USA in 1906, and he adopted his new name while working for crime boss Giuseppe Masseria. In the fall of 1928 he was arrested for robbery and used the alias Luciano. When he discovered that the police found it easier to pronounce his alias than his surname, he adopted it. The following year he was abducted, badly beaten, and left for dead. He lived on, however, and because he was the only person ever known to have survived the gangland ritual of being "taken for a ride," he adopted the alliterative nickname "Lucky." From 1933 to 1936 he lived at the Waldorf-Astoria Towers, New York, under the alias Charles Ross.

Lasse **Lucidor:** Lars Johansson (1638–1674), Swe. lyric poet. The poet's adopted name was presumably intended to mean "giving light," from Latin *lux, lucis,* "light," and Greek *dōron,* "gift."

Jon **Lucien:** John Lucien Harrigan (1942–2007), West Indian soul singer, working in U.S.

Lucile: [Lady] Lucy Duff Gordon, earlier Kennedy, née Sutherland (1863–1935), Eng. fashion designer.

Lúcio: Lucimar da Silva Ferreira (1978–), Brazilian footballer.

Lucius II: Gherardo Caccianemici (?–1145), It. pope.

Lucius III: Ubaldo Allucingoli (*c*.1110–1185), It. pope.

Luck & Flaw: Peter Fluck (1941–), Eng. caricaturist, animator + Roger Law (1941–), Eng. caricaturist, writer. The two men gained fame for the grotesque animated puppets they created for the weekly satirical TV program *Spitting Image* (1984–95). Their joint name not only puns on their real names but hints at the mercurial nature of the satirist's art.

Aunt **Lucy:** Lucy Elizabeth Bather (1836–1864), Eng. children's writer.

Sahir **Ludhianvi:** Abdul Hayee (1921–1980), Ind. movie songwriter, poet. The lyricist, born in Ludhiana, Punjab, adopted a new first name meaning "famous."

Geoffrey **Ludlow** *see* A. Stephen **Tring**

Johnny **Ludlow:** Ellen Wood, née Price (1814–1887), Eng. novelist. Mrs. Henry Wood (as she is still commonly known) used this name for her series of tales which appeared in the *Argosy* magazine from 1868. She did not admit to their authorship until 1879.

Emil **Ludwig:** Emil Ludwig Cohn (1881–1948), Ger.-born Swiss writer, biographer, working in U.S.

William **Ludwig:** William Ledwidge (1847–1923), Ir. singer, working in England. The baritone fashioned his new German name from his original English surname.

Kazak Vladimir **Lugansky:** Vladimir Ivanovich Dal (1801–1872, Russ. writer, lexicographer. Russian *kazak* is "Cossack." Dal had lived in the region around the Lugan River, now in eastern Ukraine, part of the territory inhabited by the Cossacks. *See also* Andrey **Pechersky.**

Aurélien Marie **Lugné-Poe:** Aurélien Marie Lugné (1869–1940), Fr. stage actor, theatrical director.

Béla **Lugosi:** Béla Ferenc Dezsö Blaskó (1882–1956), Hung. stage, movie actor, working in U.S. The actor took his name from his birthplace, Lugos, Hungary (now Lugoj, Romania). An early stage name was Arisztid Olt.

Aleksey **Lugovoy:** Aleksey Alekseyevich Tikhonov (1853–1915), Russ. writer. The writer adopted a pseudonym for distinction from his brother, V.A. Tikhonov, also a writer.

Luigi: Eugene Louis Facciuto (1925–), U.S. ballet dancer, teacher. An italianization of the dancer's second name.

Marcel **Luipart:** Marcel Fenchel (1912–1989), Ger.-Austr. ballet dancer, choreographer, teacher.

Luisillo: Luis Perez Davilla (1928–), Mexican ballet dancer, choreographer.

Luizão: Luiz Carlos Goulart (1975–), Brazilian

footballer. A form of the player's first name with an augmentative ("big") suffix.

Paul **Lukas:** Pál Lukács (1894 or 1887–1971), Hung.-born U.S. movie actor.

Lukía: Ioanu Kokinioti Lukía (1915–), Gk. ballet dancer.

Lukie D: Michael Kennedy (1972–), Jamaican reggae singer.

Lev **Lukin:** Lev Ivanovich Saks (1892–1961), Russ. ballet director.

Lula: Luiz Inácio da Silva (1945–), Brazilian politician. The man who became Brazil's president in 2003 adopted his pet name (from "Luiz"), which for campaigning purposes he added to his legal name.

Jean-Baptiste **Lully:** Giovanni Battista Lulli (1632–1687), It.-born Fr. composer. The composer, born in Florence, gallicized his name after being brought to Paris, France, in 1646.

Lulu: Marie McDonald McLaughlin Lawrie (1948–), Sc. popular singer, stage, TV actress. When the singer was 14 she was appearing at various clubs in Glasgow. At one such club, the Lindella, she was recommended to record agent Tony Gordon by his sister-in-law, Marian Massey, Lulu's future manager. "Tony and Marian were determined to find me a new name. Marie McDonald McLaughlin Lawrie just didn't do it for them.... Tony was sitting at the piano, while Marian paced up and down. Finally, in exasperation she said, 'Well, all I know is that she's a real lulu of a kid.' They looked at each other. Both had the same thought. It was short, cute and sounded American. I wrinkled my nose when they told me. I repeated it several times in my head, as if trying it on for size. 'You could be Lulu and the Luvvers,' said Tony.... It was a bit daft as names go, but so what?" [Lulu, *I Don't Want to Fight*, 2002].

Lulu Belle: Myrtle Eleanor Cooper (1913–1999), U.S. country singer, teaming with **Scotty.**

Benjamin **Lumley:** Benjamin Levy (1811–1875), Eng. theatrical manager, writer, of Can. Jewish descent. The future manager of Her Majesty's Theatre, a leading London opera house, adopted his new name early in life. He later turned to writing, and adopted the name "Hermes" as the author of *Another World, or Fragments from the Star City of Montallayah* (1873), describing a utopia set on Mars.

Lun: John Rich (1692–1761), Eng. actor, theater manager. The actor, who popularized pantomime, used this name when playing Harlequin. He later engaged the young actor John Woodward (1717–1777), who took the name Lun Junior and who in turn played Harlequin in pantomime.

Diego **Luna:** Diego Luna Alexander (1979–), Mexican movie actor.

Lydia **Lunch:** Lydia Koch (1959–), U.S. rock musician, photographer.

Karin **Lund** *see* Greta **Garbo**

Karl **Lund** *see* Greta **Garbo**

Carl Elof **Lund-Quist:** Carl Elof Lundquist (1908–1963), U.S. Lutheran clergyman, of Swe. descent. In 1932 Lundquist entered a theological seminary in Rock Island, Illinois, and while there hyphenated his name as Lund-Quist, observing the tradition whereby many young Swedish pastors altered the spellings of their surnames in order to be distinguished from others of the same name. Lundquist's change was minimal, however, and his name retained its obvious Swedish origin.

Chang **Lung** *see* Robert **Jordan**

Magda **Lupescu:** Magda Wolff (?1896–1977), Rom. adventuress. The mistress of King Carol II of Romania adopted a name that was equivalent of the German original (Romanian *lupu*, "wolf," with patronymic suffix *-escu*).

Larry **Lurex** *see* Freddie **Mercury**

Othmar **Luscinius:** Othmar Nachtigall (1487–1537), Ger. organist, composer. As was the fashion in his day, the musician came to be known by the Latin equivalent of his native German name, meaning "nightingale."

Vicente **Lusitano:** Vicente de Olivença (?–after 1553), Port. composer. In around 1550 the musician settled in Rome, Italy, where he gained his Italian name, meaning "Vincent the Portuguese."

Sidney **Luska:** Henry Harland (1861–1905), U.S. novelist, short-story writer, working in U.K.. Harland liked to pose as a writer of Russian origin, claiming he was born in St. Petersburg and educated in Europe. He used this name for his novels about Jewish immigrants to the USA, beginning with *As It Was Written: A Jewish Musician's Story* (1885). Despite his Jewish-sounding pseudonym, Harland was in fact a Gentile.

Lux Interior: Erick Lee Purkhiser (1946–2009), U.S. rock singer. The front man of the trash rock band the Cramps took his stage name from a line in an auto ad, itself probably meant to mean "inner luxury" (although equally suggesting "inner light"). Lux's wife, Kristy Wallace, was also in the band, styling herself Poison Ivy, a name she claimed came to her in a dream.

Maksim **Luzhanin:** Aleksandr Amvrosyevich Karatay (1909–?), Belorussian poet, translator. The writer has explained the origin of his name, meaning "meadowland dweller": "I feel that a poet's name should bear the scent and charm of his birthplace. I was born by the Sluch River. There are fine water meadows and dry meadows there with such hay that I can smell it every time I write the word. As for my first name, that was a tribute to Maksim Bogdanovich [(1891–1917)]. When I was young I felt specially drawn to him, our native poet, who died when he was 25. And that was how Maksim Luzhanin first appeared in 1925 in the newspaper *Savetskaya Belarus* ['Soviet Belorussia'] " [Dmitriyev, p.105].

Vasily **Luzhsky:** Vasily Vasilyevich Kaluzhsky (1869–1931), Russ. stage actor, theatrical director.

Annabella **Lwin:** Myant Myant Aye (1966–), Burmese-born Br. rock singer.

Martyn **Lyadov:** Martyn Nikolayevich Mandelshtam (Mandelstam) (1872–1947), Russ. revolutionary, historian.

David **Lyall:** (1) Ellen Mathews (1853–1920), Eng. novelist; (2) Annie Shepherd Smith, née Swan (1859–1943), Sc. novelist, children's writer.

Edna **Lyall:** Ada Ellen Bayly (1857–1903), Eng. novelist. The nine letters of the writer's pseudonym can be readily extracted from her original name.

Nikolay **Lyashko:** Nikolay Nikolayevich Lyashchenko (1884–1953), Russ. writer.

Le **Lycanthrope** *see* Petrus **Borel**

Lycosthenes: Conrad Wolffhart (1518–1561), Swiss philologist, theologian. The scholar adopted a Greek equivalent of his German name (*lykos*, "wolf" + *sthenos*, "strength").

Lydian: Jason Lyon (1968–), Br. crossword compiler. The setter adopted his pastoral pseudonym when contributing puzzles to *Country Life* magazine. It also reflects his musical interests and partly puns on his surname.

Viola **Lyel:** Violet Watson (1900–1972), Eng. stage, movie actress.

Lykke Li: Lykke Timotej Zachrisson (1986–), Swe. pop singer.

Abe **Lyman:** Abraham Simon (1897–1957), U.S. bandleader, drummer.

John **Lymington:** John Newton Chance (1911–1983), Br. SF writer.

[Dame] Moura **Lympany:** Mary Johnstone (1916–2005), Eng. concert pianist, working in U.S. The musician's change of name was made as a 12-year-old prodigy by orchestral conductor Basil Cameron, who favored a more exotic-sounding name. Her Cornish mother's maiden name, Limpenny, was thus altered to Lympany, and her first name replaced by its Russian diminutive, as a tribute to her mother's affection for pre–Revolutionary St. Petersburg, where she had taught the daughters of aristocrats.

Jacquie **Lyn:** Jacquelyn Duffon (1928–2002), Br.-born U.S. child movie actress.

B. Suárez **Lynch** *see* Honorio Bustos **Domecq**

Lawrence L. **Lynch:** Emma Murdoch Van Deventer (*fl.*1900), U.S. novelist.

Barré **Lyndon:** Alfred Edgar (1896–1972), Br. playwright, screenwriter, working in U.S. Edgar's pen name was presumably based on that of the hero of Thackeray's novel *The Luck of Barry Lyndon* (1844).

David **Lyndsay** *see* Walter Sholto **Douglas**

Carol **Lynley:** Carolyn Jones (1942–), U.S. movie actress. The actress began her career as a model under the name Carolyn Lee, and her screen name evolved from this.

Barbara **Lynn:** Barbara Lynn Ozen (1942–), U.S. blues singer.

Cheryl **Lynn:** Cheryl Lynn Smith (1957–), U.S. black pop singer.

Cora **Lynn** *see* Edwige **Feuillère**

Diana **Lynn:** Dolores Loehr (1926–1971), U.S. movie, stage, TV comedienne. The actress was billed as Dolly Loehr as a teenager in her earliest movies.

Dr. H.S. **Lynn:** Hugh Simmons (1836–1899), Eng. conjuror, working in U.S.

Ethel **Lynn:** Ethelinda Beers, née Eliot (1827–1879), U.S. poet. The writer used this name for her early contributions to magazines. After her marriage at age 19 she published under the name Ethyl Lynn Beers.

Irene **Lynn** *see* Fenton **Brockley**

Jeffrey **Lynn:** Ragnar Godfrey Lind (1909–1995), U.S. movie actor.

Judy **Lynn:** Judy Voiten (1936–), U.S. country singer, songwriter.

[Dame] Vera **Lynn:** Vera Margaret Lewis, née Welch (1917–), Eng. popular singer ("The Forces' Sweetheart"). The singer explains how she arrived at her new name: "I ought to adopt a more comfortable name than Vera Welch. My main concern was to find something that was short, easily remembered, and that would stand out on a bill — something that would allow for plenty of space round each letter. We held a kind of family conference about it, and we found the answer within the family too. My grandmother's maiden name had been Lynn; it seemed to be everything a stage name ought to be, but at the same time it was a real one. From then on, I was to be Vera Lynn" [Vera Lynn, *Vocal Refrain: An Autobiography*, 1975].

Carole **Lynne:** Helen Violet Carolyn Heymen (1918–2008), Br. stage actress. The actress's third name nicely served as a full new stage name. In 1946 she married Bernard **Delfont**, becoming Lady Delfont after he was knighted in 1974.

Gillian **Lynne:** Gillian Land, née Pyrke (1926–), Eng. ballet dancer, director, choreographer.

Shelby **Lynne:** Shelby Lynn Moore (1968–), U.S. country singer.

Everett **Lynton** *see* Horatio **Nicholls**

[Professor] Norbert **Lynton:** Norbert Caspar

Loewenstein (1927–2007), Ger.-born Br. art critic, historian. The scholar's father, Jewish publisher Paul Loewenstein, changed the family name to Lynton in 1944.

Lynwood Slim: Richard Duran (1953–), U.S. blues musician.

Larry Lynx: Arthur J. Sarl (?–1946), Eng. sporting writer, editor. The former actor used this name for his contributions on racing to *The People*. The lynx is traditionally noted for its keenness of sight, a faculty that a racing correspondent should have as a spotter of form.

Leonard Lyons: Leonard Sucher (1906–1976), U.S. columnist.

Lypsinka: John Epperson (1955–), U.S. drag artist. The performer's act consists in lip-synching (mouthing recorded songs), and he adopted his name in 1982. He respelled "lip-syncher" for the sake of individuality, giving a one-word name suggesting that of a fashion model such as **Verushka**.

Carmen Lyra: María Isabel Carvajal (1888–1951), Costa Rican writer. The writer formed her pen name from two Latin words both meaning "song."

Christian Lys: Percy James Brebner (1864–1922), Eng. novelist.

Charles Lysberg: Charles Samuel Bovy (1821–1873), Swiss pianist, composer. Bovy adopted the name of his birthplace, Lysberg, near Geneva, for his compositions, in case they did not succeed and he was seen to be a failure.

Vera Lysenko: Vera Lesik (1910–1975), Can. writer, of Ukr. parentage. The writer sought to emphasize her national ancestry by taking the typical and distinctive Ukrainian name Lysenko. She was the first Ukrainian-Canadian to write in English.

Jimmy Lytell: James Sarrapede (1904–1972), U.S. jazz clarinetist. The musician adopted the surname of movie actor Bert Lytell (1888–1954).

Bulwer Lytton: Edward George Earle Bulwer-Lytton, 1st Baron Lytton (1803–1873), Eng. novelist, playwright, esssyist, poet, politician. "How to term this author is an initial problem" [Sutherland, p. 388]. Bulwer Lytton was born in London the son of William Earle Bulwer (1776–1807) and Elizabeth Barbara Bulwer, née Lytton (1773–1843), the heiress of Knebworth, Hertfordshire. He was created a baronet in 1838 and in 1843 succeeded to the Knebworth estate, when he added his mother's maiden name of Lytton, optionally hyphenated to his original surname. He should not be confused with his son, diplomat and poet Edward Robert Bulwer Lytton, 1st Earl of Lytton, Viscount Knebworth, 2nd Baron Lytton of Knebworth (1831–1891), better known by his pseudonym of Owen **Meredith**.

Doris Lytton: Doris Partington (1893–1953),

Br. stage actress. The actress took her mother's maiden name as her stage name.

[Sir] Henry Lytton: Henry Alfred Jones (1865–1936), Eng. stage actor, opera singer. The actor first performed in 1882 in a review in which he met his future wife, Louie Webber (1865–1947), who was appearing under the stage name Louie Henri. They married in 1884, when she helped him gain a small part with the D'Oyly Carte Opera Company in a Gilbert and Sullivan opera, in which he sang as H.A. Henri. In 1887 he was understudy to George Grossmith and took over his part when the actor fell ill. As a result of his success in the role, Gilbert himself suggested he adopt the name Lytton, a famous name familiar to the public from the diplomat and poet Edward Robert Bulwer Lytton (*see* Owen **Meredith**).

Yevsey Lyubimov-Lanskoy: Yevsey Osipovich Gelibter (Geliebter) (1883–1943), Russ. stage actor, theatrical director. The Russian name Lyubimov means "beloved" as does the original German.

Dora Maar: Henriette Theodora Markovitch (1907–1997), Yugoslav photographer, painter, artist's model. Maar was Pablo Picasso's mistress over the period 1936–43.

Maarten Maartens: Joost Marius Willem van der Poorten-Schwartz (1858–1915), Du.-born Br. novelist, of Ger. Jewish/Du. parentage. The writer's first novel, *The Black Box Murder* (1889), was published anonymously. He first used his pseudonym for his second, *The Sin of Joost Avelingh* (1890).

Mab Cernyw: John Hobson Mathews (1858–1914), Welsh historian. The scholar was the son of a Cornishman. Hence his name, meaning "son of Cornwall."

Jackie "Moms" Mabley: Loretta Mary Aiken (?1894–1975), U.S. black comedienne. Aiken became engaged to a Canadian, Jack Mabley, whom she did not marry but whose name she took because, as she explained, "he took a lot off me and that was the least I could do." Her nickname, "Moms," was said to have been given her for her mothering instinct toward performers.

Mabon: William Abraham (1842–1922), Welsh politician, miners' leader. The former miner took his bardic name from Mabon, the Celtic (Welsh) god of youth, identified with Apollo. St. Mabon is also the patron saint of Llanafan, Glamorganshire, the historical mining county in which Abraham was born.

Jan Mabuse: Jan Gossaert (or Gossart) (c.1478–c.1532), Flemish painter. The artist adopted his name from Maubeuge, the town in northern France where his family made their home. Hence also his latinized name of Jan Malbodius.

Mac: Stanley McMurtry (1936–), Sc. cartoonist, illustrator, writer. A near generic nickname for a

Scotsman, as well as a short form of this particular Scotsman's name.

Alison **Mac:** Alison McMonagle (1980–), Br. TV actress. The actress's surname was originally shortened when she began her career as a model.

Annie **Mac:** Anne MacManus (1978–), Ir.-born Br. DJ, TV presenter.

Bernie **Mac:** Bernard Jeffrey McCullough (1957–2008), U.S. black comedian.

Uncle **Mac:** Derek McCulloch (1897–1967), Eng. children's author, broadcaster.

Macarius: (1) Mikhail (c.1482–1563), Russ. churchman, metropolitan of Moscow and All Russia; (2) Mikhail Petrovich Bulgakov (1816–1882), Russ. churchman, ecclesiastical historian; (3) Mikhail Yakovlevich Glukharyov (1792–1847), Russ. churchman, missionary, translator. All three men adopted their new name on taking their monastic vows. The name, meaning "blessed," specifically honors the 4th-century saint Macarius the Great (Macarius of Egypt). Macarius (1) was himself canonized in 1988. Compare [Archbishop] **Makarios III**.

McArone: George Arnold (1834–1865), U.S. poet, humorist. In enjoying the (macaronic?) pun, do not overlook the echo of the humorist's real surname.

Allan **M'Aulay:** Charlotte Stewart (1863–1918), Eng. novelist, of Sc. descent.

Tony **Macauley:** Anthony Instone (1944–), Br. pop composer.

Jock **McAvoy:** Joseph Bamford (1908–1971), Eng. boxer.

Ed **McBain:** Salvatore Albert Lombino (1926–2005), U.S. crime, SF writer. The author formally adopted the name Evan **Hunter** before taking this name. He devised it in 1956 when Pocket Books offered him a three-book contract to replace Erle Stanley Gardner, the creator of Perry Mason. Hunter had to choose a new name for these dime crime novels. "'I finished *Cop Hater* and I typed the title page: "*Cop Hater*, by..." and I did not have a pseudonym. I went out to the kitchen where my wife was feeding our twin sons, and I said, "How's Ed McBain?" She thought it was good, so I went back and typed it. Ed McBain sounds like someone who would be writing crime novels, who had a crime beat or was a retired detective'" [James Bone, "Adventures in Copland," *The Times Magazine*, April 18, 1998]. In 2001 Evan Hunter teamed up with Ed McBain to write *Candyland: A Novel in Two Parts*, of which McBain commented: "I think it's one of the best books we ever wrote."

Anthony **McCall:** Henry Kane (1918–), U.S. detective novelist. Kane also wrote as Kenneth R. McKay and Mario J. Sagola.

Cash **McCall:** Maurice Dollison (1941–), U.S. R&B singer.

C.W. **McCall:** William Fries (1928–), U.S. country singer. The singer adopted the name that he created "out of thin air" for a truck driver he played in a 1973 advertising campaign for the Metz bread company.

J.P. **McCall:** Peter Dawson (1882–1961), Austral. concert singer, popular songwriter, working in U.K. Dawson adopted this name for his most popular song, "Boots" (1928), to words by Rudyard Kipling. As well as under his own name, he recorded light songs as Frank Danby, music-hall songs as Will Strong, and material by the Scottish comedian and singer Harry Lauder as Hector Grant. Other names used by Dawson were Peter Allison, Geoffrey Baxter, Evelyn Byrd, Arnold Flint, Alison Miller, Gilbert Mundy, Denton Thomas, and Charles Webber.

Sidney **McCall:** Mary McNeil Fenollosa (1879–1954), U.S. poet, writer.

Edson **McCann** *see* Lester **del Rey**

Greg **McClure:** Dale Easton (1918–), U.S. movie actor. An instance where the actor's real name looks more like a screen name.

Ewan **MacColl:** James Henry Miller (1915–1989), Sc.-born Br. folksinger, songwriter, playwright. In 1945 the singer adopted the name of an admired predecessor, Scottish-born Canadian poet Evan McColl (1808–1898). MacColl's autobiography makes no mention of his name change, although his third wife, U.S. musician Peggy Seeger, in her introduction, notes: "He was one of a select group of Scots writers and poets who initiated the Lallans Movement in the late 1940s. Most of these men and women took the names of poets and writers from the past and Ewan did the same" [Ewan MacColl, *Journeyman: An Autobiography*, 1990]. MacColl's daughter was the popular singer Kirsty MacColl (1959–2000).

Kent **McCord:** Kent McWhirter (1942–), U.S. TV actor.

F.J. **McCormick:** Peter Judge (1891–1947), Ir. stage, movie actor.

Frank **McCown** *see* Rory **Calhoun**

Kid **McCoy:** Norman Selby (1873–1940), U.S. boxer. The boxer adopted his new name for distinction from another fighter of the same name.

Robert Lee **McCoy** *see* Robert **Nighthawk**

Sylvester **McCoy:** Percy James Patrick Kent-Smith (1943–), Sc. TV actor. The actor took his name from a stage show he was once in, *Sylvester McCoy, The Human Bomb*.

Jimmy **McCracklin:** James David Walker (1921–), U.S. blues, soul musician.

Mickey **McCune:** Mickey Kuhn (c.1931–), U.S. child movie actor. The actor adopted this name in place of his undesirable German-sounding one in 1941 but by 1944 had reverted to Kuhn.

G.H. Macdermott: Gilbert Hastings Farrell (1845–1901), Eng. music-hall singer, comedian. Farrell first appeared on the stage in 1869 as Gilbert Hastings, but then took the name G.H. Macdermott.

Ruth McDevitt: Ruth Shoecraft (1895–1976), U.S. movie actress.

Hugh MacDiarmid: Christopher Murray Grieve (1892–1978), Sc. poet, critic, translator. The origin of the writer's best-known pen name remains a mystery. He first used it in 1922, when supporting the revival of the Scots dialect as a literary medium. He commented: "It was an immediate realization of this ultimate reach of the implications of my experiment in writing in Scots which made me adopt, when I began writing Scots poetry, the Gaelic pseudonym of Hugh MacDiarmid (Hugh has a traditional association and essential rightness in conjunction with MacDiarmid)" [*The Times*, September 11, 1978].

Babe McDonald: Patrick Joseph McDonnell (1878–1954), Ir.-born U.S. athlete. McDonnell emigrated to the United States in 1901, when immigration officers misspelled his surname. He received the ironic nickname "Babe" (standing 6 ft 5 in and weighing 300 lbs) on joining the Irish-American Athletic Club.

Golden MacDonald: Margaret Wise Brown (1910–1952), U.S. children's writer. Brown adopted this whimsical name (of obvious commercial inspiration) for *The Little Island* (1947), one of the picturebooks for young children that made her famous. Similar names were Timothy Hay and Juniper Sage, and she created further pen names for her magazine and anthology writings. "The passionate energy with which she wrote and the casual way she selected and used pseudonyms reflect her personality as others knew it" [Lillian S. Robinson in Garraty and Carnes, vol. 3, p. 713].

Jock Macdonald: James Williamson Galloway (1897–1960), Sc.-born Can. painter. The artist assumed an archetypal Scottish name.

Marie McDonald: Cora Marie Frye (1923–1965), U.S. movie actress ("The Body").

Murray Macdonald: Walter MacDonald Honeyman (1899–?), Sc. stage director, manager.

Ross Macdonald: Kenneth Millar (1915–1983), U.S. detective novelist. In 1944, when Millar began writing, his wife, Margaret Millar (1915–1995), had already gained notice as a mystery writer. He thus had a family reason for adopting a pseudonym. He originally wrote as John Macdonald, in memory of his late father, John Macdonald Millar, but following a protest from suspense writer John D. MacDonald (*see* Scott **O'Hara**) amended the name first to John Ross Macdonald, then (from 1956) to Ross Macdonald.

Andie MacDowell: Rosalie Anderson MacDowell (1958–), U.S. movie actress.

John MacDowell: Timothy Harold Parks (1954–), Eng. novelist, translator. The academic, noted for his translations from Italian, used this name for *Cara Massimina* (1990).

Malcolm McDowell: Malcolm John Taylor (1943–), Eng. movie actor. The actor adopted his mother's maiden name at the start of his career on discovering there was already an actor named Malcolm Taylor.

Brother Jack McDuff: Eugene McDuffy (1926–2001), U.S. jazz musician.

Rita Macedo: María Concepción Macedo Guzman (1928–1993), Mexican movie actress.

Natascha McElhone: Natascha Taylor (1971–), Br. movie actress. Although mainly playing Irish parts, the actress is actually English.

Geraldine McEwan: Geraldine Crutwell, née McKeown (1932–), Eng. stage, TV actress.

Bernarr Macfadden: Bernard Adolphus McFadden (1868–1955), physical culturist, writer. McFadden modified his name to a form that he believed looked stronger and more distinctive.

Stephen MacFarlane: John Keir Cross (1911–1967), Sc. fantasy fiction, children's writer. The author used this name as a partial pseudonym, so that some of his books, such as *The Angry Planet* (1945), appeared under his real name but were "based on notes and manuscripts by Stephen MacFarlane."

Peader Mac Fhionnghaile: Peter MacGinley (1857–1940), Ir. writer. The protagonist of the Irish language, president of the Gaelic League from 1923 to 1925, adopted the Irish equivalent of his originally English name.

McG: Joseph McGinty Mitchell (*c*.1970–), U.S. movie director.

Darren McGavin: William Lyle Richardson (1922–2006), U.S. TV actor.

Mike McGear: Peter Michael McCartney (1944–), Eng. pop musician. The singer adopted his name to avoid unwarranted associations with his stepbrother, Paul McCartney of the Beatles. At the same time, it matched those of John Gorman and Roger McGough, whom he joined in 1962 to form The Scaffold. It probably also hinted at "gear" in the slang sense of "hip." "Fab gear" was a phrase current in the 1960s to refer to fashionable ("fabulous") clothes or drugs, and the Beatles were known as the "Fab Four." McCartney subsequently reverted to his original name.

Fibber McGee: James Jordan (1896–1988), U.S. movie actor, radio comedian, teaming with Molly **McGee**, his wife.

Molly **McGee**: Marion Jordan (1898–1967), U.S. movie actress, radio comedienne.

Donald **McGill**: Fraser Gould (1875–1962), Eng. comic-postcard artist.

McFaddyen O'Flathery **McGinnis** *see* **Nunquam**

William **McGinnis**: William Ellsworth ("Elzy") Lay (1868–1934), U.S. outlaw. The Wild Bunch member, a close friend and ally of Butch **Cassidy**, was sentenced to life imprisonment for a train robbery under this alias in 1899. He retained the alias after being granted a governor's pardon in 1909.

John **McGiver**: George Morris (1913–1975), U.S. movie actor.

Terence **M'Grath**: [Sir] Henry Arthur Blake (1840–1918), Ir. colonial governor, writer.

Tim **McGraw**: Samuel Timothy Smith (1967–), U.S. country singer. The singer was raised by a single mother and was originally known by her name. At the age of 11 he discovered that his father was the famous baseball player Tug McGraw, and accordingly adopted his name.

MacGregor: Leslie Gilbert Illingworth (1902–1979), Welsh-born Br. political cartoonist. The artist adopted his mother's maiden name for his cartoons appearing in the *Daily Mail* for 30 years from 1939.

Byron **MacGregor**: Gary Mack (1948–1995), Can. broadcaster.

Malcolm **MacGregor**: [Rev.] William Mason (1724–1797), Eng. lyrical dramatist, writer of church music. Mason adopted this name as author of *An Heroic Epistle to Sir William Chambers* (1773).

Jimmy **McGriff**: James Herrell (1936–), U.S. jazz organist.

Jack **McGurn**: Jack Vincenzo de Mora (1904–1936), U.S. gangster. The Chicago gangster's assumed name was apparently suggested by "machine gun."

Machaquito: Rafael Gonzáles Madrid (1880–1955), Sp. bullfighter. The matador's name means "little fellow," referring to his small stature. "In front of the bulls I'm half a lance taller," he quipped.

Arthur **Machen**: Arthur Llewellyn Jones (1863–1947), Welsh-born Br. novelist. The writer's family adopted his mother's maiden name "in order to please her Scottish relations" [*Dictionary of National Biography*]. Machen used the name Leolinus Siluriensis for his early work, *The Anatomy of Tobacco; or Smoking Methodised, Divided, and Considered after a New Fashion* (1884), following the pseudonym with the fanciful qualification "Professor of Fumifical Philosophy in the University of Brentford." Machen was born in Caerleon, Monmouthshire (now Newport), and his name refers to this town and the region of Wales inhabited by the ancient people known as the Silures. Compare the name of **Silurist**.

Machiavelli: Joyce Cansfield, née Patrick (1929–), Br. crossword compiler. The pseudonym refers to the cunning deployed by setters of cryptic crosswords, evoking the slyness associated with Niccolò **Machiavelli**. Appropriately, the name was chosen for her by **Ximenes**.

Niccolò **Machiavelli**: Niccolò Machiavegli (1469–1527), It. politician, writer. The writer signed himself in various ways but generally favored the Tuscan original, Machiavegli. An early letter, of April 29, 1499, bears the Medieval Latin signature "Nicholaus Maclavellus." The name derives from Latin *malus*, "bad," and a diminutive form of *clavus*, "nail." A "bad nail" is generally said to be one that nailed Christ to the cross, although some authorities see an allusion to a poor sexual performance. Whatever the case, the family adopted a cross-and-nails symbol.

Machito: Frank Raúl Grillo (1909–1984), U.S. bandleader, Afro-Cuban jazz musician. Grillo was nicknamed "Macho" as a child because he was the first son after three daughters. He adopted a diminutive form of the name on marrying in 1940.

Sasha **Machov**: František Matha (1903–1951), Cz. ballet dancer.

Stuart **McHugh** *see* Fenton **Brockley**

Bunny **Mack**: Cecil Bunting MacCormack (*c.*1940–), African singer.

Connie **Mack**: Cornelius Alexander McGillicuddy (1862–1956), U.S. baseball player, manager, of Ir. parentage. The entry for the famous player in *The World's All Sports Who's Who for 1950*, compiled by Herbert Kyle Turner, spells his original name with one "d," as does his appended facsimile autograph.

Eddie **Mack**: Mack Edmundson (*fl.* late 1940s/early 1950s), U.S. blues singer.

Helen **Mack**: Helen McDougall (1913–1986), U.S. movie actress.

Hughie **Mack**: Hugh McGowan (1884–1927), U.S. movie comedian.

Jack **Mack**: James MacKenzie (1911–1971), U.S. conjuror.

Lee **Mack**: Lee McKillop (1968–), Eng. comedian.

Lonnie **Mack**: Lonnie McIntosh (1941–), U.S. blues guitarist, "rockabilly" musician.

Marion **Mack**: Joanne Marion McCreery (1902–1989), U.S. movie actress.

Ted **Mack**: William E. Maguiness (1904–1976), U.S. radio, TV host.

Warner **Mack**: Warner McPherson (1938–), U.S. country singer. The singer is said to have gained his name through a mistake on a record label.

Mack 10: D. Rolison (1971–), U.S. black "gangsta" rapper.

Jim **McKay:** James Kenneth McManus (1921–2008), U.S. sportscaster, journalist

Kenneth R. **McKay** *see* Antony **McCall**

Scotty **McKay:** Max Karl Lipscomb (1937–1991), U.S. "rockabilly" guitarist, singer, movie actor.

Steele **MacKaye:** James Morrison Steele McKay (1842–1894), U.S. playwright, actor.

Sinclair **MacKellar** *see* Carter **Brown**

Kenneth **McKenna:** Leo Mielziner (1899–1962), U.S. movie actor, director. The actor adopted his mother's middle name as his stage name.

Siobhan **McKenna:** Siobhán Giolla Mhuire nic Cionaoith (1923–1986), Ir. stage, movie actress. The actress was raised in an Irish-speaking family and made her acting debut in the Irish language. She later broadened her repertoire to English-language plays and anglicized her name accordingly. (Her middle name gave English Gilmore, while Irish *nic*, "daughter," equates to *mac*, "son," in Mc- or Mac- names.)

Alexander Slidell **Mackenzie:** Alexander Slidell (1803–1848), U.S. naval officer, writer. Slidell kept his original family name until 1838, when he successfully petitioned the New York legislature to adopt his mother's maiden name as a surname in order to benefit from the legacy of a childless maternal uncle.

[Sir] Compton **Mackenzie:** Edward Montague Compton (1883–1972), Eng.-born Sc. novelist. The writer assumed (or reverted to) the original family name Mackenzie to emphasize his Scottish ancestry. His maternal grandfather was the actor Henry **Compton** and his sister the actress Fay **Compton**.

Scott **McKenzie:** Philip Blondheim (1944–), U.S. rock musician.

Charles **Macklin:** Charles M'Laughlin (or McLaughlin) (*c*.1700–1797), Ir. actor, playwright. The actor dropped the middle syllable of his name on establishing himself on the London stage in the 1730s.

Jason "Q.T." **McKnight:** Michael Cuccione (1985–2001), U.S. TV, movie actor.

Bridget **MacLagan:** Mary Borden (1886–1968), U.S.-born Eng. novelist.

Shirley **MacLaine:** Shirley MacLean Beaty (1934–), U.S. movie actress, sister of Warren **Beatty**. The actress dropped her surname and adapted the spelling of her mother's maiden name for her screen name.

Ian **Maclaren:** John Watson (1850–1907), Sc. presbyterian minister, writer. The minister first used the pseudonym, an adoption of his mother's maiden name, for his highly popular collection of sketches on Scottish rural life, *Beside the Bonnie Brier Bush* (1894). Watson was actually born in England, but came from pure Highland stock. ("Ian" is a Scottish equivalent of "John.")

Mona **McLennan:** Dorothy Cochrane Logan (*fl.*1920s), Br. swimmer. "Dr. Dorothy Cochrane Logan, of Harley Street, daughter of the late Colonel Logan, who adopts the name of Miss Mona McLennan for swimming purposes, has wrested the [English] Channel swimming 'record' for women from America" [*The Times*, October 12, 1927]. Dr. Logan later admitted she had fabricated her "record" time of 13 hrs 10 mins to swim from Cap Gris Nez, France, to Folkestone, England.

Fiona **Macleod:** William Sharp (1855–1905), Sc. author. The writer used the female name for his mystic Celtic tales and romances of peasant life in the manner of the "Celtic twilight" movement. The name Fiona, now a familiar girls' name, was first popularized by Sharp, and is based on Gaelic *fionn*, "white," "fair." Sharp maintained the fiction of "Fiona Macleod" until his death, and even had a bogus entry for the lady in *Who's Who*, in which he described "her" recreations as "boating, hill-climbing, and listening." He received many letters addressed to her, including a proposal of marriage from an ardent admirer of "her" poetry. The proposal was rejected "with a gravity befitting the occasion."

Sharp described the creation of the name in a letter to his friend Mrs. Janvier: "You have asked me once or twice about F.M., why I took her name.... The name was born naturally: (of course I had associations with the name Macleod) it, Fiona, is very rare now. Most Highlanders would tell you it was extinct — even as the diminutive of Fionaghal (Flora). But it is not. It is an old Celtic name (meaning "a fair maid") still occasionally to be found. I know a little girl, the daughter of a Highland clergyman, who is called Fiona ... I can write out of my heart in a way I could not do as William Sharp, and indeed I could not do so if I were the woman Fiona Macleod is supposed to be, unless veiled in scrupulous anonymity" [Elizabeth A. Sharp, *William Sharp (Fiona Macleod): A Memoir*, 1910].

Sharp's friend Grant Allen (*see* Olive Pratt **Raynor**) soon smelled a rat, and voiced his doubts in a letter to Sharp about his novel *A Fellowe and His Wife* (1892), coauthored with U.S. writer Blanche Willis Howard: "I was not quite satisfied you were not taking us in, especially as your book with Blanche Willis Howard had shown how womanly a tone you could adopt when it suited you; and I shan't feel absolutely at rest on the subject till I have seen the 'beautiful lassie' in person. If she turns out to be William Sharp in disguise, I shall owe you a bad one for it" [ibid.].

Mrs. Alick **MacLeod:** Catherine Edith Macauley Martin, née Mackay (1847–1937), Sc.-born Austral. novelist. Catherine Martin usually published anonymously or under a pseudonym. She was Mrs. Alick MacLeod for *The Silent Sea* (1892) but C.E.M. Martin for *The Incredible Journey* (1923). Her early novel *An Australian Girl* (1890) appeared anonymously, but the 1894 edition used the MacLeod name.

Mícheál **Mac Liammóir:** Alfred Willmore (1899–1978), Eng.-born Ir. stage, movie actor. As a juvenile the actor performed under his English name. In the 1920s he adopted a more romantic-sounding Gaelic name on joining the Gaelic League, an organization founded in 1893 with the purpose of keeping the Irish language spoken in Ireland. His surname, pronounced roughly "Macleemer," corresponds to the English original, but his first name is the Irish form of Michael.

The actor's *Who's Who* entry claims that he was born in Cork, Ireland, and that Alfred Willmore was his stage name. But it was actually his real name, and he was born in Willesden, London. The entry also says that he studied painting at the Slade School of Fine Art, London, but he was in fact a student at the Willesden Polytechnic, which is not quite the same.

Frank **McLowery** *see* Wes **Hardin**

Edward **MacLysaght:** Edward Lysaght (1888–1986), Eng.-born Ir. historian, genealogist. The First Herald of Ireland was born in England, a fact that he was reluctant to reveal. On completing his education at Oxford, he moved to Ireland and gradually became involved with the "Irish Ireland" political movement. In 1920 he added "Mac-" to his name to indicate its Gaelic origin more obviously.

Katie **McMullen:** Catherine Cookson (1906–1998), Eng. novelist. The popular writer adopted this name for her American readers. "When her agent [John Smith] persuaded a US publisher to try some of his client's books on the American market Catherine demanded they abandon the irritating [Catherine] **Marchant** pseudonym. Instead she delved into her childhood for a new — and 'more honest' — pen name.... Her American books, Catherine decided, should be issued under her childhood name of Katie McMullen" [Cliff Goodwin, *The Catherine Cookson Companion*, 1999]. Cookson was an illegitimate child and was raised by her mother, Rose McMullen, and her stepfather, John McMullen. The name by which she became known was that of her husband, Thomas Henry Cookson, whom she married in 1940.

Andy **McNab:** ? (1959–), Br. writer. The identity of the author of *Bravo Two Zero* (1994), his bestselling account of the capture and torture of members of his SAS (Special Air Service) patrol during the 1991 Gulf War, has never been fixed, as like all SAS personnel his safety is at risk. Nor does he reveal it in his autobiography, *Immediate Action* (1995). He was

abandoned newborn outside Guy's Hospital, London, and adopted at age five by a local couple. His name, probably falsely, suggests a Scottish origin.

Frances **MacNab:** Agnes D. Fraser (1859–1944), Eng. writer.

Brinsley **MacNamara:** John Weldon (1890–1963), Ir. stage actor, novelist, dramatist. Weldon also wrote as Oliver Blyth.

Gerald **MacNamara:** Harry C. Morrow (1866–1938), Ir. playwright, stage actor.

Gus **McNaughton:** Augustus Howard (1884–1969), Br. movie actor.

Pierre **Mac Orlan:** Pierre Dumarchey (1882–1970), Fr. novelist. The writer claimed to take his pen name from a Scottish grandmother, although she was entirely fictitious.

Elle **MacPherson:** Eleanor MacPherson Gow (1964–), Austral. model, TV actress. "Elle" from "Eleanor," though MacPherson did model for *Elle* magazine.

Butterfly **McQueen:** Thelma McQueen (1911–1995), U.S. black stage, movie actress. The actress's first name originated as a nickname following a production of *A Midsummer Night's Dream* in which she danced in the Butterfly Ballet. She then adopted it permanently.

Mark **Macrabin:** Allan Cunningham (1784–1842), Sc. writer, poet, songwriter. Cunningham used this name for a series of short stories called *The Recollections of Mark Macrabin, the Cameronian*, published in *Blackwood's Magazine* (1819–21).

Arthur **Macrae:** Arthur Schroepfer (1908–1962), Br. stage actor, playwright.

Ellen **McRae** *see* Ellen **Burstyn**

Georgius **Macropedius:** Joris van Lankveldt (1476–1558), Du. humanist. The scholar rendered his name into a classical equivalent, in the manner of his day. Latin Georgius (English "George") is Dutch Joris, while Greek-derived Macropedius (English "long field") is Dutch Lankveldt.

Seán **MacStiofáin:** John Edward Drayton Stephenson (1928–2001), Br.-born Ir. militant. The first chief of the Provisional IRA adopted the Irish equivalent of his English name some time before settling in Ireland in 1959.

Blind Willie **McTell:** William Samuel McTier (1901–1959), U.S. blues guitarist.

Ralph **McTell:** Ralph May (1944–), Br. folk songwriter.

Bill **Macy:** William Macy Garber (1922–), U.S. TV actor.

Madame ... For names beginning thus, see the following name, e.g. for Madame **Agnès** see **Agnès**, for Madame Floresta A. Brasileira see **Brasileira**, etc.

Juhan **Madarik:** Johannes Lauristin (1899–1941), Estonian writer. The writer's adopted plant name means "lady's bedstraw" (*Galium verum*), the Estonian word for which is *madar*.

Mad Cobra: Ewart Everton Brown (1968–), Jamaican reggae singer.

Minnie **Maddern** *see* Minnie Maddern **Fiske**

Rose **Maddox:** Roselea Arbana Brogden (1925–1998), U.S. country singer.

Jean **Madeira:** Jean Browning (1918–1972), U.S. opera singer.

Madeleine: Noor Inayat Khan (1914–1944), Br. wartime agent, working in France, of U.S.–Ind. parentage. Noor's full personal name was Noor-un-Nisa, "light of the women." Her mother, Begum Sharada Ameena, born Ora Ray Baker in 1890, married Inayat Khan in 1913.

[Sister] Mary **Madeleva:** Mary Evaline Wolff (1887–1964), U.S. nun, poet, educator.

Madge: [Mrs.] C.E. Humphry, née Graham (?–1925), Ir. journalist. The author used this name for her contributions to *Truth* and for her writings on etiquette, morals, and the like.

Madhavikutty: Kamala Das (1934–2009), Ind. poet, writer. Das adopted this pseudonym, from Madhavi, a name of the goddess Lakshmi, wife of Vishnu, and Malayalam *kutty*, "child," for her stories, novels, and plays. At the age of 67 she converted to Islam under the name Kamala Suraiyya, the latter name from Arabic *thurayya*, "the many little ones," a name of the Pleiades, the stars in the constellation Taurus, so called because there are many of them within a small area.

Madhubala: Begum Mumtaz Jehan (1933–1969), Ind. movie actress (the "Venus of India"). The Sanskrit screen name means "sweet child," "honey girl."

Haki R. **Madhubuti:** Don Luther Lee (1942–), U.S. black writer, critic. Lee adopted his Swahili name in 1973 as a result of the ideological influences of the Black Arts movement, of which he was a leading member.

Madilu System: Jean Bialu Madilu (1950–2007), Congolese musician.

Guy **Madison:** Robert Ozel Moseley (1922–1996), U.S. movie actor.

Hank **Madison** *see* Fenton **Brockley**

Noël **Madison:** Nathaniel Moscovitch (1898–1975), U.S. movie actor, of Russ. parentage.

Mad Lion: Oswald Preist (*c.*1970–), Br. black ragga, hip-hop musician. Mad Lion claims that his name is an acronym for "Musical Assassin Delivering Lyrical Intelligence Over Nations."

Madonella: Mary Astell (1668–1731), Eng. feminist, religious writer. The pseudonym can probably be understood as "little Madonna."

Madonna: Madonna Luisa Veronica Ciccone (1958–), U.S. pop singer, movie actress, of It. descent. The singer capitalized on her real first name with her 1984 hit, "Like a Virgin," a title intentionally at odds with her then hedonistic persona. Later titles also reflected the name, such as the 1991 compilation *The Immaculate Collection*.

Ron **Mael:** Ronald Day (1950–), U.S. rock musician, teaming with Russell **Mael**, his brother. The two brothers formed the rock group Sparks in 1971.

Russell **Mael:** Dwight Russell Day (1953–), U.S. rock musician.

K.H. **Maepen** *see* C.L. **Moore**

Johnny **Maestro:** John Mastrangelo (1939–2010), U.S. pop singer.

Magic Dick: Richard Salwitz (1945–), U.S. rock harmonica player.

Magic Sam: Samuel Gene Maghett (1937–1969), U.S. black blues musician. The singer and guitarist's stage name may have been suggested by his real name, Sam Maghett giving Magic Sam.

Magic Slim: Morris Holt (1937–), U.S. black blues musician. Holt was so named by **Magic Sam**.

Hyacinthe **Maglanowich:** Prosper Mérimée (1803–1870), Fr. novelist, historian. Just one of the pseudonyms adopted by the writer who also deluded his readers as Clara **Gazul**. He used it for *La Guzla* (1827), a book of ballads about murder, revenge, and vampires supposedly translated from the Illyrian.

Vasily **Magnitsky:** Vasily Konstantinovich Velelepov (1839–1901), Russ. historian, ethnographer, folklorist.

Philip **Magnus:** [Sir] Philip Magnus-Allcroft (1906–), Eng. biographer.

Magnus **Magnusson:** Magnus Sigursteinsson (1929–2007), Icelandic-born Br. broadcaster, writer. The popular TV quizmaster was born in Scotland to Icelandic parents. His father, the Icelandic consul-general for Scotland, was Sigursteinn Magnusson, and according to the traditional Icelandic practice, Magnus automatically acquired a surname directly based on his father's first name, as Sigursteinsson ("son of Sigursteinn"). However, he instead adopted his father's own surname, for ease of memorability and pronunciation (as well as alliteration). Just as sons add *-son* to their father's first name, so daughters add *-dóttir* (Magnus's mother was Ingibjorg Sigurdardóttir), and Icelandic women do not change their name on marriage, as conventionally elsewhere in the Western world.

Mr. **Magoo:** Mark Goodliffe (1965–), Br. crossword compiler. A pseudonym representing the setter's real name, while evoking the myopic cartoon character.

Lyudvig Ignatyevich **Magyar:** Lajos Milhover

(or Milgorf) (1891–1940), Hung.-born Russ. revolutionary, historian. The activist fought for the establishment of Soviet rule in Hungary. Hence his adopted name, the Hungarian word for "Hungarian."

[Venerable] **Mahaghosananda:** Va Yay (between 1922 and 1929–2007), Cambodian Buddhist monk. The Buddhist patriarch received his Sanskrit title, meaning "great shout of joy," on being awarded his doctoral degree in 1979.

Taj **Mahal:** Henry Saint Clair Fredericks (1940–), U.S. black blues musician. The musician's name is said to have appeared to him in a dream, although his musical style has little in common with the famous Indian mausoleum.

Mahalalel: Abraham Baer Gottlober (1811–1899), Russ. writer, working in Hebrew and Yiddish. Mahalalel is a biblical character, an Old Testament patriarch.

Maharaj Ji: Prem Pal Singh Rawat (1957–), Ind. guru. The leader of the Divine Light Mission (later Elan Vital) assumed a Sanskrit title meaning "perfect master." He became leader in 1966 at the age of eight on the death of his father, Shri Hans Ji Maharaj, who had founded the Mission in 1960, and subsequently shortened his name to Maharaji.

Maharal: Judah Loew (c.1529–1609), Jewish leader, legal expert. The name is an acronym of *Mo*renu *Ha*rav *Ra*bbi *Lo*ew, "Our Teacher Rabbi Loew."

Maharam: Meir ben Baruch (c.1215–1293), Jewish scholar, community leader. The name is an acronym of *Mo*renu *Ha*rav *Ra*bbi *M*eir, "Our Teacher Rabbi Meir."

Gurgen **Mahari:** Gurgen Grigoryevich Adzhemyan (1903–1969), Armenian writer. The writer began his career by writing pessimistic poems, and adopted a name to match, meaning "deathward" (Armenian *mah*, "death"). His verse brought him fame, and he kept the name even when writing much more positively.

Maharishi Mahesh Yogi: Mahesh Prasad Varma (1911 or 1917–2008), Ind. spiritual guru. The founder of Transcendental Meditation (1957) adopted a Sanskrit title meaning "great sage."

Maharsha: Samuel Eliezer ben Judah Halevi Edels (1555–1631), Jewish Talmudic commentator. The name is an acronym of *Mo*renu *Ha*rav *Ra*bbi *Sh*muel, "Our Teacher Rabbi Samuel."

Maharshal: Solomon ben Jehiel Luria (c.1510–1574), Jewish Talmudic commentator. The name is an acronym of *Mo*renu *Ha*rav *Ra*bbi *Sh*elomo Luria, "Our Teacher Rabbi Solomon Luria."

Mahlathini: Simon Nkabinde (1938–1999), S.A. black musician. The musician's professional name translates approximately from the Zulu as "bush on his head," a reference to his striking physical appearance and the rural roots of his upbringing.

Jock **Mahoney:** Jacques O'Mahoney (1919–1989), U.S. movie actor. The actor's screen name did not settle to Jock Mahoney until the mid–1950s. Before this time, from the mid–1940s, he was billed variously as Jacques J. O'Mahoney, Jock O'Mahoney, or Jack Mahoney.

Solomon **Maimon:** Solomon Heiman (1753–1800), Lithuanian-born German Jewish philosopher. The philosopher was attracted to the teachings of Maimonides (*see* **Rambam**), and adopted his name accordingly.

Maimonides *see* **Rambam**

Marjorie **Main:** Mary Tomlinson Krebs (1890–1975), U.S. movie actress. The actress, famous in her role as "Ma Kettle," took her screen name from the title of Sinclair Lewis's novel *Main Street* (1920). She was a minister's daughter, and changed her name to avoid embarrassing her family when she joined a local stock company.

Mainbocher: Main Rousseau Bocher (1891–1976), U.S.-born Fr. fashion designer.

Charles Eric **Maine:** David McIlwaine (1921–1981), Br. SF writer.

Marie-François-Pierre **Maine de Biran:** Marie-François-Pierre Gonthier de Biran (1766–1824), Fr. philosopher. The statesman and writer adopted the name Maine from Le Maine, his father's estate.

Máire: Séamus Ó Grianna (1889–1969), Ir. writer.

Antonio **Mairena:** Antonio Cruz García (1909–1983), Sp. flamenco singer. The singer's adopted name comes from his birthplace, Mairena del Alcor, near Madrid.

Maironis: Jonas Maciulis (1862–1932), Lithuanian poet. The poet adopted a plant name meaning "marjoram."

Ivan Mikhaylovich **Maisky:** Ivan Mikhaylovich Lyakhovitsky (1884–1975), Russ. ambassador to U.K.

John Wilson **Maitland:** [Sir] William Watson (1858–1935), Eng. poet.

Ruth **Maitland:** Ruth Erskine (1880–1961), Br. stage actress.

Thomas **Maitland:** Robert Williams Buchanan (1841–1901), Eng. poet, novelist. The writer used the name for his article "The Fleshly School of Poetry," attacking Pre-Raphaelites, and especially Dante Gabriel **Rossetti**, in the October 1871 edition of the *Contemporary Review.*

Maître Adam: Adam Billaut (1602–1662), Fr. carpenter, poet.

Marie **Majerová:** Marie Stívinová, née Bartošová (1882–1967), Cz. novelist.

MaJiKer: Matthew John Ker (1980–), Br. pop musician, working in France. "MaJiKer, like his name, is an amalgam of influences. His grandfather lived in Bangalore, making him Scottish by way of India, just as Ker is Birmingham by way of Paris" [*The Times*, September 25, 2009].

Tom **Major:** Abraham Thomas Ball (1879–1963), Eng. circus performer, vaudeville manager. The actor adopted his stage name in 1901 on taking up a career in variety. He was the father of John Major (1943–), British prime minister (1990–7), who kept the name.

Earl **Majors:** Alan Garreth (1953–1978), Eng. motorcycle stunt rider.

Lee **Majors:** Harvey Lee Yeary II (1940–), U.S. movie actor.

[Archbishop] **Makarios III:** Mikhail Khristodolou Mouskos (1913–1977), Cypriot head of state. The religious name (English Macarius) adopted by the archbishop is the Greek word for "blessed" and honors the 4th-century St. Macarius (*see* **Macarius**).

Nestor **Makhno:** Nestor Ivanovich Mikhnenko (1889–1935), Ukr. anarchist, military leader.

Mako: Makoto Iwamatsu (1933–2006), Jap.-born U.S. movie actor.

Adam **Makowicz:** Adam Matyszkowicz (1940–), Czech-born jazz pianist, of Pol. parentage, working in U.S. The musician began to use his new surname, a reduced form of the original, in the late 1960s. He became an American citizen in 1986.

Makriyannis: Yannis Triandafillos (1797–1864), Gk. memoirist.

Vladimir Yemelyanovich **Maksimov:** Lev Alekseyevich Samsonov (1930–1995), Russ. writer, editor. The writer emigrated to the West in 1974.

Ray **Mala:** Ray Wise (1906–1952), U.S.–Inuit (Eskimo) movie actor, cinematographer. The actor was also known by the native name Chee-ak.

Damiano **Malabaila:** Primo Levi (1919–1987), It. Jewish writer. Levi used this name when first publishing his collection of SF stories *Storie naturali* (1966).

Malachi **Malagrowther:** [Sir] Walter Scott (1771–1832), Sc. poet, novelist. Scott adopted his pen name, which he used for letters to the *Edinburgh Weekly Journal*, from Sir Mungo Malagrowther in his own novel *The Fortunes of Nigel* (1822), in which he is "a man of birth and talents, but naturally unamiable, and soured by misfortune, who now, mutilated by accident, and grown old, and deaf, and peevish, endeavours by the unsparing exercise of a malicious penetration and a caustic wit ... to retaliate on an unfriendly world, and to reduce its happier inhabitants to a momentary level with himself."

Patrick **Malahide:** Patrick G. Duggan (1945–),

Eng. TV actor. The actor long concealed his real name but used it for a radio play *Pleas and Directions* (2002), leading at least one reviewer to take it for his pen name: "It is written by P.G. Duggan — a pseudonym for the actor Patrick Malahide, who also stars" [Chris Campling in *The Times*, October 4, 2002].

Curzio **Malaparte:** Kurt Erich Suckert (1898–1957), It. writer, journalist. The writer adopted a surname that was intended to suggest the converse of that of Napoleon Bonaparte (or Buonaparte). The emperor's own name derives from a Corsican "auspicious" first name, meaning "goodly portion."

Malbim: Meir Laib ben Yehiel Michal (1809–1879), Russ. rabbi, biblical scholar. The Rabbinic scholar adopted an acronymic name formed from the initial letters of his Hebrew name.

John **Malcolm:** John Malcolm Andrews (1936–), Br. crime writer.

Malcolm X *see* Malcolm **X**

Karl **Malden:** Karl Mladen Sekulovich (1912–2009), U.S. movie, TV actor, of Cz.-Serbian parentage. "Malden had never been entirely happy at being forced to change his name and when he became a star he would encourage directors to feature the name Sekulovich somewhere in the film in honour of his father and his ethnic roots" [*The Times*, July 3, 2009].

Luigi **Malerba:** Luigi Bonardi (1927–), It. novelist, children's writer.

Lucas **Malet:** Mary St. Leger Harrison, née Kingsley (1852–1931), Eng. novelist. The daughter of novelist Charles Kingsley (1819–1875) took her (male) pseudonym from the surnames of her grandmother and great-grandmother, saying she "did not think it right to trade on the Kingsley name" [Marble, p.213]. She first used it for her second novel, *Colonel Enderby's Wife* (1885).

La **Malibran:** María de la Felicidad García (1808–1836), Fr.-born Sp. opera singer. The mezzosoprano came to be known by the name of her first husband, Eugène Malibran.

Peter **Malin** *see* Rearden **Conner**

Max **Malini:** Max K. Breit (1873–1942), Pol.-born U.S. magician. The illusionist's name, suggesting "bad," "evil," matched his unprepossessing appearance and crude acting style.

David **Mallet:** David Malloch (?1705–1765), Sc. poet, writer. The poet adopted an anglicized version of his Scottish name in 1724, writing in a letter to a friend at the time that "there is not one Englishman that can pronounce [Malloch]." Dr. Johnson strongly disapproved of this change, and referred to it in his definition of the word "alias" in his *Dictionary* (1755): "*alias* means otherwise, as Mallet *alias* Malloch, that is, otherwise Malloch."

Françoise **Mallet-Joris:** Françoise-Eugénie-Julienne Lilar (1930–), Belg.-born Fr. writer. The writer adopted the maiden name of her mother, Belgian novelist Suzanne Lilar (1901–1988).

Mathilde **Mallinger:** Mathilde Lichtenegger (1847–1920), Croatian opera singer.

Jay **Mallory** *see* Joyce **Carey**

Gina **Malo:** Janet Flynn (1909–1963), Ir.-Ger.–U.S. stage, movie actress, working in U.K.

Andrew E. **Malone:** Lawrence Patrick Byrne (1888–1939), Ir. theater critic, journalist.

Dorothy **Malone:** Dorothy Eloise Maloney (1925–), U.S. movie, TV actress. The actress modified her name on joining Warner Bros. in 1945.

Louis **Malone:** Louis MacNeice (1907–1963), Ir. dramatist, poet. The writer took his early pen name from his birthplace, Malone Road, Belfast, using it for his novel *Roundabout Way* (1932).

Molly **Malone:** Edith R. Greaves (?1897–?1952), U.S. movie actress. Many of the actress's biographical details remain uncertain. Her "real" name, given here, is perhaps her married name. Molly Malone is the subject of an anonymous Irish folksong ("In Dublin's fair city, where girls are so pretty, / I first set my eyes on sweet Molly Malone").

Ruth **Malone** *see* Craig **Rice**

Shaun **Malory:** Reginald James Kingston Russell (1883–1943), Eng. editor, writer.

Conrad **Malte-Brun:** Malte Conrad Bruun (1775–1826), Dan.-born Fr. geographer.

Therese **Malten:** Therese Müller (1855–1930), Ger. soprano.

Yelizar **Maltsev:** Yelizar Yuryevich Pupko (1917–), Russ. writer. The writer adopted a more euphonious name than his original surname (suggesting Russian *pup*, "navel").

Eily **Malyon:** Eileen Lees-Craston (1879–1961), Eng. movie actress, working in U.S.

Cheb **Mami:** Khelifati Muhammad (1966–), Algerian singer. The "prince of rai" (as distinct from **Khaled**, the "king of rai") adopted an Arabic name meaning "young mourner."

Dmitry **Mamin-Sibiryak:** Dmitry Narkisovich Mamin (1852–1912), Russ. writer. The addition to the writer's name means "Siberian." He was born near Yekaterinburg, just east of the Urals, and originally trained for the priesthood. He explains how friends gave his name: "I first tried out the names Rasskazov [Russian *rasskaz*, "story"] and Tomsky [*tom*, "volume"], but they weren't right! My name was an object of fun to my fellow ordinands: why were we Mamin ["momma's boys"], not Tyatin ["daddy's boys"]? They decided the best pseudonym was Sibiryak. After all, Yekaterinburg is the other side of the Urals, and Russians regard everywhere beyond the Urals, including Siberia, as all one!" [Dmitriyev, p.92].

Mammootty: Mohammed Kutty (1953–), Ind. movie actor.

Felix **Man:** Hans Felix Sigismund Baumann (1893–1985), Ger. pioneer photojournalist, working in U.K.

Mana-Zucca: Gizella Zuccamanov (1885–1981), U.S. pianist, singer, of Pol. parentage. The musician's adopted name was a rearrangement of her surname. (Her father, Samuel Shepard Zuccamanov, later changed the family name to Zuccaman.)

Manchecourt: Henri Léon Emile Lavedan (1859–1940), Fr. playwright, novelist. The writer presumably took his name from the village of Manchecourt, south of Paris.

Thomas **Mancinus:** Thomas Mencken (1550–c.1630), Ger. composer.

Kevin **Mancuso** *see* Joe **D'Amato**

Georges **Mandel:** Louis-Georges Rothschild (1885–1943), Fr. political leader.

Sammy **Mandell:** Samuel Mandella (1904–1967), It.-born U.S. boxer.

Sir John **Mandeville:** Jehan de Bourgogne (Jehan à la Barbe) (*c.*1300–1372), Flemish traveler. The name is that of the author of *The Voiage and Travaile of Sir John Maudervile, Kt.*, a book of (mainly fictitious) travels originally published in French between 1357 and 1371. The work was first published in English in 1499 and "Mandeville" was lauded as the "father of English prose" until 1725, when a French origin for the account was established, and the author tentatively identified as above.

Mané-Katz: Emanuel Katz (1894–1962), Ukr.-born Fr. painter. "Mané" is a pet form of "Emanuel."

Frederick **Manfred:** Frederick Feikema (1912–1994), U.S. novelist, of Frisian descent. The writer called himself Feike Feikema from 1944 through 1951.

Nino **Manfredi:** Nino Saturnino (1921–2004), It. movie actor. Some sources give the actor's original name as Castro dei Volsci.

Fanny **Manieux** *see* Jehanne **d'Alcy**

Barry **Manilow:** Barry Alan Pinkus (1946–), U.S. popular singer. The singer assumed the name of his paternal grandmother. Manilow's father, Harold Kelliher, was of Irish descent, and changed his name to Pinkus to avoid conflict with the singer's grandmother, who would not have been pleased to learn that her daughter, Edna Manilow, was marrying out of the Jewish religion. Barry's father left the family when the boy was only two years old, and Edna changed his last name to Manilow when he was 13 [Stambler, p.438].

Handsome Dick **Manitoba:** Richard Blum (1954–), U.S. rock singer.

Mankind: Michael Francis Foley (1965–), U.S. wrestler. Foley originally wrestled as Cactus Jack (presumably from the nickname of U.S. vice president John Nance Garner, who was a Texas rancher) and Dude Love. He then changed Cactus Jack to Cactus Jack Manson, after the serial killer Charles **Manson**, but in 1996 was signed up by the World Wrestling Federation as a new masked character who was originally to be called Manson the Mutilator but who settled less contentiously as Mankind.

Abby **Mann**: Abraham Goodman (1927–2008), U.S. movie, TV scriptwriter, of Eastern European parentage.

Abel **Mann** *see* Gordon **Ashe**

Al **Mann**: Gilbert Aleman (1920–1999), U.S. magician.

Anthony **Mann**: Emil Anton Bundesmann (1906–1967), U.S. movie director.

Barry **Mann**: Barry Iberman (1939–), U.S. pop songwriter.

Daniel **Mann**: Daniel Chugermann (1912–1991), U.S. movie director.

Hank **Mann**: David W. Lieberman (or Lieberman) (1887–1971), U.S. movie comedian.

Herbie **Mann**: Herbert Jay Solomon (1930–2003), U.S. jazz flutist.

Kal **Mann**: Kalman Cohen (1917–2001), U.S. pop musician, songwriter. Originally a comedy writer, the cofounder of Cameo Records sometimes used the name John Sheldon for his songwriting.

Manfred **Mann**: Michael Lubowitz (1940–), S.A.-born Eng. pop musician. The new name has echoes of German legend and literature, from the Faustian figure Manfred who forms the subject of Byron's 1817 poetic drama, and the German writer Thomas Mann (1875–1955).

Theodore **Mann**: Theodore Goldman (1924–), U.S. stage producer, director.

Mary **Mannering**: Florence Friend (1876–1953), Eng. stage actress, working in U.S.

Max **Mannering** *see* Timothy **Titcomb**

Charles **Manners**: Southcote Mansergh (1857–1935), Ir. opera singer, working in England.

David **Manners**: Rauff de Ryther Duan Acklom (1901–1998), Can. stage, movie actor, novelist.

Miss **Manners**: Judith Sylvia Martin, née Perlman (1938–), U.S. writer on etiquette.

Mrs. Horace **Manners**: Algernon Charles Swinburne (1837–1909), Eng. poet. The poet used this name for his novel *A Year's Letters*, originally serialized in 1877 but republished in 1905 as *Love's Cross Currents*.

Bob **Manning**: Manny Levin (1926–), U.S. ballad singer.

David **Manning** *see* Max **Brand**

Dick **Manning**: Samuel Medoff (1912–1991), Russ.-born U.S. songwriter.

Irene **Manning**: Inez Harvuot (1912–2004), U.S. movie actress, singer. The actress made her screen debut in *The Old Corral* (1936) under the name Hope Manning, from the first of her four husbands, Het Manheim, head of publicity at Republic Studios.

Manolete: Manuel Laureano Rodríguez Sánchez (1917–1947), Sp. bullfighter. The matador's ring name means "Little Manuel."

Manolo: Manuel Martínez Hugué (1872–1945), Sp. sculptor. "Manolo" is a pet form of "Manuel."

Man Ray: Emmanuel Rabinovich Radnitsky (1890–1976), U.S. surrealist painter, photographer, of Russ. Jewish parentage. Radnitsky adopted his new name when at art school in Manhattan. "Emmanuel had passed his twenty-first birthday and ... still harbored bitter memories of having been teased at school because of his foreign name.... Many people called Emmanuel 'Manny' for short, and he had been toying with his signature initials on recent work, changing them to 'MR' occasionally. The two brothers [Emmanuel and Samuel] came up with 'Ray' as a direct shortening, an abbreviation for Radnitsky. Despite sister Dora's protestations when she found out, too late, that it sounded 'too Irish'— she would have preferred something like 'Radin'— the whole family, not just Emmanuel, took the new name" [Neil Baldwin, *Man Ray*, 1988]. The artist's real name long remained unknown, and was publicly revealed only after his death. His adopted name is often regarded as a first name (Man) and last name (Ray), but Man Ray himself preferred to list it as a single unit.

Henry Hugo **Mansfeldt** *see* Henry Hugo **Pierson**

[Sir] James **Mansfield**: James Manfield (1733–1821), Eng. lawyer. The Lord Chief Justice of the Court of Common Pleas inserted the "s" in his name when at Cambridge University, thus creating a regular English name from what was said to have originally been a non-English one (perhaps Manfeld).

Jayne **Mansfield**: Vera Jayne Palmer (1933–1967), U.S. movie actress. The actress's screen surname is that of her first husband, Paul Mansfield (married 1950, divorced 1956).

Katherine **Mansfield**: Kathleen Mansfield Murry, née Beauchamp (1888–1923), N.Z.-born Br. novelist, short-story writer.

Portia **Mansfield**: Portia Mansfield Swett (1887–1979), U.S. dance educator, choreographer. The dancer changed her name from Portia Swett to Portia Mansfield in 1921.

Charles **Manson**: Charles Miles Maddox (1934–). U.S. cult leader, serial killer. The name of Manson's biological father is uncertain. His mother was Kathleen Maddox, who subsequently married William Manson, and the boy was given his name.

Marilyn **Manson:** Brian Hugh Warner (1969–), U.S. rock singer. The "shock rocker" took his stage name from the first name of Marilyn **Monroe** and last name of Charles **Manson**. Other members of his group Marilyn Manson and the Spooky Kids patterned their stage names on Manson's: Scott Mitchell Putesky became Daisy Berkowitz, Stephen Bier, Jr., was reincarnated as Madonna Wayne Gacy, and Fred Streithorst II gained a new persona as Sara Lee Lucas. Manson made part of his first record in the Hollywood house where the eponymous cult leader had murdered the pregnant actress Sharon Tate and four of her friends in 1969, the year when Warner was born. "To call Marilyn Manson — admire the combo of all–American victim and all–American killer — one of the bad boys of rock 'n' roll is inadequate" [Andrew Billen, "Brian and the beast," *The Times*, September 16, 2002].

Erich von **Manstein:** Erich von Lewinski (1887–1973), Ger. field marshal. The military commander's surname is that of General Georg von Manstein, who adopted the boy following the untimely death of his parents.

Abdullah **Mansur:** George Wyman Bury (1874–1920), Eng. explorer, naturalist. The author assumed this Arabic name for his book *The Land of Uz* (1911), an account of his travels in Aden, then a British colony.

Tsetsiliya **Mansurova:** Tsetsiliya Lvovna Vollershteyn (Wallerstein) (1897–?), Russ. stage actress.

Paul **Mantee:** Paul Marianetti (1936–), U.S. movie actor.

Hilary **Mantel:** Hilary Mary McEwen, née Thompson (1952–), Br. novelist. The writer adopted the name of her stepfather, Jack Mantel.

Peter **Manton** *see* Gordon **Ashe**

Mantovani: Annunzio Paolo (1905–1980), It.-born Br. conductor, musical arranger, working in U.S. The musician adopted his mother's maiden name as his sole name at the age of 16, when he began his professional career as a violinist.

Manuel: Manuel R. Thomas (1886–1934), U.S. vaudeville artist, conjuror.

E. **Manuel:** Ernest L'Épine (1826–1893), Fr. writer. A potentially misleading pseudonym, since it suggests the French poet and dramatist Eugène Manuel (1823–1901), who wrote under his real name.

Roland **Manuel:** Roland Alexis Lévy (1891–1966), Fr. composer, music critic.

Manuelito: Hashkeh Naabah (?1818–1893), U.S. American Indian chief. The Navaho leader was given his Indian war name, meaning Angry Warrior, for his prowess against the Mexicans, who in turn gave him his Spanish name. His earlier name was Ch'ilhaajinii (Black Weeds).

[Sir] Edward **Manville:** Edward Mosley (1862–1933), Eng. electrical engineer, automobile manufacturer, of Jewish parentage. The industrialist's father changed the family's surname of Mosley to Manville in the 1870s.

Phil **Manzanera:** Philip Targett-Adams (1951–), Br. rock musician, of Eng.-Colombian parentage.

Manzhelli: Pavel Afanasyevich Shevchenko (1872–1948), Russ. circus artist, horseman. The performer's Italian-style name (Mangelli) probably derives from Russian *manezh*, "riding school" (from French *manège*) with the common Italian name suffix *-elli*. His sons inherited the name as jockeys.

Giacomo **Manzù:** Giacomo Manzoni (1908–1991), It. sculptor.

Mao Dun: Shen Yan-bing (1896–1981), Chin. novelist. The writer's pseudonym puns on Chinese *máodùn*, "contradiction," alluding to his stance in 1930 following the break between the Kuomintang, his previous employers, and the Chinese Communist Party.

Maori: James Inglis (1845–1908), Sc.-born N.Z. author, journalist, politician.

Le **Mapah:** Simon Ganneau (1805–1851), Fr. sculptor, religious leader. The Frenchman was the originator of *Évadisme*, a quasireligion founded in about 1835 that exalted the standing of woman and preached equality of the sexes. Its name is based on the first two letters of "Eve" and "Adam," while "Mapah" derives from the first two letters of Latin *mater*, "mother," and *pater*, "father."

T.M. **Maple:** Jim Burke (1956–1994), Can. comic letter writer. Burke was originally nicknamed "The Mad Maple," and the first two words of this gave his initials. The maple is the Canadian national tree.

Anna **Mar:** Anna Yakovlevna Lenshina, née Brovar (1887–1917), Russ. writer, screenwriter. Mar wrote a column for the *Zhurnal dlya zhenshchin* ("Women's Journal") as Printsessa Grëza ("Princess Daydream"), answering readers' inquiries.

Adele **Mara:** Adelaida Delgado (1923–), Sp.-U.S. dancer, movie actress.

Sally **Mara:** Raymond Queneau (1903–1976), Fr. writer.

Jean **Marais:** Jean Alfred Villain-Marais (1913–1998), Fr. stage, movie actor.

Marc: Charles Mark Edward Boxer (1931–1988), Eng. cartoonist.

Conrad **Marca-Relli:** Corrado Marcarelli (1913–), U.S. Abstract Expressionist painter, of It. parentage.

Félicien **Marceau:** Louis Carette (1913–), Belg. novelist, dramatist.

Marcel **Marceau:** Marcel Mangel (1923–2007), Fr. mime. The artist was of Jewish parentage and decided to adopt a less obviously Jewish name on joining the Resistance in World War II. His new name, which blended nicely with his existing first name, came from that of the French Revolutionary general François Séverin Marceau (originally Marceau-Desgraviers) (1769–1796).

Sophie Marceau: Sophie Danièle Sylvie Maupu (1966–), Fr. movie actress. Maupu took her screen name at age 13 when driving with her parents along the Avenue Marceau, Paris, to her first audition, for the teen drama *La Boum* ("The Party") (1980).

Marcelin: Émile-Marcelin-Isidore Planet (1829–1887), Fr. writer, book illustrator.

Marcellus II: Marcello Cervini degli Spannochi (1501–1555), It. pope. The pontiff chose to retain his baptismal name.

Anne March: Constance Fenimore Woolson (1850–1894), U.S. writer. Woolson used this name for a young person's novel, *The Old Stone House* (1872).

Elspeth March: Elspeth Mackenzie (1911–1999), Br. stage actress.

Fredric March: Ernest Frederick McIntyre Bickel (1897–1975), U.S. stage, movie actor. The actor changed his name in 1924 at the suggestion of movie director John Cromwell, who felt that "Bickel" sounded too much like "pickle." So the star of *A Star Is Born* (1937) adapted his mother's maiden name of Marcher as his screen surname. Some years later he commented, "I wish I'd left it as it was — after all, [movie actor] Theodore Bickel did all right."

Jane March: Jane March Horwood (1973–), Br. movie actress.

Little Peggy March: Margaret Battavio (1948–), U.S. pop singer, songwriter. The singer's stage name evolved from her first appearance at the age of five.

Maxwell March: Margery Allingham (1904–1966), Br. crime novelist.

William March: William Edward Campbell (1893–1954), U.S. writer, business executive. The writer first used his pen name, adopted from his mother's maiden name, for stories published in various little magazines in the late 1920s.

Georges Marchal: Georges-Louis Lucot (1920–1997), Fr. movie actor.

Bobby Marchan: Oscar James Gibson (1930–1999), U.S. R&B singer.

Catherine Marchant: Catherine Cookson (1906–1998), Eng. novelist. The popular writer adopted this name for her romantic magazine stories, the first of which appeared in 1961. "John Smith, her agent, had been asked if his client would consider writing a romantic novel ... 'I couldn't think of a name so John said he would find me one,' explained Catherine. 'In the end he came up with Marchant. I

thought it was terrible. I hated it'" [Cliff Goodwin, *The Catherine Cookson Companion*, 1999]. *See also* Katie **McMullen.**

Samuel Marchbanks: Robertson Davies (1913–1995), Can. novelist, playwright. The writer adopted this name for a regular column in the *Examiner* and other papers.

Martin Marches: Martin Aleksandrovich Myuller (Müller) (1894–1961), Hung.-born Russ. illusionist.

Rocky Marciano: Rocco Francis Marchegiano (1923–1969), U.S. heavyweight boxer. The boxer had one fight as an amateur under the name "Rocky Mack" in 1947 before turning professional the following year under his familiar ring name. He is sometimes confused with Rocky **Graziano.**

Theophilus Marcliffe: William Godwin (1756–1836), Eng. philosopher, novelist, dramatist. The author of *Caleb Williams* (1794) used this name for *The Looking Glass; A True History of the Early History of an Artist* (1805). His new first name is a Greek equivalent of his original surname, meaning "friend of God." His main pen name was Edward **Baldwin.**

Marco: Edward Dooley (?–1908), U.S. magician. The illusionist was usually billed as "Marco the Magician."

Marcos: Marcos Roberto Silveira Reis (1974–), Brazilian footballer.

Subcommandante Marcos: Rafael Sebastián Guillén (1958–), Mexican guerrilla.

Louis Marcoussis: Louis Markus (1878–1941), Pol.-born Fr. painter. The artist's pseudonym, although close to his original name, was suggested to him by the poet **Apollinaire,** and came from the village of Marcoussis near Paris.

Marcus Aurelius: Marcus Annius Verus (AD 121–180), Roman emperor, philosopher. When Marcus was adopted at the age of 17 by his uncle, the emperor Antoninus Pius, earlier named Titus Aurelius Antoninus, his name was changed to Marcus Aelius Aurelius Verus. He succeeded Antoninus as emperor in 161, when he adopted the full name and imperial title of Imperator Caesar Marcus Aurelius Antoninus Augustus.

Luis Marden: Annibale Luigi Paragallo (1913–2003), U.S. photographer, explorer.

Mardoni: Clayton Hines (1904–1987), U.S. conjuror, "mentalist."

Marevna: Maria Vorobieva (1892–1984), Russ. painter, working in France, U.K. The artist was given her professional name, based on her real name, by Maxim **Gorky.**

Margery: Mina Crandon (1886–1941), U.S. medium.

Margo: María Marguerita Guadelupe Teresa

Estela Bolado Castilla y O'Donnell (1918–1985), Mexican-born stage, movie actress, dancer, working in U.S.

[Sor] **María de Jesús de Ágreda:** María Fernández Coronel (1602–1665), Sp. abbess, mystic. The abbess was the head of the Franciscan monastery in the Spanish town of Ágreda, where she was also born and where she died.

Maria del Occidente: Abigail Gowen (*c.*1795–1845), U.S. poet. Following her father's death in 1809, Abigail came under the care of her widowed brother-in-law, John Brooks. They married the following year, when she was about 15 and he almost 50, and in 1819 she changed her name legally to Mary Abigail Brooks. Soon after, she began calling herself Maria Gowen Brooks. Traveling in England in 1831, she met the poet Robert Southey, to whom she had earlier sent copies of her poems, and he offered to find an English publisher for her poem *Zóphiël*, the first canto of which had appeared in Boston, Massachusetts, in 1825. In 1833 it was published in both England and the United States under the Italian (or Spanish) pseudonym "Maria del Occidente" ("Mary of the West"), a name that Brooks had apparently adopted before her meeting with Southey.

Edna **Marian:** Edna Mannan (or Mannen, or Hannam) (1906 or 1908–1957), U.S. movie comedian.

Charlie **Mariano:** Carmino Ugo Mariano (1923–2009), U.S. jazz saxophonist, of It.–U.S. parentage. The musician originally anglicized his first names to Charles Hugo before settling on just "Charlie."

Luis **Mariano:** Mariano Eusebio González (1920–1970), Fr. movie actor, of Sp. origin.

Mother **Marie Alphonse:** Elizabeth Eppinger (1814–1867), Fr. religious. Eppinger took religious vows in 1848 and a year later founded the Daughters of the Divine Redeemer under her religious name.

Marie-Augustine de la Compassion: Marie Jamet (1820–1893), Fr. religious.

Marie de la Croix: Jeanne Jugan (1792–1879), Fr. religious. The foundress of the Little Sisters of the Poor, a community dedicated to caring for the infirm and indigent elderly, was beatified in 1982 and canonized as a saint in 2009.

Marie de l'Incarnation *see* **Mary of the Incarnation**

Marie-Jeanne: Marie-Jeanne Pelus (1920–2007), U.S. ballet dancer, of It.-Fr. parentage.

Marie Madeleine: Marie Madeleine von Puttkamer, née Marie Günther (1881–1944), Ger. poet.

Mariemma: Emma Martinez (1920–), Sp. ballet dancer. A name extracted from the dancer's original name.

Frère **Marie-Victorin:** Conrad Kirouac (1885–1944), Can. religious, naturalist.

Marilyn: Peter Robinson (1963–), Eng. pop singer. The singer, a friend of **Boy George**, affected a blond, androgynous look, vaguely reminiscent of Marilyn **Monroe**.

Jean **Marin:** Yves-André-Marie Morvan (1909–1995), Fr. journalist, radio commentator.

Marina: Malintzin (or Malinche) (*c.*1501–1550), Mexican Indian princess. The mistress of Hernán Cortés during his conquest of Mexico renounced her Indian name on her conversion to Christianity.

J.-J. **Marine:** René Oppitz (1904–1976), Belg. poet, critic, detective-story writer.

Marin-Marie: Paul Marin Durand Couppel de Saint-Front (1901–1987), Fr. yachtsman, marine painter. The name evokes St. Mary, a patron of sailors, whose own name suggests Latin *mare*, "sea."

Mario: Mario Hubert Armengol (1909–1995), Sp.-born Br. painter, cartoonist.

E.A. **Mario:** Giovanni Gaeta (1884–1961), It. dialect songwriter, poet.

Giovanni Matteo **Mario:** Mario Cavaliere di Candia (1810–1883), It. opera singer. The romantic tenor signed his first contract in 1838 with his forename alone, and thereafter adopted it as his surname, adding new first names.

Don **Marion** *see* John **Henry, Jr.**

Frances **Marion:** Marion Benson Owens (1888–1973), U.S. screenwriter. The future screenwriter was hired as an actress in 1914 by movie director Lois Weber and given the stage name Frances Marion, perhaps suggested by the revolutionary soldier Francis Marion ("Swamp Fox"). She preferred working on the other side of the screen, however, and used her name for that instead.

Joan **Marion:** Joan Nicholls (1908–1945), Br. stage actress. The actress took her mother's first name as her stage name.

Kitty **Marion:** Katherina Maria Schafer (1871–1944), Ger.-born Br. music-hall artist, suffragist.

Mona **Maris:** Maria Capdevielle (1903–1991), Fr.-Argentinian movie actress, working in U.S.

Roger **Maris:** Roger Eugene Maras (1934–1985), U.S. baseball player.

Marisol: Marisol Escobar (1930–), Fr.-born U.S. sculptor, of Venezuelan parentage. (Some sources give Marisol's full name as Escobar Marisol, but Marisol is a female Spanish forename, not a surname.)

Sari **Maritza:** Patricia Detering-Nathan (1911–1987), Eng.-Austr. movie actress.

Mariza: Mariza Nunes (1974–), Mozambiquan fado singer.

J. **Marjoram:** Ralph Hale Mottram (1883–

1971), Eng. novelist, poet. The writer used this name for two slim volumes of verse published in 1907 and 1909.

Jane **Marken:** Jane Krab (1895–1976), Fr. movie actress.

Chris **Marker:** Christian François Bouche-Villeneuve (1921–), Fr. movie director.

David **Markham:** Peter Basil Harrison (1913–1983), Eng. stage actor.

Joseph **Markham:** John Thomson Stonehouse (1925–1988), Eng. politician, fraudster. After a fine political career as a Labour minister in the second half of the 1960s, Stonehouse became a business tycoon in the growing world of fringe banking, manipulating funds to conceal mismanagement and fraud. Pride would not allow him to admit failure, so with his mistress, Mrs. Sheila Buckley, he devised an elaborate plan to "die" and then start a new life in Australia. For the purpose he obtained a copy of the birth certificate of one Joseph Markham, a man of his own age who had recently died, forged a passport application with his own photograph, and in 1974 flew to Miami, ostensibly for discussions with bank officials. On November 21, at the end of one meeting, he said he was going for a swim. A few hours later his clothes were found on the beach and he was assumed to have drowned. On Christmas Eve he was discovered in Melbourne, Australia, by police who were actually looking for the missing Lord Lucan. He was extradited, brought to trial, and jailed for seven years on fraud and conspiracy charges. He was released in 1979, divorced his wife, married Mrs. Buckley, and turned to writing thrillers.

Stonehouse's "pseudocide" is said to have been inspired by Frederick Forsyth's novel *The Day of the Jackal* (1971), about a plot to kill General de Gaulle. The story involves the obtaining of a new passport using the duplicate birth certificate of a deceased person, a classic method of assuming a new identity.

Mrs. **Markham:** Elizabeth Penrose, née Cartwright (1780–1837), Eng. novelist, children's writer. The writer took her pen name from the village of Markham, Nottinghamshire, where she visited two maiden aunts as a girl and where she met her future husband, John Penrose, whom she married in 1814.

Robert **Markham:** Kingsley Amis (1922–1995), Eng. novelist, poet, playwright, short-story writer. Amis used this name for *Colonel Sun: A James Bond Adventure* (1968). "It's easy to spell and easy to remember," he said.

Markos: Markos Vafiadis (1906–1996), Gk. Communist activist. Vafiadis was known by this *nom de guerre* as a leader of Greek resistance against Nazi invasion.

[Dame] Alicia **Markova:** Lillian Alice Marks (1910–2004), Eng. ballet dancer. The dancer was given her Russian-style name when she was still at ballet school: "After a heated discussion and references to Tolstoi and Dostoievski, we settled on the obvious *Markova*" [Arnold Haskell, *Balletomania*, 1934].

Alfred **Marks:** Alfred Edward Touchinsky (1921–1996), Br. stage, movie comedian, singer, of Pol. Jewish parentage. The actor adopted his stage name by deed poll after World War II.

Marksman: J.C. Walker (1892–1981), Welsh-born Br. cartoonist. The name is apt for an artist who aims to "hit home" in his cartoons. It was also appropriate for Walker, who was a rifle-shooting champion.

Marky Mark: Mark Wahlberg (1971–), U.S. pop singer, movie actor. The actor used this name early in his career as a rapper.

John **Marley:** Mortimer Marlieb (1907–1984), U.S. stage, movie actor, of Russ. parentage.

Marley Marl: Marlon Williams (1962–), U.S. black hip-hop musician, radio host.

Lene **Marlin:** Lene Marlin Petersen (1980–), Norw. popular singer.

Eugenie **Marlitt:** Eugenie John (1825–1887), Ger. novelist.

Ed **Marlo:** Edward Malkowski (1913–1991), U.S. conjuror.

Louis **Marlow:** Louis Umfreville Wilkinson (1881–1966), Br. novelist, biographer.

Rt. Hon. Lady Harriet **Marlow** *see* Jacquetta Agneta Mariana **Jenks**

Anthony **Marlowe:** Anthony Perredita (1913–), Eng. stage actor. The actor adopted his mother's maiden name as his stage name.

Charles **Marlowe:** Harriett Jay (1857–1932), Eng. novelist, playwright, stage actress. The writer used the male name for her plays, many coauthored with her adoptive father, the poet Robert Buchanan.

Hugh **Marlowe:** Hugh Herbert Hipple (1914–1982), U.S. movie actor.

Hugh **Marlowe** *see* Jack **Higgins**

Julia **Marlowe:** Sarah Frances Frost (1866–1950), Eng.-born U.S. stage, movie actress. The actress first appeared on stage at the age of 12 with the name Fanny Brough, the latter being the surname adopted by her family when they came to the United States in 1870. She took her melodious regular stage name on moving to New York in 1882.

June **Marlowe:** Gisela Valaria Goetten (1903–1984), U.S. movie actress.

Stephen **Marlowe:** Milton Lesser (1928–2008), U.S. mystery writer. First publishing novels under his real name, Lesser then began writing detective novels under his pen name, based on that of Philip Marlowe, the private eye in the short stories and novels of Raymond Chandler.

Vic **Marlowe**: Victor Hugh Etheridge (?–1987), Br. variety actor, dancer, teaming with Bobbie **Medlock**, his wife.

Anna **Marly**: Anna Yuryevna Betulinskaya (1917–2006), Russ.-born singer, songwriter, working in France. The singer, famous for her melody *Chant des Partisans* ("Song of the partisans"), broadcast in World War II to patriots in Nazi-occupied France, is said to have picked her name from a phone book.

Florence **Marly**: Hana Smekalova (1918–1978), Fr.-Cz. movie actress.

Richard **Marner**: Alexander Molchanoff (1921–2004), Russ.-born Br. TV actor.

Robert **Marner** *see* Algis **Budrys**

Jeanne **Marni**: Jeanne Marnière (1854–1910), Fr. writer.

Maroc: Robert S.E. Coram (*fl.*1930s–after 1970), Eng. cartoonist. A straightforward reversal.

Martin **Marprelate**: John Penry (1559–1593), Welsh Puritan writer + John Udall (?1560–1592), Eng. Puritan preacher + Henry Barrow (?–1593), Eng. church reformer + Job Throckmorton (1545–1601), Eng. Puritan. The name, with its pun on "mar prelate" (i.e. "attack the episcopacy"), was used for a number of anonymous (or pseudonymous) tracts directed against the bishops and defending the Presbyterian system of discipline. The tracts were issued from a secret press in the two years from 1588, and the suspected authors were the Puritan pamphleteers mentioned. Penry and Barrow were executed. Udall died in prison, but Throckmorton, denying his complicity, escaped punishment.

Marqueez: Laily Saldin (1918–1992), Br. exotic dancer, of part-Ceylonese parentage. The dancer's name is a variant form of French *marquise*, "marchioness."

Marquitos: Marcos Alonso Imaz (1933–), Sp. footballer. A diminutive form of the player's first name.

J.J. **Marric** *see* Gordon **Ashe**

Moore **Marriott**: George Thomas Moore-Marriott (1885–1949), Br. movie comedian.

Mlle. **Mars**: Anne-Françoise-Hippolyte Boutet (1779–1847), Fr. actress, daughter of **Monvel**.

Marjorie **Mars**: Marjorie Brown (1903–), Br. stage actress.

Beryl **Marsden**: Beryl Hogg (1947–), Eng. popular singer.

James **Marsden** *see* Gordon **Ashe**

Juan **Marsé**: Juan Fonseca (1933–), Sp. novelist. The writer's mother died at his birth, so he was adopted by the Marsé family, and took their name.

Carol **Marsh**: Norma Simpson (1926–), Br. movie actress.

Garry **Marsh**: Leslie Marsh Geraghty (1902–1981), Eng. stage, movie actor. The actor seems to have used his surname as the basis of his new first name, retaining his middle name for his new surname.

Joan **Marsh**: Nancy Ann Rosher (1913–2000), U.S. movie actress.

Marian **Marsh**: Violet Krauth (1913–2006), U.S. movie actress. In her first movies, in the early 1930s, Marsh was billed as Marilyn Morgan, but Warner Bros. insisted she change this so as not to be confused with another of their contractees, Marilyn **Miller**. The actress thus shortened "Marilyn" to "Marian" and her mother chose "Marsh" as a tribute to the silent movie actress Mae Marsh (1895–1968).

Brenda **Marshall**: Ardis Anderson Gaines (1915–1992), U.S. movie actress.

Frank **Marshall**: Frank Marzalkiewicz (*c.*1895–1969), U.S. stage puppet maker.

Garry K. **Marshall**: Garry Masciarelli (1934–), U.S. movie director, brother of Penny **Marshall**.

James **Marshall**: James Greenblatt (1969–), U.S. movie, TV actor. The actor originally changed his name to James Green. He then decided to adopt the middle name of Jimi **Hendrix** as his surname.

Owen **Marshall**: Owen Marshall Jones (1941–), N.Z. short-story writer.

Penny **Marshall**: Carole Penny Masciarelli (1942–), U.S. movie director, actress, sister of Garry K. **Marshall**.

Peter **Marshall**: Pierre LaCock (1924–), U.S. TV host, brother of Joanne **Dru**.

Raymond **Marshall** *see* James Hadley **Chase**

Tully **Marshall**: William Phillips (1864–1943), U.S. movie actor.

Richard **Marsten** *see* Evan **Hunter**

Edward **Marston**: Keith Miles (1940–), Welsh crime writer.

Charles **Martel**: (1) Thomas Delf (1812–1866), Eng. writer; (2) Karl David Hanke (1860–1945), Swiss-born U.S. librarian. Both men appear to have adopted the name of the Frankish king Charles Martel ("Charles the Hammer") (*c.*688–741). Delf specialized in translations from the French, while Hanke was the chief developer of the Library of Congress classification scheme.

Martellange: Étienne Ange Martel (1569–1641), Fr. architect, Jesuit.

Martello Tower: [Commander] Francis Martin Norman (1833–1918), Eng. writer of naval books. Martello towers are the small circular forts erected for defense purposes along the southeast coast of England during the Napoleonic Wars. They were so called from Cape Mortella, Corsica, where the French put up an effective resistance to British bombardment in 1794.

Len **Marten:** Leonard Hart (1920–1990), Br. stage, TV actor, comedian.

Paul **Martens** *see* Stephen **Southwold**

Fred **Marteny:** Feodor Neumann (1931–), Cz.-Austr. ballet dancer, choreographer.

Ralph **Marterie:** Ralph Martin (1914–1978), It.-born U.S. popular trumpeter.

Martin IV: Simon de Brie (*c.*1210–1285), Fr. pope. The pontiff took the name of France's patron saint, St. Martin, especially as he had been treasurer of St. Martin's, Tours, where the saint had been bishop and where his shrine now is.

Martin V: Oddo Colonna (1368–1431), It. pope. The pontiff took the name of St. Martin, on whose feastday (November 11, 1417) he was elected pope.

Alan Langdon **Martin** *see* Jane **Cowl**

Billy **Martin:** Alfred Manuel Pesano (1928–1989), U.S. baseball player, manager, of It. descent. "Billy" evolved from "Belli" ("beautiful"), a nickname given Martin as a young child by his Italian grandmother.

Chink **Martin:** Martin Abraham (1886–1981), U.S. jazz musician.

Claire **Martin:** Claire Montreuil (1914–), Can. writer. The writer adopted her mother's maiden name as her pen name.

David **Martin:** Ludwig Detsinyi (1915–1997), Hung.-born Austral. journalist, writer. The writer used the name Spinifex for his book of verse, *Rob the Robber, His Life and Vindication* (1954), from the Australian grass so called.

Dean **Martin:** Dino Paul Crocetti (1917–1995), U.S. movie actor, of It. parentage, teaming with Jerry **Lewis**. The actor put himself over as a "cousin" of the Metropolitan Opera star Nino Martini, although quite unrelated to him. The adoption of this particular name and ruse was suggested by band leader Ernie McKay, at Walkers Café, Columbus, Ohio [Michael Freedland, *Dino: The Dean Martin Story*, 1984].

Derek **Martin:** Derek William Rapp (1933–), Br. TV actor.

Ernest H. **Martin:** Ernest H. Markowitz (1919–), U.S. stage manager, producer.

George Madden **Martin:** Georgia May Madden (1866–1946), U.S. short-story writer, novelist.

Marty **Martin** *see* **Boxcar Willie**

Peter **Martin:** Nixon Waterman (1859–1944), U.S. poet. The writer explains how he came by his pen name: "One year I had charge of the editorial page of the Boston *Traveler*— and the fellows on the paper, knowing I went in heavy on gardening, ... suggested I start a department, called 'How does your garden grow?' and I took the name 'Peter Martin.'

The dept. attracted the atttention of the Page Co., and they paid me to write *A Little Gardening Book for a Little Girl*, which they published as one of a series.... On the title-page it said, 'By Peter Martin, Gardening Editor of the Boston *Traveler*'" [Marble, p.160].

Quinn **Martin:** Martin Cohn, Jr. (1922–1987), U.S. TV producer, scriptwriter. "Quinn" presumably represents "Cohn."

Riccardo **Martin:** Hugh Whitfield (1874–1952), U.S. opera singer.

Richard **Martin** *see* Gordon **Ashe**

Ricky **Martin:** Enrique Martin Morales (1971–), Puerto Rican pop singer, working in U.S. The singer's stage name evolved from his original first two names.

Roberta **Martin:** Roberta Evelyn Winston (1907–1969), U.S. black gospel pianist, singer. It is uncertain why Winston adopted "Martin" as her surname.

Ross **Martin:** Martin Rosenblatt (1920–1981), Pol.–U.S. movie actor.

Sara **Martin:** Sara Dunn (1884–1955), U.S. black blues, vaudeville singer.

Shane **Martin:** George Henry Johnston (1912–1970), Austral. detective novelist.

Stella **Martin:** Georgette Heyer (1902–1974), Br. author of historical romances, detective novels. The writer used this name only for her third novel, *The Transformation of Philip Jettan* (1923).

Tony **Martin:** Alvin Maris (or Morris) (1912–), U.S. cabaret singer, movie actor. The singer changed his name to Anthony Martin in 1934. His new first name then settled to its standard diminutive.

Elsa **Martinelli:** Elsa Tia (1932–), It. movie actress.

Jean Paul Égide **Martini:** Johann Paul Ägidius Schwarzendorf (1741–1816), Ger.-born Fr. composer. "His father having married again, he left for France and at Nancy found a friend in the organ builder Dupont, who advised him to adopt the Italian name of Martini" [Blom, p.350].

Al **Martino:** Alfred Cini (1927–2009), U.S. pop singer, movie actor, of It. parentage. The singer adopted his stage name from his grandfather.

Pat **Martino:** Pat Azzara (1944–), U.S. jazz guitarist, composer.

Moa **Martinson:** Helga Swartz (1890–1964), Swe. novelist. The writer's adopted name is that of her second husband, novelist Harry Martinson (1904–1978), whom she married in 1929 (divorced 1940).

György **Martinuzzi:** Juraj Utje-Šenovic (1482–1551), Hung. statesman, of Croatian-Venetian parentage. The future cardinal adopted his mother's maiden name.

Mary **Martlew:** Mary Greenhalgh (1919–), Eng. stage actress.

L. **Martov:** Yuly Osipovich Tsederbaum (1873–1923), Russ. Menshevik leader.

John **Martyn:** Iain David McGeachy (1948–2009), Br. folk-rock musician.

Manuel **Marulanda:** Pedro Antonio Marín (1930–2008), Colombian guerrilla leader. Marín took his *nom de guerre*, in full Manuel Maruenda Vélez, in memory of a Communist trade union leader murdered by government agents in 1951. He hoped his new name would replace the nickname Tirofijo ("Crackshot"), given him for his skills as a marksman, but it never did.

Ik **Marvel:** Donald Grant Mitchell (1822–1908), U.S. essayist. In 1846 Mitchell adopted the name J.K. Marvel for his contributions to the *Morning Courier* and *New York Enquirer*. This was misprinted as "Ik Marvel," and he stuck with it, taking "Ik" as a short form of "Izaak." "There was much of the poet in 'Ik Marvel,' as well as the lover of outdoors — his pseudonym seemed to combine the two writers who allured him, [English poet] Andrew Marvell [(1621–1678)] and [English writer, author of *The Compleat Angler* (1653)] I[zaa]k Walton [(1593–1683)]" [Marble, p.92].

Harry **Marvello:** Harry Hutchinson (1879–1967), Sc. magician.

Hank B. **Marvin:** Brian Rankin (1941–), Eng. rock guitarist. The musician wanted an American-style name, so based his new first name on his surname, took a middle initial from his first name, and adapted the first name of a friend called Martin for his new surname.

Marvin X *see* Marvin **X**

Sister **Mary Regis:** [Dame] Mary Maud Morant (1903–1985), Eng. religious. Mary Morant was the head of various Roman Catholic schools from 1933 to 1970, her *Who's Who* entry stipulating that she was "to be addressed as Sr Mary Regis, DBE [Dame (Commander of the Order of) the British Empire]."

Chuck **Mason** *see* Fenton **Brockley**

Chico **Marx:** Leonard Marx (1886–1961), U.S. movie comedian. The comic was the oldest of the five Marx Brothers, a team of German Jewish parentage that originally included Gummo **Marx** and Zeppo **Marx**. Each brother had a distinctive persona and stage name. Chico was always "after the chicks," Harpo **Marx** played the harp, Groucho **Marx** had a cynical view of life, or according to one theory was miserly and carried his money in a grouch bag, Gummo always had holes in his shoes and wore rubbers over them, and Zeppo was either named after a vaudevillian's chimpanzee, Mr. Zippo, or was so dubbed because he was born around the time the first Zeppelin was built. Asked about his name in a TV interview, Groucho explained: "I always had a grim visage, because I handled the money, and the others didn't have too much confidence in me, and it became Groucho, and it was a nice name" [*The Listener*, August 16, 1979]. Another theory claims that Groucho took his name from a character called Groucho Monk in the comic strip *Mager's Monks*, in which Chico, Harpo, and Gummo also appeared.

Groucho **Marx:** Julius Henry Marx (1890–1977), U.S. movie comedian, brother of Chico **Marx**.

Gummo **Marx:** Milton Marx (1893–1977), U.S. vaudeville artist, brother of Chico **Marx**.

Harpo **Marx:** Adolph (known as Arthur) Marx (1888–1964), U.S. movie comedian, brother of Chico **Marx**.

Zeppo **Marx:** Herbert Marx (1901–1979), U.S. movie comedian, brother of Chico **Marx**.

Aunt **Mary:** Mary Hughes, née Robson (*fl.*1820), Br. children's writer.

Maryan: Maria Descard (1847–1927), Fr. novelist. The writer used this pseudonym for her first novel, *Mlle. de Kervallez*, published when she was 30, taking it from the first names, Mary Ann, of her English maternal grandmother.

Mother **Mary Alphonsa:** Rose Hawthorne Lathrop (1851–1926), U.S. nun. In 1876 the daughter of novelist Nathaniel **Hawthorne** moved with her husband, George Lathrop, to New York. She converted to Catholicism in 1891, separated from her husband in 1895, and was received into the Dominican order in 1899, when she adopted her religious name. In 1901, with other members of her order, she founded the Servants of Relief for Incurable Cancer.

Mother **Mary Angela:** Ellen Hughes (1806–1866), Ir.-born U.S. nun. Ellen Hughes emigrated to the United States in 1818 and became a member of the Sisters of Charity in Maryland in 1825, when she took her religious name. In 1846 she helped establish the Sisters of Charity of Mount St. Vincent, and in 1855 became mother general.

Mother **Mary of the Cross:** Mary Helen MacKillop (1842–1909), Austral. nun, of Sc. descent. Australia's first saint, canonized in 1995, founded the Society of the Sisters of St. Joseph of the Sacred Heart (the "Little Joeys") in 1866.

Mary of the Incarnation: (1) Barbe Jeanne Acarie, née Avrillot (1566–1618), Fr. religious; (2) Marie Martin, née Guyard (1599–1672), Fr. religious. In 1604, Mme. Acarie, as she was then known, introduced the Carmelite order to France. In 1614 she entered the order herself under the name Marie de l'Incarnation ("Mary of the Incarnation"). Marie Guyard took the same name on entering an Ursuline convent in 1631. In 1639 she introduced the order to Canada. Both women had married at age 17.

Dr. Märzroth: Moritz Barach (1818–1888), Austr. writer, poet. A semianagrammatic name, meaning literally "March red."

Masaccio: Tommaso di ser Giovanni Cassai (1401–1428), It. painter. The artist's name, formed from the second syllable of his first name with the Italian pejorative ("bad") suffix *-accio*, can be understood as "slovenly Tom." Giorgio Vasari's *Lives of the Artists* (1550) writes of him thus: "He was very absent-minded and erratic, and he devoted all his mind and thoughts to art and paid little attention to himself and still less to others. He refused to give any time to worldly cares and possessions, even to the way he dressed, let alone anything else.... So instead of calling him by his proper name, which was Tommaso, everyone called him Masaccio." Compare the name of **Masolino**.

Masaniello: Tommaso Aniello d'Amalfi (1620–1647), It. political agitator. A single name formed from the bearer's first two names.

Józef **Maskoff** *see* Gabriela **Zapolska**

Masolino: Tommaso di Cristoforo Fini (*c.*1383–*c.*1447), It. painter. The artist's name, formed from the accented syllable of his first name with the Italian diminutive suffix *-olino*, can be understood to mean "little Tom." The reference is presumably to his size or stature, possibly by comparison with **Masaccio**, with whom he was closely linked, and by whom he was influenced.

Edith **Mason:** Edith Barnes (1898–1973), U.S. opera singer.

Jackie **Mason:** Yacov Moshe Maza (1934–), U.S. movie comedian. The performer's name represents a loose anglicization of his first name and a blend of his other two names.

Shirley **Mason:** Leonie Flugrath (1901–1979), U.S. movie actress, sister of Viola **Dana**.

Stuart **Mason:** Christopher Sclater Millard (1872–1927), Br. biographer. The writer used this name for his three books on Oscar Wilde (1914, 1915, 1920), but kept his real name for *The Printed Work of Claud Lovat Fraser* (1923).

Masoni: Eric Mason (?–1977), Br. magician.

Mass: Harold Massingham (1932–), Br. crossword compiler. The setter's pseudonym represents a nickname from his schooldays.

Massachusettensis: Daniel Leonard (1740–1829), U.S. Loyalist writer. The writer used this pseudoclassical pen name for a series of contributions to *The Massachusetts Gazette and Post Boy* (1774–5). These were replied to by **Novanglus**.

Lea **Massari:** Anna Maria Massatani (1933–), Fr.-It. movie actress.

Fritzi **Massary:** Friederike Massaryk (1882–1969), Austr. Jewish operetta singer, working in U.S. The soprano fled Hitler in 1933 and went to London. She later settled in California.

Ilona **Massey:** Ilona Hajmassy (1910–1974), Hung.-born U.S. movie actress.

Nick **Massi:** Nicholas Macioci (1935–2000), U.S. bass guitarist, pop singer.

Léonide **Massine:** Leonid Fedorovich Miasin (1895–1979), Russ. ballet dancer, choreographer, working in France, U.S. A gallicized form of the dancer's original name.

Hugh **Massingberd:** Hugh John Montgomery (1946–2007), Eng. writer, journalist. When the editor of *Burke's Peerage* and obituaries editor of the *Daily Telegraph* became heir presumptive to Gunby Hall, the Lincolnshire home of his great-uncle, Field Marshal Sir Archibald Montgomery-Massingberd, Montgomery was obliged to hyphenate Massingberd to his name in order to inherit the estate. He did so in 1962, becoming Hugh John Montgomery-Massingberd, but dropped his original surname in 1992.

Massive Dread: Dennis James (*c.*1960–), Jamaican reggae musician.

Charles **Masson:** James Lewis (1800–1853), Br. traveler, archaeologist. The traveler adopted his new name in the late 1820s when embarking for a ten-year period of archaeological exploration and investigation in Afghanistan.

Jane **Mast:** Mae West (1893–1980), U.S. stage, movie actress, writer. Born Mary Jane West, the entertainer adopted this name, from her middle name and the first and last two letters of her first and last names, for her popular play *Sex* (1926).

Master ... For names beginning thus, excepting the three below, see the next name, e.g. for Master Babua see **Babua**, for Master Ratan see **Ratan**, etc.

Master Juba: William Henry Lane (?1825–1852), U.S. black dancer. Lane came to be so known in 1844 after beating the reigning white minstrel dancer, John Diamond, in a series of challenge dances. The name was often given to slaves who danced the *juba*, a Negro breakdown or rustic dance in which the participants clap hands, slap their thighs, and and sing verses with "*juba*" as a refrain.

Master P: Percy Miller (1970–), U.S. black rapper.

Master Shortie: Theo Kerlin (1988–), Br. black rapper. The name refers to the rapper's stature.

Kitty **Masters:** Katherine Masterson (1902–1995), Br. popular singer.

J.B. **Masterson** *see* G.C. **Edmondson**

Carmen Nicholas **Mastren:** Carmine Niccolò Mastandrea (1913–1981), U.S. jazz musician.

Pietro **Mastri:** Pirro Masetti (1868–1932), It. poet.

Masuccio Salernitano: Tommaso Guardati (*c.*1475–*c.*1475), It. writer. The writer's first name is a diminutive of his original name, so means something like "Tommy." His second name means "of Salerno," his birthtown.

Masurao: Hiroyasu Teshima (1961–), Jap. sumo wrestler. The wrestler's fighting name means "strong and fearless man," "hero" (Japanese *masurao*).

Mata Hari: Margarethe Geertruida MacLeod, née Zelle (1876–1917), Du.-born Fr. dancer, spy. The dancer's name for her exotic Eastern temple performance on the French stage derives from Malay *matahari*, "sun," literally "eye of the day" (from *mata*, "eye," and *hari*, "day"). She took the name in 1898. Before her arrival in Paris in 1904, Zelle had been married briefly to a Dutch colonial officer, Rudolph MacLeod, and with him had stayed, equally briefly, in the Dutch East Indies. She had retained enough of the language to adopt the name for her new life in the theater.

Mata Hari's name was perhaps simply meant to evoke the Orient. But it also relates linguistically to her given name Margarethe (Margaret). This name, meaning "pearl," derives from French *marguerite*, "daisy," and English *daisy* literally means "day's eye," otherwise "eye of the day" or "sun."

Count Matchuki: Winston Cooper (*c.*1939–), Jamaican DJ, reggae musician. Cooper adopted his nickname, given him for his habit of chewing matchsticks.

Carmen Mathé: Margaretha Matheson (1938–), Sc. ballet dancer. The dancer adopted a Spanish-style name rather cleverly from her existing two names, adding "Carmen" as a clincher, the name of the alluring Spanish gypsy girl made famous by Bizet's opera.

Berkley Mather: John (later Jasper) Evan Weston-Davies (1909–1996), Eng. TV scriptwriter. The author spent many years in India as an army officer, and after World War II sold his first radio play to the BBC. To disguise his professional military status he devised a pseudonym from the (misspelled) Berkeley Grill and Mathers' drugstore, Poona (Pune), India.

Helen Mathers: Ellen Buckingham Reeves, née Mathews (1850–1920), Eng. novelist. The writer also used the name David **Lyall**. "Helen Mathers" lightly disguises "Ellen Mathews."

Mathetes: John Jones (1821–1878), Welsh Baptist minister, writer. The biblical scholar took his name from Greek *mathetes*, "learner," "disciple."

Carole Mathews: Jean Francis (1920–), U.S. movie actress.

Mat Mathews: Matthieu Schwartz (1924–), Du. jazz accordionist, working in U.S.

G.S. Mathis: Mátyás György Seiber (1905–1960), Hung.-born Br. composer, cellist. The musician used this name when writing for the accordion.

H. Ogram Matrice: Charles Francis Keary (1848–1917), Eng. novelist, historical writer. The author used this name for *A Wanderer* (1888).

Seicho Matsumoto: Matsumoto Kiyoharu (1909–1992), Jap. crime writer.

Matt: Matthew Pritchett (1964–), Eng. cartoonist.

Roberto Matta: Roberto Sebastián Antonio Matta Echuarren (1911–2002), Chilean painter, sculptor, working in France, U.S., Italy.

Matteo: Matteo Marcellus Vittucci (1919–), U.S. dancer.

Walter Matthau: Walter Matuschanskayasky (1920–2000), U.S. stage, movie actor, of Russ. Jewish parentage. Sources vary on the actor's original Slavic surname, but it seems to have been as stated here.

Albert **Matthäus** *see* Albert Paris von **Gütersloh**

Rodney **Mattheson** *see* Gordon **Ashe**

Thomas Matthew: John Rogers (*c.*1505–1555), Eng. Protestant divine, martyr. The Protestant convert used this name as editor of a revision of William Tyndale's English translation of the Bible, assuming a pseudonym for fear of meeting the same fate as Tyndale himself, burned at the stake as a heretic. But Rogers endured the same end. His edition is now known as "Matthew's Bible." Its full title ran: "The Byble, which is all the Holy Scripture: in whych are contayned the Olde and Newe Testament truly and purely translated into Englysh by Thomas Matthew, MDXXXVII."

Iain Matthews: Ian Matthew MacDonald (1946–), Eng. folk-rock musician. The musician used his middle name as a surname to avoid confusion with Ian McDonald of the group King Crimson.

Pamela **Matthews** *see* Lana **Morris**

H. Ogram Matuce: Charles Francis Keary (?–1917), Eng. novelist, historical writer.

Camille Mauclair: Séverin Faust (1872–1945), Fr. poet, novelist, art critic, of Dan. descent.

[Sir] Edward **Maufe:** Edward Brantwood Muff (1883–1974), Eng. architect. The architect changed his name by deed poll in 1908 from the common or garden Muff to the more distinctive Maufe.

Maufrigneuse *see* Joseph **Prunier**

Sharon Maughan: Sharon Mughan (1952–), Eng. TV actress.

Thierry Maulnier: Jacques Louis Talagrand (1909–1988), Fr. writer, journalist. The writer used this name for his articles in the political daily *Action Française*.

Maupin: Julie (or Emilie) d'Aubigny (*c.*1670–1707), Fr. opera singer. The soprano's (sole) stage name was her married surname.

Molly **Maureen:** Elizabeth Mary Campfield (1904–1987), Br. stage, movie actress.

Chéri **Maurice:** Charles Maurice Schwartzenberger (1805–1896), Fr.-born Ger. actor. Chéri Maurice founded the Thalia Theater, Hamburg, in 1843.

Furnley **Maurice:** Frank Leslie Thompson Wilmot (1881–1942), Austral. poet. The writer based his pseudonym on the names of two of his favorite Melbourne haunts: Ferntree Gully and Beaumaris.

Walter **Maurice:** [Sir] Walter Besant (1836–1901), Eng. novelist.

Patrick **Maurin** *see* Patrick **Dewaere**

Turk **Mauro:** Mauro Turso (1944–), U.S. jazz musician.

André **Maurois:** Émile Salomon Wilhelm Herzog (1885–1967), Fr. novelist, biographer, of Jewish parentage. The writer was a liaison officer with the British army in World War I and first used the name for *Les Silences du Colonel Bramble* (1918), a humorous depiction of British officers in their mess. In his autobiography he tells how his publisher advised him to adopt a pseudonym in order not to be recognized by the officers concerned: "I resigned myself and selected the first name André, in memory of my cousin who had been killed in action, and Maurois, the name of a village near Cambrai, because I liked its sad sonority ... André Maurois.... How strange and new those syllables sounded to me then!" [André Maurois, *Memoirs*, translated by Denver Lindley, 1970].

Max **Maven:** Phil Goldstein (1950–), Br. magician. "Maven" (or "mavin") is a slang term of Yiddish origin for an expert.

Yanka **Mavr:** Ivan Mikhaylovich Fyodorov (1883–1971), Belorussian children's writer. The writer adopted a colloquial form of his first two names.

Uncle **Max:** Charles Henry Maxwell Knight (1900–1968), Br. radio, TV naturalist.

Joey **Maxim:** Giuseppe Antonio Berardinelli (1922–2001), U.S. boxer. When the future light-heavyweight champion turned pro in 1941, his manager, Doc Kearns, replaced his lengthy Italian surname with one suggesting that the fighter's left jabs were akin to the rapid fire of a Maxim gun. His Italian first name was at the same time assimilated to its English pet equivalent.

[St.] **Maximus the Greek:** Michael Trivolis (*c.*1475–1556), Gr. churchman, translator, working in Russia. The ecclesiastic, whose surname denotes his nationality, took his religious name in 1505 as a monk on Mt. Athos, Greece, in honor of the 7th-century Greek theologian St. Maximus the Confessor. He was canonized by the Russian Orthodox Church in 1988.

Clifford **Maxwell** *see* Henry **Cecil**

Donald **Maxwell:** Donald Maxwell MacAlpine (1948–), Sc. opera singer.

Lois **Maxwell:** Lois Hooker (1927–2007), Can. movie actress, working in U.S., U.K. A name change was clearly desirable here.

Robert **Maxwell:** Jan Ludvik Hoch (1923–1991), Cz.-born Br. publisher, politician. The newspaper owner had a complex naming history. He was born near the Czech-Romanian border as the son of a Jewish peasant, Mechel Hoch, who gave him the first names Abraham Lyabi. But when the father went to register the boy at the local town hall, the Czech government official insisted on a Czech name for the record. He was thus renamed Jan Ludvik Hoch. Later, in World War II, he joined the Czech Pioneer Corps and was posted to Britain, where in 1943 he joined the North Staffordshire Regiment, taking the name of Private L.I. du Maurier, a name he had chosen from a cigarette packet in order to disguise his true identity if captured by the Germans. A year later, after the D-Day landings, he was working in the intelligence field in Paris, France, using the cover name Private Jones (although his actual rank was now higher than this).

In due course, his work so impressed the military authorities that he was promoted to second lieutenant and recommended to choose yet another name, as du Maurier and Jones were not regarded as fitting. The Scottish name of Robert Maxwell was suggested, and he adopted it, adding Ian (the English form of Jan) as a first name. He was long undecided whether to use Ian or Robert as his first name [Tom Bower, *Maxwell, the Outsider*, 1988].

Roger **Maxwell:** Roger D. Latham (1900–?), Eng. stage, movie, TV actor.

Vera **Maxwell:** Vera Huppé (1901–1995), U.S. fashion designer.

William **Maxwell:** William Maxwell Keepers (1908–2000), U.S. editor, short-story writer.

Ada **May:** Ada Mae Weeks, earlier Potter (1900–?), U.S. stage actress, dancer.

Edna **May:** Edna May Pettie (1878–1948), U.S. stage actress, singer, working in U.K.

Elaine **May:** Elaine Berlin (1932–), U.S. movie actress, director.

Joe **May:** Joseph Otto Mandel (1880–1954), Ger. movie director.

Orchard **May:** May Katherine Lanrishe (1879–?), Eng. pianist, composer.

Pamela **May:** Doris May (1917–2005), Br. ballet dancer. The ballerina was advised by dance director Ninette **de Valois** that she needed a less mundane first name. "After much thought May picked on Angela but was told she had delayed too long: the programme had already been printed as Pamela, de Valois's choice" [*The Times*, June 13, 2005].

Sophie **May:** Rebecca Sophia Clarke (1833–1906), U.S. children's writer. The author is said to have told her younger sister that she chose her new name for her first published story, printed in the *Memphis* (Tennessee) *Daily Appeal* in 1861, because "I may write again and I may not." In the event she did, producing more than 40 books for children.

Thomas **Maybank:** Hector Thomas Maybank Webb (1869–1929), Br. painter, illustrator, cartoonist.

Louis B. **Mayer:** Lazar Meir (1885–1957), Russ.-born U.S. movie producer, of Jewish parentage.

Bill **Maynard:** Walter Frederick George Williams (1928–), Eng. movie, TV actor.

Walter **Maynard:** Thomas Willert Beale (1828–1894), Eng. lawyer, musician, impresario. The writer used this name for *The Enterprising Impresario* (1867), a personal account of the world of theater managers and opera singers.

Ferdy **Mayne:** Ferdinand Mayer-Boerckel (1916–1998), Ger.-born Br. movie actor.

Leslie **Mayne:** Lionel Monckton (1861–1924), Eng. composer, music critic. The musician used this name for some popular songs.

Rutherford **Mayne:** Samuel Waddell (1878–1967), Ir. playwright, actor The writer took his name from the adventure novelist Thomas Mayne Reid (1818–1883), his mother's maternal granduncle.

Xavier **Mayne:** Edward Irenaeus Prime-Stevenson (1868–1942), U.S. writer.

Alfredo **Mayo:** Alfredo Fernández Martínez (1911–1984), Sp. movie actor.

James **Mayo:** Stephen Coulter (1914–), Br. writer of thrillers and spy novels.

Jim **Mayo** *see* Louis **L'Amour**

J.K. **Mayo:** William Hugh Charles Watson (1931–2005), Sc. novelist, playwright. Watson mainly used his real name for what he termed "serious fictions," but when these did not find a wide readership he turned to writing thrillers under a pseudonym, beginning with *The Hunting Season* (1986).

Margaret **Mayo:** Lillian Slatten (1882–1951), U.S. stage actress, playwright. The actress took her professional name on beginning her stage career at the age of 13.

Virginia **Mayo:** Virginia May Jones (1920–2005), U.S. movie actress. The actress's screen name almost certainly came from her real name, although one theory claims she took it from a pantomime horse that she appeared with as a showgirl. The front and back legs of the horse were two Mayo brothers. An old Hollywood joke says the name arose from a café counterman's call "Virginia, mayo!" when the actress ordered a (Virginia) ham sandwich with mayonnaise while waiting at a bus station.

Augusta **Maywood:** Augusta Williams (1825–1876), U.S. ballet dancer. The dancer took the name of her stepfather, theatrical manager Robert Campbell Maywood, who adopted her when she was three.

Jules **Mazarin:** Giulio Mazarini (1602–1661), It.-born Fr. cardinal, statesman.

Joseph **Mazilier:** Giulio Mazarini (1797 or 1801–1868), Fr. ballet dancer, choreographer, teacher.

Mike **Mazurki:** Mikhail Mazurski (or Mazurkiewicz) (1909–1990), U.S. movie, TV actor, of Ukr. descent.

Mc ... Names beginning Mc- are alphabetized as if beginning Mac-.

MC Brains: James DeShannon Davis (*c*.1975–), U.S. black rapper. MC in this name and those below means "master of ceremonies," a term which in hip-hop culture denotes a performer who introduces and embellishes electronic dance music.

MC Eric: Eric Martin (1970–), Welsh-born rapper, of Jamaican descent.

MC J: Jens Muller (*c*.1971–), Ger. (white) rapper, political activist, working in France.

MC Lyte: Lana Moorer (1971–), U.S. black rapper.

MC 900ft Jesus: Mark Griffin (*c*.1970–), U.S. (white) hip-hop musician. The artist's unusual name was inspired by the U.S. "televangelist" Oral Roberts, who told how a huge figure of Jesus appeared to him in the Colorado desert at a time when he despaired of raising enough money to build a sanctuary.

MC Ren: Lorenzo Patterson (*c*.1965–), U.S. black "gangsta" rapper.

MC Shan: Shawn Moltke (1965–), U.S. black hip-hop musician.

MC Trouble: Latasha Rogers (*c*.1972–), U.S. black rapper.

L.T. **Meade:** Elizabeth ("Lillie") Thomasina Toulmin Smith, née Meade (1854–1914), Ir.-born Br. writer of books for girls, mystery, detective fiction.

Audrey **Meadows:** Audrey Cotter (1929–1996), U.S. movie, TV comedienne, sister of Jayne **Meadows**.

Jayne **Meadows:** Jayne Cotter (1925–), U.S. movie actress.

Lindon **Meadows** *see* F. **Abell**

Meat Loaf: Marvin Lee Aday (1947–), U.S. rock singer. The singer was so nicknamed by his Dallas school friends on account of his gross size, with the name itself allegedly originating from a football coach. Aday landed on the coach's foot in the course of a training session, prompting a response on the lines of, "Get off me, you great hunk of meat loaf!" [Baker, p.7]. Whatever the case, the singer adopted the name, calling his first band alternately Meat Loaf

Soul and Popcorn Blizzard. The name's initials happen to match those of his first two names.

Kay Medford: Kay Regan (1918–1980), U.S. stage actress.

Medium Tem Plum: Montague Horatio Mostyn Turtle Pigott (1865–1927), Eng. lawyer, writer. The writer's assumed name should be read as Latin *medium templum*, meaning the Middle Temple, London, one of the four Inns of Court that hold the exclusive right of calling to the English bar. Pigott won a scholarship in international and constitutional law at the Middle Temple.

Bobbie Medlock: Doris Stuart (1914–2007), Eng. music-hall singer. Medlock teamed with her husband, Vic **Marlowe**, to form the variety act Medlock and Marlowe.

Carol **Medway** *see* Jill **Consey**

Joe Medwick: Joseph Medwick Veasey (1933–1992), U.S. blues singer, songwriter.

Grigory Medynsky: Grigory Aleksandrovich Pokrovsky (1899–1984), Russ. writer.

Huan Mee: Walter E. Mansfield (1870–1916), Eng. writer + Charles Herbert Mansfield (1864–?), Eng. writer, his brother. A punning representation of a spoken phrase describing the two men.

Ralph Meeker: Ralph Rathgeber (1920–1988), U.S. stage, movie actor.

Mehboob: Ramjan Khan (1906–1964), Ind. movie director. The director is also known as Mehboob Khan. The name itself means "beloved," "dear" (Arabic, Hindi *mahbub*).

Meher Baba: Merwan Shehiar Irani (1894–1969), Ind. guru, of Persian parentage. The spiritual teacher who built up a following of "Baba Lovers" in India and the West was given his name, meaning "compassionate father," by his first disciples in the early 1920s.

Mehmood: Mehmood Ali (1932–2004), Ind. movie comedian.

Deepa **Mehta:** Deepa Mehta Saltzman (1949–), Ind.-born movie director, working in Canada.

Clive Meikle: Jeremy Brooks (1926–1994), Eng. novelist, playwright.

Hannes Meinkema: Hannemieke Stamperius (1943–), Du. writer. The writer's new first name comes from her original forename and surname initial, while her new surname is formed from letters in this same forename. She kept her real name for her academic writing.

Golda Meir: Goldie Myerson, née Mabovitch (1898–1978), Russ.-born Israeli prime minister. After emigrating to the U.S. at the age of eight, Goldie Mabovitch met (in 1917) Morris Myerson, a Russian Jewish immigrant, whom she later married. Back later with her husband in Palestine, Golda changed her name to Meir at the insistence of David **Ben-Gurion** when she was appointed (1956) Israeli foreign minister. She chose a name that still suggested "Myerson" (although her marriage had by now broken up), knowing that Meir means "enlightener" in Hebrew.

George **Melachrino:** George Militiades (1909–1965), Br. danceband leader, composer, arranger, of Gk. parentage. The musician may have adopted a name meaning "dark," "swarthy," from Modern Greek *melakhroinos*.

Philipp Melanchthon: Philipp Schwartzerd (1497–1560), Ger. humanist, Protestant theologian. In the manner of his day, the theologian translated his German name (literally "black earth") into Greek.

Melanie: Melanie Safka (1947–), U.S. pop singer, songwriter, of Ukr.-It. parentage.

[Dame] Nellie **Melba:** Helen Porter Armstrong, née Mitchell (1861–1931), Austral. opera singer. The singer took her name from Melbourne, the city near which she was born. She first used the name in Brussels in 1887, for her debut as Gilda in *Rigoletto*. She in turn gave her name to those dietetic opposites, Melba toast and peach Melba, the former because she fancied it, the latter because it was as colorful as she was.

Mel-Bonis: Melanie Domange, née Bonis (1858–1937), Fr. composer.

Lauritz Melchior: Lebrecht Hommel (1890–1973), U.S. opera singer, of Dan. parentage.

Melchizedek III: Mikhail Pkhaladze (1876–1960), Georgian catholicos. The head of the Georgian Orthodox Church took the name of two of his predecessors, traditionally interpreted as "king of righteousness."

Jill **Melford:** Jill Melford-Melford (1934–), U.S. stage actress.

Melissa: Jane Brereton, née Hughes (1685–1740), Welsh poet. In the writer's only book-length publication, *Poems on Several Occasions ... with Letters to her Friends and An Account of Her Life* (1744), her anonymous biographer writes: "Her Poetical name of *Melissa* was given by a Gentleman of her Acquaintance from the Latin word 'Mell' [*sic*] as bearing some allusion to the Sweetness of her Numbers." (Latin *mel* means "honey," while the name Melissa itself is the Greek word for "bee.")

Melissanthi: Ivi Skandalaki, née Kouyia (1910–1990), Gk. poet. The poet's pen name means "honeyflower."

Paulus Melissus: Paul Schede (1539–1602), Ger. religious poet.

Marisa **Mell:** Marlies Moitzi (1929–1992), Fr. movie actress.

John **Mellencamp:** John Cougar Mellencamp (1951–), U.S. rock singer. The singer originally recorded as Johnny Cougar, then reverted to his full original name before dropping his middle name in 1989. "This man has had almost as many permutations of his name — depending on whether he feels like Mellencamp, Cougar, or Cougar Mellencamp that day — as he has had hit singles" [*The Times*, October 16, 2008].

Mellow Man Ace: Ulpiano Sergio Reyes (1967–), Cuban-born U.S. rapper.

Courtney **Melmoth:** Samuel Jackson Pratt (1749–1814), Br. poet, prose writer. The writer used the rather flamboyant name for his unsuccessful acting debut in 1773, but later adopted it more generally for his literary pennings. His wife, Charlotte Melmoth (1749–1823), was more fortunate in her stage career, appearing always as Mrs. Charlotte Melmoth after their brief marriage. Her maiden name is unknown, leading some to speculate that it may have been Melmoth.

Sebastian **Melmoth:** Oscar Wilde (1854–1900), Ir. playwright, author, poet. The writer adopted this name on fleeing to France after his release from Reading Gaol in 1897. He is said to have taken it from Charles Maturin's novel *Melmoth the Wanderer* (1820), whose hero, Melmoth, having sold his soul for the promise of prolonged life, offers relief from suffering to each of the other characters. (Maturin was a remote ancestor on Wilde's maternal side.) It is also possible that the name was suggested by Augustus Melmotte, the villain hero of Anthony Trollope's novel *The Way We Live Now* (1875).The first name Sebastian was suggested by the arrows on Wilde's prison uniform, as an allusion to paintings showing St. Sebastian being shot to death by arrows.

Maureen **Melrose** *see* Marina **Berti**

Alfred **Mels:** Martin Cohn (1829–1894), Ger. writer.

Alan **Melville:** William Melville Caverhill (1910–1983), Eng. lyric writer, dramatist.

Jean-Pierre **Melville:** Jean-Pierre Grumbach (1917–1973), Fr. movie director. The actor admired American culture and took his new name in honor of his favorite writer, Herman Melville (1819–1891).

Jennie **Melville:** Gwendoline Williams Butler (1922–), Br. mystery novelist.

Lewis **Melville:** Lewis Samuel Benjamin (1874–1932), Eng. novelist, historical writer.

Mary **Melwood:** Eileen Mary Lewis, née Hall (*c.*1920–), Br. children's writer.

Memphis Minnie: Elizabeth Douglas (1896–1973), U.S. black blues guitarist, singer. The musician, born in Louisiana and raised in Mississippi, ran away from home at the age of 13 to play music in Memphis, Tennessee. There she met guitarist and blues singer Joe McCoy, formed a duo with him, and

recorded with him for Columbia, who named McCoy "Kansas Joe" and Douglas "Memphis Minnie."

Memphis Slim: John Len Chatman (1915–1988), U.S. black blues singer, pianist. The musician, who lived in France from the 1960s after marrying a Frenchwoman, was born in Memphis, Tennessee.

Menaka: Leila Sokhay (1899–1947), Ind. ballet dancer, director. In Hindu mythology, Menaka is a heavenly dancer and sexual temptress.

Menander: Charles Langbridge Morgan (1894–1958), Br. novelist, essayist. The writer used the name for a series of articles entitled "Menander's Mirror" in the *Times Literary Supplement* during World War II. Menander was an Athenian poet of the 3d century BC.

Menantes: Christian Friedrich Hunold (1681–1721), Ger. poet, novelist.

Mendele Mokher Sefarim: Shalom Yakov Abramovich (1835–1917), Russ. Jewish writer. The creator of modern literary Yiddish adopted his name, meaning "Mendele the itinerant bookseller," in 1879. The name implies his life's aim to enlighten and educate.

Felix **Mendelssohn:** Jakob Ludwig Felix Mendelssohn-Bartholdy (1809–1847), Ger. composer. Felix's grandfather was the German Jewish philosopher Moses Mendelssohn (1729–1786), known in Jewry as Moses Dessau. His writing name, however, was Mendelssohn ("son of Mendel"), after his father, Menachem Mendel Dessau. Moses' son, Abraham Mendelssohn, adopted the Christian faith and accordingly Felix, together with his brother and two sisters, was baptized in his youth as a Lutheran Christian. The name Bartholdy was that of a family property on the Spree River held by a maternal uncle who had converted to Protestantism, and when this uncle's fortune passed to the Mendelssohns, they adopted his name. Felix thus also officially bore the name, but is now generally known without it.

Eddie **Mendoza:** Edward Middleton (1913–2004), Sc. bandleader, comedian.

Menelik II: Sahle Miriam (1844–1913), Ethiopian emperor. The ruler took his crown name from that of Menelik I, the legendary son of King Solomon and the Queen of Sheba.

Adah Isaacs **Menken:** Ada McCord (1835–1868), U.S. actress. The actress married Alexander Isaac Menken in 1856 and kept his name through all subsequent alliances and marriages. Menken was a Jew, and this may have prompted her to change her first two names to something more specifically Jewish. It is hard to sift fact from fiction in the early years of her life, and depending on circumstances she claimed to have been born either Marie Rachel Adelaide de

Vere Spencer, an Englishman's daughter, or Dolores de Ricardo Los Fuertes, of Spanish stock.

Peter **Mennin:** Peter Mennini (1923–1983), U.S. composer. The musician modified the spelling of his surname for distinction from his older brother, Louis Mennini, who was also a composer.

'Abd Allah **Menou:** Jacques-François de Baron (1750–1810), Fr. soldier. The commander of the French army in Egypt after the death of Kléber changed his name on adopting Islam in 1800.

Gerhardus **Mercator:** Gerhard Kremer (1512–1594), Flemish cartographer, mathematician. In the style of his time, the scholar translated his surname, meaning "merchant," "trader," to its Latin equivalent. This Mercator, for whom the map projection is named, should not be confused with Nicolaus **Mercator**, whose original name, though different, gave an identical Latin translation.

Nicolaus **Mercator:** Nikolaus Kauffman (c.1619–1687), Ger. mathematician, astronomer. The scholar translated his German name, meaning "merchant," "trader," to its Latin equivalent. This Mercator should not be confused with the better-known Gerhardus **Mercator**, whose original name was different.

Mabel **Mercer:** Mabel Alice Wadham (1900–1984), Eng.-born U.S. cabaret, concert singer. Mercer was the daughter of unmarried parents, Benjamin Mercer, an African-American acrobat, and Emily Wadham, an English-Welsh music-hall entertainer, and took her father's name only when in her teens.

Ismail **Merchant:** Ismail Noormohamed Haji Abdul Rehman (1936–2005), Ind.-born movie producer, director, working in U.K, teaming with U.S. director James Ivory (1928–). The moviemaker adopted his new name when a student at St. Xavier's College, Bombay.

T. **Merchant:** Thomas John Dibdin (1771–1841), Eng. playwright, operatic composer, songwriter. The writer used this punning name for some of his work, but more often wrote as Thomas Pitt, from his mother's maiden name. He was illegitimate, and only adopted his father's name of Dibdin to annoy him, as he accused him of having neglected himself and his two brothers when they were children. His elder brother, playwright Charles Pitt (1768–1833), kept his mother's name.

Vivien **Merchant:** Ada Thomson (1929–1982), Eng. stage, movie actress.

Merciless: Leonard Bartley (1971–), Jamaican reggae musician. As the singer made clear in his 1994 debut song, "Lend Out Mi Mercy": "The reason why they call mi Merciless — I len out no mercy — mi no get it back yet — you dis [show disrespect for] Merciless — well a dead."

Melina **Mercouri:** Maria Amalia Mercouris (1923–1994), Gk. movie actress, politician.

Freddie **Mercury:** Farok Bulsara (1946–1991), Zanzibar-born Br. rock singer, of Ind. parentage. Rock group Queen's flamboyant lead singer's original forename gave his school nickname "Freddie" He early used the "glam rock" name Larry Lurex. His surname has been the subject of speculation: "I had assumed Farok Bulsara had chosen the name Mercury because he imagined himself to be as uncatchable as quicksilver.... The official Queen biography says he named himself in 1970 after the messenger of the gods. [His brother-in-law] Roger [Cooke], however, insists that he chose the name because Mercury was his rising planet" [*Sunday Times Magazine*, November 17, 1996].

Anne **Meredith:** Lucy Beatrice Malleson (1899–1973), Eng. crime novelist.

Burgess **Meredith:** George Burgess (1908–1997), U.S. movie actor.

Francis **Meredith** *see* J. Calder **Ayrton**

Hal **Meredith:** Harry Blyth (1852–1898), Sc. writer of stories for boys. The author used this name for stories starring the popular detective Sexton Blake, who first appeared in *The Marvel* in December 1893.

Isabel **Meredith:** Olivia Frances Madox Agresti, née Rossetti (1875–1960), Eng. writer + Helen Maria Madox Angeli, née Rossetti (1879–1969), Eng. writer, her sister. The sisters were the daughters of art critic William Michael Rossetti (1829–1919), nieces of poet Christina Rossetti (1830–1894) and poet and painter Dante Gabriel Rossetti (1828–1882), and cousins of Ford Madox **Ford**.

Owen **Meredith:** Edward Robert Bulwer Lytton (1831–1891), Br. diplomat, poet. The son of Bulwer **Lytton** adopted his pen name for his first book, *Clytemnestra, the Earl's Return, The Artist, and Other Poems* (1855), written when he was in the diplomatic service. There was a family tradition that Anne Meredith, who had married a Lytton ancestor, was a sister or niece of Owen Tudor (c.1400–1461), Welsh founder of the English Tudor dynasty, and this is said to be the origin of the name.

Bess **Meredyth:** Helen McGlashan (1890–1969), U.S. movie scriptwriter.

Merlinus Anglicus: William Lilly (1602–1681), Eng. astrologer. Lilly used the name, meaning "English Merlin," for the many astrological almanacs he published.

Ethel **Merman:** Ethel Agnes Zimmerman (1909–1984), U.S. stage, movie actress.

Mary **Merrall:** Mary Lloyd (1890–1976), Eng. stage, movie actress. The actress almost certainly changed her name in order to avoid being confused with Marie **Lloyd**. She first appeared on the stage in 1907 as Queenie Merrall.

David **Merrick:** David Margulois (1912–2000), U.S. theatrical producer.

Leonard **Merrick:** Leonard William Miller (1864–1939), Eng. writer, of Jewish parentage. Miller changed his name by deed poll on embarking on a stage career. He later turned more successfully to fiction.

Lynn **Merrick:** Marilyn Llewelling (1919–2007), U.S. movie actress.

Judith **Merril:** Josephine Juliet Zissman, later Pohl, née Grossman (1923–1997), U.S. SF writer, working in Canada (from 1968).

Bob **Merrill:** Henry Robert Merrill Levan (1920–1998), U.S. popular composer, lyricist.

Dina **Merrill:** Nedenia Hutton Rumbough (1925–), U.S. movie, TV actress, socialite.

Helen **Merrill:** Helena Anna Milcetic (1930–), U.S. jazz singer.

Robert **Merrill:** Moishe Miller (1917–2004), U.S. opera singer.

Henry Seton **Merriman:** Hugh Stowell Scott (1862–1903), Eng. writer of historical fiction. The writer was obliged by his father to become an underwriter at Lloyds of London, a commercial position that was not to his liking. He chose the name, loosely based on his real name, in order not to incur his family's displeasure, first using it for his novel *The Phantom Future* (1888), a study of bohemian student life.

LeRoy Charles **Merritt:** LeRoy Charles Schimmelpfennig (1912–1970), U.S. librarian, educator.

Andrew **Merry:** Mildred Henrietta Gordon Darby, née Dill (1867–1932), Eng. writer, of Ir. parentage. The novelist's pseudonym is a reversal of "merry andrew," an old term for a clown or comic entertainer.

Felix **Merry:** Evert Augustus Duyckinck (1816–1878), U.S. editor, writer. The author used this name for his contributions to the New York *Literary World*, of which he was founding editor in 1847. Both Latin *felix* and English *merry* mean "happy."

Malcolm J. **Merry** *see* Malcolm J. **Errym**

Tom **Merry:** William Mecham (1853–1902), Eng. caricaturist.

Buster **Merryfield:** ? (1920–1999), Eng. TV actor. Familiar as Uncle Albert Trotter in the long-running situation comedy *Only Fools and Horses*, first screened in 1981, the actor never revealed his original name. "I have a real name," he said, "but I'll never divulge it" [*Sunday Times*, June 27, 1999]. Fans of the program generally say that "Merryfield" was his real surname and "Harry" his first name.

Billy **Merson:** William Henry Thompson (1881–1947), Eng. music-hall artist, movie actor. The actor toured Australia early in his career as a clown named Ping-Pong.

Alice **Merton:** Sarah Knowles Bolton (1841–1916), U.S. writer. The future reform activist adopted this name for her first published piece, printed in *Waverly Magazine* when she was 15.

Ambrose **Merton:** William John Thoms (1803–1885), Eng. antiquary. The founder of the academic journal *Notes and Queries* used this name for two volumes of tales and ballads published in 1846.

Paul **Merton:** Paul Martin (1957–), Br. TV humorist. The panelist and interviewer adopted the name of the London borough where he was raised. He made the change on discovering that there was another Paul Martin, a comedy magician in Leeds.

Robert King **Merton:** Meyer R. Schkolnick (1910–2003), U.S. sociologist,

Claudio **Merulo:** Claudio Merlotti (1533–1604), It. organist, composer.

William **Mervyn:** William Mervyn Pickwoad (1912–1976), Eng. stage, movie, TV actor.

Pietro **Metastasio:** Pietro Antonio Domenico Bonaventura Trapassi (1698–1782), It. poet, librettist. In 1712, when he was 13, Pietro was made the heir adoptive of Gian Vincenzo Gravina, a founder member of the Academy of Arcadia (*see* Aglauro **Cidonia**), who grecized his surname, meaning literally "transition." There is an academic pun here, as a name change is itself a metastasis or transformation.

Suzanne **Metcalf** *see* Floyd **Akers**

Method Man: Clifford Smith (1971–), U.S. black hip-hop musician. A "method man" is one who develops his style or talent by applying different methods and techniques, as Smith aimed to do.

[Sir] Algernon **Methuen:** Algernon Methuen Marshall Stedman (1856–1924), Eng. publisher. In 1889 Stedman, a former teacher of Classics and French, founded the publishing house of Methuen (using his second name) to market his own textbooks. In 1899 he changed his name from Stedman to Methuen to celebrate its first decade, so that he became Algernon Methuen Marshall Methuen.

Peter **Metro:** Donovan Harris (*c.*1960–), Jamaican DJ, reggae musician. Harris had originally intended to call himself Peter Ranking, in the same sense as for **Ranking Joe**, but on discovering another DJ of that name, based his new name on the sound (disco) Metromedia, where he was resident DJ.

Mait **Metsanurk:** Eduard Hubel (1879–1957), Estonian novelist. The writer's adopted name means "forest corner."

Metsarents: Misak Metsaturyan (1886–1908), Armenian poet.

Meudwy Môn: Owen Jones (1806–1889), Welsh writer, preacher. The writer was born on the island of Anglesey. Hence his adopted Welsh name, meaning "hermit of Anglesey."

Meuryn: Robert John Rowlands (1880–1967), Welsh poet, journalist. Meuryn is an old river name.

[Sir] Hedworth **Meux:** Hedworth Lambton (1856–1929), Eng. naval officer. In 1899 the future admiral of the fleet supplied guns as reinforcements for the defence of Ladysmith in the Boer War. His timely action met with the approval of Lady Valerie Meux, wife of brewer Sir Henry Meux, who herself sent similar guns. Lambton subsequently called on Lady Meux to return the compliment. Touched by his tribute, and after many changes of will, Lady Meux bequeathed her large fortune to Lambton on the sole condition he change his name to Meux. He did so by royal license in 1911 at the fairly late age of 55.

Giacomo **Meyerbeer:** Jakob Liebmann Beer (1791–1864), Ger. Jewish opera composer, working in Italy, France. In 1810 the composer combined his mother's maiden name (Meyer) with that of his father (Beer). Six years later he began to use the Italian equivalent of his German first name as a compliment to the country that had enabled him to embark on a musical career.

Jonathan Rhys **Meyers:** John O'Keefe (1977–), Ir. movie actor.

Maan **Meyers:** Annette Meyers (1934–), U.S. historical mystery writer + Martin Meyers (1934–), U.S. historical mystery writer. The husband-and-wife authors of novels featuring Pieter Tonneman, the Dutch sheriff of New York, chose a joint pseudonym with a Dutch-sounding first name, formed from the first two letters of their own first names.

Gustav **Meyrink:** Gustav Meyer (1868–1932), Austr. writer.

Mezz **Mezzrow:** Milton Mesirow (1899–1972), U.S. jazz musician, of Jewish parentage.

M.I.A.: Mathangi ("Maya") Arulpragasam (1977–), Br.-born Sri Lankan hip-hop artist. The musician adopted her intitialism because of its similarity to the pet form of her first name. In military parlance the letters stand for "missing in action," a phrase that the singer wryly altered to "Missing in Acton," referring to the London suburb where she lived when starting a career as an album-cover designer after "missing out" on learning English as a young child.

Miaco: Stephen Frisbie (1912–1949), U.S. magician.

Micco Spadaro: Domenico Gargiulo (1612–1675), It. painter. The artist took his name, amounting to "Mick the Knife," from his father, who made swords (Italian *spada* "sword").

Michael: Michael Donnellan (1915–1985), Ir.-born Br. fashion designer.

Father **Michael:** Philip Ellis (1652–1726), Eng. Catholic bishop.

George **Michael:** Georgios Kyriacos Panayiotou (1963–), Br. pop singer, of Gk.-Cypriot/Eng. parentage. The lead singer of the former pop duo Wham! changed his name at age 18 on updating his image, taking "George" from "Georgios" and "Michael" from his uncle's first name.

Kathleen **Michael:** Kathleen Smith (1917–), Eng. stage actress.

Ralph **Michael:** Ralph Michael Champion Shotter (1907–1994), Eng. movie actor.

Michael X *see* Michael X

Michel: José Miguel González María del Campo (1963–), Sp. footballer. An alternate form of the sportsman's second name, equating to French Michel (English Michael).

Virgil **Michel:** George Francis Michel (1890–1938), U.S. monk. Michel took the name Virgil on entering the Benedictine community in 1909.

Michelangelo: Michelagniolo di Lodovico Buonarroti Simoni (1475–1564), It. sculptor, painter, architect, poet. It is uncertain whether the artist's first name was originally Michelangelo or Michelagniolo. The former is more likely, suggesting "Michael the Archangel." The latter name means the same (Italian *angelo* and *agnolo* both mean "angel"), but also suggests "lamb" (*agnello*).

Michael **Michele:** Michael Michele Williams (1966–), U.S. black TV actress. The actress was given the (male) name Michael after a friend of her mother's, Michael Ann.

Michelito: Michel Lagravere Peniche (1998–), Mexican bullfighter. The name of the youthful matador is a diminutive form of his first name.

Ivo **Michiels:** Henri Ceuppens (1923–), Belg. author, writing in Flemish.

Miching Mallecho, Esq.: Percy Bysshe Shelley (1792–1822), Eng. poet. Shelley used this name for his satirical poem *Peter Bell the Third* (1819), a parody of Wordsworth's poem *Peter Bell* (1819). He took the name, a phrase meaning "lurking mischief," from Shakespeare's *Hamlet* (III.ii.148):

> *Ophelia.* What means this, my lord?
> *Hamlet.* Marry, this is miching mallecho; it means mischief.

Mickey and Sylvia: McHouston ("Mickey") Baker (1925–), U.S. blues guitarist + Sylvia Vanderpool, later Robinson (1936–), U.S. blues singer.

Guy **Middleton:** Guy Middleton-Powell (1906–1973), Br. movie actor.

Josephine **Middleton:** Josephine Alcock (1886–1971), U.S. stage actress.

Robert **Middleton:** Samuel G. Messer (1911–1977), U.S. movie actor.

Mrs. Mary **Midnight:** John Newbery (1713–1767), Eng. children's writer, publisher + Christopher

Smart (1722–1771), Eng. poet. The joint pseudonym was used by publisher and poet for a threepenny journal, *The Midwife, or the Old Woman's Magazine*, issued between 1751 and 1753. The name (without the "Mrs.") was also used by the poet and dramatist William Kenrick (?1725–1779) for *The So-Much Talk'd of and Expected Old Woman's Dunciad* (1751). The name itself is said to have been borrowed from a booth at London's annual Bartholomew Fair. Smart, who also wrote as Ebenezer Pentweazle, was one of Newbery's literary clients and married his stepdaughter. Alderman Pentweazle and his wife, Lady Pentweazle, are characters in Samuel Foote's play *Taste* (1752). ("Pentweazle" is apparently "pen tweazle," a little pen case, from a word related to French *étui*, "case.")

Midori: Mi Dori Goto (1971–), Jap. (female) violinist.

Ludwig Mies van der Rohe: Maria Ludwig Michael Mies (1886–1969), Ger.-born U.S. architect. The architect formed his professional name by adding his mother's maiden name (Rohe) to his family name (Mies) and inserting an artificial aristocratic "van der" between them.

Pavel Aleksandrovich Mif: Mikhail Aleksandrovich Fortus (1901–1939), Russ. Communist official, historian. The official formed his new name from the first two letters of his original first name and initial of his surname.

Toshiro Mifune: Sanchuan Minland (1920–1997), Chin.-born Jap. movie actor.

Mighty Sam: Sam McClain (1943–), U.S. blues singer.

Mighty Sparrow: Slinger Francisco (1935–), Trinidadian calypso singer. "He earned his underwhelming nickname ... by virtue of his stage performances, which involved him moving around rapidly while most other singers were stationary" [Larkin, p.851].

Migjeni: Millosh Gjergj Nikolla (1911–1938), Albanian poet, short-story writer. The writer's pen name is formed from the opening letters of each of his three names.

Luis Miguel: Luis Miguel Gallegos (1970–), Puerto Rican popular singer.

Mika: Michael Holbrook Penniman (1983–), Br. pop singer, of U.S.–Lebanese parentage. (His name is pronounced "Meeka.")

Mikey General: Michael Taylor (1963–), Br. black reggae musician, working in Jamaica.

Éphraïm Mikhaël: Georges-Éphraïm Michel (1866–1890), Fr. Symbolist poet.

Lev Mikhaylov: Lev Mikhaylovich Yelinson (1872–1928), Russ. revolutionary.

Sergeant Pyotr Mikhaylov: Peter I (the Great) (1672–1725), Russ. czar. This was the name and rank assumed by the Russian ruler when traveling incognito in western Europe in the 1690s. His full name was Pyotr Alekseyevich, the latter being a patronymic, "son of Aleksey," referring to his father, Aleksey Mikhaylovich, commonly known in English as Czar Alexis. Peter based his adopted name on his father's second name, itself a patronymic derived from his father, Peter's grandfather, Mikhail Fyodorovich, the first Romanov czar of Russia.

Solomon Mikhoels: Solomon Mikhaylovich Vovsi (1890–1948), Russ. Jewish stage actor.

Hans Mikkelsen: Ludvig von Holberg (1684–1754), Norw.-born Dan. dramatist ("Father of Danish Drama").

Zinka Milanov: Zinka Kunc (1906–1989), Croatian-born U.S. opera singer.

Annie Miles: Anne Miller (1958–), Eng. stage, TV actress.

Barry Miles: Barry Miles Silverlight (1947–), U.S. jazz musician.

Butch Miles: Charles J. Thornton, Jr. (1944–), U.S. jazz drummer.

Garry Miles: James E. Cason (1939–), U.S. popular singer.

Joanna Miles: Joanna Schiefer (1940–), U.S. movie actress.

Lizzie Miles: Elizabeth Mary Landreaux (1895–1963), U.S. black blues singer. The singer's original surname is sometimes given as Pajaud, but this was the name of her second husband, August Pajaud. Her stage name came from her first husband, J.C. Miles, who died of Spanish flu in 1918.

Miska Miles: Patricia Miles Martin (1899–1986), U.S. children's writer. The writer also used the name Jerry Lane.

Peter Miles: Gerald Richard Perreau-Saussine (1938–2002), U.S. movie actor, of Fr.–U.S. parentage, brother of Gigi **Perreau**. As a child artist, the actor was billed as Gerald Perreau until 1948, when he adopted the friendlier screen name of Peter Miles. As a writer he used the name Richard Miles.

Robert Miles: Roberto Concina (or Milani) (1969–), Swiss popular musician, "electronic composer," of It. parentage, working in Italy.

Susan Miles: Ursula Roberts, née Wyllie (1887–1970), Eng. poet, novelist, memoirist.

Vera Miles: Vera Ralston (1929–), U.S. movie actress. Miles was obliged to take a new name because of the existing movie actress Vera **Ralston**.

Lewis Milestone: Lev Milshtein (Milstein) (1895–1980), Russ.-born U.S. movie director, screenwriter. An anglicization (but not translation, which would be "millstone") of the original name.

Geo Milev: Georgi Milev Kasabov (1895–

1925), Bulg. poet. The writer adopted his father's name, which was his own patronymic (middle name).

Ray **Milland:** Reginald Alfred John Truscott-Jones (1905–1986), Welsh-born movie actor, working in U.K., U.S. The actor's first change of name was to Mullane, the surname of his stepfather after his mother's second marriage. Later, a studio publicity man suggested a further change, and recommended the name Percival Lacy. Ray (or Reg), however, was thinking back to the rural beauty of his Welsh childhood, and proposed "Mill-land." The publicity man, more reasonable this time, advised that a name with three *l*'s might present difficulties, whereupon the actor modified it to the form in which it became popularly known [Ray Milland, *Wide-Eyed in Babylon*, 1975]. He first used the name on entering British films with *The Flying Scotsman* (1929). Then, after a few more movies, he headed for Hollywood.

Mary **Millar:** Mary Wetton (1936–), Eng. stage actress, singer. The actress adopted (and adapted) her stage name from her mother's maiden name, which was Mellow.

Alison **Miller** *see* J.P. **McCall**

Ann **Miller:** Johnnie Lucille Collier (1923–2004), U.S. tap dancer, movie actress. The actress's screen name was that of her first husband, Reese Miller. (Her original first name was apparently given because her father wanted a boy. Her parents divorced when she was 10 and she then replaced it with Annie.)

Eddie **Miller:** Edward Raymond Mueller (1911–1991), U.S. jazz musician.

Freddie **Miller:** Friedrich Mueller (1911–1962), U.S. featherweight boxer, of Ger. parentage.

Gary **Miller:** Neville Williams (1924–1968), Br. popular singer, dancer.

George **Miller:** George Miliotis (1945–), Austral. movie director.

Henry **Miller:** Johann Heinrich Möller (1702–1782), Ger.-born U.S. colonial printer.

Joaquin **Miller:** Cincinnatus Hiner Miller (1839–1913), U.S. poet. The poet's adopted first name was originally a nickname, as his earliest writing defended the Mexican desperado Joaquín Murieta (1830–1853). He later preferred to spell his middle name as "Heine," perhaps in allusion to the German poet.

Jonny Lee **Miller:** Jonathan Lee (1974–), Br. movie actor, grandson of actor Bernard Lee (1908–1981).

Kristine **Miller:** Jacqueline Olivia Eskeson (1925–), Dan. movie actress, working in U.S.

Mandy **Miller:** Angie Quick (1944–), Eng. porno movie actress. The actress was renamed by producer John M. East for the movie *Emmanuelle in Soho* (1981). "East renamed her Mandy Miller in the hope

that cinemagoers would assume that she was the little deaf girl from the Ealing film [*Mandy* (1952)], all grown up" [Matthew Sweet, *Shepperton Babylon*, 2005].

Marilyn **Miller:** Mary Ellen Reynolds (1898–1936), U.S. dancer, movie actress. The actress's professional name, which gave that of Marilyn **Monroe**, is a blend of her first name (Mary), her mother's middle name (Lynn), and her stepfather's surname (Miller).

Martin **Miller:** Rudolf Müller (1899–1969), Cz.-born Br. movie actor.

Marvin **Miller:** Marvin Mueller (1913–1985), U.S. movie actor.

Max **Miller:** Thomas Henry Sargent (1895–1963), Eng. music-hall comedian (the "Cheeky Chappie"). Sargent was renamed in 1920 by his wife, singer Kathleen Marsh, perhaps with a pun on "Maximilian."

Olive Thorne **Miller:** Harriet Mann Miller (1831–1918), U.S. children's writer, naturalist. Miller first used the pen name Olive Thorne, but then added her married name to this.

Punch **Miller:** Ernest Burden (1894–1971), U.S. jazz trumpeter, singer. The musician's first name arose as a nickname, pairing the middle name of his twin sister, Ernestine Judy Burden.

Wade **Miller:** Robert Wade (1920–), U.S. mystery writer + Bill Miller (1920–1961), U.S. mystery writer.

Carl **Milles:** Wilhelm Carl Emil Andersson (1875–1955), Swe. sculptor.

Millie: Millicent Small (1942–), Jamaican pop singer.

Spike **Milligan:** Terence Alan Milligan (1918–2002), Br. humorist, comedian, of Ir. parentage. How did the oddball writer and entertainer come by his new name? "The story goes that he had been talking to [his friend] Harry Edgington about his musical ambitions. 'I'd like to play the trumpet as well as Spike Hughes does,' said the young, enthusiastic Terence. 'Oh, I see. We're going to have Spike Milligan next, are we?' So Terence became Spike" [Pauline Scudamore, *Spike Milligan*, 1985]. Jazz musician Spike Hughes (1908–1987) was born Patrick Cairns Hughes.

Powell **Millington:** [Major] Mark Synge (1871–1921), Br. soldier, military writer. The army officer used this name for his unofficial publications, his official writings being for the Indian government. He seems to have adopted his pen name from his coeval, the Irish dramatist John Millington Synge (1871–1909). They were born only nine days apart. Synge's father's surname was actually Sing.

Aurel **Milloss:** Aurel Milloss de Miholy (1906–1988), Hung.-born It. ballet dancer, choreographer.

Alan **Mills:** Albert Miller (1914–1977), Can. folk singer.

Cotton Mather **Mills, Esq.:** Elizabeth Cleghorn Gaskell, née Stevenson (1810–1865), Eng. novelist, short-story writer. Mrs. Gaskell (as she was long regularly known) used this name for her contributions to *Howitt's Journal.* Cotton Mather (1663–1728) was a prominent U.S. Puritan minister.

Donna **Mills:** Donna Jean Miller (1943–), U.S. TV actress.

Florence **Mills:** Florence Winfree (1895–1927), U.S. black entertainer.

[Sir] John **Mills:** Lewis Ernest Watts Mills (1908–2005), Br. movie actor. The actor renamed himself John when still at school because he considered his birth name "too sissy" [*Sunday Times Magazine*, August 31, 1986].

Kerry **Mills:** Frederick Allen (1869–1948), U.S. composer, lyricist.

Martin **Mills:** Martin à Beckett Boyd (1893–1972), Austral. novelist, working in U.K. Boyd used this name for his first three novels. A fourth novel, *Dearest Idol* (1929), appeared under the name Walter Beckett, after which he wrote under his real name.

Nat **Mills:** Nathan Miller (1900–1993), Br. comedian, teaming with Bobbie McCauley (?–1955), his wife.

Milly: Carla Mignone (1908–1980), It. singer, stage actress.

Mil Mascaras: Aaron Rodriguez (1942–), Mexican wrestler. The wrestler's name means "(man of a) thousand masks."

George **Milner:** George Edward Charles Hardinge, Baron Hardinge of Penshurst (1921–), Eng. crime novelist.

Rodney **Milnes:** Rodney Blumer (1936–), Eng. music critic, writer.

La **Milo:** Pansy Eggena, née Montague (*fl.*1910s), Eng. variety artist. The artist's act consisted in posing motionless, apparently (but not actually) nude, as the Venus de Milo.

Sandra **Milo:** Alessandra Marini (1935–), It. movie actress. The actress adopted her new surname when some admirers, struck by her beauty, started comparing her to the Venus de Milo.

Louis-Jacques **Milon:** Louis-Jacques Jessé (1765–1849), Fr. ballet dancer, director.

Georges **Milton:** Georges Michaud (1888–1907), Fr. movie actor, singer.

Robert **Milton:** Robert Davidor (*c.*1886–1956), Russ.-born theatrical producer, movie director, working in U.S.

Milva: Maria Ilva Biolcati (1939–), It. popular singer, stage actress.

Min: [Sir] Gordon Edward George Minhinnick (1902–1992), N.Z. cartoonist.

Mina: Anna Maria Mazzini (1940–), It. popular singer.

Johnny **Mince:** John Henry Muenzenberger (1912–1997), U.S. jazz clarinetist.

[Cardinal] József **Mindszenty:** József Pehm (1892–1975), Hung. church leader. The archbishop adopted the Magyar name in 1940 from his native village of Mindszent as a protest against Hungary's pro-Hitler stand in the 1930s. The placename itself means "All Saints" (Hungarian *mind,* "all," + *szent,* "saint"), with the final -*y* of the surname equal to "of."

Minnesota Fats *see* Minnesota **Fats**

Echo **Minott:** Noel Phillips (*c.*1962–), Jamaican reggae musician.

Nikolay **Minsky:** Nikolay Maksimovich Vilenkin (1855–1937), Russ. writer, translator. The writer adopted his name from his native city of Minsk.

Mary Miles **Minter:** Juliet Reilly (1902–1984), U.S. movie actress. The actress began her screen career as a child star, billed as "Little Juliet Shelby." When she was 13, she changed her name to Mary Miles Minter and continued under the name until 1923, when she quit films for good after a scandal involving the murder of director William Desmond Taylor, her reputed lover.

Antonio **Minturno:** Antonio Sebastiani (1500–1574), It. humanist.

Miölnir Nanteos: George Powell (1842–1882), Welsh poet. The writer became interested in Scandinavian mythology and in particular in Iceland and its struggle for independence. Hence his adopted name. Mjöllnir ("crusher") is the hammer thrown by Thor, the Nordic god of war and thunder, as his "bolt." Nanteos is the village where Powell was born.

Miou-Miou: Sylvette Arri (or Herry) (1950–), Fr. movie actress. The actress was so nicknamed early in her career by **Coluche,** whose initial verdict on her was: "Elle était un peu miou-miou" ("She was a bit of a softie").

Jean **Mirabaud:** Paul-Henri Thiry, baron d'Holbach (1723–1789), Fr. materialist, atheist writer. Holbach frequently used the names of important deceased persons as pseudonyms for his books. This one, which he used for his most important work, *Système de la nature* (1770), he took from the writer and French Academy member, Jean Baptiste de Mirabaud, who had died ten years previously.

Carmen **Miranda:** Maria do Carmo Miranda da Cunha (1909–1955), Port.-born popular singer, dancer, movie actress, working in Brazil, U.S. ("The Brazilian Bombshell"). The actress was always called "Carmen" and this became her professional first name, coupled with her surname, Miranda, her mother's maiden name. Aptly for her flamboyant, exotic roles, the name evokes the gypsy heroine of Bizet's *Carmen* and the romantic heroine of Shakespeare's *The Tempest.*

Isa Miranda: Ines Isabella Sampietro (1909–1982), It. stage, movie actress.

Mireille: Mireille Hartuch (1906–1996), Fr. stage actress, singer, composer, of Pol.-Eng. parentage. The actress was advised to drop her surname by theatrical director Firmin **Gémier**.

Miriam: Zenon Przesmycki (1861–1944), Pol. editor, writer.

Stratis Mirivilis: Efstratios Stamatopulos (1890–1969), Gk. novelist.

Mirko: Mirko Basaldella (1910–1969), It. sculptor, brother of **Afro**. A third brother, Dino Basaldella (1909–1977), preferred to retain his surname.

Panas Mirny: Afanasy Yakovlevich Rudchenko (1849–1920), Ukr. writer. The writer made it his business to expose the social injustices that existed in Ukrainian rural life. He was therefore obliged to mask his real name behind the cloak of another, disarmingly meaning "peaceful." His new first name is simply a pet form of the original.

Miroslava: Miroslava Stern (1926–1955), Cz. movie actress, working in Mexico.

Yevstigney Mirovich: Yevstigney Afinogenovich Dunayev (1878–1952), Belorussian stage actor, director, playwright.

[Dame] Helen Mirren: Ilyena Vasilievna Mironov (1945–), Br. movie actress, of Russ.-Sc. parentage. The future actress adopted her new surname at the age of 10.

Mishima Yukio: Hiraoka Kimitake (1925–1970), Jap. novelist.

Miss ... For names beginning thus, excepting the entry below, see the next word, e.g. Miss **Bluebell**, Miss **Manners**, Miss **Read**, etc.

Miss Behave: Amy Saunders (1977–), Br. performance artist, sword swallower.

Mr. ... For names beginning thus, see the next word or name, which may be a single letter, e.g. for Mr. Cee see **Cee**, for Mr. Lemon see **Lemon**, for Mr. T. see **T.**, etc.

Mistinguett: Jeanne-Marie Florentine Bourgeois (1873–1956), Fr. music-hall singer, actress. The singer, popularly known simply as "Miss," was at first named "Miss Hélyett" by a revue writer of the day, Saint-Marcel, who traveled regularly with her on the train to Enghien-les-Bains, near Paris, where she lived. Edmond Audran's light opera *Miss Hélyett* (1890) was in vogue at the time. He then suggested the variant "Miss Tinguette," rhyming this with a character in a popular song called Vertinguette. Bour-

geois adopted the name in the form "Mistinguette," later dropping the final "e" [France Vernillat and Jacques Charpentreau, *Dictionnaire de la chanson française*, 1968]. The English-style name is said to have alluded to the performer's prominent front teeth, a characteristic of the English aristocracy.

Gabriela Mistral: Lucila Godoy Alcayaga (1889–1957), Chilean poet. The poet took her pen name from the two fellow poets she admired, the Italian Gabriele **d'Annunzio** and the Provençal Frédéric Mistral (1830–1914). She began to use the name soon after Mistral's death. Thirty years later she was awarded the Nobel Prize for Literature, as he had been.

Jorge Mistral: Modesto Llosas Rosell (1920–1972), Sp. movie actor, working in Mexico.

Misugisato: Koji Okamoto (1962–), Jap. sumo wrestler. The wrestler's fighting name means "village of three cedars" (Japanese *mi*, "three" + *sugi*, "cedar" + *sato*, "village").

Barry Mitchell *see* Brad **Dexter**

Cameron Mitchell: Cameron Mizell (1918–1994), U.S. movie actor, of Sc.-Ger. parentage.

Eddy Mitchell: Claude Moine (1942–), Fr. rock singer. The singer adopted the American-style name in 1960 in order to give his persona a more "international" image.

George Mitchell: Charles Allen Pendleton (1923–2003), U.S. movie actor.

Guy Mitchell: Albert Cernick (1927–1999), U.S. pop singer, movie actor, of Yugoslav parentage. The singer had a lucky break early in his career when Frank Sinatra pulled out of a two-song deal with Columbia. Producer Mitch Miller called Cernick in as a last-minute replacement but was not keen on his Slavic name. "My name is Mitchell and you seem like a nice guy," he is alleged to have said, "so we'll call you Guy Mitchell" [*The Times*, July 13, 1999].

Joni Mitchell: Roberta Joan Anderson (1943–), Can. pop musician. Many sources give the singer's real name thus. But "Joni Mitchell" is just as real, since her first name is a pet form of "Joan" and she married fellow folksinger Chuck Mitchell in 1965 (although the couple divorced two years later).

Warren Mitchell: Warren Misell (1926–), Eng. movie, TV actor.

Yvonne Mitchell: Yvonne Joseph (1925–1979), Eng. stage, movie actress, writer. The actress adopted her mother's maiden name as her stage name.

Mitoizumi: Masato Koizumi (1962–), Jap. sumo wrestler. The wrestler originally appeared under his family name, Koizumi, but his *shikona* (fighting name) was then changed to placate the spirits that had caused him a run of bad luck, so that *Ko-* was replaced by *Mito*, the name of his hometown.

Jean **Mitry:** Jean-René-Pierre Goetgheluck Le Rouge Tillard des Acres de Presfontaines (1907–1988), Fr. movie director, film theoretician.

Mit (or Mot) **Yenda:** Timothy (or Thomas) Adney (fl.1785), Eng. poet of the Dellacruscan school. The poet simply reversed his name(s). See also **Della Crusca.**

Art **Mix** see Denver **Dixon**

Mlle. ... For names beginning thus, see the next word, e.g. Mlle. **Augusta,** Mlle. **Chantilly,** Mlle. **Clairon,** etc.

Mme. ... For names beginning thus, see the next word, e.g. Mme. **Aorena,** Mme. **Bellecour,** Mme. **d'Arblay,** etc.

Mobutu Sese Seko: Joseph-Désiré Mobutu (1930–1997), Zairean president. In 1972 Mobutu dropped his French baptismal name and expanded his surname, which officially became Mobutu Sese Seko Kuku Ngbendu wa za Banga. According to his obituary in The Times (September 9, 1997), the full name means "the all-powerful warrior who by endurance and determination will go from conquest to conquest, leaving fire in his wake." But insiders tell another tale. "'You know what his name really means?' smirked Mobutu Sese Seko Kuku Ngbendu wa za Banga's Minister of Information. 'It's not what we tell you — about him being the warrior who will never be vanquished and all that. It means "the cockerel who jumps all the chicks in the farmyard,"' he snickered. 'The old man has cuckolded all his potential opponents'" [The Times, September 9, 1997].

Moby: Richard Melville Hall (1965–), U.S. rock musician, dancer. The former punk musician and DJ was named "Moby" for his great-great-great-uncle, Herman Melville, author of Moby-Dick (1851). "It was his father, James, who first called him Moby. The couple had written his name on the birth certificate and Elizabeth, gazing down at her new-born boy in her hospital bed in Harlem, ... said, 'You know, he doesn't look like a Richard Melville Hall,' to which her husband replied, 'So let's call him Moby.' When he was a DJ in the Eighties hip-hop scene, Moby would say that his name stood for Master of the Beat Y'All. 'Everyone had to have an acronym then,' he explains. 'It was a joke'" [The Times Magazine, May 11, 2002].

Jean-Pierre **Mocky:** Jean-Paul Adam Mokiejewski (1929–), Fr. movie director, actor, of Pol. descent.

Helen **Modjeska:** Helena (originally Jadwiga) Opid (1840–1909), Pol. actress, working in U.S. The name of Modjeska's father is uncertain, and her original surname is that of Michael Opid, a music teacher who lived with her mother. Opid died around 1847, and mother and daughter were subsequently befriended by a wealthy Austrian, Gustav Sinnmayer,

who came to live with them. In theatrical circles Sinnmayer's name was Modrzejewski, and it was thus as Helena Modrzejewska that the actress made her debut in 1861 following her birth of a son, Ralph **Modjeski,** by him. She simplified her name on settling in the United States in 1876.

Ralph **Modjeski:** Rudolphe Modrzejewski (1861–1940), Pol.-born U.S. civil engineer, son of Helen **Modjeska.**

Moe: Morris Seidenstein (1909–?), U.S. conjuror.

Moebius: Jean Giraud (1938–), Fr. cartoonist. The comic-book artist also works under the name Gir, from his surname. His regular name evokes the one-sided continuous Möbius strip. Giraud began his career as an illustrator of strip westerns.

Moelona: Elizabeth Mary Jones (1878–1953), Welsh novelist. The writer took her name from her birthplace, Moylon Farm, Rhydlewis, Cardiganshire (now Ceredigion).

Paul **Moer:** Paul E. Moerschbacher (1916–), U.S. jazz pianist, composer.

The **Mofussilite:** John George Lang (1816–1864), Austral. writer. Lang's most popular novel, Too Clever By Half (1853), was written as "by the Mofussilite," from a Bengali word meaning "provincial," "yokel." The Mofussilite was also an English-language newspaper which he edited and ultimately owned.

Mogol: Giulio Rapetti (1937–), It. songwriter. The musician's adopted name means "mogul."

Léonide **Moguy:** Leonid Moguilevsky (1899–1976), Russ. newsreel producer, movie director, working in France, U.S.

W.D. **Mohammed:** Wallace D. Muhammad (1933–2008), U.S. black Muslim leader. The head of the Nation of Islam first took the name Warith Deen Mohammed, one of many changes from his birth name, before settling to the name by which he became generally known. "The renamings appeared to reflect his struggle to reconcile his triple identity of being a Muslim, an African-American and American" [The Times, September 11, 2008]. W.D.'s father, Elijah Muhammad, was a follower of Walli **Farrad,** and after the latter's disappearance in 1934 proclaimed him to be God and himself to be his messenger and prophet.

László **Moholy-Nagy:** László Weisz (1895–1946), Hung.-born U.S. artist. The artist's new name came from the town of Mohol (later in Yugoslavia), where his mother moved him and his younger brother after his father abandoned the family in 1897, and the surname of Dr. Gusztav Nagy, his maternal uncle, with whom he subsequently lived.

Benno **Moiseiwitsch:** Benno Moiseyevich (1890–1963), Russ.-born Br. pianist. The musician adopted a German spelling of his original Russian name.

Terenci **Moix:** Ramón Moix Messeguer (1942–), Sp. writer, working in Spanish and Catalan.

Johnny **Moke:** John Rowley (1945–), Br. footwear designer. The designer explains how he came by his name: "I owned a white Mini Moke car. The car became the symbol of Swinging London. In London's Chelsea district I became known as Johnny Moke. The actress Katy Manning ... was the first to actually call me Johnny Moke" [personal fax from Johnny Moke, August 25, 1995].

Stevan **Mokranjas:** Stevan Stojanovic (1856–1914), Serbian composer, folklorist.

Solomon **Molcho:** Diogo Pieres (*c.*1500–1532), Port. prophet. Pires took his new name on converting to Judaism in his mission to proclaim David Reubeni, an Arabian adventurer, as an augur of the Jewish messiah, a divinely chosen leader who would destroy the enemies of the Jews. His new name, Molcho, comes from Hebrew *melech*, "king."

Nicholas **Moldwarp:** Anne Manning (1807–1879), Eng. novelist, historian. The writer used this name for *The Lincolnshire Tragedy: Passages in the Life of the Faire Gospeller, Mistress Anne Askew* (1866), a historical novel based on the life of the Protestant martyr Anne Askew (1520–1546). Manning also wrote as Margarita **More.** "Moldwarp" is an English dialect name for the mole (the burrowing animal).

Molière: Jean-Baptiste Poquelin (1622–1673), Fr. dramatist. The classic pseudonym is also a classic poser. How did the author of *Tartuffe* and *Le Malade imaginaire* acquire his new name? We know that he must have first used it in 1643 or 1644, for it is found in a document dated June 28, 1644. It at least has more of a theatrical ring than poky-sounding Poquelin, itself related to English "pock" and "pox." The name Molière was in fact also that of a second-rank writer who died in the year that Jean-Baptiste was born. The commonly held theory is that he derived it not from his lesser namesake, but from a place of this name, or something like it, that was visited by the touring company to which Poquelin belonged. There are several French villages named Molières, for example, and at least one Molères.

Yvonne **Mollot:** Yolande Donlan (1920–), U.S. movie actress. The actress used this name for a number of movies in the first half of the 1940s.

Ferenc **Molnár:** Ferenc Neumann (1878–1952), Hung. dramatist, working in U.S. The playwright changed his German name to a Hungarian one in 1896 to emphasize his nationality.

Vyacheslav **Molotov:** Vyacheslav Mikhaylovich Skryabin (1890–1986), Russ. diplomat. The politician assumed his party name in 1906, when he became a Bolshevik. It means "hammer" (Russian *molot*), in the symbolic manner of the Bolsheviks. "In the wake of the [13th Party] Congress [of 1924], **Stalin** obtained a solid majority on the Politburo, to which were now elevated Molotov, Voroshilov, and Kalinin. Molotov was his principal assistant in the Secretariat. True to his assumed name, he was used to hammer down the organizational details of his boss's political schemes" [Adam B. Ulam, *Stalin*, 1973].

La **Môme Moineau:** Lucienne Garcia Benitz-Reixach (1905–1968), Fr. cabaret singer. The singer first found fame as a child flower-seller at Fouquet's on the Champs-Élysées, Paris. She was "discovered" in the early 1920s by couturier Paul Poiret and launched on a career in cabaret, but from time to time returned to her old trade. "Once, it is said, she failed to turn up for her show, and was discovered back at Fouquet's, selling flowers. 'I am free, free like a bird,' she explained. 'Then we shall call you "kid sparrow" [*môme moineau*],' the cabaret owner declared" [*The Times*, January 18, 1968]. Compare the name of Edith **Piaf.**

Momus: Nicholas Currie (1960–), Sc. singer, songwriter. The earthy singer presumably adopted the name of the Greek god of ridicule.

Franz **Mon:** Franz Löffelholz (1926–), Ger. writer.

Monarque: Jean Arnolis (1905–), Belg. magician. The magician's name is French for "monarch," suggesting he is "king" in his art.

Patrick **Monckton:** Patrick Arnold (1945–), Br. movie, TV actor.

Piet **Mondrian:** Pieter Cornelis Mondriaan (1872–1944), Du. painter, working in France, U.S.

Pierre **Mondy:** Pierre Cuq (1925–), Fr. movie actor.

Lireve **Monett:** Everil Worrell (1893–1969), U.S. (female) writer of horror stories. The writer's first name is a reversal of her original name, while "Monett" is a sort of graphic inversion of "Worrell."

Eddie **Money:** Edward Mahoney (1949–), U.S. rock singer.

Anne **Mongador:** Anne Chambeyron (1908–2000), Eng. circus juggler. In 1927 the performer married Georges Chambeyron, a member of the French juggling act known as the Mongadors, and adopted their stage name.

Monica: Monica Arnold (1980–), U.S. black R&B singer.

Monifah: Monifah Carter (*c.*1960–), U.S. black R&B singer.

Christopher **Monig** *see* Richard **Foster**

Phyllis **Monkman:** Phyllis Harrison (1892–?), Eng. stage actress, dancer.

Ras Prince **Monolulu:** Peter Carl McKay

(c.1880–1963), Br. black racing tipster. The exuberant tipster, famous for his cry "I gotta horse!" and his slogan "Black man for luck, white man for pluck!," came to Britain in the early 1900s. His country of origin is unknown, though he was later linked with both Abyssinia (Ethiopia) and Guyana. "Ras" (Arabic for "head") is the title of an Ethiopian prince (as originally for **Haile Selassie**). "Monolulu" was perhaps a blend of "Honolulu" and "Monomotapa," the latter being a line of African kings who ruled territory in what is now Zimbabwe and Mozambique.

Ippolite **Monplaisir**: Ippolite Georges Sornet (1821–1877), Fr. ballet dancer, director.

Matt **Monro**: Terence Edward Parsons (1930–1985), Eng. popular singer. The singer took his new first name from Matt White, the first journalist to write about him, and his second name from the first name of the father of Winifred Atwell (1914–1983), the West Indian "honkytonk" pianist who encouraged him. He had earlier performed as Al Jordan, while for a comedy record he was Fred Flange.

Armand **Monroe**: Armand Larivée (1935–), Can. entertainer, actor, gay activist. The media personality became known as "La Monroe" after Marilyn **Monroe** and subsequently adopted the name.

Marilyn **Monroe**: Norma Jean Dougherty, later Baker, née Mortensen (1926–1962), U.S. movie actress. Dougherty was the name of Monroe's first husband (married 1942, divorced 1948). Baker was a middle name of her mother, Gladys Monroe Baker Mortensen, that she used later as her "real" name. Her father has never been positively identified. When Darryl F. Zanuck of Twentieth Century–Fox signed up the actress in 1946, actor Ben Lyon wanted to change her name to Carole Lind, but this was "a rather obvious composite of an opera singer and a dead actress," and lacked the necessary resonance. Lyon and his actress wife, Bebe **Daniels**, decided they could do better. They invited Norma Jean to tea. Lyon recalled: "I finally said to her, 'I know who you are. You're Marilyn!' I told her that once there was a lovely actress named Marilyn **Miller** and that she reminded me of her. 'But what about the last name?' Marilyn said, 'My grandmother's name was Monroe and I'd like to keep that.' I said 'Great! That's got a nice flow, and two Ms should be lucky.' That's how she got her name" [Anthony Summers, *Goddess: The Secret Lives of Marilyn Monroe*, 1985].

Monrose: Claude Louis Séraphin Barizain (1783–1843), Fr. actor.

Nicholas **Monsarrat**: Nicholas John Turney Montserrat (1910–1979), Eng. novelist. The writer's name was incorrectly registered at his birth, with a spelling that was preferred by his mother, who claimed that the family went back to a French no-

bleman, the Marquis de Montserrat. In his autobiography, Monsarrat recalls that the discrepancy between spellings was to embarrass him both at school and later on joining the Royal Navy [Nicholas Monsarrat, *Life Is a Four-Letter Word*, 1966].

Monsù Desiderio: Didier Barra (c.1590–after 1647), Fr. painter + François de Normé (c.1593–after 1644), Fr. painter. The name adopted by the two rather obscure artists, who worked in Naples, Italy, and sometimes collaborated, is a local Italian form of French *Monsieur Didier*, referring to Barra.

Ashley **Montagu**: Israel Ehrenberg (1905–1999), Br.-born U.S. anthropologist, of Pol.-Russ. Jewish parentage. The scientist's full adopted name was Montague Francis Ashley Montagu. It is uncertain why he chose these particular names, which happen to be those of English aristocratic families.

Samuel **Montagu**: Montagu Samuel (1832–1911), Br. merchant banker, of Ger. Jewish descent. The parents of the future Baron Swaythling reversed his original names on the completion of his education. The rest of the family kept the surname of Samuel.

Henry James **Montague**: Henry James Mann (1844–1878), Eng.-born U.S. actor. The actor took the name Montague on beginning his stage career at the age of 20.

Bull **Montana**: Luigi Montagna (1887–1950), It.-born U.S. movie comedian, wrestler.

Country Dick **Montana**: Daniel McLain (1955–1995), U.S. rock musician.

Patsy **Montana**: Rubye Blevins (1912–1996), U.S. country singer, yodeler. Blevins was born in Arkansas, not Montana. But in 1931 she joined singing cowboy Stuart Hamblen's show, and appeared on radio and at rodeos as part of the Montana Showgirls. This gave her new surname. Hamblen renamed her Patsy as it was "a good Irish name."

Montana Slim: Wilfred Arthur Charles Carter (1904–1996), Can. country singer. ("Slim" in names of this type means "smart.")

Yves **Montand**: Ivo Livi (1921–1991), It.-born Fr. movie actor, singer. When the singer began his career in Marseille, appearing at the Alcazar, his manager told him that "Ivo Livi" was not right for a professional name: "It's too foreign and it doesn't have a proper ring to it." Montand tells how he arrived at his new name: "When I was a kid, my mother didn't like me to hang around in the street in front of our house. She spoke bad French and would shout, 'Yvo monta, Yvo monta.' ['Yvo, come up.'] That came back to me, so I frenchified my christian name, Yves, and monta became Montand" [Simone Berteaut, *Piaf*, translated by Ghislaine Boulanger, 1970].

Lorenzo **Montano**: Danilo Lebrecht (1893–1959), It writer.

Mlle. Montansier: Marguerite Brunet (1730–1820), Fr. actress, theater manager. The actress adopted the name of the aunt who raised her as her stage name.

G. Montbard: Charles Auguste Loye (1841–1901), Fr. artist, writer, working in U.K. The artist took his name from Montbard, his birthtown in east central France. The initial stands for Georges.

Mont Blong *see* **Nunquam**

Montdory: Guillaume des Gilberts (1594–1651), Fr. tragic actor.

Hilde **Monte:** Hilde Meisel (1914–1945), Ger. poet, of Jewish parentage.

Germaine **Montero:** Germain Heygele (1909–2000), Fr. singer, movie actress.

Felipa **Monterro:** Philippa Schuyler (1931–1967), U.S. concert pianist. The dark-skinned musician adopted this name for a time when performing in Europe, hoping that audiences there would take her to be Spanish or Greek. If someone recognized her, she wrote home to her mother, "I could always say that Miss Monterro developed laryngitis, or leprosy or bubonic plague or something and couldn't come at the last minute and asked me to fill in for her" [Kathryn Talalay, *Composition in Black and White: The Life of Philippa Schuyler*, 1996].

Chris **Montez:** Christopher Montanez (1943–), U.S. pop singer.

Lola **Montez:** Marie Dolores Eliza Rosanna Gilbert (1821–1861), Ir.-born adventuress, "Spanish" dancer, working in France, U.S. In 1837 the dancer married Captain Thomas James, an officer in the Indian army. She left her husband in 1840, however, and three years later adopted the Spanish name that brought her fame. "Many of us have, from time to time, improved our social status for the benefit of our listeners — or at least have wished to — but surely nobody has turned it into such an art form as did Lola Montez. Her name was Maria Dolores de Porres y Montes. That is if it wasn't Rosanna Gilbert, or Betsy Watson — something she always denied — or Betty or Eva James, or Mlle. Marie Marie, or Mrs Burton, or Mrs Heald, or — at the very end of her life — Fanny Gibbons" [James Morton, *Lola Montez: Her Life & Conquests*, 2007]. The dancer was buried in Green-Wood Cemetery, Brooklyn, as Mrs. Eliza Gilbert.

Maria **Montez:** María Africa Antonia Gracia Vidal de Santo Silas (1912–1951), Dominican Republic-born movie actress, of Sp. parentage, working in U.S., France.

Montfleury: (1) Zacharie Jacob (*c.*1600–1667), Fr. actor; (2) Antoine Jacob (1639–1685), Fr. actor, his son.

Montgomery: Matilda Valeriana Beatrix Gyllenhaal, Duchess of Orozco (1796–1863), Swe. singer, composer, of Sp. origin. The musician's assumed name is that of her second husband, J. Montgomery-Cederhejm, whom she married in 1817.

Cora **Montgomery:** Jane Cazneau (1807–1878), U.S. journalist. Cazneau, whose full name was Jane Maria Eliza McManus Storms Cazneau (she married Allen B. Storms in 1825 and William Henry Cazneau in 1849), adopted this name for articles published in the 1840s in the *New York Sun*, the *U.S. Magazine and Democratic Review*, and other journals.

Douglass **Montgomery:** Robert Douglass Montgomery (1907–1966), Can.-born U.S. movie actor. The actor began his career as Kent Douglass to avoid confusion with Robert **Montgomery**.

George **Montgomery:** George Montgomery Letz (1916–2000), U.S. movie actor, of Ukr. parentage. The actor changed his name in 1940 on signing for Twentieth Century–Fox.

K.L. Montgomery: Kathleen Montgomery (*c.*1863–1960), Ir.-born Eng. novelist, translator + Letitia Montgomery (?–1930), Ir.-born Eng. novelist, translator, her sister. The writers used this joint name for eight novels and various historical translations.

L.M. Montgomery: Lucy Maud Montgomery (1874–1942), Can. writer of novels for girls.

Marion **Montgomery:** Maud Runnels (1934–2002), U.S. jazz singer, working in U.K. The singer first performed under the name Pepi Runnels.

Robert **Montgomery:** Henry Montgomery, Jr. (1904–1981), U.S. movie actor, politician.

Diana **Monti** *see* Hildegard **Dewitz**

Sarita **Montiel:** Maria Antonia Abad Fernández (1927–), Sp. movie actress.

Tete **Montoliu:** Vincente Montoliu Massana (1933–1997), Sp. jazz pianist.

Muriel **Montrose:** Muriel Andrews (*c.*1900–?), Eng. stage actress, dancer.

Gloria **Monty:** Gloria Montemuro (1921–), U.S. TV producer.

Monvel: Jacques-Marie Boutet (1745–1812), Fr. actor, playwright, father of Mlle. **Mars**.

John **Moody:** John Cochran (?1727–1812), Ir.-born Eng. actor. Moody himself always claimed that he was born in London.

Ron **Moody:** Ronald Moodnick (1924–), Br. stage, TV comedian.

Lorna **Moon:** Helen Nora Wilson Low (1886–1930), Sc. novelist, screenwriter, working in U.S. The writer adopted the surname of her second husband, Walter Moon (1890–1971).

Sarah **Moon:** Marielle Hadengue (1941–), Br. photographer, of Fr. parentage. The artist took her new name early in her career. "She invented the name on the spur of the moment, when an editor asked her what the credit for the picture should be. 'I was still a model and I had to choose a name because I didn't want people to stop working wth me because I was doing photographs,' she says, then adds: 'It was a way of hiding'" [*Sunday Times Magazine*, October 12, 2008].

Moondog: Louis Thomas Hardin (1916–1999), U.S. blind Beat poet, street musician. The musician explains: "I began using Moondog as a pen name in 1947, in honor of a dog I had in Hurley, who used to howl at the moon more than any dog I knew of" [sleeve note on 1969 album *Moondog*]. Hardin successfully retained his name after issuing legal proceedings against DJ Alan Freed, who had claimed it for his radio show *Moondog's Rock 'N' Roll Party*.

Harry Mooney: Harry Goodchild (1889–1972), Eng. music-hall comedian.

Captain **Moonlite** *see* **Captain Moonlite**

Dmitry Moor: Dmitry Stakhiyevich Orlov (1883–1946), Russ. illustrator, poster artist.

Archie Moore: Archibald Lee Wright (1913–1998), U.S. light heavyweight boxer, movie actor. The actor took his name from an uncle who helped raise him, Cleveland Moore.

C.L. Moore: Catherine Lucille Moore (1911–1987), U.S. SF writer. In 1940 Moore married Henry Kuttner (1914–1958) and wrote many stories in collaboration with him under a range of male pseudonyms, including Paul Edmonds, Noel Gardner, James Hall, Keith Hammond, Hudson Hastings, Robert O. Kenyon, C.H. Liddell, K.H. Maepen, Scott Morgan, and Woodrow Wilson Smith.

Colleen Moore: Kathleen Morrison (1900–1988), U.S. movie actress.

Demi Moore: Demetria Guynes (1962–), U.S. movie actress. The actress's name is that of rock musician Freddy Moore, her first husband (married 1980, divorced 1984).

Edward Moore: Edwin Muir (1887–1959), Sc. poet, translator. Muir used this adaptation of his name for an early collection of aphorisms, *We Moderns* (1918).

E.J. Moore: Ernest Linebarger (1881–1957), U.S. vaudeville performer, conjuror.

Garry Moore: Thomas Garrison Morfit (1915–1993), U.S. TV comedian, linkman. The TV comic tired of people mispronouncing his surname. In 1940 a contest was therefore held to select a new name for him. A Pittsburgh woman suggested "Garry Moore" and won the prize of $50 and a trip to Chicago.

Julianne Moore: Julie Anne Smith (1960–), U.S. movie actress.

Kieron Moore: Kieron O'Hanrahan (1924–2007), Ir. movie actor.

Maggie Moore: Margaret Sullivan (1851–1926), U.S.–born stage actress, working in Australia.

Marcel Moore: Suzanne Malherbe (1892–1972), Fr. transexual illustrator, designer, partner and stepsister of Claude **Cahun**.

Marjorie Moore *see* Marjorie **Reynolds**

Michael Moore: Michael Morehouse (1925–), U.S. movie actor, director. Not to be confused with the documentary moviemaker and writer Michael Moore (1954–).

Terry Moore: Helen Koford (1929–), U.S. movie actress. The actress appeared under the names Judy Ford and Jan Ford before settling for Terry Moore in 1948.

Thelma Moore: Tsipora Miron (1923–), Ukr.-born U.S. organist, pianist, composer.

Wentworth Moore: William Hurrell Mallock (1849–1923), Eng. author, poet.

Geoffrey Moorhouse: Geoffrey Heald (1931–2009), Eng. writer. Moorhouse adopted the name of his stepfather.

Mooseman: Lloyd Roberts (*c*.1958–2000), U.S. rock bassist.

António Mora *see* Alberto **Caeiro**

Silent Mora: Louis McCord (1884–1972), U.S. magician. Despite the performer's name, only his oriental act was silent, and he otherwise spoke on stage.

Henrietta Moraes: Audrey Wendy Abbott (1931–1999), Br. model. The bohemian beauty's new name was that of her third husband, Indian poet Dom Moraes (1938–), and it was he who called her Henrietta.

Edoard Moran *see* **Trevanian**

Lois Moran: Lois Darlington Dowling (1908–1990), U.S. movie actress.

Alberto Moravia: Alberto Pincherle (1907–1990), It. novelist, short-story writer. The writer adopted the name of his maternal grandmother.

Stella Moray: Stella Morris (1923–2006), Br. stage, TV actress.

Paal Mörck: Ole Edvart Rölvaag (1876–1931), Norw.-born U.S. writer. The author, naturalized as a U.S. citizen in 1908, adopted the pseudonym for his first novel, *Amerika-Breve* ("Letter from America") (1912), and retained it for his next book, *Paar Glemte Veie* ("On Forgotten Paths") (1914).

Elinor Mordaunt: Evelyn Mary Clowes (1877–1942), Eng. popular novelist. According to some sources, the writer adopted the name of her husband, a planter named Mordaunt, but in fact she first married Maurice Wiehe (in 1898), then Robert Rawnsley Bowles (perhaps in 1933).

Mordred: Derrick Knight (1942–), Br. crossword compiler. The setter's pseudonym represents both the name of the villanous knight of Arthurian legend, punning on his own surname, and the second part of the surname of Mike Kindred, a compiler with whom he had worked earlier. It also happens to suggest "more dread," as a setter of fiendishly difficult puzzles.

Margarita **More**: Anne Manning (1807–1879), Eng. novelist, historian. The prolific writer used this name for *The Household of Sir Thomas More* (1851), a fictional account of the life of More told from the point of view of his daughter, Margaret Roper. The pen name is thus essentially that of the narrator, although also reflecting the author's mother's maiden name, Whatmore. She also wrote as Nicholas **Moldwarp**.

Jean **Moréas**: Yánnis Papadiamantópoulos (1856–1910), Gk.-born Fr. Symbolist poet. The poet abandoned his lengthy original name in favor of his mother's maiden name on moving to France in 1879.

Hégésippe **Moreau**: Pierre Jacques Rouillot (1810–1838), Fr. poet.

Eric **Morecambe**: John Eric Bartholomew (1926–1984), Eng. TV comedian, teaming with Ernie **Wise**. The comedian described how he came by his name in his and Wise's joint autobiography. "An early problem was my stage name. Nobody liked Bartholomew and Wise. [Manager] Bryan Michie wanted to call us Bartlett and Wise or Barlow and Wise. The matter was finally settled in Nottingham. My mother was talking to Adelaide Hall, the colored American singer on the bill, when her husband, Bert Hicks, came up. My mother said, 'We're trying to think of a name for Eric.' Bert ... said, 'There's this friend of mine, a colored boy who calls himself Rochester because he comes from Rochester, Minnesota. Where do you come from?' 'Morecambe.' 'That's a good name. Call him Morecambe.' My mother liked it and I liked it, and from there on I was Morecambe on the bill" [Dennis Holman, *Eric & Ernie: The Autobiography of Morecambe and Wise*, 1973].

Anthony **Morehead**: Edward Rowland Sill (1841–1887), U.S. writer. Sill adopted this name late in life for poems published in the *Century Magazine* and the *Overland Monthly*, while for poems in the *Atlantic Monthly* he wrote as Andrew Hedbrook. His use of a pseudonym was prompted as much by his family's disapproval of his literary career as by his own dislike of publicity.

André **Morell**: André Mesritz (1909–1978), Eng. stage, movie actor.

Sir Charles **Morell**: James Ridley (1736–1765), Eng. writer. Ridley used this name, purportedly that of a "one time ambassador from the British settlements in India to the Great Mogul," for his best-known work, *The Tales of the Genii* (1764), "faithfully translated from the Persian Manuscript."

Antonio **Moreno**: Antonio Garride Monteagudo (1886–1967), Sp.-born U.S. movie actor.

Rita **Moreno**: Rosita Dolores Alverio (1931–), Puerto Rican stage, movie actress, dancer. Spanish *moreno* means "brown," "dark-haired," as many West Indian people are, and Moreno was noted for her dark brown hair. She was billed as Rosita Moreno in *So Young* (1950), but "films previously credited to her before 1950 now appear to belong to another Rosita Moreno" [Quinlan 2000, p.375].

Louis **Moresby** *see* E. **Barrington**

Clara **Moreton**: Clara Sophia Jessup Bloomfield Moore (1824–1899), U.S. novelist, writer on etiquette. This was one of several pseudonyms used by the writer, others being Mrs. Bloomfield-Moore (from her husband, Bloomfield Haines Moore) and Mrs. H.O. Ward, which she used for her best-known work, *Sensible Etiquette of the Best Society* (1878).

Lee **Moreton** *see* Dion **Boucicault**

Moretto da Brescia: Alessandro Bonvicino (*c*.1498–1554), It. painter. The artist came to be known by his nickname, from Italian *moretto*, "little blackamoor," for his swarthy complexion, and his birthplace of Brescia.

John Rushton **Moreve**: John Russell Morgan (1946–1981), U.S. rock bassist.

[Sir] Charles **Morgan**: Charles Gould (1726–1806), Eng. judge. In 1756 Gould married Jane Morgan, daughter of the Lord Lieutenant of Monmouth and Brecon, and in 1792, at the rather advanced age of 66, adopted her name and coat of arms on inheriting the property of her family.

Claire **Morgan** *see* Patricia **Highsmith**

Claudia **Morgan**: Claudeigh Louise Wupperman (1912–), U.S. stage actress, daughter of Ralph **Morgan**.

Dennis **Morgan**: Stanley Morner (1910–1994), U.S. movie actor. The actor used the name Richard Stanley before settling for Dennis Morgan in 1939 on signing with Warner Bros.

De Wolfe **Morgan** *see* S.S. **Smith**

Emanuel **Morgan**: Witter Bynner (1881–1968), U.S. poet, playwright. The writer used this name for a book of verse, *Pins for Wings* (1920), and subsequent work, having originally used it, with together with fellow poet Anne **Knish**, for *Spectra: a Book of Poetic Experiments* (1916), which the coauthors favorably reviewed under their real names.

Fidelis **Morgan**: Fidelis Horswill (1952–), Br. stage, TV actress, writer. The actress adopted the name of her mother, also Fidelis Morgan.

Frank **Morgan**: Francis Philip Wupperman (1890–1949), U.S. movie actor, brother of Ralph **Morgan**.

Harry **Morgan**: Henry Bratsburg (1915–), U.S. movie actor. The actor was originally billed as Henry Morgan but became Harry Morgan from 1958 to avoid confusion with his coeval namesake, radio comedian Henry **Morgan**.

Helen **Morgan**: Helen Riggins (1900–1941), Can. movie actress, singer.

Henry **Morgan**: Henry Lerner von Ost (1915–1994), U.S. radio, TV comedian.

Jane **Morgan**: Jane Currier (1920–), U.S. popular singer

John **Morgan** *see* Mark **Carrel**

Marilyn **Morgan** *see* Marian **Marsh**

Michèle **Morgan**: Simone Roussel (1920–), Fr. movie actress. The actress is said to have called herself Michèle to please a young man of her acquaintance who liked the name. The story goes that she then took the name Morgan, for reasons of euphony, from the main branch of Morgan & Co.'s bank in the Place Vendôme, Paris.

Ralph **Morgan**: Ralph Kuhner Wupperman (1882–1956), U.S. movie actor, brother of Frank **Morgan**, father of Claudia **Morgan**.

Scott **Morgan** *see* C.L. **Moore**

Ted **Morgan**: Sanche de Gramont (1932–), Swiss-born U.S. writer, journalist.

Irmtraud **Morgner**: Irmtraud Elfriede Schreck (1933–1990), Ger. feminist writer.

Anne **Morice**: Felicity Shaw, née Worthington (1918–1989), Br. crime, thriller writer.

Mori Ogai: Mori Rintaro (1862–1922), Jap. novelist, playwright, translator. The writer used ten different pseudonyms over the course of his career.

Dick **Morland** *see* Patrick **Ruell**

Peter Henry **Morland** *see* Max **Brand**

Gaby **Morlay**: Blanche Fumoleau (1893–1964), Fr. stage, movie actress.

Angela **Morley**: Walter Stott (1924–2009), Eng. conductor, composer, arranger. In 1972 the musician underwent a sex-change operation, adopting a female first name and his mother's maiden name.

Karen **Morley**: Mildred Litton (1909–2003), U.S. movie actress.

Mrs. **Morley**: Anne (1665–1714), queen of England. This is the name that Queen Anne used for her correspondence with the Duchess of Marlborough, who called herself Mrs. **Freeman**.

Malcolm **Morley**: Malcolm Evans (1931–), Eng. painter, working in U.S.

Susan **Morley**: Sarah Frances Spedding (1836–1921), Eng. novelist.

Jacques **Mornard**: Jaime Ramón Mercader del Río Hernández (1914–1978), Sp. Communist. The assassin of Leon **Trotsky** assumed his alias when posing as a Belgian supporter of the Bolshevik leader.

Miss **Morning Glory**: Yone Noguchi (1875–1947), Jap. poet, critic, working in U.S. Noguchi adopted this female name for *The American Diary of*

a Japanese Girl (1901), a novella recounting the life of a Japanese maid.

Skip **Morr**: Charles William Coolidge (1912–1962), U.S. jazz trombonist.

Morris: Maurice de Bévère (1923–2001), Belg. cartoonist. Creator of the comic cowboy character, Lucky Luke, Maurice de Bévère adopted an English version of his first name for his professional work.

Clara **Morris**: Clara La Montagne (1848–1925), U.S. stage actress. The actress adopted the name assumed by her mother, born Sarah Jane Proctor.

Jan **Morris**: James Humphrey Morris (1926–), Br. journalist, travel writer. The writer underwent a sex-change operation in 1972, having long felt the "victim of a genetic mix-up," and thus needed a name change. She comments: "My new name, though just right for me, I thought, was sometimes itself confusing. 'I thought Jan Morris was a man,' said a jolly Australian at a *Spectator* lunch one day. 'What happened, d'you change your sex or something?' Just that, I replied" [Jan Morris, *Conundrum*, 1974].

Lana **Morris**: Avril Maureen Anita Morris (1930–1998), Br. stage, movie, TV actress. The actress made her debut in *School for Secrets* (U.S. title *Secret Flight*) (1946) under the name Pamela Matthews. She adopted her permanent screen name shortly before being cast as the Cockney maid Rosie in the 1948 romance *Spring in Park Lane*.

Lily **Morris**: Lilles Mary Crosby (1882–1952), Br. comedienne.

Peter **Morris**: John Gibson Lockhart (1794–1854), Sc. lawyer, writer. Lockhart called himself "Peter Morris the Odontist" for *Peter's Letters to His Kinsfolk* (1819), "odontist" being (facetiously) a dentist.

William **Morris**: Zelman Moses (1873–1932), U.S. theatrical agent.

[Sir] John **Morris-Jones**: John Jones (1864–1929), Welsh poet, teacher. The scholar was the son of Morris Jones, a shopkeeper, and adopted his father's name as his new surname when he was knighted in 1918.

Toni **Morrison**: Chloe Anthony Wofford (1931–), U.S. black novelist. Wofford changed her first name to Toni (from her middle name) while at Howard University, Washington, DC. Her surname is that of her husband, Jamaican architect Harold Morrison (married 1958, divorced 1964).

Morrissey: Steven Patrick Morrissey (1959–), Eng. rock musician. "Another unnerving problem is ... the difficulty of knowing how to address him. He never uses Steven, his Christian name.... He tells me that like the other boys he was called by his surname at his Manchester secondary modern [school] and came to prefer it. 'There's a certain majesty in "Morrissey." And it's certainly better than Steve.' Morrissey I shall call him" [*The Times*, May 30, 2006].

Buddy **Morrow:** Muni "Moe" Zudekoff (1919–), U.S. jazz trombonist, bandleader.

Doretta **Morrow:** Doretta Marano (1925– 1968), U.S. singer.

Laila **Morse:** Maureen Bass (1945–), Br. TV actress.

George **Morshiel:** George Shiels (1886–1949), Ir. playwright.

Geoffrey **Mortimer:** Walter Matthew Gallichan (1861–1946), Eng. journalist, husband of C. Gasquoine **Hartley**.

Philip **Mortimer:** Joseph Philip Knight (1812– 1887), Eng. composer. The musician adopted this name on publishing his first set of songs at the age of 20.

G.N. **Mortlake:** Marie Charlotte Carmichael Stopes (1880–1958), Br. writer. Marie Stopes, famous for her books on family planning, used this name for her fiction. She also wrote as Mark Arundel and Erica Fay.

Anthony **Morton** *see* Gordon **Ashe**

Howard **Morton:** Helen Macfarlane (*fl.*1850), Sc. journalist, translator. Macfarlane used this male name for socialist-oriented articles in the *Democratic Review.*

Hugh **Morton:** Charles M.S. M'Lellan (1865– 1916), U.S. playwright, working in U.K. The musician used this name for the lyrics of a number of stage musicals, such as *The Belle of New York* (1897).

Jelly Roll **Morton:** Ferdinand Joseph Lamothe (or La Menthe, or Lemott) (1890–1941), U.S. black jazz composer, pianist. To his original surname, whatever it was, the musician added Morton, the name (originally Mouton) of the porter who married his mother after her husband left her. "Jelly Roll" is a black slang term (not exclusive to Morton) implying sexual prowess.

Tex **Morton:** Robert William Lane (1916–1983), N.Z. popular musician, entertainer, working in Australia. The story goes that one day, when busking on the streets, the teenager was asked by a policeman if his name was Bobby Lane. He noticed a nearby garage sign that gave the name "Morton" and quickly informed the officer that he was Bob Morton and a street singer and entertainer. "Tex" came later when he adopted a country style of music.

Cenydd **Morus:** Kenneth Vennor Morris (1879– 1937), Welsh fantasy writer. The writer's name is a Welsh equivalent of the original.

Morus Cyfannedd: Morus Jones (1895–1982), Welsh poet. The writer's adopted name means "Morus the entertainer."

Peter **Morwood:** Robert Peter Smith (1956–), Eng. writer of adventure fantasies, working in Ireland.

Maurice **Moscovitch:** Morris Maascoff (1871– 1940), Russ.-born U.S. movie actor, father of Noël **Madison**.

Aminata **Moseka** *see* Abbey **Lincoln**

Hans **Moser:** Johann Julier (1880–1964), Austr. stage, movie actor.

Moses: (1) Loolowkin (?1829–1899), U.S. Native American chief; (2) Ron Scott (1957–), Eng. charity worker. The chief of the Columbia Sinkiuses was the son of Sulktalthscosum ("Piece Split from the Sun") and his favorite wife, Karneetsa ("Between the Robes"). He bore other names in his lifetime, the main one being that of his father, but was known to white settlers as Moses, a name given him by the Rev. Henry H. Spalding when he attended the latter's mission school at Lapwai, Idaho.

The English community volunteer changed his name by deed poll in 2002 because he felt an affinity with the biblical patriarch, who dedicated his life to God but never reached the Promised Land. "'Moses didn't get to the Promised Land because he didn't complete his work for God,' he said. 'I felt that I haven't got to the promised land. I would like to get to Heaven, but I'd like to do as much as possible down here'" [*The Times*, December 30, 2006]. Moses was appointed MBE (Member of the Order of the British Empire) in 2006 for helping to organize transport for the elderly and disabled. His honor was unusual in being the first awarded to a person with a single name. Even pop stars **Sting** and **Bono** were referred to by their full names when listed for honors.

Grandma **Moses:** Anna Mary Moses, née Robertson (1860–1961), U.S. painter. Following her "discovery" by an art collector at the age of 78, the elderly widow retained the homely name by which she was known to family and friends.

Pablo **Moses:** Pablo Henry (*c.*1953–), Jamaican reggae musician.

Moshoeshoe *see* **Mshweshwe**

Snub **Mosley:** Lawrence Leo Mosley (1905– 1981), U.S. jazz musician.

Mihály **Mosonyi:** Michael Brand (1815–1870), Hung. composer, music critic. The musician exchanged his German name for a Hungarian one in 1859 when first composing in a national style.

Monsieur **Mosse:** Raimo Jääskeläinen (1932– 1992), Finn. makeup artist. After working as a makeup artist on television in the 1950s, Jääskeläinen became "Monsieur Mosse" in 1964, when he opened his own salon.

Burt **Mossman** *see* Wes **Hardin**

Mickie **Most**: Michael Peter Hayes (1938–2003), Eng. record company director, promoter. The record producer first used the name in 1957 for a double act, the Most Brothers, with his friend Alex Murray.

Zero **Mostel**: Samuel Joel Mostel (1915–1977), U.S. stage, movie actor, of Jewish parentage. The actor adopted his school nickname, given him for his repeated zero marks.

Sydney **Mostyn** *see* Eliza Rhyl **Davies**

Mother ... For names beginning thus, see the next word(s), eg. for Mother Alphonsa see **Alphonsa**, for Mother Mary Angela see **Mary Angela**, etc.

Mounet-Sully: Jean Sully Mounet (1841–1916), Fr. tragic actor.

[Lord] Louis **Mountbatten**: [Prince] Louis Francis Albert Victor Nicholas of Battenberg (1900–1979), Eng. soldier, statesman. Queen Victoria's great-grandson adopted the English part-translation of "Battenberg" in 1917, when his father, Louis Alexander Mountbatten, formerly Prince Louis Alexander of Battenberg (1854–1921), relinquished the title amid general anti–German feeling.

The change of name was made at the request of George V in a proclamation published in the press on June 20, 1917: "The King has deemed it desirable, in the conditions brought about by the present war, that those princes of his family who are his subjects and bear German names and titles should relinquish these titles, and henceforth adopt British surnames." On July 17 George V in turn announced his intention to relinquish his German surname of Wettin and adopt the British surname of Windsor, taking it from the Berkshire town where Windsor Castle had long been a royal residence.

Mourning Dove: Christine Quintasket (?1884–1936), U.S. Native American novelist. The first traditional Native American woman novelist adopted the name Morning Dove (Humishuma) around 1912 when preparing a novel about the wide spectrum of native peoples, as against the stereotype of the brave Native American. (It was published in 1927 as *Cogewea: The Half-Blood*.) In 1921 she altered the spelling of the name to Mourning Dove to denote the tragic background to her life and work.

Mousse T: Mustafa Gündogdu (1970–), Ger. DJ, pop producer, of Turk. parentage. "If Mousse would only just change that name, people might start to take him seriously" [*The Times*, August 9, 2002].

Baba **Moustapha**: Mahamet Moustapha (1952–1982), Chadian playwright, writing in French.

Michel **Mouton** *see* François **Villon**

Movita: Movita Castenada (1915–), Mexican movie actress.

John **Mowbray** *see* John **Haslette**

May **Moxon**: Euphemia Davison, née MacDonald (1906–1996), Sc. dancer. The dancer probably adopted her stage name from her grandmother.

Natalie **Moya**: Natalie Mullaly (1900–?), Ir.-born Br. stage actress.

George **Mozart**: David Gillins (1864–1947), Eng. music-hall comedian, instrumentalist.

Mshweshwe: Lepoqo (*c*.1786–1870), African politician. In 1809, the future founder of the Sotho (Basuto) nation took a name, also spelled Moshoeshoe, meaning "he who shaves his beard," from imitative *shwe shwe*, representing the sound of a razor. The name had a figurative sense, meaning "he who captures cattle," referring to his daring raids on neighboring herds. The chief's original name meant "the dispute," as he was born at a time of unrest. His post-circumcision name was Letlama, "the binder."

Sergey **Mstislavsky**: Sergey Dmitriyevich Maslovsky (1876–1943), Russ. novelist.

MTT: Michael Tilson Thomas (1944–), U.S. orchestral conductor, pianist. The musician adopted his private initialism for public use. "He's happy about the abbreviation. 'People want to call me Maestro, but I feel so old. MTT is perfect. And of course my name had already been changed from its original form.' The family name was Thomashevsky — the surname of his illustrious grandfather, the Yiddish actor Boris Thomashevsky, who established Yiddish theatre in the US. ... MTT's father, Ted, had cut the name short for his own lively, if humbler, career [in the movies]" [*The Times*, August 25, 2007].

Muddy Waters *see* Muddy **Waters**

Leonard **Mudie**: Leonard Mudie Cheetham (1884–1965), Br. stage, movie actor, working in U.S.

Mudrooroo: Colin Johnson (1938–), Austral. novelist, of part-Aborigine origin. The writer has also used the fuller names Mudrooroo Narogin and Mudrooroo Nyoongah.

Elijah **Muhammad**: Robert Poole (1897–1975), U.S. Black Muslim leader. The meeting of Robert Poole with Walli **Farrad** started him on a career which took him to the top of the Black Muslim movement. It was he who converted, and named, both Malcolm **X** and Muhammad **Ali**.

Idris **Muhammad**: Leo Morris (1939–), U.S. black jazz drummer.

Luise **Mühlbach**: Klara Mundt, née Müller (1814–1873), Ger. writer of historical novels.

Dexter **Muir** *see* Leo **Grex**

Jean **Muir**: Jean Muir Fullarton (1911–1996), U.S. stage, movie actress. The actress originally performed in the theater under her real name, Jean Fullarton, but became Jean Muir when turning to motion pictures in the mid–1930s.

Maria **Muldaur**: Maria Grazia Rosa Domenica

d'Amato (1943–), U.S. pop singer. The singer's professional name is actually her married name, after Geoff Muldaur, whom she married in the mid–1960s. The couple were divorced in 1972.

Arthur **Mullard:** Arthur Mullord (1910–1995), Br. comic TV actor.

Adolf **Müller:** Matthies Schmid (1801–1886), Austr. composer, conductor.

Multatuli: Eduard Douwes Dekker (1820–1887), Du. writer. The writer's pen name represents Latin *multa tuli*, "I have borne many things," alluding to his personal experiences. In 1838 he went to the Dutch East Indies where he held various government posts. In 1856 he was obliged to resign when he was not supported by the colonial government in his endeavors to protect the Javanese from their own bosses. He returned to Europe and spent many years in a nomadic and impoverished existence, braving cold and hunger and losing his family in the process. His main work was the seven-volume *Ideeën* ("Ideas") (1862–77), expressing his radical views on a wide range of topics.

Claude **Muncaster:** Grahame Hall (1903–1974), Eng. landscape, marine painter. The painter changed his name to avoid being confused with his father, Oliver Hall, also an artist.

Charles **Munch:** Charles Münch (1891–1968), Ger.-born U.S. orchestral conductor. On the rise of Adolf Hitler in Germany, Munch left for Paris in 1933, and it was then that he dropped the umlaut from his name.

Baron **Münchhausen:** Rudolfe Erich Raspe (1737–1794), Ger. scientist, antiquary, writer. The author of the *Marvellous Travels and Campaigns in Russia* (1785) based his stories on the tales of a real Baron Münchhausen, who had written highly colored accounts of his adventures in the Russian war against the Turks and whose given name was Karl Friedrich Hieronymus von Münchhausen (1720–1797).

Gilbert **Mundy** *see* J.P. **McCall**

Talbot **Mundy:** William Lancaster Gribbon (1879–1940), Eng.-born U.S. writer of adventure novels, historical fantasies.

Paul **Muni:** Mehilem "Muni" Weisenfreund (1895–1967), Austr.-born U.S. stage, movie actor. In 1901 the Jewish family came to the United States, where they performed in Yiddish vaudeville and theater. In 1929 the actor was signed to a movie contract by Fox, who renamed him Paul Muni.

Scott **Muni:** Donald Allen Muñoz (1930–2004), U.S. DJ.

Kai **Munk:** Kai Harald Leininger Petersen (1898–1944), Dan. playwright, priest, patriot.

Martin **Munkacsi:** Martin Marmorstein (1896–1963), Hung.-born U.S. photographer. Marmorstein was born in Kolozsvár (now Cluj-Napoca, Romania), in the Munkacsi district of Hungary, and in 1902 his family adopted the placename as their surname.

Mihály **Munkácsy:** Leo Lieb (1844–1900), Hung. painter, working in France. Lieb adopted the name of his birth town, Munkács (now Mukacheve, Ukraine), with Mihály (Michael) presumably for euphony, as in his original alliterative name.

Alex **Munro:** Alexander Horsburgh (1911–1986), Sc. comedian.

C.K. **Munro:** Charles Walden Kirkpatrick MacMullan (1889–1973), Ir. playwright.

James **Munro:** James Wiliam Mitchell (1926–2002), Br. writer of crime fiction.

Ona **Munson:** Ona Wolcott (1906–1955), U.S. movie actress.

Jo **Munton:** Jo Gittings (1920–1997), Eng. writer, biographer.

Murad Efendi: Franz von Werner (1836–1881), Austr. poet. The poet was long in the Turkish diplomatic service, and adopted a pen name that reflected this: "Murad" was the name of several Turkish sultans, and "Efendi" was a title of respect. He may have based the name specifically on that of Murad Bey, the Egyptian Mameluke chief who fought with the French against the Turks and who died in 1801.

Grigor **Muratsan:** Grigor Ter-Ovanisyan (1854–1908), Armenian writer. Many of the writer's stories center on the injustice and poverty borne by the Armenian peasantry. Others relate to corruption in the local press. Hence his adopted name, which literally means "blackening."

F.W. **Murnau:** Friedrich Wilhelm Plumpe (1888–1931), Ger. movie director, working in U.S. The director took his name from the German town of Murnau, where he lived for some time.

Dennis Jasper **Murphy:** [Rev.] Charles Robert Maturin (1782–1824), Ir. playwright, novelist. The writer adopted the pseudonym when working as an impoverished curate in Dublin, first using it for three romances published between 1807 and 1812.

Isaac **Murphy:** Isaac Burns (1861–1896), U.S. black jockey. The horseman adopted the name of his maternal grandfather, who raised him following the death of his father in the Civil War.

John Victor **Murra:** Isak Lipschitz (1916–2006), Ukr.-born U.S. anthropologist. The scientist changed his name after immigrating to the U.S. in 1934.

Murray: Leo Norman Maurien Murray Stuart Carrington Walters (1901–1988), Austral. magician, escapologist, working in U.S., U.K.

Arthur **Murray:** Arthur Teichman (1895–1991), U.S. ballroom-dancing instructor, of Austr. Jewish parentage. Teichman dropped his family name as a teenager on becoming a dancing partner of one

Baroness de Cuddleston, whom he had met while training with Irene and Vernon **Castle**.

Bill **Murray**: William Doyle-Murray (1950–), U.S. movie actor.

Braham **Murray**: Braham Goldstein (1943–), Eng. stage director.

Brian **Murray**: Brian Bell (1937–), S.A. stage actor, working in U.K. The actor adopted his mother's maiden name as his stage name.

Cheryl **Murray**: Cheryl Frayling-Wright (1952–), Eng. TV actress.

Dee **Murray**: David Murray Oates (1946–1992), Eng. bass player, pop musician.

Edna **Murray** *see* Fenton **Brockley**

Hon. Mrs. **Murray**: Sarah Murray, later Aust, née Mease (1741–1811), Eng. travel writer. In 1783 the writer married Captain William Murray, a nobly conected Scot. But he died three years later, and most of her writing was done subsequently. The full title under which she wrote was "The Hon. Mrs. Murray, of Kensington," an impressive name vying with that of her best-known work, *A Companion and Useful Guide to the Beauties of Scotland, to the Lakes of Westmoreland, Cumberland, and Lancashire, and to the Curiosities in the District of Craven, in the West Riding of Yorkshire; to which is added a more particular Description of Scotland, especially that part of it called the Highlands* (1799). A second volume appeared in 1803 as by "Lady Murray," although the previous year she had married George Aust, a civil servant

Jan **Murray**: Murray Janofsky (1917–), U.S. comedian, TV game-show host.

John **Murray**: John McMurray (1745–1793), Eng. publisher, of Sc. descent. Murray dropped the "Mc" of his name in 1768 on setting up business as a publisher in London. The house passed down his family, until the sixth John Murray, born John Grey (1909–1993), who was a Murray on his mother's side, adopted her name in 1930 on joining the family firm.

As to the motive for the modification: "It was at a time when ... national feeling seems to have run very high, and to be a Scotchman was hardly a recommendation to a beginner, and we find that, though McMurray headed all his trade bills with a ship, as a proud testimony to his naval antecedents, he found it convenient to drop the Scotch prefix of Mc" [Henry Curwen, *A History of Booksellers*, 1873].

Ken **Murray**: Kenneth Doncourt (1903–1988), U.S. movie comedian, radio, TV entertainer.

Lieutenant **Murray**: Maturin Murray Ballou (1820–1895), U.S. writer, editor, publisher. Ballou used this name for numerous works of fiction published from the early 1840s, including the moral tale *Rosalette: or, The Flower Girl of Paris* (1848), for which he won a prize of $150. He also wrote some melo-

dramatic adventure stories as Frank Forester. (For another writer so named, *see* Frank **Forester**.)

Mae **Murray**: Marie Adrienne Koenig (1889–1965), U.S. dancer, movie actress, of Austr.-Belg. parentage. Murray first appeared under her new name in a traveling revue, *About Town* (1906).

Ruth **Murray**: [Lady] Rosa Gilbert, née Mulholland (1841–1921), Ir. novelist, short-story writer. Rosa Mulholland used this name for her first novel, *Dunmara* (1864). She then wrote under her real (maiden) name until her marriage in 1891 to Sir John Thomas Gilbert (1829–1898).

Sinclair **Murray**: Edward Alan Sullivan (1868–1947), Can. novelist.

[Sir] James **Murray-Pulteney**: James Murray (?1751–1811), Br. general. Murray added the name Pulteney to his surname on his marriage in 1794 to Henrietta Laura Pulteney, Baroness Bath, daughter of Sir William Johnstone, later Johnstone-Pulteney, "described in the journals of the day as the richest commoner and the greatest holder of American stock ever known" [*Dictionary of National Biography*].

Murugadasa: A. Muthuswamy Iyer (1900–?), Ind. movie director, producer.

Fakir **Musafar**: Roland Loomis (1930–), U.S. Modern Primitive ("body modification") leader.

Musaire: Joseph Forrest Whiteley (1894–1984), Br. entertainer, instrumentalist. The artist's chosen instrument was the theremin, with which he brought "music from the air." (The theremin is "space-controlled," meaning that it is played by movements of the hands, which do not touch the instrument.)

Gavriil **Musicescu**: Gavriil Vakulovich Musychenko (1847–1903), Russ. composer, choirmaster. The musician was fortunate to have a name that so readily adapted to indicate his profession.

Musidora: Jeanne Roques (1889–1957), Fr. music-hall singer, dancer, movie actress. The actress took her professional name at the start of her stage career (1910) from the heroine of Théophile Gautier's novel *Fortunio* (1836), an "Arabian Nights"-like tale set in Paris. The name is found in earlier literature, such as the Musidora loved by Damon in James Thomson's poem *The Seasons* ("Summer," 1727). It means "gift of the Muses," suitably enough for Roques, who also wrote novels, poems, and a play. "Musidora ... was one of the fashionable poetical soubriquets of the last century" [Charlotte M. Young, *History of Christian Names*, 1884].

P. **Mustapää**: Martti Haavio (1899–1973), Finn. poet. Haavio was professor of poetry at Helsinki university, and used his real name for his academic writing. His adopted name means "blackhead."

Mutabaruka: Allan Hope (*c*.1960–), Jamaican dub poet. The radical poet took his name from a

Rwandan term meaning "one who is always victorious."

Ornella **Muti:** Francesca Romana Rivelli (1956–), It. movie actress. The actress won her first movie role when she was 14. The schedule required her absence from school for two months: "While I was shooting in Sicily I told my teachers I was sick. To stop them finding me I changed my name from Francesca Rivelli" [*Telegraph Magazine*, July 6, 1991]. Her new name was created by Damiano Damiani, her first director. "Why 'Muti' (which in Italian means 'silent')? Probably because of that still, inert look, like a beautiful little statue. She would deny this, saying that Damiani had been inspired by the name of the theater actress Eleonora Muti" [Masi and Lancia, p.167].

Mutianus Rufus: Konrad Muth (1471–1526), Ger. humanist. The scholar latinized his name, adding "Rufus" ("red") for the color of his hair.

Eadweard **Muybridge:** Edward James Muggeridge (1830–1904), Eng.-born U.S. photographer, motion-picture pioneer. The inventor, who photographed humans and animals in motion, was born in Kingston upon Thames, Surrey, and grew up with a keen interest in local history, as many Saxon kings were said to have been crowned in his birthtown (as its name implies). His interest came to a head in 1850, when a special commemorative "coronation" stone was set up in the Market Place. On the plinth were carved the names of the kings who, it was believed, had been crowned in Kingston, among them Eadweard the Elder (crowned 900) and Eadweard the Martyr (975), their names spelled the Saxon way. "This spelling seemed a lot more romantic than plain Edward so the young man decided to adopt the Saxon version and for good measure changed his East-Anglian surname of Muggeridge ... to Muybridge. The only reason for this change of name seems to have been sheer romanticism" [Kevin MacDonnell, *Eadweard Muybridge: The Man Who Invented the Moving Picture*, 1972].

Mya: Mya Marie Harrison (1979–), U.S. black R&B singer, of Native American-It. parentage.

Ethel **Myers:** Lillian Cochran (1881–1960), U.S. sculptor. Lillian was orphaned at age three or four and adopted by Michael Klinck and his wife Alfrata, who renamed her May Ethel Klinck. In 1905 she married painter Jerome Myers and took his name.

My Fancy: Mae Rose Bawn, née Baker (1878–1933), U.S. dancer, trapeze artist, acrobat, illusionist. The music-hall performer assumed her name for her debut in Oxford, England, on March 25, 1895: "Prior to this date the artiste had been known by her family name, and we regret that we can offer no enlightenment as to the significance of the change" [Kilgarriff II, p.200]. "Mae" presumably gave "My."

Myfyr Morganwg: Evan Davies (1801–1888), Welsh poet. The poet and archdruid took a bardic name meaning "muse of Glamorgan," referring to the historical region in which he was born.

Myfyr Wyn: William Williams (1849–1900), Welsh poet, blacksmith, historian. The poet's bardic name means "fair muse."

Myles na gCopaleen: Brian O'Nolan (1912–1966), Ir. novelist. The name was used by the writer for his satirical column "Cruiskeen Lawn" in the *Irish Times* from 1940. He took it from Myles-na-Gopaleen, a minor character in Gerald Griffin's novel *The Collegians* (1829), who later became a major figure in Dion Boucicault's stage adaptation, *The Colleen Bawn* (1860). The meaning is "Myles of the ponies" (modern Irish *capaillín*, "pony").

"To begin with he called himself 'Myles na gCopaleen' ... the g before the capital C being the eclipsis which the genitive case demands. At a later stage, when he had begun to cherish the hope that he would make this persona known outside Ireland, he simplified this to Myles na Gopaleen, rather to the regret of some of the *Irish Times* staff who liked the pedantry of the eclipsis in the genitive" [Anthony Cronin, *No Laughing Matter*, 1989]. For his novels, O'Nolan used the pseudonym Flann O'Brien.

"The use of a nom de plume was important, not least because O'Nolan was a high-ranking civil servant who needed to protect his identity. Moreover, the use of the pseudonymous mask was an intrinsic part of O'Nolan's aesthetic theory — or as Myles himself wrote in 1964: "'Compartmentation of personality for the purpose of literary utterance ensures that the fundamental individual will not be credited with a certain way of thinking and fixed attitudes. No author should write under his own name nor under one permanent pen name'" [Letter to the Editor, *Times Literary Supplement*, April 17, 2009].

MynoT: Tony Martin (1929–), British crossword compiler. The pseudonym reverses letters in the setter's real name, the capital M and T representing his (reversed) initials.

Mynyddog: Richard Davies (1833–1877), Welsh poet, singer. The poet and conductor took a bardic name meaning "mountain one."

Myops: John McKie (1939–), Sc. crossword compiler. The setter's pseudonym both refers to his short-sightedness and represents the Greek word for "gadfly," used by Socrates to describe himself. A deviser of cryptic crosswords is similar, teasing and provoking his solvers.

Myrander: James Alexander Stevenson (1881–1937), Br. sculptor. The classical-style name appears to be based on the name of the artist's wife, née Ethel Myra Scott, whom he married in 1913. If so, and with a Greek sense, the meaning would be "Myra's husband."

Myrddin Fardd: John Jones (1836–1921), Welsh author, antiquary. The writer's adopted name means "Merlin the bard."

Odette **Myrtil:** Odette Quignard (1898–1978), Fr. stage actress, violinist, working in U.K., U.S.

Harriet **Myrtle:** Lydia Falconer Miller, née Fraser (1812–1876), Sc. children's writer. The same name was used by another writer, Mary Gillies, for *More Fun for our Little Friends* (1864). Gillies apparently took the name from Miller, who first used it in 1846. Hamst comments: "One person employing a pseudonym already used by another, is much to be deprecated. We have not stigmatised the above as an *allonym* [name adopted from another person], as we do not believe this lady had any intention to deceive" [p.90].

Marmaduke **Myrtle:** [Sir] Richard Steele (1672–1729), Br. essayist, dramatist. The writer used this name for his editorship of *The Lover* (1714), a periodical similar to the better-known *Spectator*.

Minnie **Myrtle:** Anna Cummings Johnson (1818–1892), U.S. writer. The writer used this name for *The Myrtle Wreath, or Stray Leaves recalled* (1854), as well as subsequent works.

Mystic Craig: William Vagell (1900–1987), U.S. vaudeville performer, magician.

Mystic Meg: Margaret Lake (1942–), Eng. astrologer. The astrologer, familiar as a fortune-teller for the weekly televised National Lottery draw, is best known by this name but also writes as Meg Markova.

Myushfik: Mikail Kadyr ogly Ismailadze (1908–1939), Azerbaijani lyrical poet. The writer's adopted name means "soft-hearted."

Ilya **Nabatov:** Ilya Semyonovich Turovsky (1896–), Russ. music-hall artist, popular versifier.

Nadar: Gaspard-Félix Tournachon (1820–1910), Fr. photographer, caricaturist. The artist's adopted name has been explained as follows: "He had also found his name: from Tournachon to Tournadar, an obscure epistemological gallic joke, referring either to his satirical *sting* [French *dard*], or else to the tongue of *flame* (also *dard*) above his brow; and thence to the more economical, and generally more marketable, Nadar. This signature now began to appear below little matchstick drawings, and at the age of 27, Nadar published a first caricature on the inside page of *Charivari*" [*The Times*, October 12, 1974].

A.A. **Nadir** *see* Achmed **Abdullah**

Nadira: (1) Makhlar-oyim (1791–1842), Uzbek poet; (2) Florence Ezekiel (1931–2006), Ind. movie actress. The poet's adopted name means "rare one." She also wrote as Kamila. The actress adopted her screen name on making her debut in 1943.

Arne **Naess:** Arne Raab (1937–2004), Ger.-born Norw. businessman. The future shipping magnate moved to Norway with his mother at the age of eight, after his parents' marriage fell apart, and took his Norwegian name, that of his uncle, two years later.

Anant **Nag:** Anant Nagarkatti (1948–), Ind. movie actor, brother of Shankar **Nag**.

Shankar **Nag:** Shankar Nagarkatti (1954–1990), Ind. movie actor, director.

Anne **Nagel:** Ann Dolan (1912–1966), U.S. movie actress.

Nahmanides *see* **Ramban**

Jimmy **Nail:** James Michael Aloysius Bradford (1954–), Br. TV actor, singer. The actor's stage name arose as a nickname given him when one day he trod on a six-inch nail while working in a glassworks.

Laurence **Naismith:** Lawrence Johnson (1908–1992), Eng. stage, movie actor.

Reggie **Nalder:** Alfred Reginald Natzler (1907–1991), Austr.-born movie actor, working in France, U.S. Nalder appeared in the porno movie *Dracula Sucks* (1979) under the name Detlef van Berg.

Nita **Naldi:** Anita Donna Dooley (1899–1961), It.-U.S. movie actress. "Nita" from "Anita."

[Sir] Lewis Bernstein **Namier:** Ludwik Bernsztajn (1888–1960), Pol.-born Br. historian, of Russ. origin. Namier's father's surname was originally Niemirowski, both his parents being Polish Jews who no longer adhered to the Jewish religion. He went to England in 1906 and was educated at Oxford University. On taking British nationality in 1913, he changed his name by deed poll to Lewis Namier, with a version of his father's name.

Nanamoli Bhikkhu: Osbert Moore (1905–1960), Eng. Buddhist. The Pali scholar discovered Buddhism through reading Julius Evola's *The Doctrine of Awakening* while serving with the army in Italy in World War II. In 1949 he went to Ceylon (Sri Lanka) and was ordained *samanera* (novice). The following year he was fully ordained as *bhikkhu* under his Buddhist name

Sister **Nancy:** Nancy Russell (*c.*1960–), Jamaican reggae singer, sister of **Brigadier Jerry**.

Nantlais: William Nantlais Williams (1874–1959), Welsh poet, hymnwriter. Nantlais is a local placename.

Joe "Tricky Sam" **Nanton:** Joseph N. Irish (1904–1946), U.S. jazz trombonist, of West Indian parentage. The origin of the musician's new surname is uncertain. He was nicknamed "Tricky Sam" because "he could always do with one hand what someone else did with two."

Alan **Napier:** Alan Napier-Clavering (1903–1988), Br. movie actor, working in U.S.

Diana **Napier:** Molly Ellis (1908–1982), Br. movie actress.

Mark **Napier:** John Laffin (1922–), Austral. novelist, journalist.

Marty **Napoleon:** Matthew Napoli (1921–), U.S. jazz pianist, nephew of Phil **Napoleon.**

Phil **Napoleon:** Filippo Napoli (1901–1990), U.S. jazz trumpeter, bandleader.

Teddy **Napoleon:** Edward George Napoli (1914–1964), U.S. jazz pianist, nephew of Phil **Napoleon.**

Raymond **Naptali:** Raymond McCook (1961–), Jamaican reggae musician, working in U.K.

Narada Mahathera: Sumanapala Perera (1898–1983), Sinhalese Buddhist. The English-educated Buddhist monk took his new name on ordination, with Mahathera ("great elder") a title given to a *bhikkhu* (fully ordained monk) of 20 years' standing.

R.K. **Narayan:** Rasipuram Krishnaswami Narayanswami Iyer (1906–2001), Ind. novelist, short-story writer. The writer's lengthy surname was shortened by the English author Graham Greene, who recommended his first novel, *Swami and Friends* (1935), to the British publisher Hamish Hamilton.

Thomas **Narcejac:** Pierre Ayraud (1908–1998), Fr. crime novelist.

Nar-Dos: Mikael Zakharyevich Ovanisyan (1867–1933), Armenian writer. When in the late 1880s the writer delivered his first novel (*Nune*) to the magazine *Nor-dar* ("New Century"), the editor told him he would have to choose a pseudonym, as was then customary. The writer recalled: "I had no objection. The secretary took a dictionary and started to pick out names. He finally came to the word 'nardos,' lavender. 'If we hyphenate it, it'll look even better!' he said. I agreed, and since then Nar-Dos has been my pen name" [Dmitriyev, pp.92–3].

Owen **Nares:** Owen Nares Ramsay (1888–1943), Br. movie actor.

Nargis: Fatima A. Rashid (1929–1981), Ind. movie actress. The actress was first on screen as Baby Rani at the age of six. In 1944 she was introduced by movie director **Mehboob** as a heroine in his film *Taqdeer* and it was he who renamed her: "Mehboob believed that stars should have the right kind of name to click with fans and he had a knack of picking such names. He had particular faith in names beginning with 'N,' which he considered lucky, so he chose for his new heroine the name of Nargis" [T.J.S. George, *The Life and Times of Nargis*, 1994]. The name itself is Hindi for "narcissus."

Nas: Nasir Ben Olu Dara Jones (1973–), U.S. black rapper, hip-hop artist.

Petroleum V. **Nasby:** David Ross Locke (1833–1888), U.S. humorous journalist. The writer adopted the droll pen name in 1861 on becoming editor of the *Findlay* (Ohio) *Jeffersonian*. The middle initial stood

for Vesuvius. The surname, that of a supposed anti-abolitionist postmaster, is of uncertain origin.

Paul **Naschy:** Jacinto Molina Alvarez (1936–), Sp. movie actor.

Daniel **Nash:** William Reginald Loader (1916–), Br. novelist.

Johnny **Nash:** John Albert Schuberg (1875–1958), U.S.–born Can. magician, movie theater owner, of Swe. parentage.

Mary **Nash:** Mary Ryan (1885–1976), U.S. movie actress.

N. Richard **Nash:** Nathan Richard Nusbaum (1913–2000), U.S. playwright, novelist.

Simon **Nash:** Raymond Chapman (1924–), Br. writer. Mainly a writer of religious works, Chapman used this pen name for his murder mysteries.

Alcofribas **Nasier:** François Rabelais (1495–1553), Fr. satirist. The writer created this anagrammatic version of his real name for *Pantagruel* (1532), one of his most famous works. He also used it for its successor, *Gargantua*, the story of Pantagruel's father, now usually read first. After that he used his real name for the third (1546) and fourth (1548) books in the series, as well as for the posthumous fifth book (1562), which may in fact not be by him. The name itself may have had some hidden significance.

Marie-José **Nat:** Marie-José Benhalassa (1940–), Fr. movie actress.

Anna **Natarova:** Anna Petrovna Chistyakova (1835–1917), Russ. circus artist, bareback rider.

John-Antoine **Nau:** Antoine Torquet (1860–1918), U.S.–born Fr. poet, novelist. The writer spent some years "before the mast," and took a surname meaning "boat" (related to English *nautical*).

Naughton and Gold *see* Jimmy **Gold**

Nauticus: (1) [Sir] William Laird Clowes (1856–1905), Eng. naval writer, historian; (2) [Sir] Owen Seaman (1861–1936), Eng. editor, humorist. The name is appropriate for both men: academically for the first, punningly for the second.

André **Navarre:** Alexander Wright (?–1940), Austral. music-hall performer.

Martina **Navratilova:** Martina Subert (1956–), Cz.-born U.S. tennis player. The sportswoman changed her surname to that of her grandfather (in its feminine form properly Navrátilová) when she was 10. She became a U.S. citizen in 1981.

Sergey **Naydyonov:** Sergey Aleksandrovich Alekseyev (1868–1922), Russ. writer.

Eliot **Naylor:** Pamela Frankau (1908–1967), Br. novelist, short-story writer, working in U.S., granddaughter of Frank **Danby**. The writer used this name for her novel *The Offshore Light* (1952).

Jerry **Naylor:** Jerry Naylor Jackson (1939–), U.S. country singer.

Alla **Nazimova:** Alla Aleksandrovna Leventon (1878–1945), Russ.-born U.S. stage, movie actress, of Jewish parentage.

Amedeo **Nazzari:** Salvatore Amedeo Buffa (1907–1979), It. movie actor.

Cheikh Aliou **Ndao:** Sidi Ahmet Alioune Ndao (1933–), Senegalese novelist, dramatist, writing in French.

Meshell **Ndegéocello:** Michelle Johnson (1968–), U.S. black rapper, R&B singer. The performer's new first name respells "Michelle," while her new surname is Swahili for "free as a bird."

[Dame] Anna **Neagle:** Marjorie Wilcox, née Robertson (1904–1986), Eng. stage, movie actress. When the actress was beginning to become established in the theater, after appearing as a chorus girl in Charles Cochran's shows, her manager commented one day: "'I think your name "Marjorie Robertson" has been too much publicized as a "Cochran Young Lady." Now you are turning to serious acting, you must change it.' I stared at him. In my childhood when I had daydreamed of a stage career, I'd invented the most incredible professional names; but now I'd spent five years putting my real name on to playbills and programs and didn't much like the idea of wasting all that publicity ... 'It's rather a long name, too,' Mr. Williams went on tentatively ... I began to see his point.... If I'd remained 'Marjorie Robertson, Chorus Girl' much longer I would have been type-cast for life ... 'My mother's name was Neagle...?' 'Nagle?' 'No — Neagle,' I protested. 'Don't worry — they'll call it Nagle,' he said. 'What about Anna Neagle?' I suggested. 'Oh, fine. That's just fine. Anna Neagle? That's it.' And so Marjorie Robertson, successful chorus girl, was quietly, and a little sadly, disposed of in a teashop on the corner of Wardour and Old Compton Streets, on August 21st, 1930. And Anna Neagle, embryo actress and star, was born" [Anna Neagle, *There's Always Tomorrow*, 1974].

Hilary **Neal:** Olive Marion Claydon Norton (1913–1973), Br. children's writer. Norton also wrote as T.R. Noon (an anagram of her surname) and Kate Norway.

Jean **Neal:** Abbie Farwell Brown (1871–1927), U.S. writer. Brown adopted this name for her regular column in the *St. Louis Globe-Democrat*, beginning in 1898.

Johann August Wilhelm **Neander:** David Mendel (1789–1850), Ger. ecclesiastical historian. The scholar was born a Jew, and adopted his new name (from the Greek meaning "new man") on being baptized a Christian in 1806.

Neb: Ronald Niebour (*c.*1902–1972), Welsh-born Br. cartoonist, art teacher.

Ivan **Nechuy-Levitsky:** Ivan Semyonovich Levitsky (1838–1918), Ukr. writer.

Nedin: Nadezhda Aleksandrovna Yanushevskaya (1896–1959), Russ. circus artist, animal trainer, wife of **Kadyr-Gulyam.**

Neera: Anna Radius Zuccari (1846–1918), It. novelist, poet.

Pola **Negri:** Barbara Apolonia Chalupiec (1897–1987), Pol.-born U.S. movie actress. "Pola" comes from the actress's middle name, while also suggesting her nationality. "Negri" comes from the Italian poet Ada Negri (1870–1965). "The very name summons up the exoticism that was her stock-in-trade" [Joseph Arkins, in Vinson, p.466].

Milutin **Nehajev:** Milutin Cihlar (1880–1930), Croatian writer.

John Gneisenau **Neihardt:** John Greenleaf Neihardt (1881–1973), U.S. poet. The poet's father named his son after the poet John Greenleaf Whittier. Neihardt did not wish to be named after another poet, however, so changed his middle name to honor the Prussian field marshal August Graf von Gneisenau.

Ross **Neil:** Isabella Neil Harwood (?1838–1888), Eng. novelist. The writer used this male name for a number of historical dramas in blank verse.

Roy William **Neill:** Roland de Gostrie (1886–1946), Ir.-born U.S. movie director.

Thomas **Neill:** Thomas Neill Cream (1850–1892), Sc. physician, murderer. The murderer poisoned his (female) victims with strychnine, using his cover name when obtaining the necessary drugs from the pharmacy.

Donald **Neilson:** Donald Nappey (1936–), Eng. murderer ("The Black Panther"). The killer took his name from an ice-cream van, mainly as he had never liked his original name, but also to avoid any future embarrassment for his daughter. (The British baby's nappy is the American diaper.) He should not be confused with Dennis Nilsen (1945–), another British murderer. (Neilson abducted and murdered a 17-year-old heiress, Lesley Whittle, in 1975. Nilsen, convicted in 1983, murdered a series of young men.)

Lilian Adelaide **Neilson:** Elizabeth Ann Brown (1846–1880), Br. actress. The actress's mother had originally had the name Brown but was later known as Mrs. Bland. Her father's name is unknown. On working as a nurse as a young woman, she learned of the somewhat dubious circumstances of her birth, and decided to make her way to London. For the purposes of this she assumed the name Lizzie Ann Bland. She began her stage career in 1865, and soon after felt confident enough to blossom forth from Lizzie Ann Bland to "Lilian Adelaide Lessont," subsequently changing this last name to "Neilson."

Perlita **Neilson:** Margaret Sowden (1933–), Eng. stage actress.

[Baron] Richard **Neimans:** Richard Pfälzer (1832–1858), Ger. traveler in Africa.

Lidiya **Nelidova:** Lidiya Richardovna Barto (1863–1929), Russ. ballet dancer, teacher.

Barry **Nelson:** Robert Haakon Nielsen (1917–2007), U.S. stage, movie actor, of Scandinavian descent.

Gene **Nelson:** Leander Berg (1920–1996), U.S. stage, movie actor, dancer.

George "Baby Face" **Nelson:** Lester Gillis (1908–1934), U.S. gunman, bank robber.

Oscar **Nelson:** Oscar Nielsen (1882–1954), Dan.-born U.S. lightweight boxer ("The Durable Dane").

Zara **Nelsova:** Zara Katznelson (1918–2002), Can.-born U.S. cellist, of Russ. parentage. The musician's name is the Russian feminine form of the stage name, Gregor Nelsov, of her father, Gregor Katznelson, a flutist.

Nemo *see* **Phiz**

Neon Park XIII: Martin Muller (1940–1993), U.S. artist. This is how the painter of album covers for Frank Zappa, Little Feat, Dr. **John**, The Beach Boys, and David **Bowie**, among others, got his name: "Martin Muller and his wife Chick were visiting friends in Mendocino in the heart of the Californian redwood forests. Stoned out of their minds, they speculated on how the local kids would react to being taken to a rock 'n' roll concert at the Fillmore in San Francisco. 'Well,' someone said, 'they'd have to be prepared.' Then Martin said, 'Well, we could asphalt one of those clear-cut places out in the woods and hang up a bunch of neon lights and call it Neon Park.' The next day Martin wrote a letter to the Canyon Cinema News declaring that he would subsequently be known as Neon Park. The XIII after his name stands for M, the thirteenth letter of the alphabet, which was used as a code for marijuana among the zoot-suiters" [Storm Thorgerson and Aubrey Powell, *100 Best Album Covers*, 1999].

Giampiero **Neri:** Giampiero Pontiggia (1927–), It. poet.

Nadia **Nerina:** Nadine Judd (1927–2008), S.A. ballet dancer, of Russ. parentage. When the dancer began her stage career, Ninette **de Valois** wanted her to adopt the name Nadia Moore. But instead she took her new surname from the nerine (pronounced "ni-rye-nee"), a scarlet flower related to the amaryllis that grew around Cape Town, where she was born. Her first name, Nadia, was a pet form of her real name, with this in turn a form of her late mother's first name, Nadezhda.

Salomeja **Neris:** Salomeja Bacinskáite-Buciene (1904–1945), Lithuanian poet. The poet took her name from the river where she lived.

Nero: Lucius Domitius Ahenobarbus (AD 37–68), Roman emperor. When the future emperor was 13, his mother married her uncle, Tiberius Claudius Drusus Nero Germanicus, otherwise the emperor Claudius, who adopted the boy and renamed him as Nero Claudius Caesar Drusus Germanicus. Nero was thus a Roman cognomen (surname), not meaning "black," as might be supposed, but "strong," "warlike" (related to English *nerve*).

Franco **Nero:** Francesco Spartanero (1941–), It. movie actor.

Peter **Nero:** Peter Bernard Nierow (1934–), U.S. popular pianist.

Pablo **Neruda:** Ricardo Eliecer Neftalí Reyes Basoalto (1904–1973), Chilean poet. The writer adopted a pen name in 1920 so as not to embarrass his father, a train conductor. He took his new first name from Pablo Picasso and his surname from the Czech writer Jan Neruda (1834–1891), whose story "At the Sign of the Three Lilies" he had greatly admired. He adopted the name legally in 1946.

Gérard de **Nerval:** Gérard Labrunie (1808–1855), Fr. poet, traveler, story writer. Nerval was the name of a property near Paris owned by the writer's parents. Further, his mother's maiden name was Laurent, and if this name is read in reverse (minus the "t" and counting "u" as "v"), one ends up with Nerval. Finally, Nerval is a sort of anagram or even reversal of the writer's original surname, Labrunie. The writer himself was deeply interested in the "hidden meaning" of language.

Jimmy **Nervo:** James Henry Holloway (1897–1975), Eng. stage comedian, teaming with Teddy **Knox**. The actor began his career in the circus, as an artist whose specialty was balancing and buffoonery, and thus falling and fractures. For such a way of life he needed "nerve." Hence his professional name.

Nervous Norvus: James Drake (1912–1968), U.S. pop-rock singer.

E. **Nesbit:** Edith Bland, née Nesbit (1858–1924), Eng. children's writer. "The use of the bare initial 'E.' led ... at least one library to assume that she was a man, which delighted her; she liked the masculine role, and assumed it happily in her writing" [Carpenter and Prichard, p.372]. Bland thus deliberately used this strategy to conceal her sex, although retained her maiden name as her true identity. She used the name Fabian **Bland** for work written jointly with her husband.

Nesimi: Seid Imadeddin (*c.*1369–1417), Azerbaijani poet, scholar. The writer's adopted Arabic name means "waft," "breath of wind."

Aziz **Nesin:** Mehmet Nusret (1915–1995), Turk.

satirical writer. The writer adopted the first name, Aziz, of his father. He had around 200 pseudonyms, since when the authorities closed the newspaper where he worked, he had to publish under a different name each time. He recalled: "On one occasion there was a real mix-up because of my pseudonyms. I published a book of children's stories combining the name of my daughter, Oya, with that of my son, Atesh. The book was included in a bibliography of Turkish women writers as the work of Oya Atesh" [Dmitriyev, p.254].

Joseph Ferdinand **Nesmüller:** Joseph Ferdinand Müller (1818–1895), Austr. writer, actor.

Sammy **Nestico:** Samuel Nistico (1924–), U.S. jazz composer.

Charles **Nestle:** Karl Ludwig Nessler (1872–1951), Ger.-born U.S. businessman. The creator of permanent waving devices for human hair visited various European countries before taking his new name in England in 1900. In 1915, still a German citizen, he left for the United States, where in 1919 he founded the company that bears his name.

Luke **Netterville:** Standish James O'Grady (1846–1928), Ir. writer. O'Grady used this name for his SF fiction.

Robert **Neuner:** Erich Kästner (1899–1974), Ger. writer. An occasional pseudonym.

Poppa **Neutrino:** David Pearlman (1933–), U.S. entrepreneur, adventurer.

Emma **Nevada:** Emma Wixom (1859–1940), U.S. opera singer. The singer was born in Alpha, near Nevada City, California, and took her name from that city. (Sources claiming she was born in Austin, Nevada, and that she is named for that state, are incorrect.) Her daughter, soprano Mignon Nevada (1886–1971), kept the name.

Aleksandr **Neverov:** Aleksandr Sergeyevich Skobelev (1886–1923), Russ. writer.

Edgar **Neville:** Edgar Neville de Romree (1899–1967), Sp. movie director.

Vladimir Ivanovich **Nevsky:** Feodosy Ivanovich Krivobokov (1876–1937), Russ. Communist official historian. The Marxist historian spent his prerevolutionary career in Petrograd (St. Petersburg). Hence his name, for the Neva River, on which that city stands.

Aunt **Newbury** *see* **Old Humphrey**

Uncle **Newbury** *see* **Old Humphrey**

Igor **Newerly:** Igor Abramow (1903–1987), Pol. writer.

Samuel Irving **Newhouse:** Solomon Irving Neuhaus (1895–1979), U.S. newspaper publisher, of Russ. Jewish parentage.

Ne Win: Maung Shu Maung (1911–2002), Burmese (Myanmar) statesman. The dictator of former Burma from 1962 through 1988 adopted his *nom de guerre* (meaning "brilliant sun") in the late 1930s, during his country's struggle for independence from Britain.

Patrick **Newley:** Patrick Nicholas Galvin (1955–2009), Ir.-born Br. writer, entertainer. The showbusiness personality adopted his stage name from his hero, actor and singer Anthony Newley (1932–1999).

Aristarchus **Newlight:** Richard Whately (1786–1863), Eng. logician, theologian. The future archbishop of Dublin used this meaningful name to attack German neologism, i.e., the German tendency to rationalistic views in religious matters. The name was thus ironic. Aristarchus was a Greek critic of the 2d century BC. The prelate used the name John Search for *Religion and Her Name* (1847).

Ernest **Newman:** William Roberts (1868–1959), Eng. music critic. Newman first used the pseudonym for his book *Gluck and the Opera* (1895). It was intended to be punningly meaningful, and indicate his innovative approach, but it also seems to have represented his attitude to life generally, because he used the name both in his private life and in his writings, although never legally adopting it.

Fred **Newman:** Manfred Neumann (1932–2008), Austr.-born Br. journalist, publisher.

Isidore **Newman:** Isidore Neumond (1837–1909), Ger.-born U.S. financier, philanthropist. Isidore's family had taken the name Neumond (German "new moon") when in 1808 Napoleon Bonaparte required all Jews in his empire to take permanent family names. He americanized his name (without actually translating it) on emigrating to the United States in 1853.

Tom **Newman:** Thomas Pratt (1894–1943), Eng. billiards player.

C.A. George **Newmann:** Christian Andrew George Naeseth (1880–1952), U.S. magician, "mentalist."

Julie **Newmar:** Julia Charlene Newmeyer (1930–), U.S. movie actress, dancer.

Thomas **Newte:** William Thomson (1746–1817), Sc. writer. Turning to a literary career in London after a spell as a church minister, Thomson used a number of pseudonyms, including this one for *Prospects and Observations on a Tour in England and Scotland, by Thomas Newte, Esq.* (1791).

Helmut **Newton:** Helmut Neustädter (1920–2004), Ger.-born fashion photographer. The photographer's English name, if read as "new town," is a rendering of the German original (*neu*, "new," *Stadt*, "town").

Juice **Newton:** Judy Kay Cohen (1952–), U.S. country singer. The progression of the first name was presumably "Judy" to "Juicy" to "Juice."

Marie **Ney:** Marie Fix (1895–1981), Eng. stage, movie actress.

N.F.B.A. *see* Madame Floresta A. **Brasileira**

Ngugi wa Thiong'o: James Ngugi (1938–), Kenyan writer. Ngugi adopted his native name when he stopped writing in English and began publishing in Kikuyu. "Both decisions wre motivated by his belief that writing in the language of the colonizer alienated Africans from their own culture" [Birch, p.715].

Ian **Niall:** John McNeillie (1916–2002), Sc.-born nature writer. The author adopted his new name for his fourth novel, *No Resting Place* (1948). "There was a strongly reclusive and self-effacing element in McNeillie's character, and it suited him to shelter behind a pen-name" [*The Times*, July 19, 2002].

Fred **Niblo:** Frederick Liedtke (1874–1948), U.S. movie director. Several sources give the director's original name as Federico Nobile, claiming an Italian ancestry, but this appears to be erroneous.

Nibor: Robin Baxter (1937–), Br. crossword compiler. The setter's pseudomym is a simple reversal of his first name.

Nibs: Frederick Drummond Niblett (*fl.*1880–after 1924), Sc.-born caricaturist, illustrator. An apt pen name for an artist, and also one punning on "his nibs" as a slang term for a self-important person.

Nicander: Morris Williams (1809–1874), Welsh hymnwriter. The writer adopted this name at the 1849 National Eisteddfod, when he won the chair. It is Greek in origin, meaning "man of victory," and was perhaps also intended as a tribute to the identically named 2d-century BC Greek poet.

Nichiren: Zennichi (1222–1282), Jap. Buddhist monk. The founder of Nichiren Buddhism, the school of Japanese Buddhism named after him, took a name meaning literally "Sun Lotus," "sun" standing for Japan and "lotus" for the *Lotus Sutra*, the form of Buddhism taught by the Buddha himself.

Nicholas II: Gérard de Bourgogne (*c.*1010–1061), Fr. pope. The pontiff named himself for Nicholas I (*c.*820–867).

Nicholas III: Giovanni Gaetano Orsini (*c.*1220–1280), It. pope. The pope took this name because he had been cardinal deacon of the church of S. Niccolò in Carcere (St. Nicholas in Prison), Rome.

Nicholas IV: Girolamo Masci (1227–1292), It. pope. The pontiff named himself for his patron, **Nicholas III**.

Nicholas V: Tommaso Parentucelli (1397–1455), It. pope. The pontiff named himself Nicholas as a mark of respect for his patron, Bishop Niccolò (Nicholas) Albergati of Bologna, whom he had served for 20 years.

Paul **Nicholas:** Paul Beuselinck (1945–), Br. TV actor, of Du. descent. Nicholas is said to have chosen his new name around one Christmas time, when it was seasonable (St. Nicholas, Santa Claus).

Horatio **Nicholls:** Lawrence Wright (1888–1964), Br. popular composer, music publisher. The musician used this and many other pseudonyms for his prodigious output of popular songs. Other names included Victor Ambroise, Haydon Augarde, Everett Lynton, Paul Paree, Gene Williams (for his big hit "Wyoming"), Betsy O'Hogan (for "Old Father Thames"), and W. Kerrigan.

Sue **Nicholls:** Susan Harmar-Nicholls (1943–), Eng. TV actress.

Barbara **Nichols:** Barbara Nickerauer (1929–1976), U.S. movie actress.

Leigh **Nichols:** Dean Koontz (1945–), U.S. fantasy, SF writer. Koontz used this name for five novels. He also wrote as Brian Coffey, Deanna Dwyer, K.R. Dwyer, John Hill, Richard Paige, Owen West, and Aaron **Wolfe.** "Q: How and why was Leigh Nichols born? A: How, I think, was by Cesarean section. Why — you'll have to ask her parents. Q: So the pen name was supposed to be a woman? A: I meant to say 'his' parents. Q: So the pen name was meant to be a man? A: I meant to say 'its' parents. Q: So Leigh Nichols was neither male nor female, it was a *thing*? A: That's right. A thing. But a *nice* thing.... Actually, Pocket Books wanted a name that could be either male or female, to draw in a wider audience. So I suggested we use 'Lee Nichols.' At the last minute, without consultation with me, they changed it to 'Leigh,' which seemed, to me, to undercut the whole idea of genderlessness. Q: But why a pen name at that point in your career? A: For the same reason that Brian Coffey, Owen West, and K.R. Dwyer were born. I have not written under pseudonyms for years and will not do so again" [Martin H. Greenberg, Bill Munster, Ed Gorman, *The Dean Koontz Companion*, 1994].

Mike **Nichols:** Michael Igor Peschkowsky (1931–), Ger.-born U.S. cabaret entertainer, movie director, of Russ. Jewish parentage. The entertainer's father anglicized his patronymic, Nikolayevich, when he left Germany on the rise of Hitler to become a physician (as Nichols) in the U.S.

Nichelle **Nichols:** Grace Nichols (1933–), U.S. black TV, movie actress. Familiar as Lieutenant Uhura in the *Star Trek* series, Nichols had always disliked her original first name as a child and asked her mother to rename her after herself, as Lishia. "She refused, instead choosing Nichelle, because it was close to Michelle, which she had wanted to name me in the first place, and because my initials would then be 'NN.'" [Nichelle Nichols, *Beyond Uhura*, 1994].

Peter **Nichols** *see* John **Christopher**

Niclas y Glais: Thomas Evan Nicholas (1878–1971), Welsh poet. The writer was a Nonconformist minister and served for ten years at Glais near Swansea. Hence his name, meaning "Nicholas of Glais."

Sorcha **Nic Leodhas:** Leclaire Gowans Alger (1898–1969), U.S. children's writer. The writer's family claimed Scottish Highland descent. Hence her pseudonym, Gaelic for "Claire, daughter of Louis."

Nico: Christa Päffgen (1938–1988), Ger. model, pop singer, movie actress. The model's new name was given her by her "mentor," German photographer Herbert Tobias: "'You cannot carry on calling yourself Christa Päffgen. Even Christa is wrong. It's not international. Krista is better, but it doesn't suit your character…. Models have one name, just like photographers and designers have one name. I am Tobias. I have a name for you, and you must use it from now on.'" He explained: "'The most wonderful man I have ever seen lives in Paris. I am in love with him…. His name is Nico Papatakis.' From that day, in the Berlin of 1956, Christa was Nico, taking the name of a man loved by another…. She recognised even then that Nico as a name was a brilliant, indefinite, ambiguous choice" [Richard Witts, *Nico: The Life and Lies of an Icon*, 1993].

Nico later offered four different versions of how she came by her name, the first being the real one: (1) she took the name from the best friend of a photographer; (2) her real name was Nico Pavlosky, but she shortened this difficult name to Nico; (3) she was so named by Salvador Dalí as an anagram of "icon"; (4) she was given the name by fashion designer Coco **Chanel**, who based it on her own name.

Nicodemus: Cecil Willington (1957–1996), Jamaican DJ, reggae musician.

Abioseh **Nicol:** Davidson Sylvester Hector Willoughby Nicol (1924–1994), Sierra Leonean diplomat, writer, working in U.K. The scholar adopted a native name in place of his English one(s).

Nicole: Françoise Parturier (1919–), Fr. journalist. The feminist writer used this name for her contributions to *Le Figaro* from 1956.

Mylène **Nicole** *see* Mylène **Demongeot**

Nicolette: Nicolette Okoh (*c.*1964–), Br. black rapper, dancer.

Nicolini (or Nicolino): Nicolò Grimaldi (1673–1732), It. male alto singer.

Ernest **Nicolini:** Ernest Nicolas (1834–1898), Fr. opera singer.

Nicolò de Malte: Nicolas Isouard (1773–1818), Maltese-born Fr. composer. The musician used this name for most of his operas, which formed the bulk of his composition. According to Warrack and West,

he was "known simply as 'Nicolò' because his family disapproved of his music" [p. 353].

Christina **Nicolson** *see* Andrew **York**

Flora **Nielsen:** Sybil Crawley (1900–1976), Can. opera singer, teacher.

Édouard **Nieuport:** Édouard de Niéport (1875–1911), Fr. aviator, airplane constructor.

Gerry **Niewood:** Gerald J. Nevidovsky (1943–), U.S. jazz musician.

Niger: Ivan Vasiliyevich Dzhanayev (1896–1947), Russ. (Ossetian) poet, literary critic. The writer's adopted name means "black," referring to his dark complexion.

Shmuel **Niger:** Shmuel Charmi (1884–1955), Russ.-born Jewish literary critic, essayist, working in U.S.

Nigger Add: Addison Jones (?1845–1926), U.S. black cowboy, broncobuster. Add's original surname is not usually given in cowboy memoirs or biographies.

Robert **Nighthawk:** Robert Lee McCollum (1909–1967), U.S. black blues guitarist. The musician took his professional name from his own 1937 release of "Prowlin' Nighthawk." On such early recordings he called himself Robert Lee McCoy, with his mother's maiden name.

William Edward **Nightingale:** William Edward Shore (1794–1874), Eng. landowner. When the father of pioneering nurse Florence Nightingale (1820–1910) came of age in 1815, he inherited the Derbyshire estates of his bachelor uncle, Peter Nightingale, and assumed his name.

Nikodim: Boris Georgievich Rotov (1929–1978), Russ. Orthodox churchman. The metropolitan of Leningrad adopted his religious name, meaning "victory of the people," on being made deacon in 1947, the choice of name almost certainly being specially significant. Compare the name of **Nikon**.

Nikolay: Ivan Dmitrievich Kasatkin (1836–1912), Russ. missionary to Japan. The Russian Orthodox missionary, raised to archbishop in 1905, is also known by the French form of his name as Père Nicolai.

Galina **Nikolayeva:** Galina Yevgenyevna Volyanskaya (1911–1963), Russ. writer.

Nikon: Nikita Minov (1605–1681), Russ. Orthodox churchman. The patriarch of Moscow and All Russia based his religious name on his original name. It would have been regarded as meaningful, from the Greek word for "victory." Compare the name of **Nikodim**.

Nikos: Nikos Kessanlis (1930–), Gk. artist.

Dorothea **Nile** *see* Ed **Noon**

Willie **Nile:** Robert Noonan (1948–), U.S. rock musician.

David K. **Niles:** David K. Neyhus (1890–1952), U.S. liberal activist, government official, of Russ. Jewish parentage. Niles never legally adopted his new name, but apparently first used it on entering politics in 1924.

Nilsson: Harry Edward Nelson III (1941–1994), U.S. pop singer, songwriter. The singer took a new name to avoid confusion with country singer Rick Nelson (originally Eric Hilliard Nelson) (1940–1985).

Christine **Nilsson:** Kristina Törnerhjelm (1843–1921), Swe. opera singer.

Harry **Nilsson:** Harry Edward Nelson III (1941–1994), U.S. pop singer, songwriter.

Nimrod: Charles James Apperley (1777–1843), Eng. sporting writer. The author of *The Chace, the Turf, and the Road* (1837), a regular contributor to *The Quarterly Review*, punningly adopted the name of the biblical Nimrod, the "mighty hunter" (Genesis 19:9). "Such a choice will be the better understood, perhaps, when it is mentioned that out of regard for the sporting tastes of his esteemed contributor, Mr. Pittman, the proprietor of the *Quarterly*, kept a stud of hunters for his especial use" [Leopold Wagner, *Names: And Their Meaning*, 1892].

Nina: Ethel Florence Nelson (1923–), Can. travel writer.

Ninjaman: Desmond Ballantine (*c*.1965–), Jamaican DJ. reggae musician. Ballantine began his career as a DJ under the name Double Ugly, but changed this to Uglyman when another DJ appeared with the same name. A second Uglyman also arrived, obliging Ballantine to create a distinctive persona, which he did by calling himself "Ninja" or "Ninjaman," the term for a trained assassin and spy in feudal Japan.

Egnate **Ninoshvili:** Egnate Fomich Ingorokva (1859–1894), Georgian writer. The writer was orphaned as a child and took his pen name from the aunt who raised him, Nina, with -*shvili* the Georgian suffix meaning "son of."

Sir Nicholas **Nipclose, Bart.:** David Garrick (1717–1779), Eng. actor, dramatist. The actor used this frivolous name for some of his farces and stage adaptations.

Red **Nirt:** Tommy Trinder (1909–1989), Eng. stage, radio comedian. The comedian used this whimsical reversal of his surname early in his career.

Shota **Nishnianidze:** Shota Georgiyevich Mamageyshvili (1929–), Georgian poet.

Udeno **Nisiely:** Benedetto Fioretti (1579–1642), It. cleric, literary scholar. The writer used this name for his five-volume *Proginnasmi poetici* (1620–39), a selective survey of Greek, Latin, and Italian writers. The name is a cryptogram for "of none if not of God" (modern Italian *di nessuno se non di Dio*).

Greta **Nissen:** Grethe Rutz-Nissen (1906–1988), Norw. movie actress, working in U.S.

Der **Nister:** Pinkhos Mendeleyevich Kaganovich (1884–1950), Ukr. Jewish writer. The writer was born in Berdichev and in 1905 moved to Zhitomir, where he became a teacher of Hebrew under an assumed name. Hence his pseudonym, Yiddish for "the hidden one."

Frank **Nitti:** Francesco Raffele Nitto (?1896–1943), It.-born U.S. gangster.

Nitty Gritty: Glen Augustus Holness (1957–1991), Jamaican reggae singer, working in U.S.

Sister **Nivedita:** Margaret Elizabeth Noble (1867–1911), Ir.-born Ind. nun. Margaret Noble began her career as a teacher in England, but in 1898 went to India to join **Vivekananda**, who named her Nivedita, Sanskrit for "given," "dedicated."

David **Niven:** James David Graham Niven (1910–1983), Eng. movie actor, writer. Some sources give the London-born actor's original name as Nevins, while "he sometimes named as his birthplace the more arresting locale of Kirriemuir, Scotland, where his father had an estate" [William Stephenson in Garraty and Carnes, vol. 16, p. 452]. Michael Munn, author of *David Niven: The Man Behind the Balloon* (2009), interviewed Niven in 1982, when the London-born actor revealed that his father was in fact the diplomat and politician Thomas Platt, later Sir Comyn Thomas-Platt, long-term lover of Niven's mother during her marriage to William Niven, who died in 1915.

Marni **Nixon:** Marni McEathron (1929–), U.S. movie actress, singer.

Mojo **Nixon:** Neill Kirby McMillan (1957–), U.S. (white) rock musician. The former cycling champion is said to have become Mojo Nixon after imbibing several green liqueurs in New Orleans.

Niyazi **Niyazi:** Niyazi Zulfugarovich Tagizade-Gadzhibekov (1912–), Georgian composer.

Kwame **Nkrumah:** Francis Nwia Kofi Nkrumah (1909–1972), Ghanaian political leader. The first president of Ghana believed that he was probably born on Saturday, September 18, 1909, and being a male child born into the Akan tribe was accordingly called Kwame, "born on Saturday." The baptizing priest recorded the date of his birth as September 21, however, and that became the official date.

Phil **Nobel** *see* Neil **Balfort**

Nobody: William Stevens (1732–1807), Eng. biographer. This, the ultimate in anonymous names, was originally used by the writer in its Hebrew equivalent form of "Ain," as the author of one of his many religious publications, *Review of the Review of a New Preface to the Second Edition of Mr. Jones's Life of Bishop Horne* (1800). The name in turn suggested his pseudonym for a collection of his pamphlets, published with the Greek and English title *Oudenos erga, Nobody's Works* (1805). At about the same time, a club was founded in Stevens' honor entitled the "Society of Nobody's Friends." Anyone who calls himself Nobody is, of course, somebody. Compare the next name below.

A. **Nobody:** Gordon Frederick Browne (1858–1932), Eng. illustrator, painter. The artist, who was the son of **Phiz**, used this mock self-deprecatory name for three books of nonsense rhymes that he wrote and illustrated.

Magali **Noël:** Magali Guiffrai (1932–), Turk.-born movie actress, working in France, Italy.

Marie **Noël:** Marie Rouget (1883–1967), Fr. writer of religious verse.

Philip **Noel-Baker:** Philip John Baker (1889–1982), Br. politician. The Labour politician married Irene Noel in 1915 and added her name to his then.

Henry **Noel-Fearn:** Henry Christmas (1811–1868), Eng. writer, numismatist. The scholar assumed his new name shortly before his death, translating his family name to its French equivalent and adding the maiden name of his mother, Jane Fearn.

Noël-Noël: Lucien Noël (1897–1989), Fr. movie comedian.

Magdalena **Noguera** *see* Florentina **del Mar**

Victor **Noir:** Yvan Salmon (1848–1870), Fr. journalist.

Mary **Nolan:** Mary Imogen Robertson (1905–1948), U.S. movie actress.

Emil **Nolde:** Emil Hansen (1867–1956), Ger. Expressionist painter. The artist was born in the village of Nolde, in what is now southern Denmark, and adopted its name on marrying in 1902.

Nomad: Norman Ellison (1893–1976), Eng. naturalist, writer, broadcaster. The name not only indicates the naturalist's "roaming" activity but also reflects his real first name.

Klaus **Nomi:** Klaus Sperber (1944–1983), Ger.-born U.S. cabaret singer. The singer formed his name as an anagram of the magazine title *Omni*.

Non Con Quill: John Cynddylan Jones (1840–1930), Welsh theologian, biblical scholar. Jones was a Nonconformist ("Noncon") minister. Hence his name, which he used for articles published in the *Western Mail*.

Nookie: Gavin Chung (*c.*1971–), Br. black hip-hop musician.

Ed **Noon:** Michael Angelo Avallone, Jr. (1924–), U.S. thriller, horror story writer. Other names used by the novelist include Troy Conway, Priscilla Dalton, Mark Dane, J.A. DePre, Dorothea Nile, Vance Stanton, and Sidney Stuart.

Jeremiah **Noon:** John Calvin (1828–1871), Br. boxer. The boxer based his name on that of Anthony

Noon, who had been killed in a fight against Owen Swift in 1834.

T.R. **Noon** *see* Hilary **Neal**

Tommy **Noonan:** Thomas Patrick Noon (1922–1958), U.S. movie comedian.

Oodgeroo **Noonuccal:** Kathleen Mary Jean Walker, née Ruska (1920–1993), Austral. Aboriginal poet. Originally writing as Kath Walker, the poet adopted her Aboriginal name in 1988 when Australia celebrated its bicentennial. Her new first name derives from a word for the paper-bark tree. Her surname was that of the Noonuccal tribe to which her parents belonged.

John **Norcross** *see* Tim **Brennan**

Max Simon **Nordau:** Max Simon Südfeld (1849–1923), Hung.-Ger. physician, writer. The name shows a swing of polarity, since the writer's original surname means "southern field," while his pen name means "northern meadow." The volte face may have been designed to represent the physician's switch from medicine to literature.

Charles **Norden:** Lawrence George Durrell (1912–1990), Br. novelist, poet. The writer adopted this name for his early novel *Panic Spring* (1937). This was actually his second novel, but as his first, *Pied Piper of Lovers* (1935), had been a failure, his publishers suggested he adopt a pseudonym as a precautionary measure. Later, the huge success of *The Alexandria Quartet* (1957–60) ensured that false names were a thing of the past.

Christine **Norden:** Mary (or Molly) Lydia Thornton (1924–1988), Br. movie actress.

Lillian **Nordica:** Lillian Norton (1857–1914), U.S. opera singer. The soprano's original surname was changed to "Nordica" by her professor at the Milan Conservatory, Antonio Sangiovanni, who said it was hard for Italians to pronounce.

Paul **Nordoff:** Paul Norman Hof Bookmyer (1909–1977), U.S. composer, music therapist. The musician studied piano under Olga **Samaroff** at the Philadelphia Conservatory and it was she who convinced him to take a new name (a blend of his two middle names) for the concert platform.

Eric **Norelius:** Erik Pehrson (1833–1916), Swe.-born U.S. Lutheran pastor, church leader. Pehrson emigrated to the United States at the age of 17 and took a new name (meaning "northern") for himself.

Norman **Norell:** Norman Levinson (1900–1972), U.S. fashion designer. The designer formed his new surname by taking the first syllable of his first name and adding a phonetic "el" for the initial of "Levinson." He then added another "l" to this, which was said to stand for "looks."

Eidé **Norena:** Kaja Hanson Eidé (1884–1968), Norw. opera singer.

Géo **Norge:** Georges Mogin (1898–1990), Belg. poet. A pseudonym extracted from the poet's original name.

Assia **Noris:** Anastasia von Gerzfeld (Herzfeld) (1912–1998), Russ.-born movie actress, of Ger.-Ukr. parentage, working in Italy.

Bebe **Norma:** Norma Ellinger (1925–1974), Eng. dancing xylophonist.

Norma Jean: Norma Jean Beasler (1938–), U.S. country singer.

Jett **Norman** see Clint **Walker**

Karyl **Norman:** George Podezzi (1897–1947), U.S. male impersonator ("The Creole Fashion Plate").

Matthew **Norman** see Craig **Brown**

Mabel **Normand:** Mabel Normand (1894–1930), U.S. movie comedienne. Many sources give Normand's "real" name as Muriel (or Mabel) Fortescue. She explained the origin of this in an interview: "'D.W. Griffith gave me a job when he brought the company back to New York from California in May 1911,' said Mabel Normand, continuing the story of her career. 'And he changed my screen name back to my real one. Vitagraph had identified the actors on the screen, but for a while Biograph, Mr. Griffith's company, gave its players funny names. Blanche **Sweet** was Daphne Wayne, I was Muriel Fortescue, and Mack **Sennett** had some trick moniker like Lionel Marchbank. As a matter of fact, his original name is Michael Sinnott and he is Irish-Canadian'" [Sidney Sutherland, "Madcap Mabel Normand. Part 2: In the Movie Money," *Liberty Magazine*, September 13, 1930].

Normski: Normon Anthony Anderson (1967–), Br. TV presenter, of Jamaican parentage. Rapper brother Kevin explains: "I just called him Normon as a kid, then he went off to America and came back with a belt saying Normski on it and started using the name all the time. It's just an aka, a street name, everyone has one. Mine is Kzee, Killer Zone" [*Sunday Times Magazine*, December 6, 1992].

Normyx: George Norman Douglas (1868–1952), Sc. novelist + Elizabeth (or Elsa) Theobaldina Douglas, née FitzGibbon, his wife (also cousin). The couple (married 1898, divorced 1904) used this joint name for *Unprofessional Tales* (1901). Until about 1908, Douglas used the name G. Norman Douglass (preserving the spelling of his father's name) for all his writings, changing this to Norman Douglas thereafter.

Norna: Mary Elizabeth Brooks, née Aiken (*fl.*1828), U.S. writer. Mrs. Brooks published poems jointly with her husband, James Gordon Brooks (1801–1841), under this name.

Nedra **Norris:** Nedra Gullette (1914–), U.S. movie actress.

Harold **Norse:** Harold George Rosen (1916–), U.S. poet, of Lithuanian-Ger. parentage. An obvious anagram, from a name that lent itself readily to this.

Andrew **North** see André **Norton**

Captain George **North:** Robert Louis Stevenson (1850–1894), Sc. essayist, novelist, poet. This was the name assumed by Stevenson for *Treasure Island* when the novel first appeared serially in the magazine *Young Folks* (1881–2). He used his real name a year later when the story was published in book form. The name may have been intended to indicate a Scot, who came from "north of the border" (with England). Or possibly he based it on the name of Christopher **North**.

Christopher **North:** John Wilson (1785–1854), Sc. literary critic. The writer used this name for his contributions to many of the dialogues that appeared in the *Noctes Ambrosianae*, published in *Blackwood's Magazine* (1822–35). "North" relates to Scotland, north of the border with England.

Danby **North:** Daniel Owen Madden (1815–1852), Ir. writer. The author used this name for *The Mildmayes, or the Clergymen's Secret* (1856).

Dudley Long **North:** Dudley Long (1748–1829), Eng. politician. "On the death, in 1789, of hs aunt Anne, ... he assumed, in compliance with the terms of her will, the name and arms of North, ... and in 1812, when his elder brother, Charles Long, ... died, he resumed the name and arms of Long, in addition to those of North" [*Dictionary of National Biography*].

Gil **North:** Geoffrey Horne (1916–), Br. writer of mystery and detective fiction.

Howard **North** see Elleston **Trevor**

Robert **North:** Robert North Dodson (1945–), U.S.–born Br. ballet dancer, choreographer.

Sheree **North:** Dawn Bethel (1933–2005), U.S. movie actress.

Theophila **North:** Dorothea Hollins (*fl.*1900s), Eng. writer. The author used this name, a mirror image of that of Theophilus **South**, for *English Bells and Bell Lore* (1895), *Twelve Trifles, Cheerful and Tearful* (1904), *The Herbs of Medea* (1904), and *Marriage of True Minds* (1906).

André **Norton:** Alice Mary Norton (1912–2005), U.S. SF, children's writer. The author legally adopted her pen name. She also used the male names Andrew North and Allen Weston.

Barry **Norton:** Alfredo de Biraben (or de Biartsen) (1905–1956), Argentinian-born U.S. movie actor.

Fleming **Norton:** Frederic Mills (1836–1895), Br. actor, entertainer.

Graham **Norton:** Graham Walker (1963–), Ir.-born Br. TV comedian, chat-show host. The entertainer was obliged to choose a new name because Equity, the actors' trade union, already had a Graham Walker on its books. He opted instead for Norton, his great-grandmother's maiden name.

Jack **Norton:** Mortimer J. Naughton (1889–1958), U.S. movie actor.

Eva **Norvind:** Eva Sakonskaya (1944–2006), Norw. movie actress, of Russ. parentage, working in Mexico, U.S. The actress later worked as a dominatrix (or, as she called it, "psychosexual counsellor") under the name Ava Taurel.

Red **Norvo:** Kenneth Norville (1908–1999), U.S. jazz musician. The musician's nickname referred to his bright red hair, which he inherited from his Scottish ancestors. His new surname arose early in his career when a reviewer repeated an MC's pronunciation error. "Grateful for publicity of any kind, Norvo decided not to bother seeking a correction" [*The Times*, April 8, 1999].

Kate **Norway** *see* Hilary **Neal**

Eille **Norwood:** Anthony Brett (1861–1948), Br. stage actor.

Jack **Norworth:** John Knauff (1879–1959), U.S. stage actor, singer, dancer.

Max **Nosseck:** Alexander Norris (1902–1972), Pol. movie director, actor, working in U.S.

Nostradamus: Michel de Nostre-Dame (1503–1566), Fr. astrologer. The name appears to be a simple latinization of Nostre-Dame (or Notre-Dame, "Our Lady"). But the astrologer could have intended something more subtle, and another possible interpretation is "we give what is ours," from Latin *nostra*, "our things," and *damus*, "we give (them)."

Notorious B.I.G.: Christopher Wallace (1973–1997), U.S. black rapper. Wallace, 6 ft 3 in tall and weighing around 300 lbs, adopted an obvious descriptive name that equally implied sexual prowess. He was also known as Biggie Smalls, a name taken from the gangster played by Calvin **Lockhart** in the 1975 movie *Let's Do It Again*.

Helga **Novak:** Helga Maria Karlsdottir (1935–), Ger. writer.

Kim **Novak:** Marilyn Pauline Novak (1933–), U.S. movie, TV actress. When the actress began her career with Columbia Pictures she was asked to rename herself Kit Marlowe. She refused, but agreed to change her first name to Kim to avoid being associated with Marilyn **Monroe**. Ironically, on moving to TV, Kit Marlowe was the name of the character she played in the series *Falcon Crest* (1986–87).

Novalis: Friedrich Leopold, Freiherr von Hardenberg (1772–1801), Ger. romantic poet, novelist. The writer's pseudonym derives from the name of the family estate of Grossenrode, itself meaning "great clearing." His ancestors devised a Latin form of this

name, from *novalis*, "fallow land," ultimately from *novus*, "new." The Hardenberg family were known as "de Novalis" as far back as the 13th century. The name is now usually accented on the second syllable (No-*va*-lis) but it has been established that the poet himself stressed the first syllable (*No*-va-lis).

Novanglus: John Adams (1735–1828), U.S. statesman, president. The name, obviously meaning "New Englander," was used by Adams for letters of his published in 1775 in the *Boston Gazette* rebutting letters by the Loyalist writer Daniel Leonard, otherwise **Massachusettensis**.

Ramon **Novarro:** Jose Ramon Gil Samaniegos (1899–1968), Mexican movie actor, working in U.S. The actor's name was given him by director Rex **Ingram**, who needed a replacement for Rudolph **Valentino** when the latter left the company. Ingram cast Samaniegos as Rupert of Henzau in his version of *The Prisoner of Zenda* (1922). The name suggests a new persona and new role in life, while perhaps intentionally evoking Spanish *varón*, "man" (in the "macho" sense).

Alec **Nove:** Alexander Novakovsky (1915–1994), Russ.-born Br. economist.

Ivor **Novello:** David Ivor Davies (1893–1951), Welsh stage actor-manager, playwright, composer. The actor inherited the Italian name from his mother, Clara Novello Davies, née Davies, whose own middle name had been given her by her father in admiration of the singer Clara Anastasia Novello (1818–1908), daughter of the English organist and music publisher Vincent Novello (1781–1861), himself the son of an Italian father and English mother. Ivor Novello's professional name thus reached him by a rather roundabout route.

Davies was known as Ivor from childhood, and in 1909 was signing himself Ivor Novello Davies as a piano teacher. He adopted the name officially by deed poll in 1927. "There were two men in that one person. There was David Ivor Davies, the dark-eyed handsome youth from Wales, and there was Ivor Novello, whom the public knew and adored and whom David Ivor Davies created. That creation was one of his major successes. So complete did it become that it was almost impossible to say where one finished and the other began" [W. Macqueen-Pope, *Ivor: The Story of an Achievement*, 1951].

Novello's play *The Rat* (1924) was coauthored with Constance **Collier** under the joint pseudonym David L'Estrange, from a combination of his original first name and her married name.

Giacomo **Noventa:** Giacomo Ca' Zorzi (1898–1960), It. poet, essayist. The writer took his pen name from his birthplace, Noventa di Piave, near Venice.

Aleksey **Novikov-Priboy:** Aleksey Silych

Novikov (1877–1944), Russ. novelist, short-story writer. The writer's fiction regularly had a naval or maritime setting. Hence his addition to his original name of Russian *priboy*, "surf."

Karel **Novy**: Karel Novák (1890–1980), Cz. novelist.

Jan **Nowak**: Zdzislaw Jezioranski (1913–2005), Pol. resistance fighter. After World War II Nowak worked as a broadcaster, first for the BBC in London, then for the U.S. station Radio Free Europe in Munich, Germany. He retired in 1976 and moved to Washington, D.C., where he became a U.S. citizen.

Owen **Nox**: Charles Barney Cory (1857–1921), U.S. ornithologist.

Nudie: Nudka Cohn (1902–1984), U.S. movie costume designer, of Russ. Jewish parentage.

Charles-Louis-Étienne **Nuitter**: Charles-Louis-Étienne Truinet (1828–1899), Fr. playwright, librettist. An anagrammatic name.

Gary **Numan**: Gary Anthony James Webb (1958–), Eng. pop singer. A symbolic name, with a new-style (nu-style) spelling. There happens also to be a British actor Gary Oldman, Numan's exact coeval.

Nunquam: Robert Peel Glanville Blatchford (1851–1943), Eng. political journalist, editor. With a Latin pseudonym meaning "never," Blatchford was one of the founders in 1891 of the left-wing periodical *The Clarion*. Other founders included his brother, Montague Blatchford, who adopted the name Mont Blong (partly from his real name, partly from a humorous English pronunciation of Mont Blanc, the French mountain), **Dangle**, Edward Fay (pen name The Bounder), and William Palmer (known as Whiffly Puncto). For a couple of novels, Blatchford used the overblown Irish name McFaddyen O'Flathery McGinnis, no doubt suggested by his early military service with the Dublin Fusiliers.

France **Nuyen**: France Nguyen Vannga (1939–), U.S. movie actress, of Fr.-Chin. parentage.

Nyanaponika Mahathera: Siegmund Feniger (1901–1994), Ger. Buddhist, of Jewish parentage. The pioneer European *bhikkhu* (fully ordained Buddhist monk) was converted to Buddhism through books. In 1936 he left Germany for Ceylon (Sri Lanka), where the following year he was ordained under his new name. Mahathera ("great elder") is a title given to a *bhikkhu* of 20 years' standing. Nyanaponika was a leading disciple of **Nyanatiloka Mahathera**.

Nyanatiloka Mahathera: Anton Gueth (1879–1957), Ger. Buddhist. After high school, the Pali scholar originally studied music in Frankfurt and Paris. He then traveled to India where he became absorbed by Buddhism and in 1904 was ordained *bhikkhu* (Buddhist monk) under his new name. Ma-

hathera ("great elder") is a title assumed by a *bhikkhu* of 20 years' standing.

Bill **Nye**: Edgar Wilson Nye (1850–1896), U.S. humorist, editor. The writer used his part-pseudonymous name for a successful series of books beginning with *Bill Nye and Boomerang* (1881). (The latter was the *Laramie Boomerang*, the Wyoming newspaper that he edited.)

Louis **Nye**: Louis Neistat (1913–2005), U.S. comedian.

Alfonsas **Nyka-Niliunas**: Alfonsas Cipkus (1919–), Lithuanian writer, critic.

Laura **Nyro**: Laura Nigro (1947–1997), U.S. pop singer, songwriter, of It. Jewish descent. The singer modified her name to avoid any racist association with "negro."

Karen **O**: Karen Lee Orzolek (1978–), U.S. pop singer, of Korean-Pol. parentage.

George Washington Ochs **Oakes**: George Washington Ochs (1861–1931), U.S. editor, publisher, of Ger. Jewish parentage. Oakes added an anglicized form of his German surname to the original without replacing it, as was more usual. His sons, John and George Oakes, did not retain the family name.

Jack **Oakie**: Lewis Delaney Offield (1903–1978), U.S. movie comedian. The actor was born in Sedalia, Missouri, but later his family moved to Muskogee, Oklahoma, where his schoolfriends nicknamed him "Oakie." He added "Jack" to this to fix himself up with a suitable screen name.

Vivian **Oakland**: Vivian Anderson (1895–1958), U.S. movie actress.

Annie **Oakley**: Phoebe Ann Moses (1860–1926), U.S. sharpshooter. The Wild West star tried out the name Annie Mozee when still a girl, but later added "Oakley" to the pet form of her middle name, so that she was billed as "Miss Annie Oakley, the Peerless Lady Wing-Shot."

Wheeler **Oakman**: Vivian Eichelberger (1890–1949), U.S. movie actor. The actor indirectly translated part of his original name, German *Eichel* meaning "acorn."

Merle **Oberon**: Estelle Merle O'Brien Thompson (1911–1979), Br. movie actress, working in U.S. The popular account of the actress's origins states that she was born in Tasmania, Australia, of Irish, French, and Dutch descent. However, it emerged in a 1983 biography (cited below) that she had invented this pedigree, and that she was actually born in Bombay, India, to a part-Irish, part-Singhalese mother, Charlotte Constance Selby, and a British army officer, Arthur Terrence O'Brien Thompson. She moved to England in 1928 and played bit parts on stage and in films under the name Queenie O'Brien. She was then discovered by Alexander **Korda**, whom she subsequently married, and adopted her permanent screen name: "She began with Merle O'Brien, then O'Bryan, then Auberon (but that was the name of a firm in Bond Street), then Overell, then Avril Oberon, then Merle Oberon" [Charles Higham and Roy Moseley, *Merle: A Biography of Merle Oberon*, 1983].

Obiter: Isaac Torbe (1918–), Br. crossword compiler. The setter's pseudonym is not only an anagram of his real name (in the form I. Torbe) but is Latin for "by the way," referring to the secondary meaning usually found in a cryptic crossword clue.

Hugh **O'Brian:** Hugh J. Krampke (1925–), U.S. movie actor.

Patrick **O'Brian:** Richard Patrick Russ (1914–2000), Br. novelist. The writer was reticent about his private life, but projected the image that he was born in Ireland, the son of wealthy Anglo-Catholic parents, and raised with relatives in Connemara and Co. Clare and with family friends in England. In 1998 a newspaper article revealed that he was in fact born in the English county of Buckinghamshire.

Dave **O'Brien:** David Barclay (1912–1969), U.S. movie actor.

David **O'Brien:** David Herd (1930–), Eng. stage actor.

Desmond B. **O'Brien** *see* **Basil**

Flann **O'Brien** *see* **Myles na gCopaleen**

John **O'Brien:** Patrick Joseph Hartigan (1878–1952), Austral. poet, balladist.

Margaret **O'Brien:** Angela Maxine O'Brien (1937–), U.S. child movie actress.

Patrick **O'Brien:** Patrick Cotter (*c*.1761–1806), Ir. giant. When a pituitary defect caused Cotter to grow to a height of 8 ft 1 in, he turned the anomaly to profitable advantage by exhibiting himself at fairs all over England. "After the manner of Irish giants he changed his name to O'Brien, claiming to be a lineal descendant of Brian [Boru], king of Ireland, and to have 'in his person and appearance all the similitude of that great and grand potentate'" [*Dictionary of National Biography*].

Richard **O'Brien:** Richard Morley-Smith (1942–), N.Z.–born Br. stage actor, writer, TV presenter. The actor adopted his mother's maiden name as his professional name.

Robert C. **O'Brien:** Robert Leslie Conly (1918–1973), U.S. writer.

W.J. **O'Bryen:** Wilfrid James Wheeler-O'Bryen (1898–?), Br. theater manager.

Dermot **O'Byrne:** [Sir] Arnold Edward Trevor Bax (1883–1953), Br. composer. Inspired by reading Yeats, Bax visited Ireland at the age of 19 and, falling under its Celtic spell, began to write. In June 1905 the name Dermod McDermott began to appear under verse written in notebooks, while in June 1908

he had two poems published over the pen name Diarmid. The pseudonym settled soon after to Dermot O'Byrne. "[The name] was the measure of his affection for things Irish and was partly a cloak to conceal his other self, Bax the musician. O'Byrne was the true projection of his Irish/Celtic self as far as he found it possible to give it form and shape" [Colin Scott-Sutherland, *Arnold Bax*, 1973].

Richard **O'Callaghan:** Richard Hayes (1945–), Br. TV actor. The actor chose a name to express his individuality and to distinguish his own career and approach from those of his mother, actress Patricia Hayes (1909–1998). He commented: "I've always had to do things my way, which is why I wanted a different name from hers. I didn't want people giving me jobs because I was her son" [*Sunday Times Magazine*, June 28, 1987].

Sean **O'Casey:** John Casey (1880–1964), Ir. dramatist. When he began writing, in 1918, the playwright used an Irish version of his name, Sean O'Cathasaigh. Later, in the early 1920s, when his plays were first produced at the Abbey Theatre, Dublin, he part-reverted to an anglicized form of this.

Jehu **O'Cataract:** John Neal (1793–1876), U.S. romantic novelist, poet. This name, a typical 19th-century American literary whimsy, originally arose as a nickname, given the writer for his impetuosity, after Jehu, the biblical king of Israel who "driveth furiously" (2 Kings 9:20). He first adopted it for two narrative poems published in 1818, *Battle of Niagara* and *Goldau, or the Maniac Harper*. His feverish, flamboyant writing and editing continued unabated until he was in his 80s.

Billy **Ocean:** Leslie Sebastian Charles (1950–), Trinidadian R&B singer, working in U.K., U.S. The singer came to Britain with his family at the age of 10 and had adopted his new name by 1975, taking it from the Ocean estate where he lived in London. Other names he used include Joshua and Sam Spade.

Humphrey **Ocean:** Humphrey Butler-Bowdon (1951–), Br. portrait artist.

Marie **Ochs:** Gloria Steinem (1934–), U.S. feminist writer. This was the name the writer adopted when infiltrating the Playboy Club as a bunny girl in 1963: "I've decided to call myself Marie Catherine Ochs. It is, may my ancestors forgive me, a family name. I have some claim to it, and I'm well versed in its European origins. Besides, it sounds much too square to be phony" [Gloria Steinem, *Outrageous Acts and Everyday Rebellions*, 1983].

Billy **O'Connor:** Eugene Devot (1895–1974), Ir. comedy magician.

Frank **O'Connor:** Michael Francis O'Donovan (1903–1966), Ir. short-story writer. The writer adopted his mother's maiden name as his pen name.

Patrick **O'Connor:** Leonard Patrick O'Connor Wibberley (1915–1983), Ir.-born U.S. journalist, novelist, children's writer. Wibberley used this name for a series of children's stories about auto racing as well a number of teenage mysteries. Other children's books appeared under the name Christopher Webb, while Leonard Holton was the name assumed by Wibberley for adult detective novels.

Una **O'Connor:** Agnes Teresa McGlade (1880–1959), Ir. movie actress, working in U.S.

Oconomowoc: [Dr.] James Alexander Henshall (1836–1925), U.S. writer on angling. The writer adopted his pen name from the town of Oconomowoc, Wisconsin, where he moved his medical practice in 1867 from Milwaukee.

Octavian *see* Caesar **Augustus**

Anita **O'Day:** Anita Belle Colton (1919–2006), U.S. jazz singer. The singer changed her name as a teenager when competing in dance marathons.

Dawn **O'Day** *see* Anne **Shirley**

Molly **O'Day:** (1) Suzanne Dobson Noonan (1911–), U.S. movie actess; (2) Lois LaVerne Williamson (1923–1987), U.S. country musician. Williamson first called herself Mountain Fern and Dixie Lee Williamson before settling on the name by which she became well known.

O.D.B. *see* **Ol' Dirty Bastard**

Dell **O'Dell:** Nell Newton (1902–1962), U.S. magician.

Kenny **O'Dell:** Kenneth Gist, Jr. (*c.*1940–), U.S. country singer, songwriter.

Scott **O'Dell:** Odell Gabriel Scott (1898–1989), U.S. writer of children's historical fiction.

Odetta: Odetta Holmes Felious Gordon (1930–2008), U.S. black folksinger, civil rights activist. The singer's father died shortly after her birth. Her mother then married a janitor, Zadock Felious, whose surname she took. In 1959 she married Dan Gordon and added his name to the two she had already.

Odette: Odette Marie Céline Churchill, later Hallowes, earlier Sansom, née Brailly (1912–1995), Fr.-born Br. wartime agent. When training for her work in the field, Odette took the code name **Céline**. She also operated as Lise, while in prison in Paris she was Madame Odette Chambrun and in Ravensbrück women's camp, Germany, she was Frau Schurer. "Chambrun" was an alias of **Raoul**, her group leader, who later became her second husband.

Mary **Odette:** Odette Goimbault (1901–?), Fr.-born Br. movie actress.

Odips: Pierre Saint-Denis (?–1983), Fr. comedy magician, marionette artist.

Sir Morgan **O'Doherty:** William Hay Forbes (*fl.*1824), Eng. writer + John Gibson Lockhart (1794–1854), Sc. lawyer, writer + William Maginn (1793–1842), Ir. writer. The name, associated mostly with Maginn, was used for the writers' contributions to *Blackwood's Magazine* and *Fraser's Magazine*.

Cathy **O'Donnell:** Ann Steely (1923–1970), U.S. movie actress.

Cornelius **O'Dowd:** Charles James Lever (1806–1872), Ir. novelist. The author, who also wrote as Harry **Lorrequer**, used this name for his series of essays entitled *Cornelius O'Dowd upon Men, Women and Other Things in General*, published in *Blackwood's Magazine* in 1864.

Irina Vladimirovna **Odoyevtseva:** Iraida Gustavovna Geynike (Heinicke) (1901–?), Russ. writer.

Odress: Joseph Charles Mathieu Juppier (1867–1911), Fr. magician.

Odronoff: Juan Manuel Zolezzi (1889–1975), Argentinian magician, "mentalist."

Odysseus: [Sir] Charles Norton Edgcumbe Eliot (1862–1931), Br. diplomat. The diplomat, whose duties took him on travels to many parts of the world, used this significant pseudonym for *Turkey in Europe* (1901), an account of Macedonia and its different races under the old regime.

Johannes **Oecolampadius:** Johannes Huszgen (or Husschin) (1482–1531), Ger. humanist, preacher. In the manner of his day the scholar translated his German name into Greek. The equivalent of modern German *Haus* thus gave Greek *oikos*, "house," and that of *Schein* gave *lampas*, *lampados*, "light." The scholar would have also seen his preaching as bringing light (truth) into the house of God (church).

Oeconomus: Sebastian Hofmeister (1476–1533), Swiss religious leader. The Franciscan scholar adopted a Greek equivalent of his German surname, meaning literally "master of the household," from *oikos*, "house," and *nomos*, "law."

Sean **O'Faolain:** John Francis Whelan (1900–1991), Ir. writer. The writer changed his name to its Irish equivalent in order to express his political convictions and stress his links with his compatriots. "We all adopted and, like myself, most retained for the rest of our lives the ancient, original Gaelic forms of our anglicised names, so, from being Whelan, I became and remain, as my children do, O'Faoláin. It is pronounced Oh-Fay-láwn" [Sean O'Faolain, *Vive Moi!*, 1993].

Talbot **O'Farrell:** William Parrot (1878–1952), Eng. music-hall singer. The performer claimed an Irish background, although he actually came from the north of England. He earlier tried out a Scottish persona as Jock McIver.

Ofelia: Mercedes Matamoros (1851–1906), Cuban poet.

Jacques **Offenbach:** Jakob Levy Eberst (1819–1880), Ger.-born Fr. composer, of Jewish parentage.

The composer's father, Isaac Juda Eberst, a cantor at the Cologne Synagogue, was born in Offenbach, and was thus known as "Der Offenbacher." When Jakob was 14, his family moved to France, and he himself adopted his father's nickname, modifying his own first name to its French equivalent.

[Cardinal] Tomás **O'Fiaich:** Thomas Seamus Fee (1923–1990), Ir. Roman Catholic church leader. The future cardinal adopted the Irish (Gaelic) form of his name in 1977, when appointed archbishop of Armagh and Primate of All Ireland.

Ken **Ogata:** Ogata Akinobu (1937–2008), Jap. movie actor.

George **Oglethorpe:** Anthony Frederick Blunt (1907–1983), Eng. art historian, Soviet spy. Unmasked as a spy in Andrew Boyle's book *The Climate of Treason* (1979), Blunt had earlier used this name for an article on baroque art in the literary magazine *Venture* in 1929. As a spy he worked under various codenames, including "Tony," "Johnson," and "Yan." In Boyle's book Blunt was disguised as "Maurice," although his true identity was revealed soon after by the satirical magazine *Private Eye*. "Boyle, however, had decided to give Blunt a pseudonym — the not terribly subtle 'Maurice,' after the homosexual hero of an E.M. Forster novel" [Miranda Carter, *Anthony Blunt: His Lives*, 2001].

Ogdoades: [Seigneur] Guillaume du Bellay de Langey (1491–1543), Fr. soldier, writer. The general and diplomat used this name for his *Mémoires*. It represents the plural of Greek *ogdoas*, "set of eight" (*okto*, "eight"), because the work was divided into eight books. It was not printed until 1757.

Gavin **Ogilvy:** [Sir] James Matthew Barrie (1860–1937), Sc. novelist, dramatist. The author of *Peter Pan* adopted this name, from his mother's maiden name, for *When a Man's Single, A Tale of Literary Life*, published serially in the *British Weekly* over the period 1887–8.

N. **Ognev:** Mikhail Grigoryevich Rozanov (1888–1938), Russ. writer. The writer adopted a pseudonym in order to be distinguished from his brother, Sergey Grigoryevich Rozanov (1894–1957), also a writer.

George **O'Hanlon:** George Rice (1917–1989), U.S. movie actor.

Kevin **O'Hara:** Marten Cumberland (1892–1971), Br. thriller writer.

Mary **O'Hara:** Mary O'Hara Alsop (1885–1980), U.S. writer, composer. O'Hara adopted her pen name on becoming a screenwriter for MGM in the early 1920s.

Maureen **O'Hara:** Maureen FitzSimons (1920–), Ir.-born U.S. movie actress. When actor Charles Laughton cast the young actress for *Jamaica Inn* (1939) he told her that her name was too long for the marquee and she would have to change it. "My jaw dropped open and I could barely sputter a response. 'But ... but I don't want to change my name.' My protest fell on deaf ears. 'Well, I'm sorry, but you have to. You can either be Maureen O'Mara or Maureen O'Hara. Which do you prefer?' I tried to hold my ground. 'Neither. I'm Maureen FitzSimons.' Laughton dismissed my protest and made the decision for me. 'Then you're Maureen O'Hara,' and so I was and so I am" [Maureen O'Hara with John Nicoletti, *'Tis Herself: An Autobiography*, 2004].

Scott **O'Hara:** John D. MacDonald (1916–1988), U.S. mystery writer. This was just one of the many pseudonyms used by MacDonald, adopted by way of a tribute to the two writers who most influenced his style, F. Scott Fitzgerald and John O'Hara.

Pixie **O'Harris:** Rhona Olive Harris, née Pratt (1903–1991), Welsh-born Austral. children's writer, illustrator. The writer was the aunt of Australian-born entertainer and TV artist Rolf Harris (1930–).

King **Ohmy:** Joseph Smith (1854–1931), Eng. circus performer. The artist was gymnast, acrobat, and clown, and his antics helped give his stage name, since as he pretended to slip from the roof of the circus to the arena, plunging to within a few inches of the ground, he would invariably exclaim "Oh, my!"

Betsy **O'Hogan** *see* Horatio **Nicholls**

O.K.: Olga Novikova, née Kireyeva (1848–1925), Russ. political writer, working in England. The writer used this initialism for her contributions to London periodicals such as *New Review*, *Fraser's Magazine*, and *Contemporary Review*.

Okati: Étienne-Louis Pitou (1892–1950), Fr. magician. The name may relate to that of **Okito**.

Dennis **O'Keefe:** Edward Vanes Flanagan (1908–1968), U.S. movie, TV actor, of Ir. parentage. The actor appeared in several films as "Bud" Flanagan (nicknamed for English comedian Bud **Flanagan**) before changing his name to Dennis O'Keefe in 1937 on signing with MGM.

Lorenz **Oken:** Lorenz Ockenfuss (1779–1851), Ger. natural scientist, philosopher.

Okito: Theodore Bamberg (1875–1963), U.S. magician, of Du. descent. The illusionist originally wore a Japanese costume. Hence his name, as an anagram of "Tokio" (as Tokyo was sometimes spelled). His son was **Fu Manchu**.

Oklama: Jaroslav Zdarsky (1917–), Cz. conjuror.

Sonny **Okosuns:** Sunny Okosun (1947–2008), Nigerian musician.

Olaf V: Alexander Edward Christian Frederik

(1903–1991), Norw. king. The king was the son of **Haakon VII** and Princess Maud, daughter of Edward VII of England, and was actually born in England. He was christened Alexander but in 1905 was renamed Prince Olaf when his father became king of Norway and took his own new Norse name.

Pierre **Olaf**: Pierre-Olaf Trivier (1928–), Fr. stage actor.

John **Oland** *see* Anna **Wickham**

Warner **Oland**: Johan Werner Ölund (1880–1938), Swe.-born U.S. movie actor.

Ivan **Olbracht**: Kamil Zeman (1882–1952), Cz. writer, son of Antal **Stašek**.

Chauncey **Olcott**: John Chancellor (1858–1932), U.S. popular singer, composer.

Sidney **Olcott**: John Sidney Alcott (1873–1949), Ir.-Can. movie director, working in U.S. The slight spelling change was probably made to ensure the surname's correct pronunciation.

Maria **Olczewska**: Marie Berchtenbreitner (1892–1969), Ger. opera singer.

Cedric **Oldacre**: [Rev.] John Wood Warter (1806–1878), Eng. antiquary. This is the short form of the name adopted by Warter for *The Last of the Old Squires; A Sketch. By Cedric Oldacre, of Sax-Normanbury, sometime of Christ Church, Oxon* (1854). Warter actually was a student at Christ Church, Oxford, graduating in 1827. Hence his other pseudonym, A Graduate of Oxford, used earlier for translations of Aristophanes.

Old Anthony *see* **Old Humphrey**

Old Block: Alonzo Delano (?1801–1874), U.S. playwright, humorist. The writer used this name, somewhat predictably, for *Penknife Sketches, or Chips of the Old Block* (1853).

An **Old Boy**: Thomas Hughes (1822–1896), Eng. author. This was the name under which the writer first published his famous novel of school life, *Tom Brown's Schooldays* (1857). It was semiautobiographical, evoking Rugby School, which Hughes had himself attended as a boy.

Humphrey **Oldcastle**: (1) Henry St. John (1672–1751), Eng. writer; (2) Nicholas Amhurst (1697–1742), Eng. poet, politician. Henry St. John, Viscount Bolingbroke, contributed to *The Craftsman* under this pen name, as did the magazine's originator, Nicholas Amhurst, who actually founded it as Caleb **D'Anvers**. There is still some doubt about the precise authorship of the articles attributed to Amhurst.

John **Oldcastle**: Wilfrid Meynell (1852–1948), Br. writer, poet. The writer used this name for *Journals and Journalism* (1880). The name punningly refers to his birth city, Newcastle upon Tyne.

Old Humphrey: George Mogridge (1787–1854), Eng. writer of moral and religious works for children and adults. Mogridge used several pseudonyms. His best known was Peter **Parley**, but he also wrote as Jeremy Jaunt, Carlton Bruce, Uncle Adam, Old Anthony, Ephraim Holding, Uncle Newbury, and Aunt Newbury, as for *Old Anthony's Hints to Young People* (1844) and *Ephraim Holding's Homely Hints to Sunday School Teachers* (1864). As Old Humphrey he wrote over 40 tracts or tales. He probably took the name from some literary character, although it is uncertain who this was.

Ol' Dirty Bastard: Russell Tyrone Jones (1968–2004), U.S. black rapper. Jones hit America with hip-hop in the early 1980s. "By the end of the decade he had taken the name ODB and formed All In Together Now with his cousins Robert Diggs (who took the name RZA or Prince Rakeem) and Gary Grice (Genius or GZA). With the addition of further members Raekwon (Corey Woods), **Method Man** (Clifford Smith), Ghostface Killah (Dennis Coles), Inspectah Deck (Jason Hunter), U-God (Lamont Hawkins) and Masta Killa (Elgin Turner), they became the rap collective Wu-Tang Clan" [*The Times*, November 16, 2004].

Old Jonathan: [Rev.] David Alfred Doudney (1811–1894), Eng. educationist, writer.

An **Old Maid**: Lydia F. March Phillips (*fl.*1860s), Eng. writer. Miss Phillips used this name for *My Life, and what shall I do with it? A question for young gentlewomen* (1860). As L.F.M. she later wrote *English Matrons and Their Profession* (1873).

Old Moore: Francis Moore (1657–1714), Eng. astrologer, physician. The name became familiar from *Old Moore's Almanac*, first published in 1697 under the title *Vox Stellarum; being an Almanack for 1698 with Astrological Observations*. The publication long outlived its creator, and is still issued.

Old Possum: T.S. Eliot (1888–1965), U.S.-born Br. poet, critic, dramatist. Eliot used this name for *Old Possum's Book of Practical Cats* (1939). It was created by his friend Ezra Pound, who when Eliot was a banker early in his career described him as a poet "playing possum," or pretending to be other than he really was. By the time the children's book appeared he was over 50, so a relatively "old" possum.

Old Sailor: Matthew Henry Barker (1790–1846), Eng. writer of sea stories. As his name implies, the writer spent much of the first part of his life at sea.

Jonathan **Oldstyle**: Washington Irving (1783–1859), U.S. essayist, short-story writer, historian. This was an early pseudonym used by the writer, who later wrote as (alone) Geoffrey **Crayon** and (jointly) Launcelot **Langstaff**. He used it for the *Letters of Jonathan Oldstyle, Gent.*, a series of satires on New

York society which appeared in the New York *Morning Chronicle* over the period 1802–3.

Ole & Axel: Carl Schenstrøm (1881–1942), Dan. movie actor + Harald Madsen (1890–1949), Dan. movie actor. The comedy duo were popular in the 1920s as a sort of early **Laurel** and **Hardy**, Schenstrøm being tall and lean, and Madsen short and fat. They were known by these names in the USA. In their native Denmark, they were Fyrtårnet og Bivognen ("Lighthouse and Trailer"), or Fy og Bi for short. In Germany and Austria they were Pat und Patachon, in France Doublepatte et Patachon, in the Netherlands Watt en Watt, in Sweden Telegrafstolpen och Tilherngeren ("Telegraph Pole and Trailer"), and in the UK Long and Short.

Adam Olearius: Adam Ölschlegel (1599–1671), Ger. writer, scholar. The writer's adopted name is a Latin rendering of his original German name (literally "oil beater").

Patrick O'Leary: [Count] Albert-Marie Edmond Guérisse (1911–1989), Belg. army officer, serving in U.K. Guérisse adopted this name from a peacetime Canadian friend in 1940, when he became first officer of the Royal Navy "Q" ship *Fidelity* with the rank of lieutenant commander under the *nom de guerre* of Patrick Albert O'Leary. Under this cover name, he set up an escape line along which at least 600 Allied prisoners made their way to Britain during World War II. He later rose to the rank of major general in the Belgian army, and in 1986 was granted the title of count by the King of the Belgians.

Ole Luk-Oie: [Sir] Ernest Dunlop Swinton (1868–1951), Br. army officer, writer. The pseudonym is a Danish phrase meaning roughly "Olaf Shut-Eye." As Ole Lukkøje it is the name of the title character of Hans Christian Andersen's 1841 fairy tale translated variously into English as "Willie Winkie," "The Sandman," "The Dustman," or (misleadingly) "Old Luke." Swinton adopted the name for his book of short stories *The Green Curve* (1909) and other writings. He also wrote as **Backsight-Forethought**.

Olenka: Olga Augusta Maria Savary (1933–), Brazilian poet, writer, of Russ. parentage. The writer's adopted name is a diminutive of her original Russian first name.

Corilla Olimpica: Maria Maddalena Morelli Fernandez (1727–1800), It. poet. Italy's foremost improvisatory poet, official poetess to the grand ducal count in Florence, adopted this as her Arcadian name (*see* Aglauro **Cidonia**).

Konstantin Olimpov: Konstantin Konstantinovich Fofanov (1889–1940), Russ. Decadent poet. The poet adopted a somewhat outlandish name (implying Olympic prowess) to be distinguished from his father, Konstantin Mikhaylovich Fofanov (1862–1911), also a poet.

Stig Olin: Stig Högberg (1920–2008), Swe. movie actor, singer.

Jules Olitski: Yevel Demikovsky (1922–), Russ.-born U.S. painter.

Oliver: William Oliver Swofford (1945–2000), U.S. folk-rock singer.

Edith Oliver: Edith Goldsmith (1913–), U.S. drama critic. The critic took her new surname from the first name of the dramatist whose surname she shared, Oliver Goldsmith (1728–1784).

Edna May Oliver: Edna May Cox-Oliver, née Nutter (1883–1942), U.S. movie actress.

George Oliver: George Oliver Onions (1873–1961), Eng. novelist, short-story writer. This was not the adoption of a pseudonym but a legal name change, made in 1918.

Jane Oliver: Helen Rees (1903–1970), Sc. novelist.

Pen Oliver: [Sir] Henry Thompson (1820–1904), Eng. surgeon, medical writer. The author used this name for two novels: *Charley Kingston's Aunt* (1884), about the life of a medical student, and "*All But.*" *A Chronicle of Laxenford Life* (1886).

Stephen Oliver: (1) William Andrew Chatto (1799–1864), Eng. writer; (2) Stephen John Walzig (*c.*1950–), U.S. juvenile TV actor. Chatto's pen name first appeared for *Scenes and Recollections of Fly-fishing in Northumberland, Cumberland, and Westmoreland, by Stephen Oliver the younger, of Aldwark in Com. Ebor.* (1834) ("Com. Ebor." is the Latin abbreviation of "County of Yorkshire"). For a later book, *A Paper:— of Tobacco* (1839) (illustrated by **Phiz**), he was Joseph Fume.

Susan Oliver: Charlotte Gercke (1937–1990), U.S. movie, TV actress, director, aviator.

Vic Oliver: Viktor Oliver van Samek (1898–1964), Austr.-born Br. comedian, musician.

Olivia: (1) Emily Pomona Briggs, née Edson (1830–1910), U.S. journalist; (2) Dorothy Bussy, née Strachey (1866–1960), Br. novelist, translator, working in France. Briggs took the name when first writing for the *Philadelphia Press*. Bussy used it for her sole novel *Olivia* (1949), a fictional autobiography of a French schoolgirl, preceded by an outline of her earlier years. The account covers a year, involves a passionate affair, and ends in the narrator's suicide. The name Olivia has long been regarded as romantic, and even suggests "I love you" if spoken rapidly.

Iris Olkyrn: Alice Milligan (1866–1953), Ir. poet.

Ollie: Clive Hugh Austin Collins (1942–), Eng. cartoonist, illustrator. A name based on the artist's surname.

Mikhail **Olminsky:** Mikhail Stepanovich Aleksandrov (1863–1933), Russ. revolutionary, writer, historian. In 1898 the activist was exiled to the Siberian town of Olyokminsk, and this gave the name by which he became regularly known. A prerevolutionary name used by the writer was **Galyorka.**

John **Olms:** Richard Lischke (1880–1955), Ger. magician, working in U.S.

Olnem: Varvara Nikolayevna Tsekhovskaya, née Menshchikova (1872–?), Russ. writer. The writer created her pen name from the second syllable of her patronymic (middle name) and the first syllable, reversed, of her maiden name.

John **O'London:** Wilfred Whitten (?–1942), Br. editor, author. Whitten founded the popular periodical *John O'London's Weekly* in 1919, but it ceased publication in 1936.

April **Olrich:** Edith April Oelrichs (1941–), Br. stage, movie, TV actress.

[Rev.] Leslie **Olsberg:** Eliezer Mordechai ben Dov HaLevi (1922–2008), Br. Jewish minister.

Maria **Olszewska:** Marie Berchtenbreitner (1892–1969), Ger. opera singer. The mezzosoprano's professional name is often misspelled "Olczewska" in English-language sources.

Ipaty **Olyk:** Ipaty Stepanovich Stepanov (1912–1943), Russ. (Mari) poet. The poet adopted a surname meaning "meadow."

Omar: Omar Lye Fook (1969–), Br. soul musician, of Chin.-Jamaican/Ind.-Jamaican parentage.

Omar Khayyám: Ghiyath ad-Din Abu al-Fath 'Omar ibn Ibrahim al-Khayyami (*c.*1048–*c.*1122), Persian poet, astronomer. The author of the *Rubáiyát* ("Quatrains") has a name meaning "Omar Tentmaker," the latter probably indicating his father's trade. (The second half of his name, as given here, spells this out more fully as "Omar son of Ibrahim the Tentmaker.")

Sydney **Omarr:** Sidney Kimmelman (1926–2003), U.S. astrologer. "At the age of 15 he changed his name to ensure greater success and fame, choosing the surname after being inspired by a film whose protagonist was Omar, and selecting the rest according to numerological principles" [*The Times*, February 25, 2003].

Jacob **Omnium:** Matthew James Higgins (1810–1868), Ir. journalist. The writer took his name from the title of his first published article "Jacob Omnium, the Merchant Prince," a satire on commercial dishonesty, printed in the *New Monthly Magazine* in 1845.

Innokenty **Omulevsky:** Innokenty Vasilyevich Fyodorov (1836–1883), Russ. writer. The writer lived in Irkutsk, not far from Lake Baykal. His adopted name derives from Russian *omul,'* "omul," a fish of the salmon family found in that lake.

Ondine: Bob Olivio (1937–), U.S. "underground" movie actor, associate of Andy **Warhol.**

Anny **Ondra:** Anna Sofia Ondráková (1903–1987), Ger.-Cz. movie actress, working in U.K. The actress adopted the simplified version of her original name in the late 1920s.

Regan **O'Neal** *see* Robert **Jordan**

Siri **O'Neal:** Siri Willow Ceridwen Neal (1972–), Welsh stage, movie, TV actress. The actress adopted her family's original name of O'Neal in 1996. This was her grandmother's name, which her mother had altered to Neal.

Zibby **Oneal:** Elizabeth Oneal, née Bisgard (1934–), U.S. writer for young adults.

Philothée **O'Neddy:** Théophile Dondey (1811–1875), Fr. poet, critic. To the author's literary accomplishments one could add "anagrammatist." He was fortunate in having a classical-style first name that could be inverted like this, from "loved of God" (in the original Greek) to "loving God."

Sigrid **Onegin:** Sigrid Elisabeth Elfriede Emilie Hoffmann (1889–1943), Swe.-born Russ. opera singer, of Ger.-Fr. parentage. The singer took her first husband's adopted name of Onegin as her professional name.

Carolan **O'Neil:** Shafto Justin Adair Fitz-Gerald (1859–1925), Eng. novelist, dramatist.

Sally **O'Neil:** Virginia Louise Concepta Noonan (1908–1968), U.S. movie actress.

Egan **O'Neill** *see* Dell **Shannon**

Máire **O'Neill:** Molly Allgood (1887–1952), Ir. stage actress.

Moira **O'Neill:** Agnes Nesta Skrine, née Higginson (1865–1955), Ir. poet, mother of M.J. **Farrell.**

One of the Boys: Percy Hetherington Fitzgerald (1834–1925), Ir. musician, artist, writer.

One of the Fancy *see* Thomas **Brown, the Younger**

L. **Onerva:** Hilja Onerva Lehtinen (1882–1971), Finn. writer. The initial "L." could derive either from the writer's first name or from the initial of her maiden name.

Colette **O'Niel:** [Lady] Constance Malleson, née Annesley (1886–1975), Ir. stage actress, writer, wife of English actor Miles Malleson (1888–1969).

Onkel Adam: Carl Anton Wetterbergh (1804–1889), Swe. writer.

Onokuni: Yasushi Aoki (1962–), Jap. sumo wrestler. The wrestler's fighting name means "big country" (Japanese *o-*, "great" + *no*, "of" + *kuni*, "country").

Oku **Onuora:** Orlando Wong (1952–), Jamaican poet, reggae musician.

David **Opatoshu:** David Opatovsky (1918–1996), U.S. movie actor.

Marcel **Ophüls:** Hans Marcel Oppenheimer (1927–), Ger. movie director, son of Max **Ophüls**.

Max **Ophüls:** Max Oppenheimer (1902–1957), Ger.-born Fr. movie director, father of Marcel **Ophüls**. The moviemaker began his career as a stage actor at the age of 17 and changed his name then to avoid embarrassing his parents.

George August **Oppen:** George August Oppenheimer (1908–1984), U.S. poet. The Jewish family shortened their name in 1927, the year that Oppen married.

Oliver **Optic:** William Taylor Adams (1822–1897), U.S. novelist, children's writer. The author, who wrote around 1,000 articles and short stories and more than 120 novels, adopted a name that humorously denotes an observer, who keeps an eye ("optic") on the world. He first used it in 1851 but it became widely known from *Oliver Optic's Magazine (Our Boys and Girls)*, which he founded in 1867 and led until it ceased publication in 1875. He reserved the name for his children's writing. His other main pseudonyms were Irving Brown for romantic novels and Clinham Hunter, M.D., for travel writing.

Michael **O'Quillo** *see* **Xariffa**

Blanche **Oram:** Roma White (1866–1930), Eng. journalist, novelist. The writer's pseudonym puns on her real name, inverting surname and forename ("Blanche" for "White," "Oram" for "Roma").

L'**Orbetto:** Alessandro Turchi (*c*.1578–1650), It. painter.

William **Orbit:** William Wainwright (1959–), Br. composer, arranger, record company owner. The musician was nicknamed "Orbit" as a teenager by his peers, who regarded him as a "space cadet," out of touch with reality. Orbit has also used the name Bass-O-Matic for dance music.

Andrea **Orcagna:** Andrea di Cione (*c*.1308–*c*.1368), It. painter, sculptor, architect. The artist is known by his nickname, said to derive from a local form of Italian *arcangelo*, "archangel." The reference is presumably to his religious paintings, or to his appearance or nature.

Beryl **Orde:** Marjorie Stapleton (1914–1966), Eng. variety impressionist.

Robin **Ordell:** Robert Dowe (1918–1942), Austral. juvenile movie actor. The actor was the son of the popular writer and comedian Athol Dowe, who worked under the name Tal Ordell. Later in his short life (he was shot down as a pilot in World War II) he took the full name Robert Athol Buntine.

Ronnie **Ordex** *see* Frankie **Howerd**

Ordovex: John Humphreys (or Humffreys) Parry (1786–1825), Welsh editor. The writer used this name for his journalism. It means "Ordovician," that is, a member of the pre–Roman Ordovices tribe

who inhabited northern Wales. Parry was born in Mold, Flintshire, in this part of Wales.

Ordubady: Mamed Hadzha-aga ogly (1872–1950), Azerbaijani writer. The writer adopted the name of his birthtown, Ordubad.

Rebecca **Ore:** Rebecca B. Brown (1948–), U.S. writer of fantasy fiction.

Katherine **O'Regan:** Kathleen Melville (1903–), Ir. stage actress.

Miles **O'Reilly:** Charles Graham Halpine (1829–1868), Ir. humorist, soldier, working in U.S. The writer used the name for his humorous description of Civil War events, *The Life and Adventures, Songs, Services, and Speeches of Private Miles O'Reilly, 47th Regiment, New York Volunteers* (1864).

Max **O'Rell:** Léon Paul Blouet (1848–1903), Fr.-born humorous writer, working in U.K. Blouet first used the name for *John Bull et son île* (1883), an account of English eccentricities and national characteristics, translated (as *John Bull and his Island*) by his English wife.

Orelsan: Aurélien Cotentin (1982–), Fr. (white) rapper.

Zaharije **Orfelin:** Zaharije Stefanovic (1726–1785), Serbian scholar, writer, historian.

Orhan Kemal: Mehmet Raşit Ogutçü (1914–1970), Turk. writer.

Seán **O'Riada:** John Reidy (1931–1971), Ir. composer. An Irish form of the musician's original name.

Orinda: Katherine Philips, née Fowler (1632–1664), Eng. poet, letter-writer. The poet adopted the name Orinda as her pseudonym, and this in turn gave her literary sobriquet, the "Matchless Orinda." She moved in a society where it was the fashion to adopt a colorful, classical-style name. Her husband, James Philips, was thus "Antenor," and her friends included "Lucasia" (Anne Owen), "Rosania" (Mary Aubrey), "Silvander" (Sir Edward Dering), "Cratander" (John Berkenhead), and "**Poliarchus**" (Sir Charles Cotterell). "In her seventeenth year she married a [59-year-old] Royalist gentleman of Wales, Mr. James Philips, of Cardigan Priory.... She seems to have adopted the melodious pseudonym by which she has become known to posterity in 1651" [Edmund Gosse, *Gossip in a Library*, 1891]. Unlike the other names above, "Orinda" apparently has no precedent in literature and was possibly created by Philips herself. It may be an altered form of Latin *oranda*, "worthy to be entreated."

Orion: (1) [Rev.] W.W. Tulloch (1846–1920), Sc. writer; (2) Jimmy Hodges Ellis (1945–1998), U.S. rock singer. This is the best known of Tulloch's pen names, which he used for his "Tangled Talk" contributions to the *Glasgow Citizen*. He also wrote as Bonar Bridge, from the Scottish village of this name;

as Arthur Hill, from the English equivalent of his Scottish surname (Gaelic *tulach* means "hill"), and perhaps also from the maiden name of his first wife, Margaret Hill; as Gregory Goosequill, possibly a blend of the names of Sir Gregory **Gander** and Arthur **Crowquill**; as The Booktaster, with a presumed pun on *poetaster*; as The Paperknife; and as Sailil, seemingly a sort of anagram of "alias."

Ellis, a famous Elvis Presley lookalike and soundalike, is said to have adopted his name after a call from a woman who had written a book titled *Orion*, a fictionalized account of the Presley story. The original Orion was a great hunter in Greek mythology.

Władysław **Orkan:** Franciszek Smreczynski (1875–1930), Pol. writer. The writer adopted a name meaning "hurricane," "whirlwind."

Orlan: ? (1947–), Fr. performance artist. The body artist (or "carnal artist," as she calls herself) adopted her new name, evoking "Orlando" or "Orléans," at the age of 15. Her true identity is unknown.

Tony **Orlando:** Michael Anthony Orlando Cassavitis (1944–), U.S. rock singer, of Gk.-Puerto Rican descent.

Pavel **Orlenev:** Pavel Nikolayevich Orlov (1869–1932), Russ. actor.

Boris **Orlovsky:** Boris Ivanovich Smirnov (1796–1837), Russ. sculptor.

Ormonde: Andrew Omond (1841–1902), Eng. magician.

Eugene **Ormandy:** Jenö Ormandy Blau (1899–1985), Hung.-born U.S. orchestral conductor.

Benjamin **Orme** *see* H.A. **Page**

Mary **Orme:** Mary Sargeant Nichols, earlier Gove, née Neal (1810–1884), U.S. writer, health reformer. Nichols used this name as author of the novel *Uncle John* (1846).

Andreas **Ornithoparchus:** Andreas Vogelsang (*fl.*1516), Ger. musicologist. The musician's original name is traditionally recorded as here, although it may have been Vogelhofer, Vogelmaier, or even Vogelstätter. Whatever it was, its bearer recast it as a classical equivalent, so that German *Vogel*, "bird," is represented by Greek *ornis, ornithos*, with the rest of the name having a disputed interpretation.

Orpheus Junior: William Vaughan (1575–1641), Welsh colonial pioneer, writer. Vaughan used this name, referring to the poet of Greek mythology, for a compilation entitled *Golden Fleece* (1626).

A. **Orr:** Alice Ingram Orr Sprague (1950–), U.S. writer of fantasy fiction.

Benjamin **Orr:** Benjamin Orzechowski (1947–2000), U.S. rock bass player, of Russ. parentage.

Robin **Orr:** Robert Kemsley (1909–?), Sc. composer, organist.

Orris: Jean Ingelow (1820–1897), Eng. poet, novelist. The writer first used her pseudonym for children's tales published in the 1850s. "Orris" is both the name of a type of iris and the word for a former kind of gold or silver lace.

Orry-Kelly: Walter John Orry Kelly (1897–1964), Austral.-born U.S. movie costume designer.

Giulio **Orsini:** Domenico Gnoli (1838–1915), It. poet. Gnoli used this name for his collection of verse *Fra terra ed astri* ("'Twixt Earth and Stars") (1903). He also wrote as Dario Gaddi.

Jiří **Orten:** Jiří Ohrenstein (1918–1941), Cz. poet.

Orwell: Walter Chalmers Smith (1824–1908), Sc. poet, preacher. The Free Church of Scotland minister took his name from the parish of Orwell, Kinross-shire, to which he was appointed in 1853. He used this name for *The Bishop's Walk* (1861) and that of Hermann Kunst for *Olrig Grange* (1872).

George **Orwell:** Eric Arthur Blair (1903–1950), Eng. novelist, satirist. The writer first used his pen name for *Down and Out in Paris and London* (1933). He felt that Eric was too "Norse" and Blair too Scottish, and that a more suitable English name was one composed of the name of the patron saint of England and that of the river in Suffolk on whose banks he had lived. He also said that he wished to avoid embarrassing his parents, although friends felt that he was really trying to escape from his genteel middleclass background. Mixed motives, therefore, seem to have prompted him to take a new name.

The reviewer of a book on Rebecca **West** summarized his choice of name: "George Orwell — a commonplace Christian name and an English river — together name the plain-speaking Englishman that Eric Blair chose to be in his work" [Samuel Hynes, "In communion with reality," *Times Literary Supplement*, December 21, 1973]. Blair had initially considered other names, among them P.S. Burton, Kenneth Miles, and H. Lewis Allways. Some sources, such as Peter Stansky and William Abrahams, in *Orwell: The Transformation* (1979), claim that Blair's publisher, Victor Gollancz, made the final choice of name. Reviewing T.R. Fyvel's *George Orwell: A Personal Memoir*, Richard Mayne wrote: "It's good to learn that in conversation ... Orwell could make people laugh. I've sometimes wondered whether he concealed a pun in his pen-name: jaw-jaw well." [*Times Literary Supplement*, November 26, 1982].

A later writer, noting that Orwell admired the novels of George Gissing, adduces a further reason for Orwell's adoption of the river name. "Why 'George Orwell'? When one notices that Gissing is the name of a Norfolk village within a day's tramping of Southwold, where Orwell was mostly based in the early 1930s, a persuasive answer suggests itself. Not only is there a Suffolk river called the Orwell, but an identically named Cambridgeshire village through which Orwell must have tramped on his way to visit his girlfriend Brenda Salkeld, who lived in Bedford. This is a far more plausible explanation for the origin of the name than any other on offer" [*Times Literary Supplement*, January 2, 2004].

Early in his career, Orwell was asked by novelist Anthony Powell whether he had considered legally adopting his pseudonym. "Well, I have," he replied, "but then, of course, I'd have to *write* under another name if I did" [Goodman, p.41].

Ozzy **Osbourne**: John Michael Osbourne (1948–), Br. rock musician. The name arose as a nickname.

Henry **Oscar**: Henry Oscar Wale (1891–1969), Br. stage actor, director.

O'Shan: Yves Chaillot (1926–), Fr. magician, "mentalist."

Andreas **Osiander**: Andreas Hosemann (1498–1552), Ger. Protestant theologian.

N. **Osinsky**: Valerian Valerianovich Obolensky (1887–1938), Russ. Communist official, economist.

Wanda **Osiris**: Anna Menzio (1905–1994), It. revue actress, singer.

Mikhail **Osorgin**: Mikhail Andreyevich Ilyin (1878–1943), Russ. writer, working in France.

Ossian: James Macpherson (1736–1796), Sc. poet, forger. In 1762 Macpherson published *Fingal*, a purported translation from the ancient Gaelic of an epic poem by the legendary Gaelic bard Ossian, in the process transforming the mythical (or possibly historical) Irish hero Finn, or Finn Mac Cool, into the Scottish Fingal, supposedly Ossian's father. The work was in fact Macpherson's fabrication, based loosely on various old ballads and fragments. An entirely invented work, *Temora*, followed in 1763 as a similar claimed translation from the Gaelic. The forgery was only fully exposed after Macpherson's death, but the authenticity of *Fingal* was doubted by Dr. Johnson in the writer's lifetime. (Macpherson was not of course claiming to *be* Ossian, but his use of the name qualifies as a quasi-pseudonym.)

Ossian Gwent: John Davies (1839–1892), Welsh poet. The poet's name means "Ossian of Gwent," from Ossian, the legendary Gaelic bard, and Gwent, the region of southeast Wales in which he was raised.

Count **Ossie**: Oswald Williams (*c.*1928–), Jamaican pop musician.

Ossit: [Baronne] Madeleine Annette Edmé Angélique Vivier Deslandes (1866–1929), Fr. literary hostess, novelist. The origin of the writer's adopted name is uncertain.

Franz **Osten**: Franz Ostermayer (1876–1956), Ger. movie director, working in India.

Juliusz **Osterwa**: Juliusz Maluszek (1885–1947), Pol. stage actor, director.

Aleksandr **Ostuzhev**: Aleksandr Alekseyevich Pozharov (1874–1953), Russ. stage actor. The actor appears to have chosen a name suggesting a converse of the original: Russian *pozharit'* means "to burn," while *ostuzhat'* means "to cool."

Gilbert **O'Sullivan**: Raymond Edward O'Sullivan (1946–), Ir. pop musician. The musician originally intended to call himself simply "Gilbert," but his manager, Gordon Mills, who also produced the name of Engelbert **Humperdinck**, suggested he keep his surname, no doubt seeking to retain the association with Gilbert and Sullivan, the operetta writers.

Séumas **O'Sullivan**: James Sullivan Starkey (1879–1958), Ir. poet, literary editor. "Séumas" is an Irish form of "James."

Richard **Oswald**: Richard Ornstein (1880–1963), Austr.-born. movie director, working in U.K., France, U.S.

Ossi **Oswalda**: Oswalda Stäglich (1897–1948), Ger. movie actress. The actress adopted a pet form of her first name as her new first name and her original first name as her new surname.

La Belle **Otero**: Caroline Puentovalga (1868–1965), Sp. courtesan, dancer. The dancer's stage name ("The Beautiful Otero") apparently derives from her husband, an Italian tenor whom she married when she was 14.

James **Otis**: James Otis Kaler (1848–1912), U.S. writer of stories for boys.

Johnny **Otis**: John Veliotes (1921–), U.S. R&B musician, of Gk. parentage.

Nikolay **Otrada**: Nikolay Karpovich Turochkin (1918–1940), Russ. poet. The poet's adopted surname means "joy," "delight." One of his first works was a collection of verse entitled *Happiness* (1939). Ironically, he was killed in World War II on the Finnish frontier.

Rudolf **Otreb** *see* Joachim **Frizius**

Ulrike **Ottinger**: Ulrike Weinberg (1942–), Ger. moviemaker.

Piero **Ottone**: Pier Leone Mignanego (1924–), It. journalist, writer.

Eoghan **Ó Tuairisc**: Eugene Watters (1919–1982), Ir. writer.

Ouida: Marie Louise de la Ramée (1839–1908), Eng.-Fr. novelist. The writer was actually born Louise Ramé but began to style herself socially "de la Ramée" in the 1860s when she first became famous. Her pen name represents her childhood pronunciation of "Louise."

Oum Kalsoum *see* **Umm Kulthum**

Gérard **Oury:** Max-Gérard Houry Tannenbaum (1919–2006), Fr. Jewish movie actor, director.

Mosheh **Oved:** Edward Goodack (1885–1958), Pol.-born Br. antiquary, writer. The jeweler's name was the one by which he was known in London's Polish Jewish community. His original name was shortened by a London signwriter to Edward Good.

Jan **Overbeek** *see* Jakov **Lind**

George **Ovey:** George Overton Odell (1870–1951), U.S. movie comedian.

Owain Alaw: John Owen (1821–1883), Welsh singer, composer. The musician's adopted name means "Owen of melody." Alaw is a forename in its own right.

Owain Myfyr: Owen Jones (1741–1814), Welsh antiquary. The writer took his name from his birthplace, the village of Llanfihangel Glyn Myfyr, Denbighshire (now Conwy).

Ashford **Owen:** Anne Charlotte Ogle (1832–1918), Eng. novelist. The writer's pen name preserves her initials, if not her gender.

Bill **Owen:** William John Owen Rowbotham (1914–1999), Eng. stage, movie, TV actor. The actor began his career as Bill Rowbotham and adopted his familiar name only late in his career.

Jean A. **Owen:** Jean A. Visger, earlier Owen, née Pinder (?–1922), Eng. writer, journalist.The writer, an inveterate traveler until World War I, used the name of her first husband, George Newton Owen, for her earlier writings, such as *From San Francisco to New York* (1869) and *Our Honolulu Boys* (1877). Later writings appeared under the name A Son of the Marshes, "that title having been chosen by Mrs. Visger to cover the collaborated work of a working naturalist in Surrey and herself" [*Who's Who*]. The naturalist in question was Denham Jordan (1836–1920).

John Pickard **Owen:** Samuel Butler (1835–1902), Eng. writer, painter. Butler used this name for *The Fair Haven* (1873), subtitled *A Work in Defence of the Miraculous Element of Our Lord's Ministry upon Earth*: "By the Late John Pickard Owen. With a Memoir by William Bickersteth Owen." The second edition of this work, an ironic attack on the Resurrection, had the author's real name. "Butler's anonymity was due in part to Swift's **Bickerstaff** tradition of mystification, and partly due to his unwillingness to provoke further controversy with his father" [*Dictionary of National Biography*]. A year earlier Butler had anonymously published his famous satirical novel *Erewhon*, although here, too, a second edition bore his real name.

Philip **Owen** *see* Hugh **Pentecost**

Seena **Owen:** Signe Auen (1894–1966), U.S. movie actress, of Dan. descent. A phonetic simplification of a Scandinavian name that some might wonder how to pronounce.

Sid **Owen:** David John Sutton (1972–), Eng. movie, TV actor.

Owen Gwyrfai: Owen Williams (1790–1874), Welsh poet. The poet's adopted name is that of the river near his home village of Waunfawr, Carnarvonshire (now Gwynedd).

Jesse **Owens:** James Cleveland Owens (1913–1980), U.S. black athlete. Around 1920 the athlete's family moved from Oakville, Alabama, to Cleveland, Ohio, where the nickname "Jesse" arose when a schoolteacher mispronounced Owens' drawled "J.C."

Rochelle **Owens:** Rochelle Bass (1936–), U.S. dramatist.

Robert **Owenson:** Robert MacOwen (1744–1812), Ir. actor. The actor anglicized his name when broadening his repertoire from the Dublin stage to that of London.

Dr. **Owlglass:** Hans Erich Blaich (1873–1945), Ger. journalist, comic poet. The name is an English translation of German *Eulenspiegel*, familiar from Till Eulenspiegel, a famous practical joker in German literature based on a real person of the same name who lived in the 14th century.

Owzat: Tim Moorey (1940–), Br. crossword compiler. The setter is a cricket lover, and chose for his pseudonym the appeal of a fielder ("How's that?") to the umpire to give the batsman out.

Elsie J. **Oxenham:** Elsie Jeanette Dunkerley (*c*.1879–1960), Br. writer of stories for girls, daughter of John **Oxenham**.

John **Oxenham:** William Arthur Dunkerley (1852–1941), Eng. poet, novelist. The motive for the writer's change of name is uncertain, and it may not have been for authorial reasons. He took the name itself from John Oxenham, a seaman adventurer in Charles Kingsley's novel *Westward Ho!* (1855).

Oxoniensis: Thomas Herbert Parry-Williams (1887–1975), Welsh poet, essayist. The Welsh scholar's adopted Latin name means "of Oxford," referring to Jesus College, Oxford, where he studied.

Platon **Oyunsky:** Platon Alekseyevich Sleptsov (1893–1939), Russ. (Yakut) writer, politician. The writer based his name on a local word *oyun*, "wizard," "shaman," with direct reference to his own verse play *The Red Shaman* (1918). This concerned the "reforging" of one such cult leader. Shamans played a key role in Yakut society.

Amos **Oz:** Amos Klausner (1939–), Israeli novelist, short-story writer, of Russ. Jewish parentage. At the age of 15, following his mother's suicide, the future writer left his native Jerusalem to live in the kibbutz Hulda, where he adopted his new name, Hebrew for "strength."

Frank **Oz:** Frank Richard Oznowicz (1944–), U.S. puppeteer, movie director.

Ozutsu: Takeshi Matsumoto (1956–), Jap. sumo wrestler. The wrestler's fighting name means "great gun," "cannon" (Japanese *ozutsu*).

Piet **Paaltjens:** François Haverschmidt (1835–1894), Du. preacher, poet.

Augustus **Pablo:** Horace Swaby (1952–1999), Jamaican dub, reggae musician. The performer was renamed in 1971 by local record producer Herman Chin-Loy. The new name caused confusion in later years as another musician was already using it.

Pach-Pach: Pavel Maksimovich Yesikovsky (originally Yesikov) (1900–1961), Russ. circus artist, horseman, movie actor. The name is a reduplicated shortening of the performer's first two names. He would have been known as Pavel Maksimovich as a standard form of address and in rapid speech ("Pal Maksimich" or colloquially "Pal Mich") this would have been shortened even further to "Pach."

Pacificus: Alexander Hamilton (1757–1804), U.S. statesman, lawyer ("King of the Feds"). Latin *pacificus* means "peaceful."

Suzanne **Packer:** Suzanne Jackson (1962–), Br. black TV actress. The actress took her grandmother's maiden name as her professional name.

Vin **Packer** *see* M.E. **Kerr**

George **Padmore:** Malcolm Nurse (1902–1959), West Indian-born political activist, writer. Nurse emigrated to the United States in 1924 and changed his name on joining the Communist Party in 1927.

Paduci: Françoise Lefebvre (Sister Paul-du-Crucifix) (1912–1991), Can. composer. The musician's professional name appears to have been created from letters in her religious title.

Anita **Page:** Anita Pomares (1910–2008), U.S. movie actress.

Annette **Page:** Annette Hynd, née Lees (1932–), Eng. ballet dancer, wife of Ronald **Hynd**. The dancer adopted her mother's maiden name as her stage name.

Ashley **Page:** Ashley Laverty (1956–), Br. ballet dancer.

Emma **Page:** Honoria Tirbutt, née O'Mahoney (1921–), Br. mystery writer.

Gale **Page:** Sally Perkins Rutter (1911–1983), U.S. movie actress.

Geneviève **Page:** Geneviève Bonjean (1931–), Fr. stage, movie actress.

Gilbert H. **Page:** Ella D'Arcy (1856 or 1857–1937), Eng. short-story writer, of Ir. parentage. D'Arcy used this male name for some stories published in *The Yellow Book* in the 1890s.

H.A. **Page:** Alexander Hay Japp (1837–1905), Sc. writer, publisher, editor. This is probably the most familiar of the writer's pseudonyms, as a free reversal of his initials and surname. He also wrote as E. Conder Gray, Benjamin Orme, A.F. Scot, and A.N. Mount Rose, while one work, *Lights on the Way* (1878), appeared under a double pseudonym, as it was "by the late J.H. Alexander, B.A.; with an explanatory note by H.A. Page." Of these, E. Conder Gray may hint at his first two names, A.F. Scot perhaps stands for "A Forfarshire Scot," and A.N. Mount Rose probably points to the town of Montrose, near which he was born and in which he was raised.

Harold **Page:** Harold Littledale Power (1833–1901), Eng. actor. Harold Power was the grandfather of the U.S. movie actor Tyrone Power (1914–1958), who first married **Annabella**, then Linda **Christian**, and who had liaisons with Judy **Garland** and Lana **Turner**.

Joy **Page:** Joy Cervette Paige (1924–2008), U.S. movie actress, daughter of Don **Alvarado**. The actress modified her last name for her appearance in the movie *Casablanca* (1943).

Larry **Page:** Leonard Davies (*c*.1938–), Eng. pop musician. The musician changed his name as a teenager in honor of the U.S. movie actor Larry **Parks**, star of *The Jolson Story*. *See also* **Larry**.

Lorna **Page** *see* Fenton **Brockley**

Marco **Page:** Harry Kurnitz (1909–1968), U.S. playwright, novelist, moviewriter.

Patti **Page:** Clara Ann Fowler (1927–), U.S. popular singer. The singer may have taken her new first name from the surname of Adelina Patti, the (Spanish-born) Italian operatic soprano who died in 1919. She was given her new surname by the Page Milk Company, a dairy in Tulsa, Oklahoma, when she appeared in a show that they sponsored, KTUL's *Meet Patti Page Show*.

Debra **Paget:** Debralee Griffin (1933–), U.S. movie actress. The actress is said to have taken her screen name from the aristocratic Paget family of England, from whom she claimed descent.

Nicola **Pagett:** Nicola Mary Scott (1945–), Eng. TV actress. The actress was obliged to change her name on discovering that Nicola Scott, daughter of ornithologist Sir Peter Scott (1909–1989), was a stage manager at the Chichester Festival Theatre. She chose a family name instead.

Pagu: Patricia Galvão (1910–1962), Brazilian poet, novelist. The writer's pen name is based on the first syllables of her original names.

Elaine **Paige:** Elaine Bickerstaff (1948–), Eng. singer, actress. The actress changed her name in drama school.

Janis **Paige:** Donna Mae Tjaden (1922–), U.S. movie actress, singer. The actress took her new first name from the musical comedy star Elsie **Janis** and her surname from a grandparent.

Richard **Paige** *see* Leigh **Nichols**

Robert **Paige:** John Arthur Page (1910–1987), U.S. movie actor. The actor began his screen career in the mid–1930s under the name David Carlyle.

Baburao **Painter:** Baburao Krishnarao Mestri (1890–1954), Ind. movie director. The director, born into a family of traditional craftsmen, taught himself to paint (and sculpt). Hence his adopted surname.

Teuvo **Pakkala:** Teodor Oskar Frosterus (1862–1925), Finn. writer. The writer adopted an equivalent of his original Swedish name, Finnish *pakkanen* meaning "frost." He also wrote as Taustan Kalle (Swedish *kall*, "cold").

Pal: Jean de Paléologue (1860–1942), Rom.-born caricaturist, illustrator, working in U.K., France, U.S.

Lucila **Palacios:** Mercedes Carvajal de Arocha (1902–), Venezuelan writer. The writer adopted her pen name in 1932.

Jack **Palance:** Vladimir Palahnuik (1919–2006), U.S. movie actor, of Russ. or Ukr. parentage. "Proceed with caution, since there are a handful of versions of his true name" [Thomson 2003, p.665].

Madame **Palatine:** Elisabeth-Charlotte von der Pfalz (1652–1722), Fr. writer, of Ger. origin. French *Palatine* translates German *Pfalz*.

Aldo **Palazzeschi:** Aldo Giurlani (1885–1974), It. poet, novelist.

Peter **Palette:** Thomas Onwhyn (1814–1886), Br. illustrator, cartoonist. The artist used this name, of obvious origin, for his etchings in an unauthorized edition of Dickens's *Nicholas Nickleby* published in 1838. He had earlier used the name Sam Weller for a similar edition of *Pickwick Papers*, the name being that of a leading character in this work.

[Sir] Francis **Palgrave:** Francis Cohen (1788–1861), Eng. historian. The father of poet and critic Francis Turner Palgrave (1824–1897), compiler of Palgrave's *Golden Treasury*, was born a Jew. He changed his name from Cohen to Palgrave, his mother-in-law's maiden name, on converting to Christianity at the time of his marriage to Elizabeth Turner in 1823.

Palinurus: Cyril Vernon Connolly (1903–1974), Br. literary critic, novelist. The writer used the name for *The Unquiet Grave* (1944), which he described as "a word-cycle in three or four rhythms: art, love, nature and religion." In classical mythology, Palinurus was the pilot of Aeneas's ship, famous for his fall from the ship into the sea. Connolly thought Palinurus fell through the typically modern will to failure.

Pal Joey: Joey Longo (c.1964–), U.S. house musician. The artist has recorded under a number of names, including Earth People, Soho, House Conductor, Espresso, and Dream House.

Andrea **Palladio:** Andrea di Pietro della Gondola (1508–1580), It. architect. The artist was named by his patron, humanist poet and scholar Gian Giorgio Trissino, in allusion both to the Greek goddess Pallas Athene and to a character in Trissino's own poem, *L'Italia liberata dai Goti* ("Italy Liberated from the Goths") (1527–47). The name also aimed to indicate the hopes that Trissino had for his protégé.

Jackie **Pallo:** Jack Gutteridge (1926–2006), Br. wrestler, entertainer. The popular TV villain took his ring name from a brother-in-law in the U.S.

Betsy **Palmer:** Patricia Brumek (1929–), U.S. movie actress, TV panelist.

Don **Palmer** *see* Carolyn **Keene**

F.H. **Palmer:** Emma Sophie Amalie Hartmann, née Linn (1807–1851), Dan. composer.

Gregg **Palmer:** Palmer Lee (1927–), U.S. movie actor.

Joseph **Palmer:** Joseph Budworth (1756–1815), Eng. writer. Following an army career, Budworth married an Irishwoman, Elizabeth Palmer, and in 1811, on the death of her brother, succeeded in her right to the estates and name of Palmer. His contributions to the *Gentleman's Magazine* were mostly signed "Rambler," beginning with *A Fortnight's Ramble to the Lakes in Westmoreland, Lancashire, and Cumberland. By a Rambler* (1792).

Lillie **Palmer:** Lillie Marie Peiser (1911–1986), Ger. movie actress.

Patsy **Palmer:** Julie Harris (1972–), Eng. TV actress. The actress adopted her mother's maiden name as her professional name.

Tom **Palmer:** Tony Andruzzi (1925–1991), U.S. magician. The conjuror was born Antonio C. Andruzzi but took the name Tom Palmer, later adopted legally in the full form Thomas S. Palmer.

Luciana **Paluzzi:** Luciana Paoluzzi (1937–), It. movie actress.

Hermes **Pan:** Hermes Panagiotopoulos (1905–1990), U.S. ballet dancer, choreographer, of U.S.–Gk. parentage. A name that is not only a desirable shortening of a lengthy surname, but that evokes two famous Greek gods: Pan, the god of pastures, was the son of Hermes, herald and messenger of the gods.

Petro **Panch:** Pyotr Iosifovich Panchenko (1891–1978), Ukr. writer.

Vijaya Lakshmi **Pandit:** Swarup Kumari Nehru (1900–1990), Ind. politician, diplomat. The political leader's new last name is that of her husband, Ranjit Sitaram Pandit, whom she married in 1921. At the same time, in accordance with Hindu custom, she changed the rest of her name to reflect her husband's clan.

Pan Head: Anthony Johnson (1966–1993), Jamaican DJ, reggae musician.

Breece D'J **Pancake:** Breece Dexter Pancake (1952–1979), U.S. writer. When Pancake converted from Methodism to Catholicism in 1977, he chose John as his confirmation name, giving Breece D.J. Pancake as the name under which he planned to publish his stories. When a typesetter accidentally altered "D.J." to "D'J" he decided to let the error remain uncorrected.

Anton **Pann:** Antonie Pantoleon Petroveanu (1796–1854), Rom. poet, folklorist, composer.

Paññavaddho: Peter Morgan (1925–), Welsh Buddhist. Born in India to British parents, Morgan turned to Buddhism and in 1956 was ordained *bhikkhu* (monk) in Thailand under his new name.

Pansy: Isabella MacDonald Alden (1841–1930), U.S. children's magazine editor. The writer, noted for her sentimental religious fiction, used the pet name by which she was known in childhood.

L. **Panteleyev:** Aleksey Ivanovich Yeremeyev (1908–), Russ. writer.

Peter **Panter** *see* Ignaz **Wrobel**

Pantycelyn: William Williams (1717–1791), Welsh hymnwriter. The writer adopted his name from that of a neighboring farm where his mother had lived before her marriage. The name itself means "holly valley."

Paul **Panzer:** Paul Wolfgang Panzerbeiter (1872–1958), Ger.-born U.S. movie actor.

Dria **Paola:** Etra Pitteo (1909–), It. movie actress.

Betty **Paoli:** Barbara Elisabeth Glück (1815–1894), Austr. poet, of Jewish descent.

Irene **Papas:** Irene Lelekou (1926–), Gk. movie actress. The actress's screen name is that of her first husband, Alkis Papas (married 1947, divorced 1951).

Papa San: Tyrone Thompson (1966–), Jamaican reggae DJ.

Papillon: Henri Charrière (1906–1973), Fr. criminal. The alleged murderer, author of the 1969 bestseller titled with his name, adopted the nickname given him for the design of a butterfly (French *papillon*) tattooed on his chest.

Joseph **Papp:** Yosl Papirofsky (1921–1991), U.S. theater producer, director, of East European Jewish parentage. Papirofsky began using the short form of his name in the 1950s and legally adopted it in 1959.

Papus: Gérard Anaclet Vincent Encausse (1865–1916), Fr. occultist. The practitioner took his name from the genius of medicine in Apollonius of Tyana's *Nyktemeron* ("Night and Day") (1st century AD).

El **Paquiro:** Francisco Montes Reina (1804–1851), Sp. bullfighter. In more recent times the name was adopted by Adolfo Ávila Ramires (1941–).

Paracelsus: Philippus Aureolus Theophrastus Bombastus von Hohenheim (1493–1541), Swiss-Ger. physician, alchemist. The medical genius and philosopher regarded himself as greater than the Roman 1st-century physician Celsus. He was therefore "beyond Celsus" (Greek *para*, "beyond"). Equally, the name could allude to his original surname (a placename), as Latin *celsus* and German *hohen* both mean "high," "lofty." Paracelsus appears to have fancied the *para-* prefix, and used it in the titles of his *Paramirum* and *Paragranum*. (In his original name, Bombastus was a nickname for his bombastic and often erroneous statements.)

Sergei **Paradjanov:** Sarkis Paradjanian (1924–1990), Georgian movie director.

Domenico **Paradies:** Pietro Domenico Paradisi (1701–1791), It. composer, working in England.

Swami **Paramarubyananda:** Jules Monchanin (1895–1957), Fr. priest. In 1939, after serving as a chaplain to the poor, Monchanin left for India, where he was joined by a fellow priest, Henri Le Saux. Together they founded an ashram, Monchanin taking the name Paramarubyananda, "bliss of the supreme spirit," from Sanskrit *parama*, "supreme," *arubya*, "spirit," and *ananda*, "bliss." Le Saux himself took the name **Abhishiktananda**. Swami is a title meaning "master," "prince."

Paul **Paray:** M.A. Charles (1886–1979), Fr. orchestral conductor, composer.

M. **Pardoe:** Margot Mary Pardoe (1902–after 1960), Br. children's writer.

Paul **Paree** *see* Horatio **Nicholls**

Judith **Paris:** Judith Franklin (1944–), Br. stage, TV actress. The actress appears to have adopted the name of one of the main characters in the series of popular historical novels by Hugh Walpole, including *Judith Paris* (1931) itself.

Mica **Paris:** Michelle Wallen (1969–), Br. black soul singer, of Caribbean parentage.

Frank **Parish** *see* Rosalind **Erskine**

Harry **Parke** *see* **Parkyakarkus**

Cecil **Parker:** Cecil Schwabe (1897–1971), Br. movie actor.

Eric **Parker:** Frederick Moore Searle (1870–1955), Eng. journalist, writer.

Errol **Parker:** Raphael Schecroun (1925–1998), Algerian-born jazz musician, working in France, U.S. The musician changed his name in 1960 to avoid litigation while simultaneously recording for two different labels.

Frank **Parker:** Franciszek A. Pajkowski (1916–1997), U.S. tennis player.

Jean **Parker:** Luise-Stephanie Zelinska (1912–2005), U.S. movie actress, of Pol.-Fr. descent.

John **Parker:** Jacob Solomons (1875–1952), U.S.-born Br. theater historian, of Pol.-Welsh parentage. The editor and compiler of *Who's Who in the Theatre,* first published in 1912, changed his Jewish name on the advice of his mother. He legalized it in 1917.

Leslie **Parker:** Angela Margaret Thirkell, earlier McInnes, née Mackail (1890–1961), Eng. novelist. The writer adopted this male name for an early book, *Trooper to the Southern Cross* (1934), based on her passage to Australia on board a troopship with her second husband in 1920.

Lew **Parker:** Austin Lewis Jacobs (1907–1972), U.S. stage actor.

Suzy **Parker:** Cecilia Ann Renee Parker (1933–2003), U.S. model, movie actress. Parker's parents at first opposed the use of the family name in what they regarded as the vulgar industry of modeling, as they did for her older sister, Dorien **Leigh,** but had dropped their objections by the time she made her name in the 1950s.

"Colonel" Tom **Parker:** Andreas Cornelius van Kuijk (1909–1997), Du.-born U.S. music promoter. The promoter, famously Elvis Presley's manager (from 1955), stowed away at the age of 16 and sailed for America, where he reinvented himself under his new name. His honorary title of "Colonel" was bestowed on him in 1948 by Louisiana governor Jimmie Davis.

Trey **Parker:** Donald McKay Parker III (1972–), U.S. movie actor, director, songwriter.

Willard **Parker:** Worster van Eps (1912–1996), U.S. movie actor.

Lucas **Parkes** *see* John **Wyndham**

Norman **Parkinson:** Ronald William Parkinson Smith (1913–1990), Eng. photographer. The society photographer derived his name from the Norman Parkinson Portrait Studio that he set up with a colleague in 1934. The first name was that of the colleague, Norman Kibblewhite; the surname was his own third name. The business was short-lived, but when it ended he continued to use the name himself.

Bert **Parks:** Bert Jacobson (1914–1992), U.S. entertainer. The perennial master of ceremonies for the Miss America pageant changed his name to fit a marquee sign.

Larry **Parks:** Sam Kleusman Lawrence Parks (1914–1975), U.S. movie actor.

Parkyakarkus: Harry Einstein (1904–1958), U.S. radio, movie comedian, father of Albert **Brooks.** Einstein originally worked as Harry Parke. Later, he expanded and embellished this surname to "Parkyakarkus." He reckoned this would be a name easily remembered by Americans, who would recognize it as an invitation to take a seat: "Park your carcase!"

Peter **Parley:** (1) Samuel Griswold Goodrich (1793–1860), U.S. bookseller, writer of moral tales for children; (2) Thomas Tegg (1776–1845), Eng. bookseller, publisher; (3) George Mogridge (*see* **Old Humphrey**); (4) William Martin (1801–1867), Eng. children's writer; (5) John Bennett (1865–1956), U.S. writer of books for boys. A popular name for tellers of children's tales, as the name itself suggests. Goodrich was the first to use it, however, beginning with *The Tales of Peter Parley About America* (1827), which opens with the words, "Here I am! My name is Peter Parley! I am an old man. I am very gray and lame." It was then adopted by other writers on both sides of the Atlantic (first by Tegg in 1832 in England), which did not please its originator. Goodrich may have based the name itself on *Parley the Porter*, a moral tract by the English writer Hannah More, although according to his daughter he took it from French *parler*, "to talk."

"In the history of the world it would be impossible, we think, to find a more popular pseudonym than that of Peter Parley. Since 1828, one hundred and seventy volumes, bearing that name, or edited under it, have been issued. Of all these about 7,000,000 of volumes have been sold: about 300,000 volumes are now sold annually. Our plan precludes our giving the titles of these works, on almost every subject; but the curious reader will find a complete list in S.A. Allibone's *Cricitcal Dictionary of English Literature*, 1859" [Hamst, p. 96].

Dita **Parlo:** Grethe Gerda Kornstädt (1906–1971), Ger. movie actress. The name seems to have a reference to speaking (Italian *parlo*, "I speak"), perhaps in connection with the "talkies." It was adopted by rock singer **Madonna** for her persona in the 1992 album *Erotica* and for the narrator in her book *Sex*, published later that year, and in part gave the name of Dita **von Teese.**

Martine **Parmain:** Martine Hemmerdinger (1942–), Fr. ballet dancer. Hemmerdinger was born in the village of Parmain, north of Paris, and took her name from there.

Parmigianino: Girolamo Francesco Mazzola (1503–1540), It. painter. The artist took his name from Parma, the city of his birth. (The word is strictly speaking the adjectival diminutive of the name, so equates to "little Parmesan.")

Feliks **Parnell:** Feliks Grzibek (1898–?), Pol. ballet dancer.

Kostas **Paroritis:** Leonidas Sureas (1878–1931), Gk. writer.

Robert **Parr** *see* A.A. **Fair**

Aulus Janus **Parrhasius:** Giovan Paolo Parisio (1470–1522), It. philologist. The scholar assumed an approximate classical equivalent of his Italian name, apparently influenced by the 5th-century BC Greek painter Parrhasius.

Rebecca **Parris**: Ruth Blair MacCloskey (1951–), U.S. jazz singer.

Julie **Parrish**: Ruby Joyce Wilbar (1940–2003), U.S. movie actress.

Maxfield **Parrish**: Frederick Parrish (1870–1966), U.S. artist. Parrish initially took his paternal grandmother's maiden name, Maxfield, as his middle name. He then dropped his original first name.

Ellen **Parsons** *see* Crescent **Dragonwagon**

Gram **Parsons**: Ingram Cecil Connor III (1946–1973), U.S. country-rock musician. Connor's father committed suicide when he was only 13. His mother then married Robert Ellis Parsons, who shortened his stepson's first name to "Gram" and provided him with a new surname at the same time.

Louella **Parsons**: Louella Rose Oettinger (1884–1972), U.S. gossip columnist, movie actress.

Fidalma **Partenide**: Petronilla Paolini Massimi (1663–1726), It. poet. The poet's pseudonym is her Arcadian name (*see* Aglauro **Cidonia**).

Mrs. **Partington**: Benjamin Penhallow Shillaber (1814–1890), U.S. humorist. The humorist created this lady as a kind of Mrs. Malaprop for his *Life and Sayings of Mrs. Partington* (1854) and other books in which Mrs. Partington chats pleasantly yet ignorantly on a whole range of topics. There had been a real Mrs. Partington, it seems, who during a storm at Sidmouth, England (in 1824), had tried to brush back the sea with her mop. References to her abortive effort became legendary and metaphorical, so that the House of Lords was compared to her in a speech (1831) attacking that body's opposition to the progress of reform. Shillaber admitted that he borrowed his own character from the English archetype. He first used her in 1847 for a newspaper on which he was employed.

Anthony **Partridge**: Edward Phillips Oppenheim (1866–1946), Eng. novelist. Oppenheim wrote many thrillers under his real name, but used this pseudonym for five novels published between 1908 and 1912.

Elli **Parvo**: Elvira Gobbo (1915–), It. movie actress. The actress's screen name evolved from an earlier name, Elli Pardo, which she romanized because of its Jewish echoes. To an Italian ear, the earlier name would suggest *il leopardo*, "the leopard." "It was a name that recalled the pounce of a leopard, perfect for a woman who brandished her breasts with barbarous energy" [Masi and Lancia, p. 55].

Gabriel **Pascal**: Gabor Lehöl (1894–1954), Rom.-born movie producer, director, working in U.K.

Gisèle **Pascal**: Gisèle Tallone (1923–), Fr. stage, movie actress.

Paschal II: Rainerius (?–1118), It. pope.

Jules **Pascin**: Julius Pincas (1885–1930), Bulg.-born U.S. painter, of It.-Serbian/Sp. Jewish parentage, working in France. The artist adopted a more obviously French first name, then anagrammatized his surname likewise.

Teixeira de **Pascoaes**: Joaquim Pereira Teixeira de Vasconcelos (1877–1952), Port. writer.

Kalla **Pasha**: Joseph T. Rickard (?1877–1933), U.S. movie comedian.

La **Pasionaria**: Dolores Ibárruri (1895–1989), Sp. Communist leader, writer. The politician first used the name, literally "Passion Flower," when writing an anticlerical diatribe in the local Communist paper that was to appear in Passion Week. The name also implied her "impassioned" stance generally regarding social conditions and injustices. She herself was a miner's daughter.

Anthony **Pasquin**: John Williams (1761–1818), Eng. critic, satirist, working in U.S. The writer took the name from the statue called Pasquin in Rome. This was unearthed in 1501 as an incomplete Roman bust, and a habit became established of attaching satirical Latin verses to it on St. Mark's Day. From this practice came the term "pasquinade" to apply to any brief but anonymous satirical comment. It is not certain how the statue itself acquired its name. One theory is that it was named after a local shopkeeper whose premises were near the site where it was discovered.

Joe **Pass**: Joseph Anthony Jacobi Passalaqua (1929–1994), U.S. jazz guitarist.

Stève **Passeur**: Étienne Morin (1899–1966), Fr. journalist, playwright.

Passo: Pavel Alekseyevich Sokolov (1876–1947), Russ. conjurer. The illusionist also performed as Sokolov-Passo. His name represents syllables from his first and last names, but also suggests French *passe*, "pass," a word associated with card games and tricks, Sokolov's specialty.

Colonel **Passy**: André Lucien Charles Daniel Dewavrin (1911–1998), Fr. secret agent, working in England. When head of the second and third bureaux of the Free French Forces, handling intelligence and operations, the French colonel took his undercover name from the Passy Métro station in Paris.

George **Paston**: Emily Morse Symonds (*c*.1860–1936), Br. novelist, dramatist, cousin of writer John Addington Symonds (1840–1893).

Tony **Pastor**: (1) Antonio Pastori (1832–1908), U.S. variety performer, impresario; (2) Antonio Pestritto (1907–1969), U.S. jazz musician.

Pastorini: Charles Walmsley (1722–1797), Ir. Roman Catholic bishop, prophetic writer.

Giovanni **Pastrone**: Piero Fosco (1883–1959), It. movie director, producer.

Nee-Daku **Patato:** Darku Adams (1932–1995), Br. black conga drummer.

Patch: Sexton (*fl.*1530s), Eng. court jester. The name originated as a nickname for the household jester for Cardinal Wolsey, who "donated" him to Henry VIII. It probably derives from Italian *pazzo*, "fool," rather than the patches on the jester's clothes, and in turn gave a generic term for a domestic fool. "I know of no evidence to support the common view among Shakespeare's editors that the word derives from what they suppose to have been the 'patched dress' worn by fools of the time" [John Southworth, *Fools and Jesters at the English Court*, 1998].

Wally **Patch:** Walter Vinnicombe (1888–1971), Eng. stage, movie comedian.

P.V. **Pathy:** Pithamandalam Venkatachalapathy (1906–1961), Ind. maker of documentary movies.

Aunt **Patience:** Hanna Tracy Cutler (1815–1896), U.S. women's right leader, physician. Cutler supplemented her income in the medical profession by writing for local papers, using this name for a column of advice to farmgirls in the *Ohio Cultivator*.

Patra: Dorothy Smith (1972–), Jamaican DJ, reggae singer.

Jason **Patric:** Jason Patric Miller, Jr. (1966–), U.S. movie actor.

Gail **Patrick:** Margaret LaVelle Fitzpatrick (1911–1980), U.S. movie actress, TV producer.

John **Patrick:** John Patrick Goggan (1905–1995), U.S. playwright, screenwriter.

Nigel **Patrick:** Nigel Dennis Wemyss (1913–1981), Eng. stage actor, director.

Q. **Patrick:** Hugh Callingham Wheeler (1912–1987), Eng.-born U.S. playwright, mystery novelist. Wheeler used this pseudonym for nine mystery novels written with Richard Wilson Webb over the period 1936 to 1965. Another nine were coauthored under the name Jonathan Stagge, while Wheeler alone wrote 17 novels as Patrick Quentin.

Cissy **Patterson:** Elinor Josephine Pattison (1881–1948), U.S. editor, publisher. The businesswoman who in 1930 became editor and publisher of the *Washington Herald* altered the spelling of her first name to Eleanor and adopted Medill, her mother's maiden name, as her middle name before settling to Cissy Patterson, as the younger sister of the newspaper publisher Joseph Medill Patterson (1879–1946).

Olive **Patterson** *see* Fenton **Brockley**

Mike **Patto:** Michael Patrick McGrath (1942–1979), Sc.-born Br. rock musician.

Ted **Pauker:** George Robert Acworth Conquest (1917–), Eng. poet, editor, writer on Russia. This is the standard pen name of the British editor and writer Robert Conquest. Its exact origin is not clear, al-

though *Pauker* is German for "kettledrummer" and also has a slang sense "schoolteacher," "crammer." Conquest had some of his poems included under this name in *The New Oxford Book of Light Verse* (1978). Shortly before his contribution, there appears in the book a selection of limericks by one Victor Gray, who is given the same birth year as Pauker (1917). A *Sunday Times* columnist, in an informal review of the book (June 4, 1978), noticed that the name of the unknown rhymester contains the initials of Conquest's first three names, and that if you move these to the front of the name you get G.R.A. Victory, with a victory of course being a conquest. This sleuthwork may not have pleased the venerable Oxford University Press, which must have been congratulating itself on its connivance over the pun.

Juozas **Paukstēlis:** Juozas Ptasìnskas (1899–1981), Lithuanian writer.

Paul: Ray Hildebrand (1940–), U.S. pop singer, teaming with **Paula**.

[St.] **Paul:** Saul (AD *c.*1–*c.*69), Christian theologian, missionary. When the disciple and missionary was still a Jew he was known by the name of Saul. After his dramatic conversion he took the Roman name Paul, which he used for preference as a proud Roman citizen. (His binominal state is alluded to in Acts 13:9: "Saul, also called Paul.") Why did Saul choose this particular name? In Hebrew "Saul" means "asked for"; in Latin "Paul" (Paulus) means "little," and as such was a standard Roman name. The meaning of the new name may perhaps have been significant in some way, possibly as a sign of humility, but Paul could have chosen it simply because it was close in sound to his previous name. It certainly marked a transition: not only from Jew to Christian but also to Paul's new role as leader when Barnabas, the former leader, delegated it to him.

Paul II: Pietro Barbo (1417–1471), It. pope. Barbo took a new name that not only honored St. **Paul** but that avoided repeating the name of St. Peter, first bishop of Rome.

Paul III: Alessandro Farnese (1468–1549), It. pope.

Paul IV: Gian Pietro Carafa (1476–1559), It. pope.

Paul V: Camillo Borghese (1552–1621), It. pope.

Paul VI: Giovanni Battista Montini (1897–1978), It. pope. The pontiff chose a name intended to suggest an "outgoing" approach, like that of the missionary St. **Paul**, who was "all things to all men" (1 Corinthians 9:22), and put his resolve into practice by traveling more widely than any previous pope.

Andrew **Paul:** Paul Andrew Herman (1961–), Eng. movie, TV actor.

Billy **Paul:** Paul Williams (1934–), U.S. pop singer. The singer reversed his name, then substituted "Billy" for "William(s)." The change was necessary because there were two well-known namesakes: Paul Williams of the Temptations (1939–1973) and U.S. movie actor and singer Paul Williams (1940–).

Clarence **Paul:** Clarence Pauling (1928–1995), U.S. black Motown songwriter.

John **Paul:** Charles Henry Webb (1834–1905), U.S. journalist, editor. Webb first used this name in 1873 for the letters he wrote for the *New York Tribune*. The letters were published a year later as *John Paul's Book*, with the result that Webb became equally well known by this pseudonym.

Les **Paul:** Lester William Polfuss (1915–2009), U.S. jazz guitarist, teaming with Mary **Ford**, his wife.

Sean **Paul:** Sean Paul Henriques (1973–), Jamaican reggae musician.

Paula: Jill Jackson (1942–), U.S. pop singer, teaming with **Paul**. Paul and Paula originally teamed up to sing for a radio station's charity drive in Texas in the early 1960s, becoming a popular attraction with their matching sweaters embroidered with the letter "P."

Mme. **Paulette:** Pauline de la Bruyère, née Adam (1900–1984), Fr. milliner. The designer adopted the name Paulette on opening her second hat shop in 1929.

Father **Paulinus:** Johann Philipp Werdin (1748–1805), Austr. orientalist.

[St.] **Paul of the Cross:** Paolo Francesco Danei (1694–1775), It. priest. The founder in 1737 of the Passionists, formally the Congregation of Discalced Clerks of the Most Holy Cross and Passion of our Lord Jesus Christ, is known in his native Italy as S. Paolo della Croce.

Paulus: Paul Habans (1845–1908), Fr. music-hall performer.

Rose **Pauly:** Rose Pollak (1894–1975), Hung. opera singer.

Pauvre Lélian: Paul Verlaine (1844–1896), Fr. poet. This name, as if meaning "Poor Lélian," is an anagram of the poet's real name, which he assumed in his prose work *Les Poètes maudits* ("The Cursed Poets") (1884), short biographical studies of six poets, one being himself.

Pav: Francis Minet (1913–), Eng. cartoonist, stained glass artist.

Marisa **Pavan:** Marisa Pierangeli (1932–), It. movie actress, working in U.S., sister of Pier **Angeli**.

[Patriarch] **Pavle:** Gojko Stoycevic (1914–2009), Serbian churchman. The head of the Serbian Orthodox Church took his religious name (the equivalent of English Paul) on being tonsured a monk in 1948.

Lalita **Pawar:** Ambika Sagun (1918–1998), Ind. movie actress.

Pax: Mary Cholmondeley (1859–1925), Br. novelist.

Katina **Paxinou:** Katina Konstandopolou (1900–1973), Gk. stage, movie actress, working in U.S.

Philip **Paxton:** Samuel Adams Hammett (1816–1865), U.S. humorist, writer of adventure stories. Hammett introduced this pseudonym for his first book, *A Stray Yankee in Texas* (1853).

Johnny **PayCheck:** Donald Eugene Lytle (1938–2003), U.S. country musician. The singer's name is sometimes said to pun on that of his fellow country singer Johnny Cash (1932–2003). In fact he took it in 1965 from John Austin Paycheck, a Chicago prizefighter knocked out by Joe Louis in 1940.

Robert **Paye** *see* Marjorie **Bowen**

Alexander **Payne:** Alexander Papadopoulos (1961–), U.S. movie director.

Payrav: Atadzhan Sulaymoni (1899–1933), Tajik poet. The poet adopted a name meaning "faithful follower."

Howard **Payson:** Edward L. Stratemeyer (1862–1930), U.S. writer. The Stratemeyer Literary Syndicate set up in 1906 used this name for stories for boys featuring Boy Scouts.

Barbara **Payton:** Barbara Lee Redfield (1927–1967), U.S. movie actress.

Olyona **Pchilka:** Olga Petrovna Kosach, née Dragomanova (1849–1930), Ukr. writer. The writer's adopted name means "little bee," with Olyona a pet form of her first name Olga. She was the mother of Lesya **Ukrainka**.

Cora **Pearl:** Emma Elizabeth Crouch (1842–1886), Eng. socialite, courtesan. Emma Crouch was educated in France until the age of 13. "Coming to England in 1856, she was misled by an elderly admirer into a life of dissipation, and took the name of Cora Pearl" [*Dictionary of National Biography*].

Minnie **Pearl:** Sarah Ophelia Colley Cannon (1912–1996), U.S. country singer, entertainer.

Martin **Pearson** *see* David **Grinnell**

Harold **Peary:** Harold José Pereira de Faria (1908–1985), U.S. radio, movie comedian.

Andrey **Pechersky:** Pavel Ivanovich Melnikov (1818–1883), Russian writer. In 1852 Melnikov read his friend Vladimir Dal a story he had written. Dal liked the story, but the question then arose, how should its author sign himself? "'Father said he didn't want to sign with his real name,' recalls Melnikov's daughter. 'Use a pen name!' said Dal. 'What sort of pen name can I have? You lived by the Lugan River and called yourself Vladimir **Lugansky**. I live in Nizhny Novgorod, but it would be awkward to call myself "Nizhny Novgorodian."' Dal recalled that

Melnikov had signed an article in the *Nizhny Novgorod Provincial Gazette* as Andrey Pechersky, since he lived in a house owned by one Andreyev on Pechersky Street. He therefore advised him to adopt that as his name" [Dmitriyev, p. 92].

Santo Joseph Pecora: Santo Joseph Pecoraro (1902–1984), U.S. jazz trombonist.

Pedr Fardd: Peter Jones (1775–1845), Welsh hymnwriter, poet. The writer's bardic name means simply "Peter the bard."

Pedr Hir: Peter Williams (1847–1922), Welsh literary figure. The writer's name arose as a nickname meaning "tall Peter."

Pedrog: John Owen Williams (1853–1932), Welsh poet. The writer took his name from the village of Llanpedrog ("St. Petroc's church"), where he was raised.

John Peel: John Robert Parker Ravenscroft (1939–2004), Eng. DJ. Following radio work in the U.S., where he was obliged to drop the "s" from his awkward surname, the DJ needed a radically new name. "Now the whole surname was for the chop. It was suggested that three syllables might be trimmed to one.... The story as John always told it was that a secretary in the Radio London office ... uttered those words that were to change a man, a name and a way of life: 'Why don't you call him "John Peel"?' ... Once John was Peel, he never considered switching back to Ravenscroft in his professional life" [John Peel and Sheila Ravenscroft, *Margrave of the Marshes*, 2005]. The name is familiar to the British from the hunting character in John Woodcock Graves's 1820 poem so titled, with lines: "D'ye ken John Peel with his coat so gay? / D'ye ken John Peel at the break of the day? / D'ye ken John Peel when he's far, far away / With his hounds and his horn in the morning?" A DJ is often active "at the break of the day" with his "hounds" (enthusiasts) and his "horn" (music). But the reasoning may not have been this subtle.

Jan Peerce: Jacob Pincus Perelmuth (1904–1984), U.S. opera singer, of Russ. Jewish parentage. The tenor began singing regularly at Radio City Music Hall in 1933 and adopted his new name, after various provisional permutations, at the suggestion of theatrical entrepreneur Samuel **Rothafel**.

Bill Peet: William Bartlett Peed (1915–2002), U.S. movie animator, illustrator, children's writer.

Pegasus: Stanley Agate (1921–2005), Br. sports journalist. A stock name for a racing correspondent, from the flying horse of classical mythology. Agate joined the London *News of the World* in 1960.

Baby **Peggy** *see* Baby **Peggy**

Peg Leg Sam: Arthur Jackson (1911–1977), U.S. black blues musician. The singer and harmonica player wore a wooden leg as the result of an accident involving a train in 1930.

Pelé: Edson Arantes do Nascimento (1940–), Brazilian footballer. The player claimed that he never knew the origin of his "game name," and that it has no meaning in any language known to him. He was apparently nicknamed thus from the age of seven. He points out that it is easy to say in many languages [Pelé and Robert L. Fish, *My Life and the Beautiful Game*, 1977].

More detailed explanations exist. "The Brazilians have a penchant for pet nicknames, and Edson Arantes do Nascimento is a bit of a mouthful. His gift was recognized by many when he was a young boy playing in the back streets of Rio de Janeiro and Pelé affectionately means "ragamuffin" or "street urchin" [*The Times*, June 21, 2004]. However: "'Pelé' has no other meaning in Portuguese, which increases the sense that it is an international brand name, like Kodak or Compaq. The etymological origin of 'Pelé' is much discussed but still unclear. Edson was known as Dico at home. When he joined Santos [football club] he was called Gasolina, *Gasoline*. Then he became 'Pelé'" [Bellos, p.229].

Pelé has his own private theory. "There have been lots of stories that claim to explain how the name came about.... Does it come from the Gaelic for football? A nice story, but unlikely. Was it to do with a Turkish immigrant in Bauru, seeing me handball during a match and mangling the Portuguese for 'The foot, stupid!' Again, it seems far-fetched.

I can never be 100 per cent certain about the origin of Pelé, but the most probable version is this. It all started with a team-mate of my father's when he played for Vasco de São Lourenço. The team-mate was known as 'Bilé,' for complicated and very Brazilian reasons.... [As a young boy] I used to nip into the goal and play around, and whenever I managed to stop a shot I'd shout, 'Good one, Bilé!' or 'Great save, Bilé!' Because I was only young I somehow distorted the nickname and said that when I grew up I wanted to be a goalie like 'Pilé.' When we moved to Bauru, this 'Pilé' became 'Pelé.' Either I changed it myself or ... it was because of my thick Minas Gerais accent.... And then one boy ... started to tease me by calling me 'Pelé.' So thanks to that goalie Bilé ... I became Pelé" [Pelé with Orlando Duarte and Alex Bellos, *Pelé: The Autobiography*, translated from the Portuguese by Daniel Hahn, 2006].

Mrs. **Pelham:** Edith Juliet Rich Isaacs (1878–1956), U.S. editor, theater critic. Isaacs often used this name for articles in women's magazines such as the *Ladies' Home Journal*.

Mrs. (or Miss) Margaret **Pelham** *see* Abbé **Bossut**

Konrad **Pelicanus:** Konrad Kürschner (1478–1556), Swiss scholar. The theologian and librarian translated his German name, meaning "furrier," to a Latin equivalent (Late Latin *pellicia*, "cloak," which gave modern French *pelisse*, "fur-lined coat").

Pellegrin: Friedrich Heinrich Karl Fouqué, Freiherr de la Motte (1777–1843), Ger. romanticist, of Fr. descent. The writer used this name, meaning "pilgrim" (Italian *pellegrino*, French *pèlerin*), for some of his dramatic sketches.

A. **Pen, Esq.:** John Leech (1817–1864), Eng. caricaturist. An early name for the artist's sketches.

Pencerdd Gwalia: John Thomas (1826–1913), Welsh harpist. The musician's name means "chief poet of Wales." Pencerdd has long been the title of an officer of the Bardic Order who is in the employ of the king. Thomas was himself appointed harpist to Queen Victoria in 1871 and played for many of the royal courts of Europe. Gwalia is a half-Latin, half-Welsh name for Wales.

A.R. **Penck:** Ralf Winkler (1939–), Ger. artist.

Arthur **Pendenys:** Arthur L. Humphreys (1865–1946), Eng. editor, local historian. Humphreys adopted this name for his contributions to *Books of Today and Tomorrow*, of which he was editor from 1894 to 1924.

Mike **Pender:** Michael Prendergast (1942–), Eng. pop musician.

Dic **Penderyn:** Richard Lewis (*c.*1807–1831), Welsh martyr. Lewis, from the village of Penderyn, was hanged for his part in the Merthyr Rising of 1831 although widely believed to be innocent.

Pendragon: Henry Sampson (1841–1891), Eng. newspaper proprietor, editor, sporting writer. Pendragon was the title given to an ancient British or Welsh chief, and meant literally "head dragon," the "dragon" being the war standard. Sampson may have used the name with an implied pun on "dragon with a pen."

Amabel **Penfeather:** Susan Fenimore Cooper (1813–1894), U.S. novelist, writer. The daughter of James Fenimore **Cooper** used this name for her first novel, *Elinor Wyllys; or, the Young Folk of Longbridge* (1845). The name itself suggests the writer of a romantic tale, which she effectively was.

Richard **Penlake:** Percy R. Salmon (1872–1959), Eng. journalist, writer on photography.

Dan **Penn:** Wallace Daniel Pennington (1941–), U.S. popular songwriter.

Joe **Penner:** Joe Pinter (1904–1941), Hung.-U.S. radio comedian, movie actor.

Patience **Pennington:** Elizabeth Waties Allston Pringle (1845–1921), U.S. writer. Pringle used this name for letters about her life and work on a South Carolina rice plantation, published weekly in the *New York Sun* from 1904 to 1907.

Guy **Penseval** *see* Geoffrey **Crayon, jun.**

Pennsylvania Farmer: John Dickinson (1732–1800), U.S. lawyer, political writer. The Philadelphia lawyer led the conservative group in the Pennsylvania legislature during the debates on proprietary government, and used the name for his *Letters from a Farmer in Pennsylvania* (1768), published in the *Pennsylvania Chronicle*. The letters criticized England's continuing assertion of its rights of taxation, saying that this was contrary to that country's own constitutional principles.

Margaret **Penrose** *see* Clarence **Young**

Richard **Penrose:** Richard James Jackson Pace (1941–), Br. psychiatrist. The specialist adopted his mother's maiden name by deed poll in 1968.

Hugh **Pentecost:** Judson Pentecost Philips (1903–1989), U.S. crime, mystery writer. Philips took his pseudonym on winning the Dodd Mead "Red Badge" prize competition in 1939 with *Cancelled in Red*. He also wrote as Philip Owen.

Ebenezer **Pentweazle** *see* Mrs. Mary **Midnight**

Willie **Pep:** Gugliermo Papaleo (1922–2006), U.S. featherweight boxer. Better "Pep" (for vigor) than "Pap" (for softness).

Pepe: Juan Alberto Schiaffino (1925–2002), Uruguayan footballer.

Pepe-Hillo: José Delgado y Gálvez (1754–1801), Sp. bullfighter.

Pepete: José Rodríguez y Rodríguez (1824–1862), Sp. bullfighter, great-uncle of **Manolete**. The name later passed to other matadors, such as José Claro (1883–1915) and José Puerta (1924–1955).

K.N. **Pepper:** James W. Morris (*fl.*1858), U.S. journalist, humorist. The writer used this name for *The K.N. Pepper Papers* (1858), the name itself a fairly obvious pun on "cayenne pepper," implying pungency and wit.

Paul **Peppergrass:** [Rev. Dr.] John Boyce (1810–1864), Ir. novelist, working in U.S.

Pip **Pepperpod:** Charles Warren Stoddard (1843–1909), U.S. traveler, poet.

Percerdd Eos Alban: Antoinette MacKinlay, née Sterling (1843–1904), U.S.–born Br. concert singer. This is the Welsh bardic name as it appears in *Who's Who* for Madame Antoinette Sterling, as she came to be known. Percerdd is apparently an error for Welsh *pencerdd*, "head poet," an early bardic title (as for **Pencerdd Gwalia**), while *eos* is "nightingale" and *alban* "solstice."

Philemon **Perch:** Richard Malcolm Johnson (1822–1909), U.S. humorous writer, educator.

Percival: Julian Ralph (1853–1903), U.S. journalist.

Charles Henry **Percy** *see* C.L. **Anthony**

Edward **Percy:** Edward Percy Smith (1891–1968), Br. playwright, novelist.

Florence **Percy:** Elizabeth Allen, formerly Akers, earlier Taylor, née Chase (1832–1911), U.S. poet, literary editor. The author used this name for her first book of poems, *Forest Buds, from the Woods of Maine* (1856), and subsequently for her most famous single poem, "Rock Me to Sleep, Mother," first printed in the *Saturday Evening Post* in 1860. The pseudonym used for this sentimental hymn to motherhood sparked a dispute over its authorship, which Mrs. Akers had to fight hard to win.

Elizabeth Ann Chase had three husbands: Marshall Taylor (married 1851, divorced 1857), Benjamin "Paul" Akers (married 1860, he died 1861), Elijah M. Allen (married 1865).

Reuben **Percy:** Thomas Byerley (?–1826), Eng. writer, journalist. Together with Joseph Clinton Robertson (1788–1852), who adopted the name Sholto Percy, Byerley published the popular *Percy Anecdotes*, which appeared in 20 volumes from 1821 to 1823. The cover announced that the collection was by "Sholto and Reuben Percy, brothers of the Benedictine monastery of Mount Benger." The name actually came from the Percy coffee house in Rathbone Place, London, where the two men regularly met. Byerley also used the name Stephen Collet for another collection, *Relics of Literature* (1823).

Sholto **Percy** *see* Reuben **Percy**

Thomas **Percy:** Thomas Piercy (1729–1811), Eng. churchman, poet. The literary scholar, famous for his collection of ballads, sonnets, historical songs, and metrical romances entitled *Reliques of Ancient English Poetry*, popularly, "Percy's *Reliques*" (1765), was a selfmade man who rose to be bishop of Dromore (in Ireland). The slight but subtle name change enabled him to claim descent from the aristocratic Percy family.

Essayist **Alpha of the Plough** commented: "I have never thought so well of Bishop Percy ... since I discovered that his real name was Piercy, and that, being the son of a grocer, he knocked his 'i' out and went into the Church, in order to set up a claim to belong to the house of the Duke of Northumberland. He even put the Percy arms on his monument in Dromore Cathedral, and, not content with changing his own name, altered the maiden name of his wife from Gutteridge to Godriche. I am afaid Bishop Percy was a snob" ["On Being Called Thompson," *Leaves in the Wind*, 1920].

Perdita: (1) Charlotte Lennox, née Ramsay (*c*.1730–1804), Eng. writer; (2) Mary Robinson, née Darby (1758–1800), Eng. actress, writer. The name is familiar in literature as that of the heroine of Shakespeare's *The Winter's Tale*, so called because she was abandoned as an infant by order of her father, Leontes, and was thus "the lost one" (Latin *perdita*).

On December 3, 1779, Mary Robinson played the part of Perdita in the play and her performance so charmed the 18-year-old Prince of Wales (later George IV) that he fell in love with her and permanently nicknamed her after the character. She adopted the name as a pseudonym, calling the Prince "Florizel," after Perdita's suitor in the play. Other well-known names adopted by Robinson were Tabitha **Bramble** and Anne Frances **Randall**, while a third was Laura Maria, combining her own name with that of the woman who inspired Petrarch's poetry.

Père ... For names beginning thus, see the next word, e.g. for Père Anselme see **Anselme**, for Père Duchesne see **Duchesne**, for Père Hippolyte see **Hippolyte**, etc.

La **Peregrina:** Gertrudis Gómez de Avellaneda (1814–1873), Cuban-born Sp. playwright, poet. The writer adopted this name, meaning "The Pilgrim," for her early poems, collected in 1841.

Valery **Pereleshin:** Valery Frantsevich Salatko-Petrishche (1913–1992), Russ. poet, working in China, Brazil.

Shimon **Peres:** Shimon Perski (1923–), Pol.-born Israeli prime minister.

Peret: Pedro Pubill Calaf (1935–). Sp. (Catalan) gypsy singer.

Danilo **Perez:** Danilo Enrico Perez Samudio (1966–), Panamanian-born jazz pianist, composer, working in U.S.

Giovanni Battista **Pergolesi:** Giovanni Battista Draghi (1710–1736), It. composer. The musician was born in the family home at Jesi, near Ancona. When the family moved to Pergola, however, they became known as *i Pergolesi*, the "Pergola people."

Nick **Perido** *see* Perry **Como**

François **Périer:** François-Gabriel-Marie Pilu (1919–2002), Fr. stage, movie actor.

Perino del Vaga: Pietro Bonaccorsi (*c*.1501–1547), It. painter. The artist adopted the name of a minor painter with whom he worked after studying with Ridolfo Ghirlandaio, son of Domenico **Ghirlandaio**.

Paul **Periwinkle:** Percy Bolingbroke St. John (1821–1889), Eng. journalist, newspaper editor.

Jacobus **Perizonius:** Jakob Voorbroek (1651–1715), Du. classical scholar. The scholar adopted a Greek equivalent of his family name, meaning "belted around," "aproned."

Carl **Perkins:** Carl Lee Perkings (1932–1998), U.S. country, "rockabilly" singer.

Eli **Perkins:** Melville De Lancey Landon (1839–1910), U.S. journalist, humorous lecturer. The humorist was given his pseudonym by Artemus **Ward**, who associated the name with someone who had "dry philosophical ideas, original and startling."

Elizabeth **Perkins:** Elizabeth Pisperikos (1960–), U.S. movie actress, of Gk. parentage.

Perley: Benjamin Perley Poore (1820–1897), U.S. journalist, author, biographer.

Barry **Perowne:** Philip Atkey (1908–1985), Eng. crime, adventure, mystery-story writer. The author adopted his uncle's name as his pen name.

Gigi **Perreau:** Ghislaine Elizabeth Marie Thérèse Perreau-Saussine (1941–), U.S. movie actress, of Fr.–U.S. parentage, sister of Peter **Miles.**

Lynne **Perrie:** Jean Dudley (1931–2006), Eng. TV actress, cabaret singer.

Jacques **Perrin:** Jacques Simonet (1941–), Fr. movie director, producer.

Anne **Perry:** Juliet Marion Hulme (1938–), Br. crime novelist. Hulme took a new identity after serving a prison sentence of just over five years for murder as a 15-year-old schoolgirl in New Zealand. (She and her best friend, Pauline Parker, killed Pauline's mother so that Pauline would be sent to live with Juliet. Their story is told in the 1994 movie *Heavenly Creatures*, with Kate Winslet playing Perry.)

Edgar A. **Perry:** Edgar Allan Poe (1809–1849), U.S. poet, short-story writer. This was the name under which the writer enlisted in the U.S. Army in 1827, after publishing a booklet titled *Tamerlane and Other Poems*, "By a Bostonian," after his birth town. Although now generally known as Edgar Allan Poe (his middle name was that of John Allan, who became his guardian when he was three years old), he invariably signed his writings as Edgar A. Poe.

Katy **Perry:** Katheryn Elizabeth Hudson (1984–), U.S. pop singer. The singer adopted her mother's maiden name so as not to be confused with U.S. movie actress Kate Hudson (1979–).

Luke **Perry:** Coy Luther Perry III (1964–), U.S. movie actor.

Margaret **Perry:** Margaret Hall Frueauff (1913–), U.S. stage actress, theatrical director. The actress took her mother's maiden name as her stage name.

Peregrine **Persic:** James Justinian Morier (1780–1849), Turk.-born Eng. traveler, writer. The writer used this name for his oriental tale *The Adventures of Hajji Baba of Ispahan* (1824). The name itself means "Persian pilgrim."

Louis **Persuis:** Luc de Loiseau (1769–1819), Fr. composer, violinist.

Camille **Pert:** Louise Hortense Grillet (1865–1952), Fr. romantic novelist.

Pertinax: Charles Joseph André Géraud (1882–1974), Fr. press correspondent, journalist, writing in French and English. The Latin byname means "holding fast," implying one who has firm opinions.

Perugino: Pietro di Cristoforo Vannucci (*c.*1448–1523), It. painter. The artist was mainly active in the city of Perugia, near which he was born. Hence his name.

Leonid Solomonovich **Pervomaysky:** Ilya Shlyomovich Gurevich (1908–1973), Ukr. writer. The writer's assumed name means "Mayday." He was born on May 4.

M. **Pery:** Maria Pauline Augusta Pferdemenges (1872–?), Ger. organist, concert pianist, composer.

Ladislav **Pešek:** Ladislav Pech (1906–), Cz. movie actor.

Pesellino: Francesco di Stefano (*c.*1422–1457), It. painter. The artist was raised by his grandfather, Giuliano il Pesello, who also painted, and worked as his assistant until the old man's death in 1446. His name comes from him, with the diminutive *-ino* suffix implying "little."

Rose **Pesotta:** Rachelle Peisoty (1896–1965), Ukr.-born U.S. labor organizer, autobiographer. In 1913 the union officer emigrated to the United States, where her name was changed at Ellis Island.

[St.] **Peter:** Simon (or Simeon) (AD ?–*c.*64), Christian leader, pope. Peter was the first of the disciples to be called by Jesus, and his "primacy" was affirmed at Caesarea Philippi when, as Simon, son of Jonah, he acknowledged Jesus as "the Christ, the Son of the living God" (Matthew 16:16). It was then that he was given his new name, with Jesus saying to him, "Blessed art thou, Simon Bar-jona: for flesh and blood hath not revealed it unto thee, but my Father which is in heaven. And I say unto thee, That thou art Peter, and upon this rock I will build my church" (17–18). The name is a play on words, for Greek *petros*, Latin *petrus*, and Aramaic (Christ's vernacular tongue) *képha* all mean "rock." The Aramaic word gave Peter's alternate name: "And when Jesus beheld him, he said, Thou art Simon, the son of Jona: thou shalt be called Cephas, which is by interpretation, A stone" (John 1:42).

Rhoda **Peter** *see* **H.D.**

Peter III: Karl Peter Ulrich (Herzog) von Holstein-Gottorp (1728–1762), Ger.-born Russ. emperor. The heir to the Russian throne was renamed in 1742 on being received into the Russian Orthodox Church. He was the grandson of Peter the Great, and already bore his name.

Peter and Gordon: Peter Asher (1944–), Eng. pop musician + Gordon Waller (1945–), Sc. pop musician.

David **Peterley:** Richard Pennington (1904–?), Eng. writer.

Peter Martyr: (1) Pietro Martire d'Anghiera (1457–1526), It. historian; (2) Pietro Martire Vermigli (1500–1562), It. ecclesiastic. Both men have come to be known by the English equivalent of their two first names. Vermigli's father had lost many children and had vowed to dedicate to the 13th-century St. Peter Martyr any that lived.

Peter, Paul and Mary: Peter Yarrow (1938–), U.S. folk musician + Noel "Paul" Stookey (1937–), U.S. folk musician + Mary Allin Travers (1936–2009), U.S. folksinger. The trio made their debut in 1961, basing their stage name on the song "Peter, Paul and Moses Playing Ring Around the Roses."

Bernadette Peters: Bernadette Lazzara (1948–), U.S. stage actress, singer, of It.–U.S. parentage. The actress changed her name at the age of 10.

Brock Peters: George Brock Fisher (1927–2005), U.S. black movie actor.

Elizabeth Peters: Barbara Louise Mertz, née Gross (1927–), U.S. mystery writer.

Ellis Peters: Edith Mary Pargeter (1913–1995), Br. crime writer, historical novelist. Pargeter reserved this name for her detective fiction, begining with *Death Mask* (1959). Ellis was the name of her brother, while Peters came from Petra, the name of the daughter of a close friend in Czechoslovakia whom she had met in World War II while serving in the Women's Royal Naval Service. She also wrote as Peter Benedict, Jolyon Carr, and John Redfern.

Ludovic Peters: Peter Ludwig Brent (1931–1984), Br. writer.

Roberta Peters: Roberta Petermann (1930–), U.S. opera singer.

Susan Peters: Suzanne Carnahan (1921–1952), U.S. movie actress.

Peters and Lee: Leonard Sergeant (1933–1992), Eng. popular singer + Dianne Lee (*c.*1950–), Eng. popular singer. The pop duo, noted for their romantic ballads, were not husband and wife, as sometimes said.

Master Joe Petersen: Mary Lethbridge, née O'Rourke (1913–1964), Sc. "boy" soprano. As a teenager, Mary O'Rourke went to live in London with her aunt Minnie Irvine and her husband Edward Stebbings. In his youth, Stebbings had performed on the halls as "Master Edward Frisby," and was training his son to take up a similar singing career. When the son's voice broke in 1933, Stebbings persuaded Mary Lethbridge (as she now was) to impersonate a boy's voice under his tutelage. She did so, and between 1933 and 1942 made several recordings as "Master Joe Petersen, the Phenomenal Boy Singer."

Miska Petersham: Mihaly Petrezselyen (1888–1960), Hung.-born U.S. writer, illustrator of children's books. Petersham worked jointly with his U.S. wife, Maud Sylvia Petersham, née Fuller (1889–1971).

Gilles Peterson: Gilles Moerhle (1964–), Br. rock musician, of Fr.-Swiss parentage.

Olaus Petri: Olof Peterson (1493–1552), Swe. clergyman.

Rhone Petrie *see* Clare **Curzon**

Ivailo Petrov: Prodan Kyuchukov (1923–), Bulg. writer.

Ivan Petrov: Ivan Ivanovich Krause (1920–), Russ. opera singer.

Valeri Petrov: Valeri Nisim Mevorakh (1920–), Bulg. screenwriter, poet.

Vladimir Petrov: Afanasy Shorokov (1907–1991), Russ. spy, working in Australia. Following his defection, the former consul at the Soviet Australian embassy lived under the name Sven Allyson.

Ye. Petrov: Yevgeny Petrovich Katayev (1903–1942), Russ. satirical writer, teaming with I. **Ilf.**

Olga Petrova: Muriel Harding (1886–1977), Br.-born movie actress, working in U.S.

Ludmila Petrowa: Ludmila Petrovna Nacheyeva (1942–), Russ. ballet dancer, teacher, working in Austria. The dancer dropped her surname for professional purposes, then modified her patronymic (middle name) to resemble a surname, with a westernized spelling ("w" for "v").

Gypsy Petulengro: Walter Leon Lloyd (?–1957), Br. herbalist, broadcaster. The identity of the "BBC Gypsy," as he came to be known, was long uncertain but was probably as given here. His childhood was spent in Hungary and Romania, and it is possible he was born there. He claimed to be the grandson of the English gypsy Ambrose Smith (1804–1878), fictionalized as Jasper Petulengro in George Borrow's novels *Lavengro* (1851) and *The Romany Rye* (1857). He spent some time in the United States, where he sold herbal remedies under the name Professor Thompson-Thompson. The name Petulengro itself means "shoe-smith," so equates to Smith's surname.

Borrow's *Lavengro* means "wordsmith," and was the nickname given Borrow himself in his youth by Smith: "'We'll no longer call you Sap-engro [Snake Master], brother,' said he, 'but rather Lav-engro, which in the language of the Gorgios meaneth Word Master.'"

K.M. Peyton: Kathleen Wendy Peyton, née Herald (1929–), Eng. children's writer. Peyton completed her first novel, *Sabre, The Horse from the Sea*, at the age of 15, and it was published four years later under her maiden name of Kathleen Herald. By then she was studying at Manchester Art School, where she eloped with a fellow student, Michael Peyton. They married in 1950 and began producing "potboiler" adventure stories together for a Boy Scout magazine, and these were published under the name of K. and M. Peyton. Three of the stories were subsequently published in book form, but their publisher did not want two authors' names on the title page, so they were stated to be by K.M. Peyton.

Peyo: Pierre Culliford (1928–1992), Belg. cartoonist.

Carlos **Pezoa Véliz**: Carlos Moyano Yaña (1879–1908), Chilean poet.

Phelix: Hugh Burnett (1924–), Eng. TV producer, cartoonist, writer. The artist adopted this name for his work as a freelance cartoonist.

Elizabeth Stuart **Phelps**: Mary Gray Phelps (1844–1911), U.S. feminist, writer. The writer assumed her mother's name at some point after the latter's death in 1852. In 1888 Phelps married Herbert Dickinson Ward but generally remains known by her maiden name.

Phi: Paul Henderson (1959–), Br. crossword compiler. The setter's pseudonym is the name of the Greek letter represented in English by *ph*, his initials.

Phiber Optik: Mark Abene (1972–), U.S. computer hacker. The telephone and computer technician took a (respelled) self-descriptive name. Fiber optics play a key role in telecommunications.

Jacob **Philadelphia**: Jacob Meyer (1721–*c*.1800), U.S.–born conjuror, of Pol. Jewish parentage, working in Germany. The magician adopted the name of his home town.

Philanactophil: Edmund Bolton (?1575–after 1634), Eng. historian, poet. The academic created this name for *The Roman Histories of Lucius Julius Florus* (1619). As for the name itself, at the end of the dedication to the Duke of Buckingham: "This word, which Bolton often used afterwards, was invented by himself, and may be interpreted 'friend of the king's friend'" [*Dictionary of National Biography*].

Philander von Sittewald: Johann Michael Moscherosch (1601–1669), Ger. satirist. The Lutheran writer used this name for his best-known work, *Die Wunderliche and Wahrhaftige Gesichte Philanders von Sittewald* ("The Wondrous and True Visions of Philander von Sittewald") (1641–3), based on *Los sueños* ("The Dreams") (1627) by the Spanish writer Francisco de Quevedo y Villegas. Philander ("loving a man," from the Greek, an epithet properly applied to a woman, but popularly taken as "loving man") is a name found in literature from the 16th century. Thus in Ariosto's *Orlando Furioso* (1532) Filandro is loved (and ruined) by Gabrina, while in John Fletcher's comedy *The Laws of Candy* (1647) one of the characters is defined as "Philander Prince of Cyprus, passionately in love with Erota." In 17th-century ballads, Philander is traditionally paired with the country maiden Phyllis, as in *The faithful Lovers Downfal; or, The Death of Fair Phillis Who Killed her self for loss of her Philander* (*c*.1682).

Philaretus: Arnold Geulincx (1624–1669), Flemish philosopher. The metaphysician's mock-Greek pseudonym means "lover of virtue." One of his principal works was *De Virtute* ("On Virtue") (1665).

Kim **Philby**: Harold Adrian Russell Philby (1912–1988), Br. intelligence officer, Soviet spy. Philby was born in India as the son of an English officer of the Indian Civil Service. "Kim" was a childhood nickname, alluding to the eponymous young hero of Rudyard Kipling's *Kim* (1901), who passes as a native Indian boy and later becomes a secret agent on behalf of the British government.

Phileleutharus Devoniensis: Thomas Northmore (1766–1851), Eng. scientist, local historian. Northmore was born in the county of Devon. Hence his classical-style name, meaning "Devon freedom-lover," which he used for *Memoirs of Planetes; or, A Sketch of the Laws and Manners of Makar* (1795).

Phileleutharus Norfolciensis: [Dr.] Samuel Parr (1747–1825), Eng. pedagogue, classical scholar. Most of Parr's works were virtually unreadable in his own time, let alone today. But this is just one of the typical classical pseudonyms that he used, in this instance for a *Discourse on the Late Fast* (1781), in which the theme (or one of them) is the American Revolution. The part-Greek, part-Latin name means "Norfolk freedom-lover." At the time of writing, Parr was a curate in Norwich in that county. For a later work, published in 1809, he was Philopatris Varvicensis, otherwise "Warwick country-lover."

Philenia: Sarah Wentworth Morton, née Apthorp (1759–1846), U.S. novelist, poet. Mrs. Morton used the full pen name "Philenia, a Lady of Boston" for *Ouâbi; or, The Virtues of Nature* (1790), a tale in four cantos celebrating the Native American as "noble savage," as well as other, similar works. The name Philenia is perhaps based on Greek *philenor*, "affectionate" (literally "loving one's husband"). She earlier used the name Constantia for her first poems, published in the *Massachusetts Magazine* in 1789.

François-André **Philidor**: François-André Danican (1726–1795), Fr. composer, chessplayer. Both François-André and his father André took their name from the sobriquet, Philidor, originally given to an ancestor, Michel Danican (?–*c*.1659), by Louis XIII as a compliment to his musical skill. The name itself was that of Filidori, a famous Italian oboist. As a name in its own right, Philidor can be appropriately understood to mean "fond of giving," "bountiful."

Philip: (1) Metacom (?–1676), U.S. Native American chief; (2) John Randolph (1773–1833), U.S. senator ("John Randolph of Roanoke"). The leader of the Wampanoag tribe of New England was renamed Philip by English colonists in 1662, while his elder brother, Wamsutta, became Alexander, the names being those of the rulers of ancient Macedonia. Philip's subsequent battle against the colonists became known as King Philip's War (1675–6). Randolph, a keen horse breeder and racehorse owner, adopted his pen name, meaning "horse lover," for his writings on horses in *The American Farmer* and *American Turf Register and Sporting Magazine.*

Gérard **Philipe:** Gérard Philip (1922–1959), Fr. movie actor.

Philippe: Jacques Talon (1802–1878), Fr. magician.

Maître **Philippe de Lyon:** Nizier Anthelme Philippe Vachot (1849–1905), Fr. healer. Although born in Savoy, the so-called miracle worker lived for most of his life near Lyon, in southeastern France.

Frederick **Philipse:** Vrydrych Flypse (1626–1702), Du.-born U.S. merchant, political leader.

Conrad **Phillips:** Conrad Philip Havord (1925–), Eng. movie, TV actor.

Esther **Phillips:** Esther Mae Jones (1935–1984), U.S. black R&B singer. The singer's career began in 1949, at age 13, when she won a talent contest in Los Angeles, singing under the name Little Esther. She was then out of show business for much of the 1950s, and on resuming her career in the early 1960s was too old to continue as Little Esther. She thus needed a new name, and is said to have picked it after noticing a Phillips 66 gasoline billboard at a gas station.

Flip **Phillips:** Joseph Edward Filipelli (1915–2001), U.S. jazz musician.

John **Phillips:** William John Vassall (1920–1996), Eng. Soviet spy. The former British Embassy official was convicted of espionage in 1962 and adopted this unremarkable name on his release from jail ten years later.

Leon **Phillips** *see* Samuel **Edwards**

Lou Diamond **Phillips:** Lou Diamond Upchurch (1962–), U.S. movie actor, director, of multiracial origin. The actor was born in the Philippines.

Rog **Phillips:** Roger Phillips Graham (1909–1965), U.S. SF writer.

Utah **Phillips:** Bruce Duncan Phillips (1935–2008), U.S. folksinger. The singer, born in Ohio but raised in Utah, adopted his name (originally in the form U. Utah Phillips) in honor of one of his musical heroes, country singer T. Texas **Tyler**.

William **Phillips:** William Livitsky (1907–2002), U.S. political editor, of East European Jewish parentage. Phillips' coeditor on the leftwing *Partisan Review* was Philip **Rahv**.

Philokuon: Arthur Croxton Smith (1865–1952), Eng. authority on dogs. Smith adopted this name, Greek for "dog lover," for a number of articles on canine subjects.

René **Philombe:** Philippe-Louis Ombede (1930–), Cameroonian author, writing in French.

Philomela: Elizabeth Rowe, née Singer (1674–1737), Eng. writer, poet. Elizabeth Singer used this name for a succession of poems published between 1691 and 1697 and collected in *Poems on Several Occasions, by Philomela* (1696). The name is that of Philomela in Greek mythology, who was changed into a nightingale, a bird noted for its song. Hence her name, from Greek words meaning "love of song." The name is appropriate for any poet, and for Rowe happens to accord well with her maiden name.

Philomena: Florence Fenwick Miller (1854–1935), Eng. writer. Florence Miller was born on the day of the Battle of Inkerman in the Crimean War and was named for Florence Nightingale. Hence her adoption of her pseudonym, from an alternate name of **Philomela** in classical mythology.

Philomneste Junior: Pierre-Gustave Brunet (1807–1896), Fr. bibliographer. Brunet used this name, apparently intended to mean "lover of courtship," for two books: *Les Fous littéraires* ("Literary Madmen") (1880) and *Livres perdus* ("Lost Books") (1882). Together with a fellow bibliographer, Octave Delpierre, he edited a work called *Bibliothèque Bibliophilo-Facétieuse* ("Bibliophilo-Facetious Library") under the joint name Les frères Gébéodé, representing the French spoken form of the two men's initials (G.B., O.D.).

Philo Pacificus: Noah Worcester (1758–1837), U.S. clergyman, editor, pacifist. The classical-style name means "peacelover," and was used by Worcester for his pamphlet *A Solemn Review of the Custom of War* (1814) as well as other pacifist works.

Philopatris Varvicensis *see* **Phileleutharus Norfolciensis**

Joan **Phipson:** Joan Margaret Fitzhardinge (1912–), Austral. children's writer.

Phiz: Hablôt Knight Browne (1815–1882), Eng. painter, illustrator, cartoonist. The artist originally used the name Nemo (Latin for "nobody") to illustrate some plates for Charles Dickens's *Pickwick Papers* (1836). Later, he chose a name designed to match Dickens's own pseudonym, **Boz**. At the same time, "phiz" is (or was) a colloquial word meaning "face" ("physiognomy"), so is appropriate in its own right for one who draws portraits and concentrates on facial expressions. Phiz's son was A. **Nobody**.

Joaquin **Phoenix:** Joaquin Bottom (1974–), U.S. movie actor. The actor's hippie parents, John Bottom and Arlyn Sharon Dunetz, who had met in California in the 1960s, changed their name to Phoenix in 1977 to mark a new beginning on returning to the States from South America. Movie actor River Phoenix (1970–1993), originally River Bottom, was their firstborn, named after the river of life in Herman Hesse's counterculture novel *Siddhartha* (1922). Daughter Rain followed in 1972, Joaquin three years later, another daughter, Liberty, in 1976, and a third daughter, Summer, in 1978.

As a toddler, Joaquin took to calling himself Leaf. "I was probably around five and I went outside and saw my dad was raking leaves. He was always raking leaves. I'm told that's why I decided on the name, but I have difficulty in believing that. It was more to do with the fact that no one could pronounce my name ... I'd have to say it a few times and that was an annoyance. 'No, it's not "walkin" or "walking"'" [*Sunday Times Magazine*, September 1, 2002]. So why change it back? "Well, when I was 15 I went to Mexico, so I had the opposite problem because Leaf would not work in Spanish. Leaf in Spanish is *oja* and then *ajo* is garlic and *ojo* is eye. So I would always get them confused and introduce myself either as garlic or eye, and then I would be known as *el stupido*. By the time I was doing [the 1995 movie] *To Die For*, I had switched to Joaquin and I remember [director] Gus [Van Sant] saying, 'So you're going for the big shift. Now you're Joaquin.' But I hadn't seen it that way. To be honest, I think I just really like my name" [ibid.].

John **Phoenix** *see* **Squibob**

Pat **Phoenix**: Patricia Pilkington (1923–1986), Ir.-born Br. TV actress. The actress who became familiar to millions as the brassy Elsie Tanner in *Coronation Street*, British television's longest-running soap opera, originally acted under her own name, Pat Pilkington. (She was actually the illegitimate daughter of a man named Mansfield, who claimed to have been married to her mother for 16 years while remaining the husband of his first wife, whom he had never divorced. Later, Pat's mother married Richard Pilkington.)

In 1955, the actress temporarily changed her name from Pilkington to Dean so as not to embarrass family and friends when she appeared in the lead role in the sex-crime play *A Girl Called Sadie* that year, at the same time dyeing her hair blonde to complete the physical disguise. She later fell on hard times, and even attempted suicide. But she felt that a change of name might change her fortune, and as she later recounted, "Pat Pilkington did, after all, officially die in London. I changed my name to Phoenix. I took the new name from the book I was reading, Marguerite Steen's *Phoenix Rising*" [*TV Times*, November 1–7, 1986]. The change did seem to help, for she began to get small parts in movies and stage shows from then on, rising slowly but surely phoenix-like from her days of depression and hunger in her London basement apartment.

River **Phoenix** *see* Joaquin **Phoenix**

Phranc: Susan Gottlieb (1957–), U.S. Jewish folksinger. The singer changed her name symbolically (in sense and spelling) when she came out as a lesbian at the age of 17, at the same time leaving home, dropping out of high school, and cutting off her waist-length hair. For a time she was involved in punk rock, but later progressed to a gentler and more meaningful role as a folksinger, although still calling herself Phranc.

Duncan **Phyfe**: Duncan Fife (1768–1854), Sc.-born U.S. furniture designer. The cabinetmaker changed the spelling of his name around 1793, after moving to New York City from Albany, New York.

Edith **Piaf**: Edith Giovanna Gassion (1915–1963), Fr. singer, actress. The entertainer was given her stage name in 1935 by Paris nightclub owner Louis Leplée. After an audition one day, he asked her her name. When she told him (all three names), he protested that a name like that was not a show business name: "'The name is very important. What's your real name again?' 'Edith Gassion, but when I sing I call myself Huguette Elias.' He swept these names aside with a wave of his hand ... 'Well, *mon petit*, I've got a name for you—*la môme Piaf* [Kid Sparrow].' We weren't wild about *la môme Piaf*, it didn't sound very artistic. That evening, Edith asked [her half-sister], 'Do you like *la môme Piaf*?' 'Not much.' Then she started to think. 'You know, Momone, *la môme Piaf* doesn't sound all that bad. I think Piaf has style. It's cute, it's musical, it's gay, it's like spring, it's like us. That Leplée isn't so dumb after all'" [Simone Berteaut, *Piaf*, translated by Ghislaine Boulanger, 1970]. Compare La **Môme Moineau**. (Berteaut herself, author of the above text, is the half-sister mentioned.)

Thus the small singer, under 5 ft tall and around 90 lbs in weight, became the "little sparrow of Paris." She adopted the name Edith in memory of Edith Cavell (1865–1915), the British nurse executed by the Germans (a matter of weeks before Piaf was born) for harboring allied soldiers and helping them escape.

Piano Red: William Lee Perryman (1911–1985), U.S. black blues musician. The pianist based his name on that of his elder brother, blues musician **Speckled Red**, with "Piano" distinguishing him. Perryman was an albino with pink eyes, which justified the "Red."

Piano Slim: Robert T. Smith (1928–), U.S. black blues musician.

Picander: Christian Friedrich Henrici (1700–1764), Ger. poet, satirist, playwright. The name presumably means "bitter man" (Greek *pikros*, "sharp," "bitter," and *anēr*, *andros*, "man"), a suitable sobriquet for a satirist. If so, it is the equivalent of the name of Maxim **Gorky**.

Alfred **Piccaver**: Alfred Peckover (1884–1958), Br. opera singer.

Pichichi: Rafael Moreno Aranzadi (1892–1922), Sp. footballer.

Dan **Pickett:** James Founty (1907–1967), U.S. black blues singer.

Jack **Pickford:** Jack Smith (1896–1933), Can. movie actor, brother of Mary **Pickford.**

Mary **Pickford:** Gladys Marie Smith (1892–1979), Can.-born U.S. movie actress ("America's Sweetheart"). Pickford was first on stage at the age of five as "Baby Gladys Smith." In 1907, Broadway impresario David Belasco convinced the teenager to change her name, so she adopted a family name that was more distinctive than plain "Smith." Her namesake, Canadian-born U.S. movie actress Gladys Smith (1921–1993), changed her first name to Alexis.

Pickle: Alastair Ruadh Macdonell (*c.*1725–1761), Sc. spy. The secret agent used this name for his communications with the government on the activities of Prince Charles Edward Stuart ("The Young Pretender") and the Jacobites. He is usually known as "Pickle the Spy," as in the title of Andrew Lang's 1897 book about him.

Peregrine **Pickle:** George Putnam Upton (1834–1919), U.S. journalist, music critic. The writer adopted the name of the eponymous hero of Tobias Smollett's *Adventures of Peregrine Pickle* (1751).

Peter Patricius **Pickle-Herring** *see* Geoffrey **Crayon, jun.**

Howard **Pickup:** Howard Boak (1951–1997), Br. punk guitarist.

Molly **Picon:** Margaret Pyckoon (1898–1992), U.S. Jewish stage, movie actress, singer. The actress apparently changed the spelling of her surname around 1917, when she left Philadelphia to tour the vaudeville circuit with an act called "The Four Seasons."

Bernard **Picton:** Bernard Knight (1931–), Welsh novelist. Professionally a forensic pathologist, as well as a qualified physician and lawyer, the writer adopted this name for his crime novels, as distinct from his historical novels on Welsh subjects.

Pictor Ignotus: William Blake (1757–1827), Eng. artist, poet, mystic. The name is Latin for "Painter Unknown," used on paintings that cannot be confidently attributed to a particular artist. Blake used it occasionally, just as the Anglo-American etcher Joseph Pennell (1857–1926) later used the initials "A.U." ("Artist Unknown").

Pieman: Simon Athony (1973–), Br. crossword compiler. The pseudonym refers to the setter's first name, from the nursery rhyme with the first line, "Simple Simon met a pieman."

De De **Pierce:** Joseph De Lacrois Pierce (1904–1973), U.S. jazz musician, teaming with Billie Pierce, née Wilhelmina Goodson (1907–1974), U.S. jazz musician, his wife.

Piero di Cosimo: Piero di Lorenzo di Chimenti (1462–1521), It. painter. The artist took his name from his master, Cosimo Rosselli (1439–1507), whom he assisted in work on certain frescoes in the Sistine Chapel.

Abbé **Pierre:** Henri Antoine Groués (1912–2007), Fr. priest, Resistance fighter.

DBC **Pierre:** Peter Warren Finlay (1961–), Austral. novelist. The initials in the name adopted by the winner of the 2003 Man Booker prize for his debut novel *Vernon God Little* are properly written without punctuation. Raised in Mexico City, the writer was long involved in debts and drugs. "Finlay took on his pseudonym, which stands for 'Dirty But Clean' Pierre, as a wry play on the nickname his friends conferred on him. Taken from an Australian cartoon character, Dirty Pierre, it was meant to signal that Finlay had put his murky, buccaneering past behind him" [*The Guardian*, October 15, 2003].

Pierre de St. André: Jean Antoine Rampalle (1624–1671), Fr. ecclesiastical writer.

Pierre de St. Louis: Jean Louis Barthélemi (1626–1684), Fr. poet.

Pierre et Gilles: Pierre Commoy (*c.*1950–), Fr. pop artist + Gilles Blanchard (*c.*1950–), Fr. pop artist. The name happens to suggest Pierrot and Gilles, two traditional French clowns or pantomime characters.

Henry Hugh (Heinrich Hugo) **Pierson:** Henry Hugh Pearson (1815–1873), Br.-born Ger. composer. "Pierson married a German lady of talent, the 'improvisatrice' Caroline Leonhardt. In Vienna he borrowed from his wife's connections the pseudonym of 'Mansfeldt.' This was done at the request of his father, who objected to his writing operatic music under his own name. Later he resumed his family name, changing the spelling to Pierson" [*Dictionary of National Biography*].

Pietro da Cortona: Pietro Berrettini (1596–1669), It. painter, architect. The artist adopted the name of his birthtown, Cortona, northwest of Perugia, central Italy.

Pigault-Lebrun: Charles-Antoine-Guillaume Pigault de l'Épinoy (1753–1835), Fr. playwright, novelist. "This author returned to Calais on one occasion to find that his disgusted father had published a notice of his death. Thereafter he called himself Pigault-Lebrun" [Harvey and Heseltine, p.557].

Alexandra **Pigg:** Sandra McKibbin (1963–), Br. TV actress. The actress's screen name presumably evolved from a nickname (as a form of her surname, rendered humorously "McPiggin").

Pigpen: Ronald McKernan (1946–1973), U.S. rock musician. The name arose as a nickname, alluding to the singer's gross and untidy habits. (Britons usually call a pigpen a "pigsty.")

Christopher **Pike:** Kevin McFadden (?–), U.S.

writer of thrillers for teenagers. Pike took his name from Captain Christopher Pike, a character in the *Star Trek* TV series.

Jimmy **Pike**: Kurnti Kurjarra (*c*.1940–2002), Austral. Aboriginal artist. The artist and activist was named after the legendary Jimmy Pike, jockey of the star Australian racehorse Phar Lap, winner of 14 consecutive races, including the 1930 Melbourne Cup.

Morton **Pike**: David Harold Parry (1868–1950), Eng. writer of boys' stories, military articles. The author used this name for stories about highwaymen and Robin Hood. He also wrote as Captain Wilton Blake.

Robert L. **Pike**: Robert Lloyd Fish (1912–1981), U.S. crime writer.

Nova **Pilbeam**: Margery Pilbeam (1919–), Br. movie actress. The actress had the same first name as her mother, so changed it to Nova, for her mother's family associations with Nova Scotia. It is also, of course, a "new" name in the literal sense.

Anne **Pilgrim** *see* Jean **Estoril**

David **Pilgrim**: John Leslie Palmer (1895–1944), Br. thriller writer + Hilary Aidan St. George Saunders (1895–1951), Br. thriller writer. A particular sort of pilgrim is a "palmer," who has been to the Holy Land and returns bearing a palm branch. Hence the punning name. The two men also wrote jointly as Francis **Beeding**.

Boris **Pilnyak**: Boris Andreyevich Vogau (1894–1937), Russ. novelist, short-story writer, of Volga Ger.-Russ. parentage.

Jeannette **Pilou**: Joanna Pilós (1931–), Gk.-born It. opera singer.

Pimen: Sergey Mikhaylovich Izvekov (1910–1990), Russ. churchman, patriarch of Moscow and All Russia. The head of the Russian Orthodox Church adopted his religious name on taking monastic vows in 1927. The name itself comes from Greek *poimēn*, "shepherd," "pastor."

Bronson **Pinchot**: Bronson Poncharovsky (1959–), U.S. movie actor.

Paul **Pindar**: John Yonge Akerman (1806–1873), Eng. antiquary, numismatist. The scholar presumably adopted a pen name based on that of Peter **Pindar**. There were others of the same name.

Peter **Pindar**: John Wolcot (1738–1819), Eng. satirical verse writer. The name was adopted by more than one writer, but notably by Wolcot. Pindar was a Greek lyric poet of the 4th century B.C., and in his first book, *Lyric Odes to the Royal Academicians for 1782*, Wolcot described himself as "a distant relation of the poet of Thebes." Most of the other Peter Pindars were imitators of Wolcot, some very palely so.

Theodore **Pine**: Emil Petaja (1915–2000), U.S. SF writer, of Finn. descent. "Theodore" was the writer's middle name, while *petaja* is Finnish for "pine."

[Sir] Arthur Wing **Pinero**: Arthur Wing Pinheiro (1855–1934), Br. dramatist, stage actor, of Port. Jewish descent.

Pink: Alecia Beth Moore (1979–), U.S. (white) R&B singer. The singer's name does not refer to her distinctively dyed hair but originated as a teenage nickname, supposedly given because she blushed bright pink when her pants were pulled off at summer camp.

Leo **Pinsker**: Judah Leib (1821–1891), Russ. Jewish physician, nationalist.

Harold **Pinta**: Harold Pinter (1930–2008), Eng. playwright. The writer used this spelling of his name for four poems printed in the magazine *Poetry London* between summer 1950 and winter 1951. "The poems were published under the name of Harold Pinta largely because one of his aunts was convinced — against all the evidence — that the family came from distinguished Portuguese ancestors, the da Pintas" [Michael Billington, *The Life and Work of Harold Pinter*, 1996].

George Frederic **Pinto**: George Frederic Saunders (1786–1806), Eng. violinist, composer. The musician adopted the name of his maternal grandfather, Thomas Pinto (?1710–1783), a violinist of Italian descent.

Pinturicchio: Bernardino di Betto di Biago (*c*.1454–1513), It. painter. The artist's name originated as a diminutive nickname, meaning either "little painter," referring to his small stature, "rich painter," from his liking for gold leaf and rich colors, or even "poor painter, "dauber."

Padre **Pio**: Francesco Forgione (1887–1968), It. stigmatic friar, spiritual healer. The future priest entered a Franciscan friary at the age of 16 and took the religious name of the father provincial, Pio da Benevento. In 2002 he was canonized as St. Pio of Pietrelcina, after his birthplace.

Lazarus **Piot**: Anthony Munday (1553–1633), Eng. poet, playwright.

Jacki **Piper**: Jacki Crump (1948–), Eng. movie, TV actress.

Jeems **Pipes of Pipesville**: Stephen G. Massett (1820–1898), U.S. writer. The author used this name for *Drifting About; or, What Jeems Pipes of Pipeville Saw-and-Did: An Autobiography* (1863).

Nelson **Piquet**: Nelson Souto Maior (1952–), Brazilian racing driver. When the sportsman began his racing career in karting he adopted his mother's maiden name of Piquet but spelled it "Piket" so that his parents would not know of his exploits. When they found out anyway, he reverted to the proper spelling.

Pirri: José Martínez Sanchez (1945–), Sp. footballer.

Ugo Pirro: Ugo Mattone (1920–2008), It. screenwriter, author.

Pisanello: Antonio Pisano (*c*.1395–1455), It. painter. The artist's name is a diminutive of his original name, itself indicating that his family came from Pisa. He actually spent his early years in Verona and was associated with that city for most of the rest of his life.

Piscator: William Elliott (1788–1863), U.S. planter, writer, sportsman. Elliott used this name, Latin for "fisherman," "angler," for many of his sporting sketches. He also wrote as Venator ("hunter").

Nikolaas Piscator: Nikolaas Johannes Visscher (*c*.1586–1652), Du. publisher, engraver. The publisher translated his name, meaning "fisherman," into Latin, as was the custom in his day.

Marie-France Pisier: Claudia Chauchat (1944–), Fr. movie actress.

Pistocchio: Francesco Antonio Mamiliano Pistocchi (1659–1726), It. male soprano singer. The singer's name arose as an emotive nickname formed from his surname.

Pitcher: Arthur Morris Binstead (1861–1914), Eng. humorist, sporting writer. The name presumably alludes to someone who sets out his pitch, or who "pitches" (throws out) his offerings. Or possibly it relates to a pitcher (jug) and its mixed contents. Binstead founded and edited the gossip magazine *Town Topics.*

Molly Pitcher: Mary McCauly (*c*.1753–1832), U.S. battle heroine. The intrepid woman was so nicknamed because she carried a pitcher of water back and forth to the weary and wounded American soldiers at the Battle of Monmouth (June 28, 1778), having accompanied her first husband, William Hays, a gunner in a Pennsylvania artillery regiment. Her real original name is uncertain. That given above is of her second husband, John McCauly, whom she married in 1793.

Pitigrilli: Dino Segre (1893–1975), It. writer of erotic novels, short stories.

[Metropolitan] **Pitirim:** Konstantin Vladimirovich Nechayev (1926–2003), Russ. prelate.

Il Pitocchetto: Giacomo Ceruti (1698–1767), It. painter. Although the artist is usually referred to by his real name, he is also known by his not entirely flattering nickname, meaning "the little miser."

Limerno **Pitocco** *see* Merlin **Cocai**

Ingrid **Pitt:** Ingoushka Petrova (1944–), Pol. movie actress, of Russ. parentage, working in U.K.

Thomas **Pitt** *see* T. **Merchant**

Augustus Henry Pitt-Rivers: Augustus Henry Lane Fox (1827–1900), Eng. soldier, archaeologist.

The soldier and scholar was known by his father's name of Fox until 1880, when he eventually inherited the estates of his great-uncle, George Pitt, 2d Baron Rivers, and assumed his name (and title).

ZaSu Pitts: Eliza Susan Pitts (1898–1963), U.S. movie, stage actress. The actress's original name is frequently given as here, but she really had her unusual name from the first. It was formed from syllables of the first names, Eliza and Susan, of her father's sisters (not her own sisters, as sometimes stated). "I bounded out of the car and caught up with her as she reached the corner of Hollywood and Gower. 'What is your name, please?' 'Zasu. Last of Eliza, first of Susie'" [King Vidor, quoted in Thomson 2003, p. 686].

Pius II: Enea Silvio (or Aeneas Silvius) Piccolomini (1405–1464), It. pope. The pontiff chose the name Pius in memory of Virgil's *pius Aeneas,* "dutiful Aeneas."

Pius III: Francesco Todeschini Piccolomini (*c*.1440–1503), It. pope. The pontiff was the nephew of **Pius II**, and took his name.

Pius IV: Giovanni Angelo de' Medici (1499–1565), It. pope.

[St.] **Pius V:** Antonio Michele Ghislieri (1504–1572), It. pope.

Pius VI: Giovanni Angelo Braschi (1717–1799), It. pope.

Pius VII: Gregorio Luigi Barnaba Chiaramonti (1742–1823), It. pope.

Pius VIII: Francesco Saverio Castiglione (1761–1830), It. pope. The pontiff took the name of **Pius VII**, whom he regarded as his exemplar.

Pius IX: Giovanni Maria Mastai-Ferretti (1792–1878), It. pope. *Pio Nono*, as he is mellifluously known in Italy, took his name in memory of **Pius VII**, who had been his friend and who, like him, had been bishop of Imola.

[St.] **Pius X:** Giuseppe Melchiorre Sarto (1835–1914), It. pope.

Pius XI: Ambrogio Damiano Achille Ratti (1857–1939), It. pope. The pontiff took his papal name in honor of **Pius X**, who had appointed him to the Vatican Library, Rome, in 1911.

Pius XII: Eugenio Maria Giuseppe Giovanni Pacelli (1876–1958), It. pope.

Benjamin Place: Edward Thring (1821–1887), Eng. schoolmaster, educationist. The headmaster of Uppingham School used this name for one of his early works, *Thoughts on Life Science* (1869). He took it from the name of the house, Ben Place, Grasmere, in the Lake District, where he went for his summer vacations and where he wrote much of the book.

Plácido: Gabriel de la Concepción Valdés (1809–1844), Cuban poet. The poet adopted a name meaning "mild," "placid."

Jean **Plaidy**: Eleanor Alice Hibbert, née Burford (1906–1993), Br. novelist, mystery writer. The prolific writer used a range of pseudonyms for her different genres of historical, romantic, and "Gothic" novels. Her best known is the one given here. Plaidy is the name of a beach in Cornwall, where she lived, while she chose Jean for its brevity. Other names were Victoria Holt, Philippa Carr, Ellalice Tate, Elbur Ford, and Kathleen Kellow. According to the author's *Daily Telegraph* obituary (January 21, 1993), the first of these was a pseudonym taken from the name of her bank. The third and fourth names, more obviously, had their genesis in her original name.

Platina: Bartolomeo Sacchi (1421–1481), It. historian. The author of the *Liber de vita Christi ac de vitis summorum pontificum omnium* (1479), known in English as *Lives of the Popes*, came to be called by the Latin form of the name of his birthplace, Piadena, near Mantua.

Andrey **Platonov**: Andrey Platonovich Klimentov (1899–1951), Russ. writer.

Yuliya **Platonova**: Yuliya Fyodorovna Tvaneva, née Garder (1841–1892), Russ. opera singer.

A. Monmouth **Platts** *see* Anthony **Berkeley**

Plausus: David Dare-Plumpton (1943–), Br. crossword compiler. The setter is a classics scholar and his pseudonym has an appropriate Latin origin, from the first two letters of his nickname, "Plum," plus *ausus*, "enterprise," or overall from *plausus*, "clapping."

Robert **Player**: Robert Furneaux Jordan (1905–1978), Eng. crime writer. Professionally an architect, Jordan adopted this name for his novels.

King **Pleasure**: Clarence Beeks (1922–1981), U.S. jazz singer, songwriter.

Martha **Plimpton**: Martha Carradine (1971–), U.S. movie actress.

Ploutos: Michael Charles Christopher Rich (1940–2002), Eng. crossword compiler. As with many crosswordists, Rich's pseudonym puns on his original name, with Greek *ploutos*, "wealth," equating to his surname. At the school Rich attended, classics were taught by **Ximenes**.

Jacques **Plowert**: Paul Adam (1862–1920), Fr. novelist. The pen name was only an occasional one, and was used by the writer in particular for his *Petit Glossaire pour servir à l'intelligence des auteurs décadents et symbolistes* (1888).

Vilis **Pludonis**: Vilis Janovic Lejnieks (1874–1940), Latvian poet.

Edith **Plummer** *see* Madame **Yevonde**

James **Plunkett**: James Plunkett Kelly (1920–), Ir. novelist, short-story writer.

Peter **Plymley**: Sydney Smith (1771–1845), Eng. clergyman, essayist. The writer assumed this name for *The Letters of Peter Plymley* (1807), defending Catholic emancipation, with the letters themselves purporting to have been written by Peter Plymley to his brother in the country, Rev. Abraham Plymley.

Pocahontas: Matoaka (?1595–1617), Native American princess. Matoaka, famous for saving the life of the English colonist John Smith, was nicknamed Pocahontas, "sportive," and assumed this name on her marriage (1614) to the Englishman John Rolfe. Little might have been heard of her had she not gone with him to England in 1616, where she died the following year of smallpox. She had been converted to Christianity in 1612 and renamed Rebecca. Hence the entry in the parish register of St. George's church, Gravesend, the town where she died: "1616, May 2j, Rebecca Wrothe, wyff of Thomas Wroth, gent., a Virginia lady borne, here was buried in ye chauncell" [*Dictionary of National Biography*].

Fernando **Poe**: Ronald Allan Kelley Poe (1939–2004), Filipino actor, politician. The actor appears to have based his new name on that of the Portuguese navigator Fernão do Pó, popularly known as Fernando Po, who in 1472 discovered the island named for him (now Bioko) off the West Africa coast.

William **Poel**: William Pole (1852–1934), Br. stage actor, director. The actor respelled his surname when his father, an engineer and musician, disapproved of his chosen profession.

Nikolay **Pogodin**: Nikolay Fyodorovich Stukalov (1900–1962), Russ. playwright, screenwriter.

Antony **Pogorelsky**: Aleksey Alekseyevich Perovsky (1787–1836), Russ. writer. The writer, the illegitimate son of Count Razumovsky, based his name on that of his estate, Pogoreltsy.

Robert **Pointon**: Daphne Rooke (1914–), S.A. novelist. The writer used this male name for her first novel, *The Sea Hath Bounds*, published in 1946. Four years later it was reissued under her real name with the title *A Grove of Fever Trees*.

Jean **Poiret**: Jean-Gustave Poiré (1926–1992), Fr. movie actor, screenwriter.

Poison Ivy *see* **Lux Interior**

David **Poitier**: David Hampton (1964–), U.S. black impostor. Hampton used this name to enter New York high society, posing as the son of movie star Sidney Poitier (1924–). (This despite the fact that Poitier had six daughters but no sons.) At first his ruse was a success, enabling him to dine free on "Dad's" account and gain access to Melanie Griffith's apartment on the grounds that he was a friend of her husband. But he repeated the scam too often, using other names from an address book he had acquired from a college student, and was finally arrested. His story was told in the movie *Six Degrees of Separation* (1993), in which he was played by Will Smith. (The movie title refers to the theory that each person in the world can trace a connection to any other person which will involve no more than six intermediary links. Everyone is thus joined by a maximum six degrees of separation to everyone else.)

La **Polaire:** Émilie-Marie Bouchard, née Zouzé (1877–1939), Algerian-born Fr. music-hall artist. "Her stage name she chose in Algiers, where she was born, after the Pole Star she could see in the sky" [Jacques Pessis and Jacques Crépineau, *The Moulin Rouge*, 1990].

Lou **Polan:** Lou Polansky (1904–), U.S. stage director.

Roman **Polanski:** Roman Liebling (1933–), Fr.-born movie director. Polanski was raised in Poland but following his first full-length feature *Nóż w wodzie* ("Knife in the water") (1962) pursued a career in the U.S. and U.K. until 1978, when he settled in France.

Michael **Polanyi:** Mihály Pollacsek (1891–1976), Hung.-born Br. chemist, philosopher.

Yan **Poldi:** Ivan Konstantinovich Podrezov (1889–1913), Russ. circus artist, trick cyclist. The name Poldi was originally used for a group of acrobatic cyclists formed by Podrezov in 1909. He was killed performing one of his acts.

Poldowski: [Lady] Irene Regine Paul, née Wieniawska (1880–1932), Br. pianist, composer, of Pol. parentage. The writer of popular ballads, daughter of the Polish violinist Henryk Wieniawski (1835–1880), married the English army officer Sir Aubrey Edward Henry Dean Paul (1869–1961) in 1901 and created a pseudonym based on his name.

Pole: Stefan Berke (1967–), Ger. experimental rock musician. Berke took his recording name from the Waldorf 4-pole filter used to create the electronic effects that form the basis of his music.

Boris **Polevoy:** Boris Nikolayevich Kampov (1908–1981), Russ. novelist, journalist. The writer's original name, Kampov, was changed by the editor of the newspaper *Tverskaya Pravda*, in which he had had an article published (using the name B. Ovod) as a 14-year-old schoolboy. The editor regarded Kampov as too "Latin," so he russianized it as Polevoy, translating Latin *campus*, "field," by the adjectival form of equivalent Russian *pole*.

Poliarchus: [Sir] Charles Cotterell (1615–?1687), Eng. politician, courtier. The courtier used this Greek name, meaning "ruler of many," for his correspondence with **Orinda**.

Polidor: Ferdinando Guillaume (1887–1977), Fr. movie comedian, stage clown. The performer's stage and screen name means "many-gifted," "multi-talented."

Polidoro da Caravaggio: Polidoro Calda

(*c.*1500–1543), It. painter. The artist came to be known from his birthplace, Caravaggio, a town which would later make famous the name of **Caravaggio**.

Polin: Pierre-Paul Marsalès (1863–1927), Fr. music-hall artist, stage actor.

Politian *see* Angelo **Poliziano**

Kosmas **Politis:** Paris Taveloudis (1888–1974), Gk. novelist. The writer's name seems to suggest "cosmopolitan," literally "citizen of the world."

Angelo **Poliziano:** Angelo Ambrogini (1454–1494), It. poet, scholar. Often known in English as Politian, the poet adopted the Roman name of his birthplace, the town of Montepulciano near Siena.

Antonio **Pollaiuolo:** Antonio di Jacopo d'Antonio Benci (1433–1498), It. painter, sculptor, engraver. The name was borne by both Antonio and his elder brother Piero (1443–1496), who worked together as artists, and is said to derive from Italian *pollaio*, "henhouse," since their father is supposed to have been a poulterer. Records indicate, however, that he was probably a goldsmith.

Daphne **Pollard:** Daphne Trott (1890–1978), Austral. movie actress, working in U.S.

Harry "Snub" **Pollard:** Harold Fraser (1886–1962), Austral.-born U.S. movie comedian.

Michael J. **Pollard:** Michael J. Pollack (1939–), U.S. movie actor.

Bernhard **Pollini:** Baruch Pohl (1838–1897), Ger. opera singer, impresario.

Jackson **Pollock:** Paul Jackson Pollock (1912–1956), U.S. artist. The artist began using his middle name as his first name when training with the Art Students' League in New York. The family surname was originally McCoy, but his father had changed this when in his 20s. As a teenager, Pollock called himself Hugo for a time.

Mary **Pollock:** Enid Blyton (1897–1968), Eng. children's writer. The popular author used this name for some books published in the 1940s.

Vyacheslav **Polonsky:** Vyacheslav Pavlovich Gusin (1886–1932), Russ. critic, journalist, historian. The writer adopted the name of the poet Yakov Petrovich Polonsky (1819–1898), with whom he felt he had an affinity.

Pol Pot: Saloth Sar (1925–1998), Khmer political leader.

Dimitr **Polyanov:** Dimĭtr Ivanov Popov (1876–1953), Bulg. poet.

Polypus *see* Cervantes **Hogg, F.S.M.**

Pomare IV: Aimata (1813–1877), Tahitian queen. The first bearer of the dynastic name was King Pomare I (reigned 1797–1803), originally Vairaatoa. The name itself means "night of the cough," from Tahitian *po*, "night," and *mare*, "cough." The king was seized by a coughing fit one night when waging war. It was ladies in the court of Queen Pomare IV who gave the name of the French writer Pierre **Loti**.

Jay **Pomeroy**: Joseph Pomeranz (1895–1955), Russ.-born Br. theatrical director. Pomeranz went to England in 1915 and became a naturalized British subject in 1929. The name change is more subtle than it appears, since Pomeranz comes from a word meaning "orange," while Pomeroy derives from a source meaning "apple."

Édouard de **Pomiane**: Edward Pomian Pozerski (1875–1964), Fr. dietician, food writer.

Aleksandr **Pomorsky**: Aleksandr Nikolayevich Linovsky (1891–1977), Russ. poet. At the start of his career the writer lived on the coast near St. Petersburg. Hence his name, meaning "coast dweller" (Russian *pomor*).

Doc **Pomus**: Jerome Solon Felder (1925–1991), U.S. (white) blues musician. The musician was already performing at jazz and blues clubs at age 15 and adopted his new name to avoid telling his parents of his activities. They found out two years later anyway.

Rosa **Ponselle**: Rosa Melba Ponzillo (1897–1981), U.S. opera singer.

Miranda **Ponsonby**: Rhodri Davies (1933–), Br. aristocrat. The former guardsman and gentleman farmer underwent a sex-change operation in the 1980s, adopting her mother's maiden name.

Pont: Gavin Graham Laidler (1908–1940), Br. cartoonist. The artist originally intended to take up a career as an architect, and to this end adopted the name Pontifex Maximus, literally "great bridge-builder," the title of the Roman pontiff or president, which was already a family nickname for him after he had paid an early visit to Italy. This later became shortened to "Pont," a name familiar to readers of *Punch*, where his cartoons appeared. He did not thus adopt his name from London's Pont Street, as has been sometimes suggested [R.G.G. Price, *A History of Punch*, 1957].

Jakob **Pontanus**: Jakob Spanmüller (1542–1626), Ger. theologian, schoolbook writer. Spanmüller was born in Brüx, now Most, Czech Republic, a name meaning "bridge" that gave his own name, from Latin *pons*, *pontis* in this sense.

Lorenzo da **Ponte** *see* Lorenzo **da Ponte**

Henry T. **Pontet**: Theodore Piccolomini (1835–1902), Eng. popular songwriter.

Clara **Pontoppidan**: Clara Wieth (1883–1975), Dan. stage, movie actress.

Pontormo: Jacopo Carucci (1494–1556), It. painter. The artist took his name from his birthplace, the village of Pontorme, near Empoli, west of Florence.

Josephine **Poole**: Jane Penelope Josephine Helyar (1933–), Br. writer of fantasy fiction for teenagers.

Poor Richard: Benjamin Franklin (1709–1790), U.S. statesman, philosopher. Franklin was the author and publisher of *Poor Richard's Almanack* (1733–58), the most famous of the American almanacs, although he signed the prefaces as "Richard Saunders." The name was almost certainly based on that of the English *Poor Robin's Almanack* (*see* **Poor Robin**), especially as Richard Saunders was the name of the English editor of *Apollo Anglicanus*.

Poor Robin: William Winstanley (?1628–1698), Eng. compiler. The precise identity of the author of the various works by "Poor Robin," especially the almanacs published in England from about 1663, is uncertain. William Winstanley seems the most likely candidate, although some support his brother, Robert Winstanley, possibly simply through the similarity between the names Robert and Robin. Others suggest that the actual author was the poet Robert Herrick. Either way, the title almost certainly inspired the name of its American equivalent, *Poor Richard's Almanack* (*see* **Poor Richard**).

Denniz **Pop**: Dag Volle (1963–1998), Swe. record producer.

Iggy **Pop**: James Newell Osterberg, Jr. (1947–), U.S. rock musician. Osterberg was nicknamed "Iggy" in 1967 when playing as drummer with the Iguanas. The following year he left the group and joined the Prime Movers, when he adopted the name Iggy Pop, the latter coming from a local junkie, Jim Popp.

Popa Chubby: Ted Horowitz (1948–), U.S. blues musician.

Faith **Popcorn**: Faith Plotkin (1948–), U.S. business consultant. The cultural-trend watcher explains how she came by her name: "I was born Faith Plotkin but in my first job my boss called me Popcorn and it stuck. I made up a story that when my great-grandfather came from Italy with the name Corne, he was so old that everyone called him Papa and that's where Poppacorne came from. The truth is that my nickname felt so much more me. I changed my name legally to Popcorn" [*Sunday Times Magazine*, February 13, 1994].

Generoso **Pope**: Generoso Papa (1891–1950), It.-born U.S. businessman, newspaper publisher. Papa emigrated to the United States in 1906 and in 1915 became an American citizen. He married a year later, and around this time altered his name from Italian Papa to its English equivalent.

Nils **Poppe**: Nils Joensson (1908–2000), Swe. stage, movie actor.

Poppi: Francesco Morandini (1544–1597), It. painter. The artist is often referred to by the name of his birthplace, the mountain village of Poppi in central Italy.

Miss **Poppy**: Elaine Addison (1965–), U.S.

childcare consultant. The author of *Miss Poppy's Guide to Raising Perfectly Happy Children* (2005) came by her pseudonym when she was employed as nanny to Rose Onassis, granddaughter of U.S. first lady Jacqueline Onassis. "As an editor at Doubleday, Onassis urged Addison to become 'the Martha Stewart of nannying.' After Addison went to a fancy dress party in New York dressed as [the fictional children's nanny] Mary Poppins ... Onassis's boss, Nancy Evans, suggested she write a Miss Poppy column for a parenting magazine (the name, she admits, was chosen in homage to Mary Poppins)" [*Sunday Times*, January 30, 2005].

Popski: Vladimir Peniakoff (1897–1951), Belg. military commander, of Russ. parentage. The name was a cover name used for military intelligence work in World War II. Peniakoff published an account of this work in *Popski's Private Army* (1950), and the book publicized the name. It was in fact in use before the war for a cartoon character, a little Russian with a beard holding a bomb, created by **Low** in the London *Evening Standard*.

Lasgush **Poradeci:** Lazar Gusho (1899–1985), Albanian poet.

Il **Porcellio:** Giannantonio de' Pandoni (before 1409–after 1485), It. humanist. The writer's nickname means "the little pig."

Publius **Porcius:** Johannes Leo Placentius (*c.*1500–1548), Flemish historian. The Dominican monk used this name for an alliterative Latin poem called *Pugna Porcorum* ("Battle of the Pigs") (1530), in which every word begins with "P." It begins: "Plaudite, Porcelli, porcorum pigra propago," which may be translated (using an English personal name for the Latin one), "Praise, Paul, prize pig's progeny."

Peter **Porcupine:** William Cobbett (1763–1835), Eng. journalist, politician. The writer used this name for *The Life and Adventures of Peter Porcupine* (1796), published in Philadelphia, a provocatively pro–English work. A porcupine has prickly spines that "sting."

Pordenone: Giovanni Antonio de' Sacchis (*c.*1483–1539), It. painter. The artist is named for his birthplace, the town of Pordenone, near Venice.

Porphyry: Malchas (*c.*234–*c.*305), Gk. scholar. The scholar's original Syrian name of Malchas meant "king." This was hellenized at Athens by Cassius Longinus, his teacher of logic, to Porphyry, meaning "purple," alluding to the imperial color (royal purple) associated with kings.

Selvaggio **Porpora:** Cornelio Bentivoglio (1668–1732), It. cardinal, scholar. The writer used this name for his blank verse translation of Statius's *Thebaid* (1729).

Porporino: Antonio Uberti (1697–1783), It.

male soprano singer. The singer took his name from Nicola Porpora (1686–1768), the composer and chapelmaster in whose class he had studied in Naples.

Genesis **P-Orridge:** Neil Andrew Megson (1949–), Br. performance artist, rock musician. The founder of the anarchic group Throbbing Gristle (in 1976) legally adopted his stage name in 1970. It arose as a school nickname, but was not suggested by the rock band Genesis, which had not then been formed.

Antonio **Porta:** Leo Paolazzi (1935–1989), It. poet, novelist.

Porte-Crayon: David Hunter Strother (1816–1888), U.S. artist, writer. Strother used his (literal) pen name, French for "pencil-holder," for his illustrations in *Harper's New Monthly Magazine*.

Alvin **Porter** *see* Fenton **Brockley**

Donald Clayton **Porter** *see* Samuel **Edwards**

Katherine Anne **Porter:** Callie Russell Porter (1890–1980), U.S. writer. On divorcing her first husband, John Henry Koontz, in 1915, Porter adopted (with a small change) the name of her paternal grandmother, Catherine Anne Porter, an important person in her life.

Diana **Portis** *see* Clemence **Dane**

Natalie **Portman:** Natalie Hershlag (1981–), Israeli-born U.S. stage, movie actress. The actress adopted her grandmother's maiden name as her stage name.

S.F. **Porter:** Sylvia Porter (1913–1991), U.S. financial writer. Porter adopted this name for her contributions to financial journals, the initials concealing the fact that she was a woman. ("S." was for Sylvia, "F." for Field, her maiden name, originally Feldman.) Although her gender became known through her radio broadcasts, and her first books were published under her real name, the *New York Post*, which hired her as a columnist in 1935, did not reveal her identity until 1942, when her reputation as a financial advisor had become assured.

Sandy **Posey:** Martha Sharp (1945–), U.S. country-pop singer, songwriter.

George **Posford:** Benjamin George Ashwell (1906–1976), Br. popular composer, conductor.

Adrienne **Posta:** Adrienne Poster (1948–), Eng. juvenile movie actress.

Posy: Rosemary Elizabeth Simmonds (1945–), Eng. cartoonist, illustrator. An adoption of the artist's pet name, from her first name.

Gillie **Potter:** Hugh William Peel (1888–1975), Eng. humorist, stage, radio comedian.

Paul Meredith **Potter:** Walter Arthur MacLean (1853–1921), Eng.-born U.S. playwright. A scandal obliged the former journalist to change his name and emigrate to the United States, where in 1876 he became foreign editor of the *New York Herald*.

Arthur **Pougin:** François Auguste Arthur Paroisse-Pougin (1834–1921), Fr. musical biographer, critic. As well as simplifying his original name, the writer also used the pseudonym Pol Dax.

Jean **Pougny:** Ivan Puni (1894–1956), Russ.-born Fr. painter, of It. descent. The artist was the grandson of the Italian composer Cesare Pugni.

Liane de **Pougy:** Marie Chassaigne, later Princess Ghika (*c*.1870–1950), Fr. novelist, courtesan.

Virgina **Pound** *see* Adrian **Booth**

Gaspard **Poussin:** Gaspard Dughet (1613–1675), Fr. painter. The artist was a pupil of Nicolas Poussin (1594–1665), who married his sister in 1630 and whose surname he adopted.

Elizabeth **Powell:** Effie Sandery (1895–1986), Austral. children's writer.

Jane **Powell:** Suzanne Burce (1929–), U.S. movie actress, singer, dancer.

Mary **Powell:** Anne Manning (1807–1879), Eng. writer. In 1849 Anne Manning published anonymously *The Maiden and Married Life of Mary Powell, afterwards Mistress Milton*. This was so popular that she identified herself on future works as "The Author of Mary Powell" and became generally known by the name of her heroine. The work itself was attributed by many to Hannah Mary Rathbone, née Reynolds (1798–1878), author of the somewhat similar *Diary of Lady Willoughby* (1844), and some sources thus attribute the pseudonym "Mary Powell" to Rathbone instead of Manning.

Mel **Powell:** Melvin Epstein (1923–1998), U.S. jazz musician.

Richard Stillman **Powell:** Ralph Henry Barbour (1870–1944), U.S. novelist, writer of boys' stories. The writer explains the origin of his name: "As I recall it, I simply picked three names from the contents table of a *Century Magazine* which happened to be in my hands at the moment of inspiration ... and arranged them in a sequence that satisfied my ear. Richard Powell Stillman *looked* just as good but it didn't *sound* so well!" [Marble, p.177].

Teddy **Powell:** Alfred Paolella (1905–?), U.S. jazz musician, bandleader. Powell wrote some of his best-known hits under the name Freddy James.

Vince **Powell:** Vincent Smith (1928–2009), Eng. TV comedy writer.

Cat **Power:** Charlyn "Chan" Marshall (1971–), U.S. black blues singer. The singer took her stage name after seeing an old man in a pizza restaurant wearing a cap with the logo "CAT Diesel Power." "Mention Cat Power to music fans and they will either purr, dreamy-eyed, with approval ... or, in some cases, simply look baffled and ask what it's got to do with cats" [*Sunday Times*, January 27, 2008].

Cecil **Power** *see* Olive Pratt **Rayner**

James T. **Powers:** James McGovern (1862–1943), U.S. stage comedian, singer.

Stefanie **Powers:** Stefania Zofia Federkiewicz (1942–), U.S. movie, TV actress.

Stephen **Powys:** Virginia Bolton, née de Lanty (1907–), U.S. playwright, short-story writer.

Poy: Percy Hutton Fearon (1874–1948), Eng. political cartoonist, editor. The artist's name is said to have originated from the American pronunciation of his first name (as "Poycee") when he was a student at the Chase School of Art in New York.

Albany **Poyntz:** Catherine Grace Frances Gore, née Moody (1800–1861), Eng. novelist. The writer used this name for a series of articles published in *Bentley's Miscellany* in 1841.

Launce **Poyntz:** Frederick Whittaker (1838–1889), U.S. writer of adventure stories. The name suggests a pun on "lance" and "points."

P.P.C.R.: Thomas Watts (1811–1869), Eng. bibliographer, librarian. The writer, keeper of printed books in the British Museum, London, used these initials for letters published in the *Mechanics' Magazine* (1836) regarding improvements to the British Museum Library. The initials themselves stood for "Peerless Pool, City Road," referring to an open-air swimming pool owned by the Watts family in Islington, north London. According to John Stow's *Survay of London* (1598), it was originally "a cleere water, called Perillous Pond, because divers youths, by swimming therein, have been drowned." A London jeweler named William Kemp converted it to a proper swimming bath in 1743, however, and changed its ill-omened name "to the more agreeable name of Peerless Pool, that is, Matchless Bath, a name which carries its own reason with it" [William Maitland, *The History of London*, 1775].

Swami **Prabhavananda:** Abinadra Nath Ghosh (1893–1976), Ind.-born U.S. religious leader. The founder of the Vedanta Society of Southern California was a disciple of Swami Brahmananda, himself a direct disciple of the Bengali saint **Ramakrishna**, and was given his honorific name, meaning literally "lord master bliss," by his teacher in 1921.

Swami **Prabhupada:** Abhay Charanaravinda Bhaktivedanta (1896–1977), Ind. religious leader, working in U.S. The founder in 1965 of the Hare Krishna movement is commonly known by his Sanskrit religious title, literally meaning "lord master footstep." This never entirely replaced his original name, however, which is usually cited with the first two names as initials (A.C. Bhaktivedanta).

Michael **Praed:** Michael Prince (1960–), Eng. movie, TV actor.

Johannes **Praetorius:** Johannes Schulze (1630–

1680), Ger. scholar, poet. The scholar's original surname was the title of a village headman, from words related to modern German *Schuld*, "debt," and *heissen*, "to call," denoting a person who collected dues and paid them to the lord of the manor. Latin *praetorius* serves as an equivalent, from *praetor*, the title of various Roman officials.

Michael **Praetorius:** Michael Schultheiss (or Schulz) (1571–1621), Ger. musician, composer. The musician latinized his name in the manner explained above for Johannes **Praetorius**.

Lama Dorje **Prajñananda:** Frederic Fletcher (1879–1950), Eng. Buddhist. The first Westerner to be ordained in Tibetan Buddhism became a monk in Ceylon (Sri Lanka) in 1924 under his Buddhist name, meaning "joy of wisdom" (Sanskrit *prajña*, "wisdom," and *ananda*, "joy," "happiness").

Prapawadee Jaroenrattanatarakoon: Chanpim Jantatian (1984–), Thai weightlifter. In 2007 the athlete was advised by a fortune-telling nun to change her name if she wished to enter the Olympics. She did so with a vengeance.

Pras: Prakazrel Michel (1972–), U.S. black hip-hop musician.

L.V. **Prasad:** Akkineni Lakshmi Vara Prasada Rao (1908–1994), Ind. movie director, producer.

Rosa von **Praunheim:** Holger Mischwitzky (1942–), Ger. movie director, gay activist. The filmmaker, who grew up in the Frankfurt suburb of Praunheim, chose his new first name to remind people of the pink triangle ("Rosa Winkel") that homosexuals had to wear in Nazi concentration camps.

Patty **Pravo:** Nicoletta Strambelli (1948–), It. popular singer, the first to promote beat music in Italy.

George R. **Preedy** *see* Marjorie **Bowen**

Prem Chand: Dhanpat Rai Srivastava (1880–1936), Ind. novelist, short-story writer. The writer adopted a symbolic name meaning "moon of love" (Hindi *prem*, "love," and *cand*, "moon").

Paul **Prendergast:** Douglas William Jerrold (1803–1857), Eng. novelist, journalist, playwright. The writer used the name for *Heads of the People* (1840–1), a series of sketches. He had earlier made contributions to various papers as Henry Brownrigg as well as under his own name.

Paula **Prentiss:** Paula Ragusa (1939–), U.S. movie actress.

Dray **Prescot** *see* Alan Burt **Akers**

E. Livingston **Prescott:** Edith Katharine Hargrave, née Spicer-Jay (?1869–1901), Br. novelist. The writer took her pseudonym from family members. Her father, Samuel Jay, was the nephew of Major Alexander Livingston, while she herself was the great-granddaughter of Sir George Prescott. She also wrote as L. Parry Truscott.

John **Presland:** Gladys Bendit, earlier Skelton, née Williams (1889–1975), Austral. novelist. The writer explained the rationale behind her choice of male name: "Presland was my mother's name.... When I began to publish I was anxious to enter the lists as anonymously as possible. I disliked all kinds of publicity ... and I thought that if sex, as well as personality, were hidden behind a pseudonym, the author stood a better chance of being judged solely on merit" [Marble, p.217].

Micheline **Presle:** Micheline Chassagne (1922–), Fr. movie actress. The actress made her screen debut in 1938 under the name Micheline Michel, and in her first U.S. movies was billed as Micheline Prelle.

Hovis **Presley:** Richard Henry McFarlane (1960–2005), Eng. comic, poet. The doleful performer and writer adopted a quirky name that combined a British make of bread with the U.S. singer Elvis Presley.

Preston: Samuel Preston (1982–), Eng. rock singer.

George F. **Preston:** John Byrne Leicester Warren, Baron de Tabley (1835–1895), Eng. poet. Warren used this name for some volumes of verse published between 1859 and 1862. The first part of the name is almost certainly a tribute to his close friend and fellow student at Oxford, George Fortescue, who was killed in an accident in 1859. He also wrote as William P. Lancaster, and both pseudonyms appear to derive from the Lancashire cities of Preston and Lancaster, not far from his native Cheshire.

Johnny **Preston:** John Preston Courville (1939–), U.S. pop, rock singer.

Kelly **Preston:** Kelly Palzis (1962–), U.S. movie actress.

Mike **Preston:** Jack Davis (1934–), Eng. pop singer. The singer was given his stage name in a competition by readers of a regular pop music column in the *Daily Mirror*. Presumably readers were told he had been discovered by London agent Dennis Preston.

Robert **Preston:** Robert Preston Meservey (1918–1987), U.S. stage, movie actor.

Préville: Pierre-Louis Dibus (1721–1799), Fr. comic actor.

André **Previn:** Andreas Ludwig Priwin (1929–), Ger.-born pianist, conductor, of Russ. Jewish descent, working in U.S., U.K.

Francis **Prevost:** Henry Francis Prevost Battersby (1862–1949), Eng. writer.

Marie **Prévost:** Mary Bickford Dunn (1898–1937), Can.-born U.S. movie actress.

Voranc **Prezihov:** Lovro Kuhar (1893–1950), Slovenian poet.

Dennis **Price:** Dennistoun John Franklyn Rose-Price (1915–1973), Eng. stage, movie actor.

Evadne **Price:** Helen Zenna Smith (1896–1985), Eng. journalist, children's writer. The writer used this name for a series of books for children about a mischievous little girl called Jane, beginning with *Just Jane* (1928).

Dickie **Pride:** Richard Charles Knellar (1941–1969), Eng. pop singer ("The Sheik of Shake"). Knellar was "discovered" by Russ **Conway** singing rock 'n' roll in a pub in 1958 and passed on by him to impresario Larry Parnes, who renamed him.

Maxi **Priest:** Max Alfred Elliott (1962–), Br. black reggae singer. The musician adopted his new name on his conversion to Rastafarianism, taking it from the Old Testament priest Levi, the eponymous ancestor of the tribe of Levi and the Levites. His first name, Max, had been given him by his mother, a fan of Max **Bygraves**.

A **Prig:** Thomas Longueville (1844–1922), Welsh banker, writer. The writer used this name for *The Life of a Prig. By a Prig* (1880), as well as for *Egosophy* (1892) and *Platitudes of a Pessimist* (1897).

Prim: Suzanne Arduini (1895–1991), Fr. movie, stage, actress.

Alberta **Prime** *see* Josephine **Beatty**

Dorothy **Primrose:** Dorothy Buckley (1916–), Sc. stage actress.

Prince: Prince Rogers Nelson (1958–), U.S. black rock musician. The artist was originally named for the Prince Rogers Trio, of which his father, John L. Nelson, was a member. On June 7, 1993, his 35th birthday, he changed his name to an unpronounceable but supposedly significant symbol, "explained by fanzines as covering the masculine and feminine sides of his personality" [Beech, p.223]. The Artist Formerly Known As Prince (TAFKAP), as the media thereafter referred to him, commented: "Changing my name's made perfect sense to me. I'm not Nel's son, Nelson, that's a slave name. I was ridiculed for that, but they did the same to Muhammad **Ali** and Malcolm **X**....What should you call me? My wife just says, 'Hey.' If she said, 'Prince, get me a cup of tea,' I'd probably drop the cup'" [*Sunday Times Magazine*, December 22, 1996].

Over the course of his career the singer has assumed other identities. "Under a variety of pen names he has created alter egos such as Alexander Nevermind, who wrote the song "Sugar Walls" for Sheena **Easton**; Christopher, who gave the hit "Manic Monday" to the Bangles; and Camille, credited as a vocalist on some of his songs" [*Sunday Times*, August 5, 2007].

"Has anyone made such a titanic fool of himself as the artist formerly known as Prince? When he started messing about with his name, he became an instant and continuing international joke, even though he later changed what he misleadingly calls his mind" [*The Times*, November 20, 2009].

Richard **Prince:** Richard Miller Archer (1858–?), Eng. actor. The performer's growing grudge against William **Terriss** eventually unhinged his mind and drove him to murder the popular actor.

Prince Allah: Keith Blake (1950–), Jamaican reggae singer. The singer adopted his name after becoming closely involved with the Rastafarian movement in 1969.

Prince Be: Attrell Cordes (1970–), U.S. black "hip-hop" musician, "daisy-age" rapper, brother of DJ **Minute Mix**.

Prince Buster: Cecil Bustamante Campbell (1938–), Jamaican rock singer. The singer was named after Jamaican prime minister Alexander **Bustamante**. "In 1938 ... rioting broke out across the island [of Jamaica], and on 24th May, Kingston was almost rent asunder. Then ... an incident of great courage took place. Sir William Bustamante, leader of the Jamaica Labour Party, stepped in front of the police pointing firearms at demonstrators. 'Shoot me,' he offered himself, 'and save the innocent people of Jamaica' ... It was on this auspicious day that one Cecil Campbell was born, and it was hardly surprising that as a consequence he should have been given the nickname of 'Buster'" [Chris Salewicz and Adrian Boot, *Reggae Explosion: The Story of Jamaican Music*, 2001].

Prince Far I: Michael Williams (*c*.1944–1983), Jamaican DJ, reggae rapper. The musician was originally given the name "King Cry-Cry" but soon renamed himself as "Prince Far I."

Prince Hammer: Beresford Simpson (*c*.1962–), Jamaican reggae musician.

Prince Jazzbo: Linval Carter (*c*.1950–), Jamaican reggae musician.

Prince Mohammed: George Nooks (*c*.1958–), Jamaican DJ, reggae musician.

Prince Paul: Paul E. Huston (1967–), U.S. black rapper.

Prince-Rigadin: Charles Petit-Demange (1872–1933), Fr. comic stage, movie actor. The actor was first "Prince" on stage, then "Rigadin" in movies. He later combined one persona with the other. Before World War I he was known by different names in different countries. He was Whiffles in England and the Commonwealth, Moritz in Germany, Maurice in Romania, Salustiano in Spain, Tartufini in Italy, Prenz in Scandinavian and Slav countries, and Rigadin everywhere else. The latter name suggests a blend of French *rigaudon*, "rigadoon" (a lively dance) and *rigolade*, "fun and games."

Princess Menorah: Steven Cohen (1962–), S.A. gay artist. A menorah is a candelabrum with (usually) seven branches, used in Jewish religious cermony. As such it brings light, as Cohen aimed to do in his art.

Princess Olive: Olivia Serres, née Wilmot (1772–1834), Eng. impostor. In 1806 Olivia Serres was appointed landscape painter to George, Prince of Wales (later George IV). In 1817 she claimed to be an illegitimate daughter of the Duke of Cumberland, brother of George III, and in 1821 had herself rechristened as Princess Olive, legitimate daughter of the duke and his first wife, Olive. Her claims were found to be baseless and she died in prison.

Princess Sharifa: Michelle Gibb (1969–), Br. black reggae singer, songwriter. The musician's adopted Arabic name means "noble," "honorable."

Aileen Pringle: Aileen Bisbee (1895–1989), U.S. movie actress. The actress adopted the name of her first husband, Sir Charles MacKenzie Pringle. She made her screen debut in 1919 as Aileen Savage.

Andrew Seth Pringle-Pattison: Andrew Seth (1856–1931), Sc. philosopher. Born in Edinburgh, Seth added his hyphenated name in 1898 as a condition of accepting the bequest of an estate known as The Haining, near Selkirk, where he and his family lived from then on and where he died.

Yvonne Printemps: Yvonne Wigniolle-Dupré (1894–1977), Fr. singer, movie, stage comedienne.

Freddie Prinze: Frederick Pruetzel (1954–1977), U.S. comedian, TV actor, of Hung. Jewish/Puerto Rican Catholic parentage. (Prinze later referred to himself as "Hungarican.")

James Prior: James Prior Kirk (1851–1922), Eng. novelist.

Samuel Prior *see* Rev. T. **Clark**

Pro: Peter Clive Probyn (1915–1991), Eng. cartoonist, animator. The artist's name not only represents his surname but also implies one who is a "pro," or a professional.

Probus: Charlotte Forman (1716–1787), Eng. journalist, writer, of Ir. parentage. The writer used this name for various contributions to the *London Chronicle*. It represents Latin *probus*, "good," and was not exclusive to Forman.

P.J. Proby: James Marcus Smith (1938–), U.S. rock singer. The singer began his performing career as Jett Powers, an arbitrary "dynamic" name, and the reversed initials of this gave "P.J." "Proby" appears to have originated as some kind of nickname, although it could have tied in with the name of his friend Elvis Presley, who dated his sister. He first used it in 1963.

Procope-Couteau: Michel Coltelli (1684–1753), Fr. physician, humorous writer. Procope-Couteau was the son of François Procope, originally Francesco Procopio di Coltelli, an impoverished Sicilian nobleman living in Paris who some time before

1700 opened the famous Café Procope, the foremost literary and political coffee house of its day.

Professor Longhair: Henry Roeland Byrd (1918–1980), U.S. black blues pianist, singer. The musician took his professional name in 1948. The name was traditional for piano players at that time, and all of the members of Byrd's band, the Four Hairs Combo, wore their hair long. Byrd recalled: "We had long hair in those days and it was [so long it was] almost against the law."

André Prokovsky: André Porkovsky (1939–2009), Fr. ballet dancer, of Russ. parentage.

Sofya Prokofyeva: Sofya Leonidovna Korovina (1928–), Russ. children's writer. The writer probably sought to avoid a name suggesting "cow" (Russian *korova*), so altered it to one with apter associations.

Lozania Prole: Ursula Bloom (1893–1984), Eng. novelist. The pen name was one of the more unusual adopted by the writer, who mainly used conventional names such as Sheila Burnes, Mary Essex, and Rachel Harvey.

Proof: DeShaun Holton (1975–2006), U.S. black rapper.

Marjorie Proops: Rebecca Marjorie Israel (*c.*1911–1996), Br. journalist. The popular "agony aunt" changed her surname to Rayle and dropped her first name at a time of anti–Semitic abuse. Proops was her married name. She began her career with the *Daily Mirror* as a fashion artist under the byline Silvaine: "I was horrified. It made me sound like a flower shop," said "Marje."

Michael Prophet: Michael George Haynes (1957–), Jamaican reggae singer.

Perch Proshyan: Ovanes Stepanovich Ter-Arakelyan (1837–1907), Armenian writer, teacher.

Robert Prosky: Robert Joseph Porzuczek (1930–2008), U.S. stage, movie actor.

Proteus: William Scawen Blunt (1840–1922), Eng. writer, poet, traveler. The writer took this name for his first volume of poetry, *Sonnets and Songs by Proteus* (1875), addressing various women.

John Keith Prothero *see* Sheridan **Jones**

Walter Proudfoot *see* John **Haslette**

Father Prout: Francis Sylvester Mahony (1804–1866), Ir. humorist, journalist. Mahony adopted the name for his contributions to *Fraser's Magazine*, collected in *The Reliques of Father Prout* (1837). He began his career as a teacher, with the aim of becoming a Jesuit, but in 1830 abandoned his vocation when obliged to resign after taking the boys on a drunken spree. He adopted his literary name from a real Father Prout whom he had known as a boy, and who had died in 1830, the year of his resignation. In 1846 he became Rome correspondent for *The Daily News* and his writings there, collected as *Facts and Figures from*

Italy (1847), were published under the pseudonym Don Jeremy Savanarola, basing the name on that of the 15th-century Italian reformer Girolamo Savonarola.

Marcel **Provence**: Marcel Jouhandeau (1888–1979), Fr. novelist, short-story writer, playwright. The writer took his name from Provence, where he was born, disguising his native town of Guéret in his works as "Chaminadour."

Joseph **Prunier**: Guy de Maupassant (1850–1893), Fr. short-story writer. Maupassant used this name for his first story, *La Main d'écorché* (1875). Other occasional names used by him were Guy de Valmont and Maufrigneuse.

Boleslaw **Prus**: Aleksander Glowacki (1847–1912), Pol. novelist.

Kozma **Prutkov**: Aleksey Konstantinovich Tolstoy (1817–1875), Russ. writer + Aleksey Mikhaylovich Zhemchuzhnikov (1821–1908), Russ. poet, his brother + Vladimir Mikhaylovich Zhemchuzhnikov (1830–1884), Russ. poet, his brother. The three men first combined under this name in 1854 when contributing verse and literary parodies to the journal *Sovremennik* ("Contemporary"). Kozma Prutkov was presented as a civil servant turned comic poet, well-intentioned and benign, but smug and unimaginative, judging everything from an official point of view. His character was popularly enhanced by an "autobiography" and he even had his portrait painted. His name was adopted from that of the brothers' valet.

Paul **Pry**: William Heath (1795–1840), Eng. caricaturist, illustrator. The artist's name implies one who "pries" into society. It was originally that of a popular stage character, the hero of John Poole's comedy of the same name (1825). Heath adopted the name in 1827 but abandoned it two years later when it became plagiarized.

Jonathan **Pryce**: Jonathan Price (1947–), Br. stage, TV actor.

Anthony **Pryde**: Agnes Russell Weekes (1880–1940), Eng. novelist. The writer gained her pseudonym by chance. In 1919 her publisher brought out both her own first American novel and James Branch Cabell's *Jurgen*, with particularly high hopes for the latter. However, Cabell's novel was suppressed by the reformer Anthony Comstock. So, "Pride goes before a fall," and Anthony Comstrock caused that fall, just as in history Mark Antony caused his own downfall. Hence the name, which she used jointly with her sister, Rose Kirkpatrick Weekes (1874–1956), for *The Purple Pearl* (1923), then alone for *The Secret Room* (1929).

Maureen **Pryor**: Maureen Pook (1924–1977), Ir. stage, movie, TV actress.

Nicholas **Pryor**: Nicholas David Probst (1935–), U.S. movie actor.

George **Psalmanazar**: ? (*c.*1679–1763), Fr. (or Swiss) literary impostor. The impostor claimed to be from Formosa (modern Taiwan), then little known, and in 1704 published *An History and Geographical Description of Formosa, with Accounts of the Religion, Customs, and Manners of the Inhabitants, by George Psalmanazar, a Native of the said Isle.* The enterprising work included a grammar of the language spoken there and a depiction of its alphabet. Both were complete fabrications, and in due course were revealed to be such by Catholic missionaries, who had actually visited the island. Psalmanazar apparently took his name from the Assyrian king Shalmaneser, adding an initial "P."

"The most extraordinary impostor on record. He himself would never divulge his real name, wishing only to be known as an impostor. So degraded and vagabondish had his life been, that he assumed the above name, and bore it with him to the grave, having faithfully kept the secret of his birth and parentage" [Hamst, p. 104].

Pseudoplutarch: John Milton (1608–1674), Eng. poet. Milton used this name for addressing Charles II in his *Pro Populo Anglicano Defensio* (1651), written in Latin, in which he replied to the *Defensio Regia* (1649) by the French scholar Salmasius (Claude de Saumaise). The overall work was written under his real name, however.

Publius: Alexander Hamilton (1757–1804), U.S. statesman + James Madison (1751–1804), U.S. statesman, president + John Jay (1745–1829), U.S. lawyer, statesman. The joint name was adopted by the three influential men for their essays in *The Federalist* in support of the Constitution. These were published in collected form in 1788. The name "Publius" referred to the intention of the writers to address New York voters publicly, and to persuade them to accept the Constitution. The three had earlier used the name A **Citizen of New York**.

Puck: John Proctor (1836–after 1898), Sc.-born Br. cartoonist, illustrator. The artist first used the familiar Shakespearean name in the late 1850s for some children's book illustrations. Those for the fantasy tales of Roland **Quiz** were almost as well known as the stories themselves.

Don Diego **Puede-Ser**: James Mabbe (1572–1642), Eng. diplomat, Spanish scholar. Mabbe used this name, meaning "James May-Be," punning on his real name, for various translations from the Spanish.

Puff Daddy *see* P. **Diddy**

Charles **Puffy**: Karoly Huszar (1884–1942), Hung.-born U.S. movie comedian.

Punjabee: William Delafield Arnold (1828–1859), Eng. novelist. The Anglo-Indian official was in India as an army officer from 1848, and subsequently became a commissioner in the Punjab. His pseudonym relates to this, and was adopted for his best-known work, *Oakfield; or, Fellowship in the East* (1853). He was the brother of the poet Matthew Arnold (1822–1888).

Giovanni Punto: Jan Václav Stic (or Johann Wenzel Stich) (1746–1803), Bohemian horn player. The musician italianized his name, with Giovanni the equivalent of Jan ("John"), and Punto translating German Stich ("stitch").

Rev. Francis Purcell *see* Charles de **Cresseron**

Reginald Purdell: Reginald Grasdorf (1896–1953), Br. stage, music-hall, movie actor. The actor adopted his mother's maiden name as his stage name.

Bobby Purify: Robert Lee Dickey (1939–), U.S. black soul singer, teaming with cousin James Purify. The two teamed up as a duo in 1965, with Bobby assuming his cousin's (real) name.

Yazep Pushcha: Iosif Pavlovich Plashchinsky (1902–1964), Belorussian poet.

Eleanor Putnam: Harriet Leonora Bates, née Vose (1856–1886), U.S. writer. The author's husband was the novelist Arlo Bates (1850–1918), with whom she wrote *Prince Vance* (completed 1886, published 1888).

Isra Putnam: Greye La Spina, née Fanny Greye Bragg (1880–1969), U.S. horror-story writer. The writer apparently based her name on that of Israel Putnam (1718–1790), the U.S. Revolutionary commander.

Vladimir Alekseyevich Pyast: Vladimir Alekseyevich Pestovsky (1886–1940), Russ. poet. The poet presumably based his pseudonym on his real name.

Iosif Pyatnitsky: Iosif (or Osip) Aronovich Tarshis (1882–1938), Russ. revolutionary.

Edward Pygge *see* Dan **Kavanagh**

Q: (1) (1) Douglas William Jerrold (1803–1857), Br. playwright, humorist; (2) Arthur Thomas Quiller-Couch (1863–1944), Br. novelist, short-story writer. "Q" as a pseudonym often means "query," otherwise "guess who wrote this." (Compare **Q.Q.**) In the case of Quiller-Couch it was his genuine initial. Jerrold also used the name Paul **Prendergast**, keeping "Q" for sociopolitical contributions to the humorous journal *Punch*, with which he was associated from its launch in 1841.

Shu Qi: Lin-Hui Li (1976–), Taiwanese movie actress.

Qorpo Santo: José Joaquím Campos Leão (1829–1889), Brazilian dramatist.

Q.Q.: Jane Taylor (1783–1824), Eng. children's writer. Taylor used this name, probably meaning "query (first name), query (surname)," for her contributions to *The Youth's Magazine*, an evangelical periodical published monthly from 1805 through 1865.

M. Quad: Charles Bertrand Lewis (1842–1924), U.S. printer, journalist, humorist. The pseudonym reveals the writer's original profession, since an "M quad" is a block of type metal the width of a capital "M" used in printing for spacing.

John Quade: John William Saunders (1938–2009), U.S. movie, TV actor.

John Qualen: Johan Oleson, later Johan Oleson Kvalen (1899–1987), Can. movie actor, of Norw. parentage, working in U.S.

Quallon: S.H. Bradbury (*fl.* 1860), Br. poet.

Quark: Eric Burge (1926–), Br. crossword compiler. As a former physics lecturer, the setter chose a term from that science for his pseudonym.

Martin Quatermass *see* John T. **Chance**

Suzi Quatro: Susan Kay Quatrocchio (1950–), U.S. rock singer, guitarist, of It. descent, working in U.K. Quatro began her career at age 14 as a TV gogo dancer called Susi Soul, a name she retained for a while with her group Suzi Soul and the Pleasure Seekers.

Adela Quebec: Sir Gerald Hugh Tyrwhitt-Wilson, Lord Berners (1883–1950), Eng. diplomat, composer, novelist, painter. Lord **Berners** used this female name for his prose lampoon *The Girls of Radcliff Hall* (1935), its title punning on the name of Radclyffe **Hall**.

Ellery Queen: Frederic Dannay (1905–1982), U.S. crime novelist + Manfred Bennington Lee (1905–1971), U.S. crime novelist The two authors were first cousins, of immigrant Jewish stock, in Brooklyn, New York. Their original names were respectively Daniel Nathan and Manford Lepofsky. Dannay's first name came from the the composer Frédéric Chopin, whom he admired, while his last name combined the first syllables of "Daniel" and "Nathan." Lee's first name came from "Manford" and his last name from the first syllable of "Lepofsky."

The duo based the name Ellery Queen on a mutual boyhood friend called Ellery. To this they added "Queen" as they reasoned this would make the name memorable, especially as it occurs throughout their books as the name of the main detective. They had considered other names, such as James Griffen and Wilbur See, but eventually rejected these. For stories involving their second detective, Drury Lane, the pair wrote as Barnaby Ross.

Queen Ida: Ida Lewis (1929–), U.S. black blues musician, sister of Al **Rapone**.

Queen Latifah: Dana Elaine Owens (1970–), U.S. black movie actress, rapper. "Her name is an amalgam of two stages in her self-invention.... The title of Queen she bestowed on herself once she started rapping professionally.... Latifah is the Muslim name she gave herself while perusing a book with a

Muslim cousin when she was eight. 'When I read what it meant, I knew that was me. Latifah: "Delicate, sensitive, kind"'" [*The Times*, May 29, 2003].

Rita de **Queluz**: Rachel de Queiróz (1910–), Brazilian novelist.

Patrick **Quentin** *see* Q. **Patrick**

Peter **Query, Esq.**: Martin Farquhar Tupper (1810–1889), Eng. versifier. The author of the once popular *Proverbial Philosophy* (1838–76, 4 series), a bestseller on both sides of the Atlantic for more than a generation, used this name for *Rides and Reveries of the Late Mr. Aesop Smith* (1858), now long forgotten, like all his other works. (The title-page wording was actually "Edited by Peter Query, F.S.A.," but Tupper was the sole author of the text.) The name is a transparent attempt to disguise a real name.

Quevedo Redivivus: George Gordon Byron (1788–1824), Eng. poet. Byron used this name for *The Vision of Judgment* (1822), a parody of Southey's identically named poem published in 1821. The name means "Quevedo renewed," referring to the Spanish poet and satirist Francisco Gómez de Quevedo y Villegas (1580–1645), imprisoned for his political attacks. Byron also wrote as Horace **Hornem**.

Quex: George Herbert Fosdike Nichols (?–1933), Eng. journalist, editor. The name is perhaps a blend of "query" and "X," suggesting anonymity.

La **Quica**: Francisca González (1907–1967), Sp. ballet dancer, teacher. The flamenco dancer adopted a name that probably arose as a nickname, from a form of Portuguese *cuica*, the four-eyed opossum, with its distinctive big head and small body. The dancer made her debut as a child in a café chantant and was presumably fancifully compared to this animal.

Amanda **Quick**: Jayne Ann Krentz, née Castle (1948–), U.S. romantic novelist.

George **Quiet** *see* Captain Rawdon **Crawley**

John **Quill** *see* Max **Adeler**

Dan **Quin**: Alfred Henry Lewis (c.1858–1914), U.S. journalist, novelist. The writer used this name for his volumes of "Wolfville" stories, presenting a series of whimsical reminiscences of cowboy and mining life in the Southwest by an "Old Cattleman." The first to appear was *Wolfville* itself (1897).

Peter **Quince**: (1) Isaac Story (1774–1803), U.S. satirist, poet; (2) John William McWean Thompson (1920–), Eng. newspaper editor, writer. Story adopted his name from Shakespeare's *A Midsummer Night's Dream*, in which Peter Quince, the carpenter, is stage manager of the "Pyramus and Thisbe" interlude. It seems likely that Thompson used the same source, rather than taking the pseudonym from his American namesake. He used the name for his book *Country Life* (1975).

Freddy **Quinn**: Manfred Petz (1932–), Austr. popular guitarist.

Harley **Quinn**: Wilfrid Thorley (1878–1963), Eng. poet, translator. A name of obvious origin used for diverting works such as *A Caboodle of Beasts* (1945) and *Quinn's Quiz: Rhymed Riddles on a Variety of Subjects for Children or Their Parents* (1957).

Julia **Quinn**: Julie Pitinger, née Cotter (1970–), U.S. writer of historical romances. The writer claims she chose her name so as to be found on bookstore and library shelves next to Amanda **Quick**.

Simon **Quinn**: Martin Cruz Smith (1942–), U.S. mystery writer.

Tony **Quinn**: Anthony Quin (1899–1967), Ir.-born Br. stage, movie actor. Not, of course, to be confused with Mexican-born U.S. movie actor Anthony Quinn (1915–2001).

A.J. **Quinnell**: Philip Nicholson (1940–2005), Eng. thriller writer.

Quino: Joaquin Salvador Lavado (1932–), Argentinian artist, humorist. A pet form of the first name.

Quiz: (1) Charles Dickens (1812–1870), Eng. novelist, short-story writer; (2) [Sir] Max Beerbohm (1872–1956), Eng. essayist, caricaturist; (3) Powys Arthur Lenthall Evans (1899–1981), Eng. caricaturist, painter, of Welsh parentage. The name is a patent disguise or simply a token anonymity. Dickens used the name for *Sketches of Young Couples* (1840). The name happens to blend in well with his better-known pseudonym, **Boz**, as well as with that of his illustrator, **Phiz**.

Roland **Quiz**: Richard Martin Howard Quittenton (1833–1914), Eng. writer of stories for young children. The author's fantasy tales of giants, fairies, magicians, and the like, were illustrated by **Puck**.

John **Quod**: John Treat Irving (1812–1906), U.S. writer on frontier life, nephew of Washington Irving (1783–1859). The writer used this name for *The Quod Correspondence* (1842), also titled *The Attorney*, a novel about legal affairs. For the name itself he may have had the generic name "John Q. Public" or "John Q. Citizen" in mind. These themselves are said to be based on the name of John Quincy Adams (1767–1848), sixth U.S. president.

Richard **Quongti**: Thomas Babington Macaulay (1800–1859), Eng. writer, statesman. The name occurs in "A Prophetic Account of a Grand National Epic Poem, to be entitled 'The Wellingtoniad,' and to be published 2824," in volume 1 of the author's *Miscellaneous Writings and Speeches* (1860): "Richard Quongti will be born at Westminster on the 1st of July, 2786. He will be the younger son of the younger branch of one of the most respectable families in England. He will be linearly descended from Quongti, the famous Chinese liberal, who, after the failure of the heroic attempt of his family to obtain a constitution from the Emperor Fim Fam, will take refuge in England, in the twenty-third century."

Paco **Rabanne**: Francisco Rabaneda y Cuervo (1934–), Sp.-born Fr. fashion designer, esotericist. Paco is a regular Spanish pet form of Francisco.

William **Rabbit**: Katay Don Sasorith (1904–1959), Laotian nationalist, writer of resistance pamphlets. Sasorith adopted the English name from his own name, as "Katay" is Laotian for "rabbit." He used the pseudonym for *Contribution à l'histoire du mouvement d'indépendance national Lao* (1948).

Peer **Raben**: Wilhelm Rabenauer (1940–2007), Ger. movie music composer.

Istvan **Rabovsky**: Istvan Rab (1930–), Hung.–U.S. ballet dancer, teacher.

Rachel: Rachel Blaustein (1890–1931), Russ.-born Israeli poet.

Mlle. **Rachel**: Élisabeth Rachel Félix (1820–1858), Fr. tragic actress of Jewish descent. The actress's sisters also took stage names: Sophie (1819–1877) was Sarah, Adelaide (1828–1872) was Lia, Rachel (1829–1854) was Rebecca, Mélanie Émilie (1836–1909) was Dinah, all of these assumed names being Jewish and biblically interrelated. (Sarah was the mother of Isaac, whose wife, Rebecca, was the sister of Laban, the father of Leah, the mother of Dinah by Jacob, and of Rachel.) Her brother Raphaël (1825–1872) acted under his real name.

Rachilde: Marguerite Vallette, née Eymery (1860–1953), Fr. novelist, literary critic. The writer claimed that her androgynous pseudonym came to her from a 16th-century Swedish medium in a seance.

Koco **Racin**: Kosta Apostolov Solev (1908–1943), Macedonian poet, novelist.

John **Rackham**: John Thomas Phillifent (1916–1976), Br. SF writer.

Radak: David Kimhi (c.1160–1215), Jewish grammarian. The scholar came to be known by an acronymic name formed from the initial letters of *R*abbi *Da*vid *K*imhi.

Radbaz: David ben Zimra (1479–1573), Egyptian Jewish scholar. The Halakhic authority came to be known by an acronymic name formed from the initial letters of *R*abbi *D*avid *b*en *Z*imra.

Carl **Raddatz**: Werner Fritz (1912–), Ger. movie actor.

Karl **Radek**: Karl Berngardovich Sobelsohn (1885–?1939), Russ. Communist propagandist, of Pol. Jewish parentage.

Jack **Radics**: Jordan Bailey (c.1960–), Jamaican reggae singer. The singer's adopted name is a form of "radical," implying a return to one's black roots (Latin *radix*, "root"). A popular Jamaican session band of the 1980s was Roots Radics.

Sowell **Radics**: Noel Bailey (1953–), Jamaican reggae singer. The singer's new first name is based on the original, while his last name is as for Jack **Radics**.

Sheila **Radley**: Sheila Mary Robinson (1928–), Eng. crime writer.

Charlotte **Rae**: Charlotte Rae Lubotsky (1926–), U.S. stage, TV actress, singer.

Johnny **Rae**: John Anthony Pompeo (1934–), U.S. jazz musician.

Anna **Raeburn**: Sally Taylor (1944–), Eng. "agony aunt." The name is not quite such a disguise as it seems. The journalist began life as Sally Taylor, but later changed Sally to "Anna" in order to avoid confusion with a roommate. She then married Michael Raeburn, so that she had a new surname. She subsequently remarried, but by then was well established as Anna Raeburn, so kept this name.

Boyd **Raeburn**: Boyde Albert Raden (1913–1966), U.S. jazz bandleader. The reason for the musician's change of name is unknown.

Raël: Claude Vorilhon (1946–), Fr. cult leader. Vorilhon claims that in 1973 a UFO landed near him in France and that he was invited aboard by an alien. "The man, who called himself 'Yahweh Elohim,' explained that the human race was created by aliens using DNA technology. The aliens wanted Vorilhon to establish an embassy near Jerusalem so they could return to Earth. As a mark of his mission, Vorilhon was given the name Raël (messenger)" [*The Times*, August 17, 2002]. In 1997 Raël founded the company Clonaid, which in 2002 claimed to have genetically engineered the world's first human clone, a baby girl named Eve born on December 26 as an identical clone of her 31-year-old mother.

Gideon **Rafael**: Gideon Ruffer (1913–1999), Ger.-born Israeli diplomat.

Raff: William John Hooper (1916–1996), Eng. cartoonist, writer, broadcaster. The artist adopted the name of his dog, which he had when serving in the Royal Air Force (RAF) in World War II. As a dog name, it also appropriately suggests a bark.

Chips **Rafferty**: John William Goffage (1909–1971), Austral. movie actor. The actor originally considered the name Slab O'Flaherty, but later rejected this in favor of the name by which he became popularly established as a "rugged" character actor.

Pat **Rafferty**: Henry Browne (1861–1952), Ir. popular songwriter.

Raffi: Akop Melik-Akopyan (Hakob Meliq-Hakobian) (1835–1888), Armenian novelist. The writer adopted a name meaning "teacher" (related to English *rabbi*), as which he began his career.

George **Raft**: George Ranft (1895–1980), U.S. movie actor, of Ger.-It. parentage. The actor modified his name in 1917.

Ragini Devi: Esther Luella Sherman (1897–1982), U.S. dancer. The exponent of Indian dance, who claimed to have been a Hindu in her previous birth, took her Hindi name soon after meeting her husband-to-be, Indian chemistry student Ramlal Balaram Bajpai, whom she married in 1921. Their daughter, Indrani, became a leading Indian classical dancer.

James **Raglan:** Thomas James Raglan Cornewall-Walker (1901–1961), Eng. stage actor.

A.R. **Rahman:** A.S. Dileep Kumar (1966–), Ind. composer. The musician took his new name, Allah Rakha Rahman, on converting to Islam in 1988.

Philip **Rahv:** Ivan Greenberg (1908–1973), Ukr.-born U.S. literary critic, editor. Greenberg took the pen name Rahv, Hebrew for "rabbi," on joining the Communist Party in 1933.

Rai: Raimundo Souza Vieira de Oliveira (1965–), Brazilian footballer.

C.E. **Raimond:** Elizabeth Parks, née Robins (1862–1952), U.S.-born Br. actress, novelist. At the age of 18, Robins moved from Zanesville, Ohio, to New York City, where she became an actress under the stage name of Claire Raimond, the surname honoring her brother, Raymond, to whom she was devoted. She later modified this for her writing to C.E. Raimond, the initials being those of her father, Charles Ephraim Robins.

Raimu: Jules-Auguste-César Muraire (1883–1946), Fr. stage, movie actor. The actor formed his professional name from his surname, inverting the first two syllables.

Ferdinand **Raimund:** Ferdinand Jakob Raimann (1790–1836), Austr. playwright, actor.

Rain: Jung Ji Hoon (1982–), South Korean pop singer, movie actor.

Allen **Raine:** Anne Adalisa Puddicombe, née Evans (1836–1908), Welsh novelist. The writer's pseudonym is said to have been suggested to her in a dream. She began writing late in life, and used it for her first and best-known novel, *A Welsh Singer* (1897), a simple love story.

Richard **Raine** *see* Colin **Forbes**

Ella **Raines:** Ella Wallace Raubes (1921–1988), U.S. movie actress.

"Ma" **Rainey:** Gertrude Malissa Nix Pridgett (1886–1939), U.S. black blues singer. Rainey was actually the singer's married name, that of William "Pa" Rainey, who married her in 1904 when he was already an established dancer, singer, and comedian. The couple toured as Rainey & Rainey. "Ma" was a compliment to her authority as "Mother of the Blues," while also hinting at her mature style. She did not make her first recording until she was 37.

W.B. **Rainey:** Wyatt Rainey Blassingame (1909–1985), U.S. writer of children's books, reference works. A switching of initials enabled the writer to use his middle name as a new surname.

Ralph **Rainger:** Ralph Reichenthal (1901–1942), U.S songwriter.

Jānis **Rainis:** Jānis Pliekšāns (1865–1929), Latvian poet, playwright. The poet adopted the name of the hamlet of Raini that he noticed one day on a roadside signpost. His wife was **Aspazija**.

Marvin **Rainwater:** Marvin Karlton Percy (1925–), U.S. country singer, of Cherokee descent. The singer adopted his mother's maiden name as his professional name.

Rosa **Raisa:** Rose Burchstein (1893–1963), Pol.-born U.S. opera singer.

Rajendranath: Rajendra Nath Malhotra (1932–2008), Ind. comic movie actor.

Rajkumar: Muthuraj Singanalluru Puttaswamayya (1929–2006), Ind. movie actor. The actor's screen name, Hindi for "prince," was given him by H.L.N. Simha, the director who gave him his first break.

Bhagwan Shree **Rajneesh:** Chandra Mohan Jain (1931–1990), Ind. cult leader, "sex guru." Sources differ regarding the cultist's original name, but it is usually given as above. It may equally have been Rajneesh Chandra Mohan. Bhagwan represents the Hindi word for "god," Shree is a Sanskrit title of respect meaning literally "majesty," and "Rajneesh" means "ruler of the night," denoting the moon (the meaning of the name Chandra). Rajneesh took his new name in 1970 on settling in Poona (Pune) with seven disciples, obliging them to change their name as he had done. Jane Smith thus became Ma Prem Hasyo. Bhagwan came to the U.S. in 1981 but was expelled in 1985 and returned to Poona, where he dropped the honorific Bhagwan and instead adopted the name Osho, "teacher."

Sabit **Rakhman:** Sabit Kerim ogly Makhmudov (1910–1970), Azerbaijani writer.

David **Raksin:** John Sartain (1912–), U.S. movie music composer, conductor.

Ralbag: Levi ben Gershom (1288–1344), Jewish philosopher. The scholar became known by an acronymic name formed from the initial latters of *R*abbi *L*evi *b*en *G*ershom. He is also known as Gersonides, a Medieval Latin form of his original name, in which the Greek suffix *-ides*, meaning "son of," translates Hebrew *ben*.

Radoi **Ralin:** Dimitar Stefanov Stoyanov (1923–2004), Bulg. poet, dissident.

Børge **Ralov:** Børge Peterson (1908–1981), Dan. ballet dancer.

Jessie **Ralph:** Jessie Ralph Chambers (1864–1944), U.S. movie actress.

Jan **Ralston** *see* Elisabeth **Kyle**

Jobyna **Ralston:** Jobyna Raulston (1901–1967), U.S. movie actress.

Vera **Ralston:** Vera Helena Hruba (1919–2003), Cz. ice skater, movie actress, working in U.S. Fearing Americans would have problems pronouncing her birth name, Ralston took a new name from a make of breakfast cereal in 1943 when she was offered a movie contract by Herbert J. Yates of Republic Pictures. It was because of Ralston that Vera **Miles** was obliged to take a new name.

Ramah: Meir Abulafia (?1170–1244), Sp. Jewish Talmudic scholar. The scholar came to be known by an acronymic name formed from the initial letters of *R*abbi *M*eir *ha*-Levi, "Rabbi Meir the Levite."

Ramakrishna: Gadadhar Chatterji (or Gadadhar Chattopadhyaya) (1836–1886), Bengali saint, mystic. The holy man's name combines those of Rama and Krishna, respectively the seventh and eight avatars (incarnations), each meaning "dark one," of the god Vishnu. Rama and Krishna were formerly two of the most widely worshipped Hindu deities. The Ramakrishna Missionary Society that bears the mystic's name was founded in Calcutta in 1897 by **Vivekananda**, his most important disciple.

Walter **Ramal:** Walter de la Mare (1873–1956), Eng. poet, short-story writer. The writer used the name, a reversal of his surname, for an early volume of poems for children, *Songs of Childhood* (1902).

Ramana Maharshi: Venkataraman Aiyer (1879–1950), Ind. Hindu philosopher, yogi. The guru's name is properly a title meaning "Raman the great sage," from Hindi *maha*, "great," and *rishi*, "sage."

Ramatirtha: Tirath Rama (1873–1906), Ind. Hindu religious leader.

Rambam: Moshe ben Maimon (1135–1204), Sp. Jewish thinker. The Talmudic authority came to be known by an acronymic name formed from the initial letters of *R*abbi *M*oshe *b*en *M*aimon. He is also known as Maimonides, a Medieval Latin form of his original name, in which the Greek suffix *-ides*, meaning "son of," translates Hebrew *ben*. Compare the name below.

Ramban: Moshe ben Nahman (1194–1270), Sp. Jewish kabbalist.The scholar came to be known by an acronymic name formed from the initial latters of *R*abbi *M*oshe *b*en *N*ahman. He is also known as Nahmanides, a Medieval Latin form of his original name, with the Greek suffix *-ides*, meaning "son of," translating Hebrew *ben*. Compare the name above.

Eddie **Rambeau:** Edward Cletus Fluri (1943–), U.S. pop singer.

Marie **Rambert:** Myriam Ramberg (1888–1982), Pol.-born Br. ballet dancer, teacher. The dancer's birth certificate showed her first name to be Cyvia. Myriam was thus originally a nickname, given her by her French poet friend, Edmée Delbecque. Myriam's father's family name was Rambam, and her father and his brothers had this name changed to make them seem only children, and so escape military service. One son thus retained the name Rambam, one (her father) took the name Ramberg, one took Rambert, as Myriam herself did, and the fourth, to represent their Polish nationality, assumed the name Warszawski ("of Warsaw") [Marie Rambert, *Quicksilver: An Autobiography*, 1972]. *See also* **Rambam**.

A **Rambler** *see* Joseph **Palmer**

Dack **Rambo:** Norman Rambeau (1941–1994), U.S. TV actor. Rambeau was raised on a cotton farm with his twin brother Orman. The two decided to change their names to Dack and Dirk and launched themselves on a singing career in the mold of the Everley Brothers as the Rambo Twins. Dirk was killed in an auto accident in 1967.

Natacha **Rambova:** Winifred Shaunessy Hudnut (1897–1966), U.S. dance teacher, movie actress.

Ramhal: Moses Hayyim Luzzatto (1707–1747), It. Jewish kabbalist. The scholar, one of the founders of modern Hebrew poetry, came to be known by an acronymic name formed from the initial letters of *R*abbi *M*oses *Ha*yyim *L*uzzatto.

Roger "Ram" **Ramirez:** Roeger Ameres (1913–1994), Puerto Rican jazz pianist. The musician hispanicized his name, with his nickname of "Ram" in turn derived from this.

Rammelzee: Jean Michel Basquiet (*c*.1960–), Fr. hip-hop musician. The former graffiti artist compiled his mystic name from "Ramm," "Elevation," and "Z" (zee), the latter said to denote two-way energy.

Laon **Ramon:** Leon Janney (1917–1980), U.S. juvenile movie actor. The actor was given his screen name by his mother, using her own maiden name. In 1928, however, a numerologist advised her that this was not an auspicious name, and he reverted to the original.

Paul **Ramon:** Paul McCartney (1942–), Eng. pop musician. The former Beatles member adopted this name when the group (then called the Silver Beatles) toured Scotland in 1959. "'It was exciting changing your name,' says Paul. 'It made it all seem real and professional. It sort of proved you did a real act, if you had a stage name.' Paul turned himself into Paul Ramon. He can't remember where he got the Ramon bit from. 'I must have heard it somewhere. I thought it sounded really glamorous, sort of **Valentino**-ish.' George [Harrison] became Carl Harrison after one of his heroes, Carl Perkins. Stu [Sutcliffe] became Stu de Stijl, after the art movement.

John [Lennon] can't remember what he called himself, if anything, but others remember him as Johnny Silver" [Hunter Davies, *The Beatles*, 1968].

Dee Dee **Ramone:** Douglas Glenn Colvin (1952–2002), U.S. punk rock musician, teaming with Joey, Johnny, and Tommy **Ramone** to form the Ramones. The group took their collective name in 1974 from Paul McCartney of the Beatles, who called himself Paul **Ramon** when with the earlier Silver Beatles.

Joey **Ramone:** Jeffrey Hyman (1951–2001), U.S. punk rock musician (*see* Dee Dee **Ramone**).

Johnny **Ramone:** John Cummings (1948–2004), U.S. punk rock musician (*see* Dee Dee **Ramone**).

Tommy **Ramone:** Tom Erdelyi (1952–), Hung.-born U.S. punk rock musician (*see* Dee Dee **Ramone**).

Tuesday Lobsang **Rampa:** Cyril Henry Hoskin (1911–1981), Eng. novelist. In 1956 the former plumber's assistant published a romantic tale, *The Third Eye*, telling of a Tibetan youth from Lhasa who had a hole made in his head (a "third eye") that endowed him with all manner of mystic powers. It emerged that the author, who claimed to be the youth in question, spoke not a word of Tibetan and had not even visited the country. Other novels followed under the same exotic pen name, and more and more readers lapped up their magic and mystery. Hoskin was also known as Dr. Carl Kuon Suo.

Anne **Rampling** *see* A.N. **Roquelaure**

Edogawa **Rampo:** Taro Hirai (1894–1965), Jap. mystery, horror-story writer. Rampo was inspired by the U.S. writer Edgar Allan Poe and adopted the Japanese form of his name as his own pseudonym.

Grace **Ramsay:** Kathleen O'Meara (1839–1888), Ir. biographer, novelist, working in France. The writer reserved this name for her novels.

Ranavanola I: Ramavo (*c*.1800–1861), queen of Madagascar. The wife of King Radama I, who ruled alone after his death in 1828, took a name meaning "she who has been bent," from *Ra* a name indicator for Malagasy males, and *avàlone*, "who is bent," from *vàlona*, "bend," "fold." The name seems to imply that following the death of her husband, the queen was "bent" to the will of the prime minister. The name was borne by two later queens, Ranavanola II and III, the latter being deposed and exiled by the French in 1897.

Ayn **Rand:** Alisa Zinovyevna Rosenbaum (1905–1982), Russ.-born U.S. novelist, screenwriter. In 1926 Rosenbaum left the Soviet Union for America, renaming herself "Ayn" (rhyming with "nine") from the Finnish writer Eino **Leino** (whom she had never read), and "Rand" from the Remington-Rand typewriter that she brought with her.

Sally **Rand:** Helen Gould Beck (1904–1979), U.S. fan dancer, movie actress. Rand's stage name was apparently given her by Cecil B. De Mille, who took it from the Rand McNally atlas.

Anne Frances **Randall:** Mary Robinson, née Darby (1758–1800), Eng. actress, writer. Robinson adopted this name for *A Letter to the Women of England, on the Injustice of Mental Subordination* (1799), perhaps taking it from Ann Randall, a supposed prostitute imprisoned for shoplifting in 1783, whose story had been reported in the press of the day.

Tony **Randall:** Leonard Rosenberg (1920–2004), U.S. movie actor. The actor's new surname is an approximate anagram of his original first name.

Robert **Randau:** Robert Arnaud (1873–1950), Algerian novelist, working in French. A simple anagram.

James **Randi:** Randall James Hamilton Zwinge (1928–), Can.-born U.S. magician, lecturer.

Frank **Randle:** Arthur McEvoy (1901–1957), Eng. music-hall comedian, movie actor.

Ellen **Randolph** *see* Marilyn **Ross**

Elsie **Randolph:** Elsie Florence Killick (1901–1982), Br. revue artist.

Jane **Randolph:** Jane Roermer (1919–), U.S. movie actress.

John **Randolph:** Emanuel Hirsch Cohen (1915–2004), U.S. movie actor, of Rom. parentage.

Alex **Random** *see* Fenton **Brockley**

Ken **Ranger** *see* Gordon **Ashe**

Otto **Rank:** Otto Rosenfeld (1884–1939), Austr.-born U.S. psychologist. The psychologist assumed his pen name in adolescence and formalized it a few years later, seeing it as symbolizing self-creation.

Rankin: John Rankin Waddell (1966–), Sc. photographer.

Ranking Joe: Joe Jackson (*c*.1960–), Jamaican reggae musician. "Ranking" implies excellence, as for Shabba **Ranks**.

Cutty **Ranks:** Philip Thomas (1965–), Jamaican DJ, reggae musician. Thomas's nickname may have sprung from his early career as a butcher. At first he literally wielded a cleaver, but now cut through rhythms and other DJs as if they were slices of meat. "Ranks" implies excellence, as for Shabba **Ranks**.

Shabba **Ranks:** Rexton Rawlston Fernando Gordon (1966–), Jamaican reggae musician. The singer adopted the name Shabba as a youth: "I was 15 when I got this name. It comes from King Shabba of Africa. It is a revolutionary name and a powerful name" [*Sunday Times Magazine*, December 13, 1992]. "Ranks" was partly suggested by "Rexton," in which "Rex" is already "king," but also implies "ranks" in the black teenage slang sense "highly regarded person" (one who "ranks" or is excellent). The African king referred to was a late 16th-century Nupe ruler.

Abram Ranovich: Abram Borisovich Rabinovich (1885–1948), Russ. ancient historian.

Stephen Ransome: Frederick C. Davis (1902–1977), U.S. crime novelist.

Raoul: (1) Peter Morland Churchill (1909–1972), Br. wartime agent, working in France; (2) Hugh Duff McLaughlan (1920–), Sc. music-hall dancer, teaming with **Babette**, his wife. Churchill led the group joined by **Odette**, and both were captured by the Gestapo. She saved him by claiming to be his wife, and was herself spared because the Germans believed she was the niece of Winston Churchill. The two in fact married in 1947, but both later remarried. "On the 28th of August, 1942, Captain Peter Morland Churchill, *alias* Monsieur Pierre Chauvet, *alias* Monsieur Pierre Chambrun, known in the field as 'Raoul,' had arrived in France for the third time since the outbreak of hostilities" [Jerrard Tickell, *Odette: The Story of a British Agent*, 1949].

Raphael: Raffaello Sanzio (1483–1520), It. painter, architect. Known universally by his first name, the artist's surname came from his father, Giovanni Santi (*c.*1440–1494).

Al Rapone: Al Lewis (1937–), U.S. black blues musician, brother of **Queen Ida**. A variant on "Al Capone."

Dizzee Rascal: Dylan Mills (1985–), Br. black rapper.

Renato Rascel: Renato Ranucci (1912–1991), It. movie actor.

Rashba: Solomon ben Abraham Adret (1235–1310), Sp. rabbi, theologian. The name by which the Jewish authority came to be known is an acronym of the initial letters of *Ra*bbi *Sh*lomo *b*en *A*braham *A*dret. Compare the three names below.

Rashbam: Samuel ben Meir (*c.*1080–*c.*1174), Fr. rabbi, biblical commentator. The scholar's name is an acronym of his Hebrew name: *Ra*bbi *Sh*muel *b*en *M*eir. Compare the name above and the two below.

Rashbaz: Simeon ben Zemah Duran (1361–1444), Sp. rabbi. The scholar's name is acronymic, from the initial letters of *Ra*bbi *S*imeon *b*en *Z*emah. Compare the two names above and the one below.

Rashi: Solomon ben Isaac (*c.*1040–1105), Fr. rabbi, biblical commentator. The scholar's name represents the initial letters of his Hebrew name: *Ra*bbi *Sh*lomo *Yi*tzhaki. Compare the three names above.

Atilla Rasikh: Atilla Kadyrovich Rasulev (1916–), Russ. (Tatar) writer.

Ras Michael: Michael George Henry (*c.*1943–), Jamaican drummer, reggae musician. Henry grew up in a Rastafarian community. Hence "Ras."

Grigory Rasputin: Grigoriy Yefimovich Novykh

(?1864–1916), Russ. monk, court favorite, religious fanatic. Rasputin was born in Siberia as the son of a peasant named Yefim Novykh. He came to lead a dissolute life, and was given the name by which he became known and which he adopted as a surname. It derives from Russian *rasputnyy*, "dissolute." An earlier uncomplimentary nickname had been "Varnak," a Siberian word meaning "vagabond" [Prince Yousoupoff, *Rasputin*, 1974].

Alexis Rassine: Alexis Rays (1919–1992), Lithuanian-Br. ballet dancer. The dancer may have based his name on that of Leonid **Massine**.

Thalmus Rasulala: Jack Crowder (1939–1991), U.S. black movie actor.

Rasul Rza: Rasul Ibragim ogly Rzayev (1910–1981), Azerbaijani poet. The poet adopted a conventional curtailment of his original name.

Eomot RaSun: Ezra Lee Blakely, Jr. (1945–), U.S. black blues singer, harmonica player. In 1973 Blakely changed his name and began to study African history. His new first name is said to mean "the child comes home unto himself." His last name refers to the ancient Egyptian sun god Ra, and is thus identical to the name of **Sun Ra**.

Master Ratan: Syed Nazir Ali (1942–), Ind. child movie actor. The name Ratan means "jewel" (Sanskrit *ratna*).

Jonatan Ratosch: Uriel Halpern (1909–), Pol. Jewish poet, working in Israel. The writer also used the name Uriel Schelach.

Rattlebrain: George F. Halse (*fl.*1864), Eng. writer. Halse used this name for *Sir Guy de Guy: a Stirring Romaunt* (1864). A rattlebrain is a shallow, voluble person.

Morgan Rattler: Percival Weldon Banks (1806–1850), Ir. lawyer, journalist. Banks used this name for contributions to *Fraser's Magazine*. The name is too early to have been suggested by the main character of R.M. Ballantyne's novel *Martin Rattler* (1858).

Rattlesnake Annie: Rosanne McGowan, née Gallimore (1941–), U.S. country singer, of Cherokee descent. The singer acquired her name as a nickname, for the rattlesnake's tail that she took to wearing on her right ear.

Simon Rattray *see* Elleston **Trevor**

Mlle. Raucourt: Françoise-Marie-Antoinette-Josèphe Saucerotte (1756–1815), Fr. actress. The actress appears to have based her stage name on her surname.

Rausch: Francis Peter Whitford (1941–), Eng. cartoonist, illustrator. The artist's name may have arisen from some incident or personal characteristic. German *Rausch* means "intoxication," "ecstasy."

Ravachol: François Claudius Kœnigstein

(1859–1892), Fr. anarchist. The anarchist, guillotined for his many assassination attempts, adopted his mother's maiden name.

Genya **Ravan**: Goldie Zelkowitz (1942–), Pol.-born U.S. rock musician.

Charlotte **Raven** *see* Craig **Brown**

Eddie **Raven**: Edward Garvin Futch (1944–), U.S. country musician.

Mike **Raven**: Churton Fairman (1927–1997), Eng. radio DJ, movie actor.

Ray: Raymond Wilson Chesterton (1912–), Eng. cartoonist, illustrator, writer.

Aldo **Ray**: Aldo da Re (1926–1991), U.S. movie actor.

Cyril **Ray**: Cyril Rotenberg (1908–1991), Eng. writer on wine. Ray's father, Albert Benson Ray, changed the family name from Rotenberg to Ray in 1913.

Jean **Ray**: Jean-Raymond De Kremer (1887–1964), Belg. novelist, short-story writer.

Man **Ray** *see* **Man Ray**

Michel **Ray**: Michel Ray Popper (1944–), Br. juvenile movie actor, working in U.S.

Nicholas **Ray**: Raymond Nicholas Kienzle, Jr. (1911–1979), U.S. movie director, of Norw. descent.

René **Ray**: Irene Creese (1911–1993), Eng. stage, movie actress.

Ted **Ray**: Charles Olden (1905–1977), Eng. comedian, violinist, father of actors Robin Ray (1934–1998) and Andrew Ray (1939–2003). The comedian's original name remains uncertain. His surname at birth seems to have been Alden, changed by his parents when he was still a boy to Olden. It is known that Olden appeared early in his career as Hugh Neek ("The Unique Entertainer"), then as Nedlo ("The Gypsy Violinist"), reversing his surname. Not long after, he selected his permanent stage name, adopting it from a noted golfer of the day, Ted Ray, British winner of the 1920 U.S. Open Championship.

Rayanne: Winifred L. Martens-Moore (1918–), Br. "mental telepathist."

Raybeez: Raymond Barbieri (1961–1997), U.S. rock singer.

Carol **Raye**: Kathleen Mary Corkrey (1923–), Br. stage, movie actress.

Don **Raye**: Donald McRae Wilhoite, Jr. (1909–1985), U.S. popular singer, songwriter.

Martha **Raye**: Margaret Teresa Yvonne Reed (1916–1994), U.S. radio, TV comedienne, singer.

Raymond: Peter Raymond (originally Raymondo Pietro Carlo Bessone) (1911–1992), Eng. hair stylist, of It. parentage ("Mr. Teazy-Weazy"). The coiffeur later gallicized his first two original names and added a second "Raymond" as a surname, so that his full name was Raymond Pierre Carlo Bessone Raymond.

Derek **Raymond**: Robert William Arthur Cook (1931–1994), Br. crime writer. The writer adopted the name of a drinking companion in order to avoid being confused with Robin Cook, U.S. author of medical thrillers.

Fred **Raymond**: Friedrich Vesely (1900–1954), Austr. popular composer, lyricist.

Gene **Raymond**: Raymond Guion (1908–1998), U.S. stage, movie, TV actor. The actor made his debut on Broadway as a juvenile stage performer under his original Gallic-sounding name. He then switched this around for a more all-American name when he arrived in Hollywood in 1931.

Henry Augustus **Raymond**: Sarah Scott, née Robinson (1723–1795), Eng. writer. Scott adopted this male name as author of *The History of Gustavus Ericson, King of Sweden* (1761).

Jack **Raymond**: John Caines (1892–1953), Br. movie director, producer.

John T. **Raymond**: John O'Brien (1836–1887), U.S. comedian. It is uncertain when or why the comic actor chose his stage name.

Paula **Raymond**: Paula Ramona Wright (1923–2003), U.S. movie actress. Wright was billed as Paula Rae Wright in her first movie, *Keep Smiling* (1938).

Paul **Raymond**: Geoffrey Anthony Quinn (1925–2008), Br. impresario, nightclub owner, of Ir. parentage. Quinn adopted his new name in 1947, when he had his first break in a pierhead variety show at the seaside resort of Clacton, Essex. His partner had the name Gaye Dawn, and the pair were billed as Mr. and Mrs. Tree, a name suggesting "mystery."

Elizabeth **Rayner** *see* Philip **Curtin**

[Rabbi] John **Rayner**: Hans Sigismund Rahmer (1924–2005), Ger. born Br.Jewish pastor, scholar.

Olive Pratt **Rayner**: Charles Grant Blairfindie Allen (1848–1899), Can.-born Br. writer, novelist. Grant Allen, as he usually called himself, used this name for such novels as *The Type-Writer Girl* (1897) and *Rosalba; The Story of Her Development* (1899). He also wrote short stories for magazines as J. Arbuthnot Wilson and was Cecil Power for his first novel, *Philistia* (1884).

Adam **Rayski**: Abraham Rajgrodski (1913–2008), Pol. Jewish Communist activist, spy, journalist.

Andy **Razaf**: Andreamenentania Paul Razafinkeriefo (1895–1973), U.S. songwriter, of Madagascan descent. Madagascan personal names (and placenames) are notoriously lengthy, and in this case a radical curtailment was clearly desirable. It was made, originally as Andrea Razaf, in 1913.

Razzle: Nicholas Dingley (1963–1984), Br. rock drummer.

Miss **Read**: Dora Jessie Saint, née Shafe (1913–),

Eng. writer. The author, a former schoolteacher, became popular for her gentle accounts of life centering on a village school, beginning with *Village School* (1955) itself. She has described how she chose her pen name: "That book, *Village School*, was being written in the first person and I remember trying to think of an ordinary kind of name by which this central character [of a village schoolmistress] would be known. My mother's maiden name was Read. There seemed no reason to seek further. When the time came for it to be published, Robert Lusty, one of the directors of the firm of Michael Joseph which was to publish this book, ... suggested that it would be a good idea to let it appear under the pseudonym of 'Miss Read,' thus creating a modest secret ... Miss Read was my *alter ego*, and I answered as readily to my assumed spinster's name as my married one. As the years passed, the secrecy began to wear a little thin. In any case, my immediate circle knew who I was, and if readers wrote to me I always answered, signing myself 'Dora Saint (Miss Read)'" [Dora Saint, "The Birth of Miss Read," *The Countryman*, Vol. 83, No. 4, Winter 1978].

Janet **Reade**: Helen Rulon (1910–), U.S. movie actress.

Pauline **Réage** *see* Dominique **Aury**

Sam **Reaves**: Samuel Allen Salter (1954–), U.S. thriller writer.

Hugues **Rebell**: Georges Grassal (1867–1905), Fr. poet, novelist.

Ivan **Rebroff**: Hans-Rolf Rippert (1931–2008), Ger. folksinger. The singer claimed Russian ancestry and accordingly fashioned himself a Russian name.

Danny **Red**: Daniel Clarke (*c.*1962–), Br. black DJ, reggae musician. Clarke originally toured Europe under the name Danny Dread, but then moved to Jamaica and changed his name to Danny Red to avoid confusion with another DJ using the Dread name.

Sonny **Red**: Sylvester Kyner (1932–1981), U.S. jazz saxophonist.

John **Redfern** *see* Ellis **Peters**

Martin **Redfield**: Alice Brown (1857–1948), U.S. novelist, short-story writer, playwright. The author used this name for her early books, explaining that she did so because "the publishers told me I would have better sale for my first novel if I took a man's name" [Marble, p.227].

Redman: Reggie Noble (1974–), U.S. black rapper. The rapper is said to have come by his nickname at age 11 when his face turned red after being hit by a snowball.

Red Rat: Wallace Wilson (1978–), Jamaican DJ, reggae musician. Wilson began his DJ career under the name of Mice, a nickname given him by

his football coach. On learning of another DJ of this name, he became Red Rat, following the personal comment, "Yah red and yah look like a rat." (In West Indian slang, "red" means "red-eyed," often as a result of taking marijuana.)

Red River Dave: Dave McEnery (1914–2002), U.S. cowboy singer.

Anthony **Red Rose**: Anthony Cameron (*c.*1962–), Jamaican reggae musician. Reggae singer Michael Rose originally performed as Tony Rose, leading Cameron to call himself Red Rose to avoid confusion.

Sumner **Redstone**: Sumner Rothstein (1923–), U.S. businessman. The Viacom chief executive officer and chairman adopted a literal translation of his German Jewish name.

Red Thunder Cloud: Carlos Westez (1919–1996), U.S. Native American storyteller.

Ralph **Redway** *see* Frank **Richards**

Alex **Redwood** *see* George **Sava**

L.A. **Reece** *see* Rhys **Adrian**

A.C. **Reed**: Aaron Corthen (1926–2004), U.S. black blues musician. Corthen's new name is said to pay tribute to the music of Jimmy **Reed**, whose half-brother he sometimes claimed to be.

Alan **Reed**: Edward Bergman (1908–1977), U.S. movie actor.

Donna **Reed**: Donna Belle Mullenger (1921–1986), U.S. movie, TV actress, hostess. The actress used the name Donna Adams when she began her screen career, later changing the second name to Reed.

Eliot **Reed**: Eric Ambler (1909–1998), Eng. crime writer + Percival Charles Rodda (1891–1976), Austral. novelist. The writers used this name for two coauthored novels. Rodda also wrote as Gavin Holt and Gardner Low.

Florence **Reed** *see* Theodore Moses **Tobani**

Jerry **Reed**: Jerry Reed Hubbard (1937–), U.S. country singer, guitarist.

Jimmy **Reed**: Mathis James Reed Leland (1925–1976), U.S. black blues musician.

Lou **Reed**: Louis Allen Firbank (1943–), U.S. rock musician. The musician may not have changed his name at all, and many sources have his original name as Louis Allen Reed.

Robert **Reed**: John Robert Rietz, Jr. (1932–1992), U.S. TV actor.

Walter **Reed**: Walter Reed Smith (1916–2001), U.S. movie actor.

Harry **Reems**: Herbert Streicher (1947–), U.S. porno movie actor.

Dilwyn **Rees**: Glyn Edmund Daniel (1914–1986), Welsh archaeologist, writer. The archaeologist, a popularizer of his specialty on radio and TV, used this pseudonym for two detective novels: *The Cambridge Murders* (1945) and *Welcome Death* (1954).

Robert **Rees:** Alfred Neobard Palmer (1847–1915), Welsh historian. The scholar used this pseudonym for his novel *Owen Tanat* (1897).

Della **Reese:** Dellareese Taliaferro, née Early (1931–), U.S. black gospel, pop singer.

Ada **Reeve:** Adelaide Mary Isaacs (1874–1966), Eng. music-hall artist, of Fr.-Du. Jewish parentage. The singer was registered at birth as above, although her father had already changed his name: "Father was born in Norwich as Samuel Isaacs, but he changed his name to Charles Reeves when he left home at the age of sixteen to go on the stage.... He once told me that he chose the name of Reeves because of his mother's friendship with [John] Sim[s] Reeves, the great tenor of those days. Looking at some old programmes I find myself billed as 'Little Ada Reeves,' with the final 's' to my name, and it was not until some years later that it disappeared and I finally became Ada R*eeve*. I do not recollect how or why this came about — it just happened" [Ada Reeve, *Take It For a Fact*, 1954].

George **Reeves:** George Brewer (1914–1959), U.S. movie actor.

Vic **Reeves:** James Roderick Moir (1959–), Br. entertainer, teaming with Bob Mortimer (1959–). The comedian comments: "Jim Moir is not a showbiz name. In the first place, it's hard to say and it's also difficult to spell. Anyway, the head of BBC Light Entertainment is called Jim Moir. I think Vic Reeves is a good name. It was the first that came into my head" [*Telegraph Magazine*, July 6, 1991]. The choice of name seems right for his role as entertainer: "It is ... an inspired invention, suggesting a pally but sleazy master of ceremonies at a holiday camp, a man well out of date in whatever he finds himself" [*Sunday Times*, April 4, 1999]. According to some sources he actually took the name from two of his favorite singers, Vic **Damone** and Jim Reeves (1923–1964).

Erik **Reger:** Heinrich Dannenberger (1893–1954), Ger. novelist.

Seeley **Regester:** Metta Victoria Victor, née Fuller (1831–1885), U.S. writer. Metta Victor first used her pen name for the first American detective novel, *The Dead Letter*, serialized in 1866.

Reggae George: George Daley (*c*.1950–), Jamaican reggae musician.

Regina di Luanto: Guendalina Lipperini (1862–1914), It. novelist.

Régine: Rachel Zylberberg (1929–), Fr. nightclub owner.

José **Régio:** José Maria dos Reis Pereira (1901–1969), Port. poet.

Regiomontanus: Johannes Müller (1436–1476), Ger. astronomer, mathematician. The name is the latinized equivalent, meaning "king's mountain," of the astronomer's birthplace, now the small town of Königsberg in Bavaria, near Schweinfurt (not the better-known city of Königsberg that is now Kaliningrad in western Russia, as stated by some sources).

Frédéric **Regnal:** [Baron] Frédéric d'Erlanger: (1868–1943), Br. composer, of Ger.–U.S. parentage. The composer, a banker by profession, used this royal-looking reversal of most of his surname for some early works.

Ada **Rehan:** Ada Delia Crehan (1857–1916), Ir.-born U.S. stage actress. During the actress's first season at the Arch Street Theatre, Philadelphia, in 1873, a printing error in the program listed her as "Ada C. Rehan," and she kept the name.

Frank **Reicher:** Franz Reichert (1875–1965), Ger.-born U.S. movie actor.

Christian **Reid:** Frances Christine Fisher Tiernan (1846–1920), U.S. novelist. Following the death of her mother, and the loss of her father in 1861 during the Civil War, Christine Fisher decided to write for her living, protecting her privacy with a pseudonym. She chose "Christian" as a sexually ambiguous variant of her first name and "Reid" because it seemed modest and unassuming.

Virginia **Reid** *see* Lynne **Carver**

Sidney **Reilly:** Shlomo (later Sigmund) Rosenblum (1874–1925), Russ.-born Br. spy, of Ukr. Jewish parentage. Rosenblum came to England in 1895 and three years later adopted the persona of an Anglo-Irish gentleman named Sidney George Reilly on marrying an Irishwoman, Margaret Thomas, after arranging her husband's death by poisoning. Following further bigamous marriages he was lured back to Moscow, where he was arrested and executed. He would subsequently be the inspiration for English writer Ian Fleming's fictional masterspy James Bond.

William K. **Reilly** *see* Gordon **Ashe**

Max **Reiner** *see* Taylor **Caldwell**

Max **Reinhardt:** Max Goldmann (1873–1943), Austr. stage actor, manager, director, working in U.S. The actor replaced his Orthodox Jewish name by one that would not be regarded as specifically Jewish.

Gert **Reinholm:** Gert Schmidt (1926–), Ger. ballet dancer, director.

Harald **Reinl:** Karl Reiner (1908–1986), Ger. movie director.

Hans **Reinmar:** Hans Wochinz (1895–1961), Austr. opera singer, working in Germany.

Ricardo **Reis** *see* Alberto **Caeiro**

Réjane: Gabrielle-Charlotte Réju (1857–1920), Fr. stage actress, theater manager.

Rema: Moses ben Israel Isserles (*c*.1530–1572), Pol. Jewish legal authority. The scholar came to be known by an acronymic name formed from the initial letters of *R*abbi *M*oses ben Israel.

Vaclav Remar: Vaclav Svadlena (1914–), Cz. ballet dancer.

Erich Maria Remarque: Erich Paul Remark (1898–1970), Ger. novelist, working in U.S. According to some sources, the writer's original name was Kramer, which he inverted to give Remark. He was granted American citizenship in 1947.

Ede Reményi: Eduard Hoffmann (1828–1898), Hung. violinist. The player adopted a Hungarian equivalent of his German name: Hungarian *remény* means "hope," and German *hoffen*, "to hope."

Uncle Remus: Joel Chandler Harris (1848–1908), U.S. writer. The white writer created the character of Uncle Remus, a wise and friendly old Negro, who told stories about Brer Rabbit, Brer Fox, and other animals to the small son of a plantation owner. The formula was new, and was immensely popular. Harris's first Uncle Remus story appeared in the *Atlanta Constitution* in 1879. In 1907 he founded his own *Uncle Remus's Magazine*.

Colonel Rémy: Gilbert Renault (1904–1984), Fr. Resistance hero, writer, politician.

Kid Rena: Henry René (1898–1949), U.S. black jazz trumpeter.

Duncan Renaldo: Renault Renaldo Duncan (1904–1980), U.S. movie actor, painter.

Renaud: Renaud Séchan (1952–), Fr. singer, songwriter.

Maurice Renaud: Maurice Arnold Croneau (1861–1933), Fr. opera singer.

Mary Renault: Eileen Mary Challans (1905–1983), Br. novelist, working in South Africa. Mary Challans began writing when still a nurse. Reviewing her novel *The Praise Singer* (1978), Philippa Toomey wrote: "Why does she use a pen name? When she started to write, she had to keep it fairly secret — Matron, that presiding deity, being almost stronger than Athene and definitely more vengeful, might not have approved. 'So I chose the name from [a character in the *Chroniques* of the 14th-century French writer] Froissart — I never thought of the car!'" [*The Times*, June 7, 1980]. An article of July 2, 1994 in this same paper, however, claimed she took the name from Renault, the French leader of a group of conspirators in Thomas Otway's play *Venice Preserv'd* (1682). She pronounced the name "Renolt."

Liz Renay: Pearl Elizabeth Dobbins (1934–), U.S. movie actress.

W.S. Rendra: Willibrodus Surendra Broto (1935–), Indonesian poet, playwright.

Renée: Renée Gertrude Taylor, née Jones (1929–), N.Z. playwright, novelist. The writer re-

jected her married name in 1981, and instead adopted just her (aptly meaningful) first name.

Nadine Renee: Nadine Shamir (1872–2004), U.S. R&B singer.

Ludwig Renn: Arnold Friedrich Vieth von Golßenau (1889–1979), Ger. novelist. Ludwig Renn is the narrator and central character of Vieth's first successful novel, *Krieg* ("War") (1928), and his name appeared as that of the author on the title page. Vieth adopted the name for his subsequent works.

Rennequin: René Suarem (1645–1708), Belg. engineer. The engineer came to be known either as Rennequin, the French diminutive of his first name, René, or as Renkin, its Flemish (Dutch) equivalent

Jean Reno: Juan Moreno Errere y Rimenes (1948–), Moroccan-born movie actor, of Sp. parentage, working in France.

Res: Shareese Renee Ballard (1978–), U.S. black popular singer. The singer's stage name, pronounced "Reese," represents a pet form of her first name.

Lutea Reseda: Marie Charlotte Carmichael Stopes (1846–1929), Sc. Shakespeare scholar, suffragist, mother of G.M. **Mortlake**. Stopes used this name, inverting the botanical plant name Reseda lutea (the wild mignonette), for contributions to *The Attempt*, journal of the Edinburgh Essay Society.

Samuel Herman Reshevsky: Samuel Herman Rzeszewski (1909–1992), Pol.-born U.S. chess player. The young chess prodigy left Poland for America in 1920 and became a naturalized U.S. citizen in 1925.

Miss Resistor: Lillian Belfield, née Ellis (1906–?), Eng. stage artist. The entertainer's act involved resisting the attempts of strongmen volunteers from the audience to lift her in the air. Her variety artist husband, Jack Belfield, performed under the name Jack Volta.

Madame Restell: Ann Trow Lohman (1811–1878), Eng.-born U.S. abortionist.

Nicolas Restif de la Bretonne: Nicolas-Edmé Rétif (1734–1806), Fr. novelist. The writer's new surname is a historical form of his original name, suffixed by the name of the farm where he was born, La Bretonne, southeast of Paris.

Jean de Reszke: Jan Mieczyslaw (1850–1925), Pol. opera singer. The tenor began his singing career in Italy as a baritone under the name Giovanni di Reschi. This was later modified to a French form.

Sir John Retcliffe: Hermann O.F. Goedsche (1815–1878), Ger. writer.

Elisabeth Rethberg: Lisbeth Sättler (1894–1976), Ger. opera singer, working in U.S.

Ret Marut *see* B. **Traven**

Werdna Retnyw: Andrew Wynter (1819–1876), Eng. physician, writer on medicine. The writer used this name, a reversal of the original, for books such as *Odds and Ends from an Old Drawer* (1855) and *Pictures of Town from my Mental Camera* (1855).

[Freiherr von] Paul Julius **Reuter:** Israel Beer Josaphat (or Jisroel-Ber Josafat) (1816–1899), Ger. journalist. The founder of Reuters news agency, originally a Jew, was baptized a Christian in 1844 and adopted the name of Reuter, substituting Christian names for Jewish. It is uncertain why he chose this particular surname.

Jean-François **Revel:** Jean-François Ricard (1924–2006), Fr. philosopher, journalist. The intellectual adopted the name Revel when working for the Resistance in World War II.

Reverend Ike: Frederick Joseph Eikerenkoetter (1935–2009), U.S. black evangelist.

Reginald **Reverie:** Grenville Mellen (1799–1841), U.S. author, poet.

Imre **Révész:** Imre Csebray (1859–1945), Hung. painter.

Dorothy **Revier:** Doris Velegra (1904–1994), U.S. movie actress. The actress's new surname is that of her first husband, Harry J. Revier, who directed her first film, *Broadway Madonna* (1922).

Alvino **Rey:** Alvin McBurney (1908–2004), U.S. guitarist, bandleader. The musician adopted his new name on moving in 1928 from Cleveland, Ohio, to New York City, in recognition of the city's craze for Latin music.

Fernando **Rey:** Fernando Casado Arambillet Veiga (1917–1994), Sp. movie actor. Taken literally, the actor's screen name means "King Ferdinand." Rey actually played kings in several films, including Philip I and Philip II.

Florián **Rey:** Antonio Martínez del Castillo (1894–1962), Sp. movie director.

H.A. **Rey:** Hans Augusto Reyersbach (1898–1977), Ger.-born U.S. children's writer, illustrator, working jointly with Margret Elisabeth Rey, née Waldstein (1906–1996), his wife.

Jan **Rey:** Jan Reimoser (1904–1979), Cz. ballet critic, teacher.

Monte **Rey:** James Montgomery Fife (1900–1982), Sc. radio singer. The singer's name reflects his second name, while punning on Monterrey, the Mexican city.

Ernest **Reyer:** Louis Étienne Ernst Rey (1823–1909), Fr. composer, music critic.

Judith **Reyn:** Judith Fisher (1944–), Rhodesian-born Eng. ballet dancer.

Beatrice **Reynolds** *see* E. **Berger**

Debbie **Reynolds:** Mary Frances Reynolds (1932–), U.S. movie actress. The actress's new first name was given her by Jack **Warner**, of Warner Bros., when she was starting her stage career in 1948. She is said to have disliked it from the first.

Gene **Reynolds:** Eugene Reynolds Blumenthal (1923–), U.S. juvenile movie actor.

Marjorie **Reynolds:** Marjorie Goodspeed (1921–1997), U.S. movie actress. The actress, a child star of silent films, was billed as Marjorie Moore in the early 1930s. She settled as Marjorie Reynolds in 1937.

Peter **Reynolds:** Peter Horrocks (1926–1975), Br. movie actor.

William **Reynolds:** William Regnolds (1931–), U.S. movie actor.

Václav **Řezáč:** Václav Voňavka (1901–1956), Cz. novelist.

Rhäticus: Georg Joachim von Lauchen (or de Porris) (1514–1576), Austr. astronomer, mathematician. The astronomer adopted a name derived from his native district of Rhaetia.

Nicholas **Rhea:** Peter Norman Walker (1936–), Br. crime writer.

Rhené-Bâton: René Bâton (1879–1940), Fr. orchestral conductor, composer.

Rhené-Jaque: Marguerite Cartier (1918–), Can. cellist, composer. The musician's adopted name is an approximate rearrangement of her religious name, Sister Jacques-René.

Robert Barnwell **Rhett:** Robert Barnwell Smith (1800–1876), U.S. secessionist politician. In 1837 Robert and his brothers changed the family name to Rhett to honor an ancestor whose male line was extinguished.

John **Rhode:** [Major] Cecil John Charles Street (1884–1965), Br. detective novelist. The pun of the name is fairly transparent. Street also wrote as Miles Burton.

Billie **Rhodes:** Levita Axelrod (1894–1988), U.S. movie comedienne. There is some doubt about the actress's name and nationality. An article in *Picture Show* of July 18, 1919, claims she was English-born and named Billie because her British parents were expecting a son, to be called after his father.

Erik **Rhodes:** Ernest Sharpe (1906–1990), U.S. movie comedian.

Marjorie **Rhodes:** Marjorie Rhodes Wise (1902–1979), Br. movie actress.

Sonny **Rhodes:** Clarence Edward Smith (1940–), U.S. black blues guitarist.

Lord **R'Hoone** *see* Honoré de **Balzac**

Owen **Rhoscomyl** *see* Arthur Owen **Vaughan**

Madlyn **Rhue:** Madeleine Roche (1934–2003), U.S. movie actress.

Siôn **Rhydderch:** John Roderick (1673–1735), Welsh grammarian, publisher. The name is the Welsh equivalent of the English original.

Busta **Rhymes:** Trevor Smith, Jr. (1972–), U.S. black rapper. Rhymes was named by Chuck **D** of the New York black rap group Public Enemy, with

"Busta" after the exuberant American football player George "Buster" Rhymes.

Jean **Rhys:** Ella Gwendolyn Rees Williams (1890–1979), Br. novelist, of Creole-Welsh parentage. The writer was given her pen name by Ford Madox **Ford,** who admired her (unpublished) fictionalized diary of the years 1910–19 and who encouraged her to publish her first book, *The Left Bank and Other Stories* (1927).

Ribal: Isaac Baer Levinsohn (1788–1860), Russ. Jewish writer. The author came to be known by an acronymic name formed from the initials of *R*abbi *I*saac *Ba*er *L*evinsohn.

Ricardinho: Ricardo Luís Pozzi Rodrigues (1976–), Brazilian footballer. A diminutive form of the player's first name.

Paul **Ricca:** Felice Delucia (1897–1972), It.-born U.S. gangster.

Ruggiero **Ricci:** Woodrow Wilson (later, Roger) Rich (1918–), U.S. concert violinist, of It. descent. The musician's father italianized Roger Rich to Ruggiero Ricci, hoping that such a professional-looking name would bring "riches."

Il **Riccio:** Andrea Briosco (1470–1532), It. sculptor. The artist came to be known by his nickname, meaning "the curlyhead." He was also known as Andrea Crispus, from the Latin equivalent.

Craig **Rice:** Georgiana Ann Randolph Craig (1908–1957), U.S. thriller, short-story writer. The writer took her new surname from that of the aunt who raised her, Mrs. Elton Rice, with her original surname serving as her new forename. She also wrote as Daphne Saunders, Ruth Malone, and Michael Venning.

Dan **Rice:** Daniel McLaren (1823–1900), U.S. clown, circus owner. The reason for McLaren's choice of name is uncertain.

Elmer **Rice:** Elmer Leopold Reizenstein (1892–1967), U.S. playwright, novelist. "In 1918, after prolonged deliberation, Reizenstein shortened his name to Rice. Accused in some quarters of attempting to disguise his Jewish roots by this move, he was quick to deny the charge. In addition to being difficult to spell, the original name, he believed, carried too heavy a reminder of the Old World" [Malcolm Goldstein in Garraty and Carnes, vol. 18, p. 410].

Barbara **Rich** *see* Laura **Riding**

Elizabeth **Rich:** Betsy Talbot Blackwell (?1905–1985), U.S. fashion editor. Blackwell adopted this name as beauty editor of the magazine *Mademoiselle,* of which she became fashion editor under her real name in 1935.

Irene **Rich:** Irene Luther (1891–1988), U.S. movie actress.

Matty **Rich:** Matthew Richardson (1971–), U.S. movie director.

Robert **Rich:** Dalton Trumbo (1905–1976), U.S. screenwriter, novelist. Robert Rich and Sam Jackson were two of the best-known pseudonyms adopted by Trumbo after he was blacklisted in 1947 as one of the "Hollywood Ten" and unable to sell screenplays under his own name. As Robert Rich he won an Oscar for scripting *The Brave One* (1956) but did not attend the awards ceremony. In 1975 he was finally given the trophy he had earned.

Tony **Rich:** Anthony Jeffries (1971–), U.S. R&B musician.

[Sir] Cliff **Richard:** Harold Rodger Webb (1940–), Eng. pop musician. The star came by his new name as the result of an impromptu "think tank" in London after he and his group the Drifters were booked by agent Harry Greatorex to appear at a dancehall in Derby. "We all went off to a pub round the corner in Old Compton Street called the Swiss, sat down with some drinks and went through names. Someone suggested Russ Clifford and I said, 'No thanks.' Then came Cliff Russard. I said, 'Cliff sounds good ... rock face, rock 'n' roll....' Then someone suggested Richards with an 's' on the end, and Ian Samwell said, 'Wait a minute. Why don't you drop the "s," then you've got two Christian names, Cliff and Richard, which is unusual so people will remember it, and it can also be a tribute to **Little Richard.**' I thought, Perfect, it's all very rock 'n' roll; and 'Cliff Richard and the Drifters' sounded good.

Why didn't I want to use my real name? It just never felt right; there was no magic in it. It was too ordinary—I wanted something special. We were competing with names like Jerry Lee Lewis, Buddy **Holly** and Elvis Presley. Harry Webb didn't come close.... Even now I hear names in show business and I think: Why didn't you change your name? They are either unspellable or unpronounceable or too commonplace, or the name sounds as though it belongs to an accountant.... Of course, in the end, creatively and artistically it doesn't matter what your name is; but there is an imagery that is part of rock 'n' roll" [Cliff Richard, *My Life, My Way,* 2008].

Francis **Richard:** Frank R. Stockton (1834–1902), U.S. novelist, short-story writer.

Keith **Richard:** Keith Richards (1943–), Eng. rock musician. The founder and lead guitarist of the Rolling Stones dropped the "s" from his name early in his career as it "looked more pop" without it. Today, however, he is usually known with it.

Pierre **Richard:** Pierre-Richard Maurice Charles Léopold Defays (1934–), Fr. movie actor, director.

Wendy **Richard:** Wendy Emerton (1943–2009), Eng. TV actress. "I changed my stage name [*sic*] to Richard for the sole reason it was short and clear. A decision that proved to be right, for I remember one of my earliest showbiz bosses, David Croft remarking 'Never choose a long stage name should you want your name in lights — they won't like paying for all the bulbs!'" [Wendy Richard with Lizzie Wiggins, *Wendy Richard ... No 'S,'* 2000].

Richard-Lenoir: François Richard (1765–1839), Fr. industrialist. Together with a colleague, Joseph Lenoir-Dufresne (1768–1806), Richard perfected the manufacture of cotton fabric. On the death of his companion he added the first part of the latter's name to his own to commemorate their collaboration.

Clay **Richards** *see* Richard **Foster**

Emil **Richards:** Emilio Joseph Radocchia (1932–), U.S. jazz musician.

Frank **Richards:** Charles Harold St. John Hamilton (1875–1961), Eng. author of school stories. This was the best-known pseudonym of the creator of Billy Bunter and a host of other immortal characters who peopled the writer's fictional Greyfriars School. The choice of the name may appear arbitrary, but in fact the author took much trouble over its selection, as he has recorded: "The chief thing was to select a name totally different from those under which he had hitherto written: so that when he used the name, he would feel like a different person, and in consequence write from a somewhat different angle. I have been told — by men who do not write — that this is all fanciful.... This only means that they don't understand" [*The Autobiography of Frank Richards,* 1952]. He introduced the name for the first Greyfriars story, published in the school-story magazine *The Magnet* in 1908.

Hamilton derived the name itself from Frank Osbaldistone, a character in Sir Walter Scott's *Rob Roy,* and his own brother Richard. He identified so closely with it that his entry in *Who's Who* appeared under the name, and he even used it for his autobiography, as already seen. Among other pseudonyms used by Hamilton were Owen Conquest, Martin Clifford, Ralph Redway, and Hilda Richards, this last for some stories featuring Bessie Bunter, Billy Bunter's sister. Hamilton's characterization of Bessie was too crude for his girl readers, however, and he was replaced by other writers, who continued the stories under his adopted female name.

Hilda **Richards** *see* Frank **Richards**

James Brinsley **Richards:** Reginald Temple S.C. Grenville Nugent Grenville-Murray (1846–1892), Eng. journalist, novelist. The writer was the son of Mark **Hope,** himself the illegitimate son of Richard Grenville, 2d Duke of Buckingham and Chandos, and understandably decided to change his overblown aristocratic name to something simpler and more proletarian.

Jeff **Richards:** Richard Mansfield Taylor (1922–1989), U.S. movie actor.

Johnny **Richards:** John Cascales (1911–1968), U.S. jazz musician.

Renee **Richards:** Richard Raskind (1935–), U.S. transexual. The tennis-playing ophthalmologist underwent a much publicized "gender reassignment" in 1975. The new first name is significant, as Renee means "reborn." "*The New York Times* ... cheerfully changed not only the name of Renee Richards (and other transsexuals) but also the gender of every single pronoun in news stories" [Gloria Steinem, *Outrageous Acts and Everyday Rebellions,* 1984]. The first transexual to make her sex change public was Christine **Jorgensen.**

Ron **Richards:** Ronald Richard Pratley (1929–2009), Eng. record producer.

Stan **Richards:** Stanley Richardson (1930–2005), Eng. stage, movie, TV actor.

Stephen **Richards:** Mark (originally Richard) Stevens (1915–1994), U.S. movie actor. Stevens used this name for his small roles in early movies of the 1940s.

W.V. **Richards** *see* Kenneth J. **Alford**

Ferdinand **Richardson:** Ferdinand Heybourne (?1558–1618), Eng. composer.

Flavia **Richardson** *see* Dair **Alexander**

Henry Handel **Richardson:** Ethel Florence Lindesay Robertson, née Richardson (1870–1946), Austral. novelist, short-story writer. The writer adopted a male name (that of an uncle on the Irish side of her family) on the basis that "there had been much talk in the press about the ease with which a woman's work could be distinguished from a man's; and I wanted to try out the truth of the assertion." She first used it for the novel *Maurice Guest* (1908).

Johnnie **Richardson:** Johnnie Louise Sanders (1940–1988), U.S. black R&B singer.

Lee **Richardson:** Lee David Richard (1926–), U.S. TV actor.

Pierre **Richard-Willm:** Pierre-Alexandre Richard (1895–1983), Fr. movie actor. The actor added his mother's maiden name to his original surname.

Richelieu: William Erigena Robinson (1814–1892), U.S. journalist, politician. Robinson used this name, that of the famous French cardinal and statesman, for his writings in the *New York Tribune.*

Shane **Richie:** Shane Patrick Roche (1964–), Br. TV presenter, actor, of Ir. parentage The performer starred as Shane Ryan and Shane Skywalker before taking a regular stage name when backing comedian Lenny Henry in a 1983 variety show. "'Listen, I need to change my act Lenny,' I started to explain.... 'More important than that, Shane, you need to change your name.' I was puzzled. 'What do you mean? It's a funny name; it means I'm out of this world.' 'It doesn't matter,' he explained patiently.... 'Do you really want to be appearing on television in 20 years' time as Shane Skywalker?' ... As Lenny advised I came up with a name I would keep for the rest of my life: Shane Richie.... The singer Lionel Richie was big at the time. I liked his name and it sounded not a million miles from my nickname at school, which was Rochey, so I went with that'" [Shane Richie with Sue Crawford, *Rags to Richie*, 2003].

Harry Richman: Harold Reichman (1895–1972), U.S. entertainer, movie actor.

Fiona Richmond: Julia Montgomery, née Harrison (1947–), Eng. model, stage, movie actress. "Julia Montgomery is a well-spoken lady who runs boutique guesthouses in Wiltshire and Grenada with her husband. In the 1970s she was Fiona Richmond, glamour model and actress and Paul **Raymond**'s girlfriend" [*Sunday Times Magazine*, August 17, 2008].

John Peter Richmond *see* John **Carradine**

Kane Richmond: Frederick W. Bowditch (1906–1973), U.S. movie actor.

Charles Francis Richter: Charles Francis Kinsiger (1900–1985), U.S. seismologist. The inventor of the Richter scale took his new name from his maternal grandfather, Charles Otto Richter, who raised him.

Harry Rickards: Benjamin Leete (1843–1911), Br. music-hall artist.

Jehan Rictus: Gabriel Randon de Saint-Amand (1867–1938), Fr. poet, novelist, dramatist.

John Riddell: Corey Ford (1902–1969), U.S. humorist, playwright. The writer described the genesis of his name in typical whimsical style: "Unfortunately, its origin is not the least mysterious nor significant. To be perfectly frank, I neither dreamt it in a dream, chose it after my dead great-grandmother, nor formed it by spelling backward the letters of my name. It happened that when I decided to do critical parodies for *Vanity Fair*, I thought it might be more successful if their author were anonymous. I wanted some name that sounded as if it might be a real person, and so I turned to that magnificent compendium of real names, the New York Telephone Directory. I lit a small jar of incense, closed all the windows and summoned three Dyak witch doctors to beat on drums. I then blindfolded myself, took three paces, flung open the telephone book, and placed my forefinger on a name (any name) then removed the blindfold, turned on the light and saw the name was none other than Runkleschmelz. In as much as Runkleschmelz was not a very good name for a reviewer, I dismissed the witch doctors and went backward through the telephone book until I found Riddell. The name John I thought of myself" [Marble, pp.82–3].

William Pett Ridge: Warwick Simpson (1860–1930), Eng. novelist.

John Ridgely: John Huntington Rea (1909–1968), U.S. movie actor.

Laura Riding: Laura Jackson, née Reichenthal (1901–1991), U.S. writer, poet, of U.S.–Austrian parentage. The author adopted her new surname in 1927, writing as Laura Riding until 1941, when she married Schuyler B. Jackson as her second husband. Thereafter she wrote as Laura (Riding) Jackson. Two pen names were Barbara Rich and Madeleine Vara.

Dean Riesner: Dean Reisner (1918–2002), U.S. screenwriter. The scriptwriter was the son of movie director Charles Reisner (1887–1962), who was sometimes credited as Charles F. Riesner, and he decided to stick with this spelling. He made his acting debut at the age of five and was a child actor under the name Dinky Dean. His first screen credit, for *Code of the Secret Service* (1939), was made under the name Dean Franklin, and he was credited again under this name for *The Fighting 69th* (1940).

Robert Rietty: Robert Rietti (1923–), Eng. stage actor, playwright, director.

Rif: Isaac ben Jacob Alfasi (1013–1103), Sp. Jewish scholar. The Talmudic scholar came to be known by an acronymic name formed from the initial letters of *R*abbi *I*saac *F*asi. The latter name relates to Fez, Morocco, where Alfasi lived for most of his life.

Edward Rigby: Edward Coke (1879–1951), Eng. stage, movie actor. The actor took his mother's maiden name as his stage name.

Rigolboche: Marguerite Badel (*fl.*1850s), Fr. variety actress, dancer. The performer's stage name is a slang word meaning "comic."

Rihanna: Robyn Rihanna Fenty (1988–), Barbadian-born U.S. pop singer, model.

Charles Valentine Riley: Charles Valentine Wylde (1843–1895), Eng.-born U.S. entomologist. Riley, the illegitimate son of an Anglican clergyman, was raised by his mother, Mary Louisa Cannon, who selected his new surname.

Ted Riley *see* Gordon **Ashe**

Carlo Rim: Jean-Marius Richard (1905–1985), Fr. screenwriter, movie director, novelist. The writer's new first name is the Italian equivalent of Charles. He created his new surname by altering the order of his initials from JMR to RJM, then replacing "J" by "I." He also worked as hyphenated Carlo-Rim.

Cheikha Rimitti: Saadia Reliziana (1923–2006), Algerian rai singer, songwriter, working in France. The singer cut her first record in 1952 under the name Cheikha Remettez Reliziana, basing the first name on Cheikh, the title (French for "sheikh") adopted by the Algerian musician of the day who became her patron, Cheikh Mohammed Ould Ennems.

It is not clear how she came by her second name. "According to legend, at a festival in Western Algeria she was invited into a tented bar normally reserved for Europeans. Enjoying the hospitality to the full, she kept repeatedly shouting: 'Remettez panaché, remettez, remettez!' (another shandy, another and another). A crowd gathered outside and began shouting: 'It's the singer Rimitti,' and the name stuck" [*The Times*, May 17, 2006]. She subsequently shortened the name to the first word alone.

W.J. Rimmer *see* Fenton **Brockley**

Montague **Ring:** Amanda Ira Aldridge (1866–1956), Br. black pianist, composer.

Joachim **Ringelnatz:** Hans Bötticher (1883–1934), Ger. poet, novelist. The writer's adopted name means "grass snake" (*Natrix natrix*), a suitable name for a humorist or satirist, who "stings" harmlessly.

Jeremiah **Ringletub:** John Styles (1770–1860), Eng. preacher. The writer used this name for *The Legend of the Velvet Cushion* (1815), a reply to the Rev. J.W. Cunningham's *The Velvet Cushion*, published the previous year.

John **Ringling:** John Rüngeling (1866–1936), U.S. circus impresario, of Ger. parentage.

Johnny Ringo *see* Wes **Hardin**

Ringuet: [Dr.] Philippe Panneton (1895–1960), Can. novelist, working in French.

Takster **Rinpoche:** Thubten Jigme Norbu (1922–2008), Tibetan scholar, reincarnate lama. According to custom, the original name of the Dalai Lama's eldest brother was changed when he entered the religious life. His new first name, meaning "roaring tiger," was taken from the village in which he was born. His second name, meaning "precious one," is a title given to spiritual masters.

Henry **Rip** *see* **Xariffa**

A. **Riposte:** Elinor Mordaunt, née Evelyn May Clowes (1877–1942), Eng. novelist, travel writer. The author used this name for the U.S. edition, entitled *Gin and Bitters*, of her novel *Full Circle* (1931). The book was intended as a counterblast ("riposte") to Somerset Maugham's *Cakes and Ale* (1930). She hardly carried the guns, however, for this daring assault.

Arthur **Riscoe:** Arthur Boorman (1896–1954), Br. stage, movie comedian.

Elizabeth **Risdon:** Elizabeth Evans (1887–1958), Br. stage, movie actress.

Rita: Eliza Margaret Jane Humphreys, earlier Booth, née Gollan (1850–1938), Sc. novelist. The writer's pen name, which she took to honor her idol, **Ouida**, reflects her second name of Margaret, and may well have been her pet name among family and friends. She also wrote as E. Jayne Gilbert.

Ritba: Yom Tov ben Avraham Ishbili (?–1330), Sp. Jewish scholar. The Talmudic and Halakhic authority came to be known by an acronymic name formed from the initial letters of *R*abbi *Y*om *T*ov *b*en *A*vraham. (Ishbili is a locational suffix meaning "of Seville.")

Tex Ritter: Woodward Maurice Ritter (1905–1974), U.S. movie actor, singing cowboy. Born in Murvaul, Texas, and steeped in Texas history and tradition, Ritter could hardly be called anything other than "Tex."

Théodore **Ritter:** Théodore Bennet (1841–1886), Fr. pianist, composer.

Al **Ritz:** Al Joachim (1901–1965), U.S. stage, movie comedian, of Austr. parentage, teaming with Harry **Ritz** and Jimmy **Ritz** as The Ritz Brothers. Acccording to one account, the brothers adopted the name of the famous hotelkeeper, César Ritz, for their first proper vaudeville act in 1925, although another story claims they took it from the side of a passing truck. The two origins need not be mutually exclusive, since César Ritz's company had its own trucks. Either way, the brothers' agent suggested that "Joachim" would be too hard for audiences to remember.

Harry **Ritz:** Herschel Joachim (1907–1986), U.S. stage, movie comedian, brother of Al **Ritz** and Jimmy **Ritz**.

Jimmy **Ritz:** James Joachim (1904–1985), U.S. stage, movie comedian, brother of Al **Ritz** and Harry **Ritz**.

Sally Ritz *see* Rosa **Henderson**

Rivaldo: Rivaldo Vitor Borba Ferreira (1972–), Brazilian footballer.

Zacharias **Rivander:** Zacharias Bachmann (1553–1597), Ger. Lutheran theologian. The scholar's adopted name translates his German name, meaning literally "stream man," from Latin *rivus*, "stream" and Greek *anēr, andros*, "man." Compare the name of Augustus Quirinus **Rivinus**.

Chita **Rivera:** Dolores Conchita Figueroa del Rivero (1933–), U.S. stage, movie actress, dancer.

Jorge **Rivero:** Jorge Pous Ribe (1938–), Mexican movie actor. The actor is also credited as George Rivero or George Rivers.

Georgia **Rivers:** Marjorie Clark (?–1989), Austral. journalist, short-story writer.

Joan **Rivers:** Joan Alexandra Rosenberg, née Molinsky (1933–), U.S. TV comedienne, chat-show host.

Johnny **Rivers:** John Ramistella (1942–), U.S. pop musician, record company executive. The musician's new name was suggested by DJ Alan Freed, who felt it would suggest the river bayou country where he was raised (Baton Rouge, Louisiana).

Larry **Rivers:** Yitzroch Loiza Grossberg (1923–

2002), U.S. painter, jazz musician, moviemaker, of Ukr. Jewish parentage. Grossberg was already playing the jazz saxophone professionally as a teenager, and one night a comedian introduced him and his group on stage as "Larry Rivers and the Mudcats." He liked the name, and it stuck [*The Times*, August 17, 2002].

Pearl Rivers: Eliza Jane Poitevent Holbrook Nicholson (1849–1896), U.S. newpaper publisher, poet. Eliza began writing poetry in her teens, but it was not until after her graduation in 1867 that her first published work appeared under the name Pearl Rivers, from the river near her Mississippi home.

Yakov Rives: Jakov Yudovich Baskin (1886–1975), Russ. Jewish writer.

Augustus Quirinus Rivinus: Augustus Quirinus Bachmann (1652–1723), Ger. botanist. The scholar translated his German surname, meaning "stream dweller," to the Latin equivalent (German *Bach*, Latin *rivus*, "stream"). Compare the name of Zacharias **Rivander**.

Donna **Rix** *see* Fenton **Brockley**

Robb: Andrew Robb (*c.*1907–?), Sc. fashion illustrator.

Sue Robbie: Susan Jennifer Robinson (1949–), Eng. TV presenter.

Harold Robbins: Francis Kane (1916–1997), U.S. novelist. The writer was a foundling, and his original name of Francis Kane was given him by the Paulist fathers in a Catholic orphanage. (He would use the name for the main character in his 1948 novel *Never Love a Stranger*.) In 1927 he was placed with a Jewish family by the name of Rubin, and subsequently adopted (but also adapted) their surname.

Jerome Robbins: Jerome Wilson Rabinowitz (1918–1998), U.S. ballet dancer, choreographer.

Marty Robbins: Martin David Robinson (1925–1982), U.S. country singer, of Pol. parentage. The singer's father, John Robinson, was a Polish immigrant to the USA originally named Mazinski.

Rob Donn: Robert Mackay (1714–1778), Sc. Gaelic poet. The poet's name means "Rob the Brown," referring to his brown hair and brown eyes, which distinguished him from the red-headed highlanders. Compare **Rob Roy**.

Robert ap Gwilym Ddu: Robert Williams (1766–1850), Welsh poet, hymnwriter. The writer's bardic name means "Robert son of Black William."

Robert-Houdin: Jean-Eugène Robert (1805–1871), Fr. conjuror. The illusionist married Josèphe Cécile Houdin in 1830, and added his wife's maiden name to his own to give his stage name. He in turn gave the name of **Houdini**.

Bart Roberts: Rex Reason (1928–), U.S. movie actor. The actor used this name for some movies in the mid–1950s.

Ben Roberts: Benjamin Eisenberg (1916–1984), U.S. screenwriter.

Davis Roberts: Robert A. Davis, Jr. (1917–1883), U.S. black movie actor.

Ewan Roberts: Thomas McEwan Hutchison (1914–1983), Sc. stage, movie actor.

Gillian Roberts: Judith Greber (1939–), U.S. mystery writer.

James Hall Roberts: Robert Lipscomb Duncan (1927–), U.S. thriller writer.

Joan Roberts: Josephine Seagrist (1920–), U.S. stage actress, singer. The actress adopted her mother's maiden name as her stage name.

Julia Roberts: Julie Fiona Roberts (1967–), U.S. movie actress. The star modified her first name on discovering an existing actress Julie Roberts.

Kiki Roberts: Marion Strasmick (1909–), U.S. showgirl, mistress of bootlegger Jack "Legs" Diamond.

Lionel Roberts: Robert Lionel Fanthorpe (1935–), Eng. SF writer.

Luckey Roberts: Charles Luckyeth (1887–1968), U.S. black jazz pianist.

Lynne Roberts: Theda May Roberts (1919–1978), U.S. movie actress. Roberts adopted the name Mary Hart for a number of low-budget westerns in the late 1930s.

Tanya Roberts: Tanya Boum (1954–), U.S. movie actress.

Robertson: Etienne-Gaspard Robert (1763–1837), Fr. illusionist.

Bob Robertson: Sergio Leone (1929–1989), It. movie director. Leone first used this name for *Fistful of Dollars* (1964) as a tribute to his movie director father, Vincenzo Leone (1879–1958), who had begun his career on the stage as Roberto Roberti, a name chosen in imitation of the actor Ruggero Ruggeri (1871–1953). Sergio's name thus meant "Bob (Robert) son of Robert." From 1965 he produced movies under his own name [Christopher Frayling, *Sergio Leone: Something To Do With Death*, 2000].

E. Arnot Robertson: [Lady] Eileen Arbuthnot Turner, née Robertson (1903–1961), Eng. novelist.

Gilles Roberval: Gilles Peronnier (or Personne) (1602–1675), Fr. mathematician. The academic took his name from his birthplace, Roberval, near Beauvais, northern France.

[Sir] George **Robey:** George Edward Wade (1869–1954), Eng. stage, movie comedian ("The Prime Minister of Mirth"). Wade's family disapproved when he began appearing in amateur theatrical performances at an early age. He therefore decided to adopt another name, and took "Robey" (originally "Roby") from a builder's business in Birmingham, where he was employed as a clerk in a streetcar company. He liked the name for its simple, robust appearance and its ease of pronunciation, and later adopted it by deed poll [*Dictionary of National Biography*].

Henri **Robin**: Henrik Joseph Donckel (1811–1874), Du. illusionist, working in France ("The French Wizard").

Denise **Robins**: Denise Naomi Klein (1897–1985), Br. romantic novelist, of Latvian Jewish descent. The writer's regular name is that of her first husband, Arthur Robins (married 1918, divorced 1938). Her many novels appeared under such names as Denise Chesterton, Ashley French, Harriet Gray, Hervey Hamilton, Julia Kane, and Francesca Wright. She first used pen names for her short stories. "Soon I was writing under three *nom-de-plumes* ... I wrote so much that it couldn't all be published under one name. I still have these early publications. I'm really quite surprised by the variety of these efforts; by 'Denise Chesterton'—'Eve Vaill'—'Anne Llewellyn'—my pseudonyms" [Denise Robins, *Stranger than Fiction*, 1965].

Edward H. **Robins**: Edward Haas (1880–1951), U.S. stage actor. The actor took his mother's maiden name for his stage surname. His middle initial represents his original surname.

Seelin **Robins** *see* James Fenimore Cooper **Adams**

Mr. and Master **Robinson**: Henry Hawley Crippen (1868–1910), Br. murderer + Ethel Le Neve (1893–1967), his mistress. Following the murder of his wife in London in 1910, Dr. Crippen and his mistress fled to the U.S., of which he was a citizen. They boarded a boat to Quebec with Ethel Le Neve posing as "Master Robinson" and Crippen as "his" father. The master of the ship, however, saw through her disguise and sent a message to the ship's owners in Liverpool. On the ship's arrival in Quebec, the couple were arrested by the police. Crippen was subsequently executed.

Various other aliases were used throughout the affair. Crippen's wife (1873–1910), the daughter of a German mother and a Polish father, was christened Kunigunde Mackamotzki. When she was in her late teens in Brooklyn, she began calling herself Cora Turner. Soon after marrying Crippen, she used the name Cora Motzki, hoping this would help with a proposed operatic career. For a time she also appeared on the stage as Belle Elmore. Ethel Le Neve, meanwhile, called herself "Miss Allen" when she again sailed for North America after the trial, and "Miss Nelson" when she returned to England in World War I. Under this latter name she married one Stanley Smith.

Cardew **Robinson**: Douglas Robinson (1917–

1992), Br. stage comedian ("Cardew the Cad"). The actor enjoyed novels of school life and took his stage name from Ralph Reckless Cardew, a character in the stories about St. Jim's written by Frank **Richards** under the name of Martin Clifford.

Edward G. **Robinson**: Emanuel Goldenberg (1893–1973), Rom.-born U.S. movie actor. The creation of the actor's professional name is described in his autobiography. Given the need for a change, since Emanuel Goldenberg was "not a name for an actor, ... too long, too foreign and ... too Jewish, ... the obvious ploy was translation, but Emanuel Goldenhill didn't work and Goldenmount was too pretentious ... I continued to debate lists of names in the phone book, catalogs, and encyclopedias I picked up in the Astor Place Library [in Manhattan] ... and none would satisfy me. Then one night I went to see a play, a highly urbane English drawing room comedy, and from my perch in the rear of the second balcony I heard a butler on stage announce to a lady..., 'Madame, a gentleman to see you—a Mr. Robinson.' Mr. Robinson! I liked the ring and strength of it. And, furthermore, it was a common change. I knew many Rosenbergs, Rabinowitzes, and Roths who'd switched to Robinson. Yes, that was it. From this time forward I would be Robinson—Emanuel Robinson. That decision was greeted at the [American] Academy [of Dramatic Arts] with something less than enthusiasm. Emanuel and Robinson were an odd coupling. What other names began with *E*? Edgar? Egbert? Ellery? Ethan? Edward? Why not Edward, then King of England? ... Edward Robinson. But I could not desert the Goldenberg entirely. That became the *G*, my private treaty with my past. But that wasn't enough. Some managers didn't like the *G*, and quite arbitrarily one of them translated it to Gould. And so, if you ever look at the early programs, you will see me billed as Edward Gould Robinson ... Edward G. or Edward Gould, let me confess right off the bat that deep down in my deepest heart, I am, and have always been, Emanuel Goldenberg" [Edward G. Robinson with Leonard Spigelglass, *All My Yesterdays: An Autobiography*, 1973].

Madeleine **Robinson**: Madeleine Svoboda (1916–2004), Fr. stage, movie actress, of Cz. origin.

Ralph **Robinson**: George III (1738–1820), king of England ("Farmer George"). George III used this name, that of his shepherd at Windsor, for his contributions to the *Annals of Agriculture*, the monthly journal published from 1784 to 1809 by the agriculturist Arthur Young. The king was a keen, progressive farmer. Hence his nickname.

Sugar Ray **Robinson**: Walker Smith, Jr. (1922–1989), U.S. black middleweight boxer. The boxer turned professional in 1940 and acquired his new name that year. Watching a small promotion from ringside one day, he was suddenly asked to substitute for a fighter named Ray Robinson, who had failed to turn up for one of the bouts. Smith won in style, and assumed that boxer's name himself. Later, an observer remarked to Robinson's trainer, George Gainford, that he seemed to have a "sweet" fighter. "Yes," replied Gainford, "he's as sweet as sugar." Hence Robinson's first name.

Rob Roy: (1) Robert MacGregor (1671–1734), Sc. outlaw; (2) John MacGregor (1825–1892), Eng. traveler, writer, canoe designer. The usual explanation behind the outlaw's name is that he signed himself "Rob Roy," that is, "Red Rob," with reference to his thick, dark red hair (compare **Rob Donn**), a feature described in Sir Walter Scott's romanticized account of his life, *Rob Roy* (1818): "His hair was dark red, thick, and frizzled, and curled short around the face." But the motto of the MacGregors is "My race is royal," and "Roy" could have derived from this.

John MacGregor originally applied the name to the canoe he designed in 1865, which was built of oak but covered fore and aft in cedar, a red wood. The name then came to be applied to MacGregor himself, whose accounts of his solo voyages in it began with *A Thousand Miles in the Rob Roy Canoe* (1866).

Frederick Robson: Thomas Robson Brownhill (1821–1864), Eng. music-hall actor.

May Robson: Mary Jeanette Robison (1858–1942), Austral.-born U.S. stage, movie actress.

Stuart Robson: Henry Robson Stuart (1836–1903), U.S. comic actor.

Robyn Ddu Eryri: Robert Parry (1804–1892), Welsh poet. The poet may have based his bardic name, meaning "Black Robin of Snowdon," on that of an earlier poet, Robyn Ddu (*fl.*1450), about whom little is known.

Patricia Roc: Felicia Miriam Ursula Herold (1915–2003), Eng. movie actress. The adoptive daughter of a Belgian businessman, André Riese, Roc is said to have gained her new surname from the Roc Film Studios, apparently choosing her new first name herself. But accounts vary. "Roc was born Felicia Reise [*sic*], but that soon changed when she was spotted in a West End Revue by a pair of Alexander **Korda**'s talent scouts, who rechristened her over supper at the Berkeley Grill. ('Anne Kent,' she recalled, was a near miss.)" [Matthew Sweet, *Shepperton Babylon*, 2005].

Blas Roca: Francesco Calderío (1908–1987), Cuban government official. When the political activist joined the Communist Party in 1929, he took the name "Roca," Spanish for "rock." This evokes the names of other Communist leaders, such as **Kamenev** (stone) and **Stalin** (steel).

J.W. **Rochester:** Vera Ivanovna Kryzhanovskaya (1861–1924), Russ. novelist, short-story writer.

Mark **Rochester:** William Charles Mark Kent (1823–1902), Eng. author, journalist. Charles Kent (as he was usually known) became editor of the evening newspaper *The Sun* in 1845, and used his pen name for political sketches that he published separately, such as *The Derby Ministry* (1858), later reissued as *Conservative Statesmen*. The name presumably alludes to the town of Rochester in the county of Kent.

The **Rock:** Dwayne Douglas Johnson (1972–), U.S. black wrestler. Johnson first entered the ring under his real name, but then felt he needed to pinpoint his persona. "He decided to spend his time thinking of a new ring name — something that was wrestling related, but also gave a hint of who he was. So Johnson came up with ... Flex Kavana? OK, so it wasn't the best of names. He chose 'Flex' because it was a muscle-related word and 'Kavana' because of its Samoan origin. Not the best of choices, but then again, Johnson wasn't the best of wrestlers at the time, either" [Picarello, p.125]. He then wrestled as Rocky Maivia, after his grandfather, Peter Maivia, but this was still not quite right. "He now simply wanted to be called 'The Rock!' 'Just take a look at me, I'm handsome, well-built, in better physical shape than many wrestlers,' he explained. 'I have everything going for me and that's why they call me The Rock! I am solid muscle, I am practically undefeated'" [ibid.].

Clark **Rockefeller:** Christian Carl Gerhartsreiter (1962–), Ger. impostor. Gerhartsreiter went to the United States as a 17-year-old exchange student and never returned. After living with a family in Connecticut, he obtained U.S. residency by marrying an American, Amy Jersild, whom he left a day later. He then moved to California and adopted the name Christopher Chichester in a bid to become an actor. Suspected of involvement in the disappearance of a San Marino couple, Jonathan and Linda Sohus, who rented him a guesthouse, he left town before he could be questioned, but in 1988 received a traffic ticket in Connecticut while driving Mr. Sohus's car. Back on the East Coast, he worked in a brokerage house under the name Christopher Crowe. Eventually adopting the prestigious name Clark Rockefeller, in 1995 he married Sandra Boss, with whom he had a daughter, Reigh. The couple divorced in 2007 and the girl moved with her mother to London. In 2009 Gerhartsreiter was accused of abducting Reigh during a supervised visit to Boston, Massachusetts, and went on trial in that city charged not only with parental kidnap but on two counts of assault and battery and giving a false name to the police. Asked in an interview with NBC television whether Ms. Boss really believed he was a Rockefeller, he replied: "No. Clearly not.... But she wanted to keep the appearance of it going. For her, it was much."

Johnny **Rocket:** John Pearce (1961–), Austral-born Br. jewelry designer. When still in Australia, Pearce worked as a tour manager for various pop groups, and on encountering uncooperative promoters, venue arrangers, and others, would "give them a rocket" (a sharp verbal rebuke). The name originated as a nickname given by his wife, and he kept it when setting up business as a jewelry designer in England [personal e-mail from Johnny Rocket, July 4, 2002].

Rockin' Dopsie: Alton Jay Rubin, Sr. (1932–1993), U.S. black zydeco singer, accordionist. Rubin was nicknamed Dopsie or Dupsee from an early age, after a Chicago dancer known as Doopsie.

Rockin' Sidney: Sidney Simien (1938–1998), U.S. black zydeco musician.

Knute **Rockne:** Knute Kenneth Rokne (1888–1931), Norw.-born U.S. college football player, coach. Rockne's father came to the United States in 1893 and the rest of the family followed soon after, when they added the "c" to their surname.

William **Rockstro:** William Smith Rackstraw (1823–1895), Eng. organist, composer. Early in life the musician adopted an older (but corrupt) spelling of his original surname.

Rockwell: Kenneth Gordy (1964–), U.S. rock musician, son of Motown Records head Berry Gordy. The singer adopted the name of his school band, itself no doubt implying players who "rock well."

Matt **Rockwell** *see* Fenton **Brockley**

J.I. **Rodale:** Jerome Irving Cohen (1898–1971), U.S. health-food publisher, of Pol. Jewish parentage. Cohen adopted a new name because in the 1920s Jews were excluded from the New York publishing world. He took a combination of family names for his surname with the initials of his original names.

Alexander **Roda Roda:** Sándór Friedrich Rosenfeld (1872–1945), Hung.-born Austr. humorist, working in U.S. Rosenfeld's father had adopted the name Roda in 1870, and his son added another "Roda" to this from his Hungarian first name, of which "Alexander" is the equivalent.

Emily **Rodda:** Jennifer Rowe (1948–), Austral. children's writer.

Fred **Rodell:** Alfred M. Rodelheim (1907–1980), U.S. legal educator. Rodell's parents divorced when he was four and he and his younger brother went with his mother to live with his uncle, Howard Loeb. Avoiding contact with his father after he turned 16, he changed his name to Fred Rodell in 1928.

Zoë von **Rodenbach** *see* Charlotte **Arand**

Julius **Rodenberg:** Julius Levy (1831–1914), Ger. journalist, novelist. The writer assumed the name of his birthplace, Rodenberg, in western Germany.

Jimmy **Rodgers:** James Snow (1933–), U.S. folksinger. The singer took his name in memory of the country singer Jimmie Rodgers (1897–1933), the "Singing Brakeman," who died in the year that Snow was born. Neither should be confused with bluesman Jimmy **Rogers**.

Simon **Rodia:** Sabato Rodia (*c.*1879–1965), It.-born U.S. artist. Rodia's altered first name (which he never actually used himself) arose from a 1937 article in the *Los Angeles Times* in which, among other errors, he was called "Simon Rodilla" by a reporter. His surname was given correctly in other articles, but the incorrect first name Simon stuck.

Red **Rodney:** Robert Rodney Chudnick (1927–1994), U.S. jazz trumpeter.

Utto **Rodolph:** Yambo Ouologuem (1940–), Malian author, writing in French. Ouologuem used this name for his erotic novel *Les Mille et une bibles du sexe* ("The Thousand and One Bibles of Sex") (1969).

Jean-Joseph **Rodolphe:** Johann Joseph Rudolph (1730–1812), Fr. composer. The musician, born in the former German city of Strasbourg, adopted a French form of his original German name.

William **Roerick:** William Roehrich (1912–1995), U.S. playwright, stage actor.

Jean **Roger-Ducasse:** Jean Jules Aimable Roger Ducasse (1873–1954), Fr. composer.

Roger of Taizé: Roger Louis Schutz-Marsauche (1915–2005), Fr.-born Swiss priest. In 1940 Brother Roger, the son of a Protestant pastor, went to the French hamlet of Taizé, between Cluny and Cîteaux, to found a community devoted to reconciliation and peace in church and society.

Ginger **Rogers:** Virginia Katherine McMath (1911–1995), U.S. stage, movie actress, dancer. The actress's first name evolved from "Virginia," the creation being the work of a young cousin who could not pronounce the letter "v." She was thus first "Dinda," then "Ginger." Her surname came from her mother's second marriage to John Rogers in 1920.

Gregory **Rogers** *see* Melville **Crossman**

Jean **Rogers:** Eleanor Lovegren (1916–1991), U.S. movie actress.

Jimmy **Rogers:** James A. Lane (1924–1997), U.S. black blues musician.

Julie **Rogers:** Julie Rolls (1943–), Br. popular singer.

Kasey **Rogers:** Imogene Rogers (1925–2006), U.S. movie actress. The actress was a sporty girl and was nicknamed Kasey after baseball player Casey Stengel (1890–1975). She took to the name, although in her early movies appeared as Laura Elliott. She had reverted to her real surname by the 1950s.

Roy **Rogers:** Leonard Franklin Slye (1911–1998), U.S. movie actor. Originally a singer under his real name, the future cowboy star called himself Dick Wesson on joining the Sons of Pioneers singing group. He later adopted the name Roy Rogers, which may have been prompted by either Ginger **Rogers** or, more likely, Will Rogers (1879–1935), the movie actor who had formerly been a cowboy.

Shorty **Rogers:** Milton Michael Rajonsky (1924–1994), U.S. jazz musician, of Rom.-Russ. parentage. Rogers acquired his nickname, "Shorty," when in high school. He adopted an anglicized version of his Slavic surname in 1946, when he and his newly-wed wife moved to Burbank, California.

Sunny **Rogers:** Jessie Mary Rogerson (1913–2005), Br. variety artist. The TV performer took her new first name from her nickname, given her as a child for her smile.

Terri **Rogers:** Ivan Southgate (1937–1999), Br. ventriloquist, magician. The entertainer underwent a sex-change operation in the early 1960s.

Mikhail **Rogov:** Mikhail Ivanovich Ivanov (1880–1942), Russ. revolutionary, Communist official.

Criena **Rohan:** Deidre Cash (1925–1963), Austral. novelist, of Ir. parentage.

Eric **Rohmer:** Maurice Henri Joseph Schérer (1920–2010), Fr. movie director.

Sax **Rohmer:** Arthur Sarsfield Ward (1883–1959), Eng. writer of mystery stories. The creator of the Chinese master villain Fu Manchu was born Arthur Henry Ward, but substituted Sarsfield for Henry when he was 15. His pen name, which he later adopted in real life, has a somewhat convoluted origin. "Sax" came from what he believed was the Anglo-Saxon word for "blade" (which may have given the name of the Saxons themselves, as the word for their weapon, although made of stone, not steel). "Rohmer" he interpreted as meaning "roamer," "wanderer." In other words, he was a "roaming blade," otherwise a freelance.

Pablo de **Rokha:** Carlos Díaz Loyola (1894–1968), Chilean poet.

Betty **Roland:** Elizabeth Maclean (1903–1996), Austral. writer. The writer adopted her father's first name as her new surname.

Gilbert **Roland:** Luis Antonio Dámaso de Alonso (1905–1994), Mexican-born U.S. movie, TV actor. The actor devised his screen name from the names of two of his favorite movie stars, John **Gilbert** and Ruth Roland (1892–1937).

Nicholas **Roland:** Arnold Robert Walmsley (1912–2000), Eng. diplomat. Walmsley used this name for three novels: *The Great One* (1967), *Natural Causes* (1969), and *Who Came by Night* (1971).

Roland-Manuel: Roland Alexis Manuel Lévy (1891–1966), Fr. composer, critic.

Rolant o Fôn: Rowland Jones (1909–1962), Welsh poet. The writer's name means "Roland of Anglesey," alluding to the island where he was born and where he spent his professional life as a solicitor (lawyer).

Fr. **Rolfe** *see* Baron **Corvo**

Henry **Rollins:** Henry Garfield (1961–), U.S. punk musician, poet.

Anthony **Rolls:** Colwyn Edward Vulliamy (1886–1971), Welsh writer. Vulliamy used his pen name for four novels. He also used the Welsh name Twm Teg ("Handsome Tom") for a comic novel of Welsh village life: *Jones, A Gentleman of Wales* (1954).

C.H. **Rolph:** Cecil Rolph Hewitt (1901–1994), Eng. writer, editor.

Henri **Rol-Tanguy:** Henri Tanguy (1908–2002), Fr. Resistance leader. After the capitulation of France to Nazi Germany in 1940, Tanguy went underground, taking the Resistance name Rol after a close comrade, Théo Rol, who had fallen in the Spanish Civil War. "Colonel Rol," as the leader was known, added his friend's name to his own after the liberation of Paris in 1944.

Ole Edvart **Rölvaag:** Ole Jakobsen (1876–1931), Norw.-born U.S. writer. Jakobsen was born on the island of Dønna, off the coast of northern Norway, and adopted the name of a nearby cove on emigrating to the USA in 1896 and settling with his uncle in Elk Point, South Dakota.

Yvonne **Romain:** Yvonne Warren (1938–), Br.-born movie actress, raised in France.

Jules **Romains:** Louis-Henri-Jean Farigoule (1885–1972), Fr. playwright, novelist, poet. Provençal *farigoule* means "thyme." "Il faut prendre garde aux pseudonymes. Il a toujours semblé que le masque romain tenait mal, et que la farigoule perçait sous le marbre antique" ("One must take care with pen names. The Roman mask always seemed to be slipping, and thyme breaking through the ancient marble") [Michel Tournier, *Le pied de la lettre*, 1994].

Stella **Roman:** Florica Vierica Alma Stela Blasu (1904–1992), Rom.-born U.S. opera singer. The singer's stage name denotes her nationality.

Viviane **Romance:** Pauline Ronacher Ortmans (1909 or 1912–1991), Austr.-born Fr. movie actress. The actress's new surname neatly combines her real second name and surname. As her name implies, she starred in romantic roles, such as the alluring but faithless wife in *La Belle Équipe*, screened in the U.S. as *They Were Five* (1936).

La **Romanina:** Vittoria Archilei, née Concarini (1550–after 1618), It. lutenist, composer. The musician was born in Rome. Hence her adopted name, meaning "the young woman of Rome."

Michael (or Mike) **Romanoff:** Harry F. Gerguson (*c.*1892–1971), Lithuanian-born U.S. impostor. Harry Gerguson posed (to 1958) as His Imperial Highness Prince Michael Alexandrovitch Dmitry Obolensky Romanoff. Any émigré Russian will tell you what weight such names carried in the old regime. (Earlier, he had tried out the noble names William Wellington, Arthur Wellesley, and Count Gladstone.) When once at a party in his royal role, someone addressed him in Russian. He turned away and said to a friend, "How vulgar, we only spoke French at court."

Romany: [Rev.] George Bramwell Evens (1884–1943), Eng. Methodist minister, writer, broadcaster on the countryside. "Romany" suggests gypsies, of course, as well as someone who roams romantically over the country. In her biography of her late husband, who was of Gypsy descent, Evens's widow describes how he got his name: "When the day of my husband's first [radio] engagement arrived [in 1932], he was received by the organizer and asked, 'How do you wish to be announced?' for, at that time, all those who took part were either Uncles or Aunties. This came as a shock. Certainly not 'Uncle Bramwell' nor 'The Rev. Bramwell Evens.' On the spur of the moment he replied, 'Romany,' and Romany he became. What a fortunate choice it was! ... The only person who disapproved of it was our small nine-year-old daughter, who had been christened Romany June, for she felt that she had a prior claim to it" [Eunice Evens, *Through the Years with Romany*, 1946]. Romany June's first husband was theater critic Richard **Findlater** (married 1948, divorced 1961).

Romário: Romário de Souza Farias (1966–), Brazilian footballer.

Romark: Ronald Markham (1927–1982), Eng. TV hypnotist. The entertainer formed his professional name from the respective first syllables of his first name and surname.

Jacob **Rombro:** Filip Krantz (1858–1922), Pol.-born U.S. labor leader, writer.

Stewart **Rome:** Septimus William Ryott (1887–1965), Br. movie actor.

Max **Romeo:** Max Smith (*c.*1947–), Jamaican reggae musician.

A.B. **Romney:** Anna Beatrice Rambault (?–1944), Eng. painter, writer.

Edana **Romney:** Edana Rubenstein (1919–), S.A. movie actress.

[Sir] Landon **Ronald:** Landon Ronald Russell (1873–1938), Eng. orchestral conductor, composer.

William **Ronald:** William Ronald Smith (1926–), Can. painter, radio, TV presenter, working in U.S.

Ronnie **Ronalde:** Ronald Charles Waldron (1923–), Br. musical whistler, bird impressionist.

Ronaldinho: Ronaldo de Assis Moreira (1980–), Brazilian footballer. The player was earlier Ronaldinho Gaúcho, adding the second word to the diminutive form of his first name for distinction from **Ronaldo**, formerly known as Ronaldinho. The addition, from American Spanish *gaúcho*, "cowboy of the pampas," denoted that he came from the south of Brazil, as he was born in Pôrto Alegre, capital of the state of Rio Grande do Sul.

The Portuguese suffixes -*inho* and -*ão*, meaning respectively "little" and "big," are common in Brazil and are used to distinguish between individuals of the same name. "In the 1990s many Ronaldos played for the national side. The first three were easy to name: Ronaldão, Ronaldinho and Ronaldo, *Big, Little and Regular-sized Ronaldo*. But in 1999 another Ronaldinho turned up. What was left? Would he be nicknamed Ronaldinhozinho, *Even Littler Ronaldo*? No. He was first called Ronaldinho Gaúcho, *Little Ronaldo from Rio Grande do Sul*. Then, since he was no longer so little, the original Ronaldinho graduated to Ronaldo ... and so Ronaldinho Gaúcho became Ronaldinho" [Bellos, p. 233].

Ronaldo: Ronaldo Luiz Nazário de Lima (1976–), Brazilian footballer. The player was formerly known as Ronaldinho, a diminutive form of his first name.

Rondart: Ronald Tomlinson (1929–), Eng. variety artist. The entertainer's specialty was blowing darts. Hence his stage name.

Gene **Rondo:** Winston Lara (1943–1994), Jamaican reggae musician.

Edward **Ronns:** Edward Sidney Aarons (1916–1975), U.S. mystery writer. Aarons used this name for several novels, such as *Death in a Lighthouse* (1938), *Murder Money* (1938), and *The Corpse Hangs High* (1939). He also wrote as Paul Ayres.

Valentine **Rooke:** Valentine Brooke (1912–), Eng. stage actor.

William Michael **Rooke:** William Michael Rourke (1794–1847), Ir. composer. "In 1813 Rourke, being freed by the death of his father from an uncongenial trade, adopted music as a profession, and modified his surname to Rooke" [*Dictionary of National Biography*].

Mickey **Rooney:** Joe Yule, Jr. (1920–), U.S. movie actor. The actor's original screen name was Mickey McGuire, which he legally adopted from the comic-strip character he played as a child in two-reel comedies. In 1932 he took the name by which he became famous. According to Rooney himself, it was suggested by Kenneth Wilson, a publicity man at Universal Studios, when they needed him for a part in a new movie but wanted to distinguish him from Mickey McGuire: "'How about "Mickey Yule"?' He savored it for a moment. 'Nah. It doesn't sound right. The rhythm is wrong. I like Mickey. But Yule? No. We need another last name. Something with a "y" in it. That would sound better. Mickey Maloney? Mickey Downey? Mickey Looney?' ... 'How about Rooney?' asked my mother. 'I knew a guy in vaudeville, Pat Rooney.' 'Not bad,' said Wilson. 'Mickey Rooney. I'll run it by my boss and see what he says.' He never bothered to ask me whether *I* liked it ... Wilson returned a few minutes later with a smile on his face. 'Well, kid, that's your new name — Mickey Rooney'" [Mickey Rooney, *Life Is Too Short*, 1991].

Henry Root: Charles William Donaldson (1935–2005), Eng. writer. The writer adopted this name for his epistolary spoof, *The Henry Root Letters* (1980), which, together with its sequel, *The Further Letters of Henry Root* (1980), reproduced correspondence between the author and various celebrities and government officials. Root himself was created in the guise of a jingoistic retired wet-fish merchant, with wife, Doris, 19-year-old daughter, Doreen, and 15-year-old son, Henry Jr. Only a very few recipients of the letters suspected the actual legpull. Other pseudonyms used by Donaldson were Talbot Church, Liz Reed, and Jean-Luc Legris.

Root Boy Slim: Foster MacKenzie III (1945–1993), U.S. black R&B musician.

Levi Roots: Keith Valentine Graham (1958–), Jamaican reggae musician, entrepreneur. "The life and music of the 'Duppy Conqueror' [Bob Marley] has fascinated me ever since I first heard the album *Natty Dread* when I had just left school. I was 16 and feeling something was wrong with my birth name, Keith Graham, which I found out was Scottish — I don't look very Scottish. So I went off on a search for my roots and culture and I found them through Marley's music. One of the first things to go as a result was my slave name" [*The Times*, October 24, 2009].

Roots Manuva: Rodney Hylton Smith (1972–), Br. hip-hop musician, of Jamaican parentage. The name may be meant to suggest a musician who seeks to "maneuver his roots," or create a new image for himself and his black heritage.

Rex Roper: Charles Victor Knight (1919–), Br. variety cowboy actor. The performer's act made a special feature of rope-spinning.

V. Ropshin: Boris Viktorovich Savinkov (1879–1925), Russ. revolutionary.

A.N. Roquelaure: Anne Rice, née Howard Allen O'Brien (1941–), U.S. novelist. Changing her first name to Anne during her first year at school, Rice adopted her pseudonym for her pornographic trilogy *The Claiming of Sleeping Beauty* (1983),

Beauty's Punishment (1984), and *Beauty's Release* (1985). A roquelaure is a knee-length cloak worn in the 18th and early 19th century, named after the Duc de Roquelaure (1656–1738). Rice has also written erotica as Anne Rampling.

Noël Roquevert: Noël Benevent (1894–1973), Fr. movie actor.

Amanda Ros: Amanda Anna Margaret Ross, née McKittrick (1860–1939), Ir. novelist, poet. The writer claimed to have been originally named Amanda Malvina Fitzalan Anna Margaret McLelland McKittrick, but some of these names are in fact from Regina Maria Roche's sentimental novel, *Children of the Abbey* (1796), a favorite book from Ross's childhood.

Carl Rosa: Karl August Nikolaus Rose (1842–1889), Ger. conductor, impresario, working in England. "In 1875 he formed in London ... the Carl Rosa Opera Company, when he changed his name to Rosa, in order, it is said, to avoid confusion in pronunciation" [*Dictionary of National Biography*]. (The German name would have been pronounced as "Rosa," not as English "Rose.")

Rosa Rosà: Edyth von Haynau (1884–?1978), Austr.-born It. futurist poet, illustrator.

Rosalie: Marie Claude Josèphe Levasseur (1749–1826), Fr. opera singer. The soprano used this name early in her career. "She first appeared on the stage in Paris in small parts and under the name of Rosalie, using her own name from 1775" [Blom, p. 316].

Rosa Matilda: Charlotte Byrne, née King (*c*.1772–1825), Eng. "Gothic" novelist.

Rosamond: Rosamond Clifford (1157–1176), Eng. mistress of Henry II. The tragic figure known as "Fair Rosamond," supposedly poisoned by Eleanor of Aquitaine, Henry's queen, has been the subject of numerous literary and musical works. According to Dryden, in his epilogue to John Bancroft's play *Henry II, King of England, with the Death of Rosamond* (1693), her first name was really Jane: "Jane Clifford was her Name, as Books aver: / Fair *Rosamond* was but her *Nom de Guerre*."

Rosario: Florencia Pérez Podilla (1918–), Sp. ballet dancer, teaming with cousin **Antonio**.

Carolina Rosati: Carolina Galletti (1826–1905), It. ballet dancer.

Françoise Rosay: Françoise Bandy de Nalèche (1891–1974), Fr. stage, movie actress.

Charles Roscoe *see* Fenton **Brockley**

Alex Rose: Olesh Royz (1898–1976), Pol.-born U.S. Labor leader.

Axl Rose: William Bailey (1962–), U.S. rock singer. Rose is the singer's real name, which he discovered when he was 17, having been raised under the name of his stepfather, L. Stephen Bailey. He called himself Axl after a band for which he played in his home state of Indiana. (The band was renamed Rose after him but he left to play with another band named LA Guns, founded by guitarist Tracii Guns. In 1985 the two bands merged to form Guns N' Roses, a characteristic "hard-and-soft" name like that of Iron Butterfly.) It is said to be no coincidence that Axl Rose's name is an anagram of "oral sex."

Billy Rose: William Samuel Rosenberg (1899–1966), U.S. theater manager, composer. Some sources give the impresario's original name as Samuel Wolf Rosenberg, although "William" more readily gives "Billy."

Calypso Rose: McCartha Lewis (1940–), Tobagan calypso singer.

George Arthur **Rose** *see* Baron **Corvo**

Philip Rose: Philip Rosenberg (1921–), U.S. stage producer.

Roseanne: Roseanne Barr, later Arnold (1952–), U.S. TV comedienne. The stand-up comic was originally known by her married name but following the breakup of her second marriage (to Tom Arnold) and her remarriage in 1995 (to Ben Thomas) chose to be billed by her first name alone.

Peter Rosegger: Petri Kettenfeier Rosegger (1843–1918), Austr. poet, novelist. Until 1894, the year when his collected works began to be published, the writer was known as P.K. Rosegger.

Fedora Roselli: Edith Dora Bernard, née Hodges (1896–1950), Eng. opera singer. The singer was the mother of writer Jeffrey **Bernard**.

Rose Matilda *see* Charlotte **Dacre**

Julius Rosen: Nikolaus Duffek (1833–1892), Cz. poet.

Anastasius Lagrantinus Rosenstengel: Catharina Margaretha Linck (*c*.1694–1721), Ger. lesbian. Adopting a name with female and phallic connotations (Rosenstengel translates as "rose stem"), Linck was executed when aged around 27 for attempting to pass as a man and for marrying another woman.

[St.] **Rose of Lima:** Isabel de Santa Maria de Flores (1586–1617), Peruvian virgin visionary, of Sp. parentage. Born in Lima, the first saint of the New World took the name Rosa at her confirmation.

Rosh: Asher ben Jehiel (*c*.1250–1327), Ger. Jewish scholar. The Talmudic authority came to be known by an an acronymic name formed from letters in *Rabbi Ash*er.

Nikolay Roshchin-Insarov: Nikolay Petrovich Pashenny (1861–1899), Russ. actor.

Rosimond: Claude La Roze (*c*.1640–1686), Fr. actor.

Carl Rosini: John Rosen (1882–?), Pol.-born magician, working in Germany, U.S.

Emperor Rosko: Michael Pasternak (1942–), Eng. radio DJ.

Natalia **Roslavleva:** Natalia Petrovna René (1907–1977), Russ.-born Br. writer on ballet. The writer used the name for her contributions to the journal *Ballet Today* in the 1940s, so commemorating the Russian dancer Lyubov Roslavleva (1874–1904).

Ernst Rosmer: Elsa Bernstein (1866–1925), Ger. playwright. The dramatist was influenced by Ibsen, and adopted her name from his *Rosmersholm* (1886). British writer Rebecca **West** took her name from a character in the same play.

Milton Rosmer: Arthur Milton Lunt (1881–1971), Br. stage, movie actor, director. The actor took his stage name from that of Johannes Rosmer, the central character in Henrik Ibsen's play *Rosmersholm* (1886). For a similar borrowing, compare the name of Rebecca **West**.

J.-H. Rosny: Joseph-Henri Boex ("Rosny aîné") (1856–1940), Belg.-born Fr. novelist + Séraphin Justin François Boex ("Rosny jeune") (1859–1948), Belg.-born Fr. novelist, his brother. The initials are those of the elder brother, who took his new name in memory of a stay in Rosny-sous-Bois, now a suburb of Paris.

Ross: Harry Ross Thomson (1938–), Sc. cartoonist, illustrator. The artist adopted the shortest of his names for his work, signing it distinctively as "roSS."

Adrian Ross: Arthur Reed Ropes (1859–1933), Eng. lyricist, librettist. Ropes used the name Arthur Reed for the libretto of a vaudeville entertainment, *A Double Event* (1884), written jointly (a "double event") with Arthur Law. He later adopted the name Adrian Ross, first using it for the libretto of *Joan of Arc* (1891).

Annie Ross: Annabelle McCauley Allan Lynch, née Short (1930–), Br.-born U.S. jazz singer, songwriter. Ross was taken to the U.S. at the age of three by her aunt, singer and actress Ella **Logan**. Her brother was the actor Jimmy **Logan**.

Barnaby **Ross** *see* Ellery **Queen**

Barney Ross: Barnet David Rosofsky (1909–1967), U.S. welterweight boxer. The boxer first fought his amateur bouts in 1926 while working as a clerk at Sears, Roebuck, and took the name "Barney Ross" so his mother would not know.

Clarissa **Ross** *see* Marilyn **Ross**

Dana Fuller **Ross** *see* Samuel **Edwards**

Edward Ross: Rossano Brazzi (1916–1994), It.-born U.S. movie actor, director. The famed "Latin lover" used this English name as director of two 1968 movies: *Salvare la faccia* ("To save his face") (U.S. title *Psychout for Murder*) and *Sette homini e un cervello* ("Seven men and one brain").

Jerry Ross: Jerold Rosenberg (1926–1955), U.S. popular composer, lyricist.

John **Ross:** Kohn Dix (1824–1864), Eng. writer, working in U.S.

John Hume **Ross:** Thomas Edward Lawrence (1888–1935), Eng. soldier, archaeologist, writer ("Lawrence of Arabia"). This was the name chosen by Lawrence to escape publicity when he enlisted in the Royal Air Force in 1922. A year later he joined the Tank Corps as T.E. Shaw, adopting the name by deed poll in 1927. The latter name was intended as a mark of respect to George Bernard Shaw. "We record with much regret the death, which took place yesterday morning, of Mr. T.E. Shaw, the name formally adopted some years ago by Colonel Lawrence, the legendary hero of the Arab War" [Obituary, *The Times*, May 20, 1935].

Jonathan **Ross:** John Rossiter (1916–), Br. detective novelist.

Leonard Q. **Ross:** Leo Calvin Rosten (1908–1997), Pol.-born U.S. writer. Rosten used this name for his best-known book, *The Education of Hyman Kaplan* (1937), a humorous account of the torments unwittingly inflicted on the English language and his long-suffering English teacher by the immigrant student of the title.

Marilyn **Ross:** William Edward Daniel Ross (1912–1995), Can.-born U.S. novelist. Other (female) names used by the writer include Marilyn Carter, Rose Dana, Ruth Dorset, Ann Gilmer, Ellen Randolph, Clarissa Ross, Olin Ross, and Jane Rossiter, this last for his first novel, *Summer Season* (1962).

Martin **Ross:** Violet Florence Martin (1861–1915), Ir. author. The writer used her surname as her first name, taking "Ross" from her birthplace, Ross House, Co. Galway. In collaboration with her cousin, Edith Anna Œnone Somerville (1858–1949), she wrote many books and stories about Irish life under the joint name of Somerville and Ross. *See also* Viva **Graham**, Geilles **Herring**.

Mike **Ross:** Colin John Novelle (1948–), Br. radio DJ.

Mother **Ross:** Christian Davies (1667–1739), Ir. soldier. When Davies's husband, Richard Welsh, mysteriously disappeared, then wrote to say he had joined the army in Flanders, she went in search of him, enlisting under the name Christopher Welsh. She finally found him, but so relished army life that she continued to serve, posing as his brother. Her sex was revealed during an operation for a broken skull, after which she reverted to female dress. When Welsh was killed at the battle of Malplaquet (1709), she herself found his body, "and her lamentations at the discovery were so extravagant as to excite the open commiseration of a captain Ross, whence, it is said, she gained the sobriquet of Mother Ross, by which she was known for the rest of her life" [*Dictionary of National Biography*].

Olin **Ross** *see* Marilyn **Ross**

Oriel **Ross:** Muriel Swinstead (1907–1994), Br. stage actress.

Peggy **Ross:** Margaret Campbell (1912–), Can. movie actress.

Shirley **Ross:** Bernice Gaunt (1909–1975), U.S. pianist, singer, movie actress.

Steven J. **Ross:** Steven Rechnitz (1927–1992), U.S. business executive, of Russ. Jewish parentage. The family name of the future Warner Communications chief was changed by his father when the latter sought a job selling oil burners in Depression-era New York.

Ted **Ross:** Theodore Ross Roberts (1934–2002), U.S. movie actor.

Robert **Rossen:** Robert Rosen (1908–1966), U.S. movie director, screenwriter, of Russ. Jewish parentage.

Dante Gabriel **Rossetti:** Gabriel Charles Dante Rossetti (1828–1882), Eng. painter, poet, of It. parentage. The Pre-Raphaelite painter rearranged his forenames for artistic effect

Francesco Antonio **Rossetti:** Franz Anton Rössler (*c*.1750–1792), Bohemian musical director, composer. The musician created an Italian form of his German name for his compositions.

Minerva **Rossetti** *see* Fenton **Brockley**

Tino **Rossi:** Constantino Rossi (1907–1983), Corsican-born Fr. popular singer. "One morning, [French composer Vincent] Scotto brought me a little Corsican with gold-flecked eyes and the faint smile of a hungry bruiser. 'You can rely on this fellow, he'll go far. He's from Ajaccio, like Napoleon, which says it all. As for his voice, you've never heard anything like it.... His name'll mean nothing to you, but you've got to start somewhere!' Vincent turned to the young man. 'Tell him your name.' 'Constantino Rossi, but I think Tino sounds better than Constantino...' Vincent approved, waxed lyrical: 'Tino Rossi! A name that will soar like a rocket! Women who hear it will go absolutely wild!' So it was that Tino Rossi ... started out in the movies" [Carlo Rim, *Mémoires d'une vieille vague*, translated by A.R., 1961].

Eleonora **Rossi-Drago:** Palmira Omiccioli (1925–), It. movie actress. The actress became Eleonora Rossi on marrying Cesare Rossi, then added "Drago" to avoid confusion with the actress Luisa Rossi. Later credits often give the name without the hyphen.

Rossini: Pyotr Akimovich Ogluzdin (1887–1939), Russ. circus artist, acrobat. Members of the performer's family followed in his footsteps under the same name, itself first used in 1902 for the three Rossini Brothers.

Jane **Rossiter** *see* Marilyn **Ross**

Rosso Fiorentino: Giovanni Battista di Jacopo (1494–1540), It. painter. The artist, born in Florence, came to be known by a descriptive nickname meaning "the Florentine redhead."

Helge **Roswaenge:** Helge Rosenving-Hansen (1897–1972), Dan. opera singer.

Nino **Rota:** Nino Rinaldi (1911–1979), It. composer.

Gene **Roth:** Gene Stuttenroth (1903–1976), U.S. movie actor.

Lillian **Roth:** Lillian Rutstein (1910–1980), U.S. movie actress, singer.

Paul **Rotha:** Roscoe Treeve Fawcett Thompson (1907–1984), Br. documentary movie producer, director, film critic. The filmmaker's parents altered his first name to Paul at an early age. He then changed his name by deed poll to Paul Rotha when starting a career as an artist, the new surname apparently based on the first syllables of his original first name and surname.

Samuel "Roxy" **Rothafel:** Samuel Lionel Rothapfel (1881–1936), U.S. movie exhibitor. The family dropped the "p" from their name at the end of World War I, when Germanic names were in disfavor. It was Rothafel's nickname that gave the name of the Roxy movie theater chain.

Mark **Rothko:** Marcus Rothkovitch (1903–1970), Latvian-born U.S. artist. When the future painter arrived as a young child in the U.S. in 1913 with his mother and older sister to join the rest of their family in Oregon, the immigration authorities at Ellis Island "yiddishized" their Jewish surname to Rothkowitz, while the manifest of the ship that brought them had him down as Markus Rotkowicz. He first used the name Rothko around 1940, after becoming a U.S. citizen, but did not settle on the new form of his first name for some time. He legally adopted the name only in 1958.

Contessa Anna **Roti:** Regina di Luanto (c.1862–1914), It. novelist. The writer's assumed name (but not title) is a part-anagram of her real name.

Ola **Rotimi:** Emmanuel Gladstone Olawole (1938–), Nigerian playwright.

Johnny **Rotten:** John Joseph Lydon (1956–), Br. punk rock musician, of Ir. parentage. The former Sex Pistols member explains: "I got the name Rotten because I had green teeth. It was [guitarist] Steve [Jones]'s nickname for me: "You're fucking Rotten!" That's what he used to say. It was, and it wasn't an affectionate nickname" [John Lydon with Keith and Kent Zimmerman, *Rotten: No Irish, No Blacks, No Dogs*, 1993].

The antiestablishment name chimed with those of his fellow punk rockers, as instanced in a contemporary news item: "They call themselves names designed to alienate society: Rat **Scabies**, Dee **Generate**, Johnny **Rotten**, Sid **Vicious**" [*Sunday Mirror*, June 12, 1977]. After the group's breakup in 1978, followed soon after by the death of Vicious, Lydon reverted to his real name and formed his own group, Public Image Limited (PiL).

Dick **Roughsey:** Goobalathaldin (1924–1985), Austral. children's writer. Roughsey was a full-blooded Aborigine, whose tribal or "skin" name meant "rough sea." Hence his adopted English surname.

Joseph **Rovan:** Joseph Rosenthal (1918–2004), Ger.-born Fr. historian The man regarded as the architect of Franco-German reconciliation adopted his new name on joining the French Resistance in World War II.

Rover: Ian Morgan (1932–), Welsh crossword compiler. The pseudonym puns on two senses of "setter," both as a dog (with Rover a common dog name) and as a person who compiles crosswords.

Roland W. ("Tiny") **Rowland:** Roland Walter Fuhrhop (1917–1998), Br. businessman, newspaper owner, of part-Ger. parentage The entrepreneur adopted (and slightly adapted) his own first name as his new surname in 1939. His nickname, "Tiny," was humorously ironic, as he was a tall, handsome man.

Effie Adelaide **Rowlands:** Effie Marie Albanesi, née Henderson (1859–1936), Br. romantic novelist ("Madame Albanesi").

Jimmy **Rowles:** James Polk Hunter (1918–1996), U.S. jazz pianist, composer. The musician adopted his stepfather's name as his professional name. Some sources give his original middle name as George.

Richard **Rowley:** Richard Valentine Williams (1877–1947), Ir. poet, playwright, publisher.

Thomas **Rowley:** Thomas Chatterton (1752–1770), Eng. poet, writer. The precocious poet, a suicide at age 18, adopted the name and persona of Thomas Rowley, an imaginary 15th-century monk, "prieste of St. Johan's, Bristowe," for a number of his poems. It is possible he selected the surname after reading about Charles II, who was nicknamed "Old Rowley" (after a prize racehorse), but it is more likely he took the complete name from a memorial in the church mentioned (St. John's, Bristol) to Thomas Rowley, a merchant who died in 1478.

J.K. **Rowling:** Joanne Kathleen Rowling (1965–), Eng. children's writer. The author of the popular books featuring Harry Potter, the schoolboy who discovers he is a wizard, reportedly decided to publish with her initials in order to deter undue male interest.

Patricia **Roxburgh:** Sylvia Rafael (1937–2005), Israeli secret agent. This was the name under which the agent was sent to France in the guise of a freelance journalist with a Canadian passport.

Alexander **Roy:** Udo Badstübner (1935–), Ger.-born Br. ballet dancer.

Brandon **Roy:** Florence Louisa Barclay, née Charlesworth (1862–1920), Eng. writer. A clergyman's wife and daughter, Barclay used this male name for a number of novels, beginning with *Guy Mervyn* (1891).

Claude **Roy:** Claude Orland (1915–1997), Fr. poet, essayist.

Harry **Roy:** Harry Lipman (1900–1971), Br. danceband leader.

Jack **Roy** *see* Rodney **Dangerfield**

John **Roy:** [Sir] Henry Mortimer Durand (1850–1924), Eng. civil servant, writer, working in India. The diplomat used this name for a three-volume novel, *Helen Treveryan; or, The Ruling Race* (1892).

Manabendra Nath **Roy:** Narendranath Bhattacharya (1887–1954), Ind. Communist leader. The politician changed his name on seeking support in San Francisco in 1916.

Nirupa **Roy:** Kokila Kishorechandra Balsara (1931–), Ind. movie actress.

Frank **Royde:** Frank Howroyd (1882–?), Eng. stage actor.

Roy **Royston:** Roy Charles Crowden (or Chown) (1899–1976), Br. juvenile stage, movie actor.

Marie **Roze:** Hippolyte Ponsin (1846–1926), Fr. opera singer.

Gennady **Rozhdestvensky:** Gennady Nikolayevich Anosov (1931–), Russ. orchestral conductor. The musician adopted his mother's maiden name to avoid trading on the reputation of his father, conductor Nikolay Anosov (1900–1962).

Alma **Rubens:** Alma Smith (1897–1931), U.S. movie actress. The actress was also billed early in her career as Alma Reuben or Alma Reubens.

Crotus **Rubianus:** Johannes Jäger (?1480–c.1539), Ger. humanist.

David **Rubio:** David Spink (1934–2000), Br. maker of musical instruments. The craftsman gained the name "Rubio" (for his red beard) while making a meager living as a flamenco guitarist in Spain early in his career.

Harry **Ruby:** Harry Rubenstein (1895–1974), U.S. stage, movie songwriter.

Jack L. **Ruby:** Jacob Rubenstein (1911–1967), U.S. assassin, of Pol. Jewish parentage. Ruby adopted his new name in 1947 on moving to Dallas, Texas, from Chicago, where he had been selling novelties.

Steele **Rudd:** Arthur Hoey Davis (1868–1935), Austral. novelist, playwright. The writer began contributing magazine articles in about 1890 under the name Steele Rudder, the first word expressing his admiration for the essayist Sir Richard Steele, the second

alluding to his love of boating. The second word was soon shortened to "Rudd."

Dane **Rudhyar:** Daniel Chennevière (1895–1985), Fr.-born U.S. composer. The musician went to the USA with a group of dancers in 1916 and settled there the following year. He subsequently became deeply interested in Indian theosophy and accordingly adopted a Hindi name meaning "popular friend."

Patrick **Ruell:** Reginald Charles Hill (1936–), Br. crime novelist. Other names used by the writer include Dick Morland and Charles Underhill.

Bruce **Ruffin:** Bernardo Constantine Balderamus (1952–), Jamaican pop, reggae musician.

Titta **Ruffo:** Ruffo Titta (1877–1953), It. opera singer. Unusually, the baritone's name was taken from a family pet dog. Oreste Titta frequently took his dog, Ruffo, out hunting. One day, on such an expedition, the dog was accidentally shot and killed. Grief-stricken, his master vowed to preserve the dog's name, and later, when his son was born, named him Ruffo commemoratively. In due course the boy grew up and started an operatic career. He had come to dislike his dog-derived name, but not wishing to offend his father, created a stage name by simply turning his original name around. Thus Ruffo Titta became Titta Ruffo, family honor was satisfied, and the canine connection was preserved.

Rufus: Roger F. Squires (1932–), Br. crossword compiler. The name represents the setter's initials.

Sig **Ruman:** Siegfried Alban Rumann (1884–1967), Ger. movie actor, working in U.S.

Boris **Runin:** Boris Mikhailovich Rubinshteyn (Rubinstein) (1912–), Russ. movie critic.

Damon **Runyon:** Alfred Damon Runyan (1880–1946), U.S. journalist, short-story writer. A printer's error in Runyon's first byline in 1895 caused his surname to be misspelled with "o" for "a."

RuPaul: RuPaul Andre Charles (1960–), U.S. black drag performer, singer.

Jia **Ruskaya:** Eugenia Borisenko (1902–1970), Russ.-It. ballet dancer. The dancer adopted a name that indicated her Russian parentage, with "Jia" an Italian pet form of her first name.

Anna **Russell:** Anna Claudia Russell-Brown (1911–2006), Br. singer, musical satirist.

Billy **Russell:** Adam George Brown (1893–1972), Eng. music-hall comedian.

Craig **Russell:** Russell Craig Eadie (1948–1990), Can. female impersonator.

Fred **Russell:** Thomas Frederic Parnell (1862–1957), Eng. ventriloquist, variety artist. The performer changed his name to avoid any undesirable associations with the Irish politician Charles Parnell (1846–1891), who had been involved in a scandal with

Kitty O'Shea, the wife of a prominent party member. He took the name Russell from his local Member of Parliament, Charles Russell (1832–1900), later Lord Russell of Killowen and Lord Chief Justice of England.

Hal **Russell**: Harold Russell Luttenbacher (1926–), U.S. jazz saxophonist.

Johnny **Russell**: John Russell Countryman (1933–), U.S. child movie actor.

Leon **Russell**: Claude Russell Bridges (1941–), U.S. rock musician. Some sources give Russell's original name as Hank Wilson.

Lillian **Russell**: Helen Louise Leonard (1861–1922), U.S. stage actress, singer. The actress was renamed in 1879 by impresario Tony **Pastor**, who gave her a list of new names to choose from. She chose "Lillian Russell" because she liked all the "l's" in it.

Mark **Russell**: Mark Ruslander (1932–), U.S. comedian.

Sarah **Russell** *see* Marghanita **Laski**

Theresa **Russell**: Theresa Paup (1957–), U.S. movie actress.

Van **Russell**: Thomas Bowyer (1902–1949), Br.-born Can. magician.

William **Russell**: William Lerche (1884–1929), U.S. movie actor.

Russo: Pyotr Dmitriyevich Poluparnev (1894–1972), Russ. circus artist, clown.

Renato **Russo**: Renato Manfredini Júnior (1960–1996), Brazilian rock singer, songwriter, of It. descent.

An **Rutgers**: An Rutgers van der Loeff-Basenau (1910–1990), Du. children's writer.

Douglas **Rutherford**: James Douglas Rutherford McConnell (1915–1988), Ir.-born Br. thriller writer.

John **Rutherford**: Beulah Marie Dix (1876–1970), U.S. playwright, screenwriter. Dix coauthored a number of plays with Evelyn Sutherland under this name, "using a male pseudonym ... in order to make the play more acceptable to English audiences" [Tamara Horn in Garraty and Carnes, vol. 6, p. 634].

Mark **Rutherford**: William Hale White (1831–1913), Eng. novelist, religious writer. Rutherford also wrote as Reuben Shapcott, and used both names for his first major work, *The Autobiography of Mark Rutherford, Dissenting Minister: Edited by his Friend, Reuben Shapcott* (1881).

Joseph Jakob **Rütten**: Joseph Jakob Kindskopf (1805–1878), Ger. bookseller.

Salomon van **Ruysdael**: Salomon de Goyer (*c.*1600–1670), Du. painter.

Ward **Ruyslinck**: Raimond de Belser (1929–), Belg. writer.

Il **Ruzzante**: Angelo Beolco (*c.*1496–1542), It. comic actor, playwright. The actor's stage name means "the chatterbox."

Irene **Ryan**: Irene Riordan (1903–1973), U.S. movie comedienne.

Meg **Ryan**: Margaret Mary Emily Anne Hyra (1961–), U.S. movie actress. The actress adopted her mother's maiden name before her screen debut in *Rich and Famous* (1981).

Sheila **Ryan**: Katherine Elizabeth McLaughlin (1921–1975), U.S. movie actress.

Tommy **Ryan**: Joseph Youngs (1870–1948), U.S. boxer.

David **Ryazanov**: David Borisovich Goldendakh (Goldendach) (1870–1938), Russ. revolutionary.

Bobby **Rydell**: Robert Ridarelli (1942–), U.S. pop musician.

Alfred **Ryder**: Alfred Jacob Corn (1919–), U.S. stage actor, director.

Red **Ryder** *see* Reed **Hadley**

Mitch **Ryder**: William Levise, Jr. (1945–), U.S. (white) soul singer. Levise was urged by his record company to find a more original name: "Any name's better than yours." He is said to have taken the name from a Detroit phone book.

Winona **Ryder**: Winona Laura Horowitz (1971–), U.S. movie actress. Born near Winona, Minnesota, the budding actress needed a new name for her first movie, *Lucas* (1986). Her father was listening to a Mitch **Ryder** album at the time, and she decided that would make a suitable surname.

Anthony **Rye** *see* John **Christopher**

Mark **Rylance**: David Mark Rylance Waters (1960–), Eng. stage, movie, TV actor, director. The actor took his stage name on learning that there was already a Mark Waters registered with Equity, the trade union for the British acting profession, which will not accept identically named members.

Xavier **Rynne**: Francis X. Murphy (1914–2002), U.S. Roman Catholic priest, historian, of Ir. parentage. Fr. Murphy used this name, based on his own middle name and his mother's maiden name, for his celebrated insider's account of the Second Vatican Council, *Letters from Vatican City* (1968). The 13 letters had earlier been individually published in the *New Yorker* under the same pseudonym.

Ryogoku: Kobayashi Hideaki (1962–), Jap. sumo wrestler. The wrestler adopted the name of a predecessor in his *heya* (stable), Ryogoku Kajinosuke.

Poul **Rytter**: Parmo Carl Ploug (1813–1894), Dan. poet, politician.

Svend Otto **S.**: Svend Otto Sörensen (1916–1996), Dan. illustrator of fairy tales.

Saadi (or Sa'di): Musharrif od-Din Muslih od-Din (*c.*1213–1292), Persian poet. The poet took his name in honor of the ruler of Shiraz, his contemporary, Abu Bakr ibn-Sa'd ibn-Zangi (ruled 1231–1260), and alludes to him by name in his book of ethics in verse *Bustan* ("The Orchard") (1257). The name itself means "happy," "lucky."

Martha **Saalfeld**: Martha vom Scheidt (1898–1976), Ger. writer.

Umberto **Saba**: Umberto Poli (1883–1957), It. poet. The poet's Jewish mother was deserted by her husband on the birth of her son, and Umberto did not get to know his father until he was an adult. He did not accept his name, Poli, however, but instead adopted the name of his nurse, Saba, the biblical Sheba. He first used it for his collection of poems *Poesie* (1910).

Sabicas: Agustín Castellón (1917–1990), Sp. flamenco guitarist. The musician's name evolved from a nickname. As a child he was known as *el niño de las habicas*, "the little broad-bean boy," for his liking for this vegetable. The last two words of this were subsequently smoothed to the single word "Sabicas."

Georg **Sabinus**: Georg Schuler (1508–1560), Ger. humanist, poet.

Sabir: Mirza Alekper Tairzade (1862–1911), Azerbaijani satirical writer, poet. The writer's adopted name means "patient," alluding indirectly to the potential censorship that he risked for his criticism of the repressive society of his day.

Sable: Rena Mero (1967–), U.S. wrestler. The name reflects the black evening gown in which the wrestler made her first appearance in the ring.

Sabre: Andrew Bremner (1951–), Br. crossword compiler, working in U.S.

Sabrina: Norma Sykes (1928–), Eng. movie, TV actress. The actress may have taken her name arbitrarily, rather than from Samuel A. Taylor's play (or the movie based on it) *Sabrina Fair* (1954).

Sabu: Sabu Dastagir (1924–1963), Ind. juvenile movie actor, working in U.K., U.S. Some sources give the actor's original name as Selar Shaik Sabu. In 1944 Sabu became an American citizen.

Sacharissa: [Lady] Dorothy Sidney (1617–1684), Eng. aristocrat. The poet Edmund Waller paid court to Lady Dorothy by this name following the death of his first wife in childbirth in 1634. The name was formed, "as he used to say pleasantly," from Latin *saccharum*, "sugar." (It was perhaps also influenced by the name Melissa, as if from Greek *meli*, "honey," plus *-issa*, rather than from *melissa*, "bee.").

Maurice **Sachs**: Jean-Maurice Ettinghausen (1906–?1944), Fr. essayist, novelist, of Alsatian Jewish origin.

George John **Sackville-West**: George John West (1791–1869), Eng. aristocrat. In 1813 the 5th Earl De la Warr married 17-year-old Lady Elizabeth Sackville, younger daughter of the 3d Duke of Dorset, and added her name to his.

Sade: Helen Folasade Adu (1959–), Br. pop singer, of Nigerian-Eng. parentage. Because people in her native Ibadan refused to address her by her English first name, the singer's parents began calling her Sade, a shortened form of her Yoruba middle name, pronounced "Shah-day."

Yitzhak **Sadeh**: Yitzhak Landsberg (1890–1952), Russ.-born Jewish military leader. Landsberg took his new name from the *plugot sadeh*, "field units," that he commanded in Palestine during the Arab rebellion of 1936–9.

Sa'di *see* **Saadi**

Michael **Sadleir**: Michael Thomas Harvey Sadler (1888–1957), Br. writer, publisher. The writer adopted an earlier spelling of the family name to be distinguished from his father, Sir Michael Sadler (1861–1943), educationist and art patron.

Miloš **Sádlo**: Miloš Zátvrzský (1912–2003), Cz. cellist. The musician adopted the name of his teacher, K.P. Sádlo.

Nikolay **Sadovsky**: Nikolay Karpovich Tobilevich (1856–1933), Ukr. stage actor, director, brother of Ivan **Karpenko-Kary** and Panas **Saksagansky**.

Prov **Sadovsky**: Prov Mikhaylovich Yermilov (1818–1872), Russ. actor. Following the death of his father, the actor was reared and trained by his mother's brothers, provincial actors G.V. and D.V. Sadovsky, and adopted their name as his stage name.

William **Safire**: William Lewis Safir (1929–2009), U.S. political commentator, linguist, of Jewish parentage. The widely-read pundit added an "e" to his original surname to make it look more American.

Françoise **Sagan**: Françoise Quoirez (1935–2004), Fr. novelist. On publishing her first novel, the internationally acclaimed *Bonjour Tristesse* (1954), the writer was urged by her editor to assume a pen name. She took it, somewhat at random, from a work on Marcel Proust mentioning the Prince de Sagan. Boson de Talleyrand-Périgord, Prince de Sagan, was actually an acquaintance of Proust, who in part used him as a model for the Duc de Guermantes in *À la recherche du temps perdu* (1913–27).

Leontine **Sagan**: Leontine Schlesinger (1889–1974), Austr. stage actress, theater, movie director, working in U.K., South Africa.

Ramanand **Sagar**: Ramanand Shankardas Chopra (1917–), Ind. movie director, producer.

Juniper **Sage** *see* Golden **MacDonald**

Sagittarius: Olga Miller, née Katzin (1896–1987), Br. author, satirist, of Russ. Jewish parentage. Miller used this name for satirical verses in the weekly *New Statesman* (from 1934). These were "barbed," like the arrows shot by the mythological Sagittarius, the Archer. Known to her friends as "Saj," Miller used other names for her satirical sociopolitical contributions to other publications. For *Time and Tide* she wrote as Fiddlestick, for the *Manchester Guardian* she was Mercutio, and in the *Daily Herald* she appeared as Scorpio.

Henricus **Sagittarius:** Heinrich Schütz (1585–1672), Ger. church music composer. Schütz translated his German name into Latin (German *Schütze*, Latin *sagittarius*, "archer") in the manner of his time.

Amo **Sagiyan:** Amayak Saakovich Grigoryan (1915–), Armenian poet.

Mario J. **Sagola** *see* Anthony **McCall**

Sahajanand Swami: Chapaiya (1781–1830), Ind. religious leader. The guru, who began his mission at the age of 21, was popularly known as Swaminarayan, from Hindi *swami*, "lord," "master," and Narayan, a name of the Hindu god Vishnu meaning "son of man."

Alexandru **Sahia:** Alexandru Stanescu (1908–1937), Rom. writer.

Sai Baba: Sathyanarayana Ratnakara Raju (1926–), Ind. spiritual leader. The modern yogi claimed to be the reincarnation of the Hindu saint Sai Baba of Shirdi (1856–1916), and assumed his name, meaning roughly "holy father," at the age of 14 on recovering from an illness.

Saib Tebrizi: Mirza Mukhammed Ali (1601–1677), Azerbaijani poet. The poet's adopted name is that of his birthplace, the city of Tabriz, northwestern Iran.

Monsieur Léon **Saint-Amans Fils:** Louise Geneviève La Hye, née Rousseau (1810–1838), Fr. organist, pianist, composer, grandniece of Jean-Jacques Rousseau. The musician adopted the name of her teacher, Léon Saint-Amans, as if his son (*fils*).

Horace de **Saint-Aubin** *see* Honoré de **Balzac**

Alan **St. Aubyn:** Frances L. Marshall, née Bridges (?–1922), Eng. novelist, archaeologist. The writer took her male pseudonym from the name of her husband's house, St. Aubyn's, near Tiverton, Devon.

Reginald **St. Barbe:** Douglas Brooke Wheelton Sladen (1856–1947), Eng. editor, novelist.

Alex **St. Clair:** Alexis Clair Snouffer (1941–2006), U.S. blues musician.

Georges **Saint-Clair:** Joseph Coudurier de Chassaigne (1878–1961), Fr. writer, journalist.

William **St. Clair:** William Ford (1821–1905), Eng. colonial civil servant, novelist. Ford used this name for his writing.

Marian **St. Claire:** Marian Beare, née Allsopp (1946–), Br. ballet dancer.

Lili **St. Cyr:** Willis Marie Van Schaak (1917–1999), U.S. striptease artist, movie actress.

Renée **St. Cyr:** Marie-Louise Vittoré (1904–2004), Fr. movie actress.

Leopold **St. Damian:** Frederic Horace Clark (?1860–1917), U.S. pianist, inventor. The musician used this pseudonym for his written works.

Michel **Saint-Denis:** Jacques Duchesne (1897–1971), Fr. theater director, playwright, actor.

Ruth **St. Denis:** Ruth Dennis (1879–1968), U.S. ballet dancer, choreographer. The joint founder, with her husband, Ted Shawn, of the Denishawn School of Dancing, changed her name at the suggestion of producer-director David Belasco when she premiered her first "Hindu ballet," *Radha*, in 1906.

Teddie **St. Denis:** June Catherine Church Denham (1909–?), Sc. variety artist, singer.

Christian **St. Forget** *see* Justin **de Villeneuve**

Saint-Georges de Bouhélier: Stéphane-Georges de Bouhélier-Lepelletier (1889–1942), Fr. poet, playwright.

Ivy **St. Helier:** Ivy Aitchison (1890–1971), Br. popular composer, singer, actress. The actress was born in the Channel Islands and took her stage name from her birthtown, St. Helier, Jersey.

Marco de **St. Hilaire:** Émile Marc Hilaire (1790–?), Fr. writer.

Antoinette **Saint-Huberty:** Antoinette Cécile Clavel (1756–1812), Fr. soprano.

Joseph-Xavier **Saintine:** Joseph-Xavier Boniface (1798–1865), Fr. popular novelist.

Raymond **St. Jacques:** James Arthur Johnson (1930–1990), U.S. black movie actor. The actor explained that he took his name from a white French boy who later became a "milkman in New Haven."

Susan **Saint James:** Susan Jane Miller (1946–), U.S. movie, TV actress. The actress has said that her name was "French-inspired." It evolved following a high-school year on a French student-exchange program.

Betta **St. John:** Betty Streidler (1930–), U.S. movie actress.

Christopher Marie **St. John:** Christabel Marshall (*c.*1875–1960), Br. novelist, playwright, biographer.

Dick **St. John:** Richard Gosting (1940–2003), U.S. pop singer.

Jeff **St. John:** Jeff Newton (1946–), Austral. soul singer.

J. Hector **St. John** *see* J. Hector St. John de **Crèvecoeur**

Jill **St. John:** Jill Oppenheim (1940–), U.S. movie actress.

Mabel **St. John:** Henry St. John Cooper (1869–1926), Eng. novelist. Cooper wrote both under this assumed female name and his original name.

Philip **St. John** *see* Lester **del Rey**

Saint-John Perse: Marie-René-Auguste-Alexis Saint-Léger Léger (1887–1975), Fr. poet, diplomat.

The writer may have taken his pseudonym from the Roman satirical poet Persius (French *Perse*).

Humphrey **St. Kayne** *see* John **Dangerfield**

Alfred **St. Laurence:** Alfred Laurence Felkin (1856–1942), Eng. writer.

Cécil **Saint-Laurent:** Jacques Laurent-Cély (1919–2000), Fr. novelist. The writer used this name for his bestselling series beginning with *Caroline chérie* (1948). He published a number of essays under the name Albéric Varenne.

Evelyn **St. Leger:** Evelyn St. Leger Randolph, née Savile (1861–1944), Eng. writer of romantic fiction.

Arthur **Saint-Léon:** Charles Victor Arthur Michel (1821–1870), Fr. ballet dancer, director.

Jean de **Saint-Luc** *see* Sylvia **Bayer**

Saint-Marc Girardin: Marc Girardin (1801–1873), Fr. politician, literary critic.

Sister **Saint Mary Magdalen:** Eliza Healy (1846–1919), U.S. college superior. Eliza Healy entered the novitiate of the Congregation of Notre Dame in Montreal, Canada, in 1874 and received her religious name two years later on making her first profession.

Crispian **St. Peters:** Robin Peter Smith (1939–2010), Eng. pop musician.

Niki de **Saint-Phalle:** Catherine Marie Agnès Fal de Saint-Phalle (1930–2002), Fr. sculptor, moviemaker. The artist called herself "Niki" from the age of seven.

Saint-Pol Roux: Pierre-Paul Roux (1861–1940), Fr. poet.

St. Vincent: Annie Clark (1982–), U.S. singer, songwriter.

Sakahoko: Yoshiaki Fukuzono (1961–), Jap. sumo wrestler, brother of **Terao**.

S.Z. **Sakall:** Eugene Geró Szakáll (1884–1955), Hung. movie actor, working in U.S. ("Cuddles"). The actor was originally a comedian on the Central European stage and screen under the name Szöke Szakáll (literally, "Blond Beard"), and his subsequent screen initials evolved from this.

Alexander **Sakharoff:** Alexander Zuckermann (1886–1963), Russ. ballet dancer, teacher, working in Italy. The dancer translated his name from German to Russian, i.e. from *Zucker* ("sugar") to *sakhar*.

Saki: Hector Hugh Munro (1870–1916), Eng. short-story writer. The writer, killed in France in World War I, first used the name for his short-story collection *Reginald* (1904). "One theory of the origin of Munro's *nom de plume* (advanced by his sister), is that he took it from the name of the cup bearer in the *Rubaiyat of Omar Khayyam*; another is that the pet ape owned by the eponymous hero of 'The Remoulding of Groby Lington,' which Saki describes as superficially gentle yet capable of extreme arousal,

was intended to be a saki; a silent, long-tailed monkey from South America. If the latter is the case, then what better and more circumspect way of indicating the author's own unutterable allegiance [to his homosexuality]? If the former is the case, well, in terms of gay iconography the Rubaiyat is almost *de trop*" [Will Self, Introduction to Saki, *The Unrest Cure and Other Beastly Tales*, 2000].

A third explanation saw the name as a contraction of "Sakya Muni," one of the names of the Buddha. Saki himself should have the last word. "'On assuming the pen name of Saki, there were at once two of me,' Munro wrote. 'It was something of a shell, of course, providing a desirable kind of anonymity'" [*The Times*, April 30, 2007].

Panas **Saksagansky:** Afanasy Karpovich Tobilevich (1859–1940), Ukr. stage actor, director, brother of Ivan **Karpenko-Kary** and Nikolay **Sadovsky**.

Kalamu ya **Salaam:** Vallery Ferdinand III (1947–), U.S. black poet, playwright, activist.

Saladin: William Stewart Ross (1844–1906), Sc. poet, writer on agnosticism. Ross used this name for his contributions to the *Agnostic Journal and Secular Review*, of which he was editor. The name is symbolic, as that of the 12th-century sultan of Egypt who invaded Palestine and defeated the Christians.

Salamanca: Michael Freeman (1948–), Br. crossword compiler. The setter's pseudonym refers to the University of Salamanca, Spain, attended as a student by the grand inquisitor Francisco Jiménez de Cisneros (whose better-known name gave that of **Ximenes**).

Freddie **Sales:** Frederick Harry Walker (1920–1995), Br. character comedian.

Soupy **Sales:** Milton Hines (1926–2009), U.S. TV entertainer, movie actor. The actor was nicknamed "Soupy" as a child because his surname, Hines, sounded like "Heinz." He changed his surname to "Sales" to match this, and adopted his new name as his screen name in 1952.

Elfreda **Salisbury** *see* Cicely **Hamilton**

Richard Anthony **Salisbury:** Richard Anthony Markham (1761–1829), Eng. botanist, horticulturist. The new name was the price of a generous gift. "In 1780 ... he became acquainted with an elderly lady, Miss Anna Salisbury, a connection of his maternal grandmother, Hester Salisbury, and in 1785 she gave him ten thousand pounds in three percents to enable him to pursue his studies in botany and gardening, on condition of his assuming the sole surname of Salisbury" [*Dictionary of National Biography*].

Ralph David **Sallon:** Rachmiel David Zelon (1899–1999), Pol.-born Br. caricaturist.

Salmasius: Claude de Saumaise (1588–1653), Fr. scholar.

Gaspare da **Salò**: Gaspare di Bertoletti (1540–1609), It. violin maker. The craftsman came to be known by the name of his native town, Salò, near Brescia, northern Italy.

Felix **Salten**: Siegmund Salzmann (1869–1945), Hung.-born Ger. Jewish novelist, journalist, art critic, working in Switzerland. German *Salz* is English *salt*.

Salt-n-Pepa: Cheryle James (1964–), U.S. black rapper + Sandi Denton (1969–), Jamaican rapper. The two women were nicknamed from their appearance by producer Herby "Lovebug" Azor, the name itself coming either from the title of the 1968 Sammy Davis, Jr., movie *Salt and Pepper* or, more likely, from a line in "The Showstopper (Is Stupid Fresh)," an answer record to Doug E. Fresh and **Slick Rick**'s hip-hop hit "The Show" [Haskins, p.91].

Cecchino **Salviati**: Francesco de' Rossi (1510–1563), It. painter. The artist entered the service of Cardinal Giovanni Salviati around 1531 and adopted his name. (Cecchino is a pet form of Francesco.)

Carlos **Salzedo**: Léon Carlos Salzédo (1885–1961), Fr.-born U.S. harpist, composer, of Sp. descent. The musician preferred to be known by the Spanish form of his French name.

Madame de **Saman**: Hortense Allart (1801–1879), Fr. literary socialite. The writer used this name for an autobiographical novel, *Les Enchantements de Prudence* ("The Enchantments of Prudence") (1873).

Sam and Dave: Samuel Moore (1935–), U.S. black soul singer + David Prater (1937–1988), U.S. black soul singer.

Antonina **Samarina**: Antonina Nikolayevna Sobolshchikova-Samarina (1896–1971), Russ. stage actress. The actress was the daughter of the actor and theatrical director Nikolay **Sobolshchikov-Samarin**, and adopted the name that he added to his original surname (and that had thus passed to her).

Olga **Samaroff**: Lucie Marie Olga Agnes Hickenlooper (1882–1969), U.S. concert pianist. The musician adopted her new name in 1905, at the start of her concert career, at the suggestion of New York concert manager Henry Wolfsohn. The name was that of a remote Russian ancestor.

Gregor **Samarow**: Oskar Meding (1828–1903), Ger. historical novelist.

Emma **Samms**: Emma Samuelson (1960–), Eng.-born U.S. TV actress.

David **Samoylov**: David Samuilovich Kaufman (1920–), Russ. poet. The writer adopted a russianized form of his Jewish patronymic (middle name) as his new surname.

Nikos **Sampson**: Nikos Gheorghiades (1924–2001), Greek Cypriot journalist, nationalist.

Savanna **Samson**: Natalie Oliveros (1967–), U.S. porno movie actress.

Samson **Samsonov**: Samson Iosifovich Edelshteyn (Edelstein) (1921–2002), Russ. movie director.

Galina **Samsova**: Galina Ursuliak, later Prokovsky, née Samtsova (1937–), Russ.-born ballet dancer, working in Canada.

Hiroyuki **Sanada**: Hiroyuki Shimosawa (1960–), Jap. movie actor.

Sonia **Sanchez**: Wilsonia Benita Driver (1934–), U.S. black poet, playwright, activist. "Sonia" from "Wilsonia," and Sanchez as the name of the writer's Puerto Rican husband.

George **Sand**: Amandine-Aurore-Lucile Dudevant, née Dupin (1804–1876), Fr. writer. The novelist derived her pen name from her liaison with the writer Jules Sandeau (1811–1883), and, according to one popular account, "it was on S. *George*'s Day that she first — on his advice — started to write on her own account; hence the *nom de guerre*" [Dawson, p. 260]. But this origin is negated by the author's own words, which associated the the name with its literal Greek meaning of "farmer." "George," she would write later, she chose spontaneously, "because George seemed to me to be synonymous with *Berrichon* [a native of Berry, the agricultural region of central France where she was born]." (There may have been an implicit connection with Virgil's *Georgics* in this respect.) The spelling of French *Georges* without the final "s," in the English manner, may have been an intended compliment to England, or more specifically to the English nuns of the Augustinian convent in Paris that she attended. "On the covers of the *Revue des Deux Mondes*, I have remarked, observes Charles Joliet, that after the title of her novel these words follow:— M. George Sand and not 'Mme.'" [Hamst, p. 111].

Dudevant first used the name in 1831 for writing done jointly with Sandeau, including some articles for *Le Figaro* and their first joint novel *Rose et Blanche*. She herself first used the name independently the following year, for her novel *Indiana*. Earlier she had used the name Blaise Bonnain, taken from a carpenter she had known as a girl. The abbreviated form "Sand" was devised by Jules, and used both by him (as Jules Sand) and by Maurice Sand, George Sand's son. "The question of a name seems little to have preoccupied her. Clear that she wanted to remain anonymous, the question of a name must have seemed relatively unimportant. What mattered was that the *change* of name represented the beginning of a new life: the life of George Sand" [Belinda Jack, *George Sand: A Woman's Life Writ Large*, 1999].

Inge **Sand**: Inge Sand Sørensen (1928–1974), Dan. ballet dancer, choreographer, director.

Paul **Sand**: Paul Sanchez (1944–), U.S. movie actor.

Dominique **Sanda:** Dominique Varaigne (1951–), Fr.-born U.S. movie actress.

Charles A. **Sandburg:** Carl August Sandburg (1878–1967), U.S. poet, writer, of Swe. parentage. Sandburg americanized his name in first grade and retained it for his early writing. On marrying in 1908, his wife persuaded him to reclaim his native Swedish name, and he was Carl Sandburg from then on.

Cora **Sandel:** Sara Fabricius (1880–1974), Norw. novelist, short-story writer.

Aksel **Sandemose:** Aksel Nielsen (1899–1965), Dan.-born Norw. novelist.

Pharoah **Sanders:** Farrell Saunders (1940–), U.S. black jazz saxophonist.

Janet **Sandison** *see* Jane **Duncan**

Eugen **Sandow:** Friedrich Wilhelm Müller (1867–1925), Ger. physical culturist, working in U.K., U.S. ("The Monarch of Muscle").

Mark **Sandrich:** Mark Goldstein (1900–1945), U.S. movie director.

George Windle **Sands** *see* John **Dangerfield**

Baby **Sandy** *see* **Baby Sandy**

Frederick **Sandys:** Anthony Frederick Augustus Sands (1829–1904), Eng. painter. The Pre-Raphaelite artist is said to have modified his name in order to imply a blood relationship with the aristocratic Sandys family.

Oliver **Sandys:** Marguerite Florence Barclay, later Evans, née Jervis (1894–1964), Eng. romantic novelist. Barclay also wrote as Countess Hélène **Barcynska**.

Lord George **Sanger:** George Sanger (1825–1911), Eng. circus proprietor, showman. "Lord" was neither an official title nor an added first name, but a response to the growing rivalry of U.S. showmen. "In 1887 he took the title of 'Lord' George Sanger by way of challenge to 'the Hon.' William Cody ('**Buffalo Bill**'), who was touring England with his 'Wild West' show" [*Dictionary of National Biography*]. Sanger's wife, née Ellen Chapman (*c*.1832–1899), was a lion tamer under the name Pauline de Vere ("Lady of the Lions").

Sangharakshita: Dennis Philip Edward Lingwood (1925–), Eng. Buddhist monk. The founder of the Friends of the Western Buddhist Order (1967) first went east in 1943 when serving in the army. He was already attracted to Buddhism, and on leaving the army in 1946 met with Buddhist gurus in India and abandoned his English name to call himself by the Sanskrit name Dharmapriya, "lover of the law," i.e., of the ideal truth as set forth in the teachings of the Buddha. His constant companion was Satyapriya, "lover of truth," an Indian convert to Buddhism originally named Rabindra Kumar Banerjee. In 1949 both men were ordained into the Buddhist religion,

Dharmapriya receiving the name Sangharakshita, "protected by the community," and Satyapriya becoming Buddharakshita, "protected by the Buddha."

In 1962 Sangharakshita had been given the new name Urgyen by the Indian guru Khachu Rimpoche. This is the Tibetan form of *Udyana*, the Sanskrit name of a land (now Swat, Pakistan) in northwestern India where the legendary Buddhist mystic Padmasambhava is said to have reigned. Sangharakshita did not adopt it then, but began using it in 1985, on the occasion of his 60th birthday. A life of Sangharakshita, *Bringing Buddhism to the West* (1995), has been written by his former personal secretary, Subhuti ("good fortune"), an English Buddhist born Alex Kennedy in 1947.

Aleksandr **Sanin:** Aleksandr Akimovich Shenberg (Schoenberg) (1869–1956), Russ. stage, movie actor, director.

Andrea **Sansovino:** Andrea Contucci (*c*.1467–1529), It. sculptor, architect. The artist took his name from his birthplace, near Monte San Savino, Florence. He gave his adopted name in turn to his pupil, Jacopo **Sansovino**.

Jacopo **Sansovino:** Jacopo Tatti (1486–1570), It. sculptor, architect. The artist trained under Andrea **Sansovino** from the age of 16 and adopted the name of his master out of admiration for his work.

Santana: Carlos Santana (1947–), U.S. rock musician.

Steve **Santana:** Stephen Campbell (*c*.1970–), Jamaican reggae musician. Campbell originally performed as Santana, but then preceded this by "Steve" to avoid confusion with the U.S. band formed in 1966 by Carlos **Santana**.

Bernardo **Santareno:** António Martinho do Rosário (1924–1980), Port. poet, playwright. The writer's adopted name comes from his birthplace, the city of Santarém, central Portugal.

George **Santayana:** Jorge Augustín Nicolás Ruiz de Santayana y Borrais (1863–1952), Sp.-born U.S. writer, philosopher.

Fernando **Santiván:** Fernández Santibáñez Puga (1898–?), Chilean writer.

Joseph **Santley:** Joseph Mansfield (1889–1971), U.S. movie director. The filmmaker adopted the name of his stepfather, veteran stage actor Eugene Santley.

Santogold: Santi White (1976–), U.S. black pop singer.

Rodrigo **Santoro:** Rodrigo Junqueira dos Reis (1975–), Brazilian movie actor.

Lucia de Jesus de los **Santos:** Lucia Abobora (1907–2005), Port. nun.

Alejandro **Sanz:** Alejandro Sánchez Pizarro (1968–), Sp. pop singer, songwriter.

Rahel **Sanzara:** Johanna Bleschke (1894–1936), Ger. novelist.

Vera **Sapoukhyn:** Molly Elliot Seawell (1860–1916), U.S. novelist, short-story writer. Seawell adopted several pen names early in her career, including this one for a series of stories set in Russia, published in *Lippincott's Magazine.* For her political novels she wrote as Foxcroft Davis.

Sapper: Herman Cyril McNeile (1888–1937), Eng. novelist. The creator of Bulldog Drummond, the ex-army officer who foils the activities of the international crook, Carl Peterson, adopted his pseudonym when an officer in the Royal Engineers, a sapper being a soldier who digs saps (tunnels or trenches to conceal an approach to a fortified place). (In the Royal Engineers, "sapper" is still the official term for a private.) The name was suggested by Lord Northcliffe, proprietor of the *Daily Mail,* in which the author's war stories first appeared, as no regular serving officer was allowed to publish under his real name. McNeile attempted to use his real name after World War I, but the public would have none of it, and demanded their familiar "Sapper."

Sapphira: Mary Barber (1690–1757), Ir. poet. The name was perhaps intended for one who wrote the truth, unlike the biblical Sapphira, who fell down dead when her deception was discovered.

Sapphire: Ramona Lofton (1950–), U.S. black lesbian writer. The writer's name echoes that of Sappho, the 7th-century BC Greek poet associated with female homosexuality who lived on Lesbos.

Mia **Sara:** Mia Sarapoccielo (1967–), U.S. movie actress.

Susan **Sarandon:** Susan Abigail Tomalin (1946–), U.S. movie actress. The actress's screen name is that of her former husband, actor Chris Sarandon (1942–) (married 1967, divorced 1979).

Vasily **Saratovets:** Vasily Frolovich Yefimov (1885–1912), Russ. revolutionary. The Bolshevik worker's name means "(native) of Saratov." He was born near that city and was politically active there.

Gene **Sarazen:** Eugenio Saraceni (1902–1999), U.S. golfer, of It. parentage.

Sarban: John William Wall (1910–1989), Br. writer of fantasy fiction. Wall was a career diplomat from 1933 through 1966 and used this name for just three books: *Ringstones, and Other Curious Tales* (1951), *The Doll Maker, and Other Tales of the Uncanny* (1953), and *The Sound of His Horn* (1952).

Dick **Sargent:** Richard Cox (1933–1994), U.S. movie actor.

Joseph **Sargent:** Giuseppe Danielle Sargente (1925–), U.S. movie director.

Frank **Sargeson:** Norris Frank Davey (1903–1982), N.Z. novelist, short-story writer. The writer

adopted his uncle's surname on assuming a new identity following a court case in 1929.

Michael **Sarne:** Michael Schener (1940–), Br. TV, movie actor, singer.

Sarnicol: Thomas Jacob Thomas (1873–1945), Welsh poet. The writer's bardic name is derived from a local placename.

Leslie **Sarony:** Leslie Legge Sarony Frye (1897–1985), Eng. songwriter, entertainer. The music-hall artist adopted his mother's maiden name (his own third name) at the age of 14, when he became a professional entertainer in juvenile variety acts.

Andrea del **Sarto** *see* **Andrea del Sarto**

Sasha: Alexander Coe (1969–), Welsh DJ, rock producer.

Marie **Sass:** Marie Constance Saxe (1838–1907), Belg. soprano.

Sassetta: Stefano di Giovanni di Consolo da Cortona (*c.*1400–1450), It. painter. The name by which the artist came to be known was apparently first used only in the 18th century. It presumably evolved as a pet form of his first name.

Sasshunada: Katsuyuki Yoshikazi (1957–), Jap. sumo wrestler. The wrestler's fighting name means "sea of Sasshu" (Japanese *nada,* "sea").

Panfilo **Sasso:** Sasso de Sassi (*c.*1455–1527), It. poet.

Sassoferrato: Giovanni Battista Salvi (1609–1685), It. painter. The artist took his name from the town of his birth near Urbino in central Italy.

Swami **Satchidananda:** Ramaswamy (1914–2002), Ind. guru, working in U.S. The yoga master was ordained as a monk in 1949 by Swami **Sivananda** and took his new name then, from Sanskrit *sat,* "being," *cit,* "consciousness," and *ananda,* "bliss," itself a threefold characterization of Brahman, the one supreme Spirit or impersonal Absolute in Hinduism. "Swami" is a religious title meaning "master."

Lu **Säuberlich:** Liselotte Säuberlich-Lauke (1911–1976), Ger. stage, movie actress.

Henri **Sauguet:** Jean-Pierre Poupard (1901–1989), Fr. composer. The composer adopted his mother's maiden name so that his repute as a writer of modern music would not embarrass his father.

Daphne **Saunders** *see* Craig **Rice**

Ernest **Saunders:** Ernest Walter Schleyer (1935–), Austr.-born Br. businessman. The former Guinness chairman, jailed in 1990 for fraud, fled with his Jewish family from Vienna to England in 1938 to escape Hitler. When he was bullied at school in World War II because of his German name, his family adopted the English name of Saunders. They chose this name because they all liked it and because it "seemed to go with Schleyer" [*Sunday Times,* February 11, 1990].

Joe **Saunders:** George Leybourne (1842–1884), Eng. music-hall artist ("Champagne Charlie"). The performer honed his original act under this name but then reverted to his family name.

Marshall **Saunders:** Margaret Marshall Saunders (1861–1947), Can. writer of animal stories for children.

Richard **Saunders** *see* **Poor Richard**

Marc **Sauval:** Marcelle Fanny Henriette Soulage (1894–?), Fr. pianist, music critic, composer. "Marc" from "Marcelle."

George **Sava:** Georgi Alexei Bankoff (1901–1996), Bulg.-born Br. author, consulting surgeon. The prolific writer of medical mystery novels claimed to have been born George Alexis Milkomanovich Milkomane, a name allegedly acquired from his uncle, Prince Alexander Milkomanovich Milkomane. In fact he was fostered when five years old by his mother's brother, General Alexis Ignatiev, who took him to Russia. His two best-known pseudonyms were George Sava and George Borodin, but he also wrote as George Braddin, Peter Conway, and Alex Redwood, as well as under his real name of George Bankoff.

Ann **Savage:** Bernie Lyon (1921–), U.S. movie actress.

John **Savage:** John Youngs (1949–), U.S. movie actor.

Laura **Savage:** Frederic George Stephens (1828–1907), Eng. art critic. The writer used this name for some early contributions on Italian painting to the Pre-Raphaelite journal *The Germ* (1850). He also used the name John Seward for his papers that this organ published.

Michael **Savage:** Michael Alan Weiner (1942–), U.S. radio talk host, "shock jock." The name suits the forcefulness of the broadcaster's nationalistic views, which his original name (suggesting "whiner") would hardly have expressed.

George **Savage-Armstrong:** George Armstrong (1845–1906), Ir. poet. "In 1891, consequent on the death of a maternal uncle, assumed the surname of Savage in addition to that of Armstrong, as representative of the Glastry branch of the old Anglo-Norman family of the Lords Savage of the Ards" [*Who's Who*].

Dany **Saval:** Danielle Nadine Suzanne Salle (1940–), Fr. movie actress.

Don Jeremy **Savanarola** *see* Father **Prout**

Saveen: Albert Saveen (1914–1994), Br. ventriloquist (with dummy "Daisy May").

Victor **Saville:** Victor Salberg (1897–1979), Br. movie director, working in U.S.

Alberto **Savinio:** Andrea de Chirico (1891–1952), It. writer, composer, painter. The musician adopted his new name in 1912 for distinction from his brother, painter Giorgio de Chirico (1888–1978).

Alfred **Savoir:** Alfred Posznanski (1883–1934), Fr. playwright, of Pol. origin. The writer's new name is a punning equivalent of the original (French *savoir* and Polish *poznanie* both mean "knowledge"), which really derives from the city of Poznań.

Lee **Savold:** Lee Hulver (?1914–1972), U.S. heavyweight boxer.

Bert **Savoy:** Everett Mackenzie (1888–1923), U.S. female impersonator.

Emil **Savundra:** Michael Marion Emil Anecletus Savundranayagam (1923–1976), Sinhalese swindler.

Hanna **Sawicka:** Anna Krystyna Szapiro (1917–1943), Pol. World War II resistance worker.

Joseph **Sawyer:** Joseph Sauer (1901–1982), U.S. movie comedy actor.

John **Saxon:** Carmen Orrico (1935–), U.S. movie actor, of It. parentage.

Peter **Saxon:** Wilfred McNeilly (1921–), Sc. SF, occult fiction writer.

Sky **Saxon:** Richard Marsh (1937–2009), U.S. rock musician. The pioneer of "garage rock" began his singing career in the early 1960s as Little Richie Marsh. In 1962 he formed his first band, the Electra-Fires, later renamed as Sky Saxon and the Soul Rockers, giving his regular stage name.

Sayat-Nova: Aruthin Sayadian (1712–1795), Armenian troubadour. The poet, famous for his love songs, adopted his melodious nickname, meaning "king of song" or "master of music."

Leo **Sayer:** Gerard Hugh Sayer (1948–), Eng. rock singer. "Often one of the first things that has to change when a star is being made is the star-to-be's name. Leo Sayer was Gerard Hughes [*sic*] Sayer when he met Adam **Faith**—but he didn't stay that way for long. Leo said: 'When Adam's wife first met me, I had a long mane of hair. She said "Hey, he's like a little lion." So I became Leo. It was unusual and short—and it stuck'" [*Reveille*, January 12, 1979].

Syd **Saylor:** Leo Sailor (1895–1962), U.S. movie comedian.

Scaasi: Arnold Martin Isaacs (1931–), Can.-born U.S. fashion designer. The designer's adopted name is a reverse spelling of his original surname.

Rat **Scabies:** Christopher Miller (1957–), Eng. punk rock drummer.

Greta **Scacchi:** Greta Gracco (1958–), It.-born movie actress, of It.-Eng. parentage.

Scaeva: John Stubbes (1541–1600), Eng. Puritan zealot. Stubbes published a pamphlet titled *The Discovery of a Gaping Gulf* (1579) condemning Queen Elizabeth's proposed marriage with Henry, Duke of Anjou. For this traitorous act, his right (writing) hand was cut off. *Scaeva* is Latin for "left-handed." The story is reminiscent of the legendary Roman hero Gaius Mucius, said to have saved Rome in *c.*509 BC from conquest by the Roman king Lars Porsena. Having volunteered to assassinate Porsena, Mucius killed his secretary by mistake. Threatened with death by fire unless he revealed the details of a conspiracy, he thrust his right hand into the fire prepared for him and burned it off. Deeply impressed, and fearing another assassination attempt, Porsena order Mucius to be freed. According to this story, Mucius was rewarded with a grant of land beyond the Tiber and given the name Scaevola, "left-handed." But the tale was almost certainly an attempt to explain the origin of Rome's famous Scaevola family

Boz Scaggs: William Royce Scaggs (1944–), U.S. rock musician. The musician spent his boyhood in Dallas, Texas, where he was nicknamed Boxley. This evolved into Boz, which replaced his original first names.

Gia Scala: Giovanna Scoglio (1934–1972), Br. movie actress, of Ir.-It. parentage, working in U.S.

Prunella Scales: Prunella Margaret Rumney West, née Illingworth (1932–), Eng. stage, TV actress. The actress adopted her mother's maiden name when she became a professional. Her mother had been on the stage before her marriage, and "I felt my father's name of Illingworth was rather long with Prunella" [personal letter from Prunella Scales, October 6, 1988].

Julius Caesar Scaliger: Julius Caesar Bordone (1484–1558), It. physician, scholar. Bordone claimed descent from the Veronese della Scala family, whose latinized name was Scaligerus, and changed his name accordingly.

Vernon Scannell: John Vernon Bain (1922–2007), Eng. poet. The poet assumed his new name as an army deserter after World War II. "But how did he acquire his surname? ... [Scannell's painter friend Cliff] Holden recalls that it was provided by a prostitute, who worked for a brothel-owner friend" [Paul Trewhela, "Painter and poet," *Times Literary Supplement*, December 7, 2007].

Scarface: Brad Jordan (1969–), U.S. black rapper.

William Scarff *see* Algis **Budrys**

Scarsellino: Ippolito Scarsella (*c.*1551–1620), It. painter. The artist's name is a diminutive form of his original family name.

Scatman John: John Larkin (1942–1999), U.S. jazz musician.

Schadenfreude: John Harrington (1944–), Br. crossword compiler. The setter chose a pseudonym that both fascinated him as a word and that seemed to encapsulate the nature of a deviser of cryptic crosswords, as someone who takes a malicious delight in the misfortunes of others.

Oda Schaefer: Oda Lange, née Kraus (1900–1988), Ger. poet, writer.

P.V. Schartenmeyer: Friedrich Theodor Vischer (1807–1887), Ger. writer. Vischer used this name for *Der deutsche Krieg* ("The German War") (1874), a comic epic on the war of 1870. Earlier, in 1862, he had published a satire on Goethe's *Faust* under the name Deutobold Symbolizetti Allegorowitsch Mystifizinsky.

Fritzi Scheff: Friederike Yager (1879–1954), Austr.-born U.S. operetta singer, actress.

Joe Schermie: Joseph Edward Schermetzler, Jr. (1948–2002), U.S. rock musician.

Andrea Schiavone: Andrea Meldolla (*c.*1510–1563), It. painter. The artist's adopted name means "Slav," referring to his provenance from Zara, Dalmatia (now Zadar, Croatia), then under Venetian jurisdiction, although his family came from Meldola, near Rimini.

Leon Schiller: Leon de Schildenfeld (1887–1954), Pol. theatrical director, designer.

Tito Schipa: Raffaele Attilio Amadeo (1888–1965), It. opera singer.

Dr. Schmidt: Johann Christoph Friedrich von Schiller (1759–1805), Ger. poet, playwright. The dramatist was originally a military surgeon in a Württemberg regiment. In 1781 he went absent without leave to attend a performance of his first play, *Die Räuber*. He was arrested by order of the regimental commander-in-chief, the Duke of Württemberg, and condemned to publish nothing but medical treatises. However, the following year he escaped from the duke under the assumed name of Dr. Schmidt and spent several years, his so-called *Wanderjahre*, outside the country. The choice of name was arbitrary.

Evald Schmidt: [Dame] Ethel Mary Smyth (1858–1944), Eng. composer, conductor, writer. Smyth studied music in Germany and her adopted male name is a Germanic equivalent of her original names.

Wilhelm Schmidtbonn: Wilhelm Schmidt (1876–1952), Ger. playwright, novelist. The writer added the name of his birthplace, Bonn, to his surname.

Karl Schmidt-Rottluff: Karl Schmidt (1884–1976), Ger. Expressionist painter. The artist added the name of his birthplace, Rottluff, near Chemnitz, to his surname in 1906.

Alexander Schneider: Abram Sznejder (1908–1993), Lithuanian violinist, orchestral conductor, working in U.S. The musician began his career in Germany and germanicized his name accordingly.

Romy Schneider: Rosemarie Magdalena Albach-Retty (1938–1982), Austr. movie actress. The actress's father was actor Wolf Albach-Retty, her mother stage and screen star Magda Schneider. Rosemarie (pet name Romy) adopted her mother's name on making her movie debut in 1953. Her career took off at once, and by 1955 Magda Schneider was playing supporting roles to those of her daughter.

Arnold Schoenberg: Arnold Schönberg (1874–1951), Austr.-born U.S. composer. The composer dropped the umlaut from his name as soon as he arrived in the U.S. in 1933. In a letter of June 25, 1947, he said that his name should be written with "oe" because few printers had the necessary "ö" and he wanted to avoid the spelling "Schonberg." German speakers still spell his name Schönberg, however, whereas English speakers (and many French) use the American form of his name.

Matitjahu Schoham: Matithau Poliakewitsch (1893–1937), Pol. Jewish playwright.

A **Scholar:** Samuel Wesley (1662–1735), Eng. clergyman, poet. The father of John Wesley, the founder of Methodism, used this name for *Maggots: or, Poems on Several Subjects, never before handled. By a Schollar*, a collection of verse published in 1685, when he was a student at Oxford.

Lotte Schöne: Charlotte Bodenstein (1891–1977), Austr.-born Fr. opera singer.

Schoolboy Cleve: Cleveland White (1925–2008), U.S. blues musician. The artist is said to have gained his name from a nickname given him when he first learned to play harmonica: "People used to say: 'Have you heard that schoolboy?'" [*The Times*, April 2, 2008].

Schoolly D: Jesse B. Weaver, Jr. (1966–), U.S. black "gangsta" rapper.

Paul Schott: Erich Wolfgang Korngold (1897–1957), Cz.-born U.S. composer + Julius Korngold (1860–1945), Cz. music critic, his father. The composer used this name for the libretto that he and his father jointly wrote for his opera *Die Tote Stadt* ("The Dead City") (1920).

Ossip Schubin: Aloysia Kirschner (1854–1934), Ger. writer. Kirschner took her name from Osip Shubin, a character in the works of the Russian writer Ivan Turgenev, whom she admired and whom she had met in Paris.

Dutch Schultz: Arthur Flegenheimer (1902–1935), U.S. gangster. The underworld entrepreneur cultivated his reputation as a hardened tough and adopted the name of a former street brawler in the Bronx, New York City, where he was born. He enjoyed reading about himself in the newspapers and reportedly took the name because it was short enough for the headlines.

Schulze-Aenesidemus: Gottlob Ernst Schulze (1761–1833), Ger. philosopher. The second part of the pen name derives from the 1st-century BC Greek Skeptic philosopher Aenesidimus.

Berthold Schwarz: Konstantin Anklitzen (*fl.*1320), Ger. monk. The developer of gunpowder for use in firearms gained the name Schwarz ("black") from his chemical experiments.

Hanns Schwarz: Ignatz Schwartz (1890–1945), Austr. movie director, working in U.K., U.S.

Scientist: Overton Brown (*c.*1960–), Jamaican reggae musician. Brown began his career as a studio engineer, where he gained a reputation for his sophisticated mixing style. Hence his nickname.

Scipione: Gino Bonichi (1904–1933), It. painter. The artist was the son of a soldier and adopted his name in 1927 in honor of Scipio Africanus, the 2d-century BC Roman general who defeated Hannibal.

Errol Scorcher: Errol Archer (1956–), Jamaican DJ. A nickname punning on the DJ's real name.

Agnes Neill Scott: Wilhelmina ("Willa") Johnston Muir, née Anderson (1890–1970), Sc. writer, translator. The author used this name for her translations.

Allan Scott: Allan George Shiach (1941–), Sc. screenwriter, movie producer, teaming with Chris **Bryant**.

Anthony **Scott** *see* Brett **Halliday**

Bon Scott: Ronald Belford (1946–1980), Sc. rock musician, working in Australia.

Evelyn Scott: Elsie Dunn (1893–1963), U.S. writer. In 1913, as a university student, Dunn ran off to England with an older, married man, Frederick Creighton Wellman. Assuming the names Evelyn Scott and Cyril Kay-Scott, the couple managed to evade searchers and in 1914 settled in Brazil. Returning to the United States in 1919 and leaving her common-law husband, Scott used the name Ernest Souza for an adventure story, "Blue Rum" (1930). This was set in Portugal, so merited a Portuguese-style alias.

Gabriel Scott: Holst Jensen (1874–1958), Norw. writer.

Gery Scott: Diana Geraldine Whitburn (1923–2005), Br. jazz, cabaret singer

Gordon Scott: Gordon M. Werschkul (1927–2007), U.S. movie actor.

Hennie Scott: Hendrik Momberg (1948–), Br. juvenile movie actor, of S.A. parentage.

Jack Scott: Giovanni Dominico Scafone, Jr. (1936–), Can. rock singer, working in U.S.

Jack S. Scott: Jonathan Escott (1922–), Br. crime novelist. The writer's assumed middle initial and last name phonetically reproduce his original surname.

Jay Scott: Jeffrey Scott Beaven (1949–1993), Can.-born U.S. movie critic.

Leader **Scott:** Lucy Baxter, née Barnes (1837–1902), Eng. writer on art. The writer derived her pen name from the maiden surnames of her two grandmothers: Isabel Leader was her mother's mother and Grace Scott her father's.

Linda **Scott:** Linda Joy Sampson (1945–), U.S. pop singer.

Lizabeth **Scott:** Emma Matzo (1922–), U.S. movie actress.

Norford **Scott** *see* Fenton **Brockley**

Randolph **Scott:** Randolph Scott (?1898–1987), U.S. movie actor. The actor's original name is given in many sources as Randolph Crane, but Crane was his mother's maiden name.

Raymond **Scott:** Harry Warnow (1908–1994), U.S. popular music composer, bandleader.

Robin **Scott:** Robin Hugh Scutt (1920–2000), Br. radio program maker. The broadcasting executive modified his surname when working with French nationals in World War II, on the basis that his original name proved tricky for French tongues.

Ronnie **Scott:** Ronald Schatt (1927–1996), Eng. jazz-club owner. A desirable name change.

Sheila **Scott:** Sheila Christine Hopkins (1927–1988), Eng. aviator. Although best-known as an aviator, Sheila Hopkins spent a year on the stage after World War II and first used her new name then.

Tony **Scott:** Anthony J. Sciacca (1921–2007), U.S. jazz musician, of It. origin.

Sir Walter **Scott:** James Kirke Paulding (1779–1860), U.S. author. Several writers and plagiarists adopted the name of the Scottish author for their own works. Paulding, a close friend of Washington Irving, used the name for *The Lay of the Scotch Fiddle, a Tale of Havre de Grace* (1813), which was thus itself a "Scotch fiddle." A joint pseudonym shared by Paulding was Launcelot **Langstaff**.

Valerie **Scott** *see* Fenton **Brockley**

Walter **Scott:** Walter Notheis, Jr. (1943–1993), U.S. rock musician.

Warwick **Scott** *see* Elleston **Trevor**

Scotty: (1) Scott Wiseman (1909–1981), U.S. country singer, teaming with **Lulu Belle**; (2) David Scott (*c*.1950–), Jamaican DJ, ragga musician.

The **Scout:** Clive Graham (1913–1974), Eng. racing correspondent. The journalist assumed the byname used by Cyril Luckham, his predecessor on the *Daily Express*. Graham began his career as Bendex in 1931.

Annibal **Scratch:** Samuel Collings (*fl*.1780–1793), Eng. painter, caricaturist. The name is appropriate for an engraver of humorous plates, as Collings was.

Screwdriver: Dalton Lindo (*c*.1960–), Jamaican reggae musician. The musician's name was chosen to blend with fellow singers Pinchers, Pliers, Spanner Banner, and **Tenor Saw**.

Simon **Scribe:** Adam Black (1784–1874), Sc. publisher. An obvious name for a writer.

H. **Scriblerus Secundus:** Henry Fielding (1707–1754), Eng. novelist, playwright. Fielding adopted this name for *The Tragedy of Tragedies, or Tom Thumb the Great* (1731), taking it from the name Martinus Scriblerus used by members of the so-called Scriblerus Club. This was a group of writers, including Pope, Swift, and Arbuthnot, formed in about 1713 with the aim of discussing topics of the day, enjoying witty conversation, and ridiculing "all false tastes in learning." They invented a character called Martinus Scriblerus, a pedantic hack, whose intellectual limitations and literary lapses were the central theme of their joint *Memoirs of the Extraordinary Life, Works, and Discoveries of Martinus Scriblerus* (1741). The character's name was based on a punning nickname given Swift when at Oxford University. (The martin is a bird resembling the swift.)

While Fielding was Scriblerus Secundus, as the second of the name, Scriblerus Tertius and Scriblerus Quartus were both names used by the poet and pamphleteer Thomas Cooke (1703–1756). Martinus Scriblerus was also used by the satirist Thomas James Mathias (1754–1835), among other writers.

Mark **Scrivener:** Marcus Andrew Hislop Clarke (1846–1881), Eng.-born Austral. novelist. Clarke adopted the nickname (originally "Marcus Scrivener") given him by his schoolmate, English poet Gerard Manley Hopkins (1844–1889). A scrivener, of course, is a clerk.

George Julius Poulett **Scrope:** George Julius Poulett Thomson (1797–1876), Eng. geologist, politician. The scientist and political economist married Emma Phipps Scrope, heiress of William Scrope, in 1821, and thereupon assumed her name and the Scrope family's arms. William Scrope was the last of the old earls of Wiltshire, and had inherited not only his own father's family estates but those of another branch of the family in Lincolnshire. These all now passed to Emma, and so to the former George Thomson.

Thomas **Scrutiny:** Samuel De Wilde (1748–1832), Du.-born Br. painter, caricaturist. The artist used this name for his political caricatures in the *Satirist* in the early years of the 19th century.

Barbara **Seagull** *see* Barbara **Hershey**

Seal: Henry Olumide Samuel (1963–), Br.-born black rock musician, of Nigerian-Brazilian parentage. The performer is said to have taken his name from his collection of porcelain seals. But it may have arisen as a nickname variant of his original surname, perhaps with reference to Sammy the Seal, the main character in a children's reading book of this name (1960) by the U.S. writer Syd Hoff. Some sources give his original first name as Sealhenry, but this appears to be a blend of the two names.

Basil Seal *see* Dan **Kavanagh**

Charles Sealsfield: Carl Magnus Postl (1793–1864), Austr.-born U.S. novelist. The writer was originally a monk, but in 1823 fled the monastery and went to the U.S. His adopted name was revealed to be a pseudonym only after his death.

Lewis Sealy: William Armiger Sealy Lewis (1850–1931), Ir. actor, showman.

Alexander Search *see* Alberto **Caeiro**

Edward Search: Abraham Tucker (1705–1774), Eng. philosopher. The writer first used this significant name for his short work, *Freewill, Foreknowledge, and Fate: A Fragment* (1763), and subsequently for the work by which he is best known, *The Light of Nature Pursued* (1768–78). Similar names were used by other thinkers and writers, such as Richard Whately, Archbishop of Dublin, who published *Religion and her Name; A Metrical Tract, with Notes* (1847) as John Search. Tucker used the name Cuthbert Comment, Gent., for a facetious pamphlet, *Man in Quest of Himself* (1763), written in reply to some criticisms of his *Freewill, Foreknowledge, and Fate.*

John Search: Thomas Binney (1798–1874), Eng. Congregationalist cleric.

John Search *see* Aristarchus **Newlight**

Nicholas Seare *see* **Trevanian**

January Searle: George Searle Phillips (1815–1889), Eng. writer, working in U.S. The writer was born in January. Hence his nickname and assumed writing name.

Carl Emil Seashore: Carl Emil Sjöstrand (1866–1949), Swe.-born U.S. psychologist. The Swedish family emigrated to the United States in 1869 and anglicized their name by means of a literal translation.

Seasick Steve: Steve Wold (1940–), U.S. blues singer. The singer's name refers to a queasy fishing trip he once experienced.

Victor Seastrom: Victor Sjöström (1879–1960), Swe. movie actor, director.

George Seaton: George Stenius (1911–1979), U.S. screenwriter, movie director, of Swe. parentage. When Stenius was at first unlucky in finding work as an actor, he started sending stories to magazines such as *True Confessions*. On striking lucky with a a story he sent off as "George Seaton," a name he had taken from a character in Philip Barry's play *Holiday* (1928), he kept the name for professional use.

Gregory Seaworthy: George Higby Throop (1818–1896), U.S. novelist. The writer first used his

pen name for *Nag's Head: or, Two Months among "The Bankers." A Story of Sea-Shore Life and Manners* (1850), a fictionalized memoir of his summer at Nags Head on the North Carolina Outer Banks.

Henry Second: Henry Sydnor Harrison (1880–1930), U.S. journalist, writer. Harrison used this name for his first novel, *Captivating Mary Carstairs* (1910).

Solomon Secondsight: James McHenry (1785–1845), Ir.-born U.S. poet, novelist, literary critic. The author used this name for a historical romance, *The Wilderness*, published in London in 1823.

John Sedges: Pearl S. Buck (1892–1973), U.S. novelist, biographer. The writer used this male name for five novels published in the 1940s and 1950s.

Paul Sédir: Yvon Le Loup (1871–1926), Fr. occultist. The practitioner's new surname is an anagram of French *désir*, "desire."

Kate Sedley: Brenda Margaret Lilian Clarke, née Honeyman (1926–), Br. historical mystery writer.

George Seferis: Giorgios Stylianou Seferiades (1900–1971), Gk. poet, essayist, diplomat.

Catherine Sefton: Martin Waddell (1941–), Ir. children's writer. Waddell adopted his grandmother's name as his pen name.

Anna Seghers: Netti Radványi, née Reiling (1900–1983), Ger. novelist, working in U.S. The writer took her name from the Flemish painter Hercules Seghers (1589–*c.*1638), a pupil of Rembrandt, whom she had always admired. She also used the name in an early story.

Adolphus Segrave: Philip Gilbert Hamerton (1834–1894), Eng. art critic, writer. Hamerton used this name for his novel *Marmorne* (1878), set in the Franco-Prussian war.

Bart Segundo *see* Fenton **Brockley**

Compay Segundo *see* **Compay Segundo**

Lea Seidl: Caroline Mayrseidl (1895–1987), Austr. stage, movie actress, singer, working in U.K.

Victor Séjour: Juan Victor Séjour Marcou et Ferrand (1817–1874), U.S. black dramatist, poet.

Steve Sekely: Istvan Szekely (1899–1979), Hung. movie director, working in U.S.

George Augustus Sekon: George Augustus Nokes (1867–1948), Eng. writer on railroads. A simple reversal here to produce an effective pen name.

Rrose Sélavy: Marchel Duchamp (1887–1968), Fr. artist. Duchamp assumed this name for much of his output, and appears in the guise of his female persona in a photograph taken by **Man Ray** in 1921. The name itself has been variously interpreted, but can perhaps be read as French *Eros, c'est la vie*, "Eros, that's life," meaning that love is all there is to it.

P.T. Selbit: Percy Thomas Tibbles (1881–1938), Eng. magician. A little juggling with the illusionist's surname, and lo, a new name emerges (but with his original initials). Before World War I, the magician presented an act with an Egyptian theme under the name Joad Heteb, "The Wizard of the Sphinx." "Heteb" may be an anagram of "Thebe," referring to the ancient Egyptian city of Thebes.

Percival M. **Selby**: Percival M. Short (1886–1955), Br. stage actor, theatrical manager.

Camille **Selden**: Elise Krinitz (1830–1897), Austr. writer. Krinitz used this name for *Les Derniers Jours de Henri Heine* ("The Last Days of Heinrich Heine") (1883), her recollections of the poet, whom she visited regularly in the last months of his life when he was bedridden. He knew her as "Mouche."

George **Selden**: George Selden Thompson (1929–1989), U.S. biographer, children's writer.

Selena: Selena Quintanilla-Pérez (1971–1995), U.S. "Tex-Mex" singer.

Connie **Sellecca**: Concetta Sellecchia (1955–), U.S. TV actress.

Arthur **Sellings**: Robert Arthur Ley (1921–1968), Br. SF writer.

Selmar: [Baron] Karl Gustav von Brinckman (1764–1847), Swe. diplomat, poet.

Morton **Selten**: Morton Richard Stubbs (1860–1939), Eng. stage, movie actor.

Lewis J. **Selznick**: Lewis Zeleznik (1870–1933), Russ.-born U.S. movie distributor, impresario, father of movie producers David O. Selznick (1902–1965) (who added the middle initial "O" for effect as a teen-ager) and Myron Selznick (1898–1944).

Sem: Georges Goursat (1863–1934), Fr. caricaturist, portrait painter, working in U.K. The artist took his pseudonym, the French form of "Shem," in honor of **Cham**, whom he greatly admired. Shem and Ham were two of the sons of the biblical Noah.

Marcella **Sembrich**: Praxede Marcelline Kochanska (1858–1935), Pol.-born U.S. opera singer. The soprano adopted her mother's maiden name for performance purposes.

Allen **Semi** *see* Nella **Larsen**

Semprini: Fernando Riccardo Alberto Semprini (1908–1990), Br. popular pianist, entertainer, of It. parentage.

Sempronia: Mary Ann Lamb (1764–1847), Eng. children's writer, poet. Most of Lamb's writing was done in collaboration with her brother, essayist and critic Charles Lamb (1775–1834), and her pen name was merely occasional.

Joe **Seneca**: Joseph McGee (1919–1996), U.S. popular singer, songwriter, stage, movie actor

Senesino: (1) Francesco Bernardi (*c*.1680–*c*.1750), It. singer; (2) Giusto Ferdinando Tenducci (*c.* 1736–1790), It. singer. Both men were male sopranos born in Siena. Hence the name by which each came to be known, meaning "little Sienese."

Mack **Sennett**: Michael (or Mikall) Sinnott (1880–1960), Can.-born U.S. comedy movie director, producer, actor, of Ir. parentage. (See also quote under Mabel **Normand**.)

Captain **Sensible** *see* **Captain Sensible**

John A. **Sentry** *see* Algis **Budrys**

Sequoyah: George Gist (*c*.1770–1843), Native American scholar, of Br. extraction. The creator of the Cherokee writing system, for whom the genus of gigantic Californian redwoods is named, is said to have been the son of a British trader named Nathaniel Gist (or Guess) and a Cherokee mother.

[St.] **Serafim Sarovsky**: Prokhor Isidorovich Moshnin (1759–1833), Russ. monk. The holy hermit, one of Russia's most popular saints, made his monastic vows at an early age, adopting the name Serafim. The second word of his name is the adjectival form of Sarov, the location of the monastery southeast of Moscow where he lived until 1825 and where he died. He was canonized in 1903 by order of Czar Nicholas II.

Aleksandr **Serafimovich**: Aleksandr Serafimovich Popov (1863–1949), Russ. writer. The writer adopted his own patronymic (middle name) as his pen name, but changed the stress (accent) from the third syllable (Sera-*fi*-movich) to the fourth (Serafi-*mo*-vich).

David **Serafin**: Ian David Lewis Michael (1936–), Br. crime writer.

Seranus: Susie Frances Harrison, née Riley (1859–1935), Can. writer. The writer's Latin-looking name may have been created from letters in her original name.

Seraphim: Vissarion Tikas (1913–1998), Gk. archbishop, head of the Orthodox Church in Greece (from 1974).

Séraphine: Séraphine Louis (1864–1934), Fr. painter. The artist is also known as Séraphine de Senlis, from the name of the town where she was in domestic service before being "discovered" in 1912.

Massimo **Serato**: Giuseppe Segato (1917–1989), It. movie actor.

Octave **Séré**: Jean Marie Octave Géraud Poueigh (1876–1958), Fr. music critic, composer. Poueigh used this name as author of *Musiciens français d'aujourd'hui* ("French Musicians of Today") (1921).

Victor **Serge**: Viktor Kibalchich (1890–1947) Belg.-born Fr. revolutionary politician, of Russ. parentage, father of **Vlady**.

Mark **Sergeyev**: Mark Davidovich Gantvarger (Handwarger) (1926–), Russ. writer. The writer replaced his Jewish surname by a regular Russian one.

Sergey **Sergeyev-Tsensky**: Sergey Nikolayevich Sergeyev (1875–1958), Russ. novelist. The writer was born and raised in Tambov, on the Tsna River. Hence the addition to his original surname, as the adjectival form of the river name.

Sergius: (1) Varfolomey Kirillovich (1314–1392), Russ. saint, monk ("Sergius of Radonezh"); (2) Ivan Nikolayevich Stragorodsky (1867–1944), Russ. churchman, patriarch of Moscow and All Russia. St. Sergius of Radonezh was one of Russia's most important spiritual leaders, and was subsequently regarded as the saint protector of Russia. Stragorodsky almost certainly took his religious name in his honor. This means that the monk must have taken his own name from an earlier Sergius. He was possibly the 3d-century Christian martyr St. Sergius, who with St. Bacchus was put to death by the Romans in about 303. Sergius of Radonezh adopted his religious name in 1337, on taking monastic vows. Stragorodsky similarly took his name in 1890. See also the next name below.

Sergius IV: Pietro Buccaporci (?–1012), It. pope. The pope's original surname was actually a nickname, meaning "pig mouth," and referring to his appearance. He would have been ready enough to take a name used by three popes before him, and would not have kept his original name in any case, out of respect for St. Peter, leader of the apostles and first bishop of Rome. According to D'Israeli, quoting **Platina**, Sergius IV was the first pope to change his name, his original name being "very unsuitable with the pomp of the tiara" [p.200], but **John II** was actually the first, five centuries earlier.

Sergo: (1) Grigory Konstantinovich Ordzhonikidze (1886–1937), Georgian revolutionary; (2) Aleksey Ivanovich Sergeyev (1915–1976), Russ. circus artist, clown. This was the revolutionary's underground name.

Mikhail Sergeyevich **Sergushev:** Markel Prokopyevich Aksyonov (1886–1930), Russ. revolutionary.

Yahoo **Serious:** Greg Pead (1954–), Austral. comic movie actor, screenwriter, director.

Junípero **Serra:** Miguel José Serra (1713–1784), Sp. missionary, working in Mexico, U.S. The founder of the Californian missions adopted his religious name in 1731 on entering the Franciscan order, identifying himself with the original Junipero, a companion of St. Francis noted for his simplicity and good humor. He was beatified in 1988.

German **Serrano:** José Ricardo Ruíz (1960–1992), Salvadorean guerrilla commander.

Jean Nicolas **Servan:** Giovanni Niccolò Servandoni (1695–1766), It. architect, working in France. The artist gallicized his name on settling in France.

Mishshi **Sespel:** Mikhail Kuzmich Kuzmin (1899–1922), Russ. (Chuvash) poet. The founder of Chuvash poetry took a plant name meaning "snow-

drop," with Mishshi a Chuvash form of his original Russian name Mikhail (Michael).

Sesshu: Oda (1420–1506), Jap. artist. The artist's original personal name is unknown, but his family name was Oda. In 1431, when he was ten, he was enrolled at a local Zen temple and given the name Toyo, "willowlike," perhaps because he was graceful and slender. In about 1466 he became chief priest of a temple in Yamaguchi, and it was then that he began calling himself Sesshu, literally "snow boat."

John **Sessions:** John Gibb Marshall (1953–), Sc.-born Br. stage, TV comedian.

Bola **Sete:** Djalma de Andrade (1928–1987), Brazilian jazz musician, working in U.S.

Ernest Thompson **Seton:** Ernest Evan Thompson (1860–1946), Eng.-born author, artist, naturalist, working in Canada, U.S. Ernest's father, Joseph Logan Thompson, claimed aristocratic Scottish ancestry, including a title, never legally established, deriving from the fifth and last earl of Winton, George Seton (died 1749). His son describes subsequent events: "When I came of age I carried out my original plan ... and on the first day of February 1883 my full and proper legal style became Ernest Evan Thompson Seton. Under this name I wrote all of my first articles; under this name I illustrated the *Century Dictionary*" [Ernest Thompson Seton, *Trail of an Artist-Naturalist: An Autobiography*, 1940]. Some years later, his parents requested he change his name back to Thompson: "It was agreed I was to wear the name 'Seton-Thompson' as a nom de plume as long as mother was alive ... and I continued 'Seton-Thompson' until the death of my mother in 1897" [ibid.], when he reverted to Ernest Thompson Seton. But this caused problems with copyrights: "On November 28, 1901, the Supreme Court of New York decided the question. In a word, 'Seton-Thompson' was a nom de plume; 'Seton' is my family name" [ibid.]. In 1930 Seton became an American citizen and settled in New Mexico.

Gabriel **Setoun:** Thomas Nicoll Hepburn (1861–1930), Sc. novelist, biographer.

Setsquare: Ray Dawson (1923–2002), Eng. Sinologist, crossword compiler. The setter used this neat name for his lifelong contributions to the *New Statesman*, where his first puzzle appeared in 1951.

Michel **Seuphor:** Michael Berckelaers (1901–1989), Belg. photographer, working in France. The artist's adopted name is an anagram of "Orpheus," the musician and poet of Greek mythology.

Dr. **Seuss:** Theodor Seuss Geisel (1904–1991), U.S. children's writer, illustrator. The popular author called himself "Dr." by way of a self-conferred title. In 1955, however, his old college, Dartmouth, awarded him a genuine doctorate. His name as a whole to some young readers would suggest "Dr. Sweet" as an added allure. Seuss wrote verse as Theo le Sieg, reversing his surname.

Paruyr **Sevak**: Paruyr Rafaelovich Kazaryan (1924–1971), Armenian poet, literary critic. The poet's name means "black-eyed," describing his appearance. Compare the next entry below.

Ruben **Sevak**: Ruben Chilinkaryan (1885–1915), Armenian writer. The writer's name means "black-eyed," as this is what he was. Compare the entry above.

Steve **Severin**: Steven Bailey (1955–), Br. punk rock musician. The bassist member of Siouxsie and the Banshees, with lead singer Siouxsie **Sioux**, took his new name from Séverin, the narrator of Leopold von Sacher-Masoch's perverse novel *Venus in Furs* (1870).

Séverine: Caroline Guebhard, née Rémy (1855–1929), Fr. journalist, novelist.

David **Severn**: David Storr Unwin (1918–2010), Eng. novelist, children's writer.

Igor **Severyanin**: Igor Vasilyevich Lotarev (1887–1941), Russ. poet, working in Estonia. The poet was born in St. Petersburg. Hence his new surname, meaning "Northerner." He is the best known of this name, which was adopted by other writers similarly.

Carmen **Sevilla**: María del Carmen García Galisteo (1930–), Sp. movie actress, dancer, singer. The actress took her stage name from her birthplace, Seville.

David **Seville**: Ross S. Bagdasarian, Sr. (1919–1972), U.S. music, record company executive, of Armenian parentage. The creator of the Chipmunks, the musical cartoon singing group, used a number of pseudonyms, of which this is the best known.

Gagerin **Sevunts**: Gagerin Seviyevich Grigoryan (1911–1969), Armenian writer.

John **Seward** *see* Laura **Savage**

Lady Algernon **Seymour**: Jeanne-Françoise Dacquin (1811–1895), Fr. writer. The *litteratrice* used this English name when writing to the author Prosper Mérimée after reading his novel *Chronique du règne de Charles IX* (1829). The two kept up a correspondence until his death in 1870, and she was the subject of his *Lettres à une inconnue* ("Letters to an Unknown Lady"), published posthumously in 1873.

Anne **Seymour**: (1) Anne Ekert (1909–1988), U.S. movie actress; (2) Phyllis Digby Morton, née Panting (?–1984), Eng. journalist, broadcaster.

Carolyn **Seymour**: Carolyn von Benckendorff (c.1955–), Br. movie, TV actress.

David **Seymour** *see* **Chim**

Gordon **Seymour**: [Sir] Charles Waldstein (later, Watson) (1856–1927), U.S.-born Br. archaeologist.

Jane **Seymour**: Joyce Penelope Wilhelmina Frankenberg (1951–), Eng. movie, TV actress, working in U.S. Seymour's screen name is presumably derived from the wife of Henry VIII, but perhaps also compliments fellow actress Jane Seymour Fonda. "A schoolgirl from Wimbledon, Joyce Frankenberg changed her name to Henry VIII's third wife and earned a king's ransom from American television after using [James] Bond as a stepping stone [in *Live and Let Die* (1973)]" [*Sunday Times*, August 11, 2002].

Lynn **Seymour**: Lynn Berta Springbett (1939–), Can. ballet dancer. Despite the possible aptness of her real surname (though it does suggest "bedsprings"), the dancer was advised to find a new name by choreographer Kenneth MacMillan. It was he who proposed "Seymour." The name seems to appeal as a pseudonym (see the entries above and that below). If its attraction does not stem from Jane Seymour, Henry VIII's third wife, possibly the lure lies in its suggestion of "see more," which could be regarded as promising or propitious. It is also an English aristocratic name in its own right, as that of the dukes of Somerset and marquises of Hertford.

Robert **Seymour** *see* Elijah **Jenkins**

William **Seymour**: William Gorman Cunningham (1855–1933), U.S. stage actor.

Mary **Seyton** *see* Lady Caroline **Lascelles**

Y **Sgolor Mawr**: Robert Roberts (1834–1885), Welsh cleric, scholar. Roberts earned a formidable reputation for his erudition. Hence his name, meaning "The Great Scholar."

Betty **Shabazz**: Betty Sanders (1936–1997), U.S. black educator, civil rights activist.

Shabba-Doo: Adolfo Quinones (1955–), U.S. black movie actor, dancer. The performer is presumably named Shabba from the same source as Shabba **Ranks**.

Shadal: Samuel David Luzzatto (1800–1865), It. Jewish writer, scholar. The writer came to be known by an acronymic name formed from the initial letters of his Hebrew name (*Sh*muel *D*avid *L*uzzatto).

John **Shadow**: John Byrom (1692–1763), Eng. poet. The poet used this appropriate name for two papers on dreams that he contributed to the *Spectator* (Nos. 586, 593) in 1714.

Mighty **Shadow**: Winston Bailey (c.1939–), U.S. black calypso singer. The singer is usually known simply as Shadow.

Ivan **Shadr**: Ivan Dmitriyevich Ivanov (1887–1941), Russ. sculptor. The artist took his name from his birthplace, the town of Shadrinsk, southern Russia.

Shag: Anatoly Sergeyevich Novozhilov (1910–), Russ. conjuror, circus artist. The performer originally teamed up with a colleague named Shvetsov as a pair of acrobats, calling their act "Dva Moreno" ("The Two Morenos"). This then became "Dva Shaga" ("The Two Steps"), and Novozhilov kept the name in the singular for his solo acts.

Shaggy: Orville Richard Burrell (1968–), Jamaican-born U.S. ragga musician. Burrell adopted the nickname given him for his hair, which made him look like the dog Shaggy in the Scooby Doo cartoons.

Harmonica Shah: Thaddeus Hall (1946–), U.S. black blues harmonica player. The musician legally changed his name to Seward Shah.

Abdulla Shaik: Abdulla Mustafa ogly Talybzade (1881–1959), Azerbaijani novelist, poet, critic.

Shakara: Shakara Ledard (*c*.1975–), Bahamanian model. Not to be confused with **Shakira**.

Shakey Jake: James D. Harris (1921–1990), U.S. blues musician. When not playing harmonica Harris was a professional gambler. Hence his name, from the crapshooters' call "Shake 'em, Jake."

Galina Shakhovskaya: Galina Aleksandrovna Rzhepishevskaya (1908–), Russ. ballet director.

Shakin' Stevens *see* Shakin' **Stevens**

Shakira: Shakira Isabel Mebarak Ripoll (1977–), Colombian pop singer, songwriter, of Lebanese–U.S./Colombian parentage. The singer, known to her friends as Shaki, has an Arabic name meaning "grateful."

Tupac Shakur: Lesane Parish Crooks (1971–1996), U.S. black rapper. The artist, also known as "2Pac," was the son of Black Panther members Billy Garland and Afeni Shakur. Some time after his birth, his mother renamed him Tupac Amaru, after the last Inca ruler, ancestor of the Peruvian Indian revolutionary **Tupac Amaru II**. He originally rapped under the name MC New York, and following his fatal shooting while leaving a Mike Tyson fight released a posthumous album under the name Makaveli.

Shaky *see* Shakin' **Stevens**

Yitzhak Shamir: Yitzhak Jazernicki (or Yezernitzky) (1915–), Pol.-born Zionist leader. The future Israeli prime minister adopted his new name, Hebrew for "thorn,"on emigrating to Palestine in 1935.

Bo Shane *see* Bo **Derek**

Ntozake Shange: Paulette Williams (1948–), U.S. black playwright, poet, novelist. The writer, who gained national fame with her 1974 feminist drama *for colored girls who have considered suicide / when the rainbow is enuf,* adopted her Zulu name in 1971 after two South African friends baptized her in the Pacific Ocean. Ntozake (pronounced "Entozakee") means "she who brings her own things," and Shange (pronounced "Shong-gay") means "one who walks with lions."

Shanice: Shanice Wilson (1973–), U.S. soul, R&B singer.

Bud Shank: Clifford Everett, Jr. (1926–), U.S. jazz musician.

Shannon: Shannon Greene (1958–), U.S. pop singer.

Del Shannon: Charles Weedon Westover (1939–1990), U.S. popular singer, songwriter. The musician is said to have derived his first name from his boss's car, a Cadillac Coupe de Ville, and his surname from a wrestler that he met in a night club, Mark Shannon. The name is virtually identical to that of Dell **Shannon**, and this cannot surely be a coincidence.

Dell Shannon: Barbara Elizabeth Linington (1921–1988), U.S. mystery writer. Other names used by Linington were Anne Blaisdell, Lesley Egan, and Egan O'Neill.

Peggy Shannon: Winona Sammon (1909–1941), U.S. stage, movie actress.

Levon Shant: Levon Segbosyan (1869–1951), Armenian writer.

Roxanne Shanté: Lolita Shanté Gooden (1970–), U.S. black rapper. The singer adopted her name in response to UTFO's "Roxanne, Roxanne" (1985), titling her first single "Roxanne's Revenge."

Reuben Shapcott *see* Mark **Rutherford**

Omar Sharif: Michael Shalhoub (1932–), Egyptian movie actor, of Syrian-Lebanese descent. The actor explains how he arrived at his screen name: "I'd changed my name to do 'The Blazing Sun.' At birth, I was Michael Shalhoub. My first name, Michael, annoyed me. Anybody could be a Michael. I'd tried to come up with something that sounded Middle Eastern and that could still be spelled in every language. Omar! Two syllables that had a good ring to them and reminded Americans of General Omar Bradley. Next I thought of combining Omar with the Arabic [princely title] Sherif, but I realized that this would evoke the word 'sheriff,' which was bit too cowboyish. So I opted for a variant — I became Omar Sharif" [Omar Sharif with Marie-Thérèse Guinchard, *The Eternal Male*, 1977]. The actor was actually billed in *The Blazing Sun* (1954) as Omar el Cherif, then until 1962 as Omar Cherif.

Jack Sharkey: Joseph Paul Zukauskas (1902–1994), U.S. boxer, of Lithuanian parentage. The boxer took his name from a former leading heavyweight, Sailor Tom Sharkey. Like him, Zukauskas was a sailor before entering the ring.

Ariel Sharon: Ariel Scheinerman (1928–), Israeli general, politician. The Israeli prime minister (2001–06) took his Hebrew name from the Plain of Sharon, the region of western Palestine (now Israel) where he was born.

Dee Sharp: Derrick Trought (1956–), Br. black reggae musician.

Dee Dee Sharp: Diana (or Dione) LaRue

(1945–), U.S. soul singer. The singer's name may pun on the musical note (D sharp).

Luke **Sharp**: Robert Barr (1850–1912), Sc. novelist, working in Canada, U.K. A name in the same facetious category as Justin **Case**. The writer was popular for his spoofs, and and one novel written under this name was *The Adventures of Sherlaw Kombs* (1892).

Lester **Sharpe**: Leslie Patrick Molloy (1918–1994), Eng. magician, teaming with wife Iris. The magician's name points to his sleight-of-hand tricks.

[Sir] Edward Albert **Sharpey-Shafer**: Edward Albert Schafer (1850–1935), Eng. physiologist. Schafer was a pupil of William Sharpey (1802–1880), regarded as the founder of English physiology, and added his teacher's name to his own in 1918 as a mark of his indebtedness.

Sharpshooter: John Phillips (*fl.*1825–1842), Eng. caricaturist, illustrator. The name is apt for a caricaturist, who aims to "score a hit" on his subject.

Omar **Sharriff**: David Alexander (1938–), U.S. black blues musician. Alexander adopted his name after converting to Islam in 1960. Compare the name of Omar **Sharif**.

Mikhail **Shatrov**: Mikhail Filippovich Marshak (1932–), Russ. playwright.

Will **Shatter**: Russell Wilkinson (1956–1987), U.S. punk musician.

Samuel **Shattock**: Samuel George Betty (1852–1924), Eng. pathologist. The medical specialist changed his name in about 1882, presumably in order to claim a kinship with a bearer of the new name.

Truly **Shattuck**: Clarice Etrulia de Bucharde (1876–1954), U.S. variety artist ("The California Nightingale"). "Why ... should Clarice Etrulia de Bucharde have selected for her stage alias a first name of such coy affectation and a second of such consonantal ugliness?" [Kilgarriff II, p.239]. The performer's new first name is a pet form of "Etrulia." Her new second name is more problematical.

Frank **Shaul** *see* Fenton **Brockley**

Arnold **Shaw**: Arnold Shukotoff (1909–1989), U.S. music business executive, of Russ. Jewish descent. Shukotoff shortened and anglicized his name on divorcing his first wife, Hanna Wiltchik.

Artie **Shaw**: Arthur Jacob Arshawsky (1910–2004), U.S. jazz musician, of Russ.-Austr. parentage.

Brian **Shaw**: Brian Earnshaw (1928–1992), Eng. ballet dancer.

Fiona **Shaw**: Fiona Mary Wilson (1958–), Ir.-born Br. stage actress. The actress discovered there was another Fiona Wilson when she was about to leave the Royal Academy of Dramatic Art. "I wanted a name that connected my Irish family with me and

passing the statue of George Bernard Shaw on the lower staircase and knowing there were many Shaws in my family, I opted for its short succinctness ... I have never regretted it. It is easy to spell, to pronounce and identifies my family and nation the way Wilson never would" [(undated) personal letter from Fiona Shaw (received October 5, 1995)].

Hank **Shaw**: Henry Shalofsky (1926–2006), Br. jazz trumpeter.

Irwin **Shaw**: Irwin Gilbert Shamoroff (1913–1984), U.S. writer, of Russ. Jewish/Lithuanian Jewish descent. Shaw's father adopted the shortened, anglicized version of his name in 1923 on setting up a real estate brokerage with his brothers.

Jane **Shaw**: Jean Bell Shaw Patrick (1910–), Sc. writer of books for girls. Shaw was the writer's mother's maiden name, as well as her own third name.

Martin **Shaw** *see* Christopher **Beck**

Roger **Shaw**: Roger Ollerearnshaw (1931–), Eng. TV announcer.

[Sir] Run Run **Shaw**: Yifu Shao (1913–1991), Chin. movie producer, working in Hong Kong.

Sandie **Shaw**: Sandra Goodrich (1947–), Eng. pop singer. A pleasantly punning seaside name, with "Sandie," of course, from her first name. The name was given by her first manager, Eve Taylor. The singer often appeared on stage barefoot, as if walking along the shore.

Susan **Shaw**: Patsy Sloots (1929–1978), Eng. movie actress. The future actress was spotted at a London Camera Club demonstration by a film agent, who changed her name to Pat Fanshawe and secured her a test. After a year's "grooming," she was given a small part in *The Upturned Glass* (1947), for which she was further renamed Susan Shaw.

T.E. **Shaw** *see* John Hume **Ross**

Victoria **Shaw**: Jeanette Elphick (1935–1988), Austral. movie actress, working in U.S.

Vincent **Shaw**: Ronald George Shaw (1925–2002), Eng. theatrical agent. The impresario began his career as an actor under the stage name Peter Vanning.

Wini **Shaw**: Winfred Lei Momi (1899–1982), U.S. movie actress, singer, of Hawaiian descent.

Dick **Shawn**: Richard Schulefand (1928–1987), U.S. movie comedian. The actor made his debut in 1948 as Richy Shawn.

William **Shawn**: William Chon (1907–1992), U.S. journalist, editor. Shawn changed his name early in his career because he thought the new name sounded more "writerly" and was less likely to be taken for an Asian name.

Robert **Shayne**: Robert Shaen Dawe (1900–1992), U.S. movie actor.

Tamara **Shayne:** Tamara Nikoulin (1897–1983), Russ.–U.S. movie actress.

Shneur Zalman **Shazar:** Shneur Zalman Rubashov (1889–1974), Russ.-born Israeli politician. The third president of Israel formed his new surname from the Hebrew initials of his original name.

N. **Shchedrin:** Mikhail Yevgrafovich Saltykov(-Shchedrin) (1826–1889), Russ. writer. Saltykov's son has explained how his father came by his pen name, which is based on the Russian word *shchedryy*, "generous": "It was like this. When he was in government service, he was advised that it was not done to sign one's work with one's real name. So he had to find a pen name, but could not hit on anything suitable. My mother suggested that he should choose a pseudonym based on the word 'shchedryy,' as in his writings he was extraordinarily generous with any kind of sarcasm. My father liked his wife's idea, and from then on he called himself Shchedrin." It is possible, however, that the name could have come from a servant in the employ of Saltykov's family, or from a local merchant T. Shchedrin, or some acquaintance of Saltykov, or it could even derive from the word *shchedrina* "pockmarks," with reference to the "pockmarks" on the face of Russia at the time (1870s) [Dmitriyev, pp.58–9].

Al **Shean:** Albert Schoenberg (1868–1949), Ger.-born U.S. comedian, actor, teaming with Ed Gallagher (?1872–1929) as Gallagher and Shean. The Schoenberg family immigrated to the United States in 1876. Albert changed his name in 1884 on setting up a vaudeville act called the Manhattan Comedy Four.

Moira **Shearer:** Moira Shearer King (1926–2006), Sc. ballet dancer, stage, movie actress.

Norma **Shearer:** Edith Norma Fisher (1900–1983), Can. movie actress.

Joseph **Shearing** *see* Marjorie **Bowen**

Gloria **Sheaves:** Marjorie Gwendoline Allard (1913–2005), Eng. dancer. Sheaves was the last member of the "Bluebell Girls" dance troupe, founded by Miss **Bluebell**.

Shed: John Young (1959–), Br. crossword compiler. The setter's pseudonym was originally his nickname as a student, given him for his sloping walk and untidy appearance.

Francis **Sheehy-Skeffington:** Francis Joseph Christopher Skeffington (1878–1916), Ir. pacifist, journalist. In 1903 Skeffington married the feminist and republican activist Hanna Sheehy (1877–1946), adding her name to his, as she added his to her maiden name.

Charlie **Sheen:** Carlos Irwin Estévez (1965–), U.S. movie actor, son of Martin **Sheen**. Sheen's elder brother, actor Emilio Estévez (1960–), retained the family name.

Fulton **Sheen:** Peter John Sheen (1895–1979), U.S. Roman Catholic bishop, electronic evangelist. Although Sheen was baptized Peter, he adopted his mother's maiden name as a youth and retained it throughout his religious career.

Martin **Sheen:** Ramón Gerardo Antonio Estévez (1940–), U.S. stage, movie, TV actor, of Sp.-It. parentage. The actor adopted the maiden name of his wife, née Janet Sheen.

Reggie **Sheffield** *see* Eric **Desmond**

Sheila: Anna Chancel (1946–), Fr. pop singer. The singer took her name in 1962 when she sang a version of Tommy Roe's hit "Sheila."

Jon **Sheldon** *see* Kal **Mann**

Raccoona **Sheldon** *see* James **Tiptree, Jr.**

Sidney **Sheldon:** Sidney Schechtel (1917–2007), U.S. novelist, screenwriter.

Barbara **Shelley:** Barbara Kowin (1933–), Br. movie actress.

Frank **Shelley:** Mario Francelli (1912–2004), Br. stage actor, manager. The actor created his professional name from his original Italian surname.

John **Shelley:** John Philip Bernhard Seales (1932–), Br. photographer.

Paul **Shelley:** Paul Matthews (1942–), Eng. stage, TV actor.

Pete **Shelley:** Peter Campbell McNeish (1955–), Eng. "electro-pop" musician. The musician's new name, adopted in 1976, was the one that his parents would have given him if he had been born a girl.

Peter **Shelley** *see* Brett **Halliday**

Anne **Shelton:** Patricia Sibley (1923–1994), Eng. popular singer.

John **Shelton:** John Price (1917–1972), U.S. movie actor.

Paul **Shelving:** Paul North (*c*.1889–1968), Br. theatrical designer.

Sam **Shepard:** Samuel Shepard Rogers VII (1943–), U.S. playwright, movie actor.

Michael **Shepley:** Michael Shepley-Smith (1907–1961), Br. stage, movie actor.

T.G. **Sheppard:** William Browder (1944–), U.S. country singer. The origin of the singer's name is told as follows: "T.G. was loathe [*sic*] to use his real name, Bill Browder, feeling that it might conflict with his promotion work. Inspiration struck when looking out of his office window across the street, he saw some dogs of the German Shepherd breed. An office colleague jokingly suggested he call himself 'The German Shepherd.' T.G. was amused at the thought, but on later reflection, decided he liked the idea" [Kash, p.408]. Another account claims he saw the name as "The Good Shepherd."

John **Shepperd:** Shepperd Strudwick (1907–1983), U.S. movie actor.

Robert Harborough **Sherard**: Robert Harborough Kennedy (1861–1943), Eng. biographer. The great-grandson of William Wordsworth adopted his father's middle name in place of his original surname.

Ann **Sheridan**: Clara Lou Sheridan (1915–1967), U.S. movie actress ("The Oomph Girl"). The actress played under her real name until 1935, when she appeared as Ann Sheridan in *Rocky Mountain Mystery*.

Dinah **Sheridan**: Dinah Mec (1920–), Br. movie actress, of Ger.-Russ. parentage.

Lee **Sheridan** *see* Dick **James**

Mary **Sheridan**: Daphne Graham (1903–), Eng. stage, movie actress.

Tony **Sheridan**: Anthony Sheridan McGinnity (1940–), Eng. pop musician.

Paul **Sheriff**: Paul Schouvalov (or Schouvaloff) (1903–1962), Russ.-born movie art director, working in U.K.

Allan **Sherman**: Allan Copelon (1924–1973), U.S. comedian, folk humorist.

Bim **Sherman**: Jarret Tomlinson (1950–2000), Jamaican reggae singer. According to his obituary in *The Times* (December 19, 2000), the musician was born Lloyd Vincent. "Nobody seems to recall where his adopted name came from but he was already using it by 1973."

Vincent **Sherman**: Abraham Orovitz (1906–2006), U.S. movie director, of Russ. parentage.

Shorty **Sherock**: Clarence Francis Cherock (1915–1980), U.S. jazz trumpeter.

Sherrick: Lamotte Smith (1957–1999), U.S. R&B musician. The musician was given his stage name by Raymona Gordy, the former wife of record producer Berry Gordy, Jr.

Billy **Sherrill**: Philip Campbell (1936–), U.S. pop, country musician.

Hymie **Shertzer**: Herman Schertzer (1909–1977), U.S. jazz saxophonist.

Lydia **Sherwood**: Lily Shavelson (1906–1989), Br. stage, movie actress.

Madeleine **Sherwood**: Madeleine Thornton (1922–), Can. movie actress.

Lev **Shestov**: Lev Isaakovich Shvartsman (Schwarzman) (1866–1938), Russ. existentialist philosopher, man of letters, working in Germany, France.

Bobby **Shew**: Robert Joratz Shewhorn (1941–), U.S. jazz musician.

Ella **Shields**: Ella Buscher (1879–1952), U.S.-born Br. music-hall singer, male impersonator.

George **Shiels**: George Morsheil (1881–1949), Ir. playwright.

Harry **Shiels**: Thomas Dowell (1906–1980), Br. variety artist.

Sahib **Shihab**: Edmund Gregory (1925–1989), U.S. jazz musician. The musician changed his name in 1947 on adopting the Muslim faith. The Arabic name Shihab means "meteor," "shooting star."

Shih Kien: Shek Wing Cheung (1913–2009), Chin. movie actor. Shih's name was styled in various ways but his birth name appears to have been as given here.

Nat **Shilkret**: Nathaniel Schüldkraut (1889–1982), U.S. popular music composer, arranger, conductor.

Takashi **Shimura**: Shoji Shiazaki (1905–1982), Jap. movie actor.

Shinehead: Edmund Carl Aitken (1962–), Br.-born black rapper, working in U.S. Aitken adopted his nickname, given him for his distinctive, closely cropped hairstyle.

Mother **Shipton**: Ursula Shipton, née Southill (or Southiel) (1488–*c*.1560), Eng. witch. The prophetess may well have been fictional, but her popular biographical data are as given here.

Ovanes **Shiraz**: Ovanes Tatevosovich Karapetyan (1914–1984), Armenian poet. The poet adopted as his new name that of the Iranian city of Shiraz, birthplace of two famous Persian poets, **Saadi** and **Hafez**.

Talia **Shire**: Talia Rosa Coppola (1946–), U.S. movie actress, sister of director Francis Ford Coppola (1939–). The actress was first billed under the name of her (then) husband David Shire, in *The Godfather* (1972).

Shirley: [Sir] John Skelton (1831–1897), Sc. lawyer, author, literary critic. The writer adopted his pen name from the title character of *Shirley* (1849), the novel by Charlotte Brontë, whose earlier *Jane Eyre* (1847) he had favorably reviewed. (Miss Brontë had written to thank him.) He used the name for his essays and reviews in *The Guardian*, a short-lived Edinburgh periodical, as well as for contributions to the longer-lived *Fraser's Magazine*. A pseudonym was necessary in order not to jeopardize his professional prospects as an up-and-coming lawyer.

Anne **Shirley**: Dawn Evelyeen Paris (1918–1993), U.S. movie actress. Shirley began her career in 1922 as a child actress under the name Dawn O'Day. In 1934, aged 16, she was given the title role in a screen version of L.M. **Montgomery**'s novel *Anne of Green Gables*, and legally adopted the name of the spirited young girl who is its heroine.

Steve **Shirley**: Vera Stephanie Shirley, earlier Brook, née Buchthal (1933–), Ger.-born Br. businesswoman. The former company executive went to England as a child refugee in 1939, changing her name later on naturalization to Brook in honor of the English World War I poet Rupert Brooke (1887–1915). In 1959 she married an Englishman and conventionally took his name.

Shirley and Lee: Shirley Goodman, née Pixley (1936–), U.S. R&B singer + Leonard Lee (1935–1976), U.S. black R&B singer.

Aleksandr **Shirvanzade:** Aleksandr Minasovich Movsisyan (1858–1935), Armenian writer. The writer was born in Shemakha, historic capital of the khanate of Shirvan. Hence his adopted name, with the Azerbaijani patronymic suffix -*zade*, so that he was a "son of Shirvan."

Shiva Sharan: Alain Daniélou (1907–1994), Fr. musician, religious scholar. In 1932, after an initial career as a dancer, Daniélou visited India, where he took up a university post in Sanskrit literature. He subsequently converted to Hinduism, taking the name Shiva Sharan, after Shiva (Siva), the third god of the Hindu Trinity, and Sharan, a name of Vishnu, the second god of the Trinity. (The first is Brahma.)

M. **Shketan:** Yakov Pavlovich Mayorov (1898–1937), Russ. (Mari) writer. Mayorov was the first Mari prose writer. Hence his adopted name, meaning "lonely."

Michelle **Shocked:** Karen Michelle Schacht (1962–), U.S. folksinger. The singer adopted her new name when she ran away from her Mormon parents at the age of 15. In 1996, on settling a legal dispute with her record company, Mercury Records, she adopted a softer, more "spiritual" persona, prompting one commentator to quip: "At this rate she might even have to change her name again — although Michelle Mellowed doesn't have quite the same ring" [*The Times*, November 22, 1996]. Some sources give her original name as Johnston, claiming she took her new name when jailed for a political protest.

Sholem Aleichem: Sholem (or Shalom) Yakov Rabinowitz (1859–1916), Russ.-born Jewish novelist, working in U.S. The name is a familiar Yiddish greeting meaning "peace [be] on you" The writer adopted the name in 1883, the year he decided to abandon Hebrew as a literary medium and instead write stories and sketches in Yiddish (then regarded as bad form).

Georgy **Sholokhov-Sinyavsky:** Georgy Filippovich Sholokhov (1901–1967), Russ. writer. The writer was born in the hamlet of Sinyavsky, and added its name to his original surname.

Troy **Shondell:** Gary Shelton (1940–), U.S. pop singer, producer.

Dinah **Shore:** Frances Rose Shore (1917–1994), U.S. cabaret singer, radio, TV actress. The singer's change of name was initially prompted when "everybody down in Nashville" suggested she adopt her childhood nickname, Fanny Rose, quipping and quoting: "Fanny sat on a tack. Fanny rose. Fanny Rose sat on a tack. Did Fanny rise?" "I had to do something," sighed Shore, and in 1944 legally replaced

this name with "Dinah," from her association with the popular song of that name.

Bob **Short:** (1) Alexander Pope (1688–1744), Eng. poet; (2) Augustus Baldwin Longstreet (1790–1870), U.S. lawyer, educationist, author. Pope used the name for some contributions to the short-lived periodical *The Guardian* (1713), and it is possible that Longstreet borrowed the pseudonym from him, enjoying the pun on his own surname. Other writers also used the name.

Bobby **Short:** Robert Waltrip (1926–), U.S. popular singer, pianist.

Luke **Short:** Frederick Dilley Glidden (1908–1975), U.S. writer of westerns. Glidden adopted his new name after selling his first story in 1935, apparently without realizing that there had been a real-life Dodge City gambler and gunfighter of the same name.

Ras **Short I:** Garfield Blackman (1941–2000), West Indian calypso, soca singer. The singer was originally nicknamed "Lord Shorty" in ironic reference to his 6 ft 4 in stature. When he converted to Rastafarianism in 1981 he modified this to "Ras Shorty."

Lionel **Shriver:** Margaret Ann Shriver (1957–), U.S. novelist. The writer explains her change of name: "I was Margaret Ann at home and Margaret at school, and I didn't like either name.... The name change came about capriciously — I had to fill in a name tag for a study programme, and I just didn't want to write Margaret Ann one more time. Lionel was just a name, out of the air.... I think I liked it because I didn't know anybody called Lionel. It could have been Harold. But the fact I've stuck with it suggests it suits me" [*Sunday Times Magazine*, August 12, 2007].

Eddi **Shu:** Edward Shulman (1918–1986), U.S. jazz musician.

Lee **Shubert:** Levi Szemanski (?1873–1953), Lithuanian-born U.S. theatrical manager.

Abel **Shufflebottom:** Robert Southey (1774–1843), Eng. poet. A frivolous name used by the poet for some minor love poems.

Shukhrat: Gulyam Alimov (1918–), Uzbek writer. The writer's pen name means "glory," "fame."

Sergey **Shumsky:** Sergey Vasilyevich Chesnokov (1820–1878), Russ. actor.

Yury **Shumsky:** Yury Vasilyevich Shomin (1887–1954), Ukr. actor.

Arthur Asahel **Shurcliff:** Arthur Asahel Shurtleff (1870–1957), U.S. landscape architect. Shurcliff changed his name in 1930 to conform to what he claimed was the original spelling of the family name.

Robert **Shurtleff:** Deborah Sampson (1760–1827), U.S. revolutionary heroine. In 1782, after teaching school for three years in Middleborough,

Massachusetts, Sampson donned men's clothes and enlisted in the Massachusetts militia forces under the name Timothy Thayer. She was exposed, and forced to resign, but later that year resumed her male dress and enlisted in the Fourth Massachusetts Regiment as Robert Shurtleff. She fought in several battles, but fell sick and was hospitalized before being given an honorary discharge in 1783. In 1784 she married a farmer, Benjamin Gannett, with whom she had three children.

Nevil **Shute:** Nevil Shute Norway (1899–1960), Br. novelist, working in Australia. "My full name is Nevil Shute Norway," runs an "Author's Note" prefacing the writer's autobiography. "Readers will find on page 71 an explanation of the reasons that made me use my Christian names alone when writing my books." Here is that explanation: "During the daytime I was working in a fairly important position on a very important engineering job.... It seemed to me that Vickers would probably take a poor view of an employee who wrote novels on the side.... For these reasons I made up my mind to do what many other authors in a similar case have done in the past, and to write under my Christian names ... Nevil Shute was quite a good, euphonious name for a novelist, and Mr. Norway could go on untroubled by his other interest and build up a sound reputation as an engineer. So it started, and so it has gone on to this day" [Nevil Shute, *Slide Rule: The Autobiography of an Engineer,* 1954].

Timothy **Shy:** Dominic Bevan Wyndham Lewis (1891–1969), Br. journalist, novelist, biographer. The writer used this pseudonym for his contributions to the *News Chronicle* from 1936. His better-known pen name was **Beachcomber.**

M. Night **Shyamalan:** Manoj Nelliyattu Shyamalan (1970–), Ind.-born U.S. movie director. Shyamalan's altered middle name represents the nickname by which he was known as a student at New York University's Tisch School of the Arts. It happens to be apt for a director of "shock horror" movies.

Shystie: Chanelle Calica (1983–), Br. black rapper.

Siamanto: Atom Yardzhanyan (1878–1915), Armenian poet.

Siamas Gwynedd: Edward Charles (1757–1828), Welsh controversialist. The writer's name means "James of Gwynedd," referring to the historic region of northern Wales in which he was born.

Josephine **Siao:** Siao Fong-fong (1947–), Chin. movie actress, working in Hong Kong.

Abbé **Sicard:** Roch Ambroise Cucurron (1742–1822), Fr. priest, educationist.

Sice: Simon Rowbottom (1969–), Eng. rock musician.

Edward William **Sidney:** Nathaniel Beverley Tucker (1784–1851), U.S. novelist.

George **Sidney:** Samuel Greenfield (1878–1945), U.S. movie comedian.

Margaret **Sidney:** Harriet Mulford Lothrop, née Stone (1844–1924), U.S. children's writer. The writer adopted her daughter's name as her first name, with Sidney simply a name that she liked.

Sylvia **Sidney:** Sophia Kosow (1910–1999), U.S. stage, movie actress, of Russ. Jewish parentage. The actress adopted her stepfather's name, Sidney, as her professional surname, adapting her first name at the same time to harmonize with it.

Siface: Giovanni Francesco Grossi (1653–1697), It. singer. The male soprano sang so superbly in a 1678 performance of Cavalli's opera *Scipione Africano* in Venice that he came to be known by the part he took, that of Siface (Syphax).

Siful Sifadda: Henrik Arnold Wergeland (1808–1845), Norw. poet. Norway's national poet used this name for some early satirical farces. The name suggests that of Sulin-Sifadda, one of the two horses owned by the Irish hero Cuthullin (Cuchullin) in James Macpherson's long poem *Fingal* (1762), purportedly translated from the original by **Ossian.** In this work, Cuthullin is defeated by Swaran, king of Lochlin (Lochlainn), a Celtic name for Scandinavia, and especially Norway.

Sigma: [Sir] Douglas Straight (1844–1914). Eng. author. The writer's pen name represents the Greek letter corresponding to the initial "S" of his surname.

Simone **Signoret:** Simone Henriette Charlotte Kaminker (1921–1985), Ger.-born Fr. movie actress. The actress adopted her mother's maiden name during the German occupation of France in World War II in place of her original Jewish name. Her second husband (married 1950) was Yves **Montand.**

Sikhkhat: Abbasguli Ali-abbas ogly Mekhtizade (1874–1918), Azerbaijani poet, translator. The writer's adopted name means "truthful," "upright."

Albert **Siklós:** Albert Schönwald (1878–1942), Hung. cellist, composer.

Silacara Bhikkhu: J.F. McKechnie (1871–1950), Eng. Buddhist. The pioneer British *bhikkhu* (fully ordained Buddhist monk) initially worked in the garment industry, then emigrated to the USA, where he worked on farms. He later went to Burma (Myanmar), where he became interested in Buddhism and in 1906 was ordained there under his Buddhist name.

The **Silent Traveller:** Chiang Yee (1903–1977), Chin.-born Eng. writer of popular travel books. The writer, famous for his travel books in the series *The Silent Traveller in ...* (London, Oxford, New York, Edinburgh, etc.) derived his English pen name from his Chinese pseudonym, Yahsin-che, meaning "dumb walking man." (The name has the British spelling of "traveller" with a double "l.")

Anja **Silja:** Anja Silja Regina Langwagen (1940–), Ger. opera singer.

Garnett **Silk:** Garnett Smith (c.1967–1994), Jamaican reggae musician.

Silkk the Shocker: Vyshonne Miller (1980–), U.S. black rapper.

Beverly **Sills:** Belle Miriam Greenough, née Silverman (1929–2007), U.S. opera singer, of Russ. Jewish descent. The soprano's professional name is based on her original first name and maiden name. "The name 'Beverly Sills' came from a friend of her mother who 'thought that some day it might look better on a marquee than Belle Silverman'" [*The Times*, July 4, 2007]. As a child, Sills performed as Bubbles, either as a pet form of her first name or because (it was said) she was born blowing bubbles.

Ignazio **Silone:** Secondo Tranquilli (1900–1978), It. antifascist writer, novelist. The writer took a pseudonym to protect his family from Fascist persecution. He subsequently adopted it as his legal name.

Silurist: Henry Vaughan (1622–1695), Welsh poet. The poet was born in Breconshire (now Powys), in a historic region of southern Wales named for the people known as the Silures. Hence his pseudonym, first used for *Olor Iscanus* ("The Swan of Usk") (1851), his second collection of poems and translations from the Latin (the language of the title). It is uncertain why Vaughan identified himself with the named people. "His adoption of the title ... is puzzling. It is unlikely either to reflect the fighting prowess of the Silures or to proffer an alternative to 'Welsh'" [Stephens, p.614].

James **Silvain:** James Sullivan (?–1856), Eng. ballet dancer, working in France, U.S.

Ron **Silver:** Ron Zimelman (1946–), U.S. movie, TV actor.

Jay **Silverheels:** Harold J. Smith (1919–1980), Can. Native American movie actor. The actor's name alludes to his roles in westerns, famously as Tonto in the long-running TV series *The Lone Ranger*.

Silverpen: Eliza Meteyard (1816–1879), Eng. novelist, writer. The writer was given the name by editor Douglas Jerrold when she contributed an article to the first number of *Douglas Jerrold's Weekly Newspaper* (1846).

Phil **Silvers:** Philip Silver (1912–1985), U.S. movie, TV comedian, of Russ. Jewish parentage.

Silvester II *see* **Sylvester II**

Silvester III *see* **Sylvester III**

Lilia **Silvi:** Silvana Musitelli (1922–), It. movie actress.

Silvia: Zanetta-Rosa-Giovanni Benozzi (c.1701–1758), It. actress.

Silyn: Robert Roberts (1871–1930), Welsh poet. The writer took his name from Cwm Silyn, the name of a valley in his native Carnarvonshire (now in Gwynedd). The name is now a forename in its own right.

Georges **Sim:** Georges-Joseph-Christian Simenon (1903–1989), Belg. detective fiction writer. This name and Christian Brulls are probably the best-known of the 24 registered pseudonyms used by Simenon. Georges Sim simply shortens his full name, while Christian Brulls combines part of his first name with his mother's maiden name. At first he was regularly published as Georges Sim. "Although Georges Simenon was a master of publicity very few people knew his real name, even in private life, and when [publisher] Arthème Fayard finally decided that the 'Maigrets' should be published, but under a different name to the previous pulps, and that this time they would use the writer's real name, he had to ask what this was. Most people thought he was called Georges Sim ... and in Italy, when early 'Maigrets' started appearing in translation, one reviewer pointed out that Simenon was the *nom de plume* of the much better known Georges Sim" [Patrick Marnham, *The Man Who Wasn't Maigret*, 1992].

Simeon Polotsky: Samuil Yemelyanovich Petrovsky-Sitnianovich (1629–1680), Belorussian-born Russ. ecclesiastic, poet, playwright. The writer, also known as Simeon of Polotsk, adopted his name in 1656 on taking his monastic vows in his birthtown of Polotsk.

John **Simm:** John Simmon (1920–), U.S. theater critic.

Al **Simmons:** Alois Szymanski (1902–1956), U.S. baseball player, of Pol. parentage. The player adopted his new name, already similar to his family name, from a hardware company billboard.

Dawn **Simmons:** Gordon Langley Hall (c.1923–2000), Br. author. The writer was the illegitimate son of Jack Copper, chauffeur to the English writer Vita Sackville-West, and a young woman of aristocratic parentage. When he was 16, he fled to Canada to escape his bullying father, then moved to New York, where he underwent a sex change in 1968, renaming himself Dawn Pepita, in memory of Vita Sackville-West. Hall's new surname was that of her husband, John-Paul Simmons, a 22-year-old black folk artist.

Gene **Simmons:** Chaim Witz (1949–), Israeli-born Br. rock musician. The musician adopted a name that paid tribute to his favorite film star, English actress Jean Simmons (1929–2010).

Ginny **Simms:** Virginia Sims (1916–1994), U.S. singer, movie actress.

Hilda **Simms:** Hilda Moses (1920–), U.S. stage actress.

Ed **Simon:** Edward Simon Morillo (1969–), Venezuelan-born U.S. jazz pianist

Jules **Simon:** Jules-François-Simon Suisse (1814–1896), Fr. philosopher, politician.

Simone **Simon:** Simone Thérèse Fernande Simone (1910–2005), Fr. movie actress.

Tito **Simon:** Keith Foster (c.1948–), Jamaican reggae musician. Other aliases under which Foster has recorded include Lance Hannibal, Jackie Foster, Les Foster, and Calva L. Foster. He began his career in the 1960s as one half of the duo Sugar and Dandy, formed with Dandy **Livingstone.**

Simon and Garfunkel: Paul Simon (1941–), U.S. folkrock musician + Arthur Garfunkel (1941–), U.S. folkrock musician. The duo called themselves Tom and Jerry for three years from 1956, having started in show business as Tom Graph and Jerry Landis. In 1959 they vanished from the music scene until 1964, when they re-emerged as Simon and Garfunkel. The pair name Tom and Jerry, familar from the cartoon cat and mouse, dates from 1821, when Pierce Egan, an English sports writer, published *Life in London; or, The Day and Night Scenes of Jerry Hawthorn, Esq., and his Elegant Friend Corinthian Tom.* The names thus originally came to typify a couple of roistering young men-about-town.

Madame **Simone:** Pauline Benda Porché (1877–1985), Fr. stage actress, author. The actress, whose stage and writing career lasted almost a century, married the actor Charles le Bargy in 1897, and it was he who persuaded her to adopt a stage name from the Alfred de Musset heroine.

Nina **Simone:** Eunice Kathleen Waymon (1933–2003), U.S. black jazz singer, pianist, composer. The musician's adopted first name, based on "Eunice," was taken to mean "little one" (as Spanish *niña*, "little girl," "child"), while her new surname was taken from the first name of Simone **Signoret.** The change of name, made after landing a nightclub spot in 1954, "was an attempt to hide the way she was earning her living, singing in bars to an audience of drunks, from her mother" [*The Times Magazine*, June 26, 1999]. Spoken indistinctly, "Eunice Waymon" in fact sounds something like "Nina Simone."

Simonetta: [Duchesa] Simonetta Colonna di Cesaro (1912–), It. fashion designer.

Simpleton: Christopher Harrison (c.1975–), Jamaican DJ, reggae musician. In 1990 **Ninjaman** had a hit with "Heartical Don." Performing as Dracula, Harrison changed the lyrics and the title to "Simpleton," then following favorable audience response adopted this as his stage name.

Simplex: Mary O'Brien (1944–), Ir. crossword compiler. The setter took over the pseudonym of a previous compiler (real name Basil Peterson) on his

death in 1986. The word itself is not only a linguistic term for a single word but denotes a "simple X," or easy crossword (which may well not be).

Simplicissimus: Georgy Valentinovich Plekhanov (1857–1918), Russ. revolutionary. A name adopted for a while by the Marxist philosopher, who also wrote as A. Volgin (*see* Vladimir Ilyich **Lenin**). It derives from the title of the best-known book by the 17th-century German novelist Hans Jakob Christoffel von Grimmelshausen, *Der Abenteuerliche Simplicissimus Teutsch, das ist: Beschreibung des Lebens eines Seltzamen Vagantens Genannt Melchior Sternfels von Fuchshaim* ("The Adventurous German Simpleton, that is: Description of the Life of a Strange Wanderer Named Melchior Sternfels von Fuchshaim") (1669). Canny readers will have noticed that the name of the hero is an anagram of that of the author. Moreover, the book was supposedly published by one Hermann Scheifhaim von Sulsfort, a similarly anagrammatic name. And as if this wasn't enough, the author purported to be a certain Samuel Greifensohn **von Hirschfeld.** The book itself is a picaresque tale of the adventures of a simple youth in various guises (soldier, robber, slave) and gives a vivid picture of the havoc wreaked in Germany by the Thirty Years' War (1618–48).

John **Simpson:** John Cody Fidler-Simpson (1944–), Eng. TV journalist, political editor.

Warwick **Simpson:** William Pett Ridge (1860–1930), Eng. humorist, novelist. The writer used this name for an early novel, *Eighteen of Them* (1894).

Will **Sin:** William Sinnott (1960–1991), Sc. techno-pop musician.

Rogelio **Sinán:** Bernardo Domínguez Alba (1902–1994), Panamanian writer.

Sinbad: Aylward Edward Dingle (?–1947), Eng. writer. An appropriate name for a man whose life from the age of 14 to 40 was spent at sea.

Alexander (or Terry) **Sinclair:** Terence Clark (1945–1983), N.Z. criminal. The drug trafficker was a partner-in-crime of Robert **Trimbole.**

Arthur **Sinclair:** Francis Quinto McDonnell (1883–1951), Ir. stage actor.

Clive **Sinclair:** Joshua Smolinsky (1948–), Br. novelist, short-story writer, of Pol. Jewish parentage. The writer recalls: "My mother's father came from Stashev in South-West Poland. How the family got there no one knows. His name in Hebrew was Joshua, though he was known as Shia, its Yiddish diminutive. When he settled in England it was Anglicized and he became Charles. I am named after him, the initial letter sufficing.... My father's mother was named Shaindel. In England Shane became plain Jane. My middle name, John, comes from her. Smolinsky was her married name, which my father changed to Sinclair when he joined the army in 1939. Thus my disguise, my *nom de vivre,* Clive Sinclair. Joshua Smolinsky (whom I might have been) lives, but only in my stories, as a down-at-heel private eye on the seamy side of Los Angeles. Joshua Ben David, by which I am known to God, has not been heard since ... my bar mitzvah.... The last named ought to be the essential me, but isn't. I am stuck as Clive Sinclair, because my mother tongue is English" [*Times Literary Supplement,* May 3, 1985].

Dennis **Sinclair** *see* Carter **Brown**

Jo **Sinclair:** Ruth Seid (1913–), U.S. writer, of Russ. Jewish parentage.

Michael **Sinclair:** Michael Sinclair MacAuslan Shea (1938–2009), Sc.diplomat, writer of spy fiction. Shea used this name to distinguish his literary activities from his professional career as a diplomat. From 1978 to 1987 he was press secretary to Queen Elizabeth II.

Ronald **Sinclair:** (1) Reginald Teague-Jones (1889–1988), Eng. intelligence officer, working in India, Russia; (2) Richard Arthur Hould (1924–1992), N.Z.–born juvenile movie actor, of N.Z.–Eng. parentage, working in U.S. Teague-Jones became so closely associated with his pseudonym that his obituary was published under it in *The Times* of November 22, 1988. A revised obituary, giving his true identity and the reason for his change of name (his implication in the execution of the 26 Baku commissars in 1918), appeared three days later: "Born Reginald Teague-Jones, he changed his name to Ronald Sinclair.... The reason was his fear ... of being liquidated by Bolshevik agents, or even of being kidnapped and brought back to the Soviet Union for trial" [Peter Hopkirk, "Ronald Sinclair: Carrying his true identity to the grave," *The Times,* November 25, 1988].

Bob **Sinclar:** Christopher le Friant (1968–), Fr. rock musician. The recording artist, head of the Yellow Productions label, took his name from a character in the French movie *Le Magnifique.*

Isaac Bashevis **Singer:** Icek-Hersz Zinger (1904–1991), Pol.-born U.S. author, writing in Yiddish. Singer published his first short story in 1927 under the pseudonym Tse, Yiddish for "Z," his initial. Later that year he published two more stories, this time as Isaac Bashevis, a name derived from his mother's first name, Bathsheva, in order to be distinguished from his brother, Israel Joseph **Singer**.

Israel Joseph **Singer:** Yisroel Yehoshua Zinger (1893–1944), Pol.-born U.S. author, writing in Yiddish, brother of Isaac Bashevis **Singer**.

Anne **Singleton:** Ruth Benedict, née Fulton (1887–1948), U.S. anthropologist, poet.

Mary **Singleton:** Frances Brooke, née Moore (1724–1789), Eng. novelist, dramatist. Frances Brooke

used this name as an essayist in her own weekly periodical, *The Old Maid,* and for a four-volume novel, *The History of Emily Montague* (1769).

Penny **Singleton:** Mariana Dorothy Agnes Letitia McNulty (1908–2003), U.S. movie actress. The actress took her professional surname from her first husband and her new first name from the coins she collected. She began her career young, and at the age of eight was performing as Baby Dorothy.

Sinitta: Sinitta Renay Malone (1966–), U.S. black pop singer.

John **Sinjohn:** John Galsworthy (1867–1933), Eng. novelist, playwright. This was an early name used by Galsworthy for his collection of stories, *From the Four Winds* (1897). The name itself refers to his identically named father, John Galsworthy, with "Sin-" apparently intended to mean "son."

Siôn Lleyn: John Roberts (1749–1817), Welsh poet. The poet's name means "John of Lleyn," referring to the Lleyn district of northwest Wales where he was born.

Siôn Wyn o Eifion: John Thomas (1786–1859), Welsh poet. The poet's name means "Fair John of Eifionydd," the latter being the historic region in northwest Wales where he was born and where many poets lived.

Siouxsie **Sioux:** Susan Janet Ballion (1957–), Eng. punk rock singer, wife (married 1991, divorced 2007) of **Budgie**. The lead singer of the group Siouxsie and the Banshees created the American Indian form of her name from "Susy," as which she had always been known to family and friends.

Siranuysh: Merobe Kantardzhyan (1857–1932), Armenian actress.

Siras: Amayak Saakovich Voskanyan (1902–), Armenian writer.

Sirdani: Sidney Daniels (1900–1982), S.A.–born comedy magician. The conjuror affected an Italian accent to explain his tricks, which he performed on radio.

Sirin: Vladimir Vladimirovich Nabokov (1899–1977), Russ.-born U.S. novelist. This was an early pseudonym used by the author when he was still writing in Russian, although already an immigrant resident in the U.S. (from 1919). "In modern times *sirin* is one of the Russian names of the Snowy Owl, the terror of tundra rodents, and is also applied to the handsome Hawk Owl, but in old Russian mythology it is a multicolored bird, with a woman's face and bust, no doubt identical with the 'siren,' a Greek deity, transporter of souls and teaser of sailors" [Vladimir Nabokov, *Strong Opinions,* 1973]. Nabokov used the name to avoid being confused with his father, Vladimir Dmitriyevich Nabokov (1869–1922), one of the founders of the Kadets, the Constitutional Democratic Party led by Pavel Milyukov.

Douglas **Sirk**: Claus (later Hans) Detlef Sierck (1897–1987), Ger. movie director, of Dan. parentage, working in U.S. "Claus" gave "Douglas."

Sirone: Norris Jones (1940–), U.S. jazz musician. A virtual reversal of the musician's original first name, with a suggestion of his surname thrown in.

Sisqo: Mark Andrews (1978–), U.S. pop singer. The singer's name suggests a respelled "Cisco."

Sista Monica: Monica Parker (1956–), U.S. black blues singer.

Sister ... For names beginning thus, see the next word, e.g. for Sister Albertina see **Albertina**, for Sister Anthony see **Anthony**, for Sister Dora see **Dora**, etc.

Sitting Bull: Tatanka Iyotanka (*c.*1831–1890), U.S. Native American chief. The future Sioux chief, the son of Sitting Bull and Her Holy Door, was originally known by a name translating as Jumping Badger. He joined his first war party at age 14, when he was given the same name as his father. The name itself connotes a buffalo bull of great strength and endurance planted solidly on its haunches to fight to the death. On giving his name to the boy, the father himself took the name Jumping Bull.

Swami **Sivananda**: Kuppuswami Iyer (1887–1963), Ind. guru. The founder of the Divine Life Mission in 1936 took a name meaning "bliss of Siva," after Siva (Shiva), the third major god in the Hindu Trinity. "Swami" is a religious title meaning "master." (The Divine Life Mission is not to be confused with the Divine Light Mission, founded by the father of **Maharaj Ji**.)

Sixtus IV: Francesco della Rovere (1414–1484), It. pope. This is the pope who built the Sistine Chapel, the papal chapel in the Vatican, named for him (Italian *Sisto*, "Sixtus").

Sixtus V: Felice Peretti (1520–1590), It. pope. The pontiff took the name out of regard for **Sixtus IV**, who had been a Franciscan, like himself.

Roni **Size**: Ryan Williams (1969–), Eng. rock drummer, bassist.

Sizzla: Miguel Collins (*c.*1970–), Jamaican reggae musician.

Skanderbeg: Gjergj (or George) Kastrioti (1405–1468), Albanian national hero. The national leader acquired this name when, as Iskander (for Alexander the Great), he was converted to Islam with the rank of bey. Hence "Skander*beg*." He subsequently rejected the Muslim faith and embraced Christianity. Compare **Iskander**.

Violet **Skelton**: Isobel Dunlop (1901–1975), Sc. violinist, composer.

Arthur **Sketchley**: George Rose (1817–1882), Eng. cleric, playwright, humorist. The writer used this name for his stage comedies and witty sketches (hence perhaps the name) published in such period-icals as *Fun* and *Cassell's Magazine*. Many of them involved the doings of an illiterate old woman called Mrs. Brown.

Skin: Deborah Dyer (1967–), Br. rock singer, of Jamaican parentage. The lead singer of the group Skunk Anansie selected a stage name to suit her awesome physical presence.

Frank **Skinner**: Christopher Collins (1957–), Eng. TV comedian, actor, chat-show host. The entertainer is said to have taken his stage name from a member of his father's local dominoes team.

Alison **Skipworth**: Alison Groom (1863–1952), Eng. movie actress, working in U.S. The actress adopted her husband's name as her screen name.

Stepan **Skitalets**: Stepan Gavrilovich Petrov (1869–1941), Russ. writer. The writer's name means "wanderer," "rover." He relates: "In 1897 I submitted my first, unsigned article to a newspaper and asked if I should sign with my real name or devise a pen name. The editor replied that for topical articles a pseudonym was necessary. But that day I was in a real hurry somewhere and didn't have a moment to think of a name. 'You think one up, I can't stop!' I said, and left. The next day I saw my first piece printed in the paper over the name Rover. 'Is that the name you gave me?' I asked the editor. 'Yes,' he replied. 'We all of us here in the office discussed the matter and in view of your article decided to call you Rover. From now on you'll be a Rover in literature just as I expect you've been a rover in real life.... Do you like the name?' 'Not bad!' I replied. 'It's a good name!' 'So, you can carry on now under that pen name.' And I set to in earnest..." [Dmitriyev, p. 93].

Skitt: Hardin Edwards Taliaferro (1811–1875), U.S. writer, Baptist minister. The pseudonym arose out of a boyhood nickname. Taliaferro (pronounced "Tolliver") was born Mark Hardin Taliaferro but changed Mark Hardin to Hardin Edwards at the age of 18 to avoid being confused with a relative. He was Skitt for humorous sketches in the *Southern Literary Messenger* of Richmond, Virginia.

Skye: Shirley Edwards (1972–), Br. rock singer. A member of the group Morcheeba, the singer has children Jaeger and Kiki, as she explained to interviewer Alan Jackson: "*AJ*: Quite some names your children have. No James or Sophie for you. But then Skye's hardly standard issue either. *Skye*: It's actually something I made up for myself from four very boring names. S, K, Y and E are my initials. *AJ*: Very boring names beginning with those letters? Let me see. Susan. Karen. Yootha. Elsie ... *S*: [laughing] Wrong. If you must know, I'm Shirley Klarisse Yonavive Edwards. *AJ*: I'd hardly call Klarisse and Yonavive boring" [*The Times Magazine*, August 5, 2000].

Ione **Skye**: Ione Skye Leitch (1971–), Br. movie

actress, working in U.S. The actress is the out-of-wedlock daughter of rock singer **Donovan**, whom she never met, and an American mother. Her second name refers to the Scottish island that was the location of her conception. Her first name presumably relates to the island of Iona. Both islands lie off Scotland's west coast.

Sunny **Skylar**: Selig Shaftel (1913–2009), U.S. songwriter, of Russ. parentage.

Gurney **Slade**: Stephen Bartlett (?–1956), Austral. children's writer.

Victoria **Sladen**: Victoria May Schlageter (1910–1999), Br. opera singer, of Ger. parentage.

Andrej **Sládkovic**: Ondrej Braxatoris (1820–1872), Slovakian poet.

Rudolf **Slánský**: Rudolf Salzmann (1901–1952), Cz. Communist politician.

Slash: Saul Hudson (1965–), Br.-born U.S. rock musician. The name was originally a nickname, given the Guns N' Roses guitarist by a friend's father because he was always dashing around.

Christian **Slater**: Christian Hawkins (1969–), U.S. movie actor. The actor adopted his mother's maiden name as his screen name.

Mia **Slavenska**: Mia Corak (1914–2002), Croatian ballerina, working in U.S. The dancer took her stage name from her birthplace, Slavonski Brod, near Belgrade. The name also happens to indicate her Slavic origins.

Olga **Slawska**: Olga Prorubnikowa (1915–), Pol. ballet dancer, teacher.

Patsy **Sledd**: Patsy Randolph (1944–), U.S. country musician.

Si **Sledlength** *see* Josh **Billings**

Robert **Slender**: Philip Morin Freneau (1752–1832), U.S. poet, of Fr.-Sc. descent. The "Poet of the American Revolution," as he came to be known, used this name for a series of essays published in the Philadelphia *Aurora* between 1799 and 1801. The persona he adopted was that of a simple countryman, whose scant knowledge of politics was based on what he had managed to glean from his newspaper.

Kenneth **Slessor**: Kenneth Adolphe Schloesser (1901–1971), Austral. poet, journalist.

Grace **Slick**: Grace Wing (1939–), U.S. rock singer.

Jonathan **Slick**: Ann Sophia Stephens (1810–1886), U.S. historical novelist. The writer used this name for her quite different *High Life in New York* (1842), based on typical Down East humor.

Sam **Slick**: Thomas Chandler Haliburton (1796–1865), Can. lawyer, humorist. The name first appeared in 1835 for a series of articles in the *Nova Scotian*, with Sam Slick supposedly a Yankee pedlar. These were then collected, and published in 1837 as

The Clockmaker; or, The Sayings and Doings of Samuel Slick, of Slickville. Haliburton emigrated to England in 1856.

Slick Rick: Ricky Walters (1965–), Br.-born U.S. black rapper.

Slim: For names ending thus, see the previous word(s), e.g. for Bumble Bee Slim see **Bumble Bee**, for Drifting Slim see **Drifting**, for Fatboy Slim see **Fatboy**, etc.

Slim Dusty: David Gordon Kirkpatrick (1927–2003), Austral. country singer. The singer wrote his first song at the age of 10 and took his stage name a year later.

Slim Harpo: James Isaac Moore (1924–1970), U.S. black harmonica player, singer, brother-in-law of **Lightnin' Slim**. The musician first performed as Harmonica Slim before adopting a neater version of the name, suggested by producer Jay Miller. ("Harpo" is standard slang for a harmonica player.)

Slim Pickens: Louis Bert Lindley, Jr. (1919–1983), U.S. rodeo performer, movie actor. Lindley acquired his pseudonym on joining the rodeo circuit as a teenager. The name "Slim Pickens" (i.e. "slim pickings") was apparently suggested by a colleague, "'cause that's shore what your prize money'll be."

Slim Ray Evans: Otis L. Neirouter (1902–1976), U.S. jazz musician.

Slim Shady *see* **Eminem**

Slim Summerville: George J. Sommerville (1892–1946), U.S. movie comedian.

Slim Whitman: Otis Dewey, Jr. (1924–), U.S. country singer, yodeler. The singer was a self-styled protégé of **Montana Slim**.

Jonathan Freke **Slingsby**: John Francis Waller (1809–1894), Ir. journalist, poet. The writer used this name, based partly on his real name, for his contributions to the *Dublin University Magazine*, of which he was a founder member. These were collected as *The Slingsby Papers* (1852).

Philip **Slingsby**: Nathaniel Parker Willis (1806–1867), U.S. writer, editor, brother of Fanny **Fern**.

Xero **Slingsby**: Matthew Coe (1957–1988), Br. jazz musician. The musician's name is a typical creation of the punk rock era.

Barrie **Sloan**: Barrie Yielding (1931–2007), Br. circus performer, working in U.S. The stiltwalker has related how his family name was changed: "The family was very large, and they were all equestrians. One time they all met in London and began to argue about who took what engagement. My father reached into his pocket for matches to light his cigar. The matchbox had an advertisement for Sloan's Linament [*sic*], and he said that from then on Sloan was his name" [*The Times*, April 9, 2007].

P.F. **Sloan**: Phillip Gary Schlein (1944–), U.S.

pop musician. Perhaps "P" for "Phillip" and "F" for the initial sound of this name.

Tod Sloan: James Forman Sloan (1874–1933), U.S. jockey. The rider accounted for his new first name by saying that his original name was James Todhunter Sloan. It actually came from his nickname, "Toad," given him for his appearance when in his "monkey crouch" riding style, with disproportionately short legs. His winning name gave British rhyming slang "on one's tod," meaning "one one's own." Todhunter would in the event have been an apt name for a horse rider, as it literally means "foxhunter."

Eric Sloane: Everard Jean Hinrichs (1905–1985), U.S. artist, writer, meteorologist. The artist took his name from the U.S. Ashcan School painter John Sloan (1871–1951), who had influenced him as a student, substituting "Eric" for "Everard" and adding an "e" to the other artist's surname.

Olive Sloane: Olive Atkins (1896–1963), Eng. music-hall artist, movie actress. The actress began her career as a child performer called Baby Pearl. She later appeared with a partner as the Sisters Love.

Ally Sloper: Charles Henry Ross (?1842–1897), Eng. humorist. The writer was the original creator of this name, which was soon well known as that of a popular comic cartoon character who was "noted for his dishonest or bungling practices" [*Oxford English Dictionary*]. The character's full name was Alexander Sloper F.O.M., the letters standing for "Friend of Man." He and his partner in various adventures, Isaac Moses, popularly known as "Ikey Mo," were seedy conmen who planned to become rich but who never did. The character of the name seems to have appeared in a fullpage strip entitled "Some of the Mysteries of Loan and Discount," published in the comic paper *Judy* in 1867. It was not long before Ross's name and that of Ally Sloper became synonymous, especially through the titles of such comics as *Ally Sloper's Half Holiday*, published from 1844 to 1914. Ross's son, Charles Ross, Jr., wrote for this particular comic under the name of Tootsie Sloper. "Sloper" itself implies someone who "slopes," that is, sneaks off or departs furtively, as after or when planning some misdeed.

Sly and Robbie: Lowell Charles ("Sly") Dunbar (1952–), Jamaican reggae musician + Robbie Shakespeare (1953–), Jamaican reggae musician. Dunbar was nicknamed "Sly" from his fondness for the black rock group Sly and the Family Stone, formed by Sly **Stone**.

Jimmy Slyde: James Titus Godbolt (1927–2008), U.S. black tap dancer. "It was while hoofing clubs with Jimmy Mitchell, aka Sir Slyde, that the two men were dubbed the Slyde Brothers, hence James Godbolt's new-found moniker, Jimmy Slyde" [*The Times*, June 18, 2008].

Tony Slydini: Quintino Marucci (1901–1991), It.-born U.S. magician. The illusionist first performed as Tony Foolem before adopting his regular stage name, evoking "sly." **Cardini** has a similar name.

Jurkšas Smalausys: Antanas Baranauskas (1835–1902), Lithuanian poet, linguist.

Miss Susan Small: Cherry Marshall (1923–2006), Br. model. The model's assumed name referred to her tiny 22-inch waist, which at one time held the record in the fashion world as the smallest in London.

Biggie Smalls *see* **Notorious B.I.G.**

Chas Smash: Cathal Smyth (1959–), Br. rock musician.

Smectymnuus: Stephen Marshall (?1594–1655), Eng. Presbyterian leader + Edmund Calamy (1600–1666), Eng. clergyman + Thomas Young (1587–1655), Sc. clergyman + Matthew Newcomen (?1610–1669), Eng. clergyman + William Spurstow (?1605–1666), Eng. clergyman. A composite pseudonym for the five English authors of a pamphlet of 1641 attacking Bishop Joseph Hall's *Humble Remonstrance* (1640–1), claiming divine right for the episcopacy. The name was formed from the men's initials (the "W" of Spurstow's "William" gave the double "u"), and happens to suggest Latin *smecticus*, from Greek *smekhein*, "to cleanse." It was abbreviated by other writers, as in Samuel Butler's satire *Hudibras* (1663): "The Handkerchief about the neck / Canonical Crabat of Smeck."

Wentworth Smee: George Brown Burgin (1856–1944), Eng. novelist, journalist, critic. The journalist used the name for his contributions to the *Sunday Sun*.

Saul Smiff: Tristram Coutts (*fl.*1890s), Eng. writer. The name is particularly associated with *The Pottle Papers* (1898).

Smilby: Francis Wilford-Smith (1927–2009), Eng. cartoonist. When at art school after World War II, Wilford-Smith became romantically involved with a fellow student, Pamela Kilby, and the pair were jointly nicknamed "the Smilbys." They married, and Wilford-Smith adopted a singular form of the nickname for his work.

Smiley Culture: David Emmanuel (*c.*1960–), Br. reggae musician, of Jamaican–S.A. parentage. The singer was given his nickname at school for his method of chatting up girls: he simply asked for a smile.

Khristo Smirnenski: Khristo Dimitrov Izmirliyev (1898–1923), Bulg. poet.

Yakov Smirnoff: Yakov Pokhis (1951–), U.S. TV comedian.

Nikolay Smirnov-Sokolsky: Nikolay Pavlovich Smirnov (1898–1962), Russ. music-hall artist, writer.

The writer added his stage name (Sokolsky) to his original surname, if only to be distinguished from the many other Smirnovs.

Al Smith: Albert Schmidt (1902–1986), U.S. cartoonist.

Alexis Smith *see* Mary **Pickford**

Alice Smith *see* Greta **Garbo**

Anna Nicole Smith: Vickie Lynn Hogan (1967–2007), U.S. model. The model's adopted surname was that of her first husband, Billy Wayne Smith, whom she married when she was 17.

Bernard Smith: Bernhard Schmidt (*c.*1630–1708), Ger.-born Eng. organ builder ("Father Smith").

Betty Smith: Elizabeth Keogh (1896–1972), U.S. novelist.

Caesar Smith *see* Elleston **Trevor**

Cal Smith: Calvin Grant Shofner (1932–), U.S. country singer.

Cordwainer Smith: Paul Myron Anthony Linebarger (1913–1966), U.S. SF writer.

Denis Smith: Dorothy Lawrence (*fl.*1915), Eng. adventuress. Lawrence enlisted as a soldier under this name with the aim of writing about army life on the Western front. In 1915 she became Sapper Denis Smith and served for a few days with the British Expeditionary Force before revealing her true identity to her commanding officer. She was interrogated, but before being shipped back to England was made to pledge she would not make her experiences public. She complied, and waited until 1919 before publishing her memoirs.

Emma Smith: Elspeth Hallsmith (1923–), Eng. writer.

Gamaliel Smith: Jeremy Bentham (1748–1832), Eng. jurist, philosopher. The writer used this name for *Not Paul but Jesus* (1823), a didactic work setting out to prove that St. Paul had distorted true Christianity as taught and practiced by Christ. Gamaliel, in the Bible, is the man who had taught Paul (Acts 22:3).

Jimmy Smith: James Mellilo (1882–1946), U.S. bowler.

Joe Smith: Joseph Sultzer (1884–1981), U.S. vaudeville comedian, teaming with Charles **Dale**.

John Smith: Robert Earl Van Orden (1931–1995), U.S. movie, TV actor. The actor adopted this particular name so as to be "the only John Smith in the business."

John Christopher Smith: Johann Christoph Schmidt (1712–1795), Ger.-born Eng. composer.

Johnston Smith: Stephen Crane (1871–1900), U.S. fiction writer. Crane used this name for his first novel, *Maggie: A Girl of the Streets*, published privately in 1893.

Martin Cruz Smith: Martin William Smith (1942–), U.S. crime, mystery writer. The novelist used his original name for *The Indians Won* (1970), about an imaginary American Indian nation. An editor suggested he capitalize on his Native American ancestry by substituting his Pueblo Indian maternal grandmother's name, Cruz, for his middle name. He thus appeared as Martin Cruz Smith on the title page of his first bestseller, *Nightwing* (1977), about vampire bats in a Hopi reservation. He had earlier used the pseudonym Jake Logan for all-action westerns.

Pete Smith: Peter Schmidt (1892–1979), U.S. movie producer.

Rosamond Smith: Joyce Carol Oates (1938–), U.S. novelist, poet, playwright. The prolific novelist first used this name for her distinctive thriller *Kindred Passions* (1987), basing it on that of her husband, Raymond Smith (married 1961). Her eighth thriller under this name, *The Barrens* (2002), appeared as by "Joyce Carol Oates writing as Rosamond Smith," a duality which prompted its reviewer to comment: "This schizophrenic gesture oddly suits the Smith novels' preoccupation with murderous *doppelgängers*; with titles such as *Lives of the Twins* and *Double Delight*, these books obsessively re-enact the invention of alter egos" [Sarah Churchwell in *Times Literary Supplement*, June 28, 2002].

Shelley Smith: Nancy Hermione Bodington (1912–1998), Eng. crime novelist.

S.S. Smith: Thames Ross Williamson (1894–after 1984), U.S. writer. The author used this name for mystery stories, basing it on the name of Simmons and Smith College, where he had taught for a time after graduating from the University of Iowa (1917) and studying at Harvard. Other names used by Williamson, mainly for children's stories, include Edward Dragonet, Waldo Fleming, De Wolfe Morgan, and Gregory Trent.

Stevie Smith: Florence Margaret Smith (1902–1971), Eng. poet. The poet's new first name arose from an incident one day in the 1920s when she was riding over a London common. "Some boys called out 'Come on, Steve,' alluding to the well-known jockey, Steve Donaghue, whose fringe stood on end when he rode, and the friend with her thought the name apt. Steve became Stevie, a sobriquet that took over from 'Peggy,' the name by which up till then she had been known to family and friends" [Frances Spalding, *Stevie Smith: A Critical Biography*, 1988]. Steve Donoghue [*sic*] rode six Derby winners.

William Henry Smith: William Henry Sedley (1806–1872), Welsh-born U.S. actor, theater manager. Sedley ran away from home at the age of 14 and joined a troupe of itinerant players under the name of Smith, which he retained thereafter. His stage career in America began in 1827.

Willie "The Lion" **Smith:** William Henry Joseph Bonaparte Bertholoff (1897–1973), U.S. black jazz pianist. The musician's new surname came from his stepfather, John Smith.

Woodrow Wilson **Smith** *see* C.L. **Moore**

James **Smithson:** James Lewes Macie (1765–1829), Eng. chemist, mineralogist. The provider of funds for the founding in 1849 of the Smithsonian Institution, Washington, DC, was the illegitimate son of Hugh Smithson Percy (originally Hugh Smithson), 1st Duke of Northumberland, and Elizabeth Keate Macie. It was through his mother's family that Macie inherited his substantial fortune. It is uncertain when he received royal permission to change his name, but it first occurs publicly in a scientific publication of 1802. It is believed his bequest to the United States was prompted by his illegitimacy, which he resented, and he is on record as stating: "My name shall live in the memory of man when the titles of the Northumberlands and Percys are extinct and forgotten."

Smokey: David Crossland (1948–), Br. crossword compiler. The setter adopted the name of his dog as his pseudonym.

Smoky Babe: Robert Brown (1927–1976), U.S. black blues musician.

Harry **Smolka:** Harry Peter Smollett (1912–), Austr.-born Eng. author, journalist.

Ján **Smrek:** Ján Cietek (1898–1982), Slovakian poet.

Conn **Smythe:** Constantine Falkland Cary (1895–1980), Can. ice hockey player. The player was also known as Karry Smythe.

Reg **Smythe:** Reginald Smyth (1917–1998), Eng. cartoonist. *See also* Andy **Capp**.

Snaffles: Charles Johnson Payne (1884–1967), Eng. sporting artist, caricaturist. The artist probably took his name from a character in the sporting novels of R.S. Surtees. A snaffle is a type of horse's bit.

Snakefinger: Philip Charles Lithman (1949–1987), Br. rock musician, working in U.S.

The **Snark:** Starr Wood (1870–1944), Eng. cartoonist. The artist adopted the name of the creature in Lewis Carroll's nonsense poem *The Hunting of the Snark* (1876).

Moshe **Sneh:** Moshe Kleinbaum (1909–1972), Pol.-born Israeli politician. The Communist politician adopted a Hebrew name equivalent to the German original (literally "little tree"), referring to the biblical burning bush seen by Moses on Mount Sinai (Exodus 3:2).

Heinrich Yale **Snekul** *see* **Erratic Enrique**

Lemony **Snicket:** Daniel Handler (1970–), U.S. children's author. The writer originally invented his name as an alias when investigating right-wing organizations for his first novel, *The Basic Eight.*

Snookums: Lawrence McKeen (1924–1933), U.S. child movie actor, of Ir. origin. The sadly short-lived actor began his screen career at the age of eighteen months under this pet name.

Snoop Dogg: Calvin Broadus (1972–), U.S. black "gangsta" rapper, movie actor. The performer was given the idea for his distinctive name by his mother, who said his long face reminded her of the cartoon dog Snoopy. His former extended name was Snoop Doggy Dogg, after his cousin's nickname, Tate Doggy Dogg. He then dropped "Doggy" following the murder of his label mate Tupac **Shakur** in 1996.

Snow: Darrin O'Brien (1971–), Can. (white) reggae DJ. O'Brien's name relates to his skin color.

Carmel **Snow:** Carmel White (1887–1961), Ir.-born U.S. fashion magazine editor.

Phoebe **Snow:** Phoebe Laub (1952–), U.S. pop musician. The singer was given her new name in 1974, when she signed up to Shelter Records.

James G. **Snyder:** Dimetrios Georgos Synodinos (1918–1996), U.S. gambler, TV personality. The gambling oddsmaker was popularly known as "Jimmy the Greek."

[Sir] Henry F.R. **Soame:** [Sir] Henry Edward Bunbury (1778–1860), Eng. historical writer. There is an apparent case of mistaken identity here. This name is usually given, as it is here, as the pseudonym of the soldier, historian, and politician Sir Henry Edward Bunbury. The *Dictionary of National Biography* points out, however, that it is the *real* name of Sir Henry Bunbury's cousin, Henry Francis Robert Soame, born ten years earlier (1768). Today neither man may seem important, but the instance is an example of the shaky historical attribution some pseudonyms can attract.

Nikolay **Sobolshchikov-Samarin:** Nikolay Ivanovich Sobolshchikov (1868–1945), Russ. theatrical director, actor. The director's actress daughter, Antonina **Samarina**, dropped the original family surname and adopted the addition.

Sócrates: Sócrates Brasileiro Sampaio de Sousa Vieira de Oliveira (1954–), Brazilian footballer.

Il **Sodoma:** Giovanni Antonio Bazzi (1477–1549), It. painter. The artist may have gained his nickname, meaning "the sodomite," simply as a joke, but Giorgio Vasari, who disliked him, explained it as follows in his *Lives* (1530): "His manner of life was licentious and dishonorable, and as he always had boys and beardless youths about him of whom he was inordinately fond, this earned him the nickname of Sodoma; but instead of feeling shame, he gloried in it, writing stanzas and verses on it, and singing them to the accompaniment of the lute." The painter, who was married and had children, seemed ready enough to use the name and signed his pictures with it.

Moses **Sofer:** Moses ben Samuel Schreiber (1763–1839), Ger. rabbi. Moses Sofer, known as Hatam Sofer ("Seal of the Scribe"), was Rabbi of Pressburg (Bratislava) until his death, when he was succeeded by his son, Abraham Samuel Benjamin Wolf (1815–1871), known as Ketav Sofer ("Writing of the Scribe"), who was succeeded by his own son, Simnah Bunem (1842–1906), known as Shevet Sofer ("Pen of the Scribe"). Simnah Bunem's son, Akiba Sofer (1878–1959), known as Daat Sofer ("Opinion of the Scribe"), succeeeded his father in the Pressburg rabbinate but in 1940 settled in Jerusalem. Moses Sofer's family name, Schreiber, also means "scribe."

Grigory **Sokolnikov:** Grigory Yakovlevich Brilliant (1888–*c*.1939), Russ. revolutionary, politician, of Jewish origin.

Lydia **Sokolova:** Hilda Munnings (1896–1974), Eng. ballet dancer. The dancer was given her name by Diaghilev himself. He told her, "I have signed your photograph ... with the name Lydia Sokolova, and I hope you will live up to the name of Sokolova, as it is that of a great dancer in Russia" [Richard Buckle, *Dancing for Diaghilev: The Memoirs of Lydia Sokolova*, 1960]. The tribute was to Yevgenia Pavlovna Sokolova (1850–1925), one of the most famous Russian ballerinas of the 1870s and 1880s, and later a noted teacher. (Munnings studied under Pavlova, who had herself been one of Sokolova's pupils.)

El **Soldado:** Luis Castro Sandoval (1912–), Mexican bullfighter. The name means "the soldier." The matador was never actually a soldier, but liked to play at soldiers as a boy. The name was apt for his courage and prowess in the ring.

Stella **Soleil:** Stella Katsoudas (*c*.1970–), U.S. popular singer. A name combining a Latin star and a French sun. The singer first recorded as Sister Soleil.

Jean Pierre **Solié:** Jean Pierre Soulier (1755–1812), Fr. singer, cellist, composer. The musician perhaps wished to escape from a surname that literally means "shoe."

M. **Solitaire:** Woldemar Nürnberger (1818–1869), Ger. physician, short-story writer. All of the writer's works appeared under this name.

El **Solitario:** Serafín Estébanez Calderón (1799–1867), Sp. writer. The writer used this name, meaning "the solitary one," for newspaper articles published in Madrid from 1930.

Philippe **Sollers:** Philippe Joyaux (1936–), Fr. writer.

Madeleine **Sologne:** Madeleine Vouillon (1912–1995), Fr. movie actress.

Fyodor **Sologub:** Fyodor Kuzmich Teternikov (1863–1927), Russ. novelist, poet. The writer based his name on that of an admired literary namesake, Count Vladimir Aleksandrovich Sollogub (1813–1882), but dropped one "l."

Solomon: Solomon Cutner (1902–1988), Br. concert pianist, of Pol. Jewish origin. The pianist was the son of Harris Cutner, a master tailor, whose original name was Schneiderman. Solomon was a prodigy, billed as "Solomon" on first performing at the age of eight and retaining the name from then on.

Ikey **Solomons, Jr.:** William Makepeace Thackeray (1811–1863), Eng. novelist. Thackeray used this name for *Catherine: A Story*, published in *Fraser's Magazine* between May 1839 and February 1840. He took the name from an early 19th-century criminal, himself said to be the model for Fagin, the "very old shrivelled Jew" who is a receiver of stolen goods in Charles Dickens's *Oliver Twist* (1838–39).

Nikolay **Solovtsov:** Nikolay Nikolayevich Fyodorov (1857–1902), Russ. actor, theatrical director.

Inna **Solovyova:** Inna Natanovna Bezilevskaya (1927–), Russ. movie critic.

Vasily **Solovyov-Sedoy:** Vasily Pavlovich Solovyov (1907–1979), Russ. composer.

Ludwik **Solski:** Ludwik Napoleon Sosnowski (1855–1954), Pol. stage actor, producer.

[Sir] Georg **Solti:** György Stern (1912–1997), Br. conductor, music director, of Hung. Jewish origin.

Jane **Somers:** Doris Lessing (1919–), Eng. novelist. Long known under her real name, Lessing used this name for *The Diary of a Good Neighbour* (1983), her aim being to see if a novel could be published on its merits, instead of on an author's name and reputation. She initially submitted it to Jonathan Cape, who rejected it, but it was subsequently published by Michael Joseph. The ruse was revealed in an article in the *Sunday Times* (September 23, 1984).

Paul **Somers** *see* Andrew **Garve**

Suzanne **Somers:** Suzanne Mahoney (1946–), U.S. TV actress. The name is that of the actress's first husband, Bruce Somers.

Franca **Somigli:** Marin Bruce Clark (1901–1974), U.S.–It. opera singer.

Elke **Sommer:** Elke Schletz (1940–), Ger. movie actress, working in U.S.

Hans **Sommer:** Hans Friedrich August Zincken (1837–1922), Ger. composer. The composer sometimes anagrammatized his original name as "Neckniz."

S.P. **Somtow:** Somtow Papinian Sucharitkul (1952–), Thai writer, composer, moviemaker.

Sonderborg: Kurt R. Hoffmann (1923–), Dan.-Ger. painter. The artist adopted the name of his home town, the Danish port of Sonderborg, as his professional name.

Sonique: Sonia Clarke (1968–), Br. black pop singer. A neat adaptation, suggesting "sonic."

Sonny: Salvatore Bono (1935–1998), U.S. pop singer, teaming with **Cher**, his (one-time) wife.

A **Son of the Marshes** *see* Jean A. **Owen**

Henriette **Sontag:** Gertrud Walpurgis Sonntag (1806–1854), Ger. opera singer.

Sony Labour Tansi: Marcel Sony (1947–), Congolese playwright, novelist, writing in French.

Jack **Soo:** Goro Suzuki (1916–1979), Jap. movie actor, working in U.S.

Evangelinus Apostolides **Sophocles:** Evangelinus Apostolides (1805 or 1807–1883), Gk.-born U.S. scholar. The future professor of Greek was nicknamed "Little Sophocles" at school for his unusual talent and later in life he added the name of the ancient Greek poet to his own.

Kaikhosru Shapurji **Sorabji:** Leon Dudley Sorabji (1892–1988), Br. pianist, composer, writer on music, of mixed parentage. Many sources give the musician's original name as Leon Dudley, and at one time he signed himself thus. But his surname was always Sorabji, that of his Parsee father, Shapurji Sorabji, whose first name he adopted as a middle name, adding Kaikhosru as his own first name.

Soraya: Soraya Raquel Lamilla Cuevas (1969–2006), U.S. pop singer, of Colombian parentage.

Jean **Sorel:** Jean de Rochbrune (1934–), Fr. movie actor.

Tabitha **Soren:** Tabitha Sornberger (1967–), U.S. TV journalist.

Juan **Soriano:** Juan Francisco Rodríguez Montoya (1920–2006), Mexican artist. The painter adopted his grandmother's maiden name as his professional name.

Agnes **Sorma:** Martha Karoline Zaremba (1865–1927), Ger. stage actress.

Ann **Sothern:** Harriette Arlene Lake (1909–2001), U.S. stage, movie actress. The actress adopted her new name in 1933 at the start of her screen career, as there were already too many Lakes in Hollywood (though not yet Veronica **Lake**). She took her new first name from her mother and her surname from the actor Edward Hugh Sothern (1859–1933).

Alain **Souchon:** Alain Kienast (*c*.1950–), Fr. pop singer.

David **Soul:** David Solberg (1943–), U.S. pop singer, TV actor.

Jimmy **Soul:** James McCleese (1942–1988), U.S. black pop singer. The singer was nicknamed "Soul" by his congregations when a boy preacher.

Suzi **Soul** *see* Suzi **Quatro**

Sister **Souljah:** Lisa Williamson (1964–), U.S. black rapper, "raptivist." The name of the artist and community activist is a blend of "soul" and "soldier."

Soulja Slim: James Tapp (1927–2003), U.S. black "gangsta" rapper.

Sousandrade: Joaquim de Sousa Andrade (1833–1902), Brazilian poet.

Angel **South:** Lucien J. Gondron (1943–1998), U.S. blues-rock guitarist.

Joe **South:** Joe Souter (1940–), U.S. popular musician.

Theophilus **South:** Edward Chitty (1804–1863), Eng. lawyer, legal writer. The lawyer used this name for *The Fly-Fisher's Text-Book* (1841), a publication quite distinct from his professional work.

Jeri **Southern:** Genevieve Hering (1926–1991), U.S. popular singer.

Southside Johnny: John Lyon (1948–), U.S. rock musician. The musician doubtless took his name from jazz jargon, where "Southside" implies playing in small bands in unpromising or unattractive locations (like Chicago's South Side, with its swarming immigrant population). Lyon himself came from New Jersey.

Nathanael **Southwell:** Nathanael Bacon (1598–1676). Eng. Jesuit. priest, younger brother of Thomas **Southwell**.

Thomas **Southwell:** Thomas Bacon (1592–1637), Eng. Jesuit priest, elder brother of Nathanael **Southwell**.

Stephen **Southwold:** Stephen Henry Critten (1887–1964), Eng. novelist, short-story writer. The writer, who also used the name Neil Bell, kept this name for his children's fiction. It alludes to his birthplace, Southwold in Suffolk, and he adopted it legally. He also wrote as S.H. Lambert and Paul Martens.

E.D.E.N. **Southworth:** Emma Dorothy Eliza Southworth, née Nevitte (1819–1899), U.S. novelist. Named simply Emma at birth, the future writer was christened Emma Dorothy Eliza Nevitte in 1824 at the request of her dying father, so giving her the initials which she used as an author to disguise her sex. She first used the name in 1846, two years after separating from her husband (married 1840).

Boris **Souvarine:** Boris Lifschitz (1895–1984), Russ.-born Fr. Communist. The political activist, who was prominent in the foundation of the French Communist party, adopted the name of the Russian nihilist Souvarine in Emile Zola's novel *Germinal* (1885). He also used the name in the form Boris Souvart. Zola himself may have based his character's name on those of two real Russian revolutionaries, Bakunin and Kropotkin, as more obviously did **Ba Jin**.

Ernest **Souza** *see* Evelyn **Scott**

Gérard **Souzay:** Gérard Marcel Tisserand (1918–2004), Fr. concert, opera singer.

Ester **Sowerman:** ? (*fl.*1617), Eng. writer. The writer is known from *Ester hath hang'd Haman: Or*

An Answere To a Lewd Pamphlet, entitled, The Arraignment of Women. With the arraignment of lewd, idle, froward, and unconstant men, and Husbands (1617), a response to Joseph Swetman's pamphlet *The Arraignment of Lewde, idle, froward, and unconstant women: Or the vanitie of them, choose you whether* (1615). The identity of the (almost certainly female) author is unknown, but the adopted first name honors the biblical Esther, who saved the Jewish people in Persia from the attacks of Haman, while the surname puns on that of Swetman (i.e. Sweetman).

Bob B. Soxx: Robert Sheen (1943–), U.S. rock musician. A punning name based on the bobbysocks (ankle socks) formerly worn by teenage girls.

Raphael Soyer: Raphael Schoar (1899–1987), Russ.-born U.S. artist. Raphael's Jewish family changed their name on immigrating to the United States in 1912.

Sissy Spacek: Mary Elizabeth Spacek (1949–), U.S. movie actress. The actress retained her kid sister's pet name "Sissy," given her by her elder brothers, for her screen name.

Kevin Spacey: Kevin Spacey Fowler (1959–), U.S. movie actor, theatrical director.

Jack Spade: Elton Box (?–1981), Eng. songwriter + Desmond Cox (1903–1966), Eng. songwriter + Lewis **Ilda**. The three men used this name for their Cockney song "Your Baby 'As Gorn Dahn the Plug-'Ole" (1944) (U.S. version "Your Baby Has Gone Down the Drainpipe"), sung by Elsa **Lanchester** in *Ditties from the Ditty Box*.

Kate Spade: Katherine Brosnahan (1964–), U.S. fashion accessory designer. The name is that of the former fashion editor's husband, Andy Spade, with whom she started her business in 1991.

Mark Spade: Nigel Marlin Balchin (1908–1970), Br. novelist. The novelist used this name for his humorous contributions to *Punch*, collected in *How to Run a Bassoon Factory, or Business Explained* (1934) and *Pleasures of Business* (1935). The name itself suggests a reference to card-playing.

Lo Spagnoletto: Jusepe de Ribera (1591–1652), Sp. painter, working in Italy. The artist's Italian name means "the little Spaniard," referring to his small stature.

Georg Spalatin: Georg Burkhardt (1484–1545), Ger. humanist, writer. The writer took his name from his birthplace, Spalt, in southern Germany.

Keith Spalding: Karl Heinz Spalt (1913–2002), Ger.-born Br. lexicographer. The future professor fled to Vienna, then to England, when Hitler came to power in 1933. He adopted an English-style name in 1940 on joining the British Army following his internment as an alien on the outbreak of World War II, but was granted a British passport in 1946.

Hina Spani: Higinia Tuñón (1896–1969), Argentinian opera singer.

Tony Spargo: Antonio Sbarbaro (1897–1969), U.S. jazz drummer.

Ned Sparks: Edward A. Sparkman (1883–1957), Can. movie comedian, working in U.S.

Timothy Sparks: Charles Dickens (1812–1870), Eng. novelist. Dickens used this name for *Sunday Under Three Heads* (1836), a pamphlet attacking the Sunday Observance Legislation promoted in parliament by Sir Andrew Agnew. The "three heads" were *As it is; as Sabbath Bills would make it; as it might be made.* He had earlier published a story, "The Bloomsbury Christening" (1834), as Godfrey Sparks.

Phil Sparrow *see* Phil **Andro**

Spartakus: Karl Liebknecht (1871–1919), Ger. lawyer, Communist leader. The activist took his name from the Spartakusbund (Spartacus League), which he and others founded in 1916 as the nucleus of the German Communist Party. It was itself named for the 1st century BC Roman slave leader, Spartacus.

Bubba Sparxxx: Warren Anderson Mathis (1978–), U.S. (white) rapper. "When times were hard in Bubba's youth, he reveals, his family smuggled moonshine. The 'xxx' from Sparxxx is a nod to this: 'The three Xs on a batch of moonshine represents the most potent you can get.' 'Bubba,' by the way, is simple Southern slang for 'dude'—it was his nickname as a kid. And Sparks? 'That's cause I'm sparky with language; that's the hip hop bit'" [*The Times Magazine*, February 28, 2004].

[Sir] Edward Spears: Edward Louis Spiers (1886–1974), Eng. army officer. The future major-general altered the spelling of his name on marrying in 1918. The aim was to ensure its correct pronunciation, since his original name was frequently mispronounced as "Spires."

Speckled Red: Rufus G. Perryman (1892–1973), U.S. black jazz pianist, brother of **Piano Red**. The name is not simply a pun on the type of poultry. Like his brother, Perryman suffered from albinism and derived his performing name from its effects on his physical appearance.

Bud Spencer: Carlo Pedersoli (1929–), It. movie actor. Pedersoli would have needed an American-sounding name for the "spaghetti westerns" he played in.

John Spencer: John Speshock (1946–2005), U.S. TV actor, of Ir.-Cz. origin.

Bruno Sperani: Beatrice Speraz (1843–1923), It. novelist. The writer, professionally a journalist, used this name for educational stories for girls and tales of working-class life.

Speranza: [Lady] Jane Francesca Wilde, née Elgee (1826–1896), Ir. writer, literary hostess, mother of Oscar Wilde. The poverty of the 1840s in Ireland prompted Jane Elgee to write political poems and essays under this name to make her mark as a rebel poet. "She had always been uneasy about her first name, which was Jane, and had modified her second name [of Frances] … into Francesca, regarding the new name as a brilliant vestige of the Elgee family's [supposed] origins in Italy…. What signature to use became a complicated matter. To tradesmen or correspondents of no consequence, she signed herself Jane Wilde. But she had another forename as well, altogether of her own devising. This was Speranza. It was part of the motto with which her notepaper was embossed: *Fidanza, Speranza, Costanza* ["Faith, Hope, Constancy"]. She first used it for verses sent to the *Nation* in 1846, signing the covering letter with the male name "John Fanshawe Ellis" instead of "Jane Francesca Elgee" [Richard Ellmann, *Oscar Wilde*, 1987].

Early in her career, Jane Elgee somehow convinced herself that her Irish family name had evolved from the Italian name Algiati, and that this was itself a variant of the name of the Florentine poet Dante Alighieri (1265–1321), from whom she accordingly claimed descent.

Sperontes: Johann Sigismund Scholze (1705–1750), Ger. poet, musicologist.

Olga **Spessiva:** Olga Aleksandrovna Spesivtseva (1895–1991), Russ.-born U.S. ballet dancer. The ballerina mostly danced under her original name.

Mikey **Spice:** Michael Theophilus Johnson (1965–), Jamaican reggae musician.

Spike: Leslie David Gibbard (1945–), N.Z.-born Br. political cartoonist, motion-picture animator. The artist used this name for his occasional work as a freelance cartoonist after his arrival in London in 1967.

Mickey **Spillane:** Frank Morrison Spillane (1918–2006), U.S. crime writer

Spinifex *see* David **Martin**

Alice **Spinner:** Augusta Zelia Fraser, née Webb (?1868–1925), Sc. writer. Fraser used this name for some stories inspired by the West Indies, beginning with *A Study in Colour* (1891). There is a play on her maiden name, a "spinner" being an alternate (and etymologically related) name for a spider, which weaves a web, with perhaps a further suggestion of a "spinner" of tales.

Spondee: Royall Tyler (1757–1826), U.S. playwright, essayist, satirist, teaming with **Colon**. A spondee is a metrical foot of two long syllables, and as such is an apt name for a (satirical) verse writer.

Mark **Spoon:** Markus Löffel (1964–2006), Ger. rock musician. The creator of the style of electronic dance music known as "trance" adopted a name that

translated the German original. He was one half of the duo Jam & Spoon, the other half being Jam El Mar (real name Rolf Ellmer), who in 1991 under the pseudonyms Trancy Spacer and Spacy Trancer released the album *Disco 2001*.

Jack **Spot:** Jack Comer (1912–), Br. criminal, of Pol. Jewish parentage. The London gangster always gave his real name thus, but the true original may have been entirely different.

Spragga Benz: Carlton Errington Grant (1969–), Jamaican rock musician. The first half of the musician's first name alludes to his interest in ragga, the second half to the Mercedes Benz insignia that he dangled from his watch chain.

Tom **Spring:** Thomas Winter (1795–1851), Eng. boxer. The popular pugilist assumed his name after winning a fight in 1814. His praises were sung by the novelist George Borrow: "Hail to thee, Tom of Bedford, or by whatever name it may please thee to be called, Spring or Winter" (*Lavengro*, 1851).

Dusty **Springfield:** Mary Isobel Catherine Bernadette O'Brien (1939–1999), Br. pop singer, of Sc.-Ir. parentage, working in U.S. The singer was nicknamed "Dusty" as a tomboy teenager, playing football with the boys. She quit school in 1955, and originally joined a vocal trio called the Lana Sisters. In 1960 she teamed up with her brother Dion, later known as Tom, and a friend of his, Tim Feild, to form a folk trio known as the Springfields, supposedly because they originally strummed their guitars in a flowery field. Dusty and Tom then adopted the group's name as their new surname [Lucy O'Brien, *Dusty*, 1989].

Rick **Springfield:** Richard Lewis Springthorpe (1949–), Austral. rock musician, movie actor.

Alice **Springs:** June Brown (1923–), Austral. photographer. Originally an actress and a model for Helmut **Newton**, the artist adopted the name of the Australian town of Alice Springs.

Zeba **Sproule** *see* (Uncle) Simeon **Toby**

Mercurius **Spur:** Cuthbert Shaw (1739–1771), Eng. poet. The poet used this name for *The Race* (1766), in which the poets of the day were made to compete for pride of place by running a race. "Mercurius" of course suggests Mercury, the fleet-footed messenger of the gods in classical mythology, and "spur" is a sporting term associated with racing.

Clinton **Spurr** *see* Fenton **Brockley**

Spy: [Sir] Leslie Matthew Ward (1851–1922), Eng. caricaturist, portrait painter. The artist made many contributions to the topical illustrated magazine *Vanity Fair*, founded in 1868 as a periodical designed to "display the vanities of the week." Ward was asked to choose a pen name by the magazine's editor, Thomas Gibson Bowles, and is said to have done so by opening a copy of Dr. Johnson's *Dictionary* at random and selecting the first word his eye fell on. This was "spy," an apt name for one whose professional job was to "spy" on society and produce his observations in pictorial form. Other artists contributing to *Vanity Fair* were **Ape**, Sir Max Beerbohm (as "Ruth," "Sulto," and "Max"), and Walter Sickert (as "Sic"). Editor Bowles wrote as "Jehu Junior," a name kept by his successors until 1929, when the magazine closed [1. Leslie Ward, *Forty Years of "Spy,"* 1915; 2. John Arlott, "Ape, Spy, and Jehu Junior," in *Late Extra: A Miscellany by "Evening News" Writers, Artists, and Photographers, c.*1952].

Squibob: George Horatio Derby (1823–1861), U.S. humorist, satirist. The writer, professionally an army officer, was a noted perpetrator of practical jokes as well as a penner of satirical verse. He thus enjoyed "squibs," or verbal attacks. He "killed off" Squibob when another writer began using the name, and from then on wrote as John Phoenix.

Ronald Squire: Ronald Lancelot Squirl (1886–1958), Eng. stage, movie actor.

Sri Chinmoy: Chinmoy Kumar Ghose (1931–), Ind. guru, working in U.S. "Sri" is an honorific title.

Sri Sri: Srirangam Srinivasa Rao (1910–1983), Ind. movie songwriter.

Staccato: Alfred Kalisch (1863–1933), Eng. music critic, librettist. An appropriate musical name.

Lilian **Stacey:** Lili Szecsi (1892–1996), Hung. refugee. The name of the longlived diplomatic negotiator is an anglicized form of that of her husband, businessman Marius Szecsi, whom she married in 1912, subsequently saving his company from expropriation and securing his freedom. (He died in 1945.) She adopted it on escaping to England in 1956 at the time of the Hungarian Revolution. The new name is an approximate equivalent of the original, which would have actually sounded like "Saichy."

Robert **Stack:** Robert Langford Modini (1919–2003), U.S. movie, TV actor.

Maria **Stader:** Maria Nolnár (1911–), Hung.-born Swiss opera singer. The soprano took the name of her Swiss adoptive parents.

Kathy **Staff:** Minnie Higginbottom (1928–2008), Eng. TV actress. The actress took the name Katherine Grant in her early stage career, then kept the pet form of this first name as a TV actress, combining it with the surname of John Staff, her husband from 1951.

Frederick **Stafford:** Friedrich Frobl von Stein (1928–1979), Austr. movie actor. Some sources give the actor's original middle name as "Strobl."

Hanely **Stafford:** Alfred John Austin (1899–1968), U.S. radio actor.

Mary **Stafford:** Flora M. Mayor (1872–1931), Eng. novelist, short-story writer.

Jonathan **Stagge** *see* Q. **Patrick**

P.-J. **Stahl:** Pierre-Jules Hetzel (1814–1886), Fr. editor, publisher. Hetzel used this name for his editions of young people's fiction, such as a French adaptation of *The Swiss Family Robinson*, by the Swiss author J.W. Wyss, originally published in German in 1812.

Stainless Stephen: Arthur Clifford Baynes (1892–1971), Eng. music-hall comedian. The artist was born in Sheffield, a city long famed for its manufacture of stainless steel. As part of his act he wore a stainless steel dicky (false shirtfront) and a bowler hat with a stainless steel ribbon.

Stakka Bo: Johan Renck (1968–), Swe. rock musician.

Joseph **Stalin:** Iosif Vissarionovich Dzhugashvili (1879–1953). Russ. Communist leader, of Georgian origin. The notorious name took some time to evolve. Dzhugashvili was contributing to Bolshevik magazines such as *Zvezda* ("Star") under the names K.S. and K. Salin, for example, two or three years before Stalin itself first appeared (in 1913). Opinions are divided regarding the symbolic intention of the name. Russian *stal'* means "steel," and certainly, after repeated arrest, banishment, and imprisonment in czarist days, Dzhugashvili's spirit was unbroken, but it is unlikely that the name was given him by **Lenin**, as legend has it, because of his "steel-like" nature.

Another early favorite pseudonym of the Bolshevik activist was Koba, said to mean "fearless," and at one time he also used the name Kato, possibly alluding to the Roman statesman Cato the Elder. Other names used by the revolutionary were David Bars, Gayoz Nizheradze, I. Besoshvili, Zakhar Gregoryan Melikyants, Ogoness Vartanovich Totomyants, K. Solin (perhaps from Russian *sol'*, "salt"), and K. Stefin. Some of these names suggest his own original Georgian name [Robert Payne, *Stalin*, 1966].

There could, however, be more to the name than meets the eye: "'Dzhuga' is said to mean 'iron' in one of the Caucasian dialects, and he was possibly drawing on his original name" [Robert Conquest, *Stalin*, 1991].

William **Stallybrass:** William Teulon Swan Sonnenschein (1883–1948), Eng. academic, college principal, of Austr. descent. In 1917, at a time when German names were out of favor, the future chancellor of Oxford University adopted the surname of his great-grandfather, Rev. Edward Stallybrass. His father, publisher and writer William Swan Sonnenschein (1855–1931), also took the name then. Despite the change, friends and colleagues of William Stallybrass, Jr., regularly called him "Sonners," with the typical Oxford "-ers" suffix.

Anton **Stamitz:** Jan Antonín Stamic (1750–after 1789), Czech composer. The musician belonged to a family who settled in Germany and adopted the German form of their surname. Anton was the son of Johann Wenzel Stamitz (Jan Václav Antonín Stamic) (1717–1757), while his brother was Karl Stamitz (Karel Stamic) (1745–1801), the latter actually being born in Germany.

John **Standing:** [Sir] John Ronald Leon (1934–), Eng. stage, movie actor, son of Kay **Hammond**. The actor adopted his mother's maiden name as his stage name.

Burt L. **Standish:** William Gilbert Patten (1866–1945), U.S. writer of dime novels. Patten took this name in 1896 when he began to write the Frank Merriwell series of juvenile tales for *Tip Top Weekly.*

Stanelli: Edward Stanley de Groot (1895–1961), Ir. variety musician, comedian.

Yemilian **Stanev:** Nikola Stoyanov (1907–1979), Bulg. writer.

Agnes **Stanfield** *see* Ada **Clare**

Sally **Stanford:** Marcia Busby (1903–1982), U.S. madam, mayor, restaurant owner. Following her separation in 1929 from her fourth husband, attorney Ernest Spagnoli, Marcia Spagnoli opened a brothel in San Francisco. To spare her ex-husband any embarrassment, she changed her name to Sally Stanford, taking "Sally" from a popular song of the day and "Stanford" from a newspaper headline reporting that Stanford had beaten California in a college football game.

Konstantin **Stanislavsky:** Konstantin Sergeyevich Alekseyev (1865–1938), Russ. stage actor, director, teacher. The actor took his new name in 1885: "It was because of the unsavory atmosphere at some of the vaudeville performances with which he became associated that Constantin Sergeyevich Alexeiev ... decided it would be wiser to conceal his identity from the public. He therefore assumed the name of Stanislavsky, which had belonged to a young amateur whom he had once known and who had stopped playing. He thought that such a Polish-sounding name would be a complete disguise" [Christine Edwards, *The Stanislavsky Heritage*, 1965].

M. **Stanitsky:** Avdotya Yakovlevna Panayeva (1819–1893), Russ. writer. The author used this male name for two novels written jointly with the poet Nikolay Nekrasov, as well as alone.

Viktor **Stanitsyn:** Viktor Yakovlevich Gëze (1897–?), Russ. actor, theatrical director.

[Sir] Albert **Stanley:** Albert Henry Knattriess (1874–1948), Br. transport chief. The future head of the London Passenger Transport Board emigrated as a small child with his family to the USA, where his father changed their surname to Stanley.

Arthur **Stanley:** Arthur Stanley Megaw (?–1961), Ir. lawyer, writer.

Florence **Stanley:** Florence Schwartz (1924–2003), U.S. stage, movie actress.

[Sir] Henry Morton **Stanley:** John Rowlands (1841–1904), Welsh-born U.S. journalist, African explorer. The explorer was the illegitimate son of John Rowlands and Elizabeth Parry, who sent him to be educated in a workhouse. In 1856 he resolved to end his crude schooling and worked his way on shipboard from Liverpool to New Orleans, where he was befriended by a merchant, Henry Hope Stanley, whose first and last names he took as his own, subsequently adding "Morton."

Kim **Stanley:** Patricia Kimberly Reid (1925–2001), U.S. stage, movie actress.

Paul **Stanley:** Paul Stanley Eisen (1950–), U.S. rock musician.

Phyllis **Stanley:** Phyllis Knapman (1914–), Eng. stage actress, singer, dancer. The actress took her new surname from the first name of her father, Stanley Evans Knapman.

Wynn **Stanley:** Worton David (1874–1940), Br. songwriter.

Frank **Stanmore:** Francis Henry Pink (1878–1943), Br. movie actor.

Coralie **Stanton:** Alice Cecil Seymour Hosken, née Keay (1877–?), Eng. novelist.

John **Stanton** *see* Christopher **Beck**

Robert **Stanton** *see* Kirby **Grant**

Vance **Stanton** *see* Ed **Noon**

Barbara **Stanwyck:** Ruby Katherine Stevens (1907–1990), U.S. movie, TV actress. The actress was given her new name by producer Willard Mack when he cast her for the stage play *The Noose* (1926). "Ruby Stevens is no name for an actress," he told her. He got the name from an old theater program, which listed Jane Stanwyck in Clyde Fitch's play *Barbara Frietchie* (1899) [Jane Ellen Wayne, *Stanwyck*, 1986].

Jean **Stapleton:** Jeanne Murray (1923–), U.S. movie, TV actress.

Jean **Star** *see* **Heldau**

Alvin **Stardust:** Bernard William Jewry (1942–), Eng. rock singer. The singer began his career under the name Shane Fenton, originally the stage name of pop singer Johnny Theakston (1944–1961). Later, he took his regular name from his favorite performers, Elvis Presley and Gene **Vincent**, adding "Stardust" both because he thought it more "1974" and to match Gary **Glitter**.

Starhawk: Miriam Simos (1951–), U.S. peace activist, witch, feminist, of Jewish parentage.

Cootie **Stark:** Johnny Miller (1927–2005), U.S. black blues musician. Miller's new surname was that of his stepfather, John Henry Stark. His new first name was a childhood nickname.

Richard **Stark:** Donald E. Westlake (1933–2008), U.S. crime writer. Westlake adopted this name for 20 novels featuring the criminal, Parker, published between 1962 and 1974. Altogether he used 11 pseudonyms, each with a different persona. As he recounted: "When I was in my twenties and thirties I churned out four to six books a year.... Publishers hate it when writers do that much. Another reason is branding. Different aliases write different books. 'Richard Stark' does all the cold emotionless stuff for me. 'Tucker Coe' writes heavy purple prose. And 'Westlake' tends to skitter around on top of the pond" [*The Times*, June 23, 2005]. *See also* J. Morgan **Cunningham**.

Barbara **Starke** *see* Patricia **Wentworth**

Edwin **Starr:** Charles Edwin Hatcher (1942–2003), U.S. black soul singer, working in U.K. The singer is said to have taken his new name when his manager in Detroit prophesied, "Kid, one day you're gonna be a star!"

Freddie **Starr:** Frederick Leslie Fowell (1943–), Eng. TV, movie entertainer. The comedian is said to have changed his name because his friends kept calling him "Foul Freddie."

Kay **Starr:** Katherine LaVerne Starks (1922–), U.S. popular radio singer.

Kenny **Starr:** Kenneth Trebbe (1953–), U.S. pop singer.

Marilyn **Starr:** Kathryn Gannon (1969–), Br. porno movie actress.

Ringo **Starr:** Richard Starkey (1940–), Eng. pop musician. The future Beatles drummer changed his name in 1961, when appearing with Rory **Storm** at Butlin's holiday camp, Skegness, Lincolnshire. "Up till then he'd been occasionally called Rings. He'd got his first ring on his 16th birthday from his mother.... By the age of 20 he was wearing up to four rings. His surname was abbreviated to Starr at Butlins so they could announce his solo drumming spot as Star Time. Rings naturally became Ringo, as it sounded better with a one-syllable surname" [Hunter Davies, *The Beatles*, 1968].

Roland **Starr** *see* Fenton **Brockley**

Ruby **Starr:** Constance Mierzwiak (1949–1995), U.S. country singer.

Lovebug **Starski:** Keven Smith (1961–), U.S. black DJ, rapper. The artist took his name from the popular TV cop show *Starsky and Hutch* (1975).

Grigory **Stary:** Grigory Ivanovich Borisov (1880–1937), Russ. Communist official. The revolutionary's adopted name means "old," presumably in some symbolic sense.

Antal **Stašek:** Antonin Zeman (1843–1931), Cz. writer.

Dakota **Staton:** Aliya Rabia (1932–), U.S. popular singer.

Vargo **Statten:** John Russell Fearn (1908–1960), Eng. SF writer.

Schuyler **Staunton** *see* Floyd **Akers**

Vladimir **Stavsky:** Vladimir Petrovich Kirpichnikov (1900–1943), Russ. writer.

Lorenzo **Stecchetti:** Olindo Guerrini (1845–1916), It. poet. The poet used this name for his collection of verse *Postuma* ("Posthumous") (1877), purportedly written by a cousin who had died of consumption. The work's explicitly erotic and blasphemous content caused something of a scandal.

Maggie **Steed:** Margaret Baker (1946–), Eng. movie, TV actress.

Byron **Steel** *see* David **Keith**

Dawn **Steel:** Dawn Spielberg (1946–1997), U.S. movie producer, studio chief. Spielberg's father was an amateur weightlifter, who changed the family name to Steel "to highlight his athletic prowess and (as he saw it) to remove any potentially damaging ethnic taint" [*The Times*, December 24, 1997].

Bob **Steele:** Robert North Bradbury, Jr. (1907–1988), U.S. movie actor. The actor took his screen name from the cowboy character he played in *The Mojave Kid* (1927).

Tommy **Steele:** Thomas Hicks (1936–), Eng. pop singer, stage, movie actor. Hicks was signed up in 1956 by two young promoters, Larry Parnes and John Kennedy, under the name of Tommy Steele. Steele devised his own stage name, although Parnes himself created the names of subsequent discoveries such as Vince **Eager**, Georgie **Fame**, Billy **Fury**, Johnny **Gentle**, Dicky **Pride**, and Marty **Wilde**. "Tommy Steele and Marty Wilde were the first of Parnes' protégés. When Larry recruited new members to his stable of stars, he always preferred to give them new names. He worked on the principal [*sic*] of finding a dynamic rock 'n' roll surname — such as Wilde and Steele — but a homely Christian name" [Vince Eager, *Vince Eager's Rock n' Roll Files*, 2007].

Paul **Stefan:** Paul Stefan-Grünfeldt (1879–1943), Austr. music critic, scholar, working in U.S.

Stefán frá Hvítadal: Stefán Sigurdsson (1887–1933), Icelandic poet. The poet's adopted name means "Stefán of Hvítadal," denoting his birthplace.

Joey **Stefano:** Nicholas Anthony Iacona, Jr. (1968–1994), U.S. porno movie actor.

Steffani: Frederick William Wisker (1904–1974), Br. boys' choir presenter. Wisker founded the Silver Songsters in 1933 and after their demise in 1947 became the manager of Ronnie **Ronalde**.

Teodor **Steffens:** Karl Helmut Dammas (1816–1885), Ger. novelist, poet, composer.

Steinn **Steinarr:** Aðalsteinn Kristmundsson (1908–1958), Icelandic poet.

Saul **Steinberg:** Saul Jacobson (1914–1998), Rom.-born U.S. cartoonist, illustrator. A substitution of one Jewish name for another, or perhaps of a generally German name for a more obviously Jewish one.

Charles Proteus **Steinmetz:** Karl August Rudolf Steinmetz (1865–1923), Ger.-born U.S. electrical engineer. The electrical pioneer immigrated to the U.S. in 1889 and anglicized his first name at this time, simultaneously replacing his two middle names by "Proteus." This was "a nickname that had been bestowed on him by his university classmates in Breslau to honor his abilities and versatility" [Joseph D. Zund in Garraty and Carnes, vol. 20, p. 643].

Henry Engelhard **Steinway:** Heinrich Engelhard Steinweg (1797–1871), Ger. piano manufacturer, working in U.S. The master piano-maker part-anglicized his name after immigrating to the United States in 1850 with his wife, three daughters, and four of his six sons.

Yury **Steklov:** Yury Mikhaylovich Nakhamkis (1873–1941), Russ. revolutionary, historian.

Stelarc: Stelios Arcadiou (1946–), Austral. performance artist, of Gk. origin.

Stella: (1) Esther Johnson (1681–1738), Eng. letter writer, correspondent of Jonathan Swift; (2) Estella Anna Lewes (1824–1880), U.S. author. Swift used this name to address Esther Johnson through his *Journal to Stella* (1710–13). The name, Latin for "star," hints at "Esther," itself popularly derived from a Persian word also meaning "star." For Lewes the name was even closer to her first name. Because of its propitious meaning, the name has been used by other writers. In the poetry of Sir Philip Sidney, "Stella," in the sonnet sequence *Astrophel and Stella* (1591), was Penelope Rich (c.1562–1607), sister of the Earl of Essex. "Astrophel" was Sidney himself. The latter name, significantly here, means "star lover." (It is more subtle than it seems. If "Philip Sidney" is abbreviated as "Phil. Sid." and taken to stand for "Philosidus," from Greek *philo-* "loving," and Latin *sidus*, "star," it only remains to devise a fully Greek equivalent, from Greek *astron*, "star," and *-phil*, "lover," to give "Astrophel.")

Georg Wilhelm **Steller:** Georg Wilhelm Stöller (1709–1746), Ger. naturalist, explorer.

Anna **Sten:** Annel (or Anjuschka) Stenska Sujakevich (1908–1993), Ukr.-born U.S. movie actress, of Swe.-Ukr. parentage.

Stendhal: Marie-Henri Beyle (1783–1842), Fr. novelist. This is the best-known pseudonym of the many used by the writer. He adopted it in 1817 from the small Prussian town of Stendal, the birthplace of Johann Joachim Winckelmann (1717–1768), an ad-

mired German archaeologist and art historian, and first used it for his travel account *Rome, Naples et Florence* (1817–26). (He added an "h" to make it look more German.) Altogether Stendhal had around 200 pen names, many of them Italian. They include: Dominique, Salviati, Cotonnet, Chamier, Baron de Cutendre, William Crocodile, Lizio, and Viscontini. For his first book, *Vies de Haydn, de Mozart et de Métastase* (1814), Beyle wrote as L.-A.-C. Bombet. (For the third composer in this title, *see* Pietro **Metastasio.**) For his autobiography, published posthumously (1890), he was Henri Brûlard, alluding to his passion (French *brûler*, "to burn").

Steno: Stefano Vanzina (1915–1988), It. movie director, screenwriter. Although obviously deriving from his first name, the writer's pseudonym also suggests "writing" itself, from the Greek element found in such words as "stenographer."

Curt **Stenvert:** Curt Steinwendner (1920–1992), Austr. photographer.

Stephan G. **Stephansson:** Stefán Guðmundarson (1853–1927), Icelandic-born Can. poet. The poet emigrated with his family to North America in 1873, settling as a farmer in Markerville, Alberta, in 1889 but always writing in Icelandic.

Stephen IX: Frederick of Lorraine (c.1000–1058), Fr. pope. The pope took the name of St. Stephen, on whose feastday (August 2, 1057) he was elected.

Martin **Stephens:** Martin Angel Keller (1948–), Br. juvenile movie actor.

Richie **Stephens:** Richard Stephenson (1966–), Jamaican reggae musician.

Tanya **Stephens:** Tanya Stephenson (1974–), Jamaican DJ, reggae singer.

Henry **Stephenson:** Henry Stephenson Garroway (1871–1956), Br. stage, movie actor, working in U.S. The actor's stage name, his own middle name, originated as his mother's maiden name.

Stepnyak: Sergey Mikhaylovich Kravchinsky (1851–1895), Russ. revolutionary, writer. The writer's name, which he later joined to his original name (as Stepnyak-Kravchinsky), means "Son of the Steppe."

Yakov **Stepovoy:** Yakov Stepanovich Yakimenko (1883–1921), Ukr. composer.

Ford **Sterling:** George Ford Stitch (or Stich) (1883–1939), U.S. stage, movie comedian.

Jan **Sterling:** Jane Sterling Adriance (1921–2004), U.S. movie actress. The actress began her screen career in 1947 under the name Jane Adrian.

Jessica **Sterling** *see* Robert **Crawford**

Richard **Sterling:** Albert G. Leggatt (1880–1959), U.S. stage actor.

Robert **Sterling:** William John Hart (1917–), U.S. movie actor.

Adolf **Stern:** Adolf Ernst (1835–1907), Ger. writer. A simple anagram converted Ernst ("serious") into Stern ("star").

Carola **Stern:** Erika Asmuss (1925–2006), Ger. writer, human rights campaigner. The writer's work as a political commentator obliged her to publish anonymously, signing articles with simply an asterism. This gave her later regular name, from German *Stern*, "star."

Daniel **Stern:** Marie Catherine Sophie de Flavigny, Comtesse d'Agoult (1805–1876), Fr. writer. The writer was the mistress of Liszt and in 1846 published her novel *Nélida*, based on her relations with him. Its title is an anagram of her new first name, rationalized as follows: "The first name was probably an allusion to the biblical story of Daniel surviving among the lions, just as she would have to survive in Paris. The last name of her new persona can be seen as a reference to the belief in protective forces (*Stern* is the German word for star). Marie continued to hope that she might have a lucky star to watch over her, as in her happy days in Italy" [Richard Bolster, *Marie d'Agoult: The Rebel Countess*, 2000].

G.B. **Stern:** Gladys Bertha Stern (1890–1973), Eng. writer, of Jewish descent. The writer later changed her middle name to Bronwyn but was known in her writing career as G.B. Stern and to her friends as "Peter." In 1919 she married a New Zealander, Geoffrey Holdsworth.

Karl **Stern:** Julia Daudet (1844–1940), Fr. poet, essayist. The writer used this male name for critical articles.

Otto **Stern:** Luise Otto-Peters (1819–1895), Ger. feminist writer.

Paul Frederick **Stern:** Paul Frederick Ernst (1899–1985), U.S. SF writer. The writer had a surname that readily lent itself to apt anagrammatization. Compare the name of Adolf **Stern.**

Stuart **Stern** *see* Robert **Crawford**

Stuart **Sterne:** Gertrude Bloede (1845–1945), Ger.-born U.S. poet. "She used this pen name in all of her published works, claiming as the reason that men's work was considered stronger than women's, and she wished her work to stand or fall on its own merits" [Ann Perkins in Garraty and Carnes, vol. 3, p. 41].

Stesichorus: Teisias (*c.*632–*c.*556 BC), Gk. lyric poet. The poet came to be known by his nickname, meaning "choir setter."

Stet: Thomas Earle Welby (1881–1933), Br. journalist, essayist, literary critic. The writer adopted the proofreader's instruction meaning "let it stand" as used for a deleted word or passage that should remain undeleted after all.

Cat **Stevens:** Steven Demetri Giorgiou (1948–), Br. folk-rock musician, of Gk. Cypriot/Swe. parentage. The singer and songwriter took his stage name from a form of his original first name preceded by a nickname given him by a girlfriend, who told him his eyes were feline. In 1976 he converted to Islam, ceased recording, and changed his name yet again to Yusuf Islam. Some 30 years later, however, he tentatively resumed recording under the simple name Yusuf.

"Cat Stevens has returned to pop as 'Yusuf.' But why doesn't his adopted surname of Islam also grace his CD covers? 'I found it awkward when I read articles with people referring to me as Islam,' he says. '"Islam says this and Islam says that." That's quite a responsibility. I haven't got shoulders big enough for that, so I thought, let's stick with first-name terms'" [*The Times*, June 16, 2009].

Connie **Stevens:** Concetta Rosalie Ann Ingolia (1938–), U.S. movie actress, of It.-Eng.-Ir. descent.

Craig **Stevens:** Gail Shekles, Jr. (1918–2000), U.S. movie actor.

Dodie **Stevens:** Geraldine Ann Pasquale (1947–), U.S. popular singer, movie actress.

Fisher **Stevens:** Steven Fisher (1963–), U.S. stage, movie, TV actor.

Francis **Stevens:** Gertrude Bennett, née Barrows (1884–?1939), U.S. SF, fantasy writer.

Inger **Stevens:** Inger Stensland (1934–1970), Swe.-born U.S. movie, TV actress.

J.D. **Stevens** *see* Fenton **Brockley**

K.T. **Stevens:** Gloria Wood (1919–1994), U.S. movie actress.

Margaret Dean **Stevens:** Bess Streeter Aldrich (1881–1954), U.S. novelist, short-story writer. Aldrich used her name down to 1918 for stories published in such popular magazines as *Colliers*, *Saturday Evening Post*, and *McCall's*. She explained: "In a sort of foolish fashion (ostrich-like) I hid behind the pen name of Margaret Dean Stevens for several years. It was a combination of my grandmother's names. I felt a timidity in having my stuff read — the typical amateur's print-fright, which is the writer's stage-fright" [Marble, p.208].

Onslow **Stevens:** Onslow Ford Stevenson (1902–1977), U.S. stage, movie actor.

Ray **Stevens:** Ray Ragsdale (1941–), U.S. country-pop writer, performer.

Risë **Stevens:** Risë Steenberg (1913–), U.S. opera singer. of Norw. parentage.

Shakin' **Stevens:** Michael Barratt (1948–), Welsh-born Br. pop singer. "Sharnalee De Silva, aged 13, of St. Albans, asks Shakin' Stevens 'What is your real name?' Shakin' replies: 'I think it's much nicer that everyone knows me as Shakin' Stevens which is now my real name. I used to play baseball in the street and one of my friends used to pick up the bat and say, "Ladies and gentlemen — Shakin' Stevens!" His name *was* Stevens. When I got into this business I thought of the guy and thought of his name and decided to use it. He can't sing, so he's quite happy'" [*Radio Times*, August 8–14, 1981]. The singer rebranded himself in the 1990s as simply "Shaky."

Stella **Stevens**: Estelle Eggleston (1936–), U.S. movie actress.

Stu **Stevens**: Wilfred Pierce (*c.*1937–), Eng. country musician.

Juliet **Stevenson**: Juliet Anne Virginia Stevens (1956–), Br. stage, movie actress.

Stevo: Steven Pearse (1962–), Eng. DJ, pop music entrepreneur.

Douglas **Stewart**: Edward Askew Sothern (1926–1981), Eng. actor. The actor used this stage name when first appearing in the provinces.

Ed **Stewart**: Edward Stewart Mainwaring (1941–), Eng. radio DJ, TV personality.

Elaine **Stewart**: Elsy Steinberg (1929–), U.S. movie actress.

Jon **Stewart**: Jonathan Stewart Leibowitz (1962–), U.S. TV talk-show host.

Marjorie **Stewart** *see* Simon **Dare**

Martha **Stewart**: Martha Haworth (1922–), U.S. movie actress, singer.

Michael **Stewart**: Michael Rubin (1924–1987), U.S. popular composer, lyricist.

Paul **Stewart**: Paul Sternberg (1908–1986), U.S. movie actor.

Jan **Stewer**: Albert John Coles (1876–?), Eng. dialect writer. The writer was born and bred in Devon, in the West Country, and adopted a name from the local ballad "Widdicombe Fair," where it is that of one of the villagers who borrowed Tom Pearse's gray mare to ride to the fair: "For I want for to go to Widdicombe Fair, / Wi' Bill Brewer, Jan Stewer, Peter Gurney, Peter Davey, Dan'l Whiddon, Harry Hawk, / Old Uncle Tom Cobbleigh and all." (The names are those of real people, and there is still an annual fair at Widecombe in the Moor, as it is now known.) Compare the name of Tom **Cobbleigh**.

Georg **Stiernhielm**: Jöran Olofsson (1598–1672), Swe. poet, scholar.

Julia **Stiles**: Julia O'Hara (1981–), U.S. movie actress. "One of the family's quirkier traits was to give Stiles her mother's maiden name as a surname (her father's, O'Hara, is her middle name); her 13-year-old sister has it the other way around. 'My brother, who is 11, had to be O'Hara too, to carry on the family name,' she says" [*Sunday Times*, March 28, 2004].

Karl **Stille**: Hermann Demme (1760–1822), Ger. poet, novelist.

Eterio **Stinfalico**: Alessandro Marcello (1684–1750), It. violinist, composer. The musician adopted this as his Arcadian name (see Aglauro **Cidonia**). The second name relates to Lake Stymphalia, near Corinth, Greece, associated in legend with the man-eating Stymphalian birds killed by Hercules.

Sting: (1) Gordon Matthew Sumner (1951–), Eng. rock singer, songwriter; (2) Steve Borden (1959–), U.S. wrestler. The musician acquired his name by way of a school nickname, referring not only to his "buzzing" energy but also to a black and yellow hooped T-shirt that he habitually wore. Borden originally wrestled as Flash before changing his ring name to Sting.

Jessica **Stirling**: Hugh C. Rae (1936–), Br. romantic novelist. The writer was advised by his publisher that women would more readily read his novels if they thought they were written by a female author.

Max **Stirner**: Johann Kaspar Schmidt (1806–1856), Ger. philosopher, translator.

Wilhelmina **Stitch**: Ruth Collie (1889–1936), Br. writer of sentimental verse.

Sonny **Stitt**: Edward Boatner (1924–1982), U.S. black jazz saxophonist. The musician adopted his stepfather's name.

Alan **Stivell**: Alan Cochevelou (1944–), Fr. folk musician. The musician's name is based on a Breton word meaning "spring," "fountain."

Anne **Stobbs**: Anne Mary Brice Latham (1922–2008), Br. writer.

Leopold **Stokowski**: Leopold Stokowski (1882–1977), Br. orchestral conductor, of Pol.-Ir. parentage, working in U.S. The conductor is sometimes said to have been born with the English name of Stokes, and his obituary notice in *The Times* mentioned that his father had so anglicized his name but that in 1905, when first working in the U.S., he had preferred to be known by his Polish name. A few days later the paper printed the following correction: "We have been asked to point out that Leopold Stokowski was registered at birth under that name and not under that of Stokes: and that, similarly, he studied at the Royal College of Music under the name of Stokowski" [*The Times*, September 24, 1977]. (Stokowski's *Who's Who* entry gives his full name as Leopold Boleslawowicz Stanislaw Antoni Stokowski, his father as Boleslaw Kopernik Stokowski, and his grandfather as Leopold Stokowski. The first of his three wives, married 1911, divorced 1923, was Olga **Samaroff**.)

[Sir] Oswald **Stoll**: Oswald Gray (1866–1942), Eng. theater manager. The impresario's mother was widowed when the boy was only three years old, but remarried when he was 13 and gave her son the name of her new Danish husband, John George Stoll.

Rosine **Stoltz**: Victoire Noël (1815–1903), Fr.

opera singer. The mezzosoprano adopted a form of her mother's maiden name of Stoll.

Teresa Stolz: Terezie Stolzová (1834–1902), Cz. opera singer.

Cliffie Stone: Clifford Gilpin Snyder (1917–1998), U.S. country musician.

George E. Stone: George Stein (1903–1967), Pol. movie actor, working in U.S. German (Jewish) *Stein* in an original name is often anglicized as "Stone," as here and in several of the names below.

Hampton Stone: Aaron Marc Stein (1906–1985), U.S. mystery writer. The author also wrote as George Bagby, perhaps adopting the real name of the humorist Mozis **Addums.**

Harold J. Stone: Harold Hochstein (1913–2005), U.S. movie actor.

I.F. Stone: Isidor Feinstein (1907–1989), U.S. journalist, newspaper owner, of Russ. Jewish parentage. Concern about rising anti–Semitism led Feinstein, as chief editorial writer of the *New York Post*, to adopt his new name in 1937, forming it from the initials of his original name with "Stein" recast as "Stone."

Irving Stone: Irving Tennenbaum (1903–1989), U.S. fictional biographer. The writer legally adopted the surname of his stepfather.

Joss Stone: Joscelyn Eve Stoker (1987–), Br. (white) soul singer, werking in U.S. The singer took her new name in 2002 for a U.S. contract. "Joss Stone is who I am on stage, and she's more confident than me, and has bigger hair and a bigger personality" [*The Times Magazine*, September 4, 2004].

Lesley Stone *see* Elleston **Trevor**

Lew Stone: Louis Steinberg (1898–1969), Br. bandleader, composer, arranger, of Jewish parentage.

Philip Stone: Philip Stones (1924–2003), Eng. stage, movie, TV actor.

Sly Stone: Sylvester Stewart (1944–), U.S. black rock musician.

Stoneclink: [Rev.] Thomas F. Dale (?–1923), Eng. sporting writer. The writer used this name for articles in the country sports magazine *The Field*.

Stonehenge: John Henry Walsh (1810–1888), Eng. sporting writer. The ancient monument of Stonehenge, on Salisbury Plain, Wiltshire, was a popular venue for hunting and riding in Victorian times. The surrounding area is now largely owned by the army, although local hunts still have the right to hold their meets there on specified occasions. Walsh first used the name for *The Greyhound: being a treatise on the Art of Breeding, Rearing, and Training Greyhounds for Public Running, their Diseases and Treatment* (1853), which long remained the standard textbook on the subject. From 1857 to the end of his life he was editor of the country sports magazine *The Field*.

[Sir] Tom Stoppard: Tomáš Straussler (1937–), Cz.-born Br. dramatist, theater critic. When the future playwright was nine years old, his mother remarried, and he took his new name from his stepfather, Major Kenneth Stoppard. Stoppard used the name William Boot for early pieces as a drama critic when writing for the magazine *Scene* (1962), taking it from the nature columnist hero of Evelyn Waugh's novel *Scoop* (1938). As a dramatist he also used the name Boot for several characters in his plays, often complemented by another character called Moon. His TV play *This Way Out with Samuel Boot* (1964) actually featured a *pair* of Boots, representing contrary attitudes toward material possessions.

Gale Storm: Josephine Owaissa Cottle (1922–2009), U.S. movie, TV actress, singer. Cottle was still in high school when she won a "Gateway to Hollywood" radio contest. She came to Hollywood on graduating and had her name changed there in the customary "Gateway" manner.

Lesley Storm: Mabel Margaret Clark, née Cowie (1904–1975), Sc. novelist, playwright.

Rory Storm: Alan Caldwell (1941–1972), Br. pop singer. The singer tried out the name Jet Storme early on in his career, then settled for a more plausible Rory Storm.

Sydney A. Story, Jr. *see* Mary **Langdon**

Harry Duffield Stovey: Harry Duffield Stow (1856–1937), U.S. baseball player. When Harry's mother forbade him to play professional baseball because players were (in her view) notorious hard-drinking rowdies, he had his name put in the newspapers as "Stovey" instead of "Stow."

Lyudmil Stoyanov: Georgi Stoyanov Zlatarov (1886–1973), Bulg. writer. The writer based his pen name on that of his father, Stoyan Zlatarov, whose first name already formed his patronymic (middle name).

Izzy Stradlin: Jeffrey Isbell (1962–), U.S. rock guitarist. Presumably a punning nickname gave this name.

Mary Strafford: Flora Macdonald Mayor (1872–1932), Eng. novelist. The writer used this name not only for her writing but for a short-lived career in her early thirties as an actress.

Edward Strahan: Earl Shinn (1838–1886), U.S. art critic. Shinn adopted this pseudonym as principal art critic for the *Nation* to protect "his father's revered name." (Earl Shinn, Sr., had written regularly on Quaker matters and his son did not wish to embarrass him posthumously by linking their name with the visual arts.)

Mark Straker: Mark Williams (1956–), Eng. movie, TV actor.

Herbert Strang: George Herbert Ely (1866–

1958), Eng. children's writer + Charles James L'Estrange (1867–1947), Eng. children's writer. The two men were staff members of the Oxford University Press, writing adventure stories and historical novels for boys in the first three decades of the 20th century. Their joint name is extracted from their real names, as can be seen. They also wrote for girls under the not very original name of Mrs. Herbert Strang.

Joseph **Strange** *see* John **Dangerfield**

Michael **Strange:** Blanche Marie Louise Oelrichs (1890–1950), U.S. actress, poet. The actress took this name for her writing. Her second husband (married 1920, divorced 1928) was John **Barrymore.**

[Sir] Robert **Strange:** Robert Strang (1721–1792), Sc. line engraver. The artist preserved what he liked to believe was the original form of the family name.

Steve **Strange:** Stephen John Harrington (1959–), Welsh rock singer. The singer was given his name by a postman: "I was living in West Hampstead [London] and my hair was white and cut spiky on top. The other girl [*sic*] I was living with, Suzy, also had white hair and so the postman used to call us Mr. and Mrs. Strange. The name just stuck" [*Observer Colour Supplement*, August 22, 1982].

Joyce **Stranger:** Joyce Muriel Wilson, née Judson (1924–), Eng. writer of animal stories for children.

Lee **Strasberg:** Israel Strassberg (1901–1982), Austr.-born U.S. theatrical director, movie actor.

Teresa **Stratas:** Anastasia Stratakis (1938–), Can. opera singer, of Gk. parentage.

Christine **Strathern:** Agnes Brysson Inglis Morrison (1903–1986), Sc. novelist, biographer. The writer adopted this pen name for her romances. Strath Earn is is the name of the valley of the Earn River near Perth, Scotland.

Dorothy **Stratten:** Dorothy Ruth Hoogstratten (1960–1980), Can. movie actress, model.

L.B. **Stratten:** Louise B. Hoogstratten (1969–), U.S. movie actress.

Eugene **Stratton:** Eugene Augustus Rühlmann (1861–1918), U.S.-born music-hall dancer, singer, of Alsatian parentage, working in U.K. The dancer began his career under the name Master Jean. He then joined a blackface group called the Four Arnolds, but decided that he was not an Arnold and instead took the name of Stratton, suggested by a fellow dancer.

Trish **Stratus:** Patricia Stratigias (1976–), Can. fitness model, TV personality.

Oscar **Straus:** Oskar Strauss (1870–1954), Austr.-born Fr. composer. The operetta composer dropped one "s" from his name so as not to be confused with the famous Strauss family of musicians.

Col. D. **Streamer:** [Captain] Harry Graham (1874–1936), Br. writer of light verse. The author joined the Coldstream Guards in 1895. Hence his punning pen name, which he used for his first and best-known work, *Ruthless Rhymes for Heartless Homes* (1899), as well as for three later collections of verse.

Meryl **Streep:** Mary Louise Streep (1949–), U.S. movie actress. The actress firmly rejected her first agent's pleas for her to change her name to "Merle Street," although she did blend her first two names into a single "Meryl."

Paul Patrick **Streeten:** Paul Patrick Hornig (1917–), Austr.-born Br. economist. The writer changed his Germanic name to an English one in 1943, under the Army Council Instruction that year which regulated some name changes. At the time he was serving in the Commandos, but returned to England on being wounded in Sicily.

E. **Streff:** Ernst Elias Niebergall (1815–1843), Ger. playwright.

Barbra **Streisand:** Barbara Joan Streisand (1942–), U.S. popular singer, movie actress. The singer dropped the middle "a" of her first name for distinctiveness and to reflect the actual pronunciaion.

Hesba **Stretton:** Sarah Smith (1832–1911), Eng. evangelical children's writer. The writer felt that her real name lacked distinctiveness, so formed a new first name from her initial and those of her siblings in order of age: Hannah, Elizabeth, Sarah, Benjamin, and Ann. (Had she been the eldest, she would have had a standard Sheba.) Her surname was from the Shropshire village of All Stretton, where Ann had been left property by her uncle. Sarah Smith adopted the name in 1858, when her writing career began.

Stijn **Streuvels:** Frank Lateur (1871–1969), Belg. novelist, writing in Flemish.

Stringbean: David Akeman (1914–1973), U.S. country singer. The singer's name arose as a nickname, referring to his gangling appearance. According to one story, this originated from a radio announcer, who came to introduce him but forgot his real name.

Strix: Peter Fleming (1907–1971), Eng. journalist, travel writer. Fleming used this name, the scientific name for the screech owl, for his contributions to the *Spectator*.

Pauline **Strogova:** Prudence Hyman (1914–1995), Br. ballet dancer.

Arnold **Strong:** Arnold Schwarzenegger (1947–), Austr.-born U.S. movie actor. The actor began his career as a bodybuilder, going on to win the Mr. World and Mr. Universe titles before becoming a box-office movie star in the 1980s. He came to America in 1968 and was billed under this name for his first film, playing the title role in *Hercules in New York* (1970). He then reverted to his original name, which despite its awkwardness and length won him world fame and fortune.

Mark **Strong:** Marco Giuseppe Salussolia (1963–), Br. movie actor, of Austr.-It. parentage.

Pat **Strong** *see* Bruce **Carter**

Patience **Strong:** Winifred Emma May (1907–1990), Eng. "inspirational" poet. The writer took her name from *Patience Strong* (1870), a homely, religion-infused (fictional) autobiography by the U.S. author Adeline D.T. Whitney (1824–1906). Winifred May was very impressed by the book and its spiritual content. "No words can describe what it did for me.... The main character, the fictitious Patience Strong, moves through the book with a simplicity that only partially hides a philosophy that is as practical as it is profound. I had found more than a pseudonym. I had turned a corner and found, by chance, my true vocation.... The charm and the power of that book, *Patience Strong*, is something I cannot define ... I place it reverently on a pedestal alongside Mrs. Gaskell's *Cranford*, Jane Austen's *Emma* and *Our Village* by Nancy Russell Mitford" [Patience Strong, *With a Poem in My Pocket*, 1981].

The import of the fictional name itself is, of course, transparent enough, and is meaningful for the book's central character, the 38-year-old spinster who shares the old New England home with her mother, and who is at a pivotal stage in her spiritual and personal life.

Will **Strong** *see* J.P. **McCall**

Albert **Stroud** *see* Algis **Budrys**

Strube: Sidney Strube (1891–1956), Br. cartoonist. The artist addressed everyone, both male and female, as "George," so it was generally assumed this was his own name. His surname rhymes with "Ruby," not "Rube."

Sheppard **Strudwick:** John Shepperd (1907–1983), U.S. movie actor.

Andrzej **Strug:** Tadeusz Galecki (1871–1937), Pol. writer.

Joe **Strummer:** John Graham Mellor (1952–2002), Eng. rock singer, songwriter. The founder-member of the punk band The Clash originally called himself Joe Cool, earning his keep by strumming on a ukulele as a London street musician.

Jan **Struther:** Joyce Placzek, earlier Maxtone Graham, née Anstruther (1901–1953), Eng. poet, short-story writer, novelist. A name created from "J. Anstruther."

Tinchy **Stryder:** Kwasi Danquah (1988–), Br. rapper, MC, of Ghanaian parentage ("The Prince of Grime"). The artist's name refers to his short stature (5 ft 1 in) as he strides around the stage. ("Tinchy" could be taken as a blend of "tiny" and "titchy.")

Binkie **Stuart:** Elizabeth Alison Fraser (1932–2001), Sc. child movie actress. The actress was billed as Fiona Stuart in her first movie, but the name of her character, Binkie, stuck with her in her short career. (Plans for her to go to Hollywood were abandoned on the outbreak of World War II.)

Esmé **Stuart:** Amélie Claire LeRoy (1851–1934), Fr.-born Br. novelist, children's writer.

Gloria **Stuart:** Gloria Frances Stewart (1910–), U.S. movie actress.

Ian **Stuart:** Alistair Maclean (1922–1987), Sc. novelist. The writer used this name for his SF writing, such as *The Dark Crusader* (1961) and *The Satan Bug* (1962).

Jeanne **Stuart:** Jeanne Sweet (1908–), Br. stage actress.

John **Stuart:** John Croall (1898–1979), Sc. movie, stage actor.

Kirk **Stuart:** Charles Kincheloe (1934–1982), U.S. jazz pianist.

Leslie **Stuart:** Thomas Augustine Barrett (1864–1928), Eng. songwriter, popular composer. The musician at first wrote songs as Lester Barrett before becoming Leslie Stuart.

Nick **Stuart:** Nicholas Pratza (1904–1973), Rom.-born U.S. movie actor.

Norman **Stuart:** [Lady] Bartle Teeling, née Lane-Clarke (?–1906), Eng. writer, composer. The daughter of the Rev. Thomas Clark and Louisa Lane adopted this name for her writing, composing and publishing music as Isola, a name apparently fashioned anagrammatically from that of her mother.

Robert **Stuart:** Robert Stuart Meikleham (*fl.*1824), Sc. engineer. Meikleham adopted his first two names as author of *A Descriptive History of the Steam Engine* (1824).

Sidney **Stuart** *see* Ed **Noon**

Tony **Stuart:** Harry Brigden (1922–2000), Eng. stage actor, dancer.

Joe **Stubbs:** Joseph Stubbles (1942–1998), U.S. black Motown singer, brother of Levi **Stubbs**.

Levi **Stubbs:** Levi Stubbles (1936–2008), U.S. black Motown singer, brother of Joe **Stubbs**. The Four Tops singer changed his name after becoming the butt of jokes about shaving.

Studebaker John: John Grimaldi (1952–), U.S. blues musician.

Student: William Sealy Gosset (1876–1937), Eng. statistician, industrial research scientist.

Theodore **Sturgeon:** Edward Hamilton Waldo (1918–1985), U.S. SF writer. In 1929, following his father's death and his mother's remarriage, the future writer's name was legally changed to that of his stepfather. "There may be hints of emotional turmoil in these name changes" [Clute and Nicholls, p.1175]. U.S. novelist Kurt Vonnegut, Jr., is said to have based his SF writer character Kilgore Trout (*see* Kilgore Trout) on Theodore Sturgeon.

Preston Sturges: Edmond Preston Biden (1898–1959), U.S. movie director, screenwriter. The writer took his new name from his mother's second husband (his stepfather), millionaire businessman Solomon Sturges, at the same time dropping his first name (which some sources spell Edmund).

Jule Styne: Julius Kerwin Stein (1905–1994), Br.-born U.S. songwriter, of Ukr. Jewish parentage. Styne changed his name around 1930 to avoid confusion with entertainment executive Jules Stein (1896–1981). The new form of his first name was pronounced "Julie."

Poly Styrene: Marion Elliott (1956–), Eng. punk rock musician. The singer, who formed the band X-Ray Spex in 1977, adopted the name because she felt it was suitable for the "plastic" culture and values of the 1970s. She abandoned punk soon after, however, and went on to become Maharani Devi, as a member of the International Society of Krishna Consciousness. The band subsequently reformed.

Styx: Leslie Clifford Harding (1914–1991), Eng. cartoonist. The artist began his career drawing sporting strips. Hence presumably his name, alluding both to the river crossed by the souls of the dead in classical mythology and the "sticks" or fences that horses jump in a steeplechase.

André Suarès: Félix-André-Yves Scantrel (1868–1948), Fr. critic, poet.

Subhuti *see* **Sangharakshita**

Nikki Sudden: Nicholas Godfrey (1956–2006), Eng. rock guitarist.

Janis Sudrabkalns: Arvids Peine (1894–1975), Latvian poet, journalist. The writer's new surname means "silver mountain." He used the name Olivereto for two books of avantgarde verse.

Edzus Sudrabu: Eduard Zilber (1860–1941), Latvian writer. The writer translated his Germanic surname, meaning "silver," to the Latvian equivalent.

Eugène Sue: Marie-Joseph Sue (1804–1857), Fr. novelist. The writer took his new first name in honor of one of his patrons, Prince Eugène de Beauharnais (1781–1824).

Mark Suffling *see* **Fenton Brockley**

Sugar Blue: James Whiting (1955–), U.S. black blues musician.

Sugar Shaft: Anthony Hardin (1970–1995), U.S. black rapper.

Suggs: Graham McPherson (1961–), Br. rock singer. The lead vocalist of the group Madness adopted his name as a teenager. "He says he was finding it hard to fit in and wanted to make himself as cool and laddish as possible. He took the name from

a musician [called Pete Suggs that] he came across in his mother's jazz encyclopedia. 'I did graffiti saying things like, "Suggs is our leader," and "Suggs is everywhere." It was preposterously self-aggrandising'" [*The Times Magazine*, August 15, 2009].

Sui Sin Far: Edith Maude Eaton (1865–1914), Eng. writer on China. The writer's Chinese-sounding name represented a Chinese pronunciation of "narcissus flower."

Ratibor Suk *see* Petr **Bezruč**

Sukarno: Kusnasosro (1901–1970), Indonesian politician. Indonesia's first president was the son of a Javanese teacher, Raden Sukemi Sosrodihardjo, and his Balinese wife, Ida Njoman Rai. He was originally named Kusnasosro, after his father, but following a series of illnesses was renamed with the more auspicious name Sukarno, "son of Karna," for a hero of the epic poem *Mahabharata*, in which he is the son of the Hindu sun god Surya. Sukarno's childhood nickname was Djago ("cock," "champion"), and as an adult revolutionary hero he was known as Bung Karno (Brother Karno, Comrade Karno).

N. Sukhanov: Nikolay Nikolayevich Gimmer (1882–1940), Russ. revolutionary, economist.

Frants Sukhoverkhov: Mikhail Ivanovich Sychyov (1883–1918), Russ. revolutionary.

Naim Suleymanoglü: Naim Suleimanov (1967–), Bulg.-Turk. weightlifter. The athlete was born a member of the Turkish minority in Bulgaria, and at an early age was forced to take a Bulgarian form of his name, Naum Shalamanov. He sought political asylum in Turkey after the 1986 World Cup, competing first for Bulgaria as Shalamanov, then for Turkey as Suleymanoglü. The -*oglü* suffix in the latter name is a form of Turkish *ogul*, meaning "son," and corresponding to the Slavic -*ov* suffix of Suleimanov (and Shalamanov). The Jewish surname itself corresponds to Salomonson.

Idrees Dawud Sulieman: Leonard Graham (1923–2002), U.S. black jazz trumpeter. Graham was an early convert to Islam, and had already adopted his Muslim name on joining Earl Hines's band in 1943.

Jean Sulivan:: [Abbé] Joseph Lemarchand (1913–1980), Fr. religious writer.

Margaret Sullavan: Margaret Brooke (1911–1960), U.S. movie actress.

Barry Sullivan: Patrick Barry (1912–1994), U.S. movie actor.

Joe Sullivan: Dennis Patrick Terence Joseph O'Sullivan (1906–1971), U.S. jazz pianist, composer.

Maxine Sullivan: Marietta Williams (1911–1987), U.S. black jazz singer.

Vernon Sullivan: Boris Vian (1920–1959), Fr. singer, songwriter, novelist. Vian wrote four novels under this name, including *J'irai cracher sur vos tombes* ("I will spit on your graves") (1946), purportedly "translated from the American" and originally written by an African-American author.

Sully Prudhomme: René-François-Armand Prudhomme (1839–1907), Fr. poet.

Majrooh **Sultanpuri:** Asrar Hussain Khan (1924–), Ind. movie songwriter. The lyricist was born in Sultanpur, Uttar Pradesh.

Salomon **Sulzer:** Salomon Loewy (1804–1890), Austr. Jewish cantor, composer.

Yma **Sumac:** Zoila Augusta Imperatriz Chavarri del Castillo (1922–2008), Peruvian-born U.S. singer. Despite reports to the contrary, the singer was *not* originally named Amy Camus. She first performed as Imma Summack, a name she is said to have adapted from a local term meaning "how beautiful." This was then altered to Yma Sumac by Capitol Records, apparently to make it look more exotic to American audiences.

Sumangalo: Harold Amos Eugene Newman (1903–1963), U.S. Buddhist. The pioneering Buddhist priest adopted his new name on his ordination while traveling in the East. He then returned to the U.S., where he performed his priestly function as a probation officer under the name of Robert Stuart Clifton. In 1951 he founded the Western Buddhist Order, but later moved to Malaya to work for Buddhism.

Donna **Summer:** LaDonna Andrea Sommer, née Gaines (1948–), U.S. pop singer. The singer married the Austrian actor Helmut Sommer when she was 19, and took his surname, but altered its spelling to make it look more English. She divorced him in 1976, but kept the anglicized name.

Charles **Summerfield:** Alfred W. Arrington (1810–1967), U.S. lawyer, writer.

Felix **Summerly:** [Sir] Henry Cole (1808–1882), Eng. art patron, educator. The artist first used the name for *Felix Summerly's Home Treasury* (1841), a series of children's stories illustrated with woodcuts based on well-known paintings. The name seems to be simply agreeable: Latin *felix* means "fruitful," "lucky," and "Summerly" obviously evokes summer. As Hamst comments: "This gentleman's pseudonym, though longer, is much pleasanter than his own name" [p.123].

Jill **Summers:** Honor Margaret Rozelle Santoi Simpson Smith (1910–1997), Br. variety artist, TV actress.

Barney **Sumner:** Bernard Dicken (1956–), Br. rock musician. This was the name used by Dicken when a member of the group New Order. Earlier, in Joy Division, he called himself Bernard Albrecht.

Sumurun: Vera Ashby (1895–1985), Br. fashion model, working in Paris, France. "When Edward Molyneux left Lucile to open his own couture house in 1919, he hired Vera Ashby as his head mannequin. He named her Sumurun, the Enchantress of the Desert" [*The Fashion Book*, 1998].

Joe **Sun:** James J. Paulson (1943–), U.S. country singer. The singer's new surname is an imaginative development of the latter half of his original surname.

Sun Bear: Vince Laduke (1929–1992), U.S. "New Age" Native American chief. "The name of 'Sun Bear' was derived from a childhood vision of a large black bear sheathed in a vivid array of rainbow colours. The bear looked steadfastly at young Vince, stood on his hind legs and gently touched him on his head" [*Daily Telegraph*, September 1, 1992, quoted in Massingberd 1997].

The **Sundance Kid:** Harry Longabaugh (1870–1909), U.S. outlaw, teaming with Butch **Cassidy**. The bank robber and gunslinger, a leader of the Wild Bunch, took his nickname from the town of Sundance, Wyoming, where he was jailed from 1887 through 1889 for stealing a horse.

Sunnyland Slim: Albert Luandrew (1907–1995), U.S. black blues musician. The pianist took his name from one of his own songs, "Sunnyland Train," about the train that ran between Memphis and St. Louis. He was also known as Sunny Land Slim, Delta Joe (for the Mississippi Delta style of blues), and Dr. Clayton's Buddy (for the singer Peter J. "Doctor" Clayton).

Sun Ra: Herman "Sonny" Blount (1914–1993), U.S. black jazz musician. The musician was nicknamed "Sonny" as a boy and this may have sown the seed of his professional name, if not his claim that he was a visitor from Saturn. "In 1952, he proclaimed his vocation: that he was not human, but rather of an angel race; that he was to serve as the Cosmic Communicator, bringing the Creator's message to benighted Planet Earth. Accordingly, he changed his name to Le Sony'r Ra-Ra after the Egyptian sun god, Le from his last name, Sony for reasons both heliocentric and mundane, and an extra r to bring the total up to a lucky 9 letters. This is the name that appears on his passport ... Sun Ra is technically his stage name. Upon changing his name, he began calling his band an Arkestra (a respelling that just happens to include "Ra" both forwards and backwards)" [Robert Campbell, in Hartmut Geerken and Bernhard Hefele, eds., *Omniverse Sun Ra*, 1994]. Sun Ra would frequently announce to concert audiences: "Some call me Mr. Ra, some call me Mr. Re, but you can call me Mr. Mystery."

Marion **Sunshine:** Mary Tunstall James (1894–1963), U.S. vaudeville, movie actress, singer, songwriter.

Supercat: William Maragh (*c.*1966–), Jamaican reggae musician, of African/East Indian descent.

Super Chikan: James Johnson (1951–), U.S. black blues musician. "Chikan" is "chicken."

Franz von **Suppé:** Francesco Ezechiele Ermenegildo, Cavaliere Suppé-Demelli (1819–1895), Dalmatian-born Austr. operetta composer, conductor, of Belg. descent.

Suraiya: Suraiya Jamal Sheikh (1929–2004). Ind. movie actress, singer.

Kamala **Suraiyya** *see* **Madhavikutty**

Master **Suresh:** Nasir Ahmed Khan (1929–), Ind. juvenile movie actor. The young actor's Sanskrit screen name means "ruler of the gods."

Surfaceman: Alexander Anderson (1845–1909), Sc. poet, librarian. The writer was 17 years a surfaceman (a worker who keeps a railroad bed in repair) on the Glasgow and South-Western Railway.

John **Surrebutter:** John Anstey (?–1819), Eng. poet. The poet used this name for "a didactic poem" entitled *The Pleader's Guide* (1796), described in the subtitle as "containing the conduct of a Suit of Law, with the Arguments of Counsellor Bother'um and Counsellor Bore'um in an action betwixt John-a-Gull and John-a-Gudgeon for assault and battery at a late contested election." The poem is witty, but the humor mainly legal. A "surrebutter" is a learned legal term for a plaintiff's reply to a defendant's rebutter, itself a reply to a plaintiff's surrejoinder, in turn a reply to a defender's rejoinder, in turn an answer to a plaintiff's reply, in turn a response to a defendant's plea (stating guilt or innocence).

Colonel **Surry:** John Esten Cooke (1830–1886), U.S. novelist, essayist. The writer used the name for a series of romances, in which the Civil War was seen through the eyes of "Colonel Surry," a fictitious aide of Stonewall Jackson.

Jacqueline **Susann:** Jacqueline Susan (1918–1974), U.S. novelist, of Lithuanian-Russ. Jewish descent. The bestselling novelist's mother, a public-school teacher, added a second "n" to the family name so that her pupils would pronounce it correctly by accenting the second syllable.

Joan **Sutherland:** Joan Maisie Kelly, née Collings (1890–1947), Eng. popular novelist. The writer began her career as a singer.

John August **Sutter:** Johann Augustus Suter (1803–1880), Ger.-born U.S. pioneer, of Swiss parentage.

Sara **Sutton:** Eugenia Sheppard (?1900–1984), U.S. journalist, author. The writer used this name for a weekly beauty column in the *New York Herald Tribune*.

Suzy: Aileen Mehle (1952–), U.S. gossip columnist, "queen of aristocratic tittle-tattle."

Han **Suyin** *see* **Han Suyin**

Karolína **Svetlá:** Johanna Rottová, née Muzáková (1830–1899), Cz. writer. The writer took her pseudonym from her husband's birthplace.

Valerian **Svetlov:** Valerian Yakovlevich Ivchenko (1860–1934), Russ. ballet critic.

Nikolay **Svetlovidov:** Nikolay Afanasyevich Sedykh (1889–1970), Russ. stage actor. The actor seems to have adopted a name related in sense to his original surname: Sedykh means literally "gray-haired," while Svetlovidov is "of fair countenance."

Feliks **Svetov:** Feliks Grigorievich Fridland (Friedland) (1927–2002), Russ. dissident writer, of Jewish descent.

Italo **Svevo:** Ettore Aron Schmitz (1861–1928), It. novelist, short-story writer, of Ger. Jewish-It. parentage. The writer's pseudonym means "Italian Swabian," and was chosen by him to express his feeling of being a hybrid: he was Italian by language, Austrian in citizenship, and German in ancestry and education. He used it defiantly on the cover of his novel *Una vita* ("A Life") (1892), when his native Trieste, then in Austria-Hungary, was torn by national rivalry between Italians, Slavs, and Germans.

Swamp Dogg: Jerry Williams, Jr. (1942–), U.S. black soul singer. The musician was at first reluctant to change his name, but then realized that the adoption of a memorable name would give him the individuality he need to express in his music. In Southern slang, a swamp fox is an alligator.

Bettye **Swann:** Betty Jean Champion (1944–), U.S. country, soul singer.

Gloria **Swanson:** Gloria May Josephine Svensson (1897–1983), U.S. movie actress, of Swe.-Pol. descent.

Miss **Swanson** *see* Greta **Garbo**

Keith **Sweat:** Keath "Sabu" Crier (1961–), U.S. black R&B singer.

Emanuel **Swedenborg:** Emanuel Swedberg (1688–1772), Swe. scientist, philosopher, religious writer. The scientist's family adopted a fuller form of their name in 1719 when they were ennobled.

Blanche **Sweet:** Sarah Blanche Sweet (1895–1986), U.S. movie actress. Many sources give the actress's "real" name as Daphne Wayne. For the origin of this, see the quote under Mabel **Normand**.

Sweet Betty: Betty Echols Journey (1949–), U.S. black blues singer.

Sweetie Irie: Derrick Bent (1971–), Br. black DJ, pop musician. "Irie" (from "high") is West Indian Rasta slang for "excellent," "euphoric," especially after smoking cannabis.

Benjamin **Swift:** William Romaine Paterson (1871–1937), Sc. writer. Paterson used this name for 14 volumes of fiction.

Tom **Swift:** Thomas Kneafcy (1928–), Br. opera singer.

Nora **Swinburne:** Nora (or Elinore) Swinburne Johnson (1902–2000), Eng. stage, movie actress.

John **Swithen:** Stephen Edward King (1947–), U.S. horror novelist. The writer used this name for an early short story, "The Fifth Quarter," published in *Cavalier* magazine in April 1972. When Richard **Bachman** was revealed to be Stephen King, fans of his writing wondered if he had used any other pen names. "Stephanie Leonard, in the April 1985 issue of [King's newsletter] *Castle Rock*, reassured the readership: 'As to whether or not he has used any other pseudonyms, except for using the name John Swithen ... he has never used any other pseudonyms'" [George Breahm, *The Stephen King Story*, 1992].

Sybilla: Sybilla Sorondo-Myelzwynska (1963–), U.S. fashion designer, of Pol.-Argentinian parentage.

Basil **Sydney:** Basil Sydney Nugent (1894–1968), Br. movie actor.

Carmen **Sylva** *see* **Carmen Sylva**

Ilena **Sylva:** Ilena Thimblethorpe (1916–), Br. stage actress. The actress based her stage name on the maiden name of her mother, Karenhappuch Silvester.

Vernon **Sylvaine:** Vernon Scotchburn (1897–1957), Eng. stage actor, playwright.

Urbanus **Sylvan:** Henry Charles Beeching (1859–1919), Eng. poet, essayist. The name was almost certainly adopted from that of Sylvanus **Urban**, and so evokes the town and the country (or forest).

Sylvander: Robert Burns (1756–1796), Sc. poet. This was the name that Burns gave himself for his correspondence with **Clarinda**. It was probably intended to mean "forest man," and resembles the Sylvanus of classical mythology as the name of different sylvan beings or deities.

Sylvester: Sylvester James (1946–1988), U.S. black disco performer, soul singer. An earlier name used by the artist was Ruby Blue.

C. **Sylvester:** [Lady] Emma Caroline Wood, née Michell (1802–1879), Eng. novelist. The pseudonym puns on the writer's married name, from Latin *silva*, "wood."

James Joseph **Sylvester:** James Joseph (1814–1897), Eng.-born U.S. mathematician. The mathematician followed the lead of his brother, who on emigrating to the United States was required to have three names. Sylvester added his third name to the family name of Joseph sometime before his matriculation at University College, London, in 1828.

Sylvester II: Gerbert of Aurillac (*c.*945–1003), Fr. pope. The first Frenchman to become pope took the name of St. Sylvester I (died 335), whose papal partnership with the Roman emperor Constantine the Great is regarded as exemplary (as his own would be with the Roman emperor Otto III).

Sylvester III: John of Sabina (?–1063), It. pope.

Sylvestris: St. George Tucker (1752–1827), U.S. jurist, writer. Tucker used this name for *Reflections on the Cession of Louisiana to the United States* (1803), published in support of Jefferson's acquisition.

Sylvia: (1) Sylvia Vanderpool (1936–), U.S. pop singer; (2) Sylvia Kirby Allen (1956–), U.S. country singer.

David **Sylvian:** David Batt (1958–), Eng. rock musician. The lead singer of the group Japan chose his new name as a tribute to Sylvain Sylvain (originally Syl Mizrahi) of the New York Dolls. He is the brother of Japan drummer Steve **Jansen**.

Sylvie: Louise Sylvain (1883–1970), Fr. movie actress.

Franciscus **Sylvius:** Franz Deleboe (or De le Boë) (1614–1672), Ger. physician, anatomist. The name is a Latin rendering of the original, meaning "of the wood."

Richard **Sympson:** Jonathan Swift (1667–1745), Ir.-born satirist, clergyman, of Eng. parentage. This was the name adopted by Swift when negotiating with the London printer and bookseller Benjamin Motte over the publication of *Gulliver's Travels* (1726). Swift was here assuming the guise of the imaginary cousin of Lemuel **Gulliver**, the supposed author of the novel, which is prefaced by "A Letter from Capt. Gulliver, to his Cousin Sympson." According to an article by R.W. Frantz in the *Huntingdon Library Quarterly*, No. 1, 1938, the name may have been intended to suggest a connection between Gulliver and Captain William Sympson, the equally fictitious author of *A New Voyage to the East-Indies* (1715), itself plagiarized from an earlier book of travels.

Sylvia **Syms:** Sylvia Blagman (1917–1992), U.S. cabaret, jazz singer, of half-Russ. parentage.

Dr. **Syntax:** William Combe (1741–1823), Eng. pamphleteer, satirist, writer. This is probably the most familiar of the many names used by the writer, famous for his verse satire *The Tour of Dr. Syntax in Search of the Picturesque* (1809), relating the comic adventures of a village schoolmaster. Other names used by Combe include Belphegor, Isaac Brandon, Johannes Scriblerus, and descriptives such as A Country Gentleman, An Italian Nun, and A Retired Officer.

Syreeta: Rita Wright (1946–), U.S. black rock singer, songwriter. The singer, who worked with (and was briefly married to) Stevie **Wonder**, elaborated her first name when the Tamla Motown label told her that her original name was not strong enough for the record-buying public.

Władysław **Syrokomla:** Ludwik Kondratowicz (1823–1862), Pol. poet.

T: Joseph Peter Thorp (1873–1962), Br. writer, biographer.

Mr. T: Laurence Tero (1952–), U.S. black TV actor. The former bodyguard was originally named Laurence Tureaud. He changed the spelling to Tero, then called himself Mr. T so people would address him as "Mister."

Svatopluk **T.:** Svatopluk Turek (1900–1972), Cz. writer.

Kamil Amin **Taabes:** Elie Cohen (1924–1965), Israeli spy. Cohen, a Jew, was given a Muslim name for his operations in the Zionist cause in Syria.

Tabarin: Antoine Girard (?–1626), Fr. street entertainer. Sources differ concerning the poser's true identity. Some say that Tabarin was his real name, and that his full name and dates were Jean Salomon Tabarin (1584–1633). Either way, his name gave the French expression *faire le tabarin*, "play the fool."

Jamaaladeen **Tacuma:** Rudy McDaniel (1956–), U.S. rock musician. The musician adopted his new name on coverting to Islam.

Tad: Thomas Dorgan (1877–1929), U.S. cartoonist. When studying at art school, Dorgan was so inspired by a teacher, Aloysius Donnegan, that he took his first name as his own middle name. His new initials, T.A.D., gave Tad as the name with which he signed his work in newspapers.

Taffrail: [Captain] Henry Taprell Dorling (1883–1968), Br. naval writer, broadcaster. The captain's name is obviously based on his middle name, but is also a nautical term for the rail around a ship's stern. Sir Walter Scott's *The Antiquary* (1816) has a Lieutenant Taffril on board H.M. gunbrig *Search*.

Tagaryu: Noboru Kurotani (1958–), Jap. sumo wrestler.

Messrs. **Tag, Rag, and Bobtail:** Isaac D'Israeli (1766–1848), Eng. writer, historian. The father of novelist and prime minister Benjamin Disraeli used this name for *Flim-Flams! or, The Life and Errors of My Uncle, and the Amours of My Aunt* (1797), with general discussions on contemporary topics.

Koki **Taiho:** Koki Naya (1940–), Jap. sumo wrestler. The athlete adopted his Japanese nickname, meaning "great bird."

Tail Dragger: James Yancey Jones (1940–), U.S. black blues singer. The singer adopted his name from the title of a song by **Howlin' Wolf**, whom he sought to emulate.

Germaine **Tailleferre:** Germaine Marcelle Taillefesse (1892–1983), Fr. composer. The musician presumably modified her name under the impression that Taillefesse had the undesirable meaning "buttocks cutter" (French *tailler*, "to cut" + *fesse*, "but-

tock"). It actually means "withy cutter" (*tailler* + *faisse*, "withy"). Tailleferre, a genuine surname, means "iron cutter."

John **Taine:** Eric Temple Bell (1883–1960), Sc.-born U.S. SF writer.

Aleksandr **Tairov:** Aleksandr Yakovlevich Kornblit (1885–1950), Russ. theatrical director.

Ken **Takakura:** Oda Goichi (1931–), Jap. movie actor.

Takamisugi: Kaneo Takashi (1961–), Jap. sumo wrestler.

Takamura Koun: Nakajima Kozo (1852–1934), Jap. sculptor. The artist studied Buddhist sculpture under Takamura Koun and subsequently adopted his master's name.

Takanofuji: Tadao Yasuda (1963–), Jap. sumo wrestler.

Takanohama: Shinji Hamada (1965–), Jap. sumo wrestler.

Taki: Mariko Taki (1940–), Jap. magician, teaming with Johnny **Aladdin**, her husband.

Takis: Panayotis Vassilakis (1925–), Gk. experimental artist.

Josef **Tal:** Josef Gruenthal (1910–), Pol.-born Israeli composer, pianist.

Talander: August Bohse (1661–1730), Ger. novelist. The Greek name may have been intended to mean "man of judiciousness," from *talanton*, "balance," "weight," and *anēr, andros*, "man." Bohse constantly sought to promote polite standards of taste.

Talbert: Talbert McLean (1906–1992), Sc. painter, cartoonist.

Howard **Talbot:** Richard Lansdale Munkittrick (1865–1928), U.S.-born Br. popular composer, of Ir. parentage. Munkittrick's father wanted his son to be a doctor and for a time he trained for this profession. He decided it was not for him, however, and instead studied music. His father disowned him, and it was at this point that he adopted his new name, taking his mother's maiden name.

Kathrine **Talbot:** Ilse Barker, née Gross (1921–2006), Ger.-born Br. novelist, translator.

Kay **Talbot** *see* Fenton **Brockley**

Lyle **Talbot:** Lysle Hollywood Henderson (1904–1987), U.S. movie actor.

Nita **Talbot:** Anita Sokol (1930–), U.S. TV comedienne.

Pierre **Tal-Coat:** Pierre Jacob (1905–1985), Fr. painter. The artist adopted his Breton name in 1926.

Dimitr **Talev:** Dimitr Talev Petrov (1898–1966), Bulg. writer.

Talfryn: Iorwerth Hefin Lloyd (1920–1986), Welsh poet. The writer's bardic name is that of his birthplace near Denbigh, northern Wales.

Talhaiarn: John Jones (1810–1869), Welsh poet.

The writer's bardic name comes from his birthplace, the village of Llanfair Talhaiarn, near Abergele, Denbighshire (now Conwy).

Hal Taliaferro: Floyd Taliaferro Alderson (1895–1980), U.S. movie actor. The actor originally appeared in silent westerns under the name Wally Wales. He then took his more durable name.

Taliesin ab Iolo: Taliesin Williams (1787–1847), Welsh poet. The writer's name means "Taliesin son of Iolo," the latter being **Iolo Morganwg**. His first name is that of the legendary 6th-century poet Taliesin.

Talis Qualis: Carl Vilhelm August Strandberg (1818–1877), Swe. poet, journalist. The pseudonym represents the Latin phrase meaning "such as it is."

S.G. Tallentyre: Evelyn Beatrice Hall (1868–1956), Eng. writer, sister-in-law of Henry Seton **Merriman**.

Talma: Mary Ann Ford (c.1870–1944), Eng. magician ("Queen of Coins"). The illusionist married the Belgian-British magician Jean Henri Servais Le Roy (1865–1953) in 1890 and performed jointly with him and Leon Bosco as Leroy-Talma-Bosco.

Richard Talmadge: Ricardo Metzetti (1896–1981), U.S. movie actor, stuntman.

Aino Talvi: Aino Augustovna Pindam (1905–), Estonian stage actress.

Talvj: Therese Albertine Louise Robinson, née von Jakob (1797–1870), Ger. author, writing in English. The writer's pseudonym represents the initials of her full maiden name, and was pronounced by her as "Talvy." Her husband was the U.S. biblical scholar Professor Edward Robinson (1794–1863).

Rabbenu Tam: Jacob ben Meir (c.1100–1171), Fr. Jewish scholar. The Talmudic authority came to be known by a name alluding to the biblical line: "Jacob was a mild man [*ish tam*], dwelling in tents" (Genesis 25:27). This is interpreted in the Rabbinic tradition to mean that Jacob was a "perfect" man, dwelling in the tents of the Torah. Hence the scholar's full name, interpreted as "Our Teacher the Perfect One." Rabbenu Tam was the grandson of **Rashi** and younger brother of **Rashbam**.

Roman Tam: Tam Pak-sin (1949–2002), Chin. entertainer, working in Hong Kong.

Tamara: Tamara Swann Drasin (1907–1943), Russ.-born U.S. stage, movie actress, singer.

Tamara Khanum: Tamara Artyomovna Petrosyan (1906–1991), Uzbek dancer, singer, of Armenian parentage.

Tamia: Tamia Washington (1975–), Can. popular singer.

Helen Tamiris: Helen Becker (1902–1966), U.S. ballet dancer, choreographer, teacher, of Russ. Jewish origin. The dancer was given her new name by a

writer with whom she became romantically involved during a tour to South America around 1920. The name itself is that of the Scythian warrior queen famous from a a line of verse by the South American poet Amongo Zegri: "Thou art Tamiris, the ruthless queen who banishes all obstacles."

A.H. Tammsaare: Anton Hansen (1878–1940), Estonian writer. The writer took the name of the farmhouse where he was born as his new surname, then added the initials of his original name.

Ta Mok: Ung Choeun (1926–2006), Cambodian military leader. The Khmer Rouge leader adopted his new name, meaning "respected grandfather," on joining the Communist Party under **Pol Pot**.

Tampa Red: Hudson Woodbridge (1904–1981), U.S. black blues musician. The singer's parents died when Woodbridge was a child and he was raised by his maternal grandmother in Tampa, Florida, so that he eventually took her last name, Whittaker. He acquired his stage name subsequently in Chicago.

Arriz Tamza: Maya Bousselmania (1957–), Algerian novelist, working in French.

V.G. Tan: Vladimir Germanovich Bogoraz (1865–1936), Russ. writer, anthropologist. The writer adopted his pseudonym from his original first name, Natan (Nathan). He spelled this out with an alternate form, N.A. Tan.

Toru Tanaka: Charles Kalani (1930–2000), Hawaiian-born U.S. wrestler. Kalani began wrestling under the name "Professor Toru Tanaka" in the 1960s.

Tancredi: Tancredi Parmeggiani (1927–1964), It. painter.

Carl Felix Tandem: Carl Spiteler (1845–1924), Swiss writer.

Neri Tanfucio: Renato Fucini (1843–1921), It. writer. Fucini used this anagrammatical pseudonym for his comic verses *Cento sonetti in vernacolo pisano* ("A Hundred Sonnets in the Pisan Dialect") (1872).

Tania (or Tanya): (1) Zoya Anatolyevna Kosmodemyanskaya (1923–1941), Russ. partisan; (2) Haydee Tamara Bunke (1937–1967), Argentinian-born Soviet agent, of Ger. parentage; (3) Patricia Campbell Shaw, née Hearst (1954–), U.S. liberationist. Tania (Tanya), a name of Russian origin (the pet form of Tatiana), was originally one of many Soviet cover names in revolutionary circles. It became more widely known from its association with Kosmodemyanskaya, executed by the Germans in World War II, who herself adopted it in memory of Tanya Solomakha, a Russian Civil War agent. It was in turn taken up by non–Russian activists such as Bunke, who worked in South America with Che **Guevara**.

In 1964, on leaving Cuba for Europe, Bunke assumed the identity of either Vittoria Pancini, the daughter of German parents living on the Italian-German border, or of Marta Iriarte, an Argentinian. When in Havana she operated as Laura Gutierrez Bauer, a name created as an Italian-Argentinian-German compromise. Like Kosmodemyanskaya, she also lost her life in the field, shot as she was crossing the Rio Grande in Bolivia. The name was later adopted in her honor by Symbionese Liberation Army agent Patty Hearst [1. *Sunday Telegraph*, July 21, 1968; 2. Marta Royas and Mirta Rodriguez Calderon, *Tania*, 1973; 3. David Boulton, *The Making of Tania: The Patty Hearst Story*, 1975; 4. V.D. Uspensky, *Zoya Kosmodemyanskaya*, 1989; 5. Christine Toomey, "Tania: lover, traitor, soldier, spy?" *Sunday Times Magazine*, August 10, 2008].

Tania Maria: Tania Maria Reis Leite (1948–), Brazilian jazz musician, working in France, U.S.

Maxim Tank: Evgeny Ivanovich Skurko (1912–1995), Belorussian revolutionary poet. The poet tells how he came by his name: "I first had my work printed in 1932 in the occasional newspaper *Na perelome* ["Turning Point"] published in Lvov. The poem was called "Factory Chimneys." I was young and green then. Almost all of the established poets that I admired had pen names. I followed their example, of course. Moreover, writing at that time under your real name was not without risk. By then I had already been using a number of undercover names: Zhenka, Viktor, Maxim.... This last was in honor of [Maxim] **Gorky**. I kept this name for my published writing. But what for a surname? I was raised in the country and at first thought of adopting a plant name. However, it turned out that many of the plant names were already bespoken by poets: **Kolas**, **Krapiva**, **Charot**, Vasilyok.... Moreover, if you follow someone's example, aren't you doing just the same? So I took something that was the opposite— powerful, steel, dynamic, something that matched, I felt, the measure and restless mood of the time. And ever since then I have been Tank. There is something rather juvenile about the name, of course. But that was how it was. Later, too, at the front, the name was actually quite appropriate" [Dmitriyev, p.217].

Tan Tan: Edward Thornton (*c*.1934–), Jamaican jazz trumpeter. The name presumably grew out of the player's surname.

Tanti: Konstantin Konstantinovich Ferroni (1888–1974), Russ. circus artist + Leon Konstantinovich Ferroni (1892–1973), Russ. circus artist, his brother. The two brothers, who performed as musical clowns, originated from an Italian circus family. Hence their Italian surname. Their ring name comes from their patronymic (middle name).

Tantia Topi: Ramchandra Panduranga (*c*.1819–1859), Ind. guerrilla leader.

Tanya *see* **Tania**

Tanymarian: [Rev.] Edward Stephen (1882–1885), Welsh hymnwriter. The musician took his name from the house in northwest Wales where he lived. The name itself means "below the strand" (Welsh *tan*, "below," *y*, "the," and *marian*, "strand").

Marguerite Taos: Marie-Louise Taos Amrouche (1913–1976), Algerian writer, working in France.

[Princess] Yelizaveta Alekseyevna Tarakanova: ? (*c*.1745–1775), Russ. adventuress. The self-styled princess pretended to the Russian throne by claiming to be the daughter of the unmarried empress Elizabeth (reigned 1741–62) and Count Aleksey Razumovsky. Her actual identity remains unknown.

Tarheel Slim: Alden Bunn (1924–1977), U.S. blues, gospel singer, guitarist. The singer came from North Carolina, the "Tarheel State."

Yury Tarich: Yury Viktorovich Alekseyev (1885–1967), Russ. movie director, screenwriter. The filmmaker's adopted name represents a casual pronunciation of his first name and patronymic (Yury Viktorovich), which would be a standard way of addressing him. (The Russian patronymic is usually shortened in speech, so that "Viktorovich" would sound as "Viktarich" or even just "Tarich.")

Mikhail Tarkhanov: Mikhail Mikhaylovich Moskvin (1877–1948), Russ. stage, movie actor.

William Tarmey: William Cleworth Piddington (1941–), Br. TV actor, singer. Advised that his original name was too long for billing purposes, the actor adopted a shorter name based on that of the U.S. singer Mel Tormé (1925–1999), whose own name is pronounced "Tarmey" by Americans.

Gerda Taro: Gerda Pohorylle (1911–1937), Pol. photographer, of Jewish parentage. Taro was the first woman known to shoot pictures in battle, and the first to die in action, working on the front line of the Spanish Civil War. She was in Paris, France, when she fell in love with Endre Friedmann, later to become Robert **Capa**. She changed her name about the same time as her lover, taking it from Taro Okamoto, a young Japanese painter working in Paris. Not only was her new name easy to pronounce, as Capa's was, but it suggested "tarot," with connotations of gypsies and fortune-telling. Moreover, the name as a whole sounded similar to that of Greta **Garbo**, who in 1936 was at the peak of her fame.

Tarsem: Tarsem Dhandwar Singh (1962–), Ind. video director, working in U.S.

Alfred Tarski: Alfred Teitelbaum (1901–1983), Pol.-born U.S. mathematician, of Jewish parentage. In 1924, the year before receiving his doctorate at the University of Warsaw, Teitelbaum changed his name to Tarski and soon after converted to Catholicism. He made the United States his home from 1939.

Niccolò **Tartaglia:** Niccolò Fontana (1499–1557), It. mathematician. During the French sacking of Brescia, his birthtown, 12-year-old Niccolò was slashed in the jaws and palate by a saber. As a result, his speech was impaired, and he was nicknamed Tartaglia, "stammerer." He later adopted the name.

Joe **Tarto:** Vincent Joseph Tortoriello (1902–1986), U.S. jazz musician.

Frank **Tashlin:** Francis Frederick von Taschlein (1913–1972), U.S. movie director.

Tashrak: Isarel Joseph Zevin (1872–1926), Belorussian-born U.S. journalist, writer.

Tasma: Jessie Catherine Couvreur, née Huybers (1848–1897), Br. novelist, journalist. The writer took her name from Tasmania, Australia, where she was raised from the age of four. Her first husband, Charles Forbes Fraser, was a Tasmanian.

Nadia **Tass:** Nadia Tassopoulos (1956–), Gk.-born movie director, producer, working in Australia.

Agostino **Tassi:** Agostino Buonamici (c.1580–1644), It. painter.

Thomas Pitt **Taswell-Langmead:** Thomas Pitt Langmead (1840–1882), Eng. historian, jurist. In 1864 the scholar added his mother's maiden name, Taswell, to his original family name.

Ellalice **Tate** see Jean **Plaidy**

Harry **Tate:** Ronald MacDonald Hutchison (1873–1940), Sc. music-hall comedian. The actor took his name from his former employers, sugar refiners Henry Tate & Sons (now Tate & Lyle).

Simon **Tate:** Simon Neil Tattersall (1956–), Br. radio presenter.

Jacques **Tati:** Jacques Tatischeff (1909–1982), Fr. comic movie actor. The actor was the grandson of Count Dmitri Tatischeff, an attaché at the Russian embassy in Paris who had married a Frenchwoman. His screen name was a shortening of his real name (in its original Russian form, Tatishchev), but also one that sounds engagingly affectionate to the French ear.

El **Tato:** Antonio Sánchez (1830–1895), Sp. bullfighter. The matador's name means "Big Brother."

Richard **Tauber:** Ernst Seiffert (1891–1948), Austr.-born Br. operetta singer, conductor. The tenor was illegitimate, and initially bore his mother's maiden name. He was later adopted by his father, Anton Richard Tauber, and took his name.

Taupi: Albie Fiore (1946–), Br. crossword compiler. The setter adopted as pseudonym the nickname (from French *taupe*, "mole") given him as a student when working during the vacation on a farm in France.

Ava **Taurel** see Eva **Norvind**

Orlando **Tavora:** António Jacinto do Amaral Martins (1924–1991), Angolan (white) poet, short-story writer, of Port. parentage.

Léo **Taxil:** Gabriel Antoine Jogand-Pagès (1854–1907), Fr. journalist, anticlerical writer. The writer appears to have based his name on that of the Greek general Taxiles.

Vic **Tayback:** Victor Tabback (1929–1990), U.S. movie actor.

Chip **Taylor:** James Wesley Voight (1940–), U.S. pop singer, composer. The brother of actor Jon Voight (1938–) and uncle of actress Angelina **Jolie** gave up his Czech surname on becoming a singer.

Dominic **Taylor** see Rosalind **Erskine**

Estelle **Taylor:** Estelle Boylan (1899–1958), U.S. stage, movie actress.

Eva **Taylor:** Irene Gibbons (1895–1977), U.S. black vaudeville singer. Gibbons took her stage name while featuring as a soloist at the Lafayette Theater, Harlem, from 1921 to 1922.

George **Taylor:** Adolf Hausrath (1837–1909), Ger. novelist.

Gwen **Taylor:** Gwendoline Allsop (1939–), Eng. stage. movie, TV actress.

John **Taylor:** Mary Anne Talbot (1778–1808), Eng. adventuress. Talbot took this male name when serving in the English military, first as a drummer boy in Flanders (1792–3), then as a cabin boy in the navy (1793–6). Her sex was discovered when she was seized by a pressgang in 1797, although she continued to dress in men's clothes even after this incident. She later became a maidservant in London.

Kent **Taylor:** Louis Weiss (1907–1987), U.S. movie actor.

Koko **Taylor:** Cora Walton (1928–2009), U.S. black blues singer. Presumably "Koko" from "Cora."

Laurette **Taylor:** Helen Laurette Magdalene Cooney (1884–1946), U.S. stage, movie actress. After making her childhood stage debut in 1896 as La Belle Laurette, the actress came to be known by the name of her first husband, Charles A. Taylor (married 1901, divorced 1910).

Little Johnny **Taylor:** Johnny Lamont Merrett (1943–2002), U.S. soul, blues singer. The singer took his name from the established soul singer, Ted Taylor (1934–1988).

Pat **Taylor:** Pat Pope (1918–), Eng. stage actress, singer.

Robert **Taylor:** Spangler Arlington Brugh (1911–1969), U.S. movie actor. The actor was given his screen name in 1934 by MGM studio chief Louis B. **Mayer.**

Theodore **Taylor:** John Camden Hotten (1832–1873), Eng. writer, publisher. The writer, whose original name was John William Hotten, and who introduced many American authors to the British public, assumed this name for a rather slight biography of Thackeray, published in 1864.

Vince **Taylor**: Brian Maurice Holden (1939–1991), Br. rock musician, working in U.S., France. "There was always tension in the air on the few occasions Vince Taylor and I worked together. My real name is Roy Taylor, which was changed to Vince **Eager** in 1958, and in the same year, Brian Maurice Holden changed his to Vince Taylor, so a certain amount of confusion developed" [Vince Eager, *Vince Eager's Rock n' Roll Files*, 2007].

Vinnie **Taylor**: Chris Donald (1948–1974), U.S. rock musician.

William Desmond **Taylor**: William Deane-Tanner (1827–1922), Eng.-Ir. movie director, working in U.S.

Taz: Peter Senerchia (1967–), U.S. wrestler.

Bram **Tchaikovsky**: Peter Bramall (1950–), Eng. rock guitarist.

André **Tchaikowsky**: Robert Andrzey Krauthammer (1936–1982), Br. pianist, of Pol. Jewish parentage. The future musician was smuggled out of Poland at the age of seven using false identity papers and brought to England by his grandmother.

Ludmila **Tcherina**: Monique Avenirovna Tchemerzine (1924–2004), Fr.-born ballet dancer, movie actress, of Fr.-Georgian parentage.

Tchichellé Tchivela: François Tchichellé (1940–), Congolese short-story wrier, working in French. The second word of the writer's name means "thunder," referring to the effect he wanted his stories to have on the conscience of those in authority.

Mrs. **Teachwell** *see* (Mrs.) Solomon **Lovechild**

Conway **Tearle**: Frederick Levy (1878–1938), U.S. movie actor.

Richard **Tee**: Richard Ten Ryk (1943–1993), U.S. jazz musician. "Tee" as the initial of "Ten Ryk."

Willie **Tee**: Willie Turbinton (1944–2007), U.S. black R&B musician. "Tee" as the initial of "Turbinton."

Brandon **Teena**: Teena Brandon (1973–1993), U.S. transexual. The young woman who wanted to live as a young man reversed her names as she reversed her gender role. Her tragic story (she was raped and murdered at age 21) was the subject of the 1999 movie *Boys Don't Cry*, in which she (he) was played by Hilary Swank.

Teena Marie: Mary Christine Brockert (1956–), U.S. (white) Motown singer. "Teena" from "Christine" and "Marie" from "Mary," with the two original names reversed.

Teffi: Nadezhda Aleksandrovna Buchinskaya, née Lokhvitskaya (1872–1952), Russ. short-story writer, poet, working in France. The writer took her pen name from Taffy, the little prehistoric girl in Rudyard Kipling's story "How the Alphabet Was Made" in the *Just So Stories* (1902).

Tegid: John Jones (1792–1852), Welsh poet, antiquary. The poet was born near Lake Bala, Merionethshire (now Gwynedd), and took his bardic name from the Welsh name of the lake, Llyn Tegid. He was also known as Ioan Tegid, with the Welsh equivalent of his first name.

Tegla: Edward Tegla Davies (1880–1967), Welsh writer, Methodist minister. The writer took his name from his birthplace, the village of Llandegla-yn-Iâl ("St. Tegla's church in Iâl"), near Denbigh.

[Sir] Eric **Teichman**: Erik Teichmann (1884–1944), Eng. diplomat, traveler, of Ger. descent. The Chinese embassy official changed his name minimally by deed poll in 1906.

Teixeira de Pascoaes: Joaquim Pereira Teixeira de Vasconcelos (1877–1952), Port. writer.

Telesilla *see* Madame Floresta A. **Brasileira**

Lou **Tellegen**: Isidor van Dameler (1881–1934), Du. movie actor, working in U.S.

Roy **Tellet**: [Rev.] Albert Eubule Evans (1839–1896), Eng. writer. Evans used this punning name for a number of popular novels.

Paul **Tell-Truth**: George Saville Carey (1743–1807), Eng. dramatist, poet. Carey adopted this name for *Liberty chastized; or, Patriotism in Chains, a Tragicomi-political Farce* (1768).

Konrad **Telmann**: Ernst Otto Konrad Zitelmann (1854–1897), Ger. poet.

Anne **Telscombe** *see* **Another Lady**

Telynog: Thomas Evans (1840–1865), Welsh poet. The poet's bardic name means "harper."

Temper: Arron Bird (1972–), Eng. graffiti artist. The artist's adopted name is short for "mad temper," implying a passionate devotion to his work.

[Dame] Marie **Tempest**: Mary Susan Etherington (1864–1942), Eng. stage actress, singer. The actress adopted her name from Lady Susan Vane-Tempest, who she claimed was her godmother.

Ann **Temple**: Penelope Ruth Mortimer, earlier Dimont, née Fletcher (1918–), Welsh novelist. The writer used this name for her "lonely hearts" column in the London *Daily Mail*. For her first novel, *Johanna* (1947), she wrote as Penelope Dimont, from her first husband, Charles Dimont (married 1937).

Hope **Temple**: Dotie Davies (1859–1938), Ir. songwriter, of Eng. parentage. The name suggests a "temple of hope." Davies married the French composer André Messager (1853–1929).

Launcelot **Temple**: John Armstrong (1709–1779), Sc. physician, poet. Armstrong used this name for *Sketches; or, Essays on Various Subjects* (1758).

Neville **Temple**: [Hon.] Julian Charles Henry Fane (1827–1870), Eng. diplomat, poet. The writer used this name (a temple is poetically a "fane") for the joint authorship, with Edward Trevor (Hon. Edward Robert Bulwer Lytton; *see* Bulwer **Lytton**), of the poem *Tannhäuser; or the Battle of the Bards* (1861).

Paul **Temple:** Francis Durbridge (1912–1998), Eng. crime writer + James Douglas Rutherford McConnell (1914–1988), Ir. crime, mystery writer. The two writers used this name for mystery novels which did *not* feature Paul Temple, the famous detective created by Durbridge.

William **Temple:** Phil Bull (1910–1989), Eng. entrepreneur. The founder of the world's largest information service for racing form operated his organization, Timeform, under his pseudonym, which he may have chosen to complement the (real) name of William Hill (1903–1971), founder of one of Britain's leading firms of bookmakers. A temple is traditionally built on a hill.

Laurence **Templeton:** [Sir] Walter Scott (1771–1832), Sc. novelist, essayist, poet. Scott used this name when dedicating *Ivanhoe* (1819) to the Rev. Dr. **Dryasdust**. Of the name itself, Scott wrote: "There was no desire or wish to pass off the supposed Mr. Templeton as a real person. But a kind of continuation of 'The Tales of My Landlord' had been recently attempted by a stranger; and it was supposed this Dedicatory Epistle might pass for some imitation of the same kind, and thus putting inquirers upon a false scent, induce them to believe they had before them the work of some new candidate for their favour" [Wheeler, p.359]. The name is similar to that of Launcelot **Temple**.

Tenella: Mary Bayard Devereux Clarke (1827–1886), U.S. poet, editor. Clarke used this name for a two-volume anthology of poems, *Wood-Notes; or, Carolina Carols: A Collection of North Carolina Poetry* (1854), taking the name from a stay in Louisiana when she and other young women began to write poetry in which they referred to each other by the names of flowers. Mary was Tenella, the name of a jasmine. Later, writing for magazines and newspapers, she called herself Betsey Bittersweet.

M. **Tenelli:** Johann Heinrich Millenet (1785–1858), Ger. theatrical director, poet, novelist. A part-anagram, part-reversal here.

William **Tenn:** Philip Klass (1920–), U.S. SF writer.

David **Tennant:** David McDonald (1971–), Sc. TV actor. The actor adopted his stage name from the singer Neil Tennant (1954–) of the Pet Shop Boys pop duo.

Jimi **Tenor:** Lassi Lehto (1965–), Finn. jazz musician. The musician felt that his real name was not sufficiently "cool" so took a name inspired by his favorite instrument, the tenor sax.

Tenor Saw: Clive Bright (1966–1988), Jamaican DJ, reggae singer. The name is presumably a punning alteration of "tenon saw."

Madison **Tensas, M.D.:** Henry Clay Lewis (1825–1850), U.S. physician, humorist. In 1846 Lewis took a job as a "swamp doctor" in Madison Parish, Louisiana, on the banks of the Tensas River, and a combination of the two placenames gave him his pseudonym as a writer.

Tenzing Norgay: Namgyal Wangdi (1914–1986), Nepalese Sherpa mountaineer. The climber, who in 1953 with Sir Edmund Hillary of New Zealand was the first person to set foot on the summit of Mt. Everest, came to be known by a Nepalese name means literally "wealthy-fortunate religion-follower."

Teoctist: Toader Arapasu (1915–2007), Rom. prelate. The head of the Romanian Orthodox Church adopted his Greek religious name (Theoktistos, "created by God") in 1935 on being tonsured as a monk.

Te Rangi Hiroa: [Sir] Peter Henry Buck (1879–1951), N.Z. anthropologist, politician, of Ir.-Maori parentage. The surgeon and athlete is often known by his Maori name.

Terao: Yoshifumi Fukuzono (1963–), Jap. sumo wrestler, brother of **Sakahoko**. The brothers' mother died while they were still at high school, leaving the family bereft. The two young men accordingly quit school to enter sumo, with Yoshifumi adopting his mother's name as his fighting name.

Teresa: Teresa Viera-Romero (1929–), U.S.–Sp. ballet dancer.

Mother **Teresa:** (1) Alice Lalor (1766–1846), Ir.-born U.S. founder of religious order; (2) Agnes Gonxha Bojaxhiu (1910–1997), Albanian-born Ind. missionary. Alice Lalor went to Philadelphia in 1795 where with two other women she founded an informal religious community. The three then went to Washington, D.C., where they opened a convent that became part of the Order of the Visitation of Holy Mary. In 1816 their community was recognized by **Pius VII** as the first U.S. foundation of the order on American terrritory, and Alice Lalor became the community's first superior as Mother Teresa.

Agnes Bojaxhiu went to Ireland in 1928 to join the Loretto Sisters, an order noted for its missionary work. She was transferred as a teacher to St. Mary's Loretto Convent High School in Calcutta, India, and when taking her vows in 1931 chose the name Teresa for St. **Theresa of Lisieux**, omitting the "h" in order to avoid confusion with another sister in the congregation. Her religious order, the Order of the Missionaries of Charity, was founded in 1950 [Anne Sebba, *Mother Teresa: Beyond the Image*, 1997].

[Blessed] **Teresa Benedicta of the Cross:** Edith Stein (1891–1942), Ger. nun. Stein was born into an Orthodox Jewish family but in 1922 converted to Catholicism after reading the autobiography of St.

Teresa of Avila (1515–1582). In 1934 she entered the Carmelite convent at Cologne, taking the religious name Teresa Benedicta of the Cross in her honor. She perished in Auschwitz, but was beatified in 1987 under the Latin name Beata Teresia Benedicta a Cruce.

Térésah: Teresa Corinna Ubertis Gray (1877–1964), It. novelist, poet.

[St.] **Teresa of Lisieux** *see* [St.] **Theresa of Lisieux**

Bryn **Terfel:** Bryn Terfel Jones (1965–), Welsh opera singer. The baritone dropped his last name on discovering that another singer Bryn Jones already existed.

Tériade: Efstratios Eleftheriades (1897–1983), Gk. art critic, editor, publisher, working in France.

Studs **Terkel:** Louis Terkel (1912–2008), U.S. writer, broadcaster. The chronicler of modern American history adopted his new first name in his twenties, taking it from Studs Lonigan, the fictional working-class Irish American hero of the novels by James T. Farrell.

Max **Terpis:** Max Pfister (1889–1958), Swiss ballet dancer, choreographer, teacher. The dancer's professional surname is a near anagram of his real name.

Stefano **Terra:** Giulio Tavernari (1917–1986), It. writer.

Tammi **Terrell:** Thomasina Montgomery (1946–1970), U.S. black R&B singer. The singer's name is usually said to come from her marriage to heavyweight boxer Ernie Terrell.

Norma **Terris:** Norma Allison (1904–1989), U.S. stage actress, singer.

Ellaline **Terriss:** Ellen Hicks, née Lewin (1871–1971), Eng. stage, movie actress, daughter of William **Terriss.**

William **Terriss:** William Charles James Lewin (1847–1897), Eng. actor. The actor's best work was done at the Adelphi Theatre, London, and consequently he was nicknamed "No. 1, Adelphi Terrace," after a nearby street. He altered "Terrace" to a spelling that more closely resembled that of a surname. The name also happens to suggest "Terry," a famous theatrical name. Terriss actually played opposite Ellen Terry (*see* Megan **Terry**). He was murdered by a deranged actor, Richard **Prince.**

Alice **Terry:** Alice Frances Taafe (1899–1987), U.S. movie actress.

C.V. **Terry:** Frank Gill Slaughter (1908–), U.S. novelist.

Don **Terry:** Donald Locher (1902–1988), U.S. movie actor.

Frank **Terry:** Nat Clifford (1871–*c.*1950), Br.-born U.S. movie comedian. The actor's assumed name was one of several that he used over the years.

Megan **Terry:** Marguerite Duffy (1932–), U.S. playwright. The writer's first name is the Welsh equivalent of her own (and her mother's) first name, Marguerite. Her surname both honors the actress Ellen Terry (1847–1928) and suggests the earth (things terrestrial).

Phillip **Terry:** Frederick Henry Kormann (1909–1993), U.S. movie actor.

Sonny **Terry:** Saunders Terrill (1911–1986), U.S. black folk-blues harmonica player.

Terry-Thomas: Thomas Terry Hoar-Stevens (1911–1990), Eng. stage, movie comedian. The gap-toothed actor began his career as Mot Snevets (a reversal), then he tried Thomas Terry. He explained: "I quite liked the sound of Thomas Terry but I decided I had to kill that one fast. I didn't want people to think I was trying to cash in on Ellen Terry's name and fame [*see* Megan **Terry**]. So I turned my christian names round and added a hyphen for an individual touch" [Terry-Thomas with Terry Daum, *Terry-Thomas Tells Tales*, 1990]. "The hyphen's the gap between my teeth," he quipped.

Peter **Terson:** Peter Patterson (1932–), Br. playwright. The writer adopted the clipped form of his name in the 1960s when he was resident dramatist at the Victoria Theatre, Stoke-on-Trent, Britain's first theater-in-the-round. Perhaps he wished to avoid the echo of "pit-a-pat" in the original.

Phillida **Terson:** Phyllis Neilson-Terry (1892–1977), Eng. stage actress. The actress's new surname combines syllables from her original surname.

Abram **Tertz:** Andrey Donatovich Sinyavsky (1925–1997), Russ. novelist, short-story writer, critic. The writer adopted this name, that of Jewish gangster from Odessa, for fiction published in the West. The choice of such a name was probably intended to imply he was an "outsider," as a criminal is.

Vaan **Teryan:** Vaan Sukiasovich Ter-Grigoryan (1885–1920), Armenian poet. The poet telescoped his surname, combining the prefixed particle Ter-, frequently found in Armenian names to denote a clerical origin, with the second half of the surname proper (itself from the first name Grigor, "Gregory").

Laurent **Terzieff:** Laurent Tchemerzine (1935–), Fr. movie actor.

Edward **Teschemacher:** Edward F. Lockton (?1876–1940), U.S. popular songwriter. Some sources treat these names as those of two separate individuals.

Teutha: William Jerdan (1782–1869), Sc. journalist, editor, writer. The writer used this name for a number of contributions to journals, taking it from the historic name of the Tweed. He was born in Kelso, which stands on this Scottish river.

Joe **Tex:** Joseph Arrington, Jr. (1933–1982),

U.S. black soul singer, composer. The musician was born in Texas, as his name implies. In 1966 he converted to the Muslim faith and took the name Yusuf Hazziez.

Texas Ruby: Ruby Agnes Owens (1908–1963), U.S. country singer. Texas-born Ruby developed her cowgirl, yodeling persona in the 1930s with the Bronco Busters band, led by her husband-to-be, country and western performer Zeke Clements.

Josephine **Tey:** Elizabeth Mackintosh (1896–1952), Sc. novelist, playwright. The writer adopted her great-grandmother's name for her best-known pen name, which she used for her detective stories. For her plays she signed herself Gordon Daviot, a name taken from Daviot, near Inverness, where her family had vacationed, and she preferred to be listed under this (male) name in *Who's Who*.

[Dame] Maggie **Teyte:** Margaret Cottingham, née Tate (1888–1976), Eng. singer. When the soprano went to Paris at the age of 20 she changed the spelling of her surname to ensure the correct pronunciation of "Tate" by the French. This led to doubts about her name's pronunciation in English-speaking countries, a situation commented on in a piece of doggerel (of American origin):

> Tell us ere it be too late,
> Art thou known as Maggie Teyte?
> Or, per contra, art thou hight
> As we figure, Maggie Teyte?

Zaré **Thalberg:** Ethel Western (1858–1915), Eng. opera singer, stage actress. The singer was a pupil of the Austrian composer Sigismond Thalberg (1812–1871) and adopted his name. After losing her singing voice, she became an actress under her real name.

Thalia: Adriane Thalia Sodi Miranda (1972–), Mexican popular singer, TV actress.

Elswyth **Thane:** Helen Ricker Beebe (1900–1984), U.S. playwright, novelist. The writer used this name before marrying naturalist and oceanographer William Beebe (1877–1962) as his second wife.

Octave **Thanet:** Alice French (1850–1934), U.S. short-story writer, novelist. The writer adopted her sexually ambiguous pen name early in her career. "Octave was the name of a school-friend of mine. It is both French and Scotch. I thought if I could find another name to go with it, that was both French and Scotch, I would adopt that. I was riding on a train one time when we stopped at a way station, and on a siding near where I sat was a freight car painted red. On the side was chalked the word, 'Thanet.' What it meant or how it got there, I have not the slightest idea, but I decided then and there to adopt it. Lots of people still think that Octave Thanet is a man and I frequently get letters like this: 'My dear

Mr. Thanet: I have read your works and I am sure you are a manly man.' They usually contain a request for a small loan, to be repaid in the near future" [Marble, p.207].

Sister Rosetta **Tharpe:** Rosetta Nubin (1915–1973), U.S. black gospel singer, guitarist. Rosetta performed publicly from childhood, when she was billed as "Little Sister" because of her small stature. In the early 1930s she married a church elder, Pastor Thorpe, and although later separating from him, kept his name as her professional name, changing one letter.

Mlle. **Théodore:** Marie-Madeleine de Crépé (or Crespé) (1760–1796), Fr. ballet dancer.

Mother **Theodore:** Anne-Thérèse Guérin (1798–1856), Fr.-born U.S. educator, religious leader. Anne-Thérèse entered the Congregation of the Sisters of Providence in 1823, taking the name Sister Theodore She became known as Mother Theodore after emigrating to the USA with five other sisters in 1840.

Theodosia: Anne Steele (1716–1778), Eng. religious poet, hymnwriter. The name, which means "gift of God," was significant for the writer, who after the death of her fiancé by drowning only a few hours before the time fixed for the wedding adopted it for *Poems on Subjects Chiefly Devotional* (1760).

Pater **Theodosius:** Anton Crispin Florentini (1808–1865), Swiss ecclesiastic, philanthropist.

[St.] **Theophanes the Hermit:** Georgy Govorov (1815–1894), Russ. prelate, theologian. The future bishop took his religious name, meaning "manifesting God," on becoming a monk in 1841. In 1866 he relinquished his episcopal duties and from 1872 lived the rest of his life as a hermit. In 1988 he was canonized by the Russian Orthodox Church.

Théophile: Théophile (de) Viau (1590–1626), Fr. poet. D'Israeli explains how the poet abandoned his last name: "A French poet of the name of Theophile *Viaut* [*sic*], finding that his surname pronounced like *veau* (calf) exposed him to the infinite jests of the minor wits, silently dropped it, by retaining the more poetic appellation of *Theophile*" [p.201]. Sources now list the poet under either first or last name.

Theophilos: Theophilos Hadjimichalis (*c*.1870–1934), Gk. painter.

Sylvanus **Theophrastus:** John Thelwall (1764–1834), Eng. reformer, politician, lecturer on elocution. The writer's pseudonym is a classical concoction, but may have had specific reference to Johannes Sylvanus, the 16th-century German reformer and theologian, and the 3d-century BC Greek philosopher Theophrastus. The latter name gained vogue from the 16th century thanks to translations of the philosopher's works, and was employed by other writers, for example as a pen name of the Scottish publisher William Creech (1745–1815) and in the title of a volume of essays by George **Eliot**, *The Impressions of Theophrastus Such* (1879).

Thérésa: Eugénie Emma Valadon (1837–1913), Fr. music-hall artist.

Mother **Theresa** *see* Mother **Teresa**

[St.] **Theresa of Lisieux:** Marie-Françoise-Thérèse Martin (1873–1897), Fr. nun, virgin. At age 15, Theresa entered the Carmelite convent at Lisieux, Normandy. She was canonized in 1925. Her full title was Theresa of the Child Jesus (Thérèse de l'Enfant Jésus) and she was popularly known as the Little Flower of Jesus.

Mère Thérèse de Jésus: Alix le Clerc (1576–1622), Fr. founder of the Nuns of Notre Dame.

Y Thesbiad: John Roose Elias (1819–1881), Welsh poet, critic.

Theta: William Thorn (1794–1870), Eng. cleric. The writer used this name, from the Greek letter representing the initial "Th" of his surname, for *The Thorn-Tree: being a History of Thorn Worship of the Twelve Tribes of Israel* (1863).

David **Thewlis:** David Wheeler (1963–), Br. stage, TV actor. The actor's stage name is his mother's maiden name.

Alan **Thicke:** Alan Jeffery (1948–), U.S. TV actor, writer. The actor adopted his stepfather's surname.

Wilhelm **Thiele:** Wilhelm Isersohn (1890–1975), Austr. movie director, scriptwriter, working in U.S.

Ursula **Thiess:** Ursula Schmidt (1924–), Ger.-born movie actress.

Thinks-I-to-Myself, Who?: [Rev.] Edward Nares (1762–1841), Eng. cleric, novelist, historian. The writer used this name for *Thinks-I-to-Myself* (1811), a "serio-ludicro-tragico-comico tale," and *I Says, Says I* (1812), a novel. Nares had himself complained when others used this pseudo-pseudonym.

Rowland **Thirlmere:** John Walker (1860–1932), Eng. cotton-mill manager, politician. The writer was born in Cumberland, a county famed for the Lake District, where one of the lakes is Thirlmere.

Bel **Thistlethwaite:** Agnes Ethelwyn Wetherald (1857–1940), Can. poet, journalist. The writer adopted her maternal grandmother's maiden name as her pen name.

Ernest **Thoinau:** Antoine Ernest Roquet (1827–1894), Fr. musician, authority on early music. Thoinau is a diminutive of Antoin, an early form of Antoine.

Caroline **Thomas:** Julia Caroline Dorr, née Ripley (1825–1913), U.S. poet, novelist. The writer adopted her mother's maiden name for her first novel, *Farmingdale* (1854). Later novels were published under her married name.

Danny **Thomas:** Muzyad Yakhoob (1912–1991) U.S. entertainer, of Lebanese parentage. When still a teenager, the actor anglicized his name for a song-and-dance act as Amos Jacobs, just as his father, Shaheed Yakhoob, had anglicized his own name as Charles Jacobs. He later adopted the anglicized first names of his two brothers to give his regular stage name.

Denton **Thomas** *see* J.P. **McCall**

E.H. Francis **Thomas:** David Tecwyn Lloyd (1914–), Welsh editor, writer. The writer used this pseudonym for two collections of short stories.

Idris **Thomas:** Robert Thomas Jenkins (1881–1969), Eng.-born Welsh historian, writer. The writer, raised at Bala, not far from the mountain Cader Idris, used this name for short stories and a novel.

Irma **Thomas:** Irma Lee (1941–), U.S. black soul singer.

Jonathan Taylor **Thomas:** Jonathan Weiss (1981–), U.S. movie actor.

Josephine **Thomas** *see* Rosa **Henderson**

J. Parnell **Thomas:** John Parnell Feeney, Jr. (1895–1970), U.S. congressman. Feeney changed his name after World War I on becoming a bond salesman with the Paine Webber Company. Court records indicate that he did so because he thought the new name would enhance his business career. The change included the substitution of a single initial in place of his original first name John.

Kid **Thomas:** (1) Thomas Valentine (1896–1987), U.S. jazz trumpeter; (2) Louis Thomas Watts (1934–1970), U.S. black blues musician.

Olive **Thomas:** Oliveretta Elaine Duffy (1884–1920), U.S. movie actress.

Piri **Thomas:** Juan Pedro Tomás (1928–), U.S. writer, moviemaker, of Puerto Rican-Cuban parentage.

Tommé **Thomas:** Grace Cecilia Ida McNaughton (1916–2003), U.S. music-hall singer, niece of Marie **Lloyd**. The performer's father, Tom MacNaughton, had wanted a son, and she adopted the name he would have given him.

Thomas à Kempis: Thomas Hemerken (c.1380–1471), Du. theologian. The reputed author of *De Imitatione Christi* takes his name from his birthtown of Kempen, near Cologne in what is now Germany.

Alfred **Thompson:** Thompson E. Jones (1831–1895), Br. musical theater librettist, artist.

Carlos **Thompson:** Juan Carlos Mundin Schafter (or Mundanschaffter) (1916–1990), Argentinian stage, movie actor, of Ger. descent.

Daley **Thompson:** Francis Morgan Thompson (1958–), Br. black athlete. The decathlete's new first name is a pet form of Ayodele, a Nigerian name given him by his father, meaning "joy comes home."

Franklin **Thompson:** Sarah Emma Evelyn Edmonds (1842–1898), U.S. adventuress. While still a teenager, Emma cut off her hair, dressed as a man, and became a Bible seller for a firm in Hartford, Connecticut, under the name Franklin Thompson. In 1861 she enlisted in a Michigan regiment, but deserted after two years and resumed her female role and dress. In 1867 she married her childhood sweetheart, Linus Seelye, and had three children.

Jack **Thompson:** John Payne (1940–), Austral. movie actor.

Kay **Thompson:** Kitty Fink (1902–1998), US. movie actress, children's writer.

Sue **Thompson:** Eva Sue McKee (1926–), U.S. pop singer.

Anna **Thomson:** Anna Levine (1957–), U.S. movie actress.

James **Thomson, B.V.:** James Thomson (1834–1882), Sc. poet. The poet added the initials to his name in order to be distinguished from the Scottish poet who was his namesake, James Thomson (1700–1748). The letters stand for "Bysshe Vanolis," the first of these names being the middle name of Percy Bysshe Shelley, the second an anagram of the name of **Novalis.** Thomson greatly admired both writers.

Henry David **Thoreau:** David Henry Thoreau (1817–1862), U.S. writer, naturalist. Thoreau switched his first two names as a young man, both because he was actually called Henry at home and because he thought the new order more euphonious.

Thomas **Thorild:** Thomas Thorén (1759–1808), Swe. journalist, poet.

Thorkelin: Grímur Jónsson (1752–1829), Icelandic scholar, antiquary, working in Denmark.

Thormanby: William Willmott Dixon (1843–1914), Eng. sporting writer. Dixon used this name, presumably that of the North Yorkshire village, for works such as *Kings of the Turf: Memoirs and Anecdotes of Distinguished Owners, Backers, Trainers, and Jockeys who have Featured on the British Turf, with Memorable Achievements of Famous Horses* (1898).

Edgar **Thorn:** Edward MácDowell (1860–1908), U.S. composer, pianist. The musician published a number of works under this pseudonym.

Geoffrey **Thorn:** Charles Townley (1843–1905), Eng. popular songwriter.

Ismay **Thorn:** Edith Caroline Pollock (*fl.*1890), Br. children's writer.

Ronald Scott **Thorn:** Ronald Scotthorn Wilkinson (1920–1996), Br. playwright, novelist. The writer used this (transparent) name early in his career for distinction from his professional work as a physician.

Helen Louise **Thorndyke** *see* Carolyn **Keene**

Guy **Thorne:** Cyril Arthur Edward Ranger-Gull (1876–1923), Eng. writer of horror and mystery novels.

Whyte **Thorne:** Richard Whiteing (1840–1928), Eng. journalist, novelist. The writer used this punning name for his first novel, *The Democracy* (1876).

Frank **Thornton:** Francis Thornton Ball (1921–), Eng. stage, TV actor. The actor adopted his mother's maiden name (his own middle name) as his stage name.

Henry **Thornton:** Henry Ford (1750–1818), Eng. theater manager.

Jim **Thorpe:** Wa-tho-huck (1888–1943), U.S. athlete, footballer. The sportsman's father was part Irish and part Native American, while his mother was part Native American and part French. His original Native American name meant "bright path." His full formal English name was James Frances Thorpe.

Linda **Thorson:** Linda Robinson (1947–), Can. stage, TV actress. The actress extracted her stage name from the surname of her first husband, Barry Bergthorson, whom she married at the age of 16.

Yodsanan **3K Battery:** Peera Pongwan (1974–), Thai boxer. Later known as Yodsanan Sor Nanthachai, the boxer changed his name to that of his sponsors, TK Battery, a locally based manufacturer of automotive and motorcycle batteries. The firm has sponsored several other boxers, who all likewise adopted their name. Medgoen Singsurat thus became Medgoen 3K Battery.

The **Three Stooges** *see* (1) Larry **Fine**; (2) Curly **Howard**

Thriller U: Eustace C. Hamilton (*c.*1962–), Jamaican reggae singer. "U" for "Eustace."

General Tom **Thumb:** Charles Sherwood Stratton (1838–1883), U.S. midget performer. Charles Stratton was rechristened "General Tom Thumb" by showman P.T. Barnum, who had discovered him at the age of four. In folklore, Tom Thumb is a plowman's son who is only as tall as his father's thumb. The name itself, as that of a dwarf or small person, goes back to at least the 16th century, with "Tom" apparently a reduplicated form of "thumb." "'Tom Thumb' is a name generally given by showmen to liliputians [*sic*]. The first holder of this 'title' was Charles Stratton, who was brought to London by Barnum" [*Daily Chronicle*, February 6, 1907].

Johnny **Thunder:** Gil Hamilton (1941–), U.S. pop singer.

Captain **Thunderbolt** *see* **Captain Thunderbolt**

Chief **Thundercloud** *see* **Chief Thundercloud**

Johnny **Thunders:** John Anthony Genzale, Jr. (1952–1991), U.S. rock musician. The guitarist first called himself Johnny Volume before settling to his regular stage name.

Mary **Thurman**: Mary Christiansen (1894 or 1895–1925), U.S. movie comedienne.

Henry J. **Thurstan**: Francis Turner Palgrave (1824–1897), Eng. poet, critic. The anthologizing editor of *Palgrave's Golden Treasury* (1861), son of the historian Sir Francis **Palgrave**, adopted this name for *The Passionate Pilgrim; or, Eros and Anteros* (1858), a series of poetic discourses.

Tian: Karoline von Günderrode (1780–1806), Ger. poet.

Lawrence **Tibbett**: Lawrence Mervil Tibbet (1896–1960), U.S. classical singer. The baritone adopted a misspelling of his surname in a 1923 Metropolitan Opera program as his professional name.

Andrew **Tibbs**: Melvin Andrew Grayson (1929–1991), U.S. black blues singer.

Tiberius: Tiberius Claudius Nero (42 BC–AD 37), Roman emperor. The emperor's original full name was as above, and was the same as that of his father. His later full name was Tiberius Caesar Augustus (or Tiberius Julius Caesar Augustus), for **Augustus**, whose stepson, adopted son, and successor he was. His own successor was **Caligula**.

Roger Charles Doughty **Tichborne**: Arthur Orton (1834–1898), Eng. impostor. The case of the "Tichborne claimant," the most celebrated in English law, dates from 1853, when Roger Tichborne, heir to an ancient baronetcy, sailed for Valparaiso, Chile. After traveling for a time in South America, he embarked on April 20, 1854, in a ship named the *Bella*, bound for Jamaica. The ship went down, and nothing more was heard of him. In October 1856, one R.C.D. Tichborne turned up at Wagga Wagga, Australia, in the person of a man known locally as Tom Castro. On December 25, 1866, he landed in England as a claimant to the Tichborne baronetcy, saying he was the lost Roger. Lady Tichborne, the real Roger's mother, claimed she recognized him, but the rest of the family were dubious. The matter went to court, where the claimant's case was found to be false and he was identified as Arthur Orton, son of a London butcher. A further trial for perjury ended in a 14-year jail sentence. Orton was released in 1884, and in 1895 confessed to the duplicity. He is said to have recanted, however, holding fast to his assumed identity, and the name engraved on his coffin was "Sir Roger Charles Doughty Tichborne."

Miss **Tickletoby**: William Makepeace Thackeray (1811–1863), Eng. novelist. Thackeray used this name for a series of contributions to *Punch* under the general heading "Miss Tickletoby's Lectures on English History." Miss Tickletoby herself comes over as a rather sinister schoolmistress who is always threatening to cane her inattentive audience. Hence her name, from *tickle* in the sense "beat" and *toby*, an early Victorian slang term for the buttocks. "Toby" was also Thackeray's nickname for his wife Isabella.

Reginald **Tierney**: Thomas O'Neill Russell (1829–1908), Ir. writer.

Tiësto: Tijs Verwest (1969–), Du. DJ.

Tiffany: Tiffany Renee Darwish (1971–), U.S. pop singer.

Pamela **Tiffin**: Pamela Wonso (1942–), U.S. movie actress, former child model.

Tiger: Norman Jackson (1960–), Jamaican DJ, reggae singer.

Dick **Tiger**: Dick Ihetu (1929–1971), Nigerian middleweight boxer.

Theobald **Tiger** *see* Ignaz **Wrobel**

[St.] **Tikhon**: Vasily Ivanovich Belavin (1865–1925), Russ. churchman, patriarch of Moscow and All Russia. The head of the Russian Orthodox Church, who was canonized in 1989, adopted his religious name on taking monastic vows in 1891. The name itself means "successful," from the Greek.

Sonny **Til**: Earlington Carl Tilghman (1925–1981), U.S. "doo-wop" singer.

Vesta **Tilley**: Matilda Alice Powles (1864–1952), Br. singing comedienne, male impersonator. The actress began her performing career at the age of three, when she was billed as Little Tilley (as a pet form of her first name, which she shared with her mother). This was a provincial debut, made at the Star Music Hall, Gloucester, where her father, Harry **Ball**, was the manager. When she was 14, she made her first London appearance, now being billed as The Great Little Tilley. It was soon after this that she adopted the name Vesta, using Tilley as a surname. That way she intrigued even more those members of her audiences, who were puzzled as to whether she was male or female. The selection of this name has been related to the type of wax match known as a "Vesta" (after the Greek goddess of the hearth).

Alice **Tilton**: Phoebe Atwood Taylor (1909–1976), U.S. detective story writer. Taylor wrote two series of novels featuring amateur detectives, one with Asey May, under her own name, and the other with Leonidas Xenophon Witherall, under her pseudonym. She also published a mystery novel, *Murder at the New York World's Fair* (1940), under the name Freeman Dana.

Tim: William Timyn (1902–1990), Austr.-born Br. cartoonist.

Timbaland: Timothy Z. Mosley (1972–), U.S. hip-hop promoter, performer. The musician adopted the nickname given him by R&B producer DeVante Swing.

Mark **Time**: Henry Crossly Irwin (1848–1924),

Eng. writer. Professionally a retired civil servant, Irwin used this transparently punning name for his imperialist "fantasy" *A Derelict Empire* (1912).

Joe Timer: Joseph Michael Theimer (1923–1955), U.S. jazz drummer.

Timothy: Timothy Birdsall (1936–1963), Eng. cartoonist, illustrator.

Timrava: Bozena Slánciková (1867–1951), Slovakian writer.

Tina: Philomena Josephine Veronica Quinn (1948–), Ir. pop singer.

Tina Louise: Tina Louise Blacker (1934–), U.S. movie actress.

Dick Tinto: Frank Booth Goodrich (1826–1894), U.S. writer, son of Peter **Parley** (1). Goodrich adopted the name of the artist who is the supposed narrator of the story told in Sir Walter Scott's *The Bride of Lammermoor* (1819).

Tintoretto: Jacopo Robusti (*c.*1518–1594), It. painter. The artist's name arose as nickname meaning "little dyer," as he was the son of a silk dyer (Italian *tintore*).

Tiny Doll *see* Tiny **Doll**

Tiny Tim: Herbert Butros Khaury (1931–1996), U.S. popular singer, of Lebanese Jewish parentage. The oddball entertainer is said to have adopted his name from an incident in 1965: "As he was shambling out of a New York night spot whose management had decided that his lanky 6 ft figure and bizarre clothes did not 'fit,' a voice from the audience called out, 'Hey, Tiny, do us a set.' Khaury returned, performed, and from that moment grew swiftly to fame as Tiny Tim" [*The Times*, December 2, 1996]. Khaury had also played Greenwich Village clubs as Darry Dover and Larry Love.

Tippa Irie: Anthony Henry (1965–), Br. black reggae singer. "Irie" as for **Sweetie Irie**.

Billy Tipton: Dorothy Lucille Tipton (1914–1989), U.S. jazz pianist, saxophonist. The musician adopted a male guise and name at the age of 19 after failing to break into the jazz scene as a woman.

James Tiptree, Jr.: Alice Sheldon, née Bradley (1915–1986), U.S. SF writer. The writer took her (male) name in 1967 from a jar of Wilkin's "Tiptree" jam that she saw in a supermarket. She also wrote as Raccoona Sheldon.

Tiradentes: Joaquim José da Silva Xavier (1748–1792), Brazilian revolutionary. The activist had many jobs as a young man, one of them being a dentist. Hence his nickname, which he adopted as his pseudonym, meaning "toothpuller" (Portuguese *tirar*, "to pull," and *dente*, "tooth").

Tiresias: Roger Swithin Green (1940–), Eng. writer. Although best known as a poet, Green also wrote prose, adopting this name for *Notes from Over-*ground (1984), a book about commuting from Oxford to London, with a title punning on Dostoyevsky's *Notes from Underground*. Tiresias, a blind prophet of Greek legend, has been a subject of poets from classical writers to the present day.

Tirso de Molina: [Fray] Gabriel Téllez (*c.*1571–1648), Sp. dramatist. When censorship threatened his work early in his career, for monks were not supposed to write plays, Téllez called himself Tirso de Molina, "Tirso of Molina."

Hans Tisdall: Hans John Knox Aufseeser (1910–1997), Ger.-born artist, designer, working in U.K.

Timothy Titcomb: Josiah Gilbert Holland (1819–1881), U.S. physician, novelist, poet, editor. The writer used this name for *Titcomb's Letters to Young People, Single and Married* (1858), among other works. He also wrote as Max Mannering.

Titian: Tiziano Vecellio (*c.*1485–1576), It. painter. Unlike some of his contemporaries, Titian did not assume (and was apparently not given) a name or nickname that differed from his original first name.

Michael Angelo Titmarsh: William Makepeace Thackeray (1811–1863), Eng. novelist. Thackeray used this name for various tales published from the 1840s. He is said to have been nicknamed "Michael Angelo" for his broken nose and his sketching talent, or according to one authority, "from his massive body, broad shoulders, and large head" [E. Cobham Brewer, *The Reader's Handbook*, 1882]. To this famous name, Thackeray then added "Titmarsh" as an absurd contrast. Samuel Titmarsh is a character in Thackeray's *The Great Hoggarty Diamond* (1848).

[Marshal] Tito: Josip Broz (1892–1980), Yugoslav revolutionary, statesman. There are various accounts claiming to explain the leader's name. One maintains that it derives from Serbo-Croat *ti to*, literally "you this," meaning "you do this," from his constant ordering about. But Tito himself is said to have adopted the name after reading books by two Serbo-Croatian writers who had Tito (the equivalent of Titus) as their first name, one perhaps being Tito Brezovacki (1754–1805). He is said to have wished to adopt the name Rudi, but someone else had already claimed it. The second of these accounts seems the more likely. In the world of partisan warfare in which Tito was involved, he had several underground names, but in Comintern communications he was always "Comrade Walter." The hazardous conditions of guerrilla combat sometimes necessitated a change of cover name as often as three times a *day* [Jules Archer, *Red Rebel: Tito of Yugoslavia*, 1968].

Giovanni Titta Rosa: Giovanni Battista Rosa (1891–1972), It. poet, literary critic. The first part of the writer's pen name represents a childish pronunciation of "Battista." (Giovanni Battista, a common Italian forename, means literally "John the Baptist.")

Titus: Antoine Titus Doschi (?–after 1849), Fr. ballet director, teacher, working in Russia.

Tivoli: Horace William Bleackley (1868–1931), Eng. writer.

Theodore Moses **Tobani:** Theodore Moses (1855–1933), Ger.-born U.S. composer, arranger. The musician began adding "Tobani" to his name in 1895, first with a hyphen, then making a legal change. His prolific output prompted his publisher to encourage him to use pen names, which he did, among them Florence Reed, F. Wohanka, and Andrew Herman (from the first names of two of his three sons).

Channing Heggie **Tobias:** Channing Heggie Robinson (1882–1961), U.S. reformer, civil rights leader. It is not known why Tobias adopted a last name different from that of his parents.

Harriet **Toby:** Harriet Katzman (1929–1952), U.S. ballet dancer.

(Uncle) Simeon **Toby:** George Trask (1798–1875), U.S. cleric, reformer. The writer used this name for *Thoughts and Stories on Tobacco, for American Lads* (1852), subtitled *Uncle Toby's Anti-Tobacco Advice to his Nephew, Billy Bruce*. Trask also used the less conventional pen name Ziba Sproule.

Toby, M.P.: [Sir] Henry William Lucy (1845–1924), Eng. journalist, humorist, satirist. The writer used this name for his contributions to *Punch*, Toby being the name of Punch's dog in the traditional "Punch and Judy" puppet show. The initials were intended to stand for "Member of Parliament," although Lucy was not an M.P. but a J.P. (Justice of the Peace). Toby was described as being the "member for Barks," punning on the county name Berkshire (abbreviated Berks, pronounced "Barks"). Lucy used the humorous pseudonym Baron de Bookworms for other articles in the magazine.

Tochinowaka: Kiyotake Kaseda (1962–), Jap. sumo wrestler. The wrestler was in the Kasugano stable, whose members usually have a fighting name prefixed with *tochi*, "horse chestnut," out of respect for Tochigiyama, their eighth *oyakata* (elder).

Tochitsukasa: Tetsu Goto (1958–), Jap. sumo wrestler. The wrestler was in the Kasugano stable, whose members usually have names prefixed *tochi* (*see* **Tochinowaka**).

Ann (E.) **Todd:** Anne Todd Mayfield (1932–), U.S. child movie actress. The actress added the middle "E." to her name in the 1940s to avoid confusion with the British actress Ann Todd (1909–1993).

James **Todd:** Clarence Rivers King (1842–1901), U.S. geologist. King assumed his new name to identify with his wife, Ada Copeland, a black nursemaid whom he married in 1888.

Mike **Todd:** Avrom Hirsch Goldbogen (1909–1958), U.S. movie producer, of Pol. Jewish parentage. When Goldbogen's father died, in 1931, he assumed the first name Michael, at the same time changing his surname to "Todd," a form of his childhood nickname, "Toat." The widescreen motion-picture system Todd-AO was named for him.

Nick **Todd:** Nicholas Boone (1935–), U.S. pop singer. The singer was signed to Dot Records, and took his stage name by reversing the company name.

Richard **Todd:** Richard Andrew Palethorpe-Todd (1919–2009), Ir.-born Br. movie actor.

Togare: Georg Kulovits (1900–1988), Hung.-born Austr. animal tamer, circus artist. Originally working as Helios, in 1925 the performer adopted the character name of his act, an exotic and fearless oriental lion tamer.

Togolok Moldo: Bayymbet Abdyrakhmanov (1860–1942), Kirgiz folk poet. The poet's adopted name was self-descriptive and means "round-faced scholar."

To Huu: Nguyen Kim Thanh (1920–2002), Vietnamese poet, politician.

To' Janggut: Muhammad Hasan bin Munas (1853–1915), Malay rebel peasant leader. Hasan came to be known by his nickname, which referred to his long white beard.

To' Kenali: Muhammad Yusof bin Ahmad (1868–1933), Malay theologian, religious teacher.

Samuel **Tolansky:** Samuel Turlausky (1907–1973), Br. physicist, of Lithuanian Jewish origin. The family name was changed for ease of pronunciation some time before 1912.

Svetlana **Toma:** Svetlana Andreyevna Fomicheva (1947–), Russ. movie actress.

Tom and Jerry *see* **Simon and Garfunkel**

Isaac **Tomkins, Gent.:** [Sir] Henry Peter Brougham, Baron Brougham and Vaux (1778–1868), Sc.-born Br. statesman, writer. The Lord Chancellor of England used this name for *We Can't Afford It!, being Thoughts on the Aristocracy of England* (1834).

F.L. **Tomline:** [Sir] William Schwenk Gilbert (1836–1911), Eng. dramatist, burlesque writer. Gilbert used this name for *The Happy Land* (1873), a burlesque version of his own "fairy comedy" *The Wicked World*. He later expanded the name as F. Latour Tomline for the comedy *The Wedding March* (1873).

[Sir] George Pretyman **Tomline:** George Pretyman (1750–1827), Eng. prelate. The bishop of Lincoln took the additional name of Tomline in 1803 when a considerable estate at Riby in Lincolnshire was left him by the will of Marmaduke Tomline. "Between the testator and legatee there was no relationship, and but very slight acquaintance, the bishop not having seen Tomline more than five or six times in his life" [*Dictionary of National Biography*].

Tommaseo: Niccolò Tomasic (1802–1874), It. (Dalmatian) writer, philologist, patriot.

Tom of Finland: Touko Laaksonen (1920–1991), Finn. artist. The artist took his name in 1957 when his "macho" drawing of a lumberjack appeared on the cover of the U.S. magazine *Physique Pictorial*.

István Tömörkény: István Steingasner (1866–1917), Hung. writer, folklorist, ethnographer.

Tomos Glyn Cothi: Thomas Evans (1764–1833), Welsh poet, writer. The writer's name derives from a local placename in his native Carmarthenshire, so means "Thomas of Glyncothi."

Graham R. Tomson: Rosamund Marriott Tomson, earlier Armytage, née Ball (1860–1911), Eng. writer. The author adopted this male name for some of her poetry, basing it on the name of her second husband, Arthur Graham Tomson, the middle initial representing her own first name.

Tone-Lōc: Anthony Terrell Smith (1966–), U.S. black rapper. The name is short for the singer's Spanish nickname, Antonio Loco ("Mad Anthony"). The macron over the vowel in "Lōc" gives it the pronunciation "Loke."

Stanley Tong: Tony Kwai-Lai (1962–), Chin. movie director, screenwriter.

Jacob Tonson: Enoch Arnold Bennett (1867–1931), Br. novelist. The writer's early pseudonym was borrowed from that of an 18th-century bookseller.

Steve Peregrine Took: Stephen Ross Porter (1949–1980), Br. rock musician. The percussionist took his name from Peregrin Took, one of the hobbits in J.R.R. Tolkien's *The Lord of the Rings* (1954).

Horne Tooke: John Horne (1736–1812), Eng. politician, philologist. In 1782 Horne added the name of William Tooke, a friend and political supporter, to his own, so that from then on he was John Horne Tooke (familiarly, Horne Tooke). Tooke had a sizeable estate in Surrey, and Horne had added his name with the intention of indicating that he would be his friend's heir. When Tooke died in 1802, however, Horne Tooke discovered that instead of making him his beneficiary, William Tooke had merely left him £500, apart from canceling certain outstanding debts.

Jean Toomer: Nathan Pinchback Toomer (1894–1967), U.S. writer, philosopher. In 1895 Toomer's father abandoned his family, whereupon he and his mother went to live with his African-American grandfather, Pinckney Benton Stewart Pinchback, who agreed to support them on condition that the boy's name be changed. Thereafter, although no legal change was made, his grandparents called him Eugene Pinchback, while in school he was known as Eugene Pinchback Toomer. Later, when beginning a career as a writer, he dropped his middle name and changed Eugene to Jean.

Too $hort: Todd Shaw (1966–), U.S. black rapper. The artist's name, based on his original name, refers to his small stature and his wish to make money by his music.

Top Cat: Anthony Codrington (c.1973–), Br. black reggae singer. The singer's nickname dates from his schooldays, when he was compared to the mischievous, fast-talking cartoon cat of the name.

Rebecca Tope: Rebecca Smith (1948–), Br. crime writer.

Topol: Chaim (or Haym) Topol (1935–), Israeli stage, movie actor. The actor made his name on the London stage playing Tevye in the U.S. musical *The Fiddler on the Roof* (1967). He dropped his first name on discovering that it confused the English.

Top Sawyer: David Davies (1818–1890), Welsh industrialist. The coalmine founder took his name from his early employment as a "top sawyer" in the timber trade, working in the upper position during the sawing process and so avoiding the sawdust. The term came to be used metaphorically for a superior or distinguished person, and Davies would have been aware of this sense.

Friedrich Torberg: Friedrich Kantor-Berg (1908–1979), Austr. novelist, essayist.

Peter Tordenskjold: Peter Wessel (1691–1720), Dan.-born Norw. naval commander, of Du. parentage. The commander was raised to the aristocracy following a battle victory in 1716 in the Great Northern War against the Swedes, and took his new name then.

Miguel Torga: Adolfo Correia da Rocha (1907–1995), Port. poet, diarist.

Peter Tork: Peter Torkelson (1942–), U.S. pop musician.

Rip Torn: Elmore Rual Torn, Jr. (1931–), U.S. stage, movie, TV actor. The actor retained his high school nickname (of obvious origin) for his professional name.

Torquemada: Edward Powys Mathers (1892–1939), Br. crossword compiler. The setter adopted the name of the infamous Spanish Grand Inquisitor, since he aimed to torture his victims, as his historic namesake had done in the 15th century. (The Inquisitor's name suggests torturing, from Latin *torquere*, "to twist," "to torture," but it actually derives from his place of origin, itself from Spanish *torre*, "tower," and *quemada*, "burnt.")

A.C. Torr *see* Fred **Leslie**

David Torrence: David Torrence Tayson (1880–1942), Sc. movie actor.

Johannes Torrentius: Jan van der Beeck (1589–1644), Du. painter. The artist translated his Dutch name (in English amounting to "John of the Brook") into a Latin equivalent.

Raquel **Torres:** Paula Marie Osterman (1908–1987), Mexican-born U.S. movie actress.

Malcolm **Torrie** *see* Stephen **Hockaby**

Traven **Torsvan** *see* B. **Traven**

Andrew **Tosh:** Andrew McIntosh (1967–), Jamaican reggae musician, son of Peter **Tosh**.

Peter **Tosh:** Winston Hubert Peter McIntosh (1944–1987), Jamaican reggae musician.

Tostão: Eduardo Gonçalves de Andrade (1947–), Brazilian footballer. The player's Portuguese name means "tanned," "sunburned" (literally "toasted").

Totius: Jakob Daniel Du Toit (1877–1953), S.A. poet, biblical scholar, writing in Afrikaans. Although based on his original surname, the writer's assumed name is also Latin for "of the whole."

Toto: Armando Novello (?–1938), Swiss circus clown. Novello took his ring name from **Totò**.

Totò: Antonio Clemente (1898–1967), It. stage, movie comedian. The actor, the illegitimate son of an impoverished noble, was in 1946 was given a title that recognized his aristocratic origin: Antonio Griffo Focas Flavio Ducas Comneno Porfirogenito Gagliardi de Curtis di Bisancio, where Ducas and Comneno are the names of two leading Byzantine families and Porfirogenito, from the Greek meaning "born in the purple," was the title of a Byzantine emperor's son. His screen name is a pet form of his first name.

Dave **Tough:** David Jarvis (1907–1948), U.S. jazz drummer.

Ali Farka **Touré:** Ali Ibrahim (1939–2006), Malian guitarist.

Askia M. **Touré:** Rolland Snellings (1938–), U.S. black poet, activist.

Kwame **Touré:** Stokely Carmichael (1941–1998), West Indian-born U.S. civil rights leader. The former Black Panthers leader changed his Western name for an African one on leaving the United States for Guinea in 1969. His new name honored two black African leaders that he admired: Kwame **Nkrumah** of Ghana and Sékou Touré (1922–1984) of Guinea.

Jennie **Tourel:** Jennie Davidovich (1899–1973), Russ.-born U.S. opera singer. The singer is said to have based her stage name on that of a teacher in Paris, Anna El-Tour, although she denied this.

Victor **Tourjansky:** Vyacheslav Turzhansky (1891–1976), Russ.-born movie director, working in France, U.S.

Maurice **Tourneur:** Maurice Tourneur Thomas (1876–1961), Fr. movie director.

Toussaint-Louverture: François Dominique Toussaint (1743–1803), Haitian black political leader. The liberator and independence fighter took his additional name in 1793 at the time of the French Revolution. It represents French *l'ouverture*, "the open-

ing," and alludes to the breaches that he bravely made in the ranks of his enemies.

Jean **Tousseul:** Olivier Degée (1890–1944), Belg. writer.

The **Tout:** P.R.G. Buchanan (1870–1950), Eng. sports cartoonist.

Rigo **Tovar:** Rigoberto Tovar Garcia (1946–2005), Mexican singer.

Martello **Tower** *see* **Martello Tower**

Robert **Towne:** Robert Schwartz (1934–), U.S. screenwriter, movie actor. Towne acted under the name Edward Wain in two films that he wrote, *The Last Woman on Earth* and *The Creature from the Haunted Sea* (both 1961).

Peter **Towry:** David Towry Piper (1918–1990), Eng. writer on art, novelist.

Toyah: Toyah Ann Willcox (1958–), Br. rock singer, stage, movie actress. The singer reverted to her full name when pursuing an acting career from the early 1990s. Her unusual first name is said to have been taken by her mother from a book she was reading about a ballerina so called.

Toyin: Toyin Adekale (1963–), Br. black (female) reggae singer.

Arthur **Tracy:** Abraham Alter Tratserofski (1899–1997), Ukr.-born U.S. popular singer.

Nitram **Tradleg:** Edmund Martin Geldart (1844–1885), Eng. religious writer. The Unitarian minister used this reversed name for *A Son of Belial: Autobiographical Sketches* (1882).

F.G. **Trafford:** Charlotte Eliza Lawson Riddell, née Cowan (1832–1906), Ir.-born Br. novelist. The author used this name for an early novel, *The Moors and the Fens* (1858), and retained it until 1864, after which she used her married name, Mrs. J.H. Riddell, as well as other pseudonyms. One was Rainey Hawthorne.

Peter **Traill:** Guy Mainwaring Morton (1896–1968), Eng. novelist, playwright.

Nick **Traina:** Nicholas John Steel (1978–1997), U.S. punk-rock musician.

Chris **Tranchell:** Christopher Peter John Small (1941–), Br. stage actor.

B. **Traven:** Albert Otto Max Feige (c.1882–1969), Ger. novelist. The writer was a recluse, revealing few personal details, and his true identity was discovered only in 1979. (He claimed he was born in Chicago, but he was probably born in Schwiebus, Germany, now Świebodzin, Poland.) From 1917 through 1920 he edited the revolutionary German magazine *Der Ziegelbrenner* ("The Tile Burner") under the name Ret Marut. The origin of this is uncertain. He also wrote as Traven Torsvan and, as a Hollywood scriptwriter, Hal Croves. He became a Mexican citizen in 1951 and died in Mexico City.

Bill **Travers:** William Lindon-Travers (1922–1994), Br. movie actor, brother of Linden **Travers**.

Graham **Travers:** Margaret Georgina Todd (1859–1918), Sc. physician, novelist. Dr. Todd used this male name for works such as *Mona Maclean, Medical Student* (1892) and *Fellow Travellers* (1896).

Henry **Travers:** Travers John Heagerty (1874–1965), Br. stage, movie actor, working in U.S.

John **Travers:** Eva Mary Bell, née Hamilton (1878–1959), Eng. novelist.

Linden **Travers:** Florence Lindon-Travers (1913–2001), Br. stage, movie actress, sister of Bill **Travers**.

P.L. **Travers:** Helen Lyndon Goff (1899–1996), Austral.-born writer, of Ir. descent, working in U.K. The creator of the fictional children's nanny Mary Poppins was so deeply influenced by her father, Travers Robert Goff, that she took his first name for her pen name. She invariably used initials for her writing, with P.L. actually standing for Pamela Lyndon.

Will **Travers** *see* Fenton **Brockley**

Michael **Travesser:** Wayne Bent (1941–), U.S. cult leader. The leader of the apocalyptic cult The Lord Our Righteousness, founded in New Mexico in 2000, was known by this name to his followers.

Nick **Travis:** Nicholas Anthony Travascio (1925–1964), U.S. jazz trumpeter.

Randy **Travis:** Randy Bruce Traywick (1959–), U.S. country singer. The singer originally performed as Randy Traywick. He then appeared as Randy Ray before adopting his eventual stage name, suggested by Martha Sharp, a director of Warner Bros. Records.

Richard **Travis:** William Justice (1913–1989), U.S. movie actor.

Will **Travis** *see* Wes **Hardin**

Tré: Tré Hardiman (*c*.1958–), U.S. black blues musician.

Arthur **Treacher:** Arthur Treacher Veary (1894–1975), Br. movie actor, working in U.S.

Lawrence **Treat:** Lawrence Arthur Goldstone (1903–1998), U.S. crime writer.

Zélia **Trebelli:** Gloria Caroline Gillebert (1834–1892), Fr. opera singer. The mezzosoprano formed her italianate stage surname by reversing her original name.

Trebor Mai: Robert Williams (1830–1877), Welsh poet. The writer's bardic name, more playful than most, reads "I am Robert" in reverse.

Pirmin **Trecu:** Pirnon Aldabaldetrecu (1930–2006), Sp. Basque ballet dancer, working in U.K.

Nye **Tredgold:** Nigel Godwin Tranter (1909–2000), Sc. historical novelist.

[Sir] Herbert Beerbohm **Tree:** Herbert Draper Beerbohm (1853–1917), Br. actor, theater manager. The actor was the son of Julius Beerbohm, a naturalized English grain merchant of Lithuanian parent-age. His stage name of "Tree" represented the English equivalent of the second half of his original surname, itself a form of German *Birnbaum*, "pear tree." He retained the original surname in his full name, which was thus Herbert Draper Beerbohm Tree, and first used the stage name Beerbohm Tree in 1876. Tree was the half-brother of the dramatist and critic Max Beerbohm (1872–1956).

Trefin: Edgar Phillips (1889–1962), Welsh poet. The writer took his bardic name from his native village of Trefin, Pembrokeshire.

Paul **Tremaine:** Georgia Blanche Douglas Johnson, née Camp (1880–1966), U.S. black poet, dramatist, literary hostess. Johnson adopted this male name for some of her short stories.

Peter **Tremayne:** Peter John Philip Berresford Ellis (1943–), Br. horror, fantasy writer. Ellis used his real name for books on Celtic history and legend.

Anthony **Trent:** Rebecca Friskin, née Clarke (1886–1979), Eng. violinist, composer.

Bruce **Trent:** William Butters (1912–1995), Br. stage actor, singer.

Gregory **Trent** *see* S.S. **Smith**

Olaf **Trent** *see* Neil **Balfort**

Robert **Tressell:** Robert P. Noonan (1870–1911), Ir. writer, working in U.K. The writer is famous for a single novel, *The Ragged-Trousered Philanthropists*, an attack on life and conditions in the building trade, published posthumously in abbreviated form in 1914 (with the pen name misspelled "Tressall") and in a full version in 1955. The author was by trade a house-painter and signwriter. The origin of his pseudonym is uncertain (possibly it was meant to suggest "trestle"), as is much about the writer's own background. His original middle name may have been Philippe.

Vladimir **Tretchikoff:** Vladimir Grigoryevich Tretyakov (1913–2006), Russ.-born S.A. artist. The painter of popular female portraits anglicized his original surname.

Trevanian: Rodney William Whitaker (1931–2005), U.S. thriller writer, academic. Whitaker adopted this name for his bestselling "airport" novels as a compliment to the English historian G.M. Trevelyan (1876–1962). He also wrote as Nicholas Seare, Benat LeCagot, and Edoard Moran.

Hilda **Trevelyan:** Hilda Marie Antoinette Anna Blow, née Tucker (1880–1959), Br. stage actress.

John **Trevena:** Ernest George Henham (1870–1946), Eng. poet, novelist, working in Canada.

Ann **Trevor:** Ann Trilnick (1899–1970), Br. movie actress.

Austin **Trevor:** Austin Trevor Schilsky (1897–1978), Ir.-born Br. movie, stage, radio actor.

Claire **Trevor:** Claire Wemlinger (1909–2000), U.S. movie actress.

Elleston **Trevor:** Trevor Dudley Smith (1920–1995), Br. spy thriller writer, working in U.S. Like many thriller writers, Smith had several pseudonyms. He used Adam Hall (said to have been taken from a phone book) for his novels featuring the British Secret Service agent Quiller. Other names were Roger Fitzalan, Trevor Burgess, Caesar Smith, Warwick Scott, Mansell Black, Simon Rattray, Howard North, and Lesley Stone.

Rose **Trevor** *see* Marie **Corelli**

William **Trevor:** William Trevor Cox (1928–), Ir.-born novelist, short-story writer, working in U.K.

Il **Tribolo:** Niccolò di Raffaello de' Pericoli (1500–1550), It. sculptor, architect.

Tricky: Adrian Thaws (1968–), Br. black rapper. The musician came by his street name as a teenager. "One time, when he was about 15, he was supposed to meet his mate outside the Broadwalk shopping centre [Bristol, England]. He didn't turn up. Instead, he went to Manchester for six weeks. When he returned, he passed by the shopping centre and, by chance, his mate happened to be standing in the arranged meeting place, so Tricky went up to him. 'And he just said, "You tricky bastard,"' Tricky recalls, 'and then everyone started calling me it real quick'" [*Sunday Times*, June 21, 1998]

Trilussa: Carlo Alberto Salustri (1871–1950), It. poet. A straight anagram of the poet's surname.

Robert **Trimbole:** Bruno Trimboli (1931–1987), It.-born Austral. criminal. Australia's most wanted man was a partner-in-crime of Alexander **Sinclair**.

A. Stephen **Tring:** Laurence Walter Meynell (1899–1989), Eng. novelist, children's writer. The author also wrote as Valerie Baxter, Robert Eton, and Geoffrey Ludlow, as well as under his real name. Tring, Eton, and Ludlow are all names of English towns.

Trinity: Wade Brammer (1954–), Jamaican reggae record producer. The artist began a new career as as singer in the late 1980s under the name Junior Brammer.

Triple H *see* Hunter Hearst **Helmsley**

Trismegistus Rustificus, D.D. *see* Thomas **Brown, the Younger**

Flora **Tristan:** Flore Tristan-Moscoso (1803–1844), Fr. feminist writer.

Tristan l'Hermite: François l'Hermite (*c.*1601–1655), Fr. dramatist, poet. The classical dramatist is said to have taken his new name through a family connection with Louis XI's counselor Tristan l'Hermite (died after 1475).

Tristão de Athayde: Alceu Amoroso Lima (1893–1983), Brazilian writer, philosopher.

Johannes **Trithemius:** Johannes von Heidenberg (1462–1516), Ger. monk, magician. The occultist

took his name from a Latin form of the name of his birthplace, Trittenheim, near Trier.

Trog: Walter ("Wally") Ernest Fawkes (1924–), Can.-born Br. cartoonist. The artist, famous for his magical creature Flook, took his name from the Troglodytes, a jazz band of which he had formerly been a member. As the name implies, the band played in a cellar.

Trois-Étoiles *see* Mark **Hope**

Frances **Trollope:** Paul Feval (1817–1887), Fr. writer of sentimental novels. The writer adopted the name of the mother of the English novelist Anthony Trollope (1815–1882).

August von **Tromlitz:** Karl August Friedrich von Witzleben (1773–1839), Ger. soldier, writer of historical romances. The writer took his name from his birthplace, Tromlitz.

Sven **Trost:** [Count] Carl Johan Gustav Snoilsky (1841–1903), Swe. lyric poet.

Henri **Trotère:** Henry Trotter (1855–1912), Eng. popular songwriter. A simple gallicization.

Leon **Trotsky:** Lev Davidovich Bronstein (1879–1940), Russ. revolutionary leader, of Jewish parentage. There has been considerable controversy as to the precise origin of this (in)famous name. A popular theory is that the revolutionary picked it at random, writing it in a blank passport handed him by friends, when emerging from exile in Siberia in 1902. It is known, however, that Trotsky was the name of a jailer in the prison at Odessa, where the young Bronstein had been before this. Trotsky is a genuine Russian name, existing in its own right. Even so, with his knowledge of German, Bronstein may have been consciously or subconsciously thinking of the German word *Trotz*, with its symbolic meaning of "defiance," "insolence," "intrepidity."

Some of Trotsky's other pseudonyms seem to be more obviously meaningful. At one stage he was Antid-Oto, a word found (*antidoto*) in an Italian dictionary when he started to weigh up different pen names, and seen by him as suitable since he "wanted to inject a Marxist antidote into the legal press." For a time in 1936 he was Crux, a name he used for articles in the *Bulletin of the Opposition*. He had also been Ensign, Arbuzov, Mr. Sedov (when leaving incognito for Europe in 1932), Pyotr Petrovich (to local Petersburg revolutionaries), Vikentyev (his "official" name in Petersburg in 1905), and Yanovsky (from Yanovka Farm, itself named for the colonel who had sold it to his father) [Joel Carmichael, *Trotsky: An Appreciation of His Life*, 1975]. Trotsky was assassinated by Frank **Jacson**.

Kilgore **Trout:** Philip José Farmer (1918–2009), U.S. SF writer. Farmer adopted this name ("There was a row about this" [Clute and Nicholls, p. 1241]), as the author of *Venus on the Half-Shell* (1975), from the fictitious SF writer in *God Bless You, Mr. Rosewater* (1965) and *Breakfast of Champions* (1973) by Kurt Vonnegut, Jr. (*see* Theodore **Sturgeon**).

Robert Trout: Robert Albert Blondheim (1909–2000), U.S. broadcast journalist.

Ben Trovato: Samuel Lover (1797–1868), Ir. songwriter, novelist, printer. The writer adopted his pseudonym from the Italian phrase *ben trovato*, literally "well found," in other words, "happy invention," like the pen name itself.

Doris Troy: Doris Higginson (1937–2004), U.S. black soul singer, songwriter.

Roger "Jellyroll" Troy: Roger McGaha (*c.*1945–1991), U.S. blues-rock bass player.

Henri Troyat: Levon Aslanovich Tarasov (1911–2007), Russ.-born Fr. novelist, of Armenian descent. The writer selected a new name at the request of his first editor, who feared that the Russian name would suggest the author of a translated work, not an original. He came up with Troyat (allegedly from a phone book), a name with the same initial as his surname. The editor then asked him to choose a more readily recognizable first name, in response to which he proposed Henri.

Nikolay Trublaini: Nikolay Petrovich Trublayevsky (1907–), Ukr. children's writer. The writer adapted his surname so that he would appear to be Italian.

Truong Chinh: Dang Xuan Khu (1907–1988), Vietnamese scholar, statesman. The leading Communist intellectual adopted a name meaning "long march," alluding to the famous Long March led by Mao Tse-tung in 1934–5 from Kiangsi to Shensi.

Basil Truro: Vassilie Trunoff (1929–1985), Austral.-born Russ. ballet dancer. During the Australian tour of the Ballet Rambert in 1948, Trunoff was invited to fill a vacancy caused when another dancer returned to England. Marie **Rambert** asked him to appear with an English stage name instead of his Russian one, thus rather unusually reversing the usual naming practice among ballet dancers.

Bruce Truscot: Edgar Allison Peers (1891–1952), Eng. authority on Spanish religious history, educationist. The academic used this pen name for two books: *Redbrick University* (1943) and *Redbrick and These Vital Days* (1945).

L. Parry Truscott *see* E. Livingston **Prescott**

H. Trusta: Elizabeth Wooster Stuart Phelps (1815–1852), U.S. novelist. The writer first used this name, an anagram of her maiden name (Stuart), for some early articles in a religious mgazine.

Sojourner Truth: Isabella Baumfree (1797–1883), U.S. black abolitionist, women's rights advocate. In 1843, the year that William Miller had

prophesied the second coming of Christ would occur, Baumfree announced that "voices" had commanded her to adopt her new name, the equivalent of "itinerant preacher," and to "travel up and down the land" singing and preaching.

Tryphé: Natalie Clifford Barney (1876–1972), U.S. writer, salon hostess. Barney wrote in French, and she used this name, Greek for "softness," "delicacy," for *Cinq petits dialogues grecs* ("Five little Greek dialogues") (1902). At the time she and her lover, Renée **Vivien**, were studying classical Greek.

Tsanko Tserkovski: Tsanko Bakalov (1869–1926), Bulg. writer. Bakalov took his pen name from his birthplace, the small town of Byala Cherkva, northern Bulgaria.

Tsuruya Namboku IV: Ebiya Genzo (1755–1829), Jap. playwright. In about 1780 the writer married the daughter of Tsuruya Namboku III, a noted actor of the day, and adopted his name in 1811.

Harriet Tubman: Araminta ("Minty") Tubman, née Ross (*c.*1820–1913), U.S. black abolitionist. The legendary Underground Railroad conductor adopted her mother's first name on escaping from a Maryland slave plantation in 1849.

Jerry Tucker: Jerry Schatz (1926–), U.S. juvenile movie actor.

Richard Tucker: Rubin Ticker (1913–1975), U.S. opera singer, of Rom. Jewish parentage. Despite the adoption of his stage name, Tucker was called "Ruby" by friends and family throughout his lifetime.

Sophie Tucker: Sophia Abuza (1884–1966), U.S. vaudeville, movie actress, of Russ. Jewish parentage. The actress's father was originally named Kalish, but when he absconded from Russian military service to go to America, he fell in with an Italian named Charles Abuza, also absent without leave. Abuza fell ill and died, whereupon Sophia's father, fearing detection by the Russian authorities, took the Italian's identity papers and adopted his name. He thus arrived in the U.S. as Charles Abuza.

In 1903 Sophia married Louis Tuck, a dancer in Hartford, Connecticut, where her family then lived. Meanwhile she had gained local success as a singer, and in 1906, when she and her husband parted, she went to New York to be auditioned by songwriter Harry **Von Tilzer**. While waiting for his verdict, she called in at the Café Monopol, on Eighth Street, and asked the proprietor if (like Little Tommy Tucker in the nursery rhyme) she could "sing for her supper," as she was hungry and low on funds. He agreed, and asked her name. She recounts: "I had my mail sent to Mrs. Louis Tuck, care of General Delivery, as of course that was my name. But 'Mrs. Tuck' didn't sound right for a singer. 'Sophie Tucker,' I told him. Right like that a career was born" [Sophie Tucker, *Some of These Days: An Autobiography*, 1948].

Tommy **Tucker**: Robert Higginbotham (1933–1982), U.S. blues singer, pianist. In the nursery rhyme, "Little Tommy Tucker / Sings for his supper," just as any singer has to do if he is to eat. Presumably the musician took his stage name from this well-known source.

Antony **Tudor**: William John Cook (1909–1987), Eng. dancer, choreographer, working in U.S. In 1928 Cook began studying ballet with Marie **Rambert**, and it was she who encouraged him to change his name.

Stepan **Tudor**: Stepan Iosifovich Oleksyuk (1892–1941), Ukr. writer.

Tasha **Tudor**: Starling Burgess (1915–2008), U.S. children's writer, illustrator. The first half of the writer's name is the pet form of Natasha, the name by which her father called her, from his liking for Natasha Rostova, the heroine of Tolstoy's *War and Peace*. She later registered the name by deed poll. The second part is the maiden name of her mother, portrait painter Rosamond Tudor.

Tenpole **Tudor**: Edward Felix Tudor-Pole (1956–), Br. actor, TV presenter, former pop singer. "Tenpole" is presumably a nickname, perhaps from an earlier "Tentpole" or from "Ted (Tudor-)Pole."

Tony **Tuff**: Winston Morris (*c.*1955–), Jamaican reggae musician.

Sonny **Tufts**: Bowen Charleston Tufts (1911–1970), U.S. movie actor.

Friedebert **Tuglas**: Friedebert Mihkelson (1886–1971), Estonian writer. The writer adopted his new name in 1923, when he became editor of the journal *Looming* ("Creation").

Nicolaes Pieterszoon **Tulp**: Nicolaes Pieterszoon (1593–1674), Du. medical writer. The anatomist took his added name from the tulip (Dutch *tulp*) carved on the front of his house. This is the Dr. Tulp portrayed in Rembrandt's famous painting *The Anatomy Lesson of Dr. Tulp* (1632).

Semyon **Tumanov**: Semyon Isayevich Tseytlin (Zeitlin) (1921–1973), Russ. movie director.

Boris **Tumarin**: Boris Tumarinson (1910–), Latvian stage actor, director, working in U.S.

Sven **Tumba**: Sven Johansson (1931–), Swe. ice hockey player. The player adopted his nickname, that of the Stockholm suburb where he was raised.

KT **Tunstall**: Kate Tunstall (1975–), Sc. rock singer, songwriter.

Tupac Amaru II: José Gabriel Condorcanqui (*c.*1740–1781), Peruvian Indian revolutionary. The hereditary chief was a maternal descendant of the last Inca ruler, Tupac Amaru ("Royal Serpent"), who was beheaded by the Spaniards in 1572, and adopted his

name in 1771. In 1780 he led a rebellion against Spanish rule and was in turn captured and beheaded.

Evgeniya **Tur**: Elizaveta Vasilyevna Salhias-de-Tournemire (1815–1892), Russ. writer, editor, critic. The writer's son tells how his mother came by her name: "It has been said that 'Evgeniya Tur' is 'Turgenev' turned round. By pure coincidence this is so, and you get an almost complete anagram. But there is no secret in this: the stories about my mother's affair with Turgenev are complete nonsense. My mother was called Elizaveta, but she was extremely fond of the names Evgeny [Eugene] and Evgeniya [Eugenia]. She was a passionate admirer of Pushkin and of *Eugene Onegin* in particular. That's where I got my own name of Evgeny.... The way her pen name came about is as follows: 'Evgeniya' was chosen with little hesitation. Then the search was on for a surname. 'Evgeniya Sal' was an abbreviation of 'Salhias,' but *sale* in French is 'dirty.' 'Evgeniya Lhias' doesn't sound well, 'Evgeniya Nemire' is too long.... Everyone liked 'Evgeniya Tur'" [Dmitriyev, p.53].

The **Tur Brothers**: Leonid Davidovich Tubelsky (1905–1961), Russ. playwright, screenwriter + Pyotr Lvovich Ryzhey (1908–1978), Russ. playwright, screenwriter. The writers' joint name comprises the first letters of their surnames.

Turlupin: Henri Legrand (*c.*1587–1637), Fr. actor. The actor used the name Belleville for serious tragic roles, keeping Turlupin for farces. The name is said to derive from a 14th-century heretical sect. Its ultimate origin is obscure, but it may be an altered form of *Tirelupin*: "By [Sir Thomas] Urquhart taken to render French *tirelupin* in Rabelais, said by [Jacques le] Duchat to be a name given in 1372 to a certain people who imitated Cynics, and lived on *lupins* which they gathered (*tiraient*) in the fields" [*Oxford English Dictionary*].

Alex Freke **Turner** see John **Dangerfield**

Ethel **Turner**: Ethel Curlewis, earlier Cope, née Burwell (1870–1958), Eng.-born Austral. children's writer. The writer adopted her stepfather's surname, as did her sister Lilian Turner (1870–1856), who also wrote for children.

Gil **Turner**: Gilbert Strunk (1933–1974), U.S. folk singer, guitarist.

Joan **Turner**: Joan Teresa Page (1922–), Northern Ireland popular singer, stage actress.

Lana **Turner**: Julia Jean Mildred Frances Turner (1921–1995), U.S. movie actress ("The Sweater Girl"). It is uncertain whether Judy Turner (as she usually called herself) chose her new first name, or whether it was given by Warner Bros. agent Mervyn LeRoy. If the latter, LeRoy is said to have taken the name from a girl he knew when he was at school. Either way, she adopted the name, which she wished to be "pronounced Lana as in lah-de-da, not lady" [Joe Morella and Edward Z. Epstein, *Lana: The Public and Private Lives of Miss Turner*, 1983].

Sammy **Turner:** Samuel Black (1932–), U.S. pop singer.

Tina **Turner:** Anna Mae Bullock (1938–), U.S. black rock singer. It is only the first name of the singer that is different, for her surname is that of her husband, Izear ("Ike") Luster Turner, Jr. (1931–2007), whom she married in 1958 and with whom she initially made her name, recording and touring as the Ike & Tina Turner Revue. It was Ike who named her Tina. He was keen on movies with "jungle girl" heroines such as Sheena, and gave his fifth wife a name to match, seeing her as a "wild woman."

Gérard de **Turnhout:** Jacques Gheert (*c*.1520–1580), Flemish composer. The musician came to be known by the name of his birthtown, Turnhout, near Antwerp, Belgium. His son, Jean de Turnhout, born Jean Jacques Gheert, also a composer, took the same name.

Christopher **Turnley:** Una Mary Ellis-Fermor (1894–1958), Eng. literary critic. The writer adopted this name for two collections of poetry in the 1930s, taking it from the first name of the dramatist Christophe Marlowe (1564–1593) and the middle name of her father, Joseph Turnley Ellis-Fermor.

Tusitala: Robert Louis Stevenson (1850–1894), Sc. essayist, novelist. In 1889 Stevenson settled in Samoa, where the Samoans acknowledged him as chief with this name, meaning "teller of tales." He accepted and approved the name, but did not adopt it for any of his writing.

Tutankhamun: Tutankhaten (*fl.*14th century BC), Egyptian pharaoh. The young king was originally known as Tutankhaten, "living image of Aten," from *tut*, "to resemble," *ankh*, "life," and *aten*, "Aten." (The name of the sun god Aten means literally "sun disk.") Later, however, he changed his name, apparently to distance himself from the Atenist heresies of the reigns of his father-in-law **Akhenaten** and of the latter's successor, Smenkhkara. His new name thus meant "living image of Amun." (Amun, otherwise Ammon, was the ram-headed god identified by the Greeks with Zeus.) Tutankhamun's wife, Ankhesenpa'aten, Akhenaten's third daughter, similarly changed her name to Ankhesenamun.

T.V. Slim: Oscar Wills (1916–1969), U.S. black blues musician. Wills adopted a name referring to his original job as a television repairman.

Mark **Twain:** Samuel Langhorne Clemens (1835–1910), U.S. humorist, writer, lecturer. It is generally believed that the writer derived his pen name from the call of pilots on the Mississippi River when they wanted a depth sounding, "Mark twain!" meaning "Mark two fathoms!." But there was a Mississippi pilot, Captain Isaiah Sellers (*c*.1802–1864), who is said to have used the name earlier for contributions to the *New Orleans Picayune*, and Twain himself claimed that he was the source of the pseudonym: "He died in 1863, and as he could no longer need that signature, I laid violent hands upon it without asking the permission of the proprietor's remains" [Kaplan, p.39]. There is no evidence, however, that Sellers actually used the name for his articles. Moreover, Sellers died over a year after Clemens began using the name. It thus seems likely that Clemens's account of how he came to be called "Mark Twain" is an invention, although it is possible he saw a false report of Sellers's death before he adopted the name. He first used it for a humorous travel account printed in the *Virginia City Territorial Enterprise* of February 3, 1863 [R. Kent Rasmussen, *Mark Twain A to Z*, 1995].

Early pen names used by Clemens included W. Epaminondas Adrastus Perkins, W. Epaminondas Adrastus Blab, Josh, Rambler, and Thomas Jefferson Snodgrass. His last novel, *Personal Recollections of Joan of Arc* (1896), was purportedly translated by Jean François Alden from the French account of Sieur Louis de Conte. Although the latter was a real person from Joan of Arc's time, he is here Mark Twain's alter ego (the initials of Sieur Louis de Conte are identical to those of Samuel Langhorne Clemens), as also is Jean François Alden, whose name may have been taken from Henry Mills Alden (1836–1919), editor of *Harper's Magazine*, in which the novel was serialized.

Shania **Twain:** Eileen Regina Edwards (1965–), Can. country singer. The singer's parents divorced when she was a toddler and in 1970 her mother married Jerry Twain, a full-blooded Ojibway Indian. At first billed as Sophyah Twain, Shania took her new first name from a half–Ojibway girl working in the wardrobe department of the *Viva Vegas* revue at Deerhurst, a resort hotel in Huntsville, Ontario. She was told the name, pronounced "Sha-*nigh*-ah," meant "on my way" but it may actually mean "silver" or "money." "[The name] was a good choice, easy to remember, both exotic and instantly familiar. Shania ... showed the Native Canadian in her and it trips off the tongue easily in a chant. Twain had a resonance all its own. Mark **Twain** was the pseudonym of writer Samuel Clemens ... Shania Twain is the sort of name a country singer should have" [Robin Eggar, *Shania Twain: The Biography*, 2001].

Tweet: Charlene Keys (1972–), U.S. black soul, hip-hop singer. The singer adopted her childhood family nickname.

Brother **Twelve:** Edward Arthur Wilson (1878–

1934), Br. cult leader, working in Canada. In 1924, while visiting France, Wilson had a vision of the "Twelfth Master," one of a group of secret chiefs believed by occultists to use magical powers to bring about the Age of Aquarius. Wilson was convinced he had been chosen to bring about the New Age and called himself "Brother Twelve" in honor of his master.

Twiggy: Lesley Lawson, née Hornby (1950–), Eng. fashion model, movie actress, singer. When the model was still at school, she was nicknamed "Sticks," for her thin and skinny appearance. This name was later revamped as "Twiggy," which she adopted professionally in 1964 for her fashion career. Her near-anorexic look was regarded as appropriate for the miniskirt modes of the day. In 1988 she married Leigh Lawson and took his name. She says: "Twiggy is a stupid name for a woman in her 40s, but it would be hard to drop. At least a full name makes me sound like a person, instead of a strange animal" [*Telegraph Magazine*, July 6, 1991]. The familiar name was again to the fore when in 2008 she presented the TV fashion program *Twiggy's Frock Exchange*.

Twinkle: Lynne Annette Ripley (1947–), Br. pop singer. Possibly the name arose as a nickname for a "little star."

Conway Twitty: Harold Lloyd Jenkins (1933–1993), U.S. country singer. Twitty tells how he came by his name: "So we started thinking about all kinds of names, and to make a long story short, what I finally wound up doing was, I got the map out and there's a place called Twitty, Texas. Then I thought if I could get something different to go with this, it might be something. I finally got the map of Arkansas and started looking through that, and there're towns in Arkansas like Baldknob, Walnut Creek, Smackover, and all kinds of crazy names like that. But right outside of Little Rock there's a town called Conway, and that's how it came about — Conway, Arkansas, and Twitty, Texas. So we all agreed that that was an unusual name, and my first record was ... under the name of Conway Twitty. I didn't agree with the idea first because my main interest was I was worried about the people in my hometown that wouldn't know who Conway Twitty is, and I wanted them all to know I had a new record out.... But I finally realized what the fellow was talking about and I decided he was right, so we went with Conway Twitty" [Shestack, p.285].

Twm Carnabwth: Thomas Rees (*c.*1806–1876), Welsh pugilist. The fighter's name, "Tom of Carnabwth," comes from that of his farm.

Twm Chwarae Teg: Thomas Williams (1737–1802), Welsh industrialist. The coppermine owner derived his name by way of a nickname. It means

"Tom Fair Play," alluding to his honest dealings with workers and rivals.

Twm o'r Nant: Thomas Edwards (1739–1810), Welsh poet, playwright. The writer's name, meaning "Tom of the brook," derives from the village of Nant Ganol, where he was raised. Its own name means "middle stream."

Twm Siôn Cati: Thomas Jones (*c.*1530–1609), Welsh poet, antiquary. The so called "Welsh Robin Hood" was popularly known by this name, which means "Tom (son of) John (and) Catherine."

Cy Twombly: Edwin Parker Twombly, Jr. (1928–), U.S. painter. The artist adopted the nickname of his father, a professional baseball player, himself so dubbed in memory of legendary pitcher Cy **Young**.

Jack Tworkov: Jacob Tworkovsky (1900–1982), Pol.-born U.S. painter, of Jewish parentage.

Twym: Alexander Stuart Boyd (1854–1930), Sc. illustrator, cartoonist. The artist used this name at the start of his career in the 1880s. It may have arisen from a nickname or represented an abbreviation.

Beverly Tyler: Beverly Jean Saul (1927–2005), U.S. movie actress.

Bonnie Tyler: Gaynor Sullivan, née Hopkins (1951–), Welsh pop singer. The singer adopted her stage name when a talent scout spotted her and gave her a new persona. She originally fronted a band under the name Sherene Davis. "Her friends call her Gaynor, her real name; she's only Bonnie on stage. So while Bonnie is flamboyant, dramatic, emotional, Gaynor is down to earth" [*The Times*, October 17, 2009].

Judy Tyler: Judith Mae Hess (1933–1957), U.S. movie actress.

Steven Tyler: Steven Tallarico (1948–), U.S. rock musician.

Toby Tyler *see* Marc **Bolan**

Tom Tyler: Vincent Markowski (1903–1954), U.S. movie actor.

T. Texas Tyler: David Luke Myrick (1916–1972), U.S. country singer. As his name implies, the singer came from Texas.

W.T. Tyler: Samuel Jennings Hamrick (1929–2008), U.S. novelist. Professionally an employee of the U.S. Foreign Service, Hamrick took his name for his spy novels from Wat Tyler, English leader of the Peasants' Revolt in 1381.

Rob Tyner: Robert Derminer (1944–1991), U.S. rock singer.

Tyotka: Eloiza (or Aloiza) Stepanovna Pashkevich (1876–1916), Belorussian poet. The poet was of peasant stock and adopted a name meaning "Auntie," identifying her with ordinary people and especially country folk. In World War I, during the German occupation, she journeyed widely helping combat a typhus epidemic, but died of the disease herself.

Jan Tyszka: Leo Jogiches (1867–1919), Lithuanian-born Pol. revolutionary, working in Germany.

Sarah Tytler: Henrietta Keddie (1827–1914), Sc. novelist. The writer's pen name is said to have been imposed on her by her publishers.

Sbrui Tyusab: Sbrui Vaganyan (1841–1901), Armenian (female) writer.

Tristan Tzara: Samuel Rosenstock (1896–1963), Rom.-born Fr. Surrealist poet. "This Romanian poet took for his *nom de guerre* a name as staccato and aggressive as the nonsensical 'Dada' ... he helped launch in 1916" [France, p.820].

Antonio Uberti: Anton Hubert (1697–1783), Ger. opera singer. The singer adopted an Italian version of his original name as appropriate for his many roles in Italian opera.

Paolo Uccello: Paolo di Dono (*c.*1397–1475), It. painter. The artist's adopted surname is the Italian word for "bird," from the nickname given him for his love of nature, and of birds in particular.

Gustav Ucicky: Gustav Klimt (1899–1961), Austr. movie director, working in Germany. The director presumably changed his name to avoid being associated with his namesake, Austrian painter Gustav Klimt (1862–1918).

Lynn Udall: John Henry Keating (1870–1963), U.S. songwriter.

Uesugi Kenshin: Nagao Torachiyo (1530–1578), Jap. military leader. The leader adopted the name of a local governor general, Uesugi Norimasa, who adopted him as his son in 1552.

Vorea Ujko: Domenico Bellizzi (1931–1989), It.-Albanian poet.

Lesya Ukrainka: Larisa Petrovna Kvitko, née Kosach (1871–1913), Ukr. poet, playwright, daughter of Olyona **Pchilka**. The writer adopted a name meaning "Ukrainian woman" to emphasize her nationality. (Lesya is a pet form of Larisa.)

Ulanhu: Yun-Tse (1906–1988), Mongolian political leader. The former vice president of the Chinese People's Republic changed his aristocratic name Yun-Tse to Ulanfu in the 1920s, this being the Wade-Giles spelling (the Pinyin spelling is Ulanhu). The change was intended as a tribute both to **Lenin**, whose family name was Ulyanov (*fu* being the Chinese character which transliterates the Russian suffix *-ov*), and to his Communist beliefs, as *ulan* is the Mongolian word for "red."

Lenore Ulric: Lenore Ulrich (1892–1970), U.S. stage, movie actress.

Ultra Violet: Isabelle Collin Dufresne (1935–), Fr. movie actress. The actress was an intimate of Andy **Warhol**. "Andy tells me I need a new name. I can't use Isabelle Collin Dufresne. No one can spell it, pronounce it, or remember it. Besides, the stars of his underground films have catchy names — International Velvet, Ingrid Superstar, **Ondine**. He suggests Poly Ester or Notre Dame for me. I tell him I'll find my own name. While reading an article on light and space in *Time* magazine, I come across the words 'ultra violet.' They leap at me ... I say the name out loud several times: 'Ultra Violet, Ultra Violet.' I stretch it out, pronounce it in five distinct syllables. I emphatically prolong each vowel. I tap the tip of my tongue forcibly against my teeth to give the consonants a staccato sound. It comes out: *Ul-tra-vi-o-let*. By luck or by choice, my name contains the five magical vowels" [Ultra Violet, *Famous for 15 Minutes: My Years with Andy Warhol*, 1988].

Umbo: Otto Maximilian Umbehr (1902–1980), Ger. photographer.

Francisco Umbral: Francisco Pérez Martínez (1935–2007), Sp. novelist.

Umm Kulthum: Fatima Ibrahim (1898–1975), Egyptian singer. Adored in the Arab world from 1922 to her death, with her long songs of love, waiting, suffering, and separation, the singer adopted a name meaning "mother of Kulthum," that of a daughter of Muhammad who married Uthman, the third Muslim caliph. The singer was also known by the French form of her name as Oum Kalsoum.

Uncle ... For names beginning thus, see the next word, e.g. for Uncle Esek see **Esek**, for Uncle Harry see **Harry**, for Uncle Mac see **Mac**, etc.

Charles Underhill *see* Patrick **Ruell**

The Undertaker: Mark Calloway (1962–), U.S. wrestler. The wrestler's adopted name alludes to the "dark and deadly" persona that he cultivated.

Michael Underwood: John Michael Evelyn (1916–1992), Eng. crime writer. Professionally a lawyer, holding the post of Assistant Director of Public Prosecutions from 1969 to 1976, the writer adopted his mother's maiden name for his crime novels, beginning with *Murder on Trial* (1954).

Miles Underwood *see* Sylvia **Bayer**

Tomi Ungerer: Jean Thomas (1931–), Fr. illustrator, political cartoonist, working in U.S., Canada.

Uranda: Lloyd Meeker (1907–1954), U.S. cult leader. The founder in 1932 of the Emissaries of Divine Light adopted this name for his writings.

Urban II: Odo (or Eudes) (*c.*1035–1099), Fr. pope.

Urban III: Uberto Crivelli (?–1187), It. pope.

Urban IV: Jacques Pantaléon (*c.*1200–1264), Fr. pope.

Urban V: Guillaume de Grimoard (1310–1370), Fr. pope.

Urban VI: Bartolomeo Prignano (*c.*1318–1389), It. pope.

Urban VII: Giambattista Castagna (1521–1590), It. pope. The pontiff consciously assumed a name (from Latin *urbanus*, "refined") that indicated his intention to treat his subjects in a civilized manner.

Urban VIII: Maffeo Vincenzo Barberini (1568–1644), It. pope.

Sylvanus **Urban:** Edward Cave (1691–1754), Eng. printer, editor. The founder of *The Gentleman's Magazine* (1731) adopted a classical-style name designed to reflect his dual interest in both town and country affairs, in other words, things "sylvan" (relating to woodland) and "urban" (relating to cities). The name was passed down to subsequent editors of the magazine until it closed in 1914. A similar name was that of Urbanus **Sylvan.**

Urbanus: Urbain Servranckx (1949–), Belg. movie actor.

Minerva **Urecal:** Minerva Holzer (1894–1966), U.S. movie actress. The actress's screen name represents a folksy form of the name of Eureka, California, her birthplace.

Chrétien **Urhan:** Chrétien Auerhahn (1790–1845), Fr. violinist, viola player.

Urmuz: Demetru Demetrescu-Buzau (1883–1923), Rom. writer. A name created from the writer's full original name.

U-Roy: Ewart Beckford (1942–), Jamaican DJ, reggae musician. "U" for "Ewart," "Roy" for "royal," a term for a West Indian or black person in general.

Usher: Usher Raymond IV (1978–), U.S. black R&B singer.

Maurice **Utrillo:** Maurice Valadon (1883–1955), Fr. painter. The artist was born as the illegitimate son of the model Suzanne Valadon. When he was eight years old, Maurice was formally adopted by the Spanish art critic Miguel Utrillo (1863–1934), who recognized him as his son in order to help him and who gave him his own name. The young artist was devoted to his mother and initially disowned his new name, signing his pictures "Maurice Valadon." Even when finally persuaded to adopt the name, he still retained his mother's initial, so that his signature was "Maurice Utrillo V."

Khveder **Uyar:** Fyodor Yermilovich Afanasyev (1914–), Russ. (Chuvash) poet. The poet's adopted surname means "bright," "shining." His new first name is a Chuvash form of his original name Fyodor (Theodore).

Uygun: Rakhmatulla Atakuziyev (1905–?), Uzbek poet, playwright. The writer's pen name means "favorable," "fitting."

Mishshi **Uyp:** Mikhail Danilovich Shumilov (1911–1970), Russ. (Chuvash) poet. The poet's adopted surname means "bullfinch," while his new first name is a Chuvash form of his original name Mikhail (Michael).

V.: Caroline Archer Clive, née Meysey-Wigley (1801–1873), Eng. novelist, poet. The writer used this name for an early work, *IX Poems by "V."* (1840), with "V" presumably from "Clive," from the Rev. Archer Clive, whom she married in the year of its publication.

Valentin **Vaala:** Valentin Ivanov (1909–1976), Finn. movie director.

Roger **Vadim:** Roger Vladimir Plemiannikov (1928–2000), Fr. movie director, of Ukr.-Fr. descent.

Vera **Vague:** Barbara Jo Allen (1905–1974), U.S. movie, radio comedienne.

Svetozar **Vajanský:** Svetozar Hurban (1847–1916), Slovakian writer.

Ladislao **Vajda:** László Vayda Weisz (1906–1965), Hung.-born Sp. movie director.

Vakeli: Iona Lukich Megrelidze (1900–?), Georgian poet, playwright. The writer's name derives from the village of his birth, Vake.

Katri **Vala:** Karin Alice Heikel, née Wadenström (1901–1944), Finn. poet.

Ricky **Valance:** David Spencer (*c.*1939–), Welsh pop singer.

G. **Valbert:** Charles Victor Cherbuliez (1829–1899), Swiss-born Fr. novelist, critic.

Val Conson: George Edward Mackenzie Skues (1858–1949), Eng. lawyer, sporting writer. Skues adopted this name, the legal abbreviation for "valuable consideration" (meaning a consideration with a monetary value), when writing for the *Fishing Gazette*, "as a hint that some small remunerations would not be unwelcome" [C.F. Walker, *The Angling Letters of G.E.M. Skues*, 1956]. The editor was apparently slow to take the hint.

Paul **Valdez** *see* Carter **Brown**

Freddie **Vale:** Frederick Veale (1925–1989), Br. stage, TV actor, theatrical agent.

Jerry **Vale:** Genaro Louis Vitaliano (1932–), U.S. popular singer.

Virginia **Vale:** Dorothy Howe (1920–), U.S. movie actress.

Ritchie **Valens:** Richard Stephen Valenzuela (1941–1959), U.S. pop guitarist, of Mexican-Native American parentage.

Dino **Valenti:** Chester Powers (1943–1994), U.S. folk-rock musician.

Barbara **Valentin:** Uschi Ledersteger (1940–2002), Ger. movie actress.

Basil **Valentin:** ? (1394–?), Ger. alchemist. The identity of the supposed monk and alchemist whose works bear his name (all edited long after his death) is unknown. The name may mask more than one person. It it clearly a pun, as it represents Greek *basileus*, "king," and Latin *valens*, "healthy." The "royal art" of alchemy centered on the philosopher's stone, which was said to reveal the "elixir of life."

Karl **Valentin**: Valentin Ludwig Fey (1882–1948), Ger. stage, movie comedian, writer.

Valentina: Valentina Nikolayevna Sanina Schlee (1899–1989), Russ.-born U.S. fashion designer.

Valentine *see* Mark **Cross**

Dickie **Valentine**: Richard Brice (1929–1971), Br. popular singer.

Douglas **Valentine**: George Valentine Williams (1883–1946), Eng. crime novelist, journalist. The writer and broadcaster used this name for *The Man with the Club Foot* (1918).

Joseph **Valentine**: Giuseppe Valentino (1900–1949), It.–U.S. cinematographer.

Valentin le Désossé: Jacques Renaudin (?–*c*.1905), Fr. music-hall dancer. By daytime a wine merchant, the dancer was so named for his supple body (French *désossé*, "boneless"). He was the regular foil of La **Goulue** at the Moulin Rouge, which he left in 1895.

Valentino: Valentino Clemente Ludovico Garavani (1932–), It. fashion designer. The designer adopted his professional name from Rudolph **Valentino**.

Rudolph **Valentino**: Rodolfo Alfonzo Raffaele Pierre Philibert Guglielmi di Valentina d'Antonguolla (1895–1926), It.-born U.S. movie actor. Of this impressive string of names, the first three (Rodolfo Alfonzo Raffaele) came from ancestors of Giovanni Gugliemi, the actor's father, while the next two (Pierre Philibert) derived from his mother's family. His cognomen (di Valentina d'Antonguolla) combined an old papal title with a claim asserted by the Guglielmis to certain estates. Thus, of all these names, the actor's basic original surname was Guglielmi. He originally called himself Rodolfo di Valentina. This then settled to the less specifically Italian Rudolph Valentino. The suggestion of "Valentine" ("sweetheart") is thus fortuitous, but suited the dark, Latin looks of the "Great Lover."

Sal **Valentino**: Sal Spampinato (1942–), U.S. pop singer.

N. **Valentinov**: Nikolay Vladislavovich Volsky (1879–?), Russ. revolutionary journalist.

Simone **Valere**: Simone Gondoff (1923–), Fr. movie actress.

Pietro **Valeriano**: Giovan Pietro Bolzani (1477–1560), It. scholar.

Johann Evangelist **Valesi**: Johann Evangelist Wallishauser (1735–1811), Ger. concert singer. The singer created an Italian name from his original name as appropriate for his performances in Italy.

Valezi: Valentina Yakovlevna Shchetinina, née Borisovna (1916–), Russ. circus artist + Yelena Pavlovna Lebedinskaya (1910–), Russ. circus artist + Zinaida Stepanovna Lesnevskaya (1911–1974), Russ. circus artist. The three bareback riders formed their joint name from the first syllables of the pet forms of their names: Valya, Lëlya, and Zina.

Leo **Valiani**: Leo Weiczen (1909–1999), It. senator, of Hung. Jewish descent. The founding father of the Italian Republic was born in Fiume, then in the Austro-Hungarian Empire, and his family italianized their name in the 1920s when the seaport and the Italian peninsula were annexed by Italy.

Peet **Vallak**: Peeter Pedajas (1893–1959), Estonian writer.

Juvencio **Valle**: Gilberto Concha Riffo (1900–), Chilean poet.

Rudy **Vallee**: Hubert Pryor Vallée (1901–1986), U.S. movie actor, musician. The popular singer took his new first name in 1920 to express his admiration for the famous saxophonist Rudy Wiedoeft.

Ramón María del **Valle-Inclán**: Ramón del Valle y Peña (1869–1936), Sp. writer. The writer changed his name to fix himself up with a fake aristocratic title.

Alwina **Valleria**: Alwina Schoening (1848–1925), U.S. opera singer.

Alida **Valli**: [Baroness] Alida Maria Laura von Altenburger von Marckenstein Freunburg (1921–2006), It. movie actress, of Austr.-It. parentage.

Frankie **Valli**: Frank Castelluccio (1937–), U.S. rock musician. As a youngster, Castelluccio was taken under the wing of the Texas country singer Jean Valley, who passed him off as his kid brother, Frankie Valley. Hence his name.

Virginia **Valli**: Virginia McSweeney (1898–1968), U.S. movie actress.

Ninon **Vallin**: Eugénie Vallin-Pardo (1886–1961), Fr. opera singer.

Guy de **Valmont** *see* Joseph **Prunier**

Valmore: Prosper Lanchantin (1793–1881), Fr. actor. The poet Marceline-Félicité-Josèphe Desbordes (1786–1859) aded the actor's stage name to her maiden name on marrying him in 1817.

Raoul **Valnay**: Aimé-Marie-Édouard Hervé (1835–1899), Fr. journalist. The writer appears to have taken the initials R.V., representing the spoken form of his surname, and formed names from these.

[Dame] Ninette de **Valois**: Edris Connell, née Stannus (1898–2001), Ir.-born Br. ballet dancer, director. Interviewed on her 90th birthday, the dancer was asked the origin of her professional name: "My mother thought of it, because our family had French connections" [*Sunday Times Magazine*, May 29, 1988]. The family claimed a distant link with the

French royal house of Valois (reigned 1328 through 1589). The dancer first used her new name on making her stage debut at age 13.

Arvo **Valton**: Arvo Vallikivi (1935–), Estonian writer.

Vamba: Luigi Bertelli (1858–1920), It. illustrator, children's writer. The writer adopted the name of Wamba, Cedric's jester in Sir Walter Scott's novel *Ivanhoe* (1820).

Vampeta: Marcos André Batista Santos (1974–), Brazilian footballer. When the future player was a young boy, he was nicknamed Vampiro from his appearance when losing his milk teeth. He was later nicknamed Capeta, after a cartoon character, a wily, joke-playing tomcat. A blend of both nicknames gave the name by which he became known as a footballer.

Vampira: Maila Nurmi (1921–), Finn.-born U.S. movie actress. The actress was best known as a presenter of late-night horror movies on TV and for her role as a "Ghoul Girl" in *Plan 9 from Outer Space* (1958), a film often hailed as the worst ever made.

Bobby **Van**: Robert King (1930–1980), U.S. dancer, singer, stage actor.

Richard **Van Allan**: Alan Philip Jones (1935–), Br. opera singer.

Jan **Van Avond**: Francis Carey Slater (1876–1958), S.A. poet, novelist.

[Dame] Irene **Vanbrugh**: Irene Barnes (1872–1949), Br. stage actress.

Violet **Vanbrugh**: Violet Augusta Mary Barnes (1867–1942), Br. stage actress. The actress adopted her stage name at the suggestion of Ellen Terry (*see* Megan **Terry**), the compliment being to the architect and dramatist Sir John Vanbrugh (1664–1726). Violet's sister Irene **Vanbrugh** followed suit.

Abigail **Van Buren**: Pauline Esther Philips, née Friedman (1918–), U.S. journalist. The advice specialist, famous for her "Dear Abby" column, was the twin of her rival "sob sister" Ann **Landers**.

Alfred Glenville **Vance**: Alfred Peck Stevens (1839–1888), Eng. music-hall actor, singer.

Charles **Vance**: Charles Ivan Goldblatt (1929–), Br. stage actor, theatrical director. The actor's stage name presumably evolved from his second name.

Clara **Vance**: Mary Andrews Denison (?1826–1911), U.S. writer. Much of the writer's vast and varied output was published under the name Mrs. Mary A. Denison, but she also wrote as Clara Vance, N.I. Edson, and other variations of her name and initials.

Ethel **Vance**: Grace Stone, née Zaring (1891–1991), U.S. novelist.

Tommy **Vance**: Richard Anthony Crispian Francis Prue Hope-West (1941–2005), Eng. DJ. Hope-West originally worked in the U.S. under the name Rick West, from the first and last elements of his original lengthy name. He got his regular name when his radio station signed a DJ named Tommy Vance who failed to turn up. The station then simply stuck the British DJ on air under the name instead.

Vivian **Vance**: Vivian Roberta Jones (1913–1979), U.S. TV actress. The actress took her stage name from her high-school acting coach, Vance Rudolph.

José **Van Dam**: Joseph Van Damme (1940–), Belg. opera singer.

Rob **Van Dam**: Robert Szatowski (1971–), U.S. wrestler.

Jean-Claude **Van Damme**: Jean-Claude Van Varenberg (1961–), Belg. movie actor, working in U.S.

Margaret **Vandegrift**: Margaret Thomson Janvier (1844–1913), U.S. writer, sister of Ivory **Black**. Janvier wrote poetry and juvenile literature under this pseudonym.

Trish **Van Devere**: Patricia Dressel (1943–), U.S. movie actress. The actress was billed as Patricia Van Devere in *The Landlord* (1970) before becoming Trish in *Where's Poppa?* (1970).

Lodewijk **van Deyssel**: Karel Joan Lodewijk Alberdingk Thijm (1864–1952), Du. writer, critic.

S.S. **Van Dine**: Willard Huntington Wright (1887–1939), U.S. literary critic, detective-story writer. "Why Willard Huntington Wright took this particular pen name he explains as well as his memory permits. Van Dyne was a family name, which he changed by inserting *i* for *y*. The reason for the 'S.S.' is lost in mystery unless it was suggested by 'steamship'" [Marble, p.201]. When the creator of the wealthy man-about-town detective Philo Vance once inquired of a bookseller who "this Van Dine" might be, he was amused to receive the reply, "They tell me he's a well-known motion-picture actor."

Frits **van Dongen** *see* Philip **Dorn**

Mamie **Van Doren**: Joan Lucille Olander (1931–), U.S. movie actress.

Edith **Van Dyne** *see* Floyd **Akers**

Derek **Vane**: [Mrs.] Blanche Eaton-Back (?–1939), Eng. romantic novelist. The prolific writer used this name for titles such as *The Sin and the Woman* (1893), *Estranged; or Love Unquenchable* (1894), *The Three Daughters of Night* (1897), *The Unguarded Hour* (1929), *Dancer's End* (1934), etc.

Sutton **Vane**: Vane Sutton-Vane (1888–1963), Eng. playwright.

Vanessa-Mae: Vanessa-Mae Nicholson (1978–), Br. violinist, of Singaporean parentage.

Peter **Van Eyck**: Götz von Eick (1913–1969), Ger. movie actor, working in U.S.

Vangelis: Evanghelos Odyssey Papathanassiou (1943–), Gk. composer, rock musician, working in U.K.

Jimmy **Van Heusen:** Edward Chester Babcock (1913–1990), U.S. composer of musicals, movie music. Told the name "Babcock" lacked flair, the musician chose "Van Heusen" from the shirt manufacturers and "James" because "it went well with Van Heusen."

Berto **Vani:** Alberto Vigevani (1918–1999), It. novelist, editor. The writer contributed to literary journals under this name before World War II in order to conceal his Jewishness.

Dave **Vanian:** David Letts (1956–), Eng. punk rock singer.

Vanilla Ice: Robert Van Winkle (1968–), U.S. rapper, of Du. descent. The singer was nicknamed "Vanilla" by his black rapping friends, from "Van" and the fact that he was white. He himself added "Ice" because it was "cool" and went well with "Vanilla."

Vanity: Denise Matthews (1958–), U.S. movie actress. The actress has also used the name D.D. Winters.

Eric **van Lhin** see Lester **del Rey.**

Joey **Vann:** Joseph Canzano (1943–1984), U.S. (white) R&B singer.

Nina **Vanna:** Nina Yazykova (1902–?), Russ.-born movie actress, working in U.K. Just before filming began of *The Man without Desire* (1923), in which the actress played a young socialite, she was persuaded by Ivor **Novello,** appearing as a Venetian aristocrat, Count Vittorio Dandolo, to change her name to "something that sounded less emetic."

Vann'Antò: Giovanni Antonio di Giacomo (1891–1960), It. poet, writing in Sicilian dialect.

Marda **Vanne:** Marda van Hulsteyn (?–1970), S.A. stage actress, working in U.K.

Peter **Vanning** see Vincent **Shaw**

Vano Romano: Ivan Mikhaylovich Panchenko (1941–), Russ. Gypsy poet. The poet's adopted Romany name means "Ivan the Gypsy."

Marian **Van Tuyl:** Marian Tubbs (1907–1987), U.S. dance educator. After her father's death in a canoeing accident, the dance teacher took the name of her mother's second husband, Frank Van Tuyl.

Kate **van Twinkle:** Kate Vannah (1855–1933), U.S. organist, pianist, composer, writer.

Nikola **Vapcarov:** Nikola Yonkov (1909–1942), Bulg. revolutionary poet.

Madeleine **Vara** see Laura **Riding**

Victor **Varconi:** Mihaly Várkonyi (1896–1976), Hung. movie actor, working in U.S.

Agnès **Varda:** Arlette Varda (1928–), Belg.-born moviemaker, of Gk.-Fr. parentage. As she grew up, the filmmaker became increasingly uncomfortable over the diminutive first name with which she had been christened and when she was 18 legally adopted a more adult-sounding replacement. "I just thought I deserved to be a real woman," she explained, "not *une petite femme*" [*The Times*, September 25, 2009].

Albéric **Varenne** see Cécil **Saint-Laurent**

Inna **Varlamova:** Klavdiya Gustavovna Landau (1922–), Russ. writer.

John Philip **Varley:** Langdon Elwyn Mitchell (1862–1935), U.S. playwright, son of Edward **Kearsley.** In 1885 Mitchell published a verse tragedy, *Sylvian and Other Poems*, under this name to avoid comparison with his father, a bestselling author.

Marcel **Varnel:** Marcel le Bozec (1894–1947), Fr.-born Br. theatrical producer.

Daniel **Varudzhan:** Daniel Chebukaryan (1884–1915), Armenian poet. The poet's adopted name means "canary." Many of his writings had the word "song" in the title.

M. **Vasalis:** Margaretha Droogleever Fortuyn-Leenmans (1909–1999), Du. poet.

S.S. **Vasan:** Thiruthiraipoondi Subramanya Srinivasan Iyer (1903–1969), Ind. movie director, producer. The director's original first name refers to his birthplace, Thiruthiraipoondi, Tamil Nadu.

Victor **Vasarely:** Győző Vásärhely (1908–1997), Hung.-born Fr. artist. The artist gallicized his name on settling in Paris, France, in 1930.

Gillan **Vase:** Elizabeth Newton, née Palmer (or Palmer Pacht) (1841–1921), Eng. novelist. The writer was born in the seaside town of Falmouth, Cornwall, and took her pseudonym from a local variant of the name of a Falmouth beach (properly Gyllyngvase).

Vasilchenko: Stepan Vasilyevich Panasenko (1879–1932), Ukr. writer.

Comte Paul **Vasili:** Juliette Adam, née Lamber (1836–1936), Fr. novelist, editor. The founder of *La Nouvelle Revue* took a name that opposed reality: she was not a count, but a commoner; not Russian, but French; not male, but female. The Cuban poet Julián del Casal (1836–1896), Adam's coeval, also wrote as Paul Vasili, and she may well have adopted the name from him.

Margarita **Vasilyeva:** Margarita Vasilyevna Rozhdestvenskaya (1889–1971), Russ. ballerina.

Gustavus **Vassa:** Olaudah Equiano (1745–1797), U.S. black abolitionist. Equiano was kidnapped in his native Africa at age 11 and sent to Barbados, then Virginia, where he was purchased by a British captain who changed his name in honor of Gustav I Vasa (1496–1560), founder of the Vasa dynasty of Swedish kings, and placed him in slave service aboard ship.

Pal **Vasvári:** Pal Fejér (1827–1849), Hung. socialist, historian.

Vatvat (or Vatvot): Rashididaddin Mohammed bin Abd al-Jalal al-Umari (1087–1182 or 1177), Persian poet. The poet's assumed name means "eagle owl."

Jeanne **Vaubernier:** Marie-Jeanne Bécu, Comtesse du Barry (1743–1793), Fr. mistress of Louis XV. This was the name adopted by the future Madame du Barry when a shop assistant in a Paris fashion house. While there, she became the mistress of the Gascon nobleman Jean du Barry, and took his name.

Arthur Owen **Vaughan:** Robert Scourfield Mills (1863–1919), Eng.-born Welsh adventurer, writer. Mills adopted this name in later life. His literary pseudonym was Owen Rhoscomyl, with a surname created from the first three letters of each of his real names in the altered form *Rho*bert *Sco*urfield *Myl*ne.

Carter A. **Vaughan** *see* Samuel **Edwards**

Frankie **Vaughan:** Francis Abelsohn (or Ableson) (1928–1999), Eng. popular singer, dancer, movie actor, of Russ. Jewish origin. "His change of name was to come about, by his own account, when he announced to his Russian grandmother that he intended to be a singer. 'Vell,' she said, 'then you vill be the best von there ever vas'" [*The Times*, September 18, 1999].

Kate **Vaughan:** Catherine Candelin (*c.*1852–1903), Br. actress, dancer, sister of Susie **Vaughan**. The sisters made their dancing debut as the Sisters Vaughan in 1870.

Peter **Vaughan:** Peter Ewart Ohm (1923–), Eng. movie, TV actor.

Richard **Vaughan:** Ernest Lewis Thomas (1904–1983), Welsh novelist.

Susie **Vaughan:** Susan Mary Charlotte Candelin (1853–1950), Br. stage actress, sister of Kate **Vaughan**.

Matthew **Vaughn:** Matthew de Vere Drummond (1971–), U.S.-born movie actor, director, working in U.K. Vaughn was brought up to believe that his father was actor Robert Vaughn (1932–), but he is really the son of George Drummond, a British aristocrat.

Jean **Vautrin:** Jean Herman (1933–), Fr. movie director, writer.

Vavá: Edvaldo Izidio Neto (1934–2002), Brazilian footballer. A pet form of the player's first name.

Kyra **Vayne:** Kyra Knopmuss (1916–2001), Russ.-born opera singer.

Vazekh: Mirza Shafi Sadykh-ogly (1796–1852), Azerbaijani poet, teacher. The poet's name means "clear," "expressive," denoting the ideal attribute of a teacher, if not necessarily of a poet.

Vazgen: Levon Karapet Baljian (1908–1994), Armenian churchman. The head of the Armenian Church took his religious name at his ordination in 1943. He was succeeded as Catholicos by **Karekin I**.

Vazha Pshavela: Luka Pavlovich Razikashvili (1861–1915), Georgian balladist. The popular poet took a name meaning "brave young Pshav" (this being the ethnic name of a Georgian mountain people).

Il **Vecchietta:** Lorenzo di Pietro (*c.*1412–1480), It. painter, sculptor, architect. The artist came to be known by his nickname, meaning "little old lady."

Vedantadesika: Venkatesa (or Venkatanatha) (1268–1370), Ind. theologian. The founder of the Vadakalai, a subsect within Sri-Vaisnavism, came to be known by a name meaning "teacher of the Vedanta," the Hindu philosophy based on the doctrine of the Upanishads.

Bobby **Vee:** Robert Thomas Velline (1943–), U.S. pop singer.

Paz **Vega:** Paz Campos Trigo (1976–), Sp. movie actress.

Johnny **Vegas:** Michael Pennington (1970–), Eng. comedian, TV, movie actor. The actor is said to have based his stage name on that of Johnny Casino in the 1970s musical *Grease*. "Vegas is not his real name. How could it be? Rather it is the nickname that became a stage name for a stand-up comedian who grew into a dark, belligerent, drunken and uncontrollable version of his alter ego, Michael Pennington. The trouble now is that only Pennington's parents and siblings call him Michael. Everyone else, even his wife, calls him Johnny, which means that a lot of people ... think he's someone he's not" [*The Times*, January 13, 2003].

Andris **Vejan:** Donat Kalnac (1927–), Latvian poet. The poet's adopted name is based on Russian *veter*, "wind."

Irina **Velembovskaya:** Irina Aleksandrovna Shukhgalter (Schuhhalter) (1922–), Russ. writer.

Lupe **Vélez:** Maria Guadalupe Vélez de Villalobos (1908–1944), Mexican movie actress.

Père **Venance:** (1) Jean François Dougados (1763–1794), Fr. priest, poet, politician; (2) J.-Albert Caron (1895–1966), Can. priest, scientific photographer, moviemaker. Caron assumed his name in 1914 when in the Capuchin novitiate, presumably in honor of Dougados, who in 1786, as a young Capuchin monk, had been sent on a fund-raising tour among the peasants and gentry of the Monts de Lacaune in southern France and who wrote of his findings in *La Quête du Blé* ("The Search for Wheat"). He was guillotined in the French Revolution for his extreme political views. The name itself honors the 6th-century saint and hymnwriter Venantius Fortunatus.

Venator *see* **Piscator**

Josef **Venatorini:** Josef Myslivecek (1737–1781), Bohemian composer.

Nick **Venet:** Nikolas Kostantinos Venetoulis (1936–1998), U.S. record producer.

Michael **Venning** *see* Craig **Rice**

Charlie **Ventura:** Charles Venturo (1916–1992), U.S. jazz saxophonist, bandleader.

Lino **Ventura:** Angiolino Giuseppe Pascal Ventura Lino Borrini (1919–1987), It.-born Fr. movie actor. The actor adopted his name as a professional wrestler.

Vik **Venus:** Jack Spector (1928–1994), U.S. DJ.

Benay **Venuta:** Venuta Rose Crooke (1911–), U.S. stage actress, singer.

Vera: (1) Charlotte Louisa Hawkins Dempster (1835–1913), Br. writer; (2) [Lady] Gertrude Elizabeth Campbell, née Blood (known as Lady Colin Campbell) (1861–1911), Ir. novelist, art critic, writer; (3) Vera Neumann (1910–1993), U.S. artist, designer. The name may have a symbolic attraction, since Latin *vera* means "true," while Russian *vera* means "faith."

Vera-Ellen: Vera-Ellen Westmeyr Rohe (1920–1981), U.S. popular singer, dancer, movie actress.

Verax: Henry Dunckley (1823–1896), Eng. journalist, editor, writer. Dunckley first used the name, Latin for "truthful," when beginning a series of letters on current topics in the *Manchester Weekly Times* in 1877. The name was used by other writers, especially for contributions to the press.

Vercors: Jean Marcel Bruller (1902–1991), Fr. writer, illustrator. The writer used this name for his secretly distributed *Le Silence de la Mer* (1942) when running an underground press in Paris. Vercors is the name of an Alpine plateau which was a Resistance center in World War II. (For a similar name, compare **Forez.**)

Verdini: Frank Hladik (1909–1994), Cz.-born Br. comedy magician.

Maribel **Verdu:** Maria Isabel Verdu Rollan (1970–), Sp. movie actress.

Fulco di **Verdura:** Fulco Santostefano della Cerda, duca di Verdura (1898–1978), It. jewelry designer.

Violette **Verdy:** Nelly Guillerm (1933–), Fr.-born U.S. ballet dancer.

Diana **Vere:** Diana Fox (1942–), Trinidadian-born Br. ballet dancer.

V. **Veresaeff:** Vikenty Vikentievich Smidovich (1867–1945), Russ. writer. The writer originally used the pen name Vikentyev, formed from his patronymic (middle name). In 1892 he adopted the name by which he was subsequently known, taking it from the name of a character in a story by the Russian writer P.P. Gnedich. He felt the name was "pleasing and unpretentious" [Dmitriyev, p.61].

Tom **Verlaine:** Thomas Miller (1949–), U.S. rock musician. The musician adopted the name of the French poet, Paul Verlaine (1844–1896), who had inspired him to write poetry before he turned his hand to lyrics.

Judith **Vermont:** Ménie Muriel Dowie (1867–1945), Eng. novelist, travel writer. This was one of a number of pseudonyms used by the writer when her work began to appear in print in the late 1880s.

Adela **Verne:** Adela Wurm (1877–1952), Br. concert pianist, of German parentage, sister of Alice **Verne** and Mathilde **Verne**. Adela was taught piano by Mathilde, and to negate the family relationship called herself "Clara Jenkins" during lessons, at the same time insisting on being treated as a stranger. A fourth sister, pianist and conductor Marie Wurm (1860–1938), kept the German family name.

Alice **Verne:** Alice Wurm (1868–1938), Br. concert pianist, sister of Adela **Verne** and Mathilde **Verne**.

Karen **Verne:** Ingabor Katrine Klinckerfuss (1915–1967), Ger. movie actress, working in U.S.

Mathilde **Verne:** Mathilde Wurm (1865–1936), Br. concert pianist, sister of Adela **Verne** and Alice **Verne**.

Oscar **Verne:** Charles Arthur Rawlings (*fl.*1890s), Eng. composer, songwriter. The pseudonym apparently relates to the writers Oscar Wilde (1856–1900) and Jules Verne (1828–1905), although it is also an anagram of Italian *conversare*, "to converse" (or *conservare*, "to conserve"). Other names used by Rawlings were Haydon Augarde, Jean Augarde, Jeanne Bartelet, Otto Bonheur, Émile Bonte, Faulkner Brandon, Louis Brandon, Henri Clermont, Auguste Cons, Eugene Delacassa, Leo Delcasse, Eileen Dore, Jean Douste, Denis Dupré, Léon du Terrail, Seymour Ellis, Robert Graham, John Gresham, Maxime Heller, Emerson James, Harrington Leigh, François Lemara, Gilbert Loewe, Angelo Martino, Alphonse Menier, Nita, Paul Perrier, Maxime Pontin, Wellington Rawlings, Vernon Rey, Carl Ritz, Carl Rubins, Émile Sachs, Hans Sachs, Ralph Seymour, Herman Straus, Maurice Telma, Gordon Temple, Paul Terrier, Thomas Thome, Claude de Vere, Beryl Vincent, Christine Williams, and Sydney West [Robert and Celia Dearling with Brian Rust, *The Guinness Book of Music Facts and Feats*, 1976].

Gerald **Verner:** Donald Stuart (1896–1980), Br. thriller writer.

Henri **Vernes:** Charles Dewisme (1918–), Belg. cartoonist, children's writer, writing in French.

Henri **Verneuil:** Achad Malakian (1920–2002), Turk. movie director, of Armenian parentage, working in France. Verneuil's refugee Armenian family arrived in France in 1924. He studied engineering, and moved from journalism to the movies at the Liberation (1944), when he adopted his pseudonym.

Anne **Vernon:** Edith Antoinette Alexandrine Vignaud (1925–), Fr. movie actress, working in U.K., U.S.

Bobby **Vernon:** Silvion de Jardin (1897–1939), U.S. movie comedian.

Dai **Vernon:** David Frederick Wingfield Werner (1894–1992), Can.-born U.S. magician.

Howard **Vernon:** Mario Lippert (1914–1996), Swiss movie actor.

John **Vernon:** Adolphus Raymondus Vernon Agopsowicz (1932–2005), Can. movie actor.

Konstanze **Vernon:** Konstanze Herzfeld (1939–), Ger. ballet dancer.

Paolo **Veronese:** Paolo Caliari (*c.*1528–1588), It. painter. The artist is named for Verona, the city of his birth. He was mainly active in Venice, however, and is considered to belong to the Venetian school.

Andrea del **Verrocchio:** Andrea di Francesco di Cioni (*c.*1435–1488), It. sculptor, painter, metalworker. The artist is said to have taken his name either from the ecclesiastic whose protégé he was or from his teacher, a goldsmith named Giuliano Verrocchi. It was in the goldsmith's trade that he was initially trained. Appropriately for an artist or craftsman, the name itself means literally "true eye."

Odile **Versois:** Katiana de Poliakoff-Baidarov (1930–1980), Fr. movie actress, of Russ. parentage, sister of actresses Marina **Vlady** and Hélène Vallier (originally Militza de Poliakoff-Baidaroff) (1932–).

Dziga **Vertov:** Denis Arkadyevich Kaufman (1896–1954), Russ. documentary movie director. The director, originally a poet and novelist, adopted a Slavic name roughly translating as "spinning top." Some sources give his original patronymic (middle name) as Abramovich.

Veruschka: [Countess] Vera von Lehndorff (1939–), Ger. fashion model, movie actress. The actress adopted her professional name when beginning her career as a model. She explains: "Veruschka was a nickname I had when I was a child. It means 'little Vera.' And as I was always too tall, I thought it would be nice to say that I'm little Vera. And it was also nice to have a Russian name because I came from the East" [Michael Gross, *Model*, 1995].

Stanley **Vestal:** Walter Stanley Campbell (1887–1957), U.S. author, educator. Campbell mostly used this name for his writings about the Southwestern frontier, and "Vestal" perhaps suggests "West."

Madame **Vestris:** Lucy Elizabeth Vestris, née Bartolozzi (1797–1856), Eng. actress, singer. As was the tradition of her day, the actress used her married name for her stage name. Her husband was the French ballet dancer Armand Vestris (1787–1825), whom she married in 1813. (He left her in 1817.)

Artyom **Vesyoly:** Nikolay Ivanovich Kochkurov (1899–1939), Russ. writer. The writer's adopted surname means "merry," although his stories of Russia rent asunder by revolution and civil war show this to be ironic.

Jack **Vettriano:** Jack Hoggan (1951–), Sc.

painter. The self-taught artist, whose working life began as a mining engineer, changed his name in 1989 on deciding to devote his life wholly to painting. "Changing his name, he says, was a wonderful marketing ploy. He adopted his mother's maiden name, Vettriano, which came from his Italian grandfather" [*The Times*, August 29, 2007].

Vetus: [Captain] Edward Sterling (1773–1847), Ir. journalist, lawyer. The writer used this name, Latin for "old," "aged," for letters to *The Times*. Six of these were published in 1812 as *The Letters of Vetus, from March 10 to May 10, 1812*. A second part, containing letters 7 through 15, followed later that year.

Pavel **Vezhinov:** Nikola Delchev Gugov (1914–1983), Bulg. novelist, short-story writer.

Lodovico **Viadana:** Lodovico Grossi (*c.*1560–1627), It. composer. The musician and friar came to be known by the name of his birthplace, Viadana, near Mantua, northern Italy.

Théophile de **Viau** *see* **Théophile**

Sid **Vicious:** John Simon Ritchie, later Beverly (1957–1979), Eng. punk rock musician. The Sex Pistols member is said to have received his antiestablishment name following an attack with a bicycle chain on a *New Nusical Express* critic, Nick Kent. However, a fellow Pistols member, Johnny **Rotten**, recounts the following in his autobiography: "I called him Sid, after my pet, ... this soppy white hamster that used to live in a cage on the corner table in my parents' living room. One day ... the hamster took a bite out of my father's hand....We dubbed Sid the hamster 'Vicious' after that. Sid's real name was Simon Ritchie or John Beverly; even he wasn't sure which. It all depended on his mother's whim at the time" [John Lydon with Keith and Kent Zimmerman, *Rotten: No Irish, No Blacks, No Dogs*, 1993].

Jon **Vickers:** Jonathan Stewart (1926–), Can. opera singer.

Martha **Vickers:** Martha MacVicar (1925–1971), U.S. movie actress.

Vicky: Victor Weisz (1913–1966), Ger.-born Br. political cartoonist, of Hung. Jewish descent. The artist used other signatures during his career, among them Pierrot and Smith.

Victizzle: Victor Akata (1991–), Br. black gospel singer.

Victor II: Gebhard of Dollnstein-Hirschberg (*c.*1018–1057), Ger. pope.

Victor III: Dauferi (later, Desiderius) (1027–1087), It. pope. The pontiff took the name Victor as a gesture of reconciliation with the emperor Henry IV, whose father, Henry III, had nominated **Victor II**.

Charles **Victor:** Charles Victor Harvey (1896–1965), Br. movie actor.

Josephine **Victor:** Josephine Guenczler (1885–?), Hung.-born U.S. stage actress.

Victor and Cazire *see* John **Fitzvictor**

Victoria: Lilli Ursula Barbara Victoria Davidson, née Commichau (1915–), Ger.-born Br. humorous illustrator.

Vesta **Victoria:** Victoria Lawrence (1873–1951), Br. music-hall singer, working in U.S., U.K. The singer based her name, and its formation, on that of Vesta **Tilley.** Like Tilley, she began her career young, appearing first as Baby Victoria, then as Little Victoria, and finally as Vesta Victoria.

Florence **Vidor:** Florence Cobb (1895–1977), U.S. movie actress. Cobb's name changed to Arto when her mother remarried and became Vidor in 1915 when she married director King Vidor (1894–1982).

Clara **Viebig:** Clara Viebig Cohn (1860–1952), Ger. novelist.

Luandino **Vieira:** José Vieira Mateus da Graça (1935–), Port.-born (white) Angolan writer. The writer's new first name relates to Luanda, where his family came to settle in 1938.

Francis **Viélé-Griffin:** Egbert Ludovicus Viele (1864–1937), U.S.-born Fr. poet.

Antanas **Vienuolis:** Antanas Zukauskas (1882–1957), Lithuanian writer. The writer explained in his autobiography: "My road through life has mostly been a lonely one, and I have had few friends. Hence my choice of the literary name Vienuolis, i.e., all on my own" [Dmitriyev, p.121].

Claude **Vigée:** Claude-André Strauss (1921–), Fr. poet. On the outbreak of World War II Strauss and his family fled their native Alsatia for a safer area of France. In 1941, while studying medicine in Toulouse, Strauss joined a Jewish resistance group, and while there adopted his new surname, intended as an inversion of French "*j'ai vie*" ("I am alive"), a phrase familiar both to Jews in the Hebrew form "*chai ani*" and to Christians from the Bible (Revelation 1:18).

Vigilans: Eric Honeywood Partridge (1894–1979), N.Z.-born Br. lexicographer. Partridge used this name, Latin for "watchful," for a slim work, *Chamber of Horrors* (1952), published by Andre Deutsch in their Language Library series, of which he was editor. Subtitled *A Glossary of Official Jargon both English and American*, the book was presented as a mild academic spoof, with the following playful blurb (in part), presumably written by Partridge himself: "The writer employs a pseudonym because he does not wish to become the victim of a man-hunt *effected* by a horde of enraged civil servants. He will, perhaps, regret it when he has to forgo the correct attribution, by more enlightened readers, of so much exhaustive research and such trenchant comment. Mr

Eric Partridge has written an introductory essay." (He italicizes *effected* as an example of official jargon.)

But this was not the sole motive for the ruse. "Coming so soon after *Usage and Abusage* [published in New York in 1942 and London in 1947] ... it would have looked a bit repetitious to have the *Chamber of Horrors* in his own name — in his own series. But the 'Vigilans' device not only relieved its author of this embarrassment but enabled him to quote himself glowingly on page after page" [Randolph Quirk, "An Adjunct to Ourself," in David Crystal, ed., *Eric Partridge In His Own Words*, 1980].

Jacomo da **Vignola:** Jacomo Barozzi (1507–1573), It. architect, painter, portraitist. The artist came to be known by the name of his birthtown of Vignola, northern Italy.

Claude **Vignon:** Noémie Cadiot (1828–1888), Fr. sculptor, novelist. The artist assumed her pseudonym on leaving her first husband and turning to writing, taking it from a character in Honoré de Balzac's novel *Béatrix* (1839), presumably itself adopted from the painter Claude Vignon (1593–1670).

Jean **Vigo:** Jean Bonaventure de Vigo Almereyda (1905–1934), Fr. movie director.

Irina **Vilde:** Darya Dmitriyevna Polotnyuk (1907–1982), Ukr. writer.

Charles **Vildrac:** Charles Messager (1882–1971), Fr. poet, novelist, dramatist. The writer adopted a literary name for his pen name, that of Roger Wildrake, the reckless cavalier ("wild rake") in Sir Walter Scott's novel *Woodstock* (1826), with the English name rendered in a French manner.

Lettie **Viljoen:** Ingrid Gouws, née Winterbach (1948–), S.A. writer.

Evald **Vilks:** Evald Latsis (1923–1976), Latvian writer. The writer was obliged to take a new name so as not to be confused with the better-known Latvian novelist Vilis Latsis (1904–1966). His new surname means "wolf."

Claudio **Villa:** Claudio Pica (1926–1987), It. popular singer.

Francisco "Pancho" **Villa:** Doroteo Arango (1878–1923), Mexican revolutionary, guerrilla leader. In 1894, aged 16, Arango fled to the hills and became a bandit. During the next 16 years he rode with the bands of Ignacio Parra, José Beltrán, and one Francisco Villa. When this last was killed in a shootout, Arango took his name to assert his authority over the gang. "Pancho" is a pet form of "Francisco."

Frank **Villard:** François Drouineau (1917–1980), Fr. movie actor.

Henry **Villard:** Ferdinand Heinrich Gustav Hilgard (1835–1900), Ger.-born U.S. financier, publisher. When Hilgard's father threatened to enlist him in the military, he emigrated to New York in 1853, changing his name after an admired schoolmate to make it difficult for his family to trace him.

Mme. de **Villedieu**: Marie-Catherine Hortense Desjardins (1631–1683), Fr. writer. The name under which the writer was regularly known was that of the man she hoped to make marry her, Antoine Boësset de Villedieu (1632–1668), but although he initially consented to her proposal, he later withdrew his acceptance. She adopted the name after his early death, apparently with the agreement of his family.

[Sir] Francis **Villeneuve-Smith**: [Sir] Francis Smith (1819–1909), Eng.-born Austral. judge. Sir Francis added his mother's maiden name of Villeneuve on retiring as Chief Justice of Tasmania in 1884.

Caroline **Villiers**: Carol Friday (1949–), Eng. stage, TV actress.

François **Villon**: François de Montcorbier (1431– after 1463), Fr. poet. Some doubt remains about the real name of the French poet, and his date of death is also not precisely known. He seems to have been born as either François de Montcorbier or François des Loges, these two "surnames" being respectively the name of a village on the borders of Burgundy where his father was born and (probably) the name of his father's farm. The name by which he is now generally known is that of the man who adopted him, Guillaume de Villon, a Paris chaplain. Villon used other pseudonyms, among them Michel Mouton.

Jacques **Villon**: Gaston Emile Duchamp (1875– 1963), Fr. painter. The brother of **Duchamp-Villon** changed his name in 1895 to express his admiration of the poet François **Villon**.

Gene **Vincent**: Eugene Vincent Craddock (1935–1971), U.S. rock musician, working in U.K.

Harl **Vincent**: Harl Vincent Schoelphfin (1893– 1968), U.S. SF writer.

Johnny **Vincent**: John Vincent Imbragulio (1927–2000), U.S. record company manager.

Walter **Vincent** *see* Walter **Vincson**

William **Vincent**: Thomas Holcroft (1745– 1809), Eng. dramatist, writer. The writer used the name (in the form "William Vincent of Gray's Inn," suggesting the author was a lawyer) for a work published in 1780 which included a "Narrative of the Late Riots in London" and an "Account of the commitment of Lord G. Gordon to the Tower."

Walter **Vincson**: Walter Vinson (1911–1975), U.S. black blues musician. Vinson also recorded as Walter Vincent and Walter Jacobs, the latter with his mother's maiden name.

Barbara **Vine**: [Baroness] Ruth Barbara Rendell, née Grasemann (1930–), Eng. crime, mystery novelist. The writer mostly uses her real name, but took another name when she was "looking for a new voice," first using it for *A Dark-Adapted Eye* (1986). It derives from her second name and the maiden name of her great-grandmother. "I know it sounds odd," says Rendell, "but I feel different when I use it. It is more feminine."

Stella **Vine**: Melissa Robson (1969–), Eng. artist. The painter of controversial celebrity portraits adopted her new name in 1995. "Stella Vine doesn't look like any of the things she's been. She doesn't look like a stripper. She doesn't look like an escort girl. And she certainly doesn't look like one of Britain's most notorious artists. Dammit, Stella Vine doesn't even look like a Stella Vine. She looks like exactly the name she was born with, Melissa Robson" [*Sunday Times Magazine*, June 10, 2007].

Aasmund **Vinje**: Aasmund Olavson (1816– 1870), Norw. poet, critic. The writer took his pen name from Vinje, the village in southern Norway where he was born.

Herr Cornelius van **Vinkbooms**: Thomas Griffiths Wainewright (1794–1852), Eng. art critic, writer, poisoner, forger. This was one of the pseudonyms used by Wainewright for his contributions to the *London Magazine*, others being Egomet Bonmot and Janus Weathercock. The name itself may have been suggested by that of the Flemish painter David Vinckboons (1576–c.1630). He used the second name for *Some Passages in the Life of Egomet Bonmot, Esq.; edited by Mr. Mwaughaim, and now first published by M E* (1827), a slim work sneering at rival authors.

Elaine **Vinson** *see* Fenton **Brockley**

Helen **Vinson**: Helen Rulfs (1907–1999), U.S. movie actress.

Charles **Vipont**: Elfrida Foulds, née Vipont (1902–1992), Br. biographer, children's writer. The author used the male name for her first children's book, *Blow the Man Down* (1939), a historical adventure tale.

Virgilius: Brian Greer (1944–), Ir.-born crossword compiler, working in U.S. The pseudonym was not apparently taken from the Roman poet (better known as Virgil) but from the byname of an 8th-century Irish scribe who inserted acrostics in his writing.

Georges **Virrès**: Henri Briers (1869–1946), Belg. writer.

Frank **Virtue**: Francis F. Virtuoso (1921–1994), U.S. record producer, bandleader.

Edvards **Virza**: Edvards Lieknis (1883–1940), Latvian poet.

Visal: Mohammed Shafi (1779–1846), Iranian poet.

Tancrède de **Visan**: Vincent Biétrix (1878– 1945), Fr. poet, literary critic.

Luchino **Visconti**: [Conte] Don Luchino Visconti di Morone (1906–1976), It. stage, movie director.

Ostap **Vishnya:** Pavel Mikhaylovich Gubenko (1889–1956), Ukr. satirical writer, humorist. The writer's assumed surname means "cherry." When he first appeared in print in a local newspaper at the age of 22, his editor, a woman named Oksana (Oxana), asked him how he wished to sign himself. He hesitated, since choosing a pen name on the spur of the moment was not so easy, then took a pen and wrote "Oksana." This female name was subsequently ousted by his male one.

E.H. **Visiak:** Edward Harold Physick (1878–1972), Br. poet, critic, writer. "Visiak" from "Physick."

Vitalis: Erik Sjöberg (1794–1828), Swe. lyric poet. The poet's adopted pen name represents Latin *vita lis*, "life [is a] struggle." He died when only 34, the struggle having been too much.

Vitamin C: Colleen Ann Fitzpatrick (1972–), U.S. pop singer, movie actress. Presumably "C" for "Colleen," and originating as a nickname.

Yuozas **Vitas:** Jonas Valunas (1899–1943), Lithuanian Communist official.

El **Viti:** Santiago Martín (1938–), Sp. bullfighter. The matador was born in the small town of Vitigudino, near Salamanca. Hence his ring name.

Vasil **Vitka:** Timofey Vasilyevich Krysko (1911–1996), Belorussian poet, playwright. The writer's adopted name means "branch," "twig."

Monica **Vitti:** Maria Luisa Ceciarelli (1931–), It. stage, movie actress.

Viva: Vivanee (earlier Janet Sue) Hoffman (1948–), U.S. movie actress, acolyte of Andy **Warhol**, mother of actress Gaby (originally Gabriela) Hoffman (1982–).

Kassandra **Vivaria:** [Donna] Magda Stuart Heinemann, née Sindici (*fl.*1890s), It.-born Br. writer. The author was the wife (married 1899, divorced 1904) of the publisher William Heinemann, who published her first novel, *Via Lucis* (1898), under this pseudonym.

Swami **Vivekananda:** Narendranath Datta (or Dutt) (1863–1902), Ind. religious leader. The Hindu sage, who propagated the teaching of his master **Ramakrishna**, took his religious name in 1883. It means "bliss of reason," from Sanskrit *viveka*, "reason," and *ananda*, "bliss." Swami is a title meaning "master," "prince."

E.C. **Vivian:** Charles Henry Cannell (1882–1947), Br. writer, editor. After changing his name, the writer used his original name as a "pseudonym" for a number of oriental adventure stories. The initials of his new name stood for Evelyn Charles.

Renée **Vivien:** Pauline Mary Tarn (1877–1909), Eng.-born Fr. poet, prose writer, of U.S.–Sc. parent-age. The poet first wrote as (genderless) "R. Vivien," then as (male) "René Vivien," and finally as (female) "Renée Vivien." She also produced works as Paule Riversdale. The revelation of her sex caused something of a scandal, since her writing was often morbidly sensual.

Vivienne: Florence Vivienne Entwistle (1887–1982), Br. portrait photographer.

Baruch Charney **Vladeck:** Baruch Nachman Charney (1886–1938), Belorussian-born U.S. journalist, civic leader. Harassed by czarist police following the 1905 revolution, Charney dropped his family name in favor of the party name Vladeck. He immigrated to the United States in 1908.

Miron **Vladimirov:** Miron Konstantinovich Sheynfinkel (Scheinfinkel) (1879–1925), Russ. revolutionary, Communist official.

Georgy **Vladimov:** Georgy Nikolayevich Volosevich (1931–2003), Russ. writer, editor.

Ignaty **Vladislavlev:** Ignaty Vladislavovich Gulbinsky (1880–1962), Russ. bibliographer.

Vladimir **Vladomirsky:** Vladimir Iosifovich Maleyko (1893–1971), Belorussian stage actor.

Vlady: Vladimir Kibalchich (1920–), Russ.-born artist, working in Mexico, son of Victor **Serge**.

Marina **Vlady:** Marina de Poliakoff-Baidarov (1938–), Fr. movie actress, of Russ. parentage, sister of Odile **Versois**. The actress began her career as a ballet dancer under the name Marina Versois. Her screen surname suggests a Russian family name such as Vladimirova.

Anton **Vodorinski:** Albert William Ketèlbey (1875–1959), Eng. composer. Some of the composer's piano works were published under this name.

Jacq Firmin **Vogelaar:** Frans Broers (1944–), Du. writer.

La **Voisin:** Catherine Monvoisin, née Deshayes (*c.*1640–1680), Fr. adventuress. The midwife and fortune teller grew wealthy through concocting poisonous potions and selling them to the ladies at the court of Louis XIV. Her crimes came to light in 1679 and she was beheaded and burned.

Volgin *see* N. **Beltov**

A. **Volgin** *see* Vladimir Ilyich **Lenin**

Boris **Volin:** Boris Mikhaylovich Fradkin (1886–1957), Russ. Communist official.

Richard von **Volkmann:** Richard Leander (1830–1889), Ger. children's writer.

Nikolay **Volkov:** Nikolay Ivanovich Ivanov (1836–1891), Russ. ballet dancer.

Ivan **Volnov:** Ivan Yegorovich Vladimirov (1885–1931), Russ. writer. The writer derived his pen name from Russian *vol'nyy*, "free," alluding to the desired freeing of peasant folk from poverty under czarist rule.

V. **Volodarsky:** Moisey Markovich Goldshteyn (Goldstein) (1891–1918), Russ. revolutionary.

Aleksandr **Volodin:** Aleksandr Moiseyevich Lifshits (1919–2001), Russ. playwright.

Vladimir **Volodin:** Vladimir Sergeyevich Ivanov (1891–1968), Russ. movie actor. The actor's new surname is based on the colloquial form, Volodya, of his own first name. He presumably adopted it for distinction from the many other Ivanovs, this being the commonest Russian surname.

Maksimilian **Voloshin:** Maksimilian Aleksandrovich Kiriyenko-Voloshin (1877–1932), Russ. poet.

Vitaly **Volsky:** Vitaly Fridrikhovich Zeydel (Seidel) (1901–?), Belorussian writer.

Voltaire: François Marie Arouet (1694–1778), Fr. writer, philosopher. The writer's pseudonym is often said to be an anagram of his surname, the initial "V" representing the "u" and the added "l" and "i" standing for *le jeune* ("the young") (taking "i" as "j"). This interpretation was first made by the essayist Thomas Carlyle. An alternate theory says that Voltaire adopted (and adapted) the name of Veauterre, a property he had acquired near Asnières-sur-Oise, north of Paris. He first used the name in 1718.

Daniele da **Volterra:** Daniele Ricciarelli (1509–1566), It. painter, sculptor. The artist's name is that of his birthplace, Volterra, Florence.

Volterrano: Baldassare Francheschini (1611–1689), It. painter. The artist was born in Volterra, near Pisa.

Claus **von Bülow:** Cecil Borberg (1926–), Dan.-born U.S. socialite. The wealthy Dane was in the news in 1983, when he was found guilty of attempting to murder his wife. He was acquitted two years later. His adopted aristocratic name matched his jet-set lifestyle.

Hans **von der Leine:** Hermann Löns (1866–1914), Ger. writer. Löns first used his pen name in 1894.

Samuel Greifensohn **von Hirschfeld:** Hans Jakob Christoffel von Grimmelshausen (?1620–1676), Ger. writer. The writer revelled in anagrammatic pseudonyms, of which this is one example. Others were Erich Stainfels von Grufensholm, Israel Fromschmit von Hugenfels, Filarhus Grossus von Trommenhaim, and even A.c.eee.ff.g.hh.ii.ll.mm.nn.oo.rr.sss.t.uu, which appeared on the title page of *Das wunderbarliche Vogel-Nest* ("The Magical Bird's Nest") (1672). His best-known pen name, however, was **Simplicissimus.**

Wilhelm **von Homburg:** Norbert Grupe (1940–2004), Ger.-born boxer, movie, TV actor, working in U.S. The actor was originally a top boxer under the name Prinz Wilhelm von Homburg.

W.O. **von Horn:** Philip Friedrich Wilhelm Örtel (1798–1867), Ger. writer of popular stories.

The writer's adopted surname means "of Horn," referring to his native town.

Rosa **von Praunheim:** Holger Mischwitzky (1942–), Latvian-born Ger. movie director, producer, actor, screenwriter. The director's assumed name hints at his militant homosexuality.

Sasha **von Scherler:** Alexandra-Xenia Elizabeth Anne Marie Fiesola von Schoeler (1939–), U.S. stage actress. The actress adopted the pet form of her first name and a simplified form of her surname.

Baron **von Schlicht:** [Count] Wolf Heinrich von Baudissin (1789–1878), Ger. literary critic, translator. No doubt significantly, German *schlicht* means "homely," "unpretentious."

Josef **von Sternberg:** Jonas Sternberg (1894–1969), Austr. Jewish movie director, working in U.S. The aristocratic "von" was added to the filmmaker's name by a Hollywood producer who thought it would look better on a marquee entrance. He made his directorial debut under the name with *The Salvation Hunters* (1924).

Erich **von Stroheim:** Erich Oswald Stroheim (1885–1957), Austr. movie actor, director, working in U.S. The actor's original name is given in some sources as Erich Oswald Hans Carl Maria von Stroheim und Nordenwall, supposedly the descendant of a noble Austrian military family. However, his real name was as stated above, and he was the son of a Jewish hatter from Prussia who had settled in Vienna.

Dita **von Teese:** Heather Renée Sweet (1972–), U.S. burlesque performer. "While still in her teens Dita became a star of the strip-club and fetish scene in LA. She assumed her nom de strip and translated her love of scant costume into a kind of performance art" [*Times Magazine*, September 20, 2008]. Her first name came from Dita **Parlo**; her last from "(strip)tease" (and a reversal of letters in her real name).

Baron Arminius **von Thunder-ten-Tronckh:** Matthew Arnold (1822–1888), Eng. poet, critic. Arnold used this early pen name for some satirical contributions to the *Pall Mall Gazette*, subsequently published collectively as *Friendship's Garland* (1871). The name is that of the principal imaginary correspondent, the descendant of a fictional baron in Voltaire's *Candide* (1759), himself named for his estate, Thunder-ten-Tronckh, an "earthly paradise."

Albert **Von Tilzer:** Albert Gumm (1878–1956), U.S. popular music publisher, songwriter. The musician changed his name following the success of his brother, Harry **Von Tilzer**, as a composer and song publisher.

Harry **Von Tilzer:** Harry Gumm (1872–1946), U.S. popular music publisher, songwriter, brother of Albert **Von Tilzer**. The composer took his mother's maiden name of Tilzer for his professional name.

Lars **Von Trier:** Lars Trier (1956–), Dan. movie drector. The controversial director "adopted the 'Von' as a jokey affectation during his film school years" [*The Times*, July 18, 2009]

Nina **Voskresenskaya** *see* Eduard **Bagritsky**

Aleksandr **Vostokov:** Aleksandr Khristoforovich Ostenek (1781–1864), Russ. philologist, poet. The writer was the illegitimate son of Count Osten-Sacken, a name that he later modified to Ostenek. His new surname is a part translation of this, as German *Ost* and Russian *vostok* both mean "east."

Marko **Vovchok:** Mariya Aleksandrovna Vilinskaya-Markovich (1833–1907), Ukr. writer, of Russ.-Pol. descent. The writer took her new surname from the village where she lived. Her new first name is a shortened form of the surname of her husband, ethnographer and political activist A.V. Markovich.

Bono **Vox** *see* **Bono**

Valentine **Vox:** ? (1894–1943), U.S. ventriloquist. There have been been at least three ventriloquists of this name, which comes from the hero of Henry Cockton's novel *The Life and Adventures of Valentine Vox, the Ventriloquist* (1840), itself inspired by the contemporary French ventriloquist Nicholas Alexandre Vattermare. The dates given here are for the second of the name. The first published *The Cabinet of Irish and Yankee Wit and Humour* (1864). The third, born Val Andrews (1926–), performed as "Val Vox" from the ages of 12 to 22, and as "Vanson" from 1948 through 1951. He wrote biographies of several magicians, including **Dante**, Horace **Goldin**, and **Chung Ling Soo**, and also *I Can See Your Lips Moving: The History and Art of Ventriloquism* (1981). "Vox," of course, is Latin for "voice."

Grigory **Voytinsky:** Grigory Naumovich Zarkhin (1893–1953), Russ. Communist, Sinologist.

Stanko **Vraz:** Jakob Frass (1810–1851), Croatian poet, critic.

Rudolf **Vrba:** Walter Rosenberg (1924–2006), Slovak Jewish writer. Walter Rosenberg and Alfred Wetzler (1918–1988) coauthored what came to be known as the "Vrba-Wetzler Report" or the "Auschwitz Protocols," a detailed description of the notorious concentration camp, where both men were prisoners. They managed to escape in 1944 and their report was published by the U.S. Government soon after. After the war, Rosenberg settled in British Columbia, where under his adopted name he became a professor of pharmacology. In 1963 Wetzler published, in Slovak, his account of his imprisonment and escape from the camp under the pseudonym Josef Lanik. Its title translated as *What Dante Did Not See* but an English translation under his real name appeared in 2007 with the title *Escape From Hell.*

Jaroslav **Vrchlický:** Emil Bohus Frída (1853–1912), Cz. poet, translator.

Theun de **Vries:** Theunis Milke (1907–), Du. poet, novelist.

Vakhtang **Vronsky:** Vakhtang Ivanovich Nadiradze (1905–), Georgian ballet master.

Azat **Vshtuni:** Azat Setovich Mamikonyan (1894–1958), Armenian poet.

Vulcana: Kate Williams (1875–1946), Welsh variety artist, "society athlete," teaming with **Atlas**, her common-law husband.

Vuokko: Nurmesniemi Vuokko (1930–), Finn. (female) fashion designer.

Samed **Vurgun:** Samed Yusif ogly Vekilov (1906–1956), Azerbaijani folk poet. The poet's adopted name means "enamored."

Vydunas: Vilius Storasta (1868–1953), Lithuanian playwright, philosopher. The writer's adopted name means "noble one."

W.E. **Wace** *see* Claudius **Clear**

Tom **Waddell:** Tom Fluabacher (1937–1987), U.S. athlete. The athlete took the name of his adoptive parents following the divorce of his natural parents.

Henry **Wade:** [Major Sir] Henry Lancelot Aubrey Fletcher (1887–1969), Eng. crime novelist. The writer adopted his mother's maiden name as his pen name.

Jane **Wade:** Nancy Mann Waddel Woodrow (?1866–1935), U.S. writer. Woodrow used this name for a single novel, *A Leaf in the Current.* Everything else she wrote appeared as by Mrs. Woodrow Wilson, from the name of her husband, James Wilson Woodrow, a distant cousin of the 28th U.S. president.

Hansa **Wadkar:** Ratan Salgaonkar (1923–1972), Ind. movie actress. The actress changed her name on her screen debut at age 11, adopting the family name of her grandmother and thus asserting her ancestry in a family of Maharashtrian courtesans.

Michael **Wager:** Emanuel Weisgal (1925–), U.S. stage actor, director.

Chuck **Wagon:** Robert Davis (*c.*1957–1981), U.S. punk-rock keyboardist.

Bunny **Wailer:** Neville O'Riley Livingston (1947–), Jamaican pop singer, songwriter. The singer was the last surviving member of The Wailers, the reggae group formed by Bob Marley in 1963.

Wakasegawa: Wataru Sato (1962–), Jap. sumo wrestler.

Tomisaburo **Wakayama:** Masaru Okamura (1929–1992), Jap. movie actor, brother of Shintaro **Katsu**.

Anton **Walbrook:** Adolf Anton Wilhelm Wohlbrück (1900–1967), Austr. movie actor, working in

U.S., U.K. The actor dropped the then unpopular first name of Adolf when in Hollywood in the 1930s.

Jersey Joe **Walcott:** Arnold Raymond Cream (1914–1994), U.S. black heavyweight boxer. Cream took his ring name from his boyhood hero, welterweight champion Joe Walcott (1873–1935), adding "Jersey" because he was born in New Jersey.

Max **Waldau:** Richard Georg Spiller von Hauenschild (1825–1855), Ger. writer.

Herwarth **Walden:** Georg Levin (1878–1941), Ger. writer, art critic, working in Russia. The writer's pseudonym was suggested by his wife, Else Lasker-Schüler (1869–1945), to whom he was married from 1903 to 1912.

Robert **Walden:** Robert Wolkowitz (1943–), U.S. TV actor.

Hugues **Waldin:** Cecile Blanc de Fontbelle (1892–?), Fr. conductor, composer.

Claire **Waldoff:** Clara Wortmann (1884–1957), Ger. music-hall artist.

Émile **Waldteufel:** Charles Émile Lévy (1837–1915), Fr. composer, conductor. The musician's assumed surname had earlier been used by his grandfather, father, and two uncles, who were all dance musicians. Its origin is uncertain. As an Alsatian surname it literally means "forest devil."

Hubert **Wales:** William Pigott (1870–1943), Br. novelist, writer on psychical research.

Josey **Wales:** Joseph Sterling (c.1960–), Jamaican DJ, reggae musician. Sterling took his name from the popular Clint Eastwood movie *The Outlaw Josey Wales* (1976).

Wally **Wales** *see* Hal **Taliaferro**

Arthur **Waley:** Arthur David Schloss (1889–1966), Eng. oriental scholar, translator. The writer's family adopted his mother's maiden name as their legal name in 1914, at the outbreak of World War I.

A'Lelia **Walker:** Lelia McWilliams (1885–1931), U.S. black businesswoman. McWilliams was born the daughter of Madame C.J. **Walker** and her first husband, Moses "Jeff" McWilliams, but adopted her mother's name (and modified her first name) on inheriting her business in 1919.

Clint **Walker:** Norman Walker (1927–), U.S. movie actor. Walker was billed as Jett Norman in the early movie *Jungle Gents* (1954).

Gary **Walker:** Gary Leeds (1944–), U.S. pop singer.

Jennie **Walker:** Charles Boyle (1951–), Br. poet. The writer adopted this female name for his first novel, *24 for 3* (2008).

Jerry Jeff **Walker:** Paul Crosby (1942–), U.S. country singer, songwriter.

John **Walker:** John Joseph Mans (1943–), U.S. pop singer.

Johnny **Walker:** Badruddin Jamaluddin Kazi (1925–2003), Ind. movie comedian. The actor took his screen name from the well-known brand of whiskey.

Junior **Walker:** Oscar G. Mixon (1931–1995), U.S. jazz, soul musician. The saxophonist adopted the nickname given him by his stepfather for his performing name.

Kath **Walker** *see* Oodgeroo **Noonuccal**

Madame C.J. **Walker:** Sarah Breedlove (1867–1919), U.S. black businesswoman. The inventor of the "Walker System" for straightening hair took her professional name at the suggestion of her future husband, Charles J. Walker, a newspaperman who helped her market and advertize her product.

Nancy **Walker:** Anna Myrtle Swoyer (1922–1992), U.S. TV actress. The actress got her stage name by accident. Richard Rodgers and his producer George Abbott were holding auditions in 1942 and Swoyer was one of those seeking a break on Broadway. Among the applicants was a singer named Helen Walker, hoping to land a minor five-line role. When Swoyer came on, she was announced in her place as "Miss Walker." The song she belted out, Ray McKinley's "Bounce Me, Brother, With a Solid Four," was not the one they had been expecting, but they changed their minds and offered her a leading part. She kept the other singer's surname, with "Nancy" a form of her real name Anna.

Scott **Walker:** Noel Scott Engel (1944–), U.S. pop musician.

Syd **Walker:** Sidney Kirman (1887–1945), Eng. radio comedian.

T-Bone **Walker:** Aaron Thibeaux Walker (1910–1975), U.S. black blues musician. Walker's new first name evolved out of his middle name.

Anton **Wall:** Christian Leberecht Heyne (1751–1821), Ger. playwright.

Max **Wall:** Maxwell George Lorimer (1908–1990), Sc.-born Br. stage, TV actor, comedian. The actor derived his stage name not from his first name, split into two, but from the short form of this name and the first half of his stepfather's name, Wallace.

Dee **Wallace:** Deanna Bowers (1948–), U.S. movie actress, dancer. The actress decided on a change of name when she moved from TV commercials to dramatic acting. She was billed as Dee Wallace until 1985, when she became Dee Wallace Stone on marrying actor Christopher Stone.

Dexter **Wallace:** Edgar Lee Masters (1869–1950), U.S. poet, lawyer. Masters used this name for some early essays and plays. In 1914, as Webster Ford, he began a series of poems about his life as a boy in western Illinois, published in *Reedy's Mirror* (St. Louis). This was the beginning of his *Spoon River An-*

thology (1915), the one work for which he is now remembered.

Edgar **Wallace:** Richard Horatio Edgar Wallace (1875–1932), Eng. novelist, playwright. The writer was born as the son of Polly Richards, née Mary Jane Blair, and Richard Horatio Edgar, both of whom were in the acting business. (His mother had married a Mr. Richards, and was known as "Polly" instead of her actual first name, Marie, which she had "upgraded" from Mary.) So how did the writer come to be "Wallace"? When Polly Richards registered her son's birth, she could not resist giving him the full name of his father, but in the paternity column of the register wrote "Walter Wallace, comedian," in order to disguise the actual identity of the father. It seems likely that "William Wallace, comedian" never existed, and no actor of this name has been traced in theatrical records. Even if he had lived, it seems unlikely that he would have agreed to give his name to a child that was certainly not his. Polly Richards was thus probably giving the boy the name of "a convenient father who could never be traced, and who had his beginning and his end solely in her own imagination" [Margaret Lane, *Edgar Wallace: The Biography of a Phenomenon*, 1939]. One of Wallace's detective plays was actually titled *The Man Who Changed His Name*. It was not a great success, and was full of improbable coincidences.

Irving **Wallace:** Irving Wallechinsky (1916–1990), U.S. novelist, encyclopedist, of Russ. descent. The writer was well known for the various editions of *The Book of Lists* (1977), among other works, with this particular publication compiled by a family foursome: Irving Wallace, David Wallechinsky (Irving's son), Amy Wallace (his daughter), and Sylvia Wallace (his wife).

Jean **Wallace:** Jean Wallasek (1923–1990), U.S. movie actress.

Julie T. **Wallace:** Julie Therese Keir (1961–), Br. stage, TV actress. The actress adopted her mother's maiden name.

Nellie **Wallace:** Eleanor Jane Liddy (1870–1948), Br. music-hall artist.

Raymond **Wallace:** Huntley Trevor (1881–1943), Eng. popular songwriter.

Sippie **Wallace:** Beulah Thomas (1898–1986), U.S. black blues singer. The singer's surname is that of her second husband, Matt Wallace. Her first name arose as a childhood nickname, given her for her lisp.

Walter Adam **Wallace:** Edward Adrian Woodruffe-Peacock (*fl.* 1890), Eng. writer.

Lester **Wallack:** John Johstone Wallack (1820–1888), U.S. actor, theatrical manager. Wallack, an actor's son, was raised and educated in England, where he originally took the stage name Allan Field

in order not to benefit unduly from his father's fame. When on tour in the provinces, he adopted the name John Lester, which he continued to use for almost two decades. He then returned to his native New York City, where he made his American debut in 1847, still as John Lester. Finally, in 1861, he appeared for the first time under the name Lester Wallack, which he retained for the rest of his career.

Fats **Waller:** Thomas Wright Waller (1904–1943), U.S. jazz pianist, composer. The musician's nickname is descriptive, given him for his girth, and until around 1931 he was billed as both "Thomas" and "Fats" (or as Thomas "Fats" Waller) in his professional work. The nickname then prevailed.

Lewis **Waller:** William Waller Lewis (1860–1915), Br. actor, theater manager. The actor was fortunate enough to have a surname that could readily be adopted as a first name for stage name use.

Max **Waller:** Léopold-Nicolas-Maurice-Édouard Warlomont (1860–1889), Belg. poet.

Thomas MacDonald **Waller:** Thomas MacDonald Armstrong (1840–1924), U.S. governor. The future Democratic governor of Connecticut was orphaned in 1848 and the following year adopted by Thomas K. Waller, whose name he subsequently adopted.

David **Walliams:** David Williams (1971–), Br. stage, TV actor. The actor modified the spelling of his name on joining Equity, the trade union of the British acting profession, one of whose members already bore his original name.

George **Wallington:** Giacinto Figlia (1924–1993), It.-born U.S. jazz pianist, composer.

A.S.C. **Wallis:** Adèle Sophia Cornelia von Antal-Opzoomer (1857–1925), Du. writer.

Walneerg: Thomas Knox (1835–1896), U.S. journalist, traveler. The writer used this name, a reversal of his birthplace, Greenlaw, New Hampshire, for *Rhymed Convictions in Song* (1852).

Raoul **Walsh:** Albert Edward Walsh (1887–1980), U.S. movie director, actor. When in his twenties, Walsh studied playwriting with a family friend, Paul Armstrong, who suggested that the actor replace his unremarkable given names with the more memorable "Raoul."

Stella **Walsh:** Stanislawa Walasiewiczowna (1911–1980), Pol.-born U.S. athlete. The athlete's original first name was Stefania. Her parents immigrated to the United States when she was only two, and her teachers, finding her Polish name difficult to pronounce, renamed her Stella Walsh. She remained a Polish citizen, competing in athletic events for Poland, until 1947, when she became a naturalized American. Even then, however, she could not try out for the 1948 Olympic team because she had belonged to the 1932 and 1936 Polish teams. She eventually became a U.S. citizen on marrying an American in 1956, by which time, at age 45, she was well past her athletic prime. A post mortem carried out following her death as the innocent victim of a shootout revealed that she was biologically male.

[Sir] Charles **Walston**: Charles Waldstein (1856–1927), U.S. archaeologist, writer, working in U.K.

Walter: Walter Goetz (1911–), Ger.-born Br. cartoonist, painter.

Bruno **Walter**: Bruno Walter Schlesinger (1876–1962), Ger.-born U.S. orchestral conductor. When working as an opera coach, Walter was advised by Theodore Loewe, director of the Breslau Stadttheater, to drop the name Schlesinger because of its frequent occurrence in the Silesian capital. He made the change in 1911 on becoming an Austrian citizen. In 1939 he moved to the U.S. and became an American citizen in 1946.

Johann **Walter** (or Walther): Johann Blankenmüller (1496–1570), Ger. composer, poet.

Judith **Walter**: Judith Gautier (?–1917), Fr. poet, novelist. The writer used this name, an anglicized form of the original, for *Le Livre de jade* (1867), a collection of poems from the Chinese.

Jess **Walters**: Josuoh Wolk (1918–2000), U.S. opera singer.

Rick **Walters** *see* Fenton **Brockley**

Joseph **Walton**: Joseph Losey (1909–1984), U.S.–born Br. movie director. This was one of the pseudonyms under which Losey worked in London in the 1950s when hoping to attract the attention of the critics. He used it for *The Intimate Stranger* (1956), having earlier directed *The Sleeping Tiger* (1954) as Victor Hanbury.

Waif **Wander**: Mary Helena Fortune, née Wilson (*c*.1833–*c*.1909), Ir.-born crime writer, novelist, poet, working in Australia. The name, suggesting a "wandering waif," was used by the writer for her romantic novels and poetry. For her crime fiction she was simply "W.W."

Walter **Wanger**: Walter Feuchtwanger (1894–1968), U.S. theater, movie producer.

Hank **Wangford**: Samuel Hutt (1940–), Br. country singer. The singer took his name from the Suffolk village where he was born. He commented: "Hank Wangford was a good name for the classic country star. He sings about pain, he sings about heartache, and that was good because Sam could go on living and being normal" [Larkin, p.1302].

David **Warbeck**: David Mitchell (1941–1997), N.Z.–born movie actor, model, of Sc. descent, working in Italy.

Artemus **Ward**: Charles Farrar Browne (1834–1867), U.S. humorist. Browne is said to have adopted his pen name not, as might be supposed, from the revolutionary war general and politician Artemas Ward (1727–1800) but from one of the figures in a Maine land dispute that drew on the surveying services of at least three generations of Browne's forebears. In 1857 he became local editor of the Cleveland *Plain Dealer* and first used the name the following year in a bogus letter to the editor:

Pitsburg, Jan. 27, 18&58

The Plane Deeler:
Sir:
    i write to no how about the show bisnes in Cleeveland i have a show consisting in part of a Calforny Bare two snakes tame foxies &c also wax works my wax works is hard to beat, all say they is life and nateral curiosities among my wax works is Our Saveyer Gen taylor and Docktor Webster in the ackt of killing Parkman. now mr. Editor scratch off few lines and tel me how is the show bisnes in your good city i shal have hanbils printed at your offis you scratch my back i will scratch your back, also git up a grate blow in the paper about my show don't forgit the wax works.
yours truly,
    ARTEMUS WARD
    Pitsburg, Penny
    p S pitsburg is a 1 horse town. A.W.

Billy **Ward**: Robert Williams (1921–2002), U.S. R&B musician.

Burt **Ward**: Herbert John Gervais, Jr. (1945–), U.S. juvenile movie actor.

E.D. **Ward**: Edward Verrall Lucas (1868–1938), Eng. essayist, writer. E.V. Lucas (as he is usually known) adopted this pseudonym, a form of his first name, for his novel *Sir Pulteney: A Fantasy* (1910).

Elizabeth Stuart Phelps **Ward**: Mary Gray Phelps (1844–1911), U.S. popular writer, feminist. When Phelps's mother died in 1852, her young daughter adopted her name, calling herself Elizabeth Stuart Phelps. In 1888 she married Herbert Dickinson Ward and conventionally added his name to her own.

Evelyn **Ward** *see* Cecil **Adair**

Fannie **Ward**: Frances Buchanan (1872–1952), U.S. stage actress.

Michael **Ward**: George Yeo (1909–1997), Br. movie comedian.

Mrs. H.O. **Ward** *see* Clara **Moreton**

Polly **Ward**: Byno Poluski (1908–1987), Br.-born movie actress.

Margaret **Warde**: Edith Kellogg Dunton (1875–1944), U.S. novelist. The writer used the name for her books about the college girl Betty Wales. She explained: "I chose a pen name because I had a sister at Smith College who, I thought, might be annoyed by a connection with anyone writing stories about college life. Also, I didn't want Smith to be embarrassed by a graduate's impressions, wholly fictional but never so regarded by one's friends. I chose Margaret because I always felt as if my name ought to have been Margaret, and Warde, with an *e*, because it wasn't in the Smith Alumnae of names. I didn't know it was so rare; a Margaret Warde in California wrote me that she had never seen it except in her own family and in one other case, Frederick Warde, and wished to trace a relationship" [Marble, p.180].

Florence **Warden:** Florence Alice James, née Price (1857–1929), Eng. romantic novelist.

Jack **Warden:** John H. Lebzelter (1920–2006), U.S. TV, movie actor. As a teenager the actor was a professional boxer under the name Johnny Costello.

Jane **Wardle:** Oliver Madox Hueffer (1877 or 1879–1931), Eng. writer. The younger brother of Ford Madox **Ford** used this female name for five volumes of fiction published between 1907 and 1910.

David **Warfield:** David Wohlfeld (1866–1951), U.S. stage actor, of Austr. Jewish parentage. Wohlfeld first used his stage name in 1890 on venturing into variety entertainment in San Francisco.

Andy **Warhol:** Andrew Varchola (1928–1987), U.S. pop artist, moviemaker, of Cz. parentage. The artist first used his modified name sporadically as a student, then adopted it permanently.

Barbara **Waring:** Barbara Gibb (1912–), Br. stage actress. The actress took her stage name from the maiden name of her mother, Louise Waring Colley.

Derek **Waring:** Derek Barton-Chapple (1927–2007), Eng. TV actor.

Richard **Waring:** (1) Richard Stephens (1912–), Eng. stage actor; (2) Brian Barton-Chapple (1925–1994), Br. TV comedy writer, brother of Derek **Waring**. Stephens adopted his mother's maiden name as his stage name.

Peter **Warlock:** Philip Arnold Heseltine (1894–1930), Eng. composer, musicologist. The musician's name, adopted around 1921, was intended to signify a change to a new, aggressive personality, one of "wine, women, and song," a warlock being a wizard, a dealer in black magic. Heseltine first used the name in 1919, after the failure of his early work and several rejects. "The name Heseltine is said to derive from 'hazel'; hence perhaps a quick switch to 'witch [hazel]' and thence by a corrective sex-change to 'warlock'" [Eric Sams, review of I.A. Copley, *The Music of Peter Warlock: A Critical Study*, *Times Literary Supplement*, July 11, 1980]. In a tippler's tip-up, Warlock recast himself as Rab Noolas for *Merry-Go-Down: A Gallery of Gorgeous Drunkards Through the Ages* (1929).

Charles **Warner:** Charles John Lickfold (1846–1909), Br. stage actor, father of H.B. **Warner**.

H.B. **Warner:** Henry Byron Warner-Lickfold (1876–1958), Br. stage, movie actor.

Jack **Warner:** Horace John Waters (1894–1981), Eng. stage, movie, TV actor. The actor changed his name to avoid trading on the name of his sisters, Elsie Waters (*c.*1895–1990) and Doris Waters (*c.*1904–1978), who teamed as radio comediennes (in the characters of Cockney gossips Gert and Daisy).

Jack L. **Warner:** Jacob Eichelbaum (1892–1978), Can.-born U.S. movie producer, of Pol. parentage. The twelve Warner children's mother was Pearl Leah Eichelbaum (1858–1934); the surname of their father, Benjamin (1857–1935), is unknown. "Ben never told anyone the original family name.... Perhaps the name was something like Varnereski. More likely it was Varna, which meant blackbird in the language spoken around [his native village of] Krasnashiltz" [Cass Warner Sperling and Cork Millner, *Hollywood Be Thy Name: The Warner Brothers Story*, 1994].

Jack was the best known of the four Warner brothers who in 1923 founded one of the world's leading motion-picture studios, Warner Brothers Pictures (from 1969 Warner Bros. Inc.). "This youngest son grew to hate the name Jacob and in his early teens changed it to Jack. He added a middle name, Leonard, because it sounded 'classy.' Jack admitted he got the name from an actor in a traveling minstrel show that had played in Baltimore. In his mind 'Jack L. Warner' had a theatrical ring to it" [ibid.]. Jack's son was the movie and TV producer Jack Warner, Jr. (1916–1995).

The other three Warner brother founders were Harry (originally Hirsch) (1881–1958), Albert (called Abe) (1884–1967), and Samuel (known as Sam) (1888–1927), who married Lina **Basquette**. The remaining eight siblings were Cecilia (1877–1881), Anna (1878–1958), Henry (1886–1890), Rose (1890–1955), Fannie (1891–1894), David (1893–1939), Sadie (1895–1959), and Milton (1896–1915).

Mary Douglas **Warre** *see* Maysie **Greig**

Betty **Warren:** Babette Hilda Hogan (1905–1990), Br. stage, movie actress.

Harry **Warren:** Salvatore Guaragna (1893–1981), U.S. movie songwriter, of It. parentage. The family name was anglicized as Warren by the time the future composer began school, where he was registered as Harry.

Leonard **Warren:** Leonard Warenoff (1911–1960), U.S. opera singer, of Russ. Jewish parentage.

Lavinia **Warren:** Mercy Lavinia Warren Bumpus (1841–1919), U.S. dwarf, wife of General Tom **Thumb**.

Rusty **Warren:** Ilene F. Goldman (1930–), U.S. variety artist.

Guy **Warren of Ghana** *see* Kofi **Ghanaba**

Price **Warung:** William Astley (1855–1911), Eng.-born Austral. novelist.

Clint **Warwick:** Albert Clinton Eccles (1940–2004), Eng. rock musician.

Dee Dee **Warwick:** Delia Mae Warrick (1945–2008), U.S. black R&B singer. The singer followed the example of her older sister, Dionne **Warwick,** changing the spelling of her surname in the early 1960s.

Dionne **Warwick:** Marie Dionne Warrick (1940–), U.S. black soul singer. The spelling in the singer's surname was altered when her first record, "Don't Make Me Over," was released in 1962.

John **Warwick:** John McIntosh Beattie (1905–1972), Austral. movie actor, working in U.K.

Richard **Warwick:** Richard Winter (1945–1997), Br. stage, TV actor. The actor changed his name to avoid confusion with another Richard Winter on the books of Equity (the actors' trade union).

Robert **Warwick:** Robert Taylor Bien (1878–1964), U.S. stage, movie actor.

Don **Was:** Donald Fagenson (1952–), U.S. rock musician. Don Was and David Was, born David Weiss (1952–), teamed as "brothers" to form the group Was (Not Was) around 1981, taking their name from a word game of Fagenson's son.

Washboard Doc: Joseph Doctor (1911–1988), U.S. black street musician.

Washboard Sam: Robert Brown (1910–1966), U.S. black washboard player, blues singer.

Washboard Slim: Robert Young (1900–1990), U.S. black street musician.

Washboard Willie: William Paden Hensley (1909–1991), U.S. black blues musician. This name and those above indicate an involvement with the washboard and its associated kitchen implements as a rhythm instrument. Washboard Slim embellished his with frying pans and cowbells.

Booker T. **Washington:** Booker Taliaferro (?1856–1915), U.S. black educator, race leader. Washington's mother gave him his first name as well as his middle name, Taliaferro. The surname of his white father is unknown, and he took the name Washington in 1870 from his slave stepfather, Washington Ferguson.

Dinah **Washington:** Ruth Lee Jones (1924–1963), U.S. black blues singer. The singer adopted her new name in 1943, when she was hired by Lionel Hampton to sing with his big band. Hampton was one of several to take the credit for suggesting the stage name.

Donna Day **Washington:** Donna Day Washington-Smith (1942–), Can. ballet dancer.

Hugo **Wast:** Gustavo Martínez Zuviría (1883–1962), Argentine novelist. The writer created his pen name from his original first name, with an added "h" and with "v" giving the "w."

William **Wastle:** John Gibson Lockhart (1794–1854), Sc. biographer, writer. The writer used this name for his contributions to *Blackwood's Magazine*, adopting it from that of Willie Wastle, a character in Robert **Burns**'s poem "Willie's Wife" (1792). This was the name under which Lockhart featured in the *Noctes Ambrosianae* (*see* Christopher **North**).

Onoto **Watana:** Winifred Eaton (1875–1954), Can. writer, of Chin.-Br. ancestry. The writer adopted a Japanese-sounding pen name.

Watcyn Wyn: Watkin Hezekiah Williams (1844–1905), Welsh poet, preacher, teacher. The poet's popular name means "Watkin the fair." It also reflects the name of the school for budding Nonconformist ministers that he set up in 1888, "Gwynfryn" ("white hill").

Waterloo: David Gribble (1932–), Br. crossword compiler. The setter's pseudonym refers to his first puzzle, which had across clues in English with entries in French, and down clues in French with entries in English. The Battle of Waterloo in 1815 involved a mix of French and English forces in the field.

Muddy **Waters:** McKinley Morganfield (1915–1983), U.S. black blues singer, guitarist. As a child the musician liked playing in the swampy puddles around the family home in Rolling Fork, Mississippi, so that his grandmother nicknamed him "Muddy." (The city is a few miles east of the Mississippi River, itself nicknamed Big Muddy or Old Muddy.) Friends added "Water" [*sic*] to this, and "the final transformation into 'Muddy Waters,' a showbiz-marquee name, came when he moved north, inevitably to Chicago" [Russell Davies, review of Robert Gordon, *Can't Be Satisfied: The Life and Times of Muddy Waters, Times Literary Supplement*, August 23, 2002].

Arena **Wati:** Dahlan bin Buyung (1925–), Malaysian writer.

Arthur **Watkyn:** Arthur Thomas Levi Watkins (1907–1965), Welsh-born Br. playwright.

Dilys **Watling:** Dilys Rhys-Jones (1946–), Eng. stage actress.

Claire **Watson:** Claire McLamore (1927–), U.S. opera singer.

Coy **Watson, Jr.:** James Caughey Watson, Jr. (1912–2009), U.S. child movie actor. "He was christened James Caughey Watson, Jr.—but his casting-director father had already tired of having his middle name pronounced 'Coffee,' and simplified it to 'Coy,' with some approximation to the Irish original" [Holmstrom, p. 56].

Robert (or Bobby) **Watson:** Robert Watson Knucher (1888–1965), U.S. movie actor.

Wylie **Watson:** John Wylie Robertson (1889–1966), Sc.-born Br. movie actor.

Majollica **Wattles** *see* Clinch **Calkins**

Jonathan **Watts:** John B. Leech (1933–), U.S. ballet dancer, teacher.

Theodore **Watts-Dunton:** Walter Theodore Watts (1832–1914), Eng. novelist. The writer added his mother's maiden name of Dunton to his original surname in 1897.

Mansie **Wauch:** David MacBeth Moir (1798–1851), Sc. physician, essayist. The writer used this name for the purported autobiography of a Dalkeith tailor, *The Life of Mansie Wauch* (1828). He also wrote as Gabriel Cowitch and Joseph Thomson, and contributed to *Blackwood's Magazine* as **Delta**.

Edward Bradwardine **Waverley:** John Wilson Croker (1780–1857), Ir.-born Br. politician, essayist. The writer adopted this name in two letters (published 1826) replying to Malachi **Malagrowther**, concocting the name itself from Edward Waverley and the Baron of Bradwardine, two characters in Scott's *Waverley*.

Ruby **Wax:** Ruby Wachs (1953–), U.S.–born comedienne, actress, interviewer, of Austr. Jewish parentage, working in U.K.

Franz **Waxman:** Franz Wachsmann (1906–1967), Ger.-born U.S. movie music composer.

Anderson **Wayne** *see* Brett **Halliday**

Carl **Wayne:** Colin David Tooley (1943–2004), Eng. pop-rock singer. The lead singer of The Move adopted his new name when taking over as vocalist for an earlier group in the mid–1960s.

Chuck **Wayne:** Charles Jagelka (1923–1997), U.S. jazz guitarist, of Cz. parentage.

David **Wayne:** (1) Wayne David McKeekan (1914–1995), U.S. stage, movie actor; (2) David Wayne Carnell (1958–2005), U.S. rock singer.

Dennis **Wayne:** Dennis Wayne Wendelken (1945–), U.S. ballet dancer.

Frances **Wayne:** Chiarina Francesca Bertocci (1919–1978), U.S. jazz singer.

John **Wayne:** Marion Robert (later Mitchell) Morrison (1907–1979), U.S. movie actor. The actor early adopted the name "Duke." This was the name of his Airedale, and the nickname used by firemen in a nearby fire station when young Morrison and dog went past. His famous screen name was prompted by Winfield Sheehan, new head of production at Fox studios, when considering Wayne for the lead role in the 1930 western *The Big Trail*. "'I don't like this name, Duke Morrison, it's no name for a leading man,' Sheehan said ... 'We got to have a good American name,' [head of production] Sol Wurtzel said. [Director Raoul] **Walsh** admired Mad Anthony Wayne, a general of the American Revolution. 'How about Anthony Wayne?' he asked. They mulled it over. 'It sounds too Italian,' Sheehan said. 'Then let's make it Tony Wayne,' Walsh said. 'Then it sounds

like a girl,' Wurtzel said. 'What's the matter with just plain John? John Wayne,' Sheehan said thoughtfully. 'John Wayne,' repeated Wurtzel. 'It's American.' 'You betcha,' Walsh said" [Maurice Zolotow, *John Wayne: Shooting Star*, 1974].

Wayne himself was at first not too keen on his new name, and he was initially confused with actors John Payne (1912–1989) and Wayne Morris (1914–1959). One one occasion John Wayne attended a party where John Payne was expected, and on another Payne flew down to Mexico to be guest of honor at a film industry soirée where Wayne was supposed to make the acceptance speech. He flew back with a silver statue with "John Wayne" engraved on it but did not give it to Wayne as he, Payne, had had to listen to all the speeches praising Wayne as "a fine actor and a great human being" [ibid.].

Johnny **Wayne:** John Louis Weingarten (1918–1990), Can. radio, TV comedian, teaming with Frank Shuster (1916–).

Kenny **Wayne:** Kenny Wayne Spruell (1944–), U.S. black blues musician.

Naunton **Wayne:** Henry Wayne Davies (1901–1970), Welsh stage, movie, radio, TV actor. The actor changed his name by deed poll in 1933.

Thomas **Wayne:** Thomas Wayne Perkins (1940–1971), U.S. pop musician.

Adam **Wazyk:** Adam Wasmann (1905–1982), Pol. writer.

Putnam **Weale:** Bertram Lenox Simpson (1877–1930), Eng. writer. Simpson's maternal grandfather, John Weale, married Sarah Hollis Putnam, granddaughter of the American Revolutionary commander Israel Putnam (1718–1790). Hence Simpson's pen name, which he used when writing about political conditions in the Far East, as in *Indiscreet Letters from Peking* (1905) and *Why China Sees Red* (1925).

Ogdred **Weary** *see* Eduard **Blutig**

Janus **Weathercock** *see* Herr Cornelius van **Vinkbooms**

Charley **Weaver:** Clifford Arquette (1905–1974), U.S. entertainer.

Doodles **Weaver:** Winstead Sheffield Weaver (1911–1983), U.S. movie comedian, uncle of Sigourney **Weaver**.

Sigourney **Weaver:** Susan Alexandra Weaver (1949–), U.S. movie actress. The actress adopted a new first name for distinctiveness when she was 14, taking it from Sigourney Howard, Jordan Baker's aunt in F. Scott Fitzgerald's novel *The Great Gatsby* (1925). "The reason, she explains, was that as a tall teenager, the diminutive versions of her name felt inappropriate. 'Sue sounds like a little person's name. So I thought, here's an interesting name. It's long, and I'm long. It's unusual. So I'll just use that for a while until I can figure out what name to use. It was like a temporary thing. But of course, now everyone calls me Sig or Siggy, which is just like Sue or Susie'" [*The Times*, July 17, 2008].

Ward **Weaver** *see* Geoffrey **Coffin**

Christopher **Webb** *see* Patrick **O'Connor**

Clifton **Webb**: Webb Parmalee Hollenbeck (?1891–1966), U.S. dancer, singer, stage, movie actor. The actor was already billed by his stage name when he appeared in the the musical comedy *The Purple Road* (1913).

Jane **Webb**: Mary Young (?–1740), Eng. pickpocket ("Jenny Diver").

Lizbeth **Webb**: [Lady] Elizabeth Campbell, née Wills-Webber (1926–), Br. stage actress, singer.

Neil **Webb** *see* Fenton **Brockley**

Charles **Webber** *see* J.P. **McCall**

Veit **Weber**: Georg Philip Ludwig Leonhard Wächter (1762–1837), Ger. writer, historian.

Katie **Webster**: Kathryn Jewel Thorne (1939–1999), U.S. black blues pianist.

Garrod **Weedy** *see* Eduard **Blutig**

Weegee: Arthur H. Fellig (1899–1968), Austr.-born U.S. news photographer. In 1910 nine-year-old Fellig and his family emigrated from Austria to New York, where officers at Ellis Island changed his original name of Usher to Arthur. In 1923 he went to Acme News Pictures (the forerunner of United Press International) and gained fame for being the first to arrive on crime and accident scenes. As a result he came to be nicknamed "Ouija" for his apparent psychic ability to sniff out a good story, after the Ouija board game that supposedly spells out messages from the spirit world. He altered this to "Weegee."

Ted **Weems**: Wilfred Theodore Weymes (1901–1963), U.S. bandleader.

Weepin' Willie: Willie Robinson (1926–), U.S. black blues singer.

Auguste **Weimar**: Auguste Goetze (1840–1908), Ger. singer, composer.

Eva **Wein** *see* Jukka **Larsson**

Hannah **Weinstein**: Hannah Dorner (1911–1984), U.S. moviemaker.

Awfly **Weirdly**: Charles Robinson (1870–1937), Eng. illustrator, cartoonist. The artist used this name for *Christmas Dreams* (1896), a book of Chrismas cards, menus, and the like, in which he parodied the mannered style of Aubrey Beardsley (1872–1898). The name is thus itself a parody of that artist's name.

Barbara **Weisberger**: Barbara Linshen (*c*.1926–), U.S. ballet dancer.

Amalie **Weiss**: Amalie Schneeweiss (1839–1898), Austr. concert singer.

Peter **Welbeck**: Harry Alan Towers (1920–2009), Br. movie, TV, radio producer, scriptwriter.

Towers often adopted this name when adapting novels for the screen.

Horace **Welby**: John Timbs (1801–1875), Eng. journalist, writer.

Mickey **Welch**: Michael Francis Walsh (1859–1941), U.S. baseball player, of Ir. parentage. Welch adopted the form of his name by which people knew him, although he never legally changed it.

Raquel **Welch**: Jo Raquel Tejada (1940–), U.S. movie actress, of Bolivian–U.S. parentage. The actress adopted and retained the name of her first husband, James W. Welch (married 1959, divorced 1964).

Ronald **Welch**: Ronald Oliver Felton (1909–1982), Welsh-born Br. children's writer. The writer took his pen name from the Welch Regiment, with which he served in World War II.

John **Welcome**: John Needham Brennan (1914–), Br. crime writer.

Tuesday **Weld**: Susan Ker Weld (1943–), U.S. movie actress. The actress has explained her first name in different ways at different times, but it seems likely that "Tuesday" is a corruption of "Susan," presumably originating as a childish pronunciation of this name in its pet form Susie.

Ben **Welden**: Benjamin Weinblatt (1901–1997), U.S. movie actor.

Ljuba **Welitsch**: Ljuba Velickova (1913–1996), Bulg.-born Austr. opera singer. The soprano's adopted name is a germanicized form of the original.

Ehm **Welk**: Thomas Trimm (1884–1966), Ger. novelist, playwright.

Colin **Welland**: Colin Williams (1934–), Eng. actor, playwright.

Sam **Weller** *see* Peter **Palette**

Samuel **Weller**: Thomas Onwhyn (?–1866), Eng. cartoonist, illustrator. The artist used this name, that of Sam Weller in Dickens' *Pickwick Papers* (1836), for his "illegitimate" illustrations to Dickens' works, including 21 of the 32 plates to *Pickwick Papers* itself.

Sylvia **Welling**: Sylvia Galloway (1901–), Br. stage actress, singer. The actress adopted her mother's maiden name as her stage name.

Brandi **Wells**: Marguerite J. Pinder Bannister (1955–2003), U.S. R&B singer.

Jacqueline **Wells** *see* Julie **Bishop**

Junior **Wells**: Amos Wells Blakemore, Jr. (1934–1998), U.S. black blues harmonica player, singer.

Kitty **Wells**: Muriel Ellen Deason (1919–), U.S. country singer. The singer's name was chosen for her by her husband, Johnny Wright, who when courting her recalled the song popularized by the Carter Family, "I'm A-Goin' to Marry Kitty Wells."

Sandra **Wells:** Ruth Lilian Clarke (1906–1992), Br. variety artist. As a flamenco dancer the performer took the name Janita, while as a ventriloquist and subsequently pantomime cat she was Joy Wilby.

Tobias **Wells:** Deloris Stanton Forbes (1923–), U.S. mystery writer.

Christopher **Welsh:** Christian Davies (1667–1739), Ir. adventuress. Christian left home at age 17 to live with an aunt, who died four years later, leaving her the owner of an inn. She married an employee, Richard Welsh, but four years later he disappeared. She went in search of him, disguising herself as Christopher Welsh and enlisting in the army. She re-enlisted in 1701 and eventually found her husband after a separation of 13 years. Her true sex and identity were discovered when she was wounded during the Battle of Ramillies (1706).

Freddie **Welsh:** Frederick Hall Thomas (1886–1927), Welsh lightweight boxer ("The Welsh Wizard"). The champion was clearly keen to stress his nationality.

Papa **Wemba:** Shungu Wembiado (1952–), Zairean musician.

Señor **Wences:** Wenceslao Moreno (1896–1999), Sp.-born U.S. ventriloquist.

Wendy and Lisa: Wendy Melvoin (*c.*1964–), U.S. pop musician + Lisa Coleman (*c.*1960–), U.S. pop musician.

John **Wengraf:** Johann Wenngraft (1897–1974), Austr. movie actor, working in U.S.

Jane **Wenham:** Jane Figgins (1930–), Eng. movie actress.

Bessie **Wentworth:** Elizabeth Andrews (1874–1901), Eng. music-hall singer.

Patricia **Wentworth:** Dora Amy Turnbull, earlier Dillon, née Elles (1878–1961), Eng. crime novelist. Another pen name used by the writer was Barbara Starke.

E. **Werner:** Elisabeth Bürstenbinder (1838–1918), Ger. novelist.

Hans **Werner:** [Baron] Ange-Henri Blaze de Bury (1813–1888), Fr. writer. Blaze de Bury used this name for his articles in the *Revue des Deux Mondes*. His Scottish wife, Baroness Marie Pauline Rose Blaze de Bury, née Stuart (*c.*1813–1894), assumed the male pen name Arthur Dudley for her writing.

Oskar **Werner:** Oskar Josef Bschließmayer (1922–1984), Austr. stage, movie actor.

Ruth **Werner:** Ursula Ruth Kuczynski (1907–2000), Ger. spy, working for Soviet Union.

Lina **Wertmüller:** Arcangela Felice Assunta Wertmüller von Elgg Espanol von Brauchich (1926–), It. movie writer, director, of Swiss descent. Wertmüller used the name George Brown for two musical comedies, *Rita la zanzara* ("Rita the Mosquito")

(1966) and *Non stuzzicate la zanzara* ("Don't Tease the Mosquito") (1967).

Mary **Wesley:** Mary Aline Mynors Siepmann, earlier Swinfen, née Farmar (1912–2002), Eng. novelist. The writer was descended from the eldest brother of Arthur Wellesley, 1st Duke of Wellington (1769–1852), whose original name was Wesley. She is said to have adopted her new name because her married name "sounded uncommercial" [Miller 1997, p.301].

Adam **West:** William West Anderson (1928–), U.S. movie actor.

Billy **West:** Roy B. Weissberg (1893–1975), Russ.-born U.S. movie comedian.

Dorothy **West** *see* Carolyn **Keene**

Dottie **West:** Dorothy Marie Marsh (1932–1991), U.S. country singer, songwriter.

Elizabeth **West:** Margaret Wilson (1882–1973), U.S. novelist, poet, missionary, working in England. The writer used this name for some early poetry. She was "An Elderly Spinster" for stories published between 1917 and 1921, when she was still single but hardly elderly. She settled in England in 1923 on marrying an Englishman she had met as a missionary in India.

Keith **West:** Keith Hopkins (1943–), Eng. pop singer.

Leslie **West:** Leslie Weinstein (1945–), U.S. rock singer, guitarist.

Nathanael **West:** Nathan Weinstein (1903–1940), U.S. novelist, screenwriter, of Lithuanian Jewish parentage. As a young man, West often wrote his name "Nathaniel von Wallenstein Weinstein," with Wallenstein being his mother's maiden name. In 1926 he changed his name to Nathanael West, using the Greek rather than the Hebraic spelling of his first name and claiming ironically that in his surname he was (literally) following newspaper editor Horace Greeley's advice to Americans to "go West."

Nigel **West:** Rupert Allason (1951–), Br. spy writer, politician. The writer chose the name before becoming a Member of Parliament in 1987. He commented: "I wanted an identity that was bland, neutral and classless. The only book I wrote under my own name did not sell at all."

Owen **West** *see* Leigh **Nichols**

[Dame] Rebecca **West:** Cicily Isabel Andrews, née Fairfield (1892–1983), Ir.-born Eng. novelist, critic. The writer took her pen name from her namesake in Ibsen's play *Rosmersholm* (1886), where "*Rebecca West*" stood for "*R*ights of *W*omen," her own cause. As she explained: "I chose the pen name of Rebecca West because when I was 18, I was contributing articles to a paper which, because of its radicalism, my mother would not let me read and something had to be done about it. I chose *that* name because at an even earlier age I played that part in Ibsen's 'Rosmerholme' [*sic*]. I have never consciously adopted it but I have never succeeded in being called anything else" [Marble, p.219].

"The brilliant and rebellious Ibsen heroine is chosen to replace Cicily Fairfield (a name that in itself seems almost too good an example of English gentility). To choose that name was to claim the ideas and the radical posture of Ibsen, and particularly his ideas about women, as one's own public identity. The choice suggests an exceptional woman, willing her life to be an example of woman's situation" [Samuel Hynes, "In Communion With Reality," *Times Literary Supplement*, December 21, 1973].

West adopted the name Corinne Andrews for *War Nurse: The True Story of a Woman who Lived, Loved and Suffered on the Western Front* (1930). She also wrote as Rachel East, and as Isabel Lancashire for a teenage novel, *The Sentinel*, that lay long undiscovered and that was first published only in 2003.

Rick **West** *see* Tommy **Vance**

Ricky **West**: Richard Allen Westfield (1943–1985), U.S. soul musician.

Westbam: Maximilian Lenz (1965–), Ger. DJ. The musician took his name from his home district of Westphalia and his DJ hero, Afrika **Bambaataa**.

Helen **Westcott**: Myrthas Helen Hickman (1928–1998), U.S. movie actress.

Netta **Westcott**: Netta Lupton (*c*.1893–1953), Br. stage actress.

Barry **Western** *see* Arthur **Gwynne**

Helen **Westley**: Henrietta Remsen Meserole Manney (1875–1942), U.S. stage, movie actress.

Mary **Westmacott**: [Dame] Agatha Christie (1890–1976), Br. detective novelist. The author used this name for six romantic novels, distinctive from her detective genre, the first being *Giant's Bread* (1930), the last *The Burden* (1956). "One may wonder why the celebrated mystery writer felt it necessary to create a separate and hidden identity as the writer of romances. One obvious reason is related to the form itself— the romance is a different medium, with an appeal to a special kind of audience" [Dick Riley and Pam McAllister, eds., *The New Bedside, Bathtub & Armchair Companion to Agatha Christie*, 1986].

Allen **Weston** *see* André **Norton**

Arthur **Weston**: Peggy Webling (*c*.1870–?), Eng. journalist, fiction writer. The writer used this name for her Canadian tales, written following a spell as an actress in Canada. She used her real name for her English fiction.

Jack **Weston**: Jack Weinstein (1925–1996), U.S. movie actor.

Paul **Weston**: Paul Wetstein (1912–1996), U.S. popular composer, pianist.

Karen **Westwood**: Karen Smith (1964–), Sc. movie, TV actress.

Agnes Ethelwyn **Wetherald**: Bel Thistlethwaite (1857–1940), Can. poet, journalist.

Elizabeth **Wetherell**: Susan Bogert Warner (1819–1885), U.S. sentimental novelist, sister of Amy **Lothrop**. The writer's adopted name, that of her great-grandmother, was perhaps intended to suggest "weather all," since her novels were mostly about young girls coping bravely with the rigors of a predominantly male world. Her first book, *The Wide Wide World* (1850), was a bestseller of its time.

Joan **Wetmore**: Joan Dixon, née Deery (1911–), Austral. stage actress.

Wolfgang **Weyrauch**: Joseph Scherer (1907–1980), Ger. writer.

Madame Groeda **Weyrd** *see* Eduard **Blutig**

Michael **Whalen**: Joseph Kenneth Shovlin (1899–1974), U.S. movie actor.

Joanne **Whalley-Kilmer**: Joanne Whalley (1964–), Eng. stage, TV, movie actress, working in U.S. The actress was billed under this name during her marriage (1988–96) to U.S. actor Val Kilmer (1959–).

Anthony **Wharton**: Alister McAllister (1877–1943), Ir. playwright, novelist. The writer also used the name Lynn Brock.

Grace **Wharton**: Katharine Thomson, née Byerley (1797–1862), Br. author. The Byerley family were descended from Colonel Anthony Byerley (?–1667), the father of Robert Byerley (1660–1714) who married Mary Wharton, great-niece of Philip, 4th Lord Wharton. Hence Mrs. Thomson's pen name, also adopted by her son, Philip **Wharton**.

Michael **Wharton**: Michael Nathan (1913–2006), Br. columnist, of Ger. Jewish descent. The writer contributed a satirical column under the Peter Simple name in the *Daily Telegraph*. He also wrote novels under the name Simon Crabtree.

Philip **Wharton**: John Cockburn Thomson (1834–1860), Br. author, son of Grace **Wharton**. Thomson used this name for two books written jointly with his mother: *Queens of Society* and *Wits and Beaux of Society* (both 1860).

William **Wharton**: Albert William du Aime (1925–2008), U.S. painter, novelist, working in France. Many of the writer's novels deal with aspects of identity and self-definition, and his pseudonym, although known to be such, long concealed his true identity.

Peetie **Wheatstraw**: William Bunch (1902–1941), U.S. black blues musician. The musician's assumed name has resonances in black folklore and literature.

Jimmy **Wheeler**: Ernest Remnant (1910–1973), Eng. music-hall comedian.

Albert **Whelan:** Albert Waxman (1875–1962), Austral. music-hall entertainer.

Arthur **Whetsol:** Arthur Parker Schiefe (1905–1940), U.S. jazz trumpeter.

Whigfield: Sannie Charlotte Carlson (1970–), Dan. pop singer. The singer adopted the surname of her singing teacher as her sole stage name.

Whim-Wham: Allen Curnow (1911–2001), N.Z. poet, critic. The writer used this name for a satirical poetry column in the *Christchurch Press* and *New Zealand Herald*. A whim-wham is a fanciful trifle.

Benedick **Whipem:** Richard Harris (1833–1906), Eng. writer.

Nancy **Whiskey:** Anne Alexandra Young Wilson (1935–2003), Sc. singer, guitarist. The singer took her new name from a Scottish folksong, "The Calton Weaver," which has a chorus "O Whiskey, whiskey, Nancy Whiskey / Whiskey, whiskey Nancy-O."

William and Robert **Whistlecraft:** John Hookham Frere (1769–1846), Eng. diplomat, author. The writer used this double pen name for his humorous poem *The Monks and the Giants* (1817–18). This itself sprang from two cantos entitled *Prospectus and Specimen of an Intended National Work, by William and Robert Whistlecraft of Stowmarket in Suffolk, Harness and Collar Makers. Intended to comprise the most interesting particulars relating to King Arthur and his Round Table* (1817). The work inspired Byron, no less, who wrote to a friend that year: "Mr. Whistlecraft has no greater admirer than myself. I have written a story in eighty-nine stanzas in imitation of him, called 'Beppo.'" Whistlecraft is a genuine Suffolk surname.

Fatima **Whitbread:** Fatima Vedad (1961–), Br. athlete, of Cypriot parentage. The javelin thrower was abandoned by her parents as a baby and raised in a children's home. Her talent was recognized by the former British international javelin thrower Margaret Whitbread, who later adopted her.

Antonia **White:** Eirene Adeline Botting (1899–1980), Eng. novelist, translator, journalist. The writer adopted her mother's maiden name, as she never considered her original name "sufficiently imposing to suit her personality" [*Times Literary Supplement*, August 26–September 1, 1988].

Babington **White** *see* Lady Caroline **Lascelles**

Barry **White:** Barry Eugene Carter (1944–2003), U.S. black R&B singer.

Chris **White:** Chris Costner Sizemore (1927–), U.S. "split personality." In 1978 an unusual autobiography was published. It was entitled *Eve*, and the author was Chris Costner Sizemore (with Elen Sain Pittillo). In it, the writer describes how she developed a multiple personality, telling the story of one woman who effectively became 12 different people, all existing within the body of a single human being. Naturally, the personalities assumed different names. The three main women were Chris White, a "sad, dowdy woman," Chris Costner, a "flamboyant party-goer," and Jane Doe, a "well-bred, refined Southern lady." (Of these, the first is Sizemore's dominant alter ego, the second her real self, with her maiden name, and the third, Jane Doe, the average woman, the female equivalent of John Doe.) Costner's case history had earlier been described by two psychiatrists, Corbett H. Thigpen and Hervey M. Cleckley. Their account was a bestseller, and was turned into a movie, *The Three Faces of Eve* (1957), in which all three women were played by Joanne Woodward.

Chrissie **White:** Ada Constance White (1895–1989), Eng. movie actress. The actress is said to have been rechristened by British producer-director Cecil Hepworth, who also renamed her husband, Henry **Edwards**. "He thought that a new arrival bore a strong resemblance to a musical comedy actress named Chrissie Bell, so Ada Constance White became Chrissie White" [Matthew Sweet, *Shepperton Babylon*, 2005].

Edmund **White:** James Blythe Patton (*fl.* 1902), Eng. writer.

George **White:** George Weitz (1890–1968), U.S. dancer, movie actor, director, producer.

Gladys **White** *see* Rosa **Henderson**

Jesse **White:** Jesse Weidenfeld (1918–1997), U.S. movie comedian.

Joseph Blanco **White:** José María Blanco y Crespo (1775–1841), Sp.-born Eng. poet, journalist, churchman. The writer fled to England as a Roman Catholic priest in 1810. There he took Anglican orders and anglicized his surname while retaining the Spanish original. He referred to this arrangement in another pseudonym, Don Leucadio Doblado, where "Don" indicates his Spanish origin, "Leucadio" (via Greek *leukos*) means "white," and Spanish "Doblado" means "doubled."

Matthew **White:** William Prynne (1600–1669), Eng. Puritan pamphleteer.

Pearl **White:** Victoria Evans White (1889–1938), U.S. movie actress.

Richard **White:** Richard Gwyn (?–1584), Welsh Roman Catholic martyr. The English surname, an equivalent of the Welsh, arose as a nickname given Gwyn by fellow students at Cambridge University.

Roma **White:** Blanche Winder, née Oram (1866–1930), Eng. novelist, children's writer. The writer translated her first name to form her new surname, then recast her maiden name to give her first name.

Thelma **White:** Thelma Wolpa (1910–2005), U.S. movie actress.

Vanna **White**: Vanna Marie Rosich (1957–), U.S. actress. The actress's adopted surname is that of her stepfather, Herbert Stackley White, Jr. (Her parents split up before she was a year old, and she was raised by her grandparents. Vanna was her grandmother's goddaughter, with a second "n" added to the original by her mother. Marie was her mother's middle name.)

Emerson **Whithorne**: Emerson Wittern (1884–1958), U.S. pianist, composer.

Alec **Whitney** *see* James **Fraser**

Harry **Whitney**: Patrick Kennedy (1801–1873), Ir. author. The writer used this name for *Legends of Mount Leinster* (1855).

Peter **Whitney**: Peter King Engle (1916–1972), U.S. movie actor.

Violet **Whyte** *see* John Strange **Winter**

Stuart Mary **Wick** *see* Minnie Maddern **Fiske**

Mary **Wickes**: Mary Isabelle Wickenhauser (1910–1995), U.S. movie comedienne.

Anna **Wickham**: Edith Alice Mary Hepburn, née Harper (1884–1947), Eng. poet. The writer grew up in Australia, and in her tenth year made a vow to her father that she would be a poet. She later took her pen name from Wickham Terrace, the Brisbane street where the vow was made. She adopted the male name John Oland for her first volume of verse, *Songs of John Oland* (1911), keeping her real name for her brief career as an opera singer.

Roger **Widdrington**: Thomas Preston (1563–1640), Eng. Benedictine monk.

Ernst **Wiechert**: Ernst Barany Bjell (1887–1950), Ger. writer.

Martina **Wied**: Alexandrine Martina Augusta Weisl, née Schnabl (1882–1957), Austr. writer.

Gerhard **Wieland**: Berta Jacobson-Lask (1878–1967), Ger. socialist writer.

Kate Douglas **Wiggin**: Kate Douglas Wiggin, née Smith (1856–1923), U.S. educator, novelist. Some sources give the writer's real name as her pen name. It was that of her first husband, Samuel Bradley Wiggin, whom she married in 1881. Following his death in 1889 she kept his name for her writing, even after her second marriage in 1895 to George Christopher Riggs.

Johnny **Wiggs**: John Wigginton Hyman (1899–1977), U.S. jazz musician, bandleader. Hyman took his new name as a high-school music teacher. "He adopted this new surname, Wiggs, so as not to offend the parish (county) school board, which disapproved of his playing 'indecent' music, that is, jazz, while still teaching children" [Barry Kernfeld in Garraty and Carnes, vol. 23, p. 356].

Mary **Wigman**: Marie Wiegmann (1886–1973), Ger. ballet dancer, choreographer.

Helene **Wildbrunn**: Helene Wehrenpfennig (1882–1972), Austr. opera singer.

Wildchild: Roger McKenzie (1971–1995), Br. pop musician.

Kim **Wilde**: Kim Smith (1960–), Eng. pop singer, songwriter, daughter of Marty **Wilde**. The singer originally found her father's fame a burden: "When I was at art college I changed my name [back] to Kim Smith because I wanted to escape. For a whole year no one knew who I was, and I found that sense of anonymity very exciting. But when I had my first hit ['Kids in America' (1981), coproduced by her father], I realised that I'd been fighting something I couldn't change and I chose to embrace being Marty's daughter completely" [*The Times*, December 4, 1995].

Marty **Wilde**: Reginald Leonard Smith (1936–), Eng. pop singer. The singer tells how he came by his new name: "I was 17 when I became Marty Wilde and I've always said that's when I really came alive. Previously I'd been Reg Smith, but Reg Smith was never me ... Larry Parnes, my manager at the time, did the name change. It was done on the toss of a coin. He tossed the coin and up came Wilde which I hated, and he tossed another coin and that decided Marty which I didn't mind but wasn't mad about. I think I wanted to be Marty Patterson after the World Heavyweight Champion, Floyd Patterson ... I might have been Reg Wilde. I still say it's important to have a name that looks fantastic in print. The Boomtown Rats — star name. Siouxsie and the Banshees — star name. Cliff **Richard** is a star-quality name ... Reg Smith isn't a star-quality name" [*TV Times Magazine*, November 28–December 4, 1981]. (For Siouxsie and the Banshees, *see* Siouxsie **Sioux**.)

Patricia **Wilde**: Patricia White (1928–), Can.-born U.S. ballet dancer. The dancer modified her name to be distinguished from her sister, Nora White, who was also a dancer.

Herman **Wildenvey**: Herman Theodor Portaas (1886–1959), Norw. poet.

Cherry **Wilder**: Cherry Barbara Grimm, née Lockett (1930–2002), N.Z.–born writer, working in Australia, Germany. The writer adopted this name for her SF and fantasy fiction.

Gene **Wilder**: Jerome Silberman (1933–), U.S. movie comedian, of Russ. Jewish parentage.

John **Wilder**: Keith Magaurn (1936–), U.S. movie, TV producer.

Will **Wildwood**: Frederick Eugene Pond (1856–1925), U.S. sporting writer. Pond was editor of *The Sportsman's Review* and *Wildwood's Review*, among other sporting publications, and was author of *The Life and Adventures of Ned Buntline* (1919) (*see* Ned **Buntline**), "written by the erratic though not erotic

W.W. Wood" [letter to Eugene V. Connett, quoted in Callahan, p.185].

Wiley: Richard Kylea Cowie (1979–), Br. black genre vocalist ("The Godfather of Grime"). A meaningful aka that reflects the artist's middle name.

Gerald Wiley: Ronnie Barker (1929–2005), Br. TV comedian. Barker devised this name for some of his material for the popular TV comedy show *The Two Ronnies* (1971–87), in which he teamed with Ronnie Corbett (1930–). He relates: "I picked this name Gerald Wiley, because most people who have a pseudonym have a glamorous name like Rock Armstrong or something wonderful. So I picked a really ugly name that no one would dream of choosing as their pseudonym" [*Sunday Times*, October 9, 2005].

Thomas Wilfred: Richard Edgar Løvstrøm (1889–1968), Dan. artist, working in U.S.

Kate Wilhelm: Kate Gertrude Wilhelm Knight, née Meredith (1928–), U.S. SF, fantasy, crime writer.

Friedrich Wilhelmi: Friedrich Wilhelm von Panwitz (1788–1852), Ger. actor.

Wilhelmina: Gertrude Wilhelmina Behmenburg Cooper (1939–1980), Du.-born U.S. fashion model, of Du.-Ger. parentage. The model began her career as Winnie Hart: "Gertrude just wouldn't do, Behmenburg was too long and awkward to remember, and her middle name, Wilhelmina, was too foreign." Subsequently, however, an agency decided that Wilhelmina was the right name after all. The model's friends knew her as Willie [Michael Gross, *Model*, 1995].

Guillaume-Louis Wilhem: Guillaume-Louis Bocquillon (1781–1842), Fr. music scholar, teacher.

Jean Willes: Jean Donahue (1922–1989), U.S. movie actress. The actress changed her billing to her married name in 1947.

Will.i.am: William James Adams, Jr. (1975–), U.S. black rapper. Not every first name lends itself to such a nice punning presentation.

Warren William: Warren William Krech (1895–1948), U.S. movie actor, of Ger. parentage.

Williams: Sidney William Martin (1919–1993), Austral. cartoonist, working in U.K. The artist used this name when drawing for *Sporting Life*.

Andy Williams: Howard Andrew (1930–), U.S. popular singer.

Barney Williams: Bernard O'Flaherty (1824–1876), U.S. actor, of Ir. parentage.

Bessie Williams *see* **Rosa Henderson**

Bill Williams: Herman William Katt (1916–1992), U.S. movie actor.

Bransby Williams: Bransby William Pharez (1870–1961), Br. music-hall actor.

Cara Williams: Bernice Kamiat (1925–), U.S. TV, radio, movie comedienne.

Charles Williams: Isaac Cozerbreit (1893–1978), Eng. movie music composer.

Daniel Williams: Daniel Grossman (1942–), U.S. ballet dancer, teacher.

Deniece Williams: Deniece Chandler (1951–), U.S. black gospel, soul singer.

F. Harald Williams: [Rev.] Frederick William Orde Ward (1843–1922), Eng. writer.

Frances Williams: Frances Jellinek (1903–1959), U.S. stage actress, singer.

Gene Williams *see* **Horatio Nicholls**

Guy Williams: Guy Catalano (1924–1989), U.S. movie, TV actor.

Joe Williams: Joseph Goreed (1918–1999), U.S. black blues singer. The singer was raised by his mother and grandmother and given the surname Williams when he was 16.

John Williams: George Mackay (1884–1913), Br. murderer, of Sc. parentage.

Mary Lou Williams: Mary Elfrieda Scruggs (1910–1981), U.S. black jazz pianist. Williams kept the name of her first husband, John Williams (married 1926, divorced 1942), for the rest of her music career.

Otis Williams: Otis Miles (1949–), U.S. black Motown singer.

Robin Williams: Robin Williams (1951–), U.S. movie comedian. "One unconfirmed source suggests that his real name may be Ralph Lipschitz" [Quinlan 2000, p.544].

Rozz Williams: Roger Alan Painter (1963–1998), U.S. rock musician.

Rubberlegs Williams: Henry Williamson (1907–1962), U.S. jazz singer, dancer.

Tennessee Williams: Thomas Lanier Williams (1911–1983), U.S. playwright, poet. Williams was born in Mississippi, not Tennessee. His Tennessee-born father, however, Cornelius Coffin Williams, was directly descended from John Williams, first senator of Tennessee, from the brother Valentine of Tennessee's first governor John Sevier (whose own name was itself changed from Xavier by the Huguenots), and from Thomas Lanier Williams I, first chancellor of the Western Territory, as Tennessee was called before it became a state. The dramatist took the new name to launch himself in New York, later explaining, "I've just indulged myself in the Southern weakness for climbing a family tree" [Tennessee Williams, *Memoirs*, 1976].

Treat Williams: Richard Williams (1952–), U.S. movie actor.

William Peere Williams-Freeman: William Peere Williams (1742–1832), Eng. admiral. Williams added Freeman to his name in 1821 on succeeding to the estate of Fawley Court, Buckinghamshire, the home of John Cook Freeman, whose sister, Mary, married his maternal grandfather, Robert Clavering, bishop of Peterborough.

Harry **Williamson:** Wulf Dietrich Christian Schmidt (1911–1992), Ger.-born Br. spy. When secured by MI5 as a double agent, Williamson was given the code name Tate, for his resemblance to the Scottish comedian Harry **Tate**.

Sonny Boy **Williamson:** Aleck Ford "Rice" Miller (1899–1965), U.S. black blues harmonica player, singer. In order to gain greater popularity, Miller claimed to be "the original Sonny Boy Williamson" following the murder of blues harmonica player John Lee "Sonny Boy" Williamson (1914–1948). (The latter was known late in his career as "Sonny Boy Williamson I" to distinguish him from Miller, who was thus referred to as "Sonny Boy Williamson II." Some artists condemned Miller for trying to cash in on the genuine Williamson's name, though most agreed he was the better musician.) Miller began by performing as "Little Boy Blue," and later played under various names, including Willie Williamson, Willie Williams, and Willie Miller. Miller was born Aleck Ford, the illegitimate child of Millie Ford, but took to using the name of his stepfather, Jim Miller.

Alexis **Willibald:** Wilhelm Häring (1798–1871), Ger. novelist.

Boxcar **Willie** *see* **Boxcar Willie**

James **Willington:** Oliver Goldsmith (1728–1784), Ir. cleric, poet, novelist, dramatist. The author of *The Vicar of Wakefield* (1766) and *She Stoops to Conquer* (1773) used this name for *The Memoirs of a Protestant, Condemned to the Galleys of France, for his Religion* (1758), a translation from the French.

Bruce **Willis:** Walter Willison (1955–), U.S. movie actor.

Brember **Wills:** Brember Le Couteur (*c.*1883–1948), Br. stage, movie actor.

Meredith **Willson:** Robert Meredith Reiniger (1902–1984), U.S. songwriter, lyricist, composer.

Willy: Henri Gauthier-Villars (1859–1931), Fr. novelist, music critic, husband of **Colette**. The name derives from the second part of the writer's surname.

August **Wilson:** Frederick August Kittel (1945–2005), U.S. black playwright, poet. The writer adopted his mother's maiden name as his new surname.

Charles **Wilson:** John Oldmixon (1673–1742), Eng. historian, pamphleteer. The writer used this name for *Memoirs of the Life, Writings, and Amours of W. Congreve, Esq. ... by Charles Wilson, Esq.* (1730).

Henry **Wilson:** Jeremiah Jones Colbath (1812–1875), U.S. statesman, abolitionist. The Republican senator and U.S. vice president was indentured as a farm laborer at the age of 10. When freed at the age

of 21 he legally changed his name, and thereafter determined to devote his life to the antislavery cause.

J. Arbuthnot **Wilson** *see* Olive Pratt **Rayner**

Jennifer **Wilson:** Jennifer Wenda Lohr (1935–), Eng. stage, movie, TV actress.

Marie **Wilson:** Katherine Elizabeth White (1916–1972), U.S. movie actress.

Meri **Wilson:** Mary Edna Edgemon (1949–2002), U.S. pop singer.

Rita **Wilson:** Margarita Ibrahimoff (1958–), U.S. movie actress.

Romer **Wilson:** Florence Roma Muir O'Brien, née Wilson (1891–1930), Br. novelist.

Whip **Wilson:** Charles Meyer (1915–1964), U.S. cowboy movie actor.

Robb **Wilton:** Robert Wilton Smith (1881–1957), Eng. music-hall, radio comedian.

John **Winch** *see* Marjorie **Bowen**

Paul **Winchell:** Paul Wilchin (1922–2005), U.S. ventriloquist.

Walter **Winchell:** Walter Winschel (1897–1972), U.S. journalist, of Russ. Jewish parentage. The "s" in the family name was dropped when Winchell was a boy. He himself later added a second "l" because he liked the way it looked in print.

Morris **Winchevsky:** Lippe Ben-Zion Novachovitch (1856–1932), Lithuanian-born U.S. Yiddish poet. The writer gained his pen name in 1884 when he produced the first of a series of socialist propaganda booklets in Yiddish containing a dialogue between two workers named Marris and Hyman. The former was held to be the author of the pamphlets, which were signed "Morris Winchesvky." Novachovitch later identified with this nom de plume, although he legally changed his name to Leopold Benedict (from his original first name and middle name).

Harry **Wincott:** Arthur J. Walden (1867–1947), Eng. popular songwriter.

Barbara **Windsor:** Barbara Anne Deeks (1937–), Eng. movie, TV actress. The actress has explained how she took her new name. "Now that I was in a long-running show, I started giving serious thought to something Aida [Foster] had mentioned to me when I joined the school. Deeks, she had said, is not a good stage name; there will come a time when you will have to change it. That time, I felt, was now [1953]. I was fed up with being asked at auditions how I spelled my name, and I wanted something simple. Mummy and I put our heads together to try to come up with a stage name that was not only uncomplicated and had a good ring to it, but meant something to us, too. We kicked around loads of ideas, but in the end it came down to two: Ellis, my mother's maiden name, and Windsor, Auntie Dolly's married name. We eventually plumped for Windsor, the name Auntie Dolly shared with the new Queen, as it seemed particularly apt in Coronation year. Daddy ... would not accept that the change was for professional reasons and accused me of turning my back on a name that had been good enough for his family for generations — and, of course, when he fought for the likes of me in the British Army. He never forgave me for changing it" [Barbara Windsor, *All of Me*, 2000].

Claire **Windsor:** Clara Viola Cronk (1898–1972), U.S. movie actress.

Marie **Windsor:** Emily Marie Bertelson (1919–2000), U.S. movie actress.

Arthur M. **Winfield:** Edward L. Stratemeyer (1863–1930), U.S. writer, of Ger. parentage. Stratemeyer used this name for various stories for boys, including the "Bound to Win" and "Old Glory" series and that with the Rover Boys. *Life* magazine carried a letter from Stratemeyer explaining its origin: "One evening when writing, with my mother sitting near sewing, I remarked that I wanted an unusual name — that I wasn't going to use my own name on the manuscript. She thought a moment and suggested Winfield. 'For then,' she said, 'you may win in that field.' I thought that good. She then supplied the first name saying, 'You are going to be an author, so why not make it Arthur?'" [Atkinson, p.viii]. Stratemeyer added the "M" himself on the grounds that as this letter stood for "thousand," it might help to sell thousands of books.

Oprah **Winfrey:** Orpah Gail Winfrey (1954–), U.S. black TV talk-show host. Winfrey's family wanted to name their child Orpah, after the biblical daughter-in-law of Naomi (Ruth 1:4). The name was spelled correctly on her birth certificate but it was commonly mispronounced, so that the spelling soon followed the pronunciation.

Mary **Wings:** Mary Geller (1949–), U.S. thriller writer. Geller adopted her new name in 1972.

Winna **Winifred:** Amelia Nielsen (1914–), Dan.-born movie actress, working in France, U.K., U.S.

Anona **Winn:** Anona Lamport (1907–1994), Austral. variety artist, radio panelist.

George **Winslow:** George Wentzlaff (1946–), U.S. child movie actor.

Bradley T. **Winter** *see* Chris **Bryant**

John Strange **Winter:** Henrietta Eliza Vaughan Stannard, née Palmer (1856–1911), Eng. novelist. The author began her literary career under the name Violet Whyte, with her first writing appearing in the *Family Herald* in 1874. In 1881 her *Cavalry Life* was published, as a collection of regimental sketches, and two years later her *Regimental Legends*. The publisher refused to issue these books under a female name, so

she selected John Strange Winter for them, this being the name of a character in the earlier work. Her readers assumed that the books were by a cavalry officer, and a jailer is said to have asked Oscar Wilde, when he was in prison, what he thought of him as a writer. "A charming person," replied Oscar, "but a lady, you know, not a man. Not a great stylist, perhaps, but a good, simple storyteller." "Thank you, Sir, I did not know he was a lady, Sir." The writer kept the name for the rest of her career.

Bernie **Winters:** Bernard Weinstein (1932–1991), Br. TV comedian, of Russ. Jewish parentage, teaming with Mike Winters (Michael Weinstein) (1930–), his brother.

D.D. **Winters** *see* **Vanity**

Linda **Winters:** Dorothy Comingore (1913–1971), U.S. movie actress. The actress was billed under this name for her early movies in the late 1930s, having first appeared in 1928 as Kay Winters.

Shelley **Winters:** Shirley Schrift (1920–2006), U.S. stage, movie actress. One day, as a teenager, the future actress was in the office of the Group Theatre in New York to read for an understudy in a play by Irwin **Shaw**. "The secretary asked me my name. 'Shirley Schrift' ... 'Shirley Schrift isn't a very good name for an actress,' she told me. 'Let's see if we can figure out another one.... What's your mother's maiden name?' 'Winter,' I told her. She wrote it down. 'Do you like "Shirley"?' she asked. 'God, no, there's millions of Shirleys all over Brooklyn, all named after Shirley Temple.' 'Well, wouldn't you like a name that sounds like Shirley in case someone calls you?' I thought for a moment. 'Shelley is my favorite poet, but that's a last name, isn't it?' She wrote it on the card in front of 'Winter.' She looked at it. 'Not anymore it isn't. Shelley Winter. That's your name.' She handed me the card, and I looked at it. It felt like me. Half poetic and half cold with fright. 'Okay,' I told her. 'Send it in.' Years later, in their infinite wisdom, Universal Studios added an *S* to 'Winter' and made me plural" [Shelley Winters, *Shelley: Also Known as Shirley*, 1981].

Eduard von **Winterstein:** Eduard von Wangenheim (1871–1961), Ger. movie actor.

John **Winton:** John Pratt (1931–2001), Eng. novelist. The writer adopted his pen name in 1959 for his first book, *We Joined the Navy*, a satire on naval training. A pseudonym was clearly desirable for the author, who was then formally Lieutenant-Commander Pratt, a Royal Navy engineer officer.

Frances **Winwar:** Francesca Vinciguerra Grebanier (1900–1985), Sicilian-born U.S. novelist. The writer, who came to the U.S. when she was seven, translated her Italian maiden name (Vinciguerra) to provide her pen name, using it for her romantic novels, popular biographies, and books on famous poets.

Estelle **Winwood:** Estelle Goodwin (1882–1984), Eng. stage, movie actress, working in U.S. A neat transposition of the two halves of the actress's surname, a slight adjustment, and a stage name emerges.

Nicky **Wire:** Nicolas Jones (1969–), Br. pop musician.

Ann **Wirt** *see* Carolyn **Keene**

Mildred **Wirt** *see* Carolyn **Keene**

[Sir] Norman **Wisdom:** Norman Wisden (1920–), Eng. stage, movie, radio comedian.

Ernie **Wise:** Ernest Wiseman (1925–1999), Eng. TV comedian, teaming with Eric **Morecambe.**

Herbert **Wise:** Herbert Weisz (1924–), Austr.-born stage actor, TV director, working in U.K.

Isaac Mayer **Wise:** Isaac Mayer Weis (1819–1900), Bohemian-born U.S. rabbi.

Stephen Samuel **Wise:** Stephen Samuel Weiss (1874–1949), U.S. social activist, Zionist leader.

Vic **Wise:** David Victor Bloom (1900–1976), Eng. music-hall comedian.

Googie **Withers:** Georgette Lizette Withers (1917–), Eng. stage, movie, TV actress. Withers has stuck by her story that the nickname "Googie" was given her by her Indian nurse during her childhood in Karachi, and that it derives from a Punjabi word meaning "dove," or else a Bengali word meaning "clown." But could it not have originated as a pet form of her first name or as a child's version of it?

Reese **Witherspoon:** Laura Jeanne Reese Witherspoon (1976–), U.S. movie actress.

Witkacy: Stanislaw Ignacy Witkiewicz (1885–1939), Pol. playwright. A pen name formed from the first part of the writer's surname and second part of his middle name.

Jah **Wobble:** John Wardle (c.1958–), Br. rock musician. The musician adopted the mangled form of his real name as voiced by Sid **Vicious.** "Wobble certainly has been prolific since the punk era, when Vicious christened him by drunkenly slurring his real name, John Wardle" [*The Times*, March 24, 2007].

George **Woden:** George Wilson Slaney (1884–1978), Eng. novelist, working in Scotland.

Dreary **Wodge** *see* Eduard **Blutig**

F. **Wohanka** *see* Theodore Moses **Tobani**

Friedrich **Wolf:** Johannes Laicus (1817–1855), Ger. scholar, writer, publisher.

Peter **Wolf:** Peter Blankfield (1946–), U.S. rock singer.

Aaron **Wolfe:** Dean Ray Koontz (1945–), U.S. fantasy, SF writer. Koontz used this name for his novel *Invasion* (1975), which many thought was by Stephen King (who wrote as Richard **Bachman**), since its foreword explained that Aaron Wolfe was a pen name. "Set in Maine, *Invasion* certainly sounded

like a King story: a rural family attacked by aliens. But its author was Dean R. Koontz, not King" [George Beahm, *The Stephen King Story*, 1992].

Humbert **Wolfe:** Umberto Wolff (1886–1940), Br. poet, of Ger.-It. Jewish parentage. The writer and civil servant adopted the new version of his name in 1918.

Ermanno **Wolf-Ferrari:** Ermanno Wolf (1876–1948), It. operatic composer, of Ger.-It. parentage. The musician added his Italian mother's maiden name to his own around 1895.

[Sir] Donald **Wolfit:** Donald Woolfitt (1902–1968), Br. stage, movie actor, theater manager.

Wolfman Jack: Robert Weston Smith (1938–1995), U.S. radio DJ, TV host. Smith changed his name several times (Daddy Jules and Roger Gordon were two of his alter egos) before finally becoming Wolfman Jack in 1963. The name alludes to the "banshee howl" that was his trademark, and that usually went out around midnight amid prurient patter.

Harry Austryn **Wolfson:** Zvi Glembotsky (1887–1974), Pol.-born U.S. scholar of Hebrew literature, historian of philosophy. Glembotsky's uncle in Cincinnati, Beryl Velvel, had taken the name "Wolfson" (from Yiddish *vel*, "wolf") so the rest of the family became Wolfsons when they arrived in the United States. Harry immigrated in 1903.

Wols: Alfred Otto Wolfgang Schulze (1913–1951), Ger. painter, working in France. The artist came by his name in his original career as a photographer. In 1937, a telegram inviting him to be official photographer at the International Exposition in Paris, France, misprinted his surname as "Wols." The curious corruption amused him, and he there and then adopted the name for his work.

Stevie **Wonder:** Steveland Judkins (or Steveland Morris Hardaway) (1950–), U.S. black soul, pop singer. The musician acquired the name Morris after his mother's remarriage. He began his career at the early age of 12, when he was dubbed "Little Stevie Wonder." Two years later, at six feet tall, he decided to keep the name, but understandably dropped "Little" [Constantine Elsner, *Stevie Wonder*, 1977].

Wayne **Wonder:** Von Wayne Charles (c.1972–), Jamaican reggae musician.

Anna May **Wong:** Wong Liu-Tsong (1905–1961), U.S. movie actress, of Chin. parentage.

Arthur **Wontner:** Arthur Smith (1875–1960), Eng. stage actor, theater manager. The actor adopted his mother's maiden name as his stage name.

John **Woo:** Yusen Wu (1946–), Chin.-born Hong Kong movie director.

Jonny **Woo:** Jonathan Wooster (1976–), Br. transvestite cabaret artist.

Brenton **Wood:** Alfred Jesse Smith (1941–), U.S.

pop singer. The singer adopted his professional name from Brenton Wood, his home district in Los Angeles.

Del **Wood:** Adelaide Hazelwood (1920–), U.S. jazz pianist, singer.

Kerry **Wood:** Edgar Allardyce Wood (1907–), U.S.-born Can. journalist, children's writer.

Natalie **Wood:** Natalia Nikolaevna Zakharenko (1938–1981), U.S. movie actress. Natalie Wood was the daughter of Russian-French immigrants who later changed their surname to Gurdin. Her own new surname came from movie director Sam Wood, a friend of her first director, Irving Pichel. She first bore it at the age of seven in *Tomorrow is Forever* (1946).

Wee Georgie **Wood:** George Bramlett (1895–1979), Eng. music-hall comedian. The entertainer was only 4 ft 9 in tall and specialized in "little boy" characters.

Woodbine Willie: [Rev.] Geoffrey Anketell Studdert Kennedy (1883–1929), Eng. priest. Studdert Kennedy was an army chaplain in World War I and came to be nicknamed for his distribution of "Woodbine" cigarettes to troops in the trenches. He used the name for a book of verse, *Rough Rhymes of a Padre* (1918).

Henry **Woodhouse:** Mario Terenzio Enrico Casalegno (1884–1970), It.-born U.S. aeronautics expert. The engineer nicely translated his Italian name into English, just as Frances **Winwar** would do later. He formally adopted his new name in 1917 and became a U.S. citizen that same year.

Holly **Woodlawn:** Harold Ajzenberg (1947–), Puerto Rican-born U.S. transvestite movie actor. The actor's first name was a nickname given by friends, after Holly Golightly, the heroine of Truman Capote's 1958 novella *Breakfast at Tiffany's*. (Woodlawn used a shrill whistle to hail cabs, like his fictional namesake.) He took his last name from the Los Angeles cemetery, posing as the sole heiress to the Woodlawn estate.

Daniel **Woodroffe:** Mary Woods, née Woodroffe (*fl.*1900s), Eng. novelist. The author used this name for *Tangled Trinities* (1901), *The Evil Eye* (1902), *The Beauty Shop* (1906), and similar novels.

Donald **Woods:** Ralph L. Zink (1904–1998), U.S. movie actor.

Sara **Woods:** Sara Bowen-Judd, née Hutton. (1922–1985), Eng.-born Can. detective novelist. The writer adopted her mother's maiden name as her pen name.

Victoria **Woolf** *see* Charlotte **Lamb**

[Sir] Peregrine **Worsthorne:** Peregrine Gerard Koch de Gooreynd (1923–), Br. newspaper editor. "He changed his name for snobbish reasons because his mother lived in a village called Worsthorne when

she was married to the governor of the Bank of England" [Nigel Dempster in *Punch*, October 26–November 1, 1996].

The genealogical background is actually as follows. Worsthorne's father, Colonel Alexander Koch de Gooreynd, assumed the name of Worsthorne by deed poll in 1921, on the birth of Peregrine's elder brother, Sir Simon Towneley, but reverted to Koch de Gooreynd in 1937. The Worsthorne name derives from Sir Simon's estate near Burnley, Lancashire. Sir Simon himself discontinued the name by deed poll and in 1955 assumed by royal license the arms of Towneley through his descent from the eldest daughter and coheiress of Colonel Charles Towneley of Towneley.

Harry **Worth:** Harold Burlon Illingsworth (1917–1989), Eng. radio, TV comedian.

Helen **Worth:** Cathryn Helen Wigglesworth (1951–), Eng. TV actress.

Irene **Worth:** Harriet Elizabeth Abrams (1915–2002), U.S. stage, TV actress.

Nicholas **Worth:** Walter Hines Page (1855–1918), U.S. journalist, diplomat.

George **Wostenholm:** George Wolstenholme (1800–1876), Eng. cutlery manufacturer. The manufacturer slightly shortened the family name to facilitate its inclusion on knife blades.

Michael **Wotruba** *see* Joe **D'Amato**

Paul **Wranitzky:** Pavel Vranický (1756–1808), Moravian composer, violinist.

John **Wray:** John Griffith Malloy (1888–1940), U.S. movie director, actor.

Reginald **Wray:** William Benjamin Home-Gall (1861–1936), Eng. writer of stories for boys. The writer used this name for such manly fiction as *Tales of the Empire, Told Round the Camp-Fire* (1901) and *Where Honour Sits* (1906). He also wrote as Captain Conyers, Reginald Drew, and Edwin Home.

Christopher **Wren:** Christopher Johnston (1947–1999), Eng. actor, choreographer. The actor presumably adopted a name that comemorated the famous architect Sir Christopher Wren (1632–1723).

Belinda **Wright:** Brenda Wright (1929–2007), Eng. ballet dancer. A small verbal uplift can work wonders for a name in this way, and "Belinda" has the added beauty of French *belle* and the neatness of Italian *linda*, highly desirable assets for a ballerina (which word is itself also suggested by the name). The dancer was advised to adopt her new forename by Marie **Rambert**.

Dale **Wright:** Harlan Dale Reiffe (1938–), U.S. pop singer.

Francesca **Wright** *see* Denise **Robins**

Frank Lloyd **Wright:** Frank Lincoln Wright (1867–1959), U.S. architect, writer. Wright's father,

William Cary Wright, was a 41-year-old widower when he married Anna Lloyd Jones, a 24-year-old schoolteacher. In 1886, Frank Lincoln Wright changed his middle name to Lloyd to mark his strong identification with his mother's Welsh family.

Kenneth **Wright** *see* Lester **del Rey**

Rowland **Wright:** Carolyn Wells (?1869–1942), U.S. author. The prolific author of humorous literature and mystery novels used this male name for *The Disappearance of Kimball Webb* (1920).

Ignaz **Wrobel:** Kurt Tucholsky (1890–1935), Ger. satirical essayist, poet, songwriter. Tucholsky also wrote under the pseudonyms Theobald Tiger, Peter Panter, and Kaspar Hauser.

József **Wronski:** József Hoene (1776–1853), Pol. mathematician, philosopher.

Stefan **Wronski:** Ferdinand Hardekopf (1876–1954), Ger. writer, translator.

Dogear **Wryde** *see* Eduard **Blutig**

Vivian **Wu:** Wu Jun Mei (1966–), Chin.-born U.S. movie actress.

Wu Ming *see* Luther **Blissett**

Gideon **Wurdz:** Charles Wayland Towne (1875–?), U.S. journalist, humorist. This punning name was used by the writer for *The Foolish Dictionary*. For *Foolish Etiquette* he was (cornily) O.B. Hayve.

Ernest **Wurmbach-Stuppach:** Stefania Vrabely-Wurmbach-Stuppachova (1849–?), Cz. pianist, composer. The musician used this name for her compositions, not her concert performances.

[Sir] Jeffry **Wyatville:** Jeffry Wyatt (1766–1840), Eng. architect. The second part of the architect's name, French for "town," was added by George IV in 1824 when the king laid the foundation stone of Wyatt's new design for the royal apartments at Windsor Castle. "The king not only augmented Wyatt's name, but added to his coat-of-arms a view of 'George IV's gateway' and the word 'Windsor' as a motto" [*Dictionary of National Biography*].

Margaret **Wycherly:** Margaret De Wolfe (1881–1956), Br. stage actress.

John **Wyckham:** John Suckling (1926–), Eng. theatrical consultant, lighting designer.

Katherine **Wylde:** Helen Hester Colvill (1854–?), Eng. novelist.

Gretchen **Wyler:** Gretchen Wienecke (1932–), U.S. stage, movie actress.

William **Wyler:** Wilhelm Weiller (1902–1981), Fr.-born U.S. movie director.

Jonathan **Wylie:** Mark Smith (1952–), Br. writer of fantasy fiction + Julia Smith (1955–), Br. writer of fantasy fiction, his wife.

Julian **Wylie:** Julian Samuelson (1878–1934), Br. theater manager.

Kythe **Wylwynne:** [Miss] M.E.F. Hyland

(*fl.*1900s), Eng. novelist, journalist, writer on domestic subjects. The author used this punning name for such titles as *The Dream Woman* (1901), *The Log of the Scarlet House* (1905), and *Man Immortal* (1908).

Bill **Wyman:** William George Perks (1936–), Eng. rock musician. The Rolling Stones bassist took his new surname from Lee Whyman, a friend made in the 1950s during national service in the Royal Air Force. He adopted the name by deed poll in 1964.

Jane **Wyman:** Sarah Jane Mayfield (1914–2007), U.S. movie actress. The future actress's parents split up when she was only four years old and she was adopted by friends named Fulks, whose surname she took. She began her show career in 1933 as a radio singer named Jane Durrell. Her stage name coincided with her contract for Warner Bros. in 1936, although she was originally billed as Sarah Jane Fulks.

Patrick **Wymark:** Patrick Cheeseman (1926–1970), Eng. TV, movie actor. The actor's son, Tristram Wymark (1961–), also an actor, has preserved his father's name and explains its origin: "I'm the only one to keep Dad's original name, Cheeseman. I keep it for its nostalgia. On my passport I have a nice little a.k.a.... The name Wymark was borrowed initially from my mum's grandfather" [*Sunday Times Magazine*, August 14, 1988].

[Sir] Charles **Wyndham:** Charles Culverwell (1837–1919), Eng. actor, theater manager. The actor took his new surname in 1860, the year of his first marriage. He legalized the name change in 1886.

Esther **Wyndham:** Mary Links, née Lutyens (1908–1999), Eng. novelist. The daughter of the noted architect Sir Edwin Lutyens (1869–1944) used this name for her magazine serials.

John **Wyndham:** John Wyndham Parkes Lucas Beynon Harris (1903–1969), Eng. SF, short-story writer. The writer used all of his six names as pen names at one stage or another, the best-known apart from John Wyndham being John Beynon, Lucas Parkes, and Johnson Harris, this last denoting "John, son of Harris."

Yehudi **Wyner:** Yehudi Weiner (1929–), Can.-born U.S. Jewish composer, pianist, conductor.

Tammy **Wynette:** Virginia Wynette Byrd, née Pugh (1942–1998), U.S. country singer. The singer was asked by Billy Sherrill, her agent in Nashville, what name she wanted to use professionally. She explained: "It had never occurred to me to change my name but he said, 'I didn't think you'd want to use Byrd since you're getting a divorce, and Pugh doesn't fit you.' I said, 'Well, what does fit me?' He thought for a minute, then said, 'With that blond ponytail you look like a Tammy to me,' I said, 'Well, can I at least keep Wynette?' He said, 'Sure. How about

Tammy Wynette?' I left his office saying the name over and over under my breath. It sounded strange, but it sounded right too. 'Tammy Wynette.' I said it out loud. It didn't sound like me, but it sounded like someone I wanted to be. I sensed it was more than just a new name. I felt I was also about to start a new life" [Tammy Wynette, *Stand by Your Man*, 1979]. Some sources specifically relate the actress's new first name to the 1957 movie *Tammy and the Bachelor*, while Wynette was the name of the nurse caring for her dying father when she was born.

Peter **Wyngarde:** Cyril Louis Goldbert (1928–), Br. stage, movie, TV actor, of Eng.-Fr. parentage.

Margaret **Wynman:** Ella Nora Hepworth Dixon (1857–1932), Eng. writer. Dixon used this meaningful name for *My Flirtations* (1892), a series of comic sketches supposedly written by a coquette.

Ed **Wynn:** Isaiah Edwin Leopold (1886–1966), U.S. stage, movie, radio, TV comedian. Leopold turned his middle name into a stage name in 1904 on teaming with Jack Lewis in a vaudeville act called *Win and Lose*. His son was the actor Keenan Wynn (1916–1986).

May **Wynn:** Donna Lee Hickey (1931–), U.S. movie actress.

Anthony **Wynne:** Robert McNair Wilson (1882–1963), Sc. surgeon, medical jounalist. Wilson wrote a number of non-medical books, reserving his pseudonym for some detective stories.

Charles Whitworth **Wynne:** [Sir] Charles William Cayzer (1869–1917), Eng. businessman, poet. Professionally the director of a steamship company, Cayzer used this name for such collections of poems as *Ad Astra* (1900) and *Songs of Summer* (1903).

Esmé **Wynne** *see* Peter **de Morny**

May **Wynne:** Mabel Winifred Knowles (1875–1949), Br. writer of popular fiction.

Pamela **Wynne:** Winifred Mary Scott, née Watson (*c.*1885–1959), Eng. novelist.

Philippe **Wynne:** Philip Walker (1938–1984), U.S. black soul singer.

Wynonna: Christina Ciminella (1964–), U.S. country singer.

Dana **Wynter:** Dagmar Spencer-Marcus (1927–), Br.-born S.A. movie, TV actress, working in U.S. The actress was billed as Dagmar Wynter in her earliest movies (from 1951).

Mark **Wynter:** Terence Lewis (1943–), Eng. pop singer.

Gail **Wynters:** Nancy Gail Shivel (1942–), U.S. jazz singer.

Diana **Wynyard:** Dorothy Isobel Cox (1906–1964), Br. stage, movie actress. The actress made her debut on the stage under her new name in 1925 and officially adopted it by deed poll in 1936.

John **Wyse:** John Wise (1904–), Eng. stage actor.

Théodore de **Wyzewa:** Teodor de Wyzewski (1862–1917), Pol.-born Fr. writer, music critic.

X: Eustace Budgell (1686–1737), Br. essayist. The writer can hardly have been the first to adopt this patent disguise. He used it for contributions to the *Spectator*.

Flying Officer **X:** Herbert Ernest Bates (1905–1974), Eng. novelist. The writer used this rather obvious pseudonym for short stories about the Royal Air Force (in which he was serving as an officer in World War II) collected as *The Greatest People in the World* (1942) and *How Sleep the Brave* (1943). He usually wrote under his real name (in the form H.E. Bates).

Malcolm **X:** Malcolm Little (1925–1965), U.S. black militant leader. The noted nationalist received the conventional Muslim "X" from Elijah **Muhammad** in 1952. "As a means of getting black people to find a new identity, he had them drop their surnames, which most of them had inherited from their slave masters, and replaced them with an 'X.' X meant an unknown quantity; it also meant ex-slave, ex–Christian, ex-smoker, and ex-alcoholic" [Lawrence H. Mamiya in Garraty and Carnes, vol. 6, p.53]. In 1964 Malcolm broke from the Nation of Islam, the Black Muslim group to which he belonged, and following his hajj (pilgrimage to Mecca) that year called himself El-Hajj Malik El-Shabazz.

Marvin **X:** Marvin Ellis Jackmon (1944–), U.S. black writer. Jackmon became a Black Muslim in the 1960s under the influence of Elijah **Muhammad** and adopted the name Marvin X. He has also written as El Muhajir, "the emigrant," properly a term for one who accompanied Muhammad, the founder of Islam, in his emigration from Mecca to Medina in AD 622.

Michael **X:** Michael de Freitas (1933–1975), Br. black power leader. The Trinidad-born activist was the son of a black mother and a Portuguese father. On his conversion to the Muslim religion, his name became Michael Abdul Malik and subsequently Michael X. His self-serving autobiography, *From Michael de Freitas to Michael X*, by Michael Abdul Malik, was published in 1968.

Xanrof: Léon-Alfred Fourneau (1867–1953), Fr. composer, songwriter, by profession a lawyer. The musician's name was created by translating French *fourneau* ("furnace") into Latin *fornax* and then reversing it. Fourneau officially adopted the name in 1896.

Xariffa: Mary Ashley Townsend, née Van Voorhis (1832–1901), U.S. poet, essayist, novelist. This is the writer's best-known pen name, which she also spelled Zariffa, a rare first name of Arabic origin meaning "amiable." Townsend also wrote as Crab Crossbones, Michael O'Quillo, and Henry Rip.

Xavier: Joseph Xavier Boniface Saintine (1798–1865), Fr. novelist, poet, dramatist.

X-et: Sven Erixson (1899–1970), Swe. painter, tapisser. The artist's name means "The X."

Ximenes: Derrick Somerset Macnutt (1902–1971), Eng. crossword compiler. Perhaps one of the most imposing and appropriate of all pseudonyms, in view of the significant capital letter. Its bearer, professionally a classics teacher, was responsible for the "Everyman" and (from 1939) much more demanding "Ximenes" puzzles in *The Observer*. The name itself is that of Francisco Jiménez de Cisneros (1436–1517), better known in English as Ximenes, the Spanish prelate who became Grand Inquisitor of Castile. Macnutt assumed the name in 1943 on succeeding to the compilership vacated by doyen cruciverbalist **Torquemada**. In the 1930s he contributed crosswords to *The Listener* as Tesremos, his middle name reversed.

X.L.: Julian Field (1849–1925), Br. novelist, writer. An initialism of obvious origin, unrelated to the writer's real name.

Xmas: Noel Jones (1943–), Sc. crossword compiler. The setter adopted a pseudonym on the lines of a cryptic clue, referring to his first name as an alternate name for Christmas, to the X formed by intersecting words in a crossword (and to the first half of that word), and to *mas* as Latin for "male."

Xul Solar: Oscar Agustín Alejandro Schulz Solari (1887–1963), Argentinian painter, of Ger.-It. parentage. The artist created his pseudonym from his original multilingual name.

Wilhelmus Xylander: Wilhelm Holtzmann (1532–1576), Ger. Hellenist. The scholar adopted a Greek equivalent of his German name, meaning "woodman" (Greek *xylon*, "wood" + *anēr, andros*, "man").

Xzibit: Alvin Nathaniel Joiner (1974–), U.S. black rapper, hip-hop musician. The name represents "exhibit."

Yaabetz (or Yabez): Jacob Israel Emden (1697–1776), Jewish Talmudic scholar. The name is an acronym of *Ja*cob *be*n *Ze*bi, the scholar's original name.

Yabby You: Vivian Jackson (1950–), Jamaican reggae musician. Jackson got his nickname from the drawn-out, chanting refrain "Be you, yabby yabby you" on his 1972 debut single, "Conquering Lion."

Yigael Yadin: Yigael Sukenik (1917–1984), Israeli archaeologist, military leader.

Genrikh Grigoryevich **Yagoda:** Heinrich Yehuda (1891–1938), Russ. Jewish police chief.

Yakov **Yakovlev:** Yakov Arkadyevich Epshteyn (Epstein) (1896–1938), Russ. Communist official.

Koji **Yakusho:** Koji Hashimoto (1956–), Jap. movie actor.

Stomu **Yamash'ta:** Tsutomu Yamashita (1947–), Jap. percussionist, composer.

Yambo: Enrico Novelli (1876–1943), It. children's writer, illustrator.

Mari **Yan:** María Flora Yáñez de Echeverria (1898–?), Chilean novelist, short-story writer.

Vasily **Yan:** Vasily Grigoryevich Yanchevetsky (1874–1954), Russ. writer. A radical pruning of an original surname.

Yana: Pamela Guard (1932–1989), Br. stage, movie actress, TV pop singer.

Tukhvat **Yanabi:** Tukhvatulla Kalimullovich Kalimullin (1894–1939), Russ. (Bashkir) poet. The poet adopted the name of his native village as his pen name.

Jean **Yanne:** Jean Gouyé (1933–2003), Fr. movie actor, director, writer.

Yanni: Yanni Chryssomallis (1954–), Gk.-born U.S. popular musician.

Yan Tsygan: Ivan Karpovich Kuksenko (1911–1958), Russ. wrestler, circus artist. The performer's name, meaning "Jan the Gypsy," hardly reflects his strongman feats, which included bending an iron girder across his shoulders and tying a necktie made of iron bars.

Yemelyan Mikhaylovich **Yaroslavsky:** Miney Izrailevich Gubelman (Hubelman) (1878–1943), Russ. historian, revolutionary, Communist. The activist abandoned his Jewish name in favor of a "Christian" one. Ironically, he was a militant atheist.

Kamil **Yashen:** Kamil Nugmanov (1909–), Uzbek writer. The writer's adopted name means "lightning."

Aleksandr **Yashin:** Aleksandr Yakovlevich Popov (1913–1968), Russ. writer. The writer's adopted name was based on Yasha, the familiar form of Yakov. This was the name of the father he had never known, for he was killed in World War I when his baby son was only one year old.

Dornford **Yates:** Cecil William Mercer (1885–1960), Eng. novelist, nephew of Anthony **Hope**. The author of a popular series of novels featuring "Berry" Pleydell and his family adopted the maiden names of his grandmothers to form his pen name. He first used it for a piece published in *Punch* in 1910.

Peyo **Yavorov:** Peyo Kracholov (1877–1914), Bulg. poet, playwright. The writer adopted a plant name meaning "sycamore."

Tom **Yawkey:** Thomas Yawkey Austin (1903–1976), U.S. baseball owner. Yawkey legally switched his middle and last names in 1918, when his mother died and he was adopted by his aunt and uncle.

Yana **Yazova:** Lyuba Gancheva (1912–1974), Bulg. poet, novelist.

Yazz: Yasmin Marie Evans (1960–), Jamaican-Eng. pop singer.

Boris **Yefimov:** Boris Fridland (Friedland) (1900–2008), Russ. satirical cartoonist. The cartoonist, famous for his lampoons of Hitler in World War II, was of Jewish parentage, as his family name implied. Hence his decision to adopt a less obviously Jewish name. He made the change in the 1920s.

Yefrem II: Grigory Shiovich Sidamonidze (1896–1972), Georgian catholicos. The head of the Georgian Orthodox Church received his name on taking monastic vows in 1922. The name itself corresponds to English Ephraim, said to mean "fruitful."

Dominik Ivanovich **Yefremov:** Mikhail Yefremovich Shteynman (Steinman) (1881–1925), Latvian-born Russ. Communist official.

D.J. **Yella:** Antoine Carraby (c.1967–), U.S. black "gangsta" rapper. "Yella" relates to the artist's vocal delivery.

Yellow Bird: John Rollin Ridge (1827–1867), U.S. writer, journalist. The writer was the son of a Cherokee and a white woman, and his pen name was the translation of his Cherokee name.

Yellowman: Winston Foster (1959–), Jamaican DJ, reggae musician. The artist's name refers to the fact that he is an albino.

C.J. **Yellowplush:** William Makepeace Thackeray (1811–1863), Eng. novelist. Thackeray used this name for *The Yellowplush Papers* (1837–8), a series of sketches in *Fraser's Magazine* purportedly written by a London West End footman named Charles James Yellowplush. The name itself was suggested by a domestic servant in the Thackeray household, "a *bona fide* manservant, an old gentleman named John Goldsworthy, formerly the Larkbeare footman, who wore faded knee-breeches in the family livery" [D.J. Taylor, *Thackeray*, 1999]. Plush was a fabric traditionally used for footmen's wear, and especially for their brightly-colored breeches. The same character appeared with a "gentrified" form of his name in *The Diary of C. Jeames de la Pluche, Esq.* (1846), and his popularity caused "Jeames" (an affected form of "James") to be used for a time as a generic name for a footman.

Donnie **Yen:** Yan Chi Tan (1966–), U.S.–born Hong Kong movie actor.

Sydney **Yendys:** Sydney Thompson Dobell (1824–1874), Eng. poet, critic. The writer was fortunate to have a first name that readily lent itself to reversal. He used it for a dramatic poem, *The Roman* (1850).

Michelle **Yeoh:** Yeo Chu-Kheng (1962–), Malaysian-born movie actress, working in Hong Kong.

Yeohlee: Yeohlee Teng (c.1955–), Malaysian fashion designer, working in U.S.

Yerukhan: Yervand Srmakeshkhanlyan: (1870–1915), Armenian writer. A practical shortening of a lengthy original name.

Yetim Emin: Magomed-Emin, son of Sevzikhan (1838–1884), Dagestani (Lezgian) poet. The writer replaced the first part of his personal name by a word meaning "hapless," "orphaned."

Irodion **Yevdoshvili:** Irodion Isakiyevich Khositashvili (1873–1916), Georgian poet. The poet based his new surname on his mother's first name, Yevdokiya (Eudocia). The Georgian suffix *-shvili* corresponds to English *-son*.

Madame **Yevonde:** Philonia Yevonde, née Cumbers (1893–1975), Eng. photographer. The society photographer is sometimes referred to as Edith Plummer, a name resulting from a researcher's error.

Paramahansa **Yogananda:** Mukunda Lal Ghosh (1893–1952), Ind. guru, working in U.S. The founder of the Self Realization Fellowship trained as a young man with Swami Sri Yukteswar Giri and was initiated by him into the Swami Order under the name Yogananda, meaning "bliss attained by yoga."

Yorick: Pietro Francesco Leopoldo Coccoluto Ferrigni (1836–1895), It. dramatic critic, writer. The writer probably adopted the name of Parson Yorick in Laurence Sterne's *Tristram Shandy* (1759–67) rather than the King of Denmark's jester recalled by Hamlet in Shakespeare's play.

Mr. **Yorick:** Laurence Sterne (1713–1768), Ir. writer. The author of *Tristram Shandy* used this name for sermons and other writings, as well as for his *Sentimental Journey* (1768), of which the full title is thus *A Sentimental Journey through France and Italy. By Mr. Yorick*. The character himself, as narrator, takes his name from the "lively, witty, sensible, and heedless parson" in the former work, who in turn believes he was probably descended from Yorick, the King of Denmark's jester recalled by Hamlet ("Alas, poor Yorick") as he moralizes on his skull in Shakespeare's play.

Alison **York** *see* Andrew **York**

Andrew **York:** Christopher Robin Nicole (1930–), Guyanese crime, mystery writer. The writer has used a range of male and female pseudonyms. The former include Daniel Adams, Leslie Arlen, Robin Cade, Peter Grange, and Mark Logan; the latter Caroline Gray, Christina Nicolson, and Alison York.

Michael **York:** Michael Hugh Johnson (1942–), Eng. movie actor.

Peter **York:** Peter Wallis (1946–), Eng. social commentator. The cocompiler (with Ann Barr) of the *Official Sloane Rangers Handbook* (1982), a guide to the lifestyle of fashionable young London women, adopted his stylish nom de plume for distinction from his main business as a management consultant.

Susannah **York**: Susannah Yolande Fletcher (1941–), Eng. movie actress. There are rival accounts to explain the name. York herself claims that it arose when she was learning about the Wars of the Roses at school and started calling herself Susannah York Fletcher, substituting "York" for her middle name. But the actress's sister has declared that she got her name by simply opening a phone book and sticking a pin in [ITV program, *This Is Your Life*, November 11, 1983]. The first version seems more plausible.

Ted **York** *see* Gordon **Ashe**

Curtis **Yorke**: [Mrs.] S. Richmond Lee, née Long (?–1930), Sc. novelist. The writer's *Who's Who* entry lists 47 titles under this name, from *That Little Girl* (1886) to *All about Judy* (1927).

Margaret **Yorke**: Margaret Beda Nicholson, née Larminie (1924–), Br. crime writer.

Stephen **Yorke**: Mary Jane Linskill (1840–1891), Eng. novelist. The writer was born in Yorkshire, and many of her novels are set in that county.

Bungo **Yoshida**: Teruo Takahasi (1934–2008), Jap. puppeteer. In 1951 the bunraku exponent entered the theater as pupil of the performer Tanagora Yoshida II. The following year, as was customary, he took his mentor's name, becoming Kotama Yoshida. In 1982 he succeeded to the prestigious stage name of Bungo Yoshida, becoming the the fifth actor so called.

Banana **Yoshimoto**: Mahoko Yoshimoto (1964–), Jap. novelist. The popular writer chose a new name with a view to a world market for her output: "It is sexless, it's funny and it can be used abroad" [*The Times Magazine*, November 9, 1996].

Bernard **Youens**: Bernard Popley (1914–1984), Br. stage, TV actor.

Alexander **Young**: Basil Alexander Youngs (1920–2000), Eng. opera singer.

Annie **Young**: Eliza Ann Dupuy (1814–1880), U.S. short-story writer, novelist. Dupy used this name for stories printed in the *New York Ledger.*

Augustus **Young**: James Hogan (1943–), Ir. poet.

Burt **Young**: Jerry de Louise (1940–), U.S. movie actor.

Chic **Young**: Murat Bernard Young (1901–1973), U.S. cartoonist. The creator of "Blondie" adopted his nickname, said to have been given him in high school for his native city of Chicago.

Clarence **Young**: Howard Roger Garis (1873–1962), U.S. writer. Garis took this name when signed up by the Stratemeyer Literary Syndicate to write stories for boys about the Motor Boys. He was also recruited to write the Motor Girls series, for which he was renamed as Margaret Penrose.

Cy **Young**: Denton True Young (1867–1955), U.S. baseball player. The player adopted his nick-

name, short for "Cyclone," referring to the power and speed of his fastballs. *See also* Cy **Twombly**.

George Ernest **Young**: George Ernest Opalisky, Jr. (1937–), U.S. jazz musician.

Gig **Young**: Byron Ellsworth Barr (1913–1978), U.S. stage, movie, TV actor. The actor took his name from the character that he played in *The Gay Sisters* (1942), his first important role. He had earlier used the name Bryant Fleming. The change was necessary because there was another actor using the name Byron Barr. Screen name and real name are each distinctively evocative: "'Gig Young' is hyperbolically cute and immediate — yet imagine a Gig Young at forty, or fifty? Won't a giggle creep in among those watching? On the other hand, 'Byron Barr' feels just as fabricated, but gentile [*sic*] romantic, raised to higher hopes than life ever comes close to making. 'Byron Barr' could be the awful, mocking real name for the aghast MC in [the 1969 movie] *They Shoot Horses, Don't They?*" [Thomson 2003, p.955].

Jesse Colin **Young**: Perry Miller (1944–), U.S. rock musician. The musician's new name honors three men: U.S. outlaw Jesse James (1847–1882), British racing driver Colin Chapman (1928–1982), and U.S. desperado Cole Younger (1844–1916).

Loretta **Young**: Gretchen Michaela Young (1913–2000), U.S. movie actress, sister of Sally **Blane**. When Colleen **Moore** discovered Young as a 14-year-old extra in *Her Wild Oat* (1928), she changed her first name to Loretta after "the most beautiful doll I ever had."

Marian **Young**: Martha Deane (1908–1973), U.S. radio host.

Ruth **Young**: Ruth Youkelson (1916–1986), U.S. labor leader, of Ukr. Jewish parentage. The activist changed her name when she first started working because "they weren't hiring Jews."

Stephen **Young**: Stephen Levy (1939–), Can. movie actor.

Irving **Younger**: Irving Yoskowitz (1932–1988), U.S. lawyer, writer.

Marguerite **Yourcenar**: Marguerite Antoinette Jeanne Marie Ghislaine Cleenewerck de Crayencour (1903–1987), Belg.-born Fr. historical novelist, working in U.S. The writer's father assisted in the creation of her (near) anagrammatical pen name, which she adopted as her legal name in 1947 on becoming a naturalized U.S. citizen.

Youth: Martin Glover (1960–), African popular music producer. A name with a limited lifespan.

Sakari **Yrjö-Koskinen**: Georg Zacharias Forsman (1830–1903), Finn. historian, politician. The politician adopted his native name when he was made a baron. (Sakari equates to Zacharias.)

Richard **Yrvid**: Richard d'Ivry (1829–1903), Fr.

composer. For some reason the musician decided to reverse his name for his compositions, which include a number of operas.

Ysgafell: Jane Williams (1806–1885), Eng.-born Welsh writer. The writer was a distant relative of the Puritan preacher Henry Williams (1624–1684) and took her pseudonym from the name of his farm, Ysgafell, near Newtown, Montgomeryshire (now Powys). The name itself is Welsh for "ledge."

P.B. Yuill: Gordon Maclean Williams (1934–), Sc. journalist, crime writer + Terry Venables (1943–), Br. footballer (later, football manager), crime writer. The joint name is said to be that of the uncle of both men.

Yuki: Gnyuki Torimaru (1937–), Jap. fashion designer.

David Yulee: David Levy (1810–1886), U.S. politician, businessman. America's first Jewish senator converted to Christianity after his marriage in 1846, taking a name used by his Moroccan forebears.

Yuriko: Yuriko Kikuchi (1920–), U.S. ballerina, teacher, choreographer, of Jap. parentage.

Blanche Yurka: Blanche Jurka (1887–1974), U.S. stage, movie actress. Presumably the actress modified the spelling of her surname to ensure its proper pronunciation, i.e. not as "Jerker."

Timi Yuro: Rosemarie Timotea Aurro (1940–2004), U.S. pop singer.

Yuss: Brian Ford (1937–2007), Welsh-born cartoonist, working in Zambia.

Yusuf *see* Cat **Stevens**

Aleksandr **Yuzhin:** Aleksandr Ivanovich Sumbatov (1857–1927), Russ. playwright, actor, theatrical director.

Yvaral: Jean-Pierre Vasarely (1934–), Fr. painter, son of Hung.-born Fr. artist Victor Vasarely (1908–1997). The artist's adopted name is formed from letters in his original surname.

Y.Y.: Robert Lynd (1879–1949), Ir. essayist. The witty writer used this name for his contributions to weekly magazines, first in the *Nation*, then in the *New Statesman*. Presumably he intended it to be read as "wise" (or more subtly "two eyes").

Rachel Z: Rachel C. Nicolazzo (1962–), U.S. jazz musician.

Stefan Zachary: Stefan Hedley Zacharkiewicz (1948–), Br. interior designer.

Zack: Gwendoline Keats (?–1910), Eng. novelist, short-story writer. The name is possibly a sort of reversal or anagram of the writer's surname.

Zadkiel: Richard James Morrison (1795–1874), Eng. naval officer, astrologer. The writer used the name for his astrological predictions, published in *Zadkiel's Almanack*. The name itself is that of the angel of the planet Jupiter in Rabbinical angelology.

Pia **Zadora:** Pia Schipani (1954–), U.S. movie actress, singer.

Zaeo: Adelaide Wieland (1863–1906), Eng. circus artist, tightrope walker.

Zagorka: Maria Juric (1873–1957), Croatian novelist, playwright.

Vladimir **Zagorsky:** Vladimir Mikhaylovich Lubotsky (1883–1919), Russ. revolutionary.

[Sir] Basil **Zaharoff:** Basileios Zacharias (1849–1936), Turk.-born Fr. armament dealer, financier, of Gk. parentage. Zaharoff's parents russified the family name during years spent in exile in Russia.

Tony **Zale:** Anthony Florian Zaleski (1913–1997), U.S. middleweight boxer, of Pol. descent.

Máté **Zalka:** Béla Frankl (1896–1937), Hung. writer, revolutionary.

Pyotr **Zamoysky:** Pyotr Ivanovich Zevalkin (1896–1958), Russ. writer.

Julius **Zancig:** Julius Jörgensen (1857–1929), Dan. spiritualist, teaming with Agnes Zancig, née Claussen (?–1916), spiritualist, his wife. The couple made their name with a supposed psychic act billed as "Two Minds With But a Single Thought." After the death of his wife, Julius teamed with Paul Vucci, a sleight-of-hand nightclub performer under the name Paul Rosini. When in 1917 Vucci was about to be conscripted, his place was taken by 13-year-old David Bamber, who later gained fame as **Fu Manchu**.

Renato **Zanelli:** Renato Morales (1892–1935), Chilean opera singer.

Mariya **Zankovetskaya:** Mariya Konstantinovna Adasovskaya (1860–1934), Ukr. stage actress, theater manager. The actress took her stage name from the village of her birth, Zanki.

Zan Muzzina di Valle Retirada: Bartolomeo Bocchini (1604–*c*.1650), It. poet, painter. Bocchini used this name for verse and plays written in Bolognese and Venetian dialect. As a painter of theatrical scenes, he was associated with the *commedia dell'arte*, or Renaissance comedy with stock characters, one being a comic servant called *Zanni*, the Venetian form of *Gianni* ("John"). Bocchini's assumed name suggests he may have played this part at some stage. Valle Retirada is literally "Hidden Valley."

Zanne: Auguste van Dekerkove (1838–1923), Fr. occultist. The practitioner assumed his new name in 1894, claiming it had been given him by "spiritual masters."

Gabriela **Zapolska:** Maria Gabriela Janowska, née Korwin-Piotrowska (1857–1921), Pol. novelist, playwright. The writer's assumed name emphasizes her nationality. An earlier name was Józef Maskoff.

Hy **Zaret:** Hyman Harry Zaritsky (1907–2007), U.S. lyricist.

Mikhas **Zaretsky:** Mikhail Yefimovich Kosenkov (1901–?), Belorussian writer.

Pantaley **Zarev:** Pantaley Yordanov Pantov (1911–), Bulg. literary critic.

Yefrosiniya **Zarnitskaya:** Yefrosiniya Filippovna Azguridi (1867–1936), Ukr. stage actress.

Nairi **Zaryan:** Ayastan Yegiazaryan (1900–1969), Armenian writer.

Kiane **Zawadi:** Bernard McKinney (1932–), U.S. jazz musician.

Zazel: Rosa Starr, née Richter (1862–1922), Eng. variety artist, gymnast ("The Human Cannon Ball"). The name perhaps evolved as an elaboration of "Rosa." The performer was trained by Guillermo Farini, adoptive father of El Nino **Farini**.

Zazie: Isabelle Marie-Anne de Truchis de Varenne (1964–), Fr. singer, songwriter. The luxuriously named singer adopted the pet form of her first name as her performing name.

Tom **Zé:** Antônio José Santana Martins (1936–), Brazilian pop musician. A name representing pet forms of the musician's first two names.

Virginia **Zeani:** Virginia Zehan (1928–), Rom.-born It. opera singer.

Yanis **Zébgos:** Yanis Talagánes (1899–1947), Gk. Communist, historian.

Franco **Zeffirelli:** Gianfranco Corsi (1923–), It. movie director, designer, operatic producer.

Zelda: Zelda Shneurson Mishkovsky (1914–1984), Ukr.-born Israeli poet.

Zélide: Isabelle de Charrière, née Isabella Agneta Elisabeth van Tuyll van Serooskerken (1740–1805), Du.-born Swiss novelist, autobiographer. The writer gave herself the name in an early self-portrait, apparently basing it on her birthplace, Zuilen, near Utrecht. *See also* Abbé **de la Tour**.

F. **Zell:** Camillo Wälzel (1829–1895), Ger. librettist.

Morning Glory **Zell:** Diana Moore (1948–), U.S. mystic, witchcraft historian. The practitioner of pagan shamanism took her name from the U.S. pagan and visionary Oberon Zell (1942–), originally Timothy Zell, whom she married in 1974. At the age of 19, when studying the Greek goddess Diana (Artemis), Moore had changed her name legally from Diana to Morning Glory, since devotion to the goddess demanded celibacy, and Moore wanted to marry and have children.

Timothy Zell was nicknamed "Otter" as a teenager for his swimming prowess. Later, further name changes would be made, the first following the solar eclipse of 1979. "Zell decided to change his name from Tim. He had been dissatisfied with it since leaving St. Louis [in 1976], for everywhere he went, he seemed to find a prominent person named Tim, and

it made him feel awkward. He tried to forge several new names without success. In March of that year [1979], he and Morning Glory sat by the banks of the river that flows through Coeden Brith [in California] and discussed Zell's identity crisis. Morning Glory suggested his nickname, Otter. Zell rejected it, saying he wanted a name with more 'flash' that would be taken seriously by urban folk ... Morning Glory then suggested asking the Mother [Goddess] for a sign, which Zell did. At that moment, an otter popped up out of the water ... 'I hear and obey' said Zell. He also changed his last name to G'Zell, as a contraction of 'Glory' and 'Zell,' a style borrowed from Anne McCaffrey's 'Dragonrider' novels. For a time, the Zells were known as Otter G'Zell and Morning G'Zell, then they reverted to the original Zell" [Guiley, p.389]. In 1994 Zell changed his first name to Oberon, legendary guardian of the underworld, "a consequence of his performance of the role of Hades ... in the Eleusinia that year; as well as personal experiences in which he understood that he had to come to terms with his own inner underworld, the Shadow side. The new name was taken in a river baptism" [ibid.]. In 1996 the Zells and others who had joined them took the family name Ravenheart.

Zellini: Arthur Wilkinson (1887–1963), Br. variety artist.

Remigio **Zena:** Gaspare Invrea (1850–1917), It. novelist, poet.

Paul **Zenon:** Paul Collins (*c.*1950–), Br. magician. The magician was given his name by the rock band Hawkwind, with whom he made guest appearances at age 18. "Paul Collins, his real name, sounded too mundane. Their original suggestion, Xenon, ended up being mispronounced by everyone. Zenon caused fewer problems" [*The Times*, July 16, 2002].

Hermann **Zenta:** Augusta Mary Anne Holmès (1847–1903), Fr. pianist, composer, of Ir. parentage. "Although her Irish parents were against her taking up music, she played the piano and sang as a child prodigy and began to compose under the name of Hermann Zenta" [Blom, p.248]. The composer became a French citizen in 1871, when she added the accent to her original Irish name of Holmes.

Earl **Zero:** Earl Anthony Jackson (1952–), Jamaican reggae musician.

Zeta: James Anthony Froude (1818–1894), Eng. historian, biographer. The writer used this name, that of the sixth letter of the Greek alphabet (perhaps representing his surname, which begins with the sixth letter of the Roman alphabet), for an autobiographical novel, *Shadows of the Clouds* (1847).

Catherine **Zeta-Jones:** Catherine Jones (1969–), Welsh movie actress. The actress added her grandmother's first name to her (common) Welsh surname for distinction from another Catherine Jones, an existing member of the actors' trade union Equity.

Eugen Zetternam: Jos Josef Diricksens (1826–1855), Belg. writer.

Jakob Zeugheer: Jakob Zeugheer Herrmann (1803–1865), Swiss-born violinist, conductor, working in U.K.

Alexandre Zevaès: Gustave Alexandre Bourson (1873–1953), Fr. politician, lawyer, historian. The writer seems to have based his new surname on letters in his first two names (with "x" as "z").

Praskovya Zhemchugova: Praskovya Ivanovna Kovalyova (1768–1803), Russ. actress, opera singer. A name from Russian *zhemchug*, "pearl," is clearly better than one from Ukrainian *koval'*, "blacksmith."

Iosif Zhinovich: Iosif Iosifovich Zhidovich (1907–1974), Belorussian conductor, composer. The musician altered one letter of his name to avoid the suggestion of Russian *zhid*, an offensive word for a Jew (akin to English *Yid*). Zhinovich was himself Jewish.

Vladimir Zhirinovsky: Vladimir Volfovich Eydelshteyn (Edelstein) (1946–), Russ. nationalist leader. The populist politician changed his surname in 1964 to conceal his Jewish origins.

Zico: Artur Antunes Coimbra (1953–), Brazilian footballer.

Pavle Zidar: Zdravko Slamnik (1932–), Slovakian writer.

Kamen Zidarov: Todor Sibev Manov (1902–), Bulg. writer.

Anne Ziegler: Irene Frances Eastwood (1910–2003), Eng. popular singer, teaming with Webster Booth (1902–1984), whom she married in 1938.

Józef Bartlomiej Zimorowic: Józef Bartlomiej Ozimek (1597–1677), Pol. writer, historian.

Lo Zingarello: Giuseppe Zimbalo (*c*.1620–1710), It. architect. The nickname means "the little gypsy."

Grigory Zinoviev: Grigory Yevseyevich Radomyslsky (1883–1936), Russ. revolutionary, of Jewish parentage. The Comintern chief's original Jewish name was Ovsel Gershon Aronov.

Perlone Zipoli: Lorenzo Lippi (1606–1665), It. painter, poet. The writer used this anagrammatical name for his mock-heroic poem *Il Malmantile racquistato* ("Malmantile Regained") (1676).

Zippo: Martin Burton (1954–), Br. circus owner. The owner of Britain's largest traveling circus began his career in the ring as a clown, which he became by accident. "I'd been brought up in Oxford and always loved theatre. I'd also joined a mime school and we did shows on Brighton beach, where clowning just clicked and I became Zippo" [*The Times*, April 9, 2008].

Zito: José Eli de Miranda (1932–), Brazilian footballer.

Zizi: Renée Jeanmaire (1924–), Fr. dancer, singer.

Zizinho: Thomaz Soares da Silva (1921–2002), Brazilian footballer.

Zmaj: Jovan Jovanovic (1833–1904), Serbian poet. The poet adopted the name of the satirical journal for which he wrote, its own name meaning "The Snake."

Zoke: Michael Attwell (1943–), Eng. TV actor, political cartoonist. The artist devised his cartooning name from those of his children, Zoe and Jake.

Miro Zolan: Miroslav Zlochovsky (1926–), Cz.-Br. ballet dancer, choreographer.

Zoli: Zoltán Rendessy (1941–1982), Hung.-born U.S. male model.

Eugenio Zolli: Israel Zoller (1881–1956), Austr. scholar. The Semitic scholar changed his surname to Zolli after becoming chief rabbi of Trieste in 1914. In 1945 he was converted to Catholicism, and for his new first name adopted the baptismal name of **Pius XII**, whose charity he greatly admired.

William Zorach: Zorach Samovich (1889–1966), Lithuanian-born U.S. sculptor. In 1892, when Samovich's father and and oldest brother fled to the United States to avoid the persecution of the Jews, the family adopted the name Finkelstein. Samovich, his mother, and five siblings emigrated the following year, and around 1896 his name was changed to William Finkelstein by a grade school teacher who found "Zorach Finkelstein" too much of a mouthful. In 1912, Finkelstein, as he now was, married the Californian artist Marguerite Thompson and changed his legal name to William Zorach.

Zoran: Zoran Ladicorbic (1947–), Yugoslav fashion designer.

A. Zorich: Vasily Timofeyevich Lokot (1899–1937), Russ. writer.

Vera Zorina: Eva Brigitta Hartwig (1917–2003), Ger.-born Norw. ballet dancer, stage, movie actress, working in U.S. The dancer was renamed in 1934 on joining the Monte Carlo Ballets Russes of Colonel **de Basil**, who insisted she adopt a Russian-sounding name. He accordingly presented her with a list of names, and she chose the only one she could pronounce. Her first husband was George **Balanchine**,

Fritz Zorn: Fritz Angst (*c*.1944–1976), Swiss writer, working in German. The writer's name changed from *Angst* ("worry") to *Zorn* ("anger"). His posthumous autobiography, *Mars* (1977), reveals the motive, telling of his battle with cancer and the empty, stifling existence he led in middle-class Zürich.

Stefan Zoryan: Stefan Arakelyan (1890–1967), Armenian writer.

Zouzou: Danielle Ciarlet (1944–), Fr. movie actress. The actress adopted a childhood nickname as her screen name. The name itself is a characteristic pet doublet, and may have derived from the repeated second syllable of *oiseau*, "bird." If so, an English equivalent might be "Chickabiddy."

Zozimus: Michael Moran (?1794–1846), Ir. blind balladeer. The street performer took his name from a character in Bishop Antony Coyle's 19th-century "Life of St. Mary of Egypt," which he recited in a verse version. The work's full title was "The Extraordinary Life, Conversion, and Death, of the Great Penitent, St. Mary of Egypt, who was discovered in the wilderness, in the fifth century, by the pious Zozimus, an ecclesiastic, who devoted his days to solitude and devotion." (This Zozimus should not be confused with the 5th-century pope St. Zozimus, nor with the 7th-century St. Zozimus of Syracuse.)

Zucchero: Adelmo Fornaciari (1956–), It. pop singer. The singer adopted his childhood nickname, meaning "sugar."

Luciano **Zuccoli:** Luciano von Ingenheim (1868–1929), It. writer, of Swiss origin.

Leopold **Zunz:** Yom Tov Lippmann (1794–1886), Ger. Jewish historian. In his *Namen der Juden: Eine geschichtliche Untersuchung* ("Names of the Jews: A Historical Investigation") (1837), written in response to a decree issued in 1836 by Friedrich Wilhelm III that Jews should no longer adopt German Christian names, Zunz convincingly demonstrated that Jews had long used foreign first names.

Giuseppe **Zuri:** Salvatore Mannuzzu (1930–), It. writer, magistrate. The writer used this name for his first important novel, *Un dodge a fari spenti* ("A car with doused lights") (1962).

Bob **Zurke:** Boguslaw Albert Zukowski (1912–1944), U.S. jazz musician.

Z.Z.: Louis Zangwill (1869–1938), Eng. novelist, of Russ. Jewish parentage. The writer, brother of the better-known Israel Zangwill (1864–1926), adopted a name that capitalized (literally) on his initial while ensuring his exclusive position at the end of any alphabetical listing, as diametrically opposed to **A.A.**

BIBLIOGRAPHY

Agee, Patrick. *Where Are They Now?* London: Everest, 1977.

Aldrich, Robert, and Garry Wotherspoon, eds. *Who's Who in Gay and Lesbian History: From Antiquity to World War II.* London: Routledge, 2001.

_____, eds. *Who's Who in Contemporary Gay and Lesbian History: From World War II to the Present Day.* London: Routledge, 2001.

Andersen, Christopher P. *The Book of People.* New York: Perigee, 1981.

Andrews, William L., Frances Smith Foster, and Trudier Harris. *The Concise Oxford Companion to African American Literature.* New York: Oxford University Press, 2001.

Arlott, John, ed. *The Oxford Companion to Sports and Games.* London: Oxford University Press, 1975.

Arnold, Denis, gen. ed. *The New Oxford Companion to Music.* Oxford: Oxford University Press, 1983. 2 vols.

Ash, Brian. *Who's Who in Science Fiction.* Rev. ed. London: Sphere, 1977.

Ashley, Leonard R.N. "Flicks, Flacks, and Flux: Tides of Taste in the Onomasticon of the Moving Picture Industry." *Names* (*Journal of the American Name Society*) vol. 23, no. 4 (December 1975).

Ashley, Mike. *Who's Who in Horror and Fantasy Fiction.* London: Elm Tree, 1977.

_____, comp. *The Mammoth Encyclopedia of Modern Crime Fiction.* London: Robinson, 2002.

Atkinson, Frank. *Dictionary of Literary Pseudonyms.* 4th enlarged ed. London: Clive Bingley, 1987.

Bagnoli, Giorgio. *The La Scala Encyclopedia of the Opera*, trans. by Graham Fawcett. New York: Simon and Schuster, 1993.

Baker, Glenn A. *The Name Game: Their Real Names Revealed.* London: GRR/Pavilion, 1986.

Banham, Martin, ed. *The Cambridge Guide to World Theatre.* Cambridge: Cambridge University Press, 1988.

Barbier, Patrick. *Histoire des castrats* [*History of the Castrati*]. Paris: Éditions Bernard Grasset, 1989.

Baring-Gould, S. *Family Names and Their Story.* London: Seeley, 1910.

Bauer, Andrew, comp. *The Hawthorn Dictionary of Pseudonyms.* New York: Hawthorn, 1971.

Beech, Mark. *A Dictionary of Rock and Pop Names.* Barnsley: Pen and Sword, 2009.

Bego, Mark. *The Rock and Roll Almanac.* New York: Macmillan, 1996.

Bellos, Alex. *Futebol: The Brazilian Way of Life.* London: Bloomsbury, 2002.

Benét, William Rose. *The Reader's Encyclopedia.* 3d ed. London: A. and C. Black, 1988.

Bering, Dietz. *The Stigma of Names: Antisemitism in German Daily Life, 1812–1933*, trans. by Neville Plaice. Ann Arbor: University of Michigan Press, 1992.

Birch, Dinah, ed. *The Oxford Companion to English Literature.* 7th ed. Oxford: Oxford University Press, 2009.

Blackwell, Earl. *Earl Blackwell's Entertainment Celebrity Register.* New York: Visible Ink, 1991.

Blain, Virginia, Patricia Clements, and Isobel Grundy. *The Feminist Companion to Literature in English.* London: B.T. Batsford, 1990.

Blake, Lord, and C.S. Nicholls, eds. *The Dictionary of National Biography: 1971–1980.* Oxford: Oxford University Press, 1986.

_____ and _____, eds. *The Dictionary of National Biography: 1981–1985.* Oxford: Oxford University Press, 1990.

Blom, Eric, comp. *Everyman's Dictionary of Music.* Rev. by Sir Jack Westrup. London: J.M. Dent, 1962.

Bottomley, Roy. *This Is Your Life.* London: Methuen, 1993.

Bowden, John. *Who's Who in Theology: From the First Century to the Present.* London: SCM, 1990.

Bowker, John, ed. *The Oxford Dictionary of World Religions.* Oxford: Oxford University Press, 1997.

Bowman, John S., ed. *The Cambridge Dictionary of American Biography.* Cambridge: Cambridge University Press, 1995.

Boylan, Henry, ed. *A Dictionary of Irish Biography.* 3d ed. Dublin: Gill and Macmillan, 1998.

Briggs, Asa, consult. ed. *A Dictionary of Twentieth Century World Biography.* Rev. ed. Oxford: Oxford University Press, 1992.

Brigstocke, Hugh, ed. *The Oxford Companion to Western Art.* Oxford: Oxford University Press, 2001.

Brosse, Jacques. *Les maîtres spirituels* [*Religious Leaders*]. Paris: Bordas, 1988.

Browning, D.C., comp. *Everyman's Dictionary of Literary Biography, English and American.* London: Dent, 1969.

Brunskill, Ian, ed. *The Times Great Lives: A Century in Obituaries.* London: Times, 2005.

Bryant, Mark. *Dictionary of Twentieth-Century British Cartoonists and Caricaturists.* Aldershot: Ashgate, 2000.

_____, and Simon Heneage, comps. *Dictionary of British Cartoonists and Caricaturists 1730–1980.* Aldershot: Scolar, 1994.

Buck, Claire, ed. *Bloomsbury Guide to Women's Literature.* London: Bloomsbury, 1992.

Burton, Sarah. *Impostors: Six Kinds of Liar.* London: Penguin, 2001.

Busby, Roy. *The British Music Hall: An Illustrated Who's Who from 1850 to the Present Day.* London: Paul Elek, 1976.

Callahan, J. Kenneth, comp. *A Dictionary of Sporting Pen Names.* Peterborough, NH: Callahan, 1995.

Cameron-Wilson, James. *Young Hollywood.* London: B.T. Batsford, 1994.

Carpenter, Humphrey, and Mari Prichard. *The Oxford Companion to Children's Literature*. Oxford: Oxford University Press, 1984.

Carty, T.J. *A Dictionary of Literary Pseudonyms in the English Language*. London: Mansell, 1995.

Case, Brian, and Stan Britt. *The Illustrated Encyclopaedia of Jazz*. London: Salamander, 1978.

Chaneles, S., and A. Wolsky. *The Movie Makers*. London: Octopus, 1974.

Cherpillod, André. *Dictionnaire étymologique des noms d'hommes et de dieux* [*Etymological Dictionary of the Names of Men and Gods*]. Paris: Masson, 1988.

Chevalier, Tracy, ed. *Twentieth-Century Children's Writers*. Chicago: St. James Press, 3d ed., 1989.

Chilton, John. *Who's Who of Jazz*. 5th ed. London: Macmillan, 1989.

Chilvers, Ian, ed. *A Dictionary of Twentieth-Century Art*. Oxford: Oxford University Press, 1998.

_____, ed. *The Oxford Dictionary of Art*. 3d ed. Oxford: Oxford University Press, 2004.

Clarke, Donald, ed. *The Penguin Encyclopedia of Popular Music*. London: Viking Penguin, 1989.

Clarke, J.F. *Pseudonyms*. London: Elm Tree, 1977.

Clifford, Mike, consult. ed. *The Illustrated Rock Handbook*. London: Salamander, 1983.

Clute, John, and John Grant, eds. *The Encyclopedia of Fantasy*. London: Orbit, 1997.

Clute, John, and Peter Nicholls, eds. *The Encyclopedia of Science Fiction*. London: Orbit, 1999.

Cohen, Aaron I. *International Encyclopedia of Women Composers*. 2d rev. and enlarged ed. New York: Books and Music (U.S.A.), 1987. 2 vols.

Comay, Joan. *Who's Who in Jewish History after the period of the Old Testament*. New ed. rev. by Lavinia Cohn-Sherbok. London: Routledge, 1995.

The Compact Edition of the Dictionary of National Biography. Oxford: Oxford University Press, 1975 [micrographical reproduction of 22 vols. of original and of decennially published vols. covering 1901–1911, 1912–1921, 1922–1930, 1931–1940, 1941–1950, 1951–1960].

Connors, Martin, Beth A. Fhaner, and Kelly M. Cross, eds. *The VideoHound and All-Movie Guide StarGazer*. Detroit: Visible Ink, 1996.

Coston, Henri. *Dictionnaire des pseudonymes* [*Dictionary of Pseudonyms*]. Paris: Lectures Françaises, 1965 (vol. I), 1969 (vol. II).

Coulombe, Charles A. *Vicars of Christ: A History of the Popes*. New York: Citadel, 2003.

Cox, Michael, ed. *The Oxford Chronology of English Literature*. Oxford: Oxford University Press, 2002. 2 vols.

Craine, Debra, and Judith Mackrell. *The Oxford Dictionary of Dance*. Oxford: Oxford University Press, 2002.

Crosland, Margaret. *Ballet Carnival: A Companion to Ballet*. London: Arco, 1977.

Cross, F.L., and E.A. Livingstone, eds. *The Oxford Dictionary of the Christian Church*. 2d ed. Oxford: Oxford University Press, 1974.

Crowther, Jonathan. *A-Z of Crosswords*. Glasgow: Collins, 2006.

Crystal, David, ed. *The Cambridge Biographical Encyclopedia*. 2d ed. Cambridge: Cambridge University Press, 1998.

Cushing, William. *Initials and Pseudonyms: A Dictionary of Literary Disguises*. New York: Crowell, 1886.

Davidson, Gladys. *Ballet Biographies*. London: Werner Laurie, 1952.

Dawson, Lawrence H. *Nicknames and Pseudonyms: Including Sobriquets of Persons in History, Literature, and the Arts Generally, Titles Given to Monarchs, and the Nicknames of the British Regiments and the States of North America*. London: Routledge, 1908.

Delaney, John J. *Dictionary of Saints*. New York: Doubleday, 1980.

D'Israeli, Isaac. *Curiosities of Literature*. New ed. London: George Routledge, 1866.

Dmitriyev, V.G. *Pridumannyye imena (rasskazy o psevdonimakh)* [*Invented Names (Stories of Pseudonyms)*]. Moscow: Sovremennik, 1986.

_____. *Skryvshiye svoë imya (iz istorii anonimov i psevdonimov)* [*The Name Concealers (A History of Anonyms and Pseudonyms)*].2nd enlarged ed. Moscow: Nauka, 1977.

Dolgins, Adam. *Rock Names*. New York: Carol, 1993.

Doyle, Brian, comp. and ed. *The Who's Who of Children's Literature*. London: Hugh Evelyn, 1968.

Drabble, Margaret, ed. *The Oxford Companion to English Literature*. 6th ed. Oxford: Oxford University Press, 2000.

Dupuy, Trevor N., Curt Johnson, and David L. Bongard. *The Harper Encyclopedia of Military Biography*. Edison, NJ: Castle, 1995.

The Economist Dictionary of Political Biography. London: Business Books, 1991.

Elson, Howard, and John Brunton. *Whatever Happened To...? The Great Rock and Pop Nostalgia Book*. London: Proteus, 1981.

Erlewine, Michael, Vladimir Bogdanov, and Chris Woodstra, eds. *All Music Guide to Rock*. San Francisco: Miller Freeman, 1995.

Evans, Jeff. *The Penguin TV Companion*. 3d ed. London: Penguin, 2006.

Ewan, Elizabeth, Sue Innes, and Siân Reynolds, eds. *The Biographical Dictionary of Scottish Women*. Edinburgh: Edinburgh University Press, 2006.

Ewen, C. L'Estrange. *A Guide to the Origin of British Surnames*. London: John Gifford, 1938.

_____. *A History of Surnames of the British Isles*. London: Kegan Paul, 1931.

Farmer, David Hugh. *The Oxford Dictionary of Saints*. 5th ed. Oxford: Oxford University Press, 2003.

The Fashion Book. London: Phaidon, 1998.

Feather, Leonard, and Ira Gitler. *The Biographical Encyclopedia of Jazz*. New York: Oxford University Press, 1999.

Fisher, John. *Funny Way to Be a Hero*. St. Albans: Paladin, 1976.

_____. *Paul Daniels and the Story of Magic*. London: Jonathan Cape, 1987.

France, Peter, ed. *The New Oxford Companion to Literature in French*. Oxford: Clarendon, 1995.

Franklin, Charles. *Spies of the Twentieth Century*. London: Odhams, 1967.

Freedland, Jonathan. "What's in a Pseudonym?" *The Guardian*, March 29, 2006.

Freestone, Basil. *Harrap's Book of Nicknames and Their Origins*. London: Harrap, 1990.

Gammond, Peter. *The Oxford Companion to Popular Music*. Oxford: Oxford University Press, 1991.

_____, and Peter Clayton. *A Guide to Popular Music*. London: Phoenix, 1960.

Garland, Mary, ed. *The Oxford Companion to German Literature*. 3d ed. Oxford: Oxford University Press, 1997.

Garraty, John A., and Mark C. Carnes, gen. eds. *American National Biography*. New York: Oxford University Press, 1999. 24 vols.

George-Warren, Holly, and Patricia Romanowski, eds. *The*

Rolling Stone Encyclopedia of Rock and Roll. 3d ed. New York: Simon and Schuster, 2001.

Goldston, Will. *Will Goldston's Who's Who in Magic.* London: Will Goldston, n.d. [c. 1935].

Goodman, Jonathan. *Who He? Goodman's Dictionary of the Unknown Famous.* London: Buchan and Enright, 1984.

Gowing, Sir Lawrence, gen. ed. *A Biographical Dictionary of Artists.* London: Grange, 1994.

Gregory, Hugh. *Who's Who in Country Music.* London: Weidenfeld and Nicolson, 1993.

Greif, Martin. *The Gay Book of Days: An Evocatively Illustrated Who's Who of Who Is, Was, May Have Been, Probably Was, and Almost Certainly Seems to Have Been Gay During the Past 5,000 Years.* London: W.H. Allen, 1985.

Gribben, Lenore. *Who's Whodunit: A List of 3,128 Detective Story Writers and Their 1,100 Pseudonyms.* Chapel Hill: University of North Carolina, 1969.

Grigorovich, Yu. N., chief ed. *Balet: Entsiklopediya [Ballet: An Encyclopedia].* Moscow: Sovetskaya Entsiklopediya, 1981.

Guinness Rockopedia. London: Guinness Publishing, 1998.

Gullen, Zoë, and Daniel Sefton, eds. *Debrett's People of Today.* 16th ed. London: Debrett's Peerage, 2002.

Hainsworth, Peter, and David Robey, eds. *The Oxford Companion to Italian Literature.* Oxford: Oxford University Press, 2002.

Halkett, Samuel, and John Laing. *Dictionary of Anonymous and Pseudonymous English Literature.* New and enlarged ed. by Dr. James Kennedy, W.A. Smith, and A.F. Johnson (vols. 1–7); by Dennis E. Rhodes and Anna E.C. Simoni (vols. 8–9). Edinburgh: Oliver and Boyd, 1926–62. 9 vols.

Hall, Tony, ed. *They Died Too Young.* Bristol: Parragon, 1996.

Halliwell, Leslie. *Halliwell's Filmgoer's Companion.* 9th ed. London: Paladin, 1988.

_____, with Philip Purser. *Halliwell's Television Companion.* 3d ed. London: Grafton, 1986.

Hamst, Olphar. *Handbook of Fictitious Names (Being a Guide to Authors, Chiefly in the Lighter Literature of the XIXth Century, Who Have Written Under Assumed Names; and to Literary Forgers, Imposters, Plagiarists, and Imitators).* London: John Russell Smith, 1868.

Hanks, Patrick, and Flavia Hodges. *A Dictionary of Surnames.* Oxford: Oxford University Press, 1988.

Hardy, Phil, and Dave Laing. *The Faber Companion to 20th-Century Popular Music.* London: Faber and Faber, 1990.

_____ and _____, eds., with additional material by Stephen Barnard and Don Perretta. *Encyclopaedia of Rock.* London: Macdonald Orbis, 1987.

Hart, James D., with revisions and additions by Phillip W. Leininger. 6th ed. *The Oxford Companion to American Literature.* Oxford: Oxford University Press, 1995.

Hartnoll, Phyllis, ed. *The Oxford Companion to the Theatre* 4th ed. Oxford: Oxford University Press, 1983.

Harvey, Sir Paul, and J.E. Heseltine, comps. and eds. *The Oxford Companion to French Literature.* Oxford: Oxford University Press, 1961.

Haskins, James: *The Story of Hip-Hop.* New York: Hyperion, 2000.

Hayward, Anthony, ed. *The Boxtree A–Z of TV Stars.* London: Boxtree, 1992.

_____, ed. *The New and Revised Guinness Who's Who of Soap Operas.* Enfield: Guinness, 1995.

_____. *Who's Who on Television.* London: Boxtree, 1996.

_____. *Who's Who on Television.* 5th ed. London: Boxtree, 1990.

_____, and Deborah Hayward. *TV Unforgettables.* Enfield: Guinness, 1993.

Heaton, David, and John Higgins, eds. *Lives Remembered: The Times Obituaries of 1991.* Pangbourne: Blewbury, 1991.

_____. *The Times Obituaries 1992.* Blewbury: Blewbury, 1992.

Henderson, Lesley, ed. *Contemporary Novelists.* 5th ed. Chicago: St. James, 1991.

Herbert, Ian, ed. *Who's Who in the Theatre.* Vol 1: Biographies. 17th ed. Detroit: Gale, 1981.

Herbert, Rosemary, ed. *The Oxford Companion to Crime and Mystery Writing.* New York: Oxford University Press, 1999.

Herbert, Stephen, and Luke McKernan, eds. *Who's Who of Victorian Cinema.* London: British Film Institute, 1996.

Hildreth, Peter. *Name Dropper.* London: McWhirter, 1970.

Hinnells, John R., ed. *Who's Who of World Religions.* New York: Simon and Schuster, 1992.

Holmstrom, John. *The Moving Picture Boy: An International Encyclopaedia from 1895 to 1995.* Wilby: Michael Russell, 1996.

Hook, J.N. *Family Names: The Origins, Meanings, Mutations, and History of More than 2,800 American Names.* New York: Macmillan, 1983.

Howard, Anthony, and David Heaton, eds. *The Times Lives Remembered: Obituaries from 1993.* Blewbury: Blewbury, 1993.

Hudd, Roy, with Philip Hindin. *Roy Hudd's Cavalcade of Variety Acts: A Who Was Who of Light Entertainment 1945–60.* London: Robson, 1997.

Hunter, Matt. *Wrestling: A Ringside Look at Wrestling Superstars.* London: Boxtree, 1999.

Hyamson, Albert M. *A Dictionary of Universal Biography of All Ages and of All Peoples.* 2d ed. London: Routledge and Kegan Paul, 1951.

Illustrated Encyclopaedia of World Theatre. London: Thames and Hudson, 1977.

International Authors and Writers Who's Who. 17th ed. Cambridge: International Biographical Centre, 2001.

Jackson, Kenneth T., ed. *The Encyclopedia of New York City.* New Haven, CT: Yale University Press, 1995.

Jacobs, Arthur. *The Penguin Dictionary of Musical Performers.* London: Penguin, 1990.

Jacobs, Louis. *The Jewish Religion: A Companion.* Oxford: Oxford University Press, 1995.

Jares, Joe. *Whatever Happened to Gorgeous George?* New York: Grosset and Dunlap, 1974.

Jennings, Gary. *Personalities of Language.* London: Victor Gollanz, 1967. [Pp. 142–162 of this book contain a popular overview of personal names, including name changes.]

Jeremy, David J., ed. *Dictionary of Business Biography.* London: Butterworths, 1984–86. 5 vols.

Jerôme, l'Archiviste. *Dictionnaire des changements de noms de 1803 à 1956 [Dictionary of Name Changes from 1803 to 1956].* Paris: Henry Coston, 1957.

_____. *Dictionnaire des changements de noms 1957–1962 [Dictionary of Name Changes 1957–1962].* Paris: La Librairie Française, 1979.

Jones, Maldwyn A. *Destination America.* London: Weidenfeld and Nicolson, 1976.

Josling, J.F. *Change of Name.* 14th ed. London: Longman, 1989.

Kaganoff, Benzion C. *A Dictionary of Jewish Names and Their History.* London: Routledge and Kegan Paul, 1978.

Kamm, Antony. *Collins Biographical Dictionary of English Literature*. Glasgow: HarperCollins, 1993.

Karney, Robyn, ed. *Who's Who in Hollywood*. London: Parragon, 1993.

Kash, Murray. *Murray Kash's Book of Country*. London: W.H. Allen, 1981.

Katz, Ephraim. *The Macmillan International Film Encyclopedia*. New ed. London: Macmillan, 1994.

Keating, H.R.F., ed. *Whodunit? A Guide to Crime, Suspense and Spy Fiction*. London: Windward, 1982.

Kelly, J.N.D., and Michael Walsh. *A Dictionary of Popes*. 2d ed. Oxford: Oxford University Press, 2010.

Kemp, Sandra, Charlotte Mitchell, and David Trotter. *Edwardian Fiction: An Oxford Companion*. Oxford: Oxford University Press, 1997.

Kennedy, Michael. *The Oxford Dictionary of Music*. rev. 2d ed. Oxford: Oxford University Press, 2006.

Kidd, Charles. *Debrett Goes to Hollywood*. New York: St. Martin's, 1986.

Kilgarriff, Michael. *Grace, Beauty and Banjos*. London: Oberon, 1998.

_____. *Sing Us One of the Old Songs: A Guide to Popular Song 1860–1920*. Oxford: Oxford University Press, 1998.

Klymasz, R.B. *A Classified Dictionary of Slavic Surname Changes in Canada*. Winnipeg: Ukrainian Free Academy of Sciences, 1961. (Onomastica No. 22.)

Koegler, Horst. *The Concise Oxford Dictionary of Ballet*. 2d rev. ed. Oxford: Oxford University Press, 1987.

Kupper, Susan J. *Surnames for Women: A Decision-Making Guide*. Jefferson, NC: McFarland, 1990.

Lamb, Geoffrey. *Magic Illustrated Dictionary*. London: Kaye and Ward, 1979.

Larkin, Colin, ed. *The Virgin Encyclopedia of Popular Music*. 4th ed. London: Virgin, 2002.

Latham, Alison, ed. *The Oxford Companion to Music*. New ed. Oxford: Oxford University Press, 2002.

Lees, Stella, and Pam Macintyre. *The Oxford Companion to Australian Children's Literature*. Melbourne: Oxford University Press, 1993.

Lloyd, Ann, and Graham Fuller, eds. *The Illustrated Who's Who of the Cinema*. London: Orbis, 1983.

Lofts, W.O.G., and D.J. Adley. *The Men Behind Boys' Fiction*. London: Howard Baker, 1970.

Maltin, Leonard, ed. *Leonard Maltin's Movie Encyclopedia*. New York: Plume, 1995.

Marble, Annie Russell. *Pen Names and Personalities*. New York: Appleton, 1930.

Marshall, Alice Kahler. *Pen Names of Women Writers from 1600 to the Present: A Compendium of the Literary Identities of 2650 Women Novelists, Playwrights, Poets, Diarists, Journalists and Miscellaneous Writers*. Camp Hill, PA: Alice Kahler Marshall, 1985.

Masanov, I.F. *Slovar' psevdonimov russkikh pisateley, uchënykh i obshchestvennykh deyateley* [*Dictionary of Pseudonyms of Russian Writers, Scholars and Public Figures*]. Moscow: Izdatel'stvo Vsesoyuznoy Knizhnoy Palaty, 1956. 4 vols.

Masi, Stafeno, and Enrico Lancia. *Italian Movie Goddesses: Over 80 of the Greatest Women in Italian Cinema*. Rome: Gremese, 1997.

Massingberd, Hugh, ed. *The Daily Telegraph Book of Obituaries: A Celebration of Eccentric Lives*. London: Macmillan, 1995.

_____, ed. *The Daily Telegraph Second Book of Obituaries: Heroes and Adventurers*. London: Macmillan, 1996.

_____, ed. *The Daily Telegraph Third Book of Obituaries: Entertainers*. London: Macmillan, 1997.

_____, ed. *The Daily Telegraph Fourth Book of Obituaries: Rogues*. London: Macmillan, 1998.

_____, ed. *The Daily Telegraph Fifth Book of Obituaries: Twentieth-Century Lives*. London: Macmillan, 1999.

Matthews, Peter, Ian Buchanan, and Bill Mallon. *The Guinness International Who's Who of Sport*. Enfield: Guinness, 1993.

McBrien, Richard P., gen. ed. *The HarperCollins Encyclopedia of Catholicism*. New York: HarperCollins, 1995.

McCauley, Martin. *Who's Who in Russia Since 1900*. London: Routledge, 1997.

McCormick, Donald. *Who's Who in Spy Fiction*. London: Elm Tree, 1977.

Meades, Jonathan. *This Is Your Life: An Insight into the Unseen Lives of Your Favourite TV Personalities*. London: Salamander, 1979.

Mencken, H.L. *The American Language*. 4th ed. New York: Alfred A. Knopf, 1936. [Pp. 474–505 of this book contain hundreds of examples of foreign surnames assimilated or changed to English names.]

Merriam-Webster's Biographical Dictionary. Rev. ed. Springfield, MA: Merriam-Webster, 1995.

Merriam-Webster's Encyclopedia of Literature. Springfield, MA: Merriam-Webster, 1995.

Miller, Compton: *Who's REALLY! Who*. Rev. ed. London: Harden's, 1997.

Miller, Maud M., ed. *Winchester's Screen Encyclopedia*. London: Winchester, 1948.

Mitchell, Glenn. *A–Z of Silent Film Comedy*. London: B.T. Batsford, 1998.

Morgan, Jane, Christopher O'Neill, and Rom Harré. *Nicknames: Their Origins and Social Consequences*. London: Routledge and Kegan Paul, 1979.

Mossman, Jennifer, ed. *New Pseudonyms and Nicknames*. Supp. to 1st ed. Detroit: Gale, 1981.

_____, ed. *Pseudonyms and Nicknames Dictionary*. 1st ed. Detroit: Gale, 1980.

Mullan, John. *Anonymity: A Secret History of English Literature*. London: Faber and Faber, 2007.

Nataf, André. *Les Maîtres de l'occultisme* [*Masters of Occultism*]. Paris: Bordas, 1988.

Neuburg, Victor E. *The Batsford Companion to Popular Literature*. London: Batsford Academic and Educational, 1982.

New Catholic Encyclopedia. New York: McGraw-Hill, 1967.

The New Encyclopædia Britannica. 15th ed. Chicago: Encyclopædia Britannica, 2002.

Nicholls, C.S., ed. *The Dictionary of National Biography: Missing Persons*. Oxford: Oxford University Press, 1993.

_____, ed. *The Dictionary of National Biography: 1986–1990*. Oxford: Oxford University Press, 1996.

_____, ed. *The Hutchinson Encyclopedia of Biography*. Oxford: Helicon, 1996.

Oates, Joyce Carol. "Success and the Pseudonymous Writer: Turning Over a New Self." *New York Times Book Review*, December 6, 1987.

O'Hara, Georgina. *The Encyclopedia of Fashion*. London: Thames and Hudson, 1986.

O'Hara Callan, Georgina. *The Thames and Hudson Dictionary of Fashion and Fashion Designers*. London, 1998.

Osborne, Harold, ed. *The Oxford Companion to Art*. Oxford: Oxford University Press, 1970.

Ousby, Ian, ed. *The Cambridge Guide to Literature in English*. Rev. ed. Cambridge: Cambridge University Press, 1993.

Panassié, Hugues, and Madeleine Gautier. *Dictionary of Jazz*. London: Cassell, 1956.

Parish, James Robert. *Great Child Stars*. New York: Ace, 1976.

Parker, John, comp. and ed. *Who's Who in the Theatre*. 10th ed. London: Sir Isaac Pitman, 1947.

Parker, Peter, ed. *The Reader's Companion to Twentieth-Century Writers*. London: Fourth Estate/Oxford: Helicon, 1995.

Parry, Melanie, ed. *Chambers Biographical Dictionary of Women*. Edinburgh: Chambers, 1996.

Partridge, Christopher, ed. *Encyclopedia of New Religions*. Oxford: Lion, 2004.

Pascall, Jeremy, and Rob Burt. *The Stars and Superstars of Black Music*. London: Phoebus, 1977.

Patmore, Angela. *The Giants of Sumo*. London: Queen Anne, 1990.

Pedder, Eddie, ed. *Who's Who on Television*. 4th ed. London: ITV, 1988.

The Penguin Biographical Dictionary of Women. London: Penguin, 1998.

Perkins, George, Barbara Perkins, and Phillip Leininger, eds. *Benét's Reader's Encyclopedia of American Literature*. Glasgow: HarperCollins, 1992.

Picarello, Robert. *Rulers of the Ring: Wrestling's Hottest Superstars*. New York: Berkley Boulevard, 2000.

The Picturegoer's Who's Who and Encyclopaedia of the Screen To-Day. 1st ed. London: Odhams, 1933.

Pine, L.G. *A Dictionary of Nicknames*. London: Routledge and Kegan Paul, 1984.

Polmar, Norman, and Thomas B. Allen. *Spy Book: Encyclopedia of Espionage*. London: Greenhill, 1997.

Pynsent, Robert B., and S.I. Kanikova, eds. *The Everyman Companion to East European Literature*. London: J.M. Dent, 1993.

Quinlan, David. *Quinlan's Film Stars*. 5th ed. Washington, DC: Brassey's, 2000.

_____. *Quinlan's Illustrated Directory of Film Character Actors*. London: B.T. Batsford, 1995.

Rajadhyaksha, Ashish, and Paul Willemen: *Encyclopaedia of Indian Cinema*. London: British Film Institute/New Delhi: New rev. ed. Oxford University Press, 1999.

Randi, James: *The Supernatural A–Z: The Truth and the Lies*. London: Hodder Headline, 1995.

Rees, Dafydd, and Luke Crampton. *The Guinness Book of Rock Stars*. 3d ed. Enfield: Guinness Publishing, 1994.

_____. *Q Encyclopedia of Rock Stars*. London: Dorling Kindersley, 1996.

Rees, Nigel, and Vernon Noble. *A Who's Who of Nicknames*. London: George Allen and Unwin, 1985.

Reyna, Ferdina. *Concise Encyclopedia of Ballet*. London: Collins, 1974.

Rigdon, Walter, ed. *The Biographical Encyclopedia and Who's Who of the American Theatre*. New York: J.H. Heinemann, 1966.

Roberts, Frank C., comp. *Obituaries from The Times 1951–1960*. Reading: Newspaper Archive Developments, 1979.

_____, comp. *Obituaries from The Times 1961–1970*. Reading: Newspaper Archive Developments, 1975.

_____, comp. *Obituaries from The Times 1971–1975*. Reading: Newspaper Archive Developments, 1978.

Robinson, Roger, comp. *Who's Hugh? An SF Reader's Guide to Pseudonyms*. Harold Wood: Beccon, 1987.

Rockwood, Camilla, ed. 8th ed. *Chambers Biographical Dictionary*. Edinburgh: Chambers, 2007.

Rogozinski, Jan. *Pirates!* New York: Facts on File, 1995.

Rose, Simon. *One FM Essential Film Guide*. Glasgow: HarperCollins, 1993.

Roxon, Lillian. *Rock Encyclopedia*. New York: Grosset and Dunlap, 1971.

Russell, Tony, and Chris Smith. *The Penguin Guide to Blues Recording*. London: Penguin, 2006.

Sachs, John, and Piers Morgan. *Private Files of the Stars*. London: Angus and Robertson, 1991.

_____. *Secret Lives*. London: Blake, 1991.

Sangharakshita. *Great Buddhists of the Twentieth Century*. Birmingham: Windhorse, 1996.

Schlueter, Paul, and June Schlueter, eds. *An Encyclopedia of British Women Writers*. Rev. and expanded ed. New Brunswick, NJ: Rutgers University Press, 1998.

Schneider, Steven Jay, gen. ed. *501 Movie Directors*. London: Cassell Illustrated, 2007.

_____. *501 Movie Stars*. London: Cassell Illustrated, 2007.

Seth, Ronald. *Encyclopedia of Espionage*. London: New English Library, 1972.

Shankle, George Earie. *American Nicknames: Their Origin and Significance*. New York: Wilson, 1955.

Share, Bernard. *Naming Names: Who, What, Where in Irish Nomenclature*. Dublin: Gill and Macmillan, 2001.

Sharp, Harold S., comp. *Handbook of Pseudonyms and Personal Nicknames*. Metuchen, NJ: Scarecrow, 1972. *First Supplement*, 1975.

Sharp, R. Farquharson. *A Dictionary of English Authors*. Rev. ed. London: Kegan Paul, Trench, Trübner, 1904.

Shestack, Melvin. *The Country Music Encyclopaedia*. London: Omnibus, 1977.

Shneyer, A. Ya., and R. Ye. Slavsky. *Tsirk. Malen'kaya entsiklopediya* [*The Circus: A Little Encyclopedia*]. Moscow: Sovetskaya Entsiklopediya, 1979.

Smith, Benjamin E., ed. *The Century Cyclopedia of Names*. London: Times/New York: Century, 1904.

Snelling, John. *The Buddhist Handbook*. New ed. London: Rider, 1992.

Stambler, Irwin. *Encyclopaedia of Pop, Rock and Soul*. New York: St. Martin's, 1989.

Stegemeyer, Anne. *Who's Who in Fashion*. 3d ed. New York: Fairchild, 1996.

Stephens, Meic, comp. and ed. *The Oxford Companion to the Literature of Wales*. Oxford: Oxford University Press, 1986.

Stetler, Susan. *Actors, Artists, Authors and Attempted Assassins*. Detroit: Visible Ink, 1991.

Stevens, Andy. *World of Stars: Your 200 Favourite Personalities*. London: Fontana, 1980.

Stoutenburgh, John, Jr. *Dictionary of the American Indian*. New York: Philosophical Library, 1960.

Stringer, Jenny, ed. *The Oxford Companion to Twentieth Century Literature in English*. Oxford: Oxford University Press, 1996.

Sutherland, John. *The Longman Companion to Victorian Fiction*. 2d ed. Harlow: Pearson, 2009.

Talevski, Nick. *Knocking on Heaven's Door*. London: Omnibus, 2006. [A biographical compendium of over 1,000 pop, rock, and popular music personalities and performers who died from the 1950s to 2006.]

Thomson, David. *A Biographical Dictionary of Film*. 3d ed. London: André Deutsch, 1994.

_____. *A Biographical Dictionary of the Cinema*. London: Secker and Warburg, 1975.

_____. *The New Biographical Dictionary of Film*. 4th ed. London: Little, Brown, 2003. ["This 2003 publication contains updating and some corrections of previous errors."]

Tobler, John, ed. *Who's Who in Rock and Roll*. London: Hamlyn, 1991.

Todd, Janet. *A Dictionary of British and American Women Writers 1660–1800*. London: Methuen, 1987.

_____, ed. *Dictionary of British Women Writers*. London: Routledge, 1989.

TV Times Who's Who on Television. London: Boxtree, 2000.

Uglow, Jennifer, comp. and ed., rev. by Maggy Hendry. *The Macmillan Dictionary of Women's Biography*. 3d ed. London: Papermac, 1999.

Unbegaun, B.O. *Russian Surnames*. Oxford: Clarendon, 1972.

Vincendeau, Ginette, ed. *Encyclopedia of European Cinema*. London: Cassell, 1995.

Vinson, James, ed. *The International Dictionary of Films and Filmmakers. Vol. III: Actors and Actresses*. London: St. James, 1986.

Walker, John, ed. *Halliwell's Who's Who in the Movies*. 4th ed. London: HarperCollins, 2006.

Walsh, Michael, ed. *Dictionary of Christian Biography*. Collegeville, MN: Liturgical, 2001.

_____. *A New Dictionary of Saints: East and West*. London: Burns and Oates, 2007.

Ward, A.C. *Longman Companion to Twentieth Century Literature*. 3d ed. London: Longman, 1981.

Warrack, John, and Ewan West. *The Oxford Dictionary of Opera*. 3d ed. Oxford: Oxford University Press, 1996.

Watkins, Dom Basil, ed. *The Book of Saints*. 7th ed. London: A. and C. Black, 2002.

Watson, Noelle, ed. *Reference Guide to Short Fiction*. Detroit: St. James, 1994.

Watson, Victor. *The Cambridge Guide to Children's Books in English*. Cambridge: Cambridge University Press, 2001.

Welch, Robert. *The Oxford Companion to Irish Literature*. Oxford: Clarendon, 1996.

Wheeler, William A. *A Dictionary of the Noted Names of Fiction (Including Also Familiar Pseudonyms, Surnames Bestowed on Eminent Men, and Analogous Popular Appellations Often Referred to in Literature and Conversation)*. London: George Bell, 1892.

Wheelwright, Julie. *Amazons and Military Maids*. London: Pandora, 1989.

Who Was Who. Volume I: 1897–1915. London: A. and C. Black, 1920.

_____. Volume II: 1916–1928. London: A. and C. Black, 1929.

_____. Volume III: 1929–1940. London: A. and C. Black, 1941.

_____. Volume IV: 1941–1950. London: A. and C. Black, 1952.

_____. Volume V: 1951–1960. London: A. and C. Black, 1961.

_____. Volume VI: 1961–1970. London: A. and C. Black, 1972.

_____. Volume VII: 1971–1980. London: A. and C. Black, 1981.

_____. Volume VIII: 1981–1990. London: A. and C. Black, 1991.

_____. Volume IX: 1991–1995. London: A. and C. Black, 1996.

_____. Volume X: 1996–2000. London: A. and C. Black, 2001.

Who Was Who in the Theatre: 1912–1976. Detroit: Gale, 1978. 4 vols.

Wilde, William H., Joy Hooton, and Barry Andrews. *The Oxford Companion to Australian Literature*. Oxford: Oxford University Press, 1995.

Williams, E.T., and C.S. Nicholls, eds. *The Dictionary of National Biography: 1961–1970*. Oxford: Oxford University Press, 1981.

Wlaschin, Ken. *The World's Great Movie Stars and Their Films*. Rev. ed. London: Peerage, 1984.

Yutkevich, S.I., chief ed. *Kino: Entsiklopedicheskiy slovar'* [*The Cinema: An Encyclopedic Dictionary*]. Moscow: Sovetskaya Entsiklopediya, 1986.

Zec, Donald. *Some Enchanted Egos*. London: Allison and Busby, 1972.

Zipes, Jack, ed. *The Oxford Companion to Fairy Tales*. Oxford: Oxford University Press, 2000.

Other Sources

Aside from the few included above, numerous articles, features, and essays on pseudonyms and name changes have appeared over the years, and readers who wish for a fuller listing than can be provided here are referred to the following bibliographies:

Lawson, Edwin D., comp. *Personal Names and Naming*. Westport, CT: Greenwood, 1987.

_____. *More Names and Naming*. Westport, CT: Greenwood, 1995.

Ruthven, Ken: "Faking Literature: The Bibliography." *Jacket* 17 (June 2002). [*Jacket* is an online-only Australian quarterly literary review, http://jacketmagazine.com.]